Alexander Adam

Roman antiquities

or, an account of the manners and customs of the Romans

Alexander Adam

Roman antiquities
or, an account of the manners and customs of the Romans

ISBN/EAN: 9783741112461

Manufactured in Europe, USA, Canada, Australia, Japa

Cover: Foto ©ninafisch / pixelio.de

Manufactured and distributed by brebook publishing software
(www.brebook.com)

Alexander Adam

Roman antiquities

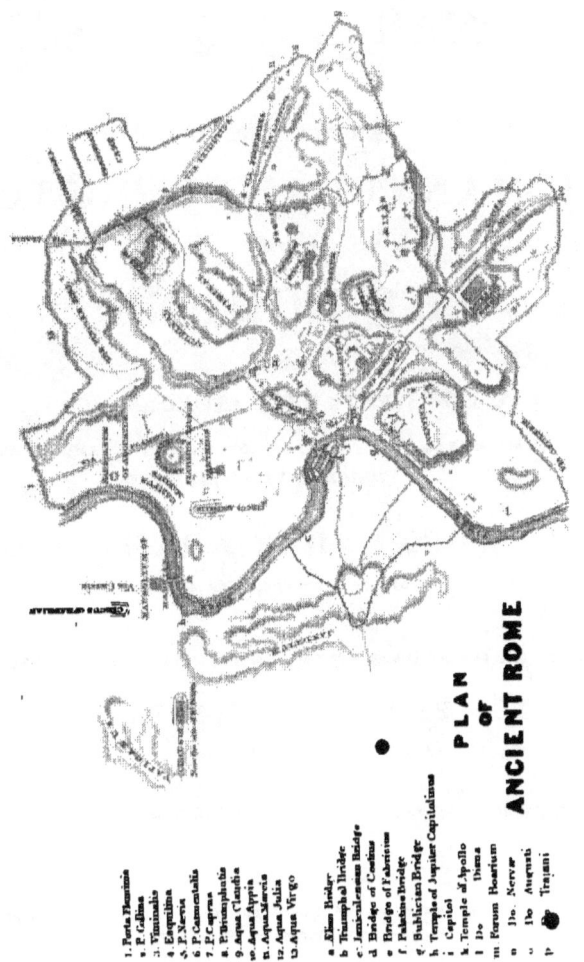

1. Porta Flaminia
2. P. Galicae
3. Viminalis
4. Esquilina
5. P. Metri
6. P. Caestalatis
7. P. Capena
8. Palanogmlanis
9. Aqua Claudia
10. Aqua Appia
11. Aqua Marcia
12. Aqua Julia
13. Aqua Virgo

a. Elian Bridge
b. Triumphal Bridge
c. Janiculum Bridge
d. Bridge of Cestius
e. Bridge of Fabricius
f. Palatine Bridge
g. Sublician Bridge
h. Temple of Jupiter Capitolinus
i. Capitol
k. Temple of Apollo
l. Do. Diana
m. Forum Boarium
n. Do. Nervæ
o. Do. Augusti
p. Do. Trajani

PLAN
OF
ANCIENT ROME

ROMAN ANTIQUITIES:

OR

AN ACCOUNT OF

THE MANNERS AND CUSTOMS

OF

THE ROMANS;

DESIGNED

TO ILLUSTRATE THE LATIN CLASSICS,

BY EXPLAINING WORDS AND PHRASES, FROM THE RITES AND CUSTOMS TO WHICH THEY REFER.

BY ALEXANDER ADAM, LL.D.,

RECTOR OF THE HIGH SCHOOL OF EDINBURGH.

WITH NUMEROUS NOTES, AND IMPROVED INDICES.

BY JAMES BOYD, LL.D.,

ONE OF THE MASTERS OF THE HIGH SCHOOL, EDINBURGH.

ILLUSTRATED BY UPWARDS OF 100 ENGRAVINGS ON WOOD AND STEEL.

BY LORENZO L. DA PONTE,

EDITOR OF THE SEVENTH, EIGHTH, NINTH, AND TENTH AMERICAN EDITIONS OF LEMPRIERE'S CLASSICAL DICTIONARY.

PHILADELPHIA:

J. B. LIPPINCOTT & CO.

1872.

TO

AGLIONBY ROSS CARSON, Esq., LL.D.,

F. R. S. and F. A. S., Edin., &c., &c.

THIS EDITION OF

ADAM'S ROMAN ANTIQUITIES,

Is respectfully dedicated,

IN TESTIMONY OF THE EDITOR'S ADMIRATION

OF THE DISTINGUISHED TALENT, SCHOLARSHIP, AND PROFESSIONAL SKILL,

BY WHICH,

As Rector of the High School of Edinburgh,

HE SUSTAINS THE REPUTATION OF THAT SEMINARY OF WHICH DR. ADAM WAS

SO LONG THE ORNAMENT AND BOAST.

ADVERTISEMENT.

Dr. Adam's elaborate "Summary of Roman Antiquities" has hitherto appeared in an octavo form, and, in consequence of its price, has not found its way into many of our classical schools. To remedy this inconvenience, the work is now presented in a more portable shape, and at little more than one-half of the original price. The editor trusts, that in thus rendering this admirable work accessible to every schoolboy, he does some service to classical literature.

The editor has availed himself of several valuable works that have appeared since the days of the learned author. Notes of considerable length will be found from Niebuhr's Roman History, from Henderson on Ancient Wines, from Blair on Slavery among the Romans, and from the works of Professor Anthon of New York. These notes in some instances correct the mistakes, and in others supply the deficiencies of the original work.

The numerous references interspersed throughout the text of former editions, have been removed to the foot of each page, which exhibits the text in a more continuous form. For the benefit of the tyro, translations have also been given of many of the Latin quotations. But to classical students, and others, who have occasion to *consult* the work, perhaps the greatest improvement will be found in the enlargement of the Indices. The Latin Index now contains fully four times more words and phrases than the former one, and embraces, it is hoped, EVERY word and phrase explained in the volume.

Six Engravings on Steel, and nearly one hundred wood cuts will be found interspersed, which have been copied from Montfaucon's L'Antiquité Expliquée, Sir William Gell's Pompeii, and other works of the highest authority.

Lastly, in order to direct attention to the most essential topics, and to facilitate examination, it is the intention of the editor to publish, as soon as possible, a complete set of QUESTIONS, which will considerably abridge the teacher's labour, and save the student's time.

With these additions and alterations, the editor humbly trusts that this edition of Adam's Antiquities may be found not altogether undeserving of public notice and patronage.

PREFACE TO FIRST EDITION.

NOTHING has more engaged the attention of literary men, since the revival of learning, than to trace, from ancient monuments, the institutions and laws, the religion, the manners and customs of the Romans, under the general name of *Roman Antiquities*. This branch of knowledge is not only curious in itself, but absolutely necessary for understanding the classics, and for reading with advantage the history of that celebrated people. It is particularly requisite for such as prosecute the study of the civil law.

Scarcely on any subject have more books been written, and many of them by persons of distinguished abilities; but they are for the most part too voluminous to be generally useful. Hence a number of abridgements have been published; of which those of Kennet and Nieuport are esteemed the best. The latter is, on the whole, better adapted than the former to illustrate the classics; but being written in Latin, and abounding with difficult phrases, is not fitted for the use of younger students. Besides, it contains nothing concerning the laws of the Romans, or the buildings of the city, which are justly reckoned among the most valuable parts in Kennet.

On these accounts, near twenty years ago, the compiler of the following pages thought of framing from both, chiefly from Nieuport, a *compendium* for his own use, with an intention to print it, if he should meet with no book on the subject to his mind. But he soon perceived, that on several important points he could not derive from either the satisfaction he wished. He therefore had recourse to other sources of information, and chiefly to the classics themselves. To enumerate the various authors he has consulted, would be tedious and useless. It is sufficient to say, that he has borrowed with freedom, from all hands, whatever he judged fit for his purpose. He has been chiefly indebted to Manutius, Brissonius, and Middleton, on the senate; to Pignorius, on slaves; to Sigonius, and Gruccbius, Manutius, Huber, Gravina, Merula, and Heineccius, on the assemblies of the people, the rights of citizens, the laws and judicial proceedings; to Lipsius, on the magistrates, the art of war, shows of the circus, and gladiators; to Schæffer, on naval affairs and carriages; to Ferrarius, on the Roman dress; to Kirchmannus, on funerals; to Arbuthnot, on coins; to Dickson, on agriculture; to Donatus, on the city; to Turnebus, Abrahamus, Rosinus, Salmasius, Hottomannus, Grævius, and Gronovius, Montfaucon, Pitiscus, Ernesti, and particularly to Gesner, in different parts of the work.

After making considerable progress in this undertaking, the compiler found the execution so difficult, that he would have willingly dropt it, could he have found any thing on the subject to answer his views. Accordingly, when Mr. Lempriere did him the favor to communicate his design of publishing that useful work, the *Classical Dictionary*, he used the freedom to suggest to him the propriety of intermingling with his plan a description of Roman Antiquities. But being informed by that gentleman that this was impracticable, and meeting with no book which joined the explanation of words and things together, he resolved to execute his original intention. It is now above three years since he began printing. This delay has been occasioned partly by the difficulty of the work, and making various alterations and additions; partly, also, by a solicitude to receive the remarks of some gentlemen of learning and taste, on whose judgment he could rely, who have been so obliging as to read over with critical attention, the sheets as they were printed.

After finishing what relates to the laws and judicial proceedings, the compiler proposed publishing that part by itself, with a kind of *syllabus* of the other parts subjoined; that he might have leisure to reprint, with improvements, a Summary of Geography and History, which he composed a few years ago for the use of scholars. But after giving an account of the deities and religious rites in his cursory manner, and without quoting authorities, he was induced, by the advice of friends, to relinquish that design, and to postpone other objects, till he should bring the present performance to a conclusion. Although he has all along studied brevity as much as regard to perspicuity would admit, the book has swelled to a much greater size than at first he imagined.

The labour he has undergone can be conceived by those only who have been conversant in such studies. But he will think his pains well bestowed, if his work answer the end intended—to facilitate the acquisition of classical learning. He has done every thing in his power to render it useful. He has endeavoured to give a just view of the constitution of the Roman government, and to point out the principal causes of the various changes which it underwent. This part, it is hoped, will be found calculated to impress on the minds of youth, just sentiments of government in general; by showing, on the one hand, the pernicious effects of aristocratic domination; and, on the other, the still more hurtful consequences of democratic licentiousness, and oligarchic tyrrany.

But it is needless to point out what has been attempted in particular parts; as it has been the compiler's great aim, throughout the whole, to convey as much useful information as possible within the limits he has prescribed to himself. Although very few things are advanced without classical authority, yet in so extensive a field, and amidst such diversity of opinions, he, no doubt, may have fallen into mistakes. These he shall esteem it the highest favour to have pointed out to him; and he earnestly entreats the assistance of the encouragers of learning to enable him to render his work more useful. He has submitted his plan to the best judges, and it has uniformly met with their approbation.

It may perhaps be thought, that in some places he has quoted too many authorities. But he is confident no one will think so, who takes the trouble to examine them. This he esteems the most valuable part of the book. It has at least been the most laborious. A work of this kind, he imagines, if properly executed, might be made to serve as a KEY to all the classics, and in some degree supersede the use of large annotations and commentaries on the different authors; which, when the same customs are alluded to, will generally be found to contain little else but a repetition of the same things.

The Compiler has now in a great measure completed what above twenty years ago he conceived to be wanting in the common plan of education in this country. His first attempt was to connect the study of Latin Grammar with that of English; which was approved of by some of the first literary characters in the kingdom. It is sufficient to mention Mr. Harris and Dr. Lowth. He has since contrived, by a new and natural arrangement, to include in the same book a vocabulary, not only of the simple and primitive words in the Latin tongue, but also of the most common derivatives and compounds, with an explanation of phrases and of tropes. His next attempt was to join the knowledge of ancient and modern geography, and the principles of history, with the study of the classics. And now he has endeavoured to explain difficult words and phrases in the Roman authors, from the customs to which they refer. How far he has succeeded in the execution he must leave others to judge. He can only say, that what he has written has proceeded from the purest desire to promote the improvement of youth; and that he should never have thought of troubling the world with his publications, if he could have found, on any of the subjects he has treated, a book adapted to his purpose. He has attained his end, if he has put it in the power of the teacher to convey instruction with more ease, and in a shorter time; and of the learner to procure, with the greater facility, instruction for himself. He has laboured long in the education of youth, and wished to show himself not unworthy of the confidence reposed in him by the public. His chief enjoyment in life has arisen from the acquisition and communication of useful knowledge; and he can truly say with Seneca, " Si cum hac exceptione detur sapientia, ut illam inclusam teneam, nec enunciem, rejiciam," Ep. 6.

Edinburgh, April, 1791.

ADVERTISEMENT TO SECOND EDITION.

THE Compiler has felt much satisfaction from the favourable reception his performance has met with. He has, in particular, been highly gratified by the approbation of several of the masters of the great schools in England, and of the professors in the universities of both kingdoms. The obliging communications he has received from them, and from other gentlemen of the first character for classical learning, he will ever remember with gratitude. Stimulated by such encouragement, he has exerted his utmost industry to improve this edition. The numerous facts and authorities he has added will show the pains he has bestowed. The index of Latin words and phrases is considerably enlarged; and an index of proper names and things is subjoined; for suggesting the utility of which, he is indebted to the authors of the Analytical Review.

There are several branches of his subject which still remain to be discussed; and in those he has treated of, he has been obliged to suppress many particulars for fear of swelling his book to too great a size. It has therefore been suggested to him, that to render this work more generally useful, it ought to be printed in two different forms: in a smaller size for the use of schools; and in a larger form, with additional observations and plates, for the use of more advanced students. This, if he find it agreeable to the public, he will endeavour to execute to the best of his ability; but it must be a work of time; and he is now obliged to direct his attention to other objects, which he considers of no less importance.

As several of the classics, both Greek and Latin, are differently divided by different editors, it will be proper to mention what editions of these have been followed in the quotations: Cæsar, by Clarke, or in usum Delphini: Pliny, by Brotier; Quinctilian and the writers on husbandry, by Gesner; Petronius Arbiter, by Burmannus; Dionysius of Halicarnassus, by Reiske; Plutarch's Morals, by Xylander; and Dio Cassius, by Reimarus. It is needless to mention the editions of such authors as are always divided in the same manner. Those not divided into chapters, as Appian, Strabo, Plutarch's Lives, &c. are quoted by books and pages.

Edinburgh, May 21st, 1792.

CONTENTS.

2

LIST OF STEEL ENGRAVINGS.

LIST OF WOOD ENGRAVINGS.

PRINCIPAL ABBREVIATIONS.

Cæs. Cæsar ; Gal. de Bello Gallico ; Civ. de Bello Civili ; Afr. de Bello Africano ; Hisp. de Bello Hispaniensi.

Cic. Cicero ; Or. de Oratore ; Legg. de Legibus ; Fin. de Finibus ; Top. Topica ; Off. de Officiis ; Tusc. Tusculanæ Disputationes ; Senec. de Senectute ; Inv. de Inventione ; Nat. D. de Natura Deorum ; Acad. Academicæ Quæstiones, &c.

Colum. Columella.

Corn. Nep. Cornelius Nepos.

Dio. Dion Cassius.

Diony. Dionysius of Halicarnassus.

Eur. Euripides ; Med. Medea.

Fest. Festus.

Flor. Florus.

Gell. Aulus Gellius.

Herodot. Herodotus.

Hesych. Hesychius.

Hor. Horatius ; Od. Odæ ; Epod. Epodi ; Sat. Satyræ ; Ep. Epistolæ ; Art. P. de Arte Poetica ; Car. Sec. Carmen Seculare.

Juv. Sat. Juvenalis Satyræ.

Lactan. Lactantius.

Liv. Livius.

Luc. Lucanus.

Lucr. Lucretius.

Mart. Martialis.

Ov. Ovidius ; Met. Metamorphoses ; Fast. Fasti ; Trist. Tristia ; Her. Heroides ; Pont. Epistolæ de Ponto ; Art. Am. de Arte Amandi ; Rem. Am. de Remedio Amoris.

Plaut. Plautus ; Amph. Amphitruo ; As. Asinaria ; Aul. Aulularia ; Capt. Captivi ; Curc. Curculio ; Cas. Casina ; Cist. Cistellaria ; Ep. Epidicus ; Bacch. Bacchides ; Most. Mostellaria ; Men. Menæchmi ; Mil. Glor. Miles Gloriosus ; Merc. Mercator ;

Pseud. Pseudolus ; Pœn. Pœnulus ; Pers. Persa ; Rud. Rudens ; Stich. Stichus ; Trin. Trinummus ; Truc. Triuculentus.

Plin. Plinius ; Nat. Hist. Naturalis Historia ; Paneg. Panegyricus ; Ep. Epistolæ.

Plut. Plutarchus.

Sal. Sallustius ; Cat. Bellum Catilinarium ; Jug. Bellum Jugurthinum.

Sen. Seneca ; Nat. Naturales Quæstiones ; Brev. Vit. de Brevitate Vitæ ; Ep. Epistolæ ; Ir. de Ira ; Ben. de Beneficiis ; Herc. Fur. Hercules Furens ; Tranq. An. de Tranquillitate Animi ; Clem. de Clementia ; Prov. de Providentia ; Vit. Beat. de Vita Beata.

Stat. Statius ; Silv. Silvæ ; Theb. Thebais.

Strab. Strabo.

Suet. Suetonius ; Jul. Julius ; Cæs. Cæsar ; Aug. Augustus ; Tib. Tiberius ; Cal. Caligula ; Claud. Claudius ; Ner. Nero ; Gal. Galba ; Oth. Otho ; Vit. Vitellius ; Vesp. Vespasian ; Tit. Titus ; Dom. Domitian.

Tac. Tacitus ; Ann. Annales ; Hist. Historia ; Agric. Agricola ; Mor. Ger. de Moribus Germanorum.

Ter. Terentius ; And. Andria ; Eun. Eunuchus ; Heat. Heautontimorumenos ; Adel. Adelphi ; Phor. Phormio ; Hec. Hecyra.

Theoph. Theophrastus.

Val. Max. Valerius Maximus.

Varr. Varro ; L. L. de Latina Lingua ; R. R. de Re Rustica.

Veget. Vegetius.

Vel. Paterc. Velleius Paterculus.

Virg. Virgilius ; Æn. Æneis ; Geo. Georgica ; Ecl. Eclogæ.

Xenoph. Xenophon ; Cyr. Cyropedia ; Anab. Anabasis.

A SUMMARY

ROMAN ANTIQUITIES.

FOUNDATION OF THE CITY, AND DIVISION OF THE PEOPLE.

Rome was founded by Romulus and a colony from Alba Longa, 753 years, as it is commonly thought, before the birth of Christ. They began to build on the 21st day of April, which was called *Palilia*, from Pales, the goddess of shepherds, to whom it was consecrated, and was ever after held as a festival.[1] *See App. a.*

Romulus divided the people of Rome into three TRIBES: and each tribe into ten CURIÆ. The number of tribes was afterwards increased by degrees to thirty-five. They were divided into country and city tribes.[2] The number of the curiæ always remained the same. Each curia anciently had a chapel or temple for the performance of sacred rites.[3] He who presided over one curia was called CURIO;[4] he who presided over them all, CURIO MAXIMUS.

From each tribe Romulus chose 1000 foot-soldiers, and 100 horse. These 3000 foot and 300 horse were called LEGIO, a legion, because the most warlike were chosen.[5] Hence one of the thousand which each tribe furnished was called MILES.[6] The commander of a tribe was called TRIBUNUS, φυλαρχος vel τριτυαρχος.[7]

The whole territory of Rome, then very small, was also divided into three parts, but not equal. One part was allotted for the service of religion, and for building temples; another, for the king's revenue, and the uses of the state; the third and most considerable part was divided into thirty portions, to answer to the thirty curiæ.[8]

The people were divided into two ranks,[9] PATRICIANS and PLEBIANS; connected together as PATRONS and CLIENTS.[10] In aftertimes a third order was added, namely, the EQUITES.

THE SENATE.

1. INSTITUTION AND NUMBER OF THE SENATE.

The Senate was instituted by Romulus, to be the perpetual council of the republic.[11] It consisted at first only of 100. They were chosen

---

1 dies natalis urbis Romæ. Vell. Pat. l. 8. Ov. F. iv. 806.
2 rusticæ et urbanæ.
3 Var. de Lat. iv. 32.

4 Tac. Ann. xil. 24. Diony. ii. 23.
4 quia sacra curabat, Fes.
5 Put. in Rom.

6 Varro de Lat. iv. 16. unus ex mille, Isid. ix.
8.
7 Diony. ii. 7. Veg. li. 7.
8 Diony. ii. 7.

9 ordines.
10 Diony. ii. 9.
11 Consilium reipublicæ sempiternum. Cic. pro Sex. 65.

from among the patricians ; three were nominated by each tribe, and three
by each curia.[1] To these ninety-nine Romulus himself added one, to preside in the senate, and have the care of the city in his absence. The
senators were called PATRES, either upon account of their age, or their paternal care of the state ; certainly out of respect ;[2] and their offspring, PA-
TRICII.[3] After the Sabines were assumed into the city, another hundred
was chosen from them, by the suffrages of the curiæ.[4] But, according to
Livy, there were only 100 senators at the death of Romulus, and their
number was increased by Tullus Hostilius, after the destruction of Alba.[5]
Tarquinius Priscus, the fifth king of Rome, added 100 more, who were
called PATRES MINORUM GENTIUM. Those created by Romulus, were
called PATRES MAJORUM GENTIUM,[6] and their posterity, *Patricii Majorum
Gentium.* This number of 300 continued, with small variation, to the
times of Sylla, who increased it ; but how many he added is uncertain.
It appears there were at least above 400.[7]

In the time of Julius Cæsar, the number of senators was increased to
900, and after his death to 1000 ; many worthless persons having been admitted into the senate during the civil wars,[8] one of whom is called by
Cicero self-chosen.[9] But Augustus reduced the number to 600.[10]

Such as were chosen into the senate by Brutus, after the expulsion of
Tarquin the Proud, to supply the place of those whom that king had slain,
were called CONSCRIPTI, *i. e.* persons *written* or *enrolled together with* the
old senators, who alone were properly styled *Patres.* Hence the custom
of summoning to the senate those who were *Patres,* and who were *Conscripti.*[11] Hence, also, the name *Patres Conscripti,* (sc. *et*) was afterwards
usually applied to all the senators.

2. CHOOSING OF SENATORS.

PERSONS were chosen into the senate first by the kings,[12] and after their
expulsion, by the CONSULS, and by the military tribunes; but from the year
of the city 310, by the censors : at first only from the patricians, but afterwards also from the plebeians,[13] chiefly, however, from the equites ;
whence that order was called *seminarium senatus.*[14]

Some think that the senate was supplied from the annual magistrates,
chosen by the people, all of whom had, of course, admittance into the
senate ; but that their senatorial character was not esteemed complete, till
they were enrolled by the censors at the next *Lustrum ;* at which time,
also, the most eminent private citizens were added to complete the number.[15]

After the overthrow at the battle of Cannæ, a dictator was created for
choosing the senate. After the subversion of liberty, the emperors conferred the dignity of the senator on whom they thought fit. Augustus created three men to choose the senate, and other three to review the equites,
in place of the censors.[16]

He whose name was first entered in the censor's books, was called PRIN-
CEPS SENATUS, which title used to be given to the person who of those

1 Diony. ii. 12.
2 Liv. i. 8.
3 qui patrem clere pos-
sent, i. e. ingenui. Liv.
x. 6. Diony. ii. 6. Fest.
4 Diony. ii. 47.
5 Liv. i. 17. and 30.

6 Tac. Ann. xi. 25.
7 Cic. ad Att. i. 14.2
8 Dio. xliii. 47. lii. 42.
9 lectus ipse a se. Phil.
xiii. 13.
10 Suet. Aug. 35. Dio.
liv. 14.

11 ita appellabant in no-
vum senatum lectos.
Liv. ii. 1.
12 Senatus legebatur.
Liv. xl. 51. vel in sena-
tum legebantur, Cic.
Clu. 47. Liv. i. 8. 30. 35.

13 Liv. ii. 1. 32. v. 12.
Festus in Prœteriti se-
natores.
14 Liv. xlii. 61.
15 Middleton on Senate.
16 Liv. xxiii. 22. Suet.
Aug. 37. Dio. lv. 13.

alive had been censor first,[1] but after the year 544, to him whom the censors thought most worthy. This dignity, although it conferred no command or emolument, was esteemed the very highest and was usually retained for life.[2] It is called PRINCIPATUS; and hence afterwards the emperor was named *Princeps*, which word properly denotes only rank, and not power.

In choosing senators, regard was had not only to their rank, but also to their age and fortune.—The age at which one might be chosen a senator,[3] is not sufficiently ascertained; although it appears that there was a certain age requisite.[4] Anciently senators seem to have been men advanced in years, as their name imports.[5] But in after times the case was otherwise. It seems probable, however, that the age required for a senator was not below thirty; from certain laws given to foreign nations, at different times, in imitation of the Romans,[6] for there is no positive assertion on this subject in the classics.

The first civil office which gave one admission into the senate was the quæstorship, which some have imagined might be enjoyed at twenty-five, and consequently that one might then be chosen a senator.[7] Others think at twenty-seven, in the authority of Polybius, vi. 17. who says, that the Romans were obliged to serve ten years in the army before they could pretend to any civil magistracy; and as the military age was seventeen, of consequence that one might be made quæstor at twenty-seven. But few obtained that office so early; and Cicero, who often boasts that he had acquired all the honours of the city, without a repulse in any, and each in his proper year,[8] or as soon as he could pretend to it by law, had passed his thirtieth year before he obtained the quæstorship, which he administered the year following in Sicily. So that the usual age of enjoying the quæstorship,[9] and of course of being chosen a senator, in the time of Cicero, seems to have been thirty-one.

But although a person had enjoyed the quæstorship, he did not on that account become a senator, unless he was chosen into that order by the censors.[10] But he had ever after the right of coming into the senate, and of giving his opinion on any question.[11] About this, however, writers are not agreed. It is at least certain, that there were some offices which gave persons a legal title to be chosen into the senate.[12] Hence, perhaps, the senators are sometimes said to have been chosen by the people.[13] And Cicero often in his orations declares, that he owed his seat in the senate, as well as his other honours, to the favour of the people.[14] Persons also procured admission into the senate by military service.[15]

When Sylla, after the destruction occasioned by his civil wars and proscriptions, thought proper to admit into the senate about 300 equites, he allowed the people to give their vote concerning each of them in an assembly by tribes.[16] But Dionysius says, that Sylla supplied the senate with any persons that occurred to him, v. 77. and probably admitted some of the lowest rank.[17]

1 qui primus censor, ex iis qui viverent, fuisset.
2 Liv. xxvii. 13. xxxiv. 44. xxxix. 52.
3 ætas senatoria.
4 Cic. de Lege Manil.
21 Tac. Ann. xv. 28.
5 Sall. Cat. 6. Cic. de

Sen. 6. Ov. F. v. 62. Flor. i. 15.
6 Cic. in Verr. ii. 49. Plin. Ep. x. 83.
7 from Dion Cass. iii. 30.
- 8 suo anno.
9 ætas quæstoria.
10 Gell. iii. 18.
11 Cic. in Verr. v. 14.

Ep. ad. Fam. ii. 7.
12 unde in senatum legi deberent. Liv. xxii. 49.
13 lecti jussu populi. Liv. iv.4.Cic. pro Sext. 65.
14 post red. in Senat. 1. He asserts the same thing in general terms,

in Verr. iv. 11. pro Cluent. 56.
15 Senatorium per militiam auspicabantur gradum. Senec. Ep.47. So Liv. xxiii. 23. .
16 Appian. de bell. civ. vi. 413.
17 Dio. xl. 63.

The *Flamen* of Jupiter had a seat in the senate, in right of his office, a privilege which none of the other priests enjoyed.[1]

Augustus granted to the sons of senators after they assumed the *manly gown*, the right of wearing the *latus clavus*, and of being present at the debates of the senate, that thus they might become the sooner acquainted with public affairs.[2] They also had the privilege of wearing the cresent on their shoes.[3]

No one could be chosen into the senate who had exercised a low trade, or whose father had been a slave :[4] but this was not always observed. Appius Claudius Cæcus first disgraced[5] the senate, by electing into it the sons of freedmen,[6] or the grandsons, according to Suetonius, who says, that *libertini*, in the time of Appius, did not denote those who were freed, but their progeny,[7] a distinction which no where occurs in the classics. Sex. Aur. Victor calls those chosen by Appius, LIBERTINI.[8] But nobody regarded that election, whatever it was, as valid, and the next consuls called the senate in the order of the roll which had been in use before the censorship of Appius.[9] It appears, however, that freedmen were admitted into the senate, at least towards the end of the republic. For Dion Cassius, speaking of the censorship of Appius Claudius, and Piso, the father-in-law of Cæsar, A. U. 704, says that Appius excluded not only all freedmen,[10] but also many noblemen, and among the rest Sallust the historian,[11] for having been engaged in an intrigue with Fausta, the daughter of Sylla, and wife of Milo.[12] Cæsar admitted into the senate not only his officers, but even his mercenary soldiers, all of whom Augustus removed,[13] at which time he was so apprehensive of danger, that when he presided in the senate, he always wore a coat of mail under his robe, and a sword, with ten of the stoutest of his senatorian friends standing round his chair.[14]

In the year of Rome 535, a law was made that no senator, or father of a senator, should keep a bark above the burden of 300 *amphoræ*, or eight tons ; for this was reckoned sufficient to carry their grain from their farms, and it seemed below a senator, to reap advantage by merchandise.[15]

Anciently no regard seems to have been paid to the fortune of a senator,[16] and when it was first fixed does not appear. But in the flourishing state of the republic, as we learn from Seutonius, it behoved every senator to have at least *eight hundred sestertia*, or 800,000 *sestertii*, which are computed to amount to between *six and seven thousand pounds sterling ;* not annually, but for their whole fortune. Augustus raised it to 1200 *sestertia*, and supplied the deficiency to those who had not that sum.[17] Cicero also mentions a certain fortune as requisite in a senator.[18]

Every *lustrum*, i. e. at the end of every fifth year, the senate was reviewed by one of the censors ; and if any one by his behaviour had rendered himself unworthy of that high rank, or had sunk his fortune below that of a senator, his name was passed over by the censor in reading the roll of senators ; and thus he was held to be excluded from the senate.[19] But this, though disgraceful, did not render persons *infamous*, as when they were condemned at a trial ; for the *ignominy* might be removed by

1 Liv. xxvii. 8 Cic. Att. iv. 2.
2 quo celerius reipublicæ assuescerent. Suet. Aug. 38.
3 Stat. Sylv. v. 2. 28.
4 libertino patre natus. Hor. Sat. i. 6. 21. & 44.
5 inquinavit vel deformavit.
6 libertinorum filiis lectis. Liv. ix. 29. 46.
7 ingenuos ex luis procreatos. Suet. Cla. 24.
8 de vir. illust. 34.
9 Liv. ix. 46. ibid. 30.
10 ἀπελευθέροι.
11 Dio. xl. 63.
12 a quo deprehensus, virgis cæsus erat. Gell. xxii. 18. Serv. in Virg. Æn. vi. 612. Acron, in Hor. Sat. i. 2. 41.
13 Dio. xliii. 51. xliii. 20.
xlviii. 22. lii. 25. & 42.
14 Suet. Aug. 35.
15 Liv. xxi. 63. Cic. in Verr. v. 18.
16 census. Plin. xiv. 1.
17 Suet. Aug. 41.
18 Fam. xiii. 5.
19 motus e senatu.

the next censors, or they might obtain offices which again procured them admittance into the senate, as was the cause with C. Antonius, who was consul with Cicero;[1] and with P. Lentulus, who was prætor at the time of Catiline's conspiracy.[2] Thus also Sallust the historian, that he might recover his senatorian dignity, was made prætor by Cæsar,[3] and afterwards governor of Numidia, where he did not act as he wrote,[4] but by rapacity and extortion accumulated a great fortune, which he left to his grand-nephew.[5]

This indulgence of being enrolled in the senate as supernumerary members, without a formal election, was first granted to magistrates by the censors, A. U. 693.[6]

There was a list of the senators,[7] where all their names were written, which, by the appointment of Augustus, used to be annually pasted up in the senate house, and the name of any senator who had been condemned by a judicial sentence, was erased from it.[8]

3. BADGES AND PRIVILEGES OF SENATORS.

THE badges[9] of senators were, 1. The *Latus clavus*, or *Tunica laticlavia*, i. e. a tunic or waistcoat with an oblong broad stripe of purple, like a ribbon, sewed to it on the fore part. It was broad, to distinguish it from that of the equites, who wore a narrow one. 2. Black buskins reaching to the middle of the leg, with the letter C in silver on the top of the foot.[10] Hence *calceos mutare*, to become a senator.[11] 3. A particular place at the public spectacles, called ORCHESTRA, next the stage in the theatre, and next the *arena* in the amphitheatre.[12] This was first granted them by P. Cornelius Scipio the elder, in his consulship, A. U. 558. Hence *Orchestra* is put for the senate itself.[13]

In the games of the circus, the senators sat promiscuously with the other citizens, till the emperor Claudius assigned them peculiar seats there also.[14]

On solemn festivals, when sacrifices were offered to Jupiter by the magistrates,[15] the senators had the sole right of feasting publicly in the Capitol, dressed in their senatorial robes, and such as were proper to the offices which they had borne in the city.[16] When Augustus reduced the number of the senate, he reserved to those who were excluded, the badge of their dress, and the privilege of sitting in the orchestra, and of coming to these public entertainments.[17]

4. ASSEMBLING OF THE SENATE, AND TIME AND PLACE OF ITS MEETING.

THE senate was assembled[18] at first by the kings, after the expulsion of Tarquin, usually by the consuls, and in their absence by the prætors, also by the dictator, master of horse, *decemviri*, military tribunes, *interrex*, prefect of the city, and by the tribunes of the commons, who could summon,

1 Cic. pro Cluent. 42.
2 Dio. xxxviii. 30.
3 Dio. xliii. 52.
4 Ούκ ἐμιμήσατο τῳ ἐργῳ τους λογους. Id. xliii. 9.
5 Tac. Ann. iii. 30. Hor. Od. ii. 2.
6 Dio. xxxvii. 46.

7 album senatorium, Λευκωμα vel ἀναγραφη βουλευτων, 137. Tac. Ann. iv. 42.
8 Dio. lv. 3. et. Frag.
9 insignia.
10 Hor. Sat. i. 6. 28. Juv. vii. 192.

11 Cic. Phil. xiii. 13.
12 Cic. Cluent. 47.
13 Liv. xxxiv. 54. Juv. iii. 177.
14 Suet. Cl. 21. Dio. lx. 7.
15 in epulo Jovis, vel in cœna Diali.

16 Gell. xii. 8. Dio. xlviii. 52. Cic. Phil. ii. 43. Senec. contr. i. 18.
17 publice epulandi jus. Suet. Aug. 35.
18 convocabatur vel cogebatur.

the senate although the consuls were present, and even against their will.[1]
The emperors did not preside in the senate unless when invested with
consular authority.[2]

The senators were summoned[3] anciently by a public officer named VIA-
TOR, because he called the senators from the country,[4] or by a PUBLIC
CRIER, when any thing had happened about which the senators were to
be consulted hastily, and without delay,[5] but in latter times by an EDICT,
appointing the time and place, and published several days before, not only at Rome, but sometimes also in the other cities of Italy.[6] The cause
of assembling it used also to be added.[7]

If any senator refused or neglected to attend, he was punished by a fine
and distraining his goods,[8] unless he had a just excuse.' The fine was
imposed by him who held the senate, and pledges were taken till it was
paid. But after sixty or sixty-five years of age, senators might attend or
not as they pleased.[9]

The senate could not be held but in a temple, that is, in a place consecrated by the augurs, that thus their deliberations might be rendered more
solemn.[10]

Anciently there were but three places where the senate used to be
held;[11] two within the city, and the temple of Bellona without it. Afterwards there were more places, as the temples of Jupiter Stator, Appollo,
Mars, Vulcan, Tellus; of Virtue, Faith, Concord, &c. Also the Curia
Hostilia, Julia, Octavia, and Pompeia; which last was shut up after the
death of Cæsar, because he was slain in it.[12] These curiæ were consecrated as temples by the augurs, but not to any particular deity. When
Hannibal led his army to Rome, the senate was held in the camp of Flaccus the proconsul, betwixt the Porta Collina and Esquilina.[13] When a
report was brought that an ox had spoken, a thing frequently mentioned
in ancient authors, the senate was held under the open air.[14]

On two special occasions the senate was always held without the city, in
the temple of Bellona or of Apollo; for the reception of foreign ambassadors,
especially of those who came from enemies, whom they did not choose to
admit into the city; and to give audience[15] to their own generals, who
were never allowed to come within the walls while in actual command.[16]

The senate met[17] at stated times, on the kalends, nones, and ides of
every month; unless when the comitia were held. For on those days[18]
it was not lawful to hold a senate,[19] nor on unlucky days,[20] unless in dangerous conjunctures, in which case the senate might postpone the comitia.[21]

An ordinary meeting of the senate was called *senatus* LEGITIMUS.[22]
If an extraordinary senate was given to ambassadors or others for any
reason whatever, it used to be called INDICTUS or EDICTUS, and then the
senators were usually summoned by an edict, whereby anciently those

1 Liv. i. 48. Cic. Ep.
Fam. x. 12. 28. Liv. viii.
33. ill. 9. and 29. A.
Gell. xiv. 7. Cic. Ep.
Fam. x. 28. xi. 6. de
Orat. iii. 1. Gell. xiv. 9.
2 princeps præsidebat,
erat enim consul. Plin.
Ep. ii. 11. Paneg. 76.
3 arcessebantur, cita-
bantur, vocabantur, in
senatum vocabantur,
&c.
4 Cic. de. Sen. 16.

5 Liv. iii. 38.
6 Cic. Phil. ill. 8. ad Att.
ix. 17.
7 Consultandum super
re magna et atroci,
Tac. Ann. ii. 28. Edi-
cere senatum in proxi-
mum diem. Edicere ut
senatus adesset, &c.
Cic. et Liv. passim.
8 mulcta et pignoris
captiones.
9 Liv. iii. 38. Cic. Phil.
i. 5. Plin. Ep. iv. 29.

Sen. de Brev. Vitæ. 20.
Controv. i. 8. Plin. Ep.
iv. 23.
10 Gell. xiv. 7. Cic.
Dom. 51.
11 Curiæ v. Senacula.
12 Festus, Suet. Jul. 88.
13 Liv. xxvi. 10.
14 Plin. Hist. viii. 45.
15 cum senatus datus
est.
16 Liv. iii. 63. xxxi. 47.
xxxiii. 22. 24. xxxiv.
43. xxxvi. 39. xlii. 36.

Sen. Benef. v. 15.
17 conveniebat.
18 diebus comitialibus.
19 Cic. ad Frat. ii. 2. ad
Fam. i. 4.
20 diebus nefastis v.
atris.
21 Id. viii. 9. Liv.
xxxviii. 53. xxxix. 39.
Cic. Mur. 25.
22 Suet. Aug. 35.

were ordered to attend who were PATRES, and who were CONSCRIPTI,[1] but afterwards, "those who were senators, and who had a right to deliver their opinion in the senate." Qui senatores, quibusque in senatu sententiam dicere liceret, ut adessent ; and sometimes, ut adessent frequentes, AD VIII. CAL. DECEMBR., &c.[2]

No decree of the senate could be made unless there was a quorum.[3] What that was is uncertain. Before the times of Sylla, it seems to have been 100.[4] Under Augustus it was 400, which, however, that emperor altered[5]. If any one wanted to hinder a decree from being passed, and suspected there was not a quorum, he said to the magistrate presiding, NUMERA SENATUM, Count the senate.[6]

Augustus enacted, that an ordinary meeting of the senate should not be held oftener than twice a month, on the Kalends and Ides ; and in the months of September and October, that only a certain number chosen by lot should attend.[7] This regulation was made under pretext of easing the senators, but in reality with a view to diminish their authority, by giving them less frequent opportunities of exercising it. Augustus chose a council for himself every six months,[8] to consider beforehand what things should be laid before a full house.[9]

The senate met always of course on the first of January, for the inauguration of the new consuls, who entered into their office on that day, and then usually there was a crowded house.—He who had the *fasces* presided, and consulted the fathers, first, about what pertained to religion,[10] about sacrificing to the gods, expiating prodigies, celebrating games, inspecting the books of the sibyls, &c.,[11] next, about human affairs, namely, the raising of armies, the management of wars, the provinces, &c. The consuls were then said to consult the senate about the republic in general,[12] and not about particular things.[13] The same was the case in dangerous junctures, when the senate was consulted about the safety of the republic.[14] The month of February was commonly devoted to hear embassies and the demands of the provinces.[15]

5. MANNER OF HOLDING AND CONSULTING THE SENATE.

THE magistrate, who was to hold the senate, offered a sacrifice, and took the auspices, before he entered the senate-house. If the auspices were not favourable, or not rightly taken, the business was deferred to another day.[16]

Augustus ordered that each senator, before he took his seat, should pay his devotions, with an offering of frankincense and wine, at the altar of that god in whose temple the senate were assembled, that thus they might discharge their duty the more religiously.[17] When the consuls entered the senate-house, the senators commonly rose up to do them honour.[18]

The senate was consulted about every thing pertaining to the administration of the state, except the creation of magistrates, the passing of laws, and the determination of war and peace ; all which properly belonged to

1 Liv. ii. 1.
2 Cic. et Liv. passim.
3 nisi senatorum numerus legitimus adesset.
4 Liv. xxxix. 18.
5 Dio. liv. 35. lv. 3.
6 Cic. Ep. Fam. viii. 11.

Festus in Numera.
7 Suet. Aug. 35.
8 consilia semestria sortiri.
9 ad frequentem senatum, Suet. Aug. 35.
10 de rebus divinis.

11 Liv. viii. 8.
12 de republica indefinite.
13 de rebus singulis finite. Aul. Gell. xiv. 7.
14 de summa republica, v. tota. Cic. passim.

15 Cic. ad Fratr. ii. 3. 12. ad Fam. i. 4. Ascon. in Verr. i. 35.
16 Plin. Pan. 76. Gell. xiv. 7. Cic. Epist. x. 12.
17 Suet. Aug. 35.
18 Cic. Pis. 12.

the whole Roman people. The senate could not determine about the rights of Roman citizens without the order of the people.[1]

When a full house was assembled, the magistrate presiding, whether consul or prætor, &c., laid the business before them in a set form; QUOD BONUM, FAUSTUM, FELIX, FORTUNATUM SIT; REFERIMUS AD VOS, PATRES CONSCRIPTI. Then, the senators were asked their opinion in this form: DIC, SP. POSTHUMI, QUID CENSES?[2] or QUID FIERI PLACET? QUID TIBI VIDETUR?

In asking the opinions of the senators, the same order was not always observed; but usually the *princeps senatus* was first desired to deliver his opinion, unless where there were consuls elect, who were always asked first, and then the rest of the senators according to their dignity, *consulares, prætorii, ædilitii, tribunitii,* et *quæstorii,* which is also thought to have been their order in sitting.[3] The benches on which the senators sat, were probably of a long form, as that mentioned by Juvenal *longa cathedra,* ix. 52. and distinct from one another, each fit to hold all the senators of a particular description; some of them shorter, as those of the tribunes, which seem to have held only a single person.[4] The consuls sat in the most distinguished place, on their curule chairs.[5]

As the consuls elect were first asked their opinion, so the prætors, tribunes, &c. elect, seem to have had the same preference before the rest of their order. He who held the senate might ask first any one of the same order he thought proper, which he did from respect or friendship.[6] Senators were sometimes asked their opinions by private persons.[7]

The consuls used to retain through the whole year the same order which they had observed in the beginning of their office. But in later times, especially under the emperors, they were asked in what order the magistrate who presided thought proper.[8] When they were all asked their opinions, they were said *perrogari,* and the senate to be regularly consulted or the affair to be deliberated about, *ordine consuli.*[9] Augustus observed no certain rule in asking the opinions of the senators, that thereby they might be rendered the more attentive.[10]

Nothing could be laid before the senate against the will of the consuls, unless by the tribunes of the people, who might also give their negative[11] against any decree, by the solemn word VETO; which was called *interceding.*[12] This might also be done by all who had an equal or greater authority than the magistrate presiding. If any person interceded, the sentence of the senate was called SENATUS AUCTORITAS, their judgment or opinion,[13] and not *senatus consultum* or *decretum,* their command. So likewise it was, named, if the senate was held at an improper time or place,[14] or if all the formalities[15] were not observed, in which case the matter was referred to the people, or was afterwards confirmed by a formal decree of the senate.[16] But when no mention is made of intercession or informality, *auctoritas senatus* is the same with *cousultum.*[17] They are sometimes also joined; thus, *senatus consulti auctoritas,* which was the usual inscription of the decrees of the senate, and marked with these initial letters, S. C. A.[18]

1 Diony. ii. 14. Liv. xxvi. 33.
2 Liv. i. 32. ix. 8.
3 Sal. Cat. 50. Cic. Phil. v. 13. Fam. viii. 4.
4 subsellia. Cic. Cat. i. 7 Cic. Fam. iii. 9 Suet. Claud. 23.
5 Cic. Ib. & Cat. iv. 1.

6 Cic. ad Att. xii. 21. in Verr. v. 14. Cic. post redit. in Senat. 7. Liv. v. 20. Gell. iv. 10. xiv. 7.
7 multi rogabantur, atque idipsum consulibus invitis. Cic. Fam. i. 2.
8 Suet. Jul. 21. Cic. Att.

i. 13 Plin. Ep. ix. 13.
9 Liv. xxix. 16. ii. 28. and 29. Plin. Pan. 60.
10 Suet. Aug. 35.
11 moram facere.
12 intercedere.
13 Cic. Legg. iii. 3. Gell. xiv. 7. Liv. iv. 57. Cic. Fam. i. 2. viii. 8.

14 alieno tempore aut loco.
15 solemnia.
16 Dio. iv. 3. Cic. Ep. Fam. x. 12.
17 Cic. Legg. ii. 15.
18 Cic.

The senators delivered their opinion,[1] standing ; whence one was said to be raised,[2] when he was ordered to give his opinion. But when they only assented to the opinion of another, they continued sitting.[3] The principal senators might likewise give their opinion about any other thing, besides what was proposed, which they thought of advantage to the state, and require that the consul would lay it before the senate ; which Tacitus calls, *egredi relationem.* They were then said CENSERE *referendum de aliqua re,* or *relationem postulare.*[4] For no private senator, not even the consul-elect, was allowed to propose to the senate any question himself. Sometimes the whole house called out for a particular motion.[5] And if the consul hesitated or refused, which he did by saying, SE CONSIDERARE VELLE, the other magistrates, who had the right of holding the senate, might do it, even against his will, particularly the tribunes of the people.[6] Hence Augustus was, by a decree of the senate, invested with the power of tribune for life, that he might lay any one thing he pleased before the senate every meeting, although he was not consul.[7] And the succeeding emperors obtained from the senate the right of laying before them one, two, or more things at the same meeting ; which was called *jus primæ, secundæ, tertiæ, quartæ, et quintæ relationis.* In those times the senator who gave his opinion first, was called *primæ sententiæ senator.*[8]

It was not lawful for the consuls to interrupt those that spoke, although they introduced in their speech many things foreign to the subject ; which they sometimes did, that they might waste the day in speaking.[9] For no new reference could be made after the tenth hour, i. e. four o'clock afternoon according to our manner of reckoning, nor a decree passed after sunset.[10] Hence Cicero, in blaming the decrees of Antony, calls them SCTA VESPERTINA.[11] We read, however, of the senate's being assembled at midnight, upon the arrival of an express from one of the consuls, Sp. Furius, that he was besieged by the Æqui and Volsci, A. U. 290,[12] and of a person haranguing till it was so late that lights were called for.[13]

Those who grossly abused this right of speaking without interruption, were sometimes forced to give over speaking,[14] by the noise and clamor of the other senators.[15] Sometimes magistrates, when they made a disagreeable motion, were silenced in this manner.[16] So when a senator threw out abusive language against any one, as Catiline did against Cicero and others, the whole senate bawled out against him.[17]

This used also to happen under the emperors. Thus Pliny, speaking of himself, after the death of Domitian, says, *Finio. Incipit respondere Vejento ; nemo patitur ; obturbatur, obstrepitur ; adeo quidem ut diceret ;* ROGO, PATRES C., NE ME COGATIS IMPLORARE AUXILIUM TRIBUNORUM. *Et statim Murena tribunus,* PERMITTO TIBI, VIR CLARISSIME, VEJENTO, DICERE. *Tunc quoque, reclamatur.*[18] The title of CLARISSIMUS was at this time given to all the senators, but formerly only to the leading men.

1 sententiam dicebant.
2, excitari. Liv. ix. 6. Cic. ad Attic. i. 13.
3 verbo assentiebantur. Cic. Fam. v. 2. Plin. Pan. 76.
4 Sall. Cat. 50. Plin. Ep. vi. 5. Tac. Ann. xiii. 49.
5 Cic. pro Dom. 27. Sall. Cat. 48.
6 Cic. pro Leg. Manil. 19. pro Sext. 30. Epist. Fam. x. 16.
7 Dio. liii. 32.

8 Vopisc. et Capitol.
9 ut diem dicendo exi-merent, consumerent, v. tollerent. Cic. Verr. ii. 39.
10 Sen. Tranq. An. c. ult. A. Gell. xiv. 7.
11 Phil. iii. 10.
12 Diony. ix. 63. so iii. 26.
13 nocte illatis lucernis, Plin. Ep. iv. 9.
14 perorare. :
15 Cic. ad Att. iv. 2.
16 Thus, Cœptum est

referri de inducendo scto, i. e. delendo vel expungendo ; ab omni senatu reclamatum est. Cic. pro Dom. 4. Ejus orationi vehementer ab omnibus reclamatum est, Id. Fam. i. 2.
17 obstrepere omnes. Sall. Cat. 3L
18 Ep. ix. 13. "After I had finished, Vejento attempted to reply : but the general cla-

mour raised against him not permitting him to go on, 'I hope, my lords,' said he, ' you will not oblige me to implore the assistance of the tribunes.' Immediately the tribune Murena cried out, ' you have my leave, most illustrious Vejento, to proceed.' But still the clamour was renewed."

Sometimes the speeches of senators were received with shouts of applause. And the most extravagant expressions of approbation were bestowed on the speakers.[1]

The consul, or presiding magistrate, seems to have exercised different powers in the senate at different times.[2] When Cato one day, to prevent a decree from being passed, attempted to waste the day in speaking, Cæsar, then consul, ordered him to be led to prison, whereupon the house rose to follow him, which made Cæsar recall his order.[3]

If any one in delivering his opinion had included several distinct articles, some of which might be approved and others rejected, it was usual to require that the opinion might be divided, and that each particular might be proposed apart ; and therefore any senator might say, DIVIDE.[4]

In matters of very great importance, the senators sometimes delivered their opinions upon oath.[5]

Several different questions might be referred to the senate by different magistrates in the same meeting.[6]

When any magistrate made a motion, he was said VERBA FACERE ; REFERRE vel DEFERRE AD SENATUM, or CONSULERE SENATUM DE ALIQUA RE ; and the senators, if they approved of it, RELATIONEM ACCIPERE.[7]

When different opinions were delivered, the senators expressed their assent, some to one and some to another, variously, by their looks, nodding with their heads, stretching out their hands, &c.[8]

The senators who spoke usually addressed themselves to the whole house, by the title of PATRES CONSCRIPTI ; sometimes to the consul or person who presided, sometimes to both.[9] They commonly concluded their speeches in a certain form : QUARE EGO ITA CENSEO ; or, PLACET IGITUR, &c.[10] QUOD C. PANSA VERBA FECIT DE—DE EA RE ITA CENSEO ; or QUÆ CUM ITA SINT ; or QUAS OB RES, ITA CENSEO.[11] Sometimes they used to read their opinion,[12] and a decree of the senate was made according to it.[13]

When a senator did not give an entire assent to the opinion of any one, but thought that something should be added, he said, SERVILIO ASSENTIOR, ET HOC AMPLIUS CENSEO ; which was called, addere sententiæ vel in sententiam.[14]

6. MANNER OF MAKING A DECREE OF THE SENATE.

WHEN several different opinions had been offered, and each supported by a number of senators, the consul or magistrate presiding might first put to the vote which opinion he pleased,[15] or suppress altogether what he disapproved.[16] And herein consisted the chief power of the consul in the senate. But even this was sometimes contested by the tribunes.[17]

A decree of the senate was made by a separation[18] of the senators to

1 Thus, Consurgenti ad censendum acclamatum est, quod solet residentibus, Plin. Ep. iv. 9. Non fere quisquam in senatu fuit, qui non me complecteretur, exoscularetur, certatimque laude cumularet, Id. ix. 13.
2 Cic. Orat. iii. 1.
3 Gell. iv. 10.

4 Cic. Fam 1.2. Senec. Ep. 21. Ascon. in Cic. Mil. 6.
5 jurati, Liv. xxvi. 33. xxx. 40. xlii. 21. Tac. Ann. iv. 21.
6 Cic. Phil. vii. 1 Liv. xxx. 21.
7 Cic. in Pis. 13. Liv. ii. 39.
8 Tac. Hist. iv. 4.
9 Cic. et Liv. passim.

Cic. Phil. viii. 1. Liv. vi. 15.
10 Sall. Cat. ii. 52.
11 Cic. Phil. iii. 15. v. 4. ix. 7.
12 de scripto dicere, Cic. Fam. x. 13.
13 in sententiam alicujus, vel ita ut ille censebat.
14 Cic. Phil. xiii. 21. Sall. Cat. 51.

15 sententiam primam pronunciare, ut in eam discessio fieret, Cic. Fam. i. 2. x. 12.
16 negare se pronunciaturum, Cæs. Bell. Civ. i. 1.
17 ante se opportere discessionem facere, quam consules, Cic. Fam. i. 2.
18 per discessionem.

different parts of the house. He who presided said, "Let those who are of such an opinion pass over to that side ; those who think differently, to this."[1] Hence *ire pedibus in sententiam alicujus*, to agree to any one's opinion ; and *discedere* v. *transire in alia omnia*, for *contrarium sentire*.[2] *Frequentes ierunt in alia omnia*, a great majority went into the contrary opinion. *Frequens senatus in alia omnia iit, discessit*.[3] The phrase QUI ALIA OMNIA, was used instead of QUI NON CENSETIS, sc. *hoc*, from a motive of superstition.[4]

Those senators who only voted, but did not speak, or, as some say, who had the right of voting but not of speaking, were called PEDARII,[5] because they signified their opinion by their feet, and not by their tongues : or, according to others, because not having borne a curule magistracy, they went to the senate on foot.[6] But, according to Pliny, anciently all the senators went to the senate on foot ; and the privilege of being carried thither in a chariot was never granted to any one but Metellus, who had lost his sight in rescuing the *Palladium*, or image of Pallas, from the temple of Vesta when in flames.[7]

He who had first proposed the opinion,[8] or who had been the principal speaker in favour of it, the consul, or whoever it was,[9] passed over first, and those who agreed with him followed.[10] Those who differed went to a different part of the house ; and into whatever part most of the senators went, the consul said of it, "This seems to be the majority."[11] Then a decree of the senate was made according to their opinion,[12] and the names of those who had been most keen for the decree, were usually prefixed to it, which were called AUCTORITATES *perscriptæ* vel *præscriptæ*, because they stayed to see the decree made out.[13] *Senatus consultum ea perscriptione est*, of that form, to that effect.[14]

Anciently the letter T was subscribed, if the tribunes did not give their negative ; for at first the tribunes were not admitted into the senate, but sat before the senate-house on benches, till the decrees of the senate were brought to them for their approbation or rejection.[15] This, however, was the case only for a very short time ; for A. U. 310, we find Canuleius, one of their number, speaking in the senate, and Dionysius says they were admitted soon after their institution.[16]

When a decree of the senate was made, without any opinions being asked or given, the fathers were said, *pedibus ferre sententiam ;* and the decree was called SENATUS CONSULTUM PER DISCESSIONEM.[17] But when the opinions of the senators were asked, it was simply called SENATUS CONSULTUM.[18] Although it was then also made *per discessionem ;* and if the senate was unanimous, the *discessio* was said to be made *sine ulla varietate*. If the contrary, *in magna varietate sententiarum*.[19]

In decreeing a supplication to any general, the opinions of the senators were always asked ; hence Cicero blames Antony for omitting this, in the case of Lepidus.[20] Before the vote was put,[21] and while the debate was going on, the members used to take their seats near that person whose

1 qui hoc censetis, illuc transite, qui alia omnia, in hanc partem.
2 Plin. Ep. viii. 14.
3 Cic. Fam. i. 2. viii. 13. x. 12.
4 ominis causa, Fest.
5 Fest. A. Gell. iii. 18. Cic. ad Att. i. 19, 20.
6 A. Gell. iii. 18.

7 Hist.' Nat. vii. 43. s. 45.
8 qui sententiam senatui præstitisset, Cic. in Pis. 32.
9 princeps vel auctor sententiæ, Ov. Pont. ii. 3. 31.
10 Plin. Ep. ii. 11.
11 hæc pars major videtur.
12 Plin. Ep. ii 12. Cic. Or. iii. 2.
13 scribendo adfuerunt, i. e. senatus consulti conficiendi testes erant.
14 Cic. Fam. v. 2.
15 Val. Max. ii. 7.
16 Liv. iv. 1. Diony. vii. 49.

17 A. Gell. xiv. 7. Cic. Phil. iii. 9. Suet. Tib. 31.
18 Cic. in Pis. 6.
19 Cic. pro Sext. 34.
20 Phil. iii. 9.
21 ante discessionem factam.

opinion they approved, and the opinion of him who was joined by the greatest number, was called SENTENTIA MAXIME FREQUENS.[1]

Sometimes the consul brought from home in writing the decree which he wished to be passed, and the senate readily agreed to it.[2]

When secrecy was necessary, the clerks and other attendants were not admitted; but what passed was written out by some of the senators.[3] A decree made in this manner was called TACITUM.[4] Some think the *senatores pedarii* were then likewise excluded.[5]

Julius Cæsar, when consul, appointed that what was done in the senate, should be published, which also seems to have been done formerly.[6] But this was prohibited by Augustus.[7] An account of their proceedings, however, was always made out; and under the succeeding emperors we find some senator chosen for this purpose.[8]

Public registers[9] were also kept of what was done in the assemblies of the people, and courts of justice; also of births and funerals, of marriages and divorces, &c., which served as a fund of information for historians; hence DIURNA URBIS ACTA,[10] ACTA POPULI,[11] ACTA PUBLICA,[12] URBANA, usually called by the simple name ACTA.[13]

SENATUS CONSULTUM and DECRETUM are used promiscuously to denote what the senate decreed;[14] but they were also distinguished as a genus and species, decretum being sometimes put for a part of the SCTUM, as when a province, an honour, or a supplication was decreed to any one.[15] Decretum is likewise applied to others besides the senate; as *decreta consulum, augurum, pontificum, decurionum, Cæsaris, principis, judicis,* &c. so likewise consulta, but more rarely; as, *consulta sapientum,* the maxims or opinions, *consulta belli,* determinations, *Gracchi.*[16]

In writing a decree of the senate, the time and place were put first, then the names of those who were present at the engrossing of it; after that the motion, with the name of the magistrate who proposed it; to all which was subjoined what the senate decreed. Thus, SENATUS CONSULTI AUCTORITAS, PRIDIE KAL. OCTOB. IN ÆDE APOLLINIS, SCRIBENDO ADFUERUNT, L. DOMITIUS, &c. QUOD M. MARCELLUS, COS. VERBA FECIT DE PROVINCIIS CONSULARIBUS, DE EA RE ITA CENSUIT, V. CENSUERUNT, UTI, &c.[17] Hence we read, DE EA RE SENATUS CONSULTUS ITA CENSUIT, DECREVIT; also PLACERE SENATUI; SENATUM VELLE ET ÆQUUM CENSERE; SENATUM EXISTIMARE, ARBITRARI, ET JUDICARE; VIDERI SENATUI.[18]

If the tribunes interposed, it was thus marked at the end; HUIC SENATUS CONSULTO INTERCESSIT C. CŒLIUS, C. PANSA, TRIB. PLEB. Sometimes the tribunes did not actually interpose, but required some time to consider of it, and thus the matter was delayed.[19]

When the senate ordered any thing to be done, these words were commonly added, PRIMO QUOQUE TEMPORE, as soon as possible. When they praised the actions of any persons, they decreed, EOS RECTE, ATQUE ORDINE VIDERI FECISSE, if the contrary, EOS CONTRA REMPUBLICAM FECISSE VIDERI.[20]

---

1 Plin. Ep. viii. 14. ii. 11.
2 Cic. Phil. i. 1.
3 Cic. pro Sull. 14.
4 Capitolin. Gordian. 12.
5 from Valer. Max. ii. 2.
6 Diurna Acta. Suet. Jul. 20. Cic. pro Sull. 14.

7 Suet. Aug. 36.
8 Actis vel commentariis senatus conficiendis. Tac. Ann. v. 4.
9 acta, i. e. tabulæ vel commentarii.
10 Tac. Ann. xiii. 31.
11 Suet. Jul. 20.
12 Tac. Ann. xii. 24.

Suet. Tib. v. Plin. Ep. vii. 33.
13 Id. ix. 15. Cic. Fam. xii. 8. Plin. vii. 54.
14 Cic. Liv. et Sall. passim. so consulta et decreta patrum, Hor.
15 Fest.
16 Cic. Legg. i. 34. Sil.

iv. 35. vii. 34.
17 Cic. Fam. viii. 6.
18 Cic. Liv. Sall. &c. passim.
19 Cic. ibid. pro Sext. 34.
20 Liv. passim.

Orders were given to the consuls,[1] not in an absolute manner, but with some exception ; SI VIDERETUR, SI E REPUBLICA ESSE DUCERENT, QUOD COMMODO REIPUBLICÆ FIERI POSSET, UT CONSULES ALTER, AMBOVE, SI EIS VIDEATUR, AD BELLUM PROFICISCERENTUR.[2] When the consuls obeyed the orders of the senate, they were said ESSE vel FORE IN PATRUM POTESTATE ; and the senators, when they complied with the desires of the people, ESSE IN POPULI POTESTATE.[3]

When the senate asked any thing from the tribunes, the form was, SENATUS CENSUIT, UT CUM TRIBUNIS AGERETUR.[4]

The decrees of the senate, when written out, were laid up in the treasury,[5] where also the laws and other writings pertaining to the republic were kept. Anciently they were kept by the ædiles in the temple of Ceres.[6] The place where the public records were kept was called TABULARIUM. The decrees of the senate concerning the honours conferred on Cæsar were inscribed in golden letters on columns of silver.[7] Several decrees of the senate still exist, engraven on tables of brass ; particularly that recorded, Liv. xxxix. 19.

The decrees of the senate, when not carried to the treasury, were reckoned invalid.[8] Hence it was ordained, under Tiberius, that the decrees of the senate, especially concerning the capital punishment of any one, should not be carried to the treasury before the tenth day, that the emperor, if absent from the city, might have an opportunity of considering them, and, if he thought proper, of mitigating them.[9]

Before the year of the city 306, the decrees of the senate were suppressed or altered at the pleasure of the consuls. Cicero accuses Antony of forging decrees.[10]

Decrees of the senate were rarely reversed. While a question was under debate,[11] every one was at freedom to express his dissent ;[12] but when it was once determined,[13] it was looked upon as the common concern of each member to support the opinion of the majority.[14]

After every thing was finished, the magistrates presiding dismissed the senate by a set form : NON AMPLIUS VOS MORAMUR, P. C. or, NEMO VOS TENET ; NIHIL VOS MORAMUR ; CONSUL, CITATIS NOMINIBUS, ET PERACTA DICESSIONE, MITTIT SENATUM.[15]

7. POWER OF THE SENATE AT DIFFERENT PERIODS.

THE power of the senate was different at different times. Under the regal government, the senate deliberated upon such public affairs as the king proposed to them ; and the kings were said to act according to their counsel,[16] as the consuls did afterwards according to their decree.[17]

Tarquin the Proud dropped the custom handed down from his predecessors, of consulting the senate about every thing ; banished or put to death the chief men of that order, and chose no others in their room.[18] But this king was expelled from the throne for his tyranny, and the regal government abolished, A. U. 243.

After this the power of the senate was raised to the highest. Every

1 negotium datum est consulibus.
2 Liv. Cæs. Cic.
3 Liv. ii. 56. &c.
4 Liv. xxvi. 33. xxx. 41.
5 in ærarium condebantur.

6 Liv. iii. 9, 55.
7 Dio. xliv. 7.
8 Suet. Aug. 94.
9 Tac. Ann. iii. 51. Dio. Ivii. 20. Suet. Tib. 75.
10 Liv. iii. 55. Cic. Phil. v. 4.

11 re integra.
12 contradicere vel dissentire.
13 re peracta.
14 quod pluribus placuisset, cunctis tuendum, Plin. Ep. vi. 13.

15 Plin. Ep. ix. 13.
16 ex consilio patrum, Liv. i. 9.
17 ex scto. Liv. ii. 2. &c.
18 Liv. i. 49.

thing was done by its authority. The magistrates were in a manner only its ministers ;[1] no law could be passed, nor assembly of the people held, without their consent.[2]   But when the patricians began to abuse their power, and to exercise cruelties on the plebeians, especially after the death of Tarquin, A. U. 257, the multitude took arms in their own defence, made a secession from the city, seized on Mons Sacer, and created tribunes for themselves, who attacked the authority of the senate, and in process of time greatly diminished it by various means ; first, by the introduction of the comitia tributa, and the exclusion of the patricians from them ;[3] then, by a law, made by Prætorius, the tribune, that the plebian magistrates should be created at the comitia tributa ;[4] afterwards, by a law passed at the comitia centuriata, by the consuls Horatius and Valerius, that the laws passed at the comitia tributa should also bind the patricians ;[5] and lastly, by the law of Publilius the dictator, A. U. 414, and of Mœnius the tribune, A. U. 467,[6] that before the people gave their votes, the fathers should authorise whatever the people should determine at the comitia centuriatia.[7]   Whereas, formerly, whatever the people ordered was not ratified unless the senators confirmed it.[8]   But the power of the senate was most of all abridged by the right of the tribunes to render the decrees of the senate of no effect by their negative.[9]   Still, however, the authority of the senate continued to be very great ; for as power and majesty properly belonged to the people, so did authority, splendour, and dignity to the senate.[10]

The senatorian order is called by Cicero, " ordo amplissimus et sanctissimus ; summum populi Romani, populorumque et gentium omnium ac regum consilium :"[11] and the senate-house, "templum sanctitatis, amplitudinis, mentis consilii publici, caput urbis, ara sociorum, portus omnium gentium," &c.[12]   Hence, senators in foreign countries were treated with the highest respect ;[13] and as they were not allowed to leave Italy without permission, unless to Sicily and Gallia Narbonensis,[14] when they had occasion to travel abroad, they usually obtained the privilege of a free legation, as it was usually called,[15] which gave them a right to be treated every where with the honours of an ambassador.   In the provinces they had lictors to attend them ; and if they had any lawsuit there, they might require that it should be remitted to Rome.[16]   The advantages of honour and respect were the only compensation which senators received for their attention to public affairs.[17]

Although the supreme power at Rome belonged to the people, yet they seldom enacted any thing without the authority of the senate.   In all weighty affairs, the method usually observed was, that the senate should first deliberate and decree, and then the people order.[18]   But there were many things of great importance, which the senate always determined itself, unless when they were brought before the people by the interces-

---

1 quasi ministri gravissimi concilii, Cic. pro Sext. 65.
2 nisi patribus auctoribus, h. e. jubentibus v. permittentibus, Liv. vi. 42.
3 Liv. ii. 60.
4 Liv. ii. 56, 57. Diony. ix. 49.
5 plebiscita, Liv. iii. 55.
6 Liv. viii. 12. Cic. Brut. 14.

7 ut fierent auctores ejus rei quam populus jussurus esset, v. in incertum eventum comitiorum, Liv.
8 nisi patres auctores fierent, Liv. i. 17. 22. iv. 3. 49. Cic. Planc. 3.
9 intercedendo.
10 potestas in populo, auctoritas in senatu, Cic. Legg. iii. 12. locus, auctoritas, domi splen-

dor ; apud exteras nationes nomen et gratia, Id. pro. Clu. 56.
11 Dom. 28.
12 Mil. 33.
13 Cic. Verr. iv. 11.
14 sine commeatu, Cic. Att. viii. 15. Suet. Claud. 16. 23. Ner. 25. Dio. liii. 42.
15 sine mandatis, sine ullo reipublicæ munere ; ut hæreditates

aut syngraphas suas persequerentur, Cic. Legg. iii. 8. Fam. xi. 1. Att. xv. 12. Suet. Tib. 31.
16 Cic. Fam. xii. 21. xiii. 26.
17 Cic. Clu. 55.
18 senatus censuit v. decrevit, populus jussit, Liv. i. 17. iv. 49. x. 12. 45. xxxvii. 55. &c.

sioes of the tribunes. This right the senate seems to have had, not from any express law, but by the custom of their ancestors.[1]

1. The senate assumed to themselves the guardianship of the public religion ; so that no new god could be introduced, nor altar erected, nor the sibylline books consulted, without their order.[2] 2. The senate had the direction of the treasury, and distributed the public money at pleasure.[3] They appointed stipends to their generals and officers, and provisions and clothing to their armies.[4] 3. They settled the provinces, which were annually assigned to the consuls and prætors, and when it seemed fit they prolonged their command.[5] 4. They nominated out of their own body all ambassadors sent from Rome,[6] and gave to foreign ambassadors what answers they thought proper.[7] 5. They decreed all public thanksgivings for victories obtained ; and conferred the honour of an ovation or triumph, with the title of IMPERATOR, on their victorious generals.[8] 6. They could decree the title of king to any prince whom they pleased, and declare any one an enemy by a vote.[9] 7. They inquired into public crimes or treasons, either in Rome or the other parts of Italy, and heard and determined all disputes among the allied and dependent cities.[10] 8. They exercised a power, not only of interpreting the laws, but of absolving men from the obligation of them, and even of abrogating them.[11] 9. They could postpone the assemblies of the people, and prescribe a change of habit to the city in cases of any imminent danger or calamity.[12]

But the power of the senate was chiefly conspicuous in civil dissensions or dangerous tumults within the city, in which that solemn decree used to be passed, " That the consuls should take care that the public should receive no harm."[13] By which decree an absolute power was granted to the consuls, to punish and put to death whom they pleased, without a trial ; to raise forces, and carry on war without the order of the people.[14] This decree was called ULTIMUM or EXTREMUM, and "forma SCTI ultimæ necessitatis."[15] By it the republic was said to be intrusted to the consuls.[16] Sometimes the other magistrates were added.[17] Sometimes only one of the consuls is named, as in the commotion raised by C. Gracchus, " ut L. Opimius consul videret," &c. because his colleague Q. Fabius Maximus was absent.[18]

Although the decrees of the senate had not properly the force of laws, and took place chiefly in those matters which were not provided for by the laws ; yet they were understood always to have a binding force, and were therefore obeyed by all orders. The consuls themselves were obliged to submit to them.[19] They could be annulled or cancelled only by the senate itself.[20] Their force, however, in certain things was but temporary ; and the magistrates sometimes alleged, that they were binding but for one year.[21] In the last age of the republic, the authority of the senate was little regarded by the leading men and their creatures, who, by means of bribery, obtained from a corrupted populace what they de-

1 Cic. Or. i. 52.
2 Liv. ix. 45. Cic. Div. 48. 54.
3 Cic. Vat. 15. Liv. xxxvii. 54.
4 Polyb. vi. 11.
5 Cic. Dom. 9.
6 Liv. il. 15. xxx. 26. xlii. 19. et alibi passim.
7 Cic. Vat. 15. Dom. 9. Liv. vi. 26. vii. 20.

xxx. 17.
8 Cic. Phil. xiv. 4. 5. Liv. v. 23. Polyb. vi.11.
9 Cæs. Liv. Cic. passim.
10 Liv. xxx. 26. Cic. Off. i. 10. Polyb. vi. 11.
11 Cic. Dom.16. 27. Leg. Manil. 21. Legg. ii. 6. Ascon. Cic. Cornel. Plin. Ep. iv. 9.

12 Cic. Mur. 25. Att. iv. 16. Cic. Sext. 12.
13 ut consules darent operam, ne quid detrimenti respublica capere t.
14 Sall. Bell. Cat. 29.
15 Cæs. Bell. Civ. i. 4. Liv. iii. 4.
16 permitti v. commendari consulibus ; or,

permitti consulibus ut rempublicam defenderent, Cic.
17 Cæs. ibid. Liv. vi. 19.
18 Cic. Cat. i. 2. Liv. iii. 4.
19 Liv. iv. 26. xlii. 21.
20 induci, i. e. deleri, poterant. Cic. Dom. i. Att. i. 17.
21 Diony. ix. 37.

sired, in spite of the senate.[1] · Thus Cæsar, by the Vatinian law, obtained the province of Cisalpine Gaul and Illyricum, for five years, from the people ; and soon after Gallia Comata or Ulterior, from the senate ; the fathers being afraid that, if they refused it, the people would grant him that too.[2] But this corruption and contempt of the senate at last terminated in the total subversion of public liberty.

Cicero imagined, that in his consulship, he had established the authority of the senate on a solid basis, by uniting it with the equestrian order ; thus constituting what he calls OPTIMA RESPUBLICA; and ascribes the ruin of the republic to that coalition not being preserved.[3] But it was soon after broken,[4] by the senate refusing to release the equites from a disadvantageous contract concerning the Asiatic revenues,[5] which gave Cæsar, when consul, an opportunity of obliging that order, by granting their request, as he had formerly obliged the populace by an agrarian law, and thus of artfully employing the wealth of the republic to enslave it.[6] See LEGES JULIÆ. The senate and equites had been formerly united,[7] and were afterwards disjoined from similar motives. See LEGES SEMPRONIÆ, de judiciis.

Augustus, when he become master of the empire, retained the forms of the ancient republic, and the same names of the magistrates ; but left nothing of the ancient virtue and liberty.[8] While he pretended always to act by the authority of the senate, he artfully drew every thing to himself.

Tiberius apparently increased the power of the senate, by transferring the right of creating magistrates and enacting laws from the comitia to the senate.[9] In consequence of which, the decrees of the senate obtained the force of laws, and were more frequently published. But this was only a shadow of power. For the senators in giving their opinions depended entirely on the will of the prince ; and it was necessary that their decrees should be confirmed by him. An oration of the emperor was usually prefixed to them, which was not always delivered by himself, but was usually read by one of the quæstors, who were called CANDIDATI.[10] Hence what was appointed by the decrees of the senate was said to be orationes principis cautum ; and these orations are sometimes put for the decrees of the senate. To such a height did the flattery of the senators proceed, that they used to receive these speeches with loud acclamations, and never failed to assent to them ; which they commonly did by crying out OMNES, OMNES.[11]

The messages of the emperors to the senate were called EPISTOLÆ or LIBELLI ; because they were folded in the form of a letter or little book. J. Cæsar is said to have first introduced these libelli, which afterwards came to be used almost on every occasion.[12]

But the custom of referring every thing to the senate[13] was only observed till the Romans became habituated to slavery. After this, the emperors gradually began to order what they thought proper, without consulting the senate ; to abrogate old laws and introduce new ones ; and, in short, to determine every thing according to their own pleasure ; by

1 Cic. Sext. 12. App. Bell. Civ. ii. 433, &c.
2 Suet. Jul. 12. Plut. Cæs.
3 Cic. Cat. iv. 10. Pis. 3. quæ sit in potestatem optimorum, i. e.
nobilium et ditissimorum. Legg. iii. 17. ἀριστοκρατεια. Att. i.14. 16.
4 ordinum concordia disjuncta est, Cic. Att. i. 13.
5 Cic. Att. i. 17.
6 Suet. Cæs. 20. Cic. Att. i. 15. Dio. xxxviii. i. 7.
7 Sall. Jug. 42.
8 prisci et integri moris, Tac. Ann. i. 3.
9 Tac. Ann. i. 15.
10 Suet. Tit. 6. Aug. 65.
11 Plin. Pan. 75. Vopisc. Tac. 7.
12 Plut. Cæs. Suet. Jul. 56, 81. Aug. 53. 84. Tac. Ann. iv. 39.
13 Suet. Tib. 30.

their answers to the applications or petitions presented to them ;[1] by their mandates and laws,[2] &c. Vespasian appears to have been the first who made use of these rescripts and edicts. They became more frequent under Hadrian: from which time the decrees of the senate concerning private right began to be more rare ; and at length under Caracalla were entirely discontinued.

The constitutions of the emperors about punishing or rewarding individuals, which were not to serve as precedents, were called PRIVILEGIA.[3] This word anciently used to be taken in a bad sense ; for a private law about inflicting an extraordinary punishment on a certain person without a trial, as the law of Clodius against Cicero, which Cicero says was forbidden by the sacred laws and those of the twelve tables.[4] The rights or advantages[5] granted to a certain condition or class of men, used also to be called PRIVILEGIA ;[6] as the privileges of soldiers, parents, pupils, creditors, &c.

The various laws and decrees of the senate, whereby supreme power was conferred on Augustus, and which used to be repeated to the succeeding emperors upon their accession to the empire,[7] when taken together, are called the Royal law, probably in allusion to the law by which supreme power was granted to Romulus.[8]

THE EQUITES.

THE equites at first did not form a distinct order in the state. When Romulus divided the people into three tribes, he chose from each tribe 100 young men, the most distinguished for their rank, their wealth, and other accomplishments, who should serve on horseback, and whose assistance he might use for guarding his person. These 300 horsemen were called CELERES,[9] and divided into three centuries, which were distinguished by the same names with the three tribes : namely, RAMNENSES, TATIENSES, and LUCERES.

The number of the equites was afterwards increased, first by Tullus Hostilius, who chose 300 from the Albans ;[10] then by Tarquinius Priscus, who doubled their number ;[11] retaining the number and names of the centuries ; only those who were added were called *Ramnenses, Tatienses, Luceres, posteriores.* But as Livy says there were now 1800 in the three centuries, Tarquin seems to have done more than double them.[12]

Servius Tullius made eighteen centuries of equites ; he chose twelve new centuries from the chief men of the state, and made six others out of the three instituted by Romulus. Ten thousand pounds of brass were given to each of them to purchase horses ; and a tax was laid on widows, who were exempt from other contributions, for maintaining their horses.[13] Hence the origin of the equestrian order, which was of the greatest utility in the state, as an intermediate bond between the patricians and plebeians.

1 per rescripta ad libellos.
2 per edicta et constitutiones.
3 quasi privæ legis, A. Gell. x. 20.
4 leges privatis hominibus irrogari : id est enim privilegium, Cic. Legg. iii. 19. Dom. 17. Sext. 30.

5 beneficia.
6 Plin. x. 56, 57. 110.
7 tum senatus cuncta, principibus solita, Vespasiano decrevit, Tac. Hist. iv. 3.
8 lex regia, vel lex imperii, et augustum privilegium. Liv. xxxiv. 6.
9 ταχεῖς ἐπὶ τα ἔργα, ad opera veloces, Diony.

ii. 13. vel a κέλης, eques desultorius ; vel a Celere, eorum præfecto, Fest.
10 decem turmas ; turma, quasi terma dicta est, quod ter denis equitibus constaret, Varr. Fest. Liv. i. 30.
11 numero alterum tantum adjecit.

12 Liv. i. 30. Romulus probably added two hundred to each century of equites, as he added one hundred to the number of the senators, upon the admission of the Sabines into the city, Diony. ii. 47.
13 Liv. i. 43.

At what particular time the equites first began to be reckoned a distinct order, is uncertain. It seems to have been before the expulsion of the kings.[1] After this all those who served on horseback were not properly called EQUITES or knights, but such only as were chosen into the equestrian order, usually by the censor, and presented by him with a horse at the public expense, and with a gold ring.

The equites were chosen promiscuously from the patricians and plebeians. Those descended from ancient families were called ILLUSTRES, SPECIOSI, and SPLENDIDI. They were not limited to any fixed number. The age requisite was about eighteen years,[2] and the fortune,[3] at least towards the end of the republic, and under the emperors, was 400 sestertia, that is, about 3,229l. of our money.[4] According to some, every Roman citizen whose entire fortune amounted to that sum, was every lustrum enrolled, of course, in the list of equites. But this was not always the case. A certain fortune seems to have been always requisite.[5]

The badges of equites were, 1. a horse given them by the public ; hence called LEGITIMUS ;[6] 2. a gold ring, whence ANNULO AUREO DONARI,[7] to become a knight ; 3. angustus clavus, or tunica angusticlavia ; 4. a separate place at the public spectacles, according to the law made by L. Roscius Otho, a tribune of the people, A. U. 686,[8] that the equites should sit in 14 rows,[9] next to the orchestra, where the senators sat ; whence SEDERE IN QUATUORDECIM, or in EQUESTRIBUS ; or SPECTARE IN EQUITE,[10] to be a knight.

The office[11] of the equites at first was only to serve in the army ; but afterwards also to act as judges or jurymen[12] and to farm the public revenues.[13] Judges were chosen from the senate till the year of the city 631, at which time, on account of the corruption of that order, the right of judging was transferred from them to the equites, by the Sempronian law, made by C. Gracchus. It was again restored to the senate by Sylla ; but afterwards shared between the two orders.

The equites who farmed the revenues were divided into certain societies, and he who presided in such a society was called MAGISTER SOCIETATIS.[14] These farmers[15] were held in such respect at Rome, that Cicero calls them homines amplissimi, honestissimi, et ornatissimi ; flos equitum Romanorum, ornamentum civitatis, firmamentum reipublicæ.[16] But this was far from being the case in the provinces, where publicans were held in detestation,[17] especially their servants and assistants.

A great degree of splendour was added to the equestrian order by a procession[18] which they made through the city every year on the fifteenth day of July,[19] from the temple of Honour, or of Mars, without the city, to the Capitol, riding on horseback, with wreaths of olive on their heads, dressed in their togæ palmatæ, or trabeæ, of a scarlet colour, and bearing in their hands the military ornaments which they had received from their general, as a reward for their valour.[20] At this time it was not allowable to cite them before a court of justice : such was at least the case under Augustus.[21]

Every fifth year, when this procession was made, the equites rode up

1 Liv. i. 35. ii. 1.
2 Dio. lii. 20.
3 census.
4 Hor. Ep. i. 1. 57. Plin. Ep. i. 19.
5 Liv. v. 7. iii. 27.
6 Ov. F. iii. 130.

7 for inter equites legi.
8 Dio. xxxvi. 25. Juv. iii. 159. xiv. 324.
9 in xiv. gradibus.
10 for equitem esse, Suet.
11 munus.

12 ut judicarent.
13 vectigalia conducere.
14 Cic. Fam. xiii. 9.
15 publicani.
16 Leg. Manil. 7. Planc. 9.
17 Asc. Cic. Verr. ii. 3.

18 transvectione.
19 idibus Quinctilibus, Liv. ix. 46.
20 Diony. vi. 13. Plin. xv. 4, 5.
21 Suet. Aug. 38.

to the censor seated in his curule chair, before the Capitol, and dismounting, led along[1] their horses in their hands before him, and in this manner they were reviewed.[2]

If any eques was corrupt in his morals, or had diminished his fortune, or even had not taken proper care of his horse, the censor ordered him to sell his horse,[3] and thus he was reckoned to be removed from the equestrian order; hence ADIMERE EQUUM, to degrade an eques; but those whom the censor approved, were ordered to lead along[4] their horses.[5]

At this time also the censor read over a list of the equites, and such as were less culpable were degraded[6] only by passing over their names in the recital.[7] We find it mentioned as a reward, that a person should not be obliged to serve in the army, nor to maintain a public horse,[8] but this exemption could be granted only by the people.[9]

The eques whose name was first marked in the censor's books, was called EQUESTRIS ORDINIS PRINCEPS,[10] or PRINCEPS JUVENTUTIS; not that in reality the equites were all young men, for many grew old in that order, as Mæcenas and Atticus; and we find the two censors, Livius and Nero, were equites,[11] but because they had been generally so at their first institution; and among the Romans men were called *juvenes* till near fifty. Hence we find Julius Cæsar called *adolescentulus*, when he stood candidate for being high-priest, although he was then thirty-six years old, and Cicero calls himself *adolescens* when he was consul.[12] Under the emperors, the heirs of the empire were called *principes juventutis*, vel *juvenum*.[13] We find this name also applied to the whole equestrian order.[14]

PLEBEIAN OR POPULAR ORDER.

ALL the other Roman citizens, besides the patricians and equites, were called PLEBS or POPULUS. *Populus* sometimes comprehends the whole nation; as, CLEMENTIA ROMANI POPULI: or all the people except the senate; as, SENATUS POPULUSQUE ROMANUS. In which last sense *plebs* is also often used; as when we say, that the consuls were created from the plebeians, that is, from those who were not patricians. But *plebs* is usually put for the lowest common people; hence, *ad populum plebemque referre*.[15] Thus Horace: *plebs eris*, i. e. *unus e plebe*, a plebeian, not an eques; who also uses *plebs* for the whole people.[16]

The common people who lived in the country, and cultivated the ground, were called PLEBS RUSTICA.[17] Anciently the senators also did the same, but not so in after times.[18] The common people who lived in the city, merchants, mechanics, &c. were called PLEBS URBANA.[19] Both are joined, Sal. Jug. 73.

The PLEBS RUSTICA was the most respectable.[20] The PLEBS URBANA was composed of the poorer citizens, many of whom followed no trade, but were supported by the public and private largesses.[21] In the latter ages of the republic an immense quantity of corn was annually distributed

---

1 traducebant.
2 Cic.Clu. 48. Quin. 5.11. 13. recognoscebantur.
3 Gell. iv. 20. Liv. xxix. 37.
4 traducere.
5 Ov. T. ii. 89.
6 qui minora culpa tenerentur, ordine equestri

moti sunt.
7 Suet. Cal. 16.
8 ne invitus militaret, neve censor ei equum publicum assignaret.
9 Liv. xxxix. 19.
10 Plin. Cal. i. 14.
11 Liv. xxix. 37.
12 Sall. Cat. 49. Phil.ii.5.

13 Suet. Cal. 15. Ov. P. ii. 5. 41.
14 Liv. xiii. 61.
15 Cic. Fam. viii. 8.Gell. x. 10.
16 Ep. i. 1. 59. Od. iii. 14. 1.
17 Liv. xxxv. 1.
18 Cic. Sen. 16. Liv. iii.

20.
19 Cic. Off. i. 42. Sall. Cat. 37.
20 optima et modestissima, Cic. Rull. iii. 31. laudatissima, Plin. xviii. 3.
21 eos publicum malum alebat. Sall. Cat. 37.

among them at the public expense, five bushels monthly to each man.[1]
Their principal business was to attend on the tribunes and popular magistrates in their assemblies; hence they were called TURBA FORENSIS,[2] and
from their venality and corruption, OPERÆ CONDUCTÆ vel *mercenarii*, in
allusion to mercenary workmen,[3] OPERÆ CONDUCTORUM,[4] MULTITUDO
CONDUCTA,[5] CONCIONES CONDUCTÆ,[6] CONCIONALIS HIRUDO *ærarii, misera
ac jejuna* PLEBECULA,[7] FÆX ET SORDES URBIS,[8] URBANA *et perdita*
PLEBS.[9]

Cicero often opposes the populace[10] to the principal nobility.[11]   There
were leading men among the populace,[12] kept in pay by the seditious magistrates, who used for hire to stimulate them to the most daring outrages.[13]
The turbulence of the common people of Rome, the natural effect of idle-
ness and unbounded licentiousness, is justly reckoned among the chief
causes of the ruin of the republic. Trade and manufactures being considered as servile employments,[14] they had no encouragement to industry;
and the numerous spectacles which were exhibited, particularly the shows
of gladiators, served to increase their natural ferocity. Hence they were
always ready to join in any conspiracy against the state.[15]

OTHER DIVISIONS OF THE ROMAN PEOPLE.

I. PATRONS AND CLIENTS; NOBILES, NOVI, AND IGNOBILES; OPTIMATES, AND POPULARES.

THAT the patricians and plebeians might be connected together by the
strictest bonds, Romulus ordained that every plebeian should choose from
the patricians any one he pleased as his PATRON or protector, whose CLI-
ENT he was called.[16]   It was the part of the patron to advise and to defend
his client, to assist him with his interest and substance; in short to do every
thing for him that a parent uses to do for his children. The client was
obliged to pay all kind of respect to his patron, and to serve him with his
life and fortune in any extremity.[17]

It was unlawful for patrons and clients to accuse or bear witness against
each other; and whoever was found to have acted otherwise, might be
slain by any one with impunity, as a victim devoted to Pluto and the infernal gods. Hence both patrons and clients vied with one another in fidelity and observance, and for more than 600 years we find no dissensions
among them.[18] Virgil joins to the crime of beating one's parent that of
defrauding a client.[19]   It was esteemed highly honourable for a patrician
to have numerous clients, both hereditary, and acquired by his own
merit.[20]

In after times, even cities and whole nations were under the protection
of illustrious Roman families; as the Sicilians under the patronage of the
Marcelli,[21] Cyprus and Cappadocia under that of Cato,[22] the Allobroges
under the patronage of the Fabii,[23] the Bononienses, of the Antonii,[24] Lace-

---

1 Sall. Frag. ed. Cort. p. 974.
2 Liv. ix. 46.
3 Cic. Sext. 17. 27. Q. fratr. ii. 1. Att. i. 13.
4 Sext. 50.
5 Phil. i. 9.
6 Sext. 49. 53.
7 Att. i. 16.
8 Att. i. 13.
9 Id. vii. 3.
10 populus, plebs, mul-titudo, tenuiores, &c.
11 principes delecti, op-timates et optimatium principes, honesti, bo-ni, locupletes, &c. Cic. Sext. 48. 66. &c.
12 duces multitudinum.
13 Sall. Cat. 50. Cic. Sext. 37. 46.
14 Sall. Cat. 4. Diony. ix. 25.
15 Sall. Cat. 37.
16 quod eum colebat.
17 Diony. ii. 10.
18 ibid.
19 Æn. vi. 605.
20 Hor. Ep. ii. 1. 103. Juv. x. 44.
21 Cic. Cæc. 4. Ver. iii. 18.
22 Cic. Fam. xv. 4.
23 Sall. Cat. 41.
24 Suet. Aug. 17.

dæmon, of the Claudii.[1]   Thus the people of Puteoli chose Cassius and the Bruti for their patrons,[2] Capua chose Cicero.[3]   This, however, seems to have taken place also at an early period.[4]

Those whose ancestors or themselves had borne any curule magistracy, that is, had been consul, prætor, censor, or curule ædile, were called NO-BILES, and had the right of making images of themselves, which were kept with great care by their posterity, and carried before them at funerals.[5]

These images were nothing else but the busts or the effigies of persons down to the shoulders, made of wax and painted ; which they used to place in the courts of their houses,[6] enclosed in wooden cases, and seem not to have brought them out, except on solemn occasions.[7]   They were titles or inscriptions written below them, pointing out the honours they had enjoyed, and the exploits they had performed.[8]   Hence *imagines* is often put for *nobilitas*,[9] and *ceræ* for *imagines*.[10]   Anciently this right of images was peculiar to the patricians; but afterwards the plebeians also acquired it, when admitted to curule offices.

Those who were the first of their family that had raised themselves to any curule office, were called *homines* NOVI, new men or upstarts.   Hence Cicero calls himself *homo per se cognitus*.[11]

Those who had no images of their own or of their ancestors, were called IGNOBILES.

Those who favoured the interests of the senate, were called OPTIMATES,[12] and sometimes *proceres* or *principes ;* those who studied to gain the favour of the multitude, were called POPULARES, of whatever order they were.[13] This was a division of factions, and not of rank or dignity.[14]   The contests betwixt these two parties excited the greatest commotions in the state, which finally terminated in the extinction of liberty.

II. GENTES AND FAMILIÆ ; NAMES OF THE ROMANS ; INGENUI AND LIBERTINI, &c.

THE Romans were divided into various ʻclans, (GENTES), and each *gens* into several families.[15]   Thus in the gens Cornelia were the families of the Scipiones, Lentuli, Cethegi, Dolabellæ, Cinnæ, Syllæ, &c.   Those of the same gens were called GENTILES, and those of the same family AGNA-TI.[16]   But relations by the father's side were also called *agnati*, to distinguish them from *cognati*, relations only by the mother's side.   An *agnatus* might also be called *cognatus*, but not the contrary.   Thus *patruus*, the father's brother, was both an *agnatus* and *cognatus :* but *avunculus*, the mother's brother, was only a *cognatus*.[17]

Anciently patricians only were said to have a gens.[18]   Hence[19] some patricians were said to be *majorum gentium*, and others *minorum gentium*. But when the plebeians obtained the right of intermarriage with the patricians, and access to the honours of the state, they likewise received the rights of gentes, which rights were then said to be confounded by these innovations.[20]   Hence however, some gentes were patrician, and others plebeian ; and sometimes in the same gens there were some families of

1 Suet. Tib. 6.
2 Cic. Phil. ii. 41.
3 Cic. Pis. 11. Fam. xvi. 11.
4. Liv. ix. 20. &c.
5 jus imaginum, Plin. xxxv. 2.

6 atria.
7 Polyb. vi. 51.
8 Juv. Sat. viii. 69. Plin. xxxv. 2.
9 Sall. Jug. 85. Liv. iii. 58.
10. Ov. A. i. 8. 65.

11 Cat. i. 11.
12 Liv. ii. 39.
13 Cic. Sext. 45.
14 Diony. ix. 1.
15 in familias v. stirpes.
16 Cic. Top. c. 6. Fest. in voce Gentiles.

17 Digest.
18 Liv. x. 8.
19 Cic. Fam. ix. 21.
20 jura gentium, vel gentilia, Liv. iv. 1. &c.

patrician rank, and others of plebeian. Hence also *sine gente*, for *libertinus et non generosus*, ignobly born.[1]

To mark the different gentes and familiæ, and to distinguish the individuals of the same family, the Romans, at least the more noble of them, had commonly three names, the *prænomen, nomen,* and *cognomen.*[2]

The PRÆNOMEN was put first, and marked the individual. It was commonly written with one letter; as, A. for Aulus; C. Caius; D. Decimus; K. Kæso; L. Lucius; M. Marcus; M'. Manius; N. Numerius; P. Publius; Q. Quintus; T. Titus; sometimes with two letters, as, Ap. Appius; Cn. Cneius; Sp. Spurius; Ti. Tiberius; and sometimes with three, as, Mam. Mamercus; Ser. Servius; Sex. Sextus.

The NOMEN was put after the prænomen, and marked the gens and commonly ended in -ius; as, Cornelius, Fabius, Tullius, Julius, Octavius, &c. The COGNOMEN was put last, and marked the familia; as, Cicero, Cæsar, &c. Thus, in Publius Cornelius Scipio, Publius is the prænomen; Cornelius, the nomen; and Scipio, the cognomen.

Some gentes seem to have had no surname; as the Marian; thus, C. Marius, Q. Sertorius, L. Mummius.[3] Gens and familia seem sometimes to be put the one for the other: thus, *Fabia gens,* v. *familia.*[4]

Sometimes there was also a fourth name, called the AGNOMEN or cognomen, added from some illustrious action or remarkable event. Thus Scipio was named Africanus, from the conquest of Carthage and Africa. On a similar account his brother Lucius Cornelius Scipio was named Asiaticus. So Quintus Fabius Maximus was called Cunctator, from his checking the impetuosity of Hannibal by declining battle. We find likewise a second agnomen, or cognomen, added; thus, the latter Publius Cornelius Scipio Africanus is called Æmilianus, because he was the son of L. Æmilius Paulus, and adopted by the son of the great Scipio, who had no male children of his own. But he is commonly called by authors Africanus Minor, to distinguish him from the former Scipio Africanus.

The Romans at first seem to have had but one name, as, Romulus, Remus, &c., or two; as, Numa Pompilius, Tullus Hostilius, Ancus Martius, Tarquinius Priscus, Servius Tullius, Sextus Tarquinius. But when they were divided into tribes or clans and families,[5] they began commonly to have three; as, L. Junius Brutus, M. Valerius Poplicola, &c.

The three names, however, were not always used; commonly two, and sometimes only one, namely, the surname.[6] But in speaking to any one, the prænomen was generally used, as being peculiar to citizens; for slaves had no prænomen. Hence, *gaudent prænomine molles auriculæ.*[7]

The surnames were derived from various circumstances; either from some quality of the mind, as, Cato from wisdom, i. e. *catus*, wise;[8] or from the habit of the body, as, Calvus, Crassus, Macer, &c.; or from cultivating particular fruits, as, Lentulus, Piso, Cicero, &c. Certain surnames sometimes gave occasion to jests and witty allusions; thus, Asina;[9] so, Serranus Calatinus;[10] hence also in a different sense Virgil says, *vel te sulco,* Serrane, *serentem,*[11] for Q. Cincinnatus was called SERRANUS, because the ambassadors from the senate found him sowing, when they brought him notice that he was made dictator.[12]

---

1 Suet. Tib. 1. Hor. Sat.   4 Liv. ii. 49.   be soothed with flat-   10 Cic. Sext. 23.
ii. 5. 15.   5 in gentes et familias.   tering titles. Hor. Sat.   11 Æn. vi. 844.
2 Juv. v.126. Quin. viii.   6 Sall. Cat. 17. Cic. Ep.   ii. 5. 32.   12 Plin. xviii. 3.
3. 27.   passim.   8 Cic. Sen. 2. &c.
3 Plut. in Mario.   7 delicate ears love to   9 Hor. Ep. i. 13. 9.

The prænomen used to be given to boys, on the 9th day, which was called *dies lustricus,* or the day of purification, when certain religious ceremonies were performed.[1] The eldest son of the family usually got the prænomen of his father ; the rest were named from their uncles or other relations.

When there was only one daughter in a family, she used to be called from the name of the gens ; thus, Tullia, the daughter of Cicero ; Julia, the daughter of Cæsar ; Octavia, the sister of Augustus, &c. ; and they retained the same name after they were married. When there were two daughters, the one was called Major and the other Minor ; thus, Cornelia Major, Cornelia Minor. If there were more than two, they were distinguished by their number ; thus, Prima, Secunda, Tertia, Quarta, Quinta, &c.[2] or more softly, Tertulla, Quartilla, Quintilla, &c.[3] Women seem anciently to have also had prænomens, which were marked with inverted letters ; thus, ϽϽ for Caia, Ⅎ for Lucia, &c.

During the flourishing state of the republic, the names of the gentes, and surnames of the familiæ, always remained fixed and certain. They were common to all the children of a family, and descended to their posterity. But after the subversion of liberty they were changed and confounded.

Those were called LIBERI, free, who had the power of doing what they pleased. Those who were born of parents who had been always free, were called INGENUI. Slaves made free were called LIBERTI and LIBERTINI. They were called *liberti* in relation to their masters, and *libertini* in relation to freeborn citizens ; thus, *libertus meus, libertus Cæsaris,* and not *libertinus ; but libertinus homo,* i. e. *non ingenuus. Servus cum manu mittitur, fit* libertinus,[4] (*non* libertus.)

Some think that libertini were the sons of the liberti, from Suetonius, who says that they were thus called anciently ;[5] but this distinction never occurs in the classics. On the contrary, we find both words applied to the same person in writers who flourished in different ages.[6] Those whom Cicero calles libertini, Livy makes *qui servitutem servissent.*[7] Hence Seneca often contrasts *servi et liberi, ingenui et libertini.*[8]

SLAVES.

MEN became slaves among the Romans, by being taken in war, by sale, by way of punishment, or by being born in a state of servitude.[9]

1. Those enemies who voluntarily laid down their arms and surrendered themselves, retained the rights of freedom, and were called DEDITITII.[10] But those taken in the field, or in the storming of cities, were sold by auction (*sub corona,* as it was termed,[11] because they wore a crown when sold ; or *sub hasta,* because a spear was set up where the crier or auctioneer stood). They were called SERVI,[12] or MANCIPIA.[13]

2. There was a continual market for slaves at Rome. Those who dealt in that trade[14] brought them thither from various countries. The seller was

---

1 Macrob. Sat. i. 16.
Suet. Ner. 6.
2 Varr. Lat. viii. 28.
Suet. Jul. 50.
3 Cic. Att. xiv. 20.
4 Quin. viii. 3. 27.
5 Claud. 24. so Isid. ix. 4.

6 Plaut. Mil. Glor. iv. 1.
15. 16. Cic. Verr. i. 47.
7 Cic. Or. i. 9. Liv. xlv.
15.
8 Vit. Beat. 24. Ep. 31.
&c.
9 servi aut nascebantur

aut fiebant.
10 Liv. vii. 31. Cæs. i.
27.
11 Liv. v. 22. &c.
12 quot essent bello servati. Isid. ix. 4.
13 quasi manu capti,

Varr. Lat. v. 8.
14 mangones vel venalitii, Cic. Or. 70. qui venales habebant, Plaut.
Trin. ii. 2. 51.

bound to promise for the soundness of slaves, and not to conceal their faults.[1] Hence they were commonly exposed to sale[2] naked; and they carried a scroll hanging at their necks, on which their good and bad qualities were specified.[3] If the seller gave a false account, he was bound to make up the loss, or in some cases to take back the slave.[4] Those whom the seller would not warrant,[5] were sold with a kind of cap on their head.[6]

Those brought from beyond seas had their feet whitened with chalk,[7] and their ears bored.[8] Sometimes slaves were sold on that condition, that if they did not please they should be returned within a limited time.[9] Foreign slaves, when first brought to the city, were called VENALES, or SERVI NOVICII;[10] slaves who have served long, and hence were become artful, *veteratores*.[11]

It was not lawful for free-born citizens among the Romans, as among other nations, to sell themselves for slaves, much less was it allowed any other person to sell free men. But as this gave occasion to certain frauds, it was ordained by a decree of the senate, that those who allowed themselves to be sold for the sake of sharing the price, should remain in slavery. Fathers might, indeed, sell their children for slaves, but these did not on that account entirely lose the rights of citizens. For when freed from their slavery, they were held as ingenui, not libertini. The same was the case with insolvent debtors, who were given up as slaves to their creditors.[12]

3. Criminals were often reduced to slavery, by way of punishment. Thus those who had neglected to get themselves enrolled in the censor's books, or refused to enlist,[13] had their goods confiscated, and, after being scourged, when sold beyond the Tiber.[14] Those condemned to the mines, or to fight with wild beasts, or to any extreme punishment, were first deprived of liberty, and by a fiction of law, turned slaves of punishment.[15]

4. The children of any female slave became the slaves of her master. There was no regular marriage among slaves, but their connection was called CONTUBERNIUM, and themselves, *contubernales*. Those slaves who were born in the house of their masters, were called VERNÆ, or *vernaculi*; hence *lingua vernacula*, v. -*aris*, one's mother tongue. These slaves were more petulant than others, because they were commonly more indulged.[16]

The whole company of slaves in one house, was called FAMILIA,[17] and the slaves, *familiares*.[18] Hence *familiæ philosophorum*, sects;[19] *sententia, quæ familiam ducit*, HONESTUM QUOD SIT, ID ESSE SOLUM BONUM; the chief maxim of the Stoics;[20] *Lucius familiam ducit*, is the chief of the sect;[21] *accedit etiam, quod familiam ducit*, &c. is the chief ground of praise.[22]

The proprietor of slaves was called DOMINUS;[23] whence this word was put for a tyrant.[24] On this account Augustus and Tiberius refused the name.[25]

1 Hor. Sat. ii. 3. 285.
2 producebantur.
3 titules vel inscriptio, Gell. iv. 2.
4 Cic. Off. iii. 16, 17. 23.
5 præstare.
6 pileati, Gell. vii. 4.
7 cretatis v. gypsatis pedibus, Plin. Hist. xxxv. 17, 18. s. 58. Tibull. ii. 3. 64.
8 auribus perforatis, Juv. i. 104.
9 redhiberentur, Cic.

Off. iii. 24. Plaut. Most. iii. 2. 113. Fest.
10 Cic. Quin. 6. Plin. Ep. i. 21. Quin. i. 12. 2. vii. 2. 6.
11 Ter. Heaut. v. 1. 16.
12 in servitutem creditoribus addicti, Quin. vi. 3. 26. v. 10. 60.
13 qui censum aut militiam subterfugerant.
14 This must, however, have sunk into a mere form, after the exten-

sion of the Roman territories, ED.—Cic. Cæc. 24.
15 servi pœpæ fingebantur.
16 Hor. Sat. ii. 6. 66.
17 Nep. Att. 13. Cic. Par. v. 2. familia constat ex servis pluribus, Cic. Cæc. 19. quindecim liberi homines, populus est; totidom servi, familia; totidem vincti, ergastulum,

Apul. Apol.
18 Cic. Cœl. 23. Plaut. Amph. Prol. 127.
19 Cic. Fin. iv. 18. Div. ii. 1. Att. ii. 16.
20 Id. Fin. ii. 16.
21 Id. Phil. v. 11.
22 Fam. vii. 5.
23 Ter. Eun. iii. 2. 23.
24 Liv. ii. 60.
25 Suet. Aug. 53. Id. 27. Tac. Ann. ii. 27.

Slaves not only did all domestic services, but were likewise employed in various trades and manufactures. Such as had a genius for it, were sometimes instructed in literature and the liberal arts;[1] some of these were sold at a great price;[2] hence arose a principal part of the immense wealth of Crassus.[3]

Slaves employed to accompany boys to and from school, were called PÆDAGOGI; and the part of the house where those young slaves staid who were instructed in literature,[4] was called PÆDAGOGIUM.[5]

Slaves were promoted according to their behaviour; as, from being a drudge or mean slave in town,[6] to be an overseer in the country.[7]

The country farms of the wealthy Romans in latter times were cultivated chiefly by slaves.[8] But there were also free men who wrought for hire as among us.[9]

Among the Romans, masters had an absolute power over their slaves. They might scourge or put them to death at pleasure.[10] This right was exercised with so great cruelty, especially in the corrupt ages of the republic, that laws were made at different times to restrain it. The lash was the common punishment; but for certain crimes they used to be branded in the forehead, and sometimes were forced to carry a piece of wood round their necks wherever they went, which was called FURCA; and whoever had been subjected to this punishment was ever afterwards called FURCIFER.[11] A slave that had been often beaten, was called MASTIGIA, or VERBERO.[12] A slave who had been branded was called STIGMATIAS, v. -icus,[13] inscriptus,[14] literatus.[15] Slaves also by way of punishment were often shut up in a work-house, or bridewell,[16] where they were obliged to turn a mill for grinding corn.[17] Persons employed to apprehend and bring back[18] slaves who fled from their masters (FUGITIVI,)[19] were called FUGITIVARII.[20]

When slaves were beaten, they used to be suspended with a weight tied to their feet, that they might not move them.[21] To deter slaves from

---

1 artibus ingenuis, -liberalibus, v. honestis, Cic. Hor. Ep. ii. 2. 7.
2 Plin. vii. 39. s. 40. Sen. Ep. 27. Suet. Jul. 47. Cic. Rosc. Com. 10.
3 Slaves seem to have been, generally, let out under contracts between their owner and employer; but they were sometimes allowed to find work for themselves, on condition of their bringing in, all or part of their gains, to their master. The slave artisans of Crassus seem to have been managed in the former way, and this will more satisfactorily account for his wealth, than if we consider it to have arisen from their sale, as mentioned in the text,—his band of architects and masons alone exceeded 500.—Examples of the latter mode may be found in the cooks in

the Aulularia and Pseudolus of Plautus; and those of the same class mentioned by Pliny, xviii. 11. If we estimate the price of labour by the pay of a foot soldier, we find that after the reign of Domitian it amounted to 1 1-4 denarius, or 9 1 2d per day; of which sixpence might remain after stoppages—this, to the purchaser of a slave for L20, would yield a return of nearly 50 per cent. upon his capital; and Cicero seems to say that a good workman might in his time get 12 asses, or 10 2-10d a-day, but not more. Persius intimates that a slave whose daily hire amounted to no more than 3 asses, was accounted very worthless in his age.—See this subject treated more fully in Blair on Roman Slavery, p. 156.

et seq.—ED.—Plut. Cras.
4 literæ serviles, Sen. Ep. 88.
5 Plin. Ep. vii. 27.
6 mediastinus.
7 villicus, Hor. Ep. i. 14.
8 Plin. xviii. 3.
9 mercenarii, Cic. Off. i. 13. Cæc. 59.
10 Juv. Sat. vi. 219.
11 Stocks, of various kinds, and known by different names, were much used in punishing slaves. One sort, called numella, must have been very severe, if it resembled an instrument of the same name, used for fastening refractory cattle. Of a similar description with stocks, was the block of wood (cedes), to which offenders were chained by the leg; and which could sometimes be dragged after them, but was generally immovable, Blair, p. 108. —ED.

12 Ter. Adel. v. 2. 6. Phorm. iv. 4. 3.
13 i. e. notis compunctus, Cic. Off. ii. 7.
14 Mart. viii. 75. 9.
15 Plaut. Cas. ii. 6. 49. i. e. literis inscriptus: as, urna literata, Plaut. Rud. ii. 5. 21. ensiculus literatus, &c. Id. iv. 4. 112.
16 in ergastulo, v. pistrino.
17 While thus employed they were generally chained, and had a wooden collar or board (pausicape), round their necks to prevent their eating the grain. —ED.— Plaut. et Ter. passim, Sen. Ben. iv. 37.
18 retrahere, Ter. Hea. iv. 2. 65.
19 Cic. Fam. v. 9.
20 Flor. iii. 19.
21 Plaut. Asin. ii. 2. 34, &c. Aul. iv. 4. 16. Ter. Phorm. i. 4. 43.

offending, a thong[1] or a lash made of leather was commonly hung on the staircase;[2] but this was chiefly applied to younger slaves.[3]

Slaves when punished capitally were commonly crucified,[4] but this punishment was prohibited under Constantine.[5] If a master of a family was slain at his own house, and the murderer not discovered, all his domestic slaves were liable to be put to death. Hence we find no less than 400 in one family punished on this account.[6]

Slaves were not esteemed as persons, but as things, and might be transferred from one owner to another, like any other effects. Slaves could not appear as witnesses in a court of justice,[7] nor make a will, nor inherit anything;[8] but gentle masters allowed them to make a kind of will;[9] nor could slaves serve as soldiers, unless first made free,[10] except in the time of Hannibal, when, after the battle of Cannæ, 8000 slaves were armed without being freed.[11] These were called VOLONES, because they enlisted voluntarily; and afterwards obtained their freedom for their bravery.[12]

Slaves had a certain allowance granted them for their sustenance,[13] commonly four or five pecks[14] of grain a month, and five *denarii*, which was called their MENSTRUUM.[15] They likewise had a daily allowance;[16] and what they spared of this, or procured by any other means with their master's consent, was called their PECULIUM. This money, with their master's permission, they laid out at interest, or purchased with it a slave for themselves, from whose labors they might make profit. Such a slave was called *servi* VICARIUS,[17] and constituted part of the *peculium*, with which also slaves sometimes purchased their freedom. Cicero says, that sober and industrious slaves, at least such as became slaves from being captives in war, seldom remained in servitude above six years.[18] At certain times slaves were obliged to make presents to their masters out of their poor savings.[19] There was sometimes an agreement between the master and the slave, that when the slave should pay a certain sum, the master should be obliged to give him his liberty.[20]

Although the state of slaves in point of right was the same, yet their condition in families was very different, according to the pleasure of their masters and their different employments. Some were treated with indulgence; some served in chains, as janitors and door-keepers;[21] others were confined in work-houses below ground.[22]

At certain times slaves were allowed the greatest freedom; as at the feast of Saturn, in the month of December,[23] when they were served at table by their masters,[24] and on the Ides of August.[25]

1 habena.
2 in scalis, Hor. Ep. ii. 2. 15.
3 Schol. ibid. Impuberes habebantur, vel ferula plectebantur, Ulp. D. i. 33. de SC. Silan. Some here join in scalis with latuit, as Cic. Mil. 15. Phil. ii. 9.
4 Juv. vi. 219. Cic. Verr. v. 3. 64, &c.
5 Late in the empire, burning alive was employed, amongst other barbarous means of satisfying the criminal code.—Blair, p. 60, and note 19.—For a full detail of the various modes of punishing

slaves, and instruments of torture used for extracting evidence from them, among the Romans, we refer to Blair's excellent work on Roman slavery, from which most of our notes on this subject have been drawn; the inquisitive reader will there find that little new either in the instrument or method of torture has been invented by the moderns.—ED.
6 Tac. Ann. xiv. 43.
7 Ter. Phorm. ii. 62.
8 Plin. Ep. viii. 16. iv. 11.
9 quasi testamenta fa-

cere, Plin. Ep. viii. 16.
10 Id. x. 39. Serv. Virg. Æn. ix. 547.
11 Liv. xxii. 57.
12 Fest. Liv. xxiv. 16.
13 dimensum.
14 modii.
15 Donat. Ter. Phorm. i. 1. 9. Sen. Ep. 80.
16 diarium, Hor. Ep. i. 14. 40.
17 Hor. Sat. ii. 7. 79. Cic. Ver. i. 36. Plaut. Asin. ii. 4. 27. Mart. ii. 18. 7.
18 Phil. viii. 11.
19 ex eo quod de dimenso suo unciatim comparserint, Ter. ibid.
20 Plaut Aul. v. 3. Casin. ii. 5, 6. &c. Rud. iv. 2. 23. Tac. xiv. 42.

21 ostiarii; and so in the country, catenati cultores, Flor. iii. 19. vincti fossores, Luc. vii. 402. hi, sc. qui agrum colunt, vel coloni, vel. servi sunt soluti aut vincti, Colum. i. 7. See post, tit. Agriculture.
22 in ergastulis subterraneis. So Plin. vincti pedes, damnatæ manus, inscriptæque vultus, arva exercent, xviii. 3. coli rura ab ergastulis pessimum est, Ib. c. 6.
23 Hor. Sat. ii. 7. 4.
24 Auson. Fer. Rom. H. 15.
25 Fest.

The number of slaves in Rome and through Italy was immense.[1] Some rich individuals are said to have had several thousands.[2] Wars were sometimes excited by an insurrection of the slaves.[3]

There were also public slaves, who were used for various public services,[4] and especially to attend on the magistrates. Their condition was much more tolerable than that of private slaves. They had yearly allowances[5] granted them by the public.[6]

There were also persons attached to the soil;[7] concerning the state of whom writers are nót agreed.[8]

Slaves anciently bore the prænomen of their master; thus, Marcipores, Lucípores, Publipores.[9] Afterwards they got various names, either from their country, or from other circumstances; as Syrus, Davus, Geta, Parmeno, &c. in comic writers; Tiro, Laurea, Dionysius, &c. in Cicero. But slaves are usually distinguished in the classics by their different employments; as, Medici, Chirurgi, Pædagogi, Grammatici, Scribæ, Fabri, Coqui, &c.

Slaves were anciently freed by three ways, *censu, vindicta, et testamento.*[10]

1. *Per* CENSUM, when a slave with his master's knowledge, or by his order, got his name inserted in the censor's roll.[11]

2. *Per* VINDICTAM, when a master, going with his slave in his hand to the prætor or consul, and in the provinces, to the proconsul or proprætor, said; "I desire that this man be free according to the custom of the Romans;"[12] and the prætor, if he approved, putting a rod on the head of the slave,[13] pronounced, "I say that this man is free after the manner of the Romans." Whereupon the lictor or the master turning him round in a circle, (which was called VERTIGO,)[14] and giving him a blow on the cheek,[15] let him go,[16] signifying that leave was granted him to go where he pleased. The rod with which the slave was struck, was called VINDICTA, as some think, from Vindicius or Vindex, a slave of the Vitellii, who informed the senate concerning the conspiracy of the sons of Brutus and others, to restore the Tarquins, and who is said to have been first freed in this manner.[17]

3. *Per* TESTAMENTUM, when a master gives his slaves their liberty by his will. If this was done in express words,[18] as, for example, DAVUS

---

1 Juv. iii. 140.
2 Sen. Tranq. Ann. viii.
3 Flor. iii. 19, 20.
4 Liv. l. 7.
5 annua.
6 Plin. Ep. x. 30. 40.
7 adscriptitii vel glebæ adscripti.
8 Previously to the arrival of the Lombards in Italy, we do not find more than three distinct appellations for separate grades of the servile condition. 1st. *Servi,mancipia,*or *servitia,* slaves. 2d, *Adscriptitii,* or *adscripti glebæ,* bondsmen fixed to the soil. 3d, *Coloni,* husbandmen, or *inquilini,* tenants, (called sometimes *originarii,* or *originales,* originals,when born in that class.)

♦ The first only were

slaves,properly so called; the second were of nearly the same civil rank; but, with regard to them, the powers of the master were curtailed; and they stood, therefore, in a situation preferable to that of other bondsmen : the lastwere free in state,but were, to a certain extent, subjected to the owner of the landon whichtheywere bound to dwell; and theywere, consequently, in a kind of liberty inferior to that enjoyed by other freemen. There were, also, two descriptions of temporary bondage : the one was that of slaves who were about to pass into freedom ; and the other

was that of freemen who were obliged, for a time, to serve a particular individual. Persons in the state of the former were called *statuliberi,* or free in rank ; those in the situation of the latter were termed *nexi,* or bound : underthisdenomination came debtors while in the hands of their creditors, before being adjudged tothem, or sold: and also citizen captives, who, being ransomed from the enemy, could not repay the price of their redemption, and were compelled to work it out, by acting, for a time, as servants to their purchasers. Blair, p. 50, 51.—ED.

9 quasi Marci, Lucii, Publii pueri, &c. Quin. i. 4. 26.
10 Cic. Top. 2. seu 10.
11 Cic. Cæc. 34. s. 99.
12 hunc hominem liberum esse volo more vel jure Quiritium.
13 Hor. Sat. ii. 7. 76.
14 Pers. Sat. v. 75.
15 alapa, Isid. ix. 4. whence, multo majoris alapæ mecum veneunt, liberty is sold, &c. Phædr. ii. 5. 22.
16 e manu emittebat.
17 Liv. ii. 5. whence also perhaps vindicare in libertatem, to free ; mulier, modo quam vindicta redemit, a woman lately freed. Ov. A. iii. 615.
18 verbis directis.

SERVUS MEUS LIBER ESTO, such freedmen were called ORCINI or *Charoni-tæ*, because they had no patron but in the infernal regions. In allusion to which, those unworthy persons who got admission into the senate after the death of Cæsar, were by the vulgar called SENATORES ORCINI.[1] But if the testator signified his desire by way of request, thus,[2] ROGO HERE-DEM MEUM, UT DAVUM MANUMITTAT; the heir[3] retained the rights of pa-tronage.[4]

Liberty procured in any of these methods was called JUSTA LIBERTAS.

In latter times slaves used to be freed by various other methods : by letter ;[5] among friends,[6] if before five witnesses a master ordered his slave to be free : or by table,[7] if a master bid a slave eat at his table ;[8] for it was thought disgraceful to eat with slaves or mean persons, and benches[9] were assigned them, not couches. Hence *imi subsellii vir*, a person of the lowest rank.[10] There were many other methods of freeing slaves, but these did not confer complete freedom.[11] They only discharged them from servitude, but did not entitle them to the privilege of citizens ; unless afterwards the vindicta was superadded, in presence of a magis-trate.[12]

Anciently the condition of all freed slaves was the same : they obtain-ed the freedom of the city with their liberty, according to the institution of Servius Tullius.[13] They were, however, distributed among the four city tribes as being more ignoble.[14] But afterwards, when many worth-less and profligate persons,being freed by their masters, thus invaded the rights of citizens, various laws were made to check the license of manu-mitting slaves. No master was allowed to free, by his will, above a cer-tain number, in proportion to the number he had ; but not above 100, if he had even 20,000, which number, some individuals are said to have pos-sessed.[15] Hence Seneca speaks of *vasta spatia terrarum per vinctos co-lenda ; et familia bellicosis nationibus major*,[16] and Pliny, of legions of

1 Suet. Aug. 35.
2 verbis precativis.
3 hæres fiduciarius.
4 A master might, by testament, leave free-dom to his slave,in any one of three ways : di-rectly, 1st, by ordering that he should be free ; or, 2ndly, by command-ing the heir to manu-mit him ; or indirectly, 3dly, by *fideicommiss*, or simple request, addres-sed to the heir, that he would emancipate the slave. The two first modes were always in-defeasible by the heir ; the last,it wasfor some time thought optional to him to fulfil or not ; but bequests of this na-ture were put on a le-vel withdirect legacies before the time of the youngerPliny. A slave, without being made free in express terms, got liberty and citizen-ship, if he, by order of either the testator or the heir, attended his master's funeral,wear-ing the *pileus*, or fan-ned his corpse on the

bier.—Blair, p. 165.—ED.
5 per epistolam.
6 inter amicos.
7 per mensam.
8 Plin. Ep. vii. 16.
9 subsellia.
10 Plaut. Stich. iii. 4.32.
11 By the master de-signedly calling the slave his son ; this, it was sometimesargued, evinced the master's intention to adopt the slave,after such a step became practicable ; but was more properly interpreted, to mean nothing further than a wish to emanci-pate :—actual adoption of one's slave, too, made him a freeman. A master, openly de-stroying, or surrender-ing to a slave, the title-deed by which the lat-ter was held in proper-ty, annulled his own right, and set the other free. Leave given to a slave to subscribe his name as witness to any solemn deed of his master, had the effect of emancipation. Attir-

ing a slave in the pe-culiar insignia of a free-man, so as to evade a tax, put an end to his servitude. The nomi-nation of a slave as one's heir, or as tutor to one's children, though without a sepa-rate bequest of free-dom, was sufficient to infer his release from bondage. On the death of a master who had maintained his slave-girl as a concubine, she and her child-en got free, by law, in spite of any thing to the contra-ry,contained in the will of the deceased. A female slave, marrying a free person, with consent of her master, who gave her a dowry, was forthwith deemed a freedwoman. The slave who discovered the murderer of his master was declared free by the prætor, and was subject to no pa-tron. Becoming a *cubi-aularius*, or domestic of the emperor's bed-chamber, if with his

master's consent, gave freedom to a slave. If we may admit the au-thority of Rufus's Mili-tary Code, a slave, ta-ken by the.enemy, and returning severely wounded, was to be in-stantly declared free ; and,if he bore no scars, was to be given back to his former owner for-five years, upon the ex-piration of which, he was to obtain liberty. Slaves entering the Christian church with their master's approba-tion, enjoyed the bene-fits of freedom so long as they remained in the sacred profession ; and those enlisting themselves in the ar-my, had a correspond-ing advantage, Blair, p. 166—168.—ED.
12 Plin. Ep. vii. 16. 32.
13 Cic. Balb. 9. Diony. iv. 22, 23.
14 Liv. Ep. xx.
15 Athen. Deipnosoph. vi. 20.
16 Ben. viii. 10.

slaves, so that the master needed a person to tell him their names.[1] Augustus ordained by a law called *Ælia Sentia*, that no slave who had ever for the sake of a crime been bound, publicly whipt, tortured, or branded in the face, although freed by his master, should obtain the freedom of the city, but should always remain in the state of the *dedititii*, who were indeed free, but could not aspire to the advantages of Roman citizens.[2] The reason of this law may be gathered from Diony. iv. 24.

Afterwards by the law called *Junia Norbana*, because it was passed in the cousulship of L. Junius Norbanus, A. U. 771, those freed *per epistolam*, *inter amicos*, or by the other less solemn methods, did not obtain the rights of Roman citizens, but of the Latins who were transplanted into colonies. Hence they were called LATINI JUNIANI, or simply LATINI.[3]

Slaves when made free used to shave their heads in the temple of Feronia, and received a cap or hat, as a badge of liberty.[4] They also were presented with a white robe and a ring by their master. They then assumed a prænomen, and prefixed the name of their patron to their own. Thus, Marcus Tullius Tiro, the freedman of Cicero. In allusion to which Persius says, *verterit hunc dominus ; momento turbinis exit* MARCUS *Dama*.[5] Hence, *tanquam habeas tria nomina*, for *tanquam liber sis*.[6] So foreigners, when admitted into the freedom of the city, assumed the name of that person by whose favour they obtained it.[7]

Patrons retained various rights over their freedmen. If the patron was reduced to poverty, the freedman was bound, in the same manner as a son to support him, according to his abilities. And if a patron failed to support his freedman when poor, he was deprived of the rights of patronage.

If a freedman died intestate, without heirs, the patron succeeded to his effects.

Those freedmen who proved ungrateful to their patrons were condemned to the mines ;[8] and the emperor Claudius, by a law, reduced them to their former slavery.[9]

OCCUPATIONS OF SLAVES.[10]

1.—RUSTIC SLAVES.'

Villicus, steward, overseer, or bailiff.
Villica, wife of do.
Subvillicus, under steward, &c.
Agricola, cultivator or agricultural labourer.
Fossor, digger.
Sarritor vel Sartor, hoer or harrower.
Occator, ditto, ditto, or clod-breaker.
Runcator, weeder.
Arator, ploughman or tiller.
Jugarius, ditto, or ox-driver.
Messor, reaper.
Molitor, miller or grinder.

Vinitor, vine-dresser.
Vindemiator vel Vindemitor, vintager.
Olivitor, dresser of olive trees.
Capulator, spoon or ladle-man, (for oil.)
Putator, pruner.
Frondator, leaf-stripper.
Fœnisector vel Fœniseca, mower or hay-cutter.
Servus ab hortorum cultura, gardener.
Hortulanus, ditto.
Olitor, herb-man or kitchen-gardener.
Topiarius, hedge and tree clipper.
Viridiarius, lawn (or green walk) keeper.

Saltuarius, forester, rather park-keeper or ranger.
Salictarius, keeper of osier-grounds.
Luparius, wolf-killer.
Pastor, herdsman of any description.
Ovilio vel Opilio, shepherd.
Virvicarius, wether-herd.
Tonsor ovium, sheep-shearer.
Caprarius, goat-herd.
Pecori præfectus vel Pecoris magister, chief herdsman.
Custos armenti vel Pastor armentorum, neat-herd.
Superjumentarius, keeper of working cattle.
Bubulcus vel Bubsequa, ox-driver or herdsman.

---

1 nomenclator, xxxiii. 1. s. 6. so Petronius Arbiter, 37. 117.
2 Suet. Aug. 40.
3 Plin. Ep. x. 105.
4 Serv. Virg. Æn. viii. 564. Liv. xlv. 44. hence ad pileum servum vocare, for ad libertatem, Liv. ibid.

5 Suppose his master whirl him round ; in the moment of his being whirled round (*his.* in one turn of a top), he issues forth Marcus Dama.—Sat. v. 77.
6 Juv. v. 190.
7 Cic. Fam. xiii. 35, 36.
8 ad lautumias.

9 in servitutem, revocavit, Suet. Claud. 25. libertum, qui probatus fuerit patrono delatores summiissse, qui de statu ejus facerent in quæstionem, servum patroni esse jussit. L. 5. Dig. de jure Patron.
10 the following cata-

logue of slaves, divided according to their occupations, is extracted from Blair's valuable work on the "State of Slavery amongst the Romans." Edin. 1833.
—ED.

RIGHTS OF ROMAN CITIZENS,

WHILE Rome was but small, and thinly inhabited, whoever fixed their abode in the city or Roman territory, obtained the rights of citizens.

Porculator vel Porcarius, swine-herd.
Subulcus, herd for young pigs.
Gregarius, horse-herd.

II.—RUSTIC, OR URBAN SLAVES,

(According to circumstances.)

Venator, hunter.
Vestigator, game finder or tracker, sometimes of bees.
Indagator, ditto, or toil setter, sometimes of bees.
Alator, game-driver or chaser.
Auceps, fowler.
Piscator vel Piscatui, præpositus, fisherman, chief ditto.
Agitator, driver, of various descriptions.
Epistates, superintendant.
Ergastulus vel Ergastularius, work-house master.
Exactor operum, task master.
Monitor, ditto.
Lorarius, scourger.
Servus fornacarius, furnace, oven, or kiln man.
Gallinarius, hen or poultry keeper.
Aviarius, aviary keeper.
Curator vel Pastor anserum, turdorum, &c. keeper or feeder of geese, thrushes, &c.
Altiliarius vel Fartor, bird fattener or crammer.
Mansuetarius vel Domitor, tamer, or breaker of wild animals.
Ursarius, bearward.
Asinarius, ass keeper, or driver.
Mulio, muleteer.
Carrucarius, wain-driver.
Basternarius, driver of basterna, (a sort of car.)
Cisiarius, ditto of cisium, (a sort of gig.)
Junctor, yoker or groom.
Equisio vel Equitius, Equorum magister vel custos. Agaso vel Strator, horse keeper or groom.
Servus a cura canis, dog or kennel keeper.
Aquarius, water manager.
Minister fontanus, fountain man.
Servus qui curabat sterquilinia et latrinas, scavenger or manure collector.

III.—URBAN SLAVES.

1.—HOUSEHOLD SLAVES.

Coquus, cook.
Archimagirus, chief ditto.
Pulmentarius, pottage-maker.
Salmentarius, pickler.
Offarius, pastry cook.
Dulciarius, confectioner.
Lactarius, milk-dresser or dairyman.
Pomarius, fruit-dresser.
Placentarius, cake-baker.
Pistor vel Pinsor, baker.
Panicoctaria, female ditto.
Focarius, fire boy.
Focaria, fire girl.
Cellarius, pantry-keeper.
Pœnuiarius, store-keeper.
Pœnuiaria, female ditto.
Condus, store-keeper or butler.
Prómus, butler or server of pantry and cellar.
Procurator, caterer.
Mensæ præpositus, table steward.
Obsonator, orderer of bill of fare.
Servus tricliniaris vel Servus tricliniarius, banqueting-room slaves.
Tricliniarcha vel Architriclinius, chief of ditto.
Lectisterniator, couch-spreader.
Mensæ detersor, table-wiper.
Structor, arranger of dishes or ornamental confectioner.
Calator vel invitator, inviter.
Vocator, ditto, or summoner, or announcer.
Infertor, server.
Gustator vel Prægustator, taster.
Scissor, vel Carptor, vel Cheironomontar, carver.
Diribitor, distributor.
Ministrator, server or waiter.
Minister, ditto, (or servant generally.)
Pocillator, cup-bearer.
Serva ad cyathos, female ditto.
Diætarius vel Zætarius, attendant at meals.
Custos, watchman.
Ostiarius vel Janitor, porter or door-keeper.
Ostiaria vel Janitrix, female ditto.
Velarius, curtain or hanging-keeper.

Atriensis vel Atrarius, hall-keeper, or hall slave generally.
Ædituus, house-cleaner.
Scoparius, sweeper.
Mediastinus, ditto, or drudge generally.
Supellecticarius vel Servus a supellectili, furniture-keeper.
Corinthiarius vel Servus a Corinthis, keeper of brazen vases, &c.
Argento præpositus, silver-plate keeper.
Auro præpositus, gold-plate keeper.

2.—PERSONAL ATTENDANTS.

Cubicularius, bedchamber slave, valet de chambre.
Silentiarius, silence-keeper or husher.
Serv. ad somnum, sleep-watcher.
Quietis minister, ditto.
Balneator, bath-keeper or manager.
Fornacator, bath-furnace heater.
Unguentarius, ointment-maker or keeper.
Unctor, anointer.
Unctrix, female ditto.
Alipilus vel Alipilarius, hair extractor.
Tonsor, barber.
Tonstrix, female ditto.
Ornator, adorner or hair-dresser.
Ornatrix, female ditto.
Ornatrix a tutulo, female hair-dresser in the tutulus fashion
Ornatrix auriculæ vel ab auricula, ear-ring woman.
Cinerarius, hair-curler.
Ciniflo, ditto, or powderer.
Cosmeta, toilet slave, either male or female.
Vestitor, dresser.
Servus a veste vel Vestiarius, wardrobe-keeper.
Vestinria, female ditto.
Vestiplica, female dress-folder.
Vestispicus, dress inspector or keeper.
Vestispica, female ditto.
Capsarius, press or chest keeper.
Puer a matella, pot de chambre boy.

To increase the number of citizens, Romulus opened an asylum or sanctuary for fugitive slaves, insolvent debtors, and malefactors, whither great numbers flocked from the neighbouring states, because no one could be taken

---

Servus qui nunciabat horas, hour-caller.
Monitor, remembrancer.
Fartor, ditto, or prompter.
Nomenclator, namer.
Assecla, follower or attendant.
Circumpes vel Pedissiquus, Puer a pedibus vel ad pedes, foot-boy or attendant.
Pedissequa, female attendant.
Anteambulo, harbinger or running footman.
Anteambulatrix, female harbinger.
Accersitor, announcer of his master.
Adversitor, attendant abroad.
Machærophorus, sword-bearer or chasseur.
Lampadophorus, lamp or lantern-bearer.
Tædiger, torch-bearer.
Lecticarius, litter-bearer.
Cathedrarius vel Cathedralicius, cathedra or chair-bearer.
Portitor sella vel Gestator, chairman or sedan-bearer.
Cursor, runner.
Viator, ditto, or messenger.
Tabellio vel Tabellarius, letter-carrier.
Salutiger vel Salutigerulus, message or compliments-bearer.
Servus qui muscas fugaret, fly-flapper.
Flabellifer, fan-bearer.
Umbrellifer, umbrella or parasol-bearer.
Umbrellifera, female ditto.
Sandaliger vel Sandaligerulus, sandal-bearer.
Sandaligerula vel Ancilla a sandalio, female ditto.
Analecta, picker up.

3.—UPPER SERVANTS.

Actor, manager or "homme d'affaires" generally.
Adjutor, assistant to actor.
Columella vel Major domus, house-steward.
Tabularius vel Calculator vel Numerarius, -accountant.
Ratiocinator, ditto, or rather auditor.
Dispensator vel Prorogator vel Arcarius, keeper of household purse and stores.
Tesserarius, score or tally master, or token or check taker.
Procurator, purveyor or superintendant.
Servus valetudinarius vel ab ægris, hospital attendant.

4.—NURSERY SLAVES, AND ATTENDANTS OF YOUTH.

Nutritor vel Nutricius, male-nurse.
Nutrix, nurse.
Bajulus vel Gerulus, bearer or carrier
Gerula, female ditto or nursery-maid.
Cunarius, rocker or cradle boy
Cunaria, female rocker or cradle-girl.
Educator, nursery tutor.
Præceptor vel Magister, teacher.
Pædagogus, ditto, originally attendant on young persons going to school.
Capsarius, satchel carrier.

5.—SLAVES OF LUXURY.

A.—ATTACHED TO HOUSEHOLD.

Literary Slaves.

Servus a bibliothecis vel a bibliotheca, librarian.
Lector, reader.
Lectrix, female ditto.
Anagnostes, reader or man of learning in various branches.
Recitator, reader aloud or reciter.
Homerista, reciter of Homer's works.
Aretalogus vel Fabulator, story teller.
Actuarius, journal-keeper.
Amanuensis vel Servus a manu, secretary, clerk, or amanuensis.

Monsters and Buffoons.

Morio, fool or idiot.
Fatuus, idiot.
Fatua, female ditto.
Nanus vel Pumilio, dwarf.
Nana, female ditto.
Hermaphroditus, hermaphrodite.
Phagus vel Polyphagus, glutton.
Spado vel Eunuchus, eunuch.
Scurra, buffoon.
Ludio, do. masker or mummer.
Deliciæ vel Delicia, darling, smart prattling boy.

Artisans.

Lanipendia, female wool weigher.
Lania, female wool dresser.
Lanifica, female do. or spinner.
Qausillaria, female spinner,

Textor, weaver.
Textrix, female ditto.
Linteo, linen weaver, or bleacher.
Fullo, fuller.
Phrygio, embroiderer.
Sutor, shoemaker or sewer generally.
Cerdo, cobbler.
Vestificus, dressmaker.
Vestifica, female ditto.
Sartor, tailor.
Sartrix, female ditto.
Sarcinator, mender or patcher.
Sarcinatrix, female ditto.
Ferrarius, smith.
Tignarius, carpenter.
Faber carpentarius, cart-wright.
Doliarius vel Servus doliaris, cooper.
Gerulus, porter or carrier.
Aquarius vel Aquariolus vel Boccario, water carrier.
Pollinctor, anointer of the dead.
Succolator vel Vespillo vel Lecticarius, bearer of the bier.
Ustor, burner of the dead.

B.—FREQUENTLY UNATTACHED TO HOUSEHOLD.

Scientific Slaves and Artists.

Medicus, physician or medical man generally.
Medica, female physician or medical attendant.
Obstetrix vel Opstetrix, midwife.
Clinicus, physician or clinical surgeon.
Chirurgus, surgeon.   [list.
Ocularius vel ab oculis, oculist.
Iatraliptes, healer by ointment and friction.
Aliptes vel Alipta, rubber with ointment.
Tractator, shampooer.?
Tractatrix, female ditto.
Magicus puer, magician or diviner.
Grammaticus, grammarian.
Litteratus vel Litterator, ditto.
Antiquarius, antiquary.
Notarius, short-hand writer.
Notaria, female ditto.
Scriptor vel Scriba, writer, clerk, or penman.
Librarius, book writer or transcriber.
Libraria, female ditto.
Glutinator, gluer or paster of papyrus, &c.
Pumicator, polisher with pumice stone.

from thence to punishment.* Even vanquished enemies were transplanted to Rome, and became citizens. In this manner the freedom of the city was granted by Romulus to the Cœninenses, Camerini, Antemnates, Crustumini, and at last also to the Sabines. This example was imitated by his successors, who transplanted the Albans and other vanquished tribes to Rome.[1] Likewise, after the expulsion of the kings, the freedom of the city was given to a great many, especially after the taking and burning of the city by the Gauls ; at which time, that it might be rebuilt with more splendour, new citizens were assumed from the Veientes, Capenates, and Falisci.[2]

Besides those who had settled in the Roman territory, and who were divided into city and country tribes, the freedom of the city was granted to several foreign towns, which were called MUNICIPIA, and the inhabitants MUNICIPES, because they might enjoy offices at Rome.[3] When any of these fixed their abode at Rome, they became CIVES INGENUI.[4] Hence it happened that the same person might enjoy the highest honours both at Rome and in his own free town. Thus Milo, while he stood candidate for the consulship at Rome, was dictator in his own native city Lanuvium. The free town in which one was born was called *patria* GERMANA, *naturæ* vel *loci*. Rome, (qua *exceptus est*,) *patria* COMMUNIS, *civitatis* vel *juris*.[5]

But when the Roman empire was more widely extended, and the dignity of a Roman citizen of course began to be more valued, the freedom of the city[6] was more sparingly conferred, and in different degrees, according to the different merits of the allies towards the republic. To some the right of voting[7] was given, and to others not. The people of Cære were the first who obtained the freedom of the city without the right of voting, for having received the sacred things of the Roman people, the vestal virgins and priests, when they fled from the Gauls.[8] The freedom of the city was soon after given in this manner to the people of Capua, Fundi, Formiæ, Cumæ, and Sinuessa, to the inhabitants of Acerra,[9] and of Anagnia, &c.

Malleator, hammerer or beater.	Symphoniacus, singer.	cymbal player and dancer.
Ornator, ornamenter.	Acroama, ditto.	Saltator, dancer,
Miniculator vel Illuminator, illuminator.	Choraules, ditto.	Saltatrix, female ditto.
Pictor, painter.	Citharædus vel Fidicen, harper, or singer to the harp.	Funambulus vel Funirepus vel Schœnobates, rope-dancer.
Cælator, engraver or embosser.	Citharæda vel Fidicina, Citha-, ristria vel Psaltria, female	Palæstria, wrestler.
Argentarius, silversmith.	ditto.	Gladiator, gladiator.
Vasentarius, vessel maker.	Tibicen, piper.	Arenarius, ditto.
Faber a Corinthis, worker in brass.	Tibicena, female ditto.	Auriga, charioteer in the circus.
Figulus, potter or tile burner.	Fistulator, flute player.	Rhedarius, ditto.
Architectus, architect.	Hydraules vel Organarius, water-organ player or director.	
Structor, builder.		6.—MILITARY ATTENDANTS.
Histrio, player.	Sambucina vel Sambucistria, female dulcimer or sackbut player.	Armiger, armour-bearer.
Comœdus, ditto, or comedian.		Galearius, helmet-ditto.
Mimus, mime.	Tympanistria, female drummer or tambourine player.	Calvator, club-ditto.
Mima, female ditto.		Calo, soldier's boy, or drudge.
Pantomimus, pantomime.	Crotalistria vel Copa, female	Cacula, ditto.
Pantomima, female ditto.		

* "Still in ancient times this rabble cannot have been conceived to have formed any considerable part of the population: for the asylum was a small inclosure on the Capitoline hill, and in its quality of asylum, could only afford protection within its precincts."—ED.

---

1 Liv. i. 8. xxiv. 51.
Tac. Ann. iii. 60. Liv.
i. 29. 33.
2 Liv. vi. 4.

3 munia v. munera, capere poterant.
4 Cic. Brut. 75. Legg. ii.
2. Cic. Mil. 37.

5 Cic. Legg. ii. 2.
6 jus civitatis.
7 jus suffragii.

8 A. Gell. xvi. 13.
9 Liv. viii. 14. 17.

The inhabitants of Lanuvium, Aricia, Nomentum, Pedum, and Privernum,[1] received the freedom of the city with the right of voting.[2] But several cities of the Hernici preferred their own laws.[3] In process of time, this right was granted to all the allies of the Latin name ; and after the Social or Italian war, it was communicated to all the Italians south of the river Rubicon on the upper sea, and of the city Luca on the lower sea. Afterwards the same right was granted to Cisalpine Gaul, which hence began to be called Gallia Togata. Augustus was very sparing in conferring the freedom of the city ; but the succeeding emperors were more liberal, and at different times granted it to different cities and nations. At last Caracalla granted the freedom of Roman citizens to all the inhabitants of the Roman world.

Those who did not enjoy the right of citizens were anciently called HOSTES, and afterwards PEREGRINI.[4] After Rome had extended her empire, first over Latium, then over Italy, and lastly over great part of the world, the rights which the subjects of that empire enjoyed came to be divided into four kinds ; which may be called *jus Quiritium, jus Latii, jus Italicum, jus provinciarum* vel *provinciale.*

JUS QUIRITIUM comprehended all the rights of Roman citizens, which were different at different times. The rights of Roman citizens were either private or public : the former were properly called *jus Quiritium*, and the latter *jus civitatis*,[5] as with us there is a distinction between denization and naturalization.

1. PRIVATE RIGHTS OF ROMAN CITIZENS.

THE private rights of Roman citizens were, 1. *Jus libertatis*, the right of liberty ; 2. *Jus gentilitatis et familiæ*, the right of family ; 3. *Jus connubii*, the right of marriage ; 4. *Jus patrium*, the right of a father ; 5. *Jus dominii legitimi*, the right of legal property ; 6. *Jus testamenti, et hæreditatis*, the right of making a will, and of succeeding to an inheritance ; 7. *Jus tutelæ*, the right of tutelage or wardship.

1. THE RIGHT OF LIBERTY.

THIS comprehended LIBERTY, not only from the power of masters,[6] but also from the dominion of tyrants, the severity of magistrates, the cruelty of creditors, and the insolence of more powerful citizens.

After the expulsion of Tarquin, a law was made by Brutus that no one should be king at Rome, and that whoever should from a design of making himself king, might be slain with impunity. At the same time the people were bound by an oath, that they would never suffer a king to be created.

Roman citizens were secured against the tyranical treatment of magistrates, first, by the right of appealing from them to the people, and that the person who appealed should in no manner be punished, till the people determined the matter ; but chiefly, by the assistance of their tribunes.

None but the whole Roman people in the Comitia Centuriata, could pass sentence on the life of a Roman citizen. No magistrate was allowed to punish him by stripes or capitally. The single expression, " I AM A ROMAN CITIZEN," checked their severest decrees.[7]

---

1 Privernates.
2 Liv. viii. 14. 21.
3 Liv. ix. 43.
4 Cic. Off. L 12.

5 Plin. Ep. x. 4. 6. 22.
Cic. Rull. ii. 19.
6 dominorum.
7 Cic. Verr. v. 54. 57.

&c. hence, Quiritare
dicitur, qui Quiritium
fidem clamans implo-
rat. Varr. Lat. v. 7.

Cic. Fam. x. 32. Liv.
xxix. 8. Acts. xxii. 25.

By the laws of the twelve tables it was ordained, that insolvent debtors should be given up[1] to their creditors to be bound in fetters and cords,[2] whence they were called NEXI, OBÆRATI, et ADDICTI. And although they did not entirely lose the rights of freemen, yet they were in actual slavery, and often treated more harshly than even slaves themselves.[3]

If any one was indebted to several persons, and could not find a cautioner[4] within sixty days, his body[5] literally, according to some, but more probably, according to others, his effects, might be cut into pieces, and divided among his creditors.[6]   Thus *sectio* is put for the purchase of the whole booty of any place, or of the whole effects of a proscribed or condemned person,[7] or for the booty or goods themselves,[8] and *sectores* for the purchasers,[9] because they made profit by selling them in parts.[10]

To check the cruelty of usurers a law was made, A. U. 429, whereby it was provided, that no debtors should be kept in irons or in bonds; that the goods of the debtor, not his person, should be given up to his creditors.[11]

But the people, not satisfied with this, as it did not free them from prison, often afterwards demanded an entire abolition of debts, which they used to call NEW TABLES.   But this was never granted them.   At one time, indeed, by a law passed by Valerius Flaccus, silver was paid with brass, as it is expressed;[12] that is, the fourth part of the debt only was paid,[13] an *as* for a *sestertius*, and a *sestertius* for a *denarius*; or 25 for 100, and 250 for 1000. Julius Cæsar, after his victory in the civil war, enacted something of the same kind.[14]

2. THE RIGHT OF FAMILY.

EACH gens and each family had certain sacred rites peculiar to itself, which went by inheritance in the same manner as effects.[15] When heirs by the father's side of the same family[16] failed, those of the same gens[17] succeeded, in preference to relations by the mother's side[18] of the same family.[19] No one could pass from a patrician family to a plebeian, or from a plebeian to a patrician, unless by that form of adoption, which could only be made at the Comitia Curiata.   Thus Clodius, the ememy of Cicero, was adopted by a plebeian, that he might be created a tribune of the commons.[20]

3. THE RIGHT OF MARRIAGE.

No Roman citizen was permitted to marry a slave, a barbarian, or a foreigner, unless by the permission of the people.[21] By the laws of the Decemviri, intermarriages between the patricians and plebeians were prohibited.   But this restriction was soon abolished.[22]   Afterwards, however, when a patrician lady married a plebeian, she was said *patribus enubere*, and was excluded from the sacred rites of patrician ladies.[23]   When any woman married out of her clan, it was called *gentis enuptio*; which likewise seems anciently to have been forbidden.[24]   The different kinds of marriage, &c. will be treated of afterwards.

1 addicerentur.
2 compedibus et nervis.
3 Liv. ii. 23.
4 vindex vel expromissor.
5 corpus.
6 secari, A. Gell. xx. 1.
7 Cic. Phil. ii. 26.
8 Cæs. Bell. Gall. ii.
33. Cic. Inv. i. 45.
9 Ascon. Cic. Verr. i. 23.

10 a seco; hence sectores collorum et bonorum, i. e. qui proscriptos occidebant, et bona eorum emebant, Cic. Rosc. Am. 29.
11 Liv. viii. 28.
12 Sall. Cat. 33.
13 Vel. ii. 23.
14 Cæs. Bell. Civ. iii. 1. Suet. Jul. 14.

15 Liv. iv. 2.
16 agnati.
17 gentiles.
18 cognati.
19 familia.
20 Cic. Dom. 15. Att. i. 18, 19.
21 Liv. xxxviii. 36. connubium est matrimonium inter cives; inter servos autem, aut

inter civem et peregrinæ conditionis hominem, aut serviles, non est connubium, sed contubernium, Boeth. Cic. Top. 4.
22 Liv. iv. 6.
23 Liv. x. 23.
24 Liv. xxxix. 19.

4. THE RIGHT OF A FATHER.

A FATHER, among the Romans, had the power of life and death over his children. He could not only expose them when infants, which cruel custom prevailed at Rome for many ages, as among other nations,[1] and a new-born infant was not held legitimate, unless the father, or in his absence some person for him, lifted it from the ground,[2] and placed it on his bosom ; hence *tollere filium*, to educate ; *non tollere*, to expose. But even when his children were grown up, he might imprison, scourge, send them bound to work in the country, and also put them to death by any punishment he pleased, if they deserved it.[3] Hence a father is called a domestic judge, or magistrate, by Seneca ; and a sensor of his son, by Suetonius.[4] Romulus, however, at first permitted this right only in certain cases.[5]

A son could acquire no property but with his father's consent ; and what he did thus acquire was called his PECULIUM, as of a slave.[6] If he acquired it in war, it was called PECULIUM CASTRENSE.

The condition of a son was in some respects harder than that of a slave. A slave, when sold once, became free ; but a son not, unless sold three times. The power of the father was suspended, when the son was promoted to any public office, but not extinguished,[7] for it continued not only during the life of the children, but likewise extended to grandchildren and great grandchildren. None of them became their own masters[8] till the death of their father and grandfather. A daughter by marriage passed from the power of her father under that of her husband.

EMANCIPATION AND ADOPTION.

WHEN a father wished to free his son from his authority,[9] it behoved him to bring him before the prætor, or some magistrate,[10] and there sell him three times, PER ÆS ET LIBRAM, as it was termed, to some friend, who was called PATER FIDUCIARIUS, because he was bound after the third sale to sell him back[11] to the natural father. There were besides present, a LIBRIPENS, who held a brazen balance ; five witnesses, Roman citizens, past the age of puberty ; and an *antestatus*, who is supposed to be so named, because he summoned the witnesses by touching the tip of their ears.[12] In the presence of these, the natural father gave over[13] his son to the purchaser, adding these words, MANCUPO TIBI HUNC FILIUM, QUI MEUS EST. Then the purchaser, holding a brazen coin,[14] said, HUNC EGO HOMINEM EX JURE QUIRITIUM MEUM ESSE AIO, ISQUE MIHI EMPTUS EST HOC ÆRE, ÆNEAQUE LIBRA ;[15] and having struck the balance with the coin, gave it to the natural father by way of price. Then he manumitted the son in the usual form. But as by the principles of the Roman law, a son, after being manumitted once and again, fell back into the power of his father, this imaginary sale was thrice to be repeated, either on the same day, and before the same witnesses, or on different days, and before different witnesses ; and then the purchaser, instead of manumitting him, which would have conferred a *jus patronatus* on himself, sold him back to the natural father, who imme-

1 Cic. Legg. iii. 8. Ter. Heaut. iv. 1. Suet. Oct. 65. Calig. 5. Tac. Hist. iv. 5. Sen. Ben. iii. 13.
2 terra levasset.
3 Sall. Cat. 39. Liv. ii. 41. viii. 7. Diony. viii.
79.
4 Claud. 16.
5 Diony. ii. 15. ix. 22.
6 Liv. ii. 41.
7 Liv. ib.
8 sui juris.
9 emancipare.
10 apud quem legis actio erat.
11 remancipare.
12 Hor. Sat. i. 9. 76.
13 mancipabat, i. e. manu tradebat.
14 sestertius.
15 I declare this man to be mine according to the custom of the Romans, and I purchase him with his coin and a pound of brass.

diately manumitted him by the same formalities as a slave.[1] Thus the son became his own master.[2]

The custom of selling *per æs* vel *assem et libram*, took its rise from this, that the ancient Romans, when they had no coined money,[3] and afterwards when they used *asses* of a pound weight, weighed their money, and did not count it.

In emancipating a daughter, or grand-children, the same formalities were used, but only once ;[4] they were not thrice repeated as in emancipating a son. But these formalities, like others of the same kind, in process of time came to be thought troublesome. Athanasius, therefore, and Justinian, invented new modes of emancipation. Athanasius appointed, that it should be sufficient if a father showed to a judge the rescript of the emperor for emancipating his son ; and Justinian, that a father should go to any magistrate competent, and before him, with the consent of his son, signify that he freed his son from his power, by saying, HUNC SUI JURIS ESSE PATIOR, MEAQUE MANU MITTO.

. When a man had no children of his own, lest his sacred rites and names should be lost, he might assume others[5] as his children by adoption.

If the person adopted was his own master,[6] it was called ARROGATIO, because it was made at the Comitia Curiata, by proposing a bill to the people.[7]

If he was the son of another, it was properly called ADOPTIO, and was performed before the prætor or president of a province, or any other magistrate.[8] The same formalities were used as in emancipation. It might be done in any place:[9] The adopted passed into the family, the name, and sacred rites of the adopter, and also succeeded to his fortune. Cicero makes no distinction between these two forms of adoption, but calls both by the general name of *adoptio*.

5. THE RIGHT OF PROPERTY.

THINGS, with respect to property among the Romans, were variously divided. Some things were said to be of DIVINE RIGHT, others of HUMAN RIGHT : the former was called sacred ;[10] as altars, temples, or any thing publicly consecrated to the gods by the authority of the pontiffs ; or religious ;[11] as sepulchres, &c. ; or inviolable ;[12] as the walls and gates of a city.[13]

These things were subject to the law of the pontiffs, and the property of them could not be transferred. Temples were rendered sacred by inauguration, or dedication, that is, by being consecrated by the augurs.[14] Whatever was legally consecrated, was ever after inapplicable to profane uses.[15] Temples were supposed to belong to the gods, and could not be the property of a private person. Things ceased to be sacred by being unhallowed.[16]

Any place became religious by interring a dead body in it.[17] Sepulchres were held religious because they were dedicated to the infernal

---

1 libra et ære liberatum emittebat. Liv. vi. 14.
2 sui juris factus est, Liv. vii. 16.
3 Liv. iv. 60.
4 unica mancipatio sufficiebat.
5 extraneous.
6 sui juris.
7 per populi rogationem, Gell, v. 19.
8 apud quem legis actio erat.
9 Suet. Aug. 64.
10 res sacræ.
11 religiosæ.
12 sanctæ, i. e. aliqua sanctione munitæ.
13 Macrob. Sat. iii. 3.
14 consecrata inauguratæque.
15 Plin. Ep. ix. 39. x. 58, 59, 76.
16 exauguratione, Liv. i. 55.
17 I. 6. s. 4. D. de di vis, rei.

gods.[1] No sepulchre could be built or repaired without the permission of the pontiffs ; nor could the property of sepulchres be transferred, but only the right of burying in them.[2] The walls of cities were also dedicated by certain solemn ceremonies, and therefore they were held inviolable,[3] and could not be raised or repaired without the authority of the pontiffs.

Things of human right were called profane ;[4] and were either PUBLIC and COMMON, as, the air, running water, the sea, and its shores, &c. ;[5] or PRIVATE, which might be the property of individuals.

Some make a distinction between things common and public, but most writers do not. The things of which a whole society or corporation had the property, and each individual the use, were called RES UNIVERSITATIS, or more properly, RES PUBLICÆ,[6] as theatres, baths, highways, &c. And those things were called RES COMMUNES, which either could be the property of no one, as the air, light, &c.,[7] or which were the joint property of more than one, as a common wall,.a common field, &c. COMMUNE, a subst. is put for the commonwealth.[8] Hence, in commune consulere, prodesse, conferre, metuere, &c. for the public good.

Things which properly belonged to nobody, were called RES NULLIUS ; as parts of the world not yet discovered, animals not claimed, &c. To this class was referred hæreditas jacens, or an estate in the interval of time betwixt the demise of the last occupier and the entry of the successor.

Things were either MOVABLE or IMMOVABLE. The movable things of a farm were called RUTA CÆSA,[9] as sand, coals, stones, &c. which were commonly excepted,[10] or retained by the seller.[11]

Things were also divided into CORPOREAL, i. e. which might be touched ; and INCORPOREAL, as rights, servitudes, &c. The former Cicero called res quæ sunt ; the latter, res quæ intelliguntur.[12] But others, perhaps more properly, call the former, RES, things ; and the latter, JURA, rights.[13]

The division of things Horace briefly expresses thus :

> Fuit hæc sapientia quondam,
> Publica privatis secernere, sacra profanis.[14]   Art. Poet. 396

Private things[15] among the Romans, were either RES MANCIPI, or NEC MANCIPI.

RES MANCIPI were those things which might be sold and alienated, or the property of them transferred from one person to another, by a certain rite used among Roman citizens only ; so that the purchaser might take them as it were with his hand ;[16] whence he was called MANCEPS, and the things res MANCIPI, vel mancupi, contracted for mancipii. And it behoved the seller to be answerable for them to the purchaser, to secure the possession.[17]

NEC MANCIPI res, were those things which could not be thus transferred ; whence also the risk of the thing lay on the purchaser.[18] Thus, mancipium and usus, are distinguished : vitaque mancipio nulli datur, in property or perpetuity, omnibus usu.[19] So mancipium and fructus.[20]

---

1 diis manibus vel inferis.
2 jus mortuum inferendi.
3 sancti.
4 res profanæ.
5 Virg. Æn. vii. 229. Cic. Rosc. Am. 26.
6 quasi populicæ, a populo, the property of the people.
7 Ov. Met. l. 135. vi. 349.
8 Cic. Verr. ii. 46. 63. 69. Hor. Od. ii. 15. 13.
9 sc. et, i. e. eruta et cæsa.
10 recepta.
11 Cic. Top. 26. Orat. ii. 55.
12 Top. 5.
13 Quin. v. 10. 116.
14 This was accounted wisdom of old, to distinguish public from private good, things sacred from things profane.—so Cor. Nep. Them. 6.
15 res privatæ.
16 manu caperet.
17 periculum judicii, vel auctoritatem, vel evictionem præstare, &c. Cic. Mur. 2.
18 Plaut. Pers. iv. 3. 55.
19 Lucr. iii. 985.
20 Cic. Fam. vii. 29, 30.

The *res* MANCIPI, were,—1. Farms, either in town or country within Italy ;[1] or in the provinces, if any city or place had obtained the *jus Italicum.* Other farms in the provinces were called *possessiones,* not *prædia ;* and because proprietors gave in an account of their families and fortunes to the censors, they were called *prædia censui censendo.*[2]—2. Slaves.—3. Quadrupeds, trained to work with back or neck ;[3] as horses, oxen, asses, mules ; but not wild beasts, although tamed; as elephants, camels.—4. Pearls.[4]—5. The rights of country farms, called servitudes.[5]

The servitudes of farms in the country were,—1. The right of going on foot through the farm of another ;[6]—2. Of driving a beast or waggon not loaded ;[7]—3. Of driving loaded waggons ;[8]—4. Of carrying water ;[9] either by canals or leaden pipes.[10] The breadth of a *via,* when straight, was eight feet ; at a turn,[11] sixteen feet ; the breadth of an *actus* four feet ; but the breadth of an *iter* is uncertain.

To these servitudes may be added, the drawing of water ,[12] the driving of cattle to water ;[13] the right of feeding ; of making lime ;[14] and of digging sand.

Those farms which were not liable to any servitude, were called PRÆDIA LIBERA,[15] those which were,[16] PRÆDIA SERVA.[17]

Buildings in the city were called PRÆDIA URBANA, and were reckoned *res mancipi,* only by accession ;[18] for all buildings and lands were called FUNDI ; but usually buildings in the city were called *ædes,* in the country, *villæ.* A place in the city without buildings, was called AREA, in the country, AGER. A field with buildings was properly called FUNDUS.

The servitudes of the *prædia urbana,* were,—1. *Servitus* ONERIS FERENDI, when one was bound to support the house of another by his pillar or wall ;—2. *Servitus* TIGNI IMMITTENDI, when one was bound to allow a neighbour to drive a beam, a stone, or iron into his wall ; for *tignum* among lawyers signified all kind of materials for building.

Anciently, for fear of fire, it was ordered that there should be an interstice left between houses of at least two feet and a half, which was called AMBITUS,[19] or ANGIPORTUS vel *-um,* and this was usually a thoroughfare, but sometimes not.[20] For when Rome came to be crowded with houses, these interstices were only left between some houses. Nero, after the dreadful fire which happened in his time, restored the ancient mode of building houses distinct from one another.[21]

Houses which were not joined by common walls with the neighbouring houses, were called INSULÆ.[22] Sometimes *domus* and *insulæ* are distinguished, Suet. Ner. 16. 38, where *domus* is supposed to signify the houses of the great, and *insulæ* those of the poorer citizens. But anciently this was not the case, rather the contrary ; as, *insula Clodii, Luculli,* &c.[23] Under the emperors, any lodgings,[24] or houses to be let,[25] were called *insulæ,* and the inhabitants of them, *inquilini,* or *insularii ;* which last name is also applied to those who were appointed to guard the *genii* of each *insula.* The proprietors of the *insulæ* were called DOMINI INSULARUM,[26] vel PRÆ-

---

1 prædia urbana et rustica in solo Italico.
2 Cic. Flacc. 32.
3 dorso vel cervice domiti.
4 margaritæ, Plin. ix. 35. s. 60.
5 servitutes, Ulp.
6 iter.
7 actus

8 via.
9 aquæductus.
10 per canales v. fistulas plumbeas, Vitruv. viii. 7.
11 in anfractum v. in flexu.
12 aquæ haustus.
13 pecoris ad aquam appulsus.

14 calcis coquendæ.
15 optimo jure v. conditione optima.
16 quæ serviebant, servitutem debebant, vel servituti erant obnoxia.
17 Cic. Rull. iii. 2.
18 jure fundi.
19 Fest.
20 Ter. Adelph. iv. 2.

39.
21 Tac. Ann. xv. 43.
22 Fest.
23 Cic.
24 hospitia.
25 ædes mercede locandæ, vel domus conductitiis.
26 Suet. Jul. 41. Tib. 48.

DIORUM;[1] and their agents *procuratores insularum.* For want of room in the city they were commonly raised to a great height by stories,[2] which were occupied by different families, and at a great rent.[3] The upmost stories or garrets were called *cænacula.* He who rented[4] an *insula,* or any part of it, was called *inquilinus.* Hence Catiline contemptuously calls Cicero *inquilinus civis urbis Romæ.*[5]

There was also,—3. *Servitus* STILLICIDII ET FLUMINIS, whereby one was obliged to let the water which fell from his house, into the garden or area of his neighbour: or to receive the water which fell from his neighbour's house into his area.—4. *Servitus* CLOACÆ, the right of conveying a private common sewer through the property of a neighbour into the *cloaca maxima* built by Tarquin.—5. *Servitus* NON ALTIUS TOLLENDI, whereby one was bound not to raise his house above a certain height; so as not to obstruct the prospect and lights of his neighbour. The height of houses was limited by law, under Augustus, to 70 feet.[6] There was also a servitude, that one should not make new windows in his wall.[7] These servitudes of city properties, some annex to *res mancipi,* and some to *res nec mancipi.*

MODES OF ACQUIRING PROPERTY.

THE transferring of the property of the *res mancipi,*[8] was made by a certain act, called MANCIPATIO, or MANCIPIUM,[9] in which the same formalities were observed as in emancipating a son, only that it was done but once. This Cicero calls *traditio alteri nexu,*[10] thus *dare mancipio,* i. e. *ex forma* vel *lege mancipii,* to convey the property of a thing in that manner: *accipere,* to receive it.[11] *Jurat,—se fore mancipii tempus in omne tui,* devoted to you.[12] *Sui mancipii esse,* to be one's own master, to be subject to the dominion of no one.[13] So *mancipare agrum alicui,* to sell an estate to any one,[14] *emancipare fundos,* to divest one's self of the property, and convey it to another.[15]

Cicero commonly uses *mancipium* and *nexum* or *-us,* as of the same import:[16] but sometimes he distinguishes them; as de Harusp. 7. where *mancipium* implies complete property, and *nexus* only the right of obligation, as when one receives any thing by way of a pledge. Thus a creditor had his insolvent debtor *jure nexi,* but not *jure mancipii,* as he possessed his slave.

There were various other modes of acquiring legal property; as, 1. JURE CESSIO, or CESSIO IN JURE,[17] when a person gave up his effects to any one before the prætor or president of a province, who adjudged them to the person who claimed them;[18] which chiefly took place in the case of debtors, who, when they were insolvent, gave up their goods[19] to their creditors.

2. USUCAPTIO vel USUCAPIO,[20] and also *usus auctoritas,* when one obtained the property of a thing, by possessing it for a certain time without interruption, according to the law of the twelve tables; for two years, if

1 Plin. Ep. x. 44, 45.
2 contignationibus v. tabulatis.
3 Juv. iii. 166.
4 mercede conducebat.
5 A citizen who lived in a hired house.—Sall. Cat. 31.

6 Strab. v. p. 162. Suet. Aug. 89. Tac. Ann. xv. 43.
7 lumina uti nunc sunt, ita sint, Cic. Or. i. 39.
8 abalienatio, vel translatio dominii v. proprietatis.

9 Cic. Off. iii. 16. Or. i. 39.
10 Top. 5. s. 28.
11 Plaut. Curc. iv. 2. 8. Trin. ii. 4. 19.
12 Ov. Pont. iv. 5. 39.
13 Cic. Brut. 16.
14 Plin. Ep. vii. 16.

15 Id. x. 3.
16 Muren. 2. Flacc. 32. Cæc. 16.
17 Cic. Top. 5.
18 vindicanti addicebat.
19 bona cedebant.
20 Cic. Cæc. 26. Legg. i. 21.

it was a farm or immovable, and for one year, if the thing was movable.[1] But this took place only among citizens.[2] Hence Cicero says, *nihil mortales a diis usucapere possunt.* If there was any interruption in the possession, it was called USURPATIO, which, in country farms, seems to have been made by breaking off the shoot of a tree.[3] But afterwards a longer time was necessary to constitute prescription, especially in the provinces, namely, ten years among those who were present, and twenty years among those who were absent. Sometimes a length of time was required beyond remembrance. This new method of acquiring property by possession, was called LONGA POSSESSIONE CAPIO, or LONGÆ POSSESSIONIS PRÆROGATIVA, vel PRÆSCRIPTIO.

3. EMPTIO SUB CORONA, i. e. purchasing captives in war, who were sold with chaplets on their heads. See p. 23.

4. AUCTIO, whereby things were exposed to public sale,[4] when a spear being set up, and a public crier calling out the price,[5] the magistrate who was present adjudged them[6] to the highest bidder.[7] The person who bade, held up his finger.[8] The custom of setting up a spear at an auction seems to have been derived from this, that at first only those things which were taken in war were sold in that manner. Hence *hasta* is put for a public sale, and *sub hasta venire*, to be publicly sold. The day, sometimes the hour, and the terms of the auction, used to be advertised, either by a common crier,[9] or in writing.[10] Hence *tabula* is put for the auction itself ;[11] *tabulum proscribere*, for *auctionem constituere ; proscribere domum*, v. *fundum*, to advertise for sale.[12] And those whose goods were thus advertised, were said *pendere*,[13] and also the goods, *bona suspensa ;* because the advertisement[14] was affixed to a pillar[15] in some public place.[16] So *tabulas auctionarias proferre* v. *tabulam*, to publish,[17] *ad tabulam adesse*, to be present at the sale.[18] Thus also *sub titulum nostros misit avara lares*, i. e. *donum*, forced me to expose my house to sale.[19]

It behoved the auction to be made in public,[20] and there were courts in the forum where auctions were made,[21] to which Juvenal is thought to allude, Sat. vii. 7. A money-broker[22] was also present, who marked down what was bidden, and to whom the purchaser either paid down the price, or gave security for it.[23] The sale was sometimes deferred.[24]

The seller was called AUCTOR, and was said *vendere auctionem*,[25] in the same manner as a general, when he sold the whole plunder of a city, was said *vendere sectionem*.[26] The right of property conveyed to the purchaser was called AUCTORITAS ; and if that right was not complete, he was said *a malo auctore emere*, to buy from a person who had not a right to sell.[27]

5. ADJUDICATIO, which properly took place only in three cases ; *in familia herciscunda*, vel *ercto ciundo*, i. e. *hæreditate dividenda*, in dividing an inheritance among co-heirs,[28] *in communi dividendo*, in dividing a joint stock

1 ut usus auctoritas, i. e. jus dominii, quod usu paratur, fundi biennium, cæterarum rerum annuus usus esset, Plin. Ep. v. 1.
2 for adversus hostem, i. e. peregrinum, æterna, auctoritas erat ; sc. alicujus rei. Cic. Off. i. 12. i. e. res semper vindicari poterat a peregrino, et nunquam usu capi.
3 surculo defringendo,

Cic. Or. iii. 28.
4 hastæ, v. voci præconis subjiciebantur.
5 præcone pretium proclamante.
6 addicebat.
7 Cic. Phil. ii. 26.
8 digitum tollebat, Cic. Verr. i. 54. digito licitus est, iii. 11.
9 a præcone prædicari, v. conclamari, Plaut. Men. v. 9. 94.
10 tabulo proscribi Cic. Ep. ad Fratr. ii. 6.

proscribebatur sc. domus seu quis emere, seu conducere vellet, Plin. Ep. vii 27. ædes venales inscribit literis, Plaut. Trin. i. 2. 131.
11 Ib.
12 Cic.
13 Suet. Claud. ix.
14 libellus v. tabella.
15 pila v. columna.
16 Sen. Ben. iv. 12.
17 Cic. Cat. ii. 8. Phil. ii. 29.
18 Quin. 6.

19 Ov. R. A. 302.
20 Cic. ib. & Rull. i. 3.
21 atria auctionari.
22 argentarius.
23 Cic. Cæc. 6. Quin. xi. 2.
24 auctio proferebatur, Cic. Att. xiii 12.
25 Cic. Quin. 5.
26 Cæs. Bell. Gall. ii. 33.
27 Cic. Verr. v. 22. Plaut. Curc. iv. 2. 12.
28 Cic. Or. A 58. Cæc. 3.

among partners,[1] *in finibus regundis*, in settling boundaries among neighbours,[2] when the judge determined any thing to any of the heirs, partners, or neighbours, of which they got immediate property ; but arbiters were commonly appointed in settling bounds.[3] Sometimes, however, things were said to be adjudged[4] to a person, which he obtained by the sentence of a judge from any cause whatever.

6. DONATIO. Donations which were made for some cause, were called MUNERA ; as from a client or freedman to his patron, on occasion of a birth or marriage.[5] Those things which were given without any obligation, were called DONA ; but these words are often confounded.

At first presents were but rarely given among the Romans ; but afterwards, upon the increase of luxury, they became very frequent and costly. Clients and freedmen sent presents to their patrons,[6] slaves to their masters, citizens to the emperors and magistrates, friends and relations to one another, and that on various occasions ; particularly on the Kalends of January, called STRENÆ ; at the feasts of Saturn, and at public entertainments, APOPHORETA ; to guests, XENIA ; on birth-days, at marriages, &c.[7]

Those things which were acquired by any of the above mentioned methods, or by inheritance, by adoption,[8] or by law, as a legacy, &c. were said to be IN DOMINIO QUIRITARIO i. e. *justo et legitimo :* other things were said to be IN BONIS, and the proprietors of them were called BONITARII, whose right was not so good as that of the DOMINI QUIRITARII, *qui optimo jure possidere dicebantur*, who were secure against lawsuits. But Justinian abolished these distinctions. When a person had the use and enjoyment of a thing, but not the power or property of alienating, it was called USUSFRUCTUS, either in one word,[9] or in two,[10] and the person FRUCTUARIUS, or USUFRUCTUARIUS.

6. RIGHT OF TESTAMENT AND INHERITANCE.

NONE but Roman citizens[11] could make a will, or be witnesses to a testament, or inherit any thing by testament.[12]

Anciently testaments used to be made at the Comitia Curiata, which were in that case properly called *Calata*.[13]

The testament of a soldier just about to engage, was said to be made IN PROCINCTU, when in the camp, while he was girding himself, or preparing for battle, in presence of his fellow-soldiers, without writing, he named his heir.[14] So *in procinctu carmina facta*, written by Ovid at Tomi, where he was in continual danger of an attack from the Getæ.[15]

But the usual method of making a will, after the laws of the twelve tables were enacted, was PER ÆS ET LIBRAM, or *per familiæ emptionem*, as it was called ; wherein before five witnesses, a *libripens* and an *antestatus*, the testator, by an imaginary sale, disposed of his family and fortunes to one who was called FAMILIÆ EMPTOR, who was not the heir, as some have thought,[16] but only admitted for the sake of form,[17] that the testator might seem to have alienated his effects in his lifetime. This act was called FAMILIÆ MANCIPATIO ; which being finished in due form, the testator, holding

1 Cic. Ep. vii. 12.
2 Cic. Legg. i. 21.
3 Cic. Top. 10.
4 adjudicari.
5 Ter. Phorm. i. 1. 13.
6 Plin. Ep. v. 14.
7 Plin. & Martial. pas-sim.
8 arrogatione.
9 thus, unsumfructum omnium bonorum suo-rum Cæsenniæ legat, ut frueretur una cum filio, Cic. Cæc. 4.
10 as, usus enim ejus et fructus fundi testamento viri fuerat Cæsenniæ, Ib. 7.
11 sui juris.
12 Cic. Arch. 5. Dom. 32.
13 Gell. xv. 27.
14 nuncupavit, Cic. Nat. D. ii. 3. Or. i. 53.
15 Pont. i. 8. 10.
16 Suet. Ner. 4.
17 dicis causa.

the testament in his hand, said, HÆC, UTI IN HIS TABULIS CERISVE SCRIP-
TA SUNT, ITA DO, ITA LEGO, ITA TESTOR, ITAQUE VOS, QUIRITES, TESTIMO-
NIUM PRÆBITOTE. Upon which, as was usual in like cases, he gently
touched the tip of the ears of the witnesses;[1] this act was called NUNCU-
PATIO TESTAMENTI.[2] Hence *nuncupare hæredem*, for *nominare, scribere*,
or *facere*.[3] But sometimes this word signifies to name one's heir *viva
voce*, without writing ; as Horace just before his death is said to have named
Augustus. For the above mentioned formalities were not always observed,
especially in later times. It was reckoned sufficient if one subscribed his
will, or even named his heir *viva voce*, before seven witnesses. Something
similar to this seems to have prevailed anciently,[4] whence an edict about
that matter is called by Cicero, VETUS et TRANSLATICIUM, as being
usual.[5]

Sometimes the testator wrote his will wholly with his own hand, in
which case it was called *holographum.* Sometimes it was written by a
friend or by others.[6] Thus the testament of Augustus was partly written
by himself, and partly by two of his freedmen.[7] Lawyers were usually
employed in writing or drawing up wills.[8] But it was ordained under
Claudius or Nero, that the writer of another's testament (called by
lawyers *testamentarius*,) should not mark down any legacy for himself.[9]
When a testament was written by another, the testator wrote below, that he
had dictated and read it over.[10] Testaments were usually written on tables
covered over with wax, because in them a person could more easily erase
what he wished to alter.[11] Hence CERÆ is put for *tabulæ ceratæ* or *tabulæ
testamenti.*[12] PRIMA CERA, for *prima pars tabulæ*, the first part of the will,[13]
and CERA EXTREMA, or *ima*, for the last part.[14] But testaments were called TABULÆ, although written on paper or parchment.[15]

Testaments were always subscribed by the testator, and usually by the
witnesses, and sealed with their seals or rings,[16] and also with the seals
of others.[17] They were likewise tied with a thread. Hence *nec mea
subjecta convicta est gemma tabella mendacem linis imposuisse notam*, nor is
my ring, i. e. nor am I convicted of having affixed a false mark, or seal, to
the thread on a forged deed or will.[18] It was ordained that the thread
should be thrice drawn through holes, and sealed.[19]

The testator might unseal[20] his will, if he wished to alter or revise it.[21]
Sometimes he cancelled it altogether ; sometimes he only erased[22] one or
two names. Testaments, like all other civil deeds, were always written
in Latin. A legacy expressed in Greek was not valid.[23] There used to
be several copies of the same testament. Thus Tiberius made two copies
of his will, the one written by himself, and the other by one of his freedmen.[24] Testaments were deposited, either privately in the hands of a
friend, or in a temple with the keeper of it.[25] Thus Julius Cæsar is said
to have intrusted his testament to the eldest of the vestal virgins.[26]

In the first part of a will, the heir or heirs were written thus: TITIUS
MIHI HÆRES ESTO, *sit* v. *erit ;* or thus, TITIUM HÆREDEM ESSE JUBEO, vel

1 auricula tacta antes-
  tabatur, quod in ima
  aure memoriæ locus
  erat, Plin. xi. 45.
2 Plin. Ep. viii. 18.
3 Suet. & Plin. passim.
4 Cic. Verr. i. 45.
5 Ib. 44.
6 Plin. Ep. vi. 26.
7 Suet. Aug. 102.

8 Cic. Or. ii. 6. Suet.
  Ner. 32.
9 Suet. Ner. 17.
10 se id dictasse et re-
  cognovisse.
11 Quin. x. 3. 31.
12 Juv. i. 63. Mart. iv.70.
13 Hor. Sat. ii. 5. 53.
14 Cic. Ver. i. 36. Suet.
  Cæs. 83.

15 Ulp.
16 signis eorum obsig-
  nabantur, Cic. Clu. 13.
  14.
17 Cic. Att. vii. 2. Suet.
  Tib. c. ult. Plin. Ep.
  ix. 1.
18 Ov. Pont. ii. 9. 69.
19 Suet. Ner. 17.
20 resignare.

21 mutare vel recogno-
  scere.
22 inducebat v. delebat.
23 Ulp. Frag. xxv 9.
24 Suet. Tib. c. ult.
25 apud ædituum.
26 Suet. Jul. 83.

volo; also, *hæredem facio, scribo, instituo.* If there were several heirs, their different portions were marked. If a person had no children of his own, he assumed others, not only to inherit his fortune, but also to bear his name,[1] as Julius Cæsar did Augustus.[2]

If the heir or heirs who were first appointed[3] did not choose to accept,[4] or died under the age of puberty, others were substituted in their room called HÆREDES SECUNDI.[5]

A corporate city[6] could neither inherit an estate, nor receive a legacy,[7] but this was afterwards changed.

A man might disenherit[8] his own children, one or all of them, and appoint what other persons he pleased to be his heirs ; thus, TITIUS FILIUS MEUS EXHÆRES ESTO.[9] Sometimes the cause[10] was added.[11] A testament of this kind was called INOFFICIOSUM, and when the children raised an action for rescinding it, it was said to be done *per querelam* INOFFICIOSI.

Sometimes a man left his fortune in trust[12] to a friend on certain conditions, particularly that he should give it up[13] to some person or persons. Whatever was left in this manner, whether the whole estate, or any one thing, as a farm, &c. was called FIDEICOMMISSUM, a trust ; and a person to whom it was thus left, was called HÆRES FIDUCIARIUS, who might either be a citizen or a foreigner.[14] A testament of this kind was expressed in the form of request or entreaty ;[15] thus, ROGO, PETO, VOLO, MANDO, FIDEI TUÆ COMMITTO ;[16] and not by way of command,[17] as all testaments were, and might be written in any language.[18]

In the last part of the will,[18] tutors were appointed for one's children, and legacies[19] left to legatees[20] all in direct and commanding words : thus, TUTOR ESTO, vel TUTORES SUNTO ; TUTOREM V. -ES DO.[21] And to their protection the testator recommended his children.[22]

Legacies were left in four different ways, which lawyers have distinguished by the following names.—1. *Per* VINDICATIONEM ; thus, DO, LEGO ; also, CAPITO, SUMITO, V. HABETO.[23] This form was so called from the mode of claiming property.[24]—2. *Per* DAMNATIONEM : thus, HÆRES MEUS, DAMNAS ESTO DARE, &c. Let my heir be bound, &c ;[25] and so in the plural, DAMNAS SUNTO. By this form the testator was said *damnare hæredem,* to bind his heir. Hence *damnare aliquem votis,*[26] *civitas damnata voti,* bound to perform.[27] But it was otherwise expressed thus, HÆRES MEUS DATO, FACITO ; HÆREDEM MEUM DARE JUBEO.—3. SINENDI *modo ;* thus, HÆRES MEUS SINITO, vel DAMNAS ESTO SINERE LUCIUM TITIUM SUMERE ILLAM REM, V. SIBI HABERE.—4. *Per* PRÆCEPTIONEM ; thus, L. TITIUS ILLAM REM PRÆCIPITO, E MEDIO, vel E MEDIA HÆREDITATE SUMITO, SIBIQUE HABETO, vel *præcipiat,* &c. when any thing was left to any person, which he was to get before the inheritance was divided, or when any thing particular was left to any one of the co-heirs besides his own share.[28] Hence PRÆCIPERE, to receive in preference to others ; and PRÆCEPTIO, a certain legacy to be paid out of the first part

---

1 nomen suum ferre.
2 in familiam nomenque adoptavit, adscivit, Suet. assumpsit, Plin.
3 instituti.
4 hæreditatem adire, v. cernere nolient.
5 secundo loco v. gradu scripti v. substituti, Cic. Clu. 11. Hor. Sat. ii. 5. 45. Suet. Jul. 83.

6 respublica.
7 Plin. Ep. v. 7,
8 exhæredare.
9 Plin. Ep. v. 1. hence Juv. Sat. 10. codice sævo hæredes vetat esse suos.
10 elogium, i. e. causa exhæredationist.
11 Cic. Clu. 48. Quin. vii. 4. 20. decl. 2.

12 fidei committebat.
13 ut restitueret v. redderet.
14 I. 8. s. 4. D. de. acceptil.
15 verbis precativis.
16 Ter. And. ii. 5.
17 verbis imperativis.
18 in tabulis secundis.
19 legata.
20 legatariis.

21 Cic. Ep. xiii. 61. Plin. Ep. ii. 1.
22 Ov. Tr. iii. El. 14.
23 to which Virgil alludes, Æn. v. 533.
24 Ulc. Mur. 12.
25 Quin. viii. 9. 9.
26 Virg. Æn. v. 80.
27 Liv. v. 25.
28 to which Virgil alludes, Æn. ix. 271.

of the fortune of the deceased,[1] as certain creditors had a privilege to be preferred to others.[2]

When additions were made to a will, they were called CODICILLI. They were expressed in the form of a letter addressed to the heirs, sometimes also to trustees.[3] It behoved them however to be confirmed by the testament.[4]

After the death of the testator, his will was opened,[5] in presence of the witnesses who had sealed it,[6] or a majority of them.[7] And if they were absent or dead, a copy of the will was taken in presence of other respectable persons, and the authentic testimony was laid up in the public archives, that if the copy were lost, another might be taken from it.[8] Horace ridicules a miser who ordered his heirs to inscribe on his tomb the sum he left.[9]

It was esteemed honourable to be named in the testament of a friend or relation, and considered as a mark of disrespect to be passed over.[10]

It was usually required by the testament, that the heir should enter upon the inheritance within a certain time, in 60 or 100 days at most.[11] This act was called HÆREDITATIS CRETIO,[12] and was performed before witnesses in these words : CUM ME MÆVIUS HÆREDEM INSTITUERIT, EAM HÆREDITATEM CERNO ADEOQUE. After saying which,[13] the heir was said HÆREDITATEM ADISSE. But when this formality[14] was not required, one became heir by acting as such,[15] although he might, if he chose, also observe the solemn form.

If the father or grandfather succeeded, they were called *hæredes* ASCENDENTES ; if, as was natural, the children or grandchildren, DESCENDENTES ; if brothers or sisters, COLLATERALES.

If any one died without making a will,[16] his goods devolved on his nearest relations ; first to his children, failing them, to his nearest relations by the father's side,[17] and failing them, to those of the same gens.[18] At Nice, the community claimed the estate of every citizen who died intestate.[19]

The inheritance was commonly divided into twelve parts, called *unciæ*. The whole was called AS. Hence *hæres ex asse*, heir to one's whole fortune ; *hæres ex semisse, ex triente, dodrante*, &c. to the half, third, three fourths, &c.

The UNCIA was also divided into parts ; the half SEMUNCIA, the third DUELLA, or *binæ sextulæ*, the fourth SICILICUM, v. *us*, the sixth SEXTULA.[20]

7. RIGHT OF TUTELAGE OR WARDSHIP.

ANY father of a family might leave whom he pleased as guardians[21] to his children.[22] But if he died intestate, this charge devolved by law on the nearest relation by the father's side. Hence it was called TUTELA LEGITIMA. This law is generally blamed, as in later times it gave occasion to many frauds in prejudice to wards.[23]

When there was no guardian by testament, nor a legal one, then a guardian was appointed to minors and to women by the prætor, and the majo-

1 Plin. Ep. v. 7.
2 protopraxia, i. e. privilegium quo cæteris creditoribus preponantur, Id. x. 109. 110.
3 ad fideicommissarios.
4 Plin. Ep. ii. 16.
5 Hor Ep. i. 7.
6 coram signatoribus.

7 Suet. Tib. 23.
8 esset unde peti posset.
9 Sat ii. 3. 84.
10 Cic. Dom. 19. 32. Sext. 52. Phil. ii. 16. Suet. Aug. 66.
11 Cic. Att. xiii. 46. Or. i. 22. Plin. Ep. x. 79.

12 hæres cum constituit se hæredem esse, dicitur cernere, Varr. L. L. vi. 5
13 dictis cretionis verbis.
14 cretionis solemnitas.
15 pro hærede se gerendo vel gestione.

16 intestatus
17 agnatis.
18 gentilibus.
19 Plin. Ep. x. 88.
20 Cic. Cæc. 6.
21 tutores
22 Liv. i. 34.
23 pupilli, Hor. Sat. ii. 5 Juv. Sat. vi. 38.

rity of the tribunes of the people, by the Atilian law, made A. U. 443. But this law was afterwards changed.

Among the ancient Romans, women could not transact any private business of importance, without the concurrence of their parents, husbands, or guardians ;[1] and a husband at his death might appoint a guardian to his wife, as to his daughter, or leave her the choice of her own guardians.[2] Women, however, seem sometimes to have acted as guardians.[3]

If any guardian did not discharge his duty properly, or defrauded his pupil, there was an action against him.[4]

Under the emperors, guardians were obliged to give security[5] for their proper conduct.[6] A signal instance of punishment inflicted on a perfidious guardian is recorded, Suet. Galb. 9.

II. PUBLIC RIGHTS OF ROMAN CITIZENS.

THESE were *jus census, militiæ, tributorum, suffragii, honorum, et sacrorum.*

I. Jus CENSUS. The right of being enrolled in the censor's books. This will be treated of in another place.

II. Jus MILITIÆ. The right of serving in the army. At first none but citizens were enlisted, and not even those of the lowest class. But in aftertimes this was altered ; and under the emperors soldiers were taken, not only from Italy and the provinces, but also at last from barbarous nations.[7]

III. Jus TRIBUTORUM. TRIBUTUM properly was money publicly imposed on the people, which was exacted from each individual through the tribes in proportion to the valuation of his estate.[8] Money publicly exacted on any other account, or in any other manner, was called VECTIGAL.[9] But these words are not always distinguished.

There were three kinds of tribute ; one imposed equally on each person,[10] which took place under the first kings ;[11] another according to the valuation of their estate ;[12] and a third which was extraordinary, and demanded only in cases of necessity, and therefore depending on no rule.[13] It was in many instances also voluntary,[14] and an account of it was taken, that when the treasury was again enriched, it might be repaid, as was done after the second Punic war.[15]

After the expulsion of the kings, the poor were for some time freed from the burden of taxes, until the year 349, when the senate decreed, that pay should be given from the treasury to the common people in the army, who had hitherto served at their own expense ; whereupon all were forced to contribute annually according to their fortune for the pay of the soldiers.[16]

In the year of the city 586, annual tributes were remitted, on account of the immense sums brought into the treasury by L. Paulus Æmilius, after the defeat of Perseus,[17] and this immunity from taxes continued, according to Plutarch, down to the consulship of Hirtius and Pansa.

The other taxes[18] were of three kinds, *portorium, decumæ,* and *scriptura.*

1. PORTORIUM was money paid at the port for goods imported and ex-

1 Liv. xxxiv. 2. Cic. Cæc. 3.
 Flacc. 34, 35.
2 Liv. xxxix. 19.
3 Liv. xxxix. 9.
4 judicium tutelæ, Cic.
 Rosc. 6. Or. i. 36.

5 satisdare.
6 rem pupilli fore salvam, Digest.
7 Zos, iv. 30, 31.
8 pro portione census.

9 Varr. L. iv. 36.
10 in capita.
11 Diony. iv. 43.
12 ex censu, Liv. i. 43.
 iv. 60. Diony. iv. 8. 19.
13 temerarium, Fest.

14 Liv. xxvi. 35.
15 Id.
16 Liv. iv. 59, 60.
17 Cic. Off. ii. 22.
18 vectigalia.

ported, the collectors of which were called PORTITORES; or for carrying goods over a bridge, where every carriage paid a certain sum to the exacter of the toll.[1] The *portoria* were remitted A. U. 692, the year in which Pompey triumphed over Mithridates,[2] but were afterwards imposed on foreign merchandise by Cæsar.[3]

2. DECUMÆ, tithes, were the tenth part of corn, and the fifth part of other fruits, which were exacted from those who tilled the public lands, either in Italy or without it. Those who farmed the tithes were called DECUMANI, and esteemed the most honourable of the publicans or farmers general, as agriculture was esteemed the most honourable way of making a fortune among the Romans.[4] The ground from which tithes were paid was also called DECUMANUS.[5] But these lands were all sold or distributed among the citizens at different times, and the land of Capua the last, by Cæsar.[6]

3. SCRIPTURA was the tax paid from public pastures and woods; so called, because those who wished to feed their cattle there, subscribed their names before the farmer of them,[7] and paid a certain sum for each beast;[8] as was likewise done in all the tithe lands.[9]

All those taxes were let publicly by the censors at Rome.[10] Those who farmed them[11] were called PUBLICANI or MANCIPES.[12] They also gave securities to the people;[13] and had partners who shared the profit and loss with them.[14]

There was long a tax upon salt. In the second year after the expulsion of Tarquin, it was ordained that salt should not be sold by private persons, but should be furnished at a lower rate by the public.[15] A new tax was imposed on salt in the second Punic war, at the suggestion of the censors Claudius Nero and Livius, chiefly the latter; who hence got the surname of Salinator.[16] But this tax was also dropped, although it is uncertain at what time.

There was another tax which continued longer, called VICESIMA, i. e. the twentieth part of the value of any slave who was freed.[17] It was imposed by a law of the people assembled by tribes, and confirmed by the senate. What was singular, the law was passed in the camp.[18] The money raised from this tax[19] used to be kept for the last exigencies of the state.[20]

Various other taxes were invented by the emperors; as the hundredth part of things to be sold,[21] the twenty-fifth of slaves,[22] and the twentieth of inheritances,[23] by Augustus,[24] a tax on eatables,[25] by Caligula,[26] and even on urine, by Vespasian.[27]

IV. JUS SUFFRAGII, the right of voting in the different assemblies of the people.

V. JUS HONORUM, the right of bearing public offices in the state. These were either priesthoods or magistracies,[28] which at first were conferred only on patricians, but afterwards were all, except a few, shared with the plebeians.

1 Digest. Vid. Cæs. B. G. i. 18. et. iii. 1.
2 Dio. 37. 51. Cic. Att. ii. 16.
3 Suet. Jul. 43.
4 Cic. Verr. ii. 13. iii. 8.
5 Cic. Verr. iii. 6.
6 Suet. Jul. 23. Cic. Att. ii. 16.
7 coram pecuario vel scripturario, Varr.

Rust. ii. 16.
8 Fest. in scripturarius ager.
9 in agris decumanis, Cic. Verr. iii. 52. Plaut. Truc. i. 2. 44.
10 lucabantur sub hasta, Cic. Rull. i. 3.
11 redimebant v. conducebant.
12 Cic. Dom. 10.

13 prædes.
14 socii.
15 Liv. ii. 9.
16 Liv. xxix. 37.
17 Cic. Att. ii. 16.
18 Liv. vii. 16.
19 aurum vicesimarium.
20 Liv. xxvii. 10.
21 centesima, Tac. i. 78.

22 vigesima quinta mancipiorum.
23 vigesima hæreditatum.
24 Suet. Aug. 49. Dio. iv. 25.
25 pro edullis.
26 Suet 40.
27 Suet. 23, &c.
28 sacerdotia et magistratus.

VI. JUS SACRORUM. Sacred rites were either public or private. The public were those performed at the public expense : the private were those which every one privately observed at home. The vestal virgins preserved the public hearth of the city ; the *curiones* with their *curiales* kept the hearths of the thirty curiæ ; the priests of each village kept the fires of each village.[1] And because upon the public establishment of Christianity in the empire, when, by the decrees of Constantine and his sons, the profane worship of the gods was prohibited in cities, and their temples shut, those who were attached to the old superstition fled to the country, andsecretly performed their former sacred rites in the villages ; hence PAGANS came to be used for heathens,[2] or for those who were not Christians ; as anciently among the Romans those were called PAGANI who were not soldiers.[3] Thus, *pagani* et *montani*, are called *plebes urbana* by Cicero, because they were ranked among the city tribes, although they lived in the villages and mountains.[4]

Each gens had certain sacred rites peculiar to itself,[5] which they did not intermit even in the heat of a war.[6] Every father of a family had his own household-gods, whom he worshipped privately at home.

Those who came from the free towns, and settled at Rome, retained their municipal sacred rites, and the colonies retained the sacred rites of the Roman people.

No new or foreign gods could be adopted by the Romans, unless by public authority. Thus Æsculapius was publicly sent for from Epidaurus, and Cybele from Phrygia.[7] Hence, if any one had introduced foreign rites of himself, they were publicly condemned by the senate.[8] But under the emperors, all the superstition of foreign nations flocked to Rome ; as the sacred rites of Isis, Serapis, and Anubis from Egypt, &c.

These were the private and public rights of Roman citizens. It was a maxim among the Romans, that no one could be a citizen of Rome, who suffered himself to be made a citizen of any other city ;[9] which was not the case in Greece :[10] and no one could lose the freedom of the city against his will.[11] If the rights of a citizen were taken from any one, either by way of punishment, or for any other cause, some fiction always took place. Thus, when citizens were banished, they did not expel them by force, but their goods were confiscated, and themselves were forbidden the use of fire and water,[12] which obliged them to repair to some foreign place. Augustus added to this form of banishment what was called DEPORTATIO, whereby the condemned, being deprived of their rights and fortunes, were conveyed to a certain place, without leaving it to their own choice to go where they pleased.

When any one was sent away to any place, without being deprived of his rights and fortunes, it was called RELEGATIO.[13]

So captives in war did not properly lose the rights of citizens. Those rights were only suspended, and might be recovered, as it was called, *jure postliminii*, by the right of restoration or return.[14]

In like manner, if any foreigner who had got the freedom of Rome returned to his native city, and became a citizen of it, he ceased to be a Ro-

1 pagorum.
2 ἐθνικοί, Gentiles.
3 Juv. xvi. 32 Suet. Galb. 19. Plin. Ep. vii. 25.
4 Dom. 28.

5 gentilitia, Liv. v. 52.
6 Liv. v. 46.
7 Liv. xxix. 11, 12.
8 Liv. iv. 30. xxv. 1. xxxix. 16.
9 Cic. Cæc. 36. Nep.

Att. 3.
10 Cic. Arch. 5. Balb. 12.
11 Cic. Dom. 29, 30. Cæc. 33.
12 tis igne et aqua in-

terdictum est.
13 Thus Ov. Trist. ii. 137. v. 11. 21
14 Cic. Top. 6. Or. i. 40.

man citizen.[1]   This was called *postliminium*, with regard to his own country, and *rejectio civitatis* with regard to Rome.

Any loss of liberty, or of the rights of citizens, was called DIMINUTIO CAPITIS, *jus libertatis imminutum*.[2]   Hence *capitis minor*, sc. *ratione* vel *respectu*, or *capite diminutus*, lessened in his state, or degraded from the rank of a citizen.[3]   The loss of liberty, which included the loss of the city, and of one's family, was called *diminutio capitis maxima;* banishment, *diminutio media;* any change of family, *minima.*[4]

JUS LATII.

THE JUS LATII or LATINITAS,[5] was next to the *jus civitatis*. Latium anciently[6] was bounded by the rivers Tiber, Anio, Ufens, and the Tuscan sea. It contained the Albans, Rutuli, and Æqui. It was afterwards extended[7] to the river Liris, and comprehended the Osci, Ausones, and Volsci.[8]   The inhabitants of Latium were called LATINI SOCII, NOMEN LATINUM, ET SOCII LATINI NOMINIS, &c. *Socii et Latinum nomen*, means the Italians and Latins.

The JUS LATII was inferior to the *jus civitatis*, and superior to the *jus Italicum*. But the precise difference is not ascertained.

The Latins used their own laws, and were not subject to the edicts of the Roman prætor. They were permitted to adopt some of the Roman laws, if they chose it, and then they were called POPULI FUNDI. If any state did not choose it, it was said EI LEGI, v. *de ea lege* FUNDUS FIERI NOLLE, i. e. *auctor, subscriptor essee*, v. *eam probare et recipere*.[9]

The Latins were not enrolled at Rome, but in their own cities.[10]   They might be called at Rome to give their votes about any thing, but then they were not included in a certain tribe, and used to cast lots to know in what tribe they should vote;[11] and when the consuls chose, they ordered them by a decree of the senate to leave the city, which, however, rarely happened.[12]

Such Latins as had borne a civil office in their own state, became citizens of Rome;[13] but could not enjoy honours before the *lex Julia* was made,[14] by which law the right of voting and of enjoying honours was granted to those who had continued faithful to Rome in the Social war, A. U. 663; which the Latins had done. The distinction, however, betwixt the *jus Latii* and the *jus civitatis*, and the same mode of acquiring the full right of citizenship, was still retained.[15]

The Latins at first were not allowed the use of arms for their own defence, without the order of the people;[16] but afterwards they served as allies in the Roman army, and indeed constituted the principal part of its strength. They sometimes furnished two thirds of the cavalry, and also of the infantry.[17]   But they were not embodied in the legions, and were treated with more severity than Roman citizens, being punished with stripes, from which citizens were exempted by the Portian law.[18]

The Latins had certain sacred rites in common with Roman citizens; as the sacred rites of Diana at Rome, (instituted by Servius Tullius,[19] in

1 Cic. Balb. 12.
2 Cic. Mil. 36. Sall. Cat. 37.
3 Hor. Od. iii. 5. 42.
4 Dig. ii. de capite minutis.
5 Suet. Aug. 47. Cic.

Att. xiv. 12.
6 Latium Vetus.
7 Latium Novum.
8 Plin. iii. 9.
9 Cic. Balb. 8.
10 Liv. xli. 9.
11 Liv. xxv. 3.

12 Cic. Brut. 26. Sext. 15.
13 App. Bell. Civ. ii. p. 443.
14 Liv. vii. 4. xxiii. 22.
15 per Latium in civitatem veniendi. Plin.

Pan. 37. 39. Strab. iv. p. 166.
16 Liv. ii. 30. iii. 19.
17 Liv. iii. 22. xxi. 17. et alibi passim.
18 Sall. Jug. 69.
19 Liv. i. 45.

imitation of the Amphictyones-at Delphi, and of the Grecian states in Asia in the temple of Diana at Ephesus,[1]) and the Latin holy-days kept with great solemnity on the Alban mountain; first for one day, the 27th of April, and afterwards for several days. The Romans always presided at the sacrifices.[2] Besides these, the Latins had certain sacred rites, and deities peculiar to themselves, which they worshipped; as Feronia at Terracina, Jupiter at Lanuvium.[3]

They had also solemn assemblies in the grove of Ferentina,[4] which appear in ancient times to have been employed for political as well as religious purposes. From this convention all those were excluded who did not enjoy the *jus Latii*.

JUS ITALICUM.

ALL the country between the Tuscan and Hadriatic seas, to the rivers Rubicon and Macra, except Latium, was called Italy. The states of Italy, being subdued by the Romans in different wars, were received into alliance on different conditions. In many respects they were in the same state with the Latins. They enjoyed their own laws and magistrates, and were not subject to the Roman prætor. They were taxed[5] in their own cities, and furnished a certain number of soldiers according to treaty. But they had no access to the freedom of Rome, and no participation of sacred rites.

After the second Punic war, several of the Italian states, for having revolted to Hannibal, were reduced to a harder condition by the dictator Sulpicius Galba, A. U. 550; especially the Brutii, Picentini, and Lucani, who were no longer treated as allies, and did not furnish soldiers, but public slaves.[6] Capua, which a little before had been taken, lost its public buildings and territory.[7] But after a long and violent struggle in the Social, or Marsic war, all the Italians obtained the right of voting and of enjoying honours by the Julian and other laws. Sulla abridged these privileges to those who had favoured the opposite party; but this was of short continuance.[8] Augustus made various changes. He ordered the votes of the Italians to be taken at home, and sent to Rome on the day of the comitia.[9] He also granted them an exemption from furnishing soldiers.[10]

The distinction of the *jus Latii* and *Italicum*, however, still continued, and these rights were granted to various cities and states out of Italy.[11] In consequence of which, farms in those places were said to be IN SOLO ITALICO, as well as those in Italy, and were called PRÆDIA CENSUI CENSENDO,[12] and said to be *in corpore census*, i. e. to constitute part of that estate, according to the valuation of which in the censor's books every one paid taxes.[13]

PROVINCES.

THOSE countries were called provinces, which the Roman people, having conquered by arms, or reduced any other way under their power, sub-

---

1 Diony. iv. 26.
2 Liv. xxi. c. ult. xx.
1 Diony. iv. 49.
3 Liv. xxxii. 9.
4 Liv. i. 50.

5 censi.
6 A. Gell. x. 3.
7 Liv. xxiv. 16.
8 Cic. Dom. 30.
9 Suet. Aug. 46.

10 Herod. ii. 11.
11 Plin. iii. 3, 4.
12 quod in censum referri poterant, utpote res mancipi, quæ ve-

nire emique poterant jure civili, Cic. Flac. 32.
13 Juv. xvi. 53, Dio. 38. 1.

jected to be governed by magistrates sent from Rome.[1] The Senate having received letters concerning the reduction of any country, consulted what laws they thought proper should be prescribed to the conquered, and sent commonly ten ambassadors, with whose concurrence, the general who had gained the conquest might settle every thing.[2]

These laws were called the.FORM or *formula* of the province. Whatever the general, with the advice of the ten ambassadors, determined, used to be pronounced publicly by him before an assembly, after silence was made by a herald.[3] Hence, in *formulam sociorum referri*, to be enrolled among.[4] *Urbem formulæ sui juris facere*, to hold in dependence or subjection.[5] *In antiqui formulam juris restitui*, to be brought into their former state of dependence on, &c.[6]

The first country which the Romans reduced into the form of a province, was Sicily.[7]

The condition of all the provinces was not the same, nor of all the cities in the same province, but different according to their merits towards the Roman people ; as they had either spontaneously surrendered, or made a long and obstinate resistance. Some were allowed the use of their own laws, and to choose their own magistrates ; others were not. Some also were deprived of part of their territory.

Into each province was sent a Roman governor (PRÆSES),[8] to command the troops in it. and to administer justice ; together with a quæstor, to take care of the public money and taxes, and to keep an account of what was received and expended in the province. The provinces were grievously oppressed with taxes. The Romans imposed on the vanquished, either an annual tribute, which was called CENSUS CAPITIS, or deprived them of part of their grounds ; and either sent planters thither from the city, or restored them to the vanquished, on condition that they should give a certain part of the produce to the republic, which was called CENSUS SOLI.[9] The former, i. e. those who paid their taxes in money, were called STIPENDIARII, or *tributarii*, as *Gallia comata*.[10] The latter, VECTIGALES ; who are thought to have been in a better condition than the former. But these words are sometimes confounded.

The sum which the Romans annually received from the stipendiary states was always the same ; but the revenues of the *vectigales* depended on the uncertain produce of the tithes, of the taxes on the public pastures,[11] and on goods imported and exported.[12] Sometimes instead of the tenth part, if the province was less fertile, the twentieth only was exacted, as from the Spaniards.[13] Sometimes in cases of necessity, an additional tenth part was exacted above what was due ; but then money was paid for it to the husbandmen ;[14] whence it was called *frumentum emptum*, also *decumanum*, or *imperatum*.[15]

Asconius in his commentary on Cicero,[16] mentions three kinds of payment made by the provincials ; the regular or usual tax, a voluntary contribution or benevolence, and an extraordinary exaction or demand.[17]

Under the emperors a rule was made out, called CANON FRUMENTARIUS, in which was comprised what corn each province ought yearly to furnish.

1 quod eas provicit, i. e. ante vicit, Fest.
2 Liv. xlv. 17, 18.
3 Liv. xlv. 29. Cic. Verr. li. 19.
4 Liv. xliv. 16.
5 Liv. xxxviii. 9.
6 Liv. xxxii. 33. xxiv. 26.
7 Cic. Verr. li. 1.
8 Ov. Pont. iv. 7. 3.
9 Cic. Verr. iii. 6. v. 5.
10 Suet. Jul. 15.
11 scriptura.
12 portorium.
13 Liv. xliii. 2.
14 Cic. Verr. iii. 31.
15 Liv. xxxvi. 2. xxxvii. 2. 50. xiii. 31.
16 Verr. ii. 2.
17 omne genus pensitationis in hoc capite po-
aitum est,canonis,quod deberetur ; oblationis, quod opus esset ; et indictionis, quod imperaretur. In which sense indictio is used by Pliny, Pan. 29.

The corn thus received was laid up in public granaries, both at Rome and in the provinces, whence it was given out by those who had the care of provisions, to the people and soldiers. Besides a certain sum paid for the public pastures, the people of the provinces were obliged to furnish a certain number of cattle from their flocks.[1] And besides the tax paid at the port, as in Sicily, in Asia, and in Britain, they also paid a tax for journeys ;[2] especially for carrying a corpse, which could not be transported from one place to another without the permission of the high priest or of the emperor. But this tax was abolished. There was also a tax on iron, silver, and gold mines, as in Spain ; on marble in Africa ; on various mines in Macedonia, Illyricum, Thrace, Britain, and Sardinia ; and also on salt pits, as in Macedonia.[3]

MUNICIPIA, COLONIÆ, ET PRÆFECTURÆ.

MUNICIPIA were foreign towns which obtained the right of Roman citizens. Of these there were different kinds. Some possessed all the rights of Roman citizens, except such as could not be enjoyed without residing at Rome. Others enjoyed the right of serving in the Roman legion,[4] but had not the right of voting and of obtaining civil offices.

The *Municipia* used their own laws and customs, which were called LEGES MUNICIPALES ; nor were they obliged to receive the Roman laws unless they chose it.[5] And some chose to remain as confederate states,[6] rather than become Roman citizens; as the people of Heraclea and Naples.[7]

There were anciently no such free towns except in Italy, but afterwards we find them also in the provinces. Thus Pliny mentions eight in Bœtica, and thirteen in hither Spain.[8]

COLONIES were cities or lands which Roman citizens were sent to inhabit. They were transplated commonly by three commissioners,[9] sometimes by five, ten, or more. Twenty were appointed to settle the colony at Capua, by the Julian law.[10] The people determined in what manner the lands were to be divided, and to whom. The new colony marched to their destined place in the form of an army, with colours flying.[11] The lands were marked round with a plough, and his own portion assigned to every one.[12] All which was done after taking the auspices, and offering sacrifices.[13]

When a city was to be built, the founder, dressed in a Gabinian garb,[14] (i. e. with his *toga* tucked up, and the lappet of it thrown back over the

* " The colonists were mostly settled as garrisons in fortified towns taken from the enemy, with land assigned to them instead of pay and provisions. The old inhabitants were not ejected, nor was the whole mass of landed property confiscated by the ruling state. Several stories in which the ancient usage is expressed, however devoid of historical truth, prove clearly that in the case of a genuine Roman colony the general rule was for only a third of the territory of the town it occupied to be confiscated and allotted to it, and that the rest was restored to the former owners. Of course this partition extended to the domain ; unless this, as the *publicum*, passed entire into the hands of the new body, which represented the populus of the place : and assuredly what was left to the old inhabitants was not enjoyed by them free from burthens, though the confiscation of the third might serve as a redemption of the land-tax."—ED.

1 Vopisc. Prob 15.
2 Cic. Verr. ii. 72. Agrar. ii. 29. Tac. Agr. 31. Suet. Vit. 14.
3 Liv. xxxiv. 21. xlv. 29.
4 munera militaria capere poterant.
5 nisi fundi fieri vellent.
6 civitatis fœderatæ.
7 Cic. Balb. 8.
8 Hist. Nat. iii. 2.
9 per triumviros coloniæ deducendæ agroque dividundo, Liv. viii. 16.
10 Dio. xxxviii. 1.
11 sub vexillo.
12 Virg. Æn. i. 425. v. 755.
13 Cic. Phil ii 40. 42.
14 Gabino cinctu ornatus, v. Gabino cultu incinctus, Liv. v. 46.

left shoulder, and brought round under the right arm to the breast, so that it girded him, and made the *toga* shorter and closer,) yoking a cow and a bull to the plough, the coulter whereof was of brass, marked out by a deep furrow the whole compass of the city ; and these two animals, with other victims, were sacrificed on the altars. All the people or planters followed, and turned inwards the clods cut by the plough. Where they wanted a gate to be, they took up the plough and left a space. Hence PORTA, a gate.[1] And towns are said to have been called URBES from being surrounded by the plough.[2] The form of founding cities among the Greeks is described by Pausanias, v. 27, who says that the first city built was Lycosura in Arcadia, viii. 38.

When a city was solemnly destroyed, the plough was also drawn along[3] where the walls had stood.[4] We read in the sacred writings of salt being sown on the ground where cities had stood.[5] The walls of cities were looked upon by the ancients as sacred, but not the gates.[6] The gates, however, were reckoned inviolable.[7]

A space of ground was left free from buildings both within and without the walls, which was called POMŒRIUM,[8*] and was likewise held sacred.[9] Sometimes put only for the open space without the walls.[10] When the city was enlarged, the *pomœrium* also was extended.[11] These ceremonies used in building cities are said to have been borrowed from the Hetrurians.[12]

It was unlawful to plant a new colony where one had been planted before ;[13] but supplies might be sent. The colonies solemnly kept the anniversary of their first settlement.[14] Some colonies consisted of Roman citizens only, some of Latins, and others of Italians.[15] Hence their rights were different. Some think that the Roman colonies enjoyed all the rights of citizens, as they are often called Roman citizens, and were once enrolled in the censor's books at Rome.[16] But most are of opinion, that the colonies had not the right of voting, nor of bearing offices at Rome.[17] The rights of Latin colonies were more limited ; so that Roman citizens who gave their names to a Latin colony, suffered a diminution of rank.[18] The Italian colonies were in a still worse condition. The difference consisted chiefly in their different immunity from taxes.

Sylla, to reward his veterans, first introduced the custom of settling MILITARY COLONIES, which was imitated by Julius Cæsar, Augustus, and others. To those colonies whole legions were sent, with their officers, their tribunes, and centurions ; but this custom afterwards fell into disuse.[19] For the sake of distinction the other colonies were called CIVILES, PLBEIÆ, or TOGATÆ, because they consisted of citizens, or, as they were afterwards named, PAGANI, or *privati*, who were opposed to soldiers.[20]

The colonies differed from the free towns in this, that they used the

---

* " The word *pomœrium* itself seems properly to denote nothing more than a suburb taken into the city, and included within the range of its auspices. By the statement of Tacitus, that of Romulus ran from the Forum Boarium–that is, from the neighbourhood of the Janus through the valley of the Circus; then from the Septizonium to about the beginning of the Via del Colosseo, or a little below the paths of Trajan ; from thence along the top of the Velia to the chapel of the Lares ; and finally by the Via Sacra to the Forum."-ED.

1 aportando aratrum.
2 ab orbe, vel ab urvo, i. e. buri, sive aratri curvatura, Varr. Lat. L. iv. 2. Fest.
3 inducebatur.
4 Hor. Od. i. 16. hence et seges est, ubi Troja fuit, Ov. Her. i. 53.
5 Judg. ix. 45. Mic. iii. 12
6 Plut. Quæst. 26.
7 sanctæ.
8 i. e. locus circa murum, vel post murum intus et extra.
9 Liv. i. 44.
10 Flor. i. 9.
11 hi consecrati fines proferebantur, Liv. ib.
12 ibid.
13 Cic. Phil. ii. 40.
14 diem natalem coloniæ religiose colebant,
Cic. Att. iv. 1. Sext. 63.
15 Liv. xxxix. 55.
16 Id. xxix. 37.
17 Dio. xliii. 39. 50.
18 Cic. Cæc. 33. Dom. 30.
19 Tac. Ann. xiv. 72.
20 see p. 47.

laws prescribed them by the Romans, but they had almost the same kind of magistrates. Their two chief magistrates were called DUUMVIRI, and their senators DECURIONES ; because, as some say, when the colony was first planted, every tenth man was made a senator. The fortune requisite to be chosen a *decurio*, under the emperors, was a hundred thousand sestertii.[1]

The senate, or general council of Grecian cities, under the Roman empire, was called BULE ; its members, BULEUTÆ ; the place where it met at Syracuse, BULEUTERIUM ; an assembly of the people, ECCLESIA.[2] In some cities those who were chosen into the senate by their censors, paid a certain sum for their admission,[3] and that even although chosen contrary to their own inclinations. In Bithynia, they were subjected to regulations with respect to the choice of senators, similar to those at Rome.[4] An act passed by the senate or people was called PSEPHISMA.[5] It was there customary, upon a person's taking the manly robe, solemnizing his marriage, entering upon the office of a magistrate, or dedicating any public work, to invite the whole senate, together with a considerable part of the commonalty, to the number of a thousand or more, and to distribute to each of the company a dole[6] of one or two denarii. This as having the appearance of an ambitious largess,[7] was disapproved of by Trajan.[8] Each colony had commonly a patron, who took care of their interests at Rome.[9]

PRÆFECTURÆ were towns to which præfects were annually sent from Rome, to administer justice ; chosen partly by the people, and partly by the prætor.[10] Towns were reduced to this form, which had been ungrateful to the Romans ; as Calatia, Capua,[11] and others. They neither enjoyed the rights of free towns nor of colonies, and differed little from the form of provinces. Their private right depended on the edicts of their præfects, and their public right on the Roman senate, who imposed on them taxes and service in war at pleasure. Some *præfecturæ*, however, possessed greater privileges than others.

Places in the country, or towns were markets were held, and justice administered, were called FORA ; as *forum* AURELIUM, *forum* APPII,[12] *forum Cornelii, Julii, Livii*, &c. Places where assemblies were held, and justice administered, were called CONCILIABULA.[13] All other cities which were neither *municipia, coloniæ*, nor *præfecturæ*, were called Confederate States.[14] These were quite free, unless that they owed the Romans certain things, according to treaty. Such was Capua, before it revolted to Hannibal. Such were also Tarentum, Naples, Tibur, and Præneste.

FOREIGNERS.

ALL those who were not citizens were called by the ancient Romans, foreigners (PEREGRINI), wherever they lived, whether in the city or elsewhere. But after Caracalla granted the freedom of the city to all freeborn men in the Roman world, and Justinian some time after granted it also to freedmen, the name of foreigners fell into disuse ; and the inhabitants of the whole world were divided into Romans and Barbarians. The whole Roman empire itself was called ROMANIA, which name is still given

1 Plin. Ep. i. 19.
2 βουλη, consilium, Plin. Ep. x. 85. 115. Cic. Verr. ii. 21. Plin. Ep. x. 3.
3 honorarium decurionatus, Id. 114.
4 Id. 83. 115.
5 Id. x. 52, 53.
6 sportula.
7 dianome.
8 Plin Ep. x. 117, 118.
9 Diony. li. 11.
10 Fest.
11 Liv. i. 38. Diony. iii.
50. Liv. xxvi. 16.
12 Cic. Cat. i. 9. Att. ii. 10.
13 Liv. xl. 37.
14 civitates fœderatæ.

to Thrace, as being the last province which was retained by the Romans, almost until the taking of Constantinople by the Turks, A. D. 1452.

While Rome was free, the condition of foreigners was very disagreeable. They might, indeed, live in the city but they enjoyed none of the privileges of citizens. They were also subject to a particular jurisdiction, and sometimes were expelled from the city at the pleasure of the magistrates. Thus M. Junius Pennus, A. U. 627, and C. Papius Celsus, A. U. 688, both tribunes of the people, passed a law, ordering foreigners to leave the city. Augustus did the same. But afterwards an immense number of foreigners flocked to Rome from all parts,[1] so that the greatest part of the common people consisted of them; hence Rome is said to be *mundi fæce repléta.*[2]

Foreigners were neither permitted to use the Roman dress,[3] nor had they the right of legal property, or of making a will. When a foreigner died, his goods were either reduced into the treasury, as having no heir,[4] or if he had attached himself[5] to any person, as a patron, that person succeeded to his effects JURE APPLICATIONIS, as it was called.[6]

But in process of time these inconveniences were removed, and foreigners were not only advanced to the highest honours in the state, but some of them even made emperors.

ASSEMBLIES OF THE PEOPLE.

AN assembly of the whole Roman people to give their vote about any thing, was called COMITIA.[7] When a part of the people only was assembled, it was called CONCILIUM; but these words were not always distinguished.[8]

In the *Comitia*, every thing which came under the power of the people was transacted; magistrates were elected, and laws passed, particularly concerning the declaration of war, and the making of peace. Persons guilty of certain crimes were also tried in the Comitia.[9] The Comitia were always summoned by some magistrate, who presided in them, and directed every thing which came before him; and he was then said, HABERE COMITIA. When he laid any thing before the people, he was said, AGERE CUM POPULO.[10] As the votes of all the people could not be taken together, they were divided into parts.

There were three kinds of Comitia: the *Curiata*, instituted by Romulus; the *Centuriata*, instituted by Servius Tullius, the sixth king of Rome; and the *Tributa*, said to have been first introduced by the tribunes of the people at the trial of Coriolanus, A. U. 263.

The Comitia Curiata and Centuriata could not be held without taking the auspices,[11] nor without the authority of the senate, but the Tributa might.[12] The days on which the Comitia could be held were called DIES COMITIALES.[13] As in the senate, so in the Comitia, nothing could be done before the rising nor after the setting of the sun.[14]

The Comitia for creating magistrates were usually held in the Campus Martius; but for making laws, and for holding trials, sometimes also in the forum, and sometimes in the capitol.

COMITIA CURIATA.

In the Comitia Curiata, the people gave their votes, divided into thirty curiæ ;[1] and what a majority of them, namely sixteen, determined, was said to be the order of the people. At first there were no other Comitia but the Curiata, and therefore every thing of importance was determined in them.

The Comitia Curiata were held, first by the kings, and afterwards by the consuls and the other greater magistrates ; that is, they presided at them, and nothing could be brought before the people but by them. They met in a part of the forum called the COMITIUM, where the pulpit or tribunal[2] stood, whence the orators used to harangue the people. It was afterwards called ROSTRA, because it was adorned with the beaks of the ships taken from the Antiates, and also *Templum*, because consecrated by the augurs ; which was its usual name before the Antiates were subdued.[3] The Comitium was first covered the year that Hannibal came into Italy.[4] Afterwards it was adorned with pillars, statues, and paintings.

Those citizens only had a right to vote at the Comitia Curiata, who lived in the city, and were included in some curia or parish. The curia which voted first were called PRINCIPIUM.[5]

After the institution of the Comitia Centuriata and Tributa, the Comitia Curiata were more rarely assembled, and that only for passing certain laws, and for the creation of the Curio Maximus, and of the Flamines.[6] Each curia seems to have chosen its own curio ; called also *magister curiæ*.[7]

A law made by the people divided into curiæ was called LEX CURIATA. Of these, the chief we read of, were,

1. The law by which military command[8] was conferred on magistrates.[9] Without this, they were not allowed to meddle with military affairs,[10] to command an army, or carry on war ;[11] but only had a civil power,[12] or the right of administering justice. Hence the Comitia Curiata were said *rem militarem continere*,[13] and the people, to give sentence twice,[14] concerning their magistrates.[15] But in after times this law seems to have been passed only for form's sake, by the suffrage of the thirty lictors or serjeants, who formerly used to summon the curiæ, and attend on them at the Comitia.[16]

2. The law about recalling Camillus from banishment.[17]

3. That form of adoption called *arrogatio*[18] was made at the Comitia Curiata, because no one could change his state or *sacra* without the order of the people.[19]

4. Testaments were anciently made at these Comitia ; and because in time of peace they were summoned[20] by a lictor twice a year for this purpose ; hence they were also called COMITIA CALATA, which name is like-

---

1 ita dictæ quod iis rerum publicarum cura commissa sit, Fest. vel potius a κυρια, sc. εκκλησια, conventus populi apud Græcos ad jubendum vel vetandum quod e republica censeret esse.
2 suggestum.
3 Liv. viii. 14. & 35. ii.

56.
4 Liv. xxvii. 38.
5 Liv. ix. 38.
6 Liv. xxvii. 8. A. Gell. xv. 27.
7 Plaut. Aul. ii. 2, 3.
8 imperium.
9 Liv. ix. 38.
10 rem militarem attingere.
11 Cic. Phil. v. 16. Ep.

Fam. i. 9.
12 potestas.
13 Liv. v. 52.
14 bis sententiam ferre, v. binis comitiis judicare.
15 Cic. Leg. Agr. ii. 11.
16 Cic ibid populi suffragiis, ad speciem atque ad usurpationem vetustatis, per triginta

lictores auspiciorum causa adumbratis, cap. 19.
17 Liv. v. 44.
18 see p. 35, 36.
19 Cic. Sext. Dom. 15. &c. Suet. Aug. 65. Dio. xxxvii. 51.
20 calata, i. e. convocata.

wise sometimes applied to the Comitia Centuriata, because they were assembled by a *Cornicen*, who was also called *Classicus*.[1]

5. What was called DETESTATIO SACRORUM, was also made here : as
when it was denounced to an heir or legatee that he must adopt the sacred
rites which followed the inheritance.[2] Whence an inheritance without
this requisite is called by Plautus *hæreditas sine sacris*.[3]

COMITIA CENTURIATA AND CENSUS.

THE principal Comitia were the Centuriata, called also *majora*,[4] in which
the people, divided into the centuries of their classes, gave their votes ;
and what a majority of centuries decreed[5] was considered as finally determined.[6] These Comitia were held according to the *census* instituted
by Servius Tullius.

The CENSUS was a numbering of the people, with a valuation of their
fortunes.[7] To ascertain the number of the people, and the fortunes of
each individual, Servius ordained that all the Roman citizens, both in town
and country, should upon oath take an estimate of their fortunes,[8] and publicly declare that estimate to him ;[9] that they should also tell the place
of their abode, the names of their wives and children, and their own age
and that of their children, and the number of their slaves and freedmen :
that if any did otherwise, their goods should be confiscated, and themselves
scourged and sold for slaves, as persons who had deemed themselves unworthy of liberty.[10] He likewise appointed a festival, called PAGANALIA,
to be held every year in each *pagus* or village, to their tutelary gods, at
which time the peasants should every one pay into the hands of him who
presided at the sacrifices a piece of money ; the men a piece of one kind,
the women of another, and the children of a third sort.[11]

Then, according to the valuation of their estates, he divided all the citizens into SIX CLASSES, and each class into a certain number of CENTURIES.
The division by *centuries*, or hundreds, prevailed every where at Rome ;
or rather by tens, from the number of fingers on both hands.[12] The infantry and calvary, the curiæ and tribes, were divided in this manner ; and
so even the land : hence CENTENARIUS AGER.[13] At first a century contained a hundred ; but not so afterwards. Thus the number of men in the
centuries of the different classes was, without doubt, very different.

The first class consisted of those whose estates in lands and effects were
worth at least 100,000 *asses*, or pounds of brass ; or 10,000 *drachmæ* according to the Greek way of computing ; which sum is commonly reckoned equal to 322*l.* 18*s.* 4*d.* of our money : but if we suppose each pound of
brass to contain 24 *asses*, as was the case afterwards, it will amount to
7,750*l.*

This first class was subdivided into eighty centuries or companies of
foot, forty of young men,[14] that is, from seventeen to forty-six years of
age,[15] who were obliged to take the field,[16] and forty of old men,[17] who

---

1 quod classes comitiis
ad comitatum vocabat,
A. Gell. xv. 27. Varr.
L. L. iv. 16.
2 Cic. Legg. ii. 9.
3 Captiv. iv. 1, cum ali-
quid obvenerit sine ali-
qua incommoda appen-

dice, Fest.
4 Cic. post red. in Se-
nat. 2.
5 quod plures centuriæ
jussissent.
6 pro rato habebatur.
7 æstimatio ἀποτίμησις.
8 bona sua jurati cense-

rent, i. e. æstimarent.
9 apud se profiterentur.
10 qui sibi libertatem ab-
judicassent, Cic. Cæc.
34.
11 Diony. iv. 51.
12 Ov. F. iii. 123, &c.
13 Ov. ibid. & Fest.

14 juniorum.
15 Cic. Sen. 17. A. Gell.
x. 28.
16 ut foris bella gere-
rent.
17 seniorum.

should guard the city.[1]   To these were added eighteen centuries of equites, who fought on horseback : in all ninety-eight centuries.

The second class consisted of twenty centuries ; ten of young men, and
ten of old, whose estates were worth at least 75,000 *asses*.   To these
were added two centuries of artificers,[2] carpenters, smiths, &c. to manage
the engines of war.   These Livy joins to the first class.   It is hardly to
be imagined that those artificers were composed of the members of either
the first or the second class, but of their servants or dependents ; for not
only the mechanic arts, but likewise every kind of trade was esteemed dishonourable among the ancient Romans.

The third class was also divided into twenty centuries ; their estate
was 50,000 *asses*.

The fourth class likewise contained twenty centuries ; their estate was
25,000 *asses*.   To these Dionysius adds two centuries of trumpeters, vii. 59.

The fifth class was divided into thirty centuries ; their estate was 11,000
asses, but according to Dionysius, 12,500.   Among these, according to
Livy, were included the trumpeters, and corneters, or blowers of the horn,
distributed into three centuries, whom Dionysius joins as two distinct centuries to the fourth class.

The sixth class comprehended all those who either had no estates, or
were not worth so much as those of the fifth class.   The number of them
was so great as to exceed that of any of the other classes, yet they were
reckoned but as one century.

Thus the number of centuries in all the classes was, according to Livy,
191 ; and according to Dionysius, 193.   Some make the number of Livy
to amount to 194, by supposing that the trumpeters, &c. were not included
in the thirty centuries of the fifth class, but formed three distinct centuries
by themselves.

Each class had arms peculiar to itself, and a certain place in the army,
according to the valuation of their fortunes.

By this arrangement the chief power was vested in the richest citizens,
who composed the first class, which, although least in number, consisted
of more centuries than all the rest put together ; but they likewise bore
the charges of peace and war[3] in proportion.[4]   For, as the votes at the
Comitia, so likewise the quota of soldiers and taxes, depended on the number of centuries.   Accordingly, the first class, which consisted of ninety-
eight, or, according to Livy, of one hundred centuries, furnished more men
and money to the public service, than all the rest of the state besides.
But they had likewise the chief influence in the assemblies of the people
by centuries.   For the equites and the centuries of this class were called
first to give their votes, and if they were unanimous, the matter was determined ; but if not, then the centuries of the next class were called, and so
on, till a majority of centuries had voted the same thing.   And it hardly
ever happened that they came to the lowest.[5]

In after times some alteration was made, as is commonly supposed, in
favour of the plebeians, by including the centuries in the tribes ; whence
mention is often made of tribes in the Comitia Centuriata.[6]   In consequence of which, it is probable that the number of centuries as well as of
tribes was increased.[7]   But when or how this was done is not sufficiently

---

1 ad urbis custodiam ut   3 munia pacis et bel-   5 Liv. i. 43. Diony. vii.   ii. 9. Planc. 20.
  præsto essent.   li.   59.   7 Cic. Phil. ii. 82.
2 fabrum.   4 Liv. i. 42.   6 Liv. v. 18. Cic. Rull.

ascertained, only it appears to have taken place before the year of the city 358.[1]

Those of the first class were called CLASSICI, all the rest were said to be INTRA CLASSEM. Hence *classici auctores*, for the most approved authors.

Those of the lowest class who had no fortune at all were called CAPITE CENSI, rated by the head ; and those who had below a certain valuation, PROLETARII : whence *sermo proletarius*, for *vilis*, low.[3] This properly was not reckoned a class ; whence sometimes only five classes are mentioned. So *quintæ classis videntur*, of the lowest.[4]

This review of the people was made[5] at the end of every five years, first by the kings, then by the consuls, but after the year 310, by the censors, who were magistrates created for that very purpose. We do not find, however, that the census was always held at certain intervals of time. Sometimes it was omitted altogether.[6]

After the census was finished, an expiatory or purifying sacrifice[7] was made, consisting of a sow, a sheep, and a bull, which were carried round the whole assembly, and then slain ; and thus the people were said to be purified.[8] Hence also *lustrare*, signifies to go round, to survey ; and *circumferre*, to purify.[9] This sacrifice was called SUOVETAURILIA or SOLITAURILIA, and he who performed it was said CONDERE LUSTRUM. It was called *lustrum* a *luendo*, i. e. *solvendo*, because at that time all the taxes were paid by the farmers-general to the censors.[10] And because this was done at the end of every fifth year, hence LUSTRUM is often put for the space of five years ; especially by the poets, by whom it is sometimes confounded with the Greek Olympaid, which was only four years.[11] It is also used for any period of time.[12]

The census anciently was held in the forum, but after the year of the city 320, in the *villa publica*, which was a place in the Campus Martius, fitted up for public uses ; for the reception of foreign ambassadors, &c.[13] The purifying sacrifice was always made[14] in the Campus Martius.[15] The census was sometimes held without the *lustrum* being performed.[16]

1. CAUSES OF ASSEMBLING THE COMITIA CENTURIATA.

THE COMITIA CENTURIATA were held for creating magistrates, for passing laws, and for trials.

In these Comitia were created the consuls, prætors, censors, and sometimes a proconsul,[17] also the *decemviri*, military tribunes, and one priest, namely, the *rex sacrorum*. Almost all laws were passed in them which were proposed by the greater magistrates, and one kind of trial was held there, namely, for high treason, or any crime against the state, which was called JUDICIUM PERDUELLIONIS ; as when any one aimed at sovereignty, which was called *crimen regni*, or had treated a citizen as an enemy.[18] War was also declared at these Comitia.[19]

1 Liv. v. 18.
2 A. Gell. vii. 13. xix. 8.
3 Gell. xvi. 10. Plaut. Mil. Glor. iii. 1. 157.
4 Liv. iii. 30. Cic. Acad. iv. 23.
5 census habitus, v. actus est.
6 Cic. Arch. 5.
7 sacrificium lustrale.
8 lustrari.
9 Virg. Ecl. x. 55. Æn. viii. 231. x. 224. Plaut. Amph. ii. 2. 144. Virg. Æn. vi. 229.
10 Var. L. L. v. 2.
11 Hor. Od. ii. 4. 24. iv. est.
i. 6. Ov. Pont. iv. 6. 5.
Mart. iv. 45.
12 Plin. ii. 48.
13 Liv. iv. 22. xxxiii. 9. Varr. Rust. iii. 2. Luc. ii. 196.
14 lustrum conditum
15 Liv. i. 44. Diony. iv. 22.
16 Liv. iii. 22.
17 Liv. xxvi. 18.
18 Liv. vi. 20. Cic. Verr. i. 5.
19 Liv. xxxi. 6, 7. xlii. 30.

2. MAGISTRATES WHO PRESIDED AT THE COMITIA CENTURIATA; PLACE
WHERE THEY WERE HELD; MANNER OF SUMMONING THEM; AND PER-.
SONS WHO HAD A RIGHT TO VOTE AT THEM.

THE Comitia Centuriata could be held only by the superior magistrates,
i. e. the consuls, the prætor, the dictator, and *interrex*; but the last could
only hold the Comitia for creating magistrates, and not for passing laws.

The censors assembled the people by centuries; but this assembly was
not properly called Comitia, as it was not to vote about any thing. The
prætors could not hold the Comitia if the consuls were present, without
their permission; but they might in their absence,[1] especially the prætor
urbanus; and, as in the instance last quoted, without the authority of the
senate.

The consuls held the Comitia for creating the consuls, and also for creating the prætors; (for the prætors could not hold the Comitia for creating
their successors,) and for creating the censors.[2] The consuls determined
which of them should hold these Comitia, either by lot or by agreement.[3]

The Comitia for creating the first consuls were held by the præfect of
the city, Spurius Lucretius, who was also *interrex*.[4]

When a *rex sacrorum* was to be created, the Comitia are thought to have
been held by the *pontifex maximus*. But this is not quite certain.

The person presiding in the Comitia had so great influence, that he is
sometimes said to have himself created the magistrates who were elected.[5]

When, from contention between the patricians and plebeians, or between
the magistrates, or from any other cause, the Comitia for electing magistrates could not be held in due time, and not before the end of the
year, the patricians met and named[6] an *interrex* out of their own number,
who commanded only for five days;[7] and in the same manner different
persons were always created every five days, till consuls were elected,
who entered immediately on their office. The Comitia were hardly
ever held by the first *interrex*: sometimes by the second, sometimes by
the third, and sometimes not till the eleventh. In the absence of the consuls, a dictator was sometimes created to hold the Comitia.[8]

The Comitia Centuriata were always held without the city, usually
in the Campus Martius: because anciently the people went armed in
martial order[9] to hold these assemblies; and it was unlawful for an army to
be marshalled in the city.[10] But in latter times, a body of soldiers only
kept guard on the Janiculum, where an imperial standard was erected,[11] the
taking down of which denoted the conclusion of the Comitia.[12]

The Comitia Centuriata were usually assembled by an edict. It behoved
them to be summoned[13] at least seventeen days before they were held,
that the people might have time to weigh with themselves what they
should determine at the Comitia. This space of time was called TRI-
NUNDINUM, or TRINUM NUNDINUM, i. e. *tres nundinæ*, three market-days,
because the people from the country came to Rome every ninth day to
buy and sell their commodities.[14] But the Comitia were not held on the

1 Liv. xxvii. 5. xliii. 16.
xlv. 21.
2 Cic. Att. ix. 9. Liv.
vii. 22. Cic. Att. iv. 2.
3 sorte vel consensu;
sortiebantur vel com-
parabant. Liv. passim.
4 Liv. i. 60. Diony. iv.
64.

5 Liv. i. 60. ii. 2. iii. 54.
ix. 7.
6 sine suffragio populi
auspicato prodebant.
7 Cic. Dom. 14. Asc.
Cic. Liv. ix. 34.
8 Liv. ix. 7. x. 11. v. 31.
vii. 21, 22. viii. 23. ix. 7.
xxv. 2.

9 sub signis.
10 Liv. xxxix. 15. Gell.
xv. 27.
11 vexillum positum
erat.
12 Dio. xxxvii. 27, 28.
13 edici v. indici.
14 Liv. iii. 35. nundinæ
a Romanis nono quo-

que die celebratæ: in-
termediis septem die-
bus occupabantur ruri,
Diony. ii. 28. vii. 58. reliquis septem rum co-
lebant. Varr. Rust.
præf. 11.

market-days,[1] because they were ranked among the *feriæ* or holy-days, on which no business could be done with the people.[2] This, however, was not always observed.[3]

But the Comitia for creating magistrates were sometimes summoned against the first lawful day.[4] All those might be present at the Comitia Centuriata who had the full right of Roman citizens, whether they lived at Rome or in the country.

3. CANDIDATES.

THOSE who sought preferments were called CANDIDATI, from a white robe[5] worn by them, which was rendered shining[6] by the art of the fuller; for all the wealthy Romans wore a gown naturally white.[7] This, however was anciently forbidden by law.[8]

The candidates did not wear tunics or waistcoats, either that they might appear more humble, or might more easily show the scars they had received on the breast or fore part of their body.[9]

In the latter ages of the republic, no one could stand candidate who was not present, and did not declare himself within the legal days; that is, before the Comitia were summoned,[10] and whose name was not received by the magistrates: for they might refuse to admit any one they pleased,[11] but not without assigning a just cause.[12] The opposition of the consuls, however, might be overruled by the senate.[13]

For a long time before the time of election, the candidates endeavoured to gain the favour of the people by every popular art;[14] by going round their houses,[15] by shaking hands with those they met,[16] by addressing them in a kindly manner, and naming them, &c.; on which account they commonly had along with them a monitor or MOMENCLATOR, who whispered in their ears every body's name.[17] Hence Cicero calls candidates *natio officiosissima*.[18] On the market-days they used anciently to come into the assembly of the people, and take their station on a rising ground,[19] whence they might be seen by all.[20] When they went down to the Campus Martius at certain times, they were attended by their friends and dependents, who were called DEDUCTORES.[21] They had likewise persons to divide money among the people.[22] For this, although forbidden by law, was often done openly, and once against Cæsar, even with the approbation of Cato.[23] There were also persons to bargain with the people for their votes, called INTERPRETES, and others in whose hands the money promised was deposited, called SEQUESTRES.[24] Sometimes the candidates formed combinations to disappoint[25] the other competitors.[26]

Those who opposed any candidate, were said *ei refragari*, and those who favoured him, *suffragari vel suffragatores esse :* hence *suffragatio*, their interest.[27] Those who got one to be elected, were said *ei præturam gratia cam-*

---

1 nundinis.
2 Macrob. i. 16. ne plebs rustica avocaretur, lest they should be called off from their ordinary business of buying and selling. Plin. xviii. 3.
3 Cic. Att. i. 14.
4 in primum comitialem diem, Liv. xxiv. 7.
5 toga candida.

6 candens vel candida.
7 toga alba.
8 ne cui album, i. e. cretam, in vestimentum addere, petitionis causa liceret, Liv. iv. 25.
9 adverso corpore, Plut. Coriol.
10 Sall. Cat. 18. Cic. Fam. xvi. 12.
11 nomen accipere, vel

rationem ejus habere.
12 Liv. v. 3. 15. xxiv. 7, 8. Val. Max. iii. 8. 3. Vell. ii. 92.
13 Liv. iii. 21.
14 Cic. Att. i. 1.
15 ambiendo.
16 prensando.
17 Hor. Ep. i. 6. 50, &c.
18 Pis. 23.
19 in colle consistere.
20 Macrob. Sat. i. 16.

21 Cic. de pet. cons. 9.
22 divisores, Cic. Att. i.
17. Suet. Aug. 3.
23 Suet. Jul. 19.
24 Cic. Act. Verr. i. 8. 12.
25 coitiones dejicerent.
26 Cic. Att. ii. 18. Liv. iii. 35.
27 Liv. x. 13.

pestri capere,[1] or *eum trahere.*[2] Those who hindered one from being elected, were said *a consulata repellere.*[3]

4. MANNER OF PROPOSING A LAW, AND OF NAMING A DAY FOR ONE'S TRIAL.

WHEN a law was to be passed at the Comitia Centuriata, the magistrate who was to propose it,[4] having consulted with his friends and other prudent men, whether it was for the advantage of the republic, and agreeable to the customs of their ancestors, wrote it over at home ; and then, having communicated it to the senate, by their authority[5] he promulgated it ; that is, he pasted it up in public,[6] for three market-days, that so the people might have an opportunity of reading and considering it.[7]   In the mean time he himself[8] and some eloquent friend, who was called AUCTOR *legis*, or SUASOR, every market-day read it over,[9] and recommended it to the people,[10] while others who disapproved it, spoke against it.[11]   But in ancient times all these formalities were not observed : thus we find a law passed the day after it was proposed.[12]   Sometimes the person who proposed the law, if he did it by the authority of the senate, and not according to his own opinion, spoke against it.[13]

In the same manner, when one was to be tried for treason,[14] it behoved the accusation to be published for the same space of time,[15] and the day fixed when the trial was to be.[16]   In the mean time the person accused[17] changed his dress, laid aside every kind of ornament, let his hair and beard grow,[18] and in this mean garb,[19] went round and solicited the favour of the people.[20]   His nearest relations and friends also did the same.[21]   This kind of trial was generally capital, but not always so.[22]

5. MANNER OF TAKING THE AUSPICES.

ON the day of the Comitia, he who was to preside at them,[23] attended by one of the augurs,[24] pitched a tent[25] without the city to observe the omens.[26]   These Cicero calls AUGUSTA CENTURIARUM AUSPICIA.[27]   Hence the Campus Martius is said to be *consularibus auspiciis consecratus*, and the Comitia themselves were called AUSPICATA.[28]

If the TABERNACULUM, which perhaps was the same with *templum* or *arx*, the place which they chose to make their observations,[29] had not been taken in due form,[30] whatever was done at the Comitia was reckoned of no effect.[31]   Hence the usual declaration of the augurs ;[32] VITIO TABERNACULUM CAPTUM ; VITIO MAGISTRATUS CREATOS vel VITIOSOS ; VITIO LEGEM LATAM ; VITIO DIEM DICTAM.[33]   And so scrupulous were the ancient Romans about this matter, that if the augurs, at any time afterwards, upon recollec-

---

1 Liv. vii. 1.
2 thus pervicit ·Appius, ut, dejecto Fabio, fratrem traheret, Liv. xxxix 32.
3 Cic. Cat. i. 10.
4 laturus v. rogaturus.
5 ex senatus consulto.
6 publice v. in publico proponebat : promulgabat, quasi provulgabat, Fest.
7 Cic. Verr. v. 69.
8 legislator vel inventor legis, Liv. ii. 56.

9 recitabat.
10 suadebat.
11 dissuadebant.
12 Liv. iv. 24.
13 Cic. Att. i. 14.
14 cum dies perduellionis dicta est, cum actio perduellionis intendebatur, Cic. vel cum aliquis capitis v. -te anquireretur. Liv.
15 promulgatur rogatio de mea pernicie, Cic. Sext. 20.
16 prodita die, qua judi-

cium futurum sit, Cic.
17 reus.
18 promittebat.
19 sordidatus.
20 homines prensabat.
21 Liv. passim.
22 Liv. vi. 20. xliii. 16. Cic. Dom. 32. see Lex Porcia.
23 qui iis præfuturus erat.
24 augure adhibito.
25 tabernaculum cepit.
26 ad auspicia captanda, vel ad auspican-

dum.
27 Mil. 16.
28 Cic. Cat. iv. 1. Liv. xxvi. 2.
29 ad inaugurandum, Liv. i. 6. s. 7. 18.
30 parum recte captum esset.
31 pro irrito habebatur, Liv. iv. 7.
32 augurum solennis, pronunciatio.
33 Cic. & Liv. passim.

tion, declared that there had been any informality in taking the auspices,[1] the magistrates were obliged to resign their office, (as having been irregularly chosen)[2] even several months after they had entered upon it.[3] When there was nothing wrong in the auspices, the magistrates were said to be SALVIS AUSPICIIS *creati*.[4] When the consul asked the augur to attend him,[5] he said, Q. FABI, TE MIHI IN AUSPICIO ESSE VOLO. The augur replied, AUDIVI.[6]

There were two kinds of auspices which pertained to the Comitia Centuriata. The one was observing the appearances of the heavens,[7] as lightning, thunder, &c. which was chiefly attended to. The other was the inspection of birds. Those birds which gave omens by flight, were called PRÆPETES ; by singing, OSCINES ; hence the phrase, *si avis occinuerit*.[8] When the omens were favourable, the birds were said ADDICERE vel ADMITTERE ; when unfavourable, ABDICERE, NON ADDICERE, vel REFRAGARI.

Omens were also taken from the feeding of chickens. The person who kept them was called PULLARIUS. If they came too slowly out of the cage,[9] or would not feed, it was a bad omen ;[10] but if they fed greedily, so that something fell from their mouth, and struck the ground,[11] it was hence called TRIPUDIUM SOLISTIMUM,[12] and was reckoned an excellent omen.[13]

When the augur declared that the auspices were unexceptionable,[14] that is, that there was nothing to hinder the Comitia from being held, he said SILENTIUM ESSE VIDETUR ; but if not, he said ALIO DIE,[15] on which account the Comitia could not be held on that day.[16]

This declaration of the augur was called NUNTIATIO, or *obnuntiatio*. Hence Cicero says of the augurs, NOS NUNTIATIONEM SOLUM HABEMUS ; ET CONSULES ET RELIQUI MAGISTRATUS ETIAM SPECTIONEM, v. *inspectionem ;*[17] but the contrary seems to be asserted by Festus,[18] and commentators are not agreed how they should be reconciled. It is supposed there should be a different reading in both passages.[19]

Any other magistrate of equal or greater authority than he who presided, might likewise take the auspices ; especially if he wished to hinder an election, or prevent a law from being passed. If such magistrate therefore declared, SE ĎE CŒLO SERVASSE, that he had heard thunder, or seen lightning, he was said, OBNUNTIARE,[20] which he did by saying ALIO DIE: whereupon by the *Lex Ælia et Fusia*, the Comitia were broken off,[21] and deferred to another day. Hence *obnuntiare concilio* aut *comitiis*, to prevent, to adjourn; and this happened, even though he said that he had seen what he did not see,[22] because he was thought to have bound the people by a religious obligation, which must be expiated by their calamity or his own.[23] Hence in the edict whereby the Comitia were summoned, this *formula* was commonly used, NE QUIS MINOR MAGISTRATUS DE CŒLO SERVASSE VELIT : which prohibition Clodius, in his law against Cicero, extended to all the magistrates.[24]

The Comitia were also stopped, if any person, while they were holding,

1 vitium obvenisse, Cic. in auspicio vitium fuisse, Liv.
2 upote vitiosi v. vitio creati.
3 Liv. ibid. Cic. Nat. Deor. ii. 4.
4 Cic. Phil. ii. 33.
5 in auspicium adhibebat.
6 Cic. Div. ii. 34.
7 servare de cœlo vel

cœlum.
8 Liv. vi. 41. x. 40.
9 ex cavea.
10 Liv. vi. 41.
11 terram paviret, i. e. feriret.
12 quasi terripavium vel terripudium, Cic. Div. ii. 34. Fest. Puls. Liv. x. 40. Plin. 21. s. 24.
13 auspicium egregium,

vel optimum, ibid.
14 omni vitio carere.
15 Cic. Div. ii. 34. Leg. ii. 12.
16 thus, Papirio legem ferenti triste omen diem diffidit, i. e. rem in diem posterum rejicere coegit, Liv. ix. 38.
17 Cic. Phil. ii. 39.
18 in voce Spectio.
19 Vid. Abr. in Cic. Sca-

lig. in Fest.
20 augur auguri, consul consuli obnuntiavisti, al. nuntiasti, Cic. Phil. ii. 33.
21 dirimebantur.
22 si auspicia ementitus esset.
23 Cic. Phil. ii. 33.
24 Dio. xxxviii. 13.

was siezed with the falling sickness or epilepsy, which was hence called MORBUS COMITIALIS; or if a tribune of the commons interceded by the solemn word VETO,[1] or any magistrate of equal authority with him who presided, interposed, by wasting the day in speaking, or by appointing holydays, &c. and also if the standard was pulled down from the Janiculum, as in the trial of Rabirius, by Metellus the prætor.[2]

The Comitia were also broken off by a tempest arising; but so, that the election of those magistrates who were already created, was not rendered invalid,[3] unless when the Comitia were for creating censors.

6. MANNER OF HOLDING THE COMITIA CENTURIATA.

WHEN there was no obstruction to the Comitia, on the day appointed, the people met in the Campus Martius. The magistrate who was to preside, sitting in his curule chair on a tribunal,[4] used to utter a set form of prayer before he addressed the people,[5] the augur repeating over the words before him.[6] Then he made a speech to the people about what was to be done at the Comitia.

If magistrates were to be chosen, the names of the candidates were read over. But anciently the people might choose whom they pleased, whether present or absent, although they had not declared themselves candidates.[7]

If a law was to be passed, it was recited by a herald, while a secretary dictated it to him,[8] and different persons were allowed to speak for and against it.[9] A similar form was observed at trials, because application was made to the people about the punishment of any one, in the same manner as about a law. Hence *irrogare pœnam*, vel *mulctam*, to inflict or impose.

The usual beginning of all applications to the people,[10] was VELITIS, JUBEATIS, QUIRITES, and thus the people were said to be consulted, or asked,[11] and the consuls to consult or ask them.[12] Hence *jubere legem* vel *rogationem*, also DECERNERE, to pass it; *vetare*, to reject it; *rogare magistratus*; to create or elect;[13] *rogare quæsitores*, to appoint judges or inquisitors.[14] Then the magistrate said, SI VOBIS VIDETUR, DISCEDITE, QUIRITES; or ITE IN SUFFRAGIUM, BENE JUVANTIBUS DIIS, ET QUÆ PATRES CENSUERUNT, VOS JUBETE.[15] Whereupon the people, who, as usual, stood promiscuously, separated every one to his own tribe and century.[16] Hence the magistrate was said *mittere populum in suffragium;* and the people, *inire* vel *ire in suffragium*.[17]

Anciently the centuries were called to give their votes according to the institution of Servius Tullius; first the equites, and then the centuries of the first class, &c.; but afterwards it was determined by lot,[18] in what order they should vote. When this was first done is uncertain. The names of the centuries were thrown into a box,[19] and then, the box being shaken, so that the lots might lie equally,[20] the century which came out first gave

---

1 Liv. vi. 35.
2 Cic. Frat. ii. 6. Dio. xxxvii. 27.
3 ut jam creati non vitiosi redderentur, Liv. xl. 59. Cic. Div. ii. 18.
4 pro tribunali, Liv. xxxix. 32.
5 Liv. xxxix. 15.
6 augure · verba præ-

unte. Cic.
7 Liv. passim.
8 subjiciente scriba.
9 Liv. xl. 21.
10 omnium rogationum.
11 consuli vel rogari.
12 Cic. & Liv. passim.
13 Sall. Jug. 40. 29.
14 Ib. 40. so justa et vetita populi in jubendis

v. sciscendis legibus, Cic. Legg. ii. 4. quibus, sc. Silano et Murenæ, consulatus, me rogante, i. e. præsidente, datus est, Id. Mur. 1.
15 Liv. xxxi. 7.
16 Asc. Cic. Corn. Balb.
17 Cic. & Liv. passim.

18 sortitio fiebat.
19 in sitellam; sitella defertur, Cic. N. D. 1. 38. sitella allata est, ut sortirentur, Liv. xxv. 3.
20 sortibus æquatis.

its vote first, and hence was called PRÆROGATIVA. Those centuries which followed next, were called PRIMO VOCATÆ. The rest, JURE VOCATÆ.[1] But all the centuries are usually called *jure vocatæ*, except the *prærogativa*. Its vote was held of the greatest importance.[2] Hence PRÆROGATIVA is put for a sign or pledge, a favourable omen or intimation of any thing future ;[3] and also for a precedent or example, a choice, or favour,[4] and among later writers for a peculiar or exclusive privilege.

When tribes are mentioned in the Comitia Centuriata,[5] it is supposed that after the centuries were included in the tribes, the tribes first cast lots ; and that the tribe which first came out was called PRÆROGATIVA TRIBUS ; and then that the centuries of that tribe cast lots which should be the *prærogativa centuria*. Others think that in this case the names of tribes and centuries are put promiscuously the one for the other. But Cicero calls *centuria, pars tribus;* and that which is remarkable, in the Comitia Tributa.[6]

Anciently the citizens gave their votes by word of mouth ; and in creating magistrates, they seem to have each used this form, CONSULES, &c. NOMINO vel DICO ; in passing laws, UTI ROGAS, VOLO vel JUBEO.[7] The will or command of the people was expressed by VELLE, and that of the senate by CENSERE ; hence *leges magistratusque* ROGARE, to make.[8]

Sometimes a person nominated to be consul, &c. by the prærogative century, declined accepting,[9] or the magistrate presiding disapproved of their choice, and made a speech to make them alter it. Whereupon the century was recalled by a herald to give its vote anew,[10] and the rest usually voted the same way with it.[11] In the same manner, after a bill was rejected by almost all the centuries, on a subsequent day,[12] we find it unanimously enacted ; as about declaring war on Philip, AB HAC ORATIONE IN SUFFRAGIUM MISSI, UT ROGARAT, BELLUM JUSSERUNT.[13]

But in later times, that the people might have more liberty in voting, it was ordained by various laws which were called LEGES TABELLARIÆ, that they should vote by ballot ; first in conferring honours, by the Gabinian law, made A. U. 614, two years after, at all trials except for treason, by the Cassian law ; in passing laws, by the Papirian law, A. U. 622 ; and lastly by the Cœlian law, A. U. 630 ; also in trials for treason, which had been excepted by the Cassian law. The purpose of these laws was to diminish the influence of the nobility.[14]

The centuries being called by a herald in their order, moved from the place where they stood, and went each of them into an enclosure,[15] which was a place surrounded with boards,[16] and near the tribunal of the consul. Hence they were said to be *intro vocatæ*, sc. *in ovile*.[17] There was a narrow passage to it raised from the ground, called PONS or PONTICULUS, by which each century went up one after another.[18] Hence old men at sixty[19] were said DE PONTE DEJICI ; and were called DEPONTANI, because after that age they were exempted from public business,[20] to which Cicero al-

1 Liv. v. 18. x. 15. 22. xxvii. 6.
2 ut nemo unquam prior eam tulerit, quin renunciatus sit, Cic. Planc. 20. Div. ii. 40. Mur. 18. Liv. xxvi. 22.
3 supplicatio est prærogativa triumphi, Cic. Fam. xv. 5.
4 Act. Verr. 9. Plin.
vii. 16. xxxvii. 9. s. 46. Liv. iii. 51. xxi. 3.
5 Liv. x. 13.
6 Planc. 20.
7 Liv. xxiv. 8, 9. Cic. Legg. ii. 10.
8 Sall. Jug. 21. Liv. i. 17.
9 Liv. v. 18. xxvi. 22.
10 in suffragium revoca-
ta ; thus, redite in suffragium, Liv. ibid.
11 auctoritatem prærogativæ secutæ sunt ; eosdem consules ceteræ centuriæ sine variatione ulla dixerunt, Liv. xxiv. 8. 6.
12 alteris comitiis.
13 Liv. xxxi. 8.
14 Cic. Am. 12. Plin.
Ep. iii. 20. Cic. Brut. 25. 27. Legg. iii. 16. Planc. 6.
15 septum vel ovile.
16 locus tabulatis inclusus.
17 Liv. x. 13.
18 Suet. Jul. 80.
19 sexagenarii.
20 Varr. & Fest.

Indes, Rosc. Am. 35. But a very different cause is assigned for this phrase both by Varro and Festus.

There were probably as many *pontes* and *septa*, or *ovilia*, as there were tribes and centuries. Hence Cicero usually speaks of them in the plural.[1] Some think that each tribe and century voted in its own *ovile*,[2] but this does not seem consistent with what we read in other authors.

At the entrance of the *pons*, each citizen received from certain officers, called DIRIBITORES, or *distributores*, ballots,[3] on which, if magistrates were to be created, were inscribed the names of the candidates, not the whole names, but only the initial letters ;[4] and they seem to have received as many tablets as there were candidates. We read of other tables being given in than were distributed, which must have been brought from home ;[5] but as no regard was paid to them, this seldom happened. The same thing took place also under the emperors, when the right of electing magistrates was transferred from the people to the senate.[6]

If a law was to be passed, or any thing to be ordered, as in a trial, or in declaring war, &c. they received two tablets ; on the one were the letters U. R. i. e. UTI ROGAS, sc. *volo* vel *jubeo*, I am for the law ; and on the other, A. for ANTIQUO, i. e. *antiqua probo, nihil novi statui volo*, I like the old way, I am against the law. Hence *antiquare legem*, to reject it.

Of these tablets every one threw which he pleased into a chest[7] at the entrance of the *ovile*, which was pointed out to them by the ROGATORES, who asked for the ballots, and anciently for the votes, when they were given *viva voce*.[8] Then certain persons called CUSTODES, who observed that no fraud should be committed in casting lots and voting,[9] took out[10] the ballots, and counted the votes by points marked on a tablet, which was called DIRIMERE *suffragia*, or DIREMPTIO *suffragiorum* ;[11] whence *omne punctum ferre*, for *omnibus suffragiis renunciari* ; to gain every vote ; and what pleased the majority was declared by a herald to be the vote of that century. The person who told to the consul the vote of his century[12] was called ROGATOR.[13] Thus all the centuries were called one after another, till a majority of centuries agreed in the same opinion ; and what they judged was held to be ratified.

The diribitores, rogatores, and custodes, were commonly persons of the first rank, and friends to the candidates, or favourers of the law to be passed, who undertook these offices voluntarily.[14] Augustus is supposed to have selected 900 of the equestrian order to be custodes or rogatores.[15]

If the points of any century were equal, its vote was not declared, but was reckoned as nothing, except in trials, where the century which had not condemned, was supposed to have acquitted. The candidate who had most votes was immediately called by the magistrate who presided ; and after a solemn prayer, and taking an oath, was declared to be elected[16] by a herald.[17] Then he was conducted home by his friends and dependents with great pomp.

---

1 thus, pontes lex Maria facit angustos, Cic. Legg. iii. 17. operæ Clodianæ pontes occuparunt, Att. i. 14. Cæpio cum bonis viris impetum facit, pontes dejicit, Her. i. 12. cum Clodius in septa irruisset, Mil. 15. eo, misere maculavit ovilia

Rome, Luc. Phars. ii. 197.
2 Serv. Virg. Ecl. i. 34.
3 tabulæ vel tabellæ.
4 Cic. Dom. 43.
5 Suet. Jul. 50.
6 Plin. Ep. iv. 25.
7 in cistam.
8 Cic. Div. i. 17. ii. 35. Nat. D. ii. 4.

9 in sortitione et suffragiis.
10 educebant.
11 Luc. v. 393.
12 qui centuriam suam rogavit, et ejus suffragium retulit ; vel consules a centuria sua creatos renunciavit, retulit.
13 Cic. ib. Or. ii. 64.

14 Cic. Pis. 15. post red. in Sen. 11.
15 ad custodiendas cistas suffragiorum, Plin. xxxiii. 2. s. 7.
16 renunciatus est.
17 Cic. Legg. Man. 1. Mur. 1. Rull. ii. 2. Vell. ii. 92.

11

It was esteemed very honourable to be named first.[1] Those who were elected consuls usually crowned the image of their ancestors with laurels.[2]

When one gained the vote of a century, he was said *ferre centuriam*, and *non ferre* vel *perdere*, to lose it ; so *ferre repulsam* to be rejected ; but *ferre suffragium* vel *tabellam*, to vote.[3]

The magistrates created at the Comitia Centuriata were said *fieri creari, declarari, nominari, dici, renunciari, designari, rogari*, &c. In creating magistrates this addition used to be made to denote the fulness of their right : UT QUI OPTIMA LEGE FUERINT ; OPTIMO JURE ; EO JURE, QUO QUI OPTIMO.[4]

When a law was passed, it was said PERFERRI ; the centuries which voted for it, were said LEGEM JUBERE, V. ROGATIONEM ACCIPERE ;[5] those who voted against it, ANTIQUARE, VETARE, V. NON ACCIPERE. *Lex* ROGATUR, *dum fertur ;* ABROGATUR, *dum tollitur ;* DEROGATUR *legi,* v. *de lege, cum per novam legem aliquid veteri legi detrahitur ;* SUBROGATUR, *cum aliquid adjicitur ;* OBROGATUR, *cum nova lege infirmatur.*[6] *Ubi duæ contrariæ leges sunt, semper antiquæ obrogat nova,* the new law invalidates the old.[7]

Two clauses commonly used to be added to all laws :—1. SI QUID JUS NON FUIT ROGARI, UT EJUS HAC LEGE NIHIL ESSET ROGATUM :—2. SI QUID CONTRA ALIAS LEGES EJUS LEGIS ERGO LATUM ESSET, UT EI, QUI EAM LEGEM ROGASSET, IMPUNE ESSET, which clause[8] Cicero calls TRANSLATITIUM, in the law of Clodius against himself, because it was transferred from ancient laws.[9]

This sanction used also to be annexed, NE QUIS PER SATURAM ABROGATO.[10] Hence *exquirere sententias per saturam,* i. e. *passim, sine certo ordine,* by the gross or lump.[11] In many laws this sanction was added, QUI ALITER vel SECUS FAXIT V. FECERIT, SACER ESTO : i. e. *ut caput ejus, cum bonis* vel *familia, alicui deorum consecraretur* v. *sacrum esset :* that it might be lawful to kill the transgressor with impunity.[12]

When a law was passed, it was engraved on brass and carried to the treasury. It used also to be fixed up in public, in a place where it might be easily read.[13] Hence, *in capitolio legum æra liquefacta, nec verba minacia fixo ære legebantur, fixit leges pretio atque refixit,* made and unmade.[14]

After the year of the city 598, when the consuls first began to enter on their office on the first day of January, the Comitia for their election were held about the end of July, or the beginning of August, unless they were delayed by the intercession of the magistrates, or by inauspicious omens. In the time of the first Punic war, the consuls entered on their office on the Ides of March, and were created in January or February.[15] The prætors were always elected after the consuls, sometimes on the same day, or the day after, or at the distance of several days.[16] From the time of their election till they entered on their office they were called DESIGNATI.

The Comitia for enacting laws or for trials, might be held on any legal day.

CENTURIES.[17]

WITH regard to the purpose of the Servian constitution to impart an equal share in the consular government to the plebeians, every one is at liberty to think as he likes : that it granted them the right of taking part in elections and

1 Cic. Legg. Man. 1.
2 Cic. Mur. 41.
3 thus, meis comitiis tacitæ libertatis, sed vocem vivam tulistis, Cic. Rull. ii. 2.
4 Festus in optima lex, Cic. Rull. i. 11. Phil. xi. 12 Liv. ix. 34.
5 Liv. ii. 57. iii. 15. 63. & alibi passim.

6 Ulp. & Fest.
7 Liv. ix. 34.
8 caput.
9 Cic. Att. iii. 23.
10 i. e. per legem in qua conjunctim multis de rebus una rogatione populus consulebatur, Fest.
11 Sall. Jug. 29.
12 Liv. ii. 8. iii. 55. Cic. Baib. 14.

13 unde de piano, i. e. from the ground, legi posset.
14 Cic. Cat. iii. 8. Ov. M. i. 3. Virg. Æn. vi. 622 Cic. Phil. xiii. 3. Fam. xii. 1.
15 Liv. passim.
16 Liv. x. 22.
17 The above remarks tending in some measure to correct the er-

rors into which Dr. Adam, in common with other writers on Roman antiquities had fallen, are extracted from the history of Rome, by Niebuhr, the best work hitherto published on the early history of Italy and Rome.—ED.

COMITIA TRIBUTA.

In the Comitia Tributa the people voted divided into tribes, according to their regions or wards.[1]

in legislation, is universally acknowledged.

Servius (as for the sake of brevity I will call the lawgiver in accordance with the writers of antiquity) would have taken the simplest method of bestowing these rights, if he had adopted the same plan whereby the commons in feudal states obtained a station alongside of the barons, and had ordained that all national concerns should be brought both before the council of the burghers, and that of the commonalty, and that the decree of the one should not have force without the approval of the other, and should be made null by its rejection. This was the footing on which the plebeian tribes in aftertimes stood in relation to the curies: but if these two bodies had been set up over against each other from the beginning, they would have rent the state asunder; to accomplish the perfect union of which the centuries were devised by Servius. For in them he collected the patricians and their clients together with the plebeians; and along with all these that new class of their fellow-citizens which had arisen from bestowing the Roman franchise on the inhabitants of other towns, the municipals! so that nobody could in any way look upon himself as a Roman, without having some place or other, though indeed it might often be a very insignificant one, in this great assembly. The preponderance, nay the whole power in that assembly lay with the plebs; this however, excited no ill will, because no one was excluded; and provoked no opposition, because it did not decide by itself, but stood on an equipoise with the curies.

This institution of the centuries has thrown that of the tribes completely into the shade; and through the former alone has the name of king Servius maintained its renown to our days. Moreover, it has

long and universally been held to be a settled point, that this is understood with more certainty. and accuracy than any other part of the Roman constitution; because it is described by Dionysius and Livy, and that description is couched in numbers: and only a very few, who saw more clearly, have ventured to pronounce, that at all events these representations were not suited to the times of which we have a contemporary history. At present this in the main is no longer contested; and, a far more authentic record having come to light, the errors common to the two historians, and those peculiar to each, may be satisfactorily pointed out. They cannot either of them have been acquainted with the account contained in the commentaries which were ascribed to the king himself, but have written from very different and very defective reports: as to Cicero, the only reason that indisposes us to believe his having drawn immediately from the authentic source, is, that erudition of this sort was not in his way; else his statements are exceedingly accurate and trustworthy. The mistakes of the two historians need not surprise us; for they were not speaking of an institution still existing, nor even of one that had been recently changed, but of what had long since passed away. Livy says expressly, that it had nothing in common with the constitution of the centuries in his days: and this, moreover, is the very reason why he describes it, as he does the ancient tactics, in his account of the Latin war. Various other statements too must have been current, containing still greater discrepancies; for Pliny takes 110,000 asses to be the limit for the property of the first class, Gellius 125,000; numbers which can neither be regarded as blunders in the manuscripts, nor as slips in the writers.

In one point both the historians are mistaken: confounding the burghers with the commonalty, they imagine that a people, in which till then perfect union and equality had prevailed, was now divided into classes according to property, in such a manner that all the power fell into the hands of the rich, though incumbered with no slight burdens. Dionysius adds another error to this, in looking upon the eighteen equestrian centuries, which had the first rank in the constitution of Servius, as a timocratical institution.

The principle of an aristocracy is to maintain a perfect equality within its own body. The poorest and obscurest nobile of Venice, into whose family no office of dignity had come for centuries, was esteemed in the great council as the equal of those whose wealth and name encircled them with splendour. A government formed like the Roman by a large body of houses is a complete democracy within itself, just as much so as that of a canton where the population is not more numerous: an aristocracy it is solely in its relation to the commonalty. This was misunderstood by Dionysius and Livy; no change was made by Servius in this equality of the ancient burghers: his timocracy only affected those who stood entirely without the pale of that body, or those who at the utmost were attached to it, but far from partaking in the same equality.

The six equestrian centuries established by L. Tarquinius were incorporated by Servius into his comitia, and received the name of the six suffragia; so that these comprised all the patricians: among whom it cannot be conceived that in this constitution, any more than in the earlier, there existed any distinction adapted to the scale of their property. Livy, though he forgot that the six centuries had been instituted

The name of tribes was derived either from their original number, three,[1] or from paying tribute,[2] or, as others think, from τριττυς, *tertia pars tribus apud Athenienses*, Æolice τριππυς, *unde* TRIBUS.

The first three tribes were called RAMNENSES or *Ramnes*, TATIENSES or *Titienses*, and LUCERES. The first tribe was named from Romulus, and included the Roman citizens who occupied the Palatine hill :. the second from Titus Tatius, and included the Sabines, who possessed the Capitoline hill ; and the third from one Lucomo a Tuscan, or rather from the grove[3] which Romulus turned into a sanctuary,[4] and included all foreigners except the Sabines. Each of these tribes had at first its own tribune or commander,[5] and its own augur.

Tarquinius Priscus doubled the number of tribes, retaining the same names ; so that they were called *Ramnenses primi* and *Ramnenses secundi*, or *posteriores*, &c.[6]

But as the *Luceres* in a short time greatly exceeded the rest in number, Servius Tullius introduced a new arrangement, and distributed the citizens into tribes, not according to their extraction, but from their local situation. He divided the city into four regions or wards, called PALATINA SUBURRANA, COLLINA, and ESQUILINA, the inhabitants of which constituted as many tribes, and had their names from the wards which they inhabited. No one was permitted to remove from one ward to another, that the tribes might not be confounded.[7] On which account certain persons were appointed to take an account where every one dwelt, also of their age, fortune, &c. These were called city tribes,[8] and their number always remained the same. Servius at the same time divided the Roman territory into fifteen parts (some say sixteen, and some seventeen), which were called country tribes.[9]

In the year of the city 258, the number of tribes was made twenty-one, Liv. ii. 21. Here, for the first time, Livy directly takes notice of the number of tribes, although he alludes to the original institution of three tribes, x. 6. Dionysius says, that Servius instituted thirty-one tribes. But in the trial of Coriolanus, he only mentions twenty-one as having voted.[10]

The number of tribes was afterwards increased on account of the addition of new citizens at different times, to thirty-five, which number continued to the end of the republic.[11]

After the admission of the Italian states to the freedom of the city, eight

---

by Tarquinius, makes a perfectly correct distinction between them and the twelve which were added by Servius, out of the principal men in the state, as he says ; he ought to have said in the commonalty : for the patricians were in the six suffragia, nor can any of them have been admitted into the twelve centuries. Dionysius therefore should have confined himself to these twelve centuries, when he conceived that the

knights were chosen by Servius out of the richest and most illustrious families ; which notion he extends to all the eighteen : for the patricians, who unquestionably as a body were the richest as well as the leading men in the state, had all of them places in the six suffragia by birth and descent, though particular individuals among them might happen to be exceedingly poor. The prevalent opinion, that the equestrian rank from the

beginning was essentially connected with great wealth, and yet that all the knights were furnished with horses by the state, and had a yearly rent assigned for their keeping, not only charges the Roman laws with absurdity and injustice, but also overlooks Livy's express remark, which follows close upon his account of the advantages enjoyed by the knights, that all these burdens were shifted from the poor upon the rich.

---

1 a numero ternario.
2 a tributo, Liv. l. 43.
3 a luco.
4 asylum retulit, Virg. Æn. viii. 342.

5 tribunus vel præfectus, Diony. iv. 14.
6 Liv. x. 6. i. 36.
7 Diony. iv. 14.
8 tribus urbanæ.

9 tribus rusticæ, Diony. iv. 15.
10 ibid. vii. 64, the number of Livy, viii. 64.
11 Liv. vi. 5. vii. 15. viii.

17. ix. 20. x. 9. Epit. xix. Liv. xxiii. 13. Asc. Cic. Verr. i. 5. Liv. i. 43.

or ten new tribes are said to have been added, but this was of short continuance; for they were all soon distributed among the thirty-five old
tribes.

For a considerable time, according to the institution of Servius Tullius,
a tribe was nothing else but the inhabitants of a certain region or quarter
in the city or country: but afterwards this was altered; and tribes came
to be reckoned parts not of the city or country, but of the state.[1] Then
every one leaving the city tribes, wished to be ranked among the rustic
tribes. This was occasioned chiefly by the fondness of the ancient Romans
for a country life, and from the power of the censors, who could institute
new tribes, and distribute the citizens, both old and new, into whatever
tribes they pleased, without regard to the place of their habitation. But
on this subject writers are not agreed. In the year 449. Q. Fabius separated the meaner sort of people from all the tribes through which they had
been dispersed by Appius Claudius, and included them in the four city tribes.[2]
Among these were ranked all those whose fortunes were below a certain
valuation, called PROLETARII; and those who had no fortune at all, CAPITE
CENSI.[3] From this time, and perhaps before, the four city tribes began to be
esteemed less honourable than the thirty-one rustic tribes; and some
of the latter seem to have been thought more honourable than others. Hence
when the censors judged it proper to degrade a citizen, they removed him
from a more honourable to a less honourable tribe;[4] and whoever convicted
any one of bribery, upon trial, obtained by law as a reward, if he chose,
the tribe of the person condemned.[5]

The rustic tribes had their names from some place; as, tribus Aniensis,
Arniensis, Cluvia, Crustumina, Falerina, Lemonia, Mœcia, Pomptina,
Quirina, Romilia, Scaptia, &c.: or from some noble family; as, Aimilia,
Claudia, Cluentia, Cornelia, Fabia, Horatia, Julia, Minucia, Papiria, Sergia,
Terentina, Veturia, &c.

Sometimes the name of one's tribe is added to the name of a person,
as a surname; thus, L. Albius Sex. F. Quirina, M. Oppius, M. F. Terentina.[6]

The Comitia Tributa began first to be held two years after the creation
of the tribunes of the people, A. U. 263, at the trial of Coriolanus.[7] But
they were more frequently assembled after the year 282, when the Publilian law was passed, that the plebeian magistrates should be created at the
Comitia Tributa.[8]

The Comitia Tributa were held to create magistrates, to elect certain
priests, to make laws, and to hold trials.

At the Comitia Tributa were created all the inferior city magistrates, as
the ædiles, both curule and plebeian, the tribunes of the commons, quæstors, &c.; all the provincial magistrates, as the proconsuls, proprætors, &c.
also commissioners for setting colonies, &c.; the *pontifex maximus*, and
after the year 650, the other *pontifices, augures, feciales*, &c. by the Domitian law.[9] For before that, the inferior priests were all chosen by their
respective colleges.[10] But at the election of the *pontifex maximus*, and the
other priests, what was singular, only seventeen tribes were chosen by lot
to vote, and a majority of them, namely nine, determined the matter.[11]

1 non urbis, sed civita-   4 tribu movebant.   viii. 8. Att. iv. 16.   10 a collegiis suis co-op-
tis.   5 Cic. Balb. 25. Plin.   7 Diony. vii. 59.   tabantur.
2 Liv. ix. 46.   xvii. 3.   8 Liv. ii. 56.   11 Cic. Rull. ii. 7.
3 Gell. xvi. 10.   6 Cic. Quint. 6. Fam.   9 Suet. Ner. 2.

The laws passed at these Comitia were called PLEBISCITA,[1] which at first only bound the plebeians, but after the year 306, the whole Roman people.[2]

Plebiscita were made about various things; as about making peace, about granting the freedom of the city, about ordering a triumph when it was refused by the senate, about bestowing command on generals on the day of their triumph, about absolving from the laws, which in later times the senate assumed as its prerogative.[3]

There were no capital trials at the Comitia Tributa; these were held only at the Centuriata: but about imposing a fine.[4] And if any one accused of a capital crime did not appear on the day of trial, the Tributa Comitia were sufficient to decree banishment against him.[5]

All those might vote at the Comitia Tributa who had the full right of Roman citizens, whether they dwelt at Rome or not. For every one was ranked in some tribe, in which he had a right to vote.[6] Some had two tribes; one in which they were born, and another either by right of adoption, as Augustus had the Fabian and Scaptian tribes,[7] or as a reward for accusing one of bribery.[8]

At the Comitia Tributa the votes of all the citizens were of equal force, and therefore the patricians hardly ever attended them. On which account, as some think, they are said to have been entirely excluded from them.[9] But about this writers are not agreed.

The Comitia for creating tribunes and plebeian ædiles, were held by one of the tribunes to whom that charge was given, either by lot or by the consent of his colleagues;[10] but for creating curule ædiles and other inferior magistrates, by the consul, dictator, or military tribunes; for electing priests, by the consul only.[11]

The Comitia Tributa for passing laws and for trials, were held by the consuls, prætors, or tribunes of the commons. When the consul was to hold them, he by his edict summoned the whole Roman people; but the tribunes summoned only the plebeians.[12] Hence they are sometimes called Comitia *populi*, and sometimes *concilium plebis:* in the one, the phrase was *populus jussit;* in the other, *plebs scivit.* But this distinction is not always observed.

The Comitia Tributa for electing magistrates were usually held in the Campus Martius,[13] but for passing laws and for trials commonly in the forum; sometimes in the Capitol, and sometimes in the *circus Flaminius,* anciently called *prata Flaminia,* or *circus Apollinaris,* where also Q. Furius, the pontifex maximus, held the Comitia for electing the tribunes of the commons, after the expulsion of the Decemviri.[14] In the forum there were separate places for each tribe marked out with ropes.[15]

In the Campus Martius, Cicero proposed building, in Cæsar's name, marble enclosures[16] for holding the Comitia Tributa,[17] which work was prevented by various causes, and at last entirely dropped upon the breaking out of the civil wars; but it was afterwards executed by Agrippa.[18]

The same formalities almost were observed in summoning and holding

---

1 quæ plebs suo suffragio sine patribus jussit, plebeio magistratu rogante, Fest.
2 Liv. iii. 55.
3 Liv. xxxiii. 10. iii. 63. xxvi. 21. Asc. Cic. Cor. &c.

4 Liv. iv. 41.
5 Id ei justum exilium esse scivit plebs, Liv. xxvi. 3. xxv. 4.
6 Liv. xlv. 15.
7 Suet. Aug. 40.
8 legis de ambitu præmio. Cic. Balb. 25.

9 Liv. ii. 56. 60.
10 Liv. iii. 64.
11 Cic. Brut. 5.
12 Gell. xv. 17.
13 Cic. Att. i. 1. iv. 3. Ep. Fam. vii. 30.
14 Liv. xxxiii. 10. xxvii. 21. iii. 63. 64.

15 Diony. vii. 59.
16 septa marmorea.
17 Cic. Att. iv. 16.
18 Dio. liii. 23. Plin. xvi. 40.

the Comitia Tributa as in the other Comitia, only it was not requisite for them to have the authority of the senate, or that the auspicies should be taken. But if there had been thunder or lightning,[1] they could not be held that day. For it was a constant rule from the beginning of the republic, JOVE FULGENTE CUM POPULO AGI NEFAS ESSE. *Comitiorum solum vitium est fulmen.*[2]

The Comitia Tributa for electing magistrates, after the year 598, were held about the end of July or the beginning of August; for electing priests, when there was a vacancy, and for laws and trials, on all comitial days.

Julius Cæsar first abridged the liberty of the Comitia. He shared the right of electing magistrates with the people; so that, except the competitors for the consulship, whose choice he solely determined himself, the people chose one half, and he nominated[3] the other. This he did by billets dispersed through the several tribes to this effect, CÆSAR DICTATOR ILLI TRIBUI. COMMENDO VOBIS ILLUM, ET ILLUM, UT VESTRO SUFFRAGIO SUAM DIGNITATEM TENEANT.[4] Augustus restored this manner of election after it had been dropped for some time, during the civil wars which followed Cæsar's death.[5]

Tiberius deprived the people altogether of the right of election, and assuming the nomination of the consuls to himself, he pretended to refer the choice of the other magistrates to the senate, but in fact determined the whole according to his own pleasure.[6] Caligula attempted to restore the right of voting to the people, but without any permanent effect.[7] The Comitia, however, were still for form's sake retained. And the magistrates, whether nominated by the senate or the prince, appeared in the Campus Martius, attended by their friends and connections, and were appointed to their office by the people with the usual solemnities.[8]

But the method of appointing magistrates under the emperors seems to be involved in uncertainty,[9] as indeed Tacitus himself acknowledges, particularly with respect to the consuls.[10] Sometimes, especially under good emperors, the same freedom of canvassing was allowed, and the same arts practised to insure success, as under the republic.[11] Trajan restrained the infamous largesses of candidates by a law against bribery;[12] and by ordaining that no one should be admitted to sue for an office, who had not a third part of his fortune in land, which greatly raised the value of estates in Italy.[13] When the right of creating magistrates was transferred to the senate, it at first appointed them by open votes,[14] but the noise and disorder which this sometimes occasioned, made the senate in the time of Trajan adopt the method of balloting, which also was found to be attended with inconveniences, which Pliny says the emperor alone could remedy.[15] Augustus followed the mode of Julius Cæsar at the Comitia, although Mecænas, whose counsel he chiefly followed, advised him to take this power altogether from the people.[16] As often as he attended at the election of magistrates, he went round the tribes, with the candidates whom he recommended,[17] and solicited the votes of the people in the usual manner. He himself gave his vote in his own tribe, as any other citizen.[18]

---

1 si tonuisset aut fulgurasset.
2 Cic. Val. 8. Div. ii. 18.
3 edebat.
4 Suet. Cæs. 41.
5 Suet. Aug. 40. Dio. liii. 21.
6 Juv. x. 77. Ov. Pont.

iv. 9. 67. Tac. Ann. i. 15. Dio. Cas. lviii. 20.
7 Suet. Cal. 16.
8 Plin. Pan. 63.
9 Suet. Cæs. 40. 76. 80. Aug. 40. 56. Ner. 43. Vit. 11. Vesp. 5. Dom.
10 Tac. Ann. L 15.

Hist. 1. 77.
10 Ann. i. 81.
11 Plin. Ep. vi. 6. 9. viii. 23.
12 ambitus lege.
13 Id. vi. 9.
14 apertis suffragiis.
15 ad tacita suffragia.

decurrere, Plin. Ep. iii. 20. iv. 25.
16 Dio. liii. 21. lii. 30.
17 cum suis candidatis.
18 ut unus e populo, Suet. Aug. 56.

ROMAN MAGISTRATES.

DIFFERENT FORMS OF GOVERNMENT, AND DIFFERENT MAGISTRATES AT DIFFERENT TIMES.

ROME was at first governed by kings: but Tarquin the 7th king being expelled for his tyranny, A. U. 244, the regal government was abolished, and two supreme magistrates were annually created in place of a king, called CONSULS. In dangerous conjunctures, a DICTATOR was created with absolute authority ; and when there was a vacancy of magistrates, an IN-TERREX was appointed to elect new ones.

In the year of the city 301, or according to others, 302, in place of consuls, ten men[1] were chosen to draw up a body of laws.[2] But their power lasted only two years ; and the consular government was again restored.

As the consuls were at first chosen only from the patricians, and the plebeians wished to partake of that dignity ; after great contests it was at last determined, A. U. 310, that, instead of consuls, six supreme magistrates should be annually created, three from the patricians, and three from the plébeians, who were called MILITARY TRIBUNES.[3] There was not, however, always six tribunes chosen ; sometimes only three, sometimes four, and sometimes even eight.[4] Nor was one half always chosen from the patricians, and another half from the plebeians. They were, on the contrary, usually all patricians, seldom the contrary.[5] For upwards of seventy years, sometimes consuls were created, and sometimes military tribunes, as the influence of the patricians or plebeians was superior, or the public exigencies required ; till at last the plebeians prevailed, A. U. 387, that one of the consuls should be chosen from their order, and afterwards that both consuls might be plebeians ; which, however, was rarely the case, but the contrary. From this time the supreme power remained in the hands of the consuls till the usurpation of Sylla, A. U. 672, who, having vanquished the party of Marius, assumed to himself absolute authority, under the title of *dictator*, an office which had been disused above 120 years. But Sylla having voluntarily resigned his power in less than three years, the consular authority was again restored, and continued till Julius Cæsar, having defeated Pompey at the battle of Pharsalia, and having subdued the rest of his opponents, in imitation of Sylla, caused himself to be created perpetual dictator, and oppressed the liberty of his country, A. U. 706. After this, the consular authority was never again completely restored. It was indeed attempted, after the murder of Cæsar in the senate-house on the Ides of March, A. U. 710, by Brutus and Cassius and the other conspirators ; but M. Antonius, who desired to rule in Cæsar's room, prevented it. And Hirtius and Pansa, the consuls of the following year, being slain at Mutina, Octavius, who was afterwards called Augustus, Antony, and Lepidus, shared between them the provinces of the republic, and exercised absolute power under the title of TRIUMVIRI *reipublicæ constituendæ*.

The combination between Pompey, Cæsar, and Crassus, commonly called the first triumvirate, which was formed by the contrivance of Cæsar, in the consulship of Metellus and Afranius, A. U. 693,[6] is justly reckoned the original cause of this revolution, and of all the calamities attending it.

1 decemviri, Liv. iii. 33. lari potestate, Diony: 31. 35. 44. v. 1. 6 Vell. Pat. ii. 44. Hor.
2 ad leges scribendas. xi. 60, 5 Liv. iv. 25. 44. 56. v. Od. ii. 1.
3 tribuni militum consu- 4 Liv. iv. 6. 16. 25. 42. 12, 13. 16. vi. 30.

For the Romans, by submitting to their usurped authority, showed that they were prepared for servitude. It is the spirit of a nation alone which can preserve liberty. When that is sunk by general corruption of morals, laws are but feeble restraints against the encroachments of power. Julius Cæsar would never have attempted what he effected, if he had not perceived the character of the Roman people to be favourable to his designs.

After the overthrow of Brutus and Cassius at the battle of Philippi, A. U. 712, Augustus, on a slight pretext deprived Lepidus of his command, and having vanquished Antony in a sea-fight at Actium, became sole master of the Roman empire, A. U. 723, and ruled it for many years under the title of PRINCE or EMPEROR.[1] The liberty of Rome was now entirely extinguished; and although Augustus endeavoured to establish a civil monarchy, the government perpetually tended to a military despotism, equally fatal to the characters and happiness of prince and people.

In the beginning of the republic, the consuls seem to have been the only stated magistrates; but as they, being engaged almost in continual wars, could not properly attend to civil affairs, various other magistrates were appointed at different times, prætors, censors, ædiles, tribunes of the commons, &c.[2] Under the emperors various new magistrates were instituted.

OF MAGISTRATES IN GENERAL.

A MAGISTRATE is a person invested with public authority.[3] The office of a magistrate in the Roman republic was different from what it is among us. The Romans had not the same discrimination betwixt public employments that we have. The same person might regulate the police of the city, and direct the affairs of the empire, propose laws, and execute them, act as a judge or a priest, and command an army.[4] The civil authority of a magistrate was called *magistratus* or *potestas*, his judicative power, *jurisdictio*, and his military command *imperium*. Anciently all magistrates who had the command of an army were called PRÆTORES.[5]

MAGISTRATUS either signifies a magistrate, as *magistratus jussit*; or a magistracy, as *Titio magistratus datus est*.[6] So, POTESTAS, as *habere potestatem*, *gerere potestates*, *esse in v. cum potestate*, to bear an office; *Gabiorum esse potestas*, to be magistrate of Gabii.[7] MAGISTRATUS was properly a civil magistrate or magistracy in the city; and POTESTAS in the provinces.[8] But this distinction is not always observed.[9]

When a magistrate was invested with military command by the people, for the people only could do it, he was said *esse in v. cum imperio*, *in justo v. summo imperio*.[10] So, *magistratus et imparia capere*, to enjoy offices civil and military.[11] But we find *esse in imperio*, simply for *esse consulem*;[12] and all those magistrates were said *habere imperium*, who held great authority and power,[13] as the dictators, consuls, and prætors. Hence they were

---

1 princeps vel imperator.
2 Liv. iv. 4.
3 Magistratus est qui præsit, Cic. Legg. iii. 1. dicitur magistratus a magistro. Magister autem est, qui plus aliis potest, Fest.
4 Liv. x. 29. et alibi passim.
5 vel quod cæteros præirent, vel quod aliis præessent, Asc. Cic.

6 Fest.
7 Juv. x. 99. jurisdictionem tantum in urbe delegari magistratibus solitam, etiam per provincias, potestatibus demandavit, Suet. Claud. 24.
8 magistratus, vel iis, qui in potestate aliqua sint, ut puta proconsul, vel prætor, vel alii, qui provincias regunt, Ulp.
9 Sall. Jug. 63.

10 cum imperio esse dicitur, cui nominatim est a populo mandatum imperium, Fest. thus, abstinentia neque in imperiis, neque in magistratibus præstitit, i. e. neque cum exercitui præesset et jus belli gerendi haberet, neque cum munera civilia in urbe gereret, Suet. Cæs. 54. nemine cum imperio, military command;

aut magistratu, civil authority; tendens quoquam, quin Rhodum diverteret. Tib. 12.
11 Suet. Cæs. 75.
12 Liv. iv. 7.
13 qui et coercere aliquem possent, et jubere in carcerem duci, Paul. l. 2. ff. de in jus vocando.

said to do any thing *pro imperio ;*[1] whereas the inferior magistrates, the tribunes of the commons, the ædiles, and quæstors, were said *esse sine imperio*, and to act only *pro potestate.*[2] Sometimes *potestas* and *imperium* are joined, thus *togatus in republica cum potestate imperioque versatus est.*[3]

DIVISION OF MAGISTRATES.

THE Roman magistrates were variously divided ; into ordinary and extraordinary, greater and less, curule and not curule ; also patrician and plebeian, city and provincial magistrates.

The MAGISTRATUS ORDINARII were those who were created at stated times, and were constantly in the republic ; the EXTRAORDINARII not so.

The MAGISTRATUS MAJORES were those who had what were called the greater auspices.[4] The *magistratus majores ordinarii* were the consuls, prætors, and censors, who were created at the Comitia Centuriata : the *extraordinarii* were the dictator, the master of the horse,[5] the interrex, the præfect of the city, &c.

The MAGISTRATUS MINORES ORDINARII were the tribunes of the commons, the ædiles, and quæstors ; EXTRAORDINARII, the *præfectus annonæ, duumviri navales,* &c.

The MAGISTRATUS CURULES were those who had the right of using the *sella curulis* or chair of state, namely, the dictator, the consuls, prætors, censors, and curule ædiles. All the rest, who had not that right were called NON CURULES.[6] The *sella curulis* was anciently made of ivory, or at least adorned with ivory ; hence Horace calls it *curule ebur.*[7] The magistrates sat on it in their tribunal, on all solemn occasions.

In the beginning of the republic, the magistrates were chosen only from the patricians, but in process of time also from the plebeians, except the interrex alone.[8] The plebeian magistrates were the ædiles and tribunes of the commons.

Anciently there was no certain age fixed for enjoying the different offices.[9] A law was first made for this purpose[10] by L. Villius (or L. Julius), a tribune of the commons, A. U. 573, whence his family got the surname of ANNALES, although there seems to have been some regulation about that matter formerly.[11] What was the year fixed for enjoying each office is not fully ascertained.[12] It is certain that the prætorship used to be enjoyed two years after the ædileship, and that the 43d was the year fixed for the consulship.[13] If we are to judge from Cicero, who frequently boasts that he had enjoyed every office in its proper year,[14] the years appointed for the different offices by the *lex Villia* were, for the quæstorship thirty-one, for the ædileship thirty-seven, for the prætorship forty, and for the consulship forty-three. But even under the republic popular citizens were freed from these restrictions,[15] and the emperors granted that indulgence,[16] whomsoever they pleased, or the senate to gratify them. The *lex annalis*, however, was still observed.[17]

---

1 Liv. ii. 56, to which Terence alludes, Phor. i. 4. 19.
2 Liv. ii. 56. iv. 26.
3 Cic. Phil. i. 7.
4 quæ minoribus magis rata essent. Gell. xiii. 15.
5 magister equitum.

6 curules magistratus appellati sunt, quia curru vehebuntur. Fest. in quo curru sella curulis erat, supra quam considerent, Gell. iii. 18.
7 Ep. i. 6. 53.
8 quem et ipsum patri-

cium esse, et a patriciis prodi necesse erat. Cic. Dom. 14.
9 Cic. Phil. v. 17.
10 lex annalis.
11 Liv. xl. 43. xxv. 2.
12 see p. 3.
13 Cic. Fam. x. 25. Phil. v. 17.

14 se suo quemque magistratum anno gessisse.
15 ibid.
16 annos remittebant.
17 Plin. Ep. vii. 16. iii.
20. Dio. liii. 28.

It was ordained by the law of Romulus, that no one should enter on any office, unless the birds should give favourable omens.[1] And by the CORNELIAN LAW, made by Sulla, A. U. 673, that a certain order should be observed in obtaining preferments; that no one should be prætor before being quæstor, nor consul before being prætor; nor should enjoy the same office within ten years, nor two different offices in the same year.[2] But these regulations also were not strictly observed.

All magistrates were obliged, within five days after entering on their office, to swear that they would observe the laws,[3] and after the expiration of their office, they might be brought to a trial if they had done any thing amiss.[4]

KINGS.

ROME was at first governed by kings, not of absolute power nor hereditary, but limited and elective. They had no legislative authority, and could neither make war nor peace without the concurrence of the senate and people.[5]

The kings of Rome were also priests, and had the chief direction of sacred things, as among the Greeks.[6]

The badges of the kings were the *trabea*, i. e. a white robe adorned with stripes of purple, or the *toga prætexta*, a white robe fringed with purple, a golden crown, an ivory sceptre, the *sella curulis*, and twelve lictors, with the *fasces* and *secures*, i. e. carrying each of them a bundle of rods, with an axe stuck in the middle of them.

The badges of the Roman magistrates were borrowed from the Tuscans.[7] According to Pliny, Romulus used only the *trabea*. The *toga prætexta* was introduced by Tullus Hostilius, and also the *latus clavus*, after he had conquered the Tuscans.[8]

The regal government subsisted at Rome for 243 years under seven kings, Romulus, Numa Pompilius, Tullus Hostilius, Ancus Marcius, L. Tarquinius Priscus, Servius Tullius, and L. Tarquinius surnamed SUPERBUS from his behaviour; all of whom, except the last, so reigned, that they are justly thought to have laid the foundations of the Roman greatness.[9] Tarquin, being universally detested for his tyranny and cruelty, was expelled the city with his wife and family, on account of the violence offered by his son Sextus to Lucretia, a noble lady the wife of Collatinus. This revolution was brought about chiefly by means of L. Junius Brutus. The haughtiness and cruelty of Tarquin inspired the Romans with the greatest aversion to regal government, which they retained even afterwards. Hence *regie facere*, to act tyrannically, *regii spiritus, regia superbia*, &c.

The next in rank to the king was the TRIBUNUS, or PRÆFECTUS CELERUM, who commanded the horse under the king, as afterwards the *magister equitum* did under the dictator.

When there was a vacancy in the throne,[10] which happened for a whole year after the death of Romulus, on account of a dispute betwixt the Romans and Sabines, about the choice of a successor to him, the senators shar-

---

1 nisi aves addixissent vel admisissent, Liv. l. 36.
2 Ap. Bell. Civ. i. p. 412. Liv. vii. 40. xxxii. 7. Cic. Phil. xi. 5.

3 in leges jurare, Liv. xxxi. 5.
4 Liv. xxxvii. 57. Suet. Jul. 23.
5 Diony. ii. 13. Sall. Cat. 6.

6 Diony. ii. 14. Virg. Æn. iii. 80. Cic. Div. i. 40.
7 Liv. i. 8. Flor. i. 5. Sall. Cat. 51. fin. Diony. iii. 61. Strab. v. p. 220.

8 Plin. ix. 39. s. 68. viii. 48. s. 74.
9 Liv. ii. 1.
10 interregnum.

ed the government among themselves. They appointed one of their number
who should have the chief direction of affairs, with the title of INTERREX,
and all the ensigns of royal dignity, for the space of five days ; after him
another, and then another, till a king was created.[1]

Afterwards under the republic, an *interrex* was created to hold the elections when there was no consul or dictator, which happened either by their
sudden death, or when the tribunes of the commons hindred the elections by their intercession.[2]

ORDINARY MAGISTRATES.

I. CONSULS.

1. FIRST CREATION, DIFFERENT NAMES, AND BADGES, OF CONSULS.

AFTER the expulsion of the kings, A. U. 244, two supreme magistrates
were annually created with equal authority ; that they might restrain one
another, and not become insolent by the length of their command.[3]

They were anciently called PRÆTORES, also IMPERATORES, or JUDICES,[4]
afterwards CONSULES, either from their consulting for the good of the state,[5]
or from consulting the senate[6] and people,[7] or from their acting as judges.[8]
From their possessing supreme command the Greeks called them' ΥΠΑΤΘΙ.
If one of the consuls died, another was substituted[9] in his room for the
rest of the year ; but he could not hold the Comitia for electing new
consuls.[10]

The insignia of the consuls were the same with those of the king, except
the crown ; namely, the *toga pretexta, sella curulis*, the sceptre or ivory
staff,[11] and twelve lictors with the *fasces* and *secures*.

Within the city the lictors went before only one of the consuls, and that
commonly for a month alternately.[12] A public servant, called *accensus*, went
before the other consul, and the lictors followed ; which custom, after it
had been long disused, Julius Cæsar restored in his first consulship. He
who was eldest, or had most children, or who was first elected, or had most
suffrages, had the *fasces* first.[13] According to Dionysius,[14] the lictors at
first went before both consuls, and were restricted to one of them by the
law of Valerius Poplicola. We read in Livy, of 24 lictors attending the
consuls,[15] but this must be understood without the city.

2. POWER OF THE CONSULS.

As the consuls at first had almost the same badges with the kings, so
they had nearly the same power.[16] But Valerius, called POPLICOLA,[17] took
away the *securis* from the *fasces*,[18] i. e. he took from the consuls the power
of life and death, and only left them the right of scourging, at least within
the city ; for without the city, when invested with military command, they
still retained the *securis*, i. e. the right of punishing capitally.[19]

---

1 Liv. 1. 17. Diony. ii. 57.   do, Cic. Pis. 10. Flor.i. 9.   10 Liv. xii. 18.   15 ii. 55.
2 Liv. iii. 55. vi. 35.   6 a consulendo sena-   11 scipio eburneus.   16 Liv. ii. 1.
3 Cic. post red. Sen. 4.   tum, Cic. Legg. iii. 3.   12 mensibus alternis,   17 a populo colendo.
  Eutr. i. 9.   7 Varr. L. L. iv. 14.   Liv. ii. 1.   18 securim fascibus ad-
4 Liv. iii. 55. Fast. Sall.   8 a judicando, Quin. i. 9.   13 Suet. Jul. 20. Gell.   emit.
  Cat. 6. Varr. L. L. v. 7.   9 subrogatus vel suffec-   ii. 15. Liv. ix. 8.   19 Diony. v. 19. 59. Liv.
5 a reipublicæ consulen-   tus est.   14 lib. v. 2.   xxiv. 9.

When the consuls commanded different armies, each of them had the *fasces* and *secures*; but when they both commanded the same army, they commonly had them for a day alternately.[1]

Poplicola likewise made a law, granting to every one the liberty of appealing from the consuls to the people; and that no magistrate should be permitted to punish a Roman citizen who thus appealed; which law was afterwards once and again renewed, and always by persons of the Valerian family. But this privilege was also enjoyed under the kings.[2]

Poplicola likewise ordained, that when the consuls came into an assembly of the people, the lictors should lower the *fasces* in token of respect, and also that whoever usurped an office without the consent of the people might be slain with impunity.[3] But the power of the consuls was chiefly diminished by the creation of the tribunes of the commons, who had a right to give a negative to all their proceedings.[4] Still, however, the power of the consuls was very great, and the consulship was considered as the summit of all popular preferment.[5]

The consuls were at the head of the whole republic.[6] All the other magistrates were subject to them, except the tribunes of the commons. They assembled the people and the senate, laid before them what they pleased, and executed their decrees. The laws which they proposed and got passed, were commonly called by their name. They received all letters from the governors of provinces, and from foreign kings and states, and gave audience to ambassadors. The year was named after them, as it used to be at Athens from one of the Archons.[7] Thus, *M. Tullio Cicerone et L. Antonio consulibus*, marked the 690th year of Rome. Hence *numerare multos consules*, for *annos*.[8] *Bis jam pene tibi consul trigesimus instat*, you are near sixty years old.[9] And the consuls were said *aperire annum, fastosque reserare*.[10]

He who had most suffrages was called CONSUL PRIOR, and his name was marked first in the calendar.[11] He had also the *fasces* first, and usually presided at the election of magistrates for the next year.

Every body went out of the way, uncovered their heads, dismounted from horseback, or rose up to the consuls as they passed by.[12] If any one failed to do so, and the consul took notice of it, he was said to order the lictor ANIMADVERTERE.[13] Acilius the consul ordered the curule chair of Lucullus the prætor to be broken in pieces, when he was administering justice, because he had not risen up to him when passing by.[14] When a prætor happened to meet a consul, his lictors always lowered their fasces.[15]

In the time of war the consuls possessed supreme command. They levied soldiers, and provided what was necessary for their support. They appointed the military tribunes, or tribunes of the legions, (in part; for part was created by the people,)[16] the centurions, and other officers.[17]

The consuls had command over the provinces,[18] and could, when authorized by the senate, call persons from thence to Rome,[19] and punish them.[20] They were of so great authority, that kings, and foreign nations, in alliance with the republic, were considered to be under their protection.[21]

1 alternis imperitabant, Liv. xxii. 41.
2 Liv. ii. 8. iii. 55. x. 9. l. 26. viii. 35.
3 Liv. ii. 7. Diony. v. 19.
4 omnibus actis intercedere.
5 honorum populi finis. Cic. Planc. 25
6 Cic. Mur. 35.
7 Cic. Fat. 9.
8 Sen. Ep. 4.
9 Martial. i. 16. 3.
10 Plin. Pan. 58.
11 in fastis.
12 Sen. Ep. 64.
13 Liv. xxiv. 44. Suet. Jul. 80.
14 Dio. xxxvi. 10. 24.
15 Diony. viii. 14.
16 see Lex·Attilia.
17 Cic. Legg. iii. 3. Polyb. vi. 34.
18 Cic. Phil. iv. 4.
19 Romam evocare, excire, v. accire.
20 Cic. Verr. i. 38. Liv. iii. 4. xxix. 15.
21 Cic. Sext. 30.

In dangerous conjunctures the consuls were armed with absolute power by the solemn decree of the senate, UT VIDERENT, vel DARENT OPERAM, &c.[1] In any sudden tumult or sedition, the consuls called the citizens to arms in this form : QUI REMPUBLICAM SALVAM ESSE VELIT, ME SEQUATUR.[2]

Under the emperors the power of the consuls was reduced to a mere shadow ; their office then only was to consult the senate, and lay before them the ordinances[3] of the emperors, to appoint tutors, to manumit slaves, to let the public taxes, which had formerly belonged to the censors, to exhibit certain public games and shows, which they also sometimes did under the republic,[4] to mark the year by their name, &c. They retained, however, the badges of the ancient consuls, and even greater external pomp. For they wore the *toga picta* or *palmata*, and had their *fasces* wreathed with laurel, which used formerly to be done only by those who triumphed. They also added the *securis* to the *fasces*.

3. DAY ON WHICH CONSULS ENTERED ON THEIR OFFICE.

IN the beginning of the republic, the consuls entered on their office at different times ; at first, on the 23d or 24th of February,[5] the day on which Tarquin was said to have been expelled,[6] which was held as a festival, and called REGIFUGIUM ;[7] afterwards, on the first of August,[8] which was at that time the beginning of the year, i. e. of the consular, not of the civil year; which always began with January.[9] In the time of the decemviri, on the fifteenth of May.[10] About fifty years after, on the 15th of December.[11] Then on the first of July,[12] which continued till near the beginning of the second Punic war, A. U. 530, when the day came to be the 15th of March.[13] At last, A. U. 598 or 600,[14] it was transferred to the 1st of January,[15] which, continued to be the day ever after.[16]

After this the consuls were usually elected about the end of July or the beginning of August. From their election to the 1st of January, when they entered on their office, they were called CONSULES DESIGNATI ; and whatever they did in public affairs, they were said to do it by their authority, not by their power.[17] They might, however, propose edicts, and do several other things pertaining to their office.[18] Among other honours paid to them, they were always first asked their opinion in the senate.[19] The interval was made so long, that they might have time to become acquainted with what pertained to their office ; and that inquiry might be made, whether they had gained their election by bribery. If they were convicted of that crime upon trial, they were deprived of the consulship, and their competitors, who accused them, were nominated in their place.[20] They were also, besides being fined, declared incapable of bearing any office, or of coming into the senate, by the Calpurnian and other laws, as happened to Autronius and Sylla.[21] Cicero made the punishment of bribery still more severe by the Tullian law, which he passed by the authority of the senate, with the additional penalty of a ten years' exile.[22]

The first time a law was proposed to the people concerning bribery was

1 Liv. til. 4. vi. 19. see p. 15.
2 Cic. Rab. 7. Tusc. Quæst. iv. 23.
3 placita.
4 Ov. Pont. iv. 5. 18. Ep. ix. 47. Cic. Off. iii. 17.
5 vii. vel vi. Kal. Mart.
6 Ov. F. ii. 685.
7 Fest.
8 Kal. Sext.
9 Liv. iii. 6.
10 Id. Mail. ib. 36.
11 Id. Decemb. Liv. iv. 37. v. 11.
12 Kal. Quinct. Liv. v. 32. viii. 20.
13 Id. Mart.
14 Q. Fulvio et T. Annio, Coss.
15 in Kal. Jan.
16 dies solennis magistratibus, ineundis, Liv. Epit. 47. Ov. Fast. i. 81. iii. 147.
17 quod potestate nondum poterat, obtinuit
auctoritate, Cic. Pis. 4. Sext. 32.
18 Dio. xl. 66.
19 see p. 8.
20 Cic. Sull. 17. 32.
21 Cic. Corn. Mur. 23. &c. Sall. Cat. 18.
22 Mur. 32. Vat. 15. Sext. 64.

A. U. 397, by C. Pætilius, a tribune of the commons, by the authority of the senate.[1]

On the 1st of January, the senate and people waited on the new consuls[2] at their houses, (which in aftertimes was called OFFICIUM)[3] whence being conducted with great pomp, which was called PROCESSUS CONSULARIS to the Capitol, they offered up their vows,[4] and sacrificed each of them an ox to Jupiter; and then began their office,[5] by holding the senate, consulting it about the appointment of the Latin holidays, and about other things concerning religion.[6] Within five days they were obliged to swear to observe the laws, as they had done when elected.[7] And in like manner, when they resigned their office, they assembled the people, and made a speech to them about what they had performed in their consulship, and swore that they had done nothing against the laws. But any one of the tribunes might hinder them from making a speech, and only permit them to swear, as the tribune Metellus did to Cicero,[8] whereupon Cicero instantly swore with a loud voice, that he had saved the republic and the city from ruin; which the whole Roman people confirmed with a shout, and with one voice cried out, that what he had sworn was true; and then conducted him from the forum to his house with every demonstration of respect.[9]

4. PROVINCES OF THE CONSULS.

DURING the first days of their office, the consuls cast lots, or agreed among themselves about their provinces.[10]

A province,[11] in its general acceptation, is metaphorically used to signify the office or business of any one, whether private or public; thus, *O Geta*, provinciam *cepisti duram*.[12] Before the Roman empire was widely extended, the province of a consul was simply a certain charge assigned him, as a war to be carried on, &c., or a certain country in which he was to act during his consulship.[13]

Anciently these provinces used to be decreed by the senate after the consuls were elected, or had entered their office. Sometimes the same province was decreed to both consuls.[14] Thus both consuls were sent against the Samnites, and made to pass under the yoke by Pontius, general of the Samnites, at the Furcæ Caudinæ. So Paulus Æmilius and Terentius Varro were sent against Hannibal, at the battle of Cannæ.[15]

But by the Sempronian law, passed by C. Sempronius Gracchus, A. U. 631, the senate always decreed two provinces for the future consuls before their election,[16] which they, after entering on their office, divided by lot or agreement.[17] In latter times the province of a consul was some conquered country, reduced to the form of a province,[18] which each consul, after the expiration of his office, should command; for during the time of their consulship they usually remained in the city.[19]

1 auctoribus patribus; ut novorum maxime hominum ambitio, qui nundinas et conciliabula obire soliti erant, comprimeretur, Liv. vii. 15.
2 salutabant.
3 Plin. Ep. ix. 37.
4 vota nucupabant.
5 munus suum auspicabantur.
6 Ov. Pont. iv. 4. 9. Liv. xxi. 63. xxii. 1. xxvi. 26. Cic. post red.

ad Quir. 5. Rull. ii. 34. Dio. Frag. 120.
7 Liv. xxxi. 50. Plin. Pan. 64, 65.
8 Dio. xxxvii. 38.
9 Cic. Pis. 3. Ep. Fam. v. 2.
10 provincias inter se sortiobantur, aut parabant, vel comparabant: provincias partiti sunt, Liv. ii. 40. iii. 10. 22. 57. et alibi passim.
11 provincia.

12 Ter. Phorm. i. 2. 22. Heaut. iii. 2. 5.
13 Liv. ii. 40. 54. 56. iii. 10. 22. 25. v. 32. vii. 6.
12. viii. 1. 29. ix. 41. x.
15. Flor. i. 11.
14 Liv. x. 32. xxxii. 8. xxxiii. 29. xxxiv. 42. xl. 1. et alibi passim.
15 Liv. ix. 1. xxii. 40. xxv. 3. xxvii. 22, &c.
16 Cic. Dom. 9. Prov. Cons. 2. Sall. Jug. 27.
17 sorte vel compara

tione partiti sunt.
18 see p. 49, 50.
19 hence Cicero says, tum bella gerere nostri duces incipiunt, cum auspicia, i. e. consulatum et præturam, posuerunt, Nat. D. ii. 3. for propraetors and proconsuls had not the right of taking the auspices, auspicia non habebant, Cic. Div. ii. 36.

The provinces decreed to the consuls were called PROVINCIÆ CONSU-
LARES ; to the prætors, PRÆTORIÆ.

Sometimes a certain province was assigned to some one of the consuls ; as Etruria to Fabius, both by the decree of the senate, and by the
order of the people ; Sicily to P. Scipio : Greece and the war against Antiochus, to L. Scipio, by the decree of the senate. This was said to be
done *extra ordinem, extra sortem* vel *sine sorte, sine comparatione.*[1]

It properly belonged to the senate to determine the provinces of the consuls and prætors. In appointing the provinces of the prætors, the tribunes
might interpose their negative, but not in those of the consuls.[2] Sometimes the people reversed what the senate had decreed concerning the provinces. Thus the war against Jugurtha, which the senate had decreed to
Metellus, was given by the people to Marius.[3] And the attempt of Marius, by means of the tribune Sulpicius, to get the command of the war
against Mithridates transferred from Sylla to himself, by the suffrage of
the people, gave occasion to the first civil war at Rome,[4] and in fact gave
both the occasion and the example to all the rest that followed. So when
the senate, to mortify Cæsar, had decreed as provinces to him and his colleague Bibulus, the care of the woods and roads, Cæsar, by means of the
tribune Vatinius, procured from the people, by a new and extraordinary law,
the grant of Cisalpine Gaul, with the addition of Illyricum, for the term of
five years ; and soon after also Transalpine Gaul from the senate, which
important command was afterwards prolonged to him for other five years,
by the Trebonian law.[5]

No one was allowed to leave his province without the permission of the
senate, which regulation, however, was sometimes violated upon extraordinary occasions.[6]

If any one had behaved improperly, he might be recalled from his province by the senate, but his military command could only be abolished[7]
by the people.[8]

The senate might order the consuls to exchange their provinces, and
even force them to resign their command.[9]

Pompey, in his third consulship, to check bribery, passed a law, that no
one should hold a province till five years after the expiration of his magistracy ;[10] and that for these five years, while the consuls and prætors were
disqualified, the senators of consular and prætorian rank, who had never
held any foreign command, should divide the vacant provinces among themselves by lot. By which law the government of Cilicia fell to Cicero
against his will.[11] Cæsar made a law, that the prætorian provinces should
not be held longer than a year, nor the consular more than two years.
But this law, which is much praised by Cicero, was abrogated by Antony.[12]

5. FROM WHAT ORDER THE CONSULS WERE CREATED.

THE consuls were at first chosen only from among the patricians, but
afterwards also from the plebeians. This important change, although in
reality owing to weightier causes, was immediately occasioned by a trifling
circumstance. M. Fabius Ambustus, a nobleman, had two daughters, the

---

1 Liv. iii. 2. vi. 30. x. 24.
xxviii. 38. xxxvii. 1, &c.
2 Cic. Prov. Cons. 6.
3 Sall. Jug. 73.
4 Plut. Mar. & Syll.

App. Bell. Civ. 1.
5 Suet. Jul. 19. 22. Cic.
Dom. 9. Vat. 15. Suet.
Dio. xxxviii. 8. Liv. Ep.
105. Cic. Prov. Cons.

8 Ep. Fam. i. 7. see
page 15.
6 Liv. x. 18. xxvii. 43.
xxix. 19.
7 abrogari.

8 Liv. xxix. 19.
9 Liv. v. 32. xxvi. 29.
10 Dio. xl. 46.
11 Cic. Ep. Fam. iii. 2.
12 Cic. Phil. i. 8.

elder of whom was married to Sulpicius, a patrician, and the younger to
C. Licinius Stole, a plebeian. While the latter was one day visiting her
sister, the lictor of Sulpicius, who was then military tribune, happened to
strike the door with his rod, as was usual when that magistrate returned
home from the forum. The young Fabia, unacquainted with that custom,
was freightened at the noise, which made her sister laugh, and express
surprise at her ignorance. This stung her to the quick : and upon her
return home she could not conceal her uneasiness. Her father, seeing
her dejected, asked her if all was well ; but she at first would not give a
direct answer; and it was with difficulty he at last drew from her a confession that she was chagrined at being connected with a man who could
not enjoy the same honours with her sister's husband. For although it
had been ordained by law that the military tribunes should be created
promiscuously from the patricians and plebeians, yet for forty-four years
after the first institution, A. U. 311, to A. U. 355, no one plebeian had been
created, and very few afterwards.[1] Ambustus, therefore, consoled his
daughter with assurances that she should soon see the same honours at
her own house which she saw at her sister's. To effect this, he concert-
ed measures with his son-in-law, and one L. Sextius, a spirited young
man of plebeian rank, who had every thing but birth to entitle him to the
highest preferments.

Licinius and Sextius being created tribunes of the commons, got themselves continued in that office for ten years ; for five years they suffered
no curule magistrates to be created, and at last prevailed to get one of the
consuls created from among the plebeians.[2]

L. Sextius was the first plebeian consul, and the second year after
him, C. Licinius Stolo, from whom the law ordaining one of the consuls to
be a plebeian, was called LEX LICINIA.[3] Sometimes both consuls were
plebeians, which was early allowed by law. But this rarely happened ;
the patricians for the most part engrossed that honour.[4] The Latins once
required, that one of the consuls should be chosen from among them, as
did afterwards the people of Capua ;[5] but both these demands were rejected with disdain.

The first foreigner who obtained the consulship was Cornelius Balbus,[6]
a native of Cadiz ; who became so rich, that at his death, he left each of
the citizens residing at Rome, 23 drachmæ, or denarii, i. e. 16s. 1¾d.[7]

6. LEGAL AGE, AND OTHER REQUISITES FOR ENJOYING THE CONSULSHIP.

THE legal age for enjoying the consulship[8] was forty-three ;[9] and whoever was made consul at that age, was said to be made in his own year.[10]

Before one could be made consul, it was requisite to have gone through
the inferior offices of quæstor, ædile, and prætor. It behoved candidates
for this office to be present, and in a private station,[11] and no one could be
created consul a second time till after an interval of ten years.[12]

But these regulations were not always observed. In ancient times there
seems to have been no restrictions of that kind, and even after they were
made, they were often violated. Many persons were created consuls in

1 Liv. iv. 6. v. 12, 13. 18. xxiii. 31. et alibi pas- 6 Plin. viii. 43. s. 44. 10 suo anno, Cic. Rull.
vi. 30. 37. sim. Sall. Jug. 63. Cic. Vell. ii. 51. ii. 2.
2 Liv. vi. 35. 42. Rull. H. 1. 7 Dio. xlviii. 32. 11 see p. 60.
3 Liv. vii. 1, 2. 21. 5 Liv. viii. 4, 5. xxxiii. 8 ætas consularia. 12 Liv. vii. 42. x. 13.
4 Liv. vii. 18, 19. 42. 6. 9 Cic. Phil. v. 17.

their absence, and without asking it, and several below the legal age ; thus M. Valerius Corvus at twenty-three, Scipio Africanus the elder, at twenty-eight, and the younger at thirty-eight, T. Quinctius Flaminius, when not quite thirty,[1] Pompey, before he was full thirty-six years old.[2]

To some the consulship was continued for several years without intermission ; as to Marius, who was seven times consul, and once and again created in his absence.[3] Several persons were made consuls without having previously borne any curule office.[4] Many were re-elected within a less interval than of ten years.[5] And the refusal of the senate to permit Cæsar to stand candidate in his absence, or to retain his province, gave occasion to the civil war betwixt him and Pompey, which terminated in the entire extinction of liberty.[6]

7. ALTERATIONS IN THE CONDITION OF THE CONSULS UNDER THE EMPERORS.

JULIUS CÆSAR reduced the power of the consuls to a mere name. Being created perpetual dictator,[7] all the other magistrates were subject to him. Although the usual form of electing consuls was retained, he assumed the nomination of them entirely to himself. He was dictator and consul at the same time,[8] as Sylla had been before him ; but he resigned the consulship when he thought proper, and nominated whom he chose to succeed him. When about to set out against the Parthians, he settled the succession of magistrates for two years to come.[9] He introduced a custom of substituting consuls at any time, for a few months or weeks ; sometimes only for a few days, or even hours ;[10] that thus the prince might gratify a greater number with honours. Under Commodus, there were twenty-five consuls in one year.[11] The usual number in a year was twelve. But the consuls who were admitted on the first day of January gave name to the year, and had the title of ORDINARII, the others being styled SUFFECTI, or *minores*.[12]

The consuls, when appointed by the emperor, did not use any canvassing, but went through almost the same formalities in other respects as under the republic.[13] In the first meeting of the senate after their election, they returned thanks to the emperor in a set speech, when it was customary to expatiate on his virtues ; which was called HONORE, *vel* IN HONOREM PRINCIPIS CENSERE, because they delivered this speech, when they were first asked their opinion as consuls elect.[14] Pliny afterwards enlarged on the general heads, which he used on that occasion, and published them under the name of PANEGYRICUS[15] *Nervæ Trajano Augusto dictus.*

Under the emperors there were persons dignified merely with the title, without enjoying the office, of consuls ;[16] as, under the republic, persons who had never been consuls or prætors, on account of some public service, obtained the right of sitting and speaking in the senate, in the place of

---

1 Cic. Amic. 3. Liv. vii. 26. xxv. 2. xxvi. 18. xxviii. 38. Epit. xlix. Plut.
2 ex S. C. legibus solutus consul ante fiebat, quam ullum magistratum per leges capere licuisset, i. e. before by law he could be made ædile, which was the first office properly

called magistratus, although that title is often applied also to the quæstorship and tribuneship, Cic. Legg. Man. 21.
3 Liv. Epit. 67, 68. 80.
4 Liv. xxv. 42. xxxii. 7. Dio. xxxvi. 23.
5 Liv. passim.
6 Cæs. Bell. Civ. i. 2, 3.
7 Suet. 76.

8 Cic. Phil. ii. 32. Suet. Jul. 41. 76. Dio. xliii. 1.
9 consules et tribunos plebis in biennium, quos voluit, Cic. Att. xiv. 6 Dio. xliii. 51.
10 Lucan. v. 397. Suet. Jul. 76. Cic. Fam. vii. 30. Dio. xliii. 36.
11 Lamprid. 6.
12 Dio. xlviii. 35.
13 Plin. Ep. ix. 13. Pan.

63, 64, 65. 69. 77. 92.
14 Plin. Ep. iii. 13. 18. vi. 27. Pan. 2. 90, 91. 93. 54. see page 8.
15 i. e. λογος πανηγυρικος, oratio in conventu habita, a πανηγυρις, conventus, Cic. Att. i. 14.
16 consules honorarii.

those who had been consuls or prætors,[1] which was called *auctoritas* vel *sententia consularis* aut *prætoria*.[2]

Those who had been consuls were called CONSULARES ;[3] as those who had been prætors, were called PRÆTORII ; ædiles, ÆDILITII ; quæstors, QUÆSTORII.

Under Justinian, consuls ceased to be created, and the year, of consequence, to be distinguished by their name, A. U. 1293. But the emperors still continued to assume that office the first year of their sovereignty. Constantine created two consuls annually ; whose office it was to exercise supreme jurisdiction, the one at Rome, and the other at Constantinople.

II. PRÆTORS.

1. INSTITUTION AND POWER OF THE PRÆTOR.

THE name of PRÆTOR[4] was anciently common to all the magistrates ; thus the dictator is called *prætor maximus*.[5] But when the consuls, being engaged in almost continual wars, could not attend to the administration of justice, a magistrate was created for that purpose, A. U. 389, to whom the name of PRÆTOR was thenceforth appropriated. He was at first created only from among the patricians, as a kind of compensation for the consulship being communicated to the plebeians ; but afterwards, A. U. 418, also from the plebeians.[6] The prætor was next in dignity to the consuls, and was created at the Comitia Centuriata with the same auspices as the consuls, whence he was called their colleague. The first prætor was Sp. Furius Camillus, son to the great M. Furius Camillus, who died the year that his son was prætor.[7]

When one prætor was not sufficient, on account of the number of foreigners who flocked to Rome, another prætor was added, A. U. 510, to administer justice to them, or between citizens and them,[8] hence called PRÆTOR PEREGRINUS.

The two prætors, after their election, determined, by casting lots, which of the two jurisdictions each should exercise.

The prætor who administered justice only between citizens, was called PRÆTOR URBANUS, and was more honourable ; whence he was called PRÆTOR HONORATUS,[9] MAJOR :[10] and the law derived from him and his edicts is called JUS HONORARIUM. In the absence of the consuls he supplied their place.[11] He presided in the assemblies of the people, and might convene the senate : but only when something new happened.[12] He likewise exhibited certain public games, as the *Ludi Apollinares* ; the Circensian and Megalesian games ; and therefore had a particular jurisdiction over players, and such people; at least under the emperors.[13] When there was no censor, he took care, according to a decree of the senate, that the public buildings were kept in proper repair.[14] On account of these important offices, he was not allowed to be absent from the city above ten days.[15]

1 loco consulari vel prætorio, Cic. Phil. i. 6. v. 17. Liv. Epit. 116.'
2 Cic. Vat. 7. Balb. 25. so, allectus inter prætorios. Plin. Ep. i. 14. Pallanti senatus ornamenta prætoria decrevit, vii. 29. viii. 6.

3 Cic. Fam. xii. 4, &c.
4 is qui præit jure et exercitu, Varro, στρατηγος.
5 Liv. iii. 55. vii. 3. Asc. Cic.
6 Liv. viii. 15.
7 Liv. vii. 1. viii. 32. Gell. xiii. 14. Plin.

Pan. 77.
8 qui inter cives Romanos et peregrinos jus diceret, Liv. Epit. xix. —xxii. 36.
9 Ov. Fast. i. 52.
10 Festus in voce Major consul.
11 munus consulare

sustinebat, Cic. Fam. x. 12.
12 Cic. Fam. xii. 28.
13 Liv. xxvii. 23. Juv. xi. 192. Tac. Ann. i. 77.
14 sarta tecta exigebat, Cic. Ver. i. 50.
15 Cic. Phil. ii. 13.

The power of the prætor in the administration of justice was expressed in these three words, DO, DICO, ADDICO. *Prætor* DABAT *actionem et judices;* the prætor gave the form of a writ for trying and redressing a particular wrong complained of, and appointed judges or a jury to judge in the cause; DICEBAT *jus,* pronounced sentence; ADDICEBAT *bona* vel *damna,* adjudged the goods of the debtor to the creditor, &c.

The days on which the prætor administered justice were called DIES FASTI.[1] Those days on which it was unlawful to administer justice, were called NEFASTI.

> Ille nefastus erit, per quem tria verba silentur:
> Fastus erit, per quem lege licebit agi. *Ov. Fast.* i. 47.

2. EDICTS OF THE PRÆTOR.

THE *prætor urbanus,* when he entered on his office, after having sworn to the observance of the laws, published an edict,[2] or system of rules,[3] according to which he was to administer justice for that year; whence it is called by Cicero LEX ANNUA.[4] Having summoned an assembly of the people, he publicly declared[5] from the *rostra*[6] what method he was to observe[7] in administering justice.[8] This edict he ordered not only to be recited by a herald,[9] but also to be publicly pasted up in writing,[10] in large letters.[11] These words used commonly to be prefixed to the edict, BONUM FACTUM.[12]

Those edicts which the prætor copied from the edicts of his predecessors were called TRALATITIA; those which he framed himself, were called NOVA; and so any clause or part of an edict, CAPUT TRALATITIUM vel NOVUM.[13] But as the prætor often, in the course of the year, altered his edicts through favour or enmity,[14] this was forbidden, first by a decree of the senate, A. U. 686, by a law which C. Cornelius got passed, to the great offence of the nobility, UT PRÆTORES EX EDICTIS SUIS PERPETUIS, JUS DICERENT, i. e. that the prætors, in administering justice, should not deviate from the form which they prescribed to themselves in the beginning of their office.[15] From this time the law of the prætors[16] became more fixed, and lawyers began to study their edicts with particular attention, some also to comment on them.[17] By order of the emperor Hadrian, the various edicts of the prætors were collected into one, and properly arranged by the lawyer Salvius Julian, the great-grandfather of the emperor Didus Julian; which was thereafter called EDICTUM PERPETUUM, or JUS HONORARIUM, and no doubt was of the greatest service in forming that famous code of the Roman laws called the CORPUS JURIS, compiled by order of the emperor Justinian.

Beside the general edict which the prætor published when he entered on his office, he frequently published particular edicts as occasion required.[18]

An edict published at Rome was called EDICTUM URBANUM; in the provinces, PROVINCIALE, *Siciliense,*[19] &c.

Some think that the *prætor urbanus* only published an annual edict, and

---

1 a fando, quod iis diebus hæc tria verba fari licebat.
2 edictum.
3 formula.
4 Cic. Verr. i. 42.
5 edicebat.
6 cum in concionem adscendisset.

7 quæ observaturus esset.
8 Cic. Fin. li. 22.
9 Plaut. Prol. Pœn. 11.
10 scriptum in albo, i. e. in tabula dealbata, vel, ut alii dicunt, albis literis notata, publice proponi, unde de plano,

i. e. de humo, recte legi posset.
11 literis majusculis, Suet. Cal. 41.
12 Suet. Jul. 80. Vit. 14. Plaut. ibid.
13 Cic. Verr. i. 45.
14 Cic. Verr. l. 41. 46.
15 Asc. in Cic. Corn.—

Dio. Cass. 36. c. 22, 23.
16 jus præturium.
17 Cic. Legg. i. 5. Gell. xiii. 10.
18 edicta peculiaria, et repentina, Cic. Verr. iii. 14.
19 Cic. Verr. iii. 42. 46. 45, &c.

that the *prætor peregrinus* administered justice, either according to it, or according to the law of nature and nations. But we read also of the edict of the prætor peregrinus. And it appears that in certain cases he might even be appealed to for relief against the decrees of the prætor urbanus.[1]

The other magistrates published edicts as well as the prætor : the kings, the consuls, the dictator, the censor, the curule ædiles, the tribunes of the commons, and the quæstors.[2] So the provincial magistrates,[3] and under the emperors, the præfect of the city, of the prætorian cohorts, &c. So likewise the priests, as the *pontifices* and *decemviri sacrorum*, the augurs, and in particular, the *pontifex maximus*.[4] All these were called HONO-RATI, *honore honestati, honoribus honorati, honore vel honoribus usi ;*[5] and therefore the law which was derived from their edicts was also called JUS HONORARIUM. But of all these, the edicts of the prætor were the most important.

The orders and decrees of the emperors were sometimes also called *edicta*, but usually *rescripta*.[6]

The magistrates in composing their edicts took the advice of the chief men of the state ;[7] and sometimes of one another.[8]

The summoning of any one to appear in court, was likewise called *edictum*. If a person did not obey the first summons, it was repeated a second and third time ; and then what was called a peremptory summons was given,[9] and if any one neglected it, he was called contumacious, and lost his cause. Sometimes a summons of this kind was given all at once, and was called UNUM PRO OMNIBUS, or UNUM PRO TRIBUS. We read of the senators being summoned to Rome from all Italy by an edict of the prætor.[10]

Certain decrees of the prætor were called INTERDICTA ; as about acquiring, retaining, or recovering the possession of a thing ;[11] also about restoring, exhibiting, or prohibiting a thing ; whence Horace,[12] INTERDICTO *huic* (sc. insano) *omne adimat jus prætor*, i. e. *bonis interdicat*, the prætor by an interdict would take from him the management of his fortune, and appoint him a curator,[13] according to the law of the twelve tables.[14]

3. INSIGNIA OF THE PRÆTOR.

THE prætor was attended by two lictors in the city, who went before him with the *fasces*,[15] and by six lictors without the city. He wore the *toga prætexta*, which he assumed, as the consuls did, on the first day of his office, after having offered up vows[16] in the Capitol.

When the prætor heard causes, he sat in the forum or Comitium, on a TRIBUNAL,[17] which was a kind of stage or scaffold,[18] in which was placed the *sella curulis* of the prætor,[19] and a sword and a spear[20] were set up-

1 Cic. Fam. xiii. 59. Verr. i. 46. Asc. Cic. Cæs. Bell. Civ. iii. 20. Dio. xiii. 22.
2 Liv. i. 32. 44. ii. 24. 30. viii. 6. 34. xiiii. 14. Nep. Cap. i. Gell. xv. 11. Plaut. Capt. iv. 2. 43. Cic. Phil. ix. 7. Verr. ii. 41. iii. 7.
3 Cic. Epist. passim.
4 Liv. xl. 37. Val. Max. viii. 2. 1. Tac. Hist. ii. 91. Gell. ii. 28
5 Liv. xxv. 5. Ov. Pont. iv. 5. 2. Sall. Cat. 35. Vell. ii. 124. Flor. i. 13.

Cic. Flacc. 19.
6 see page 17.
7 thus, consules cum viros primarios atque amplissimos civitatis multos in consilium advocassent, de consilii sententia pronunciarunt, &c. Cic. Verr. iii. 7.
8 thus, cum collegium prætorium tribuni pleb. adhibuissent, ut rea nummaria de communi sententia constitueretur ; conscripserunt communiter edictum,

Cic. Off. iii. 20. Marius [quod communiter compositum fuerat, solus edixit, ibid.
9 edictum peremptorium dabatur, quod disceptationem perimeret, i. e. ultra tergiversari non pateretur, which admitted of no farther delay.
10 Liv. xliii. 11.
11 Cic. Cæc. 3. 14. 21. Or. i. 10. to which Cicero alludes, urbanitatis possessionem quibusvis interdictis de-

fendamus, Fam. vii. 32.
12 Sat. ii. 3. 217.
13 Hor. Ep. i. 1. 102.
14 quæ furiosis et male rem gerentibus bonis interdici jubebat, Cic. Sen. 7.
15 Plaut. Ep. i. 1. 26.
16 votis nuncupatis.
17 in, or oftener pro tribunali.
18 suggestum v. -us.
19 Cic. Verr. ii. 38. Mart. xi. 99. al. 98.
20 gladius et hasta.

right before him. The tribunal was made of wood, and movable, so large as to contain the ASSESSORES or counsel of the prætor, and others,[1] in the form of a square, as appears from ancient coins. But when spacious halls were erected round the forum, for the administration of justice, called BASILICÆ, or *regiæ*, sc. *ædes vel porticus*,[2] from their largeness and magnificence, the tribunal in them seems to have been of stone, and in the form of a semicircle, the two ends of which were called *cornua*, or *partes primores*.[3] The first *basilica* at Rome appears to have been built by M. Porcius Cato, the censor, A. U. 566, hence called Porcia.[4]

The JUDICES, or jury appointed by the prætor, sat on lower seats, called SUBSELLIA, as also did the advocates, the witnesses, and hearers.[5] Whence *subsellia* is put for the act of judging, or of pleading ; thus, *versatus in utrisque subselliis, cum summa fama et fide* ; i. e. judicem et patronum egit. *A subselliis alienus*, &c. i. e. *causidicus*, a pleader. For such were said *habitare in subselliis, a subselliis in otium se conferre*, to retire from pleading.[6]

The inferior magistrates, when they sat in judgment,[7] did not use a tribunal, but only *subsellia* ; as the tribunes, plebeian ædiles, and quæstors, &c.[8]

The benches on which the senators sat in the senate-house were likewise called *subsellia*. Hence *longi* subsellii *judicatio*, the slowness of the senate in decreeing.[9] And so also the seats in the theatres, circus, &c.; thus, *senatoria subsellia ; bis septena subsellia*, the seats of the equites.[10]

In matters of less importance, the prætor judged and passed sentence without form, at any time, or in any place, whether sitting or walking ; and then he was said COGNOSCERE, *interloqui, discutere*, E vel DE PLANO ; or, as Cicero expresses it, *ex æquo loco, non pro*, vel *e tribunali*, aut *ex superiore loco* ; which expressions are opposed.[11] But about all important affairs he judged in form on his tribunal ; whence *atque hæc agebantur in conventu palam, de sella ac de loco superiore*.[12]

The usual attendants[13] of the prætor, besides the lictors, were the SCRIBÆ, who recorded his proceedings ;[14] and the ACCENSI, who summoned persons, and proclaimed aloud when it was the third hour, or nine o'clock before noon ; when it was mid-day, and when it was the ninth hour, or three o'clock afternoon.[15]

4. NUMBER OF PRÆTORS AT DIFFERENT TIMES.

WHILE the Roman empire was limited to Italy, there were only two prætors. When Sicily and Sardinia were reduced to the form of a province, A. U. 526, two other prætors were added to govern them, and two more when Hither and Farther Spain were subdued.[16] In the year 571, only four prætors were created by the Bæbian law, which ordained, that six prætors and four should be created alternately,[17] but this regulation seems not to have been long observed.

Of these six prætors, two only remained in the city ; the other four,

---

1 Suet. Cæs. 84. Cic. Vat. 14. Or. i. 37. Brut. 84.
2 Suet. Aug. 31. Cal. 37. Stat. Silv. i. 1. 29. Βασιλικαι στοαι, Zos. v. 2. Jos. A. xvii. 11.
3 Vitr. v. 1. Tac. Ann. i. 75. Suet. Tib. 33.
4 Liv. xxxix. 44.
5 Cic. Rosc. Am. 11. Or. i. 62. Flacc. 10. Brut. 84. Suet. Aug. 56.
6 Suet. Ner. 17. Cic. Or. i. 8 62. ii. 33. Cæc. 15. Fam. xiii. 10.
7 judicia exercebant.
8 Asc. Cic. Suet. Claud.
23.
9 Cic. Cat. i. 7. Fam. iii. 9.
10 Cic. Corn. i. Mart. v. 28.
11 Cic. Fam. iii. 8. Cæc. 17 Or. 6. Suet. Tjb. 33.
12 Cic. Verr. iv. 40.
13 ministri vel appari-
tores.
14 qui acta in tabulas referrent, Cic. Verr. iii. 78, 79.
15 Verr. I. L. v. 9.
16 Liv. xxxii. 27, 28. Ep. 20.
17 Liv. xl. 44.

immediately after having entered on their office, set out for their provinces. The prætors determined their province, as the consuls, by casting lots, or by agreement.[1]

Sometimes one prætor administered justice both between citizens and foreigners; and in dangerous conjunctures, none of the prætors were exempted from military service.[2]

The prætor urbanus and peregrinus administered justice only in private or lesser causes; but in public and important causes, the people either judged themselves, or appointed persons, one or more, to preside at the trial,[3] who were called QUÆSITORES, or quæstores parricidii, whose authority lasted only till the trial was over. Sometimes a dictator was created for holding trials.[4] But A. U. 604, it was determined, that the prætor urbanus and peregrinus should continue to exercise their usual jurisdictions; and that the four other prætors should during their magistracy also remain in the city, and preside at public trials; one at trials concerning extortion;[5] another concerning bribery;[6] a third concerning crimes committed against the state;[7] and a fourth about defrauding the public treasury.[8] These were called QUÆSTIONES PERPETUÆ,[9] because they were annually assigned[10] to particular prætors, who always conducted them for the whole year,[11] according to a certain form prescribed by law; so that there was no need, as formerly, of making a new law, or of appointing extraordinary inquisitors to preside at them, who should resign their authority when the trial was ended. But still, when any thing unusual or atrocious happened, the people or senate judged about the matter themselves, or appointed inquisitors to preside at the trial; and then they were said extra ordinem quærere: as in the case of Clodius, for violating the sacred rites of the Bona Dea, or Good Goddess, and of Milo, for the murder of Clodius.[12]

L. Sulla increased the number of the quæstiones perpetuæ, by adding those de FALSO, vel de crimine falsi, concerning forgers of wills or other writs, coiners or makers of base money, &c. de SICARIS et VENEFICIS, about such as killed a person with weapons or poison; et de PARRICIDIS, on which account he created two additional prætors, A. U. 672; some say four. Julius Cæsar increased the number of prætors, first to ten, A. U. 707, then to fourteen, and afterwards to sixteen.[13] Under the triumviri, there were sixty-seven prætors in one year. Augustus reduced the number to twelve, Dio says ten; but afterwards made them sixteen. According to Tacitus, there were no more than twelve at his death. Under Tiberius, there were sometimes fifteen and sometimes sixteen.[14] Claudius added two prætors, for the cognizance of trusts.[15] The number then was eighteen; but afterwards it varied.

Upon the decline of the empire, the principal functions of the prætors were conferred on the præfectus prætorio, and other magistrates instituted by the emperors. The prætors of course sunk in their importance; under Valentinian their number was reduced to three; and this magistracy having become an empty name,[16] was at last entirely suppressed, as it is thought, under Justinian.

1 Liv. passim.
2 Liv. xxiii. 32. xxv. 3. xxvii. 38. xxxi. 1. xxxv. 41.
3 qui questioni præessent, Cic. Clu. 29. quærerent, quæstiones publicas vel judicia exercerent, Liv. iv. 51. xxxviii. 55. Sall. Jug. 40
4 Liv. ix. 26.
5 de repetundis.
6 de ambitu.
7 de majestate.
8 de peculatu.
9 Cic. Brut. 26.
10 mandabantur.
11 qui perpetuo exercerent.
12 Cic. Att. i. 13, 14. 16. Mil. &c.
13 Dio. xlii. 51. xliii. 47. 49. Tac. Hist. iii. 37.
14 Dio. xliii. 32. xlviii. 43. 53. lviii. 20. Pompon. Orig. Jur. ii. 28. Tac. Ann. i. 14.
15 qui de fidei commissis jus dicerent
16 inane nomen, Boeth. Consol. Philos. iii. 4.

III. CENSORS.

Two magistrates were first created, A. U. 312, for taking an account of the number of the people, and the value of their fortunes ;[1] whence they were called CENSORES.[2] As the consuls, being engaged in wars abroad or commotions at home, had not leisure for that business,[3] the census had been intermitted for seventeen years. The censors at first continued in office for five years.[4] But afterwards, lest they should abuse their authority, a law was passed by Mamercus Æmilius the dictator, ordaining, that they should be elected every five years ; but that their power should continue only a year and a half.[5]

The censors had all the ensigns of the consuls, except the lictors. They were usually chosen from the most respectable persons of consular dignity ; at first only from among the patricians, but afterwards likewise from the plebeians. The first plebeian censor was C. Marcius Rutilus, A. U. 404, who also had been the first plebeian dictator.[6] Afterwards a law was made, that one of the censors should always be a plebeian. Sometimes both censors were plebeians,[7] and sometimes those were created censors who had neither been consuls nor prætors,[8] but not so after the second Punic war.

The last censors, namely Paulus and Plancus, under Augustus, are said to have been private persons ;[9] not that they had never borne any public office before, but to distinguish them from the emperor; all besides him being called by that name.[10]

The power of the censors at first was small ; but afterwards it became very great. All the orders of the state were subject to them.[11] Hence the censorship is called by Plutarch the summit of all preferments,[12] and by Cicero *magistra pudoris et modestiæ*.[13] The title of censor was esteemed more honourable than that of consul, as appears from ancient coins and statues : and it was reckoned the chief ornament of nobility to be sprung from a censorian family.[14]

The office of the censors was chiefly to estimate the fortunes, and to inspect the morals of the citizens.[15]

The censors performed the census in the Campus Martius. Seated in their curule chairs, and attended by their clerks and other officers, they ordered the citizens, divided into their classes and centuries, and also into their tribes,[16] to be called[17] before them by a herald, and to give an account of their fortunes, family, &c., according to the institution of Servius Tullius.[18] At the same time they reviewed the senate and equestrian order, supplied the vacant places in both, and inflicted various marks of disgrace[19] on those who deserved it. A senator they excluded from the senate-house,[20] an eques they deprived of his public horse,[21] and any other citizen they removed from a more honourable to a less honourable tribe ;[22] or deprived

---

1 consui agendo.
2 Liv. et Fest. censor, ad cujus censionem, id est, arbitrium, censeretur populus, Var. L. L. iv. 14.
3 non consulibus operæ erat, sc. pretium, i. e. lis non vacabat id negotium agere.

4 Liv. iii. 22. iv. 8.
5 ex quinquennali annua ac semestris censura facta est, Liv. iv. 24. ix. 33.
6 Liv. vii. 22.
7 Liv. Epit. 59.
8 Liv. xxvii. 6. 11.
9 privati, Dio. liv. 2.
10 Vell. ii. 59. Suet.

' Tac. et Plin. passim.
11 censoribus subjecti, Liv. iv. 24.
12 omnium honorum apex vel fastigium, Cat. Maj.
13 Pis. 4.
14 Val. Maj. viii. 13. Tac. Ann. iii. 28. Hist. iii. 9.

15 Cic. Legg. iii. 3.
16 Liv. xxix. 37.
17 citari.
18 see p. 56.
19 notas inurebant.
20 senatu movebant vel ejiciebant, see p. 4.
21 equum adimebant, see p. 19.
22 tribu movebant.

him of all the privileges of a Roman citizen, except liberty.[1] This mark of disgrace was also inflicted on a senator or an eques, and was then always added to the mark of disgrace peculiar to their order.[2] The censors themselves did not sometimes agree about their powers in this respect.[3] They could inflict these marks of disgrace upon what evidence, and for what cause they judged proper; but, when they expelled from the senate, they commonly annexed a reason to their censure, which was called SUBSCRIPTIO CENSORIA.[4] Sometimes an appeal was made from their sentence to the people.[5] They not only could hinder one another from inflicting any censure,[6] but they might even stigmatize one another.[7]

The citizens in the colonies and free towns were there enrolled by their own censors, according to the form prescribed by the Roman censors,[8] and an account of them was transmitted to Rome; so that the senate might see at one view the wealth and condition of the whole empire.[9]

When the censors took an estimate of the fortunes of the citizens, they were said *censum agere* vel *habere*; CENSERE *populi ævitates, soboles, familias, pecuniasque, referre in censum*, or *censui ascribere*.[10] The citizens, when they gave in to the censors an estimate of their fortunes, &c. were said CENSERI *modum agri, mancipia, pecunias*, &c. sc. *secundum* vel *quod ad, profiteri, in censum deferre* vel *dedicare*,[11] *annos deferre* vel *censeri*:[12] sometimes also *censere*; thus, *prædia censere*, to give in an estimate of one's farms;[13] *prædia censui censendo*,[14] farms, of which one is the just proprietor. Hence, *censeri*, to be valued or esteemed, to be held in estimation;[15] *de quo censeris, amicus*, from whom or on whose account you are valued;[16] *privatus illis* CENSUS *erat brevis, exiguus, tenuis*, their private fortune was small;[17] *equestris, v. -ter*, the fortune of an eques; CCCC. *millia nummum*, 400,000 sesterces;[18] *senatorius*, of a senator;[19] *homo sine censu, ex censu tributa conferre, cultus major censu, dat census honores, census partus per vulnera*, a fortune procured in war;[20] *demittere censum in viscera*, i. e. *bona obligurire*, to eat up;[21] *Romani census populi*, the treasury,[22] *breves extendere census*, to make a small fortune go far.[23]

The censors divided the citizens into classes and centuries, according to their fortunes. They added new tribes to the old, when it was necessary.[24]

---

1 ærarium faciebant, Liv. qui per hoc non esset in albo centuriæ suæ, sed ad hoc esset civis tantum, ut pro capite suo tributi nomine æra penderet, Asc. Cic. or, as it is otherwise expressed, in tabulas Cæritum, vel inter Cærites referebant, i. e. jure suffragii privabant, Gell. xvi. 13. Strab. v. p. 220. hence Cærite cera digni, worthless persons, Hor. Ep. i. 6. 63, but this last phrase does not often occur. Cicero and Livy almost always use ærarium facere; in vel inter ærarios referre.
2 thus, censores Mamercum, qui fuerat dictator, tribu moverunt, octuplicatoque censu, i. e. having made the valuation of his estate

eight times more than it ought, that thus he might be obliged to pay eight times more tribute, ærarium fecerunt, Liv. iv. 24. omnes quos senatu moverunt, quibusque equos ademerunt, ærarios fecerunt, et tribu moverunt, xlii. 10.
3 Claudius negabat, suffragii lationem injussu populi censorem cuiquam homini adimere posse. Neque enim si tribu movere posset, quod sit nihil aliud quam mutare jubere tribum, ideo omnibus v. et xxx.tribubus emovere posse: id est, civitatem libertatemque eripere, non ubi censeatur finire, sed censu excludere Hæc inter ipsos disceptata, &c. Liv. xlv. 15.

4 Liv. xxxix. 42. Cic. Clu. 43, 44.
5 Plut. T. Q. Flam in.
6 ut alter de senatu moveri velit, alter retineat; ut alter in ærarios referri, aut tribu moveri jubeat, alter vetet, Cic. ibid. Tres ejecti de senatu: retinuit quosdam Lepidus a collega præteritos, Liv. xl. 51.
7 Liv. xxix. 37.
8 ex formula ab Romanis censoribus data.
9 Liv. xxix. 15. 37.
10 Cic. Legg. iii. 3. Liv. xxxix. 44. Flor. i. 6. Tac. Ann. xiii. 51.
11 Cic. Flacc. 32. s. 80. Arch. 4. Sen. Ep. 95.
12 thus, CL. annos, i. e. 150 years old, census est Claudii Cæsaris censura T. Fullonius Bononiensis; idque collatis censibus quos

ante detulerat, verum apparuit, Plin. vii. 49. s. 50.
13 Cic. Flacc. 32. Liv. xlv. 15.
14 sc. apta; i. e. quorum census conseri, pretium æstimari, ordinis et tributi causa, potest.
15 Cic. Arch. 6. Val. Max. v. 3. ext. 3. Ov. Am. ii. 15. 2. Sen. Ep. 76. Plin. Pan. 15.
16 Ov. Pont. ii. 5. 73.
17 Hor. Od. ii. 15. 13. Ep. i. 1. 43. 7. 76.
18 Plin. Ep. i. 19.
19 Suet. Vesp. 17.
20 Cic. Flacc. 52. Verr. ii. 63. Hor. Sat. ii. 3. 323. Ov. Am. iii. 8. 56. 9.
21 Ov. Met. iii. v. 846.
22 Luc. iii. 157.
23 Mart. xii. 6.
24 Liv. x. 9. Epit. 19.

14

They let the public lands and taxes,[1] and the regulations which they prescribed to the farmers-general[2] were called *leges* vel *tabulæ censoriæ*.[3]

The censors agreed with undertakers about building and repairing the public works, such as temples, porticoes, &c.;[4] which they examined when finished,[5] and caused to be kept in good repair.[6] The expenses allowed by the public for executing these works were called ULTROTRIBU-TA, hence *ultrotributa locare*, to let them, or to promise a certain 'sum for executing them ; *conducere*, to undertake them.[7]

The censors had the charge of paving the streets, and making the public roads, bridges, aqueducts, &c.[8] They likewise made contracts about furnishing the public sacrifices, and horses for the use of the curule magistrates ;[9] also about feeding the geese which were kept in the Capitol, in commemoration of their having preserved it, when the dogs had failed to give the alarm.[10] They took care that private persons should not occupy what belonged to the public. And if any one refused to obey their sentence, they could fine him, and distrain his effects till he made payment.[11]

The imposing of taxes is often ascribed to the censors ; but this was done by a decree of the senate and the order of the people ; without which the censors had not even the right of laying out the public money, nor of letting the public lands.[12] Hence the senate sometimes cancelled their leases[13] when they disapproved of them, for the senate had the chief direction in all these matters.[14]

The censor had no right to propose laws, or to lay any thing before the senate or people, unless by means of the consul or prætor, or a tribune of the commons.[15]

The power of the censors did not extend to public crimes, or to such things as came under the cognizance of the civil magistrate, and were punishable by law ; but only to matters of a private nature, and of less importance ; as, if one did not cultivate his ground properly ; if an eques did not take proper care of his horse, which was called INCURIA, or *impolitia* ;[16] if one lived too long unmarried (the fine for which was called ÆS UXORIUM), or contracted debt without cause ;[17] and particularly, if any one had not behaved with sufficient bravery in war, or was of dissolute morals ; above all, if a person had violated his oath.[18] The accused were usually permitted to make their defence.[19]

The sentence of the censors[20] only affected the rank and character of persons. It was therefore properly called IGNOMINIA,[21] and in later times had no other effect than of putting a man to the blush.[22] It was not fixed and unalterable, as the decision of a court of law,[23] but might be either taken off by the next censors, or rendered ineffectual by the verdict of a jury, or by the suffrages of the Roman people. Thus we find C. Gæta, who had been extruded the senate by the censors, A. U. 639, the very

---

1 see p. 46.
2 mancipibus v. publica-
  nis.
3 Cic. Verr. iii. 6. Rull.
  i. 2. Polyb. vi. 15.
4 opera publica ædifi-
  canda et reficienda re-
  demptoribus locabant.
5 probaverunt, i. e.
  recte et ex ordine fac-
  ta esse pronunciave-
  runt.
6 sarta tecta exigebant,

ac. et, Liv. iv. 22. xl.
  51. xlii. 3. xlv. 15.
7 Liv. xxxix. 44. xliii.
  16. Sen. Ben. iv. 1.
8 Liv. ix. 29. 43. xli. 27.
9 Plut. Cat. Liv. xxiv.
  18. Fest. in Equi cu-
  rules.
10 Cic. Rosc. Am. 20,
  Plin. x. 22. s. 26. xxix.
  4. s. 14.
11 Liv. iv. 6. xliii. 16.
12 Liv. xxvii. 11. xl. 46.

xli. 27. xliv. 16. Polyb.
  vi. 10.
12 locationes induce-
  bant.
14 Polyb. xxxix. 44.
15 Plin. Hist. Nat. xxxv.
  17. Liv. loc. cit.
16 Gell. iv. 12.
17 Fest. Val. Max. ii. 9.
18 Liv. xxiv. 18. Cic.
  Clu. 47. Off. iii. 31.
  Gell. vii. 18.
19 causam dicere, Liv.

loc. cit.
20 animadversio censo-
  ria vel judicium censo-
  ris.
21 quod in nomine tan-
  tum, i. e. dignitate ver-
  sabatur.
23 nihil fere damnato af-
  ferebat præter rubo-
  rem, Cic.
23 non pro re judicata
  habebatur.

next lustrum himself made censor.[1] Sometimes the senate added force to the feeble sentence of the censors,[2] by their decree; which imposed an additional punishment.[3]

The office of censor was once exercised by a dictator.[4] After Sylla, the election of censors was intermitted for about seventeen years.[5]

When the censors acted improperly, they might be brought to a trial, as they sometimes were, by a tribune of the commons. Nay, we find a tribune ordering a censor to be seized and led to prison, and even to be thrown from the Tarpeian rock; but both were prevented by their colleagues.[6]

Two things were peculiar to the censors.—1. No one could be elected a second time to that office, according to the law of C. Martius Rutilus, who refused a second censorship when conferred on him, hence surnamed CENSORINUS.[7]—2. If one of the censors, died, another was not substituted in his room; but his surviving colleague was obliged to resign his office.[8]

The death of a censor was esteemed ominous, because it had happened that a censor died, and another was chosen in his place, in that lustrum in which Rome was taken by the Gauls.[9]

The censors entered on their office immediately after their election. It was customary for them, when the Comitia were over, to sit down on their curule chairs in the Campus Martius before the temple of Mars.[10] Before they began to execute their office, they swore that they would do nothing through favour or hatred, but that they would act uprightly; and when they resigned their office, they swore that they had done so. Then going up to the treasury,[11] they left a list of those whom they had made *ærarii*.[12]

A record of the proceedings of the censors[13] was kept in the temple of the Nymphs, and is also said to have been preserved with great care by their descendants.[14] One of the censors, to whom it fell by lot,[15] after the census was finished, offered a solemn sacrifice[16] in the Campus Martius.[17]

The power of the censors continued unimpaired to the tribuneship of Clodius, A. U. 695, who got a law passed, ordering that no senator should be degraded by the censors, unless he had been formally accused and condemned by both censors;[18] but this law was abrogated, and the powers of the censorship restored soon after by Q. Metellus Scipio, A. U. 702.[19]

Under the emperors, the office of censor was abolished; but the chief parts of it were exercised by the emperors themselves, or by other magistrates.

Julius Cæsar made a review of the people[20] after a new manner, in the several streets, by means of the proprietors of the houses;[21] but this was not a review of the whole Roman people, but only of the poorer sort, who received a monthly gratuity of corn from the public, which used to be given them in former times, first at a low price, and afterwards, by the law of Clodius, for nought.[22]

Julius Cæsar was appointed by the senate to inspect the morals of the

1 Cic. Clu. 42. see p. 4.
2 inerti censorio notæ.
3 Liv. xxiv. 18.
4 Liv. xxiii. 22, 23.
5 Asc. Cic.
6 Liv. xxiv. 43. xliii. 15, 16. ix. 34. Epit. 59. Plin. vii. 44. s. 45. 43. s. 45.
7 Val. Max. iv. 1.

8 Liv. xxiv. 43. xxvii.
6. Plut. Q. Rom. 50.
9 Liv. v. 31. vi. 27.
10 Liv. xl. 45.
11 in ærarium ascendentes.
12 Liv. xxix. 37.
13 memoria publica recensionis tabulis publi-

cis impressa.
14 Cic. Mil. 27. Diony. i. 74.
15 Varr. L. L. v. 9.
16 lustrum condidit.
17 see p. 58.
18 Dio. xxxviii. 13.
19 Asc. Cic. Dio. xl. 57.

20 recensum populi egit.
21 vicatim per dominos insularum, Suet. Jul. 41.
22 Liv. ii. 34. Cic. Sext. 25. Asc. Cic.

citizens for three years, under the title of PRÆFECTUS MORUM vel *moribus*; afterwards for life, under the title of censor.[1] A power similar to this seems to have been conferred on Pompey in his third consulship.[2]

Augustus thrice made a review of the people; the first and last time with a colleague, and the second time alone.[3] He was invested by the senate with the same censorian power as Julius Cæsar, repeatedly for five years, according to Dion Cassius,[4] according to Suetonius for life,[5] under the title of MAGISTER MORUM.[6] Hence

> Cum tot sustineas, ac tanta negotia solus,
> Res Italas armis tuteris, *moribus* ornes,
> Legibus emendes, &c.[7]   *Hor. Ep.* ii. 1.

Augustus, however, declined the title of censor, although he is so called by Macrobius;[8] and Ovid says of him, *sic agitur* CENSURA, &c.[9] Some of the succeeding emperors had assumed this title, particularly those of the Flavian family, but most of them rejected it; as Trajan, after whom we rarely find it mentioned.[10]

Tiberius thought the censorship unfit for his time.[11] It was therefore intermitted during his government, as it was likewise during that of his successor.

A review of the people was made by Claudius and L. Vitellius, the father of the emperor A. Vitellius, A. U. 800; by Vespasian and Titus, A. U. 827;[12] but never after. Censorinus[13] says, that this review was made only seventy-five times during 650, or rather 630 years, from its first institution under Servius to the time of Vespasian; after which it was totally discontinued.

Decius endeavoured to restore the censorship in the person of Valerian, but without effect. The corrupt morals of Rome at that period could not bear such a magistrate.[14]

IV. TRIBUNES OF THE PEOPLE.

THE plebeians being oppressed by the patricians on account of debt, at the instigation of one Sicinius, made a secession to a mountain, afterwards called Mons Sacer, three miles from Rome, A. U. 260;[15] nor could they be prevailed on to return, till they obtained from the patricians a remission of debts for those who were insolvent, and liberty to such as had been given up to serve their creditors; and likewise that the plebeians should have proper magistrates of their own to protect their rights, whose persons should be sacred and inviolable.[16] They were called TRIBUNES according to Varro,[17] because they were at first created from the tribunes of the soldiers.

Two tribunes were at first created, at the assembly by curiæ, who, according to Livy, created three colleagues to themselves. In the year 283, they were first elected at the Comitia Tributa, and A. U. 297, ten

---

1 Dio. xliii. 14. xliv. 5. Suet. Jul. 76. Cic. Fam. ix. 15.
2 corrigendis moribus delectus, Tac. Ann. ii. 28.
3 Suet. Aug. 27.
4 Dion. Cass. liii. 17. Liv. ii. 10. 30.

5 recepit et morum legumque regimen perpetuum, Suet. Aug. 27.
6 Fast. Cons.
7 Since you alone support the burden of so many and such important concerns, defend Italy with your arms,

adorn it by your moral ordinances, reform it by your laws, &c.
8 Sat. ii. 4. Suet. 27.
9 Fast. vi. 647.
10 Plin. Pan. 45. Dio. liii. 18.
11 non id tempus censuræ, Tac. Ann. ii. 33.

12 Suet. Claud. 16. Vit. 2. Vesp. 8. Tit. 6.
13 de die nat. 18.
14 Treb. Poll. Val.
15 Liv. ii. 23, &c.
16 sacrosancti, Liv. iii. 33. 55. Diony. vi. 89.
17 Varr. L. L. l. iv. 14.

tribunes were created,[1] two out of each class, which number continued ever after.

No patrician could be made tribune unless first adopted into a plebeian family, as was the case with Clodius the enemy of Cicero.[2] At one time, however, we find two patricians of consular dignity elected tribunes.[3] And no one could be made tribune or plebeian ædile, whose father had borne a curule office, and was alive, nor whose father was a captive.[4]

The tribunes were at first chosen indiscriminately from among the plebeians; but it was ordained by the Atinian law, some think, A. U. 623, that no one should be made tribune who was not a senator.[5] And we read, that when there were no senatorian candidates, on account of the powers of that office being diminished, Augustus chose them from the equites.[6] But others think, that the Atinian law only ordained, that those who were made tribunes should of course be senators, and did not prescribe any restriction concerning their election.[7] It is certain, however, that under the emperors, no one but a senator had a right to stand candidate for the tribuneship.[8]

One of the tribunes chosen by lot, presided at the Comitia for electing tribunes, which charge was called *sors comitiorum*. After the abdication of the decemviri, when there were no tribunes, the pontifex maximus presided at their election. If the assembly was broken off[9], before the ten tribunes were elected, those who were created might choose[10] colleagues for themselves to complete the number. But a law was immediately passed by one Trebonius to prevent this for the future, which enacted, "That he who presided should continue the Comitia, and recal the tribes to give their votes, till ten were elected."[11]

The tribunes always entered on their office the 10th of December,[12] because the first tribunes were elected on that day.[13] In the time of Cicero, however, Asconius says, it was on the 5th.[14] But this seems not to have been so; for Cicero himself, on that day, calls Cato *tribunus designatus*.[15]

The tribunes wore no *toga prætexta*, nor had they any external mark of dignity, except a kind of beadle called *viator*, who went before them. It is thought they were not allowed to use a carriage.[16] When they administered justice, they had no tribunal, but sat on *subsellia* or benches.[17] They had, however, on all occasions, a right of precedency; and every body was obliged to rise in their presence.[18]

The power of the tribunes at first was very limited. It consisted in hindering, not in acting,[19] and was expressed by the word VETO, I forbid it. They had only the right of seizing, but not of summoning.[20] Their office was only to assist the plebeians against the patricians and magistrates.[21] Hence they were said *esse privati, sine imperio, sine magistratu*, not being dignified with the name of magistrates, as they were afterwards.[22] They were not even allowed to enter the senate.[23]

But in process of time they increased their influence to such a degree, that, under pretext of defending the rights of the people, they did almost whatever they pleased. They hindered the collection of tribute, the en-

1 Cic. Corn. l. Liv. ii. 33. c. 58. iii. 30.
2 Dom. 16. Suet. Jul. 20.
3 Liv. iii. 65.
4 Liv. xxviii. 21. xxx. 19.
5 Gell. xiv. 8. Suet. Aug. 10.
6 Suet. Aug.40. Dio. liv. 26. 30.

7 see Manut. Legg.
8 jus tribunatus petendi, Plin. Ep. ii. 9.
9 si comitia dirempta essent.
10 cooptare.
11 Liv. iii. 54. 64, 65.
12 ante diem quartum Idus Decembris.
13 Liv. xxxix. 52. Diony.

vi. 89.
14 nonis Decembris, in proœm. Verr 10.
15 Sext. 26.
16 Cic. Phil. ii. 24. Plut. Quæst. Rom. 81.
17 Asc. Cic.
18 Plin. Ep. i. 23.
19 Diony. vii. 17.
20 prehensionem sed

non vocationem habebant, Gell. xiii. 12.
21 auxilii, non pœnæ jus datum illi potestati, Liv. ii. 35. vi. 37.
22 Liv. ii. 56. Plut. Cor. Quæst. Rom. 81. Liv. iv. 2. Sall. Jug. 37.
23 see p. 11.

listing of soldiers, and the creation of magistrates, which they did at one
time for five years.[1]   They could put a negative[2] upon all the decrees of
the senate and ordinances of the people, and a single tribune, by his VETO,
could stop the proceedings of all the other magistrates, which Cæsar calls
extremum jus tribunorum.[3]   Such was the force of this word, that whoever
did not obey it, whether magistrate or private person, was immediately ordered to be led to prison by a *viator*, or a day was appointed for his trial
before the people, as a violator of the sacred power of the tribunes, the
exercise of which it was a crime to restrain.[4]   They first began with bringing the chief of the patricians to their trial before the Comitia Tributa ; as
they did Coriolanus.[5]

If any one hurt a tribune in word or deed, he was held accursed,[6] and
his goods were confiscated.[7]   Under the sanction of this law, they carried
their power to an extravagant height.   They claimed a right to prevent
consuls from setting out to their provinces, and even to pull victorious
generals from their triumphal chariot.[8]   They stopped the course of justice by putting off trials, and hindering the execution of a sentence.[9]
They sometimes ordered the military tribunes, and even the consuls themselves to prison, as the Ephori at Lacedæmon did their kings, whom the
tribunes at Rome resembled.[10]   Hence it was said, *datum sub jugum tribunitiæ potestatis consulatum fuisse.*[11]

The tribunes usually did not give their negative to a law, till leave had
been granted to speak for and against it.[12]

The only effectual method of resisting the power of the tribunes, was
to procure one or more of their number,[13] to put a negative on the proceedings of the rest ; but those who did so might afterwards be brought to a
trial before the people by their colleagues.[14]

Sometimes a tribune was prevailed on. by entreaties or threats, to withdraw his negative,[15] or he demanded time to consider it,[16] or the consuls
were armed with dictatorial power to oppose him,[17] from the terror of which,
M. Antonius and Q. Cassius Longinus, tribunes of the commons, together
with Curio and Cœlius, fled from the city to Cæsar into Gaul, and afforded
him a pretext for crossing the river Rubicon, which was the boundary of
his province, and of leading his army to Rome.[18]

We also find the senate exercising a right of limiting the power of the
tribunes, which was called CIRCUMSCRIPTIO, and of removing them from
their office,[19] as they did likewise other magistrates.[20] · On one occasion
the senate even sent a tribune to prison ; but this happened at a time when
all order was violated.[21]

The tribuneship was suspended when the decemviri were created, but
not when a dictator was appointed.[22]

The power of the tribunes was confined to the city and a mile around it,[23]
unless when they were sent any where by the senate and people ; and

1 Liv. iv. 1. v. 12. vi. 35.
2 intercedere.
3 Cic. Mil. 5. Polyb. vi.
14. Bell. Civ. i. 4. Liv.
ii. 44. iv. 6. 48. vi. 35.
· xliv. 21.
4 in ordinem cogere,
Plin. Ep. i. 23. Liv.
xxv. 3, 4. Plut. Mar.
5 Diony. vii. 65.
6 sacer.
7 Liv. iii. 55. Diony. vi.
89. viii. 17.
8 Plut. Crass.   Dio.

xxxix. 39. Cic. Cœl. 14.
9 Liv. iii. 25. xxxviii.
60. Cic. Phil. ii. 2. Vat.
14. Prov. Cons. 8.
10 Liv. iv. 26. v. 9. Epit.
48. 55. Cic. Vat. 9, 10.
Legg. iii. 7. 9. Dio.
xxxvii. 50. Nep.Paus.3.
11 Liv. iv. 26.
12 Liv. xlv. 21.
13 e collegio tribuno-
rum.
14 Liv. ii. 44. iv, 48. v.
29. vi. 35.

15 intercessione desis-
tere.
16 noctem sibi ad deli-
berandum postulavit :
se postero die moram
nullam esse facturum,
Cic. Sext. 34. Att. iv.
2. Fam. viii. 8.
17 Cæs. Bell. Civ. i. 5.
Cic. Phil. ii. 21, 22. see
p. 15.
18 Cic. Phil. ii. 21, 22.
Dio. xl. 13. App. Civ.
ii. p. 448. Plut. Cæs. p.

727. Luc. i. 273.
19 a republica removen-
di, i. e. curia et foro
interdicendi, Cic. Att.
vii. 9 Mil. 33. Cæs.
Bell. Civ. i. 32. iii. 21.
Suet. Jul. 16.
20 Cic. Phil. xiii. 9.
21 Dio. xl. 45, 46.
22 Liv. iii. 32. vi. 38.
23 neque enim provoca-
tionem esse longius ab
urbe mille passuum,
Diony.viii.87.Liv.iii.20.

then they might, in any part of the empire, seize even a proconsul at the head of his army and bring him to Rome.[1]

The tribunes were not allowed to remain all night[2] in the country, nor to be above one whole day out of town, except during the *feriæ Latinæ*; and their doors were open day and night, that they might be always ready to receive the requests and complaints of the wretched.[3]

The tribunes were addressed by the name TRIBUNI. Those who implored their assistance,[4] said A VOBIS, TRIBUNI, POSTULO, UT MIHI AUXILIO SITIS. The tribunes answered, AUXILIO ERIMUS, vel NON ERIMUS.[5]

When a law was to be passed, or a decree of the senate to be made, after the tribunes had consulted together,[6] one of their number declared,[7] SE INTERCEDERE, vel NON INTERCEDERE, aut MORAM FACERE *comitiis, delectui*, &c. Also, SE NON PASSURUS *legem ferri* vel *abrogari; relationem fieri de*, &c. *Pronunciant* PLACERE, &c. This was called DECRETUM *tribunorum*. Thus, *medio decreto jus auxilii sui expediunt*, exert their right of intercession by a moderate decree.[8]

Sometimes the tribunes sat in judgment, and what they decreed was called their EDICTUM, or *decretum*.[9] If any one differed from the rest, he likewise pronounced his decree; thus, *Tib. Gracchus ita decrevit :* QUO MINUS EX BONIS L. SCIPIONIS QUOD JUDICATUM SIT, REDIGATUR, SE NON INTERCEDERE PRÆTORI. L. SCIPIONEM NON PASSURUM IN CANCERE ET IN VINCULIS ESSE MITTIQUE EUM SE JUBERE.[10]

The tribunes early assumed the right of holding the Comitia by tribes, and of making laws[11] which bound the whole Roman people.[12] They also exercised the power of holding the senate, A. U. 298, of dismissing it when assembled by another, and of making a motion, although the consuls were present. They likewise sometimes hindered the censors in the choice of the senate.[13]

The tribunes often assembled the people merely to make harangues to them.[14] By the ICILIAN law it was forbidden, under the severest penalties, to interrupt a tribune while speaking,[15] and no one was allowed to speak in the assemblies summoned by them without their permission: hence, *concionem dare*, to grant leave to speak; *in concionem ascendere*, to mount the rostrum; *concionem habere*, to make a speech, or to hold an assembly for speaking; and so, *in concionem venire, in concionem vocare*, and *in concione stare;* but to hold an assembly for voting about any thing, was *habere comitia* vel AGERE *cum populo*.[16]

The tribunes limited the time of speaking even to the consuls themselves, and sometimes would not permit them to speak at all.[17] They could bring any one before the assembly,[18] and force them to answer what questions were put to them.[19] By these harangues the tribunes often inflamed the populace against the nobility, and prevailed on them to pass the most pernicious laws.

The laws which excited the greatest contentions were about dividing the public lands to the poorer citizens[20]—about the distribution of corn at a low

---

1 jure sacrosanctæ potestatis. Liv. lib. xxix. 20.
2 pernoctare.
3 Diony. viii. 87. Gell. iii. 2. xiii. 12. Macrob. Sat. i. 3.
4 eos appellabant vel auxilium implorabant.
5 Liv. iv. 26. xxviii. 45.
6 cum in consilium se-

cessissent.
7 ex sua collegarumque sententia vel pro collegio pronunciavit.
8 Liv. iii. 13. & alibi passim.
9 Cic. Verr. ii. 41.
10 Liv. xxxviii. 60.
11 plebiscita.
12 Liv. iii. 10. 55. see p. 69.

13 Diony. x. 21. Cic. Legg. iii. 10. Phil. vii. 1. Sext. 11. App. Bell. Civ. ii. Dio. xxxvii. 9.
14 concionem advocabant, vel populum ad concionem, Gell. xii. 14.
15 Diony. vii. 17. Cic. Sext. 37.
16 Cic. Att. iv. 2. Sext. 40. Acad. iv. 47. Gell.

xiii. 15.
17 Cic. Rab. 2. see p. 79.
18 ad concionem vel in concione producere.
19 Cic. Vat. 10. Pis. 6, 7. post red. in Sen. 6. Dio. xxxviii. 16.
20 leges agrariæ, Liv. ii. 41. iv. 48. vi. 11. Cic. Rull. *See App.* B.

price, or for nought[1]—and about the diminution of interest,[2] and the abolition of debts, either in whole or in part.[3]

But these popular laws were usually joined by the tribunes with others
respecting the aggrandizement of themselves and their order ; and when
the latter were granted, the former were often dropped.[4] At last, however,
after great struggles, the tribunes laid open the way for plebeians to all the
offices of the state.

The government of Rome was now brought to its just *æquilibrium*.
There was no obstruction to merit, and the most deserving were promoted.
The republic was managed for several ages with quiet and moderation.[5]
But when wealth and luxury were introduced, and avarice had seized all
ranks, especially after the destruction of Carthage, the more wealthy plebeians joined the patricians, and they in conjunction engrossed all the honours and emoluments of the state. The body of the people were oppressed ; and the tribunes, either overawed or gained, did not exert their influence to prevent it ; or rather, perhaps, their interposition was disregarded.[6]

At last Tiberius and Caius Gracchus, the grandsons of the great Scipio
Africanus by his daughter Cornelia, bravely undertook to assert the liberties of the people, and to check the oppression of the nobility. But proceeding with too great ardour, and not being sufficiently supported by the mul-
tude, they fell a sacrifice to the rage of their enemies. Tiberius, while
tribune, was slain in the Capitol, by the nobility, with his cousin Scipio Nasica, pontifex maximus, at their head, A. U. 620 ; and Caius, a few years
after, perished by means of the consul Opimius, who slaughtered a great
number of the plebeians. This was the first civil bloodshed at Rome,
which afterwards at different times deluged the state.[7] From this period,
when arms and violence began to be used with impunity in the legislative
assemblies, and laws enacted by force to be held as valid, we date the com-
mencement of the ruin of Roman liberty.

The fate of the Gracchi discouraged others from espousing the cause
of the people. In consequence of which, the power of the nobles was
increased, and the wretched plebeians were more oppressed than ever.[8]

But in the Jugurthine war, when, by the infamous corruption of the nobility, the republic had been basely betrayed, the plebeians, animated by
the bold eloquence of the tribune Memmius, regained the ascendancy.[9]
The contest betwixt the two orders was renewed : but the people being
misled and abused by their favourite, the faithless and ambitious Marius,[10]
the nobility again prevailed under the conduct of Sylla.

Sylla abridged, and in a manner extinguished, the power of the tribunes,
by enacting, " That whoever had been tribune, should not afterwards enjoy any other magistracy ; that there should be no appeal to the tribunes ;
that they should not be allowed to assemble the people and make harangues to them, nor to propose laws,"[11] but should only retain the right
of intercession,[12] which Cicero greatly approves.[13]*

---

*" The tribes were first made a branch of the legislature by the Publilian law. Until then they could only pass resolutions, as every other corpora-tion can, which merely bound their own body. On this, as on other points, Sylla, when he took away the right of propos-ing laws from the tribunes, was unquestionably restoring the letter of the constitution out of an age which had passed away, and which he every-where aimed to revive."—ED.

---

1 leges frumentariæ vel annonariæ, Liv. Epit. lx. lxxi. Cic. Her. l. 12. Sext. 25. Asc. Cic.
2 de levando fœnore.
3 de novis tabulis ; leges fœnebræ, Liv. vi. 27.
25. vii. 16. 42. xxxv. 7. Paterc. ii. 23. see p. 34.
4 Liv. vi. 35. 39. 42.
5 pla cide modesteque.
6 Sall. Jug. 41.
7 App. Bell. Civ. i. 349.
359. Cic. Cat. i. 1. Sall. Jug. 16. 42. Vell. ii. 3.
8 Sall. Jug. 31.
9 Sall. Jug. 40. 65. 73.84.
10 Dio. frag. xxxiv. 94.
11 Liv. Epit. 89. App. Bell. Civ. i. 413.
12 Cæs. Bell. Civ. i. 6. Injuriæ faciendæ potes-tatem ademit, auxilii ferendi reliquit.
13 Cic. Legg. iii. 9.

But after the death of Sylla, the power of the tribunes was restored. In the consulship of Cotta, A. U. 679, they obtained the right of enjoying other offices, and in the consulship of Pompey and Crassus, A. U. 683, all their former powers ; a thing which Cæsar strenuously promoted.[1]

The tribunes henceforth were employed by the leading men as the tools of their ambition. Backed by a hired mob,[2] they determined every thing by force. They made and abrogated laws at pleasure.[3] They disposed of the public lands and taxes as they thought proper, and conferred provinces and commands on those who purchased them at the highest price.[4] The assemblies of the people were converted into scenes of violence and massacre ; and the most daring always prevailed.[5]

Julius Cæsar, who had been the principal cause of these excesses, and had made a violation of the power of the tribunes a pretext for making war on his country,[6] having at last become master of the republic by force of arms, reduced that power by which he had been raised, to a mere name ; and deprived the tribunes of their office[7] at pleasure.[8]

Augustus got the tribunitian power to be conferred on himself for life, by a decree of the senate ; the exercise of it by proper magistrates, as formerly, being inconsistent with an absolute monarchy, which that artful usurper established.[9] This power gave him the right of holding the senate, of assembling the people, and of being appealed to in all cases.[10] It also rendered his person sacred and inviolable ; so that it became a capital crime[11] to injure him in word or deed, which, under the succeeding emperors, served as a pretext for cutting off numbers of the first men in the state, and proved one of the chief supports of tyranny.[12] Hence this among other powers used to be conferred on the emperors in the beginning of their reign, or upon other solemn occasions ; and then they were said to be *tribunitia potestate donati.*[13] Hence also the years of their government were called the years of their tribunitian power,[14] which are found often marked on ancient coins ; computed not from the 1st of January, nor from the 10th of December,[15] the day on which the tribunes entered on their office ; but from the day on which they assumed the empire.

The tribunes, however, still continued to be elected, although they retained only the shadow of their former power,[16] and seem to have remained to the time of Constantine, who abolished this with other ancient offices.

V. ÆDILES.

THE *ædiles* were named from their care of the buildings,[17] and were either plebeian or curule.

TWO ÆDILES PLEBEII were first created, A. U. 260, in the Comitia Curiata, at the same time with the tribunes of the commons, to be as it were their assistants, and to determine certain lesser causes, which the tribunes committed to them.[18] They were afterwards created, as the other inferior magistrates, at the Comitia Tributa.

TWO ÆDILES CURULES were created from the patricians, A. U. 387, to

---

1 Asc. Cic. Sall. Cat. 38. Cic. Verr. i. 15. Legg. iii. 11. Suet. Jul. 5.
2 a conducta plebe stipati.
3 Cic. Pis. 4. Sext. 25.
4 Cic. Sext. 5. 10. 24. 26, &c. Dom. 8. 20.

5 Cic. Sext. 35—38, &c. Dio. xxxix. 7, 8, &c.
6 see p. 94.
7 potestate privavit.
8 Suet. Jul. 79. Dio. xliv. 10. Vell. ii. 68.
9 Dio. li. 19. Suet. Aug. 27. Tac. Ann. iii. 56.
10 Dio. li. 19. liv. 3. see

p. 9.
11 crimen majestatis, Dio. liii. 17.
12 adjumenta regni, Tac. Ann. iii. 38. Suet. Tib. 58. 61. Ner. 35.
13 Capit. M. Anton.— Vop Tac. see p. 16, 17.
14 Dio. liii. 17.

15 iv. Id. Dec.
16 inanem umbram et sine honore nomen, Plin. Ep. i. 23. Pan. 10. 95. Tac. ii. 77. xiii. 28.
17 a cura ædium.
18 Diony. vi. 90.

15

perform certain public games. They were first chosen alternately from the patricians and plebeians, but afterwards promiscuously from both, at the Comitia Tributa.[1]

The curule ædiles wore the *toga prætexta*, had the right of images, and a more honourable place of giving their opinion in the senate. They used the *sella curulis* when they administered justice, whence they had their name.[2] Whereas the plebeian ædiles sat on benches ;[3] but they were inviolable[4] as the tribunes.[5]

The office of the ædiles was to take care of the city,[6] its public buildings, temples, theatres, baths, *basilicæ*, porticoes, aquæducts, common sewers, public roads, &c. especially when there were no censors : also of private buildings, lest they should become ruinous, and deform the city, or occasion danger to passengers. They likewise took care of provisions, markets, taverns, &c. They inspected those things which were exposed to sale in the Forum ; and if they were not good, they caused them to be thrown into the Tiber. They broke unjust weights and measures. They limited the expenses of funerals. They restrained the avarice of usurers. They fined or banished women of bad character, after being condemned by the senate or people. They took care that no new gods or religious ceremonies were introduced. They punished not only petulant actions, but even words.[7]

The ædiles took cognizance of these things, proposed edicts concerning them,[8] and fined delinquents. They had neither the right of summoning nor of seizing, unless by the order of the tribunes ; nor did they use lictors or *viatores*, but only public slaves. They might even be sued at law[9] by a private person.[10]

It belonged to the ædiles, particularly the curule ædiles, to exhibit public solemn games, which they sometimes did at a prodigious expense, to pave the way for future preferments.[11] They examined the plays which were to be brought on the stage, and rewarded or punished the actors as they deserved. They were bound by oath to give the palm to the most deserving.[12] Agrippa, when ædile under Augustus, banished all jugglers[13] and astrologers.

It was peculiarly the office of the plebeian ædiles, to keep the decrees of the senate, and the ordinances of the people, in the temple of Ceres, and afterwards in the treasury.[14]

Julius Cæsar added two other plebeian ædiles, called CEREALES,[15] to inspect the public stores of corn and other provisions.[16]

The free towns also had their ædiles, where sometimes they were the only magistrates, as at Arpinum.[17]

The ædiles seem to have continued, but with some variations, to the time of Constantine.

VI. QUÆSTORS.

THE Quæstors were so called,[18] because they got in the public revenues.[19]

1 Liv. vi. 42. vii. 1. Gell. vi. 9.
2 Cic. Verr. v. 14.
3 Asc. Cic.
4 sacrosancti.
5 Fest. Liv. iii. 55.
6 Cic. Legg. iii. 3.
7 Plaut. Rud. ii. 3. 42.

Juv. x. 101. Cic. Phil. ix.
7. Ov. Fast. vi. 663. Liv.
iv. 30. x. 31. 37. xxv. 2.
Tac. Ann. ii. 85. Gell. x. 6
8 Plaut. Capt. iv. 2. v. 43.
9 in jus vocari.
10 Gell. xiii. 12, 13.
11 Liv. xxiv. 43. xxvii.

6. Cic. Off. ii. 16.
12 Suet. Aug. 45. Plaut.
Trin. iv. 2. 148. Cist.
Epil. 3. Amph. Prol. 72.
13 præstigiatores, Dio.
xlix. 43.
14 Liv. iii. 55.
19 a Cerere.

16 Dio. xliii. 51. Just.
Digest. l. 2. ii. 32.
17 Juv. iii. 179. Cic.
Fam. xiii. 11.
18 a quærendo.
19 publicas pecunias
conquirebant, Varr. L.
L. iv. 14.

The institution of quæstors seems to have been nearly as ancient as the city itself. They were first appointed by the kings, according to Tacitus.[1] And then by the consuls, to the year 307, when they began to be elected by the people, at the Comitia Tributa.[2] Others say, that two quæstors were created by the people from among the patricians, soon after the expulsion of Tarquin, to take care of the treasury, according to a law passed by Valerius Poplicola.[3]

In the year 333, besides the two city quæstors, two others were created to attend the consuls in war;[4] and from this time the quæstors might be chosen indifferently from the plebeians and patricians. After all Italy was subdued, four more were added, A. U. 498, about the same time that the coining of silver was first introduced at Rome.[5] Sylla increased their number to twenty.[6] Julius Cæsar to forty.[7] Under the emperors, their number was uncertain and arbitrary.

Two quæstors only remained at Rome, and were called QUÆSTORES URBANI; the rest, PROVINCIALES or MILITARES.

The principal charge of the city quæstors was the care of the treasury, which was kept in the temple of Saturn.[8] They received and expended the public money, and entered an account of their receipts and disbursements.[9] They exacted the fines imposed by the public. The money thus raised was called ARGENTUM MULTATITIUM.[10]

The quæstors kept the military standards in the treasury, (which were generally of silver, sometimes of gold,) for the Romans did not use colours,[11] and brought them out to the consuls when going upon an expedition. They entertained foreign ambassadors, provided them with lodgings, and delivered to them the presents of the public.[12] They took care of the funeral of those who were buried at the public expense, as Menenius Agrippa and Sulpicius. They exercised a certain jurisdiction, especially among their clerks.[13]

Commanders returning from war, before they could obtain a triumph, was obliged to swear before the quæstors, that they had written to the senate a true account of the number of the enemy they had slain, and of the citizens that were missing.[14]

The provinces of the quæstors were annually distributed to them by lot,[15] after the senate had determined into what provinces quæstors should be sent. Whence SORS is often put for the office or appointment of a quæstor, as of other magistrates and public officers, or for the condition of any one.[16] Sometimes a certain province was given to a particular quæstor by the senate or people. But Pompey chose Cassius as his quæstor, and Cæsar chose Antony, of themselves.[17]

The office of the provincial quæstors was to attend the consuls or prætors into their provinces; to take care that provisions and pay were furnished to the army; to keep the money deposited by the soldiers;[18] to exact the taxes and tribute of the empire; to take care of the money and to sell the spoils taken in war; to return an account of every thing to the trea-

1 Ann. xi. 22.
2 Cic. Fam. vi. 30.
3 Plut. Popl. Diony. v. 24.
4 ut consulibus ad ministeria belli præsto essent.
5 Liv. iv. 43. Epit. xv.
6 supplendo senatui cui judicia tradiderat, Tac.

Ann. xi. 22.
7 Dion. xliii. 47.
8 Suet. Claud. 24. Plut. Quæst. Rom. 40.
9 in tabulas accepti et expensi referebant, Asc. Cic.
10 Liv. xxx. 39. xxxviii. 60. Tac. Ann. xiii. 28.
11 non velis utebantur.

12 Plin. xxxiii. 3. s. 19. Liv. iii. 69. iv. 22. vii.
23. Val. Max. v. 1.
13 Diony. vi. fin. Cic. Phil. ix. 7. Plut. Cat. Min.
14 Val. Max. ii. 8.
15 Cic. Mur. 8.
16 Cic. Verr. i. 15. Act. i. 8. Cæc. 14. Fam. ii.

19. Planc. 27. Cat. iv. 7. Liv. xxxv. 6. Hor. Sat. i. 1. 1. Ep. i. 14. 11. Suet. Aug. 19.
17 sine sorte, Liv. xxx. 33. Cic. Att. vi. 6. Phil. ii. 20.
18 nummos ad signa positos, Suet. Dom. 8. Veg. ii. 20.

sury ; and to exercise the jurisdiction assigned them by their governors.
When the governor left the province, the quæstor usually supplied his
place.[1]

There subsisted the closest connection between a proconsul or proprætor and his quæstor.[2] If a quæstor died, another was appointed by the
governor in his room, called PROQUÆSTOR.[3]

The place in the camp where the quæstor's tent was, and where he
kept his stores, was called QUÆSTORIUM, or *quæstorium forum*, so also the
place in the province, where he kept his accounts and transacted business.[4]

The city quæstor had neither lictors nor *viatores*, because they had not
the power of summoning or apprehending, and might be prosecuted by a
private person before the prætor.[5] They could, however, hold the Comitia ;
and it seems to have been a part of their office in ancient times to prosecute those guilty of treason, and punish them when condemned.[6]

The provincial quæstors were attended by lictors, at least in the absence
of the prætor, and by clerks.[7]

The quæstorship was the first step of preferment[8] which gave one admission into the senate, when he was said *adire ad rempublicam* pro *rempublicam capessere*. It was, however, sometimes held by those who had
been consuls.[9]

Under the emperors the quæstorship underwent various changes. A
distinction was introduced between the treasury of the public[10] and the
treasury of the prince ;[11] and different officers were appointed for the
management of each.

Augustus took from the quæstors the charge of the treasury, and gave it
to the prætors, or those who had been prætors ; but Claudius restored it
to the quæstors. Afterwards præfects of the treasury seem to have been
appointed.[12]

Those who had borne the quæstorship used to assemble the judges, called *centumviri*, and preside at their courts ; but Augustus appointed that this
should be done by the DECEMVIRI *litibus judicandis*. The quæstors also
chose the *judices*. Augustus gave to the quæstors the charge of the public records, which the ædiles and, as Dion Cassius says, the tribunes
had formerly exercised. But this too was afterwards transferred to
præfects.[13]

Augustus introduced a new kind of quæstors called QUÆSTORES CANDI-
DATI, or *candidati principis* vel *Augusti*, vel *Cæsaris*, who used to carry the
messages of the emperor[14] to the senate.[15] They were called *candidati*,
because they sued for higher preferments, which by the interest of the emperor they were sure to obtain ; hence *petis tanquam Cæsaris candidatus*,
i. e. carelessly.[16]

Augustus ordained by an edict, that persons might enjoy the quæstorship,
and of course be admitted into the senate, at the age of twenty-two.[17]

1 Liv. v. 26. xxvi. 47.
Plaut. Bacch. iv. 9. v.
153. Polyb. x. 19. Suet.
Jur. 7. Cic. Verr. i. 14.
38. Div. Cæc. 17. Fam.
ii. 15. 18.
2 In parentum loco
quæstoribus suis erant,
Cic. Planc. 11. Div.
Cæc. 19. Fam. xiii. 10.
26. Plin. Ep. iv. 15.

3 Cic. Verr. i. 15. 36.
4 Liv. x. 22. xli. 2. Cic.
Planc. 41.
5 Gell. xiii. 12, 13. Suet.
Jul. 23.
6 Diony. viii. 77. Liv. ii.
41. iii. 24, 25.
7 Cic. Planc. 41. Verr.
iii. 78.
8 primus gradus hono-
ris, Cic. Verr. i. 4.

9 Cic. Vell. ii. 94. Liv.
iii. 25. Diony. x. 23. see
p. 3.
10 ærarium.
11 fiscus, Suet. Aug.
102. Tac. Ann. vi. 2.
Plin. Pan. 36. Dio. lili.
16.
12 Suet. Aug. 36. Claud.
24. Dio.liii. 2. Plin. Ep.
iii. 4. Tac. Ann. xiii.

28, 29.
13 Suet. Aug. 36. Dio.
xxxix. 7. Dion. Cass.
liv. 36. Tac. loc. cit.
14 libellos, epistolas, et
orationes.
15 Suet. Aug. 56. Tit. 6.
Claud. 40. Vell. ii. 124.
see p. 16.
16 Quinct. vi. 3. 62.
17 Plin. Ep. x. 63. 64.

Under the emperors the quæstors exhibited shows of gladiators, which they seem to have done at their own expense, as a requisite for obtaining the office.[1]

Constantine instituted a new kind of quæstors, called QUÆSTORES PALATII, who were much the same with what we now call chancellors.[2]

OTHER ORDINARY MAGISTRATES.

THERE were various other ordinary magistrates ; as,

TRIUMVIRI CAPITALES, who judged concerning slaves and persons of the lowest rank, and who also had the charge of the prison, and of the execution of condemned criminals.[3]

TRIUMVIRI MONETALES, who had the charge of the mint.[4] According to the advice of Mæcenas to Augustus, it appears that only Roman coins were permitted to circulate in the provinces.[5]

NUMMULARII, vel *pecuniæ spectatores*, saymasters.[6]

TRIUMVIRI NOCTURNI, vel *tresviri*, who had the charge of preventing fires,[7] and walked round the watches in the night-time,[8] attended by eight lictors.

QUATUOR VIRI VIALES, vel *viocuri*,[9] who had the charge of the streets and public roads.

All these magistrates used to be created by the people at the Comitia Tributa.

Some add to the *magistratus ordinarii minores* the CENTUMVIRI *litibus judicandis* (vel *stlitibus judicandis*, for so it was anciently written), a body of men chosen out of every tribe (so that properly there were 105), for judging such causes as the prætor committed to their decision ; and also the DECEMVIRI *litibus judicandis.* But these were generally not reckoned magistrates, but only judges.

NEW ORDINARY MAGISTRATES UNDER THE EMPERORS.

AUGUSTUS instituted several new offices ; as *curatores operum publicorum, viarum, aquarum, alvei Tiberis*, sc. *repurgandi et laxioris faciendi, frumenti populo dividundi ;* persons who had the charge of the public works, of the roads, of bringing water to the city, of cleansing and enlarging the channel of the Tiber, and of distributing corn to the people.[10] The chief of these officers were : —

I. The governor of the city,[11] whose power was very great, and generally continued for several years.

A præfect of the city used likewise formerly to be chosen occasionally,[12] in the absence of the kings, and afterwards of the consuls. He was not chosen by the people, but appointed, first by the kings, and afterwards by the consuls.[13] He might, however, assemble the senate, even although he was not a senator, and also hold the Comitia.[14] But after the creation

1 Tac. Ann. xi. 22. Suet. Dom. 4.
2 Zos. v. Proc. Bel. Per.
3 Plaut. Aul. iii. 2. 2. Liv. xxxii.26. Sall. Cat. 55.
4 qui auro, argento, æri, fiando, feriundo præerant, which is often marked in letters, A. A. A. F. F. Dio. liv. 26. xxix. 20.
6 ad quos nummi probandi causa deferebantur, an probi essent, cujus auri, an subæra-ti, an æqui ponderis, 'an bonæ fusionis.
7 incendiis per urbem arcendis præerant.Liv. ix. 46.
8 vigilias circumibant, Plaut. Amph. i. 1. 3.
9 qui vias curabant.
10 Suet Aug. 37.
11 præfectus urbi, vel urbis, Tac. Ann. vi. 11.
12 in tempus deligebatur.
13 a regibus impositi : postea consules mandabant, Tac. ibid.
14 Gell. xiv. c. ult. Liv. i. 59.

of the prætor, he used 'only to be appointed for celebrating the *feriæ Latinæ*, or Latin holy-days.

Augustus instituted this magistracy by the advice of Mæcenas, who himself in the civil wars had been intrusted by Augustus with the charge of the city and of Italy.[1] The first præfect of the city was Messala Corvinus, only for a few days; after him Taurus Statilius, and then Piso for twenty years. He was usually chosen from among the principal men of the state.[2] His office comprehended many things, which had formerly belonged to the prætors and ædiles. He administered justice betwixt masters and slaves, freedmen and patrons; he judged of the crimes of guardians and curators; he checked the frauds of bankers and money-brokers; he had the superintendence of the shambles,[3] and of the public spectacles: in short, he took care to preserve order and public quiet, and punished all transgressions of it, not only in the city, but within a hundred miles of it.[4] He had the power of banishing persons both from the city and from Italy, and of transporting them to any island which the emperor named.[5]

The præfect of the city was, as it were, the substitute[6] of the emperor, and had one under him, who exercised jurisdiction in his absence, or by his command. He seems to have had the same insignia with the prætors.

II. The præfect of the prætorian cohorts,[7] or the commander of the emperor's body guards.

Augustus instituted two of these from the equestrian order, by the advice of Mæcenas, that they might counteract one another, if one of them attempted any innovation.[8] Their power was at first but small, and merely military: but Sejanus, being alone invested by Tiberius with this command, increased its influence,[9] by collecting the prætorian cohorts, formerly dispersed through the city, into one camp.[10]

The præfect of the prætorian bands was under the succeeding emperors made the instrument of their tyranny, and therefore that office was conferred on none but those whom they could entirely trust. They always attended the emperor to execute his commands: hence their power became so great that it was little inferior to that of the emperor himself.[11] Trials and appeals were brought before them; and from their sentence there was no appeal, unless by way of supplication to the emperor.

The prætorian præfect was appointed to his office by the emperor's delivering to him a sword.[12]

Sometimes there was but one præfect, and sometimes two. Constantine created four *præfecti prætorio*: but he changed their office very much from its original institution; for he made it civil instead of military, and divided among them the care of the whole empire. To one he gave the command of the East, to another of Illyricum, to a third of Italy and Africa, and to a fourth, of Gaul, Spain, and Britain; but he took from them the command of the soldiers, and transferred that to officers, who were called *magistri equitum*.

Under each of these *præfecti prætorio* were several substitutes,[13] who had the charge of certain districts, which were called DIŒCESES; and the chief

1 cunctis apud Romam atque Italiam præpositus, Tac. Ibid. Hor. Od. iii. 8. 17. 29. 25. Dio. iii. 21.

2 ex viris primariis vel consularibus.

3 carnis curam gere-'bat.

4 intra centesimum ab urbe lapidem, Dio. liii. 21.

5 in insulam deportandi, Ulp. Off. Præf. Urb.

6 vicarius.

7 præfectus prætorio, vel prætoriis cohortibus.

8 Dio. lii. 24.

9 vim præfecturæ modicam antea intendit.

10 Tac. Ann. iv. 2. Suet. Tib. 37.

11 ut non multum ab-fuerit, a principatu; munus proximum vel alterum ab Augusti imperio, Vict. Cæs. 9.

12 Plin. Pan. 67. Herod. iii. 2. Dio. lxviii. 33.

13 vicarii.

city in each of these, where they held their courts, was called METROPO-
LIS. Each *diœcesis* might contain several *metropoles*, and each *metropolis*
had several cities under it. But Cicero uses DIŒCESIS for the part of a
province, and calls himself EPISCOPUS, inspector or governor of the Campanian coast, as of a *diœcesis*.[1]

III. PRÆFECTUS ANNONÆ, vel *rei frumentariæ*, who had the charge of
procuring corn.

A magistrate used to be created for that purpose on extraordinary occasions under the republic : thus, L. Minutius, and so afterwards Pompey,
with great power.[2] In the time of a great scarcity, Augustus himself undertook the charge of providing corn,[3] and ordained, that for the future
two men of prætorian dignity should be annually elected to discharge
that office; afterwards he appointed four,[4] and thus it became an ordinary
magistracy. But usually there seems to have been but one *præfectus annonæ* ; it was at first an office of great dignity, but not so in after times.[5]

IV. PRÆFECTUS MILITARIS ÆRARII, a person who had the charge of the
public fund which Augustus instituted for the support of the army.[6]

V. PRÆFECTUS CLASSIS, admiral of the fleet. Augustus equipped two
fleets, which he stationed,[7] the one at Ravenna on the Hadriatic, and the
other at Misena or -um on the Tuscan sea. Each of these had its own
proper commander.[8] There were also ships stationed in other places ; as
in the Pontus Euxinus, near Alexandria, on the Rhine, and Danube.[9]

VI. PRÆFECTUS VIGILUM, the officer who commanded the soldiers who
were appointed to watch the city. Of these there were seven cohorts, one
for every two wards,[10] composed chiefly of manumitted slaves.[11] Those
who guarded adjoining houses in the night-time, carried each of them a
bell,[12] to give the alarm to one another when any thing happened.

The *præfectus vigilum* took cognizance of incendiaries, thieves, vagrants,
and the like ; and if any atrocious case happened, it was remitted to the
præfect of the city.

There were various other magistrates in the latter times of the empire,
called *comites, correctores, duces, magistri officiorum, scriniorum*, &c. who
were honoured with various epithets, according to their different degrees
of dignity ; as, *clarissimi, illustres, spectobiles, egregii, perfectissimi*, &c.
The highest title was *nobilissimus* and *gloriosissimus*.

EXTRAORDINARY MAGISTRATES.

I. DICTATOR AND MASTER OF HORSE.

THE Dictator was so called, either because he was named by the consul,[13] or rather from his publishing edicts or orders.[14] He was also called
magister populi, and *prætor maximus*. This magistracy seems to have
been borrowed from the Albans, or Latins.[15]

---

1 Cic. Att. v. 21. vii. 11.
Fam. iii. 8. xiii. 53. 67.
2 omnis potestas rei fru-
mentariæ toto orbe in
quinquennium ei data
est, Liv. iv. 12. Cic.
Att. iv. 1. Dio. xxxix.
9. Liv. Epit. 104. Plin.
Pan. 29.
3 præfecturam annonæ
suscepit.
4 Dio. liv. 1. 17.

5 Tac. Ann. i. 7. xi. 31.
Hist. iv. 68. Boeth.
Cons. Phil. iii.
6 ærarium militare cum
novis vectigalibus ad
tuendos prosequendos-
que milites, Suet. Aug.
49.
7 constituit.
8 præfectus classis Ra-
vennatis, et præfectus
classis Misenatium,

Tac. Hist. iii. 12. Veg.
iv. 32.
9 Tac. Hist. ii. 83. Ann.
98. Flor. iv. 12.
10 una cohors binis re-
gionibus.
11 libertino milite,Suet.
Aug. 25. 30.
12 κωδων, tintinnabu-
lum, Dio. liv. 4.
13 quod a consule dice-

retur, cui dicto omnes
audientes essent,Varr.
L. L. iv. 14.
14 a dictando, quod mul-
ta dictaret, i. e. edice-
ret : et homines pro
legibus haberent quæ
diceret, Suet. Jul. 77.
15 Sen. Ep. 108. Liv.
i. 23. vii. 3. Cic. Mil.
10.

It is uncertain who was first created dictator, or in what year. Livy says, that T. Lartius was first created dictator, A. U. 253, nine years after the expulsion of the kings. The first cause of creating a dictator was the fear of a domestic sedition, and of a dangerous war from the Latins. As the authority of the consuls was not sufficiently respected on account of the liberty of appeal from them, it was judged proper in dangerous conjunctures, to create a single magistrate, with absolute power, from whom there should be no appeal, and who should not be restrained by the interposition of a colleague.[1]

A dictator was afterwards created also for other causes : as, — 1. For fixing a nail[2] in the right side of the temple of Jupiter, which is supposed to have been done in those rude ages,[3] to mark the number of years. This was commonly done by the ordinary magistrate ; but in the time of a pestilence, or of any great public calamity, a dictator was created for that purpose,[4] to avert the divine wrath. — 2. For holding the Comitia. — 3. For the sake of instituting holidays, or of celebrating games when the prætor was indisposed. — 4. For holding trials.[5] — And, 5. Once for choosing senators,[6] on which occasion there were two dictators; one at Rome, and another commanding an army, which never was the case at any other time.[7]

The dictator was not created by the suffrages of the people, as the other magistrates ; but one of the consuls, by order of the senate, named as dictator whatever person of consular dignity he thought proper ; and this he did, after having taken the auspices, usually in the dead of the night.[8]

One of the military tribunes also could name a dictator ; about which Livy informs us there was some scruple. He might be nominated out of Rome, provided it was in the Roman territory, which was limited to Italy. Sometimes the people gave directions whom the consuls should name dictator.[9]

Sylla and Cæsar were made dictators at the Comitia, an interrex presiding at the creation of the former, and Lepidus the prætor at the creation of the latter.[10]

In the second Punic war, A. U. 536, after the destruction of the consul Flaminius and his army at the Thrasimene lake, when the other consul was absent from Rome, and word could not easily be sent to him, the people created Q. Fabius Maximus PRODICTATOR, and M. Minucius Rufus master of horse.[11]

The power of the dictator was supreme both in peace and war. He could raise and disband armies ; he could determine about the life and fortunes of Roman citizens, without consulting the people or senate. His edict was observed as an oracle.[12] At first there was no appeal from him, till a law was passed that no magistrate should be created without the liberty of appeal,[13] first by the consuls Horatius and Valerius, A. U. 304 ; and afterwards by the consul M. Valerius, A. U. 453.[14] But the force of this law with respect to the dictator is doubtful. It was once strongly contested,[15] but never finally decided.

---

1 Liv. ii. 18. 29. iii. 20. Cic. Legg. iii. 5. Diony. v. 70, &c.
2 clavi figendi vel pangendi causa.
3 cum literæ erant raræ.
4 quia majus imperium erat, Liv. viii. 18.

5 quæstionibus exercendis, Liv. vii. 3. 28. viii. 22. 40. ix. 7. 26. 34. xxv. 2.
6 qui senatum legeret.
7 Liv. xxiii. 22, &c.
8 nocte silentio, ut mos est, dictatorem dixit, Liv. viii. 22. ix. 38. Dio-

ny. x. 23. post mediam noctem, Fest. in voc. Silentio, Sinistrum, et Solida sella.
9 Liv. iv. 31. xxvii. 5.
10 Cic. Rull. iii. 2 Cæs. Bell. Civ. ii. 19. Dio. xli. 36.
11 Liv. xxii. 8. 31.

12 pro numine observatum, Liv. viii. 34.
13 sine provocatione.
14 Liv. iii. 55. x. 9. Fest. in voc. Optima lex.
15 Liv. viii. 33.

The dictator was attended by twenty-four lictors,[1] with the fasces and secures even in the city.[2]

When a dictator was created, all the other magistrates abdicated their authority, except the tribunes of the commons. The consuls, however, still continued to act, but in obedience to the dictator, and without any ensigns of authority in his presence.[3]

The power of the dictator was circumscribed by certain limits.

1. It only continued for the space of six months,[4] even although the business for which he had been created was not finished, and was never prolonged beyond that time, except in extreme necessity, as in the case of Camillus.[5] For Sylla and Cæsar usurped their perpetual dictatorship, in contempt of the laws of their country.

But the dictator usually resigned his command whenever he had effected the business for which he had been created. Thus Q. Cincinnatus and Mamercus Æmilius abdicated the dictatorship on the sixteenth day, Q. Servilius on the eighth day.[6]

2. The dictator could lay out none of the public money, without the authority of the senate or the order of the people.

3. A dictator was not permitted to go out of Italy ; which was only once violated, and that on account of the most urgent necessity, in Atilius Calatinus.[7]

4. The dictator was not allowed to ride on horseback, without asking the permission of the people,[8] to show, as it is thought, that the chief strength of the Roman army consisted in the infantry.

But the principal check against a dictator's abuse of power was, that he might be called to an account for his conduct, when he resigned his office.[9]

For 120 years before Sylla, the creation of a dictator was disused, but in dangerous emergencies the consuls were armed with dictatorial power. After the death of Cæsar, the dictatorship was for ever abolished from the state, by a law of Antony the consul.[10] And when Augustus was urged by the people to accept the dictatorship, he refused it with the strongest marks of aversion.[11] Possessed of the power, he wisely declined an odious appellation.[12] For ever since the usurpation of Sylla, the dictatorship was detested on account of the cruelties which that tyrant had exercised under the title of dictator.

To allay the tumults which followed the murder of Clodius by Milo, in place of a dictator, Pompey was by an unprecedented measure made sole consul, A. U. 702. He, however, on the first of August, assumed Scipio, his father-in-law, as colleague.[13]

When a dictator was created, he immediately nominated[14] a master of horse,[15] usually from among those of consular or prætorian dignity, whose proper office was to command the cavalry, and also to execute the orders

---

1 The writers on Roman antiquities, and especially Dr. Adam, assert that the dictator was attended by 24 lictors, with the fasces and secures, even in the city. In this they appear to have erred. Plutarch indeed tells us, in Fabio, that the dictator was attended by 24 lictors ; but, as J. Lipsius observes, this statement is contradicted by higher authority ; for we are told in the epitome of the 89th book of Livy, that Sylla, in assuming to himself 24 lictors, had done a thing entirely unprecedented : Sylla, dictator factus, quod nemo quidem unquam fecerat, cum fascibus viginti quatuor processit.—ANTHON.

2 so that Livy justly calls imperium dictatoris, suo ingenio vehemens, a command in itself uncontrollable, ii. 18. 30.

3 Polyb. iii. 87. Liv. iv. 27. xxii. 11.

4 semestris dictatura, Liv. ix. 34.

5 Liv. vi. 1.

6 Liv. iii. 29. iv. 34. 47. &c.

7 Liv. Epit. xix.

8 Liv. xxiii. 14.

9 Liv. vii. 4.

10 Cic. Phil. i. 1.

11 genu nixus, dejecta ab humeris toga, nudo pectore, deprecatus est, Suet. Aug. 52.

12 Dio. liv. 1.

13 Dio. xl. 50, 51.

14 dixit.

15 magister equitum.

16

of the dictator. M. Fabius Buteo, the dictator nominated to choose the senate, had no master of horse.

Sometimes a master of horse was pitched upon[1] for the dictator, by the senate, or by order of the people.[2]

The *magister equitum* might be deprived of his command by the dictator, and another nominated in his room. The people at one time made the master of the horse, Minucius, equal in command with the dictator Fabius Maximus.[3]

The master of the horse is supposed to have had much the same insignia with the prætor, six lictors, the *prætexta*, &c.[4] He had the use of a horse, which the dictator had not without the order of the people.

DICTATORSHIP.

THE appointment of the first dictator is placed in the tenth year after the first consuls; and the oldest annalists say it was T. Larcius. But there were divers contradictory statements, and the vanity of the Valerian house assigned this honour to a nephew of Publicola. According to the date just mentioned, Larcius was consul at the time, and so only received an enlargement of his power: another account related as the occasion of the appointment, what sounds probable enough, that by an unfortunate choice the republic had been placed in the hands of two consuls of the Tarquinian faction, whose names were subsequently rendered dubious by indulgence or by calumny.

That the name of dictator was of Latin origin, is acknowledged; and assuredly the character of his office, invested with regal power for a limited period, was no less so. The existence of a dictator at Tusculum in early, at Lanuvium in very late times, is matter of history; and Latin ritual books, which referred to Alban traditions, enabled Macer to assert that this magistracy had subsisted at Alba; though it is true that the preservation of any historical record concerning Alba is still more out of the question than concerning Rome before Tullus Hostilius. The Latins, however, did not merely elect dictators in their several cities, but also over the whole nation: from a fragment of Cato we learn that the Tusculan Egerius was dictator over the collective body of the Latins. Here we catch a glimmering of light; but we must follow it

with caution. If Rome and Latium were confederate states on a footing of equality, in the room of that supremacy which lasted but for a short time after the revolution, they must have possessed the chief command alternately: and this would explain why the Roman dictators were appointed for only six months; and how they came to have twenty-four lictors: namely, as a symbol that the governments of the two states were united under the same head: the consuls had only twelve between them, which went by turns from one to the other. And so the dictatorship at the beginning would be directed solely towards foreign affairs; and the continuance of the consuls along with the dictator would be accounted for: nay, the dictatorship, being distinct from the office of the *magister populi*, might sometimes be conferred on him, sometimes on one of the consuls. The object aimed at in instituting the dictatorship,—as I will call it from the first, by the name which in course of time supplanted the earlier one,—was incontestably to evade the Valerian laws, and to re-establish an unlimited authority over the plebeians even within the barriers and the mile of their liberties: for the legal appeal to the commonalty was from the sentence of the consuls, not from that of this new magistrate. Nor does such an appeal seem ever to have been introduced, not even after the power of the tribunes had grown to an inordinate excess: the Romans rather chose to let the dictatorship drop. The tradition, accordingly, is perfectly correct in recording how the ap-

pointment of a dictator alarmed the commonalty.

That even the members of the houses at the first had no right of appealing against the dictatorto their comitia,though theyhad possessed such a right even under the kings is expressly asserted by Festus: at the same time he adds that they obtained it. This is confirmed by the example of M. Fabius; who, when his son was persecuted by the ferocity of a dictator, appealed in his behalf to the populace; to his peers, the patricians in the curies.

The latter Romans had only an indistinct knowledge of the dictatorship, drawn from their earlier history. Excepting Q. Fabius Maximus in the second campaign of the second Punic war, whose election and situation, moreover, were completely at variance with ancient custom, no dictator to command an army had been appointed since 503; and even the comitia for elections had never been held by one since the beginning of the Macedonian war. As applied to the tyranny of Sylla and the monarchy of Cæsar, the title was a mere name, without any ground for such a use in the ancient constitution. Hence we can account for the error of Dion Cassius, when,overlooking the privilege of the patricians,he expressly asserts that in no instance was there a right of appealing against the dictator, and that he might condemn knights and senators to death without a trial: as well as for that of Dionysius, who fancies he decided on every measure at will, even about peace and war. Such notions, out of whichthe moderns have drawn their phrase *dictatorial power*,

II. THE DECEMVIRS.

THE laws of Rome at first, as of other ancient nations, were very few and simple.[1] It is thought there was for some time no written law.[2] Differences were determined[3] by the pleasure of the kings,[4] according to the

are suitable indeed to Sylla and Cæsar: with reference to the genuine dictatorship they are utterly mistaken.

Like ignorance as to the ancient state of things is involved in the notion of Dionysius, that, after the senate had merely resolved that a dictator was to be appointed, and which consul was to name him, the consul exercised an controled discretion in the choice: which opinion, being delivered with such positiveness, has become the prevalent one in treatises on Roman antiquities. Such might possibly be the case, if the dictator was restricted to the charge of presiding over the elections, for which purpose it mattered not who he was: in the second Punic war, in 542, the consul M. Valerius Lævinus asserted this as his right; and in the first the practice must already have been the same; for else P. Claudius Pulcher could not have insulted the republic by nominating M. Glycia. But never can the disposal of kingly power have been entrusted to the discretion of a single elector.

The pontifical law books, clothing the principles of the constitution after their manner in an historical form, preserved the true account. For what other source can have supplied Dionysius with the resolution of the senate, as it professes to be, that a citizen, whom the senate should nominate, and the people approve of, should govern for six months? The people here is the populus: it was a revival of the ancient custom for the king to be elected by the patricians: and that such was the form is established by positive testimony.

Still oftener, indeed, throughout the whole first decad of Livy, do we read of a decree of the senate whereby a dictator was appointed, without any notice of the great council of the patricians. The old mode

of electing the kings was restored in all its parts: the dictator after his appointment had to obtain the imperium from the curies. And thus, from possessing this right of conferring the imperium, the patricians might dispense with voting on the preliminary nomination of the senate. Appointing a dictator was an affair of urgency: some augury or other might interrupt the curies: it was unfortunate enough that there were but too many chances of this at the time when he was to be proclaimed by the consul, and when the law on his imperium was to be passed. And after the plebeians obtained a share in the consulate, as the senate was continually approximating to a fair mixture of the two estates, it was a gain for the freedom of the nation, provided the election could not be transferred to the centuries, to strengthen the senate's power of nominating. Under the old system a plebeian could not possibly be dictator. Now, as C. Marcius in 398 opened this office to his own order, whereas in 393 it is expressly stated that the appointment was approved by the patricians, it is almost certain that the change took place within this interval. Even in 444 the bestowal of the imperium was assuredly more than an empty form: but it became such by the Mænian law; thenceforward it was only requisite that the consul should consent to proclaim the person named by the senate. Thus after that time, in the advanced state of popular freedom, the dictatorship could occur but seldom except for trivial purposes: and if on such occasions the appointment was left to the consuls, they would naturally lay claim to it likewise in those solitary instances where the office still had real importance. However, when P. Claudius insultingly misused his privilege, the remembrance of the

ancient procedure was still fresh enough for the senate to have the power of annulling the scandalous appointment. To do so, they would not even need the legal limitation mentioned by Livy, that none but consulars were eligible. A law of those early times can only have spoken of prætors and prætorians: for which reason, the prætor continuing to be deemed a colleague of the consuls, it was not violated when L. Papirius Crassus was made dictator in 415: and the other cases which would be against the rule, if interpreted strictly of such men as had actually been consuls, might probably be explained in the same way, if we had prætorian Fasti.

In a number of passages it is distinctly stated that the master of the knights was chosen by the dictator at pleasure. But this again must have been the more recent practice: at all events his appointment in one instance is attributed to the senate no less clearly than that of the dictator: as at the origin of the office it is at least in general terms to electors: and the decree of the plebs, which in 542 raised Q. Fulvius Flaccus to the dictatorship, enjoined him to appoint P. Licinius Crassus *magister equitum.* The civil character of this officer is enveloped in total obscurity: but that he was not merely the master of the horse and the dictator's lieutenant in the field, is certain. I conjecture, that he was elected by the centuries of plebeian knights, —as the *magister populi* was by the *populus,* the six suffragia,—and that he was their protector. The dictator may have presided at the election, letting the twelve centuries vote on the person whom he proposed: this might afterwards fall into disuse, and he would then name his brother magistrate himself.—Niebuhr, Vol. i. p. 552—559.

1 Tac. Ann. iii. 26.　　2 nihil scripti juris.　　3 lites dirimæ bantur.　　4 regum arbitrio.

principles of natural equity,[1] and their decisions were held as laws.[2]   The
kings used to publish their commands either by pasting them up in public
on a white wall or tablet,[3] or by a herald.   Hence they were said, *omnia
MANU gubernare*.[4]   The kings, however, in every thing of importance, consulted the senate and likewise the people.   Hence we read of the LEGES
CURIATÆ of Romulus and of the other kings, which were also called LE-
GES REGIÆ.[5]

But the chief legislator was Servius Tullius,[6] all whose laws, however,
were abolished at once[7] by Tarquinius Superbus.

After the expulsion of Tarquin the institutions of the kings were observed, not as written law, but as customs ;[8] and the consuls determined
most causes, as the kings had done, according to their pleasure.

But justice being thus extremely uncertain, as depending on the will of
an individual,[9] C. Terentius Arsa, a tribune of the commons, proposed to
the people, that a body of laws should be drawn up, to which all should
be obliged to conform.[10]   But this was violently opposed by the patricians,
in whom the whole judicative power was vested, and to whom the knowledge of the few laws which then existed was confined.[11]

At last, however, it was determined, A. U. 299, by a decree of the senate and by the order of the people, that three ambassadors should be sent
to Athens to copy the famous laws of Solon, and to examine the institutions, customs, and laws of the other states in Greece.[12]

Upon their return, ten men[13] were created from among the patricians,
with supreme power, and without the liberty of appeal, to draw up a body
of laws,[14] all the other magistrates having first abdicated their office.*   The
decemviri at first behaved with great moderation.   They administered justice to the people each every tenth day.   The twelve fasces were carried before him who was to preside, and his nine colleagues were attended by a single officer, called ACCENSUS.[15]   They proposed ten tables of
laws, which were ratified by the people at the Comitia Centuriata.   In
composing them, they are said to have used the assistance of one HER-
MODORUS, an Ephesian exile, who served them as an interpreter.[16]

---

* The arrangement of the
ruling order agreed to was,
that the consulship should be
suspended, and that in the
mean while ten senators, like
a college of interrexes, should
be invested with consular, and
at the same time with legislative power.   Among the ten
appointed by virtue of this
agreement we find both the
consuls of the year 302: and
as these were indemnified for
the dignity they were forced
to resign, so it is probable that
the quæstors of blood and the
warden of the city, whose offices were likewise transferred
to the decemvirate, obtained

seats in it.   Thus the patricians would have four deputies appointed exclusively by
themselves, and one whose
election they had confirmed ;
while five places were left
open for the free choice of the
centuries.   As the first decemvirate represented a decury of
interrexes, the supreme power
was always lodged with one of
their body at a time, who
was called the *custos urbis ;* he
was attended by the lictors,
and presided over the senate
and the whole republic as warden of the city.   The rest, each
of whom had merely a beadle
at his orders, are said to have

acted as judges.   There is no
imaginable reason why the rotation should have followed
any other law than it would
have done in a decury of interrexes, where the kingly
power remained five days with
each : and this conjecture is
favoured by Dionysius, who
speaks in vague terms of a
certain number of days.   From
its nature as an interreign
their office had no other limit
to its duration, than the ac-
complishment of the commission they had received.   Their
successors took their seats on
the ides of May.

---

1 ex æquo et bono, Sen.
     Ep. 90.
2 Diony. x. 1.
3 7 in album relata pro-
     ponere in publico, Liv.
     i. 32. 44.
4 Pompon. l. 2. s. 3. D.
     Orig. Jur. i. e. potes-

tate et imperio., Tac.
     Agric. 9.
5 Liv. v. 1.
6 præcipuus sanctor le-
     gum, Tac. Ann. iii. 26.
7 uno edicto sublatæ,
     Diony. iv. 43.
8 tanquam mores majo-

rum.
9 in unius voluntate
     positum, Cic. Fam. ix.
     16.
10 quo omnes uti debe-
     rent.
11 Liv. iii. 9.
12 Liv. iii. 31. Plin. Ep.

viii. 24.
13 decemviri.
14 legibus scribendis.
15 Liv. iii. 32, 33.
16 Cic. Tusc. v. 36. Plin.
     xxxiv. 5. s. 10.

As two other tables seemed to be wanting, decemviri were again created for another year to make them. But these new magistrates acting
tyrannically, and wishing to retain their command beyond the legal time,
were at last forced to resign, chiefly on account of the base passion of
Appius Claudius, one of their number, for Virginia, a virgin of plebeian
rank, who was slain by her father to prevent her falling into the decemvir's hands. The decemviri all perished either in prison or in banishment.
But the laws of the twelve tables[1] continued ever after to be the rule and
foundation of public and private right through the Roman world.[2] They
were engraved on brass, and fixed up in public,[3] and even in the time of
Cicero, the noble youth who meant to apply to the study of jurisprudence,
were obliged to get them by heart as a necessary rhyme,[4] not that they
were written in verse, as some have thought ; for any set form of words,[5]
even in prose, was called CARMEN, or *carmen compositum*.[6]

III. TRIBUNI MILITUM CONSULARI POTESTATE.

THE cause of their institution has already been explained.[7] They are
so called, because those of the plebeians who had been military tribunes in
the army were the most conspicuous. Their office and insignia were much
the same with those of the consuls.

IV. INTERREX.

CONCERNING the causes of creating this magistrate, &c., see p. 76.

OTHER EXTRAORDINARY MAGISTRATES OF LESS NOTE.

THERE were several extraordinary inferior magistrates ; as DUUMVIRI
perduellionis judicandæ causa.[8] *Duumviri navales, classis ornandæ refici-
endæque causa*.[9] *Duumviri ad ædem Junoni Monetæ faciundam*.[10]

TRIUMVIRI *coloniæ deducendæ*.[11] *Triumviri bini, qui citra et ultra quin-
quagesimum lapidem in pagis forisque et conciliabulis omnem copiam ingenuo-
rum inspicerent, et idoneos ad arma ferenda conquirerent, militesque facerent*.[12]
*Triumviri bini ; uni sacris conquirendis donisque persignandis ; alteri re-
ficiendis ædibus sacris*.[13] *Triumviri mensarii, facti ob argenti penuriam*.[14]

QUINQUEVIRI, *agro Pomptino dividendo*.[15] *Quinqueviri ab dispensatione
pecuniæ* MENSARII *appellati*.[16] *Quinqueviri muris turribusque reficiendis*,[17]
minuendis publicis sumptibus.[18]

DECEMVIRI *agris inter veteranos milites dividendis*.[19]

1 leges duodecim tabu-
larum.
2 fons universi publici
privatique juris, Liv.
iii. 34. finis æqui juris,
Tac. Ann. iii. 27.
3 leges decemvirales,
quibus tabulis duode-
decim est nomen,in æs
incisas in publico pro-
posuerant, sc. consu-
les, Liv. iii. 57.
4 tanquam carmen ne-
cessarium, Cic. Legg.
ii. 23.
5 verba concepta.
6 Liv. i. 24. 26. iii. 64.
x. 36. Cic. Mur. 12.
7 see p. 72.
8 two commissioners to

pass judgment for mur-
der.
9 two naval commis-
sioners for the equip-
ping and refitting of
the fleet.
10 two commissioners
to erect a temple to
Juno Moneta, Liv. i.26.
vi. 29. vii. 28. ix. 30. xi.
16. 26. xli. 1.
11 three commissioners
to conduct a colony.
12 two sets of trium-
virs,one of whichwith-
in, and the other be-
yond, the distance of
fifty miles, should in-
spect into the number
of free-born men in all

the market towns and
villages, and enlist
such for soldiers as had
strength enough to car-
ry arms.
13 two sets of trium-
virs ; one, to search
for the effects belong-
ing to the temples, and
register the offerings :
the other, to repair the
temples.
14 three public bankers
appointed on account
of a scarcity of money,
Liv. iv. 11. vi. 26. viii.
16. ix. 28. xxi. 25. xxiii.
21. xxiv. 18. xxv. 5. 7.
xxvi. 36. xxxi.49.xxxii.
29.

15 five commissioners,
to make a distribution
of the Pomptine lands.
16 five commissioners
called bankers, from
their dealing out the
money.
17 five commissioners
for repairing the walls
and towers (of Rome).
18 five commissioners
appointed to reduce the
public expenses, Liv.
vi. 21. vii. 21. xxv. 7.
Plin. Ep. ii. 1 Pan. 62.
19 ten commissioners,
to distribute lands
among the veteran sol-
diers, Liv. xxxi. 4.

Several of these were not properly magistrates. They were all, however, chosen from the most respectable men of the state. Their office
may in general be understood from their titles.

PROVINCIAL MAGISTRATES.

THE provinces of the Roman people were at first governed by prætors,[1]
but afterwards by proconsuls and proprætors, to whom were joined quæstors and lieutenants. The usual name is PROCONSUL and PROPRÆTOR ; but
sometimes it is written *pro consule* and *pro prætore*, in two words ; so likewise *pro quæstore*.[2]

Anciently those were called proconsuls, to whom the command of
consul was prolonged[3] after their office was expired,[4] or who were invested with consular authority, either from a subordinate rank, as Marcellus,
after being prætor,[5] and Gellius, or from a private station, as Scipio.[6] This
was occasioned by some public exigence, when the ordinary magistrates
were not sufficient. The same was the case with proprætors,[7] The first
proconsul mentioned by Livy, was T. Quinctius, A. U. 290. But he seems
to have been appointed for the time. The first to whom the consular power was prolonged, was Publilius.[8] The name of proprætor was also given
to a person whom a general left to command the army in his absence.[9]

The names of consul and proconsul, prætor and proprætor, are sometimes confounded. And we find all governors of provinces called by the
general name of proconsules, as of præsides.[10]

The command of consul was prolonged, and proconsuls occasionally appointed by the Comitia Tributa, except in the case of Scipio, who was
sent as proconsul into Spain by the Comitia Centuriata.[11] But after the
empire was extended, and various countries reduced to the form of provinces, magistrates were regularly sent from Rome to govern them, according to the Sempronian law,[12] without any new appointment of the people,
Only military command was conferred on them by the Comitia Curiati.[13]

At first the provinces were annual, i. e. a proconsul had the government of a province only for one year ; and the same person could not
command different provinces. But this was violated in several instances ;
especially in the case of Julius Cæsar.[14] And it is remarkable that the
timid compliance of Cicero with the ambitious views of Cæsar, in granting him the continuation of his command, and money for the payment of
his troops, with other immoderate and unconstitutional concessions, although he secretly condemned them,[15] proved fatal to himself, as well as to
the republic.

The prætors cast lots for their provinces,[16] or settled them by agreement,[17]
in the same manner with the consuls. But sometimes provinces were
determined to both by the senate or people.[18] The senate fixed the extent and limits of the provinces, the number of soldiers to be maintained
in them, and money to pay them ; likewise the retinue of the governors,[19]
and their travelling charges.[20] And thus the governors were said ORNARI,

---

1 see p. 86, 87.
2 Cic. Acad. 4. 4. Verr.
    1. 15. 36.
3 Imperium proroga-
    tum.
4 Liv. viii. 22. 26. ix. 42.
    x. 16.
5 ex prætura, Liv. xxiii.
    30.

6 Cic. Legg. i. 90. xxvi.
    18. xxviii. 38.
7 Cic. Phil. v. 16. Suet.
    Aug. 10. Sall. Cat. 19.
8 Liv. iii. 4. viii. 23.
    26.
9 Sall Jug. 36. 103.
10 Suet. Aug. 3. 36.
11 Lix. x. 24. xxvi. 18.

xxix. 13. xxx. 27.
12 see p. 79.
13 see p. 55.
14 Suet. Jul. 22. 24. Cic.
    Fam. i. 7. see p. 16. 80.
15 Prov. Cons. & Balb.
    27. Fam. i. 7. Att. ii.
    17. x. 6.
16 provincias sortieban-

tur.
17 inter se compara-
    bant.
18 Liv. xxvii. 36. xxxiv.
    54. xxxv. 20. xxxvii. 1.
    xlv. 16, 17.
19 comitatus vel cohors.
20 viaticum.

i. e. *instrui*, to be furnished. What was assigned them for the sake of household furniture, was called VASARIUM. So *vasa*, furniture.[1]

A certain number of lieutenants was assigned to each proconsul and propraetor, who were appointed usually by the senate, or with the permission of the senate by the proconsul himself, who was then said *aliquem sibi legare*, or very rarely by an order of the people.[2] The number of lieutenants was different according to the rank of the governor, or the extent of the province.[3] Thus, Cicero in Cilicia had four, Caesar in Gaul ten, and Pompey in Asia fifteen. The least number seems to have been three; Quintus, the brother of Cicero, had no more in Asia Minor.[4]

The office of a *legatus* was very honourable; and men of praetorian and consular dignity did not think it below them to bear it. Thus Scipio Africanus served as *legatus* under his brother Lucius.[5]

The *legati* were sometimes attended by lictors, as the senators were when absent from Rome, *jure liberae legationis*,[6] but the person under whom they served, might deprive them of that privilege.[7]

In the retinue of a proconsul were comprehended his military officers,[8] and all his public and domestic attendants. Among these were young noblemen, who went with him to learn the art of war, and to see the method of conducting public business; who, on account of their intimacy, were called CONTUBERNALES.[9] From this retinue, under the republic, women were excluded, but not so under the emperors.[10]

A proconsul set out for his province in great pomp. Having offered up vows in the Capitol,[11] dressed in his military robe,[12] with twelve lictors going before him, carrying the fasces and secures, and with the other ensigns of command, he went out of the city with all his retinue. From thence he either went straightway to the province, or if he was detained by business, by the interposition of the tribunes, or by bad omens,[13] he staid for some time without the city, for he could not be within it while invested with military command. His friends, and sometimes the other citizens, out of respect, accompanied him[14] for some space out of the city with their good wishes. When he reached the province, he sent notice of his arrival to his predecessor, that, by an interview with him, he might know the state of the province; for his command commenced on the day of his arrival; and by the CORNELIAN law, the former proconsul was obliged to depart within thirty days after.[15]

A proconsul in his province had both judicial authority and military command.[16] He used so to divide the year, that he usually devoted the summer to military affairs, or going through the province, and the winter to the administration of justice.[17] He administered justice much in the same way with the praetor at Rome, according to the laws which had been prescribed to the province when first subdued, or according to the regulations which had afterwards been made concerning it by the senate or people at Rome; or finally according to his own edicts, which he published in the province concerning every thing of importance.[18] These, if he borrowed them from others, were called TRANSLATITIA vel *Tralatitia* v. *-icia*; if not

---

1 Cic. Rull. ii. 13. Pis. 35. Liv. l. 24.
2 Cic. Fam. i. 7. xii. 55. Vat. 15. Nep. Att. vi. 6.
3 Cic. Phil. ii. 15.
4 Cic. Q. fr. i. l. 3.
5 Liv. xxxvii. 1. &c. Gell. iv. 18.

6 see p. 14.
7 Liv. xxix. 9. Cic.Fam. xii. 30.
8 praefecti, Cic. Verr. ii. 10.
9 Cic. Coel. 30. Planc. 11.
10 Tac. Ann. iii. 33, 34.

Suet. Oct. 34.
11 votis in capitolio nuncupatis.
12 paludatus.
13 Plut. Crass. Cic. Div. i. 16. ii. 9. Flor. iii. 11. Dio. xxxvii. 50.
14 officii causa prose-

quebantur, Liv. xlii. 49. xlv. 59.
15 Cic. Fam. iii. 6.
16 potestatem vel jurisdictionem et imperium.
17 Bel. 1. Cic. Att. v. 14. Verr. 5. 12.
18 Cic. Att. vi. 1.

NOVA. He always published a general edict before he entered on his government, as the prætor did at Rome.

The proconsul held assizes or courts of justice,[1] in the principal cities of the province, so that he might go round the whole province in a year. He himself judged in all public and important causes; but matters of less consequence he referred to his quæstor or lieutenants, and also to others.[2]

The proconsul summoned these meetings[3] by an edict on a certain day, when such as had causes to be determined should attend.[4]

The provinces were divided into so many districts, called CONVENTUS, or *circuits*,[5] the inhabitants of which went to a certain city to get their causes determined, and to obtain justice.[6] Thus Spain was divided into seven circuits.[7]

The proconsul chose usually twenty of the most respectable men of the province, who sat with him in council,[8] and were called his council.[9] The proconsul passed sentence according to the opinion of his council.[10]

As the governors of provinces were prohibited from using any other language than the Latin, in the functions of their office, they were always attended by interpreters. The judices were chosen differently in different places, according to the rank of the litigants, and the nature of the cause.[11]

The proconsul had the disposal[12] of the corn, of the taxes, and, in short, of every thing which pertained to the province. Corn given to the proconsul by way of present, was called HONORARIUM.[13]

If a proconsul behaved well he received the highest honours,[14] as statues, temples, brazen horses, &c., which, through flattery, used indeed to be erected of course to all governors, though ever so corrupt and oppressive.

Festival days also used to be appointed; as in honour of Marcellus,[15] n Sicily, and of Q. Mucius Scævola,[16] in Asia.

If a governor did not behave well, he might afterwards be brought to his trial:—1. for extortion,[17] if he had made unjust exactions, or had even received presents.—2. for peculation,[18] if he had embezzled the public money.[19]—and, 3. for what was called *crimen* MAJESTATIS, if he had betrayed his army or province to the enemy, or led the army out of the province, and made war on any prince or state without the order of the people or the decree of the senate.

Various laws were made to secure the just administration of the provinces, but these were insufficient to check the rapacity of the Roman magistrates. Hence the provinces were miserably oppressed by their exactions. Not only the avarice of the governor was to be gratified, but that of all his officers and dependents; as his lieutenants, tribunes, præfects, &c., and even of his freedmen and favourite slaves.[20]

The pretexts for exacting money were various. The towns and villages

---

1 forum vel conventus agebat.
2 Cic. Flac. 21. Cæc. 17. Verr. ii. 18. Att. v. 21. ad Q. fratr. i. 1, 7. Suet. Jul. 7.
3 conventus idicebat.
4 Liv. xxxi. 29. to this Virgil is thought to allude, Æn. v. 578. indicitque forum, &c.
5 νομοι, Plin. Ep. x. 5.
6 disceptandi et juris obtinendi causa conveniebant.

7 in septem conventus, Plin. iii. 3. the Greeks calledconventus agere, αγοραιους αγειν sc. ημεραϛ so. in Act. Apost. xix. 38. αγοραιοι αγονται, &c. conventus aguntur, sunt procon-sules; in jus vocent se invicem. Hence, conventus circumire, Suet. Jul. 7. percur-rere, Cæs. viii. 46. for urbes circumire, ubi hi conventus agebantur.

8 qui ei in consilio ade-rant, assidebant.
9 consilium, consiliarii, assessores, et recupe-ratores. Hence, consi-lium cogere, in consi-lium advocare, adhi-bere; in consilio esse, adesse, assidere, ha-bere; in consilium ire, mittere, admittere, &c.
10 de consilii sententia decrevit, pronunciavit, &c.
11 Val. Max. ii. 2. 2.

Cic. Verr. ii. 13. 15. 17. iii. 37. Fam. xiii. 54.
12 curatio.
13 Cic. Pis. 35.
14 Cic. Att v. 21.
15 Marcellea, -orum.
16 Muces, Cic. Verr. ii. 21. 10. 13.
17 repetundarum, Plin. Ep. iv. 9.
18 peculatus.
19 hence called pecula-tor, or depeculator, Asc. Cic. Verr. i. 1.
20 Juv. viii. 87—130.

through which the governors passed, were obliged, by the JULIAN law, to supply them and their retinue with forage, and wood for firing. The wealthier cities paid large contributions for being exempted from furnishing winter-quarters to the army. Thus the inhabitants of Cyprus alone paid yearly, on this account, 200 talents, or about 40,000*l*.[1]

Anciently a proconsul, when he had gained a victory, used to have golden crowns sent him not only from the different cities of his own province, but also from the neighbouring states, which were carried before him in his triumph.[2] Afterwards the cities of the province, instead of sending crowns, paid money on this account, which was called AURUM CORONARIUM, and was sometimes exacted as a tribute.[3]

A proconsul, when the annual term of his government was elapsed, delivered up the province and army to his successor, if he arrived in time, and left the province within thirty days : but first he was obliged to deposit, in two of the principal cities of his jurisdiction, on account of the money which had passed through his own or his officers' hands, stated and balanced.[4] If his successor did not arrive, he nevertheless departed, leaving his lieutenant, or more frequently his quæstor, to command in the province.[5]

When a proconsul returned to Rome, he entered the city as a private person, unless he claimed a triumph ; in which case he did not enter the city, but gave an account of his exploits to the senate assembled in the temple of Bellona, or in some other temple without the city.[6] In the meantime, he usually waited near the city till the matter was determined, whence he was said *ad urbem esse*,[7] and retained the title of IMPERATOR, which his soldiers had given him upon his victory, with the badges of command, his lictors and fasces, &c. Appian says that in his time no one was called imperator, unless 10,000 of the enemy had been slain.[8] When any one had pretensions to a triumph, his fasces were always wreathed with laurel, as the letters were which he sent to the senate concerning his victory. Sometimes, when the matter was long of being determined, he retired to some distance from Rome.[9] If he obtained a triumph, a bill was proposed to the people that he should have military command[10] on the day of his triumph, for without this no one could have military command within the city. Then he was obliged by the JULIAN law, within thirty days, to give in to the treasury an exact copy of the accounts which he had left in the province.[11] At the same time he recommended those who deserved public rewards for their services.[12]

What has been said concerning a proconsul, took place with respect to a proprætor ; unless that a proconsul had twelve lictors, and a proprætor only six. The army and retinue of the one were likewise greater than that of the other. The provinces to which proconsuls were sent, were called PROCONSULARES ; proprætors, PRÆTORIÆ.[13]

PROVINCIAL MAGISTRATES UNDER THE EMPERORS.

AUGUSTUS made a new partition of the provinces. Those which were peaceable and less exposed to an enemy, he left to the management of the

1 Cic. Att. v. 21. v. 16.
2 Liv. xxxvii. 58.xxxviii. 37. 14. xxxix. 5. 7. 29. xl. 43. Dio. xlii. 49.
3 Cic. Pis. 37.
4 apud duas civitates, quæ maximæ videren-

tur, rationes confectas et consolidatas deponere, Cic. Fam. v. 20.
5 Cic. Fam. ii. 15. Att. vi. 5, 6.
6 Liv. iii. 63. xxxviii. 45. Dio. xlix. 15.

7 Sall. Cat. 30.
8 Bell. Civ. ii. p. 445.
9 Cic. Fam. ii. 16. Att. vii. 15. x. 10. Pis. 17.
10 ut ei imperium esset, Liv. xlv. 35. Cic. Att. iv. 16.

11 eadem rationes totidem verbis referre ad ærarium,Cic. Att. v.20.
12 in beneficiis, ad ærarium detulit, Cic. ibid. Arch. 5.
13 Dio. Illi. 14.

senate and people ; but of such as were more strong, and open to hostile
invasions, and where, of course, it was necessary to support greater armies, he undertook the goverment himself.[1] This he did under pretext
of easing the senate and people of the trouble, but in reality to increase
his own power, by assuming the command of the army entirely to himself.

The provinces under the direction of the senate and people,[2] at first were
Africa propria, or the territories of Carthage, Numidia, Cyrene, Asia,
(which, when put for a province, comprehended only the countries along
the Propontis and the Ægean sea, namely, Phrygia, Mysia, Caria, Lydia,)
Bithynia and Pontus, Græcia and Epirus, Dalmatia, Macedonia, Sicilia,
Sardinia, Creta, and Hispania Bœtica.[3]

The provinces of the emperor[4] were Hispania Tarraconensis and Lusi-
tania, Gallia, Cœlosyria, Phœnicia, Cilicis, Cyprus, Ægyptus, to which
others were afterwards added. But the condition of these provinces was
often changed ; so that they were transferred from the senate and people
to the emperor, and the contrary. The provinces of the emperor seem to
have been in a better state than those of the senate and people.[5]

The magistrates sent to govern the provinces of the senate and people
were called PROCONSULES, although sometimes only of prætorian rank,[6]
The senate appointed them by lot[7] out of those who had borne a magistracy in the city at least five years before.[8] They had the same badges of
authority as the proconsuls had formerly ; but they had only a civil power,[9]
and no military command,[10] nor disposal of the taxes. The taxes were
collected, and the soldiers in their provinces commanded by officers appointed by Augustus. Their authority lasted only for one year, and they
left the province immediately when a successor was sent.[11]

Those whom the emperor sent to command his provinces were called
LEGATI CÆSARIS *pro consule*, *propætores*, vel *pro prætore*, *consulares legati*,
consulares rectores, or simply *consulares* and *legati*,[12] also *præsides*, *præfecti*,
correctores, &c.

The governor of Egypt was usually called PRÆFECTUS, or *præfectus
Augustalis*,[13] and was the first imperatorial legate that was appointed.

There was said to be an ancient prediction concerning Egypt, that it
would recover its liberty when the Roman fasces and prætexta should come
to it.[14] Augustus, artfully converting this to his own purpose, claimed that
province to himself, and, discharging a senator from going to it without
permission,[15] he sent thither a governor of equestrian rank, without the
usual ensigns of authority.[16] To him was joined a person to assist in administering justice, called JURIDICUS ALEXANDRINÆ CIVITATIS.[17]

The first præfect of Egypt was Cornelius Gallus, celebrated by Virgil in
his last eclogue, and by Ovid.[18]

The legates of the emperor were chosen from among the senators, but
the præfect of Egypt only from the equites.[19] Tiberius gave that charge to
one of his freedmen. The legati Cæsaris wore a military dress and a

1 regendas ipse susce-
pit, Suet. Aug. 47.
2 provinciæ senatoriæ
et populares vel publi-
cæ.
3 Cic. Flac. 27. Dio.
liii. 12.
4 provinciæ imperato-
ræ, vel Cæsarum.
5 Dio. liii. 12. liv. 4. 3.

Strab. xvii. fin. Tac.
Ann. i. 76.
5 Dio. liii. 13.
7 sortito mittebant.
8 Suet. Aug. 36. Vesp.
4. Plin. Ep. ii. 12. Dio.
liii. 14.
9 potestas vel jurisdic-
tio.
10 imperium.

11 Dio. ibid.
12 Dio. liii. 13. Suet.
Tib. 32. 41. Vesp. 4. 8.
Tac. Hist. ii. 97.
13 Suet. Vesp. 6. Di-
gest.
14 Cic. Fam. i. 7. Treb.
Poll. Æmil.
15 Dio. li. 17.
16 Tac. Ann. ii. 59.

Suet. Tib. 53.
17 Pandect. b διαλαμβ-
νης, Strab. xvii. p. 797.
18 Am. i. 15. 29. hunc
primum Ægyptus Ro-
manum judicem ha-
buit, Entr. vii. 7. Suet.
Aug. 66. Dio. li. 17.
19 Tac. xii. 60. Dio. liii.
13.

sword, and were attended by soldiers instead of lictors. They had much greater powers than the proconsuls, and continued in command during the pleasure of the emperor.[1]

In each province, besides the governor, there was an officer called PRO-CURATOR CÆSARIS,[2] or *curator*, and in later times *rationalis*, who managed the affairs of the revenue,[3] and also had a judicial power in matters that concerned the revenue, whence that office was called *procuratio amplissima*.[4] These procurators were chosen from among the equites, and sometimes from freedmen. They were sent not only into the provinces of the emperor, but also into those of the senate and people.[5]

Sometimes a procurator discharged the office of a governor,[6] especially in a small province, or in a part of a large province, where the governor could not be present; as Pontius Pilate did, who was procurator or *præpositus* of Judea, which was annexed to the province of Syria. Hence he had the power of punishing capitally, which the procuratores did not usually possess.[8]

To all these magistrates and officers Augustus appointed different salaries, according to their respective dignity.[9] Those who received 200 sestertia were called DUCENARII; 100, CENTENARII; 60, SEXAGENARII, &c.[10] A certain sum was given them for mules and tents; which used formerly to be afforded at the public expense.[11]

All these alterations and arrangements were made in appearance by public authority, but in fact by the will of Augustus.

RE-ESTABLISHMENT OF MONARCHY UNDER AUGUSTUS; TITLES, BADGES, AND POWERS OF THE EMPERORS.

THE monarchial form of government established by Augustus, although different in name and external appearance, in several respects resembled that which had prevailed under the kings. Both were partly hereditary, and partly elective. The choice of the kings depended on the senate and people at large; that of the emperors, chiefly on the army. When the former abused their power they were expelled; the latter were often put to death; but the interests of the army being separate from those of the state, occasioned the continuation of despotism. According to Pomponius,[12] their rights were the same; but the account of Dionysius and others is different.[13]

As Augustus had become master of the republic by force of arms, he might have founded his right to govern it on that basis, as his grand uncle and father by adoption, Julius Cæsar, had done. But the apprehension he always entertained of Cæsar's fate made him pursue a quite different course. The dreadful destruction of the civil wars, and the savage cruelty of the Triumviri, had cut off all the keenest supporters of liberty,[14] and had so humbled the spirits of the Romans, that they were willing to submit to any form of government rather than hazard a repetition of former calamities.[15] The empire was now so widely extended, the number of those who had a right to vote in the legislative assemblies so great,

1 Dio. liii. 13. lviii. 19.
2 Tac. Agric. 15.
3 qui res fisci curabat: publicos reditus colligebat et erogabat.
4 Suet. Claud. 12. Galb. 15.
5 Dio. lii. 25. liii. 15.
6 vice præsidis fungebatur.
7 Suet. Vesp. 4.
8 Tac. Ann. iv. 15. xii. 23. xv. 43.
9 Dio. liii. 15.
10 Capitolin. in Pertinac. c. 2.
11 Suet. Aug. 36.
12 de origine juris, D. I. 2. 14. reges omnem potestatem habuisse.
13 see p. 75.
14 Tac. Ann. i. 2.
15 tuta et præsentia quam vetera et periculosa malebant, ibid.

(the Romans having never employed the modern method of diminishing that number by representation,) and the morals of the people so corrupt, that a republican form of government was no longer fitted to conduct so unwieldy a machine. The vast intermixture of inhabitants which composed the capital, and the numerous armies requisite to keep the provinces in subjection, could no longer be controlled but by the power of one. Had Augustus possessed the magnanimity and wisdom to lay himself and his successors under proper restraints against the abuse of power, his descendants might have long enjoyed that exalted station to which his wonderful good fortune, and the abilities of others had raised him. Had he, agreeably to his repeated declarations, wished for command only to promote the happiness of his fellow-citizens, he would have aimed at no more power than was necessary for that purpose. But the lust of dominion, although artfully disguised, appears to have been the ruling passion of his mind.[1]

Upon his return to Rome, after the conquest of Egypt, and the death of Antony and Cleopatra, A. U. 725, he is said to have seriously deliberated with his two chief favourites, Agrippa and Mæcenas, about resigning his power, and restoring the ancient form of government. Agrippa advised him to do so, but Mæcenas dissuaded him from it. In the speeches which Dio Cassius makes them deliver on this occasion, the principal arguments for and against a popular and monarchial government are introduced. The advice of Mæcenas prevailed.[2] Augustus, however, in the following year, having corrected the abuses which had crept in during the civil wars,[3] and having done several other popular acts, assembled the senate, and in a set speech pretended to restore every thing to them and to the people. But several members, who had been previously prepared, exclaimed against this proposal ; and all the rest, either prompted by opinion or overawed by fear, all with one voice conjured him to retain the command. Upon which, as if unequal to the load, he appeared to yield a reluctant compliance ; and that only for ten years; during which time, he might regulate the state of public affairs ;[4] thus seeming to rule, as if by constraint, at the earnest desire of his fellow-citizens ; which gave his usurpation the sanction of law.

This farce he repeated at the end of every ten years ; but the second time, A. U. 736, he accepted the government only for five years, saying that this space of time was then sufficient, and when it was elapsed, for five years more ; but after that, always for ten years.[5] He died in the first year of the fifth *decennium*, the 19th of August,[6] A. U. 767, aged near 76 years, having ruled alone near 44 years. The succeeding emperors, although at their accession they received the empire for life, yet at the beginning of every ten years used to hold a festival, as if to commemorate the renewal of the empire.[7]

As the senate by their misconduct[8] had occasioned the loss of liberty, so by their servility to Augustus they established tyranny.[9] Upon his feigned offer to resign the empire, they seem to have racked their invention to contrive new honours for him. To the names of IMPERATOR, CÆSAR, and PRINCE,[10] which they had formely conferred, they added those of AUGUS-

1 specie recusantis flagrantissime cupiverat, Tac. Ann. i. 2, 3. 10.
2 Dio. lii. 41.
3 Suet. Aug. 32.
4 rempublicam ordinaret.

5 Dio. liii. 16. 46. liv. 12. iv. 6.
6 xiv. Kal. Sept.
7 Dio, liii. 10.
8 see p. 96.
9 ruere in servitutem consules, patres, eques,

consuls, senators, and Roman knights, contended with emulation, who should be the most willing slaves ; as Tacitus says upon the accession of Tibe-

rius, Ann. i. 7.
10 princeps senatus, Dio. xliii. 44. xlvi. 47. liii. 1.

TUS[1] and *Father of his Country*.[2] This title had been first given to Cicero by the senate, after his suppression of Catiline's conspiracy,[3] by the advice of Cato, or of Catulus, as Cicero himself says.[4] It was next decreed to Julius Cæsar,[5] and some of his coins are still extant with that inscription. Cicero proposed that it should be given to Augustus, when yet very young. It was refused by Tiberius, as also the title of IMPERATOR, and DOMINUS, but most of the succeeding emperors accepted it.[6]

The title of PATER PATRIÆ denoted chiefly the paternal affection which it became the emperors to entertain towards their subjects; and also that power which, by the Roman law, a father had over his children.[7]

CÆSAR was properly a family title. According to Dio, it also denoted power.[8] In later times, it signified the person destined to succeed to the empire, or, assumed into a share of the government during the life of the emperor, who himself was always called AUGUSTUS, which was a title of splendour and dignity, not of power.[9]

Augustus is said to have first desired the name of ROMULUS, that he might be considered as a second founder of the city; but perceiving that thus he should be suspected of aiming at sovereignty, he dropped all thoughts of it, and accepted the title of AUGUSTUS, the proposer of which in the senate was Munatius Plancus. Servius says, that Virgil, in allusion to this desire of Augustus, describes him under the name of QUIRINUS.[10]

The chief title which denoted command was IMPERATOR. By this the successors of Augustus were peculiarly distinguished. It was equivalent to REX. In modern times it is reckoned superior.[11] The title of imperator, however, continued to be conferred on victorious generals as formerly; but chiefly on the emperors themselves, as all generals were supposed to act under their auspices.[12] Under the republic the appellation of imperator was put after the name; as CICERO IMPERATOR;[13] but the title of the emperors usually before, as a *prænomen*.[14] Thus, the following words are inscribed on an ancient stone, found at Ancyra, now Angouri,[15] in Asia Minor:—IMP. CÆSAR DIVI F. AUG. PONT. MAX. COS. XIV. IMP. XX. TRIBUNIC. POTEST. XXXVIII.—The emperor Cæsar, the adopted son of (Julius Cæsar, called) Divus (after his deification); Augustus the high-priest, (an office which he assumed after the death of Lepidus, A. U. 741), fourteen times consul, twenty times (saluted) imperator, (on account of his victories. Dio says he obtained this honour in all 21 times. Thus Tacitus, *Nomen* IMPERATORIS *semel atque vicies partum*), in the 38th year of his tribunician power, (from the time when he was first invested with it by the senate, A. U. 724.)[16] So that this inscription was made above five years before his death.

The night after Cæsar was called AUGUSTUS, the Tiber happened to overflow its banks, so as to render all the level parts of Rome navigable, to which Horace is supposed to allude.[17] This event was thought to prog-

---

1 venerandus v. -abilis, ab augur, quasi inauguratus vel consecratus; ideoque Diis carus; culto divino afficiendus, σεβαςτος, Paus. iii. 11. vel ab augeo; quam sua Jupiter auget ope, Ov. Fast. i. 612. Suet. Aug. 7. Dio. liii. 10.

2 pater patriæ, Suet. 58. Ov. Fast. ii. 127. Pont. iv. 9. ult. Trist. iv. 4. 13, &c.
3 Roma patrem patriæ Ciceronem libera dixit, Juv. viii. 244. Plin. vii. 30.
4 App. B. Civ. ii. 431. Plut. Cic. Pis. 3.
5 Suet. 76. Dio. xliv. 4.

6 Phil. xiii. 11. Suet. 26. 37. 67. Dio. lviii. 2. Tac. Ann. xi. 25.
7 Dio. liii. 18. Sen.Clem. i. 14.
8 Dio. ibid. xliii. 44.
Suet. Galb. 1.
9 Spart. Ælio. Vero. 3. Dio. liii. 18.
10 Dio. liii. 16. Suet. Aug.7. Vell.ii. 91. Virg.

Æn. i. 296. iii. 27.
11 Dio. xliii. 44. lili. 17.
12 Hor. Od. iv. 14. 32.
Ov. Trist. ii. 173.
13 Cic. Ep. passim.
14 Suet. Tib. 26.
15 in lapide Ancyrano: 16 Dio. li. 19. lii. 41. liv. 27. Tac. Ann. i. 9.
17 Od. i. 2. Dio. liii. 20. Tac. Ann. i. 76.

nosticate his future greatness. Among the various expressions of flattery
then used to the emperor, that of Pacuvius, a tribune of the commons,
was remarkable ; who in the senate devoted himself to Cæsar, after the
manner of the Spaniards and Gauls,[1] and exhorted the rest of the senators
to do the same. Being checked by Augustus, he rushed forth to the people, and compelled many to follow his example. Whence it became a
custom for the senators, when they congratulated any emperor on his accession to the empire, to say, that they were devoted to his service.[2]

Macrobius informs us, that it was by means of this tribune[3] that an order of the people[4] was made, appointing the month Sextilis to be called
AUGUST.[5]

The titles given to Justinian in the Corpus Juris are, in the Institutes,
SACRATISSIMUS PRINCEPS, and IMPERATORIA MAJESTAS ; in the Pandects,
DOMINUS NOSTER SACRATISSINUS PRINCEPS ; and the same in the Codex,
with this addition, PERPETUUS AUGUSTUS.

The powers conferred on Augustus as emperor were, to levy armies,
to raise money, to undertake wars, to make peace, to command all the
forces of the republic, to have the power of life and death within as well
as without the city ; and to do every thing else which the consuls and
others invested with supreme command had a right to do.[6]

In the year of the city 731, the senate decreed that Augustus should be
always proconsul, even within the city ; and in the provinces should enjoy
greater authority than the ordinary proconsuls. Accordingly, he imposed
taxes on the provinces, rewarded and punished them as they had favoured
or opposed his cause, and prescribed such regulations to them as he himself thought proper.[7]

In the year 735, it was decreed, that he should always enjoy consular
power, with twelve lictors, and sit on a curule chair between the consuls.
The senators at the same time requested that he would undertake the rec-
tifying of all abuses, and enact what laws he thought proper ; offering to
swear that they would observe them, whatever they should be. This Augustus declined, well knowing, says Dio, that they would perform what
they cordially decreed without an oath ; but not the contrary, although
they bound themselves by a thousand oaths.[8]

The multiplying of oaths always renders them less sacred, and nothing
is more pernicious to morals, than the two frequent exaction of oaths by public authority, without a necessary cause. Livy informs us, that the sanc-
tity of an oath[9] had more influence with the ancient Romans than the fear
of laws and punishments.[10] They did not, he says, as in aftertimes, when
a neglect of religion prevailed, by interpretations adapt an oath and the
laws to themselves, but conformed every one his own conduct to them.[11]

Although few of the emperors accepted the title of censor,[12] yet all of
them in part exercised the rights of that office, as also those of pontifex
maximus and tribune of the commons.[13]

The emperors were freed from the obligation of the laws,[14] so that they
might do what they pleased. Some, however, understand this only of
certain laws : for Augustus afterwards requested of the senate, that he

1 devotos illi soldurios
appellant, Cæs. Bell.
Gall. iii. 22. Vall. Max.
ii. 6. 11.
2 Dio. ibid.
3 Pacuvio tribuno ple-

bem rogante.
4 plebiscitum.
5 Sat. 1. 12.
6 Dio. liii. 17.
7 Dio. liii. 22. Liv. 7. 9.
25.

8 Dio. liv. 10.
9 fides et jusjurandum.
10 proximo legum et
pœnarum metu, Liv. i.
21. ii. 45.
11 Liv. ii. 32. iii. 20. xxii.

61. Cic. Off. iii. 30, 31.
Polyb. vi. 54. 56.
12 see p. 91, 92.
13 Dio. liii. 17. see p. 97.
14 legibus soluti.

might be freed from the Voconian law, but a person was said to be *legibus solutus* who was freed only for one law.[1]

On the first of January, every year, the senate and people renewed their oath of allegiance, or, as it was expressed, confirmed the acts of the emperors by an oath ; which custom was first introduced by the triumviri, after the death of Cæsar, repeated to Augustus, and always continued under the succeeding emperors. They not only swore that they approved of what the emperors had done, but that they would in like manner confirm whatever they should do. In this oath the acts of the preceding emperors, who were approved of, were included : and the acts of such as were not approved of were omitted, as of Tiberius, of Caligula, &c. Claudius would not allow any one to swear to his acts,[2] but not only ordered others to swear to the acts of Augustus, but swore to them also himself.[3]

It was usual to swear by the genius, the fortune, or safety of the emperor, which was first decreed in honour of Julius Cæsar, and commonly observed, so likewise by that of Augustus, even after his death. To violate this oath was esteemed a heinous crime, and more severely punished than real perjury.[4] It was reckoned a species of treason,[5] and punished by the bastinado, sometimes by cutting out the tongue.[6] So that Minutius Felix justly says, " It is less hazardous for them to swear falsely by the genius of Jove, than by that of the emperor."[7] Tiberius prohibited any one from swearing by him, but yet men swore, not only by his fortune, but also by that of Sejanus. After the death of the latter, it was decreed that no oath should be made by any other but the emperor. Caligula ordained that to all oaths these words should be added :—NEQUE ME, NEQUE MEOS LIBEROS CHARIORES HABEO, QUAM CAIUM ET SORORES EJUS, and that the women should swear by his wife Drusilla,[8] as he himself did, in his most public and solemn asseverations. So Claudius, by Livia.[9]

In imitation of the temple and divine honours appointed by the triumviri to Julius Cæsar, and confirmed by Augustus, alters were privately erected to Augustus himself, at Rome,[10] and particularly in the provinces ; but he permitted no temple to be publicly consecrated to him, unless in conjunction with the city, Rome : AUGUSTO ET URBI ROMÆ ; and that only in the provinces ; for in the city they were strictly prohibited. After his death, they were very frequent.[11]

It was likewise decreed, in honour of Augustus, that when the priests offered up vows for the safety of the people and senate, they should do the same for him, so for the succeeding emperors, particularly at the beginning of the year, on the 3d of January ; also, that, in all public and private entertainments, libations should be made to him with wishes for his safety, as to the *Lares* and other gods.[12]

On public occasions, the emperors wore a crown and a triumphal robe. They also used a particular badge, of having fire carried before them. Marcus Antoninus calls it a lamp, probably borrowed from the Persians.[13]

1 Dio. liii. 18. 28. lvi. 32. Cic. Phil. ii. 13.
2 in acta sua jurare.
3 Tac. Ann. xvi. 22. Dio. xlvii. 19. li. 20. liii. 28. lvii. 8. lviii. 17. lix. 9. lx. 4. 10.
4 Dio. xliv. 6. 50. lvii. 9. Tac. Ann. i. 73. Cod. iv. 1, 2. ii. 4. 41. Dig.

xii. 2. 13. Tert. Ap. 18.
5 majestatis.
6 D. xii. 2. 13. Gotho fred in loc.
7 c. 29. est iis (sc. Ethnicis) tutius per Jovis genium pejerare quam regis.
8 Dio. lvii. 8. lviii. 2. 6. 12. lix. 3. 9. 11.

9 Dio. i. 5. Suet. Cal. 24. Claud. 11.
10 Dio. xlvii. 18. li. 20. Virg. Ecl. i. 7. Hor. Ep. ii. 1. 16. Ov. F. i. 13.
11 Tac. Ann. i. 11. 73. iv. 37. Suet. 52. Dio. lvi. 46.
12 Dio. li. 19. lix. 24. Tac. Ann. iv. 17. xvi.

22. Ov. F. ii. 637. Pont. ii. 3. ult. Hor. Od. iv. 5. 33.
13 i. 17. Xen. Cyr. viii. iii. p. 215. Ammian. xxiii. 6. Dio. li. 20. Tac. Ann. xiii. 8. Herodiam. i. 8. 8. i. 16. 9. i. 5.

Something similar seems to have been used by the magistrates of the municipal towns ;[1] a pan of burning coals, or a portable hearth,[2] in which incense was burned ; a perfumed stove.[3]

Dioclesian, introduced the custom of kneeling to the emperors.[4] Aurelius Victor says that the same thing was done to Caligula and Domitian.[5]

Augustus, at first, used the powers conferred on him with great moderation ; as indeed all the first emperors did in the beginning of their government.[6] In his lodging and equipage he differed little from an ordinary citizen of distinguished rank, except being attended by his prætorian guards. But after he had gained the soldiers by donatives, the people by a distribution of grain, and the whole body of citizens by the sweetness of repose, he gradually increased his authority,[7] and engrossed all the powers of the state.[8] Such of the nobility as were most compliant[9] were raised to wealth and preferments. Having the command of the army and treasury, he could do every thing. For although he pretended to separate his own revenues from those of the state, yet both were disposed of equally at his pleasure.[10]

The long reign and artful conduct of Augustus so habituated the Romans to subjection, that they never afterwards so much as made one general effort to regain their liberty, nor even to mitigate the rigour of tyranny ; in consequence of which, their character became more and more degenerate. After being deprived of the right of voting, they lost all concern about public affairs ; and were only anxious, says Juvenal, about two things, bread and games.[11] Hence, from this period their history is less interesting, and, as Dio observes, less authentic ; because, when every thing was done by the will of the prince, or of his favourites and freedmen, the springs of action were less known than under the republic.[12] It is surprising that, though the Romans at different times were governed by princes of the most excellent dispositions, and of the soundest judgment, who had seen the woful effects of wicked men being invested with unlimited power, yet none of them seem ever to have thought of new-modelling the government, and of providing an effectual check against the future commission of similar enormities. Whether they thought it impracticable, or wished to transmit to their successors, unimpaired, the same powers which they had received ; or from what other cause, we know not. It is at least certain that no history of any people shows more clearly the pernicious effects of an arbitrary and elective monarchy, on the character and happiness of both prince and people, than that of the ancient Romans. Their change of government was, indeed, the natural consequence of that success with which their lust of conquest was attended ; for the force employed to enslave other nations, being turned against themselves, served at first to accomplish and afterwards to perpetuate their own servitude. And it is remarkable, that the nobility of Rome, whose rapacity and corruption had so much contributed to the loss of liberty, were the principal sufferers by this change ; for on them those savage monsters who succeeded Augustus chiefly exercised their cruelty. The bulk of the people, and particularly

1 pruna batillus v. -um.
2 focus portabilis.
3 Hor. Sat. i. 5. 36.
4 adorari se jussit, cum ante eum cuncti salutarontur, Eutr. ix.
16.
5 Cæs. c. 39. Dio. lix.
4 27, 28.
6 Dio. lvii. 8. lix. 4.
7 insurgere paulatim.
8 munia senatus, magistratum, legum in se transferre, Tac. An. i. 2.
9 quanto quis servitio promptior.
10 Dio. liii. 16.
11 panem et Circenses, i. e. largesses and spectacles, Juv. x. 80.
12 Dio. liii. 19.

the provinces, were not more oppressed than they had been under the republic.[1]

PUBLIC SERVANTS OF THE MAGISTRATES.

THE public servants[2] of the magistrates were called by the common name of APPARITORES,[3] because they were at hand to execute their commands,[4] and their service or attendance APPARITIO.[5] These were,

I. SCRIBÆ, notaries or clerks who wrote out the public accounts, the laws, and all the proceedings[6] of the magistrates. Those who exercised that office were said *scriptum facere*,[7] from *scriptus, -ûs.*. They were denominated from the magistrates whom they attended ; thus, *scribæ quæstorii, ædilitii, prætorii*, &c., and were divided into different *decuriæ*.[8] It was determined by lot what magistrate each of them should attend. This office was more honourable among the Greeks than the Romans.[9] The *scribæ* at Rome, however, were generally composed of free-born citizens ; and they became so respectable that their order is called by Cicero *honestus*.[10]

There were also *actuarii* or *notarii*, who took down in short-hand what was said or done.[11] These were different from the *scribæ* and were commonly slaves or freedmen. The *scribæ* were also called *librarii*. But *librarii* is usually put for those who transcribe books, for which purpose, the wealthy Romans, who had a taste for literature, sometimes kept several slaves.[12]

The method of writing short-hand is said to have been invented by Mæcenas ; according to Isidore, by Tiro, the favourite slave and freedman of Cicero.[13]

II. PRÆCONES, heralds or public criers, who were employed for various purposes : —

1. In all public assemblies they ordered silence,[14] by saying, SILETE vel TACETE ; and in sacred rites by a solemn form, FAVETE LINGUIS, ORE FAVETE OMNES. Hence, SACRUM *silentium*, for *altissimum* or *maximum. Ore favent*, they are silent.[15]

2. In the Comitia they called the tribes and centuries to give their votes ; they pronounced the vote of each century ; they called out the names of those who were elected.[16] When laws were to be passed, they recited them to the people.[17] In trials, they summoned the *judices*, the persons accused, their accusers, and sometimes the witnesses.

Sometimes heralds were employed to summon the people to an assembly, and the senate to the senate-house ; also the soldiers, when encamped, to hear their general make a speech.[18]

1 thus Tacitus observes, Neque provinciæ illum rerum statum abnuebant, suspecto senatus populique imperio ob certamina potentium, et avaritiam magistratuum ; invalido legum auxilio,quæ vi, ambitu, postremo pecunia turbabantur, Ann. l. 2.— The provinces acquiesced under the new establishment, weary of the mixed authority of the senate and people ; a mode of government long distracted by

contentions among the great, and in the end rendered intolerable by the avarice of public magistrates ; while the laws afforded a feeble remedy, disturbed by violence, defeated by intrigue, and undermined by bribery and corruption.
2 ministri.
3 Liv. i. 8.
4 quod iis apparebant, i. e. præsto erant ad obsequium, Serv. Virg. Æn. xii. 850.
5 Cic. Fam. xiii. 54.

6 acta.
7 Liv. ix. 46. Gell. vi. 9.
8 whence decuriam emere, for munus scribæ emere, Cic. Verr. iii. 79.
9 Cic. Cat. iv. 7. Nep. Eum. l.
10 quod eorum fidei tabulæ publicæ, periculaque magistratuum committuntur, Cic. Verr. iii. 79.
11 notis excipiebant, Suet. Jul. 55.
12 Dio. iv. 7. Fest. Cic. Att. xii. 6. Suet. Dom. 10. Nep. Att. 13.

13 Isid. l. 22. Sen. Ep. 90. Dio. lv. 7.
14 silentium indicebant vel imperabant : exsurge, præco, fac populo audientiam, Plaut. Pœn. prol. 11.
15 Hor. Od. ii. 13. 29. iii. 1. Virg. Æn. v. 71. Ov. Am. iii. 13. 29.
16 Cic. Verr. v. 15. see p. 65.
17 see p. 63.
18 see p. 6. Liv. i. 26. 59. iii. 38. iv. 32.

3. In sales by auction, they advertised them ;[1] they stood by the spear, and called out what was offered.

4. In the public games, they invited the people to attend them ; they ordered slaves and other improper persons to be removed from them ;[2] they proclaimed[3] the victors and crowned them ;[4] they invited the people to see the secular games, which were celebrated only once every 110 years, by a solemn form, CONVENITE AD LUDOS SPECTANDOS, QUOS NEC SPECTAVIT QUISQUAM, NEC SPECTATURUS EST.[5]

5. In solemn funerals, at which games sometimes used to be exhibited,[6] they invited people to attend by a certain form; EXSEQUIAS CHREMETI, QUIBUS EST COMMODUM, IRE JAM TEMPUS EST, OLLUS EFFERTUR.[7] Hence these funerals were called FUNERA INDICTIVA. The *præcones* also used to give public notice when such a person died ; thus, OLLUS QUIRIS LETO DATUS EST.[8]

6. In the infliction of capital punishment, they sometimes signified the orders of the magistrate to the lictor ; LICTOR, VIRO *forti* ADDE VIRGAS ET IN EUM LEGE *primum* AGE.[9]

7. When things were lost or stolen, they searched for them.[10]

The office of a public crier, although not honourable, was profitable.[11] They were generally freeborn, and divided into *decuriæ*.

Similar to the *præcones* were those who collected the money bidden for goods at an auction from the purchaser, called COACTORES.[12] They were servants[13] of the money-brokers, who attended at the auctions : hence, *coactiones argentarias factitare*, to exercise the trade of such a collector.[14] They seem also to have been employed by bankers to procure payment from debtors of every kind. But the collectors of the public revenues were likewise called COACTORES.[15]

III. LICTORES. The lictors were instituted by Romulus, who borrowed them from the Etruscans. They are commonly supposed to have their name[16] from their binding the hands and legs of criminals before they were scourged.[17] They carried on their shoulder rods,[18] bound with a thong in the form of a bundle,[19] and an axe jutting out in the middle of them. They went before all the greater magistrates, except the censors, one by one in a line. He who went foremost was called PRIMUS LICTOR ; he who went last, or next to the magistrate, was called PROXIMUS LICTOR, or *postremus*,[20] i. e. the chief lictor, *summus lictor*, who used to receive and execute the commands of the magistrate.

The office of the lictors was,

1. To remove the crowd,[21] by saying, CEDITE, CONSUL VENIT : DATE VIAM vel LOCUM CONSULI ; SI VOBIS VIDETUR, DISCEDITE QUIRITES, or some such words,[22] whence the lictor is called *summotor aditus*. This sometimes occasioned a good deal of noise and bustle.[23] When the magistrate

---

1 auctionem conclamabant vel prædicabant, Plaut. Men. Cic. Verr. iii. 16. Off. iii. 13. Hor. A. P. 419. see p. 40.

2 Cic. Resp. Har. 12. Liv. ii. 37.

3 prædicabant.

4 Cic. Fam. v. 12.

5 Come and be spectators of games which no one has seen, nor will see again, Suet. Claud. 21. Hero dian. iii. 8.

6 Cic. Legg. ii. 24.

7 Whoever has a mind to attend the funeral of Chremes, now is the time ; he is brought out for burial, Ter. Phorm. v. 8. 38.

8 Fest. Quir. Suet. Jul. 84.

9 Lictor, apply the rods to this man of valour, and on him first execute the law, Liv. xxvi. 15, 16.

10 Plaut. Merc. iii. 4. v. 78. Petron. Arb. c. 57. where an allusion is

supposed to be made to the custom abolished by the Æbutian law.

11 Juv. vii. 6, &c.

12 Hor. Sat. i. 6. 86. Cin. Clu. 64.

13 ministri.

14 Suet. Vesp. 1.

15 Cic. Rab. Post. 11.

16 a ligando, Liv. i. 8.

17 Gell. xii. 3.

18 virgas ulmeas, Plaut. As. ii. 2. v. 74. iii. 2. v. 29. viminei fasces virgarum, Ep. i. 1. 26. vel ex betula, Plin. xvi. 18.

s. 30.

19 bacillos loro colligatos in modum fascis.

20 Liv. xxiv. 44. Cic. Frat. i. 1. 7. Div. i. 26. Sall. Jug. 12.

21 ut turbam summoverent, Liv. iii. 11. 48. viii. 33. Hor. Od. ii. 16. 10.

22 solennis ille lictorum et prænuncius clamor, Plin. Pan. 61. Liv. ii. 56.

23 Liv. xlv. 29. passim.

returned home, a lictor knocked at the door with his rod,[1] which he also did when the magistrate went to any other house.[2]

2. To see that proper respect was paid to the magistrates.[3] What this respect was, Seneca informs us, namely, dismounting from horseback, uncovering the head, going out of the way, and also rising up to them.[4]

3. To inflict punishment on those who were condemned, which they were ordered to do in various forms : I, LICTOR, COLLIGA MANUS ; I, CAPUT OBNUBE HUJUS ; ARBORI INFELICI SUSPENDE ; VERBERATO VEL INTRA POMŒRIUM *vel extra* POMŒRIUM ; I, LICTOR, DELIGA AD PALUM ; ACCEDE, LICTOR, VIRGAS ET SECURES EXPEDI ; IN EUM LEGE AGE, i. e. *securi percute*, vel *feri*.[5]

The lictors were usually taken from the lowest of the common people, and often were the freedmen of him on whom they attended. They were different from the public slaves, who waited on the magistrates.[6]

IV. ACCENSI. These seem to have had their name from summoning[7] the people to an assembly, and those who had lawsuits to court.[8] One of them attended on the consul who had not the fasces.[9] Before the invention of clocks, one of them called out to the prætor in court when it was the third hour, or nine o clock, before noon ; when it was mid-day, and the ninth hour, or three o'clock afternoon.[10] They were commonly the freedmen of the magistrate on whom they attended ; at least in ancient times.[11] The *accensi* were also an order of soldiers, called *supernumerarii*, because not included in the legion.[12]

V. VIATORES. These were properly the officers who attended on the tribunes and ædiles.[13] Anciently they used to summon the senators from the country where they usually resided ; whence they had their name.[14]

VI. CARNIFEX. The public executioner or hangman, who executed[15] slaves, and persons of the lowest rank ; for slaves and freedmen were punished in a manner different from freeborn citizens.[16] The *carnifex* was of servile condition, and held in such contempt that he was not permitted to reside within the city, but lived without the *Porta Metia*, or *Esquilina*,[17] near the place destined for the punishment of slaves,[18] called *Sestertium*, where were erected crosses and gibbets,[19] and where also the bodies of slaves were burnt, or thrown out unburied.[20]

Some think that the *carnifex* was anciently keeper of the prison under the *triumviri capitales*, who had only the superintendence or care of it : hence *tradere* vel *trahere ad carnificem*, to imprison.[21]

LAWS OF THE ROMANS.

THE laws of any country are rules established by public authority, and enforced by sanctions, to direct the conduct and secure the rights of its inhabitants.[22]

---

1 forem, uti mos est, virga percussit, Liv. vi. 34.
2 Plin. vii. 30. s. 31.
3 animadvertere ut debitus honos iis redderetur, Suet. Jul. 80.
4 Sen. Ep. 64. Suet. Jul. 78.
5 Go, lictor, bind his arms ; cover his head ; hang him upon the gallows ; scourge him without (or within;the

Pomœrium. Go, lictor, bind him to the stake. Lictor, draw near, get ready the rods and axes. Treat him according to law,—Liv. i. 26. viii. 7. 32. xxvi. 16.
6 Liv. ii. 55. Cic. Verr. i. 26.
7 ab acciendo.
8 in jus.
9 Suet. Jul. 20. Liv. iii. 33.

10 Varr. L. L. v. 9. Plin. vii. 60.
11 Cic. Frat. i. 1. 4
12 Veg. ii. 19. Asc. Cic. Verr. i. 28. Liv. viii. 8.
10.
13 Liv. ii. 56. xxx. 39.
14 quod sæpe in via essent, Cic. Sen. 16. Columell. Præf. 1.
15 supplicio afficiebat.
16 Tac. Ann. iii. 50.
17 Cic. Rab. 5. Plaut. Pseud. i. 3. v. 98.

18 juxta locum servilibus pœnis sepositum, Tac. Ann. xv. 60. ii. 32. Plut. Galb.
19 cruces et patibula, Tac. Ann. xiv. 33.
20 Plaut. Cas. ii. 6. v. 2. Hor. Ep. v. 99.
21 Plaut. Rud. iii.6.v.19.
22 lex justi injustique regula, Sen. Ben. iv. 12. leges quid aliud sunt quam minis mixta præcepta ? Ep. 94.

The laws of Rome were ordained by the people, upon the application
of a magistrate.[1]

The great foundation of Roman law or jurisprudence[2] was that collection of laws called the law, or laws of the Twelve Tables, compiled by the
decemviri, and ratified by the people ;[3] a work, in the opinion of Cicero,
superior to all the libraries of philosophers.[4] Nothing now remains of
these laws, but scattered fragments.

The unsettled state of the Roman government, the extension of the empire, the increase of riches, and consequently of the number of crimes,
with various other circumstances, gave occasion to a great many new
laws.[5]

At first those ordinances only obtained the name of laws, which were
made by the Comitia Centuriata,[6] but afterwards those also which were
made by the Comitia Tributa,[7] when they were made binding on the whole
Roman people ; first by the Horatian law,[8] and afterwards more precisely
by the Publilian and Hortensian laws.[9]

The different laws are distinguished by the name[10] of the persons who
proposed them, and by the subject to which they refer.

Any order of the people was called LEX, whether it respected the public,[11] the right of private persons,[12] or the particular interest of an individual. But this last was properly called PRIVILEGIUM.[13]

The laws proposed by a consul were called CONSULARES, by a tribune,
TRIBUNITIÆ, by the decemviri, DECEMVIRALES.[14]

SIGNIFICATIONS OF JUS AND LEX, AND DIFFERENT SPECIES OF THE ROMAN LAW.

THE words *Jus* and *Lex* are used in various senses. They are both
expressed by the English word LAW.

Jus properly implies what is just and right in itself, or what from any
cause is binding upon us.[15] *Lex* is a written statute or ordinance.[16] *Jus*
is properly what the law ordains, or the obligation which it imposes ;[17] or,
according to the Twelve Tables, QUODCUNQUE POPULUS JUSSIT, ID JUS
ESTO, QUOD MAJOR PARS JUDICARIT, ID JUS RATUMQUE ESTO.[18] But *jus*
and *lex* have a different meaning, according to the words with which they
are joined : thus, *Jus* NATURÆ vel NATURALE, is what nature or right reason teaches to be right ; and *jus* GENTIUM, what all nations esteemed to
be right : both commonly reckoned the same.[19] *Jus civium* vel CIVILE, is
what the inhabitants of a particular country esteem to be right, either by
nature, custom, or statute.[20] When no word is added to restrict it, JUS

1 rogante magistratu,
see p. 61,63.
2 Romani juris, Liv.
xxxiv. 6.
3 see p. 108.
4 omnibus omnium phi-
losophorum bibliothe-
cis anteponendum, Or.
i. 44.
5 corruptissima republi-
ca plurimæ leges, Tac.
Ann. iii. 27.
6 populiscita, Tac. An.
iii. 58.
7 plebiscita.
8 ut quod tributim ple-
bes jussisset, populum
teneret,—that whatev-
er was ordered by the

commons collectively,
should bind the whole
people, Liv. iii. 55.
9 ut plebiscita omnes
Quirites tenerent,-that
the orders of the com-
mons should bind all
the Romans, Liv. viii.
12. Epit. xi. Plin. xvi.
10. s. 15. Gell. xv. 27.
10 nomen gentis.
11 jus publicum vel sa-
crum.
12 jus privatum vel ci-
vile.
13 Gell. x. 20. Asc. Cic.
Mil.
14 Cic. Sext. 64. Rull.
ii. 8. Liv. iii. 55—57.

15 Cic. Off. iii. 21.
16 lex, quæ scripto san-
cit, quod vult, aut ju-
bendo, aut vetando,
Cic. Legg. i. 6. a le-
gendo, quod legi solet,
ut innotescat, Varr. L.
L. v. 7. legere leges
propositas jussere,Liv.
iii. 34. vel a delectu,
Cic. Legg. i. 6. a justo
et jure legendo, i. e.
eligendo, from the
choice of what is just
and right, ii. 5. lex,
justorum injustorum-
que distinctio, ibid.
Græco nomine appel-
lata νομος, a suum cui-

que tribuendo. i. 6.
17 est enim jus quod
lex constituit, that is
law, or, that is binding
which the law ordains,
Cic. Legg. i. 15. Her. ii.
13.
18 Liv. vii. 17. ix. 33.
Cic.
19 Cic. Sext. 42. Har.
resp. 14.
20 Cic. Top. 5. Off. iii.
16, 17. Or. i. 48. hence
constituere jus, quo
omnes utantur, Dom.
cui subjecti sint, Cæc.
so jus Romanum, An-
glicum, &c.

CIVILE is put for the civil law of the Romans.   Cicero sometimes opposes *jus civile* to *jus naturale*, and sometimes to what we call criminal law.[1] *Jus* COMMUNE, what is held to be right among men in general, or among the inhabitants of any country.[2]   *Jus* PUBLICUM et PRIVATUM, what is right with respect to the people,[3] or the public at large, and with respect to individuals ; political and civil law.[4]   But *jus publicum* is also put for the right which the citizens in common enjoyed.[5]   *Jus* SENATORIUM,[6] what related to the rights and customs of the senate ; what was the power of those who might make a motion in the senate ;[7] what the privilege of those who delivered their opinion :[8] what the power of the magistrates, and the rights of the rest of the members, &c.[9]   *Jus* DIVINUM *et* HUMANUM, what is right with respect to things divine and human.[10]   *Jus* PRÆTORIUM, what the edicts of the prætor ordained to be right.[11]   *Jus* HONORARIUM.[12] *Jus* FLAVIANUM, ÆLIANUM, &c., the books of law composed by Flavius, Ælius, &c.   URBANUM, i. e. CIVILE *privatum, ex quo jus dicit prætor urbanus.*[13]   *Jus* PRÆDIATORIUM, the law observed with respect to the goods[14] of those who were sureties[15] for the farmers of the public revenues, or undertakers of the public works,[16] which were pledged to the public,[17] and sold, if the farmer or undertaker did not perform his bargain.[18]   Hence PRÆDIATOR, a person who laid out his money in purchasing these goods, and who, of course, was well acquainted with what was right or wrong in such matters.[19]   *Jus* FECIALE, the law of arms or heraldry, or the form of proclaiming war.[20]   *Jus* LEGITIMUM, the common or ordinary law, the same with *jus civile*, but *jus legitimum exigere,* to demand one's legal right, or what is legally due.[21]   *Jus* CONSUETUDINIS, what long use hath established, opposed to LEGE *jus* or *jus scriptum,* statute or written law.[22]   *Jus* PONTIFICIUM vel SACRUM, what is right with regard to religion and sacred things, much the same with what was afterwards called ecclesiastical law.[23]   So JUS *religionis, augurum, cæremoniarum, auspiciorum,* &c.   *Jus* BELLICUM vel BELLI, what may be justly done to a state at war with us, and to the conquered.[24] JURIS *disciplina,* the knowledge of law.[25]   STUDIOSI *juris,* i. e. *jurisprudentiæ,* students in law.   *Consulti, periti,* &c., lawyers.[26]   JURE et *legibus,* by common and statute law.   So Horace, *vir bonus est quis ?   Qui consulta patrum, qui leges, juraque servat,* &c.   Jura *dabat legesque viris.*[27] But JURA is often put for laws in general ; thus, *nova jura condere.*   JURA *inventa metu injusti fateare necesse est, civica jura respondere.*[28]   JUS and ÆQUITAS are distinguished, *jus* and *justitia ; jus civile* and *leges.*   So *æquum et bonum* is opposed to *callidum versutumque jus,* an artful interpretation of

---

1 jus publicum, Cic.
Sext. 42. Verr. i. 42.
Cæcin. 2. Cæcil. 5.
2 Cic. Cæc. 4. Dig. Inst.
3 quasi jus populicum.
4 Liv. iii. 34. Cic. Fam.
iv. 14. Plin. Ep. i. 22.
5 jus commune, Ter.
Phor. ii. 2. 65.
6 pars juris publici.
7 quæ potestas referentibus, see p. 8, 9.
8 quid censentibus jus.
9 Plin. Ep. viii. 14.
10 Liv. i. 18. xxxix. 16.
Tac. Ann. iii. 26. 70.
vi. 26. hence, fas et jura sinunt, laws divine and human, Virg. G. i.
269. contra jus fasque,
Sall. Cat. 15. jus fasque exuero, Tac. Hist.

iii. 5. omne jus et fas delere, Cic. quo jure,
quave injuria, right or wrong, Ter. A. i. 3. 9.
per fas et nefas, Liv.
vi. 14. jus et injuriæ,
Sall. Jug. 16 jure fieri,
jure cæsus, Suet. Jul.
76.
11 Cic. Off. i. 10. Verr.
i. 44.
12 see p. 85.
13 Liv. ix. 46. Cic. Verr.
Act. i. 1.
14 prædia vel prædia bona, Asc. Cic.
15 prædes.
16 mancipes.
17 publico obligata vel pignori opposita.
18 Cic. Balb. 20. Verr.
i. 54. Fam. v. 20. Suet.

Claud. 9.
19 juris prædiatorii peritus, Cic. Balb. 20. Att.
xii. 14. 17.
20 Cic. Off. i. 11. Liv. i.
32.
21 Cic. Dom. 13, 14.
Fam. viii. 6.
22 Cic. Inv. °ii. 22. 54.
jus civile constat aut ex scripto aut sine scripto, 1. 6. D. Just.
Jur.
23 Cic. Dom. 12—14.
Legg. ii. 18, &c. Liv.
i. 20.
24 Cæs. Bell. G. i. 27.
Cic. Off. i. 11. iii. 29.
Liv. i. 1. v. 27. hence,
leges silent inter arma,
laws are silent amidst arms, Cic. Mil. 4. ferro

jus in armis, Liv. v. 3.
facere jus ense, Luc.
iii. 821. viii. 642. ix.
1073. jusque datum sceleri, a successful usurpation, by which impunity and a sanction were given to crimes, i. 2.
25 Cic. Legg. i. 5. intelligentia, Phil. ix. 5.
interpretatio, Off. i. 11.
26 Suet Ner. 32. Gell.
xii. 13. Cic.
27 Cic. Ver. i. 42. 44.
Hor. Ep. i. 16. 40. Virg.
Æn. i. 509.
28 Liv. iii. 33. Hor. Sat.
I. iii. 111. Art. P. 122.
398. Ep. 1. 3. 23.

a written law. *Summum jus*, the rigour of the law, *summa injuria*.[1] *Summo jure agere, contendere, experiri*, &c., to try the utmost stretch of law. Jus vel JURA *Quiritium, civium,* &c.[2] JURA *sanguinis, cognationis,* &c., *necessitudo*, v. *jus necessitudinis*, relationship.[3] Jus *regni*, a right to the crown; *honorum*, to preferments ; *quibus per fraudem jus fuit*, power or authority ; *jus luxuriæ publicæ datum est*, a licence ; *quibus fallere ac furari jus erat; in jus et ditionem* vel *potestatem alicujus venire, concedere* ; *habere jus in aliquem* ; *sui juris esse ac mancipii*, i. e. *sui arbitrii et nemini parere*, to be one's own master ; *in controverso jure est*, it is a point of law not fixed or determined.[4] Jus *dicere* vel *reddere*, to administer justice. *Dare jus gratiæ*, to sacrifice justice to interest.[5] Jus is also put for the place where justice is administered ; thus, IN JUS EAMUS, i. e. *ad prætoris sellam* ; *in jure*, i. e. *apud prætorem*, in court ; *de jure currere*, from court.[6]

LEX is often taken in the same general sense with JUS : thus, *Lex est recta ratio imperandi, atque prohibendi, a numine deorum tracta ; justorum injustorumque distinctio ; æternum quiddam, quod universum mundum regit ; consensio omnium gentium lex naturæ putanda est ; non scripta sed nata lex : salus populi suprema lex esto ; fundamentum libertatis, fons æquitatis,* &c.[7]

LEGES is put, not only for the ordinances of the Roman people, but for any established regulations ; thus, of the free towns, LEGES MUNICIPALES, of the allied towns, of the provinces.[8]

When LEX is put absolutely, the law of the Twelve Tables is meant ; as, LEGE *hæreditas ad gentem Minuciam veniebat, ea ad hos redibat* LEGE *hæreditas*,[9] that estate by law fell to them.

LEGES CENSORIÆ, form of leases or regulations made by the censors ; LEX *mancipii* vel *mancipium*, the form and condition of conveying property.[10]

LEGES *venditionis* vel *venalium vendendorum, agrum,* vel *domum possidendi,* &c., rules or conditions.[11]

LEGES *historiæ, poematum, versuum,* &c., rules observed in writing.[12] Thus we say, the laws of history, of poetry, versifying, &c., and, in a similar sense, the laws of motion, magnetism, mechanics, &c.

In the Corpus Juris, LEX is put for the Christian religion ; thus, LEX *Christiana, catholica, venerabilis, sanctissima,* &c. But we in a similar sense use the word *law* for the Jewish religion ; as the *law* and the *gospel :* or for the books of Moses ; as, the *law* and the *prophets.*

JUS ROMANUM, or *Roman law*, was either written or unwritten law.[13] The several species which constituted the *jus scriptum*, were, laws, properly so called, the decrees of the senate, the edicts or decisions of magistrates, and the opinions or writings of lawyers. Unwritten law[14] comprehended natural equity and custom. Anciently *jus scriptum* only comprehended laws properly so called.[15] All these are frequently enumerated or alluded to by Cicero, who calls them FONTES ÆQUITATIS.[16]

1 Cic. Off. i. 10. iii. 16. Virg. ii. 426. Phil. ix. 5. Cæc. 23.
2 see p. 32, &c.
3 Suet. Cal. 16.
4 Liv. i. 49 iii. 55. Tac. xiv. 5. Sall. Jug. 3. Sen. Ep. 16. Suet. Ner. 16. Cic.
5 Liv.
6 Don. Ter. Phor. v. 7. 43. 66. Plaut. Rud. iii.

6. 68. Men. iv. 2. 19. Cic. Quin. 25.
7 Cic. Legg. Clu. 53.
8 Cic. Fam. vi. 18. Ver. ii. 13. 49, 50.
9 Cic. Verr. i. 45. Ter. Hecy. i. 2. 97.
10 Cic. Verr. i. 55. Ill. 7. Prov. Cons. 5. Rab. Perd. 3. Ad. Q. Fr. i. 12 Or. i. 39. Off. ill. 16.

11 Cic. Or. i. 58. Hor. Ep. ii. 2. v. 18. hence, emere, vendere hac vel illa lege, i. e. sub hac conditione vel pacto, Suet. Aug. 21. ea lege i. e. ex pacto et conventu, exierat, Cic. At. vi. 3. hac lege atque omine, Ter. A. i. 2. 29. Hes. v. 5. 10. lex vitæ qua nati sumus, Cic.

Tus. 16. mea lege utar, I will observe my rule, Ter. Phor. iii. 2. ult.
12 Cic. Legg. i. 1. Or. iii. 49.
13 jus scriptum aut non scriptum.
14 jus non scriptum.
15 Dig. Orig. Jur.
16 Top. 5, &c. Her. iii. 13.

LAWS OF THE DECEMVIRI, OR, THE XII. TABLES.

VARIOUS authors have endeavoured to collect and arrange the fragments of the Twelve Tables. Of these the most eminent is Godfrey.[1]

According to his account,

The I. table is supposed to have treated of lawsuits; the II. of thefts and robberies; III. of loans, and the right of creditors over their debtors; IV. of the right of fathers of families; V. of inheritances and guardianships; VI. of property and possession; VII. of trespasses and damages; VIII. of estates in the country; IX. of the common rights of the people; X. of funerals, and all ceremonies relating to the dead; XI. of the worship of the gods, and of religion; XII. of marriages, and the right of husbands.

Several ancient lawyers are said to have commented on these laws,[2] but their works are lost.

The fragments of the Twelve Tables have been collected from various authors, many of them from Cicero. The laws are, in general, very briefly expressed: thus,

SI IN JUS VOCET, ATQUE (i. e. *statim*) EAT.

SI MEMBRUM RUPSIT (*ruperit*), NI CUM EO PACIT (*paciscetur*), TALIO ESTO.

SI FALSUM TESTIMONIUM DICASSIT (*dixerit*) SAXO DEJICITOR.

PRIVILEGIA NE IRROGANTO; sc. *magistratus.*

DE CAPITE (*de vita, libertate, et jure*) CIVIS ROMANI, NISI PER MAXIMUM CENTURIATUM (*per comitia centuriata*) NE FERUNTO.

QUOD POSTREMUM POPULUS JUSSIT, ID JUS RATUM ESTO.

HOMINEM MORTUUM IN URBE NE SEPELITO, NEVE URITO.

AD DIVOS ADEUNTO CASTE: PIETATEM ADHIBENTO, OPES AMOVENTO. QUI SECUS FACIT, DEUS IPSE VINDEX ERIT.

FERIIS JURGIA AMOVENTO. EX PATRIIS RITIBUS OPTIMA COLUNTO.

PERJURII POENA DIVINA, EXITIUM; HUMANA, DEDECUS.

IMPIUS NE AUDETO PLACARE DONIS IRAM DEORUM.

NEQUIS AGRUM CONSECRATO, AURI, ARGENTI, EBORIS SACRANDI MODUS ESTO.

The most important particulars in the fragments of the Twelve Tables come naturally to be mentioned and explained elsewhere in various places.

After the publication of the Twelve Tables, every one understood what was his right, but did not know the way to obtain it. For this they depended on the assistance of their patrons.

From the Twelve Tables were composed certain rites and forms, which were necessary to be observed in prosecuting lawsuits,[3] called ACTIONES LEGIS. The forms used in making bargains, in transferring property, &c., were called ACTUS LEGITIMI.—There were also certain days on which a lawsuit could be raised,[4] or justice could be lawfully administered,[5] and others on which that could not be done;[6] and some on which it could be done for one part of the day, and not for another.[7] The knowledge of all these things was confined to the patricians, and chiefly to the pontifices, for many years; till one Cn. Flavius, the son of a freedman, the scribe or clerk of Appius Claudius Cæcus, a lawyer who had arranged in writing

1 Jacobus Gothofredus.
2 Cic. Legg. ii. 23. Plin.
xiv. 13.
3 quibus inter se homines disceptarent.
4 quando lege agi posset.
5 dies fasti.
6 nefasti.
7 intercisi.

these *actiones* and days, stole or copied the book which Appius had composed, and published it, A. U. 440.[1] In return for which favour he was made curule ædile by the people, and afterwards prætor. From him the book was called JUS CIVILE FLAVIANUM.[2]

The patricians, vexed at this, contrived new forms of process ; and, to prevent their being made public, expressed them in writing by certain secret marks,[3] somewhat like what are now used in writing short-hand, or, as others think, by putting one letter for another, as Augustus did,[4] or one letter for a whole word, (*per* SIGLAS, as it is called by later writers.) However, these forms also were published by Sextus Ælius Catus, who for his knowledge in the civil law, is called by Ennius *egregie cordatus homo*, a remarkably wise man.[5] His book was named JUS ÆLIANUM.

The only thing now left to the patricians was the interpretation of the law ; which was long peculiar to that order, and the means of raising several of them to the highest honours of the state.

The origin of lawyers at Rome was derived from the institution of patronage.[6] It was one of the offices of a patron to explain the law to his clients, and manage their lawsuits.

TITUS CORUNCANIUS, who was the first plebeian pontifex maximus, A. U. 500, is said to have been the first who gave his advice freely to all the citizens without distinction,[7] whom many afterwards imitated ; as Manilius, Crassus, Mucius Scævola, C. Aquilius, Gallus, Trebatius, Sulpicius, &c.

Those who professed to give advice to all promiscuously, used to walk across the forum,[8] and were applied to[9] there, or at their own houses. Such as were celebrated for their knowledge in law, often had their doors beset with clients before day-break,[10] for their gate was open to all,[11] and the house of an eminent lawyer was, as it were, the oracle of the whole city. Hence Cicero calls their power REGNUM JUDICIALE.[12]

The lawyer gave his answers from an elevated seat.[13] The client, coming up to him, said, LICET CONSULERE ?[14] The lawyer answered, CONSULE. Then the matter was proposed, and an answer returned very shortly ; thus, QUÆRO AN EXISTIMES ? vel, ID JUS EST NECNE ?—SECUNDUM EA, QUÆ PROPONUNTUR, EXISTIMO, PLACET, PUTO. Lawyers gave their opinions either by word of mouth or in writing ; commonly without any reason annexed,[15] but not always.

Sometimes, in difficult cases, the lawyers used to meet near the temple of Apollo in the forum,[16] and, after deliberating together (which was called DISPUTATIO FORI), they pronounced a joint opinion. Hence, what was determined by the lawyers, and adopted by custom, was called RECEPTA SENTENTIA, RECEPTUM JUS, RECEPTUS MOS, POST MULTAS VARIATIONES RECEPTUM ; and the rules observed in legal transactions by their consent, were called REGULÆ JURIS.

When the laws or edicts of the prætor seemed defective, the lawyers supplied what was wanting in both from natural equity ; and their opinions in process of time obtained the authority of laws. Hence lawyers were called not only *interpretes*, but also CONDITORES et AUCTORES JURIS, and their opinions JUS CIVILE, opposed to *leges*.[17]

1 fastos publicavit, et actiones primum edidit.
2 Liv. ix. 46. Cic. Or. i. 41. Mur. 11. Att. vi. 1. 1. 2. s. 7. D. Orig. Jur. Gell. vi. 9. Val. Max. li. 5. 2. Plin. xxxii.
1. s. 6.
3 notis, Cic. Mur. 11.
4 Suet. Aug. 88.
5 Cic. Or. i. 45.
6 see p. 20.
7 Liv. Epit. 18. l. 2, s.
35. 38. D. Orig. Jur.
8 transverso foro.
9 ad eos adibatur.
10 Cic. Or. iii 33. Hor. Sat. i. 1. v. 9. Ep. ii. 1. 104.
11 cunctis janua patebat, Tibul. i. 4. 78.
12 Cic.Or. i. 45. Att. i. 1.
13 ex solio, tanquam ex
tripode, Cic. Legg. i. 3. Or. ii. 33. iii. 33.
14 Cic. Mur. 13.
15 Hor. Sat. ii. 3. 192. Sen. Ep. 94.
16 Juv. 1. 128.
17 Dig. Cic. Cæc. 24. 25. Off. iii. 16.

Cicero complains that many excellent institutions had been perverted by the refinements of lawyers.[1]

Under the republic, any one that pleased might profess to give advice about matters of law ; but at first this was only done by persons of the highest rank, and such as were distinguished by their superior knowledge and wisdom. By the Cincian law, lawyers were prohibited from taking fees or presents from those who consulted them,[2] which rendered the profession of jurisprudence highly respectable, as being undertaken by men of rank and learning, not from the love of gain, but from a desire of assisting their fellow-citizens, and through their favour of rising to preferments. Augustus enforced this law by ordaining that those who transgressed it should restore fourfold.[3]

Under the emperors, lawyers were permitted to take fees[4] from their clients, but not above a certain sum,[5] and after the business was done.[6] Thus the ancient connection between patrons and clients fell into disuse, and every thing was done for hire. Persons of the lowest rank sometimes assumed the profession of lawyers,[7] pleadings became venal,[8] advocates made a shameful trade of their function by fomenting lawsuits,[9] and, instead of honour, which was formerly their only reward, lived upon the spoils of their fellow-citizens, from whom they received large and annual salaries. Various edicts[10] were published by the emperors to check this corruption, also decrees of the senate,[11] but these were artfully eluded.

Lawyers were consulted, not only by private persons, but also[12] by magistrates and judges,[13] and a certain number of them attended every proconsul and propraetor to his province.

Augustus granted the liberty of answering in questions of law only to particular persons, and restricted the judges not to deviate from their opinion, that thus he might bend the laws, and make them subservient to despotism. His successors (except Caligula) imitated this example ; till Adrian restored to lawyers their former liberty,[14] which they are supposed to have retained to the time of Severus. What alterations after that took place, is not sufficiently ascertained.

Of the lawyers who flourished under the emperors, the most remarkable were M. ANTISTIUS LABEO,[15] and C. ATEIUS CAPITO,[16] under Augustus ; and these two, from their different characters and opinions, gave rise to various sects of lawyers after them ; CASSIUS, under Claudius ;[17] SALVIUS JULIANUS, under Hadrian ; POMPONIUS, under Julian ; CAIUS, under the Antonines ; PAPINIANUS, under Severus ; ULPIANUS and PAULUS, under Alexander and Severus ; HERMOGENES, under Constantine, &c.

Under the republic, young men who intended to devote themselves to the study of jurisprudence, after finishing the usual studies of grammar, Grecian literature, and philosophy,[18] usually attached themselves to some

---

1 Mur. 12.
2 hence, turpe reos empta miseros defendere lingua, Ov. Am. i. 10. 39.
3 Dio. liv. 18.
4 honorarium, certam justamque mercedem, Suet. Ner. 17.
5 capiendis pecuniis ponunt modum (sc. Claudius) usque ad dena sestertia, Tac. Ann. xi. 7.—He (Claudius) took a middle course, and

fixed the legal perquisite at the sum of 10,000 sestercos.
6 peractis negotiis permittebat pecunias duntaxat decem millium dare,—After the cause is decided, they are permitted to accept a gratuity of 10,000 sesterces, Plin. Ep. v. 21.
7 Juv. viii. 47.
8 venire advocationes.
9 in lites coire.
10 edicta, libri, vel li-

belli.
11 Plin. Ep. v. 14. 21.
12 in concilium adhibebantur, vel assumebantur.
13 Cic. Top. 17. Mur. 13. Caec. 24. Gell. xiii. 13. Plin. Ep. iv. 22. vi. 11.
14 l. 2. s. ult. D. Orig. Jur. Suet. 34.
15 incorruptae libertatis vir,—a strenuous asserter of civil liberty, Tac. Ann. iii. 75. Gell. xiii. 12.

16 cujus obsequium dominantibus magis probabatur,—a man whose flexibility gained him greater credit with those who bore rule, ibid.
17 Cassianae scholae princeps,—the founder of the Cassian school, Plin. Ep. vii. 24.
18 Cic. Brut. 80. Off. i. 1. Suet. Clar. Rhet. l. 2. studia liberalia v. humanitatis, Plut. Luc. princ.

eminent lawyer, as Cicero did to Q. Mucius Scævola,[1] whom they always attended, that they might derive knowledge from his experience and conversation.   For these illustrious men did not open schools for teaching law, as the lawyers afterwards did under the emperors, whose scholars were called AUDITORES.[2]

The writings of several of these lawyers came to be as much respected in courts of justice[3] as the laws themselves.[4]   But this happened only by tacit consent.   Those laws only had a binding force, which were solemnly enacted by the whole Roman people assembled in the Comitia. Of these, the following are the chief :—

LAWS MADE AT DIFFERENT TIMES.

LEX ACILIA, 1. About transplanting colonies,[5] by the tribune C. Acilius, A. U. 556.[6]

2. About extortion,[7] by Manius Acilius Glabrio, a tribune (some say consul), A. U. 683.   That in trials for this crime, sentence should be passed, after the cause was once pleaded,[8] and that there should not be a second hearing.[9]

Lex ÆBUTIA, by the tribune Æbutius, prohibiting the proposer of a law concerning any charge or power, from conferring that charge or power on himself, his colleagues, or relations.[10]

Another concerning the judices, called centumviri, which is said to have diminished the obligation of the Twelve Tables, and to have abolished various customs which they ordained,[11] especially that curious custom, borrowed from the Athenians,[12]of searching for stolen goods without any clothes on but a girdle round the waist, and a mask on the face.[13]   When the goods were found, it was called FURTUM CONCEPTUM.[14]

Lex ÆLIA et FUSIA de comitiis,—two separate laws, although sometimes joined by Cicero.—The first by Q. Ælius Pætus, consul, A. U. 586, ordained that when the Comitia were held for passing laws, the magistrates, or the augurs by their authority, might take observations from the heavens ;[15] and, if the omens were unfavourable, the magistrate might prevent or dissolve the assembly,[16] and that magistrates of equal authority with the person who held the assembly, or a tribune, might give their negative to any law.[17]—The second, Lex FUSIA, or FUFIA, by P. Furius, consul, A. U. 617, or by one Fusius, or Fufius, a tribune, That it should not be lawful to enact laws on all the dies fasti.[18]

Lex ÆLIA SENTIA, by the consuls Ælius and Sentius, A. U. 756, about the manumission of slaves, and the condition of those who were made free.[19]

Lex ÆMILIA, about the censors.[20]

Lex ÆMILIA sumptuaria vel cibaria, by M. Æmilius Lepidus, consul, A. U. 675, limiting the kind and quantity of meats to be used at an entertainment.[21]   Pliny ascribes this law to Marcus Scaurus.[22]

---

1 Cic. Am. 1.
2 Sen. Contr. 25.
3 usu fori.
4 l. 2. s. 28. D. Orig. Jur.
5 de coloniis deducendis.
6 Liv. xxxiii. 29.
7 de repetundis.

8 semel dicta causa.
9 ne reus comperendinaretur. Cic. proœm. Verr. 17. i. 9. Asc. Cic.
10 Cic. Rul. ii. 8.
11 Gell. ix. 18. xvi. 10.
12 Aristoph. Nub. v.
496. Plat. Legg. xii.
13 furtorum   quæstio

cum lance et licio, Gel. ibid. Festus in lance.
14 Inst. ii. 10. 3.
15 de cœlo servarent.
16 comitiis obnunciaret.
17 legi   intercederent, Cic. Sext. 15. 53. post red. Sen. 5. Prov. Con. 19. Vat. 9. Pis. 4. Att.

ii. 9.
18 Cic. ib. see p. 62.
19 Suet. Aug. 40. see p. 29.
20 see p. 88.
21 Macrob. Sat. ii. 13. Gell. ii. 24.
22 viii. 57. Aur. Vict. Vir. illustr. 72.

Leges AGRARIÆ ; *Cassia, Licinia, Flaminia, Sempronia, Thoria, Cornelia, Servilia, Flavia, Julia, Mamilia.*

Leges de AMBITU ; *Fabia, Calpurnia, Tullia, Aufidia, Licinia, Pompeia.*

Leges ANNALES vel *Annariæ.*[1]

Lex ANTIA *sumptuaria,* by Antius Restio, the year uncertain ; limiting the expense of entertainments, and ordaining that no actual magistrate, or magistrate elect, should go any where to sup but with particular persons. Antius, seeing his wholesome regulations insufficient to check the luxury of the times, never after supped abroad, that he might not witness the violation of his own law.[2]

Leges ANTONIÆ, proposed by Antony after the death of Cæsar, about abolishing the office of dictator, confirming the acts of Cæsar,[3] planting colonies, giving away kingdoms and provinces, granting leagues and immunities, admitting officers in the army among jurymen ; allowing those condemned for violence and crimes against the state to appeal to the people, which Cicero calls the destruction of all laws, &c. ; transferring the right of choosing priests from the people to the different colleges.[4]

Leges APPULEIÆ, proposed by L. Appuleius Saturninus, A. U. 652, tribune of the commons ; about dividing the public lands among the veteran soldiers ; settling colonies ;[5] punishing crimes against the state ;[6] furnishing corn to the poor people, at $\frac{10}{12}$ of an *as*, a bushel.[7]

Saturninus also got a law passed, that all the senators should be obliged, within five days, to approve upon oath of what the people enacted, under the penalty of a heavy fine ; and the virtuous Metellus Numidicus was banished, because he alone would not comply.[8] But Saturninus himself was soon after slain for passing these laws by the command of Marius, who had at first encouraged him to propose them, and who by his artifice had effected the banishment of Metellus.[9]

Lex AQUILLIA, A. U. 672, about hurt wrongfully done.[10]——Another, about designed fraud, A. U. 687.[11]

Lex ATERIA TARPEIA, A. U. 300, that all magistrates might fine those who violated their authority, but not above two oxen and thirty sheep.[12] After the Romans began to use coined money, an ox was estimated at 100 *asses,* and a sheep at ten.[13]

Lex ATIA, by a tribune, A. U. 690, repealing the Cornelian law, and restoring the Domitian, in the election of priests.[14]

Lex ATILIA *de dedititiis,* A. U. 543.[15]——Another *de tutoribus,* A. U. 443, that guardians should be appointed for orphans and women, by the prætor and a majority of the tribunes.[16]——Another, A. U. 443, that sixteen military tribunes should be created by the people for four legions ; that is, two-thirds of the whole. For in four legions, the number which then used annually to be raised, there were twenty-four tribunes, six in each : of whom by this law four were appointed by the people, and two by the consuls. Those chosen by the people were called COMITIATI ; by the consuls, RUTILI or RUFULI. At first they seem to have been all nominated by the kings, consuls, or dictators, till the year 393, when the people assumed the right

1 see p. 74.
2 Gell. ii. 24. Macrob. ii. 13.
3 acta Cæsaris.
4 Cic. Phil. i. I. 9. ii. 3. 36—38. v. 34. xiii. 3. 5. Att. xiv. 12. Dio. Cass. xiv. 29. Ap. Bel. Civ. iii. Dio. xliv. fin.

5 Aur. Vict. Vir. illust. 73. Cic. Balb. 21.
6 de majestate, Cic. Or. ii. 25. 49.
7 semisse et triente, i. e. dextante, vel decunce : see leges Sempronia, Cic. Her. i. 12. Legg. ii. 16.

8 quod in legem vi latam jurare nollet, Cic. Sext. 16. Dom. 31. Clu. 35. Vict. Vir. illust. 62. 9 Cic. Rab. perd. xviii. Bell. Civ. i. 367.
10 de damno injuria dato, Cic. Brut. 34.

11 de dolo malo, Cic. Nat. D. iii. 30. Off. iii. 14.
12 Diony. x. 50.
13 Festus in Peculatus.
14 Dio. xxxvii. 37.
15 Liv. xxvi. 33.
16 Ulp. Fragm. Liv. xxxix. 9. see p. 44.

of annually appointing six.[1] Afterwards the manner of choosing them
varied. Sometimes the people created the whole, sometimes only a part.
But as they, through interest, often appointed improper persons, the choice
was sometimes left, especially in dangerous junctures, entirely to the
consuls.[2]

Lex ATINIA, A U. 623, about making the tribunes of the common senators.[3]——Another, that the property of things stolen could not be acquired
by possession.[4] The words of the law were, QUOD SURREPTUM ERIT, EJUS
ÆTERNA AUCTORITAS ESTO.[5]

Lex AUFIDIA *de ambitu*, A. U. 692. It contained this singular clause,
that if a candidate promised money to a tribe, and did not pay it, he should
be excused ; but if he did pay it, he should be obliged to pay to every tribe
a yearly fine of 3000 sestertii as long as he lived.[6]

Lex AURELIA *judiciaria*, by L. Aurelius Cotta, prætor, A. U. 683, that
judices or jurymen should be chosen from the senators, equites, and tribuni
ærarii. The last were officers chosen from the plebeians, who kept and
gave out the money for defraying the expenses of the army.[7]——Another,
by C. Aurelius Cotta, consul, A. U. 678, that those who had been tribunes
might enjoy other offices, which had been prohibited by Sylla.[8]

Lex BÆBIA, A. U. 574, about the number of prætors.[9]——Another
against bribery, A. U. 571.[10]

Lex CÆCILIA DIDIA, or *et Didia*, or *Didia et Cæcilia*, A. U. 655, that laws
should be promulgated for three market-days, and that several distinct
things should not be included in the same law, which was called *ferre per
saturam*.——Another against bribery.——Another, A. U. 693, about ex-
empting the city and Italy from taxes.[11]

Lex CALPURNIA, A. U. 604, against extortion, by which law the first
quæstio perpetua was established.——Another, called also *Acilia*, concerning bribery, A. U. 686.[12]

Lex CANULEIA, by a tribune, A. U. 309, about the intermarriage of the
patricians with the plebeians.[13]

Lex CASSIA, that those whom the people condemned should be excluded
from the senate.——Another about supplying the senate.——Another,
that the people should vote by ballot, &c.[14]

Lex CASSIA TERENTIA *frumentaria*, by the consuls C. Cassius and M.
Terentius, A. U. 680, ordaining, as it is thought, that five *modii* or pecks
of corn should be given monthly to each of the poor citizens, which was
not more than the allowance of slaves,[15] and that money should be annually
advanced from the treasury, for purchasing 800,000 *modii* of wheat,[16] at
four sestertii a *modius* or peck ; and a second tenth part[17] at three sestertii
a peck.[18] This corn was given to the poor people, by the Sempronian
law, at a *semis* and *triens* a *modius* or peck ; and by the Clodian law,
gratis.[19] In the time of Augustus, we read that 200,000 received corn
from the public. Julius Cæsar reduced them from 320,000 to 150,000.[20]

Lex CENTURIATA, the name of every ordinance made by the Comitia
Centuriata.[21]

1 Liv. vii. 5. ix. 30. Asc.
  Cic.
2 Liv. xlii. 31. xliii. 12.
  xliv. 21.
3 Gell. xiv. 8.
4 usucapione.
5 see p. 39. Gell. xvii.
  7. Cic. Verr. i. 42.
6 Cic. Att. i. 16.

7 Cic. Verr. 2. 69. 72.
  Phil. i. 8. Rull. i. 2.
  Asc. Planc. 6. Att. i.
  16. Fest.
8 Asc. Cic.
9 see p. 65.
10 Liv. xl. 19.
11 Cic. Att. ii. 9. Phil. v.
  3. Dom. 20. Sull. 22, 23.

Dio. xxxvii. 51.
12 Cic. Verr. iv. 25. Off.
  ii. 21. Mur. 23. Brut.
  27. Sall. Cat. 18.
13 Liv. iv. 6.
14 Asc. Cic. Corn. Tac.
  xi. 25. see p. 61.
15 Sall. Hist. Fragm. p.
  974. ed. Cortii.

16 tritici imperati.
17 alteras decumas, see
  p. 50.
18 pro decumano, Cic.
  Verr. iii. 70. v. 71.
19 see p. 133.
20 Dio. iv. 10. Suet.
  Aug. 40. 42. Jul. 41.
21 Cic. Rull. ii. 11.

Lex CINCIA *de donis et muneribus,* hence called MUNERALIS, by Cincius, a tribune, A. U. 549, that no one should take money or a present for pleading a cause.[1].

Lex CLAUDIA *de navibus,* A. U. 535, that a senator should not have a vessel above a certain burden.[2] A clause is supposed to have been added to this law prohibiting the quæstor's clerks from trading.[3]——Another, by Claudius the consul, at the request of the allies, A. U. 573, that the allies and those of the Latin name should leave Rome, and return to their own cities. According to this law the consul made an edict; and a decree of the senate was added, that for the future no person should be manumitted, unless both master and slave swore that he was not manumitted for the sake of changing his city. For the allies used to give their children as slaves to any Roman citizen on condition of their being manumitted.[4]—— Another, by the emperor Claudius, that usurers should not lend money to minors, to be paid after the death of their parents, supposed to be the same with what was called the SENATUS-CONSULTUM MACEDONIANUM, enforced by Vespasian.[5]——Another, by the consul Marcellus, A. U. 703, that no one should be allowed to stand candidate for an office while absent: thus taking from Cæsar the privilege granted him by the Pompeian law;[6] also, that the freedom of the city should be taken from the colony of *Novumcomum,* which Cæsar had planted.[7]

Leges CLODIÆ, by the tribune P. Clodius, A. U. 695.——1. That the corn which had been distributed to the people for a *semis* and *triens,* or for $1\frac{2}{3}$ of an *as, dextans,* the *modius,* or peck, should be given gratis.[8]—— 2. That the censors should not expel from the senate or inflict any mark of infamy, on any man who was not first openly accused and condemned by their joint sentence.[9]——3. That no one should take the auspices, or observe the heavens when the people were assembled on public business; and, in short, that the Ælian and Fusian laws should be abrogated.[10]—— 4. That the old companies or fraternities[11] of artificers in the city which the senate had abolished, should be restored, and new ones instituted.[12] These laws were intended to pave the way for the following:——5. That whoever had taken the life of a citizen uncondemned and without a trial, should be prohibited from fire and water: by which law Cicero, although not named, was plainly pointed at, and soon after, by means of a hired mob, his banishment was expressly decreed by a second law.[13]

Cicero had engaged Ninius, a tribune, to oppose these laws, but was prevented from using his assistance, by the artful conduct of Clodius; and Pompey, on whose protection he had reason to rely, betrayed him.[14] Cæsar, who was then without the walls with his army, ready to set out for his province of Gaul, offered to make him one of his lieutenants; but this, by the advice of Pompey, he declined. Crassus, although secretly inimical to Cicero, yet, at the persuasion of his son, who was a great admirer of Cicero's, did not openly oppose him. But Clodius declared that what he did was by the authority of the triumviri, and the interposition of the senate and equites, who, to the number of 20,000, changed their habit on Cicero's

1 Plaut. apud Festum. Cic. Sen. 4. Or. ii. 7. Att. 1.20. Tac. Ann. xi. 5. Liv. xxxiv. 4.
2 see p. 4.
3 Suet. Dom. 9.
4 ut libertini cives essent, Liv. xli. 8, 9. Cic. Balb. 23.

5 Tac. Ann. xi. 13. Ulp. Suet. 11. to this crime Horace alludes, Sat. i. 2. v. 14.
6 Cæsari privilegium eripiens vel beneficium populi adimens.
7 Suet. Jul. 28. Cic. Fam. xiii. 35.

8 Cic. Sext. 25. Asc. Cic. see p. 132.
9 Cic. ib. Pis. 5. Dio. xxxviii. 13.
10 see p. 62. Cic. Vat. 6, 7. 9. Sext. 15. 26. Prov. Cons. 19. Asc. Pis. 4.
11 collegia.
12 Cic. Pis. 4. Suet. Jul.

42.
13 Vell. ii. 45. Cic. Dom. 18—20. post red. Sen. 2. 5. &c.
14 Dio. xxxviii. 13. 17. Plut. Cic. Att. x. 4.

account, was rendered abortive by means of the consuls Piso, the father-in-law of Cæsar, and Gabinius, the creature of Pompey.[1] Cicero, therefore, after several mean compliances, putting on the habit of a criminal, and even throwing himself at the feet of Pompey, was at last obliged to leave the city, about the end of March, A. U. 695. He was prohibited from coming within 468 miles of Rome, under pain of death to himself, and to any person who entertained him.[2] He, therefore, retired to Thessalonica in Macedonia. His houses at Rome and in the country were burnt, and his furniture plundered. Cicero did not support his exile with fortitude ; but showed marks of dejection, and uttered expressions of grief unworthy of his former character.[3] He was restored with great honour, through the influence of Pompey, by a very unanimous decree of the senate, and by a law passed at the Comitia Centuriata, 4th August the next year.[4] Had Cicero acted with as much dignity and independence, after he reached the summit of his ambition, as he did with industry and integrity in aspiring to it, he needed not to have owed his safety to any one.——6. That the kingdom of Cyprus should be taken from Ptolemy, and reduced into the form of a province ; the reason of which law was to punish that king for having refused Clodius money to pay his ransom, when taken by the pirates, and to remove Cato out of the way, by appointing him to execute this order of the people, that he might not thwart the unjust proceedings of the tribune, nor the views of the triumviri, by whom Clodius was supported.[5]——7. To reward the consuls Piso and Gabinius, who had favoured Clodius in his measures, the province of Macedonia and Greece was, by the people, given to the former, and Syria to the latter.[6]——8. Another law was made by Clodius to give relief to the private members of corporate towns,[7] against the public injuries of their communities.[8]——9. Another to deprive the priest of Cybele, at Pessinus in Phrygia, of his office.[9]

Lex CŒLIA *tabellaria perduellionis*, by Cœlius a tribune.[10]

Leges CORNELIÆ, enacted by L. Cornelius Sylla, the dictator, A. U. 672.

——I. *De proscriptione et proscriptis*, against his enemies, and in favour of his friends. Sylla first introduced the method of proscription. Upon his return into the city, after having conquered the party of Marius, he wrote down the names of those whom he doomed to die, and ordered them to be fixed up on tables in the public places of the city, with the promise of a certain reward[11] for the head of each person so proscribed. New lists[12] were repeatedly exposed as new victims occurred to his memory, or were suggested to him. The first list contained the names of forty senators and 1600 equites. Incredible numbers were massacred, not only at Rome, but through all Italy.[13] Whoever harboured or assisted a proscribed person was put to death. The goods of the proscribed were confiscated, and their children declared incapable of honours.[14] The lands and fortunes of the slain were divided among the friends of Sylla, who were allowed to enjoy preferments before the legal time.[15]——*De* MUNICIPIIS, that the free towns which had sided with Marius, should be deprived of their lands, and the right of citizens ; the last of which Cicero says could not be done.[16]

1 Dio. xxxviii. 15. Cic. Q. fr. ii. 9. Sext. 11—13. 16—18. post red. Quir. 3.
2 Dio. xxxviii. 14. 17. Cic. Att. iii. 4. x. 4.
3 Cic. Planc. 41. Red. Sen. 7. 14. Dom. 24. Att. iii. 7—11. 13. 15.
19. &c. Dio. xxxviii. 18.
4 Cic. Att. iv. 1. post red. Quir.7. Sen. 11. Mil. 20. Pis. 15. Dio. xxxix. 8.
5 Cic. Dom. 8. 25. Vell. ii. 45. Sext. 18. 28. Dio. xxxviii. 30. xxxix. 22.
6 Cic. ib. 10. 24. Pis. 16.
7 municipiorum.
8 Cic. Dom. 30.
9 Cic. Sext. 26. de resp. Harusp. 13.
10 see p. 64.
11 duo talenta, two talents.
12 tabulæ proscriptionis.
13 App. Bell. Civ. 409. Dio. Frag. 137.
14 Cic. Verr. i. 47. Ros. Am. 43, 44. Rull. iii. 3. Pis. 2. Vel. Pat. ii 28.
15 Sall. Catt. 51. Cic. Ac. ii. 1.
16 quis jure Romano civitas nemini invito adimi poterat, Dom. 30. Cæc. 33.

Sylla being created dictator with extraordinary powers by L. Valerius Flaccus, the interrex, in an assembly of the people by centuries,[1] and having there got ratified whatever he had done or should do, by a special law,[2] next proceeded to regulate the state, and for that purpose made many good laws.

2. Concerning the republic, the magistrates, the provinces, the power of the tribunes.[3] That the *judices* should be chosen only from among the senators; that the priests should be elected by their respective colleges.[4]

3. Concerning various crimes:—*de* MAJESTATE,[5] *de* REPETUNDIS,[6] *de* SICARIIS *et* VENEFICIS, those who killed a person with weapons or poison; also, who took away the life of another by false accusation, &c.—One accused by this law, was asked whether he chose sentence to be passed on him by voice or by ballot?[7] *de* INCENDIARIIS, who fired houses; *de* PARRICIDIS, who killed a parent or relation; *de* FALSO, against those who forged testaments or any other deed, who debased or counterfeited the public coin.[8] Hence this law is called by Cicero, CORNELIA TESTAMENTARIA, NUMMARIA.[9]

The punishment annexed to these laws was generally *aquæ et ignis interdictio*, banishment.

Sylla also made a sumptuary law, limiting the expense of entertainments.[10]

There were other *leges* CORNELIÆ, proposed by Cornelius the tribune, A. U. 686, that the prætors in judging should not vary from their edicts.[11] That the senate should not decree about absolving any one from the obligation of the laws without a quorum of at least two hundred.[12]

Lex CURIA, by Curius Dentatus when tribune, A. U. 454, that the senate should authorize the Comitia for electing plebeian magistrates.[13]

Leges CURIATÆ, made by the people assembled by *curiæ*.[14]

Lex DECIA, A. U. 443, that *duumviri navales* should be created for equipping and refitting a fleet.[15]

Lex DIDIA *sumptuaria*, A. U. 610, limiting the expense of entertainments, and the number of guests; that the sumptuary laws should be extended to all the Italians; and not only the master of the feast, but also the guests, should incur a penalty for their offence.[16]

Lex DOMITIA *de sacerdotiis*, the author Cn. Domitius Ahenobarbus, a tribune, A. U. 650, that priests (i. e. the *pontifices, augures*, and *decemviri sacris faciendis*,) should not be chosen by the colleges, as formerly, but by the people.[17] The pontifex maximus and curio maximus were, in the first ages of the republic, always chosen by the people.[18]

Lex DUILIA, by Duilius a tribune, A. U. 304, that whoever left the people without tribunes, or created a magistrate from whom there was no appeal, should be scourged and beheaded.[19]

Lex DUILIA MÆNIA *de unciario fœnore*, A. U. 396, fixing the interest of money at one per cent.——Another, making it capital for one to call assemblies of the people at a distance from the city.[20]

1 App. Bell. Civ. i. 411.
2 sive Valeria, sive Cornelia, Cic. Rosc. Am. 43. Cic. Rul. lii. 2.
3 see p. 74, 75. 96. 112.
4 Asc. Cic. Div. Ver. 2.
5 Cic. Pis. 12. Clu. 35. Fam. iii. 11. see p. 112.

6 concerning extortion, Cic. Rab. 3. see p 87.
7 palam an clam! Cic. Clu. 20.
8 qui in aurum vitii quid addiderint vel adulterinos nummos fecerint, &c.

9 Verr. i. 42.
10 Gell. ii. 24. Macrob. Sat. ii. 13.
11 see p. 84, 85.
12 Asc. Cic. Corn.
13 Aur. Vict. 37. Cic. Or. 14.
14 see p. 55.

15 Liv. ix. 30.
16 Macrob. Sat. ii. 13.
17 see p. 69. Suet. Ner. 2. Cic. Rull. ii. 7.
18 Liv. xxv. 5. xxvii. 8.
19 Liv. iii. 55.
20 Liv. vii. 16.

Lex FABIA *de plagio* vel *plagiariis*, against kidnapping or stealing away and retaining freemen or slaves.[1] The punishment at first was a fine, but afterwards to be sent to the mines ; and for buying or selling a freeborn citizen, death.

Literary thieves, or those who stole the works of others, were also called PLAGIARII.[2]——Another, limiting the number of *sectatores* that attended candidates, when canvassing for any office. It was proposed, but did not pass.[3]

The SECTATORES, who always attended candidates, were distinguished from the SALUTATORES, who only waited on them at their houses in the morning, and then went away ; and from the DEDUCTORES, who also went down with them to the forum and Campus Martius ; hence called by Martial, ANTAMBULONES.[4]

Lex FALCIDIA *testamentaria*, A. U. 713, that the testator should leave at least the fourth part of his fortune to the person whom he named his heir.[5]

Lex FANNIA, A. U. 588, limiting the expenses of one day at festivals to 100 *asses*, whence the law is called by Lucilius, CENTUSSIS ; on ten other days every month, to thirty ; and on all other days, to ten *asses ;* also, that no other fowl should be served up,[6] except one hen, and that not fattened for the purpose.[7]

Lex FLAMINIA, A. U. 521, about dividing among the soldiers the lands of Picenum, whence the Galli Senones had been expelled ; which afterwards gave occasion to various wars.[8]

Lex FLAVIA *agraria*, the author L. Flavius a tribune, A. U. 695, for the distribution of lands among Pompey's soldiers ; which excited so great commotions, that the tribune, supported by Pompey, had the hardiness to commit the consul Metellus to prison for opposing it.[9]

Leges FRUMENTARIÆ, laws for the distribution of corn among the people, first at a low price, and then gratis ; the chief of which were the Sempronian, Appuleian, Cassian, Clodian, and Octavian laws.

Lex FUFIA, A. U. 692, that Clodius should be tried for violating the sacred rites of the Bona Dea, by the prætor, with a select bench of judges ; and not before the people, according to the decree of the senate. Thus by bribery he procured his acquittal.[10]

Lex FULVIA, A. U. 628, about giving the freedom of the city to the Italian allies ; but it did not pass.[11]

Lex FURIA, by Camillus the dictator, A. U. 385, about the creation of the curule ædiles.[12]

Lex FURIA, vel *Fusia* (for both are the same name,)[13] *de testamentis*, that no one should leave by way of legacy more than 1000 *asses*, and that he who took more should pay fourfold.[14] By the law of the Twelve Tables, one might leave what legacies he pleased.

Lex FURIA ATILIA, A. U. 617, about giving up Mancinus to the Numantines, with whom he had made peace without the order of the people or senate.[15]

Lex FUSIA *de comitiis*, A. U. 691, by a prætor, that in the Comitia Tri-

---

1 Cic. Rab. perd. 3. Quin. Fr. i. 2.
2 Mart. i. 53.
3 Cic. Mur. 34.
4 ii. 18. Cic. pet. cons. see p. 60.
5 Paul. Leg. Falc. Dio. xlviii. 33.

6 ne quid volucrium vel volucre poneretur.
7 quæ non altilis esset, Gell. ii. 24. Macrob. Sat. ii. 13. quod deinde caput translatum, per omnes leges ambulavit, Plin. x. 50. s. 71.

8 Polyb. ii. 21. Cic. Sen. 4.
9 Dion. Cass. xxxvii. 50. Cic. Att. i. 18, 19. ii. 1.
10 Cic. Att. i. 13, 14. 16. Dio. xxxvii. 46.
11 App. Bell. Civ. i. 371. Val. Max. ix. 5.

12 Liv. vi. 42.
13 Liv. iii. 4. Quinct. i. 4. 13.
14 Cic. Verr. i. 42. Balb.
8. Theo. Inst. ii. 22.
15 Cic. Off. iii. 30.

buts, the different kinds of people in each tribe should vote separately and thus the sentiments of every rank might be known.[1]

Lex FUSIA vel *Furia* CANINIA, A. U. 751, limiting the number of slaves to be manumitted, in proportion to the whole number which any one possessed ; from two to ten the half, from ten to thirty the third, from thirty to a hundred the fourth part; but not above a hundred, whatever was the number.[2]

Leges GABINIÆ, by A. Gabinius, a tribune, A. U. 685, that Pompey should get the command of the war against the pirates, with extraordinary powers.[3] That the senate should attend to the hearing of embassies the whole month of February.[4] That the people should give their votes by ballots, and not *viva voce* as formerly, in creating magistrates.[5] That the people of the provinces should not be allowed to borrow money at Rome from one person to pay another.[6]

There is another Gabinian law, mentioned by Porcius Latro[7] in his declamation against Catiline, which made it capital to hold clandestine assemblies in the city. But this author is thought to be supposititious.[8]

It is certain, however, that the Romans were always careful to prevent the meetings of any large bodies of men,[9] which they thought might be converted to the purposes of sedition. On this account, Pliny informs Trajan, that according to his directions he had prohibited the assemblies of Christians.[10]

Lex GELLIA CORNELIA, A. U. 681, confirming the right of citizens to those to whom Pompey, with the advice of his council,[11] had granted it.

Lex GENUCIA, A. U. 411, that both consuls might be chosen from the plebeians. That usury should be prohibited. That no one should enjoy the same office within ten years, nor be invested with two offices in one year.[12]

Lex GENUCIA ÆMILIA, A. U. 390, about fixing a nail in the right side of the temple of Jupiter.[13]

Lex GLAUCIA, A. U. 653, granting the right of judging to the equites, *de repetundis*.[14]

Lex GLICIA, *de inofficioso testamento*.[15]

Lex HIERONICA, vel *frumentaria*,[16] containing the conditions on which the public lands of the Roman people in Sicily were possessed by the husbandmen. It had been prescribed by Hiero, tyrant of Syracuse, to his tenants,[17] and was retained by the prætor Rupilius, with the advice of his council, among the laws which he gave to the Sicilians, when that country was reduced into the form of a province.[18] It resembled the regulations of the censors,[19] in their leases and bargains,[20] and settled the manner of collecting and ascertaining the quantity of the tithes.[21]

Lex HIRTIA, A. U. 704, that the adherents of Pompey[22] should be excluded from preferments.

Lex HORATIA, about rewarding Caia Terratia, a vestal virgin, because she had given in a present to the Roman people the Campus Tiburtinus,

---

1 Dio. xxxviii. 8.
2 Vop. Tac. 11. Paul. Sent iv. 15. see p. 28.
3 cum imperio extraordinario, Cic. Leg. Man. 17. Dio. xxxvi. 7.
4 Cic. Quin. Fr. ii. 13.
5 see p. 64.

6 versuram facere, Cic. Att. v. 21. vi. 2.
7 c. 19.
8 see Cort. Sall.
9 heteriæ.
10 Plin. Ep. x. 43. 76. 94. 97.
11 de consilii sententia,

Cic. Balb. 8. 14.
12 Liv. vii. 42.
13 Liv. vii. 3.
14 see lex Servilia, Cic. Or. 62.
15 see p. 43.
16 Cic. Verr. ii. 13.
17 iis qui agros regis

colerent.
18 Cic. Verr. iii. 8. 10.
19 leges censoriæ.
20 in locationibus et practionibus.
21 Cic. Verr. v. 28.
22 Pompeiani, Cic. Phil. xiii. 16.

or Martius. That she should be admitted to give evidence,[1] be discharged from her priesthood,[2] and might marry if she chose.[3]

Lex HORTENSIA, that the *nundinæ*, or market-days, which used to be held as *feriæ* or holydays, should be *fasti* or court-days : that the country people who came to town for market might then get their lawsuits determined.[4]

Lex HORTENSIA, *de plebiscitis.*[5]

Lex HOSTILIA, *de furtis*, about theft, is mentioned only by Justinian.[6]

Lex ICILIA, *de tribunis*, A. U. 261, that no one should contradict or interrupt a tribune[7] while speaking to the people.[8]——Another, A. U. 297, *de Aventino publicando*, that the Aventine hill should be common for the people to build upon.[9] It was a condition in the creation of the decemviri, that this law, and those relating to the tribunes,[10] should not be abrogated.

Lex JULIA, *de civitate sociis et Latinis danda* ; the author L. Julius Cæsar, A. U. 663, that the freedom of the city should be given to the Latins and all the Italian allies who chose to accept of it.[11]

Leges JULIÆ, laws made by Julius Cæsar and Augustus.

1. By C. Julius Cæsar, in his first consulship, A. U. 694, and afterwards when dictator :

Lex JULIA AGRARIA, for distributing the lands of Campania and Stella to 20,000 poor citizens, who had each three children or more.[12]

When Bibulus, Cæsar's colleague in the consulate, gave his negative to this law, he was driven from the forum by force. And next day, having complained in the senate, but not being supported, he was so discouraged, that during his continuance in office for eight months, he shut himself up at home, without doing any thing but interposing by his edicts,[13] by which means, while he wished to raise odium against his colleague, he increased his power.[14] Metellus Celer, Cato, and his great admirer[15] M. Favonius, at first refused to swear to this law ; but, constrained by the severity of the punishment annexed to it, which Appian says was capital, they at last complied.[16] This custom of obliging all citizens, particularly senators, within a limited time, to signify their approbation of a law by swearing to support it, at first introduced in the time of Marius, was now observed with respect to every ordinance of the people, however violent and absurd.[17]

—— *de* PUBLICANIS *tertia parte pucuniæ debitæ relevandis*, about remitting to the farmers-general a third part of what they had stipulated to pay.[18] When Cato opposed this law with his usual firmness, Cæsar ordered him to be hurried away to prison : but fearing lest such violence should raise odium against him, he desired one of the tribunes to interpose and free him.[19]

Dio says that this happened when Cato opposed the former law in the senate.[20] When many of the senators followed Cato, one of them, named M. Petreius, being reproved by Cæsar for going away before the house was dismissed, replied, " I had rather be with Cato in prison, than here with Cæsar."[21]

---

1 testabilis esset.
2 exaugurari posset.
3 Gell. vi. 7.
4 lites componerent, Macrob. Sat. l. 16.
5 see p. 14, 70, 124.
6 Inst. iv. 10.
7 interfari tribuno.
8 Diony. vii. 17
9 Id. x. 32. Liv. iii. 31.

10 eges lsacratæ, Liv. lii. 32.
11 qui ei legi fundi fieri vellent, Cic. Balb. 8.
Gell. iv. 4. see p. 33.48.
12 Cic. Planc. 5. Att. ii. 16. 18, 19. Vell. ii. 44. Dio. xxxviii. i. 7.
13 ut, quoad potestate abiret, domo abditus

nihil aliud quam per edicta obnuntiaret, xxxviii. 6.
14 Vell. ii. 44.
15 æmulator.
16 Bell. Civ. ii. 434. Dio. xxxviii. 7. Plut. Cato Minor.
17 see leges Appuleiæ.

Dio. xxxviii. 7. Cic. Sext. 28.
18 Suet. ib. Cic. Planc.
14. Dio. ib. App. Bell. Civ. ii. 435. see p. 16.
19 Plut. Cæs.
20 xxxviii. 3. Suet. Cæs.
20. Gell. iv. 10.
21 see p. 10.

————For the ratification of all Pompey's acts in Asia. This law was chiefly opposed by Lucullus; but Cæsar so frightened him with threatenings to bring him to an account for his conduct in Asia, that he promised compliance on his knees.[1]

———— de PROVINCIIS ORDINANDIS; an improvement on the Cornelian law about the provinces; ordaining that those who had been prætors should not command a province above one year, and those who had been consuls, not above two years. Also ordaining that Achaia, Thessaly, Athens, and all Greece should be free and use their own laws.[2]

———— de SACERDOTIIS, restoring the Domitian law, and permitting persons to be elected priests in their absence.[3]

———— JUDICIARIA, ordering the *judices* to be chosen only from the senators and equites, and not from the *tribuni ærarii*.[4]

———— de REPETUNDIS, very severe[5] against extórtion. It is said to have contained above 100 heads.[6]

———— de LEGATIONIBUS LIBERIS, limiting their duration to five years.[7] They were called *liberæ*,[8] because those who enjoyed them were at liberty to enter and leave Rome when they pleased.

———— de VI PUBLICA ET PRIVATA, ET DE MAJESTATE.[9]

———— de PECUNIIS MUTUIS, about borrowed money.[10]

———— de MODO PECUNIÆ POSSIDENDÆ, that no one should keep by him in specie above a certain sum.[11]

———— About the population of Italy, that no Roman citizen should remain abroad above three years, unless in the army, or on public business; that at least a third of those employed in pasturage should be freeborn citizens; also about increasing the punishment of crimes, dissolving all corporations or societies, except the ancient ones, granting the freedom of the city to physicians, and professors of the liberal arts, &c.

———— de RESIDUIS, about bringing those to account who retained any part of the public money in their hands.[12]

———— de LIBERIS PROSCRIPTORUM, that the children of those proscribed by Sylla should be admitted to enjoy preferments, which Cicero, when consul, had opposed.[13]

———— SUMPTUARIA.[14] It allowed 200 HS. on the *dies profesti*; 300 on the calends, nones, ides, and some other festivals; 1000 at marriage-feasts,[15] and such extraordinary entertainments. Gellius ascribes this law to Augustus, but it seems to have been enacted by both. By an edict of Augustus or Tiberius, the allowance for an entertainment was raised, in proportion to its solemnity, for 300 to 2000 HS.[16]

———— de veneficiis, about poisoning.[17]

2. The *Leges JULIÆ* made by Augustus were chiefly—

———— Concerning marriage;[18] hence called by Horace LEX MARITA.[19]

———— de ADULTERIIS, *et de pudicitia, de ambitu*, against forestalling the market.[20]

---

1 Suet. ib.
2 Cic. Phil. 1. 6. Pis. 16. Dio. xliii. 25.
3 Cic, Brut. 5.
4 Suet. Jul. 41. Cic. Phil. i. 9.
5 acerrima.
6 Cic. Fam. viii. 7. Pis. 16. 21. 37. Sext. 64. Rab. Posth. 4. Vat. 12. Att. v. 10. 16. Suet.

Jul. 43.
7 see p. 14. Cic. Att. xv. 11.
8 quod, cum velis, introire, exire licebat, ib.
9 Cic. Phil. i. 6, 9.
10 see p. 34. Dio. xli. 37. xliii. 51. Cæs. Bell. Civ. iii. 1. 20. 42.
11 sixty sestertia. Dio. xli. 38. Tac. Ann. vi.

16.
12 Suet. 42. Marc. l. 4. s. 3. Leg. Jul.
13 Suet. Jul. 41. Cic. Pis. 2.
14 Suet. Jul. 42. Cic. Att. xiii. 7. Fam. vii. 26. ix. 15.
15 nuptiis et repotiis.
16 Gell. ii. 24. Dio. liv.2.
17 Suet. Ner. 33.

18 de maritandis ordinibus, Suet. Aug. 34.
19 Hor. car. sec. v. 68. Liv. Epit. 59. Suet. 89.
20 ne quis contra annonam fecerit, societatemve coierit, quo annona carior fiat, Ulp. Plin. Ep. vi. 31. Suet. 34.

—— *de* TUTORIBUS, that guardians should be appointed for orphans in the provinces, as at Rome, by the Atilian law.[1]

Lex JULIA THEATRALIS, that those equites who themselves, their fathers, or grandfathers, had the fortune of an eques, should sit in the fourteen rows assigned by the Roscian law to that order.[2]

There are several other laws called *leges Juliæ*, which occur only in the *Corpus Juris*.

Julius Cæsar proposed revising all the laws, and reducing them to a certain form. But this, with many other noble designs of that wonderful man, was prevented by his death.[3]

Lex JUNIA, by M. Junius Pennus, a tribune, A. U. 627, about expelling foreigners from the city.[4] Against extortion, ordaining that, besides the *litis æstimatio*, or paying an estimate of the damages, the person convicted of this crime should suffer banishment.[5]

—— Another, by M. Junius Silanus the consul, A. U. 644, about diminishing the number of campaigns which soldiers should serve.[6]

Lex JUNIA LICINIA, or *Junia et Licinia*, A. U. 691, enforcing the Didian law by severer penalties.[7]

Lex JUNIA NORBANA, A. U. 771, concerning the manumission of slaves.[8]

Lex LABIENA, A. U. 691, abrogating the law of Sylla, and restoring the Domitian law in the election of priests ; which paved the way for Cæsar's being created pontifex maximus. By this law, two of the college named the candidates, and the people chose which of them they pleased.[9]

Lex AMPLA LABIENA, by two tribunes, A. U. 663, that at the Circensian games Pompey should wear a golden crown, and his triumphal robes ; and in the theatre, the prætexta and a golden crown ; which mark of distinction he used only once.[10]

Lex LÆTORIA, A. U. 292, that the plebeian magistrates should be created at the Comitia Tributa.[11]—— Another, A. U. 490, against the defrauding of minors.[12] By this law the years of minority were limited to twenty-five, and no one below that age could make a legal bargain,[13] whence it is called *lex* QUINA VICENNARIA.[14]

Leges LICINIÆ, by P. Licinius Varus, city prætor, A. U. 545, fixing the day for the *ludi Apollinares*, which before was uncertain.[15]

—— by C. Licinius Crassus, a tribune, A. U. 608, that the choice of priests should be transferred from their college to the people ; but it did not pass.[16]

This Licinius Crassus, according to Cicero, first introduced the custom of turning his face to the forum when he spoke to the people, and not to the senate, as formerly.[17] But Plutarch says this was first done by Caius Gracchus.[18]

—— by C. Licinius Stolo, A. U. 377, that no one should possess above 500 acres of land, nor keep more than 100 head of great, or 500 head of small cattle. But Licinius himself was soon after punished for violating his own law.[19]

—— by Crassus the orator, similar to the Æbutian law.[20]

---

1 Just. Inst. Atil. Tut.
2 Suet. Aug. 40. Plin. xxxiii. 2. s. 8.
3 Suet. Jul. 44.
4 see p. 54.
5 Paterc. ii. 8. Cic. Balb. 11.
6 Asc. Cic. Corn.

7 Cic. Phil. v. 3. Sext. 64. Vat. 14. Att. ii. 9. iv. 16.
8 see p. 28, 29.
9 Dio. xxxvii. 37. Cic. Phil. ii. 2.
10 Paterc. ii. 40.
11 Liv. ii. 56, 57.

12 contra adolescentium circumscriptionem, Cic. Off. iii. 15.
13 stipulari, Plaut. Rud. / v. 3. 25.
14 Plaut. Pseud. i. 3. 68.
15 Liv. xxvii. 23.
16 Cic. Am. 25.

17 primum instituit in forum versus agere cum populo, ibid.
18 Plut. Grac.
19 App. Bell. Civ. i. Liv. vi. 35. vii. 16.
20 Cic. Dom. 20.

Lex LICINIA, *de sodalitiis et de ambitu,* A. U. 698, against bribery, and assembling societies or companies for the purpose of canvassing for an office.[1] In a trial for this crime, and for it only, the accuser was allowed to name[2] the jurymen[3] from the people in general.[4]

Lex LICINIA *sumptuaria,* by the consuls P. Licinius Crassus the Rich, and Cn. Lentulus, A. U. 656, much the same with the Fannian law ; that on ordinary days there should not be more served up at table than three pounds of fresh, and one pound of salt meat ;[5] but as much of the fruits of the ground as every one pleased.[6]

Lex LICINIA CASSIA, A. U. 422, that the legionary tribunes should not be chosen that year by the people, but by the consuls and prætors.[7]

Lex LICINIA SEXTIA, A. U. 377, about debt, that what had been paid for the interest[8] should be deducted from the capital, and the remainder paid in three years by equal portions. That instead of duumviri for performing sacred rites, decemviri should be chosen ; part from the patricians, and part from the plebeians. That one of the consuls should be created from among the plebeians.[9]

Lex LICINIA JUNIA, or *Junia et Licinia,* by the two consuls, A. U. 691, enforcing the *Lex Cæcilia Didia ;* whence both laws are often joined.[10]

Lex LICINIA MUCIA, A. U. 658, that no one should pass for a citizen who was not so ; which was one principal cause of the Italic or Marsic wars.[11]

Leges LIVIÆ, proposed by M. Livius Drusus, a tribune, A. U. 662, about transplanting colonies to different places in Italy and Sicily, and granting corn to poor citizens at a low price ; also that the judices should be chosen indifferently from the senators and equites, and that the allied states of Italy should be admitted to the freedom of the city.

Drusus was a man of great eloquence, and of the most upright intentions ; but endeavouring to reconcile those whose interests were diametrically opposite, he was crushed in the attempt ; being murdered by an unknown assassin at his own house, upon his return from the forum, amidst a number of clients and friends. No inquiry was made about his death. The states of Italy considered this event as a signal of revolt and endeavoured to extort by force what they could not obtain voluntarily. Above 300,000 men fell in the contest in the space of two years. At last the Romans, although upon the whole they had the advantage, were obliged to grant the freedom of the city, first to their allies, and afterwards to all the states of Italy.[12]

This Drusus is also said to have got a law passed for mixing an eighth part of brass with silver.[13]

But the laws of Drusus,[14] as Cicero says, were soon abolished by a short decree of the senate.[15]

Drusus was grandfather to Livia, the wife of Augustus, and mother of Tiberius.

Lex LUTATIA, *de vi,* by Q. Lutatius Catulus, A. U. 675, that a person might be tried for violence on any day, festivals not excepted, on which no trials used to be held.[16]

---

1 Cic. Planc. 15, 16.
2 edere.
3 judices.
4 ex omni populo, ib. 17.
5 salsamentorum.
6 Macrob. ii. 13. Gell. ii. 24.
7 Liv. xlii. 31.
8 quod usuris pernu-

meratum esset.
9 Liv. vi. 11. 35. see p. 80, 81.
10 Cic. Vat. 4. Phil. v. 3. Sext. 64. Att. ii. 9. iv. 16.
11 Cic. Off. iii. 11. Balb. 21. 24. Asc. Cic. Corn.
12 App. Bell. Civ. i. 373,

Vel. Pat. ii. 15. Liv. Epit. 71. Cic. Brut. 28. 49. 62. Rab. 7. Planc. 14. Dom. 19.
13 Plin. xxxiii. 33.
14 leges Liviæ.
15 unoversiculo senatus puncto temporis subiatæ sunt, Cic. Legg. ii. 6. decrevit enim sena-

tus. Philippo cos. referente, contra auspicia, latas videri,—For the senate decreed, on the motion of Philippus the consul, that they had been passed inauspiciously.
16 Cic. Cæl. i. 29. Act. Verr. 10.

Lex MÆNIA, by a tribune, A. U. 467, that the senate should ratify whatever the people enacted.[1]

Lex MAJESTATIS, for punishing any crime against the people, and afterwards against the emperor, Cornelia, &c.[2]

Lex MAMILIA, *de limitibus* vel *de regundis finibus agrorum*, for regulating the bounds of farms ; whence the author of it, C. Mamilius, a tribune, A. U. 642, got the surname of LIMITANUS. It ordained, that there should be an uncultivated space of five feet broad left between farms ; and if any dispute happened about this matter, that arbiters should be appointed by the prætor to determine it. The law of the Twelve Tables required three.[3]——Another, by the same person, for punishing those who had received bribes from Jugurtha.[4]

Lex MANILIA, for conferring on Pompey the command of the war against Mithridates, proposed by the tribune C. Manilius, A. U. 687, and supported by Cicero when prætor, and by Cæsar, from different views ; but neither of them was actuated by laudable motives.[5]——Another, by the same, that freedmen might vote in all the tribes, whereas formerly they voted in some one of the four city tribes only. But this law did not pass.[6]

Leges MINILIANÆ *venalium vendendorum*, not properly laws, but regulatiations to be observed in buying and selling, to prevent fraud, called by Varro, ACTIONES.[7] They were composed by the lawyer Manilius, who was consul, A. U. 603.

The formalities of buying and selling were by the Romans used in their most solemn transactions ; as, in emancipation and adoption, marriage and testaments, in transferring property, &c.

Lex MANLIA, by a tribune, A. U. 558, about creating the *Triumviri Epulones*.[8]

—— *de* VICESIMA, by a consul, A. U. 396.[9]

Lex MARCIA, by Marcius Censorinus, that no one should be made a censor a second time.[10]

—— *de Statiellatibus* vel *Statiellis*, that the senate upon oath should appoint a person to inquire into, and redress the injuries of the *Statielli*, or *-ates*, a nation of Liguria.[11]

Lex MARIA, by C. Marius, when tribune, A. U. 634, about making the entrances to the Ovilia[12] narrower.

Lex MARIA PORCIA, by two tribunes, A. U. 691, that those commanders should be punished, who, in order to obtain a triumph, wrote to the senate a false account of the number of the enemy slain in battle, or of the citizens that were missing ; and that when they returned to the city, they should swear before the city quæstors to the truth of the account which they had sent.[13]

Lex MEMMIA vel REMMIA : by whom it was proposed, or in what year, is uncertain. It ordained, that an accusation should not be admitted against those who were absent on account of the public.[14] And if any one was convicted of false accusation,[15] that he should be branded on the forehead with a letter,[16] probably with the letter K, as anciently the name of this crime was written KALUMNIA.

1 Cic. Brut. 14. see p.   xxxvi. 26.   9 Liv. vii. 16. see p.   14 Val. Max. ill. 7. 9.
   14.   6 see p. 69. Asc. Cic.   46.   Suet. Jul. 23.
2 Cic. Pis. 21. Tac. An.   Corn. Mur. 23.   10 Plut. Cor.   15 calumniæ.
   iv. 34.   7 Cic. Or. i. 5. 58. Var. 11 Liv. xlii. 21.   16 Cic. Ros. Am. 19,
3 Cic. Legg. i. 21.   Rust. ii. 5. 11.   12 pontes, Cic. Legg. iii.   20.
4 Sall. Jug. 40.   8 Liv. xxxiii. 42. Cic.   17.
5 Cic. Legg. Man. Dio.   Or. iii. 19.   13 Val. Max. ii. 8. 1.

Lex MENENIA, A. U. 302, that, in imposing fines, a sheep should be estimated at ten *asses*, and an ox at one hundred.[1]

Lex MENSIA, that a child should be held as a foreigner, if either of the parents was so. But if both parents were Romans and married, children always obtained the rank of the father,[2] and if unmarried, of the mother.

Lex METILIA, by a tribune, A. U. 516, that Minucius, master of horse, should have equal command with Fabius the dictator.[3]——Another, as it is thought by a tribune, A. U. 535, giving directions to fullers of cloth ; proposed to the people at the desire of the censors.[4]——Another, by Metellus Nepos a prætor, A. U. 694, about freeing Rome and Italy from taxes,[5] probably those paid for goods imported.[6]

Leges MILITARES, regulations for the army. By one of these it was provided, that if a soldier was by chance enlisted into a legion, commanded by a tribune whom he could prove to be inimical to him, he might go from that legion to another.[7]

Lex MINUCIA *de triumviris mensariis*, by a tribune, A. U. 537, about appointing bankers to receive the public money.[8]

Leges NUMÆ, laws of king Numa, mentioned by different authors :—that the gods should be worshipped with corn and a salted cake :[9] that whoever knowingly killed a free man should be held as a parricide :[10] that no harlot should touch the altar of Juno ; and if she did, that she should sacrifice an ewe lamb to that goddess with dishevelled hair :[11] that whoever removed a landmark should be put to death :[12] that wine should not be poured on a funeral pile.[13]

Lex OCTAVIA *frumentaria*, by a tribune, A. U. 633, abrogating the Sempronian law, and ordaining, as it is thought, that corn should not be given at so low a price to the people. It is greatly commended by Cicero.[14]

Lex OGULNIA, by two tribunes, A. U. 453, that the number of the pontifices should be increased to eight, and of the augurs to nine ; and that four of the former, and five of the latter, should be chosen from among the plebeians.[15]

Lex OPPIA by a tribune, A. U. 540, that no woman should have in her dress above half an ounce of gold, nor wear a garment of different colours, nor ride in a carriage in the city or in any town, or within a mile of it, unless upon occasion of a public sacrifice.[16]

Lex OPTIMA, a law was so called which conferred the most complete authority,[17] as that was called *optimum jus* which bestowed complete property.

Lex ORCHIA, by a tribune, A. U. 566, limiting the number of guests at an entertainment.[18]

Lex OVINIA, that the censors should choose the most worthy of all ranks into the senate.[19] Those who had borne offices were commonly first chosen ; and that all these might be admitted, sometimes more than the limited number were elected.[20]

Lex PAPIA, by a tribune, A. U. 688, that foreigners should be expelled from Rome, and the allies of the Latin name forced to return to their cities.[21]

1 Festus in Peculatus.
2 patrem sequuntur liberi, Liv. iv. 4. Ulp.
3 Liv. xxii. 25, 26.
4 quam C. Flaminius, L. Æmilius censores dedere ad populum ferendam, Plin. xxxv. 17. s. 57.
5 τέλη, vectigalia, Dio.

xxxvii. 51.
6 portorium, Cic. Att. ii. 16.
7 Cic. Flac. 32.
8 Liv. xxxiii. 21.
9 fruge et salsa mola, Plin. xviii. 2.
10 Festus in Quæstores parricidii.
11 Id. in Pellices, Gell.

iv. 3.
12 qui terminum exarasset, et ipsum et boves sacros esse, Fest. in Termino.
13 Plin. xiv. 12, &c.
14 Cic. Brut. 62. Off. ii. 21.
15 Liv. x. 6. 9.
16 Liv. xxxiv. 1 Tac.

Ann. iii. 33.
17 Fest. in voce.
18 Fest.inOpsonitavera, Macrob. Sat. ii. 13.
19 Fest. in Præteriti senatores.
20 Dio. xxxvii. 46.
21 Cic. Off. iii. 11. Balb.
23. Arch. 5. Att. iv. 16. Dio. xxxvii. 9.

Lex PAPIA POPPÆA, about the manner of choosing[1] vestal virgins. The author of it, and the time when it passed, are uncertain.

Lex PAPIA POPPÆA *de maritandis ordinibus*, proposed by the consuls Papius and Poppæus at the desire of Augustus, A. U. 762, enforcing and enlarging the Julian law.[2] The end of it was to promote population, and repair the desolation occasioned by the civil wars. It met with great opposition from the nobility, and consisted of several distinct particulars.[3] It proposed certain rewards to marriage, and penalties against celibacy, which had always been much discouraged in the Roman state, and yet greatly prevailed, for reasons enumerated.[4] Whoever in the city had three children, in the other parts of Italy four, and in the provinces five, was entitled to certain privileges and immunities. Hence the famous JUS TRIUM LIBERO-RUM, so often mentioned by Pliny, Martial, &c., which used to be granted also to those who had no children, first by the senate, and afterwards by the emperor, not only to men, but likewise to women.[5] The privileges of having three children were, an exemption from the trouble of guardianship, a priority in bearing offices,[6] and a treble proportion of corn. Those who lived in celibacy could not succeed to an inheritance, except of their nearest relations, unless they married within 100 days after the death of the testator ; nor receive an entire legacy.[7] And what they were thus deprived of in certain cases fell as an escheat[8] to the exchequer[9] or prince's private purse.

Lex PAPIRIA, by a tribune, A. U. 563, diminishing the weight of the *as* one half.[10]

—— by a prætor, A. U. 421, granting the freedom of the city, without the right of. voting, to the people of Acerra.[11]

—— by a tribune, the year uncertain, that no edifice, land, or altar, should be consecrated without the order of the people.

—— A. U. 325, about estimating fines,[12] probably the same with *lex* MENENIA.

—— That no one should molest another without cause.[13]

—— by a tribune, A. U. 621, that tablets should be used in passing laws.[14]

—— by a tribune, A. U. 623, that the people might re-elect the same person tribune as often as they chose ; but it was rejected.[15]

Instead of Papirius, they anciently wrote Papisius. So Valesius for Valerius, Auselius for Aurelius, &c. Ap. Claudius is said to have invented the letter R, probably from his first using it in these words.[16]

Lex PEDIA, by Pedius the consul, A. U.710, decreeing banishment against the murderers.of Cæsar.[17]

Lex PEDUCÆA, by a tribune, A. U. 640, against incest.[18]

Lex PERSOLONIA, or *Pisulania*, that if a quadruped did any hurt, the owner should either repair the damage, or give up the beast.[19]

Lex PÆTELIA *de ambitu*, by a tribune, A. U. 397, that candidates should not go round to fairs and other public meetings, for the sake of canvassing.[20]

---

1 capiendi, Gell. i. 12.
2 Tac. Ann. iii. 25. 28.
3 Lex Satura.
4 Val. Max. ii. 9. Liv. xlv. 15. Epit. 59. Suet. Aug. 34. 69. Dio. lvi. 3, 4. Gell. i. 6. v. 19. Plin. xiv. Proœm. Sen. cons. Marc. 19. Plaut.

Mil. iii. 185. 111, &c.
5 Plin. Ep. ii. 13. vii. 16. x. 2. 95, 96. Mart. ii. 91, 92. Dio. lv. 2. Suet. Claud. 19.
6 Plin. Ep viii. 16.
7 legatum omne vel solidum capere.
8 caducum.

9 fisco, Juv. ix. 88. &c.
10 Plin. xxxiii. 3.
11 Liv. viii. 17.
12 Cic. Dom. 49. Liv. iv. 30.
13 Fest. in Sacramentum.
14 Cic. Legg. iii. 16.

15 Cic. Am. 25. Liv. Ep. 59.
16 D. i. 2. 2. 36. Cic. Fam. ix. 21. Var. L. L. i. 6. Fest. Quinct. i. 4.
17 Vell. Pat. ii. 69.
18 Cic. Nat. D. iii. 30.
19 Paul. Sent. i.
20 Liv. vii. 15.

—— de NEXIS, by the consuls, A. U. 429, that no one should be kept in fetters or in bonds, but for a crime that deserved it, and that only till he suffered the punishment due by law : that creditors should have a right to attach the goods, and not the person of their debtors.[1]

—— de PECULATU, by a tribune, A. U. 566, that inquiry should be made about the money taken or exacted from king Antiochus and his subjects, and how much of it had not been brought into the public treasury.[2]

Lex PETREIA, by a tribune, A. U. 668, that mutinous soldiers should be decimated, i. e. that every tenth man should be selected by lot for punishment.[3]

Lex PETRONIA, by a consul, A. U. 813, prohibiting masters from compelling their slaves to fight with wild beasts.[4]

Lex PINARIA ANNALIS, by a tribune, A. U. 622. What it was is uncertain.[5]

Lex PLAUTIA vel PLOTIA, by a tribune, A. U. 664, that the judices should be chosen both from the senators and equites ; and some also from the plebeians. By this law each tribe chose annually fifteen[6] to be judices for that year, in all 525. Some read *quinos creabant :* thus making them the same with the CENTUMVIRI.[7]

—— PLOTIA de vi, against violence.[8]

Lex POMPEIA de vi, by Pompey, when sole consul, A. U. 701, that an inquiry should be made about the murder of Clodius on the Appian way, the burning the senate-house, and the attack made on the house of M. Lepidus the interrex.[9]

—— de AMBITU, against bribery and corruption in elections, with the infliction of new and severer punishments.[10]

By these laws the method of trial was altered, and the length of them limited : three days were allowed for the examination of witnesses, and the fourth for the sentence ; on which the accuser was to have two hours only to enforce the charge ; the criminal three for his defence. This regulation was considered as a restraint on eloquence.[11]

Lex POMPEIA *judiciaria*, by the same person ; retaining the Aurelian law, but ordaining, that the judices should be chosen from among those of the highest fortune[12] in the different orders.[13]

—— de COMITIIS, that no one should be allowed to stand candidate for an office in his absence. In this law Julius Cæsar was expressly excepted.[14]

—— de repetundis,[15] de parricidis.[16]

The regulations which Pompey prescribed to the Bithynians were also called *lex* POMPEIA.[17]

Lex POMPEIA *de civitate*, by Cn. Pompeius Strabo, the consul, A. U. 665, granting the freedom of the city to the Italians and the Galli Cispadani.[18]

Lex POPILIA, about choosing the vestal virgins.[19]

Lex PORCIA, by P. Porcius Læca, a tribune, A. U. 454, that no one should bind, scourge, or kill a Roman citizen.[20]

Lex PUBLICIA, vel *Publicia de lusu*, against playing for money at any game but what required strength, as shooting, running, leaping, &c.[21]

1 Liv. viii. 28.
2 Liv. xxxviii. 54.
3 App. Bell. Civ. ii.p.457.
4 Mod. Legg. Corn. sic.
5 Cic Or. ii 65.
6 quinos denos suffragio creabant.
7 Asc. Cic. Corn.
8 Cic. Mil. 13. Fam.

viii. 8.
9 Cic. Mil. Asc.
10 Dio. xxxix. 37. xi. 52.
11 ibid. Dialog. Orat. 30.
12 ex amplissimo censu.
13 Cic. Pis. 39. Phil. i. 8. Asc. Cic. quum in judice et fortuna spectari deberet, de dignitas,—

For in a judge both his rank and fortune are to be regarded, Cic. Phil. i. 20.
14 Suet. Jul. 28. Dio. xl. 66. App. Bell. Civ. ii. p. 442. Cic. Att. viii. 3. Phil. ii. 10.
15 App. Bel. Civ. ii. 441.

16 l. l. Dig.
17 Plin. Ep. x. 83. 113. 115.
18 Plin. iii. 20.
19 Gell. i. 12.
20 Liv. x. 9. Cic. Rab. perd. 3, 4. Verr. v. 63. Sall. Cat. 51.
21 l. 3. D. de aleat.

Lex PUBLILIA.[1]

Lex PUPIA, by a tribune, that the senate should not be held on Comitial days ; and that in the month of February, their first attention should be paid to the hearing of embassies.[2]

Lex QUINCTIA, A. U. 745, about the punishment of those who hurt or spoiled the aquæducts or public reservoirs of water.[3]

Lex REGIA, conferring supreme power on Augustus.[4]

Lex REMMIA.[5]

Leges REGIÆ, laws made by the kings, which are said to have been collected by Papirius, or, as it was anciently written, Papisius, soon after the expulsion of Tarquin,[6] whence they were called *jus civile* PAPIRIANUM ; and some of them, no doubt, were copied into the Twelve Tables.

Lex RHODIA, containing the regulations of the Rhodians concerning naval affairs, which Cicero and Strabo greatly commend,[7] supposed to have been adopted by the Romans. But this is certain only with respect to one clause, *de jactu*, about throwing goods overboard in a storm.

Leges de REPETUNDIS ; Acilia, Calpurnia, Cæcilia, Cornelia, Julia, Junia, Pompeia, Servilia.

Lex ROSCIA *theatralis*, determining the fortune of the equites, and appointing them certain seats in the theatre.[8] By this law a certain place in the theatre was assigned to spendthrifts.[9] The passing of this law occasioned great tumults, which were allayed by the eloquence of Cicero the consul.[10]

Lex RUPILIA, or more properly *decretum*, containing the regulations prescribed to the Sicilians by the prætor Rupilius, with the advice of ten ambassadors, according to the decree of the senate.[11]

Leges SACRATÆ : various laws were called by that name, chiefly those concerning the tribunes, made on the Mons Sacer, because the person who violated them was consecrated to some god.[12] There was also a LEX SACRATA MILITARIS, that the name of no soldier should be erased from the muster-roll without his own consent. So among the Æqui and Volsci, the Tuscans, the Ligures, and particularly the Samnites, among whom those were called *sacrati milites*, who were enlisted by a certain oath, and with particular solemnities.[13]

Lex SATURA was a law consisting of several distinct particulars of a different nature, which ought to have been enacted separately.[14]

Lex SCATINIA, vel *Scantinia, de nefanda venere*, by a tribune, the year uncertain, against illicit amours. The punishment at first was a heavy fine,[15] but it was afterwards made capital.

Lex SCRIBONIA, by a tribune, A. U. 601, about restoring the Lusitani to freedom.[16] Another, *de servitutum usucapionibus*, by a consul under Augustus, A. U. 719, that the right of servitudes should not be acquired by prescription, which seems to have been the case in the time of Cicero.[17]

---

1 see p. 14. 69.
2 Cic. Frat. ii. 2. 13. Fam. i. 4.
3 Frontin. de aquæduct.
4 see p. 17.
5 see Lex Memmia.
6 Cic. Tusc. Quæst. iii. 1. Fam. ix. 21. Diony. ii. 36.
7 Cic. Legg. Nan. 18.

Strab. 14.
8 see p. 18. Cic. Mur. 19. Juv. xiv. 323. Liv. Epit. 99. Mart. v. 8. Dio. xxxvi. 25.
9 decoctoribus, Cic. Phil. ii. 18.
10 Cic. Att. ii. 1. Plut. Cic. to which Virgil is supposed to allude,

Æn. i. 125.
11 Cic Verr. ii. 13. 15, 16.
12 Fest. Cic. Corn. Off. iii. 31. Balb. 14, 15.
iii. 54, 55. xxxiv. 5.
13 Liv. iv. 26. vii. 41. ix. 33. 39. x. 48. xxxvi. 3.
14 Fest.

15 Cic. Fam. viii. 14. Phil. iii. 6. Juv. ii. 43. Quinct. iv. 3. vii. 4. Suet. Dom. 8.
16 Liv. Epit. 49. Cic. Brut. 23.
17 Cæc. 26. 1. 4. D. de Usuc.

I.

Leges SEMPRONIÆ, laws proposed by the Gracchi.[1]

1. TIB. GRACCHI AGRARIA, by Tib. Gracchus, A. U. 620, that no one should possess more than 500 acres of land ; and that three commissioners should be appointed to divide among the poorer people what any one had above that extent.[2]

—— *de* CIVITATE ITALIS DANDA, that the freedom of the state should be given to all the Italians.[3]

—— *de* HÆREDITATE ATTALI, that the money which Attalus had left to the Roman people, should be divided among those citizens who got lands, to purchase the instruments of husbandry. These laws excited great commotions, and brought destruction on the author of them. Of course they were not put in execution.[4]

2. C. GRACCHI FRUMENTARIA, A. U. 628, that corn should be given to the poor people at a *triens* and a *semis*, or at $\frac{1}{3}\frac{0}{2}$ of an AS, a *modius* or peck ; and that money should be advanced from the public treasury to purchase corn for that purpose. The granaries in which this corn was kept were called HORREA SEMPRONIA.[5]

Note. A *triens* and *semis* are put for a *dextans*, because the Romans had not a coin of the value of a *dextans*.

—— *de* PROVINCIIS, that the provinces should be appointed for the consuls every year before their election.[6]

—— *de* CAPITE CIVIUM, that sentence should not be passed on the life of a Roman citizen without the order of the people.[7]

—— *de* MAGISTRATIBUS, that whoever was deprived of his office by the people, should ever after be incapable of enjoying any other.[8]

—— JUDICIARIA, that the judices should be chosen from among the equites, and not from the senators as formerly.[9]

—— Against corruption in the judices.[10] Sylla afterwards included this in his law *de falso.*

—— *de* CENTURIIS EVOCANDIS, that it should be determined by lot in what order the centuries should vote.[11]

—— *de* MILITIBUS, that clothes should be afforded to soldiers by the public, and that no deduction should be made on that account from their pay ; also, that no one should be forced to enlist below the age of seventeen.[12]

—— *de* VIIS MUNIENDIS, about paving and measuring the public roads, making bridges, placing milestones, and, at smaller distances, stones to help travellers to mount their horses, for it appears the ancient Romans did not use stirrups ; and there were wooden horses placed in the Campus Martius, where the youth might be trained to mount and dismount readily. Thus Virgil, *corpora saltu subjiciunt in equos.*[13]

Caius Gracchus first introduced the custom of walking or moving about while haranguing the people, and of exposing the right arm bare, which the ancient Romans, as the Greeks, used to keep within their robe.[14]

Lex SEMPRONIA *de fænore*, by a tribune, long before the time of the Gracchi, A. U. 560, that the interest of money should be regulated by the same laws among the allies and Latins, as among Roman citizens.

1 Cic. Phil. i. 7.
2 Liv. Epit. 58. Plut. Gracc. p. 837. App. Bell. Civ. 1. 355.
3 Paterc. ii. 2, 3.
4 Liv. Epit. 58. Plut. Gracc.
5 Cic. Sext. 44. Tusc.

Quæst. iii. 20. Brut. 62. Off. ii. 21. Liv. Ep. 58. 60.
6 Cic. Prov. Co. 2. Balb. 27. Dom. 9. Fam. i. 7.
7 Cic. Rab. 4. Verr. v. 63. Cat. iv. 5.
8 Plut. Gracc.

9 App. Bell. Civ. i. 363. Dio. xxxvi. 88. Cic. Verr. i. 13.
10 nequis judicio circumveniretur, Cic. Clu. 55.
11 Sall. Cæs. Rep. Ord. see p. 63.

12 Plut. Gracc.
13 with a bound they vault on their steeds, Æn. xii. 288. Veg. i. 18.
14 veste continere, Quin. xi. 3. 138. Dio. Fragm. xxxiv. 90.

The cause of this law was, to check the fraud of usurers, who lent their money in the name of the allies,[1] at higher interest than was allowed at Rome.

Lex SERVILIA AGRARIA, by P. Servilius Rullus, a tribune, A. U. 690, that ten commissioners should be created with absolute power for five years, over all the revenues of the republic ; to buy and sell what lands they thought fit, at what price and from whom they chose ; to distribute them at pleasure to the citizens ; to settle new colonies wherever they judged proper, and particularly in Campania, &c. But this law was prevented from being passed by the eloquence of Cicero the consul.[2]

—— *de* CIVITATE, by C. Servilius Glaucia, a prætor, A. U. 653, that if any of the Latin allies accused a Roman senator, and got him condemned, he should obtain the same place among the citizens which the criminal had held.[3]

—— *de* REPETUNDIS, by the same person, ordaining severer penalties than formerly against extortion, and that the defendant should have a second hearing.[4]

—— SERVILIA JUDICIARIA, by Q. Servilius Cœpio, A. U. 647, that the right of judging, which had been exercised by the equites alone for seventeen years, according to the Sempronian law, should be shared between the senators and equites.[5]

Lex SICINIA, by a tribune, A. U. 662, that no one should contradict or interrupt a tribune while speaking to the people.[6]

Lex SILIA, by a tribune, about weights and measures.[7]

Lex SILVANI et CARBONIS, by two tribunes, A. U. 664, that whoever was admitted as a citizen by any of the confederate states, if he had a house in Italy when the law was passed, and gave in his name to the prætor,[8] within sixty days, he should enjoy all the rights of a Roman citizen.[9]

Lex SULPICIA SEMPRONIA, by the consuls, A. U. 449, that no one should dedicate a temple or altar without the order of the senate, or a majority of the tribunes.[10]

Lex SULPICIA, by a consul, A. U. 553, ordering war to be proclaimed on Philip king of Macedon.[11]

Leges SULPICIÆ *de ære alieno*, by the tribune, Serv. Sulpicius, A. U. 665, that no senator should contract debt above 2000 denarii : that the exiles who had not been allowed a trial should be recalled : that the Italian allies, who had obtained the rights of citizens, and had been formed into eight new tribes, should be distributed through the thirty-five old tribes : also that the manumitted slaves,[12] who used formerly to vote only in the four city tribes, might vote in all the tribes : that the command of the war against Mithridates should be taken from Sylla, and given to Marius.[13]

But these laws were soon abrogated by Sylla, who, returning to Rome with his army from Campania, forced Marius and Sulpicius, with their adherents, to fly from the city. Sulpicius, being betrayed by a slave, was brought back and slain. Sylla rewarded the slave with his liberty, according to promise, but immediately after ordered him to be thrown from the Tarpeian rock for betraying his master.[14]

Leges SUMPTUARIÆ ; Orchia, Fannia, Didia, Licinia, Cornelia, Æmilia, Antia, Julia.

1 In socios nomina transcribebant, Liv. xxxv. 7.
2 Cic. Rull. Pis. 2.
3 Cic. Balb. 24.
4 ut reus comperendi-naretur, Cic. Verr. i. 9. Rab. Posth. 4.
5 Cic. Brut. 43, 44. 86. Or. ii. 55. Tac. Ann. xii. 60.
6 Diony. vii. 17.
7 Fest. in Publica Pondera.
8 apud prætorem profiteretur.
9 Cic. Arch. 4.
10 Liv. ix. 46.
11 Liv. xxxi. 6.
12 cives libertini.
13 Plut. Syl. Mar. Liv. Epit. 77. Asc. Cic. Paterc. ii. 18.
14 Ibid.

Leges TABELLARIÆ, four in number.[1]

Lex TALARIA, against playing at dice at entertainments.[2]

Lex TERENTIA et CASSIA *frumentaria*.[3]

Lex TERENTILIA, by a tribune, A. U. 291, about limiting the powers of the consuls. It did not pass ; but after great contentions gave cause to the creation of the decemviri.[4]

Leges TESTAMENTARIÆ ; Cornelia, Furia, Voconia.

Lex THORIA *de vectigalibus*, by a tribune, A. U. 646, that no one should pay any rent to the people for the public lands in Italy which he possessed.[5] It also contained certain regulations about pasturage. But Appian gives a different account of this law.[6]

Lex TITIA *de quæstoribus*, by a tribune, as some think, A. U. 448, about doubling the number of quæstors, and that they should determine their provinces by lot.[7]

—— *de* MUNERIBUS, against receiving money or presents for pleading.[8]

—— AGRARIA : what it was, is not known.[9]

—— *de* LUSU, similar to the Publician law.

—— *de* TUTORIBUS, A. U. 722, the same with the Julian law ; and, as some think, one and the same law.[10]

Lex TREBONIA, by a tribune, A. U. 698, assigning provinces to the consuls for five years : Spain to Pompey ; Syria and the Parthian war to Crassus ; and prolonging Cæsar's command in Gaul for an equl time. Cato, for opposing this law, was led to prison. According to Dio, he was only dragged from the assembly.[11]

—— *de* TRIBUNIS, A. U. 305.[12]

Lex TRIBUNITIA, either a law proposed by a tribune, or a law restoring their power.[13]

Lex TRIUMPHALIS, that no one should triumph who had not killed 5000 of the enemy in one battle.[14]

Lex TULLIA, *de* AMBITU, by Cicero, when consul, A. U. 690, adding to the former punishments against bribery, banishment for ten years ; and, that no one should exhibit shows of gladiators for two years before he stood candidate for an office, unless that task was imposed on him by the testament of a friend.[15]

—— *de* LEGATIONE LIBERA, limiting the continuance of it to a year.[16]

Lex VALERIA *de provocatione*.[17]

—— *de* FORMIANIS, A. U. 562, about giving the people of Formiæ the right of voting.[18]

—— *de* SYLLA, by L. Valerius Flaccus, interrex, A. U. 671, creating Sylla dictator, and ratifying all his acts ; which Cicero calls the most unjust of all laws.[19]

—— *de* QUADRANTE, by L. Valerius Flaccus, consul, A. U. 667, that debtors should be discharged on paying one-fourth of their debts.[20]

Lex VALERIA HORATIA *de tributis comitiis ; de tribunis*, against hurting a tribune.[21]

---

1 see p. 64.
2 ut ne legi fraudem faciam talariæ, that I may not break, &c. Plaut. Mil. Glor. ii. 2. 9.
3 see lex Cassia.
4 Liv. iii. 9, 10, &c.
5 agrum publicum vectigali levavit, Cic. Brut. 36.

6 Bell. Civ. i. p. 366. Cic. Or ii. 70.
7 Cic. Mur. 8.
8 Aus. Epig. 89. Tac. Ann. xi. 13. where some read, instead of Cinciam, Titiam.
9 Cic. Or. ii. 11. Legg. ii. 6. 12. See App. B.
10 Justin. Instit. Atil. Tut.

11 xxxix. 33, 34. Liv. Epit. 104.
12 Liv. iii. 64, 65. see p. 92, 93.
13 Cic. Act. prim. Verr.
16. Rull. ii. 8. Liv. iii. 56.
14 Val. Max. ii. 8.
15 Dio. xxxvii. 29. Cic. Vat. 15. Sext. 64. Mur. 32. 34, &c.

16 Cic. Legg. iii. 8.
17 see p. 77.
18 Liv. xxxviii. 36.
19 Cic. Rull. iii. 2. 3. Rosc. 43. Legg. i. 15.
20 Paterc. ii. 23. see p. 34.
21 Liv. iii. 55. see p. 14.

Lex VARIA, by a tribune, A. U. 662, that inquiry should be made about those by whose means or advice the Italian allies had taken up arms against the Roman people.[1]

Lex VATINIA *de* PROVINCIIS,[2]

—— *de alternis consiliis rejiciendis*, that, in a trial for extortion, both the defendant and accuser might for once reject all the judices or jury; whereas formerly they could reject only a few, whose places the prætor supplied by a new choice.[3]

—— *de* COLONIS, that Cæsar should plant a colony at Novocomum in Cisalpine Gaul.[4]

Leges DE VI, *Plotia, Lutatia, et Julia.*

Lex VIARIA, *de* VIIS MUNIENDIS, by C. Curio, a tribune, A. U. 703, somewhat similar to the Agrarian law of Rullus. By this law there seems to have been a tax imposed on carriages and horses.[5]

Lex VILLIA ANNALIS.[6]

Lex VOCONIA *de* HÆREDITATIBUS *mulierum*, by a tribune, A.U. 384, that no one should make a woman his heir,[7] nor leave to any one, by way of legacy, more than to his heir or heirs.[8] But this law is supposed to have referred chiefly to those who were rich,[9] to prevent the extinction of opulent families.

Various arts were used to elude this law. Sometimes one left his fortune in trust to a friend, who should give it to a daughter or other female relation; but his friend could not be forced to do so, unless he inclined. The law itself, however, like many others, on account of its severity, fell into disuse.[10]

These are almost all the Roman laws mentioned in the classics. Augustus having become sole master of the empire, continued at first to enact laws in the ancient form, which were so many vestiges of expiring liberty,[11] as Tacitus calls them: but he afterwards, by the advice of Mæcenas, gradually introduced the custom of giving the force of laws to the decrees of the senate, and even to his own edicts.[12] His successors improved upon this example. The ancient manner of passing laws came to be entirely dropped. The decrees of the senate, indeed, for form's sake, continued for a considerable time to be published; but at last these also were laid aside, and every thing was done according to the will of the prince.

The emperors ordained laws—1. By their answers to the applications made to them at home, or from the provinces.[13]

—— 2. By their decrees in judgment or sentences in court,[14] which were either INTERLOCUTORY, i. e. such as related to any incidental point of law which might occur in the process; or DEFINITIVE, i. e. such as determined upon the merits of the cause itself, and the whole question.

——3. By their occasional ordinances,[15] and by their instructions[16] to their lieutenants and officers.

These constitutions were either general, respecting the public at large; or special, relating to one person only, and therefore properly called PRIVILEGIA, privileges; but in a sense different from what it was used in under the republic.[17]

---

1 Cic. Brut. 56. 89.
Tusc. Quæst. ii. 24.
Val. Max. v. 2.
2 see p. 80.
3 subsortitione,   Cic.
Vat. 11.
4 Suet. Jul. 28.
5 Cic. Fam. viii. 6. Att.
vi. 1.

6 see p. 74.
7 ne quis heredem virginem neque mulierem faceret, Cic. Ver. i. 42.
8 c. 43. Sen. 5. Balb. 8.
9 qui essent censi, i. e. pecuniosi vel classici, those of the first class, Asc. Cic. Gell. vii. 13.

10 Cic. Fin. ii. 17. Gell. xx. i.
11 vestigia morientis libertatis.
12 Tac Ann. i. 2. iii. 28. Dio. lii.
13 per rescripta ad libellos supplices, epistolas, vel preces.

14 per decreta.
15 per edicta vel constitutiones.
16 per mandata.
17 Plin. Ep. x. 56, 57. see p. 17.

The three great sources, therefore, of Roman jurisprudence were the laws,[1] properly so called, the decrees of the senate,[2] and the edicts of the prince.[3] To these may be added the edicts of the magistrates, chiefly the prætors, called JUS HONORARIUM,[4] the opinions of learned lawyers,[5] and custom or long usage.[6]

The titles and heads of laws, as the titles and beginnings of books,[7] used to be written with vermilion :[8] hence, RUBRICA is put for the civil law ; thus, *rubrica vetavit*, the laws have forbidden.[9]

The constitutions of the emperors were collected by different lawyers. The chief of these were Gregory and Hermogenes, who flourished under Constantine. Their collections were called CODEX GREGORIANUS, and CODEX HERMOGENIANUS. But these books were composed only by private persons. The first collection made by public authority was that of the emperor Theodosius the younger, published, A. C. 438, and called CODEX THEODOSIANUS. But it only contained the imperial constitutions from Constantine to his own time, for little more than a hundred years.

It was the emperor JUSTINIAN that first reduced the Roman law into a certain order. For this purpose he employed the assistance of the most eminent lawyers in the empire, at the head of whom was TRIBONIAN.

Justinian first published a collection of the imperial constitutions, A. C. 529, called CODEX JUSTINIANUS.

Then he ordered a collection to be made of every thing that was useful in the writings of the lawyers before his time, which are said to have amounted to 2000 volumes. This work was executed by Tribonian, and sixteen associates, in three years, although they had been allowed ten years to finish it. It was published, A. C. 533, under the title of Digests or Pandects.[10] It is sometimes called, in the singular, the Digest or Pandect.

The same year were published, the elements or first principles of the Roman law, composed by three men, Tribonian, Theophilus, and Dorotheus, and called the Institutes.[11] This book was published before the Pandects, although it was composed after them.

As the first code did not appear sufficiently complete, and contained several things inconsistent with the Pandects, Tribonian and other four men were employed to correct it. A new code, therefore, was published, xvi Kal. Dec. 534, called CODEX REPETITÆ PRÆLECTIONIS, and the former code declared to be of no further authority. Thus in six years was completed what is called CORPUS JURIS, the body of Roman law.

But when new questions arose, not contained in any of the above-mentioned books, new decisions became necessary to supply what was wanting, or correct what was erroneous. These were afterwards published, under the title of Novels,[12] not only by Justinian, but also by some of the succeeding emperors. So that the *Corpus Juris Romani Civilis* is made up of these books : the Institutes, Pandects, or Digests, Code, and Novels.

The Institutes are divided into four books ; each book into several titles

---

1 leges.
2 senatus consulta.
3 constitutiones principales.
4 jus honorarium, see p. 85.
5 auctoritas vel responsa prudentum vel juris consultorem, Cic. Mur. 13. Cæc. 24.

6 consuetudo vel mos majorum, Gell. xi. 18.
7 Ov. Trist. i. 7. Mart. iii. 2.
8 rubrica vel minio.
9 Pers. v. 90, alii se ad album, i. e. jus prætorium, quia prætores edicta sua in albo proponebant, ac rubricas,

i. e. jus civile, transtulerunt, Quin. xii. 3. 11.—some have gone no farther than the records of some courts, and the titles of some law chapters, Patsall. —hence Juvenal, perlege rubras majorum leges, Sat. xiv. 193,—

study the red-lettered titles (laws) of our forefathers.
10 pandectæ vel digesta.
11 instituta.
12 novellæ, sc. constitutiones.

or chapters ; and each title into paragraphs (§), of which the first is not numbered : thus, Inst. lib. i. tit. x. princip.; or, more shortly, 1. 1. 10. pr. So, Inst. l. i. tit. x. § 2.——or, I. 1. 10. 2.

The Pandects are divided into fifty books.; each book into several titles ; each title into several laws, which are distinguished by numbers; and some-times one law into beginning (princ. for principium) and paragraphs ; thus, D. 1. 1. 5., *i. e.* Digest, first book, first title, fifth law.   If the law is divid-ed into paragraphs, a fourth number must be added ; thus D. 48. 5. 13. pr., or, 48. 5. 15. 13. 3.   Sometimes the first word of the law, not the number, is cited.   The Pandects are often marked by a double *f*; thus, *ff.*

The Code is cited in the same manner as the Pandects, by book, title, and law ; the Novels by their number, the chapters of that number, and the paragraphs, if any ; as Nov. 115, *c.* 3.

The Justinian code of law was universally received through the Roman world.   It flourished in the east until the taking of Constantinople by the Turks, A. D. 1453.   In the west it was, in a great measure, suppressed by the irruption of the barbarous nations, till it was revived in Italy in the 12th century by IRNERIUS, who had studied at Constantinople, and opened a school at Bologna, under the auspices of Frederick I., emperor of Ger-many.   He was attended by an incredible number of students from all parts, who propagated the knowledge of the Roman civil law through most countries of Europe, where it still continues to be of great authority in courts of justice ; and seems to promise, at least in point of legislation, the fulfilment of the famous prediction of the ancient Romans concerning the eternity of their empire.

JUDICIAL PROCEEDINGS OF THE ROMANS.

THE judicial proceedings[1] of the Romans were either private or public ; or, as we express it, civil or criminal.

I. JUDICIA PRIVATA, CIVIL TRIALS.

JUDICIA *privata*, or civil trials, were concerning private causes or dif-ferences between private persons.   In these at first the kings presided, then the consuls, the military tribunes and decemviri ; but, after the year 389, the prætor *urbanus* and *peregrinus.*[2]

The judicial power of the prætor *urbanus* and *peregrinus* was properly called JURISDICTIO ;[3] and of the prætors who presided at criminal trials, QUÆSTIO.[4]

The prætor might be applied to[5] on all court-days ;[6] but on certain days he attended only on petitions or requests ;[7] so the consuls ; and on others, to the examination of causes.[8]

On court-days, early in the morning, the prætor went to the forum ; and there, being seated on his tribunal, ordered an *accensus* to call out to the people around that it was the third hour, and that whoever had any cause[9] might bring it before him.   But this could only be done by a certain form.

---

1 judicia.—omnia judi-
cia aut distrahenda-
rum controversiarum
aut puniendorum mali-
ficiorum causa reperta
sunt, Cic. Cæc. 2.

2 Cic. Or. i. 38. Top. 17.
Diony. x. 1. Liv. ii. 27.
iii. 33. see p. 83, 84.
3 quæ posita erat in
edicto et ex edicto de-
cretis.

4 Cic. Verr. i. 40, 41.
46, 47, &c. ii. 48. v. 14.
Mur. 20. Flac. 3. Tac.
Agr. 6.
5 adiri poterat, copiam
vel potestatem sui fa-

ciebat.
6 diebus fastis.
7 postulationibus vaca-
bat.
8 Plin. Ep. vii. 33.
9 qui lege agere vellet.

I. VOCATIO IN JUS, OR SUMMONING TO COURT.

IF a person had a quarrel with any one, he first tried to make it up[1] in private.[2] If the matter could not be settled in this manner, the plaintiff[3] ordered his adversary to go with him before the prætor,[4] by saying, IN JUS VOCO TE : IN JUS EAMUS : IN JUS VENI : SEQUERE AD TRIBUNAL : IN JUS AMBULA, or the like.[5] If he refused, the prosecutor took some one present to witness, by saying, LICET ANTESTARI ? May I take you to witness ? If the person consented, he offered the tip of his ear,[6] which the prosecutor touched.[7] Then the plaintiff might drag the defendant[8] to court by force,[9] in any way, even by the neck,[10] according to the law of the Twelve Tables ; SI CALVITUR[11] PEDEMVE STRUIT,[12] MANUM ENDO JACITO, *injicito*. But worthless persons, as thieves, robbers, &c., might be dragged before a judge without this formality.[13]

By the law of the Twelve Tables none were excused from appearing in court ; not even the aged, the sickly, and infirm. If they could not walk, they were furnished with an open carriage.[14] But afterwards this was altered, and various persons were exempted ; as magistrates, those absent on account of the state ; also matrons, boys and girls under age, &c.[15]

It was likewise unlawful to force any person to court from his own house, because a man's house was esteemed his sanctuary.[16] But if any one lurked at home to elude a prosecution,[17] he was summoned[18] three times, with an interval of ten days between each summons, by the voice of a herald, or by letters, or by the edict of the prætor ; and if he still did not appear,[19] the prosecutor was put in possession of his effects.[20]

If the person cited found security, he was let go : SI ENSIET (*si autem sit*, sc. *aliquis,*) QUI IN JUS VOCATUM VINDICIT, (*vindicaverit,* shall be surety for his appearance,) MITTITO, let him go.

If he made up the matter by the way (ENDO VIA), the process was dropped. Hence may be explained the words of our Saviour, Matt. v. 25. Luke xii. 58.

II. POSTULATIO ACTIONIS, REQUESTING A WRIT, AND GIVING BAIL.

IF no private agreement could be made, both parties went before the prætor. Then the plaintiff proposed the action[21] which he intended to bring against the defendant,[22] and demanded a writ[23] from the prætor for that purpose. For there were certain forms,[24] or set words,[25] necessary to be used in every cause.[26] At the same time the defendant requested that an advocate or lawyer might be given him, to assist him with his counsel.

There were several actions competent for the same thing. The prosecutor chose which he pleased, and the prætor usually granted it ;[27] but he might also refuse it.

---

1 litem componere vel dijudicare.
2 intra parietes, Cic. Quinct. 5. 11. per disceptatores domesticos vel opera amicorum, Cæc. 2.
3 actor vel petitor, Liv. iv. 9.
4 in jus vocabat.
5 Ter. Phor. v. 7. 43. 88.
6 auriculam opponebat.
7 Hor. Sat. i. 9. v. 76. Plaut. Cor. v. 2. see p.

42.
8 reum.
9 in jus rapere.
10 obtorto collo, cervice adstricta, Cic. & Plaut. Pœn. iii. 5. 45. Juv. x. 88.
11 moratur.
12 fugit vel fugam adornat, Fest.
13 Plaut. Pers. iv. 9. v. 10.
14 jumentum, i. e. plaustrum vel vectabulum, Gell. xx. 1. Cic. Legg.

ii. 23. Hor. Sat. i. 9. 70.
15 D. de in jus vocand. &c. Liv. xlv. 37. Val. Max. ii. 1. 5. iii. 7. 9.
16 tutissimum refugium et receptaculum.
17 si fraudationis causa latitaret, Cic. Quin. 19.
18 evocabatur.
19 se non sisteret.
20 in bona ejus mittebatur, ib.
21 actionem edebat, vel dicam scribebat, Cic.

Verr. ii. 15.
22 quam in reum intendere vellet, Plaut. Per. iv. 9.
23 actionem postulabat.
24 formulæ.
25 verba concepta.
26 formulæ de omnibus rebus constitutæ, Cic. Rosc. Com. 6.
27 actionem vel judicium dabat vel reddebat, Cic. Cæc. 3. Quin. 22. Verr. ii. 12. 27. Hor. ii. 13.

The plaintiff, having obtained a writ from the prætor, offered it to the defendant, or dictated to him the words. This writ it was unlawful to change.[1]

The greatest caution was requisite in drawing up the writ,[2] for if there was a mistake in one word, the whole cause was lost.[3]   Hence SCRIBERE *vel* SUBSCRIBERE DICAM *alicui* vel *impingere*, to bring an action against one, or *cum aliquo* JUDICIUM SUBSCRIBERE, EI FORMULAM INTEMDERE.   But DI-CAM vel *dicas sortiri*, i. e. *judices dare sortitione, qui causam cognoscant*, to appoint judices to judge of causes.[4]

A person skilled only in framing writs and the like, is called by Cicero, LEGULEIUS,[5] and by Quinctilian, FORMULARIUS.   He attended on the ad-vocates, to suggest to them the laws and forms ; as those called PRAGMA-TICI did among the Greeks,[6] and as agents do among us.

The plaintiff required that the defendant should give bail for his ap-. pearance in court[7] on a certain day, which was usually the third day af-ter.[8]   And thus he was said VADARI REUM.[9]   This was also done in a set form prescribed by a lawyer, who was said VADIMONIUM CONCIPERE.[10]

The defendant was said VADES DARE, vel VADIMONIUM PROMITTERE.   If he did not find bail, he was obliged to go to prison.[11]   The prætor some-times put off the hearing of the cause to a more distant day.[12] But the par-ties[13] chiefly were said VADIMONIUM DIFFERRE *cum aliquo*, to put off the day of the trial.   *Res esse in vadimonium cœpit*, began to be litigated.[14]

In the mean time the defendant sometimes made up[15] the matter pri-vately with the plaintiff, and the action was dropped.[16]   In which case the plaintiff was said *decidisse* vel *pactionem fecisse cum reo, judicio reum ab-solvisse* vel *liberasse, lite contestata* vel *judicio constituto*, after the lawsuit was begun ; and the defendant, *litem redemisse*, after receiving security from the plaintiff[17] that no further demands were to be made upon him.[18] If a person was unable or unwilling to carry on a lawsuit, he was said NON POSSE vel NOLLE PROSEQUI, vel EXPERIRI, sc. *jus* vel *jure*, vel *jure summo*.[19]

When the day came, if either party when cited was not present, without a valid excuse,[20] he lost his cause.   If the defendant was absent, he was said DESERERE VADIMONIUM, and the prætor put the plaintiff in possession of his effects.[21]

If the defendant was present, he was said VADIMONIUM SISTERE *vel* OBIRE.   When cited, he said, UBI TU ES, QUI ME VADATUS ES ?   UBI TU ES, QUI ME CITASTI ?   ECCE ME TIBI SISTO, TU CONTRA ET TE MIHI SISTE. The plaintiff answered, ADSUM.   Then the defendant said, QUID AIS ?   The plaintiff said, AIO FUNDUM, QUEM POSSIDES, MEUM ESSE ; vel AIO TE MIHI DARE, FACERE, OPORTERE, or the like.[22]   This was called INTENTIO AC-TIONIS, and varied according to the nature of the action.

1 mutare formulam non licebat, Sen. Ep. 117.
2 in actione vel formula concipienda.
3 Cic. Inv. ii. 19. Her. i. 2. Quin. lii. 8. vii. 3. 17. qui plus petebat, quam debitum est, causam perdebat, Cic. Q. Rosc. 4. vel formu-la excidebat, i. e. causa cadebat, Suet. Claud. 14.
4 Cic. Verr. ii. 15. 17. Ter. Phor. ii. 3. 92.

Plin. Ep. v. 1. Suet. Vit. 7.
5 præco actionum, can-tor formularum, an-ceps syllabarum, Cic. Or. i. 55.
6 Quin. xii. 3. 11.
7 vades, qui sponderent eum adfuturum.
8 tertio die vel peren-die, Cic. Quin. 7. Mur. 12. Gell. vii. 1.
9 vades ideo dicti, quod, qui eos dederit, vaden-di, id est, discendendi

habet potestatem, Fest. Cic. Quin. 6.
10 Cic. Frat. ii. 15.
11 Plaut. Per. ii. 4. v. 18.
12 vadimonia differebat, 213.
13 litigatores.
14 Cic. Att. ii. 7. Fam. ii. 6. Quin. 14. 16.
15 rem componebat et transigebat, compro-mised.
16 Plin. Ep. v. 1.
17 cum sibi cavisset ve:

satis ab actore acce-pisset.
18 amplius a se nemi-nem petiturum, Cic. Quin. 11, 12.
19 ib. 7, &c.
20 sine morbo vel causa sontica.
21 Hor. Sat. i. 9. v. 36. Cic. Quin. 6. 20.
22 Plaut. Curc. i. 3. 5. Cic. Mur. 12.

III. DIFFERENT KINDS OF ACTIONS.

ACTIONS were either real, personal, or mixed.

1. A real action[1] was for obtaining a thing to which one had a real right,[2] but which was possessed by another.[3]

2. A personal action[4] was against a person for doing or giving something, which he was bound to do or give, by reason of a contract, or of some wrong done by him to the plaintiff.

3. A mixed action was both for a thing, and for certain personal protestations.

1. REAL ACTIONS.

ACTIONS for a thing, or real actions, were either CIVIL, arising from some law,[5] or PRÆTORIAN, depending on the edict of the prætor.

ACTIONES PRÆTORIÆ, were remedies granted by the prætor for rendering an equitable right effectual, for which there was no adequate remedy granted by the statute or common law.

A civil action for a thing[6] was called VINDICATIO ; and the person who raised it, VINDEX. But this action could not be brought, unless it was previously ascertained who ought to be the possessor. If this was contested, it was called LIS VINDICIARUM, and the prætor determined the matter by an interdict.[7]

If the question was about a slave, the person who claimed the possession of him, laying hands on the slave[8] before the prætor, said, HUNC HOMINEM EX JURE QUIRITIUM MEUM ESSE AIO, EJUSQUE VINDICIAS, i. e. *possessionem*, MIHI DARI POSTULA.[9] If the other was silent, or yielded his right,[10] the prætor adjudged the slave to the person who claimed him ;[11] that is, he decreed to him the possession, till it was determined who should be the proprietor of the slave.[12] But if the other person also claimed possession,[13] then the prætor pronounced an interdict,[14] QUI NEC VI, NEC CLAM, NEC PRE-CARIO POSSIDET, EI VINDICIAS DABO.

The laying on of hands[15] was the usual mode of claiming the property of any person, to which frequent allusion is made in the classics.[16]

In disputes of this kind,[17] the presumption always was in favour of the possessor, according to the law of the Twelve Tables, SI QUI IN JURE MA-NUM CONSERUNT, i. e. *apud judicem disceptant*, SECUNDUM EUM QUI POSSI-DET, VINDICIAS DATO.[18]

But in an action concerning liberty, the prætor always decreed possession in favour of freedom,[19] and Appius, the decemvir, by doing the contrary,[20] by decreeing that Virginia should be given up into the hands of M. Claudius, his client, who claimed her, and not to her father, who was present, brought destruction on himself and his colleagues.[21]

Whoever claimed a slave to be free[22] was said EUM LIBERALI CAUSA

---

1 actio in rem.
2 jus in re.
3 per quam rem nostram, quæ ab alio possidetur, petimus, Ulp.
4 actio in personam.
5 Cic. Cæc. 5. Or. i. 2.
6 actio civilis vel legitima in rem.
7 Cic. Verr. i. 45. Cæc. 8. 14.
8 manum el injiciendo.

9 to which Plautus alludes, Rud. iv. 3. 86.
10 jure cedebat.
11 servum addicebat vindicanti.
12 ad exitum judicii.
13 si vindicias sibi conservari postularet.
14 interdicebat.
15 manus injectio, Liv. iii. 43.
16 Ov. Ep. Herold. viii.

16. xii. 158. Am. i. 4. 40. ii. 5. 30. Fast. iv. 90. Virg. Æn. x. 419. Cic. Rosc. Com. 16. Plin. Ep. x. 19. in vera bona non est manus injectio ; animo non potest injici manus, i. e. vis fieri, Sen.
17 in litibus vindiciarum.
18 Gell. xx. 10.

19 vindicias dedit secundum libertatem.
20 decernendo vindicias secundum servitutem, vel ab libertate in servitutem contra leges vindicias dando.
21 Liv. iii. 47. 56. 58.
22 vindex, qui in libertatem vindicabat.

MANU ASSERERE ;[1] but if he claimed a free person to be a slave, he was said IN SERVITUTEM ASSERERE ; and hence was called ASSERTOR. Hence, *hæc* (sc. *præsentia gaudia*) *utraque manu, complexuque assere toto ;*[2] ASSERO, for *affirmo*, or *assevero*, is used only by later writers.

The expression MANUM CONSERERE, to fight hand to hand, is taken from war, of which the conflict between the two parties was a representation. Hence VINDICIA, i. e. *injectio* vel *correptio manus in re præsenti*, was called *vis civilis et festucaria*.[3] The two parties are said to have crossed two rods[4] before the prætor, as if in fighting, and the vanquished party to have given up his rod to his antagonist. Whence some conjecture that the first Romans determined their disputes with the point of their swords.

Others think that *vindicia* was a rod,[5] which the two parties[6] broke in their fray or mock fight before the prætor (as a straw[7] used anciently to be broken in making stipulations),[8] the consequence of which was, that . one of the parties might say, that he had been ousted or deprived of possession,[9] by the other, and therefore claim to be restored by a decree[10] of the prætor.

If the question was about a farm, a house, or the like, the prætor anciently went with the parties[11] to the place, and gave possession[12] to which of them he thought proper. But from the increase of business this soon became impracticable ; and then the parties called one another from court[13] to the spot,[14] to a farm, for instance, and brought from thence a turf,[15] which was also called VINDICIÆ, and contested about it as about the whole farm. It was delivered to the person to whom the prætor adjudged the possession.[16]

But this custom also was dropped, and the lawyers devised a new form of process in suing for possession, which Cicero pleasantly ridicules.[17] The plaintiff[18] thus addressed the defendant ;[19] FUNDUS QIU EST IN AGRO, QUI SABINUS VOCATUR, EUM EGO EX JURE QUIRITIUM MEUM ESSE AIO, INDE EGO TE EX JURE MANU CONSERTUM (to contend according to law) voco. If the defendant yielded, the prætor adjudged possession to the plaintiff. If not, the defendant thus answered the plaintiff, UNDE TU ME EX JURE MANUM CONSERTUM VOCASTI, INDE IBI EGO TE REVOCO. Then the prætor repeated his set form,[20] UTRISQUE, SUPERSTITIBUS PRÆSENTIBUS, i. e. *testibus præsentibus* (before witnesses), ISTAM VIAM DICO. INITE VIAM. Immediately they both set out, as if to go to the farm, to fetch a turf, accompanied by a lawyer to direct them.[21] Then the prætor said, REDITE VIAM ; upon which they returned. If it appeared that one of the parties had been dispossessed by the other through force, the prætor thus decreed, UNDE TU ILLUM DEJECISTI, CUM NEC VI, NEC CLAM, NEC PRECARIO POSSIDERET, EO ILLUM RESTITUAS JUBEO. If not, he thus decreed, UTI NUNC POSSIDETIS, &c. ITA POSSIDEATIS. VIM FIERI VETO.

The possessor being thus ascertained, then the action about the right of property[22] commenced. The person ousted or outed[23] first asked the defendant if he was the lawful possessor.[24] Then he claimed his right, and in the meantime required that the possessor should give security,[25] not to

---

1 to claim him by an action of freedom. Ter. Adel. ii. 1. 39. Plaut. Pæn. v. 2. Liv. 3. 44.
2 then seize it fast ; embrace it ere it flies,—Hay. Mart. l. 16. 9.
3 Gell. 20. 10.
4 festucas inter se commisisse.

5 virgula vel festuca.
6 litigantes vel disceptantes.
7 stipula.
8 Isid. v. 24.
9 possessione dejectus.
10 interdicto.
11 cum litigantibus.
12 vindicias dabat.
13 ex jure.

14 in locum vel rem præsentem.
15 glebam.
16 Fest. Gell. xx. 10.
17 Mur. 12.
18 petitor.
19 eum, unde petebatur.
20 carmen compositum.
21 qui ire viam doceret.
22 de jure dominii.

23 possessione exclusus vel dejectus, Cic. Cæc. 19.
24 quando ego te in jure conspicio, postulo an si es auctor ? i. e. possessor, unde meum jus repetere possim, Cic. Cæc. 19. Prob. Not.
25 satis daret.

do any damage to the subject in question,[1] by cutting down trees, or demolishing buildings, &c., in which case the plaintiff was said PER PRÆDES, v. -em, vel pro præde LITIS VINDICIARUM SATIS ACCIPERE.[2] If the defendant did not give security, the possession was transferred to the plaintiff, provided he gave security.

A sum of money also used to be deposited by both parties, called SACRAMENTUM, which fell to the gaining party after the cause was determined,[3] or a stipulation was made about the payment of a certain sum, called SPONSIO. The plaintiff said, QUANDO NEGAS HUNC FUNDUM ESSE MEUM, SACRAMENTO TE QUINQUAGENARIO PROVOCO. SPONDESNE QUINGENTOS, SC. nummos vel asses, SI MEUS EST? i. e. si meum esse probavero. The defendant said, SPONDEO QUINGENTOS SI TUUS SIT. Then the defendant required a correspondent stipulation from the plaintiff,[4] thus, ET TU SPONDESNE QUINGENTOS, SI TUUS SIT? i. e. si probavero tuum non esse. Then the plaintiff said, SPONDEO, SI MEUS SIT. Either party lost his cause if he refused to give this promise, or to deposit the money required.

Festus says this money was called SACRAMENTUM, because it used to be expended on sacred rites; but others, because it served as an oath,[5] to convince the judges that the lawsuit was not undertaken without cause, and thus checked wanton litigation. Hence it was called PIGNUS SPONSIONIS.[6] And hence pignore contendere, et sacramento, is the same.[7]

Sacramentum is sometimes put for the suit or cause itself,[8] sacramentum in libertatem, i. e. causa et vindiciæ libertatis, the claim of liberty. So SPONSIONEM FACERE, to raise a lawsuit; sponsione lacessere, certare, vincere, and also vincere sponsionem, or judicium, to prevail in the cause; condemnari sponsionis, to lose the cause; sponsiones, i. e. causæ, prohibitæ judicari, causes not allowed to be tried.[9]

The plaintiff was said sacramento vel sponsione provocare, rogare, quærere, et stipulari. The defendant, contendere ex provocatione vel sacramento, et restipulari.[10]

The same form was used in claiming an inheritance,[11] in claiming servitudes, &c. But, in the last, the action might be expressed both affirmatively and negatively; thus, AIO, JUS ESSE vel NON ESSE. Hence it was called actio CONFESSORIA et NEGATORIA.

2. PERSONAL ACTIONS.

PERSONAL actions, called also CONDICTIONES, were very numerous. They arose from some contract, or injury done; and required that a person should do or give certain things, or suffer a certain punishment.

Actions from contracts or obligations were about buying and selling;[12] about letting and hiring;[13] about a commission;[14] partnership;[15] a deposite;[16] a loan;[17] a pawn or pledge;[18] a wife's fortune;[19] a stipulation,[20] which

---

1 se nihil deterius in possessione facturum.
2 Cic. Ver. i. 45.
3 Fest. Varr. L. L. iv. 36.
4 restipulabatur.
5 quod instar sacramenti vel jurisjurandi esset.
6 quia violare quod quisque promittit perfidia est, Isid. Orig. v. 24.
7 Cic. Fam. vii. 22. Or. i. 10.

8 pro ipsa petitione, Cic. Cæc. 23.
9 Cic. Dom. 29. Mil. 27. Or. i. 10. Quin. 8.26,27. Verr. i. 53. iii. 57. 62. Cæc. 6. 16. 31, 32. Off. iii. 19. Rosc. Com.4, 5.
10 Cic. Rosc. Com. 13. Val. Max. ii. 8. 2. Var. L. L. iv. 36. Fest.
11 in hæreditatis petitione.
12 de emptione et venditione.
13 de locatione et con-

ductione: locabatur vel domus vel fundus, vel opus faciendum, vel vectigal; ædium conductor inquilinus, fondi colonus, operis redemptor, vectigalia publicanus vel manceps dicebatur.
14 de mandato.
15 de societate.
16 de deposito apud sequestrem.
17 de commodato vel mutuo, proprie commo-

damus vestes, libros, vasa, equos, et similia, quæ eadem redduntur; mutuo autem damus ea, pro quibus alia redduntur ejusdem generis, ut nummos, frumentum, vinum, oleum, et fere cetera, quæ pondere, numero vel mensura dari solent.
18 de hypotheca vel pignore.
19 de dote vel re uxoria.
20 de stipulatione.

took place almost in all bargains, and was made in this form :—An spondes ? Spondeo : An dabis ? Dabo : An promittis ? promitto, vel repromitto, &c.[1]

When the seller set a price on a thing, he was said indicare : thus, indica, fac pretium, and the buyer, when he offered a price, liceri, i. e.
rogare quo pretio liceret auferre.[2] At an auction, the person who bade[3]
held up his forefinger ;[4] hence digito liceri. The buyer asked, quanti
licet, sc. habere vel auferre. The seller answered, decem nummis licet, or
the like.[5] Thus some explain de Drusi hortis, quanti licuisse (sc. eas
emere), tu scribis audieram : sed quanti quanti, bene emitur quod necesse
est.[6] But most here take licere in a passive sense, to be valued or appraised ; quanti quanti, sc. licent, at whatever price.[7] So venibunt quiqui
licebunt (whoever shall be appraised, or exposed to sale, shall be sold)
præsenti peeunia, for ready money.[8] Unius assis non unquam pretio pluris
licuisse, notante judice quo nosti populo, was never reckoned worth more
than the value of one as, in the estimation of the people, &c.[9]

In verbal bargains or stipulations there were certain fixed forms[10] usually
observed between the two parties. The person who required the promise
or obligation, stipulator,[11] asked[12] him who was to give the obligation,[13]
before witnesses, if he would do or give a certain thing ; and the other always answered in correspondent words : thus, an dabis ? Dabo vel dabitur. An spondes ? Spondeo. Any material change or addition in the
answer rendered it of no effect. The person who required the promise
was said to be reus stipulandi ; he who gave it, reus promittendi.
Sometimes an oath was interposed,[14] and, for the sake of greater security,[15]
there was a second person, who required the promise or obligation to be repeated to him, therefore called astipulator,[16] and another, who joined in
giving it, adpromissor. Fide jussor vel sponsor, a surety, who said, et
ego spondeo idem hoc, or the like. Hence, astipulari irato consuli, to
humour or assist.[17] The person who promised, in his turn usually asked a correspondent obligation, which was called restipulatio ; both acts
were called sponsio.

Nothing of importance was transacted among the Romans without the
rogatio, or asking a question, and a correspondent answer :[18] hence interrogatio for stipulatio. Thus also laws were passed ; the magistrate asked, rogabat, and the people answered, uti rogas, sc. volumus.[19]

The form of mancipatio, or mancipium, per æs et libram, was sometimes
added to the stipulatio.[20]

A stipulation could only take place between those who were present.
But if it was expressed in a writing,[21] simply that a person had promised, it was supposed that every thing requisite in a stipulation had been
observed.[22]

---

1 Plaut. Pseud. iv. 6.
Bacchid. iv. 9.
2 Plaut. Per. iv. 4. 37.
Stich. i. 3. 68. Cic. Ver.
iii. 33.
3 licitator.
4 index, Cic. ib. 11.
5 Plaut. Ep. iii. 4. 35.
6 You write me how
much the seat of Drusus is valued at : I had
heard of it before ; but
be what it will, there
is no paying too dear
for a thing which one

must have,—Cic. Att.
xii. 23.
7 Mart. vi. 66. 4.
8 Plaut. Men. v. 9. 97.
9 Hor. Sat. i. 6. 13.
10 stipulationum formulæ, Cic. Legg. i. 4. vel
sponsionum, Ros.Com.
4.
11 sibi qui promitti curabat, v. sponsionem
exigebat.
12 rogabat v. interrogabat.
13 promissor vel repro

missor, Plaut. As. ii.
4. 48. Pseud. i. 1. 112.
for both words are put
—for the same thing.Cur.
v. 2. 68. v. 3. 31. 33,
Cic. Rosc. Com. 4. 13.
14 Plaut. Rud. v. 2. 47.
Pseud. i. 1. 115. iv. 6.
15. Bacch. iv. 8. 41. s.
5. Inst. de inutil. Stip.
Plaut. Trin. v. 2. 34.39.
Curc. v. 2. 74. Dig.
15 ut pacta et conventa
firmiora essent.
16 Cic. Quin. 18. Pis. 9.

qui arrogabat, Plaut.
Rud. v. 2. 45.
17 Liv. xxxix. 5. Fest.
Cic. Att. v. 1. Rosc.
Am. 9. Plaut. Trin. v.
2. 39.
18 congrua responsio.
19 Sen. Ben. iii. 16. see
p. 63. 65.
20 Cic. Legg. ii. 20. 21.
21 si in instrumento
scriptum esset.
22 Inst. iii. 20. 17. Paul.
Recep. Sent. v. 7. 2.

In buying and selling, in giving or taking a lease,[1] or the like, the bargain was finished by the simple consent of the parties : hence these contracts were called CONSENSUALES. He who gave a wrong account of a thing to be disposed of, was bound to make up the damage. An earnest penny[2] was sometimes given, not to confirm, but to prove the obligation.[3] But in all important contracts, bonds,[4] formally written out, signed, and sealed, were mutually exchanged between the parties. Thus Augustus and Antony ratified their agreement about the partition of the Roman provinces, after the overthrow of Brutus and Cassius at Philippi, by giving and taking reciprocally written obligations.[5] A difference having afterwards arisen between Cæsar, and Fulvia the wife of Antony, and Lucius his brother, who managed the affairs of Antony in Italy, an appeal was made by Cæsar to the disbanded veterans; who, having assembled in the capitol, constituted themselves judges in the cause, and appointed a day for determining it at Gabii. Augustus appeared in his defence ; but Fulvia and L. Antonius, having failed to come, although they had promised, were condemned in their absence ; and, in confirmation of the sentence, war was declared against them, which terminated in their defeat, and finally in the destruction of Antony.[6] In like manner, the articles of agreement between Augustus, Antony, and Sex. Pompeius, were written out in the form of a contract, and committed to the charge of the vestal virgins. They were farther confirmed by the parties joining their right hands, and embracing one another. But Augustus, says Dio, no longer observed this agreement, than till he found a pretext for violating it.[7]

When one sued another upon a written obligation, he was said *agere cum eo ex* SYNGRAPHA.[8]

Actions concerning bargains or obligations are usually named ACTIONES *empti, venditi, locati* vel *ex locato, conducti* vel *ex conducto mandati,* &c. They were brought[9] in this manner :—The plaintiff said, AIO TE MIHI MU-TUI COMMODATI, DEPOSITI NOMINE, DARE CENTUM OPORTERE ; AIO TE MIHI EX STIPULATU, LOCATO, DARE FACERE OPORTERE. The defendant either denied the charge, or made exceptions to it, or defences,[10] that is, he admitted part of the charge, but not the whole ; thus, NEGO ME TIBI EX STIPULATO CEN-TUM DARE OPORTERE, NISI QUOD METU, DOLO, ERRORE ADDUCTUS SPOPONDI, *vel* NISI QUOD MINOR XXV ANNIS SPOPONDI. Then followed the SPONSIO, if the defendant denied, NI DARE FACERE DEBEAT ; and the RESTIPULATIO, SI DARE FACERE DEBEAT ; but if he excepted, the *sponsio* was, NI DOLO AD-DUCTUS SPOPONDERIT ; and the *restipulatio* SI DOLO ADDUCTUS SPOPONDE-RIT.[11]

An exception was expressed by these words, SI NON, AC SI NON, AUT SI, AUT, NISI, NISI QUOD, EXTRA QUAM SI. If the plaintiff answered the defendant's exception, it was called REPLICATIO ; and if the defendant answered him, it was called DUPLICATIO. It sometimes proceeded to a TRIPLICA-TIO and QUADRUPLICATIO. The exceptions and replies used to be included in the SPONSIO.[12]

When the contract was not marked by a particular name, the action was called ACTIO PRÆSCRIPTIS VERBIS, *actio incerta* vel *incerti ;* and the

1 in locatione vel con-
ductione.
2 arrha v. arrhabo.
3 Cic. Off. iii. 16. Inst.
iii. 23. pr. Varr. L. L.
iv. 36.
4 syngraphæ.
5 γραμματεια, syngra-
phæ, Dio. xlviii. 2. 11.
6 Dio. xlvii. 12, &c.
7 Dio. xlviii. 37. 45.
8 Cic. Mur. 17.
9 intendebantur.
10 actoris intentionem
aut negabat vel inficia-
batur aut exceptione
elidebat.
11 to this Cicero al-
ludes, Inv. ii. 19. Fin.
2. 7. Att. vi. 1.
12 Liv. xxxix. 43. Cic.
Verr. i. 45. iii. 57. 59.
Cæc. 16. Val. Max. ii.
8. 2.

writ[1] was not composed by the prætor, but the words were prescribed by a lawyer.[2]

Actions were sometimes brought against a person on account of the contracts of others, and were called *adjectitia qualitatis.*

As the Romans esteemed trade and merchandise dishonourable, especially if not extensive,[3] instead of keeping shops themselves, they employed slaves, freedmen, or hirelings, to trade on their account,[4] who were called INSTITORES ;[5] and actions brought against the trader,[6] or against the employer,[7] on account of the trader's transactions, were called ACTIONES INSTITORIÆ.

In like manner, a person who sent a ship to sea at his own risk,[8] and received all the profits,[9] whether he was the proprietor[10] of the ship, or hired it,[11] whether he commanded the ship himself,[12] or employed a slave or any other person for that purpose,[13] was called *navis* EXERCITOR ; and an action lay against him[14] for the contracts made by the master of the ship, as well as by himself, called ACTIO EXERCITORIA.

An action lay against a father or master of a family, for the contracts made by his son or slave, called *actio* DE PECULIO or *actio* DE IN REM VERSO, if the contract of the slave had turned to his master's profit ; or *actio* JUSSU, if the contract had been made by the master's order.

But the father or master was bound to make restitution, not to the entire amount of the contract,[15] but to the extent of the *peculium,* and the profit which he had received.

If the master did not justly distribute the goods of the slave among his creditors, an action lay against him, called *actio* TRIBUTORIA.

An action also lay against a person in certain cases, where the contract was not expressed, but presumed by law, and therefore called *obligatio* QUASI EX CONTRACTU ; as when one, without any commission, managed the business of a person in his absence, or without his knowledge ; hence he was called NEGOTIORUM GESTOR, or VOLUNTARIUS AMICUS, vel PROCURATOR.[16]

3. PENAL ACTIONS.

ACTIONS for a private wrong were of four kinds ; EX FURTO, RAPINA, DAMNO, INJURIA ; for theft, robbery, damage, and personal injury.

1. The different punishments of thefts were borrowed from the Athenians. By the laws of the Twelve Tables, a thief in the night-time might be put to death ;[17] and also in the day-time, if he defended himself with a weapon,[18] but not without having first called out for assistance.[19]

The punishment of slaves was more severe. They were scourged and thrown from the Tarpeian rock. Slaves were so addicted to this crime, that they were anciently called FURES ;[20] and theft, SERVILE PROBRUM.

---

1 formula.
2 Val. Max. viii. 2. 2.
3 Cic. Off. i. 42.
4 negotiationibus præficiebant.
5 quod negotio gerendo instabant.
6 in negotiatorem.
7 in dominum.
8 suo periculo navem mari immittebat.
9 ad quem omnes ob-

ventiones et reditus navis pervenirent.
10 dominus.
11 navem per aversionem conduxisset.
12 sive ipse navis magister esset.
13 navi præficeret.
14 in eum competebat, erat, vel dabatur.
15 non in solidum.
16 Cic. Cæc. 5. Brut. 4.

17 si nox (noctu)furtum faxit, sim (si eum) aliquis occisit (occiderit), jure cæsus esto.
18 si luci furtum faxit, sim aliquis endo (in) ipso furto capsit (cepe-rit, verberator, illique, cui furtum factum escit (erit) addicitor, Gell. xi. ult.
19 sed non nisi is, qui

interemturus erat, quiritaret, i. e. clamaret Quirites, vestram fidem, sc. imploro, vel porro Quirites.
20 Virg. Ecl. iii. 16. quid domini faciant, audent cum talia fures !—what will masters do, when thieves are so audacious ! Hor. Ep. i. 6. 46. Tac. Hist. i. 48.

But afterwards these punishments were mitigated by various laws, and by the edicts of the prætors. One caught in manifest theft[1] was obliged to restore fourfold,[2] besides the things stolen ; for the recovery of which there was a real action[3] against the possessor, whoever he was.

If a person was not caught in the act, but so evidently guilty that he could not deny it, he was called *fur* NEC MANIFESTUS, and was punished by restoring double.[4]

When a thing stolen was, after much search, found in the possession of any one, it was called FURTUM CONCEPTUM, and by the law of the Twelve Tables was punished as manifest theft,[5] but afterwards, as *furtum nec manifestum*.

If a thief, to avoid detection, offered things stolen[6] to any one to keep, and they were found in his possession, he had an action, called *actio* FURTI OBLATI, against the person who gave him the things, whether it was the thief or another, for the triple of their value.

If any one hindered a person to search for stolen things, or did not exhibit them when found, actions were granted by the prætor against him, called *actiones* FURTI PROHIBITI *et* NON EXHIBITI ; in the last for double.[7] What the penalty was in the first is uncertain. But in whatever manner theft was punished, it was always attended with infamy.

2. Robbery[8] took place only in movable things.[9] Immovable things were said to be invaded, and the possession of them was recovered by an interdict of the prætor.

Although the crime of robbery[10] was much more pernicious than that of theft, it was, however, less severely punished.

An action[11] was granted by the prætor against the robber,[12] only for fourfold, including what he had robbed. And there was no difference whether the robber was a freeman or a slave ; only the proprietor of the slave was obliged, either to give him up,[13] or pay the damage.[14]

3. If any one slew the slave or beast of another, it was called DAMNUM INJURIA DATUM, i. e. *dolo* vel *culpa nocentis admissum*, whence ACTIO vel JUDICIUM DAMNI INJURIA, sc. *dati*,[15] whereby he was obliged to repair the damage by the Aquilian law. QUI SERVUM SERVAMVE, ALIENUM ALIENAMVE, QUADRUPEDEM vel PECUDEM INJURIA OCCIDERIT, QUANTI ID IN EO ANNO PLURIMI FUIT, (whatever its highest value was for that year,) TANTUM ÆS DARE DOMINO DAMNAS ESTO. By the same law, there was an action against a person for hurting any thing that belonged to another, and also for corrupting another man's slaves, for double if he denied.[16] There was, on account of the same crime, a prætorian action for double even against a person who confessed.[17]

4. Personal injuries or affronts[18] respected either the body, the dignity, or character of individuals.—They were variously punished at different periods of the republic.

By the Twelve Tables, smaller injuries[19] were punished with a fine of twenty-five *asses* or pounds of brass.

But if the injury was more atrocious ; as, for instance, if any one deprived another of the use of a limb,[20] he was punished by retaliation,[21] if the

---

1 in furto manifesto.	1 ablatas.	12 in raptorem.	17 l. 5. s. 2. ibid.
2 quadruplum.	7 Plaut. P. iii. 1. v. 61.	13 eum noxæ dedere.	18 injuriæ.
3 vindicatio.	8 rapina.	14 damnum præstare.	19 injuriæ leviores.
4 Gel. xi. 18.	9 in rebus mobilibus.	15 Cic. Rosc. Com. 11.	20 si membrum rupsit,
5 see p. 130. Gell. ibid.	10 crimen raptus.	16 adversus inficiantem	i. e. ruperit.
Inst. iv. i. 4.	11 actio vi bonorum rap-	in duplum, l. l. princ.	21 talione.
6 res furtivas vel furto	torum.	D. de serv. corr.	

person injured would not accept of any other satisfaction.[1] If he only
dislocated or broke a bone,[2] he paid 300 *asses*, if the sufferer was a free-
man, and 150, if a slave. If any slandered another by defamatory verses,[3]
he was beaten with a club, as some say, to death.[4]

But these laws gradually fell into disuse, and, by the edicts of the praetor, an action was granted on account of all personal injuries and affronts
only for a fine, which was proportioned to the dignity of the person, and
the nature of the injury. This, however, being found insufficient to check
licentiousness and insolence, Sylla made a new law concerning injuries,
by which, not only a civil action, but also a criminal prosecution, was appointed for certain injuries, with the punishment of exile, or working in
the mines. Tiberius ordered one who had written defamatory verses
against him to be thrown from the Tarpeian rock.[5]

An action might also be raised against a person for an injury done by
those under his power, which was called ACTIO NOXALIS; as, if a slave
committed theft, or did any damage without his master's knowledge, he
was to be given up to the injured person:[6] and so, if a beast did any
damage, the owner was obliged to offer a compensation, or give up the
beast.[7]

There was no action for ingratitude,[8] as among the Macedonians, or
rather Persians; because, says Seneca, all the courts at Rome[9] would
scarcely have been sufficient for trying it. He adds a better reason: *quia
hoc crimen in legem cadere non debet.*[10]

4. MIXED AND ARBITRARY ACTIONS.

ACTIONS by which one sued for a thing,[11] were called *actiones* REI
PERSECUTORIÆ; but actions merely for a penalty or punishment, were
called PŒNALES; for both, MIXTÆ.

Actions in which the judge was obliged to determine strictly, according
to the convention of parties, were called *actiones* STRICTI JURIS: actions
which were determined by the rules of equity,[12] were called ARBITRARIÆ,
or BONÆ FIDEI. In the former, a certain thing, or the performance of a
certain thing,[13] was required; a *sponsio* was made, and the judge was restricted to a certain *form*: in the latter, the contrary of all this was the
case. Hence, in the forms of actions *bonæ fidei* about contracts, these
words were added, EX BONA FIDE; in those trusts called *fiduciæ*, UT INTER
BONOS BENE AGIER OPORTET, ET SINE FRAUDATIONE; and in a question
about recovering a wife's portion after a divorce,[14] and in all arbitrary
actions, QUANTUM *vel* QUID ÆQUIUS, MELIUS.[15]

IV. DIFFERENT KINDS OF JUDGES; JUDICES, ARBITRI, RECUPE-
RATORES, ET CENTUMVIRI.

AFTER the form of the writ was made out,[16] and shown to the defendant, the plaintiff requested of the prætor to appoint one person or more to

---

1 see p. 127.
2 qui os ex genitali, l. e.
ex loco ubi gignitur,
fudit, Gell. xx. 1.
3 si quis aliquem pub-
lice diffamasset, eique
adversus bonos mores
convicium fecisset, af-
fronted him, vel car-
men famosum in eum

condidisset.
4 Hor. Sat. ii. 1. v. 82.
Ep. ii. 1. v. 154. Corn.
Pers. Sat. 1. Cic. Aug.
Civ. D. ii. 9. 12.
5 Gel. xx. 1. Dio. lvii.22.
6 si servus, insciente
domino, furtum faxit,
noxiamve noxit, nocu-
erit, i. e. damnum fe-

cerit, noxæ deditor.
7 si quadrupes paupe-
riem, damnum, faxit,
dominus noxæ æstimi-
am, damni æstimatio-
nem, offerto: si nolit,
quod noxit, dato.
8 actio ingrati.
9 omnia fora, sc. tria,
lr. ii. 9.

10 Sen. Ben. iii. 6. 7.
11 rem persequebatur.
12 ex æquo et bono.
13 certa præstatio.
14 in arbitrio rei uxoriæ.
15 Cic. Off. iii. 15. Q.
   Rosc. 4. Top. 17.
16 concepta actionis in-
tentione.

judge of it.[1] If he only asked one, he asked a judex, properly so called, or an arbiter ; if he asked more than one,[2] he asked either those who were called recuperatores, or centumviri.

1. A JUDEX judged both of fact and of law, but only in such cases as were easy and of smaller importance, and which he was obliged to determine according to an express law, or a certain form prescribed to him by the prætor.

2. An ARBITER judged in those causes which were called *bonæ fidei*, and arbitrary, and was not restricted by any law or form ;[3] he determined what seemed equitable, in a thing not sufficiently defined by law.[4] Hence he is called HONORARIUS. *Ad arbitrum* vel *judicem ire, adire, confugere, arbitrum, sumere, capere* ; ARBITRUM ADIGERE, i. e. *ad arbitrum agere* vel *cogere*, to force one to submit to an arbitration ; *ad arbitrum vocare* vel *appellere* ; AD vel APUD JUDICEM, *agere, experiri, litigare, petere* ; but arbiter and judex, *arbitrium* and *judicium*, are sometimes confounded ; arbiter is also sometimes put for TESTIS, or for the master or director of a feast, *arbiter, bibendi, arbiter Adriæ*, rule of the Adriatic ; *maris*, having a prospect of the sea.[5]

A person chosen by two parties by compromise,[6] to determine a difference without the appointment of the prætor, was also called arbiter, but more properly COMPROMISSARIUS.

3. RECUPERATORES were so called, because by them every one recovered his own.[7] This name at first was given to those who judged between the Roman people and foreign states about recovering and restoring private things ;[8] and hence it was transferred to those judges who were appointed by the prætor for a similar purpose in private controversies ; but afterwards they judged also about other matters.[9] They were chosen from Roman citizens at large, according to some ; but more properly, according to others, from the JUDICES SELECTI ;[10] and, in some cases only, from the senate. So in the provinces,[11] where they seemed to have judged of the same causes as the centumviri at Rome, a trial before the recuperatores was called JUDICIUM RECUPERATORIUM, *cum aliquo recuperatores sumere, vel eum ad recuperatores adducere*, to bring one to such a trial.[12]

4. CENTUMVIRI were judges chosen from the thirty-five tribes, three from each, so that properly there were 105 ; but they were always named by a round number, CENTUMVIRI.[13] The causes which came before them[14] are enumerated by Cicero. They seem to have been first instituted soon after the creation of the prætor peregrinus. They judged chiefly concerning testaments and inheritances.[15]

After the time of Augustus they formed the council of the prætor, and judged in the most important causes,[16] whence trials before them[17] are sometimes distinguished from private trials ; but these were not criminal trials, as some have thought,[18] for in a certain sense all trials were public.[19]

1 judicem vel judicium in eam a prætore postulabat.
2 judicium.
3 totius rei arbitrium habuit et potestatem.
4 Fest. Cic. Rosc. Com. 4, 5. Off. iii. 16. Top. 10. Sen. Ben. iii. 3. 7
5 Cic. Tusc. v. 41. Fat. 17. Rosc. Com. 4. 9. Off. iii. 16. Top. 10. Am. 39. Mur. 12. Quin. 3. Flac. 35. Ter. Hea. iii. 1. 94. Adel. i. 2. 42.

Plaut. Rud. iv. 3. 99. 104. Sall. Cat. 20. Liv. ii. 4. Hor. Od. i. 3. ii. 7. 23 Ep. i. 11. 96.
6 ex compromisso.
7 Theoph. Inst.
8 Fest. in reciperatio.
9 Plaut. Bacch. ii. 3. v. 36. Cic. Cæc. 1, &c. Cæcil. 17. Liv. xxvi. 48. Suet. Ner. 17. Dom. 8. Gell. xx. 1.
10 ex albo judicum, from the list of judges, Plin. Ep. iii. 20. Liv. xliii. 2.

11 ex conventu Romanorum civium, i. e. ex Romanis civibus qui juris et judiciorum causa in certum locum convenire solebant, see p. 112. Cic. Verr. ii. 13. iii. 11. 13. 28 59. v. 5. 36. 59. 69. Cæs. Bell. Civ. ii. 20. 36. iii. 21. 29.
12 Cic. Inv. ii. 20. Suet. Vesp. 3. Liv. xliii. 2.
13 Fest.

14 causæ centumvirales.
15 Cic. Or. i. 38. Cæc. 18. Val. Max. vii. 7. Quin. iv. 1. 7. Plin. iv. 8. 32.
16 Tac. Or. 38.
17 judicia centumviralia.
18 Plin Ep. i. 18. vi. 4. 33. Quin. iv. i. v. 10. Suet. Vesp. 10.
19 judicia publica, Cic. Arch. 2.

The number of the Centumviri was increased to 180, and they were divided into four councils, hence QUADRUPLEX JUDICIUM is the same as CENTUMVIRALE; sometimes only into two, and sometimes in important causes they judged all together. A cause before the centumviri could not be adjourned.[1]

Ten men[2] were appointed, five senators and five equites, to assemble these councils, and preside in them in the absence of the prætor.[3]

Trials before the centumviri were held usually in the Basilica Julia, sometimes in the forum. They had a spear set upright before them. Hence *judicium hastæ*, for CENTUMVIRALE, *centumviralem hastam cogere*, to assemble the courts of the centumviri, and preside in them. So, CENTUM GRAVIS HASTA VIRORUM, the tribunal of the centumviri. *Cessat centeni moderatrix judicis hasta.*[4]

The centumviri continued to act as judges for a whole year, but the other judices only till the particular cause was determined for which they were appointed.

The DECEMVIRI also judged in certain causes, and it is thought that in particular cases they previously took cognizance of the causes which were to come before the centumviri, and their decisions were called PRÆJUDICIA.[5]

V. THE APPOINTMENT OF A JUDGE OR JUDGES.

OF the above-mentioned judges, the plaintiff proposed to the defendant[6] such judge or judges as he thought proper according to the words of the *sponsio*, NI ITA ESSET: hence, JUDICEM vel -es FERRE ALICUI, NI ITA ESSET, to undertake to prove before a judge or jury that it was so,[7] and asked that the defendant would be content with the judge or judges whom he named, and not ask another.[8] If he approved, then the judge was said to be agreed on, CONVENIRE, and the plaintiff requested of the prætor to appoint him in these words: PRÆTOR, JUDICEM ARBITRUMVE POSTULO, UT DES IN DIEM TERTIUM SIVE PERENDINUM; and in the same manner *recuperatores* were asked.[9] Hence, *judices dare*, to appoint one to take his trial before the ordinary judices.[10] But centumviri were not asked, unless both parties subscribed to them.[11] If the defendant disapproved of the judge proposed by the plaintiff, he said, HUNC EJERO vel NOLO.[12] Sometimes the plaintiff desired the defendant to name the judge.[13]

The judge or judges agreed on by the parties were appointed[14] by the prætor, with a certain form answering to the nature of the action. In these forms the prætor always used the words SI PARET, i. e. *apparet:* thus, c. ACQUILLI; JUDEX ESTO, SI PARET, FUNDUM CAPENATEM, DE QUO SERVILIUS AGIT CUM CATULO, SERVILII ESSE EX JURE QUIRITIUM, NEQUE SI SERVILIO A CATULO RESTITUATUR, TUM CATULUM CONDEMNA. But if the defendant made an exception, it was added to the form, thus: EXTRA QUAM SI TESTAMENTUM PRODATUR, QUO APPAREAT CATULI ESSE. If the prætor refused to admit the exception, an appeal might be made to the tribunes.[15] The prætor, if he thought proper, might appoint different judges from those chosen by the parties, although he seldom did so; and no one could refuse to act as a judex, when required, without a just cause.[16]

1 Plin. Ep. i. 18. iv. 24. vi. 33. Quin. v. 2. xi. l. xii. 5. Val. Max. vii. 8. 1.
2 decemviri, see p. 101.
3 Suet. Aug. 36.
4 Plin. Ep. ii. 24. Val. Max. vii. 8. 4. Quinct. v. 2. xii. 5. Suet. Aug.

36. Mart. Epig. vii. 62.
Stat. Sylv. iv. 4. 43.
5 Sigon. Judic. Cic. Cæc. 33. Dom. 29.
6 adversario ferebat.
7 Liv. iii. 24. 57. viii. 33. Cic. Quin. 15. Or. ii. 65.
8 ne alium procaret, i. e.

posceret, Fest.
9 Cic. Verr. iii. 58. Mur. 12. Q. Rosc. 15. Clu. 43. Val. Max. ii. 8. 2.
Prob. in Notis.
10 Plin. Ep. iv. 9.
11 Plin. Ep. v. 1.
12 Cic. Or. ii. 70. Plin. Pan. 36.

13 ut judicem diceret, Liv. iii. 56.
14 dabantur vel addicebantur.
15 Cic. Acad. Quæst. iv. 30.
16 Suet. Claud. 15. Plin. Ep. iii. 20. x. 66.

The prætor next prescribed the number of witnesses to be called,[1] which commonly did not exceed ten. Then the parties, or their agents,[2] gave security[3] that what was decreed would be paid, and the sentence of the judge held ratified.[4]

In arbitrary causes, a sum of money was deposited by both parties, called COMPROMISSUM, which word is also used for a mutual agreement.[5]

In a personal action, the procuratores only gave security; those of the plaintiff, to stand to the sentence of the judge; and those of the defendant, to pay what was decreed.[6]

In certain actions the plaintiff gave security to the defendant that no more demands should be made upon him on the same account.[7]

After this followed the LITIS CONTESTATIO, or a short narration of the cause by both parties, corroborated by the testimony of witnesses.[8] The things done in court before the appointment of the judices, were properly said IN JURE FIERI; after that, IN JUDICIO: but this distinction is not always observed.

After the judex or judices were appointed, the parties warned each other to attend the third day after,[9] which was called COMPERENDINATIO, or CONDICTIO.[10] But in a cause with a foreigner, the day was called DIES STATUS.[11]

VI. MANNER OF CONDUCTING A TRIAL.

WHEN the day came, the trial went on, unless the judge, or some of the parties, was absent from a necessary cause,[12] in which case the day was put off.[13] If the judge was present, he first took an oath that he would judge according to law to the best of his judgment,[14] at the altar,[15] called PUTEAL LIBONIS, or *Scribonianum*, because that place, being struck with thunder,[16] had been expiated[17] by Scribonius Libo, who raised over it a stone covering,[18] the covering of a well,[19] open at the top,[20] in the forum; near which the tribunal of the prætor used to be, and where the usurers met. It appears to have been different from the Puteal, under which the whetstone and razor of Attius Navius were deposited, in the Comitium, at the left side of the senate-house.[21]

The Romans, in solemn oaths, used to hold a flint-stone in their right hand, saying, SI SCIENS FALLO, TUM ME DIESPITER, SALVA URBE ARCEQUE, BONIS EJICIAT, UT EGO HUNC LAPIDEM.[22] Hence, *Jovem lapidem jurare*, for *per Jovem et lapidem*. The formula of taking an oath we have in Plautus, and an account of different forms in Cicero. The most solemn oath of the Romans was by their faith or honour.[23]

The judex or judices, after having sworn, took their seats in the subsellia;[24] whence they were called JUDICES PEDANEI: and SEDERE is often put for COGNOSCERE, to judge.[25] SEDERE is also applied to an advocate while not pleading.[26]

1 quibus denunciaretur testimonium.
2 procuratores.
3 satisdabant.
4 judicatum solvi et rem ratam haberi.
5 Cic. Rosc. Com. 4. Verr. ii. 27. Q. Frat. ii. 15. Fam. xii. 30.
6 Cic. Quin. 7. Att. xvi. 15.
7 eo nomine a se neminem amplius vel postea petiturum, Cic. Brut. 5. Rosc. Com. 12. Fam. xiii. 29.

8 Cic. Att. xvi. 15. Rosc. Com. 11, 12. 18. Fest. Macrob. Sat. iii. 9.
9 inter se in perendinum diem, ut ad judicium venirent denunciabant.
10 Asc. Cic. Fest. Gell. xiv. 2.
11 Macrob. Saf. i. 16. status condictus cum hoste, i. e. cum peregrino, Cic. Off. i. 32. dies, Plaut. Curc. i. 1. 5. Gell. xvi. 4.

12 ex morbo vel causa sontica, Fest.
13 diffissus est, i. e. prolatus, Gell. xiv. 2.
14 ex animi sententia, Cic. Acad. Q. 47.
15 aram tenens, Cic. Flac. 36.
16 fulmine attactus.
17 procuratus.
18 suggestum lapideum cavum.
19 putei operculum, vel puteal.
20 superne apertum, Fest.

21 Hor. Sat. ii. 6. v. 35. Ep. i 19. 6. Cic. Sext. 8. Div. i. 17. Ov. Rem. Am. 561. Liv. i. 36.
22 Fest. in. Lapis.
23 Cic. Fam. viii. 1. 12. Acad. iv. 47. Liv. xxi. 45. xxii. 53. Gel. i. 21. Plaut. Rud. v. 2. 45. Diony. ix. 10. 48. xi. 54.
24 quasi ad pedes prætoris.
25 Plin. Ep. v. 1. vi. 33. sedere auditurus, vi. 31.
26 Plin. Ep. iii. 9. f.

The judex, especially if there was but one, assumed some lawyers to assist him with their counsel,[1] whence they were called CONSILIARII.[2]

If any of the parties were absent without a just excuse, he was summoned by an edict,[3] or lost his cause. If the prætor pronounced an unjust decree in the absence of any one, the assistance of the tribunes might be implored.[4]

If both parties were present, they were first obliged to swear that they did not carry on the lawsuit from a desire of litigation.[5]

Then the advocates were ordered to plead the cause, which they did twice, one after another, in two different methods;[6] first briefly, which was called CAUSÆ CONJECTIO,[7] and then in a formal oration[8] they explained the state of the cause, and proved their own charge[9] or defence[10] by witnesses and writings,[11] and arguments drawn from the case itself;[12] and here the orator chiefly displayed his art.[13] To prevent them, however, from being too tedious,[14] it was ordained by the Pompeian law, in imitation of the Greeks, that they should speak by an hour-glass;[15] a water-glass, somewhat like our sand-glasses. How many hours were to be allowed to each advocate, was left to the judices to determine.[16] These glasses were also used in the army. Hence *dare* vel *petere plures clepsydras*, to ask more time to speak : *quoties judico, quantum quis plurimum postulat aquæ do*, I give the advocates as much time as they require. The *clepsydræ* were of a different length ; sometimes three of them in an hour.[17]

The advocate sometimes had a person by him to suggest[18] what he should say, who was called MINISTRATOR. A forward noisy speaker was called RABULA,[19] vel *proclamator*, a brawler or wrangler.[20]

Under the emperors, advocates used to keep persons in pay[21] to procure for them an audience, or to collect hearers,[22] who attended them from court to court,[23] and applauded them, while they were pleading, as a man who stood in the middle of them gave the word.[24] Each of them for this service received his dole,[25] or a certain hire (*par merces*, usually three denarii, near 2s of our money) ; hence they were called LAUDICŒNI.[26] This custom was introduced by one Largius Licinius, who flourished under Nero and Vespasian ; and is greatly ridiculed by Pliny.[27] When a client gained his cause, he used to fix a garland of green palm[28] at his lawyer's door.

When the judges heard the parties, they were said *iis* OPERAM DARE.[29] How inattentive they sometimes were, we learn from Macrobius.[30]

VII. MANNER OF GIVING JUDGMENT.

THE pleadings being ended,[31] judgment was given after mid-day, accord-

1 sibi advocavit, ut in consilio adessent, Cic. Quin. 2. in consilium rogavit, Gell. xiv. 2.
2 Suet. Tib. 33. Claud. 12.
3 see p. 85.
4 Cic. Quin. 6. 20.
5 calumniam jurare, vel de calumnia, Liv. xxxiii. 49. Cic. Fam. viii. 6. 1. 16. D. de jur. quod injuratus in codicem referre noluit, sc. quia falsum erat, id jurare in litem non dubitet. i. e. id sibi deberi jurejurando confirmare, litis obtinendæ causa, Cic.

Rosc. Com. 1.
6 App. Bell. Civ. i. p. 663.
7 quasi causæ in breve coactio, Asc. Cic.
8 justa oratione perorabant, Gell. xvii. 2.
9 actionem.
10 inficiationem vel exceptionem.
11 testibus et tabulis.
12 ex ipsa re deductis, Cic. Quin. Rosc. Com. Gell. xiv. 2.
13 Cic. Or. ii. 42—44. 79. 81.
14 ne in immensum evagarentur.
15 ut ad clepsydram di-

cerent, i. e. vas vitreum, graciliter fistulatum, in fundo cujus erat foramen, unde aqua guttatim efflueret, atque ita tempus metiretur, Cic. Or. iii. 34.
16 Cic. Quin. 9. Plin. Ep. i. 26. iv. 9. ii. 11. 14. 1. 23. vi. 2. 5. Dia. Caus.
17 Veg. iii. 8. Cæs. Bell. G. v. 13. Plin. Ep. ii. 11. vi. 2.
18 qui subjiceret.
19 a rabie, quasi latrator.
20 Cic. Or. i. 46. ii. 75. Flac. 22.

21 conducti et redempti mancipes.
22 coronam colligere, auditores, v. audituros corrogare.
23 ex judicio in judicium.
24 quum μεσοχορος dedit signum.
25 sportula.
26 i. e. qui ob cœnam laudabant.
27 Ep. ii. 14. vi. 2.
28 virides palmæ, Juv. vii. 118.
29 1. 18. pr. D. de jud.
30 Satur. ii. 12.
31 causa utrinque perorata.

ing to the law of the Twelve Tables, POST MERIDIEM PRÆSENTI (*etiamsi unustantum præsens sit*), LITEM ADDICITO, i. e. *decidito*.[1]

If there was any difficulty in the cause, the judge sometimes took time to consider it;[2] if, after all, he remained uncertain, he said,[3] MIHI NON LIQUET, I am not clear. And thus the affair was either left undetermined,[4] or the cause was again resumed.[5]

If there were several judges, judgment was given according to the opinion of the majority;[6] but it was necessary that they should be all present. If their opinions were equal, it was left to the prætor to determine.[7] The judge commonly retired[8] with his assessors to deliberate on the case, and pronounced judgment according to their opinion.[9]

The sentence was variously expressed : in an action of freedom, thus, VIDERI SIBI HUNC HOMINEM LIBERUM ; in an action of injuries, VIDERI JURE FECISSE *vel* NON FECISSE ; in actions of contracts, if the cause was given in favour of the plaintiff, TITIUM SEIO CENTUM CONDEMNO ; if in favour of the defendant, SECUNDUM ILLUM LITEM DO.[10]

An arbiter gave judgment[11] thus : ARBITROR TE HOC MODO SATISFACERE ACTORI DEBERE. If the defendant did not submit to his decision, then the arbiter ordered the plaintiff to declare upon oath, at how much he estimated his damages,[12] and then he passed sentence,[13] and condemned the defendant to pay him that sum, thus : CENTUM DE QUIBUS ACTOR IN LITEM JURAVIT REDDE.[14]

VIII. WHAT FOLLOWED AFTER JUDGMENT WAS GIVEN.

AFTER judgment was given, and the lawsuit was determined,[15] the conquered party was obliged to do or pay what was decreed ;[16] and if he failed, or did not find securities[17] within thirty days, he was given up[18] by the prætor to his adversary,[19] and led away[20] by him to servitude. These thirty days are called, in the Twelve Tables, DIES JUSTI ; rebus jure judicatis, XXX dies justi sunto, post deinde manus injectio esto, in jus ducito.[21]

After sentence was passed the matter could not be altered : hence agere actum, to labour in vain ; *actum est ; acta est res ; perii*, all is over, I am undone ; *actum est de me*, I am ruined ; *de Servio actum rati*, that all was over with Servius, that he was slain ; *actum* (i. e. *ratum*) *habebo quod egeris*.[22]

In certain cases, especially when any mistake or fraud had been committed, the prætor reversed the sentence of the judges,[23] in which case he was said *damnatos* in integrum restituere, or judicia restituere.[24]

After the cause was decided, the defendant, when acquitted, might bring an action against the plaintiff for false accusation :[25] hence, CALUMNIA *litem*, i. e. *lites per calumniam intentæ*, unjust lawsuits ; *calumniarem metum injicere*, of false accusations ; *ferre calumniam*, i. e. *calumnia convictum esse*,

---

1 Gell. xvii. 2.
2 diem diffindi, i. e. differri jussit, ut amplius deliberaret, Ter. Phor. ii. 4. 17.
3 dixit vel juravit, Gell. xiv. 2.
4 injudicata, Gell. v. 10.
5 secunda actio institutæ est, Cic. Cæc. 2.
6 sententia lata est de plurium sententia.
7 l. 23, 36, 38. D. de re jud.

8 secessit.
9 ex consilii sententia, Plin. Ep. v. l. vi. 31.
10 Val. Max. ii. 8. 2.
11 arbitrium pronunciavit.
12 quanti litem æstimaret.
13 sententiam tulit.
14 l. 18. D. de dolo malo.
15 lite dijudicata.
16 judicatum facere vel solvere.

17 sponsores vel vindices.
18 judicatus, i. e. damnatus et addictus est.
19 to which custom Horace alludes, Od. iii. 3. 33.
20 abductus, Cic. Flac. 19. Liv. vi. 14. 34, &c. Plaut. Pœn. iii. 3. 94. As. v. 2. 87. Gell. xx. 1.
21 see p. 34.
22 Cic. Am. 22. Att. ix.

18. Fam. xiv. 3. Tus. iii. 21. Ter. Phor. ii. 2. 72. And. iii. l. 7. Adel. iii. 2. 7. Plaut. Pseud. i. 1. 63. Liv. i. 17. Suet. Ner. 42.
23 rem judicatam rescidit.
24 Cic. Verr. ii. 26. v. 6. Clu. 36. Ter. Phor. ii. 4. 11.
25 actorem calumniæ postulare, Cic. Clu. 31.

vel *calumniæ damnari* aut *de calumnia ; calumniam non effugiet,* he will not fail to be condemned for false accusation ;[1] *injuriæ existunt* CALUMNIA, i. e. *callida et malitiosa juris interpretatione ;* CALUMNIA *timoris,* the misrepresentation of fear, which always imagines things worse than they are ; *calumnia religionis,* a false pretext of ; *calumnia dicendi,* speaking to waste the time ; CALUMNIA *paucorum,* detraction.[2] So CALUMNIARI, *falsam litem intendere,* et *calumniator,* &c.

There was also an action against a judge, if he was suspected of having taken money from either of the parties, or to have wilfully given wrong judgment.[3] Corruption in a judge was, by the law of the Twelve Tables, punished with death ; but afterwards as a crime of extortion.[4]

If a judge, from partiality or enmity,[5] evidently favoured either of the parties, he was said LITEM SUAM FACERE. Cicero applies this phrase to an advocate too keenly interested for his client.[6] In certain causes the assistance of the tribunes was asked.[7] As there was an appeal[8] from an inferior to a superior magistrate, so also from one court or judge to another.[9] The appeal was said ADMITTI, RECIPI, NON RECIPI, REPUDIARI : he to whom the appeal was made, was said, DE vel EX APPELLATIONE COGNOSCERE, JUDICARE, SENTENTIAM DICERE, PRONUNCIARE APPELLATIONEM JUSTAM vel INJUSTAM ESSE.

After the subversion of the republic, a final appeal was made to the emperor, both in civil and criminal affairs, as formaly,[10] to the people in criminal trials.[11] At first this might be done freely,[12] but afterwards under a certain penalty.[13] Caligula prohibited any appeal to him.[14] Nero ordered all appeals to be made from private judges to the senate, and under the same penalty as to the emperor : so Hadrian.[15] Even the emperor might be requested, by a petition,[16] to review his own decree.[17]

II. CRIMINAL TRIALS, PUBLICA JUDICIA.

CRIMINAL trials were at first held[18] by the kings, with the assistance of a council.[19] The king judged of great crimes himself, and left smaller crimes to the judgment of the senators.

Tullus Hostilius appointed two persons[20] to try Horatius for killing his sister,[21] and allowed an appeal from their sentence to the people. Tarquinius Superbus judged of capital crimes by himself alone, without any counsellors.[22]

After the expulsion of Tarquin, the consuls at first judged and punished capital crimes.[23] But after the law of Poplicola concerning the liberty of appeal,[24] the people either judged themselves in capital affairs, or appointed certain persons for that purpose, with the concurrence of the senate, who were called QUÆSITORES, or *quæstores parricidii.*[25] Sometimes the consuls were appointed ; sometimes a dictator and master of horse,[26] who were

1 Cic. Mil. 27. Clu. 59. Fam. viii. 8. Gell. xiv. 2. Suet. Cæs. 20. Vit. 7. Dom. 9.
2 Sall. Cat. 30. Cic. Off. i. 10. Fam. i. 1. vi. 7. Att. iv. 3. Acad. iv. 1.
3 dolo malo vel imperitia.
4 repetundarum.
5 gratia vel inimicitia.
6 Or. ii. 75. Ulp. Gell. x. 1.
7 tribuni appellabantur,

Cic. Quin. 7. 20.
8 appellatio, Liv. iii. 56.
9 ab inferiore ad superius tribunal, vel ex minore ad majorem judicem, prætextu iniqui gravaminis, of a grievance, vel injustæ sententiæ, Ulp.
10 provocatio.
11 Suet. Aug. 33. Dio. iii. 33. Act. Apos. xxv. 11. Suet. Cæs. 12.

12 antea vacuum id solutumque pœna fuerat.
13 Tac. Ann. xiv. 28.
14 magistratibus liberam jurisdictionem, et sine sui provocatione concessit, Suet. Cal. 16.
15 ut ejusdem pecuniæ periculum facerent, cujus ii, qui imperatorem appellavere, Tac. ibid. Suet. Ner. 17. Dig. xliv. 2. 2.
16 libello.

17 sententiam suam retractare.
18 exercebantur.
19 cum consilio, Liv. i. 49. Diony. ii. 14.
20 duumviri.
21 qui Horatio perduellionem judicarent.
22 Liv. i. 26. 49
23 Liv. ii. 5. Diony. x. 1.
24 see p. 77.
25 see p. 87.
26 Liv. iv. 51. ix. 26.

then called QUÆSITORES. The senate also sometimes judged in capital affairs, or appointed persons to do so.[1] But after the institution of the *quæstiones perpetuæ*,[2] certain prætors always took cognizance of certain crimes, and the senate or people seldom interfered in this matter, unless by way of appeal, or on extraordinary occasions.

I. CRIMINAL TRIALS BEFORE THE PEOPLE.

TRIALS before the people[3] were at first held in the Comitia Curiata. Of this, however, we have only the example of Horatius.[4]

After the institution of the Comitia Centuriata and Tributa, all trials before the people were held in them ; capital trials in the Comitia Centuriata, and concerning a fine, in the Tributa.

Those trials were called CAPITAL, which respected the life or liberty of a Roman citizen. There was one trial of this kind held in the Comitia by tribes ; namely, of Coriolanus, but that was irregular, and conducted with violence.[5]

Sometimes a person was said to undergo a capital trial,[6] in a civil action, when, besides the loss of fortune, his character was at stake.[7] The method of proceeding in both Comitia was the same ; and it was requisite that some magistrate should be the accuser. In the Comitia Tributa, the inferior magistrates were usually the accusers, as the tribunes or ædiles. In the Comitia Centuriata, the superior magistrates, as the consuls or prætors, sometimes also the inferior, as the quæstors or tribunes.[8] But they are supposed to have acted by the authority of the consuls.

No person could be brought to a trial unless in a private station. But sometimes this rule was violated.[9]

The magistrate who was to accuse any one, having called an assembly, and mounted the rostra, declared that he would, against a certain day, accuse a particular person of a particular crime, and ordered that the person accused[10] should then be present. This was called DICERE DIEM, sc. *accusationis*, vel *diei dictio*. In the meantime the criminal was kept in custody, unless he found persons to give security for his appearance,[11] who, in a capital trial, were called VADES,[12] and for a fine, PRÆDES ;[13] thus, *præstare aliquem*, to be responsible for one ; *ego Messalam Cæsari præstabo*.[14]

When the day came, the magistrate ordered the criminal to be cited from the rostra by a herald.[15] If the criminal was absent without a valid reason,[16] he was condemned. If he was detained by indisposition or any other necessary cause, he was said to be excused,[17] and the day of trial was put off.[18] Any equal or superior magistrate might, by his negative, hinder the trial from proceeding. If the criminal appeared,[19] and no magistrate interceded, the accuser entered upon his charge,[20] which was repeated three times, with the intervention of a day between each, and supported by witnesses, writings, and other proofs. In each charge the pun-

---

1 Sall. Cat. 51, 52. Liv.
ix. 26.
2 see p. 87.
3 judicia ad populum.
4 Cic. Mil. 3.
5 Liv. ii. 35. Diony. vii.
38, &c.
6 periculum capitis adire, causam capitis vel pro capite dicere.
7 cam judicium esset

de fama fortuniæque,
Cic. Quin. 9. 13. 15.
Off. i. 12.
8 Liv. ii. 41. iii. 24, 25.
55. iv. 21. vi. 20. Val.
Max. vi. 1. 7. Gell. x.
6.
9 Cic. Flacc. 3. Liv.
xliii. 16.
10 reus.
11 sponsores eum in ju-

dicio ad diem dictam
sistendi, aut mulctam,
qua damnatus esset,
solvendi.
12 Liv. iii. 13. xxv. 4.
13 Gell. vii. 19. Aus.
Eid. 347. a præstando,
Varr. iv. 4.
14 Cic. Q. Fr. i. 1. 3. ii.
6 Att. vi. 3. Plin. Pan.
83.

15 Liv. xxxviii. 51. Suet.
Tib. 11.
16 sine causa sontica.
17 excusari, Liv. ib. 52.
18 dies prodictus vel productus est.
19 si reus se stitisset, vel se sisteretur.
20 accusationem instituebat.

24

ishment or fine was annexed, which was called ANQUISITIO. Sometimes the punishment at first proposed was afterwards mitigated or increased.[1]

The criminal usually stood under the rostra in a mean garb, where he was exposed to the scoffs and railleries[2] of the people.

After the accusation of the third day was finished, a bill[3] was published for three market-days, as concerning a law, in which the crime and the proposed punishment or fine was expressed. This was called MULCTÆ PŒNÆVE IRROGATIO; and the judgment of the people concerning it, MULC-TÆ PŒNÆVE CERTATIO.[4] For it was ordained that a capital punishment and a fine should never be joined together.[5]

On the third market-day, the accuser again repeated his charge; and the criminal, or an advocate[6] for him, was permitted to make his defence, in which every thing was introduced which could serve to gain the favour of the people, or move their compassion.[7] Then the Comitia were summoned against a certain day, in which the people, by their suffrages, should determine the fate of the criminal. If the punishment proposed was only a fine, and a tribune the accuser, he could summon the Comitia Tributa himself; but if the trial was capital, he asked a day for the Comitia Centuriata from the consul, or, in his absence, from the prætor. In a capital trial the people were called to the Comitia by a trumpet.[8]

The criminal and his friends, in the mean time, used every method to induce the accuser to drop his accusation.[9] If he did so, he appeared in the assembly of the people, and said, SEMPRONIUM NIHIL MOROR. If this could not be effected, the usual arts were tried to prevent the people from voting, or to move their compassion.[10]

The criminal, laying aside his usual robe,[11] put on a sordid, i. e. a ragged and old gown,[12] not a mourning one,[13] as some have thought; and in this garb went round and supplicated the citizens; whence *sordes* or *squalor* is put for guilt, and *sordidati* or *squalidi* for criminals. His friends and relations, and others who chose, did the same.[14] When Cicero was impeached by Clodius, not only the equites, and many young noblemen of their own accord,[15] but the whole senate, by public consent,[16] changed their habit[17] on his account, which he bitterly complains was prohibited by an edict of the consuls.[18]

The people gave their votes in the same manner in a trial as in passing a law.[19]

If any thing prevented the people from voting on the day of the Comitia, the criminal was discharged, and the trial could not again be resumed.[20] Thus Metellus Celer saved Rabirius from being condemned, who was accused of the murder of Saturnius forty years after it happened, by pulling down the standard, which used to be set up in the Janiculum,[21] and thus dissolving the assembly.[22]

If the criminal was absent on the last day of his trial, when cited by the

1 in mulcta temperarunt tribuni: quum capitis anquisissent, Liv. ii. 55. quum tribunus bis pecunia anquisisset; tertio se capitis anquirere diceret, &c. tum perduellionis se judicare Cn. Fulvio dixit that he prosecuted Fulvius for treason, Liv. xxvi. 3.

2 probris et conviciis, ibid.

3 rogatio.
4 Cic. Legg. iii. 3.
5 ne pœna capitis cum pecunia conjungeretur, Cic. Dom. 17. tribuni plebis, omissa mulctæ certatione, rei capitalis Posthumio dixerunt, Liv. xxv. 4.
6 patronus.
7 Cic. Rab. Liv. iii. 12. 58.
8 classico, Sen. Ira, i. 16. Liv. xxvi. 3. xvliii.

16.
9 accusatione desistere.
10 Liv. iv. 42. vi. 5. 20. Gell. iii. 4. see p. 62, 63.
11 toga alba.
12 sordidam et obsoletam, Liv. ii. 61. Cic. Verr. i. 58.
13 pullam vel atram.
14 Liv. iii. 58. Cic. Sext. 14.
15 privato consensu.
16 publico consilio.
17 vestem mutabant, ib.

11, 12.
18 c. 14. Pis. 8 16. post red. Sen. 7. Dio. xxxvii. 16.
19 see p. 64, 65. Liv. xxv. 4.
20 si qua res illum diem aut auspiciis aut excusatione sustulit, tota causa judiciumque sublatum est, Cic. Dom. 17.
21 see p. 59. Cic. Rab.
22 Dio. xxxvii. 27.

herald, he anciently used to be called by the sound of a trumpet, before
the door of his house, from the citadel, and round the walls of the city.[1]
If still he did not appear, he was banished;[2] or if he fled the country
through fear, his banishment was confirmed by the Comitia Tributa.[3]

II. CRIMINAL TRIALS BEFORE INQUISITORS.

INQUISITORS[4] were persons invested with a temporary authority to try
particular crimes. They were created first by the kings, then by the people, usually in the Comitia Tributa, and sometimes by the senate. In the
trial of Rabirius, they were, contrary to custom, appointed by the prætor.[5]
Their number varied. Two were usually created,[6] sometimes three, and
sometimes only one. Their authority ceased when the trial was over.[7]
The ordinary magistrates were most frequently appointed to be inquisitors;
but sometimes also private persons. There was sometimes an appeal made
from the sentence of the inquisitors to the people, as in the case of Rabirius.
Hence, *deferre judicium a subselliis in rostra*, i. e. *judicibus ad populum*.[8]

Inquisitors had the same authority, and seem to have conducted trials
with the same formalities and attendants, as the prætors did after the institution of the *quæstiones perpetuæ*.[9]

III. CRIMINAL TRIALS BEFORE THE PRÆTORS.

THE prætors at first judged only in civil causes; and only two of them
in these, the prætor Urbanus and Peregrinus. The other prætors were
sent to govern provinces. All criminal trials of importance were held by
inquisitors created on purpose. But after the institution of the *quæstiones
perpetuæ*, A. U. 604, all the prætors remained in the city during the time
of their office. After their election they determined by lot their different
jurisdictions. Two of them took cognizance of private causes, as formerly,
and the rest presided at criminal trials; one at trials concerning extortion,
another at trials concerning bribery, &c. Sometimes there were two
prætors for holding trials concerning one crime; as, on account of the
multitude of criminals, concerning violence. Sometimes one prætor presided at trials concerning two different crimes; and sometimes the prætor
peregrinus held criminal trials, as concerning extortion;[10] so also, according to some, the prætor urbanus.

The prætor was assisted in trials of importance by a council of select
judices or jurymen; the chief of whom was called JUDEX QUÆSTIONIS, or
princeps judicum. Some have thought this person the same with the prætor or quæsitor; but they were quite different.[11] The *judex quæstionis*
supplied the place of the prætor when absent, or too much engaged.

1. CHOICE OF THE JUDICES OR JURY.

THE JUDICES were at first chosen only from among the senators; then,
by the Sempronian law of C. Gracchus, only from among the equites;
afterwards, by the Servilian law of Cæpio, from both orders; then, by the
Glaucian law, only from the equites; by the Livian law of Drusus, from the
senators and equites: but, the laws of Drusus being soon after set aside

1 Varr. L. L. v. 9.
2 exilium ei sciscebatur.
3 see p. 70.
4 quæsitores.
5 Liv. i. 26. iv. 51. ix.

26. xxxviii. 54. xliii. 2.
Dio. xxxvii. 37. Suet.
Cæs. 12.
6 duumviri, Liv. vi. 20.
7 Sall. Jug. 40. Asc. Cic.
Mil. see p. 87.

8 Liv. passim. Suet.
Cæs ll. Dio. xxxvii.
27. Cic. Clu. 6.
9 to the office of quæ-
sitores Virgil alludes,
Æn. vi. 432. Asc. ac-

tion. Verr.
10 Cic. Clu. 53. Cœl. 13.
Asc. tog. cand. 2
11 Cic. & Asc. Clu. 27.
33. 58. Verr. i. 61. Quin.
viii. 3.

by a decree of the senate, the right of judging was again restored to the
equites alone : then, by the Plautian law of Silvanus, the judices were
chosen from the senators and equites. and some of them also from the
plebeians ; then, by the Cornelian law of Sylla, only from the senators ;
by the Aurelian law of Cotta, from the senators. the equites, and *tribuni
ærarii:* by the Julian law of Cæsar, only from the senators and equites ;
and by the law of Antony, also from the officers of the army.[1]

The number of the judices was different at different times : by the law
of Gracchus, 300 ; of Servilius, 450 ; of Drusus, 600 ; of Plautius, 525 ;
of Sylla and Cotta, 300, as it is thought ; of Pompey, 360.   Under the
emperors, the number of judices was greatly increased.[2]

By the Servilian law it behoved the judices to be above thirty, and below sixty years of age. By other laws it was required that they should be
at least twenty-five ;[3] but Augustus ordered that judices might be chosen
from the age of twenty.[4]

Certain persons could not be chosen judices, either from some natural
defect, as the deaf, dumb, &c. ; or by custom, as women and slaves ; or by
law, as those condemned upon trial of some infamous crime ;[5] and, by the
Julian law, those degraded from being senators ; which was not the case
formerly.[6] By the Pompeian law, the judices were chosen from among
persons of the highest fortune.

The judices were annually chosen by the prætor urbanus or peregrinus,
according to Dion Cassius, by the quæstors, and their names written down
in a list.[7] They swore to the laws, and that they would judge uprightly
to the best of their knowledge.[8] The judices were prohibited by Augustus
from entering the house of any one.[9] They sat by the prætor on benches,
whence they were called his ASSESSORES, or CONSILIUM, and CONSESSORES
to one another.[10]

The judices were divided into DECURIÆ, according to their different orders ; thus, DECURIA SENATORIA JUDICUM, *tertia*. Augustus added a fourth
decuria,[11] (because there were three before, either by the law of Antony,
or of Cotta,) consisting of persons of an inferior fortune, who were called
DUCENARII, because they had only 200,000 sesterces, the half of the estate
of an *eques*, and judged in lesser causes. Caligula added a fifty *decuria*. Galba refused to add a sixth *decuria*, although strongly urged by many to do it.[12]

The office of a judex was attended with trouble, and therefore, in the
time of Augustus, people declined it ; but not so afterwards, when their
number was greatly increased.[13]

2. ACCUSER IN A CRIMINAL TRIAL.

ANY Roman citizen might accuse another before the prætor. But it was
reckoned dishonourable to become an accuser, unless for the sake of the
republic, to defend a client, or to revenge a father's quarrel. Sometimes
young noblemen undertook the prosecution of an obnoxious magistrate, to
recommend themselves to the notice of their fellow-citizens.[14]

1 see Manutius de Leg. for Sigonius, and Helneccius, who copies him, give a wrong account of this matter.
2 Cic. Fam. viii. 8. Paterc. ii. 76. Plin. xxxiii. 1.
3 D. 4. 8.
4 a vicesimo allegit, Suet. Aug. 32. as the best commentators read the passage.

5 turpi et famoso judicio, e. g. calumniæ, prævaricationis, furti, vi bonorum raptorum, injuriarum, de dolo malo, pro socio, mandati, tutelæ, depositi.
6 Cic. Clu. 43. see p. 4.
7 in album relata, vel

albo descripta, Suet. Tib. 51. Claud. 16. Dom. 4. Sen. Ben. iii. 7. Gell. xiv. 2. Dion. Cas. xxxix. 7.
8 de animi sententia.
9 Dio. liv. 18.
10 Cic. Act. Ver. 10. Fin. ii. 19. Sen. Ben. iii, 7. Gell. xiv. 2.
11 Cic. Clu. 37. Phil. i. 8.

Verr. ii. 32. Suet. 32. Plin. xxxiii. 7.
12 Suet. 14. 16. Plin. xxxiii. i. s. 8.
13 Cic. Verr. i. 8. Suet. et Plin. ibid.
14 Cic. Off. ii. 14. Div. 20. Verr. i. 38. ii. 47. Cœl. vii. 30. Suet. Jul. 4. Plut. Luc. princ.

If there was a competition between two or more persons who should be the accuser of any one, as between Cicero and Cæcilius Judæus, which of them should prosecute Verres, who had been propraetor of Sicily, for extortion, it was determined who should be preferred by a previous trial, called DIVINATIO; because there was no question about facts, but the judices, without the help of witnesses, divined, as it were, what was fit to be done.[1] He who prevailed acted as the principal accuser;[2] those who joined in the accusation,[3] and assisted them, were called SUBSCRIPTORES; hence *subscribere judicium cum aliquo*, to commence a suit against one.[4] It appears, however, there were public prosecutors of public crimes at Rome, as in Greece.[5]

Public informers or accusers[6] were called QUADRUPLATORES,[7] either because they received as a reward the fourth part of the criminal's effects, or of the fine imposed upon him; or, as others say, because they accused persons, who, upon conviction, used to be condemned to pay fourfold;[8] as those guilty of illegal usury, gaming, or the like.[9] But mercenary and false accusers or litigants[10] chiefly were called by this name, and also those judges who, making themselves parties in the cause, decided in their own favour.[11] Seneca calls those who for small favours sought great returns, *quadruplatores beneficiorum suorum*, overrating or overvaluing them.[12]

3. MANNER OF MAKING THE ACCUSATION.

THE accuser summoned the person accused to court,[13] where he desired[14] of the inquisitor that he might be allowed to produce his charge,[15] and that the praetor would name a day for that purpose; hence, *postulare aliquem de crimine*, to accuse; LIBELLUS POSTULATIONUM, a writing containing the several articles of a charge, a libel.[16] This *postulatio* or request was sometimes made in the absence of the defendant. There were certain days on which the praetor attended to these requests, when he was said POSTULATIONIBUS VACARE.[17]

On the day appointed, both parties being present, the accuser first took[18] a solemn oath, that he did not accuse from malice,[19] and then the charge was made[20] in a set form: thus, DICO, *vel* AIO, TE IN PRÆTURA SPOLIASSE SICULOS, CONTRA LEGEM CORNELIAM, ATQUE EO NOMINE SESTERTIUM MILLIES A TE REPETO.[21] If the criminal was silent, or confessed, an estimate of damages was made out,[22] and the affair was ended; but if he denied, the accuser requested[23] that his name might be entered in the roll of criminals,[24] and thus he was said REUM *facere, lege v. legibus interrogare, postulare*: MULCTAM *aut pœnam petere et repetere*. These are equivalent to *nomen deferre*, and different from *accusare*, which properly signifies to substantiate or prove the charge, the same with *causam agere*, and opposed to *defendere*.[25] If the praetor allowed his name to be enrolled, for he might refuse it,[26] then the accuser delivered to the praetor a scroll or tablet,[27] accurately

---

1 Cic. Caec. 20. Asc. Cic. Gell. li. 4.
2 accusator.
3 causae vel accusationi subscribebant.
4 Cic. Caec. 15. Mur. 24. Fam. viii. 6. Q. Frat. iii. 4. Plin. Ep. v. 1.
5 Cic. Sext. Rosc. 20. Legg. iii. 47. Plin. Ep. iii. 9. iv. 9.
6 delatores publicorum criminum.

7 Cic. Verr. ii. 8, 9.
8 quadrupli damnari.
9 Cic. Caec. 7. 22. et ibi Asc. Paulus apud Fest. Tac. Ann. iv. 20.
10 calumniatores, Cic. Verr. ii. 7–9. Plaut. Pers. i. 2. 10.
11 qui in suam rem litem verterent; interceptores litis alienae, qui sibi controversiosam adjudicarent rem,' Liv. iii. 72. Cic. Caec. 23.

12 Sen. vii. 25.
13 in jus vocabat.
14 postulabat.
15 nomen deferre.
16 Cic. Fam. viii. 6. Plin. Ep. x. 85.
17 Cic. Frat. iii. 1. 5. Plin. Ep. vii. 33.
18 concipiebat.
19 calumniam jurabat.
20 delatio nominis fiebat.
21 Cic. Caec. 5.
22 lis ei vel ejus aesti-

mabatur.
23 postulavit.
24 ut nomen inter reos reciperetur, i. e. ut in tabulam inter reos referretur.
25 Quin. v. 13. 3. Cic. Coel. 3. Dio. xxxix. 7. Dig. l. 10. de jure patron.
26 Cic. Fam. viii. 6.
27 libellus.

written, mentioning the name of the defendant, his crime, and every circumstance relating to the crime, which the accuser subscribed,[1] or another for him, if he could not write; at the same time binding himself to submit to a certain punishment or fine, if he did not prosecute or prove his charge.[2]

There were certain crimes which were admitted to be tried in preference to others,[3] as, concerning violence or murder. And sometimes the accused brought a counter charge of this kind against his accuser, to prevent his own trial.[4] Then the prætor appointed a certain day for the trial, usually the tenth day after. Sometimes the thirtieth, as by the Licinian and Julian laws.[5] But in trials for extortion, the accuser required a longer interval. Thus, Cicero was allowed 110 days, that he might go to Sicily, in order to examine witnesses, and collect facts to support his indictment against Verres, although he accomplished it in fifty days.[6] In the mean time, the person accused changed his dress,[7] and sought out persons to defend his cause.

Of defenders,[8] Asconius mentions four kinds; PATRONI, vel *oratores*, who pleaded the cause; ADVOCATI, who assisted by their counsel and presence, the proper meaning of the word; PROCURATORES, who managed the business of a person in his absence; and COGNITORES, who defended the cause of a person when present. But a *cognitor* might also defend the cause of a person when absent; hence put for any defender.[9] The *procuratores*, however, and *cognitores*, were used only in private trials, the *patroni* and *advocati* also in public. Before the civil wars, one rarely employed more than four patrons or pleaders, but afterwards often twelve.[10]

4. MANNER OF CONDUCTING THE TRIAL.

ON the day of trial, if the prætor could not attend, the matter was put off to another day. But if he was present, both the accuser and defendant were cited by a herald. If the defendant was absent, he was exiled. Thus, Verres, after the first oration of Cicero against him, called *actio prima*, went into voluntary banishment; for the five last orations, called *libri in Verrem*, were never delivered. Verres is said to have been afterwards restored by the influence of Cicero, and, what is remarkable, perished together with Cicero in the proscription of Antony, on account of his Corinthian vessels, which he would not part with to the triumvir.[11]

If the accuser was absent, the name of the defendant was taken from the roll of criminals.[12] But if both were present, the judices or jury were first chosen, either by lot or by naming,[13] according to the nature of the crime, and the law by which it was tried. If by lot, the prætor or judex quæstionis put into an urn the names of all those who were appointed to be judices for that year, and then took out by chance[14] the number which the law prescribed. After which the defendant and accuser were allowed to reject[15] such as they did not approve, and the prætor or judex quæstionis substituted[16] others in their room, till the legal number was completed.[17]

Sometimes the law allowed the accuser and defendant to choose the judices, in which case they were said JUDICES EDERE, and the judices were

---

1 Plin Ep. i. 20. v. 1.
2 cavebat se in crimine persoveraturum usque ad sententiam.
3 extra ordinem, Plin. Ep. iii. 9.
4 Cic. Fam. viii. 8. Dio. xxxix. 18.

5 Cic. Q. Frat. ii. 13.
Vat. 14. Asc. Corn.
6 Asc. loc. Cic. Verr. Act. prim. 2.
7 see p. 61.
8 defensores.
9 Liv. ii. 55. xxxix. 5. Asc. Div. Cæc. 4. Fest.

Cic. Verr. 2. 43. Rosc.
Com. 18. Hor. Sat. ii. 5. v. 28.
10 Asc. Cic. Scaur.
11 Asc. Verr. Cic. Sen. Suas. vi. 6 Plin. xxxiv.
2. Lactant. ii. 4.
12 de reis exemptum

est, Asc. Cic.
13 per sortitionem vel editionem.
14 sorte educebat.
15 rejicere.
16 subsortiebatur.
17 Cic. Verr. Act. i. 7. Asc. Cic.

called EDITITII. Thus, by the Servilian law of Glaucia against extortion, the accuser was ordered to name from the whole number of judices a hundred, and from that hundred the defendant to choose fifty. By the Lucinian law, *de sodalitiis*, the accuser was allowed to name the jury from the people at large.[1]

The judices or jury being thus chosen, were cited by a herald. Those who could not attend, produced their excuse, which the prætor might sustain[2] or not, as he pleased.

When they were all assembled, they swore to the laws, and that they would judge uprightly ; hence called JURATI HOMINES. The prætor himself did not swear.[3] Then their names were marked down in a book,[4] and they took their seats.[5]

The trial now began, and the accuser proceeded to prove his charge, which he usually did in two actions.[6] In the first action, he produced his evidence or proofs, and in the second he enforced them. The proofs were of three kinds, the declarations of slaves extorted by torture (QUÆSTIONES), the testimony of free citizens (TESTES), and writings (TABULÆ).

1. QUÆSTIONES. The slaves of the defendant were demanded by the prosecutor to be examined by torture in several trials, chiefly for murder and violence. But slaves could not be examined in this manner against their master's life,[7] except in the case of incest, or a conspiracy against the state. Augustus, in order to elude this law, and subject the slaves of the criminal to torture, ordered that they should be sold to the public, or to himself; Tiberius, to the public prosecutor,[8] but the ancient law was afterwards restored by Adrian and the Antonines.

The slaves of others also were sometimes demanded to be examined by torture ; but not without the consent of their master, and the accuser giving security, that if they were maimed or killed during the torture, he would make up the damage.[9]

When slaves were examined by torture, they were stretched on a machine, called ECULEUS, or *equuleus*, having their legs and arms tied to it with ropes,[10] and being raised upright, as if suspended on a cross, their members were distended by means of screws,[11] sometimes till they were dislocated.[12] To increase the pain, plates of red-hot iron,[13] pincers, burning pitch, &c. were applied to them. But some give a different account to this matter.

The confessions of slaves extorted by the rack, were written down on tables, which they sealed up till they were produced in court. Private persons also sometimes examined their slaves by torture.[14] Masters frequently manumitted their slaves, that they might be exempted from this cruelty ; for no Roman citizen could be scourged or put to the rack. But the emperor Tiberius subjected free citizens to the torture.[15]

2. TESTES. Free citizens gave their testimony upon oath.[16] The form of interrogating them was, SEXTE TEMPANI, QUÆRO EX TE, ARBITRERISNE, *C. Sempronium in tempore pugnam inisse?*[17] The witness answered, ARBITROR vel NON ARBITROR.[18]

1 Cic. Mur. 23. Planc. 15. 17.
2 accipere, Cic. Phil. v. 5.
3 Cic. Rosc. Am. 3. Act. Verr. 9. 13.
4 libellis consignabantur.
5 subsellia occupabant,

Asc. Verr. act. i. 6.
6 duabus actionibus.
7 in caput domini, Cic. Top. 34. Mil. 22. Dejot. I.
8 mancipari publico actori jubet, Dio. lv. 5. Tac. Ann. ii. 30, iii. 67. D. xlviii. 18. de Quæst.

9 ibid.
10 fidiculis, Suet. Tib. 62. Cal. 33.
11 per cochleas,
12 ut ossium compago resolveretur; hence eculeum longior factus, Sen. Ep. 8.
13 laminæ candentes.

14 Cic. Mil. 22. Clu. 63. 66.
15 Liv. viii. 15. Cic. Mil. 21. Verr. v. 63. Dio. lvii. 19.
16 jurati.
17 Liv. iv. 40.
18 Cic. Acad. iv. 47. Font. 9.

Witnesses were either voluntary or involuntary.[1] With regard to both, the prosecutor[2] was said, TESTES DARE, *adhibere, citare, colligere, edere, proferre, suburnare*, vel PRODUCERE; TESTIBUS UTI. With regard to the latter, IIS TESTIMONIUM DENUNCIARE, to summon them under a penalty, as in England by a writ called a SUBPŒNA, INVITOS EVOCARE. The prosecutor only was allowed to summon witnesses against their will, and of these a different number by different laws, usually no more than ten.[3]

Witnesses were said TESTIMONIUM DICERE, *dare, perhibere, præbere*, also *pro testimonio audiri*. The phrase DEPOSITIONES *testium* is not used by the classics, but only in the civil law. Those previously engaged to give evidence in favour of any one were called ALLIGATI; if instructed what to say, SUBORNATI.[4] Persons might give evidence, although absent, by writing;[5] but it was necessary that this should be done voluntarily, and before witnesses.[6] The character and condition of witnesses were particularly attended to.[7] No one was obliged to be a witness against a near relation or friend by the Julian law,[8] and never[9] in his own cause.[10]

The witnesses of each party had particular benches in the forum, on which they sat. Great dexterity was shown in interrogating witnesses.[11]

Persons of an infamous character were not admitted to give evidence,[12] and therefore were called INTESTABILES,[13] as those likewise were, who being once called as witnesses,[14] afterwards refused to give their testimony. Women anciently were not admitted as witnesses, but in aftertimes they were.[15]

A false witness, by the law of the Twelve Tables, was thrown from the Tarpeian rock, but afterwards the punishment was arbitrary, except in war, where a false witness was beaten to death with sticks by his fellow-soldiers.[16]

3. TABULÆ. By this name were called writings of every kind, which could be of use to prove the charge; particularly account books,[17] letters, bills, or bonds, &c.[18]

In a trial for extortion, the account-books of a person accused were commonly sealed up, and afterwards at the trial delivered to the judges for their inspection.[19] The ancient Romans used to make out their private accounts,[20] and keep them with great care. They marked down the occurrences of each day first in a note-book,[21] which was kept only for a month,[22] and then transcribed them into what we call a ledger,[23] which was preserved for ever; but many dropped this custom, after the laws ordered a man's papers to be sealed up, when he was accused of certain crimes, and produced in courts as evidences against him.[24]

The prosecutor having produced these different kinds of evidence, explained and enforced them in a speech, sometimes in two or more speeches. Then the advocates of the criminal replied; and their defence sometimes lasted for several days.[25] In the end of their speeches,[26] they tried to

1 Quin. v. 7. 9.
2 actor vel accusator.
3 Cic. Verr. i. 18, 19. v. 63. Rosc. Am. 36. 38. Fin. ii. 19. Juv. xvi. 29, &c. Plin. Ep. iii. 9. v. 20. vi. 5. Val. Max. viii. 1. Front. de Limit. 5. Quin. v. 7. 9. D. de Test.
4 Cic. Frat. ii. 3. Rosc. Com. 17. Isid. v. 23. Plin. Ep. iii. 9. Suet. Claud. 15.
5 per tabulas.

6 præsentibus signatoribus, Quin. v. 7.
7 diligenter expendebantur, Cic. Flacc. 5.
8 l. 4. D. de Testib.
9 more majorum.
10 de re sua, Cic. Rosc. Am. 36.
11 Quin. v. 7. Cic. Q. Rosc. 13. Flacc. 10. Don. Ter. Eun. iv. 4. v. 33.
12 testes non adhibiti sunt.
13 Plaut. Curc. i. 5. v.

30. Hor. Sat. ii. 3. v. 181. Gell. vi. 7. vii. 18.
14 antestati, v. in testimonium adhibiti.
15 Gell. vi. 7. xv. 13. Cic. Verr. i. 37.
16 Gell. xx. 1. l. 16. D. de Testib. et Sent. v. 25. s. 2. Polyb. vi. 35.
17 tabulæ accepti et expensi.
18 syngraphæ.
19 Cic. Verr. i. 23. 61. Balb. 5.
20 tabulas, sc. accepti

et expensi conficere vel domesticas rationes scribere.
21 adversaria, -orum.
22 menstrua erant.
23 codex vel tabulæ.
24 Cic. Quin. 2. Verr. i. 23. 39. Rosc. Com. 2. Cœl. 7. Att. xii. 5. Tusc. v. 33. Suet. Cæs. 47.
25 Asc. Cic. Corn. Ver.
26 in epilogo vel peroratione.

move the compassion of the judices, and for that purpose often introduced the children of the criminal. In ancient times only one counsel was allowed to each side.[1]

In certain causes persons were brought to attest the character of the accused, called LAUDATORES.[2] If one could not produce at least ten of these, it was thought better to produce none.[3] Their declaration or that of the towns from which they came, was called LAUDATIO, which word commonly signifies a funeral oration delivered from the rostra in praise of a person deceased, by some near relation, by an orator or chief magistrate.[4] Each orator, when he finished, said DIXI; and when all the pleadings were ended, a herald called out, DIXERUNT, vel -ERE.[5] Then the prætor sent the judices to give their verdict,[6] upon which they rose and went to deliberate for a little among themselves. Sometimes they passed sentence[7] *viva voce* in open court, but usually by ballot. The prætor gave to each judex three tablets; on one was written the letter C, for *condemno*, I condemn; on another, the letter A, for *absolvo*, I acquit; and on a third, N. L., *non liquet*, sc. *mihi*, I am not clear. Each of the judices threw which of these tablets he thought proper into an urn. There was an urn for each order of judges; one for the senators, another for the equites, and a third for the *tribuni ærarii*.[8]

The prætor, having taken out and counted the ballots, pronounced sentence according to the opinion of the majority,[9] in a certain form. If a majority gave in the letter C, the prætor said VIDETUR FECISSE, i. e. guilty; if the letter A, NON VIDETUR FECISSE, i. e. not guilty; if N. L., the cause was deferred.[10] The letter A. was called LITERA SALUTARIS, and the tablet on which it was marked, TABELLA ABSOLUTORIA, and C, *litera* TRISTIS, the tablet, DAMNATORIA. Among the Greeks, the condemning letter was Θ, because it was the first letter of θανατος, death; hence called *mortiferum* and *nigrum*.[11] Their acquitting letter is uncertain.

It was anciently the custom to use white and black pebbles,[12] in voting at trials:[13] hence *causa paucorum calculorum*, a cause of small importance, where there were few judges to vote; *omnis calculus immitem demittitur ater in urnam*, and only black stones were thrown into the merciless urn; i. e. he is condemned by all the judges; *reportare calculum deteriorum*, to be condemned: *meliorem*, to be acquitted; *errori album calculum adjicere*, to pardon or excuse.[14] To this Horace is thought to allude, Sat. ii. 3. 246, *creta an carbone notandi?* are they to be approved or condemned? and Persius, Sat. v. 108; but more probably to the Roman custom of marking in their calendar unlucky days with black,[15] and lucky days with white ·[16] hence *notare* vel *signare diem lactea gemma* vel *alba, melioribus lapillis*, vel *albis calculis*, to mark a day as fortunate.[17] This custom is said to have been

1 Cic. Sext. 69. Plin. Ep. l. 20.
2 Cic. Balb. 18. Clu. 59. Fam. i. 9. Fin. ii. 21. Suet. Aug. 56.
3 quam illum quasi legitimum numerum consuetudinis non explere, Cic. Verr. v. 22.
4 Cic. Fam. iii. 8. 6. Or. ii. 84. Liv. v. 50. Suet. Cæs. vi. 84. Aug. 101. Tib. 6. Tac. Ann. v. 1. xvi. 6. Plin. Ep. ii. 1.

5 Asc. Cic. Dom. Ter. Phor. ii 3. 90. sc. 4.
6 in consilium mittebat, ut sententiam ferrent vel dicerent, Cic. Verr. i. 9. Clu. 27. 30.
7 sententias ferebant.
8 Cæs. Bel. Civ. iii. 83. Cic. Q. Frat. ii. 6.
9 ex plurium sententia.
10 causa ampliata est, Asc. Cic. Verr. v. 6. Acad. iv. 47.
11 Per. Sat. 4. v. 13. Cic.

Mil. 6. Suet. Aug. 33.
Mart. vii. 36.
12 lapilli vel calculi.
13 mos erat antiquis niveis atrisque lapillis, his damnare reos, illis, absolvere culpa,—It was the custom of old to decide in criminal causes with black and white stones, the first condemned the accused, the other declared him innocent, Ov. Met. xv. 41.
14 Plin. Ep. i. 2. Quin.

viii. 3. 14. Ov. ib. 44. Corp. Juris.
15 carbone, with charcoal, whence dies atri for infausti.
16 creta vel cressa nota, with chalk, Hor. Od. i. 36. 10. called Creta, or terra Cressa vel Cretica, because it was brought from that island.
17 Mart. viii. 45. ix. 53. xi. 37. Pers. Sat. ii. 1. Plin. Ep. vi. 11.

borrowed from the Thracians or Scythians, who, every evening before they slept, threw into an urn or quiver a white pebble, if the day had passed agreeably ; but if not, a black one : and at their death, by counting the pebbles, their life was judged to have been happy or unhappy.[1] To this Martial beautifully alludes, xii. 34.

The Athenians, in voting about the banishment of a citizen who was suspected to be too powerful, used shells,[2] on which those who were for banishing him wrote his name, and threw each his shell into an urn. This was done in a popular assembly ; and if the number of shells amounted to 6000, he was banished for ten years,[3] by an OSTRACISM, as it was called. Diodorus says, for five years.[4]

When the number of judges who condemned, and of those who acquitted, was equal, the criminal was acquitted,[5] CALCULO MINERVÆ, by the vote of Minerva, as it was termed ; because when Orestes was tried before the Areopagus at Athens for the murder of his mother, and the judges were divided, he was acquitted by the determination[6] of that goddess.[7] In allusion to this, a privilege was granted to Augustus, if the number of the judices, who condemned, was but one more than of those that acquitted, of adding his vote to make an equality : and thus of acquitting the criminal.[8]

While the judices were putting the ballots into the urn, the criminal and his friends threw themselves at their feet, and used every method to move their compassion.[9]

The prætor, when about to pronounce a sentence of condemnation, used to lay aside his *toga prætexta.*[10]

In a trial for extortion, sentence was not passed after the first action was finished ; that is, after the accuser had finished his pleading, and the defender had replied ; but the cause was a second time resumed,[11] after the interval of a day, or sometimes more, especially if a festival intervened, as in the case of Verres, which was called COMPERENDINATIO, or *-atus, -tûs.*[12] Then the defender spoke first, and the accuser replied ; after which sentence was passed. This was done, although the cause was perfectly clear, by the Glaucian law ; but before that, by the Acilian law, criminals were condemned after one hearing.[13]

When there was any obscurity in the cause, and the judices were uncertain whether to condemn or acquit the criminal, which they expressed by giving in the tablets, on which the letters N. L. were written, and the prætor, by pronouncing AMPLIUS, the cause was deferred to any day the prætor chose to name. This was called AMPLIATIO, and the criminal or cause was said *ampliari ;* which sometimes was done several times, and the cause pleaded each time anew.[14] Sometimes the prætor, to gratify the criminal or his friends, put off the trial till he should resign his office, and thus not have it in his power to pass sentence[15] upon him.

If the criminal was acquitted, he went home and resumed his usual dress.[16] If there was ground for it, he might bring his accuser to a trial

1 Plin. vii. 40.
2 οστρακα, testæ vel testulæ.
3 testarum suffragiis.
4 xi. 55. Nep. Them. 8. Arist. 1. Cim. 3.
5 Cic. Clu. 27. Plut. Mar. see p. 65.
6 sententia.
7 Cic. Mil. 3. et ibi

Lambin. Æsch. Eum. v. 738.
8 Dio. li. 19.
9 Val. Max. viii. 1. 6. Asc. Cic. M. Scaur.
10 Plut. Cic. Sen. Ira, i. 16.
11 causa iterum dicebatur vel agebatur.
12 Cic. Verr. i. 7. 9. et

ibi Asc. &c.
13 semel dicta causa, semel auditis testibus.
14 Cic. ib. Brut. 22. bis ampliatus, tertio absolutus est reus, Liv. xliii. 2. iv. 44. causa L. Cottæ septies ampliata, et ad ultimum octavo judicio

absoluta est, Val. Max. viii. 1. 11.
15 ne diceret jus, Liv. xli. 22.
16 sordido habitu posito, albam togam resumebat.

for false accusation,[1] or for what was called PRÆVARICATIO ; that is, betraying the cause of one's client, and, by neglect or collusion, assisting his opponent.[2]

PRÆVARICARI[3] signifies properly to straddle, to stand or walk wide, with the feet too far removed from one another, not to go straight.[4] Hence, to shuffle, to play fast and loose, to act deceitfully.[5] If the criminal was condemned, he was punished by law according to the nature of his crime.

Under the emperors, most criminal causes were tried in the senate,[6] who could either mitigate or extend the rigour of the laws,[7] although this was sometimes contested.[8]

If a person was charged with a particular crime, comprehended in a particular law, select judges were appointed ; but if the crimes were various, and of an atrocious nature, the senate itself judged of them, as the people did formerly ; whose power Tiberius, by the suppression of the Comitia, transferred to the senate.[9] When any province complained of their governors, and sent ambassadors to prosecute them,[10] the cause was tried in the senate, who appointed certain persons of their own number to be advocates, commonly such as the province requested.[11]

When the senate took cognizance of a cause, it was said *suscipere* vel *recipere cognitionem*, and *dare inquisitionem*, when it appointed certain persons to plead any cause, DARE ADVOCATOS, V. PATRONOS. So the emperor. When several advocates either proposed or excused themselves, it was determined by lot who should manage the cause.[12] When the criminal was brought into the senate-house, by the lictors, he was said *esse* INDUCTUS. So the prosecutors.[13] When an advocate began to plead, he was said *descendere ut acturus*, *ad agendum* vel *ad accusandum*, because, perhaps, he stood in a lower place than that in which the judges sat, or came from a place of ease and safety to a place of difficulty and danger : thus *descendere in aciem* v. *prælium*, *in campum* v. *forum*, &c. to go on and finish the cause, *causam peragere* v. *perferre*. If an advocate betrayed the cause of his client,[14] he was suspended from the exercise of his profession,[15] or otherwise punished.[16]

An experienced advocate commonly assumed a young one in the same cause with him, to introduce him at the bar and recommend him to notice.[17] After the senate passed sentence, criminals used to be executed without delay. But Tiberius caused a decree to be made, that no one condemned by the senate should be put to death within ten days ; that the emperor, if absent from the city, might have time to consider their sentence, and prevent the execution of it, if he thought proper.[18]

5. DIFFERENT KINDS OF PUNISHMENTS.

PUNISHMENTS among the Romans were of eight kinds :—

1. MULCTA vel *damnum*, a fine, which at first never exceeded two oxen

---

1 calumniæ.
2 Cic. Top. 36. Plin. Ep. i. 20. iii. 9. Quin. ix. 2.
3 comp. of præ et varico, v. -or, from varus, bow or bandy-legged, crura incurva habens.
4 arator, nisi incurvus, prævaricatur, i. e. non rectum sulcum agit, vel a recto sulco divertit, Plin.

5 in contrariis causis quasi varie esse positus, Cic. ib.
6 Dio. lvii. 16. et alibi passim.
7 mitigare leges et intendere, Plin. Ep. ii. -11. iv. 9.
8 aliis cognitionem senatus lege conclusam, aliis liberam solutamque dicentibus, id.
9 Tac. Ann. i. 15. Plin. 20.

ii. 10.
10 legatos vel inquisitores mittebant, qui in eos inquisitionem postularent.
11 Plin. Ep. ii. 11. iii. 4. 9.
12 nomina in urnam conjecta sunt, Plin. Ep. ii. 11. iii. 4. vi. 29. vii. 6. 33. x. 20.
13 Id. ii. 11, 12. v. 4. 13. 20.

14 si prævaricatus esset.
15 ei advocationibus interdictum est.
16 Id. v. 13.
17 producere, ostendere famæ et assignare famæ, Plin. Ep. vi. 23.
18 Dio. lvii. 20. lviii. 27. Tac. Ann. iii. 51. Suet. Tib. 75. Sen. tranq. an. 14.

and thirty sheep, or the valuation of them ;[1] but afterwards it was increased.

2. VINCULA, bonds, which included public and private custody ; public, in prison, into which criminals were thrown after confession or conviction ; and private, when they were delivered to magistrates, or even to private persons, to be kept at their houses (*in libera custodia*, as it was called) till they should be tried.[2]

A prison[3] was first built by Ancus Martius, and enlarged by Servius Tullius ; whence that part of it below ground, built by him, was called TULLIANUM,[4] or LAUTUMIÆ,[5] in allusion to a place of the same kind built by Dionysius at Syracuse. Another part, or, as some think, the same part, from its security and strength, was called ROBUR, or *robus*.[6]

Under the name of *vincula* were comprehended *catenæ*, chains ; *compedes* vel *pedicæ*, fetters or bonds for the feet ; *manicæ*, manacles or bonds for the hands ; NERVUS, an iron bond or shackle for the feet or neck ;[7] also a wooden frame with holes, in which the feet were put and fastened, the stocks : sometimes also the hands and neck : called likewise COLUMBAR. *Boiæ*, leathern thongs, and also iron chains, for tying the neck or feet.[8]

3. VERBERA, beating or scourging, with sticks or staves ;[9] with rods ;[10] with whips or lashes.[11] But the first were in a manner peculiar to the camp, where the punishment was called FUSTUARIUM, and the last to slaves. Rods only were applied to citizens, and these too were removed by the Porcian law.[12] But under the emperors citizens were punished with these and more severe instruments, as with whips loaded with lead, &c.[13]

4. TALIO,[14] a punishment similar to the injury, an eye for an eye, a limb for a limb, &c. But this punishment, although mentioned in the Twelve Tables, seems very rarely to have been inflicted, because by law the removal of it could be purchased by a pecuniary compensation.[15]

5. IGNOMINIA vel *infamia*. Disgrace or infamy was inflicted,[16] either by the censors or by law, and by the edict of the prætor. Those made infamous by a judicial sentence, were deprived of their dignity, and rendered incapable of enjoying public offices, sometimes also of being witnesses, or of making a testament ; hence called INTESTABILES.[17]

6. EXILIUM, banishment. This word was not used in a judicial sentence, but AQUÆ ET IGNIS INTERDICTIO, forbidding one the use of fire and water, whereby a person was banished from Italy, but might go to any other place he chose. Augustus introduced two new forms of banishment, called DEPORTATIO, perpetual banishment to a certain place ; and RELEGATIO, either a temporal or perpetual banishment of a person to a certain place, without depriving him of his rights and fortunes.[18] Sometimes persons were only banished from Italy[19] for a limited time.

7. SERVITUS, slavery. Those were sold as slaves, who did not give in their names to be enrolled in the censor's books, or refused to enlist as

---

1 see lex Ateria, Liv.
iv. 30.
2 Cic. Div. i. 25. Tac.
iii. 51. vi. 3. Sall. Cat.
47. Liv. xxxix. 14.
3 carcer.
4 Sall. Cat. 55. Varr. L.
L. iv. 32. Liv. i. 33.
5 i. e. loca ex quibus
lapides excisi sunt,

Fest. in voce, Liv.
xxvi. 27. xxxii. 26.
xxxvii. 5. xxxix. 44.
6 Fest. in voce, Liv.
xxxviii. 59. Val. Max.
vi. 3. 1. Tac. Ann. iv.
29. Cic. Verr. v. 27. 55.
7 Fest. in voce.
8 Plaut. As. iii. 3. 5.
Rud. iii. 6. 30. Liv. viii.

28.
9 fustibus.
10 virgis.
11 flagellis.
12 Hor. Ep. 4. Cic. Rab.
perd. 4. Juv. x. 109.
Cic. Verr. iii. 29. Liv.
x. 9. Sall. Cat. 51.
13 plumbatis.
14 similitudo supplicii

vel vindictæ, hostimentum.
15 talio vel pœna redimi poterat, Gell. xx. 1.
16 inurebatur vel irrogabatur.
17 Digest.
18 see p. 47.
19 iis Italia interdictum, Plin. Ep. iii. 9.

soldiers ; because thus they were supposed to have voluntarily renounced the rights of citizens.[1]

8. Mors, death, was either civil or natural. Banishment and slavery were called a civil death. Only the most heinous crimes were punished by a violent death.

In ancient times it seems to have been most usual to hang malefactors,[2] afterwards, to scourge[3] and behead them,[4] to throw them from the Tarpeian rock,[5] or from that place in the prison called ROBUR, also to strangle them[6] in prison.

The bodies of criminals, when executed, were not burned or buried ; but exposed before the prison, usually on certain stairs, called GEMONIÆ sc. scalæ, vel. GEMONII gradus ;[7] and then dragged with a hook,[8] and thrown into the Tiber.[9] Sometimes, however, the friends purchased the right of burying them.

Under the emperors, several new and more severe punishments were contrived ; as, exposing to wild beasts,[10] burning alive,[11] &c. When criminals were burned, they were dressed in a tunic besmeared with pitch and other combustible matter, called TUNICA MOLESTA,[12] as the Christians are supposed to have been put to death. Pitch is mentioned among the instruments of torture in more ancient times.[13] Sometimes persons were condemned to the public works, to engage with wild beasts, or fight as gladiators, or were employed as public slaves in attending on the public baths, in cleansing common sewers, or repairing the streets and highways.[14]

Slaves after being scourged[15] were crucified,[16] usually with a label or inscription on their breast, intimating their crime, or the cause of their punishment, as was commonly done to other criminals, when executed. Thus Pilate put a title or superscription on the cross of our Saviour.[17] The form of the cross is described by Dionysius, vii. 69. Vedius Pollio, one of the friends of Augustus, devised a new species of cruelty to slaves, throwing them into a fish-pond to be devoured by lampreys.[18]

A person guilty of parricide, that is, of murdering a parent or any near relation, after being severely scourged,[19] was sewed up in a sack,[20] with a dog, a cock, a viper, and an ape, and then thrown into the sea or a deep river.[21]

RELIGION OF THE ROMANS.

I. THE GODS WHOM THEY WORSHIPPED.

THESE were very numerous, and divided into *Dii majorum gentium*, and *Minorum gentium, in allusion* to the division of senators.[22] The DII MAJORUM GENTIUM were the great celestial deities, and those called DII SELECTI. The great celestial deities were twelve in number.[23]

1. JUPITER,[24] the king of gods and men ; the son of Saturn and Rhea or

1 Cic. Cæc. 34. see p.48.
2 Infelici arbori suspendere, Liv. i. 26.
3 virgis cædere.
4 securi percutere, Liv. ii. 5. vii. 19. xxvi. 15.
5 de saxo Tarpeio dejicere, Id. vi. 20.
6 laqueo gulam, guttur, vel cervicem frangere, Fest. Val. Max. v. 4. 7. vi. 31. Sall. Cat.

7 55. Cic. Vat. 11. Luc. ii. 154.
7 quod gemitus locus esset.
8 unco tracti.
9 Suet. Tib. 53. 61. 75. Vit. 17. Tac. Hist. iii. 74. Plin. viii. 40. s. 61. Val. Max. vi. 3. 3. Juv. x. 66.
10 ad bestias damnatio.
11 vivicomburium.

12 Sen. Ep. 14. Juv. viii. 235. l. 155. Mart. x. 25. 5.
13 Tac. Ann. xv. 44. Plaut. Capt. iii. 4. 65.
14 Plin. Ep. x. 40.
15 sub furca cæsi.
16 in crucem acti sunt.
17 Matt. xxvii. 37. John xix. 19. Dio. liv. 3. Suet. Cal. 32. Dom. 10.

18 murænæ, Plin. ix. 23. s. 39. Dio. liv. 23.
19 sanguineis virgis cæsus.
20 culeo insutus.
21 Cic. Rosc. Am. ii. 25, 26. Sen. Clem. i. 23.
22 see p. 2. Cic. Tusc. i. 13.
23 Diony. vii. 72.
24 Ζεὺς Πατὴρ voc. Ζεὺ Πατερ.

Ops, the goddess of the earth ; born and educated in the island of Crete ; supposed to have dethroned his father, and to have divided his kingdom with his brothers ; so that he himself obtained the air and earth, Neptune the sea, and Pluto the infernal regions : usually represented as sitting on an ivory throne, holding a sceptre in his left hand, and a thunderbolt[1] in his right, with an eagle ; and Hebe the daughter of Juno, and goddess of youth, or the boy Ganymedes, the son of Tros, his cup-bearer,[2] attending on him ; called JUPITER FERETRIUS,[3] ELICIUS,[4] STATOR, CAPITOLINUS, and TONANS, which two were different, and had different temples ;[5] TARPEIUS, LATIALIS, DIESPITER[6] OPTIMUS MAXIMUS, OLYMPICUS, SUMMUS, &c. *Sub Jove frigido, sub dio,* under the cold air ; *dextro Jove,* by the favour of Jupiter ; *incolumi Jove,* i. e. *capitolio, ubi Jupiter colebatur.*[7]

2. JUNO, the wife and sister of Jupiter, queen of the gods, the goddess of marriage and of child-birth, called JUNO REGINA vel *regia ;* PRONUBA,[8] MATRONA, LUCINA,[9] MONETA,[10] because, when an earthquake happened, a voice was uttered from her temple, advising the Romans to make expiation by sacrificing a pregnant sow ;[11] represented in a long robe[12] and magnificent dress ; sometimes sitting or standing in a light car, drawn by peacocks, attended by the AURÆ, or air-nymphs, as by IRIS, the goddess of the rainbow. *Junone secunda,* by the favour of.[13]

3. MINERVA or PALLAS, the goddess of wisdom ; hence said to have sprung[14] from the brain of Jupiter by the stroke of Vulcan ; also of war and of arms ; said to be the inventress of spinning and weaving,[15] of the olive, and of warlike chariots ; called Armipotens, Tritonia virgo, because she was first seen near the lake Tritonis in Africa ; Attica *vel* Cecropia, because she was chiefly worshipped at Athens ;—represented as an armed virgin, beautiful, but stern and dark coloured, with azure or sky-coloured eyes,[16] shining like the eyes of a cat or an owl,[17] having a helmet on her head, and a plume nodding formidably in the air ; holding in her right hand a spear, and in her left a shield, covered with the skin of the goat Amalthea, by which she was nursed (hence called ÆGIS), given her by Jupiter, whose shield had the same name, in the middle of which was the head of the Gorgon Medusa, a monster with snaky hair, which turned every one who looked at it into stone.[18]

There was a statue of Minerva,[19] supposed to have fallen from heaven, which was religiously kept in her temple by the Trojans, and stolen from thence by Ulysses and Diomedes. *Tolerare colo vitam tenuique Minerva,* i. e. *lanificio non quæstuoso,* to earn a living by spinning and weaving, which bring small profit ; *invita Minerva,* i. e. *adversante et repugnante natura,* against nature or natural genius ;[20] *agere aliquid pingui Minerva,* simply, bluntly, without art ; *abnormis sapiens, crassaque Minerva,* a philosopher without rules, and of strong rough common sense ; *sus Minervam,* sc. *docet,* a proverb against a person who pretends to teach those who are

---

1 fulmen.
2 pincerna vel pocillator.
3 a ferendo,quod ei spolia opima afferebantur ferculo vel feretro gesta,Liv. l. 10. vel a feriendo, Plut. in Romulo, omine quod certo dux ferit ense ducem,Prop. iv. 11. 46. Diony. i. 34.
4 quod se illum certo carmine e cœlo elicere

posse credebant, Ov. F. iii. 327. ut edoceret, quomodo prodigia fulminibus, aliove quo viso missa, curarentur, vel expiarentur, ibid. & Liv. i. 20.
5 Dio. liv. 4. Suet. Aug. 29. 91.
6 diei et lucis pater.
7 Hor. Od. l. 1. 25. li. 3. 23. iii. 5. 12. Pers. v. 114.

8 quod nubentibus præesset, Serv. Virg. Æn. iv. 166. Ov. Ep. vi. 43.
Sacris præfecta maritis, i. e. nuptialibus solemnitatibus, xii. 65.
9 quod lucem nascentibus daret.
10 a monendo.
11 Cic. Div. i. 45. ii. 32.
12 stola.
13 Virg. Æn. iv. 45.
14 cum clypeo prosilu-

isse, Ov. F. iii. 841.
15 lanificii et texturæ, Ter. Heaut. v. 4. 13. Ov. ib.
16 glaucis oculis, γλαυκωπις Αθηνη.
17 γλαυξ, -κος, noctua, Gell. ii. 26.
18 Virg. Æn. viii. 354. & ibi Serv.
19 palladium.
20 Virg. Æn. viii. 409. Cic. Off. i. 31.

wiser than himself, or to teach a thing of which he himself is ignorant. Pallas is also put for oil,[1] because she is said first to have taught the use of it.

4. VESTA, the goddess of fire. Two of this name are mentioned by the poets ; one the mother, and the other the daughter of Saturn, who are often confounded. But the latter chiefly was worshipped at Rome. In her sanctuary was supposed to be preserved the Palladium of Troy,[2] and a fire kept continually burning by a number of virgins, called the Vestal virgins ; brought by Æneas from Troy ;[3] hence *hic locus est Vestæ, qui* PALLADA *servat* et IGNEM,[4] near which was the palace of Numa.[5]

5. CERES, the goddess of corn and husbandry, the sister of Jupiter ; worshipped chiefly at Eleusis in Greece, and in Sicily : her sacred rites were kept very secret.—She is represented with her head crowned with the ears of corn or poppies, and her robes falling down to her feet, holding a torch in her hand. She is said to have wandered over the whole earth with a torch in her hand, which she lighted at Mount Ætna,[6] in quest of her daughter Proserpina, who was carried off by Pluto. PLUTUS, the god of riches, is supposed to be the son of Ceres.

Ceres is called Legifera, the lawgiver, because laws were the effect of husbandry, and Arcana, because her sacred rites were celebrated with great secrecy,[7] and with torches ;[8] particularly at Eleusis in Attica,[9] from which, by the voice of a herald, the wicked were excluded ; and even Nero, while in Greece, dared not to profane them. Whoever entered without being initiated, although ignorant of this prohibition, was put to death.[10] Those initiated were called MYSTÆ,[11] whence *mysterium*. A pregnant sow was sacrificed to Ceres, because that animal was hurtful to the corn-fields.[12] And a fox was burnt to death at her sacred rites, with torches tied round it ; because a fox wrapt round with stubble and hay set on fire, being let go by a boy, once burnt the growing corn of the people of Carseoli, a town of the Æqui, as the foxes of Samson did the standing corn of the Philistines.[13]

Ceres is often put for corn or bread ; as *sine Cerere et Baccho friget Venus*, without bread and wine love grows cold.[14]

6. NEPTUNE,[15] the god of the sea, and brother of Jupiter ; represented with a trident in his right hand, and a dolphin in his left ; one of his feet resting on part of a ship ; his aspect majestic and serene ; sometimes in a chariot drawn by sea-horses, with a triton on each side ; called ÆGÆUS ; because worshipped at Ægea, a town in the island of Eubœa.[16] *Uterque Neptunus*, the *mare superum* and *inferum*, on both sides of Italy ; or, Neptune who presides over both salt and fresh water.[17] *Neptunia arva* vel *regna*, the sea. *Neptunius dux*, Sex. Pompeius, who, from his power at sea, called himself the son of Neptune. *Neptunia Pergama* vel *Troja*, because its walls were said to have been built by Neptune and Apollo,[18] at

1 Ov. Ep. xix. 44. Cic. Acad. i. 4. Fest. Hor. Sat. ii. 2. Columel. i. pr. 33. xi. 1. 31.
2 fatale pignus imperii Romani,—the fatal pledge of the Roman empire, Liv. xxvi. 27.
3 Virg. Æn. ii. 297.
4 this is the place (temple) of Vesta, in which the palladium is kept, and the perpetual fire, Ov. Trist. iii. 1. 39.
5 ib. 40. Hor. Od. i. 2.

16.
6 hinc Cereris sacris nunc quoque tæda datur,—hence it is that in the sacrifices of Ceres, a lighted torch is still given to those who perform the ceremony, Ov. F. iv. 494.
7 Plin. viii. 56. Hor. Od. iii. 2. 27.
8 whence, et per tædifera mystica sacra. Dea,—and by the sacred mysteries of the

torch-bearing goddess, Ov. Ep. ii. 42.
9 sacra Eleusinia.
10 Suet. Ner. 34. Liv. xxxi. 14.
11 Ov. F. iv. 556. a μυω, premo.
12 Ov. Pont. ii. 9. 30. Met. xv. 111.
13 Judg. xv. 4. Ov. F. iv. 681. to 712.
14 Ter. Eun. iv. 5. 6. Cic. Nat. D. ii. 23.
15 a nando, Cic. Nat. D. ii. 26. vel quod ma-

re terras obnuit, ut nubos cælum ; a nuptu, id est opertione : unde nuptiæ, Varr. L. L. iv. 10.
16 Virg. Æn. iii. 74. Hom. ll. v. 29.
17 liquentibus stagnis marique salso, Catul. xxix. 3.
18 Ov. F. i. 5. 5. Virg. Æn. ii. 625. viii. 695. Hor. Ep. ix. 7. Dio. xlviii. 19.

the request of Laomedon, the father of Priam, who defrauded them of their promised hire,[1] that is, he applied to that purpose the money which he had vowed to their service.　On which account Neptune was ever after hostile to the Trojans, and also to the Romans.　Apollo was afterwards reconciled by proper atonement ; being also offended at the Greeks for their treatment of Chryseis, the daughter of his priest Chryses, whom Agamemnon made a captive.　The wife of Neptune was Amphitrite, sometimes put for the sea.[2]　Besides Neptune, there were other sea gods and goddesses ; Oceanus, and his wife Tethys ; Nereus, and his wife Doris, the Nereides, Thetis, Doto, Galatea, &c.　Triton, Proteus, Portumnus, the son of Matuta or Aurora and Glaucus, Ino, Palemon, &c.

7.　VENUS, the goddess of love and beauty, said to have been produced from the foam of the sea, near the island Cythera ; hence called Cytherea, Marina, and by the Greeks Αφροδιτη, ab αφρος, spuma ; according to others, the daughter of Jupiter and the nymph Dione ; hence called Dionæa mater, by her son Æneas, and Julius Cæsar Dionæus ; as being descended from Iulus, the son of Æneas.　Dionæo sub antro, under the cave of Venus,—the wife of Vulcan, but unfaithful to him ;[3] worshipped chiefly at Paphos, Amathus, -untis, and Idalia v. -ium in Cyprus ; at Eryx in Sicily, and at Cnidus in Caria ; hence called Cypris, -idis, Dea, Paphia ; Amathusia Venus ; Venus Idalia, and ERYCINA ; Regina Cnidia ; Venus Cnidia.[4]　Alma, decens, aurea, formosa, &c. also Cloucina or Cluacina, from cluere, anciently the same with luere or purgare, because her temple was built in that place, where the Romans and Sabines, after laying aside their arms, and concluding an agreement, purified themselves.　Also supposed to be the same with Libitina, the goddess of funerals, whom some make the same with Proserpine,—often put for love, or the indulgence of it ; damnosa Venus, pernicious venery.　Sera juvenum Venus, eoque inexhausta pubertas, the youths partake late of the pleasures of love, and hence pass the age of puberty unexhausted ; for a mistress ; for beauty, comeliness, or grace.　Tabulæ pictæ Venus, vel Venustas, quam Græci χαριτα vocant ; dicendi Veneres, the graces ; Venerem habere.　Cicero says there were more than one Venus.[5]

The tree most acceptable to Venus was the myrtle, hence she was called MYRTEA, and by corruption MURCIA, and the month most agreeable to her was April, because it produced flowers ; hence called mensis VENERIS, on the first day of which the matrons, crowned with myrtle, used to bathe themselves in the Tiber, near the temple of FORTUNA VIRILIS, to whom they offered frankincense, that she would conceal their defects from their husbands.[6]

The attendants of Venus were her son CUPID ; or rather the Cupids, for there were many of them ; but two most remarkable, one, Eros, who caused love, and the other, Anteros, who made it cease, or produced mutual love ; painted with wings, a quiver, bow, and darts : the three GRACES, (Gratiæ vel Charites), Anglaia or Pasithea, Thalia, and Euphrosyne, re-

1 pacta mercede destituit, Hor. Od. iii. 3. 22.
2 Ov. Met. i. 14. Rem. Am. 469. Hom. Il. 1. Serv. Virg. Æn. ii. 610. G. i 502.
3 Hor. Od. i. 4, 5. ii. 1. 39. Virg. Æn. iii. 19. 26. 5. iv. 128. Ecl. ix. 47. Ov. Met. iv. 171.

4 Tac. Ann. iii. 62. Cic. Verr. ii. 8. iv. 60. Div. i. 13. Hor. Od. i. 30. 1. 2. 33. Virg. Æn. v. 760.
5 Nat. D. iii. 23. Venus dicta, quod ad omnes res veniret ; atque ex ea venustas,—called Venus, because she had an influence upon

all things ; and from her the word venustas, ii. 27. et Venerii, i. e. servi Veneris, Cæc. 17. Plin. xv. 29. s. 36. xxxv. 10. s. 26. Diony. iv. 15. Plut. Num. 67. Hor. Ep. i. 18. 21 Sat. i. 2. 119. 4. 113. Tac. Mor. Ger. 20. Virg. Ecl. iii. 66. Plaut. Stic.

ii. 1. 5. Quin. x. 1. Sen. Ben. ii. 28.
6 Ov. F. iv. 139, &c. Hor. Od. iv. 11. 15. Virg. Ec. vii. 62. Serv. in loc. Æn. v. 72. viii. 635. Plin. xv. s. 36. Plut. Quæst. Rom. 20. Varr. L. L. iv. 32.

presented generally naked, with their hands joined together ; and NYMPHS dancing with the Graces, and Venus at their head.[1]

8. VULCANUS vel *Mulciber*, the god of fire[2] and of smiths ; the son of Jupiter and Juno, and husband of Venus : represented as a lame blacksmith, hardened from the forge, with a fiery red face while at work, and tired and heated after it. He is generally the subject of pity or ridicule to the other gods, as a cuckold and lame. Vulcan is said to have had his workshop[3] chiefly in Lemnos, and in the Æolian or Lipari islands near Sicily, or in a cave of mount Ætna. His workmen were the Cyclopes, giants with one eye in their forehead, who were usually employed in making the thunderbolts of Jupiter.[4] Hence Vulcan is represented in spring as eagerly lighting up the fires in their toilsome or strong smelling workshops,[5] to provide plenty of thunderbolts for Jupiter to throw in summer, called *avidus*, greedy, as Virgil calls *ignis*, fire, *edax*, from its devouring all things ; sometimes put for fire ; called *luteus*, from its colour ; from *luteum* v. *lutum*, woad, the same with *glastum* ;[6] which dyes yellow ;[7] or rather from *lutum*, clay, *luteus*, dirty. Cicero also mentions more than one Vulcan,[8] as indeed he does in speaking of most of the gods.

9. MARS or *Mavors*, the god of war and son of Juno ; worshipped by the Thracians, Getæ, and Scythians, and especially by the Romans, as the father of Romulus, their founder, called Gradivus,[9] painted with a fierce aspect, riding in a chariot, or on horseback, with a helmet and a spear. Mars, when peaceable, was called QUIRINUS.[10] BELLONA, the goddess of war, was the wife or sister of Mars.

A round shield[11] is said to have fallen from heaven in the reign of Numa, supposed to be the shield of Mars ; which was kept with great care in his sanctuary, as a symbol of the perpetuity of the empire, by the priests of Mars ; who were called SALII ; and that it might not be stolen, eleven others were made quite like it.[12]

The animals sacred to Mars were the horse, wolf, and the wood-pecker.[13] Mars is often, by a metonymy, put for war or the fortune of war ; thus, *æquo, vario, ancipite, incerto Marte pugnatum est*, with equal, various, doubtful success ; *Mars communis*, the uncertain events of war ; *accendere Martem cantu*, to kindle the rage of war by martial sounds ; i. e. *pugnam vel milites ad pugnam tuba ; collato Marte et eminus pugnare*, to contend in close battle, and from a distance ; *invadunt Martem clypeis*, they rush to the combat with shields, i. e. *pugnam ineunt ; nostro Marte aliquid peragere*, by our own strength, without assistance ; *verecundiæ erat, equitem suo alienoque Marte pugnare*, on horseback and on foot ; *valere Marte forensi*, to be a good pleader ; *dicere difficile est, quid Mars tuus egerit illic*, i. e. *bellica virtus*, valour or courage ; *nostra Marte*, by our army or soldiers ; *altero Marte*, in a second battle ; *Mars tuus*, your manner of fighting ; *incursu gemini Martis*, by land and sea.[14]

10. MERCURIUS, the son of Jupiter and Maia, the daughter of Atlas ; the messenger of Jupiter and of the gods ; the god of eloquence ; the patron of

---

1 Hor. Od. i. 4. 5.—30.
6. ii. 8. 13. Sen. Ben. i.
3.
2 Ignipotens, Virg. Æn.
x. 243.
3 officina.
4 Virg. Æn. viii. 416.
5 graves ardens urit officinas.
6 Cæs. B. G. v. 14. Hor.

Od. i. 4. 7. iii. 58. Sat.
i. 5. 74. Plaut. Amph.
i. 1. 185. Juv. x. 133.
Virg. Æn. ii. 758. 311.
v. 662. vii. 77.
7 herba qua cæruleum inficiunt, Vitr. vii. 14.
Plin. xxxiii. 5. s. 26.
croceo mutabit vellora
luto,—shall tinge his

fleece with saffron dye,
Virg. Ecl v. 44. luteum ovi, the yolk of an
egg, Plin. x. 53.
8 Nat. D. ii. 23.
9 a gradiendo, Ov. F. ii.
861.
10 Serv. Virg. i. 296.
11 ancile quod ab omni
parte recisum est, Ov.

F. iii. 377.
12 ancilia, -ium, vel
-iorum.
13 picus.
14 Luc. vi. 269. Virg.
Cic. Liv. iii. 62. Ov.
Pont. iv. 6. 39. 7. 45.
Art. Am. i. 212. Hor.
Od. iii. 5. 24. 34.

merchants and of gain, whence his name (according to others, *quasi* Medicurrius, *quod* medius *inter deos et homines* currebat); the inventor of the lyre and of the harp; the protector of poets or men of genius,[1] of musicians, wrestlers, &c.; the conductor of souls or departed ghosts to their proper mansions; also the god of ingenuity and of thieves, called Cyllenius vel Cyllenia proles, from Cyllene, a mountain in Arcadia on which he was born; and Tegeæus, from Tegea, a city near it.

The distinguishing attributes of Mercury are his petasus, or winged cap; the talaria, or winged sandals for his feet; and a caduceus, or wand[2] with two serpents about it, in his hand; sometimes as the god of merchants he bears a purse.[3]

Images of Mercury[4] used to be erected where several roads met,[5] to point out the way; on sepulchres, in the porches of temples and houses, &c. *Ex quovis ligno non fit Mercurius*, every one cannot become a scholar.

11. APOLLO, the son of Jupiter and Latona, born in the island Delos; the god of poetry, music, medicine, augury, and archery; called also Phœbus and Sol. He had oracles in many places, the chief one at Delphi in Phocis; called by various names from the places where he was worshipped, Cynthius from Cynthus, a mountain in Delos; Patareus, or -æus, from Patara, a city in Lycia; Latous, son of Latona; Thymbræus, Grynæus, &c.; also Pythius, from having slain the serpent Python.[6]

Apollo is usually represented as a beautiful beardless young man, with long hair (hence called *intonsus* et *crinitus*),[7] holding a bow and arrows in his right hand, and in his left hand a lyre or harp. He is crowned with laurel, which was sacred to him, as were the hawk and raven among the birds.

The son of Apollo was ÆSCULAPIUS, the god of physic, worshipped formerly at Epidaurus in Argolis, under the form of a serpent, or leaning on a staff, round which a serpent was entwined :—represented as an old man, with a long beard, dressed in a loose robe, with a staff in his hand.

Connected with Apollo and Minerva were the nine MUSES, said to be the daughters of Jupiter and Mnemosyne or memory; Calliope, the muse of heroic poetry; Clio, of history; Melpomene, of tragedy; Thalia, of comedy and pastorals; Erato, of love-songs and hymns; Euterpe, of playing on the flute; Terpsichore, of the harp; Polyhymnia, of gesture and delivery, also of the three-stringed instruments called barbitos, vel -on; and Urania, of astronomy.[8]

The muses frequented the mountains Parnassus, Helicon, Pierus, &c., the fountains Castalius, Aganippe, or Hippocrene, &c., whence they had various names, Heliconides, Parnassides, Pierides, Castalides, Thespiades, Pimpliades, &c.

12. DIANA, the sister of Apollo, goddess of the woods and of hunting; called Diana on earth, Luna in heaven, and Hecate in hell: hence *tergemina, diva triformis, tria virginis ora Dianæ;* also Lucina, Ilithya, et Genitalis seu Genetyllis, because she assisted women in child-birth; Noctiluca, and *siderum regina*,[9] Trivia, from her statues standing where three ways met.

Diana is represented as a tall, beautiful virgin, with a quiver on her

1 Mercurialium virorum.
2 virga.
3 marsupium, Hor. i. 10. Virg. Æn. iv. 239.

viii. 138.
4 Hermæ truncl, shapeless posts with a marble head of Mercury on them, Juv. viii. 53.

5 in compitis.
6 vel a πυθεσθαι, quod consuleretur.
7 Ov. Trist. iii. 1. 60.
8 Aus. Eid. 20. Diod.

iv. 7. Phurnutus de Natura Deorum.
9 Virg. Æn. iv. 52. Hor.

shoulder, and a javelin or a bow in her right hand, chasing deer or other animals.

These twelve deities were called CONSENTES, -um,[1] and are comprehended in these two verses of Ennius, as quoted by Apuleius, *de Deo Socratis :*

> Juno, Vesta, Minerva, Ceres, Diana, Venus, Mars,
> Mercurius, Jovi', Neptunus, Vulcanus, Apollo.

On ancient inscriptions they are thus marked :—J. O. M. i. e. *Jovi optimo maximo,* CETERISQ. DIS CONSENTIBUS. They were also called DII MAGNI, and CŒLESTES, or NOBILES, and are represented as occupying a different part of heaven from the inferior gods, who are called PLEBS.[2]

THE DII SELECTI WERE EIGHT IN NUMBER.

1. SATURNUS, the god of time; the son of ~~Cœlus~~ or Uranus, and ~~Terra~~ Vesta. Titan his brother resigned the kingdom to him on this condition, that he should rear no male offspring. On which account he is feigned by the poets to have devoured his sons as soon as they were born. But Rhea found means to deceive him, and bring up by stealth Jupiter and his two brothers.

Saturn, being dethroned by his son Jupiter, fled into Italy, and gave name to Latium, from his lurking there.[3] He was kindly received by Janus, king of that country. Under Saturn is supposed to have been the golden age, when the earth produced food in abundance spontaneously, when all things were in common, and when there was an intercourse between the gods and men upon earth; which ceased in the brazen and iron ages, when even the virgin Astrea, or goddess of justice herself, who remained on earth longer than the other gods, at last, provoked by the wickedness of men, left it. The only goddess then left was Hope.[4] Saturn is painted as a decrepit old man, with a scythe in his hand, or a serpent biting off its own tail.

2. JANUS, the god of the year, who presided over the gates of heaven, and also over peace and war. He is painted with two faces.[5] His temple was open in time of war, and shut in time of peace. A street in Rome, contiguous to the forum, where bankers lived, was called by his name, thus *Janus summus ab imo,* the street Janus from top to bottom ; *medius,* the middle part of it.[6] Thoroughfares[7] from him were called Jani, and the gates at the entrance of private houses, Januæ ; thus, *dextro* JANO *portæ* CARMENTALIS. through the right hand postern of the Carmental gate.[8]

3. RHEA, the wife of Saturn ; called also Ops, Cybele, Magna Mater, Mater Deorum, Berecynthia, Idæa, and Dindymene, from three mountains in Phrygia. She was painted as a matron, crowned with towers,[9] sitting in a chariot drawn by lions.[10]

Cybele, or a sacred stone, called by the inhabitants the mother of the gods, was brought from Pessinus in Phrygia to Rome, in the time of the second Punic war.[11]

4. PLUTO, the brother of Jupiter, and king of the infernal regions ; called

---

1 Varr. L. L. vii. 38. qua in consilium Jovis adhibebantur, Augustin. de Civit. Dei, iv. 23. duodecim enim deos advocat. Sen. Q. Nat. ii. 41. a consensu,
quasi consentientes, vel a censendo, i. e. consulo. 2 Virg. Æn. i. 391. ill. 11. Ov. Am. iii. 6. Met. i. 172. Vitru. i. 8. Cic. Legg. ii. 8.
3 a latendo. 4 Virg. G. i. 125. Ov. Met. i. 150. Pont. i. 6. 99. 5 bifrons vel biceps. 6 Hor. Ep. i. i. 54. Sat. iii. 3. 18. Cic. Phil. vi.
5. Liv. i. 19. 7 transitiones perviæ. 8 Cic. N. D. ii. 27. Liv. ii. 49. 9 turrita. 10 Ov. F. iv. 249, &c. 11 Liv. xxix. 11. 14.

also Orcus, Jupiter *infernus et Stygius.* The wife of Pluto was PROSER-
PINA, the daughter of Ceres, whom he carried off, as she was gathering
flowers in the plains of Enna, in Sicily ; called *Juna inferna* or *Stygia,* often confounded with Hecate and Luna, or Diana ; supposed to preside over
sorceries or incantations.[1]

There were many other infernal deities, of whom the chief were the
FATES or Destinies,[2] the daughters of Jupiter and Themis, or of Erebus and
Nox, three in number ; Clotho, Lachesis, and Atropos, supposed to determine the life of men by spinning. Clotho held the distaff, Lachesis spun,
and Atropos cut the thread : when there was nothing on the distaff to spin,
it was attended with the same effect. Sometimes they are all represented as employed in breaking the threads.[3] The FURIES,[4] also three in
number, Alecto, Tisiphone, and Megæra ; represented with wings and
snakes twisted in their hair : holding in their hands a torch, and a whip to
torment the wicked ; MORS vel *Lethum,* death ; SOMNUS, sleep, &c. The
punishments of the infernal regions were sometimes represented in pictures, to deter men from crimes.[5]

5. BACCHUS, the god of wine, the son of Jupiter and Semele ; called
also Liber or Lyæus, because wine frees the minds of men from care :
described as the conqueror of India) represented always young, crowned
with vine or ivy leaves, sometimes with horns ; hence called CORNIGER,[6]
holding in his hand a thyrsus, or spear bound with ivy : his chariot was
drawn by tigers, lions, or lynxes, attended by Silenus, his nurse and preceptor, bacchanals,[7] and satyrs. The sacred rites of Bacchus[8] were celebrated every third year[9] in the night-time, chiefly on Cithæron, and Isme-
nus, in Bœotia, on Ismarus, Rhodope, and Edon in Thrace.

PRIAPUS, the god of gardens, was the son of Bacchus and Venus.[10]

6. SOL, the sun, the same with Apollo ; but sometimes also distinguished, and then supposed to be the son of Hyperion, one of the Titans or giants
produced by the earth ; who is also put for the sun. Sol was painted in a
juvenile form, having his head surrounded with rays, and riding in a chariot drawn by four horses, attended by the Horæ or four seasons : Ver, the
spring ; Æstas, the summer ; Autumnus, the autumn ; and Hiems, the winter.[11] The sun was worshipped chiefly by the Persians under the name of
Mithras.

7. LUNA, the moon, as one of the *Dii Selecti,* was the daughter of Hyperion and sister of Sol. Her chariot was drawn only by two horses.

8. GENIUS, the *dæmon* or tutelary god, who was supposed to take care of
every one from his birth during the whole of life. Places and cities, as
well as men, had their particular Genii. It was generally believed that
every person had two genii, the one good, and the other bad. *Defraudare
genium suum, to pinch one's appetite ; indulgere genio, to indulge it.*

Nearly allied to the genii were the LARES and PENATES, household-gods,
who presided over families.

The *Lares* of the Romans appear to have been the manes of their ancestors.[13] Small waxen images of them, clothed with a skin of a dog,
were placed round the hearth in the hall.[14] On festivals they were

---

1 veneficiis præesse.
2 Parcæ, a parcendo,
vel antiphrasin quod
nemini parcant.
3 Luc. iii. 18. Ov. Pont.
l. 8. 64. Ep. xii. 3. Am.
ii. 6. 46.

4 Furiæ vel Diræ, Eu-
menides vel Erinnyes.
5 Plaut. Capt. v. 4. 1.
6 Ov. Ep. xiii. 33.
7 frantic women, Bac.
chæ, Thyades vel Mæ-
nades, Ov. F. iii. 715

—770. Ep. iv. 47.
8 Bacchanalia, orgia,
vel Dionysia.
9 hence called trieta-
rica.
10 Serv. Virg. G. iv.
3.

11 Ov. Met. ii. 25.
12 Ter. Phor. i. 1. 10
Pers. v. 151.
13 Virg. Æn. ix. 255.
14 in atrio.

p. 189

crowned with garlands, and sacrifices were offered to them.[1] There were not only *Lares domestici et familiares*, but also *compitales et viales, militares et marini*, &c.

The *Penates*[2] were worshipped in the innermost part of the house, which was called *penetralia* : also *impluvium, or compluvium*. There were likewise *publici Penates*, worshipped in the capitol, under whose protection the city and temples were. These Æneas brought with him from Troy. Hence *patrii Penates, familiaresque*.[3]

Some have thought the Lares and Penates the same; and they seem sometimes to be confounded. They were, however, different.[4] The Penates were of divine origin ; the Lares, of human. Certain persons were admitted to the worship of the Lares, who were not to that of the Penates. The Penates were worshipped only in the innermost part of the house, the Lares also in the public roads, in the camp, and on sea.

Lar is often put for a house or dwelling : *apto cum lare fundus*,[5] a farm with a suitable dwelling. So *Penates* : thus, *nostris succede Penatibus hospes*,[6] come under our roof as our guest.

DII MINORUM GENTIUM, OR INFERIOR DEITIES.

THESE were of various kinds :

1. *Dii* INDIGETES, or heroes, ranked among the gods on account of their virtue and merits ; of whom the chief were,—

HERCULES, the son of Jupiter, and Alcmena wife of Amphitryon, king of Thebes ; famous for his twelve labours, and other exploits : squeezing two serpents to death in his cradle, killing the lion in the Nemæan wood, the hydra of the lake Lerna, the boar of Erymanthus, the brazen-footed stag on mount Menalus, the harpies in the lake of Stymphalus, Diomedes, and his horses, who were fed on human flesh, the wild bull in the island of Crete, cleansing the stables of Augeas, subduing the Amazons and Centaurs, dragging the dog Cerberus from hell, carrying off the oxen of the three-bodied Geryon from Spain, fixing pillars in the *fretum Gaditanum*, or straits of Gibraltar, bringing away the golden apples of the Hesperides, and killing the dragon which guarded them, slaying the giant Antæus, and the monstrous thief Cacus, &c.

Hercules was called Alcides, from Alcæus the father of Amphitryon ; and Tirynthius, from Tiryns, the town where he was born ; Œtæus, from mount Œte, where he died. Being consumed by a poisoned robe, sent him by his wife Dejanira in a fit of jealousy, which he could not pull off, he laid himself on a funeral pile, and ordered it to be set on fire. Hercules is represented of prodigious strength, holding a club in his right hand, and clothed in the skin of the Nemæan lion. Men used to swear by Hercules in their asseverations : *Hercle, Mehercle, vel -es ; so under the title of Dius Fidius, i. e. Deus fidei*, the god of faith or honour : thus, *per Dium Fidium, me Dius fidius, sc. juvet*.[7] Hercules was supposed to preside too over treasures hence *dives amico Hercule*, being made rich by propitious Hercules ; *dextro Hercule*, by the favour of Hercules.[8] Hence

1 Plaut. Trin. i. 1. Juv. xii. 89. Suet. Aug. 31.
2 sive a penu ; est enim omne quo vescuntur homines penus ; sive quod penitus insident, —either from penus, all kinds of human provisions ; or because they reside within, Cic. Nat. Deor. ii. 27. Dii per quos penitus spiramus. Macrob. Sat. iii. 4. idem ac Magni Dii, Jupiter, Juno, Minerva, Serv. Virg. Æn.

ii. 296.
3 Cic. Dom. 57. Suet. Aug. 92. Liv. iii. 17. Virg. Æn. ii. 293. 717. iii. 148. iv. 598.
4 Liv. i. 29. Cic. Quin. 26, 27. Verr. iv. 22.
5 Hor. Od. i 12. 44. Ov.

F. vi. 95. 362. 529.
6 Virg. Æn. viii. 123. Plin. Pan. 47
7 Plaut. Sal. Cat. 35.
8 Hor. Sat. ii. 6. 12. Per. ii. 11.

those who obtained great riches consecrated[1] the tenth part to Hercules.[2]

CASTOR and POLLUX, sons of Jupiter and Leda, the wife of Tyndarus, king of Sparta, brothers of Helena and Clytemnestra, said to have been produced from two eggs; from one of which came Pollux and Helena, and from the other, Castor and Clytemnestra. But Horace makes Castor and Pollux to spring from the same egg. He, however, also calls them FRATRES HELENÆ, the god of mariners, because their constellation was much observed at sea; called Tyndaridæ, Gemini, &c. Castor was remarkable for riding, and Pollux for boxing; represented as riding on white horses, with a star over the head of each, and covered with a cap; hence called FRATRES PILEATI. There was a temple at Rome dedicated to both jointly, but called the temple only of Castor.[3]

Æneas, called Jupiter Indiges; and Romulus, QUIRINUS, after being ranked among the gods either from *quiris* a spear, or Cures, a city of the Sabines.[4]

The Roman emperors also after their death were ranked among the gods.

2. There were certain gods called SEMONES;[5] as,

PAN, the god of shepherds, the inventor of the flute; said to be the son of Mercury and Penelope, worshipped chiefly in Arcadia; hence called *Arcadius,* and *Mænalius,* vel.-*ides,* et *Lyceus,* from two mountains there; *Tegeæus,* from a city, &c. called by the Romans *Inuus;*—represented with horns and goat's feet. Pan was supposed to be the author of sudden frights or causeless alarms; from him called *Panici terrores.*[6]

FAUNUS and SYLVANUS, supposed to be the same with Pan. The wife or daughter of Faunus was Fauna or Fatua, called also Marica and BONA DEA.[7]

There were several rural deities called FAUNI, who were believed to occasion the nightmare.[8]

VERTUMNUS, who presided over the change of seasons and merchandise;—supposed to transform himself into different shapes. Hence *Vertumnis natus iniquis,* an inconstant man.[9]

POMONA, the goddess of gardens and fruits; the wife of Vertumnus.[10]

FLORA, the goddess of flowers; called Chloris by the Greeks.[11]

TERMINUS, the god of boundaries; whose temple was always open at the top.[12] And when, before the building of the capitol, all the temples of the other gods were unhallowed,[13] it alone could not,[14] which was reckoned an omen of the perpetuity of the empire.

PALES, a god or goddess who presided over flocks and herds; usually feminine, *pastoria* PALES.[15]

HYMEN *vel* HYMENÆUS, the god of marriage.

LAVERNA, the goddess of thieves.[16]

VACUNA, who presided over vacation, or respite from business.[17]

AVERRUNCUS, the god who averted mischiefs.[18]   There were several of these.

1 pollucebant.
2 Cic. Nat. D. iii. 36. Plaut. Stich. i. 3. 60. Bacch. iv. 14, 15. Plut. Crass. init.
3 Hor. Sat. ii. 1. 26. Od. i. 3. 2. 12. 26. Dio. xxxvii. 8. Suet. Cæs. 10. Fest. Cat. 35.
4 Ov. F. ii. 475—480.
5 quasi semihomines,

'minores diis at majores hominibus,—inferior to the supreme gods, but superior to men, Liv. viii. 26.
6 Cic. Diony. v. 16.
7 Macrob. Sat. i. 12.
8 ludibria noctis vel ephialten immittere, Plin. xxv. 4.
9 Prop. iv. 2. Hor. Sat.

ii. 7. 14.
10 Ov. Met. xiv. 623.
11 Lact. i. 26. Ov. F. v. 195.
12 Fest. se supra ne quid nisi sidera cernat, —that he might see nothing above him but the stars, Ov. F. ii. 671.
13 exangurarentur.

14 Liv. i. 55. v. 54. Jovi ipsi regi noluit concedere,—he would not give place to great Jove himself, Gell. xii. 6 Liv. ib.
15 Flor i. 20.
16 Hor. Ep. i. 16. 60.
17 Ov. F. vi. 307.
18 mala averruncabat, Var. vi. 5.

FASCINUS, who prevented fascination or enchantment.

ROBIGUS, the god, and RUBIGO, or ROBIGO, the goddess who preserved corn from blight.[1] Ovid mentions only the goddess ROBIGO.[2]

MEPHITIS, the goddess of bad smells.[3] CLOACINA, of the *cloacæ*, or common sewers.

Under the Semones were comprehended the NYMPHS,[4] female deities, who presided over all parts of the earth : over mountains, Oreades ; woods, Dryades, Hamadryades, Napææ ; rivers and fountains, Naïades *vel* Naiädes ; the sea, Nereides, Oceanitides, &c.—Each river was supposed to have a particular deity, who presided over it ; as Tiberinus over the Tiber ;[5] Eridanus over the Po ; *taurino vultu*, with the countenance of a bull, and horns ; as all rivers were represented.[6] The sources of rivers were particularly sacred to some divinity, and cultivated with religious ceremonies. Temples were erected ; as to Clitumnus, to Ilissus ;[7] small pieces of money were thrown into them, to render the presiding deities propitious ; and no person was allowed to swim near the head of the spring, because the touch of a naked body was supposed to pollute the consecrated waters.[8] Thus no boat was allowed to be on the *lacus Vadimonis*, in which were several floating islands. Sacrifices were also offered to fountains ; as by Horace to that of Bandusia, whence the rivulet Digentia probably flowed.[9]

Under the SEMONES were also included the judges in the infernal regions, Minos, Æacus, and Rhadamanthus ; CHARON, the ferryman of hell,[10] who conducted the souls of the dead in a boat over the rivers Styx and Acheron, and exacted from each his *portorium* or freight,[11] which he gave an account of to Pluto ; hence called, PORTITOR : the dog CERBERUS, a three-headed monster, who guarded the entrance of hell.

The Romans also worshipped the virtues and affections of the mind, and the like ; as Piety, Faith, Hope, Concord, Fortune, Fame, &c., even vices and diseases ; and under the emperors likewise foreign deities ; as Isis, Osiris, Anubis, of the Egyptians ;[12] also the winds and the tempests : Eurus, the east wind ; Auster or Notus, the south wind ; Zephyrus, the west wind ; Boreas, the north wind ; Africus, the south-west ; Corus, the north-west ; and ÆOLUS, the god of the winds, who was supposed to reside in the Lipari islands, hence called Insulæ Æoliæ : AURÆ, the air-nymphs or sylphs, &c.

The Romans worshipped certain gods that they might do them good, and others that they might not hurt them ; as Averruncus and Robigus. There was both a good Jupiter and a bad ; the former was called DIJOVIS,[13] or Diespiter, and the latter, VEJOVIS, or VEDIUS. But Ovid makes Vejovis the same with *Jupiter parvus*, or *non magnus*.[14]

II. MINISTRI SACRORUM, THE MINISTERS OF SACRED THINGS.

THE ministers of religion, among the Romans, did not form a distinct order from the other citizens.[15] They were usually chosen from the most

1 a rubigine, Gell. v. 13.
2 Fast. iv. 911.
3 Serv. Virg. Æn. vii. 84.
4 nymphæ.
5 Virg. Æn. viii. 31. 77.
6 quod flumina sunt atrocia ut tauri, Fest. vel propter impetus et

mugitus aquarum, Vet. Schol. Hor. Od. iv. 14. 25. sic tauriformis volvitur Aufidus, — so bull-formed Aufidus rolls, Virg. G. iv. 371. Ov. Met. ix pr. Ælia. ii. 33. Claud. cons. Prob. 214, &c.

7 Sen. Ep. 41. Plin. Ep. viii 8. Paus. i. 19.
8 Tac. Ann. xiv. 22.
9 Od iii. 13. Ep. i. 18. 104. Plin. ii. 95. a. 96. Ep. viii. 20.
10 portitor, Virg. Æn. vi. 298. porthmeus, -eos, Juv. iii. 266.

11 naulum.
12 Cic. Nat. D. ii. 22. iii. 25. Legg. ii. 14. Juv. i. 113. Luc. viii. 831.
13 a juvando.
14 Fast. iii. 445, &c. Gell. v. 12.
15 see p. 73.

honourable men in the state. Some of them were common to all the gods ;[1] others appropriated to a particular deity.[2] Of the former kind were,

I. The PONTIFICES,[3] who were first instituted by Numa, and chosen from among the patricians, were four in number till the year of the city 454, when four more were created from the plebeians. Some think that originally there was only one pontifex ; as no more are mentioned in Livy, i. 20 ; ii. 2. Sylla increased their number to fifteen ; they were divided into MAJORES and MINORES. Some suppose the seven added by Sylla and their successors to have been called minores ; and the eight old ones, and such as were chosen in their room, MAJORES. Others think the majores were patricians, and the minores plebeians. Whatever be in this, the cause of the distinction certainly existed before the time of Sylla. The whole number of the pontifices was called COLLEGIUM.[4]

The pontifices judged in all causes relating to sacred things ; and, in cases where there was no written law, they prescribed what regulations they thought proper. Such as neglected their mandates, they could fine according to the magnitude of the offence. Dionysius says, that they were not subject to the power of any one, nor bound to give an account of their conduct even to the senate, or people. But this must be understood with some limitations ; for we learn from Cicero, that the tribunes of the commons might oblige them, even against their will, to perform certain parts of their office, and an appeal might be made from their decree, as from all others, to the people. It is certain, however, that their authority was very great. It particularly belonged to them to see that the inferior priests did their duty. From the different parts of their office, the Greeks called them ἱεροδιδάσκαλοι, ἱερονομοι, ἱεροφύλακες, ἱεροφανται, sacrorum doctores, administratores, custodes, et interpretes.[5]

From the time of Numa, the vacant places in the number of pontifices were supplied by the college, till the year 650 ; when Domitius, a tribune, transferred that right to the people. Sylla abrogated this law ; but it was restored by Labienus, a tribune, through the influence of Julius Cæsar. Antony again transferred the right of election from the people to the priests ;[6] thus Lepidus was chosen pontifex maximus irregularly.[7] Pansa once more restored the right of election to the people. After the battle of Actium, permission was granted to Augustus to add to all the fraternities of priests as many above the usual number as he thought proper ; which power the succeeding emperors exercised, so that the number of priests was thenceforth very uncertain.[8]

The chief of the pontifices was called PONTIFEX MAXIMUS ;[9] which name is first mentioned by Livy, iii. 54. He was created by the people, while the other pontifices were chosen by the college, commonly from among those who had borne the first offices in the state. The first plebeian pontifex maximus was T. Coruncanius.[10]

This was an office of great dignity and power. The pontifex maximus was supreme judge and arbiter in all religious matters. He took care

1 omnium deorum sacerdotes.

2 uni alicui numini addicti.

3 a posse facere, quia illis jus erat sacra faciendi. vel potius a ponte faciendo, nam ab iis sublicius est factus primum et restitutus sæpe, cum ideo sacra

et uls et cis Tiberim fiant, Varr. L. L. iv. 15 Diony. li. 73. iii. 45.
4 Liv. iv. 4. x. 6. xxii.
57 Ep. 69. Diony. ii. ·73. Cic. Har. R. 6. Dom. 19.
5 Diony. li. 73. Cic. Dom. l. 45. 51. Har. R. 10. Asc. Mil. 12.
6 Dio. xliv. fin. xxxvii.

37. Diony. li. 73. Suet. Ner. 2. Asc. Cic. Cæc.
3 Rull. ii. 7. Vell. ii. 12.
7 ib. furto creatus, Vel. ii. 61. in confusione rerum ac tumultu, pontificatum maximum intercepit, Liv. Ep. 117.
8 Cic. Ep. Brut. 5. Dio. li. 29. liii. 17.

9 quod maximus rerum, quæ ad sacra, et religiones pertinent, judex sit, Fest. judex atque arbiter rerum divinarum atque humanarum, id. in ordo sacerdotum.
10 Liv. xxv. 5. Ep. xvii.

that sacred rites were properly performed; and, for that purpose, all the other priests were subject to him. He could hinder any of them from leaving the city; although invested with consular authority, and fine such as transgressed his orders, even although they were magistrates.[1]

How much the ancient Romans respected religion and its ministers we may judge from this; that they imposed a fine on Tremellius, a tribune of the commons, for having, in a dispute, used injurious language to Lepidus the pontifex maximus.[2] But the pontifices appear, at least in the time of Cicero, to have been, in some respects, subject to the tribunes.[3]

It was particularly incumbent on the pontifex maximus to take care of the sacred rites of Vesta. If any of the priestesses neglected their duty, he reprimanded or punished them, sometimes by a sentence of the college, capitally.[4]

The presence of the pontifex maximus was requisite in public and solemn religious acts; as when magistrates vowed games or the like, made a prayer, or dedicated a temple, also when a general devoted himself for his army,[5] to repeat over before them the form of words proper to be used,[6] which Seneca calls PONTIFICALE CARMEN. It was of importance that he pronounced the words without hesitation. He attended at the Comitia, especially when priests were created, that he might inaugurate them, likewise when adoptions or testaments were made.[7] At these the other pontifices also attended: hence the Comitia were said to be held, or what was decreed in them to be done, *apud pontifices*, vel *pro collegio pontificum*, in presence of; *solennia pro pontifice suspicere*, to perform the due sacred rites in the presence, or according to the direction, of the pontifex maximus. Any thing done in this manner was also said *pontificio jure fieri*. And when the pontifex maximus pronounced any decree of the college in their presence, he was said PRO COLLEGIO RESPONDERE.[8] The decision of the college was sometimes contrary to his own opinion. He, however, was bound to obey it. What only three pontifices determined was held valid. But, in certain cases, as in dedicating a temple, the approbation of the senate, or of a majority of the tribunes of the commons, was requisite.[9] The people, whose power was supreme in every thing,[10] might confer the dedication of a temple on whatever person they pleased, and force the pontifex maximus to officiate, even against his will; as they did in the case of Flavius. In some cases the *flamines* and *rex sacrorum* seemed to have judged together with the pontifices, and even to have been reckoned of the same college.[11] It was particularly the province of the pontifices to judge concerning marriages.[12]

The pontifex maximus and his college had the care of regulating the year, and the public calendar, called FASTI KALENDARES, because the days of each month, from kalends to kalends, or from beginning to end, were marked in them through the whole year, what days were *fasti*, and what *nefasti*, &c., the knowledge of which was confined to the pontifices and patricians,[13] till C. Flavius divulged them.[14] In the *fasti* of each year were

1 Liv. i. 20. ii. 2. ix. 46. Ep. xix. i. xxxvii. 5. xl. 2. 42. Cic. Phil. xi. 8. Tac. Ann. iii. 58. 51. 2 sacrorumque quam magistratuum ejus potentiæ fuit, Liv. Ep. xlvii. Cic. Dom. 45. 4 Ov. F. iii. 417. Gell. i. 12. Sen. Con. i. 2. Liv. iv. 44. viii. 15.

xxii. 57. xxxviii. 11. Cic. Har. resp. 7. Legg. ii. 9. 5 Liv. iv. 27. viii. 9. ix. 46. x. 7. 28. xxxi. 9. xxxvi. 2. 6 iis verba prætre, v. carmen præfari, ib. v. 41. 7 Cons. Marc. 13. Val. Max. viii. 13. 2. Liv. xxvii. 8. xl. 42. Tac.

Hist. i. 15. Gell. v. 19. xv. 27. Cic. Dom. 13. Plin. Pan. 37. 8 Cic. Dom. 14. 53. Liv. ii. 27. 9 Liv. ix. 46. xxxi. 9. resp. Har. 6. 10 cujus est summa potestas omnium rerum, Cic. ib. 11 Cic. Dom. 49. 52. Liv. 12 Tac. Ann. i. 10. Dio.

xlvii. 44. 13 Liv. iv. 3. Fest. Suet. Jul. 40. Aug. 31. Macr. Sat. i. 14. 14 fastos circa forum in albo proposuit,— he hung up to public view, around the forum, the calendar on white tablets, Liv. ix. 46. see p. 127.

also marked the name of the magistrates, particularly of the consuls. Thus, *enumeratio fastorum*, quasi *annorum ;* FASTI *memores*, permanent records; *picti*, variegated with different colours; *signantes tempora*.[1] Hence a list of the consuls, engraved on marble, in the time of Constantius, the son of Constantine, as it is thought, and found accidentally by some persons digging in the forum, A. D. 1545, are called FASTI CONSULARES, or the *Capitolian marbles*, because beautified, and placed in the Capitol, by cardinal Alexander Farnese.

In latter times it became customary to add, on particular days, after the name of the festival, some remarkable occurrence. Thus, on the *Lupercalia*, it was marked[2] that Antony had offered the crown to Cæsar. To have one's name thus marked[3] was reckoned the highest honour (whence, probably, the origin of canonization in the church of Rome); as it was the greatest disgrace to have one's name erased from the *fasti*.[4]

The books of Ovid, which describe the causes of the Roman festival for the whole year, are called FASTI.[5] The first six of them only are extent.

In ancient times, the pontifex maximus used to draw up a short account of the public transactions of every year in a book,[6] and to expose this register in an open place at his house, where the people might come and read it;[7] which continued to be done to the time of Mucus Scævola, who was slain in the massacre of Marius and Cinna. These records were called, in the time of Cicero, ANNALES *maximi*,[8] as having been composed by the pontifex maximus.

The annals composed by the pontifex before Rome was taken by the Gauls, called also COMMENTARII, perished most of them with the city. After the time of Sylla, the pontifices seem to have dropped the custom of compiling annals ; but several private persons composed historical accounts of the Roman affairs ; which from their resemblance to the pontifical records in the simplicity of their narration, they likewise styled ANNALS ; as Cato, Pictor, Piso, Hortensius, and Tacitus.[9]

The memoirs[10] which a person wrote concerning his own actions were properly called COMMENTARII, as Julius Cæsar modestly called the books he wrote concerning his wars ;[11] and Gellius calls Xenophon's book concerning the words and actions of Socrates[12] *Memorabilia Socratis*. But this name was applied to any thing which a person wrote or ordered to be written as a memorandum for himself or others,[13] as the heads of a discourse which one was to deliver, notes taken from the discourse or book of another, or any book whatever in which short notes or memorandums were written : thus, *commentarii regis Numæ, Servii Tullii, Eumenis, regum, Cæsaris, Trajani.* Hence *a commentariis*, a clerk or secretary. Cœlius, in writing to Cicero, calls the *acta publica*, or public registers of the city, COMMENTARIUS RERUM URBANARUM.[14]

In certain cases the pontifex maximus and his college had the power of life and death ; but their sentence might be reversed by the people.[15]

1 Liv. ix. 18. Val. Max. vi. 2. Cic. Sext. 14. At. iv. 8. Pis. 13. Fam. v. 12. Tusc. i. 28. Hor. Od. iii. 17. 4. iv. 14. 4. Ov. F. i. 11. 657.
2 adscriptum est, Cic. Phil. ii. 34.
3 adscriptum.
4 Cic. Ep. Brut. 15. Pis. 13. Sext. 14. Verr. ii. 53. iv. fin. Tac. Ann. i. 15. iii. 17. Ov. F. i. 9.

5 Ov. F. i. 7. Fastorum libri appellantur, in quibus totius anni fit descriptio, Fest. quia de consulibus et regibus editi sunt, laid. vi. 8.
6 in album efferebat, vel potius referebat.
7 proponebat tabulam domi, potestas ut esset populo cognoscendi.
8 Cic. Or. ii. 12. Gel. iv.

5.
9 Cic. ib. Liv. i. 44. 45. ii. 40. 58. vi. 1. x. 9. 37, &c. Diony. iv. 7. 15. Gell. i. 19. Vell. ii. 16.
10 ὑπομνήματα.
11 Cic. Brut 75. Fam. v. 12. Syl. 16. Ver. v. 21. Suet. Aug. 74. Tib. 61. Cæs. 56.
12 ἀπομνημονευματα, xiv. 3.
13 quæ commeminisse

opus esset, notes to help the memory.
14 Cic. Brut. 44. Rab. perd. 5. Att. xiv. 14. Fam. viii. 11. Plin. Ep. x. 106. Gruter, p 89. Quin. ii. 11. 7. iii. 8. 67. iv. 1. 69. x. 7. 30. Liv. i. 31, 32. 60. xl. 11. 6.
15 Asc. Cic. Mil. 12. Harl resp. 7. Legg. ii. 9. Liv. xxxvii. 51. xl. 2.

The pontifex maximus, although possessed of so great power, is called by Cicero PRIVATUS, as not being a magistrate. But some think that the title pontifex maximus is here applied to Scipio by anticipation, he not having then obtained that office, according to Paterculus, contrary to the account of Appian, and Cicero himself elsewhere calls him simply a private person. Livy expressly opposes pontifices to *privatus*.[1]

The pontifices wore a robe bordered with purple,[2] and a woollen cap,[3] in the form of a cone, with a small rod[4] wrapt round with wool, and a tuft or tassel on the top of it, called APEX, often put for the whole cap; thus, *iratos tremere regum apices*, to fear the tiara nodding on the head of an enraged Persian monarch; or for a woollen bandage tied round the head, which the priests used instead of a cap for the sake of coolness.[5] Sulpicius Galba was deprived of his office on account of his cap having fallen[6] from his head in the time of a sacrifice. Hence *apex* is put for the top of any thing; as, *montis apex*, the summit of the mountain; or for the highest honour or ornament; as, *apex senectutis est auctoritas*, authority is the crown of old age.[7]

In ancient times the pontifex maximus was not permitted to leave Italy. The first pontifex maximus freed from that restriction was P. Licinius Crassus, A. U. 618; so afterwards Cæsar.[8]

The office of pontifex maximus was for life, on which account Augustus never assumed that dignity while Lepidus was alive, which Tiberius and Seneca impute to his clemency; but with what justice, we may learn from the manner in which Augustus behaved to Lepidus in other respects. For, after depriving him of his share in the Triumvirate, A. U. 718, and confining him for a long time to Circeji under custody, he forced him to come to Rome, against his will, A. U. 736, and treated him with great indignity.[9] After the death of Lepidus, A. U. 741, Augustus assumed the office of pontifex maximus, which was ever after held by his successors, and the title even by Christian emperors till the time of Gratian, or rather of Theodosius; for on one of the coins of Gratian this title is annexed. When there were two or more emperors, Dio informs us that one of them only was pontifex maximus; but this rule was soon after violated.[10] The hierarchy of the church of Rome is thought to have been established partly on the model of the pontifex maximus and the college of pontifices.

The pontifices maximi always resided in a public house,[11] called REGIA.[12] Thus, when Augustus became pontifex maximus, he made public a part of his house, and gave the REGIA (which Dio calls the house of the *rex sacrorum*) to the vestal virgins, to whose residence it was contiguous; whence some suppose it the same with the *regia Numæ*, the palace of Numa, to which Horace is supposed to allude under the name of *monumenta regis*, Od. i. 2, 15; and Augustus, Suet. 76; said afterwards to sustain the *atrium* of Vesta, called ATRIUM REGIUM. Others suppose it different. It appears to have been the same with that *regia* mentioned by Festus in EQUUS oc-

1 Cic. Cat. i. 2. Off. i. 22. Paterc. ii. 3. App. Bell. Civ. i. p. 539. Liv. v. 52.
2 toga pretexta, Liv. xxxiii. 28. Lamp. Alex. Sev. 40.
3 galerus, pileus vel tutulus, Fest. & Var. vi. 3.

4 virgula.
5 Serv. Virg. Æn. ii. 683. viii. 664. x. 70. Cic. Legg. i. 1. Liv. vi. 41. Hor. Od. iii. 21. 19.
6 apex prolapsus.
7 Val. Max. i. 1. 4. Sil. xii. 709. Cic. Sen. 17.
8 Liv. xxviii. 38. 44. Ep.

59. Dio. frag. 62. Suet. 22.
9 Dio. xlix. 12. liv. 15. lvi. 30. lxix. 15. Suet. 16. Aug. 31. Sen. Cic. i. 10.
10 ib. 27. Ov. F. iii. 420. Zos. iv. 36. Dio. liii. 17. Cap. Balb. 8.
11 habitavit, sc. Cæsar,

in sacra via, domo publica, Suet. Cæs. 46.
12 Plin. Ep. iv. 11. 6. quod in ea sacra a rege sacrificulo erant solita usurpa i, Fest. vel, quod in ea rex sacrificulus habitare consuesset, Serv. Virg. Æn. viii. 363.

TOBER, in which was the sanctuary of Mars ; for we learn from Dio that the arms of Mars, i. e. the *ancilia*, were kept at the house of Cæsar, as being pontifex maximus.[1] Macrobius says that a ram used to be sacrificed in it to Jupiter every *nundinæ* or market-day,, by the wife of the *flamen dialis*.[2]

A pontifex maximus was thought to be polluted by touching, and even by seeing, a dead body ; as was an augur. So the high priest among the Jews. Even the statue of Augustus was removed from its place, that it might not be violated by the sight of slaughter. But Dio seems to think that the pontifex maximus was violated only by touching a dead body.[3]

II. AUGURES, anciently called AUSPICES,[4] whose office it was to foretel future events, chiefly from the flight, chirping, or feeding of birds,[5] and also from other appearances ; a body of priests[6] of the greatest authority in the Roman state, because nothing of importance was done respecting the public, either at home or abroad, in peace or in war, without consulting them,[7] and anciently in affairs of great consequence they were equally scrupulous in private.[8]

AUGUR is often put for any one who foretold futurity. So, *augur Apollo*, i. e. *qui augurio præest*, the god of augury.[9] AUSPEX denoted a person who observed and interpreted omens,[10] particularly the priest who officiated at marriages. In later times, when the custom of consulting the auspices was in a great measure dropped, those employed to witness the signing of the marriage-contract, and to see that every thing was rightly performed, were called AUSPICES NUPTIARUM, otherwise *proxenetæ, conciliatores, παρανυμφιοι, pronubi*. Hence auspex is put for a favourer or director ; thus, *auspex legis*, one who patronised a law ; *auspices cœptorum operum*, favourers ; *diis auspicibus*, under the direction or conduct of ; so *auspice musa*, the muse-inspiring ; *Teucro*, Teucer being your leader.[11]

AUGURIUM and AUSPICIUM are commonly used promiscuously ; but they are sometimes distinguished. *Auspicium* was properly the foretelling of future events from the inspection of birds ; *augurium*, from any omen or prodigies whatever ; but each of these words is often put for the omen itself. AUGURIUM SALUTIS, when the augurs were consulted whether it was lawful to ask safety from the gods.[12] The omens were also called *ostenta, portenta, monstra, prodigia*.[13] The auspices taken before passing a river were called PEREMNIA,[14] from the beaks of birds, as it is thought, or from the points of weapons,[15] a kind of auspices peculiar to war, both of which had fallen into disuse in the time of Cicero.

The Romans derived their knowledge of augury chiefly from the Tuscans : and anciently their youth used to be instructed as carefully in this art as afterwards they were in the Greek literature. For this purpose, by a decree of the senate, six of the sons of the leading men at Rome were

1 Ov. F. vi. 263. Trist. iii. l. 30. Dio, xliv. 17. liv. 27. Liv. xxvi. 27. Gell. iv. 6. Plut. Q. Rom. 98.
2 flaminica, Sat. l. 16.
3 San. cons. Marc. 15. Tac. Ann. i. 62. Levit. xxi. 11. Dio, liv. 28. 35. lvi. 31. lx. 13.
4 Plut. Q. Rom. 72.
5 ex avium gestu vel garritu et spectione,

Fest. Cic. Fam. vi. 6. Hor. Od. iii. 27, &c.
6 amplissimi sacerdotii collegium, Cic. Fam. iii. 10.
7 nisi auspicato, Liv. l. 36. vi. 41. sine auspiciis, Cic. Div. l. 2. nisi augurio acto, 17. ii. 36. Ver. v. 6. vel capto, 8 Cic. Div. i. 16.
9 Cic. Div. ii. 3, 4. Fam.

vi. 6. Hor. Od. i. 2. 32. Virg. Æn. iv. 376.
10 auspicia vel omina, Hor. Od. iii. 27. 8.
11 Od. i. 7. 27. Ep. i. 3. 13. Liv. xlii. 12. Juv. x. 336. Cic. Clu. 5. Nat. D. i. 15. ii. 3. Legg. ii. 13. Div. i. 16. Att. ii. 7. Virg. Æn. iii. 20. iv. 45. Plaut. Cas. prol. 86. Suet. Claud. 26.

12 Dio. xxxvii. 24. ll. 21. Suet. Aug. 31. Tac. Ann. xii. 23. Cic. Div. i. 47. Nat. D. ii. 3. Non. v. 30. Virg. Æn. i. 392. iii. 89. 499.
13 quia ostendunt, portendunt, monstrant, prædicunt, Cic. Div. i. 42.
14 Fest. Cic. Nat. D. ii. 3. Div. ii. 36.
15 ex acuminibus, Ib.

sent to each of the twelve states of Etruria to be taught. Valerius Maximus says ten.[1] It should probably be, in both authors, one to each.

Before the city of Rome was founded, Romulus and Remus are said to have agreed to determine by augury[2] who should give name to the new city, and who should govern it when built. Romulus chose the Palatine hill, and Remus the Aventine, as places to make their observations.[3] Six vultures first appeared as an omen or augury[4] to Remus: and after this omen was announced or formally declared,[5] twelve vultures appeared to Romulus. Whereupon each was saluted king by his own party. The partisans of Remus claimed the crown to him from his having seen the omen first; those of Romulus, from the number of birds. Through the keenness of the contest they came to blows, and in the scuffle Remus fell. The common report is, that Remus was slain by Romulus for having, in derision, lept over his walls.[6]

After Romulus, it became customary that no one should enter upon an office without consulting the auspices. But Dionysius informs us that, in his time, this custom was observed merely for form's sake. In the morning of the day on which those elected were to enter on their magistracy, they rose about twilight, and repeated certain prayers under the open air, attended by an augur, who told them that lightning had appeared on the left, which was esteemed a good omen, although no such thing had happened. This verbal declaration, although false, was reckoned sufficient.[7]

The augurs are supposed to have been first instituted by Romulus, three in number, one to each tribe, as the haruspices, and confirmed by Numa. A fourth was added, probably by Servius Tullius, when he increased the number of tribes, and divided the city into four tribes. The augurs were at first all patricians; till A. U. 454, when five plebeians were added. Sylla increased their number to fifteen. They were at first chosen, as the other priests, by the Comitia Curiata, and afterwards underwent the same changes as the pontifices.[8] The chief of the augurs was called MAGISTER COLLEGII. The augurs enjoyed this singular privilege, that, of whatever crime they were guilty, they could not be deprived of their office; because, as Plutarch says, they were intrusted with the secrets of the empire. The laws of friendship were anciently observed with great care among the augurs, and no one was admitted into their number who was known to be inimical to any of the college. In delivering their opinions about any thing in the college, the precedency was always given to age.[9]

As the pontifices prescribed solemn forms and ceremonies, so the augurs explained all omens.[10] They derived tokens[11] of futurity chiefly from five sources: from appearances in the heavens, as thunder or lightning; from the singing or flight of birds;[12] from the eating of chickens; from quadrupeds; and from uncommon accidents, called diræ, v. -a. The birds which gave omens by singing,[13] were the raven,[14] the crow,[15] the owl,[16] the cock;[17] by flight,[18] were the eagle, vulture, &c.; by feeding, chickens,[19] much attended to in war;[20] and contempt of their intimations was supposed to occasion signal misfortunes; as in the case of P. Claudius in the

1 l. 1. Liv. ix. 36. Cic. Legg. ii. 9. Div. i. 41.
2 auguriis legere.
3 templa ad inaugurandum.
4 augurium.
5 nunciato augurio, or, as Cicero calls it, decantato, Div. i. 47. see p. 63.

6 Liv. i. 7.
7 DIony. li. 6. iii. 35.
8 Liv. i. 13. iii. 37. x. 6.
9 Ep. lxxxix. Diony. ii. 22. 64. iv. 34. see p. 192.
10 Plin. Ep. iv. 8. Plut. Q. Rom. 97.

10 Cic. Har. 9.
11 signa.
12 Stat. Theb. iii. 482.
13 oscines.
14 corvus.
15 cornix.
16 noctua vel bubo.
17 gallus gallinaceus, &c. Fest. Plin. x. 20.

s. 22. 29. s. 42.
18 alites vel praepetes, Gell. vi. 6. Serv. Virg. Æn. iii. 361. Cic. Div. i. 47. Nat. D. ii. 64.
19 pulli, Cic. Div. ii. 34. see p. 62.
20 Plin. x. 22. s. 24. Liv. x. 40.

first Punic war, who, when the person who had the charge of the chickens[1] told him that they would not eat, which was esteemed a bad omen, ordered them to be thrown into the sex, saying, Then let them drink. After which, engaging the enemy, he was defeated with the loss of his fleet.[2] Concerning ominous birds, &c. see Stat. Theb. iii. 502, &c.

The badges of the augurs[3] were, 1. A kind of robe, called TRABEA, striped with purples,[4] according to Servius, made of purple and scarlet.[5] So Dionysius, speaking of the dress of the Salii, describes it as fastened with clasps;[6] hence *dibaphum*[7] *cogitare*, to desire to be made an augur; *dibapho vestire*, to make one. 2. A cap of a conical shape, like that of the pontifices.[8] 3. A crooked staff, which they carried in their right hand, to mark out the quarters of the heavens,[9] called LITUUS.[10]

An augur made his observations on the heavens[11] usually in the dead of the night,[12] or about twilight.[13] He took his station on an elevated place, called ARX or TEMPLUM, *vel* TABERNACULUM, which Plutarch calls σκηνη,[14] where the view was open on all sides; and, to make it so, buildings were sometimes pulled down. Having first offered up sacrifices, and uttered a solemn prayer,[15] he sat down[16] with his head covered,[17] and, according to Livy, i. 18, with his face turned to the east; so that the parts towards the south were on the right,[18] and those towards the north on the left.[19] Then he determined with his *lituus* the regions of the heavens from east to west, and marked in his mind some objects straight forward,[20] at as great a distance as his eyes could reach; within which boundaries he should make his observation.[21] This space was also called TEMPLUM.[22] Dionysius and Hyginus give the same description with Livy of the position of the augur, and of the quarters of the heavens. But Varro makes the augur look towards the south, which he calls *pars antica*; consequently the *pars sinistra* was on the east, and *dextra* on the west: that on the north he calls *postica*.[23] In whatever position the augur stood, omens on the left among the Romans were reckoned lucky; but sometimes omens on the left are called unlucky,[24] in imitation of the Greeks, among whom augurs stood with their faces to the north: and then the east, which was the lucky quarter, was on the right.[25] Hence *dexter* is often put for *felix* vel *faustus*, lucky or propitious, and *sinister* for *infelix*, *infaustus*, vel *funestus*, unlucky or unfavourable. Thunder on the left was a good omen for every thing else but holding the Comitia.[26] The croaking of a raven[27] on the right, and

1 pullarius.
2 Cic. Nat. D. ii. 3. Div. i. 16. Liv. Ep. 19. Val. Max. i. 4. 3.
3 ornamenta auguralia, Liv. x. 7.
4 virgata vel palmata, a trabibus dicta.
5 ex purpura et cocco mistum, Virg. Æn. vii. 612.
6 ii. 70.
7 i. e. purpuram bis tinctam.
8 Cic. Fam. ii. 16. Att. ii. 9.
9 quo regiones cœli determinarent.
10 baculus, v. -um, sine nodo aduncus, Liv. i. 18. Incurvum et leviter a summo inflexum bacillum quod ab ejus litui, quo canitur, similitudine novem inve-

nit, Cic. Div. i. 17 virga brevis, in parte qua robustior est, incurva, Gell. v. 8.
11 servabat de cœlo, v. cœlum, Cic. Div. ii. 35. Dom. 15. Phil. ii. 32. Luc. i. 601, v. 395.
12 post mediam noctem, Gell. iii. 2. media nocte, Liv. xxxiv. 14. cum est silentium, Fest. nocte silentio, Liv. ix. 38. viii. 23. aperto cœlo. ita ut apertis uti liceat lucernis, Plut. Q. R. 71. id silentium dicimus in auspicio, quod omni vitio caret, Cic. Div. ii. 44.
13 Diony. ii. 5.
14 Marc. p. 300. Liv. i. 18. iv. 7. Cic. Div. ii. 35.

15 effata, plur. Serv. Virg. Æn. vi. 197. whence effari templum, to consecrate, Cic. Att. xiii. 42. hinc fana nominata, quod pontifices in sacrando, fati aut finem, Varr. L. L. v. 7.
16 sedem cepit in solida sella.
17 capite velato.
18 partes dextræ.
19 lævæ.
20 signum contra animo finivit.
21 Liv. i. 18.
22 a tuendo; locus augurii aut auspicii causa quibusdam conceptis verbis finitus Var. L. L. vi. 5. Don. Ter. iii. 5. 42.
23 Dion. ii. 5. Hyg. de limit.

24 Plaut. Pseud. ii. 4. 72. Ep. ii. 2. 1. Serv. Virg. Æn. ii. 693. ix. 631. Stat. Theb. iii. 493. Cic. Legg. ii. 3. Div. ii. 35. Gell. v. 12. Ov. Trist. i. 8. 49. iv. 3. 69. Ep. ii. 113. Virg. Ecl. i. 18. ix. 15. Suet. Claud. 7. Vii. 9. Diony. ii. 3.
25 sinistrum, quod bonum sit, nostri nominaverunt, externi, sc. Græci, dextrum, Cic. Div. ii. 36.
26 Virg. Æn. iv. 579. viii. 302. i. 444. Plin. Ep. i. 9. vii. 98. Tac. Hist. v. 5. Cic. Div. 18. 35.
27 corvus.

of a crow[1] on the left, was reckoned fortunate, and *vice versa*. In short, the whole art of augury among the Romans was involved in uncertainty.[2] It seems to have been at first contrived, and afterwards cultivated, chiefly to increase the influence of the leading men over the multitude.

The Romans took omens[3] also from quadrupeds crossing the way, or appearing in an unaccustomed place;[4] from sneezing,[5] spilling salt on the table, and other accidents of that kind, which were called DIRA, sc. *signa*, or DIRÆ. These the augurs explained, and taught how they should be expiated. When they did so, they were said *commentari*.[6] If the omen was good, the phrase was, IMPETRITUM, INAUGURATUM EST, and hence it was called *augurium impetrativum* vel *optatum*. Many curious instances of Roman superstition, with respect to omens and other things, are enumerated by Pliny, as among the Greeks by Pausanias.[7] Cæsar, in landing at Adrumetum in Africa with his army, happened to fall on his face, which was reckoned a bad omen; but he, with great presence of mind, turned it to the contrary; for, taking hold of the ground with his right hand, and kissing it, as if he had fallen on purpose, he exclaimed, *I take possession of thee, O Africa!*[8]

Future events were also prognosticated by drawing lots;[9] thus, *oracula sortibus æquatis ducuntur*, that is, being so adjusted that they had all an equal chance of coming out first.[10] These lots were a kind of dice[11] made of wood, gold, or other matter, with certain letters, words, or marks inscribed on them. They were thrown commonly into an urn, sometimes filled with water,[12] and drawn out by the hand of a boy, or of the person who consulted the oracle. The priests of the temple explained the import of them. The lots were sometimes thrown like common dice, and the throws esteemed favourable or not, as in playing. SORTES denotes not only the lots themselves, and the answer returned from the explanation of them, *sortes ipsas et cetera*, *quæ erant ad sortem*, i. e. ad responsum reddendum, *parata, disturbavit, simia*,[13] but also any verbal responses whatever of an oracle;[14] thus, ORACULUM is put both for the temple, and the answer given in it.[15] Tacitus calls by the name of *sortes* the manner in which the Germans used to form conjectures about futurity. They cut the branch of a tree into small parts or slips,[16] and, distinguishing these slips by certain marks, scattered them at random[17] on a white cloth. Then a priest, if the presage was made for the public;[18] if in private, the master of a family, having prayed to the gods, and looking to heaven, took up each of the slips three times, and interpreted it according to the mark impressed on it. Of prophetic lots, those of Præneste were the most famous.[19] Livy mentions among unlucky omens the lots of Cære to have been diminished in their bulk,[20] and of Falerii. Omens of futurity were also taken from names.[21] Those who foretold futurity by lots or in any manner whatever, were called SORTILEGI, which name Isidorus applies to

1 cornix.
2 Cic. Div. i. 7. 39.
3 omnes optabant.
4 Juv. xiii. 62. Hor. Od. iii. 27. Liv. xxi. nit. xxii. 1.
5 ex sternutatione.
6 Cic. Am. 2. Div. i. 16. ii. 40. Dio. xl. 18. Ov. Am. i. 12.
7 Paus. iv. 13. Plin. xxviii. 2. Plaut. As. ii. 11. Serv. Virg. Æn. v.

190.
6 teneo te, Africa, Dio. xlii. fin. Suet. Jul. 59.
9 sortibus ducendis, Cic. Div. ii. 33. i. 18.
10 Plaut. Cas. ii. 6. 35.
11 tali v. tesseræ.
12 Plaut. Cas. ii. 6. 98. 32, 33. 46. Suet. Tib. Paus. Mes. iv. 4. Elis. v. 25. Cic. Div. ii. 41.
13 Cic. Div. i. 34. Liv. viii. 24. Suet. Tib. 14.

Prop. iv. 9. 19.
14 sortes quæ vaticinatione funduntur, quæ oracla verius dicimus, Cic. Div. ii. 33. 56. dictæ per carmina sortes, Hor. Art. P. 403. Liv. i. 56. v. 15. Viry. Æn. iv. 346. vi. 72. Ov. Met. i. 368. 381.
15 Cic. Font. 10. Div. i. 1. 34. 51.Ep. Brut. 2.
16 in surculos.

17 temere ac fortuito.
18 si publice consuleretur.
19 Tac. Mor. G. 10. Cic. Div. ii. 41. Suet. Tib. 63. Dom. 15. Stat. Syl. i. 3. 80.
20 extenuatæ, xxi. 62. xxii. 1.
21 Plaut. Pers. iv. 4. 72. Bacch. ii. 3. 50.

those who, upon opening any book at random, formed conjectures from the
meaning of the first line or passage which happened to cast up :[1] hence,
in later writers, we read of the sortes virgilianæ, Homericæ, &c.
Sometimes select verses were written on slips of paper,[2] and, being thrown
into an urn, were drawn out like common lots ; whence of these it was
said, sors excidit. Those who foretold future events by observing the
stars, were called astrologi, mathematici, genethliaci,[3] from genesis,
vel genitura, the nativity or natal hour of any one, or the star which happened to be then rising,[4] and which was supposed to determine his future
fortune : called also horoscopus ;[5] thus, geminos, horoscope, varo (for vario)
producis genio ; O natal hour ! although one and the same, thou producest
twins of different dispositions. Hence a person was said habere imperato-
riam genesim, to whom an astrologer had foretold at his birth that he would
be emperor. Those astrologers were also called chaldæi or babylonii,
because they came originally from Chaldæa or Babylonia, or Mesopotamia,
i. e. the country between the conflux of the Euphrates and Tigris ; hence
Chaldaicis rationibus eruditus, skilled in astrology ; Babylonica doctrina,
astrology ; nec Babylonios tentaris numeros, and do not try astrological cal-
culations, i. e. do not consult an astrologer,[6] who used to have a book,[7]
in which the rising and setting, the conjunction, and other appearances of
the stars were calculated. Some persons were so superstitious, that in
the most trivial affairs of life they had recourse to such books,[8] which
Juvenal ridicules, vi. 576. An Asiatic astrologer,[9] skilled in astronomy,[10]
was consulted by the rich ; the poor applied to common fortune-tellers,[11]
who usually sat in the Circus Maximus, which is therefore called by Horace fallax.[12]

Those who foretold future events by interpreting dreams were called
conjectores ; by apparent inspiration, harioli vel divini, vates vel vaticina-
tores, &c.

Persons disordered in their mind[13] were supposed to possess the faculty
of presaging future events. These were called by various other names ;
cerriti or Ceriti, because Ceres was supposed sometimes to deprive her
worshippers of their reason ;[14] also larvati,[15] and lymphatici or lymphati,[16]
because the nymphs made those who saw them mad.[17] Isidore makes lym-
phaticus the same with one seized with the hydrophobia.[18] Pavor lympha-
ticus, a panic fear ; nummi auri lymphatici, burning in the pocket, as eager
to get out, or to be spent ; mens lymphata mareotica, intoxicated. As helle-
bore was used in curing those who were mad, hence elleborosus, for insa-
nus. Those transported with religious enthusiasm were called fanatici,[19]
from fanum, a fari, because it was consecrated by a set form of words,[20]
or from faunus.[21] From the influence of the moon on persons labour-

1 viii. 9. Lac. ix. 581.
2 In pittaciis.
3 Spart. Adr. 2. Lamp.
Alex. Sev. 14. Cic. Div.
i. 38, 39. ii. 42. Verr. ii.
52. Suet. Aug. 91. Tib.
Cal. 57. Tac. Hist. i. 22.
Juv. vi. 561. xiv. 248.
Gell. xiv. 1.
4 sidus natalitium, Cic.
Div. ii. 42. Juv. xiv.
243. Suet. Tit. 9.
5 ab hora inspicienda.
6 Hor. Od. i. 11. Pers.
vi. 18. Suet. Vesp. 14.
Dom. 10. Strab. xvi.
739. Plin. vi. 28. Cic.

Div. ii. 47. Lucr. v. 726.
Diod. ii. 29.
7 ephemeris, v. plur,
-idos.
8 Plin. xxix. 1.
9 Phryx Augur et In-
dus.
10 astrorum mundique
peritus.
11 sortilegi vel divini.
12 Sat. i. 6. 113. If the
predictions of astrolo-
gers proved false, they
were sometimes put to
death ; but if true, they
were richly rewarded,
and highly respected,

Suet. Tib. 14. Tac. An.
vi 20. 26. Dic. lv. 11.
13 melancholici, cardi-
aci, et phrenetici.
14 Non. i. 213. Plaut. A.
ii. 2. 141. Hor. Sat. ii.
3. 278.
15 Larvarum plebi. i. e.
furiosi et mente moti,
quasi larvis et spectris
exterriti. Fest. Plaut.
Men. v. 4. 2.
16 Virg. Æn. vii. 377
Liv. vii. 17. a nymphis
in furorem acti, νυμφο-
ληπτοι, Varr. L. L. vi.
5. qui speciem quan-

dam e fonte, id est effi-
giem nymphæ, vide-
rint, Fest.
17 Ov. F. iv. 49.
18 qui aquam timent,
ὑδροφοβοι, x. Etera L.
19 Liv. x. 28. Sen. Ep.
11. Plaut. Pœn. i. 2. 132.
Rud. iv. 3. 67. Hor. Od.
i. 37. 14. Juv. ii. 112. iv.
123. Cic. Div. ii. 57.
Dom. 60.
20 fando, Fest. Var. L.
L. v. 7.
21 qui primus fani con-
ditor fuit. Serv. Virg.
G. i. 10.

ing under certain kinds of insanity, they are called by later writers LUNA-TICI.

HARUSPICES,[1] called also EXTISPICES, who examined the victims and their entrails after they were sacrificed, and from thence derived omens of futurity ; also from the flame, smoke, and other circumstances attending the sacrifice ; as if the victim came to the altar without resistance, stood there quietly, fell by one stroke, bled freely, &c. These were favourable signs. The contrary are enumerated. They also explained prodigies.[2] Their office resembled that of the augurs ; but they were not esteemed so honourable : hence, when Julius Cæsar admitted Ruspina, one of them, into the senate, Cicero represents it as an indignity to the order. Their art was called HARUSPICINA, vel *haruspicum disciplina*, derived from Etruria, where it is said to have been discovered by one Tagus, and whence *haruspices* were often sent for to Rome. They sometimes came from the East ; thus, *Armenius* vel *Comagenus haruspex*,[3] an Armenian or Commagenian sooth-sayer. Females also practised this art.[4] The college of the *haruspices* was instituted by Romulus. Of what number it consisted is uncertain. Their chief was called SUMMUS HARUSPEX.[5] Cato used to say, he was surprised that the *haruspices* did not laugh when they saw one another, their art was so ridiculous ; and yet wonderful instances are recorded of the truth of their predictions.[6]

III. QUINDECEMVIRI *sacris faciundis*, who had the charge of the Sibyl-line books, inspected them, by the appointment of the senate, in dangerous junctures, and performed the sacrifices which they enjoined. It belong-ed to them in particular to celebrate the secular games, and those of Apol-lo.[7] They are said to have been instituted on the following occasion :—

A certain woman, called Amalthæa, from a foreign country, is said to have come to Tarquinius Superbus, wishing to sell nine books of Sybilline or prophetic oracles. But upon Tarquin's refusal to give her the price which she asked, she went away, and burned three of them. Returning soon af-ter, she sought the same price for the remaining six. Whereupon, being ridiculed by the king as a senseless old woman, she went and burned other three ; and coming back, still demanded the same price for the three which remained Gellius says that the books were burned in the king's presence. Tarquin, surprised at the strange conduct of the woman, con-sulted the augurs what to do. They, regretting the loss of the books which had been destroyed, advised the king to give the price required. The woman, therefore, having delivered the books, and having desired them to be carefully kept, disappeared, and was never afterwards seen. Pliny says she burned two books and only preserved one. Tarquin committed the care of these books, called LIBRI SIBYLLINI, or VERSUS,[8] to two men[9] of illustrious birth ; one of whom, called Atilius, or Tullius,[10] he is said to have punished, for being unfaithful to his trust, by ordering him to be sewed up alive in a sack,[11] and thrown into the sea, the punishment afterwards in-flicted on parricides.[12] In the year 387, ten men[13] were appointed for this

1 ab *haruga*, i. e. ab hostia, Don. Ter. Phor. iv. 4. 28. vel potius a victima, aut extis vic-timarum in ara inspi-ciendis.
2 Cic. Cat. iii. 8. Div. i. 3. ii. 11. Non. i. 53. Stat. Theb. iii. 456. Virg. G. iii. 486. Luc. i. 609. Suet. Aug. 29.

Plin. vii. 3.
3 Juv. vi. 519. Cic. Fam. vi. 18. Div. i. 2
41. ii. 23. Cat. iii. 8. Ov. Met. xv. 553. Luc. i. 584. 637. Censorin. Nat. D. 4. Liv. v. 15. xxvii. 37. Mart. iii. 24. 3.
4 aruspicæ, Plaut. Mil. Glor. iii. 1. 93.

5 Cic. Div. ii. 24. Diony. ii. 22.
6 Cic. Nat. D. 1 26. Div. ii. 24. Liv. xxv. 16. Sall. Jug. 63. Tac. H. i. 27. Suet. Galb. 19. Cæs. 81. Dio. xliv. 18.
7 Dio. liv. 19. Hor. Car. Sæc. 72. Tac. Ann. ii. 11. vi. 12.
8 Hor. Car. Sæc. 5.

Cic. Verr. iv. 49. Gell. i. 19. Diony. iv. 62. Lact. i. 6. Plin. xiii. 13. s. 27.
9 duumviri.
10 Diony. ib. Val. Max. i. i. 13.
11 in culeum insui, ib.
12 Cic. Ros. Am. 25.
13 decemviri.

purpose, five 'patricians and five plebeians, afterwards fifteen, as it is thought by Sylla. Julius Cæsar made them sixteen. They were created in the same manner as the pontifices. The chief of them was called MAGISTER COLLEGII.[1]

These Sibylline books were supposed to contain the fate of the Roman empire; and, therefore, in public danger or calamity, the keepers of them were frequently ordered by the senate to inspect[2] them. They were kept in a stone chest, below ground, in the temple of Jupiter Capitolinus. But the Capitol being burned in the Marsic war, the Sibylline books were destroyed together with it, A. U. 670. Whereupon ambassadors were sent everywhere to collect the oracles of the Sibyls; for there were other prophetic women besides the one who came to Tarquin; Lactantius, from Varro, mentions ten; Ælian, four. Pliny says there were statues of three Sibyls near the rostra in the forum.[3] The chief was the Sibyl of Cumæ,[4] whom Æneas is supposed' to have consulted; called by Virgil *Deiphobe*, from her age, *longæva*, *vivax*,[5] and the Sibyl of Erythræ, a city of Ionia,[6] who used to utter her oracles with such ambiguity, that whatever happened, she might seem to have predicted it, as the priestess of Apollo at Delphi;[7] the verses, however, were so contrived, that the first letters of them joined together made some sense; hence called ACROSTICHIS, or in the plural *achrostichides*.[8] Christian writers often quote Sibylline verses in support of Christianity; as Lactantius, i. 6, ii. 11, 12, iv. 6; but these appear to have been fabricated.

From the various Sibylline verses thus collected, the Quindecemviri made out new books; which Augustus (after having burned all other prophetic books,[9] both Greek and Latin, above 2000), deposited in two gilt cases,[10] under the base of the statue of Apollo, in the temple of that god on the Palatine hill, to which Virgil alludes, Æn. vi. 69, &c., having first caused the priests to write over with their own hands a new copy of them, because the former books were fading with age.[11]

The quindecemviri were exempted from the obligation of serving in the army, and from other offices in the city. Their priesthood was for life.[12] They were properly the priests of Apollo; and hence each of them had at his house a brazen tripod,[13] as being sacred to Apollo, similar to that on which the priestess of Delphi sat; which Servius makes a three-footed stool or table,[14] but others, a vase with three feet and a covering, properly called *cortina*,[15] which also signifies a large round caldron, often put for the whole tripod, or for the oracle: hence, *tripodas sentire*, to understand the oracles of Apollo. When tripods are said to have been given in a present, vases or cups supported on three feet are understood,[16] such as are to be seen on ancient coins.'

IV. SEPTEMVIRI *epulonum*, who prepared the sacred feasts at games, processions, and other solemn occasions.

It was customary among the Romans to decree feasts to the gods, in

---

1 Liv. vi. 37. 42. Serv. Virg. Æn. vi. 73. Dio. xlii. 51. xliii. 51. liv. 19. Plin. xxviii. 2. see Lex Domitia.
2 adire, inspicere, v. consulere, Liv. iii. 10. v. 13. vii. 27. xi. 12. xxi. 62. xxii. 9. xxiv. 10. xxxvi. 27. xxxviii. 45. xli. 21.

3 xxxiv. 5. s. 10. Tac. Ann. vi. 12. Paus. x. 12. Lac. i. 6. Æl. xii. 35.
4 Sibylla Cumæa.
5 Æn. vi. 36, 68, 391. Ov. Met. xiv. 104.
6 Erythræa Sibylla, Cic. Div. i. 18.
7 Id. ii. 54. Paus. iv. 12.
8 αϰϱοστιχϵις, Diony. iv.

62.
9 fatidici libri.
10 forulis auratis.
11 Suet. Aug. 31. Dio. liv. 17.
12 Diony. iv. 62.
13 cortina vel tripus, Serv. Virg. Æn. iii. 332. Val. Flac. i. 5.
14 mensa, ib. 360.

15 ὅλμος.
16 Plin. xxxiv. 3. s. 8. xxxv. 11. s. 41. Varr. L. L. vi. 3. Virg. Æn. iii. 92. v. 110. vi. 347. Ov. Met. xv. 635. Her. iii. 32. Suet. Aug. 52. Hor. Od. iv. 8. 3. Nep. Paus. I.

order to appease their wrath, especially to Jupiter,[1] during the public games.[2] These sacred entertainments became so numerous, that the pontifices could no longer attend to them; on which account this order of priests was instituted, to act as their assistants. They were first created A. U. 557, three in number,[3] and were allowed to wear the *toga prætexta*, as the pontifices.[4] Their number was increased to seven, it is thought by Sylla.[5] If any thing had been neglected or wrongly performed in the public games, the Epulones reported it[6] to the pontifices; by whose decree the games on that account were sometimes celebrated anew. The sacred feasts were prepared with great magnificence; hence, *cænæ pontificum, vel pontificales*, et *augurales*, for sumptuous entertainments.[7]

The pontifices, augures, septemviri, epulones, and quindecemviri, were called the four colleges of priests.[8] When divine honours were decreed to Augustus, after his death, a fifth college was added, composed of his priests: hence called COLLEGIUM SODALIUM AUGUSTALIUM. So FLAVIALIUM *collegium*, the priests of Titus and Vespasian. But the name of COLLEGIUM was applied not only to some other fraternities of priests, but to any number of men joined in the same office; as the consuls, prætors, quæstors, and tribunes, also to any body of merchants or mechanics, to those who lived in the Capitol, even to an assemblage of the meanest citizens or slaves.[9]

To each of the colleges of pontifices, augures, and quindecemviri, Julius Cæsar added one, and to the septemviri, three. After the battle of Actium, a power was granted to Augustus, of adding to these colleges as many extraordinary members as he thought proper; which power was exercised by the succeeding emperors, so that the number of those colleges was thenceforth very uncertain. They seem, however, to have retained their ancient names; thus, Tacitus calls himself *quindecemvirali sacerdotio præditus*, and Pliny mentions a SEPTEMVIR EPULONUM.[10]

It was anciently ordained by law, that two persons of the same family[11] should not enjoy the same priesthood.[12] But under the emperors this regulation was disregarded.

The other fraternities of priests were less considerable, although composed of persons of distinguished rank.

1. FRATRES AMBARVALES, twelve in number, who offered up sacrifices for the fertility of the ground,[13] which were called *sacra Ambarvalia*, because the victim was carried round the fields.[14] Hence they were said *agros lustrare* et *purgare*, and the victim was called HOSTIA AMBARVALIS,[16] attended with a crowd of country people having their temples bound with garlands of oak leaves, dancing and singing the praises of Ceres; to whom libations were made of honey diluted with milk and wine:[16] these sacred rites were performed before they began to reap, privately as well as publicly.

This order of priests is said to have been instituted by Romulus, in ho-

1 epulum Jovis, v. -l.
2 ludorum causa, Liv. xxv. 2. xxvii. 38. xxix. 38. fin. xxx. 39. xxxi. 4. xxxii. 7.
3 triumviri epulones, Liv. xxxiii. 44. Cic. Or. iii. 19.
4 ib. in the sing. triumvir epulo, xl. 42.
5 Gell. i. 12. sing. septemvirque epulis festis.

Luc. i. 602.
6 afferebant.
7 Cic. Har. 10. Liv. ib. Hor. Od. ii. 14. 28. Macrob. Sat. ii. 9.
8 τεσσαρες ιερωσυναι, Dio. liii. 1. sacerdotes summorum collegiorum, Suet. Aug. 101.
9 Tac. Ann. iii. 63. Dio. lvi. 46. lviii. 12. Suet. Dom. 4. Claud. 24. Liv.

ii. 27. v. 50. 52. x. 22. 24. xxxvi. 3. Plin. xxxiv. 1. Ep. x. 42. Cic. post red. Sen. 13. Sext. 25. Pis. 4. Dom. 18. 28. Off. iii. 20.
10 Ep. iii. 11. Tac. Ann. xi. 11. Dio. xlii. 51. fin. li. 20. liii 17.
11 εκ της αυτης συγγενειας,
12 Dio. xxxix. 17.

13 ut arva fruges ferrent, Varr. iv. 15.
14 arva ambiebat, ter circum ibat hostia fruges, Virg. G. i. 345.
15 Id. Ecl. v. 75. Tibull. ii. 1. 1. 17. Macrob. Sat. iii. 5. Fest.
16 cui tu lacte favos, i. e. mel, et miti dilue Baccho, Virg. G. i. 344. 347.

nour of his nurse Acca Laurentia, who had twelve sons,'and when one of them died, Romulus, to console her, offered to supply his place, and called himself and the rest of her sons, FRATRES ARVALES. Their office was for life, and continued even in captivity and exile. They wore a crown made of the ears of corn,[1] and a white woollen wreath round their temples.[2]

INFULÆ *erant filamenta lanea, quibus sacerdotes et hostiæ templaque velabantur*.[3] The *infulæ* were broad woollen bandages tied with ribands,[4] used not only by priests to cover their heads, but also by suppliants.[5]

2. CURIONES, the priests who performed'the public sacred rites in each *curia*, thirty in number.[6] Heralds who notified the orders of the prince or people at the spectacles were also called CURIONES. Plautus calls a lean lamb *curio*, i. e. *qui cura macet*, which is lean with care.[7]

3. FECIALES, vel *Fetiales*, sacred persons employed in declaring war and making peace.[8] The fecialis, who took the oath in the name of the Roman people in concluding a treaty of peace, was called PATER PATRATUS.[9] The feciales[10] were instituted by Numa Pompilius, borrowed, as Dionysius thinks, from the Greeks: they are supposed to have been twenty in number. They judged concerning every thing which related to the proclaiming of war, and the making of treaties: the forms they used were instituted by Ancus.[11] They were sent to the enemy to demand the restitution of effects:[12] they always carried in their hands, or wreathed round their temples, vervain,[13] a kind of sacred grass or clean herbs,[14] plucked from a particular place in the capitol, with the earth in which it grew;[15] hence the chief of them was called VERBENARIUS.[16] If they were sent to make a treaty, each of them carried vervain as an emblem of peace, and a flint stone to strike the animal which was sacrificed.[17]

4. SODALES *Titii*, vel *Titienses*, priests appointed by Titus Tatius to preserve the sacred rites of the Sabines; or by Romulus, in honour of Tatius himself; in imitation of whom the priests instituted to Augustus after his death were called SODALES.[18]

5. REX *sacrorum*, vel *rex sacrificulus*, a priest appointed, after the expulsion of Tarquin, to perform the sacred rites, which the kings themselves used formerly to perform; an office of small importance, and subject to the pontifex maximus, as all the other priests were. Before a person was admitted to this priesthood, he was obliged to resign any other office he bore. His wife was called REGINA, and his house anciently REGIA.[19]

PRIESTS OF PARTICULAR GODS.

THE priests of particular gods were called FLAMINES, from a cap or fillet[20] which they wore on their head.[21] The chief of these were:—

1. *Flamen* DIALIS, the priest of Jupiter, who was distinguished by a lictor, *sella curulis*, and *toga prætexta*, and had a right from his office of coming into the senate. *Flamen* MARTIALIS, the priest of Mars, QUIRINALIS,

1 corona spicea.
2 infula alba, Gell. vi. 17. Plin. xviii. 2.
3 Fest.
4 vittæ, Virg. G. iii. 487. Æn. x 538. Ov. Pont. iii. 2. 74.
5 Cæs. Bell. Civ. ii. 12. Liv. xxiv. 30. xxv. 25. Tac. Hist. i. 66. Cic. Verr. iv. 50. Luc. v. 142.
6 see p. 1.

7 Aul. iii. 6. 27. Plin. Ep. iv. 7. Mart. Præf. ii.
8 Liv. ix. 5
9 quod jusjurandum pro toto populo patrabat, i. e. præstabat, vel peragebat, Liv. i. 24
10 collegium fecialium, Liv. xxxvi. 3.
11 Diony. i. 21. ii. 72. Varr. apud. Non. xii. 43. Cic. Legg. ii. 9.

Liv. i. 32.
12 clarigatum, i. e. res raptas clare repetitum.
13 verbena, Serv. Virg. xii. 120. vel verbenaca.
14 sagmina, v. herbæ puræ.
15 gramen ex arce cum sua terra evulsum.
16 Plin. xxii. 3. xxx. 9. s. 69.
17 privos lapides silices,

privasque verbenas, Liv. xxx. 43.
18 Tac. Ann. i. 54. Hist. ii. 95. Suet. Claud. 6. Galb. 8.
19 Liv. ii. 2. xl. 52. Macrob. Sat. i. 15. Serv. Virg. Æn. viii. 363. Diony. iv. 74. v. 1.
20 a filo vel pileo.
21 Varr. L. L. iv. 15.

of Romulus, &c. These three were always chosen from the patricians. They were first instituted by Numa, who had himself performed the sacred rites, which afterwards belonged to the *flamen Dialis*. They were afterwards created by the people, when they were said to be *electi, designata, creati*, vel *destinati*, and inaugurated, or solemnly admitted to their office, by the pontifex maximus and the augurs, when they were said *inaugurari, prodi*, vel *capi*. The pontifex maximus seems to have nominated three persons to the people, of whom they chose one.

The flamines wore a purple robe called LÆNA, which seems to have been thrown over their toga ; hence called by Festus *duplex amictus*, and a conical cap, called APEX. *Lanigerosque* APICES, the sacred caps tufted with wool. Although not pontifices, they seem to have had a seat in that college. Other flamines were afterwards created, called MINORES, who might be plebeians, as the flamen of Carmenta, the mother of Evander. The emperors also, after their consecration, had each of them their flamines, and likewise colleges of priests, who were called *sodales*. Thus, FLAMEN CÆSARIS, sc. Antonius.[2]

The flamen of Jupiter was an office of great dignity,[3] but subjected to many restrictions, as, that he should not ride on horseback, nor stay one night without the city, nor take an oath, and several others.[4] His wife[5] was likewise under particular restrictions ; but she could not be divorced : and if she died the flamen resigned his office, because he could not perform certain sacred rites without her assistance.[6]

From the death of Merula, who killed himself in the temple of Jupiter,[7] Cicero says in the temple of Vesta, to avoid the cruelty of Cinna, A. U. 666, there was no flamen Dialis for seventy-two years, (Dio makes it seventy-seven years, but it seems not consistent), and the duties of his function were performed by the pontifices, till Augustus made Servius Maluginensis priest of Jupiter.[8] Julius Cæsar had indeed been elected[9] to that office at seventeen,[10] but, not having been inaugurated, was soon after deprived of it by Sylla.

II. SALII, the priests of Mars, twelve in number, instituted by Numa ; so called, because on solemn occasions they used to go through the city dancing,[11] dressed in an embroidered tunic,[12] bound with a brazen belt, and a toga prætexta or trabea ; having on their head a cap rising to a considerable height, in the form of a cone,[13] with a sword by their side ; in their right hand a spear, a rod, or the like ; and in their left, one of the ancilia, or shields of Mars.[14] Lucan says it hung from their neck.[15] Seneca resembles the leaping of the Salii[16] to that of fullers of cloth.[17] They used to go to the capitol, through the forum and other public parts of the city, singing as they went sacred songs,[18] said to have been composed by Nu-

---

1 Tac. Ann. iv. 16. Liv. i. 20. xxvii. 8. xxx. 26. Diony. ii. 64. Gell. xv. 27. Vell. ii 43. Suet. Cal. 12. Val. Max. vi. 9. 3. Cic. Dom. 14. Mil. 10, 17. Phil. ii. 43. Brut. 1.
2 Cic. Phil. ii. 43. Brut. 14. Har. 6. Dom. 9. Suet. Claud. Jul. 74. *Dio. xi. iv. 6. Luc. i. 604. Virg. Æn. viii. 664. Fest.
3 maxima dignationis inter xv flamines, Fest.
4 Gell. x. 15. Plut. Q.

Rom. 39. 43. 107, 108. Fest. 5. Plin. xxviii. 9. Liv. v. 52. xxxi. 50. Tac. Ann. iii. 58.
5 flaminica.
6 Plut. Q. Rom. 49. Ov. F. vi. 226. Tac. Ann. iv. 16.
7 incisis venis, superfusoque altaribus, sanguine,—his veins being opened, and the blood sprinkled on the altar.
8 Cic Or. iii. 3. Flor. iii. 21. Vell. ii. 22. Dio. liv. 24. 36. Tac. Ann.

iii. 58. Suet. Aug. 31. 9 destinatus, Suet. I. creatus, Vell. ii. 43.
10 pene puer, ib.
11 a saltu nomina ducunt, Ov. F. iii. 387. exsultantes Salii, Virg. Æn. viii. 663. a saltando, quod facere in comitio in sacris quotannis solent et debent, Varr. iv. 15.
12 tunica picta.
13 apex, κυρβασια.
14 Diony. ii. 70.
15 et Salius læto portians ancilia collo, L

603.—' the Salii blithe, with bucklers on the neck.'—Rowe.
16 saltus Saliaris.
17 saltus fullonius, Ep. ; 15.
18 per urbem ibant canentes carmina cum tripudiis solemnique saltatu,—they went in procession through the city, singing hymns, with leaping and solemn dancing, Liv. i. 20. Hor. Od. i. 36. 12. iv. l. 28.

ma,[1] which, in the time of Horace, could hardly be understood by any one, scarcely by the priests themselves.[2] Festus called these verses AXA-MENTA, vel *assamenta*, because they were written on tablets.

The most solemn procession of the Salii was on the first of March, in commemoration of the time when the sacred shield was believed to have fallen from heaven, in the reign of Numa. They resembled the armed dancers of the Greeks, called Curetes, from Crete, where that manner of dancing called PYRRICHE had its origin ; whether invented by Minerva, or, according to the fables of the poets, by the Curetes, who, being intrusted with the care of Jupiter in his infancy, to prevent his being discovered by Saturn his father, drowned his cries by the sound of their arms and cymbals. It was certainly common among the Greeks in the time of Homer.[3]

No one could be admitted into the order of the Salii unless a native of the place, and freeborn, whose father and mother were alive. Lucan calls them *lecta juventus patricia*, young patricians, because chosen from that order. The Salii, after finishing their procession, had a splendid entertainment prepared for them ; hence SALIARES *dapes*, costly dishes ; *epu lari Saliarem in modum*, to feast luxuriously ;[4] their chief was called PRÆ-SUL,[5] who seems to have gone foremost in the procession ; their principal musician, VATES ; and he who admitted new members, MAGISTER. According to Dionysius,[6] Tullus Hostilius added twelve other Salii, who were called AGONALES, -*enses*, or *Collini*, from having their chapel on the Colline hill. Those instituted by Numa had their chapel on the Palatine hill ; hence, for the sake of distinction, they were called PALA-TINI.[7]

III. LUPERCI, the priests of Pan ; so called[8] from a wolf, because that god was supposed to keep the wolves from the sheep. Hence the place where he was worshipped was called *Lupercal*, and his festival *Lupercalia*, which was celebrated in February ; at which time the *Luperci* ran up and down the city naked, having only a girdle of goats' skins round their waist, and thongs of the same in their hands, with which they struck those whom they met, particularly married women, who were thence supposed to be rendered prolific.[9]

There were three companies[10] of Luperci ; two ancient, called FABIANI and QUINTILIANI,[11] and a third, called JULII, instituted in honour of Julius Cæsar, whose first chief was Antony ; and, therefore, in that capacity, at the festival of the Lupercalia, although consul, he went almost naked into the *forum Julium*, attended by his lictors, and having made a harangue to the people[12] from the rostra, he, according to concert, as it is believed, presented a crown to Cæsar, who was sitting there in a golden chair, dressed in a purple robe, with a golden diadem, which had been decreed him, surrounded by the whole senate and people. Antony attempted repeatedly to put the crown on his head, addressing him by the title of king, and declaring that what he said and did was at the desire of his fellow-citizens. But Cæsar, perceiving the strongest marks of aversion in the people, rejected it, saying, that Jupiter alone was king of Rome, and therefore sent the

---

1 Saliare Numæ carmen. Hor. Ep. ii. 1. 86. Tac. An. ii. 83.
2 Quin. i. 6. 40.
3 Il. vi. v. 494. Strab. x. 467, 468. fin. Diony. ii. 70. vii. 72. Hygin. 139.
Serv. Virg. iv. 151.
4 Luc. ix. 478. Suet. Claud. 33. Hor. Od. i. 37. 2. Cic. Att. v. 9.
5 i. e. qui ante alios salit.
6 ill. 32. Cic. Div. i. 26.
ii. 66. Capitol. Anton. Philos. 4.
7 Id. ii. 70.
8 a lupo.
9 Serv. Virg. Æn. viii. 343. Ov. F. ii. 427.
445. v. 101.
10 sodalitates.
11 a Fabio et Quintilio præpositis suis, Fest.
12 nudus concionatus est, Cic. Phil. ii. 34. 43.

crown to the Capitol, as a present to that god.[1] It is remarkable that none of the succeeding emperors, in the plenitude of their power, ever ventured to assume the name of *rex*, king.

As the Luperci were the most ancient order of priests, said to have been first instituted by Evander,[2] so they continued the longest, not being abolished till the time of Anastasius, who died A. D. 518.

IV. POTITII and PINARII, the priests of Hercules, instituted by Evander, when he built an altar to Hercules, called MAXIMA, after that hero had slain Cacus; said to have been instructed in the sacred rites by Hercules himself,[3] being then two of the most illustrious families in that place. The Pinarii, happening to come too late to the sacrifice, after the entrails were eaten up,[4] were, by the appointment of Hercules, never after permitted to taste the entrails;[5] so that they only acted as assistants in performing the sacred rites.[6] The *Potitii*, being taught by Evander, continued to preside at the sacrifices of Hercules for many ages;[7] till the Pinarii, by the authority or advice of Appius Claudius, the censor, having delegated their ministry to public slaves, the whole race,[8] consisting of twelve *familiæ*, became extinct within a year; and some time after Appius lost his sight; a warning, says Livy, against making innovations in religion.[9]

V. GALLI, the priests of Cybele, the mother of the gods; so called from GALLUS, a river in Phrygia, which was supposed to make those who drank it mad, so that they castrated themselves, as the priests of Cybele did,[10] in imitation of Attys, -yis, Attis, -idis, v. Attin, -inis;[11] called also CURETES, CORYBANTES, their chief, ARCHIGALLUS; all of Phrygian extraction;[12] who used to carry round the image of Cybele, with the gestures of mad people, rolling their heads, beating their breasts to the sound of the flute,[13] making a great noise with drums and cymbals; sometimes also cutting their arms, and uttering dreadful predictions. During the festival called HILARIA, at the vernal equinox,[14] they washed with certain solemnities the image of Cybele, her chariot, her lions, and all her sacred things in the Tiber, at the conflux of the Almo.[15] They annually went round the villages, asking an alms,[16] which all other priests were prohibited to do.[17] All the circumstances relating to Cybele and her sacred rites are poetically detailed by Ovid, Fast iv. 181, 373. The rites of Cybele were disgraced by great indecency of expression.[18]

VIRGINES VESTALES,[19] virgins consecrated to the worship of Vesta, a priesthood derived from Alba, for Rhea Sylvia, the mother of Romulus, was a vestal, were originally from Troy, first instituted at Rome by Numa, and were four in number; two were added by Tarquinius Priscus, or by Servius Tullius, which continued to be the number ever after.[20]

The Vestal virgins were chosen first by the kings,[21] and after their ex-

1 Dio. xiv. 31. 44. xlvi. 5. 12. Suet. Cæs. 79. Cic. Phil. ii. 5. v. 14. xiii. 8. 15. 19. Vell. ii. 56. Plut. Cæs. p. 736, Anton. p. 921. App. Bell. Civ. ii. p. 496.
2 Ov. F. ii. 279. Liv. i. 5.
3 Cic. Dom. 52. Serv. Virg. Æn. viii. 269, 270. Liv. i. 7.
4 extis adesis.
5 Diony. i. 40.
6 et domus Herculei custos Pinaria sacri— and the Pinarian family, the depository of

this institution sacred to Hercules, Virg. ib.
7 antistites sacri ejus fuerunt, Liv. ib. primusque potitius auctor, Virg. ib.
8 genus omne, v. gens, potitiorum.
9 quod dimovendis statu suo sacris religionem facere possct, ix. 29.
10 Fest. Herodian. i. 11. Ov. F. iv. 361. genitalia sibi abscindebant cultris lapideis vel Samia testa, with

knives of stone or Samian brick, Juv. ii. 116. vi. 513. Mart. iii. 81. 3. Plin. xi. 49. s. 109. xxxv. 12. s. 46.
11 Ov. F. iv. 223. Met. x. 104. Arnob.
12 Lucr. ii. 629. Hor. Od. i 18. 8. Serv. Virg. ix. 116. Plin. xxxv. 10. s. 36. Diony. ii. 19.
13 tibiæ Berecynthiæ, v. buxi.
14 viii. Kal. April. Macrob. Sat. i. 21. Hor. Od. i. 16. 7. Virg. Æn. ix. 619. Luc. i. 585.

Sen. Med. 804.
15 Ov. F. iv. 337.
16 stipem emendicantes, ib. 350. Pont. i. 1. 40. Diony. ii. 19.
17 Cic. Legg. ii. 9. 16.
18 Juv. ii. 110. August. Civ. Dei, ii 14.
19 Παρθένοι Ἑστιάδες.
20 Liv. i. 3. 20. Diony. ii. 64, 65. iii. 67. Virg. Æn. ii. 296. Plut. Num. Fest. Sex.
21 Diony. ib.

pulsion, by the pontifex maximus; who, according to the Papian law, when a vacancy was to be supplied, selected from among the people twenty girls above six, and below sixteen years of age, free from any bodily defect, which was a requisite in all priests,[1] whose father and mother were both alive, and freeborn citizens. It was determined by lot in an assembly of the people, which of these twenty should be appointed. Then the pontifex maximus went and took her on whom the lot fell, from her parents, as a captive in war,[2] addressing her thus, TE, AMATA, CAPIO; that being, according to A. Gellius, the name of the first who was chosen a Vestal: hence CAPERE *virginem Vestalem*, to choose a Vestal virgin; which word was also applied to the *flamen dialis*, to the pontifices and augurs.[3] But afterwards this mode of casting lots was not necessary. The pontifex maximus might chose any one he thought proper, with the consent of her parents, and the requisite qualifications.[4] If none offered voluntarily, the method of casting lots was used.[5]

The Vestal virgins were bound to their ministry for thirty years. For the first ten years they learned the sacred rites; for the next ten, they performed them; and for the last ten, taught the younger virgins. They were all said *præsidere sacris, ut assiduæ templi* ANTISTITES, v. -*tæ*, that they might, without interruption, attend to the business of the temple.[6] The oldest[7] was called MAXIMA.[8] After thirty years' service they might leave the temple and marry; which, however, was seldom done, and always reckoned ominous.[9]

The office of the Vestal virgins was,—1. To keep the sacred fire always burning,[10] whence *æternæque Vestæ oblitus*, forgetting the fire of eternal Vesta; watching it in the night-time alternately,[11] and whoever allowed it to go out was scourged[12] by the pontifex maximus,[13] or by his order. This accident was always esteemed unlucky, and expiated by offering extraordinary sacrifices.[14] The fire was lighted up again, not from another fire, but from the rays of the sun, in which manner it was renewed every year on the first of March; that day being anciently the beginning of the year.[15]— 2. To keep the sacred pledge of the empire, supposed to have been the Palladium, or the *Penates* of the Roman people, called by Dio τα ιερα; kept in the innermost recess of the temple, visible only to the virgins, or rather to the *Vestalis maxima* alone;[16] sometimes removed from the temple of Vesta by the virgins, when tumult and slaughter prevailed in the city, or in case of a fire, rescued by Metellus the pontifex maximus when the temple was in flames, A. U. 512, at the hazard of his life, and with the loss of his sight, and consequently of his priesthood, for which a statue was erected to him in the capitol, and other honours conferred on him,[17]—and, 3. To perform constantly the sacred rites of the goddess. Their prayers and vows were always thought to have great influence with the gods. In their devotions they worshipped the god Fascinus to guard them from envy.[18]

---

1 sacerdos integer sit. Sen. con. iv. 2. Plut. Q. Rom. 72.
2 manu prehensam a parenti, veluti bello captam abducebat.
3 Gell. i. 12.
4 cujus ratio haberi posset, ibid, Tac. Ann. ii. 86.
5 Suet. Aug. 31.
6 Liv. i. 20. Tac. Ann. ii. 86. Sen. Vit. beat.

29. Diony. ii. 67.
7 Vestalium vetustissima, Tac. Ann. xi. 32.
8 Suet. Jul. 83. ἡ πρεσβεύουσα, Dio, li.
9 Diony. h. 67.
10 Flor. i. 2. custodiunto ignem foci publici sempiternum, Cic. Legg. ii. 8.
11 Liv. xxxviii. 31. Hor. Od. iii. 5. 11.
12 flagris cædebatur.

13 Val. Max. i. 6. Diony. ii. 67. nuda quidem, sed obscuro loco et velo medio interposito, Plut. Num. p. 67. Liv. xxviii. 11.
14 hostiis majoribus, procurari, ib.
15 Plut. ib. Macrob. Sat. i. 12. Ov. F. iii. 143.
16 Liv. v. 52. xxvi. 27. Tac. Ann. xv. 41. Luc. i. 598. ix. 994. Diony.

ii. 66. Herodian. i. 14.
17 see p. 11. Diony. ii. 66. Liv. 24. Ep. xix. Dio, xlii. 31. Ov. F. iv. 437. Plin. vii. 43. Sen. Contr. iv. 2.
18 Sen. prov. 5. Hor. Od. i. 2. 28. Cic. Font. 17. Dio, xlviii. 19. Plin. xxviii. 4. s. 7.

The Vestal virgins wore a long white robe, bordered with purple ; their heads were decorated with fillets[1] and ribands ;[2] hence the *Vestalis maxima* is called VITTATA SACERDOS, and simply VITTATA, the head-dress, SUFFIBULUM, described by Prudentius.[3] When first chosen, their hair was cut off and buried under an old *lotos* or lote-tree in the city,[4] but it was afterwards allowed to grow.

The Vestal virgins enjoyed singular honours and privileges. The prætors and consuls, when they met them in the street, lowered their fasces, and went out of the way, to show them respect. They had a lictor to attend them in public, at least after the time of the triumvirate ;[5] Plutarch says always ; they rode in a chariot ;[6] sat in a distinguished place at the spectacles ; were not forced to swear,[7] unless they inclined, and by none other but Vesta. They might make their testament, although under age ; for they were not subject to the power of a parent or guardian, as other women. They could free a criminal from punishment, if they met him accidentally ; and their interposition was always greatly respected. They had a salary from the public.[8] They were held in such veneration, that testaments and the most important deeds were committed to their care, and they enjoyed all the privileges of matrons who had three children.[9]

When the Vestal virgins were forced through indisposition to leave the ATRIUM VESTÆ, probably a house adjoining to the temple, and to the palace of Numa, REGIA parva NUMÆ, if not a part of it, where the virgins lived, they were intrusted to the care of some venerable matron.[10]

If any Vestal violated her vow of chastity, after being tried and sentenced by the pontifices, she was buried alive with funeral solemnities in a place called the CAMPUS SCELERATUS, near the Porta Collina, and her paramour scourged to death in the forum ; which method of punishment is said to have been first contrived by Tarquinius Priscus. The commission of this crime was thought to forbode some dreadful calamity to the state, and, therefore, was always expiated with extraordinary sacrifices. The suspected virtue of some virgins is said to have been miraculously cleared.[11]

These were the principal divisions of the Roman priests. Concerning their emoluments the classics leave us very much in the dark ; as they also do with respect to those of the magistrates. When Romulus first divided the Roman territory, he set apart what was sufficient for the performance of sacred rites, and for the support of temples.[12] So Livy informs us, that Numa, who instituted the greatest number of priests and sacrifices, provided a fund for defraying these expenses,[13] but appointed a public stipend[14] to none but the Vestal virgins. Dionysius, speaking of Romulus, says, that while other nations were negligent about the choice of their priests, some exposing that office to sale, and others determining it by lot ; Romulus made a law that two men, above fifty, of distinguished rank and virtue, without bodily defect, and possessed of a competent fortune, should be chosen from each curia, to officiate as priests in that curia or parish for life ; being exempted by age from military service, and by

1 infulæ,   στεμματα,   Mum.
Diony. ii. 67. viii. 89.
2 vittæ, Ov. F. iii. 30.
3 contra Sym. ii. 1093.
Luc. i. 597. Juv. iv. 10.
Fest.
4 Plin. xvi. 44. s. 85.
5 Sen. contr. i. 2. vi. 8.
Dio. xlvii. 19.
6 carpento v. pilento,
Tac. Ann. xii. 42. Plut.

7 Id. iv. 16. Suet. Aug.
44. Gell. x. 15.
8 Liv. i. 20. Suet. Aug.
31. Jul. 1. Tib. 2. Vit.
16. Tac. Ann. ii. 34. xi.
22. Hist. iii. 81. Cic.
Font. 17. Agr. ii. 36.
Plut. Num. Sen. ib.
Gell. ib.
9 Suet. Jul. 83. Aug.

102. Tac. Ann. i. 8. iv.
16. Dio. xlviii. 12. 37.
46. lvi. 10.
10 Ov. Trist. iii. 1. 30.
Fast. vi. 263. Plin. Ep.
vii. 19.
11 Val. Max viii. 1. 5.
Liv. viii. 15. xiv. xxii.
57. xxix. 14. lxiii. Plin.
vii. 35. Ep. iv. 11.
Diony. i. 78. ii. 67. viii.

89. ix. 40. Dio. fragm.
91. 92. Plut. Q. Rom.
83. Asc. Mil. 12. Suet.
Dom. 8. Juv. iv. 10.
12 Diony. ii. 7.
13 unde in eos sumptus
pecunia erogaretur, i.
20.
14 stipendium de publico statuit, ib.

law from the troublesome business of the city. There is no mention of
any annual salary. In after ages the priests claimed an immunity from
taxes, which the pontifices and augurs for several years did not pay. At
last, however, the quæstors wanting money for public exigencies, forced
them, after appealing in vain to the tribunes, to pay up their arrears.[1] Augustus increased both the dignity and emoluments[2] of the priests, particularly of the Vestal virgins ; as he likewise first fixed the salaries of the
provincial magistrates,[3] whence we read of a sum of money[4] being given
to those who were disappointed of a province.[5] But we read of no fixed
salary for the priests ; as for the teachers of the liberal arts, and for
others.[6] When Theodosius the Great abolished the heathen worship at
Rome, Zosimus mentions only his refusing to grant the public money for
sacrifices, and expelling the priests of both sexes from the temples.[7] It
is certain however, that sufficient provision was made, in whatever manner, for the maintenance of those who devoted themselves wholly to sacred functions. Honour, perhaps, was the chief reward of the dignified
priests, who attended only occasionally, and whose rank and fortune raised them above desiring any pecuniary gratification. There is a passage
in the life of Aurelian by Vopiscus,[8] which some apply to this subject ;
although it seems to be restricted to the priests of a particular temple,
pontifices roboravit, sc. *Aurelianus*, i. e. he endowed the chief priests with
salaries, *decrevit etiam emolumenta ministris*, and granted certain emoluments to their servants, the inferior priests who took care of the temples.
The priests are by later writers sometimes divided into three classes, the
antistites, or chief priests, the *sacerdotes* or ordinary priests, and the *ministri* or meanest priests, whom Manilius calls *auctoratos in tertia jura
ministros*, but for the most part only into two classes, the *pontifices* or
sacerdotes, and the *ministri*.[9]

SERVANTS OF THE PRIESTS.

THE priests who had children employed them to assist in performing
sacred rites : but those who had no children procured free-born boys and
girls to serve them, the boys to the age of puberty, and the girls till they
were married. These were called *Camilli* and *Camillæ*.[10]

Those who took care of the temples were called ÆDITUI or *æditumni*,
those who brought the victims to the altar and slew them, POPÆ, *victimarii*
and *cultrarii ;* to whom in particular the name of MINISTRI was properly
applied. The boys who assisted the flamines in sacred rites were called
FLAMINII ; and the girls, FLAMINÆ. There were various kinds of musicians, *tibicines, tubicines, fidicines,* &c.[11]

III. PLACES AND RITES OF SACRED THINGS.

THE places dedicated to the worship of the gods were called temples,
TEMPLA,[12] and consecrated by the augurs ; hence called Augusta. A
temple built by Aprippa in the time of Augustus, and dedicated to all the
gods, was called Pantheon.[13]

A small temple or chapel was called *sacellum* or *ædicula*. A wood or

---

1 annorum, per quos
non dederant. stipen-
dium exactum est,
Liv. xxxiii. 42. s. 44.
Diony. ii. 21.
2 commoda, Suet. Aug.
31.

3 Dio. lii. 23. 25. liii. 15.
4 salarium.
5 Id. 78. 22, xliii. 4.
lxxviii. 22. Tac. Agr.
42.
6 Suet. Tib. 46. Vesp.
18. Ner. 10. Digest.

7 v. 38.
8 c. 15.
9 Man. v. 350. Leg. 14.
Cod. Theod. de Pagan.
Sacrif. et Templis.
10 Diony. ii. 24.
11 Liv. ix. 30. Fest. Ov.

F. i. 319. iv. 637. Met.
ii. 717. Virg. G. iii. 486,
Juv. xii. 14.
12 fana, delubra, sacra-
ria, ædes sacræ.
13 Dio. liii. 27.

thicket of trees consecrated to religious worship was called *lucus*, a grove.[1]
The gods were supposed to frequent woods and fountains; hence, *esse
locis superos testatur silva per omnem sola virens Libyen*.[2]

The worship of the gods consisted chiefly in prayers, vows, and sacrifices.

No act of religious worship was performed without prayer. The words
used were thought of the greatest importance, and varied according to the
nature of the sacrifice.[3] Hence the supposed force of charms and incantations.[4] When in doubt about the name of any god, lest they should mistake, they used to say, QUISQUIS ES. Whatever occurred to a person in
doubt what to say, was supposed to be suggested by some divinity.[5] In
the daytime the gods were thought to remain for the most part in heaven,
but to go up and down the earth during the night to observe the actions
of men. The stars were supposed to do the contrary.[6]

Those who prayed stood usually with their heads covered,[7] looking towards the east; a priest pronounced the words before them;[8] they frequently touched the altars or the knees of the images of the gods ; turning
themselves round in a circle,[9] towards the right,[10] sometimes they put
their right hand to their mouth,[11] and also prostrated themselves on the
ground.[12]

The ancient Romans used with the same solemnity to offer up vows.[13]
They vowed temples, games (thence called *ludi votivi*), sacrifices, gifts, a
certain part of the plunder of a city, &c. Also what was called VER SA-
CRUM, that is, all the cattle which were produced from the first of March
to the end of April.[14] In this vow among the Samnites, men were included.[15] Sometimes they used to write their vows on paper or waxen
tablets, to seal them up,[16] and fasten them with wax to the knees of the
images of the gods ; that being supposed to be the seat of mercy : hence
genua incerare deorum,[17] to cover with wax the knees of the gods. When
the things for which they offered up vows were granted, the vows were
said *valere, esse rata*, &c., but if not, *cadere, esse irrita*, &c.

The person who made vows was said *esse voti reus ;* and when he obtained his wish,[18] *voti vel voto damnatus*, bound to make good his vow, till
he performed it. Hence *damnabis tu quoque votis*, i. e. *obligabis ad vota
solvenda*, shalt bind men to perform their vows by granting what they
prayed for ; *reddere* vel *solvere vota*, to perform. *Pars prædæ debita*,[19] *debiti* vel *meriti honores, merita dona*, &c. A vowed feast[20] was called POL-
LUCTUM, from *pollucere*, to consecrate ; hence *pollucibiliter cœnare*, to feast
sumptuously.[21] Those who implored the aid of the gods, used to lie[22] in
their temples, as if to receive from them responses in their sleep. The
sick in particular did so in the temple of Æsculapius.[23]

Those saved from shipwreck used to hang up their clothes in the temple of Neptune, with a picture[24] representing the circumstances of their
danger and escape.[25] So soldiers, when discharged, used to suspend their

1 Plin. xii. 6.
2 Luc. ix. 552.—Here, and here only, through wide Libya's space, Tall trees, the land, and verdant herbage grace.—Rowe.
3 Val. Max. i. 1.
4 verba et incantamenta carminum, Plin. xxviii. 2. Hor. Ep. i. i. 34.
5 Plaut. Most. iii. 1. 137.

Rud. i. 4. 37. Virg. Æn. iv. 577. Apul. de Deo Socratis.
6 Plaut Rud. Prol. 8.
7 capite velato vel operto.
8 verba præibat.
9 in gyrum se convertebant, Liv. v. 21.
10 Plaut. Curc. i. i. 70.
11 dextram ori admovebant, whence adoratio.
12 procumbebant aris

advoluti.
13 vovere, vota facere, suscipere, concipere, nuncupare, &c.
14 Liv. xxii. 9, 10. xxxiv. 44.
15 Fest. in Mamertini.
16 obsignare.
17 Juv. x. 55.
18 voti compos.
19 Liv. Macrob. Sat. iii. 2. Virg. Ecl. v. 80.
20 epulum votivum.

21 Plaut. Rud. v. 3. 63. Stich. i. 3. 80. Most. i. 1. 23.
22 incubare.
23 Serv. Virg. vii. 88. Cic. Div. i. 43. Plaut. Curc. i. 1. 61. ii. 2. 10.
24 tabula votiva.
25 Virg. xii. 768. Hor. Od. i. 5. Cic. Nat. D. iii. 37.

arms to Mars, gladiators their swords to Hercules, and poets, when they
finished a work, the fillets of their hair to Apollo. A person who had suffered shipwreck, used sometimes to support himself by begging, and for
the sake of moving compassion to show a picture of his misfortunes.[1]

Augustus having lost a number of his ships in a storm, expressed his
resentment against Neptune, by ordering that his image should not be
carried in procession with those of the other gods at the next solemnity
of the Circensian games.[2]

Thanksgivings[3] used always to be made to the gods for benefits received, and upon all fortunate events. It was, however, believed that the
gods, after remarkable success, used to send on men, by the agency of
NEMESIS,[4] a reverse of fortune.[5] To avoid which, as it is thought, Augustus, in consequence of a dream, every year, on a certain day, begged
an alms from the people, holding out his hand to such as offered him.[6]

When a general had obtained a signal victory, a thanksgiving[7] was decreed by the senate to be made in all the temples ; and what was called
a LECTISTERNIUM, when couches were spread[8] for the gods, as if about to
feast, and their images taken down from their pedestals, and placed upon
these couches round the altars, which were loaded with the richest dishes.
Hence, *ad omnia pulvinaria sacrificatum*, sacrifices were offered at all the
shrines ; *supplicatio decreta est*,[9] a thanksgiving was decreed. This
honour was decreed to Cicero for having suppressed the conspiracy of
Catiline, which he often boasted had never been conferred on any other
person without laying aside his robe of peace.[10] The author of the decree
was L. Cotta. A supplication was also decreed in times of danger or
public distress ; when the women prostrating themselves on the ground,
sometimes swept the temples with their hair. The Lectisternium was
first introduced in the time of a pestilence, A. U. 356.[11]

In sacrifices it was requisite that those who offered them should come
chaste and pure ; that they should bathe themselves ; be dressed in white
robes, and crowned with the leaves of that tree which was thought most
acceptable to the god whom they worshipped. Sometimes also in the garb
of suppliants, with dishevelled hair, loose robes, and barefooted. Vows
and prayers were always made before the sacrifice.

It was necessary that the animals to be sacrificed[12] should be without
spot and blemish,[13] never yoked in the plough, and therefore they were
chosen from a flock or herd, approved by the priests, and marked with
chalk,[14] whence they were called *egregiæ*,

eximiæ, lectæ. They were adorned with
fillets and ribands,[15] and crowns ; and
their horns were gilt.

The victim was led to the altar by the
popæ, with their clothes tucked up, and
naked to the waist,[16] with a slack rope,
that it might not seem to be brought by
force, which was reckoned a bad omen.

1 Hor. Ep. i. 1. 4. Stat.
Silv. iv. 4. 92. Juv.
xiv. 301. Phædr. iv. 21.
24.
2 Suet. Aug. 16.
3 gratiarum actiones.
4 ultrix facinorum im-
piorum bonorumque
præmiatrix, — the re-
venger of impious

deeds, and rewarder
of good, Marc. xiv. 11.
5 Liv. xlv. 41.
6 cavum manum asses
porrigentibus præbens,
Suet. Aug. 91. Dio. liv.
35.
7 supplicatio vel sup-
plicium, Liv. iii. 63.
8 lecti vel pulvinaria

sternebantur.
9 Cic. Cat. iii. 10. Liv.
xxii. 1.
10 togatus, Dio. 37. 36.
Cic. Pis. 3. Cat. iii. 6.
10.
11 Cic. Phil. ii. 6. xiv. 8.
Liv. iii. 7. v. 13.
12 hostiæ vel victimæ,
Ov. F. i. 335.

13 decoræ et integræ
vel intactæ.
14 Juv. x. 66.
15 infulis et vittis, Liv.
ii. 54.
16 qui succincti erant et
ad illa nudi, Suet. Cal.
32.

For the same reason it was allowed to stand loose before the altar ; and it was a very bad omen if it fled away. Then after silence was ordered,[1] a salted cake[2] was sprinkled[3] on the head of the beast, and frankincense and wine poured between its horns, the priest having first tasted the wine himself, and given it to be tasted by those that stood next him, which was called LIBATIO ; and thus the victim was said *esse macta*, i. e. *magis aucta :* hence *immolare* et *mactare*, to sacrifice ; for the Romans carefully avoided words of a bad omen ; as, *cædere, jugulare*, &c. The priest plucked the highest hairs between the horns, and threw them into the fire ; which was called LIBAMINA PRIMA.[4] The victim was struck by the *cultrarius*, with an axe or a mall,[5] by the order of the priest, whom he asked thus, AGONE ? and the priest answered, HOC AGE.[6] Then it was stabbed[7] with knives ; and the blood being caught[8] in goblets, was poured on the altar. It was then flayed and dissected. Sometimes it was all burned, and called HOLOCAUSTUM,[9] but usually only a part; and what remained was divided between the priests and the person who offered the sacrifice.[10] The person who cut up the animal, and divided it into different parts, was said *prosecare exta*, and the entrails thus divided were called PROSICIÆ or PROSECTA. These rites were common to the Romans with the Greeks ; whence Dionysius concludes that the Romans were of Greek extraction.[11]

Then the *aruspices* inspected the entrails ;[12] and if the signs were favourable,[13] they were said to have offered up an acceptable sacrifice, or to have pacified the gods ;[14] if not,[15] another victim was offered up,[16] and sometimes several.[17] The liver was the part chiefly inspected, and supposed to give the most certain presages of futurity ; hence termed CAPUT EXTORUM. It was divided into two parts, called *pars* FAMILIARIS, and *pars* HOSTILIS vel *inimica*. From the former they conjectured what was to happen to themselves ; and from the latter, what was to happen to an enemy. Each of these parts had what was called CAPUT,[18] which seems to have been a protuberance at the entrance of the blood-vessels and nerves, which the ancients distinguished by the name of fibres.[19] A liver without this protuberance,[20] or cut off,[21] was reckoned a very bad omen ;[22] or when the heart of the victim could not be found; for although it was known that an animal could not live without the heart, yet it was believed sometimes to be wanting ; as happened to Cæsar, a little before his death, while he was sacrificing, on that day on which he first appeared in his golden chair and purple robe, whereupon the haruspex Spurinna warned him to beware of the ides of March.[23] The principal fissure or devision of the liver,[24] was likewise particularly attended to, as also its fibres or parts, and those of the lungs.[25] After the haruspices had inspected the entrails,

1 Cic. Div. i. 45. see p. 201.
2 mola salsa, vel fruges salsæ, Virg. Æn. ii. 133. far et mica salis, Ov. & Hor. i. e. far tostum, comminutum, et sale mistum, bran or meal mixed with salt.
3 Inspergebatur.
4 Serv. Virg. Æn. iv. 57. vi. 246.
5 malleo, Suet. Cal. 32.
6 Ov. F. i. 323. Suet. Cal. 51.
7 jugulabatur.'
8 excepta.
9 ex ὅλος totus, et καιω

uro, Virg. vi. 25.
10 qui sacra v. sacrificium faciebat, v. sacris operavatur, Virg. G. i. 393. ac. Ann. ii. 14.
11 vii. 72. Liv. v. 21.θv. F. vi. 168. Plaut. Pœn. ii. 1. 8.
12 exta consulebant, Virg. iv. 64.
13 si exta bona essent.
14 diis latasse.
15 si exta non bona vel prava et tristia essent.
16 sacrificium instaurabatur, vel victima succedanea mactabatur.
17 Cic. Div. ii. 36. 38. Suet. Cæs. 81. Liv.

xxv. 16. Serv. Virg. iv. 50. v. 94.
18 Plin. xi. 37. s. 73. Liv. viii. 9. Cic. Div. ii. 12, 13. Luc. i. 621.
19 thus, in ima fibra, Suet. Aug. 95. ecce videt capiti fibrarum increscere molem Alterius capitis, Luc. i. 627. en capita paribus bina consurgunt toris, Sen. Œdip. 356. caput jecinoris duplex, Val. Max. i. 6. 9. i. e. two lobes, one on each side of the fissure or cavity, commonly called porta, v. -tæ, Cic. Nat. D.

ii. 55. which Livy calls auctum in jecinore, xxvii. 26. s. 26.
20 jecur sine capite.
21 caput jecinore cæsum.
22 nihil tristius, Cic. Div. i. 52. ii. 13. 16. Liv. viii. 9.
23 Cic. Div. i. 52. ii. 16. Val. Max. i. 6. 13. Suet. Jul. 81.
24 fissum jecoris familiare et vitale.
25 Cic. Nat. D. iii. 6. Virg. G. i. 484. Æn. iv. 6. x. 176.

then the parts which fell to the gods were sprinkled with meal, wine, and frankincense, and burned[1] on the altar. The entrails were said *diis dari, reddi, et porrici*,[2] when they were placed on the altars,[3] or when, in sacrificing to the *dii marini*, they were thrown into the sea.[4] Hence, if any thing unlucky fell out to prevent a person from doing what he had resolved on, or the like, it was said to happen *inter cæsa* (sc. *exta*) *et porrecta*, between the time of killing the victim and burning the entrails, i. e. between the time of forming the resolution and executing it.[5]

When the sacrifice was finished, the priest having washed his hands and uttered certain prayers, again made a libation, and then the people were dismissed in a set form; ILICET, or *ire licet*.

After the sacrifice followed a feast,[6] which in public sacrifices was sumptuously prepared by the *septemviri epulones*. In private sacrifices, the persons who offered them feasted on the parts which fell to them, with their friends.[7]

On certain solemn occasions, especially at funerals, a distribution of raw flesh used to be made to the people, called VISCERATIO :[8] for *viscera* signifies not only the intestines, but whatever is under the hide : particularly the flesh between the bones and the skin.[9]

The sacrifices offered to the celestial gods differed from those offered to the infernal deities in several particulars. The victims sacrificed to the former were white, brought chiefly from the river Clitumnus, in the country of the Falisci ;[10] their neck was bent upwards,[11] the knife was applied from above,[12] and the blood was sprinkled on the altar, or caught in cups. The victims offered to the infernal gods were black ; they were killed with their faces bent downwards,[13] the knife was applied from below,[14] and the blood was poured into a ditch.

Those who sacrificed to the celestial gods were clothed in white, bathed the whole body, made libations by heaving the liquor out of the cup,[15] and prayed with the palms of their hands raised to heaven. Those who sacrificed to the infernal gods were clothed in black ; only sprinkled their body with water, made libations by turning the hand,[16] and threw the cup into the fire, prayed with their palms turned downwards, and striking the ground with their feet.[17]

Sacrifices were of different kinds ; some were stated,[18] others occasional ;[19] as, those called expiatory, for averting bad omens,[20] making atonement for a crime,[21] and the like.

Human sacrifices were also offered among the Romans. — By an ancient law of Romulus (which Dionysius calls *νομος προδοσιας, lex proditionis*, ii. 10), persons guilty of certain crimes, as treachery or sedition, were devoted to Pluto and the infernal gods, and therefore any one might slay them with impunity. In after times, a consul, dictator, or prætor, might devote not only himself, but any one of the legion,[22] and slay him as an expiatory

---

1 adolebantur vel cremabantur.
2 quasi porrigi, vel porro jaci.
3 cum aris vel flammis imponerentur, Virg. Æn. vi. 252. xii. 214.
4 Ib. v. 774.
5 Cic. Att. v. 18.
6 epulæ sacrificiales.
7 sacra tulere suam (partem). pars est data cetera mensis,—the sacrifice had its own

share: the rest is for the table, Ov. Met. xii. 154.
8 Liv. viii. 22. xxxix. 46.
xli. 28. Cic. Off. ii. 16. Suet. Cæs. 38.
9 Serv. Virg. Æn. i. 211. iii. 622. vi. 253. Suet. Vit. 13.
10 Ov. Pont. iv. 8. 41. Juv. xii. 13. Virg. G. ii. 146.
11 sursum reflectebatur.
12 imponebatur.

13 pronæ.
14 supponebatur.
15 fundendo manu supina.
16 invergendo, ita ut manu in sinistram partem versa patera converteretur.
17 Serv. Virg. Æn. vi. 244. Cic. Tusc. Q. ii. 25.
18 stata et solemnia.
19 fortuita et ex accidente nata.

20 ad portenta vel prodigia procuranda, expianda et avertenda vel averruncanda.
21 sacrificia piacularia, ad crimem expiandum.
22 ex legione Romana, called Scripta, because perhaps the soldiers not included in the legion, the Velites, Subitarii, Tumultuarii, &c. were excepted.

victim.[1] In the first ages of the republic human sacrifices seem to have been offered annually,[2] and it was not till the year 657, that a decree of the senate was made to prohibit it.[3] Mankind, says Pliny, are under inexpressible obligations to the Romans for abolishing so horrid a practice.[4] We read, however, of two men who were slain as victims with the usual solemnities in the Campus Martius by the pontifices and flamen of Mars, as late as the time of Julius Cæsar, A. U. 708. Whence it is supposed that the decree of the senate mentioned by Pliny respected only private and magical sacred rites, and those alluded to, Horat. Epod, 5. Augustus, after he had compelled L. Antonius to a surrender at Perusia, ordered 400 senators and equites, who had sided with Antony, to be sacrificed as victims on the altar of Julius Cæsar, on the ides of March, A. U. 713. Suetonius makes them only 300. To this savage action Seneca alludes, de Clem. i. 11. In like manner, Sex. Pompeius threw into the sea not only horses, but also men alive, as victims to Neptune. Boys used to be cruelly put to death, even in the time of Cicero and Horace, for magical purposes.[5]

A place reared for offering sacrifices, was called ARA or ALTARE, an altar.[6] In the phrase, *pro aris et focis*, ARA is put for the altar in the *impluvium* or middle of the house, where the *Penates* were worshipped; and FOCUS, for the hearth in the *atrium* or hall, where the *Lares* were worshipped. A secret place in the temple, where none but priests entered, was called ADYTUM, universally revered.[7]

Altars used to be covered with leaves and grass, called VERBENA, i. e. herba sacra,[8] adorned with flowers, and bound with woollen fillets, therefore called *nexæ torques*, i. e. *coronæ*.[9]

Altars and temples afforded an asylum or place of refuge among the Greeks and Romans, as among the Jews,[10] chiefly to slaves from the cruelty of their masters, to insolvent debtors and criminals, where it was reckoned impious to touch them,[11] and whence it was unlawful to drag them,[12] but sometimes they put fire and combustible materials around the place, that the person might appear to be forced away, not by men, but by a gód (Vulcan), or shut up the temple and unroofed it,[13] that he might perish under the open air, hence *ara* is put for *refugium*.[14]

The triumviri consecrated a chapel to Cæsar in the forum, on the place where he was burned; and ordained that no person who fled thither for sanctuary should be taken from thence to punishment; a thing which, says Dio, had been granted to no one before, not even to any divinity; except the asylum of Romulus, which remained only in name, being so blocked

1 piaculum, i. e. in piaculum, hostiam cædere, Liv. viii. 10.
2 Macrob, Sat i. 7.
3 ne homo immolaretur, Plin. xxx. l. s. 3.
4 qui sustulere monstra, in quibus hominem occidere religiosissimum erat, mandi vero etiam saluberrimum, ib.
5 Cic. Vat. 14. Hor. Ep. 5. Dio. xliii. 24. xlviii. 14. 48. Suet.

Aug. 15.
6 altaria, ab altitudine, tantum diis superis consecrabantur; aræ et diis superis et inferis,—Altaria, so called ab altitudine from their height, were consecrated only to the supernal deities: aræ, both to the supernal and infernal, Serv. Virg. Ecl. v. 66. Æn. ii. 515.
7 Paus. x. 32. Cæs. B.

C. iii. 105. Sal. Cat. 52. Cic. Dej. 3. Phil. ii. 30. Sext. 42. Dom. 40, 41.
8 Serv. Virg. Æn. xii. 120. Ecl. viii. 65. Don. Ter. iv. 4, 5. Hor. Od. iv. 117.
9 Ov. Trist. iii. 13. 15. Stat. Theb. viii. 298. Sil. xvi. 309. Prop. iv. 6. 6. Virg. Æn. iv. 459. G. iv. 276.
10 Nep. Paus. 4. Cic. Nat. D. iii. 10. Q. Ros.

Kings, l. 50.
11 Cic. Tusc. i. 36. Virg. Æn. i. 349. ii. 513. 550. Ter. Heaut. v. 2. 22. Plaut. Rud. iii. 4. 18. Most. v. i. 45. Tac. Ann. iii. 60.
12 Cic. Dom. 41. Plaut. Most. v. i. 65
13 tectum sunt demoliti.
14 Nep. Paus. 5. p. 63. Ov. Trist. iv. 5. 2.
2. Ov. Trist. v. 2. 43. 1.

up that no one could enter it.   But the shrine of Julius was not always
esteemed inviolable ; the son of Antony was slain by Augustus, although
he fled to it.[1]

There were various vessels and instruments used in sacrifices ; as *acerra*
vel *thuribulum*, a censor for burning incense ; *simpulum* vel *simpuvium*,
guttum, *capis*, *-idis*, *patera*, cups used in libations, *ollæ*, pots ; *tripodes*,
tripods ; *secures* vel *bipennes*, axes ; *cultri* vel *secespitæ*, knives, &c.   But
these will be better understood by the representation below, than by description :—

THE ROMAN YEAR.

Romulus is said to have divided the year into ten months ; the first of
which was called *Martius*, March, from Mars, his supposed father ; the
second *Aprilis*, either from the Greek name of Venus ($A\varphi\varrho o\delta\iota\tau\eta$),[2] or because then trees and flowers open[3] their buds ; the third, *Maius*, May,
from *Maia*, the mother of Mercury ; and the fourth, *Junius*, June, from the
goddess *Juno*, or in honour of the young ;[4] and May of the old.[5]   The
rest were named from their number, *Quintilis*, *Sextilis*, *September*, *October*,
November, *December*.   *Quintilis* was afterwards called *Julius*, from Julius
Cæsar, and *Sextilis Augustus*, from Augustus Cæsar ; because in it he had
first been made consul, and had obtained remarkable victories,[6] in particular, he had become master of Alexandria in Egypt, A. U. 724, and fifteen
years after,[7] on the same day, probably the 29th of August, had vanquished the Rhæti, by means of Tiberius.   Other emperors gave their names
to particular months, but these were forgotten after their death.[8]

Numa added two months, called *Januarius*, from *Janus ;* and *Februarius*,
because then the people were purified,[9] by an expiatory sacrifice,[10] from
the sins of the whole year ; for this anciently was the last month in the
year.[11]

Numa, in imitation of the Greeks, divided the year into twelve months,
according to the course of the moon, consisting in all of 354 days ; he
added one day more, to make the number odd, which was thought the more
fortunate.   But as ten days, five hours, forty-nine minutes, (or rather forty-
eight minutes, fifty-seven seconds), were wanting to make the lunar year

1 Dio. xlvii. 19. Suet.   Ov. F. iv. 87.   lv. 6.   gabatur vel lustraba-
   Aug. 17.   4 juniorum.   7 lustro tertio.   tur.
2 Ov. F. i. 39. iii. 75. 98. 5 majorum, Ov. F. v. 8 Hor. Od. iv. 4. Suet. 10 februalia.
   Hor. Od. iv. 11.   427.   Dom. 13. Plin. Pan. 54.   11 Cic. Legg. ii. 21. Ov.
3 se aperiunt, Plut. Na. 6 ib. i. 41. Suet. 31. Dio. 9 februabatur, i. e. pur- F. ii. 49. Tibull. iii. 1. 2.

correspond to the course of the sun, he appointed that every other year an extraordinary month, called *mensis intercalaris*, or *Macedonius*, should be inserted between the 23d and 24th day of February.[1] The intercalating of this month was left to the discretion[2] of the pontifices; who, by inserting more or fewer days, used to make the current year longer or shorter, as was most convenient for themselves or their friends; for instance, that a magistrate might sooner or later resign his office, or contractors for the revenue might have longer or shorter time to collect the taxes. In consequence of this licence, the months were transposed from their stated seasons; the winter months carried back into autumn, and the autumnal into summer.[3]

Julius Cæsar, when he became master of the state, resolved to put an end to this disorder, by abolishing the source of it, the use of the intercalations; and for that purpose, A.U.707, adjusted the year according to the course of the sun, and assigned to each month the number of days which they still contain. To make matters proceed regularly from the 1st of the ensuing January, he inserted in the current year, besides the intercalary month of twenty-three days, which fell into it of course, two extraordinary months between November and December, the one of thirty-three, and the other of thirty-four days; so that this year, which was called the last year of confusion, consisted of sixteen months, or 445 days.[4]

All this was effected by the care and skill of Sosigenes, a celebrated astronomer of Alexandria, whom Cæsar had brought to Rome for that purpose; and a new calendar was formed from his arrangement by Flavius, a scribe, digested according to the order of the Roman festivals, and the old manner of computing the days by kalends, nones, and ides; which was published and authorized by the dictator's edict.

This is the famous JULIAN or solar year, which continues in use to this day in all Christian countries, without any other variation than that of the old and new style; which was occasioned by a regulation of pope Gregory, A. D. 1582, who, observing that the vernal equinox, which, at the time of the council of Nice, A. D. 325, had been on the 21st of March, then happened on the 10th, by the advice of astronomers, caused ten days to be entirely sunk and thrown out of the current year, between the 4th and 15th of October; and to make the civil year for the future to agree with the real one, or with the annual revolution of the earth round the sun; or, as it was then expressed, with the annual motion of the sun round the ecliptic, which is completed in 365 days, five hours, forty-nine minutes, he ordained that every 100th year should not be leap year, excepting the 400th; so that the difference will hardly amount to a day in 7000 years; or, according to a more accurate computation of the length of the year, to a day in 5200 years.

This alteration of the style was immediately adopted in all the Roman Catholic countries, but not in Britain till the year 1752, when eleven days were dropped between the 2d and 14th September, so that the month contained only nineteen days; and thenceforth the new style was adopted as it had been before in the other countries of Europe. The same year also another alteration was made in England, that the legal year, which before had begun the 25th of March, should begin upon the 1st of January, which first took place 1st January, 1752.

---

1 Plin. xxxiv. 7. Liv. i. 19.   3 Cic. Legg. ii. 12. Fam.   Cæs. 40. Dio, xl. 62.   4 Suet. Cæs. 40. Plin.
2 arbitrio.   vii. 3. 12. viii. 6. At. v.   Censorin. 20. Macrob.   xviii. 25. Macrob. Sat.i.
9. 13. vi. 1. x. 17. Suet.   Sat. i. 13.   14.Cens.de Die Nat. 20.

The Romans divided their months into three parts by kalends, nones, and ides. The first day was called KALENDÆ vel *calendæ*,[1] from a priest calling out to the people that it was new moon ; the fifth day, NONÆ, the nones ; the thirteenth, IDUS, the ides, from the obsolete verb *iduare*, to divide, because the ides divided the month. The nones were so called, because, counting inclusively, they were nine days from the ides.

In March, May, July, and October, the nones fell on the seventh, and the ides on the fifteenth. The first day of the intercalary month was called CALENDÆ INTERCALARES, of the former of those inserted by Cæsar, KAL. INTERCALARES PRIORES. *Intra septimas calendas*, in seven months. *Sextæ kalendæ*, i. e. *kalendæ sexti mensis*, the first day of June.[2]

Cæsar was led to this method of regulating the year by observing the manner of computing time among the Egyptians ; who divided the year into twelve months, each consisting of thirty days, and added five intercalary days at the end of the year, and every fourth year six days.[3] These supernumerary days Cæsar disposed of among those months which now consist of thirty-one days, and also the two days which he took from February ; having adjusted the year so exactly to the course of the sun, says Dio, that the insertion of one intercalary day in 1461 years would make up the difference,[4] which, however, was found to be ten days less than the truth. Another difference between the Egyptian and Julian year was, that the former began with September, and the latter with January.

The ancient Romans did not divide their time into weeks, as we do, in imitation of the Jews. The country people came to Rome every ninth day,[5] whence these days were called NUNDINÆ *quasi* NOVENDINÆ, having seven intermediate days for working, but there seems to have been no word to denote this space of time. The time, indeed, between the promulgation and passing of a law was called TRINUM NUNDINUM, or TRINUN-DINUM ;[6] but this might include from seventeen to thirty days, according to the time when the table containing the business to be determined[7] was hung up, and the Comitia were held. The classics never put *nundinum* by itself for a space of time. Under the later emperors, indeed, it was used to denote the time that the consuls remained in office, which then probably was two months,[8] so that there were twelve consuls each year ; hence *nundinum* is also put for the two consuls themselves.[9]

The custom of dividing time into weeks[10] was introduced under the emperors. Dio, who flourished under Severus, says, it first took place a little before his time, being derived from the Egyptians ; and universally prevailed. The days of the week were named from the planets, as they still are ; *dies Solis*, Sunday ; *Lunæ*, Monday ; *Martis*, Tuesday ; *Mercurii*, Wednesday ; *Jovis*, Thursday ; *Veneris*, Friday ; *Saturni*, Saturday.

The Romans, in marking the days of the month, counted backwards. Thus, they called the last day of December *pridie kalendas*, sc. *ante*, or *pridie kalendarum Januarii*, marked shortly, *prid. kal. Jan.* the day before that, or the 30th of December, *tertio kal. Jan.* sc. *die ante*, or *ante diem tertium kal. Jan.* and so through the whole year : thus,

1 a calando vel vocan-   3 Herodot, ii. 4.   Phil. v. 3. Fam.xvi. 12.   Vop. Tac. 9.
do.   4 Dio, xliii. 26.   7 tabula promulgationis.   10 hebdomades, v. -dæ
2 Ov. F. vi. 181. Cic.   5 see p. 59.   8 Lamprid. in Alex.   vel septimanæ.
Quint. 25. Fam. vi. 14.   6 Liv. iii. 35. Macrob.   Sever. 28. 43.
Mart. i. 100. 6.   i. 16. Cic. Dom. 16, 17.   9 collegium consulum,

A TABLE OF THE KALENDS, NONES, AND IDES.

Days of the Month.	April, June, Sept., November.	January, Aug. December.	March, May, July, Oct.	February.
1	Kalendæ.	Kalendæ.	Kalendæ.	Kalendæ.
2	IV.	IV.	VI.	IV.
3	III.	III.	V.	III.
4	Prid. Non.	Prid. Non.	IV.	Prid. Non.
5	Nonæ.	Nonæ.	III.	Nonæ.
6	VIII.	VIII.	Prid. Non.	VIII.
7	VII.	VII.	Nonæ.	VII.
8	VI.	VI.	VIII.	VI.
9	V.	V.	VII.	V.
10	IV.	IV.	VI.	IV.
11	III.	III.	V.	III.
12	Prid. Id.	Prid. Id.	IV.	Prid. Id.
13	Idus.	Idus.	III.	Idus.
14	XVIII.	XIX.	Prid. Id.	XVI.
15	XVII.	XVIII.	Idus.	XV.
16	XVI.	XVII.	XVII.	VIV.
17	XV.	XVI.	XVI.	XIII.
18	XIV.	XV.	XV.	XII.
19	XIII.	XIV.	XIV.	XI.
20	XII.	XIII.	XIII.	X.
21	XI.	XII.	XII.	IX.
22	X.	XI.	XI.	VIII.
23	IX.	X.	X.	VII.
24	VIII.	IX.	IX.	VI.
25	VII.	VIII.	VIII.	V.
26	VI.	VII.	VII.	IV.
27	V.	VI.	VI.	III.
28	IV.	V.	V.	Prid. Kal.
29	III.	IV.	IV.	Martii.
30	Prid. Kal.	III.	III.	
31	mens. seq.	Prid. Kal. mens. seq.	Prid. Kal. mens. seq.	

In leap year, that is, when February has twenty-nine days, which happens every fourth year, both the 24th and 25th days of that month were marked *sexto kalendis Martii* or *Martias ;* and hence this year is called BISSEXTILIS.

The names of all the months are used as substantives or adjectives, except *Aprilis*, which is used only as a substantive.

The Greeks had no calends in their way of reckoning, but called the first day of the month νουμηνια, or new moon ; hence *ad Græcas kalendas solvere,* for *nunquam.*[1]

The day among the Romans was either civil or natural.

The civil day[2] was from midnight to midnight. The parts of which were, 1. *media nox ;* 2. *mediæ noctis inclinatio,* vel *de media nocte ;* 3. *gallicinium,* cock-crow, or cock-crowing, the time when the cocks begin to crow ; 4. *conticinium,* when they give over crowing ; 5. *diluculum,* the dawn ; 6. *mane,* the morning ; 7. *antemeridianum tempus,* the forenoon ; 8. *meridies,* noon, or mid-day ; 9. *tempus pomeridianum,* vel *meridiei inclinatio,* afternoon ; 10. *solis occasus,* sunset ; 11. *vespera,* the evening ; 12. *crepusculum,* the twilight ;[3] 13. *prima fax,* when candles were lighted, called also *primæ tenebræ, prima lumina ;* 14. *concubia nox,* vel *concubium,* bedtime ; 15. *intempesta nox,* or *silentium noctis,* far on in the night ; 16. *inclinatio ad mediam noctem.*[4]

---

1 Suet. Aug. 87.   3 dubium tempus, noc-   dubia res crepera dic-   4 Liv. xxv. 9. Conso .
2 dies civilis.   tis an diei sit: ideo   tæ, Varr. L. L. vi. 4.   Die Nat. c. 24. Hor.

The natural day[1] was from the rising to the setting of the sun. It was
divided into twelve hours, which were of a different length at different seasons : hence *hora hiberna* for *brevissima*.[2]

The night was divided into four watches,[3] each consisting of three
hours, which were likewise of a different length at different times of the
year : thus, *hora sexta noctis*, midnight ; *septima*, one o'clock in the morning ; *octava*, two, &c.[4]

Before the use of dials[5] was known at Rome, there was no division of
the day into hours ; nor does that word occur in the Twelve Tables.
They only mention sunrising and sunsetting, before and after mid-day.
According to Pliny, mid-day was not added till some years after,[6] an *accensus* of the consuls being appointed to call out that time,[7] when he saw
the sun from the senate-house, between the rostra and the place called
GRÆCOSTASIS, where ambassadors from Greece and other foreign countries used to stand.[8]

Anaximander or Anaximenes of Miletus, is said to have invented dials
at Lacedæmon in the time of Cyrus the Great. The first dial is said to
have been set up at Rome by L. Papirius Cursor, A. U. 447, and the next
near the rostra, by M. Valerius Messala the consul, who brought it from
Catana in Sicily, in the first Punic war, A. U. 481 : hence *ad solarium
versari*, for *in foro*. Scipio Nasica first measured time by water, or by a
clepsydra, which served by night as well as by day, A. U. 595.[9] The use
of clocks and watches was unknown to the Romans.

DIVISION OF DAYS AND ROMAN FESTIVALS.

DAYS among the Romans were either dedicated to religious purposes,[10]
or assigned to ordinary business.[11] There were some partly the one, and
partly the other,[12] half holidays.

On the *dies festi* sacrifices were performed, feasts and games were celebrated, or there was at least a cessation from business. The days on
which there was a cessation from business were called FERIÆ, holidays,[13]
and were either public or private.

Public *feriæ* or festivals were either stated,[14] or annually fixed on a certain day by the magistrates or priests,[15] or occasionally appointed by order
of the consul, the prætor, or pontifex maximus.[16] The stated festivals
were chiefly the following :

1. In January, AGONALIA, in honour of Janus, on the 9th,[17] and also of
the 20th of May ; CARMENTALIA, in honour of Carmenta, the mother of
Evander, on the 11th.[18] But this was a half holiday ;[19] for after mid-day
it was *dies profestus*, a common work-day. On the 13th,[20] a wether[21] was
sacrificed to Jupiter. On this day the name of AUGUSTUS was conferred
on Cæsar Octavianus.[22] On the first day of this month people used to
wish one another health and prosperity,[23] and to send presents to their
friends.[24] Most of the magistrates entered on their office, and artists
thought it lucky to begin any work they had to perform.[25]

---

1 dies naturalis.
2 Plaut. Pseud. v. 2. 11.
3 vigilia prima, secun-
da, &c.
4 Plin. Ep. iii. 4.
5 horologia solaria vel
sciaterica.
6 vii. 60. Censorin. 23.
7 accenso consulum id
pronunciante.

8 Plin ib. Varr. L. L.
iv. 32. Cic Q. Fr. il. 1.
9 see p. 166. Plin. il. 76.
vii. 60. Gell. ex Plaut.
iii 3. Cic. Quint. 18.
10 dies festi.
11 dies profesti.
12 dies intercisi, i. e. ex
pare festi, et ex parte
profesti.

13 Cic. Legg. ii. 8. Div.
i. 45.
14 statæ.
15 conceptivæ.
16 imperativæ.
17 v Id. Ov. F. i. 318.
18 III. Id. Ov. ib. 461.
19 interciaus.
20 Idibus.
21 vervex vel ovis se-

mimas, -aris.
22 Ov. F. i. 588. 590.
23 omnia fausta, Plin.
xxviii. 2. s. 5.
24 see p. 4f.
25 opera auspicabantur,
Sen. Ep. 83. Ov. Mart.
passim.

2. In February, FAUNALIA, to the god Faunus, on the 13th ;[1] LUPERCA-
LIA, to Lycæan Pan, on the 15th ;[2] QUIRINALIA, to Romulus, on the 17th ;
FERALIA,[3] to the *dii Manes*, on the 21st (Ovid says the 17th), and sometimes continued for several days ; after which friends and relations kept
a feast of peace and love,[4] for settling differences and quarrels among one
another, if any such existed ;[5] TERMINALIA, to Terminus ; REGIFUGIUM,
vel *regis fuga*, in commemoration of the flight of king Tarquin, on the 24th ;
EQUIRIA, horse-races in the Campus Martius, in honour of Mars, on the
27th.

3. In March, MATRONALIA, celebrated by the matrons for various reasons, but chiefly in memery of the war terminated between the Romans
and Sabines, on the first day ; when presents used to be given by husbands to their wives ;[6] *festum* ANCILIORUM, on the same day, and the three
following, when the shields of Mars were carried through the city by the
Salii, who used then to be entertained with sumptuous feasts ; whence
saliares dapes vel *cœnæ*, for *lautæ, opiparæ, opulentæ*, splendid banquets ;[7]
LIBERALIA, to Bacchus, on the 18th,[8] when young men used to put on the
toga virilis, or manly gown ; QUINQUATRUS, *-uum* vel *quinquatria*, in honour of Minerva, on the 19th, at first only for one day, but afterwards for
five ; whence they got their name.[9] At this time boys brought presents
to their masters, called *Minervalia*. On the last day of this festival, and
also on the 23d March,[10] the trumpets used in sacred rites were purified[11]
by sacrificing a lamb ; hence it was called TUBILUSTRIUM, vel -IA ;[12] HILA-
RIA, in honour of the mother of the gods, on the 25th.

4. In April, MEGALESIA, or *Megalenses*, to the great mother of the gods,
on the 4th or 5th ; CEREALIA, or *ludi Cereales*, to Ceres, on the 9th ; FORDI-
CIDIA, on the 15th, when pregnant cows were sacrificed ;[13] PALILA vel *Pa-
rilia*, to Pales, the 21st.[14] On this day Cæsar appointed Circensian games
to be annually celebrated ever after, because the news of his last victory
over Labienus and the sons of Pompey at Munda in Spain had reached
Rome the evening before this festival ;[15] ROBIGALIA, to Robigus,[16] that he
would preserve the corn from mildew,[17] on the 25th ; FLORALIA, to Flora
or Chloris,[18] begun on the 28th, and continued to the end of the month,
attended with great indecency, which is said to have been once checked
by the presence of Cato.[19]

5. In May, on the kalends, were performed the sacred rites of the *Bona
Dea*, by the Vestal virgins, and by women only,[20] in the house of the consuls and prætors, for the safety of the people.[21] On this day also an altar
was erected,[22] and a sacrifice offered to the Lares called *Præstites* ;[23] on
the 2d, COMPITALIA, to the Lares in the public ways, at which time boys
are said anciently to have been sacrificed to Mania, the mother of the
Lares : but this cruel custom was abolished by Junius Brutus ;[24] on the
9th, LEMURIA, to the Lemures, hobgoblins, or spectres in the dark, which
were believed to be the souls of their deceased friends.[25] Sacred rites
were performed to them for three nights, not successively, but alternately,

1 Idibus.
2 xv. kal. Mart.
3 quod tum epulas ad sepulchra amicorum ferebant, vel pecudes feriebant, Fest.
4 charistia.
5 Val. Max. ii. 1. 6. Ov. Fast. ii. 631.
6 Ov. F. iii. 170. Plaut. Mil. iii. 197. Tibul. iii.

1. Suet. Vesp. 19.
7 Hor. Od. i. 37. 2.
8 xv. kal. Apr.
9 Ov. F. iii. 810. Gell. ii. 21.
10 x. kal. April.
11 lustrabantur.
12 Ov. F. iii. 489. v. 725.
13 fordæ boves, i. e. gra-vidæ, quæ in ventre fe-runt, Ov. F. vi. 5. 632.

14 see p. 1.
15 Dio, xliii. 42.
16 or rather to Robigo, a goddess, Ov. F. iv. 911.
17 a rubigine.
18 ut omnia bene deflo-rescerent, shed their blossoms, Plin. xviii.29.
19 Sen. Ep. 97. Mart. i. 3. & præf. Val. Max.

ii. 10. 8. Lact. i. 20. 10. Scholiast. Juv. vi.249.
20 cum omne mascu-lum expellebatur, Juv. vi. 339.
21 Dio. xxxvii. 35. 45.
22 constituta.
23 quod omnia tuta præstant, Ov. F.v.132.
24 Macrob. Sat. i. 7.
25 manes paterni.

for six days ;[1] on the 13th, or the ides, the images of thirty men made of rushes,[2] called Argei, were thrown from the Sublician bridge by the Vestal virgins, attended by the magistrates and priests, in place of that number of old men, which used anciently to be thrown from the same bridge into the Tiber ;[3] on the same day was the festival of merchants,[4] when they offered up prayers and sacred rites to Mercury ; on the 23d,[5] VULCANALIA, to Vulcan, called *tubilustria*, because then the sacred trumpets were purified.[6]

6. In June, on the kalends, were the festivals of the goddess CARNA,[7] of MARS *extramuraneous*, whose temple was without the porta Capena, and of JUNO *moneta* ; on the 4th, of BELLONA ; on the 7th, *ludi piscatorii* ; the 9th, VESTALIA, to Vesta ; 10th, MATRALIA, to mother Matuta, &c. With the festivals of June, the six books of Ovid, called *Fasti*, end ; the other six are lost.

7. In July, on the kalends, people removed[8] from hired lodgings ; the 4th, the festival of female Fortune, in memory of Coriolanus withdrawing his army from the city ; on the 5th, LUDI APOLLINARES ;[9] the 12th, the birthday of Julius Cæsar ; the 15th or ides, the procession of the equites ;[10] the 16th, DIES ALLIENSIS, on which the Romans were defeated by the Gauls ;[11] the 23d, NEPTUNALIA.

8. In August, on the 13th or ides, the festival of Diana ; 19th, VINALIA, when a libation of new wine was made to Jupiter and Venus ; 18th, CONSUALIA, games in honour of Consus, the god of counsel, or of equestrian Neptune, at which the Sabine women were carried off by the Romans ; the 23d, VULCANALIA.[12]

9. In September, on the 4th,[13] *ludi* MAGNA or ROMANI, in honour of the great gods, Jupiter, Juno, and Minerva, for the safety of the city ; on the 13th, the consul, or dictator,[14] used anciently to fix a nail in the temple of Jupiter ; the 30th, MEDITRINALIA, to Meditrina, the goddess of curing or healing,[15] when they first drank new wine.

10. In October, on the 12th, AUGUSTALIA, vel *ludi Augustales;* the 13th, FAUNALIA ; the 15th, or ides, a horse was sacrificed, called *equus Octobris*, v. -*ber*, because Troy was supposed to have been taken in this month by means of a horse. The tail was brought with great speed to the regia or house of the pontifex maximus, that its blood might drop on the hearth.[16]

11. In November, on the 13th, there was a sacred feast called *epulum Jovis;* on the 27th, sacred rites were performed on account of two Greeks and two Gauls, a man and woman of each, who were buried alive in the ox-market.[17]

12. In December, on the 5th or nones, FAUNALIA ; on the 17th,[18] SATURNALIA, the feasts of Saturn, the most celebrated of the whole year, when all orders were devoted to mirth and feasting, friends sent presents to one another, and masters treated their slaves upon an equal footing, at first for one day, afterwards for three, and, by the order of Caligula and Claudius,[19] for five days. Two days were added, SIGILLARIA,[20] from small images,

---

1 Ov. F. v. 429. 492.
2 simulacra scirpea virorum.
3 Festus in Depontani. Varr. L. L. vii. 3. Ov. F. v. 621.
4 festum mercatorum.
5 x. kal. Jun.
6 ib. 725.
7 quæ vitalibus huma-

nis præerant.
8 commigrabant.
9 Liv. ii. 40. xxv. 12.
xxvii. 23. Cic. Q. Frat. ii. 3. Fam. xiii. 2. Suet. Tib. 35.
10 see p. 18.
11 dies ater et funestus, Cic. Att. ix. 5. Suet. Vit. 2.

12 Plin. xviii. 29. Ep. iii. 5. Liv. i. 9.
13 prid. non.
14 prætor   maximus, Liv. vii. 3.
15 medendi.
16 Fest. Tac. Ann. i. 15.
17 Liv. xxii. 57. Plut. Q. 83. & Marcello. Plin. xxviii. 2. s. 3.

18 xvi. kal. Jan.
19 Dio, lix. 6. lx. 25. Suet. Aug. 75. Vesp.
19. Claud. 17. Macrob. Sat. ii. 10. Stat. Silv. iv. 9. Liv. ii. 21. xxii. 1.
20 a sigillis.

which then used to be sent as presents, especially by parents to their children; on the 23d, LAURENTINALIA, in honour of Laurentia Acca, the wife of Faustulus, and nurse of Romulus.[1]

The FERIÆ CONCEPTIVÆ, which were annually appointed[2] by the magistrates on a certain day, were—

1. FERIÆ LATINÆ, the Latin holidays, first appointed by Tarquin for one day. After the expulsion of the kings they were continued for two, then for three, and at last for four days.[3] The consuls always celebrated the Latin *feriæ* before they set out to their provinces; and if they had not been rightly performed, or if any thing had been omitted, it was necessary that they should be again repeated.[4]

2. PAGANALIA, celebrated in the villages,[5] to the tutelary gods of the rustic tribes.[6]

3. SEMENTIVÆ, in seed time, for a good crop.[7]

4. COMPITALIA, to the Lares, in places where several ways met.[8]

FERIÆ IMPERATIVÆ were holidays appointed occasionally; as, when it was said to have rained stones,*sacrum* NOVENDIALE vel *feriæ per novem dies*, for nine days, for expiating other prodigies,[9] on account of a victory, &c., to which may be added JUSTITIUM,[10] a cessation from business on account of some public calamity, as a dangerous war, the death of an emperor, &c.[11] SUPPLICATIO et LECTISTERNIUM, &c.[12]

Feriæ were privately observed by families and individuals on account of birthdays, prodigies, &c. The birthday of the emperors was celebrated with sacrifices and various games, as that of Augustus the 23d September. The games then celebrated were called AUGUSTALIA,[13] as well as those on the 12th of October,[14] in commemoration of his return to Rome, which Dio says continued to be observed in his time, under Severus.[15]

DIES PROFESTI were either *fasti* or *nefasti*, &c.[16] *Nundinæ*, quasi *novendinæ*,[17] market-days, which happened every ninth day: when they fell on the first day of the year, it was reckoned unlucky, and therefore Augustus, who was very superstitious, used to insert a day in the foregoing year, to prevent it, which day was taken away from the subsequent year, that the time might agree with the arrangement of Julius Cæsar;[18] PRÆLIARES, fighting days, and *non præliares;* as the days after the kalends, nones, and ides; for they believed there was something unlucky in the word post, after, and therefore they were called *dies religiosi, atri,* vel *infausti,* as those days were, on which any remarkable disaster had happened; as *dies Alliensis,* &c.[19] The ides of March, or the 15th, was called PARRICIDIUM; because on that day Cæsar, who had been called PATER PATRIÆ, was slain in the senate-house.[20]

As most of the year was taken up with sacrifices and holidays, to the great loss of the public, Claudius abridged their number.[21]

1 Macrob. ib. Varr. L. v. 3.	7 Varr. ib.	12 see p. 212.	Suet. Aug. 32. Macrob. Sat. i. 13.
2 concipiebantur vel indicebantur.	8 in compitis. 9 Liv. i. 31. iii. 5. xxxv. 40. xlii. 2.	13 Dio, lii. 8. 25. 34. lvi. 29.	19 Ov. F. i. 58. Liv. vi.1. 20 Suet. Cæs. 85. 88. conclave, in qua cæsus fuerat, obstructum et in latrinum conversum. Dio. xlvii. 19.
3 see p. 49. Liv. i. 55. vi. 42.	10 cum jure stant. 11 Liv. iii. 3. 27. iv. 26.	14 iv. Id. Octob. 15 Dio. liv. 10. 34. lvi. 46.	
4 instaurari, Liv. pass.	31. vi. 2. 7. vii. 6. 28.	16 see p. 220.	
5 in pagis.	ix. 7. x. 4. 21. Tac.	17 see p. 59.	
6 see p. 56.	Ann. ii. 32.	18 Dio. xi. 47. xlviii. 33.	21 Dio. lx. 17.

ROMAN GAMES.

GAMES among the ancient Romans constituted a part of religious worship. They were of different kinds at different periods of the republic. At first they were always consecrated to some god ; and were either stated (*ludi* STATI), the chief of which have been already enumerated among the Roman festivals ; or vowed by generals in war (VOTIVI) ; or celebrated on extraordinary occasions (EXTRAORDINARII).

At the end of every 110 years, games were celebrated for the safety of the empire, for three days and three nights, to Apollo and Diana, called *ludi* SÆCULARES.[1] But they were not regularly performed at these periods.

The most famous games were those celebrated in the Circus Maximus ; hence called *ludi Circenses;* of which the chief were *ludi Romani* vel *magni.*[2]

I. LUDI CIRCENSES.

THE Circus Maximus was first built by Tarquinius Priscus, and afterwards at different times magnificently adorned. It lay betwixt the Palatine and Aventine hills, and was of an oblong circular form, whence it had its name. The length of it was three *stadia* (or furlongs) and a half, i. e. 437½ paces, or 2187½ feet; the breadth little more than one *stadium*, with rows of seats all round, called *fori* or *spectacula*,[3] rising one above another, the lowest of stone, and the highest of wood, where separate places were allotted to each curia, and also to the senators and to the equites ; but these last under the republic sat promiscuously with the rest of the people.[4] It is said to have contained at least 150,000 persons, or, according to others, above double that number ; according to Pliny, 250,000.[5] Some moderns say, 380,000. Its circumference was a mile. It was surrounded by a ditch or canal, called *Euripus*, ten feet broad, and ten feet deep ; and with porticoes three stories high,[6] both the work of Julius Cæsar. In different parts there were proper places for the people to go in and out without disturbance. On one end there were several openings,[7] from which the horses and chariots started,[8] called CARCERES vel *repagula*, and sometimes *carcer*,[9] first built, A. U. 425.[10] Before the *carceres* stood two small statues of Mercury,[11] holding a chain or rope to keep in the horses,[12] in place of which there seems sometimes to have been a white line,[13] or a cross furrow filled with chalk or lime, at which the horses were made to stand in a straight row,[14] by persons called MORATORES, mentioned in some ancient inscriptions. But this line, called also CRETA or CALX, seems to have been drawn chiefly to mark the end of the course, or limit of victory,[15] to which Horace beautifully alludes, *mors ultima linea rerum est*, death is the end of all human miseries.[16]

On this end of the circus, which was in the form of a semicircle, were three balconies, or open galleries, one in the middle, and one in each corner ; called MÆNIANA, from one Mænius, who, when he sold his house ad-

---

1 see p. 122.
2 Liv. i. 35.
3 i. e. sedilia unde spectarent.
4 see p. 5.
5 Diony. iii. 68. Plin. xxxvi. 15. s. 24.

6 στοαι τριστεγαι.
7 ostia.
8 emittebantur.
9 quud equos coercebat, ne exirent, priusquam magistratus signum mitteret, Varr. L.

L. iv. 32.
10 Liv. viii. 20.
11 Hermuli.
12 Cassiodor. Var. Ep. iii. 51.
13 alba linea.
14 frontibus æquaban-

tur, ib.
15 ad victoriæ notam, Plin. xxxv. 17. s. 58. Isid. xviii. 37.
16 Ep. i. 16. fin.

joining to the forum, to Cato and Flaccus the censors, reserved to himself
the right of one pillar, where he might build a projection, whence he and
his posterity might view the shows of gladiators, which were then exhibited in the forum.[1]

In the middle of the circus, for almost the whole length of it, there was
a brick wall, about twelve feet broad, and four feet high, called SPINA,[2] at
both the extremities of which there were three columns or pyramids on
one base, called METÆ, or goals, round which the horses and chariots
turned,[3] so that they always had the *spina* and *meta* on their left hand,
contrary to the manner of running among us. Whence *a carceribus ad
metam* vel *calcem*, from the beginning to the end.[4]

In the middle of the spina, Augustus erected an obelisk, 132 feet high,
brought from Egypt ; and at a small distance, another, 88 feet high. Near
the first meta, whence the horses set off, there were seven other pillars,
either of an oval form or having oval spheres on their top, called OVA,
which were raised, or rather taken down, to denote how many rounds the
charioteers had completed, one for each round ; for they usually ran seven
times round the course. Above each of these *ova* was engraved the figure
of a dolphin. These pillars were called FALÆ or PHALÆ. Some think there
were two different kinds of pillars, one with the figure of an *ovum* on the
top, which were erected at the *meta prima*; and another with the figure of
a dolphin, which stood at the *meta ultima*. Juvenal joins them together, *con-
sulit ante falas delphinorumque columnas*, consults before the phalæ and the
pillars of the dolphins.[5] They are said to have been first constructed, A. U.
721, by Agrippa, but *ova ad metes* (al. notas) *curriculis numerandis* are mentioned by Livy long before, A. U. 577, as they are near 600 years after by Cassiodorus.[6] The figure of an egg was chosen in honour of Castor and Pollux,[7]
and of a dolphin in honour of Neptune, also as being the swiftest of animals.[8]

Before the games began, the images of the gods were led along in procession on carriages and in frames,[9] or on men's shoulders, with a great
train of attendants, part on horseback, and part on foot. Next followed the
combatants, dancers, musicians, &c. When the procession was over, the
consuls and priests performed sacred rites.[10]

The shows[11] exhibited in the Circus Maximus were chiefly the following :

1. Chariot and horse-races, of which the Romans were extravagantly fond.

The charioteers[12] were distributed into four parties[13] or factions, from
their different dress or livery ; *factio alba* vel *albata*, the white ; *russata*,
the red ; *veneta*, the sky-coloured or sea-coloured ; and *prasina*, the green
faction ; to which Domitian added two, called the golden and purple
(*factio aurata et purpurea*.)[14] The spectators favoured one or the other
colour, as humour or caprice inclined them. It was not the swiftness of
the horses, nor the art of the men, that attracted them; but merely the
dress.[15] In the time of Justinian, no less than 30,000 men are said to
have lost their lives at Constantinople in a tumult raised by contention
among the partisans of these several colours.[16]

The order in which the chariots or horses stood was determined by lot ;

1 Asc. Cic. Suet. Cal.18.
2 Schol. Juv. vi. 587.
Cassiod. Ep. iii. 51.
3 flectebant.
4 Ov. Am. ii. 65. Luc.
viii. 200. Cic. Am. 27.
Sen. 23.
5 tollebantur, Var. R. l.

2. 11. Juv. vi. 589.
6 iii. Var. Ep. 51. Liv.
xli. 27. Dio. xlix. 43.
7 Dioscuri, i. e. Jove
nati, Cic. Nat. D. iii.
21. agonum præsides.
8 Tertul. Spectac. 8.
Plin. ix. 8.

9 in thensis et ferculla,
Suet. Jul. 76. Ov. Am.
iii. 2. 44. Cic. Verr. 5.
72.
10 Diony. vii. 72.
11 spectacula.
12 axitatores vel aurigæ.
13 greges.

14 Suet. Dom. 7.
15 nunc favent panno,
pannum amant,—now
it is the dress they fa-
vour ; it is the dress
that captivates them,
Plin. Ep. ix. 6.
16 Proc. Bel. Pers.

and the person who presided at the games gave the signal for starting by dropping a napkin or cloth.[1] *   Then the chain of the *Hermuli* being withdrawn, they sprang forward, and whoever first run seven times round the course was victor.[2]   This was called one match,[3] for the matter was almost always determined at one heat ; and usually there were twenty five of these in one day, so that when there were four factions, and one of these started at each time, 100 chariots ran in one day,[4] sometimes many more ; but then the horses commonly went only five times round the course.[5]

The victor, being proclaimed by the voice of a herald, was crowned, and received a prize in money of considerable value.[6]

Palms were first given to the victors at games, after the manner of the Greeks, and those who had received crowns for their bravery in war, first wore them at the games, A. U. 459.[7]   The palm-tree was chosen for this purpose, because it rises against a weight placed on it ;[8] hence it is put for any token or prize of victory, or for victory itself.[9]   *Palma lemniscata*, a palm crown, with ribands[10] hanging down from it ; *huic consilio palma do*, I value myself chiefly on account of this contrivance.[11]

2. Contests of agility and strength, of which there were five kinds : running,[12] leaping,[13] boxing,[14] wrestling,[15] and throwing the *discus* or quoit,[16] (represented in the subjoined cut) ; hence called *pentathlum*,[17] vel *-on*, or *certamen athleticum* vel *gymnicum*, because they contended naked,[18] with nothing on but trowsers or drawers,[19] whence GYMNASIUM, a place of exercise, or a school.   This covering, which went from the waist downwards, and supplied the place of a tunic, was called CAMPESTRE,[20] because

---

* The person at whose expense the games were given, sat over the middle entrance. It was from hence that the signal was made for the chariots to start. At first torches were used ; but afterwards a napkin or cloth was lowered.   It was the business of the consul to make the signal, and in his absence the prætor gave it. In the time of the emperors it was the prætor's office : he let a napkin fall from the balcony ; and it is said, that the custom arose from an order of   Nero, who was dining, and the people became so impatient for the games to begin, that he ordered his own napkin to be thrown down as a signal.   A trumpet also sounded, as at the Olimpic games.

---

1 mappa vel panno misso.
2 Prop. ii. 25, 26   Sen. Ep. 30. Ov. Hal. 68.
3 unus missus, -ûs.
4 Serv. Virg. G. iii. 18. centum quadrijugi.
5 Suet. Claud. 21. Ner. 22. Dom. 4.

6 Suet. Cal. 32.   Virg. Æn. iii. 245. Mart. L. 50. 74. Juv. vii. 113.
7 Liv. x. 47.
8 adversus pondus resurgit, et sursum nititur, Gell. iii. 6. Plin. xvi. 42. s. 81. 13.
9 Hor. Od. l. 1. 5. Juv.

xi. 181. Virg. G. iii. 49.
Ov. Trist. iv. 8. 19.
10 lemnisci.
11 Ter. Heaut. iv. 3. 31. Cic. Rosc. Am. 35.
12 cursus.
13 saltus.
14 pugilatus.
15 lucta.

16 disci jactus.
17 Latine quinquertium, Fest.
18 γυμνοι.
19 subligaribus tantum velati. *
20 Hor. Ep. l. 11. 18. περίζωμα, Paus. l. 44.

it was used in the exercises of the Campus Martius, and those who used it, *Campestrati*. So anciently at the Olympic games.[1]

The *athletæ* were anointed with a glutinous ointment called CEROMA, by slaves called aliptæ; whence *liquida* PALÆSTRA, *uncta* PALÆSTRA, and wore a coarse shaggy garment called ENDRO-MIS, *-idis*,[2] used of finer stuff by women, also by those who played at that kind of hand-ball,[3] called TRIGON or HARPASTUM. The combatants[4] were previously trained in a place of exercise,[5] and restricted to a particular diet. In winter they were exercised in a covered place called XYSTUS, vel *-um*, surrounded with a row of pillars, PERISTY-LIUM.[6] But *xystum* generally signifies a walk under the open air,[7] laid with sand or gravel, and planted with trees, joined to a *gymnasium*.[8]

Boxers covered their hands with a kind of gloves,[9] which had lead or iron sewed into them, to make the strokes fall with a greater weight, called CÆSTUS vel *cestus*.[10] The persons thus exercised were called *palæstritæ*, or *xystici* ; and he who exercised them, EXERCITATOR, *magister* vel *doctor palæstricus, gymnasiarchus*, vel *-a, xystarchus*, vel *-es.* From the attention of Antony to gymnastic exercises at Alexandria, he was called *gymnasiarcha* by Augustus.[11]

PALÆSTRA was properly a school for wrestling,[12] but is put for any place

1 Aug. Civ. Dei, xiv. 17.   3 pila.   Poet. 413. 1 Corinth.   Plin. Ep. ii. 17. ix. 36.
Thucyd. i. 6.   4 athletæ.   ix. 25.   9 chirothecæ.
2 Mart. vii. 31. 9. iv. 4.   5 in palæstro vel gym-   7 ambulatio hypæthra   10 Virg. Æn. v. 379. 400.
19. xi. 48. Juv. vi. 245.   nasio, Plaut. Bacch. iii.   vel subdialis.   11 Plin. xxiii. 7. s. 63.
Cic. i. 9. 35. Ov. Ep.   3. 14.   8 Cic. Att. i. 8. Acad.   Dio. L. 27.
xix. 11. Luc. ix. 661.   6 Vitr. v. 2. Hor. Art.   iv. 3. Suet. Aug. 72.   12 a παλη luctatio.

of exercise, or the exercise itself; hence *palæstram discere*, to learn the exercise; *unctæ dona palæstræ*, exercises.[1] These gymnastic games[2] were very hurtful to morals.

The athletic games among the Greeks were called ISELASTIC,[3] because the victors,[4] drawn by white horses, and wearing crowns on their heads; of olive, if victors at the Olympic games;[5] of laurel, at the Pythian; parsley, at the Nemean; and of pine at the Isthmian; were conducted with great pomp into their respective cities which they entered through a breach in the walls made for that purpose; intimating, as Plutarch observes, that a city which produced such brave citizens had little occasion for the defence of walls. They received for life an annual stipend[6] from the public.[7]

3. LUDUS TROJÆ, a mock fight, performed by young noblemen on horseback, revived by Julius Cæsar, and frequently celebrated by the succeeding emperors,[8] described by Virgil, Æn. v. 561, &c.

4. What was called VENATIO, or the fighting of wild beasts with one another, or with men called *bestiarii*, who were either forced to this by way of punishment, as the primitive Christians often were; or fought voluntarily, either from a natural ferocity of disposition, or induced by hire.[9*] An incredible number of animals of various kinds was brought from all quarters, for the entertainment of the people, and at an immense expense. They were kept in inclosures, called VIVARIA, till the day of exhibition. Pompey, in his second consulship, exhibited at once 500 lions, who were all despatched in five days; also eighteen elephants.[10]

5. The representation of a horse and foot battle, and also of an encampment or a siege.[11]

6. The representation of a sea-fight,[12] which was at first made in the Circus Maximus, but afterwards oftener elsewhere. Augustus dug a lake near the Tiber for that purpose, and Domitian built a naval theatre, which was called *naumachia Domitiani*. Those who fought were called *naumachiarii*. They were usually composed of captives or condemned malefactors, who fought to death, unless saved by the clemency of the emperor.[13†]

---

* It was in the course of the second Punic war that wild beasts were first exhibited at all, as before that time there was a decree of the senate, prohibiting the importation of beasts from Africa. At first they were only shown to the people, and not hunted or killed. The earliest account we have of such an exhibition was U. C. 502, when one hundred and forty-two elephants were produced, which were taken in Sicily. Pliny, who gives us this information, tells us, that he could not ascertain whether they were put to death in the Circus, or merely exhibited there. But these animals had been seen in Rome, twenty-three years before, in the triumph of M. C. Dentatus over Pyrrhus. According to Seneca, Pompey was the first person who gave a combat of elephants. If we may believe Suetonius, Galba introduced them in the games dancing or walking upon ropes. Lions first appeared in any number U. C 652, but these were not turned loose. In the year 661, Sylla brought forward one hundred, when he was prætor, and had some African hunters sent on purpose to shoot them. In the year 696, besides lions, elephants, bears, etc., one hundred and fifty panthers were shown for the first time.

† The *Naumachia* of Augustus was on the other side of the Tiber, and was 1800 feet in length, and 200 in width, so that thirty ships of war could engage in it. Caligula constructed one, as did Domitian and others. That of Domitian was on the site of the present *Piazza di Spagna*. Elagabalus upon one occasion filled the Euripus with wine, and had naval exhibitions performed in it. P. Victor mentions ten *Naumachiæ*.

---

1 Cic. Or. iii. 22. Op. Ep. xix. 11.
2 gymnici agones, Plin. iv. 22.
3 from εισελαυνω, invehor.
4 hieronicæ, Suet. Ner. 24, 25.
5 Virg. G. iii. 18.
6 opsonia.
7 Plin. Ep. x. 119. Vitr. ix. Præf.
8 Dio. xliii. 23. xlviii. 20. li. 22. Suet. 19. Aug. 43. Tib. 6. Cal. 18. Claud. 21. Ner. 7.
9 auctoramento, Cic. Tusc. Quæst. ii. 17. Fam. vii. 1. Off. ii. 16. Vat. 17.
10 Cic. Fam. viii. 2. 4. 6. Dio. xxxix. 38. Plin. viii. 7.
11 Suet. Jul. 39. Claud.
21. Dom. 4.
12 naumachia.
13 Suet. Aug. 43. Claud. 21. Tib. 72. Dom. 5. Dio. ix. 33. Tac. Ann. xii. 56.

If any thing unlucky happened at the games, they were renewed,[1] often more than once.

II. SHOWS OF GLADIATORS.

THE shows[2] of gladiators were properly called *munera*, and the person that exhibited[3] them, *munerarius*, vel *-ator*, *editor* et *dominus* ; who, although in a private station, enjoyed, during the days of the exhibition, the ensigns of magistracy. They seem to have taken their rise from the custom of slaughtering captives at the tombs of those slain in battle to appease their manes.[4]

Gladiators were first publicly exhibited[5] at Rome by two brothers called Bruti at the funeral of their father, A. U. 490,[6] and for some time they were exhibited only on such occasions ; but afterwards also by the magistrates, to entertain the people, chiefly at the Saturnalia and feasts of Minerva. Incredible numbers of men were destoyed in this manner. After the triumph of Trajan over the Dacians, spectacles were exhibited for 123 days, in which 11,000 animals of different kinds were killed, and 10,000 gladiators fought ; whence we may judge of other instances. The emperor Claudius, although naturally of a gentle disposition, is said to have been rendered cruel by often attending the spectacles.[7]

Gladiators were kept and maintained in schools[8] by persons called LANISTÆ, who purchased and trained them. The whole number under one lanista was called FAMILIA. They were plentifully fed on strong food ; hence *sagina gladiatoria*, the gladiator's mess.[9]

A lanistra, when he instructed young gladiators,[10] delivered to them his lessons and rules[11] in writing, and then he was said *commentari*, when he gave over his employment, *a gladiis recessisse*.[12]

The gladiators, when they were exercised, fenced with wooden swords.[13] When a person was confuted by weak arguments, or easily convicted, he was said, *plumbeo gladio jugulari*, to have his throat cut with a sword of lead. *Jugulo hunc suo sibi gladio*, I foil him with his own weapons, I silence him with his own arguments. *O plumbeum pugionem !* O feeble or inconclusive reasoning![14]

Gladiators were at first composed of captives and slaves, or of condemned malefactors. Of these some were said to be *ad gladium damnati*, condemned to the sword, who were to be despatched within a year : this, however, was prohibited by Augustus ;[15] and others, *ad ludum damnati*, condemned to public exhibition, who might be liberated after a certain time. But afterwards also freeborn citizens, induced by hire or by inclination, fought on the arena, some even of noble birth, and what is still more wonderful, women of quality,[16] and dwarfs.[17]

1 instaurabantur, Dio. lvi. 27. lx. 6.
2 spectacula.
3 edebat.
4 Cic Att. ii. 19. Leg. ii. 24. Virg. Æn. x. 518.
5 dati sunt.
6 Liv. Ep. xvi. Val. Max. ii. 4. 7.
7 Dio. xlviii. 15. lx. 14.
8 in ludis.
9 Suet. Jul. 26. Aug. 42. Tac. Hist. ii. 88.,
10 tirones.
11 dictata et leges.

12 Suet. Jul. 26. Juv. xi. 8. Cic. Or. iii. 23. Ros. Am. 40.
13 rudibus batuebant ; whence batualia, a battle, Cic. ib. Suet. Cal. 32. 54.
14 Cic. At. i. 16. Fin. iv. 18. Ter. Adel. v. 8. 34. —At first they were exercised against stakes fastened in the ground (exerceri ad palos) ; afterwards they fought against each other. It was then that their

masters (lanistæ) encouraged them by crying, adtolle, cæde, declina, percute. urge.— Vide de Bello Africano, 71.
15 gladiatores sine missione edi prohibuit, Suet. Aug. 45.
16 Juv. ii. 43. vi. 254. viii. 191. Liv. xxviii. 2. Suet. Ner. 12. Dom. 4. Tac Ann. xv. 32.
17 nani, Stat. Sylv. 1. vi. 57.—When a gladiator had vanquished

his adversary, or received a wound, he was sometimes excused, in compliance with the wish of the people, or of the emperor, or in virtue of his engagement, from continuing the combat, or from fighting again the same day ; but the victor never obtained his discharge, if by his engagement he was bound to combat to the death : in this case he

Freemen who became gladiators for hire were said *esse auctorati*, and their hire, *auctoramentum*, or *gladiatorium*, and an oath was administered to them :[1] *uri, vinciri, verberari, necari.*

Gladiators were distinguished by their armour and manner of fighting. Some were called SECUTORES, whose arms were a helmet, a shield, and a sword, or a leaden bullet.[2] With them were usually matched[3] the RE-TIARII. A combatant of this kind was dressed in a short tunic, but wore nothing on his head.[4] He bore in his left hand a three-pointed lance, called *tridens* or *fuscina*, and in his right a net,[5] with which he attempted to entangle[6] his adversary, by casting it over his head and suddenly drawing it together, and then with his trident he usually slew him. But if he missed his aim, by either throwing the net too short or too far, he instantly betook himself to flight, and endeavoured to prepare his net for a second cast; while his antagonist as swiftly pursued, (whence the name Secutor), to prevent his design by despatching him.

Some gladiators were called MIRMILLONES,[7] because they carried the image of a fish on their helmet ; hence a *retiarius*, when engaged with one of them, said, " I do not aim at you, I throw at your fish." NON TE PETO, PISCEM PETO : QUID ME FUGIS, GALLE ?[8] The *Mirmillo* was armed like a Gaul, with a buckler[9] and a hooked sword or cutlass,[10] and was usually matched with a Thracian.[11] *Quis Myrmilloni componitur æquimanus? Threx.*

Certain gladiators from their armour was called SAMNITES, and also *hoplomachi.* Some *dimachæri*, because they fought with two swords ; and others *laquearii*, because they used a noose to entangle their adversaries.[12]

There was a kind of gladiators who fought from chariots,[13] after the manner of the Britons or Gauls, called ESSEDARII,[14] and also from horseback, with, what was curious, their eyes shut,[15] who were called ANDABATÆ. Hence *andabatarum more pugnare*, to fight in the dark or blindfold.[16]

Gladiators who were substituted[17] in place of those who were conquered or fatigued, were called SUPPOSITITII, or SUBDITITII. Those who were asked by the people, from the emperor, on account of their dexterity and skill in fighting, were called POSTULATITII : such were maintained at the emperor's private charge, and hence called FISCALES or *Cæsariani.* Those who were produced and fought in the ordinary manner were called ORDI-NARII.[18] When a number fought together,[19] and not in pairs, they were called CATERVARII ; those produced at mid-day, who were generally untrained, MERIDIANI.[20]

The person who was to exhibit gladiators[21] some time before announced

---

was under the necessity of continuing his occupation, and often even of fighting the same day against a new opponent. Augustus prohibited this ; but Caracalla compelled the gladiators to submit to it. Hence the expression, gladiatori læso missionem petere, Martial, xii. 29. 7. modo vulneribus tantum, modo sine missione etiam, sometimes permitting the combatants to go no farther than

wounds, at other times to proceed to extremities, Liv. 41. 20. To this practice Seneca makes a beautiful allusion, Ep. 37. Quid prodest, paucos dies aut annos lucri facere ? sine missione nascimur.
1 Pet. Arbiter. 117. Hor. Sat. ii. 7. 5. Suet. Tib. 7. Liv. xliv. 31.
2 massa plumbea, Isid. xviii. 55.
3 committebantur vel componebantur.
4 Suet. Cal. 30. Claud. 34. Juv. viii. 205.

5 rete.
6 irretire.
7 a μορμυρος, piscis.
8 Festus.
9 parma vel pelta.
10 sica vel harpe, i. e. gladio incurvo et felcato.
11 Threx vel Thrax, i. e. Threcidicis armis ornatus, Cic. Phil. vii. 6. Liv. xli. 20. Hor. Sat. ii. 6. 44. Suet.Cal. 32.Juv. viii. 201. Aus. Monos. 102.
12 Isid. xviii. 56. Liv. ix. 40. Cic. Sext. 64. Suet. Cal. 35.

13 ex essedis.
14 Cic. Fam. vii. 6. Suet. Cal. 35. Cæs. B. G. v. 24.
15 clausis oculis.
16 Hieruny. Cic. Fam. vii. 10.
17 supponebantur.
18 Mart. v. 25. 8. Suet. Aug.44. Dom. 4.
19 gregatim, temere, ac sine arte.
20 Suet. Aug. 45. Cal. 30. Claud. 34. Sen. Ep. 7.
21 editor.

the show,[1] by an advertisement or bill pasted up in public,[2] in which he mentioned the number and names of the most distinguished gladiators. Sometimes these things seem to have been represented in a picture.[3]

Gladiators were exhibited sometimes at the funeral pile, often in the forum, which was then adorned with statutes and pictures, but usually in an amphitheatre; so called, because it was seated all around, like two theatres joined.[4]

AMPHITHEATRES were at first temporary, and made of wood. The first durable one of stone was built by Statilius Taurus, at the desire of Augustus, which seems likewise to have been partly of wood. The largest amphitheatre was that begun by Vespasian and completed by Titus, now called COLISÆUM, from the colossus or large statue of Nero which stood near it. It was of an oval form, and is said to have contained 87,000 spectators. Its ruins still remain. The place where the gladiators fought was called ARENA, because it was covered 'with sand or sawdust, to 'prevent the gladiators from sliding, and to absorb the blood; and the persons who fought *arenarii*. But *arena* is also put for the whole amphitheatre, or the show,[5] also for the seat of war,[6] or for one's peculiar province.[7]

PLAN OF THE AMPHITHEATRE AT POMPEII.

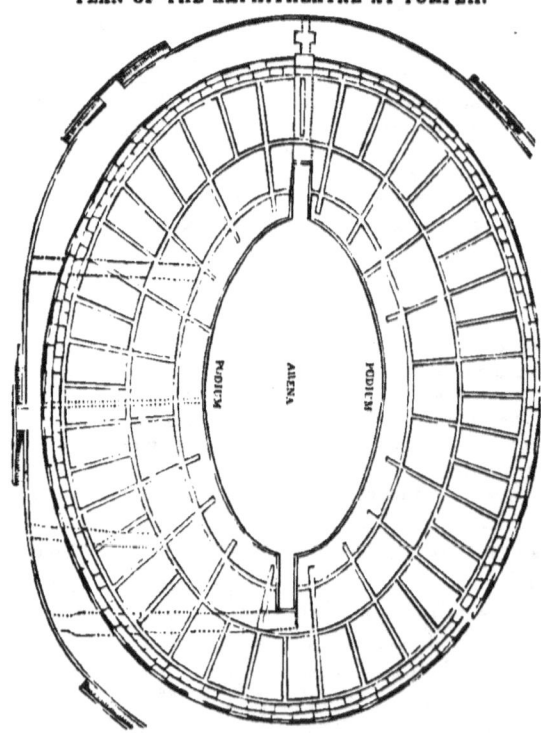

1 munus edicebat, Sen. Ep. 117. ostendebat, pronunciabat, proponebat, &c. Cic. Fam. ii. 8. ix. 8. Suet. Jul. 26.

Tit. 8. 2 per libellum publice affixum. 3 Hor. Sat. ii. 7. 95. Plin. xxxv. 7. s. 33.

4 Cic. Verr. i. 22. Plin. xxxvi. 14 16, &c. 5 Suet. Aug. 29. Juv. iii. 34. 6 prima belli civilis are-

na Italia fuit,—the first field of the civil war was Italy, Flor. iii. 20, 21. iv. 2. Luc. vi. 62. 7 Plin. Ep. vi. 12.

The part next the arena was called PODIUM, where the senators sat, and
the ambassabors of foreign nations ; and where also was the place of the
emperor,[1] elevated like a pulpit or tribunal,[2] and covered with a canopy
like a pavilion ;[3] likewise of a person who exhibited the games,[4] and of
the Vestal virgins.[5]

The *podium* projected over the wall which surrounded the arena, and
was raised between twelve and fifteen feet above it ; secured with a breast-
work or parapet[6] against the irruption of wild beasts. As a further defence, the arena was surrounded with an iron rail,[7] and a canal.[8]

The equites sat in fourteen rows behind the senators. The seats[9] of
both were covered with cushions,[10] first used in the time of Caligula.
The rest of the people sat behind, on the bare stone, and their seats were
called POPULARIA.[11]   The entrances to these seats were called VOMITORIA ;
the passages[12] by which they ascended to the seats were called *scalæ* or
scalaria ; and the seats between two passages were, from their form, called *cuneus,* a wedge : for, like the section of a circle, this space gradually
widened from the arena to the top. Hence, *cuneis innotuit res omnibus,*
the affair was known to all the spectators.[13]

Sometimes a particular place was publicly granted to certain persons
by way of honour, and the *editor* seems to have been allowed to assign a
more honourable seat to any person he inclined.[14]

There were certain persons called DESIGNATORES or *dissignatores,* masters of ceremonies, who assigned to every one his proper place, as undertakers did at funerals ; and when they removed any one from his place,
they were said *eum excitare* vel *suscitare.*[15] The *designatores* are thought
by some to have been the same with what were called LOCARII ;[16] but these
according to others, properly were poor people, who came early and took
possession of a seat, which they afterwards parted with to some rich person who came late, for hire.[17]

Anciently women were not allowed to see the gladiators, without the
permission of those in whose power they were. But afterwards this restriction was removed. Augustus assigned them a particular place in the
highest seats of the amphitheatre.[18]

There were in the amphitheatres secret tubes, from which the spectators were besprinkled with perfumes,[19] issuing from certain figures ;[20] and
in rain or excessive heat there were coverings[21] to draw over them ;[22] for
which purposes there were holes in the top of the outer wall, in which
poles were fixed to support them. But when the wind did not permit
these coverings to be spread, they used broad-brimmed hats or caps,[23] and
umbrellas.[24]

By secret springs, certain wood machines called PEGMATA, vel -*mæ,*
were raised to a great height, to appearance spontaneously, and elevated
or depressed, diminished or enlarged, at pleasure. Gladiators were sometimes set on them, hence called *pegmares,*[25] and sometimes boys.[26] But
pegmata is put by Cicero for the shelves[27] in which books were kept.[28]

1 suggestus, vel -um.
2 Suet. Jul. 76. Plin.
Pan. 51.
3 cubiculum vel papilio,
 Suet. Ner. 12.
4 editoris tribunal.
5 Suet. Aug. 44.
6 lorica.
7 ferreis clathris.
8 euripo, Plin. viii. 7.
9 gradus vel sedilia.
10 pulvillis, Juv. iii. 152.

11 Suet. Clau. 25. Dom.
4. Dio. lix. 7.
12 viæ.
13 Phædr. v. 7. 35. Juv.
vi. 61. Suet. Aug. 44.
14 Cic. Phil. ix. 7. Att.ii.
1.
15 Plaut. Pœn. Prol. 19.
Cic. Att. iv. 3. Hor.
Ep. i. 7. 5. Mart. iii. 95.
v. 14. vi. 9.
16 quia sedes vel spec-
tacula locabant.
17 Mart. v. 25.
18 Val. Max. vi. 3. 12.
Suet. Aug. 44. Ov. A.
ii. 7. 3.
19 croco diluto aut aliis
fragrantibus,liquoribus,
Mart. v. 26. de Spect.
3.
20 signa, Luc. ix. 808.
21 vela vel velaria.
22 Juv. iv. 122.

23 causiæ vel pilei.
24 Dio. lix. 7. Mart. xiv.
27, 29.
25 Mart. Spect. ii. 16.
viii. 33. Sen. Ep. 88.
Suet. Claud. 34. Cal.26.
26 et pueros inde ad ve-
laria raptos,—and boys
snatched up to the co-
verings, Juv. iv. 122.
27 pro loculis.
28 Att. iv. 8.

Nigh to the amphitheatre was a place called SPOLIARIUM, to which those who were killed or mortally wounded were dragged by a hook.[1]

On the day of the exhibition the gladiators were led along the arena in procession. Then they were matched by pairs,[2] and their swords examined[3] by the exhibiter of the games.[4]

The gladiators, as a prelude to the battle,[5] at first fought with wooden swords or the like, flourishing[6] their arms with great dexterity.[7] Then upon a signal given with a trumpet,[8] they laid aside these,[9] and assumed their proper arms.[10] They adjusted themselves[11] with great care, and stood in a particular posture.[12] Hence *moveri, dejici, vel deturbari de statu mentis : depelli, dejici, vel demoveri gradu,* &c.[13] Then they pushed at one another,[14] and repeated the thrust.[15] They not only pushed with the point,[16] but also struck with the edge.[17] It was more easy to parry or avoid[18] direct thrusts,[19] than back or side strokes.[20] They therefore took particular care to defend their side ;[21] hence *latere tecto abscedere,* to get off safe ; *per alterius latus peti, latus apertum* vel *nudum dare,* to expose one's self to danger. Some gladiators had the faculty of not winking. Two such, belonging to the emperor Claudius, were on that account invincible.[22]

The rewards given to the victors were a palm (hence *plurimarum palmarum gladiator,* who had frequently conquered ; *alias suas palmas cognoscet, i. e. cædes ;*[23] *palma lemniscata,* a palm crown, with ribands[24] of dif-

---

THE annexed cut represents two armed gladiators, from a painting at Pompeii.—The first wears a helmet having a vizor, much ornamented, with the long buckler (scutum). It is persumed that he should have for offensive weapon a sword, but the sculptor has neglected to represent it. Like all the other gladiators he wears the *subligaculum,* a short apron of red or white stuff fixed above the hips by a girdle of bronze or embroidered leather. On the right leg is a kind of buskin, commonly made of coloured leather, on the left an ocrea or greave, not reaching

to the knee. The left leg is thus armed, because that side of the body was the most exposed by the ancients, whose guard on account of the buckler, was the reverse of the modern guard ; the rest of the body is entirely naked. The other figure is armed with a helmet ornamented with wings, a smaller buckler, thighpieces formed of plates of iron, and on each leg the high greave, called by the Greeks κνημίς. These figures appear to represent one of the light-armed class, called Veles, and a Samnite (Samnis,) so called because they were armed after

the old Samnite fashion. The former, who has been sixteen times a conqueror in various games, has at last encountered a more fortunate, or a more skilful adversary. He is wounded in the breast, and has let fall his buckler, avowing himself conquered ; at the same time he implores the pity of the people by raising his finger towards them— for it was thus that the gladiators begged their life. Behind him the Samnite awaits the answering sign from the spectators, that he may spare his antagonist, or strike the deathblow, as they decree.

---

1 unco trahebantur, Plin. Pan. 36. Sen. Ep. 93. Lampr. Commod. fin.
2 paria inter se componebantur, vel comparabantur, Hor. Sat. l. vii. 20.
3 explorabantur.
4 Suet. Tit. 9.
5 præludentes vel proludentes.
6 ventilantes.
7 Cic. Or. ii. 78. Sen. Ep. 117. Ov. Art. Am. iii.

515. 589.
8 sonebant ferali clangore tuba.
9 arma lusoria, rudes vel gladios habetes ponebant, v. abjiciebant.
10 arma pugnatoria vel decretoria, i. e. gladios acutos sumebant, Quin. x. 5. 20. Suet. Cal. 54. 11 se ad pugnam componebant, Gell. vii. 3. 12 in statu vel gradu stabant, Plaut. Mil. iv.

9. 13.
13 Cic. Off. i. 23. Att. xvi. 15. Hep. Them. 5. Liv. vi. 32.
14 petebant.
15 repetebant, Suet. Cal. 58.
16 punctim.
17 cæsim.
18 cavere, propulsare, exire, effugere, excedere, eludere.
19 ictus adversos, et rectas ac simplices manus.

20 manus vel petitiones aversus testasque, Quin. v. 13. 54. ix. 1. 20. Virg. ix. 439. Cic. Cat. i. 6.
21 latus tegere.
22 Ter. Heaut. iv. 2. 5. Cic. Vat. 5. Tibull. l. 4. 46. Plin. xi. 37. s. 54. Sen. Ir. ii. 4.
23 Mart. Spect. 32. Cic. Rosc. Am. 6. 30.
24 lemnisci.

ferent colours hanging from it ;[1] *sexta palma urbana etiam in gladiatore
difficilis*), money,[2] and a rod or wooden sword,[3] as a sign of their being
discharged from fighting ; which was granted by the *editor*, at the desire of
the people, to an old gladiator, or even to a novice, for some uncommon
act of courage.   Those who receive it[4] were called RUDIARII, and fixed
their arms in the temple of Hercules.[5]   But they sometimes were afterwards induced by a great hire[6] again to engage.   Those who were dismissed on account of age or weakness, were said *delusisse*.[7]

When any gladiator was wounded, the people exclaimed, HABET, sc.
vulnus, vel *hoc habet*, he has got it.   The gladiator lowered[8] his arms as a
sign of his being vanquished : but his fate depended on the pleasure of the
people, who, if they wished him to be saved, pressed down their thumbs ;[9]

if to be slain, they turned up their thumbs,[10] and ordered him to receive the
sword,[11] which gladiators usually submitted to with amazing fortitude.
Sometimes a gladiator was rescued by the entrance of the emperor,[12] or by
the will of the *editor*.

The spectators expressed the same eagerness by betting[13] on the different gladiators, as in the circus.[14]

Till the year 693, the people used to remain all day at an exhibition of
gladiators without intermission till it was finished ; but then for the first
time they were dismissed to take dinner, which custom was afterwards observed at all the spectacles exhibited by the emperors.   Horace calls inter-
missions given to gladiators in the time of fighting, or a delay of the combat, DILUDIA, *-orum*.[15]

Shows of gladiators[16] were prohibited by Constantine, but not entirely
suppressed till the time of Honorius.[17]

III. DRAMATIC ENTERTAINMENTS.

DRAMATIC entertainments, or stage plays,[18] were first introduced at
Rome, on account of a pestilence, to appease the divine wrath, A. U. 391.[19]
Before that time there had only been the games of the circus.   They were
called LUDI SCENICI, because they were first acted in a shade,[20] formed by

1 Ib. 35. Festus.
2 Cic. Phil. xi. 5. Juv.
   vii. ult. Suet. Clau. 21.
3 rudis.
4 rude donati.
5 Hor. Ep. i. 1. Ov. Trist.
   iv. 8. 24.
6 ingente auctoramen-
   to.
7 Suet. Tib. vii. Plin.

xxxvi. 27.
8 submittebat.
9 pollicem premebant,
   Hor. Ep. i. 18. 66.
10 pollicem vertebant,
   Juv. iii. 36. hence lau-
   dare utroque pollice, i.
   e. valde, to applaud
   greatly, Hor. Ep. i. 18.
   66. Plin. 28: 2. s. 5.

11 ferrum recipere.
12 Ov. Pont. ii. 8. 53.
   Cic. Sext. 37. Tusc. ii.
17. Mil. 34. Sen. Ep. 7.
177. Tranquil. Animi,
   c. 11. Const. Sap. 16.
13 sponsionibus.
14 Suet. Tit. 8. Dom.
10. Mart. ix. 68.
15 Ep. i. 19. 47. Schol.

in loc. Dio. xxxvii. 46.
   Suet.
16 cruenta spectacula.
17 Const. Cod. xi. 43.
   Prudent. contraSymm.
   ii. 11. 21.
18 ludi scenici.
19 Liv. vii. 2.
20 σκια, umbra.

the branches and leaves of trees,[1] or in a tent.[2]   Hence afterwards the front of the theatre, where the actors stood, was called SCENA, and the actors SCENICI, or SCENICI ARTIFICES.[3]

Stage-plays were borrowed from Etruria ; whence players[4] were called HISTRIONES, from a Tuscan word *hister*, i. e. *ludio* ; for players also were sent for from that country.[5]   These Tuscans did nothing at first but dance to a flute,[6] without any verse or corresponding action.   They did not speak, because the Romans did not understand their language.[7]

The Roman youth began to imitate them at solemn festivals, especially at harvest home, throwing out raillery against one another in unpolished verse, with gestures adapted to the sense.   These verses were called VERSUS FESCENNINI, from Fescennia, or -ium, a city of Etruria.[8]

Afterwards, by frequent use, the entertainment was improved,[9] and a new kind of dramatic composition was contrived, called SATYRÆ or SATURÆ, *satires*, because they were filled with various matter, and written in various kinds of verse, in allusion to what was called LANX SATURA, a platter or charger filled with various kinds of fruits, which they yearly offered to the gods at their festivals, as the *primitiæ*, or first gatherings of the season. Some derive the name from the petulance of the Satyrs.

These satires were set to music, and repeated with suitable gestures, accompanied with the flute and dancing.   They had every thing that was agreeable in the Fescennine verses, without their obscenity.   They contained much ridicule and smart repartee ; whence those poems afterwards written to expose vice got the name of satires ; as, the satires of Horace, of Juvenal, and Persius.

It was LIVIUS ANDRONICUS, the freedman of M. Livius Salinator, and the preceptor of his sons, who giving up satires,[10] first ventured to write a regular play,[11] A. U. 512, some say, 514 ; the year before Ennius was born, above 160 years after the death of Sophocles and Euripides, and about fifty-two years after that of Menander.[12]   He was the actor of his own compositions, as all then were.   Being obliged by the audience frequently to repeat the same part, and thus becoming hoarse,[13] he asked permission to employ a boy to sing to the flute, whilst he acted what was sung,[14] which he did with the greater animation, as he was not hindered by using his voice.   Hence actors used always to have a person at hand to sing to them, and the colloquial part[15] only was left them to repeat.   It appears there was commonly a song at the end of every act.[16]

Plays were afterwards greatly improved at Rome from the model of the Greeks, by NÆVIUS, ENNIUS, PLAUTUS, CÆCILIUS, TERENCE, AFRANIUS, PACUVIUS, ACCIUS, &c.

After playing was gradually converted into an art,[17] the Roman youth, leaving regular plays to be acted by professed players, reserved to themselves the acting of ludicrous pieces or farces, interlarded with much ribaldry and buffoonery, called EXODIA, because they were usually introduced after the play, when the players and musicians had left the stage, to remove the painful impressions of tragic scenes, or FABELLÆ ATELLANÆ,

1 Ov. Art. Am. i. 105.
  Serv. Virg. Æn. i. 164.
2 σκηνη, tabernaculum.
3 Suet. Tib. 34. Cæs. 84.
  Cic. Planc. 11. Ver. iii.
  79.
4 ludiones.

5 Liv. vii. 2.
6 ad tibicinis modos.
7 ibid.
8 Hor. Ep. II. i. 145.
9 sæpius usurpando res
  excitata est.
10 ub saturis, i. e. satu-

ris relictis.
11 argumento fabulam
  serere.
12 Cic. Brut. 18. Gell.
  xvii. 21.
13 quum vocem obtu-
  disset.

14 canticum agebat.
15 diverbia.
16 Liv. vii. 2.' Plaut.
  Pseud. ii. ult.
17 ludus in artem paula-
  tim verterat.

or LUDI OSCI, LUDICRUM OSCUM,[1] from Atella, a town of the Osci in Campania, where they were first invented and very much used.

The actors of these farces[2] retained the rights of citizens,[3] and might serve in the army, which was not the case with common actors, who were not respected among the Romans as among the Greeks, but were held infamous.[4]

Dramatic entertainments, in their improved state, were chiefly of three kinds, comedy, tragedy, and pantomimes.

I. Comedy[5] was a representation of common life,[6] written in a familiar style, and usually with a happy issue. The design of it was to expose vice and folly to ridicule.

Comedy, among the Greeks, was divided into old, middle, and new. In the first, real characters and names were represented; in the second, real characters, but fictitious names; and in the third, both fictitious characters and names. Eupolis, Cratinus, and Aristophanes excelled in the old comedy, and Menander in the new.[7] Nothing was ever known at Rome but the new comedy.

The Roman comic writers, Nævius, Afranius, Plautus, Cæcilius, and Terence, copied from the Greek, chiefly from MENANDER, who is esteemed the best writer of comedies that ever existed;[8] but only a few fragments of his works now remain. We may, however, judge of his excellence from Terence, his principal imitator.

Comedies, among the Romans, were distinguished by the character and dress of the persons introduced on the stage. Thus comedies were called TOGATÆ, in which the characters and dress were Roman, from the Roman toga, so *carmen togatum*, a poem about Roman affairs. PRÆTEXTATÆ, vel *prætextæ*, when magistrates and persons of dignity were introduced; but some take these for tragedies;[9] TRABEATÆ, when generals and officers were introduced; TABERNARIÆ, when the characters were of low rank; PALLIATÆ, when the characters were Grecian, from *pallium*, the robe of the Greeks; MOTORIÆ, when there were a great many striking incidents, much action, and passionate expressions; STATARIÆ, when there was not much bustle to stir, and little or nothing to agitate the passions; and MIX-

1 Tac. Ann. iv. 14. Liv. vii. 2. Cic. Fam. vii. 1. Schol. Juv. iii. 175. vi. 71. Suet. Tib. 45. Dom. 10.
2 atellani vel atellanarum actores.
3 non tribu moti sunt.
4 Ulp. 1, 2. s. 5. D. de his qui not. infam.—Nep. Præf. Suet. Tib. 35.—In the time of Cicero, actors were ranked among the lowest classes of the people. Those who performed the Comœdiæ Atellanæ (a national spectacle) were alone classed as citizens in the tribes of Rome. No other actor was ever permitted to serve, even as a common soldier. We see, from several passages of Plautus, that actors were whipt with rods as other slaves, Cistell. act. 5. Caterva. Under Augustus, a de-

cree of the senate prohibited the equites and the senators from appearing on the stage, Suet. Aug. 45: and, even under the immoral government of Tiberius, the senators were prohibited from witnessing the performances of the pantomimes, and the equites from accompanying them on the streets, Suet. Tib. Tac. Ann. i. 1. We should deceive ourselves then, were we to regard as honour rendered to a degraded profession the marks of esteem bestowed on some comedians on account of their merit. These exceptions, few in number, had reference only to individuals. What Cicero says, in two of his orations in honour of the comedian Roscius,

proves only that the Roman people knew how to render justice to merit even on the stage, Cic. Rosc. Com. l. c. 6. We know with what familiarity Pylades the pantomime spoke to Augustus. Some instances prove also the influence which the theatre exercised over the Romans : at the time of the banishment of Cicero, a comedian thought himself authorised to represent to the Roman people their ingratitude and their inconstancy ; the people suffered the reprimand. The actor, emboldened by the patience of the people, sought to awaken their feelings, and the tears flowed. In the tragedy of Brutus, Cicero was proclaimed

by name the saviour of the commonwealth, and a thousand voices repeated the homage, (Sext. 56) while the malevolence of his enemies, who were present and still in power, durst not manifest itself in opposition to their acclamations of gratitude.—See Meicrotto, on the Manners and Life of the Romans, &c. Part. I. p. 122.
5 comœdia, quasi κωμης ωδη, the song of the village.
6 quotidianæ vitæ speculum.
7 Hor. Sat. i. 4. Ep. ii. 1. 57. Quin. x. 1.
8 Quin. x. 1.
9 Juv. i. 3. Hor. A. P. 281. Stat. Silv. ii. 7. 53.

TÆ, when some parts were gentle and quiet, and others the contrary.[1] The representations of the *atellani* were called *comœdia atellanœ*.

The actors of comedy wore a low-heeled shoe, called *soccus*.

Those who wrote a play, were said *docere* vel *facere fabulam*; if it was approved, it was said *stare, stare recto talo, placere*, &c. if not, *cadere, exigi, exsibilari*, &c.

II. TRAGEDY is the representation of some one serious and important action, in which illustrious persons are introduced, as, heroes, kings, &c. written in an elevated style, and generally with an unhappy issue. The great end of tragedy was to excite the passions, chiefly pity and horror; to inspire the love of virtue, and an abhorrence of vice. It had its name, according to Horace, from τραγος, a goat, ωδη, a song; because a goat was the prize of the person who produced the best poem, or was the best actor,[2] to which Virgil alludes, Ecl. iii. 22; according to others, because such a poem was acted at the festival of Bacchus after vintage, to whom a goat was then sacrificed, as being the destroyer of the vines; and therefore it was called τραγωδια, the goat's song. *Primi ludi theatrales ex liberalibus nati sunt*, from the feasts of Bacchus.[3]

THESPIS, a native of Attica, is said to have been the inventor of tragedy, about 536 years before Christ. He went about with his actors from village to village in a cart, on which a temporary stage was erected, where they played and sung, having their faces besmeared with the lees of wine,[4] whence according to some, the name of tragedy, (from τρυξ, -υγος, new wine not refined, or the lees of wine, and ωδος, a singer; hence τρυγωδης, a singer thus besmeared, who threw out scoffs and raillery against people.)

Thespis was contemporary with Solon, who was a great enemy to his dramatic representations.[5]

Thespis was succeeded by Æschylus, who erected a permanent stage,[6] and was the inventor of the mask,[7] of the long flowing robe,[8] and of the

MASKS.

CLEMENS Alexandrinus informs us, that masks were mentioned in the poems of Orpheus and Linus, whence we may judge of their antiquity. On the other hand it is certain, that theatrical masks only came into use in the time of Æschylus; that is, about the 70th Olympiad, and consequently above seven or eight hundred years later. The first masks of which Clemens Alexandrinus speaks, were not different from those we now use; whereas the masks for the theatre were a sort of head-

---

1 Suet. Gram. 21. Hor. A. P. 225. Ter. Heaut. prol. 26. Don. Ter. Cic. Brut. 116. 2 Cic. Or. i. 51. Hor. A. P. 220. 3 Serv. Virg. G. ii. 381. 4 peruncti læcibus ora, Hor. de Art. Poet. 275. 5 Plut. in Solone. 6 modicis instravit pulpita tignis. 7 persona. 8 palla, stola, vel syrma.

high-heeled shoe or buskin,[1] which tragedians wore : whence these words are put for a tragic style, or for tragedy itself, as *soccus* is put for a comedy or a familiar style. *Nec comœdia in cothurnos assurgit, nec contra tragœdia socco ingreditur*, comedy does not strut in buskins, neither does tragedy trip along in slippers.[2]

pieces that covered the whole head, and represented not only the features of a face, but the beard, ears, hair, and even all the ornaments in a woman's head-dress. At least this is the account we have of them from Festus, Pollux, Aulus Gellius, and all the authors who mention them. This is likewise the idea Phædrus gives of them in his Fable of the Mask and the Fox. And it is moreover a fact which an infinity of bas-reliefs and engraved stones put beyond all doubt.

We must not, however, imagine, that the theatrical masks had always the same form ; for it is certain they were very gradually brought to this perfection. All writers agree, that at first they were very imperfect. At first the actors only disguised themselves by bedaubing their faces with the lees of wine ; and it was in that manner the pieces of Thespis were acted. —Qui canerent agerentve peruncti fæcibus ora.—Who played and sung their pieces, having their faces stained with lees of wine.—Hor. Art. Poet. 277.

They continued afterwards to make a sort of masks with the leaves of the arcion, a plant which the Greeks called for that reason προσωπιον ; and it was likewise called sometimes among the Latins, personata, as appears from this passage in Pliny,—quidam arcion personatam vocant, cujus folio nullum est latius.

In fine, after dramatic poetry was become complete in all its parts, the necessity the actors found of imagining some way of changing their figure and mien in an instant, in order to represent personages of different ages and characters, put them on contriving the masks we are now speaking of. But it is not easy to trace them to their first inventor ; for authors are divided into various opinions on that head. Suidas and Athenæus

give the honour of the invention to the poet Chœrilus, contemporary with Thespis. Horace, on the other hand, gives it to Æschylus.—Post hunc personæ pallæque repertor honestæ Æschylus.—Æschylus, the inventor of the mask and decent robe.—Hor. Art. Poet. 278. And Aristotle, who in all probability must have been better instructed in this matter, tells us in the 5th chapter of his poetics, that it was unknown in his time to whom the glory of the invention was due.

But though we cannot precisely determine by whom this kind of masks was invented, yet the names of those are preserved to us who first introduced any particular kind of them upon the theatre. Suidas, for instance, informs us, it was the poet Phrynicus who first brought a female mask into use : and Neophron of Sicyon first introduced one for that kind of domestic among the ancients, who was charged with the care of their children, from whose appellation we have the word pedagogue. Athenæus relates, that it was Æschylus who first dared to bring upon the stage drunken personages in his Καβειροι : and that it was an actor of Megara, called Maison, who invented the comic masks for a valet and a cook. We read in Pausanius, that Æschylus introduced the use of hideous frightful masks in his Eumenides : but that it was Euripides who first adventured to add serpents to them.

Masks were not always made of the same materials. The first were of the bark of trees.—Oraque corticibus sumunt horrenda cavatis.—And put on horrid masks made of barks of trees.—Virg. Geo. 1. 2. 387.

We learn from Pollux, that afterwards some were made of leather lined with linen or some stuff. But these masks being easily spoiled, they came at last, according to He-

sychius, to make them wholly of wood. And they were formed by sculptors according to the ideas of the poets, as we may see from the Fable of Phædrus we 'have' already quoted.

Though Pollux enters into a very long detail of the theatrical masks, yet he only distinguishes three sorts ; the comic, tragic, and satiric ; and in his description he gives to each kind as much deformity as it was possibly susceptible of ; that is, features carricatured to the most extravagant pitch of fancy, a hideous absurd air, and a wide extended mouth, ever open to devour the spectators, so to speak.

But there being upon an infinity of ancient monuments, masks of a quite opposite form and character, that is to say, which have natural and agreeable faces, and nothing like that large gaping mouth which renders others so frightful ; I was long at a loss to what class I should refer them ; and I have consulted the most learned in these matters for my information to no purpose ; they are so divided on this subject, that I have not been able to draw any satisfaction from them about it.

But if we reflect on the one hand, that some authors speak of a fourth sort of masks not mentioned by Pollux, I mean those of the dancers ; and if we consider on the other hand, that in such masks there was no occasion for that large ouverture which rendered the others so deformed, and which was certainly not given to them by the ancients, without some very necessary reason, I am apt to think the masks in question were of this fourth kind ; and the more I have considered them, the more I am confirmed in this opinion. As probable however as it appeared to me, it was but a conjecture, and some positive authority was wanting, before it could be laid down as truth : and this is what I have at last

As the ancients did not wear breeches, the players always wore under the tunics a girdle or covering.[1]

After Æschylus, followed SOPHOCLES and EURIPIDES, who brought tragedy to the highest perfection. In their time comedy began first to be considered as a distinct composition from tragedy; but at Rome comedy

found in a passage of Lucian, which leaves no room for further scepticism on the subject.

It is in his dialogue upon dancing, where after having spoken of the ugliness of other masks, and of that wide mouth in particular common to them all, he tells us that those of the dancers were of a quite different make, and had none of these deformities. "With regard," saith he, "to the equipage of the dancers, it is needless to go about to prove its aptitude and conveniency; that one must be blind not to allow. As for their masks nothing can be more agreeable, they have not that wide hideous mouth of the others; but are perfectly natural, and correspondent to their use."

It is therefore unquestionably to this class that we must refer the masks now under our consideration. And we can no longer doubt, that there was besides the three kinds mentioned by Pollux, a fourth, which they called Orchestric, and sometimes mute masks, ορχηστρικα και αφωνα προσωπεια.

But this is not the only omission Pollux may be reproached with on the subject of masks. Even of those which he mentions, there are three sorts he hath not distinguished, which had, however, their different denominations, προσωπειον, μορμολυκειον, γοργονειον. For though those names were in process of time used promiscuously, to signify all sorts of masks, yet it is probable that the Greeks first employed them to distinguish three different kinds: and we find in fact in their pieces three sorts, the different forms and characters of which, answer exactly to the different meanings of these three terms.

The first and more common sort were those which represented real life, and they were properly denominated προσωπειον. The two other sorts were not so common; and hence it was that the term προσωπειοι being more used, became the general name for

them all. One sort represented the shades, and being frequently employed in tragedy, and having something frightful in their appearance, the Greeks called them μορμόλυκειον. The last kind were contrived on purpose to terrify, and only represented horrible figures, such as Gorgons and Furies, whence they had the name of γοργονειον.

It is possible that these terms did not loose their original signification till the masks had entirely changed their first form; that is, in the time of the new comedy: for till then there was a sensible difference amongst them. But at last the several kinds were confounded: the comic and tragic only differed in size and in ugliness, and the dancers' masks alone preserved their first appearance.

Pollux not only tells us in general, that the comic masks were ridiculous, but we learn from the detail of them he has left us, that the greater part of them were extravagant to absurdity. There was hardly any of them which had not distorted eyes, a wry mouth, hanging cheeks, or some such other deformity.

With respect to the tragic masks they were yet more hideous; for over and above their enormous size, and that gaping mouth which threatened to devour the spectators, they generally had a furious air, a threatening aspect, the hair standing upright, and a kind of tumour on the forehead, which only served to disfigure them, and render them yet more terrible.

Thus, in a letter to Zena and Serenus, falsely ascribed to Justin Martyr, but very ancient, we have the following passage:—"In like manner as he who roars out with all his strength in representing Orestes, appears huge and terrible to the gaping spectators, because of his buskins with their high heels, his false belly, his long training robe, and his frightful mask."

And in the work of Lucian already quoted, we meet with this description of a tragedian:—"Can any thing be more shocking or frightful? a man of huge stature, mounted upon high heels, and carrying on his head an enormous mask, the very sight of which fills with dread and horror; for it gapes as if it were to swallow the spectators."

In fine, the satiric sort was the absurdest of them all, and having no other foundation but in the caprice of poets, there were no imaginable odd figures which these masks did not exhibit; for besides fawns and satyrs, whence they had their names, some of them represented Cyclopes, Centaurs, &c. In one word, there is no monster in fable which was not exhibited in some of these pieces by proper masks. And therefore we may say, it was the kind of dramatic entertainments in which the use of masks was most necessary.

Not but that they were indispensably so in tragedy likewise, to give the heroes and demigods that air of grandeur and majesty they were supposed to have really had. For it is no matter whence that prejudice came; or whether they were really of a supernatural size: it was sufficient that this was the received opinion, and that the people believed it, to make it necessary to represent them as such; they could not have been otherwise exhibited without transgressing against probability; and by consequence, it was impossible to bring them on the stage without the assistance of masks.

But what rendered it impossible for the actors to perform their parts without them, was their being obliged to represent personages not only of different kinds and characters, but likewise of different ages and sexes; I say different sexes, for it must be remembered there were no actresses among the ancients; the fewas long cultivated, before any attempt was made to compose tragedies. Nor have we any Roman tragedies extant, except a few, which bear the name of Seneca. Nothing remains of the works of Ennius, Pacuvius, Accius, &c. but a few fragments.

Every regular play, at least among the Romans, was divided into five acts ;[1] the subdivision into scenes is thought to be a modern invention.

Between the acts of a tragedy were introduced a number of singers, called the CHORUS, who indeed appear to have been always present on the stage. The chief of them, who spoke for the rest, was called *choragus* or *coryphæus.* But CHORAGUS is usually put for the person who furnished the dresses, and took care of all the apparatus of the stage,[2] and *choragium* for the apparatus itself,[3] *choragia* for *choragi ;* hence *falsæ choragium gloriæ,* something that one may boast of.[4]

The chorus was introduced in the ancient comedy, as we see from Aristophanes ; but when its excessive licence was suppressed by law, the chorus likewise was silenced. In Plautus a choragus appears and makes a speech.[5]

The music chiefly used was that of the flute, which at first was small and simple, and of few holes ;[6] but afterwards it was bound with brass, had more notes, and a louder sound.

Some flutes were double, and of various forms. Those most frequently mentioned are the *tibiæ dextræ* and *sinistræ, pares* and *impares,* which have occasioned so much disputation among critics, and still appear not to be sufficiently ascertained. The most probable opinion is, that the double flute consisted of two tubes, which were so joined together as to have but one mouth, and so were both blown at once. That which the musician played on with his right hand was called *tibia dextra,* the right-handed flute ; with his left, *tibia sinistra,*

male characters in their pieces were acted by men.

From what hath been said, it results, that three things made the use of masks absolutely necessary on the theatre. First, the want of actresses to act the parts of women. Secondly, that extraordinary size of which tragic personages were in possession. And thirdly, the very nature and genius of the satyric kind.

But, besides the indispensable necessity of each of those sorts of masks in particular ; there were some general advantages which accrued from

them, all of no small consideration. For first, as every piece had its own mask proper to it, and therefore the same actor could, by changing his mask, act several parts in the same piece, without being perceived to do so. The spectators, by this means, were not cloyed with always seeing the same faces, and the actors were, so to speak, multiplied to all the necessary variety, at a very easy rate.

And as they used them likewise to represent the faces of the persons intended to be represented, it was a method of

rendering the representation more natural than it could otherwise have been, especially in pieces where the intrigue turned upon a perfect resemblance of faces, as in the Amphitryon and the Menechmi. It was with the faces of the actors then as it is now with respect to the ornaments in our scenes, which must be magnified to have their due effect at a certain distance.—Boindin's Discourse on Masks, delivered to the Academy of Inscriptions and Belles Lettres, July 1st, 1712.

1 Hor. Art. Poet. 189.　Art. Poet. 193.　15.　Plaut. Curc. iv. 1.
2 Plaut. Pers. i. 3. 79. 3 instrumentum scena- 4 Vitr. v. 9. Cic. Herr. 6 Hor. A. P. 202.
Trinumm. iv. 2. 16. rum, Fest. Plaut. Cap. iv. 50.
Suet. Aug. 70. Hor. prol. 61. Plin. xxxvi. 5 Hor. Art. Poet. 283.

the left-handed flute. The latter had but few holes, and sounded a deep serious bass; the other had more holes, and a sharper and more lively tone.[1] When two right or two left-handed flutes were joined together, they were called *tibiæ pares dextræ*, or *tibiæ pares sinistræ*. The flutes of different sorts were called *tibiæ impares*, or *tibiæ dextræ et sinistræ*. The right-handed flutes were the same with what were called the Lydian flutes,[2] and the left-handed with the Tyrian flutes.[3] Hence Virgil, *biforem dat tibia cantum*, i. e. *bisonum, imparem*, Æn. ix. 618. Sometimes the flute was crooked, and is then called *tibia Phrygia* or *cornu*.[4]

III. PANTOMIMES were representations by dumb-show, in which the actors, who were called by the same name with their performances (*mimi vel pantomimi,*) expressed every thing by their dancing and gestures without speaking;[5] hence called also *chironomi*.[6] But *pantomimi* is always put for the actors, who were likewise called *planipedes*, because they were without shoes.[7] They wore, however, a kind of wooden or iron sandals, called SCABILLA or *scabella*, which made a rattling noise when they danced.[8]

The pantomimes are said to have been the invention of Augustus; for before his time the *mimi* both spoke and acted.

MIMUS is put both for the actor and for what he acted, not only on the stage, but elsewhere.[9]

The most celebrated composers of mimical performances or farces[10] were Laberius and Publius Syrus, in the time of Julius Cæsar. The most famous pantomimes under Augustus were Pylades and Bathyllus, the favourite of Mæcenas.[11] He is called by the scholiast on Persius, v. 123, his freedman;[12] and by Juvenal, *mollis*, vi. 63. Between them there was a constant emulation. Pylades being once reproved by Augustus on this account, replied, "It is expedient for you, that the attention of the people should be engaged about us." Pylades was the great favourite of the public. He was once banished by the power of the opposite party, but soon afterwards restored. The factions of the different players sometimes carried their discords to such a length, that they terminated in bloodshed.[13]

The Romans had rope-dancers,[14] who used to be introduced in the time of the play,[15] and persons who seemed to fly in the air,[16] who darted[17] their bodies from a machine called *petaurum*, vel *-us*; also interludes or musical

---

1 Plin. xvi. 36. s. 66. Varr. R. R. 1, 2. 15.

2 tibiæ Lydiæ.

3 tibiæ Tyriæ vel Sarranæ, vel Serranæ.

4 Virg. Æn. vii. 737. Ov. Met. iii. 532. Pont. I. i. 32. Fast. iv. 181.— Among the Romans and other nations, the flute was employed on almost every occasion, and at every solemnity. It was made use of in triumphs (Censorin. de die Nat. c. 12.) C. Duilius, who first obtained the honour of a triumph, for a naval victory over the Carthaginians (triumphum navalem), was constantly accompanied in commemoration of that event (quasi quotidie triumpharet.) by a flute player (tibicen), who walked before him

when he returned to his house, every time that he supped abroad, Flor. ii. 2. Val. Max. iii. 6. Cui nocturnus honos, funalia clara, sæcerque, post epulas, tibicen adest, Sil. Ital. lib. 6. Cic. de Senat. They sang the praises of the gods, and offered up to them their prayers, to the sound of the flute (tibiæ), Is. ii. 15. Stat. Theb. lib. 8. They employed it in religious ceremonies and in sacrifices, Ovid. Fast. lib. 6. Prop. lib. 4. 6. It was equally to the sound of the flute that they harangued the people, that they read poetry, and that they sang the praises of heroes in feasts and at funerals; orators sought, by the

aid of the flute, to give modulation and suitable accent to their voices. Poets, and above all, lyric poets, availed themselves of it as much when they read their verses; hence, si neque tibias Euterpe cohibet, nec Polyhymnia Lesbæum refugit tendere barbiton, Hor. i. Od. i.; on which Christoph. Landinus makes the following remark; si Musæ, quasi per Euterpen unam ex iis, designat, non prohibentur a tibia, id est. a versibus, qui tibia canuntur.

5 loquaci manu.

6 Juv. xiii. 110. vi. 63. Ov. Trist. ii. 515. Mart. iii. 86. Hor. i. 18. 13. ii. 2. 125. Man. v. 474. Suet. Ner. 54.

7 excalceati, Sen. Ep. 8.

Quin. v. 11. Juv. viii. 191. Gell. i. 11.

8 Cic. Cœl. 27. Suet. Cal. 54.

9 Cic. Cœl. 57. Ver. iii. 36. Rab. Post. 12. Phil. ii. 27. Suet. Cæs. 39. Ner. 4. Oth. 3. Cal. 45. Aug. 45. 100. Sen. Ep. 80. Juv. viii. 198.

10 mimographi.

11 Suet. Jul. 39. Hor. Sat. i. 10. 6. Gell. xvii.

14 Tac. Ann. i. 54.

12 libertus Mæcenatis.

13 Suet. Tib. 37. Dio. liv. 17. Macrob. Sat. ii. 7. Sen. Ep. 47. Nat. Q. vii. 32. Petron. 5.

14 funambuli, schœnobatæ vel neurobatæ.

15 Ter. Hec. Prol. 4. 34. Juv. iii 77.

16 petauristæ.

17 jactabant vel excutiebant.

entertainments, called EMBOLIA, or ACROAMATA ; but this last word is usually put for the actors, musicians, or repeaters themselves, who were also employed at private entertainments.[1]

The plays were often interrupted likewise by the people calling out for various shows to be exhibited ; as the representation of battles, triumphal processions, gladiators, uncommon animals, and wild beasts, &c. The noise which the people made on these occasions is compared by Horace to the raging of the sea.[2] In like manner, their approbation[3] and disapprobation,[4] which at all times were so much regarded.[5]

Those who acted the principal parts of a play were called *actores primarum partium* ; the second, *secundarum partium;* the third, *tertiarum*, &c.[6]

The actors were applauded or hissed as they performed their parts, or pleased the spectators. When the play was ended, an actor always said PLAUDITE.[7]

The actors who were most approved received crowns, &c. as at other games ; at first composed of leaves or flowers, tied round the head with strings, called STRUPPI, *strophia*, v. *-iola*,[8] afterwards of thin plates of brass gilt,[9] called COROLLÆ or *corollaria ;* first made by Crassus of gold and silver.[10] Hence COROLLARIUM, a reward given to players over and above their just hire,[11] or any thing given above what was promised:[12] The emperor M. Antoninus ordained that players should receive from five to ten gold pieces,[13] but not more.[14]

The place where dramatic representations were exhibited was called THEATRUM, a theatre.[15] In ancient times the people viewed the entertainments standing ; hence *stantes* for spectators ;[16] and A. U. 599, a decree of the senate was made, prohibiting any one to make seats for that purpose in the city, or within a mile of it. At the same time a theatre, which was building, was by the appointment of the censors, ordered to be pulled down, as a thing hurtful to good morals.[17]

Afterwards temporary theatres were occasionally erected. The most splendid was that of M. Æmilius Scaurus, when ædile. which contained 80,000 persons, and was adorned with amazing magnificence, and at an incredible expense.[18]

Curio, the partisan of Cæsar, at the funeral exhibition in honour of his father,[19] made two large theatres of wood, adjoining to one another, suspended each on hinges,[20] and looking opposite ways,[21] so that the scenes should not disturb each other by their noise ;[22] in both of which he acted stage plays in the former part of the day ; then having suddenly wheeled them round, so that they stood over against one another, and thus formed an amphitheatre, he exhibited shows of gladiators in the afternoon.[23]

Pompey first reared a theatre of hewn stone in his second consulship, which contained 40,000 ; but that he might not incur the animadversion of the censors, he dedicated it as a temple to Venus. There were afterwards

1 Fest. Juv. xiv. 265. Man. iii. 438. Mart. ii. 86. Cic. Sext. 54. Ver. iv. 22. Arch. 9. Suet. Aug. 77. Macrob. Sat. ii. 4. Nep. Att. 14.
2 Ep. II. i. 185.
3 plausus.
4 sibilus, strepitus, fremitus, clamor, tonitruum, Cic. Fam. viii. 2. fistula pastoritia, At. 16.

5 Cic. Pis. 27. Sext. 54 —56. Hor. Od. i. 20. li. 17.
6 Ter. Phor. prol. 28. Cic. Cæc. 15. Asc. loc.
7 Quin. vi. 1. Cic. Rosc. Com. 2. At. i. 3. 16. Ter.
8 Fest. Plin. xxi. 1.
9 e lamina ærea tenui inaurata aut inargentata.
10 Plin. xxi. 2, 3.

11 additum præterquam quod debitum est, Var. L. L. iv. 36. Plin. Ep. vii. 24. Cic. Verr. iii. 79. iv. 22. Suet. Aug. 45.
12 Cic. Verr. iii. 50. Plin. ix. 35. s. 57.
13 aurei.
14 Capitolin. 11.
15 a Ξεαομαι, video.
16 Cic. Am. 7.
17 nociturum publicis

moribus, Liv. Ep. xlviii. Val. Max. ii. 4. 3.
18 Plin. xxxvi. 15. s. 24. 8.
19 funebri patris munere.
20 cardinum singulorum versatili suspensa libramento.
21 inter se aversa.
22 ne invicem obstreperent.
23 Plin. xxxvi. 15.

several theatres, and in particular those of Marcellus and of Balbus, near that of Pompey; hence called *tria theatra*, the three theatres.[1]

Theatres at first were open at top, and, in excessive heat or rain, coverings were drawn over them, as over the amphitheatre, but in later times they were roofed.[2]

Among the Greeks, public assemblies were held in the theatre; and among the Romans it was usual to scourge malefactors on the stage.[3] This the Greeks called θεατρίζειν et παραδειγματίζειν.

The theatre was of an oblong semicircular form, like the half of an

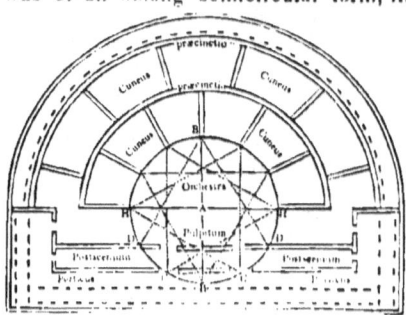

THEATRE.

In the Roman theatre, the construction of the orchestra and stage was as follows.—The former was bounded towards the cavea by a semicircle. Complete the circle, draw the diameters BB, HH, perpendicular to each other, and inscribe four equilateral triangles, whose vertices shall fall severally upon the ends of the diameters; the twelve angles of the triangles will divide the circumference into twelve equal portions. The side of the triangle opposite to the angle at B will be parallel to the diameter HH, and determines the place of the scene, as HH determines the front of the stage, or pulpitum. By this construction the stage is brought nearer to the audience, and made considerably deeper than in the Greek theatre, its depth being determined at a quarter of the diameter of the orchestra, which itself was usually a third, or somewhat more, of the diameter of the whole building. The length of the stage was twice the diameter of the orchestra. The increased depth of the stage was rendered necessary by the greater number of persons assembled on it; the cho-

rus and musicians being placed here by the Romans. A further consequence of the construction is, that the circumference of the cavea could not exceed one hundred and eighty degrees. Sometimes, however, the capacity of the theatre was increased by throwing the stage further back, and continuing the seats in right lines perpendicular to the diameter of the orchestra. This is the case in the great theatre at Pompeii. Within the orchestra were circular ranges of seats for the senate and other distinguished persons, leaving a level platform in the centre. The seven angles which fall within the circumference of the orchestra mark the places at which staircases up to the first præcinctio, or landing, were to be placed; those leading from thence to the second, if there were more than one, were placed intermediately opposite to the centre of each cunous. The number of staircases, whether seven, five, or three, of course depended on the size of the theatre. In the great theatres of Rome, the space between the orchestra and first præcinctio, usually consisting of fourteen seats, was reserv-

ed for the equestrian order, tribunes, &c.; all above these were the seats of the plebeians. Women were appointed by Augustus to sit in the portico, which encompassed the whole. The lowest range of seats was raised above the area of the orchestra one-sixth of its diameter; the height of each seat is directed not to exceed one foot four inches, nor to be less than one foot three. The breadth is not to exceed two feet four inches, nor to be less than one foot ten. The stage, to consult the convenience of those who sit in the orchestra, is only elevated five feet, less than half the height given to the Grecian stage. The five angles of the triangles not yet disposed of, determine the disposition of the scene. Opposite the centre one are the regal doors; on each side are those by which the secondary characters entered. Behind the scene, as in the Greek theatre, there were apartments for the actors to retire into, and the whole was usually surrounded with porticoes and gardens. These porticoes were generally used for rehearsal.

1 Suet. Claud. 21. Aug. 45. Tertull. Spect. 10. Plin. viii. 7. Dio. xxxix. 36. Dio. xliii. 49. Tac.   xiv. 19. Ov. Trist. iii. 12. 13. 24. Am. ii. 7, 3. Art. iii. 394.   2 Stat. Sylv. iii. 5. 91.   Plin. xix. 1. s. 6. xxxvi. 15. s. 24. Lucr. iv. 73. vi. 108.   3 Suet. Aug. 47. Tac. ii.   80. Sen. Ep. 108. Cic. Flacc. 7.

amphitheatre.[1] The benches or seats,[2] rose above one another, and were distributed to the different orders in the same manner as in the amphitheatre. The foremost rows next the stage, called *orchestra*, were assigned to the senators and ambassadors of foreign states ; fourteen rows behind them to the equites, and the rest to the people. The whole was called CAVEA. The foremost rows were called *cavea prima*, or *ima; the last, cavea ultima* or *summa ;* the middle, *cavea media.*[3]

The parts of the theatre allotted to the performers were called *scena, postscenium, proscenium, pulpitum,* and *orchestra.*

1. SCENA, the scene, was adorned with columns, statues, and pictures of various kinds, according to the nature of the plays exhibited, to which Virgil alludes, Æn. i. 166, 432. The ornaments sometimes were inconceivably magnificent.[4]

When the scene was suddenly changed by certain machines, it was called SCENA VERSATILIS ; when it was drawn aside, SCENA DUCTILIS.[5]

The scenery was concealed by a curtain,[6] which contrary to the modern custom, was dropt[7] or drawn down, as among us the blinds of a carriage, when the play began, and raised[8] or drawn up when the play was over ; sometimes also between the acts. The machine by which this was done was called EXOSTRA. Curtains and hangings of tapestry were also used in private houses, called *aulæa Attalica*, because said to have been first invented at the court of Attalus, king of Pergamus, in Asia Minor.[9]

2. POSTSCENIUM, the place behind the scene, where the actors dressed and undressed ; and where those things were supposed to be done which could not with propriety be exhibited on the stage.[10]

3. PROSCENIUM, the place before the scene, where the actors appeared. The place where the actors recited their parts was called PULPITUM ; and the place where they danced ORCHESTRA, which was about five feet lower than the *pulpitum.* Hence *ludibria scena et pulpito digna*, buffooneries fit only for the stage.[11]

MILITARY AFFAIRS OF THE ROMANS.

I. LEVYING OF SOLDIERS.

THE Romans were a nation of warriors. Every citizen was obliged to enlist as a soldier when the public service required, from the age of seventeen to forty-six ; nor at first could any one enjoy an office in the city who had not served ten campaigns. Every foot soldier was obliged to serve twenty campaigns, and every horseman ten. At first none of the lowest class were enlisted as soldiers, nor freedmen, unless in dangerous junctures. But this was afterwards altered by Marius.[12]

The Romans, during the existence of their republic, were almost always engaged in wars ; first with the different states of Italy for near 500 years, and then for about 200 years more in subduing the various countries which composed that immense empire.

The Romans never carried on any war without solemnly proclaiming it. This was done by a set of priests called FECIALES.

1 Plin. xxxvi. 16.
2 gradus vel cunei.
3 Suet. Aug. 44. Cic. Sen. 14.
4 Vitr. v. 6. Val. Max. ii. 4. 6. Plin. xxxvi. 15. s. 24.

5 Serv. Virg. G. iii. 24.
6 aulæum vel siparium, oftener plural -a.
7 premebatur.
8 tollebatur.
9 Hor. Ep. ii. 189. Art. Poet. 154. Od. iii. 29.

15. Sat. ii. 8. 54. Ov. Met. iii. 111. Juv. vi. 166. Cic. prov. cons. 6. Prop. ii. 23. 46. Serv. Virg. Æn. i. 701.
10 Hor. Art. Poet. 182. Lucret. iv. 1176.

11 Vitrav. v. 6. Plin. Ep. iv. 25.
12 Polyb. vi. 17. Liv. x. 21. xxii. 11. 57. Sall. Jug. 86. Gell. xvi. 10.

When the Romans thought themselves injured by any nation, they sent one or more of these feciales to demand redress ;[1] and if it was not immediately given, thirty-three days were granted to consider the matter, after which, war might be justly declared.   Then the feciales again went to their confines, and having thrown a bloody spear into them, formally declared war against that nation.[2]   The form of words which he pronounced before he threw the spear was called CLARIGATIO.[3]   Afterwards, when the empire was enlarged, and wars carried on with distant nations, this ceremony was performed in a certain field near the city, which was called AGER HOSTILIS.   Thus Augustus declared war professedly against Cleopatra, but in reality against Antony.   So Marcus Antoninus, before he set out to the war against the Scythians, shot a bloody spear from the temple of Bellona into the *ager hostilis*.[4]

In the first ages of the republic, four legions for the most part were annually raised, two to each consul ; for two legions composed a consular army.   But oftener a greater number was raised, ten, eighteen, twenty, twenty-one, twenty-three.[5]   Under Tiberius twenty-five, even in time of peace, besides the troops in Italy, and the forces of the allies : under Adrian thirty.   In the 529th year of the city, upon a report of a Gallic tumult, Italy alone is said to have armed 80,000 cavalry, and 700,000 foot.[6]   But in after-times, when the lands were cultivated chiefly by slaves,[7] it was not so easy to procure soldiers.   Hence, after the destruction of Quintilius Varus and his army in Germany, A. U. 763, Augustus could not raise forces even to defend Italy and Rome, which he was afraid the Germans and Gauls would attack, without using the greatest rigour.[8]

The consuls, after they entered on their office, appointed a day,[9] on which all those who were of the military age, should be present in the capitol.[10]

On the day appointed, the consuls, seated in their curule chairs,[11] held a levy,[12] by the assistance of the military or legionary tribunes, unless hindered by the tribunes of the commons.[13]   It was determined by lot in what manner the tribes should be called.

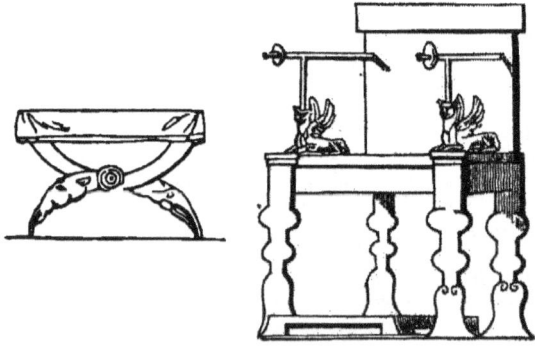

1 ad res repedentas, Liv. iv. 30. xxxviii. 45. Var. L. L. iv. 15. Diony. ii. 72.
2 Liv. i. 32.
3 a clara voce qua utebatur, Serv. Virg. Æn. ix. 52. x. 14. Plin. xxii.

2.
4 Ov. F. vi. 205. Dio. lxxi. 53. i. 4.
5 Liv. ii. 30. vi. 12. vii. 35. xx. 1. xxiv. 11. xxvi. 28. xxvii. 24. xxviii. 38. xxx. 2.
6 Tac. An. Spartian, 15.

Plin. iii. 20. s. 24.
7 Liv. vi. 12.
8 Dio. lxi. 23.
9 diem edicebant, vel indicebant.
10 Liv. xxvi. 31. Polyb. vi. 17.
11 The first of the above

curule chairs was found in Herculaneum, the second is taken from a drawing found in Pompeii.
12 delectum habebant.
13 Liv. iii. 51. iv. 1.

The consuls ordered such as they pleased to be cited out of each tribe,
and every one was obliged to answer to his name under a severe penalty.[1]
They were careful to choose[2] those first, who had what were thought
lucky names,[3] as, Valerius, Salvius, Statorius, &c.[4] Their names were
written down on tables ; hence *scribere*, to enlist, to levy or raise.

In certain wars, and under certain commanders, there was the greatest
alacrity to enlist,[5] but this was not always the case. Sometimes compulsion[6]
was requisite ; and those who refused[7] were forced to enlist[8] by fines and
corporal punishment.[9] Sometimes they were thrown into prison or sold
as slaves. Some cut off their thumbs or fingers to render themselves unfit for service : hence *pollice trunci*, poltroons. But this did not screen
them from punishment. On one occasion, Augustus put some of the
most refractory to death.[10]

There were, however, several just causes of exemption from military
service,[11] of which the chief were, age,[12] if above fifty ; disease or in-
firmity :[13] office,[14] being a magistrate or priest; favour or indulgence[15]
granted by the senate or people.[16]

Those also were excused who had served out their time.[17] Such as
claimed this exemption, applied to the tribunes of the commons,[18] who judged of the justice of the claims,[19] and interposed in their behalf or not, as
they judged proper. But this was sometimes forbidden by a decree of
the senate. And the tribunes themselves sometimes referred the matter
to the consuls.[20]

In sudden emergencies, or in dangerous wars, as a war in Italy, or
against the Gauls, which was called TUMULTUS,[21] no regard was had to
these excuses.[22] Two flags were displayed[23] from the capitol, the one
red,[24] to summon the infantry,[25] and the other green,[26] to summon the cavalry.[27]

On such occasions, as there was not time to go through the usual forms,
the consul said, QUI REMPUBLICAM SALVAM ESSE VULT, ME SEQUATUR.
This was called CONJURATIO, or *evocatio*, and men thus raised, CONJURATI,
who were not considered as regular soldiers.[28]

Soldiers raised upon a sudden alarm[29] were called SUBITARII,[30] or TU-
MULTUARII, not only at Rome, but also in the provinces, when the sickly
or infirm were forced to enlist, who were called CAUSARII.[31] If slaves
were found to have obtruded themselves into the service,[32] they were
sometimes punished capitally.[33]

The cavalry where chosen from the body of the equites, and each had
a horse and money to support him, given them by the public.[34]

On extraordinary occasions, some equites served on their own horses.[35]

1 Liv. iii. 11. 41. Gell.
xi. 5. Val. Max. vi. 3, 4.
2 legere.
3 bona nomina.
4 Cic. Div. i. 45. Fest.
in voce Lacus Lucri-
nus.
5 nomina dare, Liv. x.
25. xlii. 32.
6 coercitio.
7 refractarii, qui mili-
tiam detrectabant.
8 sacramento adacti.
9 damno et virgis, Liv.
iv. 53. vii. 4.
10 Dio. lvi. 23. Diony.
vii. Cic. Cæc. 34. Suet.
Aug. 24. Val. Max. vi.

3. 3.
11 vacationis militiæ
vel a militia.
12 ætas, Liv. xlii. 33,
34.
13 morbus vel vitium,
Suet. Aug. 24.
14 honor, Plut. Camil.
vers. fin.
15 beneficium.
16 Cic. Phil. v. 19. Nat.
D. ii. 2. Liv. xxxix. 19.
17 emeriti, qui stipen-
dia explevissent vel
defuncti, Ov. Am. ii. 9.
24.
18 Liv. ii. 55.
19 causas   cognosce-

bant.
20 Liv. xxxiv. 56. xlii.
32, 33.
21 quasi timor multus,
vel a tumeo, Cic. Phil.
v. 31.viii. l.Quin. vii. 3.
22 delectus sine vaca-
tionibus habitus est,
Liv. vii. 11. 28. viii. 20.
x. 21.
23 vexilla sublata vel
prolata sunt.)
24 roseum.
25 ad pedites evocan-
dos.
26 ceruleum.
27 Serv. Virg. Æn. viii.
4.

28 Liv. xxii. 38. xlv. 2.
Cæs. Bell. G. vii. 1.
29 in tumultu : nam tu-
multus nonnunquam
levior quam bellum,
Liv. ii. 26.
30 ita repentina auxilia
appellabant, Liv. iii. 4.
30.
31 Liv. i. 37. vi. 6. xxxv.
2. xl. 26.
32 inter tirones.
33 in eos animadversum
est, Plin. Ep. x. 38, 39.
34 Liv. i. 43.
35 Liv. 7.

But that was not usually done ; nor were there, as some have thought, any horse in the Roman army, but from the equites, till the time of Marius, who made a great alteration in the military system of the Romans in this, as well as in other respects.

After that period, the cavalry was composed not merely of Roman equites, as formerly, but of horsemen raised from Italy, and the other provinces ; and the infantry consisted chiefly of the poorer citizens, or of mercenary soldiers, which is justly reckoned one of the chief causes of the ruin of the republic.

After the levy was completed, one soldier was chosen to repeat over the words of the military oath,[1] and the rest swore after him.[2] Every one as he passed along said, IDEM IN ME.[3]

The form of the oath does not seem to have been always the same. The substance of it was, that they would obey their commander, and not desert their standards, &c. Sometimes those below seventeen were obliged to take the military oath.[4]

Without this oath no one could justly fight with the enemy. Hence *sacramenta* is put for a military life. Livy says, that it was first legally exacted in the second Punic war,[5] where he seems to make a distinction between the oath (SACRAMENTUM) which formerly was taken voluntarily, when the troops were embodied, and each decuria of cavalry, and century of foot, swore among themselves (*inter se equites decuriati, pedites centuriati conjurabant,*) to act like good soldiers, (*sese fugæ ac formidinis ergo non abituros, neque ex ordine recessuros,*) and the oath (JUSJURANDUM) which was exacted by the military tribunes, after the levy, (*ex voluntario inter ipsos fœdere a tribunis ad legitimam jurisjurandi actionem translatum.* On occasion of a mutiny, the military oath was taken anew.[6]

Under the emperors, the name of a prince was inserted in the military oath, and this oath used to be renewed every year on their birth-day, by the soldiers, and the people in the provinces, also on the kalends of January.[7] On certain occasions, persons were sent up and down the country to raise soldiers, called CONQUISITORES, and the force used for that purpose, COERCITIO vel *conquisitio,* a press or impress.[8] Sometimes particular commissioners[9] were appointed for that purpose.

Veteran soldiers who had served out their time,[10] were often induced again to enlist, who were then called EVOCATI. Galba gave this name to a body of equites, whom he appointed to guard his person.[11] The evocati were exempted from all the drudgery of military service.[12]

After Latium and the states of Italy were subdued, or admitted into alliance, they always furnished at least an equal number of infantry with the Romans, and the double of cavalry, sometimes more.[13] The consuls, when about to make a levy, sent them notice what number of troops they required,[14] and at the same time appointed the day and place of assembling.[15]

The forces of the allies seem to have been raised,[16] much in the same

---

1 qui reliquis verba sacramenti præiret.
2 in verba ejus jurabant.
3 Festus in præjurationes, Liv. ii. 45. Polyb. vi. 19.
4 sacramento vel -um dicere, Liv. iii. 20. xxi. 38. xxii. 57. xxv. 5. Gell. xvi. 4.

5 xxii. 38. Cic. Off. i. 11. Juv. xvi. 35.
6 Liv. xxviii. 29.
7 Suet. Galb. 16. Tac. Ann. xvi. 22. Hist. i. 12. iv. 31. Plin. Ep. x. 60. Pan. 68.
8 Liv. xxi. 11. xxiii. 32. Cic. prov. cons. 2 Att. vii. 21. Hist. Bell. Alex. 2.

9 triumviri, Liv. xxv. 5.
10 homines meritis, stipendiis.
11 Suet. Galb. 10. Liv. xxxvii. 4. Cic. Fam. iii. 7. Cæs. Bell. Civ. iii. 53. Sall. Jug. 84. Dio. xlv. 12.
12 cæterorum immunes, nisi propulsandi hostis, Tac. Ann. i. 36.

13 Liv. viii. 8. xxii. 36. see p. 48.
14 ad socios Latinumque nomen ad milites ex formula accipiendos mittunt, arma, tela, alia parari jubent, Liv. xxii. 57.
15 quo convenirent, Liv. xxxiv. 56. xxxvii. 4.
16 scripti vel conscripti.

manner with those of the Romans. They were paid by their own states, and received nothing from the Romans but corn ; on which account they had a paymaster (*quæstor*) of their own.[1] But when all the Italians were admitted into the freedom of the city, their forces were incorporated with those of the republic.

The troops sent by foreign kings and states were called auxiliaries.[2] They usually received pay and clothing from the republic, although they sometimes were supported by those who sent them.

The first mercenary soldiers in the Roman army are said to have been the Celtiberians in Spain, A. U. 537. But those must have been different from the auxiliaries, who are often mentioned before that time.[3]

Under the emperors the Roman armies were in a great measure composed of foreigners ; and the provinces saw with regret the flower of their youth carried off for that purpose.[4] Each district was obliged to furnish a certain number of men, in proportion to its extent and opulence.

II. DIVISION OF THE TROOPS IN THE ROMAN ARMY; THEIR ARMS, OFFICERS, AND DRESS.

AFTER the levy was completed, and the military oath administered, the troops were formed into legions.[5] Each legion was divided into ten cohorts, each cohort into three *maniples*, and each *maniple* into two centuries.[6] So that there were thirty maniples, and sixty centuries in a legion ;[7] and if there had always been 100 men in each century, as its name imports, the legion would have consisted of 6000 men. But this was not the case.

The number of men in a legion was different at different times.[8] In the time of Polybius it was 4200.

There were usually 300 cavalry joined to each legion, called JUSTUS EQUITATUS, or ALA.[9] They were divided into ten *turmæ* or troops ; and each *turma* into three *decuriæ*, or bodies of ten men.

The different kinds of infantry which composed the legion were three, the *hastati, principes,* and *triarii*.

The HASTATI were so called, because they first fought with long spears,[10] which were afterwards laid aside as inconvenient. They consisted of young men in the flower of life, and formed the first line in battle.[11]

The PRINCIPES were men of middle age in the vigour of life : they occupied the second line. Anciently they seem to have been posted first : whence their name.

The TRIARII were old soldiers of approved valour, who formed the third line ; whence their name.[12] They were also called PILANI from the *pilum* or javelin which they used ; and the *hastati* and *principes*, who stood before them, ANTEPILANI.

There was a fourth kind of troops called VELITES, from their swiftness and agility,[13] the light-armed soldiers,[14] first instituted in the second Punic war.

1 Prolyb. vi. Liv. xxvii. 9. 11.
2 auxiliares milites vel auxilia, ab augeo, Cic. Att. vi. 5. Var. Fest.
3 Liv. xxi. 46. 48. 55, 56. xxii. 22. xxiv. 49.
4 Tac. Hist. vi. 14. Agric. 31.
5 legio a legendo, quia

milites in delectu legebantur, Varr. l.. L. iv. 16. which word is sometimes put for an army, Liv. ii. 26. Sall. Jug. 79.
6 manipulus, ex manipulo vel fasciculo fœni, hastæ vel perticæ longæ alligato, quem

pro signo primum gerebat, Ov. F. iii. 117.
7 Gell. xvi. 4.
8 Liv. vii. 25. viii. 8. xxvi. 28. xxix. 24. xlii. 31. xliii. 12. Cæs. B. C. iii. 106. B. Al. 69.
9 Liv. iii. 62.
10 hasta.
11 Var. L. L. iv. 16.

Liv. viii. 8.
12 Diony. viii. 86.
13 a volando vel velocitate.
14 milites levis armaturæ, vel expediti, vel levis armatura,Liv.xxvi. 4.

These did not form a part of the legion, and had no certain post assigned them ; but fought in scattered parties where occasion required, usually before the lines. To them were joined the slingers and archers.[1]

The light-armed troops were anciently called *ferentarii, rorarii*,[2] and, according to some, *accensi*. Others make the *accensi* supernumerary soldiers, who attended the army to supply the place of those legionary soldiers who died or were slain.[3] In the meantime, however, they were ranked among the light-armed troops. These were formed into distinct companies,[4] and are sometimes opposed to the legionary cohorts.[5]

The soldiers were often denominated, especially under the emperors, from the number of the legion in which they were ; thus, *primani*, the soldiers of the first legion ; *secundani, tertiani, quartani, quintani, decimani, tertiadecimani, vicesimani, duodevicesimani, duo et vicesimani*, &c.[6]

The *velites* were equipped with bows, slings, seven javelins or spears with slender points like arrows, so that when thrown they bent and could not easily be returned by the enemy ;[7] a Spanish sword, having both edge and point ;[8] a round buckler (PARMA) about three feet in diameter, made of wood and covered with leather ; and a helmet or casque for the head (GALEA vel *galerus*), generally made of the skin of some wild beast, to appear the more terrible.[9]

1 Funditores, Baleares, Achæi, &c. Liv. xxi. 21, xxviii. 37. xxxviii, 29. 31. Sagittarii, Cretenses, Arabes, &c. Liv. xxxvii. 40. xlii. 35.— The sling was much used by many nations. The Balearians, or the people of the islands now called Majorca and Minorca, excelled at the sling. They were so attentive in exercising their youth in the use of it, that they did not give them their food in the morning till they had hit a mark. The Balearians were very much employed in the armies of the Carthaginians and Romans, and greatly contributed to the gaining of victories. Livy mentions some cities of Achaia, Egium, Patræ, and Dymæ, whose inhabitants were still more dexterous at the sling than the Balearians. They threw stones farther, and with greater force and certainty, never failing to hit what part of the face they pleased. Their slings discharged the stones with so much force, that neither buckler nor head-piece could resist their impetuosity ; and the address of those who managed them was such, according to the scrip-

ture, (Judg. xx. 16.) that they could hit a hair, without the stones going either on one side or the other. Instead of stones they sometimes charged the sling with balls of lead, which it carried much farther.—Bows and arrows are of the most remote antiquity. There were few nations who did not use them. The Cretans were esteemed excellent archers. We do not find that the Romans used the bow in the earliest times of the republic. They introduced it afterwards; but it appears, that they had scarce any

archers, except those of the auxiliary troops. 2 quod ante rorat quam pluit, Varr. L. L. vi. 3. 3 Festus in adcensi et adscriptitii, Var. ib. 4 expediti manipuli et expeditæ cohortes. 5 Sall. Jug. 46. 90. 100. 6 Tac. Hist. iv. 36, 37. iii. 27. v. 1. Suet. Jul. 70. 7 quorum telum inhabile ad remittendum imperitis est,—whose weapon is of such a kind that it cannot well be thrown back, except by experienced hands, Liv. xxiv. 34. 8 quo cæsim et punctim potebant, Liv. 9 Polyb. vi. 20.

The arms of the *hastati, principes,* and *triarii,* both defensive[1] and offensive,[2] were in a great measure the same:

1. An oblong shield (SCUTUM), with an iron boss (UMBO) jutting out in the middle, four feet long and two feet and a half broad, made of wood, joined together with little plates of iron, and the whole covered with a bull's hide : sometimes a round shield (CLYPEUS) of a smaller size.

2. A head-piece (GALEA vel *cassis* v. -*ida*) of brass or iron, coming down to the shoulders, but leaving the face uncovered, whence the command of Cæsar at the battle of Pharsalia, which in a great measure determined the fortune of the day, FACIEM FERI, MILES—soldier, strike the face.[3] Pompey's cavalry being chiefly composed of young men of rank, who were as much afraid of having their visages disfigured as of death. Upon the top of the helmet was the crest (CRISTA), adorned with plumes of feathers of various colours.

3. A coat of mail (LORICA), generally made of leather, covered with plates of iron in the form of scales, or iron rings twisted within one another like chains.[4] Instead of the coat of mail, most used only a plate of brass on the breast (*thorax* vel *pectorale*).

4. Greaves for the legs (OCREÆ)[5] sometimes only on the right leg, and a kind of shoe or covering for the feet, called *caliga,* set with nails,[6] used chiefly by the common

soldiers,[7] whence the emperor Caligula had his name. Hence *caligatus,* a common soldier ; Marius *a* caliga *ad consulatum perductus,* from being a common soldier.[8]

---

1 arma ad tegendum.
2 tela ad petendum,
  Polyb. vi. 20. 22.
3 Flor. iv. 2.

4 hamis conserta.
5 Liv. ix. 40. tegmina
  crurum, Virg. Æn. xi.
  777.

6 Juv. xvi. 24. Veg. i.
  20.
7 gregarii vel manipulares milites.

8 Sen. Ben. v. 16. Suet.
  Cal. ix. 52. Aug. 25.
  Tac. Ann. i. 41. Cic.
  Att. ii. 3.

5. A sword (*gladius* vel *ensis*) and two long javelins (PILA).

The cavalry at first used only their ordinary clothing for the sake of agility, that they might more easily mount their horses ; for they had no stirrups (STAPIÆ vel STAPEDÆ, as they were afterwards called.) When they were first used is uncertain. There is no mention of them in the classics, nor do they appear on ancient coins and statues. Neither had the Romans saddles such as ours, but certain coverings of cloth[1] to sit on, called EPHIPPIA, vel STRATA, with which a horse was said to be CONSTRATUS. These the Germans despised. The Numidian horse had no bridles.[2]

But the Roman cavalry afterwards imitated the manner of the Greeks, and used nearly the same armour with the foot. Thus, Pliny wrote a book *de jaculatione equestri*, about the art of using the javelin on horseback.[3]

Horsemen armed *cap-a-piè*, that is, completely from head to foot, were called LORICATI or CATAPHRACTI.[4]

In each legion there were six military tribunes,[5] who commanded under the consul, each in his turn, usually month about. In battle, a tribune seems to have had the charge of ten centuries, or about a thousand men, hence called in Greek χιλιαρχος, vel -ης. Under the emperors they were chosen chiefly from among the senators and equites ; hence called LATICLAVII and ANGUSTICLAVII. One of these seems to be called TRIBUNUS COHORTIS, and their command to have lasted only six months ; hence called SEMESTRIS TRIBUNATUS, or SEMESTRE AURUM,[6] because they had the right of wearing a golden ring.

The tribunes chose the officers who commanded the centuries,[7] from among the common soldiers, according to their merit.[8] But this office[9] was sometimes disposed of by the consul or proconsul through favour, and even for money.[10]

The badge of a centurion was a vine-rod or sapling (VITIS) : hence *vite donari*, to be made a centurion ; *vitem poscere*, to ask that office ; *gerere*, to bear it.[11]

There were two centurions in each maniple called by the same name, but distinguished by the title *prior*, former, and *posterior*, latter, because the one was chosen and ranked before the other.[12] Under the emperors persons were made centurions all at once through interest.[13]

The centurion of the first century of the first maniple of the *triarii*, was called *centurio primi pili*, vel *primi ordinis*, or *primus pilus*, *primipilus*, or *primopilus*, also *primus centurio, qui primum pilum ducebat, dux legionis* (ὁ ἡγεμων του ταγματος.)[14] He presided over all the other centurions, and had the charge of the eagle,[15] or chief standard of the legion, whereby he obtained both profit and dignity, being ranked among the equites. He had

1 vestis stragula.
2 Hor. Ep. i. 14. 44. Liv. xxi. 54. xxxv. 11. Cæs. B. G. iv. 2.
3 Polyb. vi. 23. Plin. Ep. iii. 4.
4 Liv. xxv. 48. xxxvii. 40.

5 see p. 131.
6 Juv. vii. 8. Plin. Ep. iii. 9. iv. 4. Suet. Oth. 10. Liv. xl. 41. Hor. Sat. i. 6. 48.
7 centuriones vel ordinum ductores.
8 Liv. xlii. 34. Cæs. vi.

39. Luc. i. 645. vi. 145.
9 centurionatus.
10 Cic. Pis. 36.
11 Luc. vi. 146. Juv. xiv. 193. viii. 247. Plin xiv. 1. s. 3. Tac. i. 23. Ov. Art. Am. i. 527.

12 Tac. Ann. i. 32. Diony. ix. 10.
13 Dio. lii. 25.
14 Diony. ix. 10. Liv. vii. 13. 41. xxv. 19. Cæs. B. G. ii. 25.
15 aquila.

a place in the council of war with the consul and tribunes. The other centurions were called *minores ordine*.[1]

The centurion of the second century of the first maniple of the *triarii*, was called *primipilus posterior*, so the two centurions of the second maniple of the *triarii, prior centurio*, and *posterior centurio secundi pili*, and so on to the tenth, who was called *centurio decimi pili, prior* et *posterior.* In like manner, *primus princeps, secundus princeps*, &c. *Primus hastatus*, &c. Thus there was a large field for promotion in the Roman army, from a common soldier to a centurion ; from being the lowest centurion of the tenth maniple of *hastati*,[2] to the rank of *primipilus*. Any one of the chief centurions was said *ducere honestum ordinem*, to hold an honourable rank ; as Virginius, Liv. iii. 44.

The centurions chose each two assistants or lieutenants, called OPTI-ONES, *uragi*, or *succenturiones* ;[3] and two standard-bearers or ensigns (SIGNIFERI vel *vexillarii*.)[4]

He who commanded the cavalry of a legion was called PRÆFECTUS ALÆ.[5]

Each *turma* had three DECURIONES or commanders of ten, but he who was first elected commanded the troop, and he was called DUX TURMÆ. Each *decurio* had an *optio* or deputy under him.[6]

The troops of the allies (which, as well as the horse, were called ALÆ, from their being stationed on the wings), had præfects (PRÆFECTI) appointed them, who commanded in the same manner as the legionary tribunes. They were divided into cohorts, as the Roman infantry.[7] A third part of the horse, and a fifth of the foot of the allies, were selected and posted near the consul, under the name of EXTRAORDINARII, and one troop called ABLECTI or *selecti*, to serve as his life-guards.[8]

It is probable that the arms and inferior officers of the allied troops were much the same with those of the Romans.

Two legions, with the due number of cavalry,[9] and the allies, formed what was called a consular army,[10] about 20,000 men, in the time of Polybius, 18,600.[11]

The consul appointed lieutenant-generals (LEGATI) under him, one or more, according to the importance of the war.[12]

When the consul performed any thing in person, he was said to do it by his own conduct and auspices ;[13] but if his *legatus* or any other person did it by his command, it was said to be done[14] by the auspices of the consul and conduct of the *legatus*. In this manner the emperors were said to do every thing by their auspices, although they remained at Rome ;[15] hence *auspicia*, the conduct.

The military robe or cloak of the general was called PALUDAMENTUM, or *chlamys*, of a scarlet colour, bordered with purple ; sometimes worn also by the chief officers,[16] and, according to some, by the lictors who attended

1 Tac. Hist. lii. 22. Val. Max. i. 6. 11. Juv. xiv. 197. Mart. i. 32. Ov. Am. iii. 8. 20. Pont. iv. 7. 15. 49.

2 decimus hastatus posterior, Liv. xiii. 34.

3 Liv. viii. 8. Festus. in optio.

4 Liv. vi. 8. xxxv. 5. Tac. Ann. ii. 61. Hist. i. 41. iii. 17. Cic. Div. i. 77.

5 Plin. Ep. iii. 4.
6 Varr. L. L. iv. 16. Polyb. vi. 23. Sal. Jug. 38.
7 Sal. Jug. 58. Liv. xxxi. 21. Gell. xvi. 4. Cæs. B. G. i. 39. Suet. Aug. 38. Claud. 35. Plin. Ep. x. 19.
8 Liv. xxxv. 5. Polyb. vi. 26.
9 cum justo equitatu.
10 exercitus consularis.

11 Polyb. vi. 24.
12 Liv. ii. 29. 59. iv. 17. x. 40. 43. Sall. Cat. 59. Jug. 28. Cæs. B. C. ii. 17. iii. 55.
13 ductu vel imperio, et auspicio suo, Liv. iii. l. 17. 42. xli. 17. 28. Plaut. Amph. i. 1. 41. ji. 2. 25. Hor. i. 7. 27.
14 auspicio consulis, et ductu legati.
15 ductu Germanici, aus-

piciis Tiberii,—under the conduct of Germanicus and the auspices of Tiberius, Tac. Ann. ii. 41. Hor. Od. iv. 14.
16. 33. Ov. Trist. ii. 173. Liv. iii. 60.
16 Liv. i. 26. Plin. xvi. 3. Tac. Ann. xii. 56, cum paludatis ducibus, officers in red coats, Juv. vi. 399.

Paludamentum.

Sagum.

the consul in war.[1] CHLAMYS was likewise the name of a travelling dress ;[2] hence *chlamydatus*, a traveller or foreigner.[3]

The military cloak of the officers and soldiers was called SAGUM, also *chlamys*, an open robe drawn over the other clothes, and fastened with a clasp,[4] opposed to *toga*, the robe of peace. When there was a war in Italy,[5] all the citizens put on the *sagum :* hence *est in sagis civitas, sumere saga, ad saga ire :* et *redire ad togas,* also put for the general's robe ; thus, *punico lugubre mutavit sagum,* i. e. *deposuit coccineam chlamydem* Antonius, *et accepit nigram,* laid aside his purple robe and put on mourning.[6]

III. DISCIPLINE OF THE ROMANS, THEIR MARCHES AND ENCAMPMENTS.

THE discipline of the Romans was chiefly conspicuous in their marches and encampments. They never passed a night, even in the longest marches, without pitching a camp, and fortifying it with a rampart and ditch.[7] Persons were always sent before to choose and mark out a place for that purpose ;[8] hence called METATORES ; thus, *alteris castris vel secundis,* is put for *altero die,* the second day ; *tertiis castris, quintis castris,* &c.[9]

When the army staid but one night in the same camp, or even two or three nights, it was simply called *castra,* and in later ages MANSIO; which word is also put for the journey of one day, or for an inn,[10] as σταθμος among the Greeks.

When an army remained for a considerable time in the same place, it was called *castra* STATIVA, a standing camp, ÆSTIVA, a summer camp ; and HIBERNA, a winter camp (which was first used in the siege of Veji).[11]

The winter quarters of the Romans were strongly fortified, and furnished, particularly under the emperors, with every accommodation like a

1 Liv. xli. 10. xlv. 30.   Rud. ii. 2. 9.   7 Liv. xliv. 39. Sall. 10 Suet. Tit. 10. Plin.
2 vestis viatoria.   5 in tumultu.   Jug. 45. 91.   xii. 14.
3 Plaut. Pseud. iv. 2. sc. 6 Cic. Phil. v. 12. viii. 8 castra metari.   11 Liv. v. 2. hibernacula
7. 49.   11. xiv. 1. Hor. Ep. ix. 9 Tac. Hist. iii. 15. iv. ædificavit, xxiii.
4 Suet. Aug. 26. Plaut. 27.   71. Cæs. B. G. vii. 36.

city, as storehouses,[1] workshops,[2] an infirmary,[3] &c. Hence from them many towns in Europe are supposed to have had their origin; in England particularly, those whose names end in *cester* or *chester*.

The form of the Roman camp was a square,[4] and always of the same figure. In later ages, in imitation of the Greeks, they sometimes made it circular, or adapted it to the nature of the ground.[5] It was surrounded with a ditch,[6] usually nine feet deep and twelve feet broad, and a rampart,[7] composed of the earth dug from the ditch,[8] and sharp stakes[9] stuck into it.[10]

The camp had four gates, one on each side, called *porta* PRÆTORIA, vel *extraordinaria*, next the enemy; DECUMANA, opposite to the former,[11] *porta* PRINCIPALIS DEXTRA and PRINCIPALIS SINISTRA.[12]

The camp was divided into two parts, called the upper and lower.

The upper part[13] was that next the *porta prætoria,* in which was the ge-

---

PLAN OF A POLYBIAN OR CONSULAR CAMP.

Section of the Vallum, and Agger, with Fascines.

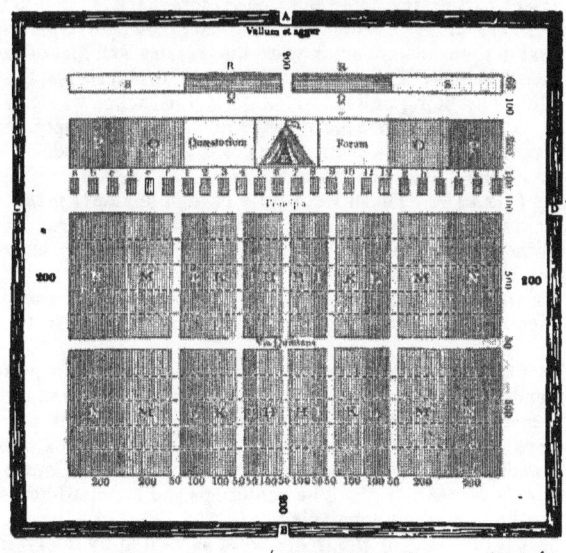

REFERENCES.	nistra.	M Cavalry of allies.	sional allies.
The dotted lines across the cavalry, &c. denote the divisions of troops or maniples.	D Porta principalis dextra.	N Infantry of allies.	1 2 3 4 5 6 7 8 9 10 11 12
	E Prætorium.	O Consul's and Quæstor's horse guards.	The twelve tribunes.
	H Roman cavalry.	P Do. foot guards.	a b c d e f g h i j k l,
A Prætorian gate.	I Triarii.	Q Extraordinary cavalry of the allies.	The prefects of allies.
B Decuman gate.	K Principes and Velites.	R Do. foot of the allies.	₊*₊ The figures on the right, and bottom, are
C Porta principalis si-	L Hastati and Velites.	S Strangers and occa-	the measures of length in feet.

1 armaria.	6 fossa.	xvii. 14, 15.	12 Liv. xl. 27.
2 fabricæ.	7 vallum.	11 ab tergo castrorum et hosti aversa, vel ab hoste, Liv. iii. 5. x. 32.	13 pars castrorum superior.
3 valetudinarium.	8 agger.		
4 quadrata.	9 sudes, valli vel pali.		
5 Veg. i. 23. Polyb. vi. 25.	10 Virg. G. ii. 25. Cæs. B. C. ii. 1. 15. Polyb.	Cæs. B. G. ii. 24. Cir. iii. 79.	

neral's tent,[1] called PRÆTORIUM, also AUGURALE,[2] from that part of it where he took the auspices,[3] or AUGUSTALE, with a sufficient space around for his retinue, the prætorian cohort, &c. On one side of the *prætorium* were the tents of lieutenant-generals, and on the other that of the quæstor, QUÆS-TORIUM, which seems anciently to have been near the *porta decumana*, hence called *quæstoria*. Hard by the quæstor's tent, was the FORUM, called also QUINTANA, where things were sold and meetings held.[4] In this part of the camp were also the tents of the tribunes, prefects of the allies, the *evocati*, *ablecti*, and *extraordinarii*, both horse and foot. But in what order they were placed does not appear from the classics. We only know that a particular place was assigned both to officers and men, with which they were all perfectly acquainted.

The lower part of the camp was separated from the upper by a broad open space, which extended the whole breadth of the camp, called PRINCI-PIA, where the tribunal of the general was erected, when he either adminis-tered justice, or harangued the army,[5] where the tribunes held their courts,[6] and punishments were inflicted, the principal standards of the army, and the altars of the gods stood ; also the images of the emperors, by which the soldiers swore,[7] and deposited their money at the standards,[8] as in a sacred place, each a certain part of his pay, and the half of a donative, which was not restored till the end of the war.[9]

In the lower part of the camp the troops were disposed in this manner : the cavalry in the middle : on both sides of them the *triarii*, *principes*, and *hastati ;* next to them on both sides were the cavalry and foot of the allies, who, it is observable, were always posted in separate places, lest they should form any plots[10] by being united. It is not agreed what was the place of the *velites*. They are supposed to have occupied the empty space be-tween the ramparts and the tents, which was 200 feet broad. The same may be said of the slaves (CALONES vel *servi*), and retainers or followers of the camp (LIXÆ).[11] These were little used in ancient times. A com-mon soldier was not allowed a slave, but the officers were. The *lixæ* were sometimes altogether prohibited.[12] At other times they seem to have staid without the camp, in what was called PROCESTRIA.[13]

The tents (*tentoria*) were covered with leather or skins extended with ropes : hence *sub pellibus hiemare, durare, haberi, retineri*, in tents, or in camp.[14]

In each tent were usually ten soldiers, with their *decanus* or petty officer who commanded them ;[15] which was properly called CONTUBERNIUM, and they *contubernales*. Hence young noblemen, under the general's particu-lar care, were said to serve in his tent,[16] and were called his CONTUBER-NALES. Hence, *vivere in contubernio alicujus*, to live in one's family. *Contubernalis*, a companion.[17] The centurions and standard-bearers were posted at the head of their companies.

The different divisions of the troops were separated by intervals, called VIÆ. Of these there were five longwise,[18] i. e. running from the *decuman*

1 ducis tabernaculum.
2 Tac. Ann. ii. 13. xv. 30.
3 auguraculum, Fest. vel auguratorium, Hyg. de Castramet.
4 Quin. viii. 2. 6. Liv. x. 32. xxxiv. 47. xli. 2. Suet. Ner. 26. Polyb. vi. 38.
5 Liv. vii. 12. Tac. An.

i. 67. Hist. iii. 13.
6 jura reddebant, Liv. xxviii. 24.
7 Suet. Oth. i. Aug. 24. Liv. viii. 32. ix. 16. xxvi. 48. Tac. Ann. i. 39. iv. 2. xv. 29. Hor. Od. iv. 5. Ep. ii. 1. 16.
8 ad vel apud signa.
9 Veg. ii. 20. Suet. Dom. 7.

10 nequid novæ rei mo-lirentur.
11 qui excercitum se-quebantur, quæstus, gratia, Fest. Liv. xxiii. 16.
12 Sal. Jug. 45.
13 ædificia extra castra, Fest. Tac. Hist. iv. 22.
14 Flor. i. 12. Liv. v. 2. 37. 39. Tac. Ann. 13.

35. Cic. Acad. iv. 2.
15 qui iis præfuit.
16 contubernio ejus mi-litare.
17 Suet. Jul. 42. Cic. Cœl. 30. Planc. 21. Sall. Jug. 64. Plin. Ep. i. 19. vii. 24. x. 3.
18 in longum.

towards the *prætorian* side; and three across, one in the lower part of the camp, called *quintana*, and two in the upper, namely, the *principia* already described, and another between the *prætorium* and the prætorian gate. The rows of tents between the *viæ* were called STRIGÆ.[1]

In pitching the camp, different divisions of the army were appointed to execute different parts of the work, under the inspection of the tribunes or centurions,[2] as they likewise were during the encampment to perform different services,[3] to procure water, forage, wood, &c. From these, certain persons were exempted,[4] either by law or custom, as the equites, the evocati and veterans,[5] or by the favour[6] of their commander; hence called BENEFICIARII.[7] But afterwards this exemption used to be purchased from the centurions, which proved most pernicious to military discipline. The soldiers obliged to perform these services were called MUNIFICES.[8]

Under the emperors there was a particular officer in each legion who had the charge of the camp, called PRÆFECTUS CASTRORUM.[9]

A certain number of maniples was appointed to keep guard at the gates, on the rampart, and in other places of the camp, before the *prætorium*, the tents of the legati, quæstor, and tribunes, both by day and by night,[10] who were changed every three hours.[11]

EXCUBIÆ denotes watches either by day or night; VIGILIÆ, only by night. Guards placed before the gates were properly called STATIONES, on the ramparts CUSTODIÆ. But *statio* is also put for any post; hence, *vetat Pythagoras injussu imperatoris, id est, Dei, de præsidio et statione vitæ decedere*, Pythagoras forbids us to quit our post and station in life without the command of the governor, that is, of God. Whoever deserted his station was punished with death.[12]

Every evening before the watches were set,[13] the watch-word (*symbolum*) or private signal, by which they might distinguish friends from foes,[14] was distributed through the army by means of a square tablet of wood in the form of a die, called TESSERA from its four corners.[15] On it was inscribed whatever word or words the general chose, which he seems to have varied every night.[16]

A frequent watch-word of Marius was LAR DEUS; of Sylla, APOLLO DELPHICUS; and of Cæsar, VENUS GENITRIX, &c.; of Brutus, LIBERTAS.[17] It was given[18] by the general to the tribunes and præfects of the allies, by them to the centurions, and by them to the soldiers. The person who carried the tessera from the tribunes to the centurions was called TESSE-RARIUS.[19]

In this manner also the particular commands of the general were made known to the troops, which seems likewise sometimes to have been done *viva voce*.[20]

Every evening when the general dismissed his chief officers and friends,[21] after giving them his commands, all the trumpets sounded.[22]

Certain persons were every night appointed to go round[23] the watches; hence called CIRCUITORES, vel *circitores*. This seems to have been at

---

1 ῥύμαι.
2 Juv. vii. 147.
3 ministeria.
4 immunes operum militarium, in unum pugnæ laborem reservati, —excused from military works, being reserved entirely for the single labour of fighting, Liv. vii. 7.

5 Val. Max. ii. 9. 7. Tac. Ann. i. 36.
6 beneficio.
7 Fest. Cæs. B. C. i. 75.
8 Veg.ii.7. 19. Tac. Ann. i. 17. Hist. i. 46.
9 Tac. Ann. i 20. xiv. 37. Hist. ii. 29. Veg. ii. 10.
10 agere excubias vel stationes et vigilias.

11 Polyb. vi. 33.
12 Suet. Aug. 24. Cic. Sen. 20. Liv. xxv. 10. xliv. 33.
13 antequam vigiliæ disponerentur.
14 Dio. xliii. 34.
15 τέσσαρες, -α, quatuor.
16 Polyb. vi. 32.
17 Serv. Virg. Æn. vii. 637. Dio. 47. 43.

18 tessera data est.
19 Tac. Hist. i. 25.
20 Liv. vii. 35. ix. 32. xxvii. 46. xxviii. 14. xliv. 33. Suet. Galb. 6.
21 cum prætorium dimittebat.
22 Liv. xxx. 5. xxi. 54. xxvi. 15. xxxvii. 5.
23 circumire vel obire.

first done by the equites and tribunes, on extraordinary occasions by the legati and general himself. At last particular persons were chosen for that purpose by the tribunes.[1]

The Romans used only wind-instruments of music in the army. Those were the TUBA, straight like our trumpet ; CORNU, the horn, bent almost round ; BUCCINA, similar to the horn, commonly used by the watches ; LI-TUUS, the clarion, bent a little at the end, like the augur's staff or *lituus*; all of brass : whence those who blew them were called ÆNEATORES. The *tuba* was used as a signal for the foot, the *lituus* for the horse ; but they are sometimes confounded, and both called *concha*, because first made of shells.[2]

The signal was given for changing the watches[3] with a trumpet or horn (*taba*),[4] hence *ad tertiam buccinam*, for *vigiliam*,[5] and the time was determined by hour-glasses.[6]

A principal part of the discipline of the camp consisted in exercises (whence the army was called EXERCITUS), walking and running[7] completely armed ; leaping, swimming ;[8] vaulting[9] upon horses of wood ; shooting the arrow, and throwing the javelin ; attacking a wooden figure of a man as a real enemy ;[10] the carrying of weights, &c.[11]

When the general thought proper to decamp,[12] he gave the signal for collecting their baggage,[13] whereupon all took down their tents,[14] but not till they saw this done to the tents of the general and tribunes.[15] Upon the next signal they put their baggage on the beasts of burden, and upon the third signal began to march ; first the *extraordinarii* and the allies of the right wing with their baggage ; then the legions ; and last of all the allies of the left wing, with a party of horse in the rear, (*ad agmen cogendum*, i. e. *colligendum*, to prevent straggling,) and sometimes on the flanks, in such order[16] that they might readily be formed into a line of battle if an enemy attacked them.

An army in close array was called AGMEN PILATUM, vel *justum*.[17] When under no apprehension of an enemy, they were less guarded.[18]

The form of the army on march, however, varied, according to circumstances and the nature of the ground. It was sometimes disposed into a square (AGMEN QUADRATUM), with the baggage in the middle.[19]

Scouts (*speculatores*) were always sent before to reconnoitre the ground.[20] A certain kind of soldiers under the emperors were called SPECULATORES.[21]

The soldiers were trained with great care to observe the military pace,[22] and to follow the standards.[23] For that purpose, when encamped, they were led out thrice a month, sometimes ten, sometimes twenty miles, less or more, as the general inclined. They usually marched at the rate of twenty miles in five hours, sometimes with a quickened pace[24] twenty-four miles in that time.

---

1 Liv. xxii. 1. xxviii. 24. Sall. Jug. 45. Veg. iii. 8.
2 Suet. Jul. 32. Acron. Hor. Od. i. 1. 23. Virg. Æn. vi. 167. 171.
3 vigiliis mutandis.
4 tuba, Luc. viii. 24. buccinna, Liv. vii. 35. Tac. Hist. v. 22.
5 Liv. xxvi. 15.
6 per clepsydras, Veg. iii. 8. see p. 166.
7 decursio.

8 Liv. xxiii. 35. xxvi. 51. xxix. 22. Polyb. vi. 20. Suet. Aug. 65.
9 salitio, Veg. i. 18.
10 exercitus ad palum, vel palaris, Juv. vi. 346.
11 Virg. G. iii. 346.
12 castra movere.
13 colligendi vasa.
14 tabernacula detendebant.
15 Polyb. vi.
16 composito agmine,

non itineri magis apto, quam prælio.
17 Serv. Virg. Æn. xii. 121. Tac. Hist. i. 68.
18 agmine incauto, i. e. minus munito, ut into-pacatosducebat.ac.consul,—theconsul marched in a careless manner, as through a tract where no hostility was to be apprehended, Liv. xxxv. 4.
19 Liv. xxxi. 37. xxxv.

4. 27, 28. xxxix. 30. Hirt. Bell. Gall. viii. 8. Tac. Ann. i. 51.
20 ad omnia exploranda, Suet. Jul. 58. Sall Jug. 46.
21 Tac. Hist. i. 24, 25. 27. ii 11. 33 73. Suet. Claud. 35. Oth. 5.
22 gradu militari incedere.
23 signa sequi.
24 gradu vel agmine citato, Veg. i. 9.

35

The load which a Roman soldier carried is almost
incredible: victuals[1] for fifteen days, sometimes
more,[2] usually corn, as being lighter, sometimes
dressed food,[3] utensils,[4] a saw, a basket, a mattock,[5]
an axe, a hook, and leathern thong,[6] a chain, a pot,
&c., stakes usually three or four, sometimes twelve,[7]
the whole amounting to sixty pounds weight, besides
arms ; for a Roman soldier considered these not as a
burden, but as a part of himself.[8] Under this load
they commonly marched twenty miles a day, sometimes more.[9] There were beasts of burden for carrying the tents, mills, baggage, &c. (JUMENTA SARCI-
NARIA.) The ancient Romans rarely used waggons,
as being more cumbersome.[10]

The general usually marched in the centre, sometimes in the rear, or wherever his presence was necessary.[11]

When they came near the place of encampment, some tribunes and centurions, with proper persons appointed for that service,[12] were sent before
to mark out the ground, and assign to each his proper quarters, which they
did by erecting flags[13] of different colours in the several parts.

The place for the general's tent was marked with a white flag, and
when it was once fixed, the places of the rest followed of course, as being
ascertained and known.[14] When the troops came up, they immediately
set about making the rampart,[15] while part of the army kept guard[16] to
prevent surprise. The camp was always marked out in the same manner,
and fortified, if they were to continue in it only for a single night.[17]

IV. THE ORDER OF BATTLE AND THE DIFFERENT
STANDARDS.

THE Roman army was usually drawn up in three lines,[18] each several
rows deep.

The *hastati* were placed in the first line ;[19] the *principes* in the second ;
and the *triarii* or *pilani* in the third ; at proper distances from one another.
The principes are supposed anciently to have stood foremost. Hence *post
principia*, behind the first line ; *transvorsis principiis*, the front or first line
being turned into the flank.[20]

A maniple of each kind of troops was placed behind one another, so
that each legion had ten maniples in front. They were not placed directly
behind one another as on march,[21] but obliquely, in the form of what is
called a *quincunx*, unless when they had to contend with elephants, as at
the battle of Zama.[22] There were certain intervals or spaces,[23] not only
between the lines, but likewise between the maniples. Hence *ordines*

1 cibaria.
2 Virg. G. iii. 346. Hor.
Sat. ii. 10. Cic. Tusc.
ii. 15, 16. Liv. Ep 57.
3 coctus cibus, Liv. ii.
27.
4 utensilia, ib. 42.
5 rutrum.
6 falx et lorum ad pabu-
landum.

7 Liv. iii. 27. xxviii. 45.
Hor. Ep. ix. 13.
8 arma membra milites
ducebant, Cic. Tusc.ii.
16.
9 Veg. i. 10. Spart.
Adrian. 10.
10 Cæs. B. C. l. 81.
11 Sall. Jug. 45. Polyb.
x. 22.

12 cum metatoribus.
13 vexilla.
14 Polyb. vi. 39.
15 vallum jaciebant.
16 præsidium agitabant.
17 Josep. Bel. Jud. iii. 6.
18 triplice acie, vel tri-
plicibus subsidiis, Sall.
Jug. 49.
19 in prima acie, vel in

principiis.
20 Ter. Eun. iv. 7. 11.
Liv. ii. 65. iii. 22. vili.
8. 10. xxxvii. 39. Sall
Jug. 49.
21 agmine quadrato.
22 Virg. G. ii. 279. Liv.
xxx. 33. Polyb. xv. 9.
App.
23 viæ.

explicare, to arrange in order of battle, and in the maniples each man had a free space of at least three feet, both on the side and behind.[1]

The *velites* were placed in the spaces or intervals,[2] between the maniples, or on the wings.[3]

The Roman legions possessed the centre,[4] the allies and auxiliaries the right and left wings.[5] The cavalry were sometimes placed behind the foot, whence they were suddenly led out on the enemy through the intervals between the maniples, but they were commonly posted on the wings; hence called ALÆ,[6] which name is commonly applied to the cavalry of the allies,[7] when distinguished from the cavalry of the legions,[8] and likewise to the auxiliary infantry.[9]

This arrangement, however, was not always observed. Sometimes all the different kinds of troops were placed in the same line. For instance, when there were two legions, the one legion and its allies were placed in the first line, and the other behind as a body of reserve.[10] This was called ACIES DUPLEX, when there was only one line, ACIES SIMPLEX. Some think, that in later times an army was drawn up in order of battle, without any regard to the division of soldiers into different ranks. In the description of Cæsar's battles there is no mention made of the soldiers being divided into *hastati, principes*, and *triarii*, but only of a certain number of legions and cohorts, which Cæsar generally drew up in three lines.[11] In the battle of Pharsalia he formed a body of reserve, which he calls a fourth line,[12] to oppose the cavalry of Pompey, which indeed determined the fortune of the day. This was properly called ACIES QUADRUPLEX.[13]

In the time of Cæsar the bravest troops were commonly placed in the front,[14] contrary to the ancient custom. This and various other alterations in the military art are ascribed to Marius.

ACIES is put not only for the whole or part of an army in order of battle; as, *aciem instruere, æquare, exornare, explicare, extenuare, firmare, perturbare, instaurare, restituere, redintegrare*, &c., but also for the battle itself; *commissam aciem secutus est terræ tremor*, there happened an earthquake after the fight was begun; *post acies primas*, after the first battle.[15]

Each century, or at least each maniple, had its proper standard and standard-bearer. Hence *milites signi unius*, of one maniple or century;[16] *reliqua signa in subsidio artius collocat*, he places the rest of his troops as a body of reserve or in the second line more closely; *signa inferre*, to advance; *convertere*, to face about; *efferre*, to go out of the camp; *a signis discedere*, to desert;[17] *referre*, to retreat, also to cover the standards; *signa conferre*, vel *signis collatis confligere*, to engage; *signis infestis inferri, ire* vel *incedere*, to march against the enemy; *urbem intrare sub signis*, to enter the city in military array; *sub signis legiones ducere*, in battle order; *signa infesta ferre*, to advance as if to an attack.[18]

---

1 Liv. iii. 60. Polyb. xvii. 26.
2 in viis.
3 Liv. xxx. 33. xlii. 58. Sall. Jug. 49.
4 mediam aciem tenebant.
5 cornua, Liv. xxxvii.
6 Liv. x. 5. xxviii. 14. Gell. xvi. 4. Plin. Ep. 7. 30.
7 alarii vel alarii equi-

tes, Liv. xxxv. Cic. Fam. ii. 17.
8 equites legionarii, Liv. xl. 40. Cæs. B. G. i. 41.
9 cohortes alares vel alariæ, Liv. x. 40. 42. Cæs. B. C. i. 65. ii. 16.
10 in subsidiis vel præsidiis, Liv. xxvii. 2. 12. xxix. 8. xxx. 18. Cæs. B. C. i. 75. B. G.

iii. 25. Afr. 12. 53. Sall. Cat. 59.
11 Cæs. B. G. i. 19. 41. ii. 22. iv. 11. B. C. i. 57. 75. iii. 74. Afr. 53. Sall. Cat. 59. Tac. Hist. 24.
12 quartam aciem instituit.
13 B. Afr. 58. B. C. iii. 76.
14 Sall. Cæs. ib.

15 Cic. Fam. vi. 3. Suet. Aug 20. Flor. ii. 6. Ov. Met. xiii. 207.
16 Var. L. L. iv. 16. Liv. viii. 8. Vig. ii. 23.
17 Liv. xxv. 23. xxxiii. 24. 1. 9. Sall. Cat. 59. Cæs. B. G. i. 25. Liv. xxv. 4.
18 Liv. iii. 51. xxv. 20. Virg. Æn. v. 582. vi. 826. Cic. Att. xvi. 6.

The ensign of a *manipulus* was anciently a bundle of hay on the top of a pole,[1] whence *miles manipularis*, a common soldier; afterwards a spear with a cross piece of wood on the top, sometimes the figure of a hand above, probably in allusion to the word *manipulus ;* and below, a small round or oval shield. commonly of silver, also of gold, on which were represented the images of the warlike deities, as Mars or Minerva; and after the extinction of liberty, of the emperors, or of their favourites.[2] Hence the standards were called *numina legionum*, and worshipped with religious adoration. The soldiers swore by them.[3]

We read also of the standard of the cohorts, as of præfects or commanders of the cohorts. But then a whole is supposed to be put for a part, *cohortes* for *manipuli* or *ordines*, which were properly said *ad signa convenire et contineri.* The divisions of the legion, however, seem to have been different at different times. Cæsar mentions 120 chosen men of the same century,[4] and Vegetius (ii. 13) makes *manipulus* the same with *contubernium*. It is at least certain that there always was a diversity of ranks,[5] and a gradation of preferments.[6] The divisions most frequently mentioned are COHORTES, battalions of foot, and TURMÆ, troops of horse. *Cohors* is sometimes applied to the auxiliaries, and opposed to the legions. It is also, although more rarely, applied to cavalry.[7]

The standards of the different divisions had certain letters inscribed on them, to distinguish the one from the other.[8]

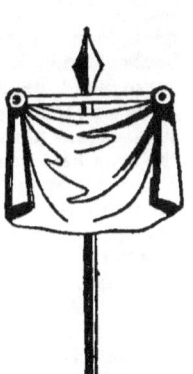

The standard of the cavalry was called VEXILLUM, a flag or banner, i. e. a square piece of cloth fixed on the end of a spear, used also by the foot,[9] particularly by the veterans who had served out their time, but under the emperors were still retained in the army, and fought in bodies distinct from the legion, under a particular standard of their own (*sub vexillo*, hence called VEXILLARII.) But *vexillum* or *vexillatio* is also put for any number of troops following one standard.[10] To lose the standards was always esteemed disgraceful,[11] particularly to the standard-bearer, sometimes a capital crime. Hence to animate the soldiers, the standards were sometimes thrown among the enemy.[12]

A silver eagle with expanded wings, on the top of a spear, sometimes holding a thunderbolt in its claws, with the figure of a small chapel above it, was the common standard of the legion, at least after the time of Marius, for

1 see p. 248.
2 Ov. F. iii. 116. Plin. xxxiii. 3. Herodian. iv. 7. Tac. Ann. i. 43. Hist. i. 41. iv. 62.
3 Suet. Tib. 48. Cal. 14. Vit. 2. Tac. Ann. i. 39. Veg. ii. 6. Luc. i. 374.
4 Liv. xxvii. 15. Cæs. B. G. ii. 25. vi. 1. 31.

37. B. C. ii. 13. iii. 76. Tac. Ann. i. 18. Hist. i. 41. Sall. Jug. 46.
5 ordines inferiores et superiores, Cæs. B. G. vi. 34. Tac. Hist. i. 52. iv. 59.
6 ordines vel gradus militiæ, ib. Cæs. B. C. i. 44. Suet. Claud. 25.

7 Cic. Marc. 2. Fam. xv. 2. Att. vi. 2. Tac. Hist. ii. 89. v. 18. Plin. Ep. x. 107.
8 Verg. ii. 13.
9 Liv. Cæs. B. G. vi. 33. 37.
10 Tac. Ann. i. 17. 26. 36. 38. Hist. i. 31. 70. Suet. Galb. 18. Stat.

Theb. xii. 782.
11 magnum perdere crimen erat, Ov. F. iii. 12 Cæs. B. C. iv. 23. v. 29. B. C. i. 54. Liv. ii. 59. iii. 70. vi. 8. xxv. 14. xxvi. 5.

before that the figures of other animals were used. Hence AQUILA is put for a legion,[1] and *aquila signaque* for all the standards of a legion. It was anciently carried before the first maniple of the triarii; but after the time of Marius, in the first line, and near it was the ordinary place of the general, almost in the centre of the army; thus MEDIO DUX AGMINE *Turnus vertitur arma tenens*, in the centre king Turnus moves, wielding his arms,[2] usually on horseback. So likewise the legati and tribunes.[3]

· The soldiers who fought before the standards, or in the first line, were called ANTESIGNANI;[4] those behind the standards,[5] POSTSIGNANI, vel SUBSIGNANI; but the *subsignani* seem to have been the same with the *vexillarii*, or privileged veterans.[6]

The general was usually attended by a select band, called COHORS PRÆTORIA, first instituted by Scipio Africanus; but something similar was used long before that time, not mentioned in Cæsar, unless by the by.[7]

When a general, after having consulted the auspices, had determined to lead forth his troops against the enemy, a red flag was displayed,[8] on a spear from the top of the prætorium,[9] which was the signal to prepare for battle. Then having called an assembly by the sound of a trumpet,[10] he harangued[11] the soldiers, who usually signified their approbation by shouts, by raising their right hands, or by beating on their shields with their spears. Silence was a mark of timidity.[12] This address was sometimes made in the open field from a tribunal raised of turf.[13] A general always addressed his troops by the title of *milites*; hence Cæsar greatly mortified the soldiers of the tenth legion, when they demanded their discharge, by calling them QUIRITES instead of MILITES.

After the harangue all the trumpets sounded,[14] which was the signal for marching. At the same time the soldiers called out *to arms*.[15] The standards which stood fixed in the ground were pulled up.[16] If this was done easily, it was reckoned a good omen; if not, the contrary. Hence, *aquilæ prodire nolentes*, the eagles unwilling to move.[17] The watch-word was given,[18] either *viva voce*, or by means of a *tessera*, as other orders were communicated.[19] In the meantime many of the soldiers made their testaments (*in procinctu*.)[20]

When the army was advanced near the enemy,[21] the general riding round the ranks again exhorted them to courage, and then gave the signal to engage. Upon which all the trumpets sounded, and the soldiers rushed for-

1 Dio. xl. 18. Plin. x. 4. s. 5. Cæs. Hisp. 30.
2 Virg Æn. ix. 28. Tac. passim. Sall. Cat, 59.
3 Liv. vi. 7. Sall. Cat. 59. Cæs. Gall. i. 25. ib. Cæs. vii. 65.
4 Liv. ii. 20. iv. 37. vii. 16. 33. ix. 32. 39. xxii. 5. xxx. 33. Cæs. B. C. i. 41. 52.
5 post signa, Liv. viii. 11. Front. Strat. i. 2. 17.
6 Tac. Hist. i. 70. iv.

7 33. Ann. i. 36.
7 Cic. Cat. ii. 11. Fam. x. 30. Sall. Cat.60. Jug. 98. Fest. Liv. ii. 20. B. G. i. 40.
8 vexillum vel signum pugnæ proponebatur.
9 Cæs. Bell. G. ii. 20. Liv. xxii. 45.
10 classico, i. e. tuba concione advocata, Liv. iii. 62. vii. 36. viii. 7. 32.
11 alloquebatur.
12 Luc. i. 386. ii. 596.

13 e tribunali cespititio aut viridi cespite exstructo, Tac. Ann. i.
16 Plin. Pan. 56. Stat. Silv. v. 2. 144. Dio. xlii.
53 Suet. Cæs. 70.
14 signa canebant, Luc. ii. 597.
15 ad arma conclamatum est.
16 convellebantur, Liv. iii. 50. 54. vi. 28. Virg. Æn. ix. 19.
17 Flor. ii. 6. Dio. xl. 18.

Liv. xxii. 3. Cic. Div. i. 35. Val. Max. i. 211. Luc. vii. 162.
18 signum datum est.
19 Liv. v. 36. xxi. 14. Cæs. B. C. ii. 20. B. Afric. 83.
20 see p 41. Gell. xv. 27.
21 intra teli conjectum, unde a ferentariis prælium committi posset.

ward to the charge with a great shout,[1] which they did to animate one another and intimidate the enemy. Hence *primus clamor atque impetus rem decrevit*, when the enemy were easily conquered.[2]

The *velites* first began the battle; and when repulsed retreated either through the intervals between the files,[3] or by the flanks of the army, and rallied in the rear. Then the hastati advanced; and if they were defeated, they retired slowly[4] into the intervals of the ranks of the principes, or if greatly fatigued, behind them. Then the principes engaged; and if they too were defeated, the triarii rose up;[5] for hitherto they continued in a stooping posture,[6] leaning on their right knee, with their left leg stretched out, and protected with their shields: hence, AD TRIARIOS VENTUM EST, it is come to the last push.[7]

The triarii receiving the hastati and principes into the void spaces between their manipuli, and closing their ranks,[8] without leaving any space between them, in one compact body,[9] renewed the combat. Thus the enemy had several fresh attacks to sustain before they gained the victory. If the triarii were defeated, the day was lost, and a retreat was sounded.[10]

This was the usual manner of attack before the time of Marius. After that several alterations took place, which, however, are not exactly ascertained.

The legions sometimes drew lots about the order of their march, and the place they were to occupy in the field.[11]

The Romans varied the line of battle by advancing or withdrawing particular parts. They usually engaged with a straight front[12] (ACIES DIRECTA). Sometimes the wings were advanced before the centre (ACIES SINUATA), which was the usual method; or the contrary (ACIES GIBBERA, vel *flexa*), which Hannibal used in the battle of Cannæ.[13] Sometimes they formed themselves into the figure of a wedge, (CUNEUS vel *trigonum*, a triangle,) called by the soldiers CAPUT PORCINUM, like the Greek letter delta, *Δ*. This method of war was also adopted by the Germans and Spaniards.[14] But *cuneus* is also put for any close body, as the Macedonian phalanx. Sometimes they formed themselves to receive the *cuneus*, in the form a FORCEPS or scissars; thus, V.[15]

When surrounded by the enemy, they often formed themselves into a round body, (ORBIS vel GLOBUS, hence *orbes facere* vel *volvere; in orbem se tutari* vel *conglobare*).[16] When they advanced or retreated in separate parties, without remaining in any fixed position, it was called SERRA.[17]

When the Romans gained a victory, the soldiers with shouts of joy saluted their general by the title of IMPERATOR.[18] His lictors wreathed their *fasces* with laurel, as did also the soldiers their spears and javelins.[19] He immediately sent letters wrapped round with laurel[20] to the senate, to inform them of his success,[21] and if the victory was considerable, to demand a triumph, to which Persius alludes, vi. 43. These kind of letters were

1 maximo clamore procurrebant cum signis vel pilis infestis, i. e. in hostem versis vel directis, Sall. Cat. 60. Cæs. B. C. iii. 92. Liv. vi. 8. &c. Dio. xxxvi. 39.
2 Liv. xxv. 4.
3 per intervalla ordinum.
4 presso pede.

5 consurgebant.
6 subsidebant, hinc dicti subsidia, Fest.
7 Liv. viii. 8.
8 compressis ordinibus.
9 uno continente agmine.
10 receptui cecinerunt, Liv. viii. 8, 9.
11 Tac. Hist. ii. 41.
12 recta fronte, Festus;

vel æquatis, frontibus, Tibull. iv. i. 103.
13 Liv. xxii. 47. xxviii.
14. Sen. Beat. Vit. 4. Plut Mar.
14 Liv. viii. 10. xxxix. 31. Quinc. ii. 13. Virg. xii. 269. 457. Cæs. vi. 39. Tac. Mor. G. 6.
15 Liv. xxxii. 17. Gell. x. 9. Veg. ii. 19.
16 Sall. Jug. 97. Liv. ii.

50. iv. 28. 39. xxiii. 27. Cæs. B. G. iv. 37. Tac. Ann. ii. 11.
17 Festus.
18 see p. 113.
19 Stat. Sylv. vii. 92. Mart. viii. 5, 6. Plin. xv. 30. Plut. Lucul.
20 literæ laureatæ.
21 to which Ovid alludes, Am. ii. 11. 25.

seldom sent under the emperors.[1] If the senate approved, they decreed a thanksgiving[2] to the gods, and confirmed to the general the title of IMPERATOR, which he retained till his triumph or return to the city. In the mean time his lictors, having the fasces wreathed with laurel, attended him.[3]

V. MILITARY REWARDS.

AFTER a victory the general assembled his troops, and, in presence of the whole army, bestowed rewards on those who deserved them. These were of various kinds.

The highest reward was the civic crown (CORONA CIVICA), given to him who had saved the life of a citi-zen, with this inscription, OB CIVEM SERVATUM, vel *cives servatos*,[4] made of oak leaves,[5] hence called *quercus civilis*, and by the appointment of the general presented by the person who had been saved to his preserver, whom he ever after respected as a parent.[6] Under the emperors it was always bestowed by the prince.[7] It was attended with particular honours. The person who received it wore it at the spectacles, and sat next the senate. When he entered, the audience rose up, as a mark of respect.[8] Among the honours decreed to Augustus and Claudius by the senate was this, that a civic crown should be suspended from the top of their house, between two laurel branches, which were set up in the vestibule before the gate, as if they were the perpetual preservers of the citizens, and the conquerors of their enemies.[9] Hence, in some of the coins of Augustus, there is a civic crown, with these words inscribed, OB CIVES SERVATOS.

To the person who first mounted the rampart, or entered the camp of the enemy, was given by the general a golden crown, called CORONA VALLARIS vel CASTRENSIS ; to him who first scaled the walls of a city in an assault, CORONA MURALIS ; who first boarded the ship of an enemy, CORONA NAVALIS.[10]

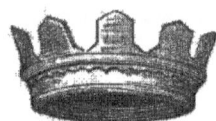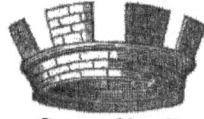

Corona Vallaris.   **Corona Muralis.**   *Corona Navalis.*

Augustus gave to Agrippa, after defeating Sextus Pompeius in a sea-fight near Sicily, a golden crown, adorned with figures of the beaks of ships, hence called ROSTRATA, said to have been never given to any other person ; but according to Festus and Pliny, it was also given to M. Varro in the war against the pirates by Pompey ; but they seem to confound the *corona rostrata* and *navalis*, which others make different.[11]

---

1 Dio. liv. 11. Tac. Agr. 18. Liv. xlv. 1. Cic. Pis. 17. Att. v. 20. Fam. ii. 10. App. B. Mithrid. p. 223.
2 supplicatio, vel supplicium, vel gratulatio, Cic. Marc. 4. Fam. ii. 18.
3 Cic. Phil. xiv. 3—5. 4 Gell. v. 6. Liv. vi 20. x. 46. Sen. Clem. i. 26. 5 e fronde querna. 6 Cic. Planc. 30. Virg. Æn. vi. 772. 7 imperatoria manu, Tac. Ann. iii.21. xv. 12. 8 ineunti etiam ab se-

natu assurgebatur, Plin. xxi. 4. 9 Suet. 17. Dio. liii. 16. Val. Max. ii. 8. fin. Ov. F. i. 614. iv. 958. Trist. iii. 1. 35—48. 10 Val. Max. i. 8. Liv. xxvi. 48. Gell. v. 6. Fest.

11 Suet. Claud. 17. Virg. viii. 684. Liv. Ep. 129. Paterc. ii. 81. Dio. xlix. 14. Fest. in voc. navali, Plin. vii. 20. xvi. 4.

When an army was freed from a blockade, the soldiers gave to their deliverer[1] a crown made of the
grass which grew in the place where they had been
blocked up; hence called *graminea corona* OBSIDIO-
NALIS. This of all military honours was esteemed
the greatest. A few, who had the singular good
fortune to obtain it, are recounted by Pliny.[2]

Golden crowns were also given to officers and soldiers who had displayed singular bravery; as to T. Manlius Torquatus, and M. Valerius
Corvus, who each of them slew a Gaul in single combat; to P. Decius,
who preserved the Roman army from being surrounded by the Samnites,[3]
and to others.

There were smaller rewards[4] of various kinds; as a spear without any
iron on it (HASTA PURA);[5] a flag or banner, i. e. a streamer on the end of a
lance or spear (VEXILLUM),[6] of different colours, with or without embroidery;[7] trappings (PHALERÆ), ornaments for horses and for men; golden
chains[8] (*aureæ* TORQUES), which went round the neck, whereas the *phaleræ* hung down to the breast; bracelets (ARMILLÆ), ornaments for the
arms; CORNICULA, ornaments for the helmet in the form of horns;[9] CA-
TELLÆ vel *catennulæ*, chains composed of rings; whereas the *torques* were
twisted[10] like a rope; FIBULÆ, clasps or buckles for fastening a belt or garment.[11]

These presents were conferred by the general in presence of the army;
and such as received them, after being publicly praised, were placed next
him. They ever after kept them with great care, and wore them at the
spectacles and on all public occasions. They first wore them at the games,
A. U. 459.[12]

The spoils (SPOLIA vel *exuviæ*), taken from the enemy were fixed up on
their door-posts, or in the most conspicuous part of their houses.[13]

When the general of the Romans slew the general of the enemy in sin
gle combat, the spoils which he took from him[14] were called SPOLIA OPI-
MA,[15] and hung up in the temple of Jupiter Feretrius, built by Romulus, and
repaired by Augustus, by the advice of Atticus.[16]   These spoils were obtained only thrice before the fall of the republic; the first by Romulus, who
slew Acron, king of the Cæninenses; the next by A. Cornelius Cossus,
who slew Lar Tolumnius, king of the Vejentes, A. U. 318; and the third
by M. Claudius Marcellus, who slew Viridomarus, king of the Gauls, A.
U. 530.[17]

Florus calls the spoils OPIMA, which Scipio Æmilianus, when in a subordinate rank, took from the king of the Turduli and Vaccæi in Spain,
whom he slew in single combat; but the *spolia opima* could properly be
obtained only by a person invested with supreme command.[18]

Sometimes soldiers, on account of their bravery, received a double share
of corn,[19] which they might give away to whom they pleased; hence called DUPLICARII, also double pay,[20] clothes, &c., called by Cicero DIARIA.[21]

1 ei duci, qui liberavit,   7 auratum vel purum,   11 Liv. xxxix. 31.   17 Liv. i. 10. iv. 20. Ep.
Gell. v. 6.   Sall. Jug. 85. Suet.   12 Sall. Jug. 54. Liv. x.   xx. Virg. Æn. vi. 859.
2 Liv. vii. 37. Plin.   Aug 25.   47. xxiv. 16. Cic. Phil.   Plut. Marc.Prop. iv. 11.
xvii. 4—6.   8 Tac. Ann. ii. 9. iii. 21.   v. 13 17.   18 Flor. ii. 17. Dio. li.
3 Liv. vii. 10. 26. x. 44. Juv. xvi. 60. Virg. Æn.   13 Virg. Æn. ii. 504.   24.
xxvi. 21. xxx. 16.   v. 310. Liv. ix. 46. xxii.   Liv. xxiii. 23.   19 duplex frumentum.
4 præmia minora.   52. Cic. Att. xvi. 17.   14 quæ dux duci detra-   20 duplex stipendium,
5 Virg. Æn. vi. 760.   Verr. iii. 60. iv. 12.   xit.   Liv. ii. 59. vii. 37.
Suet. Claud. 28.   9 Sil. Ital. xv. 52. Liv.   15 ab ope vel opibus,   21 Att. viii. 14. Cæs. B.
6 quasi parvum velum,   x. 44.   Fest. Liv. iv. 20.   C. iii. 53.
Serv. Virg. Æn. viii. 1.   10 tortæ.   16 Nep. Vit. 20.

TRIUMPHAL PROCESSION.

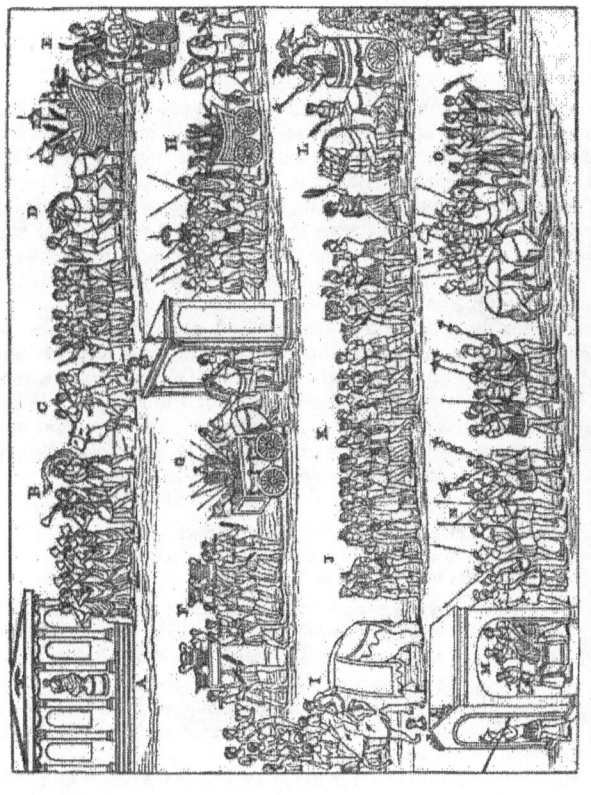

A. Temple of Jupiter Capitolinus. B. Musicians. C. Victims. D. Models of the conquered Cities. E. Bullion. F. Money. G. Arms of the vanquished Nations. H. Statues and Pictures. I. Elephants of the vanquished Nations. J. Captive Kings with their Families. K. Captives. L. General Triumphing. M. Sacrifice at the Gate. N. Victorious Army. O. General's Children and Kinsmen. P. Perfumes.

VI. A TRIUMPH.

THE highest military honour which could be obtained in the Roman state was a triumph, or solemn procession, with which a victorious general and his army advanced through the city to the capitol ; so called from Θριαμβος, the Greek name of Bacchus, who is said to have been the inventor of such processions. It had its origin at Rome, from Romulus carrying the spolia opima in procession to the capitol ;[1] and the first who entered the city in the form of a regular triumph was Tarquinius Priscus, the next P. Valerius ; and the first who triumphed after the expiration of his magistracy,[2] was Q. Publilius Philo.[3]

A triumph was decreed by the senate,[4] and sometimes by the people against the will of the senate, to the general who, in a just war with foreigners,[5] and in one battle, had slain above 5000 enemies of the republic, and by that victory had enlarged the limits of the empire. Whence a triumph was called *justus*, which was fairly won. And a general was said *triumphare*, et *agere* vel *deportare triumphum de* vel *ex aliquo ; triumphare aliquem* vel *aliquid*,[6] *ducere*, *portare* vel *agere eum in triumpho.*

There was no just triumph for a victory in a civil war ; hence,

Bella geri placuit nullos habitura triumphos ? *Luc.* i. 12.

Could you in wars like these provoke your fate ?
Wars where no triumphs on the victor wait ! *Rowe.*

although this was not always observed, nor when one had been first defeated, and afterwards only recovered what was lost, nor anciently could one enjoy that honour, who was invested with an extraordinary command, as Scipio in Spain,[7] nor unless he left his province in a state of peace, and brought from thence his army to Rome along with him, to be present at the triumph. But these rules were sometimes violated, particularly in the case of Pompey.[8]

There are instances of a triumph being celebrated without either the authority of the senate, or the order of the people, and also when no war was carried on.[9]

Those who were refused a triumph at Rome by public authority, sometimes celebrated it on the Alban mountain. This was first done by Papirius Naso, A. U. 522, whom several afterwards imitated.[10]

As no person could enter the city while invested with military command, generals, on the day of their triumph, were, by a particular order of the people, freed from that restriction.[11]

The triumphal procession began from the Campus Martius, and went from thence along the Via Triumphalis, through the Campus and Circus Flaminius to the Porta Triumphalis, and thence through the most public places of the city to the capitol.

The streets were strewed with flowers, and the altars smoked with incense.[12]

First went musicians of various kinds, singing and playing triumphal

1 Varr. L. L. v. 7. Plin. vii. 56. s. 57. Diony. ii. 34.
2 acto honore.
3 Liv. i. 38. ii. 7. viii. 26.
4 Liv. iii. 63. vii. 17.
5 justo et hostili bello, Cic. Dej. 5.
6 Virg. Æn. vi. 836.

Plin. v. 5. Val. Max. ii. 6. Cic. Pis. 19. Hor. Od. i. 12. 54.
7 Liv. xxviii. 38. xxxvi. 20. Ep. 115, 116. 133. Val. Max. ii. 8. 7. Dio. xlii. 18. xliii. 19. Flor. iv. 2. Plin. Pan. 2. Oros. iv.
8 Liv. xxvi. 21. xxxi.

49. xxxix. 29. xlv. 39. Val. Max. viii. 15. 6. Dio. xxxvii. 25.
9 Liv. x. 37. xl. 38. Oros. v. 4. Cic. Cœl. 14. Suet. Tib. 2. Val. Max. v. 4.6.
10 Val. Max. iii. 6. 5. Liv. xxvi. 21. xxxiii. 24. xlii. 21. xlv. 38.
11 ut iis, quo die urbem

triumphantes inveherentur, imperium esset, —that they might be invested with plenary authority, during the day on which they should ride through the city in triumph, Liv. xlv. 35.
12 Ov. Trist. iv. 2. 4.

songs ; next were led the oxen to be sacrificed, having their horns gilt, and their heads adorned with fillets and garlands ; then in carriages were brought the spoils taken from the enemy, statues, pictures, plate, armour, gold and silver, and brass ; also golden crowns, and other gifts sent by the allied and tributary states.[1] The titles of the vanquished nations were inscribed on wooden frames,[2] and the images or representations of the conquered countries, cities, &c.[3] The captive leaders followed in chains, with their children and attendants ; after the captives came the lictors, having their fasces[4] wreathed with laurel, followed by a great company of musicians and dancers, dressed like satyrs, and wearing crowns of gold : in the midst of whom was a pantomime, clothed in a female garb, whose business it was, with his looks and gestures, to insult the vanquished. Next followed a long train of persons carrying perfumes.[5] Then came the general (DUX) dressed in purple embroidered with gold,[6] with a crown of laurel on his head, a branch of laurel in his right hand, and in his left an ivory sceptre, with an eagle on the top, having his face painted with vermilion, in like manner as the statue of Jupiter on festival days,[7] and a golden ball[8] hanging from his neck on his breast, with some amulet in it, or magical preservative against envy,[9] standing in a gilded chariot[10] adorned with ivory,[11] and drawn by four white horses, at least after the time of Camillus, sometimes by elephants, attended by his relations,[12] and a great crowd of citizens all in white. His children used to ride in the chariot along with him,[13] and, that he might not be too much elated, a slave,[14] carrying a golden crown, sparkling with gems, stood behind him, who frequently whispered in his ear, REMEMBER THAT THOU ART A MAN ![15] After the general, followed the consuls and senators on foot, at least according to the appointment of Augustus ; for formerly they used to go before him. His legati and military tribunes commonly rode by his side.[16]

The victorious army, horse and foot, came last, all in their order, crowned with laurel, and decorated with the gifts which they had received for their valour, singing their own and their general's praises ; but sometimes throwing out railleries against him, often exclaiming, IO TRIUMPHE, in which all the citizens, as they passed along, joined.[17]

The general, when he began to turn his chariot from the forum to the capitol, ordered the captive kings and leaders of the enemy to be led to prison, and there to be slain, but not always ; and when he reached the capitol, he used to wait till he heard that these savage orders were executed.[18]

Then, after having offered up a prayer of thanksgiving to Jupiter and the other gods for his success, he commanded the victims to be sacrificed,

---

1 Virg. Æn. viii. 720. Liv. xxxiii. 24. xxxvii. , 58. xxxix. 5. 7. xl. 43. xlv. 40.
2 in ferculis, Suet. Jul. 37. Cic. Off. i. 36.
3 Liv. xxvi. 21. Quin. vi. 3. Plin. v. 5. Ov. Pont. ii. 1. 37. iii. 4. 25. Art. Am. i. 220. Flor. iv. 2.
4 the above cut represents the form of the

fasces without laurel. 5 suffimenta. 6 toga picta et tunica palmata. 7 Liv. ii. 47. x. 6. Plin. v.39. xv. 30. xxxiii. 7. s. 36. Diony. v. 47. Plut. Æn. Juv. x. 43. 8 aurea bulla. 9 Macrob. Sat. i. 6. 10 stans in curru aurato. 11 Ov. Pont. iii. 4. 35. Juv. v. 23. viii. 3.

12 Ov. Art. i. 214. Liv. v. 23. Plin. viii. 2. Suet. Tib. 2. Dom. 2. Cic. Mur. 5. 13 Juv. x. 45. Liv. xlv. 40. App. de Punic. 14 ne sibi placeret. 15 Plin. xxxiii. 1. s. 4. Juv. x. 41. Zonar. ii. Tertul. Apolog. 33. 16 Dio. li. 21. Cic. Pis. 25. 17 Hor. Od. iv. 2. 49.

Ov. Trist. iv. 2. 51. Am. i. 2. 34. Liv. v. 49. xlv. 38. Suet. Jul. 49. 51. Diony. vii. 72. Mart. i. 5. 3. 18 Cic. Ver. v. 30. Liv. xxvi. 13. xlv. 41, 42. Dio. xl. 41. xliii. 19. App. Bell. Mithrid. 253. Joseph. Bell. Jud. vii. 24.

which were always white, from the river Clitumnus,[1] and deposited his golden crown in the lap of Jupiter,[2] to whom he dedicated part of the spoils.[3] After which he gave a magnificent entertainment in the capitol to his friends and the chief men of the city. The consuls were invited, but were afterwards desired not to come,[4] that there might be no one at the feast superior to the triumphant general. After supper he was conducted home by the people with music and a great number of lamps and torches, which sometimes also were used in the triumphal procession.[5]

The gold and silver were deposited in the treasury,[6] and a certain sum was usually given as a donative to the officers and soldiers, who then were disbanded.[7] The triumphal procession sometimes took up more than one day ; that of Paulus Æmilius three.[8] When the victory was gained by sea, it was called a NAVAL TRIUMPH ; which honour was first granted to Duilius, who defeated the Carthaginian fleet near Liparæ in the first Punic war, A. U. 493, and a pillar erected to him in the forum, called COLUMNA ROSTRATA,[9] with an inscription, part of which still remains.

When a victory had been gained without difficulty, or the like, an inferior kind of triumph was granted, called OVATIO, in which the general entered the city on foot or on horseback, crowned with myrtle, not with laurel,[10] and instead of bullocks, sacrificed a sheep,[11] whence its name.[12]

After Augustus, the honour of a triumph was in a manner confined to the emperors themselves, and the generals who acted with delegated authority under their auspices only received triumphal ornaments, a kind of honour devised by Augustus.[13] Hence L. Vitellius, having taken Terracina by storm, sent a laurel branch in token of it[14] to his brother. As the emperors were so great, that they might despise triumphs, so that honour was thought above the lot of a private person ; such therefore usually declined it, although offered to them ; as Vinicius, Agrippa, and Platius.[15] We read, however, of a triumph being granted to Belisarius, the general of Justinian, for his victories in Africa, which he celebrated at Constantinople, and is the last instance of a triumph recorded in history. The last triumph celebrated at Rome was by Diocletian and Maximian, 20th Nov. A. D. 303, just before they resigned the empire.[16]

VII. MILITARY PUNISHMENTS.

THESE were of various kinds, either lighter or more severe.

The lighter punishments, or such as were attended with inconvenience, loss, or disgrace, were chiefly these, 1. Deprivation of pay, either in whole or in part,[17] the punishment of those who were often absent from their standards.[18] A soldier punished in this manner was called ÆRE DIRUTUS. Whence Cicero facetiously applies this name to a person deprived of his fortune at play, or a bankrupt by any other means.—2. Forfeiture of their spears, CENSIO HASTARIA.[19]—3. Removal from their tents,[20] sometimes to remain without the camp and without tents, or at a distance

1 Ov. ib. Virg. G. ii. 146.
2 in gremio Jovis, Sen. Helv. 10.
3 Plin. xv. 30. xxxv. 40.
4 ut venire supersederent.
5 Val. Max. ii. 8. 6. Dio. xliii. 22. Flor. ii. 2 Cic. Sen. 13. Suet. Jul. 37.
6 Liv. x. 46.
7 exauctorati et dimissi,

Liv. xxviii. 9. xxx. 45.
xxxvi. 40.
6 Plut.
9 Liv. Ep. 17. Quin. i. 7. Sil. vi. 663.
10 Gell. v. 6. Dio. liv. 8.
Plin. xv. 29. s. 38.
11 ovem.
12 Plut. Marc. Diony. v. 47. viii. 9. Liv. iii. 10.
xxvi. 21. xxxi. 30.

xxxiii. 28. xli. 28.
12 Suet. Aug. 38. Tib. 9. Dio. liv. 24. 31. lxii. 19.
23.
14 lauream prospere gestæ rei.
15 Tac. Hist. iii. 77. Flor. iv. 12. 53. Dio. liii. 26. liv. 11. 24. lx. 30.
16 Eutrop. ix. 27, 28.

Procop.
17 stipendio privari,Liv. xl. 41.
18 infrequentes, Plaut. Truc. ii. 1. 19.
19 Fest. Cic. Ver. v. 13. Phil. xiii. 12.
20 locum in quo tenderent mutare, Liv. xxv. 6.

from the winter quarters.[1]—4. Not to recline or sit at meals with the rest.[2] —5. To stand before the prætorium in a loose jacket,[3] and the centurions without their girdle,[4] or to dig in that dress.[5]—6. To get an allowance of barley instead of wheat.[6]—7. Degradation of rank ;[7] an exchange into an inferior corps or less honourable service.[8]—8. To be removed from the camp,[9] and employed in various works,[10] an imposition of labour,[11] or dismission with disgrace,[12] or EXAUCTORATIO. A. Gellius mentions a singular punishment, namely, of letting blood.[13] Sometimes a whole legion was deprived of its name, as that called AUGUSTA.[14]

The more severe punishments were, 1. To be beaten with rods,[15] or with a vine sapling.[16]—2. To be scourged and sold as a slave.—3. To be beaten to death with sticks, called FUSTUARIUM, the bastinado,[17] which was the usual punishment of theft, desertion, perjury, &c. When a soldier was to suffer this punishment, the tribune first struck him gently with a staff, on which signal, all the soldiers of the legion fell upon him with sticks and stones, and generally killed him on the spot. If he made his escape, for he might fly, he could not however return to his native country ; because no one, not even his relations, durst admit him into their houses.[18]— 4. To be overwhelmed with stones[19] and hurdles.[20]—5. To be beheaded,[21] sometimes crucified, and to be left unburied.—6. To be stabbed by the swords of the soldiers,[22] and, under the emperors, to be exposed to wild beasts, or to be burned alive, &c.

Punishments were inflicted by the legionary tribunes and præfects of the allies, with their council ; or by the general, from whom there was no appeal.[23]

When a number had been guilty of the same crime, as in the case of a mutiny, every tenth man was chosen by lot for punishment, which was called DECIMATIO, or the most culpable were selected. Sometimes only the twentieth man was punished, VICESIMATIO ; or the 100th, CENTESIMA-TIO.[24]

VIII. MILITARY PAY AND DISCHARGE.

THE Roman soldiers at first received no pay[25] from the public. Every one served at his own charges. Pay was first granted to the foot, A. U. 347, and three years after, during the siege of Veji, to the horse.[26]

It was in the time of the republic very inconsiderable, two *oboli* or three *asses* (about 2½d English) a day to a foot-soldier, the double to a centurion, and the triple to an EQUES. Julius Cæsar doubled it. Under Augustus it was ten asses (7¾d.), and Domitian increased it still more, by adding three gold pieces annually.[27] What was the pay of the tribunes is uncertain ; but it appears to have been considerable. The prætorian cohorts had double the pay of the common soldiers.[28]

Besides pay, each soldier was furnished with clothes, and received a

1 Liv. x. 4. xxvi. 1. Val. Max. ii. 7. 15.
2 cibum stantes capere, Liv. xxiv. 16.
3 Suet. Aug. 24. Val. Max. ii. 7. 9.
4 discincti, Liv. xxvii. 13.
5 Plut. Luc.
6 hordeo pasci, Liv. ib. Suet. Aug. 24.
7 gradus dejectio.
8 militiæ mutatio, Val. Max. ib.

9 n castris segregari.
10 Veg. iii. 4.
11 munerum indictio.
12 ignominiose mitti, Hirt. Bell. Afr. 54. Plin. Ep. vi. 31.
13 sanguinem mittendi, x. 8.
14 Dio. liv. 11.
15 virgis cædi.
16 vite, Val. Max. ii. 7. 4. Juv. viii. 247.
17 Liv. v. 6. Ep. 55. Cic. Phil. iii. 6. Polyb. vi.

35.
18 Polyb. ib.
19 lapidibus cooperiri.
20 sub crate necari, Liv. i. 51. iv. 50.
21 securi percuti, Liv. ii. 59. xxviii. 29. Ep. xv.
22 Tac. Ann. i. 44. Liv. xxx. 43. Val. Max. ii. 7. 15.
23 Polyb. vi. 35.
24 Capitolin. Macrin. 12. Liv. ii. 59. xxviii. 29. Cic. Clu. 46. Suet. Aug.

24. Galb. 12. Tac. Hist. i. 37. Plut. Cras. Dio. xli. 35. xlvii. 42. xlix. 27. 38.
25 stipendium.
26 Liv. iv. 59. v. 7.
27 Suet. Dom. 7. Jul. 26. Aug. 46. Tac. Ann. i. 17. Polyb. vi. 37. Plaut. Most. ii. 1. 10. Liv. v. 12.
28 Juv. iii. 132. Dio. liv. 25.

certain allowance[1] of corn, commonly four bushels a month, the centurions double, and the equites triple. But for these things a part of their pay was deducted.[2]

The allies received the same quantity of corn, except that the horse only received double of the foot. The allies were clothed and paid by their own states.[3]

Anciently there were no cooks permitted in the Roman army. The soldiers dressed their own victuals. They took food twice a day, at dinner and supper. A signal was publicly given for both. The dinner was a slight meal, which they commonly took standing. They indulged themselves a little more at supper. The ordinary drink of soldiers, as of slaves, was water mixed with vinegar, called POSCA.[4]

When the soldiers had served out their time,[5] the foot twenty years, and the horse ten, they were called EMERITI, and obtained their discharge. This was called MISSIO HONESTA vel JUSTA. When a soldier was discharged for some defect or bad health, it was called *missio* CAUSARIA ; if, from the favour of the general, he was discharged before the just time, *missio* GRATIOSA ; on account of some fault, IGNOMINIOSA.[6]

Augustus introduced a new kind of discharge, called EXAUCTORATIO, by which those who had served sixteen campaigns were exempted from all military duty except fighting. They were however retained[7] in the army, not with the other soldiers under standards,[8] but by themselves under a flag,[9] whence they were called VEXILLARII or *veterani*, sometimes also SUBSIGNANI,[10] till they should receive a full discharge and the rewards of their service,[11] either in lands or money, or both, which sometimes they never obtained. EXAUCTORARE is properly to free from the military oath, to disband.[12]

IX. METHOD OF ATTACKING AND DEFENDING TOWNS.

THE Romans attacked[13] places either by a sudden assault, or if that failed,[14] they tried to reduce them by a blockade.[15]

They first surrounded a town with their troops,[16] and by their missive

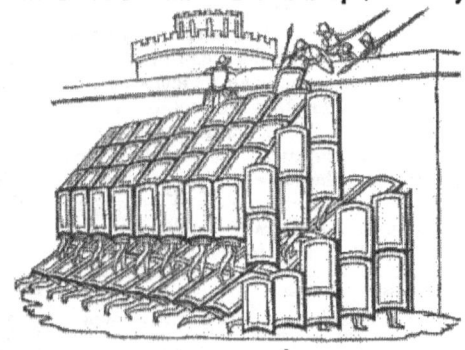

1 dimensum.
2 Tac. Ann. i. 17. Polyb, vi. 37.
3 Polyb. ib.
4 Plaut. Mil. iii. 2. 23.
5 stipendia legitima fecissent vel meruissent.
6 Luc. i. 344. Liv. xlii. 11. Hirt. Bell. Afr. 54.

D. de Re Milit. 1. 13.
7 tenebantur.
8 sub signis et aquilis.
9 sub vexillo suorum, Tac. Ann. i. 36.
10 Tac. Hist. i. 70.
11 præmia vel commoda militiæ.
12 Liv. viii. 34. xxv. 20.

Suet. Aug. 24. 49. Tib. 48. Cat. 44. Vit. 10. Cic. Phil. n. 46. Virg. Ecl. i. 71. ix 2-5. Tac. Ann. i. 17. Hor. Sat. ii. 6. 55.
13 oppugnabant.
14 si subito impetu expugnare non poterant.

15 Cæs. B. G. vii. 36.
16 corona cingebant, vel circumdabant, Liv. vii. 27. xxiii. 44. xxiv. 2. mœnia exercitu circumvenerunt, Sal. Jug. 57.

weapons endeavoured to clear the walls of defendants.[1] Then, joining their shields in the form of a *testudo* or tortoise,[2] to secure themselves from the darts of the enemy, they came up to the gates,[3] and tried either to undermine[4] the walls, or to scale them.[5]

When a place could not be taken by storm, it was invested. Two lines of fortifications or intrenchments[6] were drawn around the place, at some distance from one another, called the lines of contravallation and circumvallation : the one against the sallies of the townsmen, and the other against attacks from without.[7]

These lines were composed of a ditch and a rampart, strengthened with a parapet and battlements,[8] and sometimes a solid wall of considerable height and thickness, flanked with towers or forts at proper distances round the whole.

At the foot of the parapet, or at its junction with the rampart,[9] there sometimes was a palisade made of larger stakes cut in the form of stags' horns ; hence called CERVI, to prevent the ascent of the enemy. Before that, there were several rows of trunks of trees, or large branches, sharpened at the ends,[10] called CIPPI, fixed in trenches[11] above five feet deep. In front of these were dug pits[12] of three feet deep, intersecting one another in the form of a *quincunx*, thus,

stuck thick with strong sharp stakes, and covered over with bushes to deceive the enemy, called LILIA. Before these, were placed up and down[13] sharp stakes about a foot long (TALEÆ), fixed to the ground with iron hooks called STIMULI. In front of all these, Cæsar, at Alesia, made a ditch twenty feet wide, 400 feet from the rampart, which was secured by two ditches, each fifteen feet broad, and as many deep ; one of them filled with water. But this was merely a blockade, without any approaches or attacks on the city.[14]

Between the lines were disposed the army of the besiegers, who were thus said, *urbem obsidione claudere* vel *cingere*, to invest.

The camp was pitched in a convenient situation to communicate with the lines.

From the inner line was raised a mount,[15] composed of earth, wood, and hurdles,[16] and stone, which was gradually advanced[17] towards the town, always increasing in height, till it equalled or overtopped the walls. The mount which Cæsar raised against Avaricum or Bourges, was 330 feet broad, and 80 feet high.[18]

The *agger* or mount was secured by towers, consisting of different stories,[19] from which showers of darts and stones were discharged on the

1 nudare muros defensoribus, vel propugnatoribus.
2 testudine facta v. acta, Liv. xliv. 9. Dio. xlix. 30.
3 succedere portis.
4 subruere vel subfodere.

5 Liv. x. 43. xxvi. 45. xxxiv. 39. xliv. 9. Cæs. B. G. ii. 7. Tac. Hist. iii. 28. 31. Sall. Jug. 94.
6 ancipitia munimenta vel munitiones, Liv. ii. 11.
7 Liv. v. 1. xxxviii. 4.

8 lorica et pinnæ.
9 ad commissuras pluteorum atque aggeris.
10 præacutis cacuminibus.
11 fossæ.
12 scrobes.
13 omnibus locis disserebantur.

14 Cæs. B. G. vii. 66, 67.
15 agger exstruebatur.
16 crates.
17 promovebatur.
18 Cæs. B. G. vii. 23.
19 turres contabulatæ.

Catapulta.

townsmen by means of engines,[1] called CATAPULTÆ, BALISTÆ,[*] and SCOR-
PIONES,[2] to defend the work and workmen.[3] Of these towers Cæsar is
supposed to have erected 1561 on his lines around Alesia.[4] The labour
and industry of the Roman troops were as remarkable as their courage.

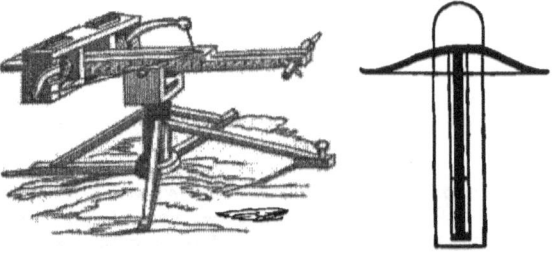

Balista.   *Scorpio.*

[*] The catapulta and balista were intended for discharging darts, arrows, and stones.
They were of different sizes,
and consequently produced
more or less effect. Some
were used in battles, and might
be called field pieces : others
were employed in sieges,
which was the use most commonly made of them. The balistæ must have been the heav-
iest and most difficult to carry,
because there was always a
greater number of catapultæ
in the armies. Livy, in his
description of the siege of
Carthage, says, that there
were a hundred and twenty
great, and more than two hundred small catapultæ taken,

with thirty-three great balistæ,
and fifty-two small ones. Josephus mentions the same difference amongst the Romans,
who had three hundred catapultæ, and forty balistæ, at the
siege of Jerusalem. These
machines had a force which it
is not easy to comprehend,
but which all good authors attest. Vegetius says, that the
balistæ discharged darts with
so much rapidity and violence,
that nothing could resist their
force. Athenæus tells us, that
Agesistratus made one of little
more than two feet in length,
which shot darts almost five
hundred paces. These ma-
chines were not unlike our
cross-bows. There were

others of much greater force,
which threw stones of three
hundred weight, upwards of a
hundred and twenty-five paces.
We find surprising effects of
them in Josephus. The darts
of the catapultæ, he tells us,
destroyed abundance of people. The stones from the balistæ beat down the battlements, and broke the angles
of the towers ; nor was there
any phalanx so deep, but one
of these stones would sweep a
whole file of it from one end to
the other. Folard, in his Commentary upon Polybus, says,
their force was very near equal
to that of artillery.

1 tormenta.
2 These engines cast,
much farther than the
human arm could throw
them, weighty javelins,
large beams of wood
headed with iron, and

heavy stones. They may
be briefly described as
gigantic cross-bows,
the most powerful of
which consisted not of
a single beam or
spring, but of two dis-

tinct beams, inserted
each into an upright
coil of ropes, tightly
twisted in such a way,
that the ends of the
arms could not be
drawn towards each

other, without increas-
ing the tension of the
ropes, so as to produce
a most violent recoil.
3 opus et administros
tutari, Sall. Jug. 76.
4 Cæs. B. G. vii. 72.

There were also moveable towers,[1] which were pushed forward[2] and brought back[3] on wheels, fixed below,[4] on the inside of the planks.[5] To prevent them from being set on fire by the enemy, they were covered with raw hides[6] and pieces of coarse cloth and mattresses.[7] They were of an immense bulk, sometimes thirty, forty, or fifty feet square, and higher than the walls, or even than the towers of the city. When they could be brought up to the walls, a place was seldom able to stand out long.[8]

But the most dreadful machine of all was the battering ram[9] (ARIES), a long beam, like the mast of a ship, and armed at one end with iron in the form of a ram's head; whence it had its name. It was suspended by the middle with ropes or chains fastened to a beam that lay across two posts, and hanging thus equally balanced, it was by a hundred men, more or less (who were frequently changed), violently thrust forward, drawn back, and

1 turres mobiles vel ambulatoriæ. — These moving towers were often, but not necessarily, combined with the ram. On the ground floor the ram exerted its destructive energy. In the middle was a bridge, the sides guarded by wicker-work, constructed so as to be suddenly lowered or thrust out upon the very battlements. In the upper stories soldiers with all sorts of missile weapons were placed, to clear the wall, and facilitate the passage of their comrades. They were mounted on numerous wheels, moved from within; probably their axles were pierced for levers like a capstan,

2 admovebantur vel adigebantur.
3 reducebantur.

and fixed in the wheels, so that when the formerwere forced round, the latter turned with them. The size of these towers was enormous; Vitruvius directs the smallest of them not to be less than ninety feet high and twenty-five broad, the top to be a fifth smaller, and to contain ten stories each, with windows. The largest was one hundred and eighty feet high, and thirty-four broad, and contained twenty stories. These engines were emphatically named Helepoleis, or city-takers, by the Greeks.

4 rotis subjectis.
5 Cæs. B. G. ii. 31. v. 42. vii. 24. Hirt. Bell. Alex. 2. Liv. xxi. 11.
6 coria.
7 centones vel cilicia, Cæs. B. C. ii. 10.
8 Liv. xxi. 11. 14. xxxii. 17. xxiii. 17.
9 The ram is said to have been first employed, in its most simple form, by the Carthaginians, to demolish the walls of Cadiz, after they had taken the place. Wanting proper iron tools for this purpose, a number of men took up a beam, and by their united force shook down the masonry. Pephasmenus, a Tyrian artificer, is said to have perceived the economy of power obtained by sus-

pending the beam from a mast, or triangle. Cetras of Calchedon conceived the idea of mounting it on wheels and a platform, and protecting those who worked it by a roof and sides. He called it (testudo) the tortoise, from the slowness of its motion, or because the ram thrust in and out its head like a tortoise from its shell. To cap the beam with iron was an obvious improvement; and the way in which a ram buts with its head readily suggested the form usually given to the instrument, as well as its name. Some of them were upwards of 100 feet long.

again pushed forward, till, by repeated strokes, it had shaken and broken down the wall with its iron head..[1]

The ram was covered with sheds or mantlets, called VINEÆ, machines constructed of wood and hurdles, and covered with earth or raw hides, or any materials which could not easily be set on fire. They were pushed forwards by wheels below.[2] Under them the besiegers either worked the ram, or tried to undermine the walls.[3]

Similar to the *vineæ* in form and use were the TESTUDINES : so called, because those under them were safe as a tortoise under its shell.[4]

Of the same kind were the PLUTEI, the MUSCULI,[5] &c.

These mantlets or sheds were used to cover the men in filling up the ditches, and for various other purposes.[6]

When the nature of the ground would not permit these machines to be erected or brought forward to the walls, the besiegers sometimes drove a

1 Veg. iv. 14. Liv. xxi. 12. xxx. 32. 46. xxxii. 23. xxxviii. 5. Joseph. Bell. Jud. iii. 9.
2 rotis subjectis age-bantur vel impelle-bantur, Sall. Jug. 76.
3 Liv. ii. 17. v. 7. x. 34. xxi. 7. 61. xxiii. 18.—The hurdles were sometimes laid for a roof on the top of posts, which the soldiers, who went under it for shelter, bore up with their hands.
4 Liv. v. 5. Cæs. B. G.

v. 41. 50. Bell. Civ. ii. 2 14.
5 Liv. xxi. 61. xxxiv. 17. Cæs. passim.—Pluteus was a movable gallery on wheels, shaped like an arched sort of waggon, for the protection of arch-ers, who were station-ed in it to clear the walls with their ar-rows, and thus facili-tate the approach of storming parties, and the erection of scaling-ladders. Musculus was

a small machine of the same description, sent in advance of the large towers, already de-scribed, to level the way for them, fill up the ditch if necessary, clear away rubbish, re-move palisades, and make a solid road to the very foot of the walls. The Romans believed that a close alliance subsisted be-tween the whale (ba-læna) and a smaller species of the same

tribe, called musculus, and that when the for-mer became blind, from the enormous weight of its eyelids dropping over and closing up the organ, the latter swam before, and guided it from all shallows which might prove injurious to it. Hence this machine was called musculus, as it explored and smoothed the way for the larger engines.
6 Cæs. B. G. vii. 58.

Pluteus.

mine[1] into the heart of the city, or in this manner intercepted the springs
of water.[2]

When they only wished to sap the foundation of the walls, they supported the part to be thrown down with wooden props, which being consumed with fire, the wall fell to the ground.

In the meantime the besieged, to frustrate the attempts of the besiegers,
met their mines with counter mines,[3] which sometimes occasioned dreadful conflicts below ground. The great object was to prevent them from
approaching the walls.[4]

The besieged also, by means of mines, endeavoured to frustrate or overturn the works of the enemy.[5] They withdrew the earth from the mount,[6]
or destroyed the works by fires below, in the same manner as the besiegers overturned the walls.[7]

Where they apprehended a breach would be made, they reared new
walls behind, with a deep ditch before them. They employed various methods to weaken or elude the force of the ram, and to defend themselves
against the engines and darts of the besiegers. But these, and every thing
else belonging to this subject, will be best understood by reading the accounts preserved to us of ancient sieges, particularly of Syracuse by Marcellus, of Ambracia by Fulvius, of Alesia by Julius Cæsar, of Marseilles
by his lieutenants, and of Jerusalem by Titus Vespasian.[8] When the
Romans besieged a town, and thought themselves sure of taking it, they
used solemnly[9] to call out of it[10] the gods, under whose protection the
place was supposed to be.* Hence when Troy was taken, the gods are
said to have left their shrines. For this reason, the Romans are said to
have kept secret their tutelary god, and the Latin name of the city.[11]

* The form of the Evocation was nearly as follows:—" If there be to Carthage a protecting god or goddess, I pray and beseech ye great gods, who have taken into your care this city, to abandon these habita-tions, these temples and these sacred places ; to forget them, to fill them with terror, and to withdraw to Rome and to our people. May our dwellings, our temples, and our sacred of-ferings find favour before you. Let it *appear that you are my protectors, the protectors of the Roman people and of my sol-diers. If you do this, I pledge myself to found temples, and to institute games in your ho-nour.*

1 cuniculum agebant.
2 Liv. v. 19. 21. Hirt. Bell. Gall. viii. 41. 43.
3 transversis cuniculis hostium cuniculos ex-cepere, Liv. xxiii. 18. xxxviii. 7.
4 apertos, sc. ab hosti-bus vel Romanis, cuni-culos morabantur, mœ-nibusque appropinqua-re prohibebant,—all which very much re-tarded the approach and kept us at a dis-tance from the place,
Cæs. B. G. vii. 22.
5 Cæs. B. G. iii. 21. vii. 22.
6 terram ad se introrsus subtrahebant.
7 Joseph. Bell. Jud. iii. 12.
8 Liv. xxiv. 33. xxxviii. 4.
xlii. 63. Cæs. B. G.vii.B.
C. ii. Joseph. Bell. Jud.
9 certo carmine.
10 evocare.
11 Liv. v. 21. Virg. Æn. ii. 351. Plin. iii. 5. s. 9. xxviii. 2. s. 4. Macrob. iii. 9.

The form of a surrender we have, Liv. i. 38, Plaut. Amph. i. 1. 71, 102, and the usual manner of plundering a city when taken, Polyb. x. 16.

NAVAL AFFAIRS OF THE ROMANS.

NAVIGATION at first was very rude, and the construction of vessels extremely simple. The most ancient nations used boats made of trunks of trees hollowed,[1] called ALVEI, LINTRES, SCAPHÆ, vel MONOXYLA,[2] or composed of beams and planks fastened together with cords or wooden pins, called RATES, or of reeds, called CANNÆ,[3] or partly of slender planks,[4] and partly of wicker-hurdles or basket-work,[5] and covered with hides, as those of the ancient Britons, and other nations, hence called NAVIGIA VITILIA, corio circumsuta, and naves sutiles, in allusion to which, Virgil calls the boat of Charon, cymba sutilis,[6] somewhat similar to the Indian canoes, which are made of the bark of trees ; or to the boats of the Icelanders and Esquimaux Indians, which are made of long poles placed cross-wise, tied together with whale sinews, and covered with the skins of sea-dogs, sewed with sinews instead of thread.

The Phœnicians, or the inhabitants of Tyre and Sidon, are said to have been the first inventors of the art of sailing, as of letters and astronomy. For Jason, to whom the poets ascribe it,[7] and the Argonauts, who first sailed under Jason from Greece to Colchis in the ship Argo, in quest of the golden fleece, that is, of commerce, flourished long after the Phœnicians were a powerful nation. But whatever be in this, navigation certainly received from them its chief improvements.

The invention of sails is by some ascribed to Æolus, the god of the winds, and by others to Dædalus ; whence he is said to have flown like a bird through the air. They seem to have been first made of skins, which the Veneti, a people of Gaul, used even in the time of Cæsar, afterwards of flax or hemp ; whence lintea and carbasa (sing. -us) are put for vela, sails. Sometimes clothes spread out were used for sails.[8]

It was long before the Romans paid any attention to naval affairs. They at first had nothing but boats made of thick planks,[9] such as they used on the Tiber, called NAVES CAUDICARIÆ ; whence Appius Claudius, who first persuaded them to fit out a fleet, A. U. 489, got the surname of CAUDEX. They are said to have taken the model of their first ship of war from a vessel of the Carthaginians, which happened to be stranded on their coasts, and to have exercised their men on land to the management of ships.[10] But this can hardly be reconciled with what Polybius says in other places, nor with what we find in Livy about the equipment and operations of a Roman fleet.[11] The first ships of war were probably built from the model of those of Antium, which, after the reduction of that city, were brought to Rome, A. U. 417.[12] It was not, however, till the first Punic war that they made any figure at sea.

---

1 ex singulis arboribus cavatis Virg. G. i. 195. 262. Plin. xvi. 41. Liv. xxvi. 26,
2 Paterc. ii. 107. Ov. F. ii. 407. Liv. i. 4. xxv. 3. Plin. vi. 23. Strab. lil. 155.
3 Juv. v. 89. Fest.

4 carinæ ac statumina, the keel and ribs, ex levi materia.
5 reliquum corpus navium viminibus contextum,
6 Æn. vi. 414. Cæs. B. C. i. 54. Luc. iv. 131. Herodot. i. 194. Dio.

xlviii. 18. Plin. iv. 16. vii. 56. xxiv. 9. a. 40.
7 Plin. v. 12. Ov. Met. vi. vers. ult. et Am. ii. 11. 1. Luc. iii. 194.
8 Diod. v. 7. Virg. Æn. vi. 15. Cæs. B. G. iii. 13. Tac. Ann. ii. 24. Hist. v. 23. Juv. xii.

66.
9 ex tabulis crassioribus, Fest.
10 Sen. Brev. Vit. 13. Varr. Vit. Rom. 11. Polyb. i. 20, 21.
11 Liv. ix. 30. 38.
12 Liv. viii. 14.

Ships of war were called NAVES LONGÆ, because they were of a longer shape than ships of burden, (*naves* ONERARIÆ, ὁλκαδες, whence hulks; or arcæ, barks,) which were more round and deep. The ships of war were driven chiefly by oars, the ships of burdens by sails,[1] and as they were more heavy,[2] and sailed more slowly, they were sometimes towed[3] after the war ships.[4]

Navis Longa.

Their ships of war were variously named from their rows or ranks of oars.[5] Those which had two rows or tiers were called *biremes;*[6] three, *triremes;* four, *quadriremes;* five, *quinqueremes* vel *penteres.*

Navis Oneraria.

The Romans scarcely had any ships of more than five banks of oars; and therefore those of six or seven banks are called by a Greek name, *hexeres, hepteres,* and above that by a circumlocution, *naves, octo, novem, decem ordinum,* vel *versuum.*[7] Thus, Livy calls a ship of sixteen rows,[8] *navis ingentis magnitudinis, quam sexdecim versus remorum agebant,* a galley of vast size, which was moved by sixteen tiers of oars. This enormous ship, however, sailed up the Tiber to Rome.[9] The ships of Antony (which Florus says resembled floating castles and towns; Virgil, floating islands or mountains,) had only from six to nine banks of oars. Dio says from four to ten rows.[10]

There are various opinions about the manner in which the rowers sat. That most generally received is, that they were placed above one another in different stages or benches[11] on one side of the ship, not in a perpendicular line, but in the form of a *quincunx.* The oars of the lowest bench were short, and those of the other benches increased in length, in proportion to their height above the water. This opinion is confirmed by several passages in the classics,[12] and by the representations which remain of ancient galleys, particularly that on Trajan's pillar at Rome. It is, however, attended with difficulties not easily reconciled.

There were three different classes of rowers, whom the Greeks called *thranitæ, zeugitæ* or *zeugioi,* and *thalamitæ,* or *-ioi,* from the different parts of the ship in which they were placed. The first sat in the highest part of the ship, next the stern; the second, in the middle; and the last in the lowest part, next the prow. Some think that there were as many oars belonging to each of these classes of rowers, as the ship was said to have ranks or banks of oars: others, that there were as many rowers to each oar, as the ship is said to have banks; and some reckon the number of

1 Cæs. B G. iv. 20. 25. v. 7. Isid. xix. i. Cic. Fam. xii. 15.
2 graviores.
3 remulco tractæ.
4 Liv. xxxii. 16.
5 ab ordinibus remorum.
6 dicrota, Cic. Att. v. 11. xvi. 4. vel dicrotæ, Hirt. B. Alex. 47.
7 Liv. xxxvii. 22. Flor.
iv. 11.
8 ἑκκαιδεκηρης, Polyb.
9 Liv. xlv. 35.
10 I. 23. 33. Flor. iv. 11. 4. Virg. Æn. viii. 691.
11 in transtris vel jugis.
12 Virg. Æn. v. 119. Luc. iii. 536. Sil. Ital. xiv. 424.

banks, by that of oars on each side. In this manner they remove the difficulty of supposing eight or ten banks óf oars above one another, and even forty ; for a ship is said by Plutarch and Athenæus to have been built by Ptolemy Philopator which had that number ;[1] but these opinions are involved in still more inextricable difficulties.

WAR GALLEYS.

IT unfortunately happens that no detailed account or explicit evidence has come down to us, whereby the mode in which the banks of oars were arranged might be satisfactorily ascertained ; the only source of information being the mere casual allusions of historians and poets, who have naturally avoided to encumber their narration with technical details of construction. Upon Trajan's column, indeed, vessels are sculptured, supposed to be those of two and three banks of oars; but the figures and mechanical proportions upon it are so confused and crowded that nothing can be safely determined from this authority. So also, in the rostrated column of Duilius, erected to commemorate his naval victory over the Carthaginians, and discovered about two centuries and a half ago at Rome, only the beaks of galleys are projected from the shaft of the pillar, and no part of the banks of oars is exhibited. Several paintings of ancient vessels have likewise been discovered in the ruins of Herculaneum, but so much effaced that nothing can be gathered from them to throw any light on the subject. In the absence, therefore, of all direct evidence, recourse has been necessarily had to conjecture.

The war vessels of the ancients were designated and rated according to the number of the banks of oars by which they were impelled. There were, generally, two classes of war galleys, one of a single line of oars, and the other of two, three, five, seven, or more banks, all of which were, at different periods, employed in naval engagements. The form of vessels of one bank of oars may be readily imagined ; but the construction of the numerous class of galleys of more than one bank, is a point fruitful of conjectures and perplexities.

After stating insuperable objections to the various solutions of these difficulties that have been proposed by Vossius, Savile, Melville, and others, Mr. Howell, in his ingenious " Essay on the War Galleys of the Ancients," lately published, advances the following theory. After detailing the inconveniences which would be found in the early war galleys of a single arrangement of oars occupying the whole vessel's length, and neither leaving a deck for the soldiers to fight upon, nor admitting of a commanding height whence to discharge their missiles, he proceeds to unfold the idea which, according to his supposition, must have struck the Erythræans, who are generally admitted to have been the first to substitute galleys of two banks for the old ones of a single tier. Suppose a vessel of the original form, pulling twenty oars, ten on each side, thus :—

o o o o o o o o o o

the Erythræans, he imagines, found, that, without adding to the length of the vessel, they could have the same number of oars in nearly one-half of the length, by placing the oars obliquely, thus, up the side of the galley :

o o
o o
o o
o o
o o

by this means the rowers being all placed in the midships, ample room would be left for an elevated deck for combat at the poop and prow. Thus, then, according to Mr. Howell, originated the creation of a bireme ; and when this idea was once started, of placing the banks of five oars each obliquely, the extension of the plan was easy to an indefinite degree, simply by adding to the length of the galley, without at all increasing her height. The oar-ports of a trireme would, for instance, appear thus :—

o o o
o o o
o o o
o o o
o o o

a quinquereme thus :—

o o o o o
o o o o o
o o o o o
o o o o o
o o o o o

and so on, until the galley of Ptolemy Philopater would count forty of these oblique ascents, behind one another from stem to stern, and each of five oars, without being necessarily higher in the water than a bireme. "That a rank or bench of oars," says Mr. Howell, "never contained more than five oars, I think can be proved, whatever the size of the galley was, whether a bireme or trireme, up to the galley of Philopater, which had forty banks, nine feet being the highest point from the water to the scalmi from which they could pull with effect. That the scalmi of Philopator's galley did not exceed this, is evident from Athenæus, lib. v. c. 37. The longest oar was 38 cubits, or 57 feet ; there could not be less than three feet from the water's edge to the lower edge of the oar-port, and eighteen inches for the width of it. That they were so wide, was necessary for the size of the oar, and we learn it also from a curious fact. Megabates, visiting the fleet, found a Grecian galley without its guard, and thus he punished the captain ; Herodotus (lib. v. cap. 33), Δια θαλαμης διελοντας της νεος. The meaning evidently is, ' he bound him to the lowest bench, with his head out of the oarport.' This he could not have done had the oar-ports been less. Now, from the lower bench to the upper bench inside, five feet is sufficient for

Ships contrived for lightness and expedition (*naves* ACTUA-RIÆ) had but one rank of oars on each side,[1] or at most two. They were of different kinds, and called by various names; as, *celoces*, i. e. *naves celeres* vel *cursoriæ*, *lembi*, *phaseli*, *myoparones*, &c. But the most re-

both man and oar. The benches being placed sloping from the lowest up to the fifth or highest, the outer edge of the upper oar-port would be four feet six inches from the upper edge of the under port, whose width is eighteen inches, so that nine feet is all that was required for the height of a bank's ascent. Adopting this idea, the difficulty of the subject is at once removed, and, when once this method of placing the oars was found out, expense or convenience were the only objects to be studied by the ancients, for nothing could be more easy than adding to the length of the galley according to the number of banks required, even up to one hundred, could such a large vessel have been easily navigated."

This theory supersedes all others in probability, and is in agreement with most of the passages referring to galleys and matters of military marine in the ancient authors. It at once obviates the absurdity contained in that monstrous supposition, that even forty banks must have been placed one over another. Nor would there be any inconvenience in the oblique ascending series of five oars in each bank. It justifies also the general title applied to war galleys—*naves longæ* ; the appropriateness of which would be utterly lost in the huge proportions of a galley of forty, or even ten banks, rising one above another ; while it agrees with the inevitable deduction from various writers, and from the imperfect representation on Trajan's

column, that there were at least several ascending tiers of oar-ports, requiring oars of various lengths. It moreover is in accordance with the appearance of the galleys on Duilius's rostrated column ; on which, in the beaks of the vessels (the only part represented) there are no oars ; leading us to conclude that these were placed only in the waist.

It remains to add, that Mr. Howell has presented the directors of the Edinburgh Academy with a model of a hexireme, constructed according to his theory, which is represented in the following cut, and to which are subjoined the Latin and Greek names of the several parts of the war galley.

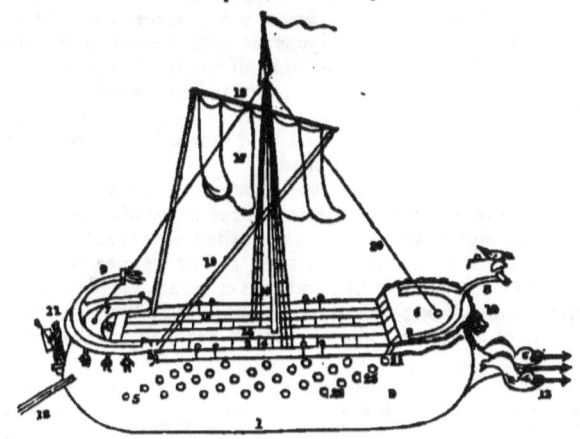

REFERENCES.

1 carina, τροπις.
2 testudo, κυτος.
3 latera, ωλευραι.
4 fori v. transtra, τοιχοι.
5 foramina remorum, εγκωπα.
6 prora, πρωρα.
7 puppis, cauda, πρυμνη, ουρα.
8 corymbi vel corona, ακροστολια et στολος.
9 corymbi, αφλαστα.
10 oculos navis, οφθαλμος.
11 tutela, επιτροπη.
12 gubernaculum, κηδαλιον.
13 rostrum, εμβολον.
14 stega, καταφραγματα.
15 catastroma, καταστρωμα.
16 malus, ιστος.
17 vela, ιστια.
18 antenna, κεραια.
19 pedes, ποδες.
20 funes qui malum sustinent, προτονοι.
21 thranitai, θρανιται.
22 juga, ζυγα.
23 thalamoi, θαλαμοι.

1 simplice ordine agebantur, μονηρεις, Tac. Hist. v. 23.

markable of these were the *naves* LIBURNÆ,[1] a kind of light galleys used by the Liburni, a people of Dalmatia, addicted to piracy. To ships of

this kind Augustus was in a great measure indebted for his victory over Antony at Actium. Hence after that time the name of *naves* LIBURNÆ was given to all quick-sailing vessels, and few ships were built but of that construction.[2]

Ships were also denominated from the country to which they belonged, and the various uses to which they were applied ; as NAVES MERCATORIÆ, *frumentariæ, vinariæ, oleariæ ;* PISCATORIÆ vel *lenunculi,* fishing-boats ; SPECULATORIÆ et *exploratoriæ,* spy-boats ; PIRATICÆ vel *prædatoriæ ;*[3] HIPPAGOGÆ, vel *hippagines,* for carrying horses and their riders ; TABELLA-RIÆ, message-boats ;[4] VECTORIÆ GRAVESQUE, transports and ships of burden ; *annotinæ privatæque,* built that or the former year for private use. Some read *annonariæ,* i. e. for carrying provisions. Each ship had its long-boat joined to it.[5]

A large Asiatic ship among the Greeks was called CERCURUS, it is supposed from the island Corcyra ; but Pliny ascribes the invention of it to the Cyprians.[6]

Galleys kept by princes and great men for amusement, were called by various names ; *triremes ceratæ* vel *æratæ, lusoriæ et cubiculatæ* vel *thalamegi,* pleasure-boats or barges ; *privæ,* i. e. *propriæ et non meritoriæ,* one's own, not hired ; sometimes of immense size, *deceres* vel *decemremes.*[7]

Each ship had a name peculiar to itself inscribed or painted on its prow ; thus, PRISTIS, SCYLLA, CENTAURUS, &c., called PARASEMON, its sign, or IN-SIGNE,[8] as its tutelary god[9] was on its stern ; whence that part of the ship was called TUTELA or *cautela,* and held sacred by the mariners. There supplications and treaties were made.[10]

In some ships the *tutela* and παρασημον were the same.[11]

Ships of burden used to have a basket suspended on the top of their mast as their sign,[12] hence they were called CORBITÆ.[13]

There was an ornament in the stern and sometimes on the prow, made of wood, like the tail of a fish, called APLUSTRE, vel plur. -*ia,* from which was erected a staff or pole with a riband or streamer[14] on the top.[15]

The ship of the commander of a fleet[16] was distinguished by a red flag,[17] and by a light.

1 Cæs. B. G. v. 1. Luc. iii. 531. Cic. et Liv. Hor. Ep. i. 1.
2 Dio. 1. 29. 32. Veg. iv. 33.
3 Cæs. B. C. ii. 39. iii. 5 Cic. Verr. v. 33. Liv. xxiii. 1. xxx. 10. xxxiv. 32. 36. xxxvi. 42.
4 Sen. Ep. 77. Plaut. Mil. Glor. iv. 1. 39. Liv. xliv. 28. Gell. x. 25. Fest.

5 Cæs. B. G. v. 7. cymbulæ onerariis adhærescebant, Plin. Ep. 8. 20.
6 vii. 56. Plaut. Merc. i. 1. 86. Stich. ii. 2. 84. iii. 1. 12.
7 Sen. Ben. vii. 20. Suet. Cæs. 52. Cal. 37. Hor. Ep. i. 1. 92.
8 Tac. Ann. vi. 34. Liv. xxxvii. 29. Herodot. viii. 89. Virg. Æn. v.

116.
9 tutela vel tutelare numen.
10 Liv. xxx.36. Sil. Ital. xiii. 76. xiv. 511. 439. Ov. Trist. i. El. 3. v. 110. 9. v. 1. Heroid. xvi. 112. Pers. vi. 30. Luc. iii. 501. Sen. Ep. 76. Petron. c. 105.
11 Serv. Virg. Æn. v. 116. Act. Apos. xxviii. 11.

12 pro signo.
13 Fest. Cic. Att. xvi. 6. Plaut. Pœn. iii. 1. 4. 40.
14 fascia vel tænia.
15 Juv. x. 136. Luc. iii. 671.
16 navis prætoria.
17 vexillum vel velum purpureum, Tac. Hist. v. 22. Plin. xix. 1. Cæs. B. C. ii. 6. Flor. iv. 8. Virg. Æn. ii. 256.

The chief parts of a ship and its appendages were, CARINA, the keel or bottom ; *statumina*, the ribs, or pieces of timber which strengthened the sides ; PRORA, the prow or fore-part, and PUPPIS, the stern or hind-part ; ALVEUS, the belly or hold of the ship : SENTINA, the pump,[1] or rather the bilge or bottom of the hold, where the water, which leaked into the ship, remained, till it was pumped out,[2] or the bilge-water itself, properly called NAUTEA. In order to keep out the water, ships were besmeared with wax and pitch ; hence called CERATÆ.[3]

On the sides[4] were holes[5] for the oars (REMI, called also by the poets *tonsæ*, the broad part or end of them, *palma* vel *palmula*), and seats[6] for the rowers.[7]

Each oar was tied to a piece of wood,[8] called SCALMUS, by thongs or

strings, called STROPPI vel *struppi ;* hence *scalmus*[9] is put for a boat; *navicula duorum scalmorum*, a boat of two oars; *actuaria*, sc. navis, *decem scalmis, quatuor scalmorum navis.* The place where the oars were put, when the rowers were done working, was called CASTERIA.[10]

On the stern was the rudder (GUBERNACULUM vel *clavus*), and the pilot (*gubernator*) who directed it.

Some ships had two rudders, one on each end, and two prows, so that they might be moved either way without turning, much used by the Germans, and on the Pontus Euxinus, or Black Sea, called CAMARÆ,[11] because in a swelling sea they were covered with boards like the vaulted roof of a house ;[12] hence *camaritæ*, the name of a people bordering on the Black Sea.[13]

In the middle of the ship was erected the mast (MALUS), which was raised[14] when the ship left the harbour, and taken down[15] when it approached the land ; the place where it stood was called MODIUS.[16] The ships of the ancients had only one mast.

On the mast were fixed the sailyards (ANTENNÆ vel *brachia*), and the sails (VELA) fastened by ropes (*funes* vel *rudentes*). *Immittere rudentes*, to loosen all the cordage ; *pandere vela*, to spread the sails.[17]

1 Cæs. B. C. iii. 25.
2 donec per antliam exhauriretur. Cic. Fam. ix. 15. Sen. 6. Mart. ix. 19. 4. Suet. Tib. 51.
3 Juv. vi. 99, Plaut. Asin. v. 2. 44. Nom. i. 25. Ov. Her. v. 42.
4 latera.
5 foramina.
6 sedilia vel transtra.
7 remiges.
8 paxillus vel lignum teres.
9 The oars employed by the ancients in rowing are not described by any of the ancient au-

thors ; it may be reckoned best, therefore, to apply for information to the moderns, and follow Isaac Vossius in his description of the oars in use in the Mediterranean galleys of his time. There was, in all probability, very little alteration in their construction from their first use until the present time. It being simple in itself, and only adapted to one object, its improvement must have been rapid, and when found

quite efficient, there was no inducement to alter it. Thus an oar of thirty-six feet long A to B, has from A to C a space of eleven feet within the galley ; it is hung upon the scalmi by the thong at C ; it is here extremely thick, nine inches in diameter, and as the hand could not grasp it, there is a handle fixed upon it, DD. It extends within to about three feet of the scalmi thong.
10 Plaut. As. iii. 1. 16.

Isid. xix. 4. Cic. Off. iii. 14. Or. ii. 34. Att. xvi.
3 Vel. ii. 43.
11 Tac. Ann. ii. 6. Mor. G. 44. Strab. xi. 496.
12 camera, Tac. Hist. iii. 47. Gell. x. 25.
13 Eustath. Diony. 700.
14 attollebatur vel erigebatur, Cic. Verr. v. 34.
15 inclinabatur vel ponebatur.
16 Virg. Æn. v. 829. Lucan. iii. 45. Isid. xix. 2.
17 Plin. Ep. viii. 4.

The sails were usually white, as being thought more lucky, sometimes coloured.[1]

The ends of the sail-yards were called CORNUA ; from which were suspended two ropes called PEDES, braces, by pulling which towards the stern, the sails were turned to the right or left. If the wind blew obliquely from the left, they pulled the rope on the right, and so on the contrary : hence *facere pedem*, to trim or adjust the sails ; *obliquat lævo pede carbasa*, he turns the sails so as to catch the wind blowing from the right ; so *obliquat sinus in ventum, currere utroque pede*, to sail with a wind right astern, or blowing directly from behind ; *in contrarium navigare prolatis pedibus*, by tacking ; *intendere brachia velis*, i. e. *vela brachiis*, to stretch the sails, or to haul them out to the yard-arms ; *dare vela ventis*, to set sail ; so *vela facere*, or to make way ; *subducere vela*, to lower the sails ;[2] *ministrare velis*, vel -*a*, i. e. *attendere*, to manage, by drawing in and letting out the opposite braces :[3] *velis remis*, sc. *et* ; i. e. *summa vi, manibus pedibusque, omnibus nervis*, with might and main ;[4] so *remigio veloque*, Plaut, Asin. 1. 3. 5. ; who puts *navales pedes* for *remiges et nautæ*, Men. ii. 2. ult.

The top-sails were called SUPPARA *velorum*, or any appendage to the main-sail.[5]

Carina puppis, and even *trabs*, a beam, are often put by the poets for the whole ship ; but never *velum*, as we use sail for one ship or many ; thus, a sail, an hundred sail.

The rigging and tackling of a ship, its sails, sail-yards, oars, ropes, &c. were called ARMAMENTA. Hence *arma* is put for the sails, *colligere arma jubet*, i. e. *vela contrahere*, he commands them to furl the sails, and for the rudder, *spoliata armis*, i. e. *clavo*,[6] despoiled of her rudder.

Ships of war,[7] and these only, had their prows armed with a sharp beak,[8] which usually had three teeth or points, whence these ships were called ROSTRATÆ, and because the beak was covered with brass, ÆRATÆ.[9]

Ships, when about to engage, had towers erected on them, whence stones and missive weapons were discharged from engines called PROPUGNACULA; hence *turritæ puppes*. Agrippa invented a kind of towers which were suddenly raised. Towers used also to be erected on ships in sieges and at other times.[10]

Some ships of war were all covered,[11] others uncovered,[12] except at the prow and stern, where those who fought stood.[13]

The planks or platforms[14] on which the mariners sat or passed from one part of the ship to another, were called FORI, gangways,[15] and the helps to mount on board, PONTES vel SCALÆ.[16] Some take *fori* for the deck (STEGA, -*æ*), others for the seats. It is at least certain they were both in the top of the ship and below. We also find *forus*, sing.[17]

1 Ov. Her. ii. 11. Catul. lxiv. 225. Plin. xix. 1. s. 5.
2 Sil. vi. 325. Luc. v. 428. Catul. iv. 21. Cic. Verr. v. 34. Plin. li. 57. s. 48. Virg. Æn. iv. 546. v. 16. 281 629, 830.
3 adducendo et remittendo vel proferendo pedes, Virg. Æn. vi. 302. x. 218.
4 Cic. Q. Frat. ii. 14. Tusc. iii. 11. Off. iii. 33. but in the last passage the best copies

have viris equisque, as Phil. viii. 7.
5 Luc. v. 429. Stat. Sylv. ii. 2. 27. Sen. Ep. 77.
6 Plaut. Merc. 1. 62. Virg. Æn. v. 15. vi. 353.
7 naves longæ vel bellicæ.
8 rostrum, oftener plur. rostra, Cæs. B. G. iii. 13. Sil. Ital. xiv. 480.
9 Virg. Æn. v. 142. viii. 690. Cæs. B. C. ii. 3. Hor. Od. ii. 16. 21. Plin. xxxii. 1.

10 Cæs. B. G. iii. 14. Flor. ii. 2. iv. 11. Plin. xxxii. 1. Plut. in Ant. Hor. Ep. i. 2. Virg. Æn. viii. 693. Serv. Virg. Liv. xxiv. 34. Tac. Ann. xv. 9. Sil. Ital. xix. 418.
11 tectæ vel constratæ, καταφρακτοί ; quæ καταστρώματα, tabulata vel constrata habebant, decks.
12 apertæ, αφρακτοί, v. -α, Cic. Att. v. 11, 12. vi. 8. 12.
13 Liv. xxx. 43. xxxvi.

42. Cæs. passim. Cic. Verr. v. 34.
14 tabulata.
15 ab eo quod incessus ferant, Serv. Virg. Æn. iv. 605.vi. 412. Cic. Sen. 6.
16 επιβαθραι v. κλιμακες Virg. Æn. x. 288. 654. 658. Stat. Sylv. iii. 2. 55.
17 Gell. xvi. 19. Plaut. Bacch. ii. 3. 44. Stich. iii. 1. 12. Sil. xiv. 425. Luc. iii. 630.

38

The anchor (ANCHORA), which moored or fastened[1] the ships, was at
first of stone, sometimes of wood filled with lead, but afterwards of iron.
It was thrown[2] from the prow by a cable, and fixed in the ground, while
the ship stood (or, as we say, rode) at anchor,[3] and raised[4] when it sailed ;
sometimes the cable[5] was cut.[6] The Veneti used iron chains instead of
ropes.[7]

The plummet for sounding depths[8] was called BOLIS or catapirates, or
MOLYBDIS, -idis, as Gronovius reads, Stat. Sylv. iii. 2. 30.

The ropes by which the ship was tied to land were called RETINACULA,
or ORÆ, or simply FUNES. Hence oram solvere, to set sail.[9]

The ancients had ropes for girding a ship in a storm,[10] which are
still used. They had also long poles,[11] to push it off rocks and
shoals.[12]

Sand, or whatever was put in a ship to keep it steady, was called
SABURRA, ballast.[13]

Ships were built[14] of fir,[15] alder,[16] cedar, pine, and cypress,[17] by the Veneti, of oak,[18] sometimes of green wood ; so that a number of ships were
put on the stocks,[19] completely equipped and launched,[20] in forty-five days
after the timber was cut down in the forest ; by Cæsar, at Arles, against the
people of Marseilles, in thirty days[21]

There was a place at Rome called the Tiber where ships lay and were
built, called NAVALIA, plur. -ium, the dock.[22]

As the Romans quickly built fleets, they as speedily manned them.
Freedmen and slaves were employed as mariners or rowers,[23] who were
also called SOCII NAVALES, and CLASSICI. The citizens and allies were
obliged to furnish a certain number of these, according to their fortune, and sometimes to supply them with provisions and pay for a limited
time.[24]

The legionary soldiers at first used to fight at sea as well as on land.
But when the Romans came to have regular and constant fleets, there was
a separate kind of soldiers raised for the marine service,[25] who were called
CLASSIARII, or EPIBATÆ ; but this service was reckoned less honourable
than that of the legionary soldiers, and was sometimes performed by manumitted slaves. The rowers also were occasionally armed.[26]

The allies and conquered states were in after times bound to furnish a
certain number of ships completely equipped and manned ; some only
stores, arms, tackling, and men.[27]

Augustus stationed a fleet on the Tuscan sea at Misenum, where Agrippa made a fine harbour called PORTUS JULIUS, by joining the Lucrine lake
and the lacus Avernus to the bay of Baiæ,[28] and another on the Hadriatic

---

1 fundabat vel alliga-
bat.
2 jaciebatur, Virg. Æn.
vi. ult.
3 ad anchoram vel in
anchora stabat, Cæs.
B. G. v. 10.
4 tollebatur vel velle-
batur, Id. iv. 23.
5 anchorale vel ancho-
ra.
6 præcidebatur,   Liv.
xxii. 19. Cic. Verr. v.
34.
7 Cæs. B. G. iii. 13.
8 ad altitudinem maris

explorandum, Isid. xix.
4.
9 Virg. Æn. iii. 639.
667. iv. 580. Liv. xxii.
19. xxviii. 36. Quinct.
Ep. Tryph. & iv. 2. 41.
10 Hor. Od. i. 14. Act.
Apost. xxvii. 17.
11 conti, perticæ, sudes
vel trudes.
12 Virg. Æn. v. 208.
13 Liv. xxxvii. 14. Virg.
G. iv. 195
14 ædificabantur.
15 abies, Virg. G. ii.
68.

16 alnus, Luc. iii. 440.
whence alni, ships, ib.
ii. 427.
17 Veg. iv. 34.
18 ex robore, Cæs. B.
G. iii. 13.
19 positæ.
20 instructæ v. ornatæ
armatæque in aquam
deductæ sint.
21 Liv. xxviii. 45. Cæs.
B. C. i. 34. Plin. xvi.
39. s. 74.
22 Liv. iii. 26. viii. 14.
xl. 51.
23 nautæ vel remiges.

24 Liv. xxi. 49, 50. xxii.
11. xxiv. 11. xxvi. 17.
35. 48. Curt. iv. 3. 18.
25 milites in classem
scripti, Liv. xxii. 57.
26 Liv. xxvi. 48. xxxii.
23. xxxvii. 16. Suet.
Galb. 12. Aug.   16.
Tac. Ann. xv. 51. Hist.
i. 87. Cæs. passim.
27 Cic. Verr. v. 17, &c.
Liv. xxviii. 45. xxxvi.
43. xlii. 48.
28 Suet. Aug. 16.

at Ravenna, and in other parts of the empire, also on rivers, as the Rhine and Danube.[1]

The admiral of the whole fleet was called DUX PRÆFECTUSQUE CLASSIS, and his ship, NAVIS PRÆTORIA,[2] which in the night-time had, as a sign,[3] three lights.[4]

At first the consuls and prætors used to command the fleets of the republic, or some one under them ; as Lælius under Scipio.[5]

The commanders of each ship was called NAVARCHI, or TRIERARCHI, i. e. *præfecti trieris* vel *triremis navis*, or MAGISTRI NAVIUM.[6] The master or proprietor of a trading vessel, NAUCLERUS, NAVICULATOR, vel ·ARIUS, who, when he did not go to sea himself, but employed another to navigate his ship, was said, *naviculariam*, sc. rem, *facere*.[7]

The person who steered the ship and directed its course was called GUBERNATOR, the pilot, sometimes also MAGISTER, or RECTOR. He sat at the helm, on the top of the stern, dressed in a particular manner,[8] and gave orders about spreading and contracting the sails,[9] plying or checking the oars,[10] &c. It was his part to know the signs of the weather, to be acquainted with ports and places, and particularly to observe the winds and the stars. For as the ancients knew not the use of the compass, they were directed in their voyages chiefly by the stars in the night-time,[11] and in the day-time by coasts and islands which they knew. In the Mediterranean, to which navigation was then chiefly confined, they could not be long out of the sight of land. When overtaken by a storm, the usual method was to drive their ships on shore,[12] and when the danger was over, to set them afloat again by the strength of arms and levers. In the ocean they only cruised along the coast.

In some ships there were two pilots, who had an assistant called PRORETA, i. e. *custos et tutela proræ*, who watched at the prow.[13]

He who had command over the rowers was called HORTATOR and PAUSARIUS,[14] or PORTISCULUS, which was also the name of the staff or mallet with which he excited or retarded them.[15] He did this also with his voice in a musical tone, that the rowers might keep time in their motions. Hence it is also applied to the commanders. Those who hauled or pulled a rope, who raised a weight, or the like, called HELCIARII, used likewise to animate one another with a loud cry, hence *nauticus clamor*, the cries or shouts of the mariners.[16]

Before a fleet, (CLASSIS) set out to sea, it was solemnly reviewed[17] like an army ; prayers were made and victims sacrificed. The auspices were consulted, and if any unlucky omen happened, as a person sneezing on the left, or swallows alighting on the ships, &c., the voyage was suspended.[18]

1 sinus Baianus, Suet. Ner. 27. vel lacus Baianus, Tac. Ann. xiv. 4. Dio. xlviii. 50. Virg. G. ii. 163.
2 Tac. Ann. iv. 5. xii. 30. Hist. i. 58. ii. 63. iv. 79. Suet. Aug. 49. Veg. iv. 31. Flor. iv. 12. 26.
3 signum nocturnum.
4 Cic. Verr. v. 34. Liv. xxix. 25.
5 Liv. xxvii. 42. xxix. 25.
6 Cic. Verr. i. 30. iii. 60. v. 34. Tac. Hist. ii. 9.

Suet. Ner. 34. Liv. xxix. 25.
7 Plaut. Mil. iv. 3. 16. Cic. Fam. xvi. 9. Att. ix. 3. Ver. ii. 55. v. 16. Man. 5.
8 Virg. Æn. iii. 161. 176. v. 176. Sil. iv. 719. Luc. viii. 167. Cic. Sen. 6. Plaut. Mil. iv. 4. 41. 45.
9 expandere vel contrahere vela.
10 incumbere remis vel eos inhibere, Virg. v. 12. x. 218. Cic. Or. i. 33. Att. xiii. 21.

11 Ov. Met. iii. 592. Luc. viii. 172. Virg. Æn. iii. 201. 269. 513. Hor. Od. ii. 16. 3.
12 in terram agere vel ejicere.
13 Ov. Met. iii. 617. Æl. ix. 40. Plaut. Rud. jv. 3. 75.
14 κελευστής, Plaut. Merc. iv. 2. 4. Sen. Ep. 56. Plaut. Asin. iii. 1. 15. Fest.
15 celeusmata vel hortamenta dabat, Plaut. Asin. iii. 1. 15. Isid. Orig. xix. 12.

16 Serv. Virg. Æn. ii. 128. v. 140. Luc. ii. 688. Sil. v. 360. Val. Flacc. i. 460. Mart. iii. 67. iv. 64. Quinct. i. 10. 16. Stat. Theb. vi. 800. Asc. Cic. Div. 17. Dio. i. 32.
17 lustrata est.
18 Cic. Phil. xii. 3. Liv. xxix. 27. xxxvi. 42. Ap. B. C. v. 110. 118. v. 772. Sil. xvii. 48. Val. Max. i. Hor. Ep. x. i. 16. 24. Poly. iii. 10. Frost. i. 12.

The mariners, when they set sail or reached the harbour, decked the stern with garlands.[1]

There was great labour in launching[2] the ships, for as the ancients seldom sailed in winter, their ships during that time were drawn up[3] on land, and stood on the shore.[4]

They were drawn to sea by ropes and levers,[5] with rollers placed below,[6] called PALANGES, vel -gæ, or SCUTULÆ, and, according to some, lapsus rotarum; but others more properly take this phrase for rotæ labentes, wheels.[7]

Archimedes invented a wonderful machine for this purpose, called HELIX.[8]

Sometimes ships were conveyed for a considerable space by land, and for that purpose they were sometimes so made, that they might be taken to pieces, a practice still in use. Augustus is said to have transported some ships from the open sea to the Ambracian gulf near Actium, on a kind of wall covered with raw hides of oxen, in like manner over the Isthmus of Corinth. So Trajan, from the Euphrates to the Tigris.[9]

The signal for embarking was given with the trumpet. They embarked[10] in a certain order, the mariners first and then the soldiers. They also sailed in a certain order, the light vessels usually foremost, then the fleet or ships of war, and after them the ships of burden; but this order was often changed.[11]

When they approached the place of their destination, they were very attentive to the objects they first saw, in the same manner as to omens at their departure.[12]

. When they reached the shore,[13] and landed[14] the troops, prayers and sacrifices again were made.

If the country was hostile, and there was no proper harbour, they made a naval camp,[15] and drew up their ships on land.[16] They did so, especially if they were to winter there.[17] But if they were to remain only for a short time, the fleet was stationed in some convenient place,[18] not far from land.[19]

Harbours, (PORTUS) were most strongly fortified, especially at the entrance.[20] The two sides of which, or the piers, were called CORNUA, or BRACHIA ; on the extremities were erected bulwarks and towers. There was usually also a watch-tower (PHAROS, plur. -i),[21] with lights to direct the course of ships in the night-time, as at Alexandria in Egypt, at Ostia and Ravenna, at Capreæ, Brundusium, and other places.[22] A chain sometimes was drawn across as a barrier or boom (claustrum).[23]

Harbours were naturally formed at the mouths of rivers; hence the name

1 Virg. Æn. iv. 418. G. i. 303.
2 in deducendo, Virg. Æn. iv. 397.
3 subductæ.
4 Hor. Od. i. 4. 2. Virg. Æn. i. 555. iii. 135. 177.
5 vectibus.
6 cylindris lignisque teretibus et rotundis subjectis.
7 Cæs. B. C. ii. iii. 34. Virg. Æn. ii. 236.
8 Athen. v. Plut. in Marcell. Sil. Ital. xiv.

352.
9 Liv. xxv. 11. Sil. xii. 441. Suet. Cal. 47. Curt. viii. 10. Just. xxxii. 3. Dio. l. 12. li. 5. Strab. viii. 335. xlviii. 28.
10 conscendebant, Luc. ii. 690.
11 Virg. Æn. v. 833. Liv. xxli. 16. xxix. 25. passim.
12 Virg. Æn. iii. 537. Liv. xxix. 27. xxx. 25.
13 terram appulerunt.
14 exposuerunt, Liv.

xxxvii. 14. 47.
15 castra navalia vel nautica.
16 subducebant, Liv. xxiii. 28. xxx. 9, 10. Cæs. B. G. iv. 21.
17 Liv. xxxvi. 45. xxxviii. 8.
18 ad anchoram stabat, vel in statione tenebatur.
19 Liv. xxiv. 17. xxxi. 23. xxxvii. 15. Cæs. B. C. ii. 6. iv. 21. B. Alex. 25.
20 aditus vel introitus;

os, ostium, vel fauces, Virg. Æn. i. 404. Cic. Liv.
21 Cic. Att. ix. 14. Luc. ii. 615. 706. Plin. Ep. vi. 31. Suet. Claud. 20.
Liv. xxxi. 26. Vitr. v. 11.
22 Cæs. B. C. iii. ult. Plin. xxxvi. 12. Suet. Tib. 74. Cal. 46. Stat. Sylv. iii. 5. 100.
23 Front. Strat. i. 5, 8;

of OSTIA at the mouth of the Tiber. Ovid calls the seven mouths of the Nile, *septem* PORTUS.[1]

Harbours made by art[2] were called COTHONES, vel -NA, -*orum*.

Adjoining to the harbour were docks (NAVALIA, -*ium*), where the ships were laid up,[3] careened and refitted.[4]

Fleets about to engage were arranged in a manner similar to armies on land. Certain ships were placed in the centre,[5] others in the right wing,[6] and others in the left ; some as a reserve.[7] We find them sometimes disposed in the form of a wedge, a forceps, and a circle, but most frequently of a semicircle or half-moon.[8]

Before the battle, sacrifices and prayers were made as on land ; the admiral sailed round the fleet in a light galley,[9] and exhorted the men.

The soldiers and sailors made ready[10] for action : they furled the sails and adjusted the rigging ; for they never chose to fight but in calm weather.[11]

A red flag was displayed from the admiral's ship, as a signal to engage. The trumpets in it and all the other ships were sounded, and a shout raised by all the crews.[12]

The combatants endeavored to disable or sink the ships of the enemy, by sweeping off[13] the oars, or by striking them with their beaks, chiefly on the sides. They grappled with them by means of certain machines called crows (CORVI), iron hands or hooks (FERREÆ MANUS),[14] drags or grappling irons (HARPAGONES),[15] &c. and fought as on land.[16] They sometimes also employed fire-ships, or threw firebrands, and pots full of coals and sulphur, with various other combustibles,[17] which were so successfully employed by Augustus at the battle of Actium, that most of Antony's fleet was thereby destroyed.[18]

In sieges they joined vessels together, and erected on them various engines, or sunk vessels to block up their harbours.[19]

The ships of the victorious fleet, when they returned home, had their prows decked with laurel, and resounded with triumphant music.[20] The prizes distributed after a victory at sea were much the same as on land.[21] Also naval punishments, pay, and provisions, &c.[22]

The trading vessels of the ancients were in general much inferior in size to those of the moderns. Cicero mentions a number of ships of burden, none of which was below 2000 *amphoræ*,[23] i. e. about fifty-six tons, which he seems to have thought a large ship.[24] There were, however, some ships of enormous bulk. One built by Ptolemy is said to have been 280 cubits, i. e. 420 feet long, and another 300 feet ; the tonnage of the former 7182, and of the latter, 3197.[25] The ship which brought from Egypt the great obelisk that stood in the Circus of the Vatican in the time of Cali-

---

1 Her. xiv. 107. Am. ll. 13. 10. Serv. Virg. Æn. v. 281. Liv. i. 33. xxvi. 19. Diony. iii. 45.
2 manu vel arte. Serv. Virg. Æn. i. 431. Fest.
3 subductæ.
4 refectæ, Cic. Off. ii. 17. Liv. xxxvii. 10. Cæs. B. C. ii. 3, 4. Virg. iv. 503. Ov. Am. ii. 9. 21.
5 media acies.
6 dextrum cornu.
7 subsidio, naves sub-

sidiariæ, Hirt. Bel. Al. 10. Liv. xxxvi. 44. xxxvii. 23. 29.
8 Polyb. i. Polyæn. iii. Thucy. ii. Veg. iv. 45. Sil. xiv. 370.
9 navis actuaria.
10 se expediebant.
11 Liv. xxvi. 39.
12 Sil. xiv. 372. Luc. iii. 540. Dio. xliii. 9.
13 detergendo.
14 Dio. l. 29. Luc. iii. 635.
15 i. e. asseres ferreo unco præfixi.

16 Flor. ii. 2. Liv. xxvi. 39. xxx. 10. Cæs. B. G. i. 52. Curt. iv. 9. Luc. xi. 712. Dio. xxxix. 43. xlix. 1. 3. &c. Hirt. B. Alex. 11.
17 stuppea flamma manu, tellisque volatile ferrum spargitur, from their hands flaming balls of tow, and from missive engines the winged steel is flung. Virg. Æn. viii. 694.
18 Dio. l. 29. 34, 35 ; hence vix una sospes

navis ab ignibus, scarcely one ship saved from the flames, Horat. Od. i. 37. 13.
19 Curt. iv. 13. Liv. xxiv. 34. xxvi. 26. xxxv. 11. 14. Cæs. B. C. iii. 34.
20 Dio. li. 5.
21 see p. 262.
22 Liv. xxiii. 21. 48.
23 quarum minor nulla erat duum millium amphorum.
24 Cic. Fam. xii. 15.
25 Athenæus.

gula, besides the obelisk itself, had 120,000 *modii* of *lentes*, lentiles, a kind of pulse, for ballast, about 1138 tons.[1]

CUSTOMS OF THE ROMANS.

I. THE ROMAN DRESS.

THE distinguishing part of the Roman dress was the TOGA or gown, as that of the Greeks was the *pallium*, and of the Gauls, *braccæ*, breeches, whence the Romans were called GENS TOGATA,[2] or TOGATI, and the Greeks, or in general those who were not Romans, PALLIATI : and *Gallia cisalpina*, when admitted unto the rights of citizens, was called TOGATA.[3]   Hence also *fabulæ togatæ et palliatæ*.[4]   As the toga was the robe of peace, *togati* is often opposed to *armati* ;[5] and as it was chiefly worn in the city,[6] it is sometimes opposed to RUSTICI.[7]

The Romans were particularly careful in foreign countries always to appear dressed in the toga, but this was not always done.   Some wore the Greek dress ; as Scipio in Sicily, and the emperor Claudius at Naples.[8]

The TOGA[9] was a loose,[10] flowing,[11] woollen robe, which covered the whole body, round and close at the bottom,[12] but open at the top down to the girdle,[13] without sleeves ; so that the right arm was at liberty, and the left supported a part (*lacinia*, a flap or lappet) of the toga, which was drawn up[14] and thrown back over the left shoulder, and thus formed what was called SINUS, a fold or cavity upon the breast, in which things might be carried, and with which the face or head might be covered.[15]   Hence Fabius, the Roman ambassador, when he denounced war in the senate of Carthage, is said to have poured out,[16] or shaken out the lap of his toga.[17]   Dionysius says the form of the toga was semicircular.[18]   The toga in later times had several folds, but anciently few or none.[19]   These folds, when collected in a knot or centre, were called UMBO, which is put for the toga itself.[20] When a person did any work, he tucked up[21] his toga, and girded it[22] round him : hence *accingere se operi* vel *ad opus*, or oftener, in the passive, *accingi*, to prepare, to make ready.[23]

The toga of the rich and noble was finer and larger[24] than of the less wealthy.   A new toga was called PEXA, when old and thread-bare, *trita*.[25] The Romans were at great pains to adjust[26] the toga, that it might sit properly,[27] and not draggle.[28]

1 Plin. xvi. 40. s. 76.
2 Suet. Aug. 40. 98. Jul. 80. Claud. 15. Plin. Ep. v. 11. Virg. Æn. i. 286.
3 Cic. Rosc. Am. 46. Ver. i. 29. ii. 62. Or. i. 24. iii. 11. Rab. Post. 9. Phil. v. 5. viii. 9. Sall. Jug. 21. Tac Hist. ii. 20. Suet. Cæs. 4. 8.
4 see p. 236.
5 Liv. iii. 10. 60. iv. 10. Cic. Cæc. 15. Off. i. 23. Pis. 3.

6 ibi, sc. rure, nulla ne cessitas togæ, Plin.Ep. v. 6.
7 Plin. vi. 30.
8 Cic. Rabir. 10. Tac. Ann. ii. 59. Dio. lxvi. 6.
9 a tegendo, quod corpus tegat, Var.
10 laxa.
11 fluitans.
12 ab imo.
13 ad cincturam.
14 subducebatur.

15 Plin. xv. 18. Gell. iv. 18. Suet. Jul. 82. Liv. viii. 9.
16 sinum effudisse, Liv. xxi. 18.
17 excussisse togæ gremium, Flor. ii. 6.
18 iii. 61.
19 veteribus nulli sinus, Quinct. xi. 3.
20 Virg. Æn. i. 324. Pers. v. 33.
21 succingebat.
22 astringebat.

23 see p. 51, 52.
24 laxior.
25 Hor. Epod. iv. 8. Epist. i. 18. 30. 95. Mart. li. 44. 58.
26 componere.
27 ne impar diesideret.
28 nec deflueret. Hor. Sat. ii. 3. 77. l. 3. 31. Epist. i. 1. 95. Quin. xi. 3. Macrob. Sat. ii. 9.

The form of the toga was different at different times. The Romans at first had no other dress. It was then strait[1] and close ; it covered the arms, and came down to the feet.

The toga was at first worn by women as well as men. But afterwards matrons wore a different robe, called STOLA, with a broad border or fringe,[2] called INSTITA, reaching to the feet, (whence *instita* is put for *matrona*), and also, as some say, when they went abroad, a loose outer robe thrown over the *stola* like a surtout, a mantle, or cloak, called PALLA, or *peplus*.[3] But the old scholiast on Horace makes *palla* here the same with *instita*, and calls it *peripodium* and *tunicæ pallium*. Some think that this fringe constituted the only distinction between the stola and toga. It is certain, however, that the outer robe of a woman was called PALLA.[4]

Matron in Stola. · *Woman in Palla.*

Courtezans, and women condemned for adultery, were not permitted to wear the *stola* ; hence called TOGATÆ, and the modesty of matrons is called *stolatus pudor*.[5]

There was a fine robe of a circular form worn by women, called CYCLAS, *-adis*.[6]

None but Roman citizens were permitted to wear the *toga* ; and banished persons were prohibited the use of it. Hence *toga* is put for the dignity of a Roman.[7]

The colour of the toga was white, and on festivals they usually had one newly cleaned ; hence they were said *festos* (sc. *dies*) ALBATI *celebrare*, to celebrate their festival days clothed in white.[8] Candidates for office wore a toga whitened by the fuller, TOGA CANDIDA.[9] The toga in mourning was of a black or dark colour, TOGA PULLA vel *atra* ; hence those in mourning were called PULLATI, or ATRATI.[10] But those were also called *pullati*, who wore a great-coat[11] instead of the toga, or a mean ragged dress,[12] as the vulgar or poor people.[13]

1 arcta, Gell. vii. 12.
2 limbus.
3 Hor. Sat. i. 2. 99. 99.
  Ov. Art. Am. i. 32.
  Tibul. i. 7. 74.
4 Virg. Æn. i. 648. xi.
  576. quod palam et foris

gerebatur, Var. L. L.
iv. 30.
5 Hor. Sat. i. 2. 82. Juv.
  ii. 70. Mart. ii. 39. vi.
  64. x. 52. Cic. Phil. 2.
  15. Mart. i. 36. 8.
6 Juv. vi. 258. Suet.

Cal. 52.
7 Plin. Ep. iv. 11. Hor.
  Od. iii. 5. 10.
8 Ov. Trist. v. 5. 7. Hor.
  Sat. ii. 2. 60.
9 see p. 60.
10 Suet. Aug. 44. Juv.

iii. 213. Cic. Vat. 12.
11 lacerna.
12 Suet. Aug. 40. Plin.
  Ep. vii. 17.
13 pullatus circulus, vel
  turba pullata, Quinc.
  ii. 12. vi. 4.

The mourning robe of women was called RICINIUM, vel -NUS, vel RICA,[1] which covered the head and shoulders, or MAVORTES, -IS, vel -TA. They seem to have had several of these above one another, that they might throw them into the funeral piles of their husbands and friends. The Twelve Tables restricted the number to three.[2]

The Romans seldom or never appeared at a feast in mourning, nor at the public spectacles, nor at festivals and sacrifices.[3]

At entertainments the more wealthy Romans laid aside the toga, and put on a particular robe, called SYNTHESIS, which they wore all the time of the *saturnalia*, because then they were continually feasting.[4] Nero wore it in[5] common.

Magistrates and certain priests wore a toga bordered with purple,[6] hence called TOGA PRÆTEXTA ; as the superior magistrates,[7] the pontifices, the augurs, the DECEMVIRI *sacris faciundis*, &c., and even private persons when they exhibited games.[8]

Generals when they triumphed wore an embroidered toga, called PICTA vel PALMATA.[9]

Young men, till they were seventeen years of age, and young women, till they were married, also wore a gown bordered with purple, TOGA PRÆ-TEXTA, whence they were called PRÆTEXTATI.[10] Hence *amicitia prætextata*, i. e. *a teneris annis*, friendship formed in youth ; but *verba prætextata* is put for *obscæna*,[11] and *mores prætextati* for *impudici* vel *corrupti*.[12]

Under the emperors the toga was in a great measure disused, unless by clients when they waited[13] on their patrons, and orators, hence called *togati*, enrobed.[14]

Boys likewise wore a hollow golden ball or boss (AUREA BULLA),[15] which hung from the neck on the breast ; as some think in the shape of a heart, to prompt them to wisdom ; according to others round, with the figure of a heart engraved on it.[16] The sons of freedmen and poorer citizens used only a leathern boss.[17] Bosses were also used as an ornament for belts or girdles.[18]

Young men usually, when they had completed the seventeenth year of their age, laid aside[19] the toga prætexta, and put on[20] the manly gown (TO-

1 quod post tergum re-jiceretur.
2 Cic. L. ii. 23. Serv. Virg. Æn. i. 268. Isid. xix. 25.
3 Cic. Vat. 12. Mart. iv. 2. Ov. F. i. 79. Hor. ii. 2. 60. Pers. ii. 40.
4 Mart. ii. 46. iv. 66. v. 80. xiv. 1. 141. Sen. Ep. 18.
5 synthesina, sc. vestis, Suet. 51.
6 limbo purpureo circumdata.
7 Cic. Red. Sen. 5. Liv. xxxiv. 7. Juv. x. 99.
8 Cic. Sext. 69. Pis. 4. Liv. xxvii. 39, &c.

9 Mart. vii. 2. 7.
10 Liv. xxii. 57. xxxiv. 7. Cic. Ver. i. 44. Cat. ii. 2. Mur. 5. Prop.iv.12. 33. Suet. Aug. 44. 94. Mart. x. 20.
11 Suet. Vesp. 22. quod nubentibus, depositis prætextis, a multitudine puerorum obscœna clamarentur, Festus, Gell. ix. 10. Macrob. Sat. ii. 1.
12 Juv. ii. 170.
13 officium faciebant.
14 Suet. Aug. 60. Mart. i. 109. ii. 57. x. 74. 3. Schol. Juv. x. 45. Sen. Const. 9. Tac. An. xi. 7.
15 The bulla was hung

on the left breast of the child, that, at the sight of it, they might consider they were men, if they had a wise heart ; and be likewise no inconsiderable incitement to courage : the purple of the gown or prætexta was also to remind them of the modesty which became them at that age. As for the word bulla, some derive it from βουλη, *consilium*, or counsel ; some from βουλομαι, *velle*, or to will ; some from βαλλειν, by a figure taken

from archers, intimating the good purpose, as a mark, that youth should aim at.—Senhouse.
16 Cic. Ver. i. 58. Asc. toc. Liv. xxvi. 6. Plaut. Rud. iv. 4. 127. Macrob. Sat. i. 6.
17 bulla scortea, vel signum de paupere loro, Juv. v. 165. Plin. xxxiii. 1.
18 Virg. Æn. xii. 942.
19 ponebant vel deponebant.
20 sumebant vel induebant.

GA VIRILIS), called *toga* PURA, because it was purely white ; and LIBERA, because they were then freed from the restraint of masters, and allowed greater liberty.[1]

The ceremony of changing the toga was performed[2] with great solemnity before the images of the *lares*, to whom the *bulla* was consecrated,[3] sometimes in the Capitol, or they immediately went thither, or to some temple, to pay their devotions to the gods.[4]

The usual time of the year for assuming the *toga virilis* was at the feasts of Bacchus in March.[5]

Then the young man was conducted by his father or principal relation to the forum, accompanied by his friends (whose attendance was called OFFICIUM SOLENNE TOGÆ VIRILIS, the ceremony of taking up the manly robe), and there recommended to some eminent orator, whom he should study to imitate,[6] whence he was said *forum attingere* vel *in forum venire*, when he began to attend to public business.[7]   This was called *dies togæ virilis*, or *dies tirocinii*, and the conducting of one to the forum, TIROCINIUM ;[8] the young men were called TIRONES, young or raw soldiers, because then they first began to serve in the army.   Hence TIRO is put for a learner or novice ; *ponere tirocinium*, to lay aside the character of a learner, and give a proof of one's parts ; to be past his noviciate.[9]

When all the formalities of this day were finished, the friends and dependants of the family were invited to a feast, and small presents distributed among them, called SPORTULÆ.   The emperors on that occasion used to give a largess to the people, CONGIARIUM, so called from *congius*, a measure of liquids.[10]

Servius appointed, that those who assumed the toga virilis should send a certain coin to the temple of Youth.[11]

Parents and guardians permitted young men to assume[12] the toga virilis, sooner or later than the age of seventeen, as they judged proper ; under the emperors, when they had completed the fourteenth year.[13]   Before this they were considered as part of the family,[14] afterwards of the state.[15]

Young men of rank, after putting on the toga virilis, commonly lived in a separate house from their parents.[16]   It was, however, customary for them, as a mark of modesty, during the first whole year, to keep[17] their right arm within the toga, and in their exercises in the Campus Martius never to expose themselves quite naked, as men come to maturity sometimes did.[18]

The ancient Romans had no other clothing but the toga ;[19] in imitation of whom, Cato used often to go dressed in this manner, and sometimes even to sit on the tribunal, when prætor.[20]   Hence *exigua toga Catonis*, the scanty gown of Cato ; *hirta*,[21] because it was strait[22] and coarse.[23] Nor did candidates for offices wear any thing but the toga.[24]

---

1 Cic. Att. v. 20. ix. 19. Ov. Trist iv. 10. 28. Fast. iii. 777. Pers. v. 30.
2 toga mutabatur, Hor. Od. i. 36. 9.
3 laribus donata pependit, Prop. iv. 132.
4 Val. Max. v. 4. 4. Suet. Claud. 2.
5 liberalibus, xii. Kal. Apr. Cic. Att. vi. 1. Ov. F. iii. 771.
6 Cic. Att. ix. 22. Am.

1. Suet. Aug. 26. Ner. 7. Tib. 54. Claud. 2. Plin. Ep. i. 9. Tac. Or. 34.
7 forensia stipendia auspicabatur, Sen. Cont. v. 6. Cic. Fam. v. 8. xiii. 10. xv. 16.
8 Suet. Aug. 26. 66. Cal. 10. 15. Claud. 2. Tib. 54.
9 Cic. Phil. xi. 15. Or. i. 50. Fam. vii. 3. Liv. xi. 35. xiv. 37. Suet.

Ner. 7.
10 Plin. Ep. x. 117, 118. Suet. Tib. 54. Tac. An. iii. 29.
11 Diony. iv. 15.
12 dabant.
13 Cic. Att. vi. 1. Suet. Aug. 8. Cal. 10. Cla. 43. Ner. 7. Tac. Ann. xii. 41. xiii. 15.
14 pars domus.
15 reipublicæ, Tac. Mor. Germ. 13.
16 Suet. Tib. 15. Dom. 2

17 cohibere.
18 Cic. Cœl. 5.
19 Gell. vii. 12
20 campestri sub toga cinctus, Asc. Cic. Val. Max. iii. 6, 7.
21 Hor. Ep. i. 19. 13. Luc. ii. 386.
22 arcta.
23 crassa vel 'pinguis, Hor. Sat. i. 3. 15. Juv. ix. 28. Mart. iv. 19.
24 see. p. 60.

The Romans afterwards wore below the toga a white woollen vest called TUNICA, which come down a little below the knees before, and to the middle of the legs behind,[1] at first without sleeves. Tunics with sleeves,[2] or reaching to the ancles,[3] were reckoned effeminate.[4] But under the emperors these came to be used with fringes at the hands,[5] from the example of Cæsar, longer or shorter according to fancy. Those who wore them were said to be MANULEATI.[6]

The tunic was fastened by a girdle or belt[7] about the waist to keep it tight, which also served as a purse,[8] in which they kept their money; hence *incinctus tunicam mercator*, the merchant with his tunic girt. The purse commonly hung from the neck, and was said *decollasse*, when it was taken off; hence *decollare*, to deceive.[9]

It was also thought effeminate to appear abroad with the tunic slackly or carelessly girded: hence the saying of Sylla concerning Cæsar to the Optimates, who interceded for his life, UT MALE PRÆCINCTUM PUERUM CAVERENT, to be upon their guard against that loose-girt boy. For this also Mæcenas was blamed.[10] Hence *cinctus, præcinctus*, and *succinctus*, are put for *industrius, expeditus* vel *gnavus*, diligent, active, clever, because they used to gird the tunic when at work,[11] and *discinctus* for *iners, mollis, ignavus*; thus, *discinctus nepos*, a dissolute spendthrift; *discincti Afri*, effeminate, or simply ungirt, for the Africans did not use a girdle.[12]

The Romans do not seem to have used the girdle at home or in private; hence *discincti ludere*, i. e. *domi*, with their tunics ungurt; *discinctaque in otia natus*, formed for soft repose,[13] for they never wore the toga at home, but an undress.[14] Hence the toga and other things which they wore only abroad were called FORENSIA, or VESTITUS FORENSIS, and VESTIMENTA FORENSIA.[15]

The tunic was worn by women as well as men; but that of the former always came down to their feet, and covered their arms. They also used girdles both before and after marriage.[16]

The Romans do not seem to have used a belt above the toga. But this point is strongly contested. Young men, when they assumed the toga virilis, and woman, when they were married, received from their parents a tunic wrought in a particular manner, called TUNICA RECTA, or REGILLA.[17]

The senators had a broad stripe of purple (or rather two stripes, *fasciæ* vel *plagulæ*) sewed on the breast of their tunic, called LATUS CLAVUS,[18] which is sometimes put for the tunic itself, or the dignity of a senator; the equites a narrow stripe, ANGUSTUS CLAVUS,[19] called also PAUPER CLAVUS.[20]

---

1 Quinc. xi. 3. 128.
2 dhirodotæ vel tunicæ manicatæ.
3 talares.
4 Cic. Cat. ii. 10. Virg. Æn. ix. 616. Gell. vii. 12.
5 ad manus fimbriatæ.
6 Suet. Jul. 45. Cal. 52. Hor. Sat. i. 2. 25. Prop. iv. 2. 28.
7 cingulum, cinctus -ûs, zona vel balteus.
8 pro marsupio vel cru-

mena.
9 Gell. xv. 2. Plaut. Merc. v. 2. 84. Truc. iii. 2. 7. Cap. iii. 1. 37. Suet. Vit. 16. Hor. Ep. ii. 2. 40. Ov. F. v. 673.
10 Suet. Jul. 46. Dio. xliii. 43. Sen. Ep. 14.
11 Hor. Sat. i. 5, 6. ii. 6. 107. 8. 10. Ov. Met. vi. 59.
12 Hor. Epod. i. 34. Pers. iii. 31. Virg. Æn. viii. 724. Sil. iii. 236.

Plaut. Pœn. v. 2. 46.
13 Hor. Sat. ii. 1. 73. Ov. Am. i. 9. 41.
14 vestis domestica, vel vestimenta, Suet. Aug. 73. Vit. 8. Cic. Fin. ii. 24. Plin. Ep. v. 6. f.
15 Columel. xii. 45. 5. Suet. Aug. 74. Cal. 17. 16 Festus in cingulum, Mart. xiv. 151. Ov. Am. i. 7. 46. Juv. vi. 445. Hor. Sat. i. 2. 95. 99.

17 Festus, Plin. viii. 48. s. 74.
18 Var. L. L. viii. 47. Hor. Sat. i. 6. 28. Ov. Trist. iv. 10. 29. 35.
19 Suet. Jul. 45. Tib. 35. Claud. 24. Vesp. 2. 4. Vell. ii. 88.
20 Stat. Silv. iv. 5. 42. v. 2. 17. arctum lumen purpuræ, see p. 6. & 18.

Augustus granted to the sons of senators the right of wearing the *latus clavus* after they assumed the toga virilis, and made them tribunes and præfects in the army ; hence called TRIBUNI ET PRÆFECTI LATICLAVII. The tribunes chosen from the equites were called ANGUSTICLAVII. They seem to have assumed the toga virilis and latus clavus on the same day.[1]

Generals, in a triumph, wore, with the *toga pacta* an embroidered tunic (TUNICA PALMATA), called also *tunica Jovis*, because the image of that god in the Capitol was clothed with it. Tunics of this kind used to be sent, by the senate, to foreign kings as a present.[2]

The poor people, who could not purchase a toga, wore nothing but a tunic ; hence called TUNICATUS POPELLUS, or TUNICATI. Foreigners at Rome seem also to have used the same dress (hence *homo tunicatus* is put for a Carthaginian), and slaves, like gladiators.[3] In the country, persons of fortune and rank used only the tunic. In winter they wore more than one tunic. Augustus used four.[4]

Under the tunic, the Romans wore another woollen covering next the skin, like our shirt, called INDUSIUM, or SUBUCULA,[5] and by later writers, *interula* and *camisia*.[6] Linen clothes[6] were not used by the ancient Romans, and are seldom mentioned in the classics. The use of linen was introduced, under the emperors, from Egypt: whence *sindon* vel *vestes Byssinæ*, fine linen. Girls wore a linen vest, or shift, called SUPPARUM vel -*us*.[7]

The Romans, in later ages, wore above the toga a kind of great-coat, called LACERNA, open before, and fastened with clasps, or buckles (FIBULÆ, which were much used to fasten all the different parts of dress, except the toga), especially at the spectacles,[8] to screen them from the weather, with a covering for the head and shoulders,[9] called CUCULLUS. They used to lay aside the *lacerna* when the emperor entered. It was at first used only in the army,[10] but afterwards also in the city.

During the civil wars, when the toga began to be disused, the lacerna came to be worn in place of it to such a degree, that Augustus one day seeing, from his tribunal, a number of citizens in the assembly dressed in the lacerna,[11] which was commonly of a dark colour, repeated with indignation from Virgil,

Romanos rerum dominos gentemque togatam ! *Æn.* i. 282.

The subject world shall Rome's dominion own,
And, prostrate, shall adore the nation of the gown ! *Dryden.*

and gave orders to the ædiles not to allow any one to appear in the forum or circus in that dress.[12] It was only used by the men, and at first was thought unbecoming in the city. It was sometimes of various colours and texture.[13]

Similar to the lacerna was the LÆNA,[14] a Grecian robe or mantle thrown over the *pallium*.[15]

The Romans had another kind of great-coat or surtout, resembling the

1 Suet. Aug. 38. Oth. 10. Galb. 10, Ner. 26. Domit. 10. Plin. Ep. viii. 23.
2 Liv. x. 7. xxvii. 4. xxx. 15. xxxi. 11. Mart. vii. 1. Plin. ix. 36. s. 60.
5 Juv. x. 38.
3 Hor. Ep. i. 7. 65. Cic. Rull. ii. 34. Plaut. Pœn. v. 3. 2. Amp. i. 1. 213.

Sen. Brev. Vit. 12. Juv. ii. 143.
4 Juv. iii. 179. Suet. Aug. 82.
5 Hor. Ep. i. 1. 95.
6 vestes lineæ, Plin. xii. 6.
7 Plin. Præf. Plaut. Rud. i. 2. 91. Luc. ii. 363. Fest.
8 Juv. ix. 29. Virg.

Æn. iv. 139. Ov. Met. viii. 318. Mart. xiv. 137.
9 capitium, quod capit pectus, Var. L. L. iv. 30.
10 Juv. vi. 118. 329. Mart. xi. 99. Suet. Claud. 6. Paterc. ii. 80. Ov. Fast. ii. 745. Prop. iii. 10. 7.

11 pullati vel lacernati.
12 Mart. xiv. 129. Suet. Aug. 40.
13 Schol. Juv. i. 52. Cic. Phil. ii. 30. Juv. i. 27. ix. 38. Mart. ii. 19.
14 χλαινη.
15 Serv. Virg. Æn. v. 262. Fest. Mart. xii. 36. xiv. 13. 136.

lacerna, but shorter and straiter, called PENULA, which was worn above the tunic,[1] having likewise a hood,[2] used chiefly on journeys and in the army, also in the city,[3] sometimes covered with a rough pile, or hair, for the sake of warmth, called GAUSAPA, *sing. et plur.* vel -*e*, or *gausapina pœnula*, of various colours, and common to men and women, sometimes made of skins, SCORTEA.[4]

The military robe of the Romans was called SAGUM, an open woollen garment, which was drawn over the other clothes, and fastened before with clasps ; in dangerous conjunctures worn also in the city, by all except those of consular dignity, as in the Italic war for two years. *Distento sago impositum in sublime jactare,* to toss in a blanket.[5]

The Romans wore neither stockings nor breeches, but used sometimes to wrap their legs and thighs with pieces of cloth (FASCIÆ, vel -*iolæ*, fillets, bands, or rollers), named, from the parts which they covered, TIBIALIA and FEMINALIA or *femoralia*,[6] similar to what are mentioned, Exod. xxviii. 42, Levit. vi. 10. xvi. 4, Ezek. xliv. 18 ; used first, probably, by persons in bad health, afterwards by the delicate and effeminate,[7] who likewise had mufflers to keep the throat and neck warm, called FOCALIA vel *focale*, sing.,[8] used chiefly by orators. Some used a handkerchief (SUDARIUM) for that purpose.[9]

Women used ornaments round their legs,[10] called PERISCELIDES.[11]

The Romans had various coverings for the feet,[12] but chiefly of two kinds. The one (CALCEUS, ὑπόδημα, a shoe), covered the whole foot, somewhat like our shoes, and was tied above with a latchet or lace, a point or string.[13] The other (SOLEA, σανδάλιον, a slipper or sandal)[14] covered only the sole

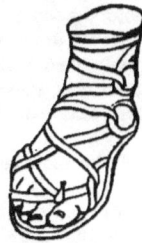 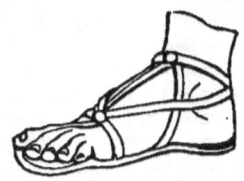

Soleæ.

of the foot, and was fastened on with leathern thongs or strings,[15] hence called VINCULA. Of the latter kind there were various sorts : CREPIDÆ, vel -DULÆ, GALLICÆ, &c. ; and those who wore them were said to be *discalceati* (ανυποδητοι) *pedibus intectis,* unshod, with feet uncovered.[16]

The Greeks wore a kind of shoes called PHÆCASIA.[17]

The calcei were always worn with the toga when a person went

1 Suet. Ner. 48.
2 caput vel capitium, Plin. xxiv. 15.
3 Cic. Att. xiii. 33. Mil. 10. Sext. 38. Juv. v. 78. Sen. Ep. 87. N. Q. iv. 6. Suet. Cic. 52. Lamp. Alex. Sev. 27.
4 Petr. 28. Ov. Art. Am. ii. 300. Pers. v. 46. Mart. vi. 59. xiv. 130. 145. 147. Fest.
5 Suet. Aug. 26. Oth. 2.

Sil. xvii. 531. Cic. Phil. viii. 11. Liv. Ep. 72, 73. Paterc. ii. 16. Mart. i. 4. 7.
6 i. e. tegumenta tibiarum et femorum, Suet. Aug. 82.
7 Cic. Brut. 60. Att. ii. 3. Har. Resp. 21. Hor. Sat. ii. 3. 255. Quinct. xi. 3. 144. Suet. Aug. 82.
8 a faucibus, Mart. iv.

41. vi. 41. xiv. 142.
9 Gell. xi. 9. Suet. Ner. 51.
10 ornamenta circa crura.
11 Hor. Ep. i. 17. 56.
12 calceamenta vel tegumenta pedum, Cic. Tusc. v. 32.
13 corrigia, lorum vel ligula, Cic. Div. ii. 40. Mart ii. 29. 57.
14 quod solo pedis subji-

ciatur, Fest.
15 teretibus habenis vel obstrigillis vincta, Gel. xiii. 21. amentis, Plin. xxxiv. 6. s. 14.
16 Tac. Ann. ii. 59 Ov. F. ii. 324. Cic. Rab. Post. 27. Phil. ii. 30. Hor. Sat. i. 3. 127. Gel. xiii. 21, &c.
17 Sen. Ben. vii. 21.

abroad;[1] whence he put them off,[2] and put on[3] slippers, when he went on a journey. Caligula permitted those who chose, to wear slippers in the theatre, as he himself did in public.[4]

Slippers (*soleæ*) were used at feasts, but they put them off when about to eat.[5] It was esteemed effeminate for a man to appear in public in slippers.[6] Slippers were worn by women in public.[7]

The shoes of senators were of a black colour, and came up to the middle of their legs. They had a golden or silver crescent (*lana* vel *lunula*, i. e. *litera* C.) on the top of the foot; hence the shoe is called *lunata pellis*, and the foot *lunata planta*. This seems to have been peculiar to patrician senators; hence it is called PATRICIA LUNA.[8]

The shoes of women were generally white,[9] sometimes red, scarlet, or purple;[10] yellow,[11] &c., adorned with embroidery and pearls, particularly the upper leathers or upper parts.[12]

Men's shoes were generally black; some wore them scarlet or red, as Julius Cæsar, and especially under the emperors, adorned with gold, silver, and precious stones. They were sometimes turned up in the point, in the form of the letter f, called *calcei repandi*.[13]

The senators are said to have used four latchets to tie their shoes, and plebeians only one.[14]

The people of ancient Latium wore shoes of unwrought leather,[15] called PERONES, as did also the Marsi, Hernici, and Vestini, who were likewise clothed in skins,[16] &c. It was long before they learned the use of tanned leather (ALUTÆ),[17] which was made of various colours.[18]

The poor people sometimes wore wooden shoes,[19] which used to be put on persons condemned for parricide.[20]

Similar to these, were a kind of shoes worn by country people, called SCULPONEÆ,[21] with which they sometimes struck one another in the face,[22] as courtesans used to treat their lovers.[23] Thus Omphale used Hercules.

The shoes of the soldiers were called CALIGÆ, sometimes shod with nails;[24] of the comedians, SOCCI, slippers, often put for *soleæ*; of the tragedians, COTHURNI.[25]

The Romans sometimes used socks, or coverings for the feet, made of wool or goats' hair, called UDONES.[26]

The Romans, also, had iron shoes[27] for mules and horses, not fixed to the hoof with nails, as among us, but fitted to the foot, so that they might be occasionally put on and off;[28] sometimes of silver or gold.[29]

Some think that the ancients did not use gloves;[30] but they are mentioned both by Greek and Roman writers,[31] with fingers,[32] and without them; what we call mittens.

1 Plin. Ep. vii. 3. Suet. Aug. 73.
2 calceos et vestimenta mutavit.
3 induebat vel induce-bat.
4 Cic. Mil. 10. Dio. lix. 7. Suet. 52.
5 Plaut. Truc. ii. 4. 13. Hor. Sat. ii. 8. 77. Ep. i. 13. 15. Mart. iii. 50.
6 soleatus, Cic. Har. Resp. 21. Ver. v. 33. Pis. 6. Liv. xxix. 19. Suet. Cal. 32.
7 Plaut. Truc. ii. 8.
8 Hor. Sat. i. 6. 26. Juv. vii. 192. Mart. i. 50. ii. 29. Schol. Juv. Stat.

Silv. v. 2. 28.
9 Ov. Art. Am. iii. 271.
10 rubri, mallei, et pur-purei, Pers. v. 169. Virg. Ecl. vii. 32. Æn. i. 341.
11 lutei vel cerei, Catul. lix. 9.
12 crepidarum obstra-gula, Plin. ix. 35. s. 56.
13 Cic. Nat. D. i. 30. Mart.ii. 29. 8. Dio. xliii. 43. Plaut. Bacch. ii. 3. 97. Sen. ii. 12. Plin. xxxvii. 2.
14 Isid. xix. 34. Sen. Tranquil. Anim. 2.
15 ex corio crudo.
16 Virg. Æn. vii. 90.

Juv. xiv. 195.
17 ex alumine (of alum), quo pelles subigeban-tur, ut molliores fie-rent.
18 Mart. ii. 29. vii. 34.
19 soleæ ligneæ.
20 Auct. Her. i. 13. Inv. ii. 50.
21 Cato de Re R. 59.
22 os batuebant, Plaut. Cas. ii. 8. 59.
23 commitigare sanda-lio caput,—to break the head with a slip-per, Ter. Eun. v. 8. 4.
24 clavis suffixæ,—see p. 250.
25 see p. 238.

26 Mart. xiv. 140.
27 soleæ ferreæ.
28 Gatul. xviii. 26. Plin. xxx. 11. s. 49. Suet. Ner. 30. Vesp. 23.
29 Poppæa conjux, Ne-ronis delicatioribus ju-mentis suis soleas ex auro quoque induere, Id. xxxiii. 11. s. 49. Dio. lxii. 28.
30 chirotheca vel ma-nicæ.
31 Hom. Odys. 24. Plin. Ep. iii. 5.
32 digitalia, -um, Varr. R. R. i. 55.

The ancient Romans went with their heads bare,[1] as we see from ancient coins and statues, except at sacred rites, games, festivals, on journeys, and in war. Hence, of all the honours decreed to Cæsar by the senate, he is said to have been chiefly pleased with that of always wearing a laurel crown, because it covered his baldness, which was reckoned a deformity among the Romans, as well as among the Jews.[2]

They used, however, in the city, as a screen from the heat or wind, to throw over their head the lappet of their gown,[3] which they took off when they met any one to whom they were bound to show respect, as the consuls, &c.[4]

The Romans veiled their heads at all sacred rites, but those of Saturn; in cases of sudden and extreme danger; in grief or despair, as when one was about to throw himself into a river, or the like.[5] Thus Cæsar, when assassinated in the senate-house; Pompey, when slain in Egypt; Crassus, when defeated by the Parthians; Appius, when he fled from the forum; and when criminals were executed.[6]

At games and festivals the Romans wore a woollen cap or bonnet, (PI-LEUS, vel -um,)[7] which was also worn by slaves, hence called PILEATI, when made free or sold,[8] whence *pileus* is put for liberty, likewise by the old and sickly.[9]

The Romans on journeys used a round cap, like a helmet, (GALERUS, vel -um,) or a broad-brimmed hat (PETASUS). Hence *petasatus*, prepared for a journey. Caligula permitted the use of a hat similar to this in the theatre, as a screen from the heat.[10]

The women used to dress their hair in the form of a helmet, or *galerus*, mixing false hair[11] with it. So likewise warriors, who sometimes also used a cap of unwrought leather (CUDO vel -on).[12]

The head-dress of women, as well as their other attire, was different at different periods. At first it was very simple. They seldom went abroad; and, when they did, they almost always had their faces veiled. But when riches and luxury increased, dress became with many the chief object of attention; hence a woman's toilette and ornaments were called MUNDUS MULIEBRIS, her world.[13]

They anointed their hair with the richest perfumes,[14] and sometimes painted it,[15] made it appear a bright yellow, with a certain composition or wash, a *lixivium* or ley,[16] but never used powder, which is a very late invention; first introduced in France about the year 1593.

The Roman women frizzled or curled their hair with hot irons,[17] and sometimes raised it to a great height by rows and stories of curls.[18] Hence AL-TUM CALIENDRUM,[19] the lofty pile of false hair; *suggestus*, vel -um *comæ*, as

1 capite aperto.
2 2 Kings. ii. 23. Suet. Jul. 45. Domit. 16. Ov. Art. Am. iii. 250. Tac. An. iv. 57. Juv. iv. 38.
3 laciniam vel sinum togæ in caput rejicere.
4 Plut. Pomp. Quæst. Rom. 10. see p. 77.
5 Serv. Virg. Æn. iii. 405. Liv. i. 26. iv. 12. Plaut. Most. ii. 1. 77. Petr. 7. 90. Hor. Sat. ii. 3. 37.
6 Suet. Cæs. 82. Dio. xlii. 4. Plut. Liv. i. 26. iii. 49. Sil. xi. 259.

7 Hor. Ep. i. 13. 15. Mart. xi. 7. xiv. 1. Suet. Ner. 57. Sen. Ep. 18. Liv. xxiv. 16. Plaut. Amph. i. 303.
8 Gell. vii. 8. see p. 24.
9 Suet. Tib. 4. Mart. ii. 48.4. Ov. Art. Am. i.783.
10 Virg. Æn. vii. 688. Suet. Aug. 82. Cic. Fam. xv. 17. Dio. lix. 7.
11 crines ficti vel suppositi.
12 Schol. Juv. vi. 120. Sil. i. 404. viii. 494. xvi. 59.
13 Liv. xxxiv. 7.

14 Ov. Met. v. 53. Tibul. iii. 428.
15 Tib. i. 9. 43. Ov. Art. Am. iii. 163, comam rutilabant vel incendebant.
16 lixivo vel -va, cinere vel cinere lixivii, Val. Max. ii. 1. 5. Plin. xiv. 20. xxviii. 12. s. 51. spuma Batava vel caustica, i. e. sapone, with soap, Mart. viii. 33. 20. xiv. 26. Suet. Cal. 47.
17 calido ferro vel calamistris vibrabant, cris-

pabant, vel intorquebant, Virg. Æn. xii. 100. Cic. Brut. 75; hence coma calamistrata, frizzled hair, Cic. Sext. 8.; homo calamistratus, by way of contempt, Cic. post red. Sen. 6. Plaut. Asin. iii. 3. 37.
18 Juv. vi. 501.
19 i. e. capillitium adulterinum vel capillamentum, Suet. Cal. 11. in galeri vel galeæ modum suggestum, Tert. Cult. Fœm. 7.

a building ; *coma in gradus formata*, into stories ;[1] *flexus cincinnorum* vel *ánnulorum*, the turning of the locks or curls ; *fimbriæ* vel *cirri*, the extremities or ends of the curls.[2] The locks seem to have been fixed by hair-pins.[3]

The slaves who assisted in frizzling and adjusting the hair[4] were called CINIFLONES or CINERARII,[5] who were in danger of punishment if a single lock was improperly placed,[6] the whip[7] was presently applied, or the mirror[8] (SPECULUM), made of polished brass or steel, of tin or silver, was

aimed at the head of the offender. A number of females attended, who did nothing but give directions.[9] Every woman of fashion had at least one female hair-dresser.[10]

The hair was adorned with gold, and pearls, and precious stones,[11] sometimes with crowns or garlands, and chaplets of flowers,[12] bound with fillets or ribands of various colours.[13]

The head-dress and ribands of matrons were different from those of virgins.[14] Ribands (VITTÆ) seem to have been peculiar to modest women ;[15] and, joined with the STOLA, were the badge of matrons.[16]

Immodest women used to cover their heads with mitres, (MITRÆ vel *mitellæ*).[17]

Mitres were likewise worn by men, although esteemed effeminate ;[18] and what was still more so, coverings for the cheeks, tied with bands[19] under the chin.[20]

1 Hor. Sat. i. 8. 48. Stat. Sylv. i. 2. 114. Suet. Ner. 51. Quinct. xii.
2 Cic. Pis. 11. Juv. xiii. 165.
3 crinalis acus, Prop. iii. 9. 52. Dio. li. 14.
4 in crine componendo.
5 Hor. Sat. i. 2. 98.
6 si unus de toto peccaverat orbe comarum annulus, incerta non bene fixus acu.
7 taurea, i. e. flagrum vel scutica de pêne taurino.
8 The above cut represents two of the most important articles of a lady's toilet table ; her mirrors and a box of pins. The former were made usually of steel, but sometimes of glass ; the latter we are told by Pliny, xxxvi. 36. were brought from Sidon.
9 Juv. vi. 491. Plin. xxxiv. 17. s. 48. Mart. ii. 66.
10 ornatrix, Ov. Am. i. 14. 16. ii. 7. 17. 23.
11 Ov. Her. xv. 75. xxi. 89. Manil. v. 516.
12 coronæ et serta, Plaut. Asin. iv. 1. 58.
13 crinales vittæ vel fasciæ, Ov. Met. i. 477. iv. 6.
14 Prop. iv. 12. 34. Virg. Æn. ii. 168.
15 hence vittæ tenues, insignæ pudoris, Ov. Art. Am. l. 31.; nil mihi cum vitta, i. e. cum muliere pudica et casta, Ov. Rem. Am. 386.
16 Ov. Trist. ii. 247. hence et vos, quis vittæ longaque vestis abest, i. e. impudicæ, Ov. Fast. iv. 184.
17 Juv. iii. 66. Serv. Virg. Æn. iv. 216. Cic. Resp. Har. 21.
18 Cic. Rabir. Post. 10.
19 redimicula vel ligamina.
20 Virg. ib. & ix. 616. Prop. ii. 29.

An embroidered net or caul[1] was used for enclosing the hair behind, called *vesica* from its thinness.[2]

Women used various cosmetics,[3] and washes or wash-balls,[4] to improve their colour.[5] They covered their face with a thick paste,[6] which they wore at home.[7]

Poppæa, the wife of Nero, invented a sort of *pomatum* or ointment to preserve her beauty, called from her name POPPÆANUM, made of asses' milk, in which she used also to bathe. Five hundred asses are said to have been daily milked for this purpose: and when she was banished from Rome, fifty asses attended her.[8] Some men imitated the women in daubing their faces; Otho is reported to have done the same.[9] Pumice-stones were used to smooth the skin.[10]

Paint (FUCUS) was used by the Roman women as early as the days of Plautus; ceruse or white lead (*cerussa*), or chalk (*creta*), to whiten the skin, and vermilion (*minium purpurissum vel rubrica*) to make it red. (Hence, *fucatæ, cerussatæ, cretatæ, et minionatæ*, painted,) in which also the men imitated them.[11]

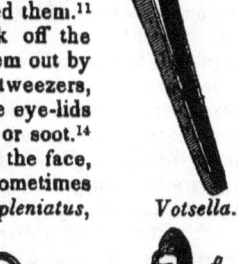

The women used a certain plaster which took off the small hairs from their cheeks; or they pulled them out by the root[12] with instruments called VOLSELLÆ, tweezers, which the men likewise did.[13] The edges of the eye-lids and eye-brows they painted with a black powder or soot.[14]

When they wanted to conceal any deformity on the face, they used a patch (SPLENIUM vel *emplastrum*), sometimes like a crescent;[15] also for mere ornament. Hence *spleniatus*, patched.[16] Regulus, a famous lawyer under Domitian, used to anoint[17] his right or left eye, and wear a white patch over the right side or the left of his forehead, as he was to plead either for the plaintiff or defendant.[18]

Votsella.

The Romans took great care of their teeth by washing and rubbing them. When they lost them, they procured artificial teeth of ivory. If loose, they bound them with gold.[19] It is said Æsculapius first invented the pulling out of teeth.[20]

The Roman ladies used ear-rings (INAU-RES)[21] of pearls,[22] three or four to each ear, sometimes of immense value;[23] (hence, *uxor tua locupletis domûs auribus censum gerit*), and

1 reticulum auratum.
2 Juv. ii. 96. Mart. viii. 33. 19.
3 medicamina vel lenocinia.
4 smegmata.
5 Ov. Med. Fac. 51. Sen. Helv. 16.
6 multo pane vel tectorio.
7 Juv. vi. 460, &c.
8 Plin. xi. 41. xxviii. 12. s. 50. Dio. lxii. 28.
9 faciem pane madido linere quotidie consuevit, Suet. Oth. 12. Juv. ii. 107.
10 Plin. xxxvi. 21. s. 42.
11 Plaut. Most. i. 3. 101. 118. Truc. ii. 11. 35.

Ov. Art. Am. iii. 199. Hor. Ep. xii. 10. Mart. ii. 41. viii. 33. 17. Cic. Pis. 11.
12 radicitus vellebant.
13 Mart. viii. 47. ix. 28. Suet. Cæs. 45. Galb. 22. Oth. 12. Quinct. l. 6. 44. v. 9. 14. viii. præem. 19,
14 fuligine collinebant, Tertul. Cult. Fœm. 5. Juv. ii. 93. Plin. Ep. vi. 9.
15 lunatum, Mart. ii. 29. 8. viii. 33. 22.
16 Plin. Ep. iv. 2. Mart. x. 22.
17 circumlinere.
18 dextrum, si a v. pro-

petitore; alterum, si a possessore esset acturus, Plin. Ep. vi. 2.
19 Cic. Legg. ii. 24. Plin. xxxi. 10. Ep. viii.
18. Mart. i. 20. 73. ii. 41. v. 44. xii. 23. xiv. 22. 56. Hor. Sat. i. 8. 46.
20 dentis evulsionem, Cic. Nat. D. iii. 57.
21 The first of these two cuts represents a gold earring, with pearl pendants. The second is a gold breastpin, to which is attached a Bacchanalian figure, with a patera in one hand and a glass in the

other. He is provided with bat's wings; and two belts or bands of grapes pass across his body. The bat's wings symbolize the drowsiness consequent upon hard drinking. They were both found in the late excavations at Pompeii, and are drawn as large as the originals.
22 margaritæ, baccæ, vel uniones, Hor. Ep. viii. 14. Sat. ii. 3. 241.
23 Plin. ix. 35. s. 56, 57. Sen. Ben. vii. 9. Suet. Jul. 50.

of precious stones ;[1] also necklaces or ornaments for the neck (MONILIA), made of gold and set with gems, which the men also used. But the ornament of the men was usually a twisted chain[2] or a circular plate of gold,[3] also a chain composed of rings,[4] used both by men and women.[5] Ornaments for the arms were called ARMILLÆ. There was a female ornament called SEGMENTUM, worn only by matrons, which some suppose to have been a kind of necklace ;[6] but others, more properly, an embroidered riband,[7] or a purple fringe[8] sewed to the clothes.[9] Hence *vestis segmentata*, an embroidered robe, or having a purple fringe.[10]

The Roman women used a broad riband round the breast called STROPHIUM, which served instead of a boddice or stays. They had a clasp, buckle, or bracelet on the left shoulder, called SPINTHER or *spinter*.[11]

The ordinary colour of clothes in the time of the republic was white ; but afterwards the women used a great variety of colours, according to the mode, or their particular taste.[12]

Silk[13] was unknown to the Romans till towards the end of the republic. It is frequently mentioned by writers after that time. The use of it was forbidden to men.[14]

Heliogabalus is said to have been the first who wore a robe of pure silk,[15] before that time it used to be mixed with some other stuff.[16] The silk, which had been closely woven in India, was unravelled, and wrought anew in a looser texture, intermixed with linen or woollen yarn,[17] so thin that the body shone through it ;[18] first fabricated in the island Cos. Hence *vestes Coæ* for *sericæ* vel *bombycinæ, tenues* vel *pellucidae ; ventus textilis*, v. *nebula*. The emperor Aurelian is said to have refused his wife a garment of pure silk, on account of its exorbitant price.[19]

Some writers distinguish between *vestis bombycina* and *serica*. The former they make to be produced by the silk-worm (*bombyx*), the latter from a tree in the country of the Seres (*sing. Ser*,) in India. But most writers confound them. It seems doubtful, however, if *sericum* was quite the same with what we now call silk.[20]

Silk-worms (*bombyces*) are said to have been first introduced at Constantinople by two monks in the time of Justinian, A. D. 551.[21] The Romans were long ignorant of the manner in which silk was made.

Clothes were distinguished not only from their different texture and colour, but also from the places where they were manufactured ; thus, *vestis aurea, aurata, picta*, embroidered with gold ; *purpurea, conchyliata*,[22] *ostro* vel *murice tincta, punicea, Tyria* vel *Sarrana, Sidonia, Assyria, Phœnicia ; Spartana, Melibœa ; Getula, Pœna* vel *Punica*, &c. PURPLE, dyed with the juice of a kind of shell-fish, called PURPURA or MUREX ; found chiefly at Tyre in Asia ; in Meninx, -ngis, an island near the Syrtis Minor, and on the Getulian shore of the Atlantic ocean, in Africa ; in Láconica in Europe. The most valued purple resembled the colour of clotted blood,

---

1 Ov. Art. Am. i. 432.
Met. x. 115. 264. Virg.
Æn. i. 658. Cic. Verr.
vi. 18. Suet. Galb. 18.
Sen. Vit. Beat. 17. Plin.
ix. 35.
2 torquis, v. -es, Virg.
Æn. vii. 351.
3 circulus auri vel aureus, Virg. Æn. v. 559.
4 catena, catella, vel catenula.
5 Liv. xxxix. 31. Hor.
Ep. i. 17. 55.

6 Val. Max. v.2. 1. Serv.
Virg. Æn. i. 658. Isid.
xix. 31.
7 fascia, tænia, vel vitta
intexta auro.
8 purpurea fimbria vel
instita.
9 Schol. Juv. ii. 124.
89. Ov. Art. Am. iii.
169.
10 a crebris sectionibus,
Symmach. Ep 4. 12. f.
11 Catul. lxii. 65. Fest.
Plaut. Men. iii. 3. 4.

12 Ov. Art. iii. 187.
13 vestis serica vel
bombycina.
14 Virg. G. ii. 121. Hor.
Ep. viii. 15. Suet. Gal.
52. Mart. iii. 82. viii.
33. 68. xi. 38. xi. 8. 27.
50. Juv. vi. 259. Tac.
Ann. ii. 33. Vop. Tac.
10.
15 vestis holoserica.
16 subsericum, Lampr.
Elag. 26. 29.
17 Plin. vi. 20.

18 ut transluceret, ibid.
19 Plin. xi. 22. s. 26.
Tibul. ii. 3. 57. Prop. i.
2. 2. Hor. Sat. i. 2. 101.
Petron. 55. Vop. Aur.
45.
20 Plin. xi. 22. s. 25.
xxiv. 12. s. 66; &c.
21 Proc. Bell. Goth. iv.
17.
22 Cic. Phil. ii. 27.

of a blackish shining appearance ; whence blood is called by Homer, *purpureus*.[1] Under Augustus the violet colour[2] came to be in request ; then the red[3] and the Tyrian twice dyed ;[4] *vestis coccinea* vel *cocco tincta*, scarlet, also put for purple ; *Melitensis, e gossypio* vel *xylo*, cotton ; COA, i. e. *serica* vel *bombycina et purpura*, fine silk and purple made in the island of Cos or Coos ;[5] *Phrygiana*, vel *-ionica*, i. e. *acu contexta et aureis filis decorata*, needle-work or embroidery ; others read here *phryxiana*, and make it a coarse shaggy cloth ; freeze, opposed to *rasa*, smoothed, without hairs ; *virgata*, striped ; *scutulata*, spotted or figured,[6] like a cobweb,[7] which Pliny calls *rete scutulatum, galbana* vel *-ina*, green or grass-coloured,[8] worn chiefly by women ; hence *galbanatus*, a man so dressed, and *galbani mores*, effeminate ; *amethystina*, of a violet or wine-colour ; prohibited by Nero, as the use of the *vestis conchyliata*, a particular kind of purple, was by Cæsar, except to certain persons and ages, and on certain days ;[9] *crocota*, a garment of a saffron-colour ;[10] *sindon*, fine linen from Egypt and Tyre ;[11] *vestis atra* vel *pulla*, black or iron-grey, used in mourning, &c. In private and public mourning the Romans laid aside their ornaments, their gold and purple.[12]

No ornament was more generally worn among the Romans than rings (ANNULI.) This custom seems to have been borrowed from the Sabines. The senators and equites wore golden rings, also the legionary tribunes. Anciently none but the senators and equites were allowed to wear gold rings.[13]

The plebeians wore iron rings, unless when presented with a golden one for their bravery in war, or for any other desert.[14] Under the emperors the right of wearing a golden ring was most liberally conferred, and often for·frivolous reasons. At last it was granted, by Justinian, to all citizens.[15] Some were so finical with respect to this piece of dress, as to have lighter rings for summer, and heavier for winter, hence called *semestres*.[16]

The ancient Romans usually wore but one ring, on the left hand, on the finger next the least, hence called DIGITUS ANNULARIS ; but, in later times, some wore several rings, some one on each finger, or more,[17] which was always esteemed a mark of effeminacy.

Rings were laid aside at night, and when they bathed, also by suppliants, and in mourning.[18]

The case[19] where rings were kept, was called DACTYLOTHECA.[20]

Rings were set with precious stones[21] of various kinds ; as jasper,[22] sardonyx, adamant, &c., on which were engraved the images of some of their ancestors or friends, of a prince or a great man, or the representation of some signal event, or the like.[23] Thus on Pompey's ring were engraved three trophies, as emblems of his three triumphs over the three parts of the

1 Plin. ix. 36. s. 60. 38. s. 62.
2 violacea purpura.
3 rubra Tarentina.
4 Tyria Dibapha, i. e. bis tincta, Plin. ix. 39. s. 63. Hor. Od. ii. 16. 35.
5 Mart. v. 24. Hor. Sat. i. 2. 101. vi. 102. 106. Od. iv. 13. 13. Cic. Ver. ii. 72. Plin.xix. 1. Suet. Tib. ii. 4. 29. Juv. viii. 101.
6 Plin. viii. 48. s. 74.

Virg. Æn. viii. 660. Juv. ii. 97.
7 aranearum tela.
8 Plin. xi. 24. Juv. ii. 97. color herbarum, Mart. v. 24.
9 Mart. i. 97. ii. 57. iii. 82. 5. xiv. 154. Juv. vii. 136. Suet. Jul. 43.
10 crocei coloris, Cic. Resp. Har. 21.
11 Mart. ii. 16. iv. 19. 12. xi. 1.
12 Liv. ix. 7. xxxiv. 7.
13 Liv. i. 11. xxiii. 12.

xxvi. 36. Ap. Bel. Pun. 63. Dio. xlviii. 45.
14 Cic. Fam. x. 31. Vel. iii. 80. Suet. Jul. 39. Stat. Silv. iii. 144. Macrob. Sat. ii. 10.
15 Novel. 78. Tac. Hist. iv. 3. Plin. xxxiii. 1. 2.
16 Juv. i. 28. vii. 89.
17 Mart. v. 11. 62. 5. xi. 60. Gell. x. 10. Macrob. vii. 13. Hor. Sat. ii. 7. 9.
18 Ter. Heaut. iv. 1. 42.

Ov. Am. ii. 15. 23. Liv. ix. 7. xliii. 16. Isid. xix. 31. Val. Max. viii. 1. 3. Suet. Aug. 101.
19 capsula.
20 Mart. xi. 60.
21 gemmæ.
22 iaspis.
23 Mart. ii. 50. v. 11. Cic. Cat. iii. 5. Fin. v. 1. Ov. Trist. i. 6. 5. Plin. xxxvii. 1. Ep. x. 16. Suet. Tib. 58. Galb. 10. Sen. Ben. iii. 26. Plaut. Curc. iii. 50.

world, Europe, Asia, and Africa; on Cæsar's ring, an armed Venus; on
that of Augustus, first a sphynx, afterwards the image of Alexander the
Great, and at last his own, which the succeeding emperors continued to
use.[1]

Nonius, a senator, is said to have been proscribed by Antony for the
sake of a gem in his ring, worth 20,000 sesterces.[2]

Rings were used chiefly for sealing letters and papers,[3] also cellars,
chests, casks, &c.[4] They were affixed to certain signs or symbols,[5] used
for tokens, like what we call tallies, or tally-sticks, and given in contracts
instead of a bill or bond, or for any sign.[6] Rings used also to be given by
those who agreed to club for an entertainment,[7] to the person commission-
ed to bespeak it,[8] from *symbola*, a shot or reckoning: hence *symbolam
dare*, to pay his reckoning. *Asymbolus ad cœnam venire*, to come to supper
without paying. The Romans anciently called a ring UNGULUS, from *un-
guis*, a nail; as the Greeks δακτυλιος from δακτυλος, a finger; afterwards
both called it *symbolus vel -um*.[9]

When a person at the point of death delivered his ring to any one, it
was esteemed a mark of particular affection.[10]

Rings were usually pulled off from the fingers of persons dying; but
they seem to have been sometimes put on again before the dead body was
burnt.[11]

Rings were worn by women as well as men, both before and after marriage. It seems any free woman might wear a golden one; and Isidorus
says, all free men, contrary to other authors. A ring used to be given by
a man to the woman he was about to marry, as a pledge of their intended
union (ANNULUS PRONUBUS;)[12] a plain iron one,[13] according to Pliny;
but others make it of gold. Those who triumphed also wore an iron
ring.[14]

The ancient Romans, like other rude nations, suffered their beards to
grow (hence called *barbati*; but *barbatus* is also put for a full-grown man,)[15]
till about the year of the city 454, one P. Ticinius Mænas, or Mæna, brought
barbers from Sicily, and first introduced the custom of shaving at Rome,
which continued to the time of Hadrian, who, to cover some excrescenses
on his chin, revived the custom of letting the beard grow,[16] but that of
shaving was soon after resumed.

The Romans usually wore their hair short, and dressed it[17] with great
care, especially in later ages, when attention to this part of dress was
carried to the greatest excess. Ointments and perfumes were used even
in the army.[18]

When young men first began to shave,[19] they were said *ponere barbam*.
The day on which they did this was held as a festival, and presents were
sent to them by their friends.[20]

---

1 Dio. xliii. 18. xliii. 43.
li. 3. Cic. Sext. 61. Pis.
13. Balb. 4. 6. Plin. vii.
26. xxxvii. 1. Suet.
Aug. 50.
2 Plin. xxxvii. 6. s. 21.
3 ad tabulas obsignan-
das, annulus signato-
rius, Macrob. Sat. vii.
13. Liv. xxviii. 28. Tac.
Ann. ii. 2. Mart. ix. 89.
4 Plaut. Cas. ii. 1. 10.
Cic. Fam. xvi. 26.
5 symbola, vel -i.
6 Plaut. Bacch. ii. 3. 29.

Pseud. i. 1. 53. ii. 2.
53. iv. 7. 104. Just. ii.
12.
7 qui colerunt, ut de
symbolis essent, i. e.
qui communi sumptu
erant una cœnaturi.
8 qui ei rei præfectus
est, Ter. Eun. iii. 4. 1.
Plaut. Stich. iii. 1. 28.
34.
9 Ter. Phorm. ii. 2. 25.
And. i. 1. 61. Gell. vi.
13. Plin. xxxiii. i. s. 4.
10 Curt. x. 5. Justin.

xii. 15. Val. Max. vii.
88.
11 Suet. Tib. 83. Cal. 12.
Prop. iv. 7. 9.
12 Hor. Od. i. 9. 23. Ter.
Hec. iv. 1. 59. v. 3. 30.
Plaut. Cas. iii. 5. 63.
Juv. vi. 27. Isid. xix. 32.
13 ferreus sine gemma.
14 Plin. xxxi. 1. xxxiii.
1. s. 4. Tertul. Apolog.
6. Isid. xix. 32.
15 Liv. v. 41. Cic. Mur.
12. Cœl. 14. Fin. iv. 23.
Juv. iv. 103. x. 66. Hor.

Sat. ii. 3. 249. Mart.
viii. 52.
16 Plin. vii. 59. Spart.
Adrian. 26.
17 cæsariem, crines, ca-
pilios, comam vel co-
mas, pectebant vel co-
mebant.
18 Sen. Brev. Vit. 12.
Suet. Cæs. 67.
19 cum barba resecta
est, Ov. Trist. iv. 10.
58.
20 Suet. Cal. 10. Juv.
iii. 187. Mart. iii. 6.

The beard was shaven for the first time, sooner or later, at pleasure ; sometimes when the toga virilis was assumed, but usually about the age of twenty-one. Augustus did not shave till twenty-five.[1] Hence young men with a long down[2] were called *juvenes barbatuli*, or *bene barbati*.[3]

The first growth of the beard[4] was consecrated to some god ;[5] thus Nero consecrated his in a golden box,[6] set with pearls, to Jupiter Capitolinus. At the same time, the hair of the head was cut and consecrated also, usually to Apollo, sometimes to Bacchus. Till then they wore it uncut, either loose,[7] or bound behind in a knot.[8] Hence they were called CAPILLATI.[9]

Both men and women among the Greeks and Romans used to let their hair grow[10] in honour of some divinity, not only in youth, but afterwards, as the Nazarites among the Jews.[11] So Paul, Acts xviii. 18.

The Britons, in the time of Cæsar, shaved the rest of their body, all except the head and upper lip.[12]

In grief and mourning the Romans allowed their hair and beard to grow,[13] or let it flow dishevelled,[14] tore it,[15] or covered it with dust and ashes. The Greeks, on the contrary, in grief cut their hair and shaved their beard, as likewise did some barbarous nations.[16] It was reckoned ignominious among the Jews to shave a person's beard.[17] Among the Catti, a nation of Germany, a young man was not allowed to shave, or cut his hair, till he had slain an enemy. So Civilis, in consequence of a vow.[18]

Those who professed philosophy also used to let their beard grow, to give them an air of gravity. Hence *barbatus magister* for Socrates ; but *liber barbatus*, i. e. *villosus*, rough ; *barbatus vivit*, without shaving.[19]

Augustus used sometimes to clip[20] his beard, and sometimes to shave it.[21] Some used to pull the hairs from the root,[22] with an instrument called VOLSELLA, nippers or small pincers, not only of the face, but the legs, &c.,[23] or to burn them out with the flame of nut-shells,[24] or of walnut-shells,[25] as the tyrant Dionysius did ; or with a certain ointment, called PSILOTHRUM vel DROPAX,[26] or with hot pitch or rosin, which Juvenal calls *calidi fascia visci*, a bandage of warm glue ; for this purpose certain women were employed, called USTRICULÆ.[27] This pulling off the hairs, however, was always reckoned a mark of great effeminacy,[28] except from the arm-pits,[29] as likewise to use a mirror when shaving.[30]

The Romans, under the emperors, began to use a kind of peruke or periwig, to cover or supply the want of hair, called CAPILLAMENTUM, or GALERUS, or GALERICULUM.[31] The false hair[32] seems to have been fixed on a skin. This contrivance does not appear to have been known in the

1 Suet. Cal. 10. Dio. xlviii. 34. Macrob. in Som. Scip. i. 6.
2 lanugo.
3 Cic. Att. i. 14. Cat. ii. 10.
4 prima barba vel lanugo.
5 Petron. 29.
6 pixide aurea.
7 Suet. Ner. 12. Mart. i. 32. Stat. Theb. viii.493. Hor. Od. ii. 5. 23. iii.20. 13. iv. 10. 3.
8 renodabant vel nodo religabant, Id. Ep. xl. 42.
9 Petron. 27.
10 pascere, alere, nutrire, permittere vel submittere.

11 Numb. vi. 5. Virg. Æn.vii. 391. Stat. Sylv. iii. Præf. carm. 4. 6. Theb. ii. 253. vi. 607. Censorin. D. N. 1. Plut. Thes.
12 Cæs. B. C. v. 10.
13 pro nittebant vel submittebant, Liv. vi. 16. Suet. Jul. 67. Aug.23. Cal. 24.
14 solvebant, Liv. i. 26. Ter. Heaut. ii. 3. 45. Virg. Æn. iii. 65. Ov. F. ii. 813.
15 lacerabant vel evellebant, Cic. Tusc. iii.
16 Suet. Cal. 5. Virg. Æn. xii. 609. Catul. xliv. 224. Sen. Ben. v.

6. Plut. in. Pelopid. et Alex. Bion Eidyl. 1.81.
17 2 Sam. x. 4.
18 Tac. Mor. Germ. 31. . Hist. iv. 61.
19 Hor. Sat. i. 3. 133. ii. 3. 35. Art. Poet. 297. Pers. iv. 1. Mart. xi.85. 18. xiv. 14.
20 tondere forfice.
21 radero novacula, i. e. radendam curaro vel facere, Suet. Aug. 79. Mart. ii. 17.
22 pilos vellere.
23 Plaut. Curc. iv. 4. 22. Suet. Cæs. 45. Jul. 45. Aug. 68. Galb. 22. Oth. 12. Mart. v. 62. viii. 46. ix. 28. Quinct. i. 6. v. 9. viii. proœm.

24 subruere nuce ardenti, Suet. Aug. 68.
25 adurere candentibus juglandium putaminibus.
26 Cic. Tusc. v. 20. Off. ii. 7. Mart. iii. 74. vi. 93. x. 65. Juv. ix. 14.
27 Tertul. de pall. 4.
28 Gell. vii. 12. Cic. Rosc. Com. 7. Plin. Ep. xrix. 1. s 8.
29 alæ vel axillæ, Hor. Ep. xii. 5. Sen. Ep. 114. Juv. xi. 157.
30 Mart. vi. 64. 4. Juv. ii. 99.
31 Juv. vi. 120. Suet. Cal. 11. Oth. 12.
32 crines ficti vel suppositi.

time of Julius Cæsar, at least not to have been used by men ; for it was used by women.[1]

In great families there were slaves for dressing the hair and for shaving (TONSORES,) and for cutting the nails ; sometimes female slaves did this (TONSTRICES.)[2]

There were, for poorer people, public barbers' shops or shades (TONSTRINÆ,) much frequented, where females also used to officiate.[3]

Slaves were dressed nearly in the same manner with the poor people,[4] in clothes of a darkish colour,[5] and slippers ;[6] hence *vestis servilis, servilis habitus.*[7]

Slaves in white are mentioned with disapprobation. They wore either a straight tunic, called EXOMIS or DIPHTHERA,[8] or a coarse frock.[9]

It was once proposed to the senate, that slaves should be distinguished from citizens by their dress ; but it appeared dangerous to discover their number.[10]

Slaves wore their beard and hair long. When manumitted they shaved their head and put on a cap.[11]

In like manner, those who had escaped from shipwreck shaved their head. In calm weather mariners neither cut their hair nor nails. So those accused of a capital crime, when acquitted, cut their hair and shaved, and went to the Capitol to return thanks to Jupiter.[12]

The ancients regarded so much the cutting of the hair, that they believed no one died, till Proserpina, either in person, or by the ministration of Atropos, cut off a hair from the head, which was considered a kind of first-fruits of consecration to Pluto.[13]

II. ROMAN ENTERTAINMENTS, EXERCISES, BATHS, AND PRIVATE GAMES.

THE principal meal of the Romans was what they called CŒNA, supper supposed by some to have been anciently their only one.[14] The usual time for the *cœna* was the ninth hour, or three o'clock, afternoon, in summer, and the tenth hour in winter. It was esteemed luxurious to sup more early.[15]

An entertainment begun before the usual time, and prolonged till late at night, was called CONVIVIUM INTEMPESTIVUM ; if prolonged till near morning, CŒNA ANTELUCANA.[16] Such as feasted in this manner, were said *epulari* vel *vivere* DE DIE, and IN DIEM *vivere* when they had no thought of futurity,[17] a thing which was subject to the animadversion of the censors.

About mid-day the Romans took another meal, called PRANDIUM, dinner, which anciently used to be called CŒNA,[18] because taken in company, and food taken in the evening,[19] VESPERNA. But when the Romans, upon the

---

1 Mart. xiv. 30. Suet. Jul. 45. Ov. Am. i. 14. 45.
2 Cic. Tusc. v. 20. Ov. Met. xi. 182. Mart. vi. 52. Plaut. Aul. ii. 4. 33. Truc. iv. 3. 59. Val. Max. iii. 2. 15. Tibull. i. 8. 11.
3 Ter. Phorm. 1. 2. 29. Hor. Ep. i. 7. 50. Mart. ii. 17.
4 see p. 288.
5 pullati.
6 crepidati.

7 Tac. Hist. iv. 36. Cic. Pis. 38.
8 Gell. vii. 12. Plaut. Cas. ii. sc. ult. Suet. Dom. 12. Hesych. 16.
9 lacerna et cucullus, Hor. Sat. ii. 7. 54. Juv. iii. 170. Mart. x. 76.
10 Sen. Clem. i. 24. Ep. 18.
11 pileus, Juv. v. 171. Plaut. Amph. 1. 1. 306. see p. 29.
12 Plaut. Rud. v. 2. 16. Juv. xii. 81. Lucian in

Ermotim. Petron. 104. Mart. ii. 74. Plin. Ep. vii. 27.
13 Virg. Æn. iv. 698. Hor. Od. i. 28. 20.
14 Isid. xx. 2.
15 Cic. Fam. ix. 26. Juv. i. 49. Mart. iv. 8. 6. Auct. Herenn. iv. 51. Plin. Ep. iii. 1. Pan. 49.
16 Cic. Cat. ii. 10. Arch. 6. Mur. 6. Verr. iii. 25. Sen. 14. Att. ix. 1. Sen. Ira. ii. 28. Suet. Cal.

45.
17 Liv. xxv. 23. Cat. xlvii. 6. Suet. Ner. 27. Curt. v. 22. Cic. Phil. ii. 34. Tusc. v. 11. Or. ii. 40. Plin. Ep. v. 5.
18 κοινη, i. e. cibus communis, a pluribus sumptus, Plus. Symp. viii. 6. Isid. xx. 2. quo Plinius alludere videtur, Ep. ii. 6.
19 cibus. vespertinus, Festus in Cœna.

increase of riches, began to devote longer time to the cœna or common meal, that it might not interfere with business, it was deferred till the evening; and food taken at mid-day was called PRANDIUM.

At the hour of dinner the people used to be dismissed from the specta-cles, which custom first began, A. U. 393.[1]

They took only a little light food[2] for dinner, without any formal pre-paration, but not always so.[3]

Sometimes the emperors gave public dinners to the whole Roman peo-ple.[4]

A dinner was called PRANDIUM CANINUM[5] vel *abstemium*, at which no wine was drunk.[6]

In the army, food taken at any time was called PRANDIUM, and the army after it, PRANSUS PARATUS.[7]

Besides the prandium and cœna, it became customary to take in the morning a breakfast (JENTACULUM,) and something delicious after supper to eat with their drink, called COMISSATIO. They used sometimes to sup in one place, and take this after-repast in another.[8]

As the entertainment after supper was often continued till late at night,[9] hence COMISSARI, to feast luxuriously, to revel, to riot.[10] COMISSATIO, a feast of that kind, revelling or rioting after supper;[11] COMISSATOR, a person who indulged in such feasting, a companion or associate in feasting and revelling. Hence Cicero calls the favourers of the conspiracy at Catiline, after it was suppressed, COMISSATORES CONJURATIONIS.[12]

Some took food betwixt dinner and supper, called MERENDA,[13] or ANTE-CŒNA, vel -*ium*.[14]

The ancient Romans lived on the simplest fare, chiefly on pottage,[15] or bread and pot-herbs; hence every thing eaten with bread, or besides bread, was afterwards named PULMENTUM, or PULMENTARIUM,[16] called in Scotland *kitchen*.[17] *Uncta pulmentaria*, i. e. *lauta et delicata fercula*, nice delicate dishes. Their chief magistrates and most illustrious generals, when out of office, cultivated the ground with their own hands, sat down at the same board, and partook of the same food with their servants; as Cato the censor. They sometimes even dressed their dinner themselves, as Curius, or had it brought them to the field by their wives.[18]

But when riches were introduced by the extension of conquest, the

1 Suet. Claud. 34. Cal. 56, 58. Dio. xxxvii. 46.
2 cibum levem et facilem sumebant. v. gustabant, Plin. Ep. iii. 4.
3 Cels. l. 3. Hor. Sat. i. 6. 127. ii. 3. 245. 4. 22. Sen. Ep. 84. Mart. xiii. 30. Plaut. Pœn. iii. 5. 14. Cic. Ver. i. 19. Suet. Claud. 33. Dom. 21.
4 Suet. Jul. 38. Tib. 20.
5 By the term *caninum prandium*, Gellius seems to understand an abstemious dinner. Erasmus does the same; but Quintus Carolus, a commentator on Gellius, interprets it differently, thus, "What is here said of a dog's not drinking wine, is equal-

ly true of a cat, or a mouse, or a fish. There are three sorts of wine, new, old, and of middle age: new wine makes us cold, old wine temperately warms, but wine of middle age inflames the blood, gets into the head, and makes people quarrel and fight like dogs." Erasmus servilely follows Gellius in his interpretation of this proverb, with no original remarks of his own. —Beloe.
6 quod canis vino caret, because a dog drinks no wine, Gell. xiii. 29.
7 Liv. xxviii. 14. Gell. xv. 12.
8 Plaut. Curc. i. 1. 72.

Most. i. 4. 5. Liv. xl.' 7. 9. Mart. xiii. 31. xiv. 223. Suet. Vit. 13. Dom. 21.
9 Suet. Tit. 7.
10 κωμάζειν a κωμη, vicus, Festus, vel potius a Κωμος, Comus, the god of nocturnal merriment and feasting among the Greeks, Hor. Od. iv. 1. 9. Quin. xi. 3. 57.
11 Cic. Cat. ii. 5. Mur. 6. Cœl. 15. Mart. xii. 48. 11.
12 Att. 1. 16. Liv. xl. 7. Ter. Adelp. v. 2. 6. Mart. iv. 5. 3. ix. 62. 15. Petron. 65. Gell. iv. 14.
13 quia vulgo dabatur iis, qui ære merebant, i. e. mercenariis, antequam labore mitteren-

tur, a domino seu conductore, — because it was commonly given to those qui ære merebant, that is, to hired labourers, before they were dismissed from work, by the master or person who hired them, Plaut. Most. iv. 2. 50.
14 Isid. xx. 22.
15 puls.
16 οψωνιον, opsonium.
17 Plin. xviii. 8. Varr. L. L. iv. 22. Hor. Sat. ii. 2. 20. Ep. i. 18. 48. Sen. Ep. 87. Phædr. iii. 7. 23. Juv. vii. 185. xiv. 171.
18 Pers. iii. 102. Plut. Plin. xix. 5. s. 26. Juv. xi. 79. Mart. iv. 64.

manners of the people were changed, luxury seized all ranks.[1] The pleasures of the table became the chief object of attention. Every thing was ransacked to gratify the appetite.[2]

The Romans at first sat at meals,[3] as did also the Greeks. Homer's heroes sat on different seats[4] around the wall, with a small table before each, on which the meat and drink were set. So the Germans and Spaniards.[5]

The custom of reclining[6] on couches (LECTI vel TORI) was introduced from the nations of the East, and at first was adopted only by the men, but afterwards allowed also to the women. It was used in Africa in the time of Scipio Africanus the elder.[7]

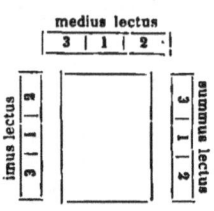

The images of the gods used to be placed in this posture in a lectister- nium ; that of Jupiter reclining on a couch, and those of Juno and Minerva erect on seats.[8]

Boys, and young men below seventeen, sat at the foot of the couch of their parents or friends,[9] at a more frugal table ;[10] sometimes also girls, and persons of low rank.[11]

The custom of reclining[12] took place only at supper. There was no formality at other meals. Persons took them alone or in company, either standing or sitting.[13]

The place where they supped was anciently called CŒNACULUM, in the higher part of the house, whence the whole upper part, or highest story, of a house was called by that name, afterwards CŒNATIO, or TRICLINIUM,[14] because three couches (τρεῖς κλίναι,

medius lectus

	3	1	2	
imus lectus 3 1 3				summus lectus 3 1 2

1 Sævior armis luxuria incubuit,victumque ulciscitur orbem, — luxury, more cruel than arms, hath invaded us, and avenges the conquered world, Juv. vi. 192.

2 vescendi causa terra marique omnia exquirere,—for the sake of gratifying the appetite, sea and land were ransacked, Sal. Cat. 13. Gustus, i. e. dapes delicatas, dainties, elementa per omnia quærunt,—they ransack, as it were, earth, air, and water, for dainties to please their taste, Juv. xi. 14.

3 Ov. F. vi. 305. Serv.

Virg. Æn. vii. 176.

4 θρόνοι, solia.

5 Odys. i. iii. &c. vii. viii. Tac. Mor. Ger. 22. Strab. ii. p. 155.

6 accumbendi.

7 Val. Max. ii. 1, 2. Liv. xxviii. 28.

8 Val. Max. ii. 1, 2.

9 in imo lecto vel subsellio, vel ad lecti fulcra assidebant, Suet. Aug. 64.

10 propria et parciore mensa, Tac. An. xiii. 16.

11 Suet. Claud. 32. Don. in Vit. Terent. Plaut. Stich. iii. 2. 32. v. 4. 21.

12 The above cut, taken from a picture found in Pompeii, represents a domestic supper party.

The young man reclining on the couch is drinking from a horn, the primitive drinking vessel, pierced at the smaller end so as to allow the wine to flow in a thin stream into his mouth. This mode of drinking, which is still practised in some parts of the Mediterranean, must require some skill in order to hit the mark exactly. The female seated beside him stretches out her hand to a servant, to receive what appears to be her myrotheca, a box of perfumes. The table and the ground are strewed with flowers.

13 Suet. Aug. 78.

14 Var. L. L. iv. 33. Liv. xxix. 40. Suet. Vit. 7. Ner. 31. Cæs. 43. Tib. 72. Cic. Att. 52. Juv. vii. 183.—The second cut represents the summer triclinium in the small garden of the house of Sallust, lately found at Pompeii. The couches are of masonry, intended to be covered with matresses and rich tapestry ; the round table in the centre was of marble. In the reign of Tiberius, such couches were veneered with costly wood and tortoise shell.

tres lecti, triclinares vel *discubitorii*) were spread[1] around the table, on which the guests might recline.[2]

On each couch there were commonly three. They lay with the upper part of the body reclined on the left arm, the head a little raised, the back supported by cushions,[3] and the limbs stretched out at full length, or a little bent; the feet of the first behind the back of the second, and his feet behind the back of the third, with a pillow between each. The head of the second was opposite to the breast of the first, so that, if he wanted to speak to him, especially if the thing was to be secret, he was obliged to lean upon his bosom,[4] thus, John xiii. 23. In conversation, those who spoke raised themselves almost upright, supported by cushions. When they ate, they raised themselves on their elbow,[5] and made use of the right hand, sometimes of both hands; for we do not read of their using either knives or forks.[6]

He who reclined at the top[7] was called SUMMUS vel *primus*, the highest; at the foot, IMUS vel *ultimus*, the lowest; between them, MEDIUS, which was esteemed the most honourable place.[8]

If a consul was present at a feast, his place was the lowest on the middle couch, which was hence called LOCUS CONSULARIS, because there he could most conveniently receive any messages that were sent to him.[9] The master of the feast reclined at the top of the lowest couch, next to the consul.

Sometimes in one couch there were only two, sometimes four. It was reckoned sordid to have more.[10] Sometimes there were only two couches in a room; hence called BICLINIUM.[11]

. The number of couches depended on that of the guests, which Varro said ought not to be below the number of the Graces, nor above that of the Muses. So, in the time of Plautus, the number of those who reclined on couches did not exceed nine. The persons whom those who were invited had liberty to bring with them, were called UMBRÆ, uninvited guests.[12]

The bedsteads (SPONDÆ) and feet (FULCRA vel *pedes*) were made of wood, sometimes of silver or gold,[13] or adorned with plates[14] of silver. On the couch was laid a mattress or quilt (CULCITA vel MATTA,) stuffed with feathers or wool,[15] anciently with hay or chaff.[16] All kinds of stuffing[17] were called TOMENTUM.[18]

A couch with coarse stuffing,[19] a pallet, was called *tomentum* CIRCENSE, because such were used in the circus; opposed to *tomentum* LINGONICUM, v. LEUCONICUM.[20]

At first couches seem to have been covered with herbs or leaves,[21] hence LECTUS, a couch,[22] vel TORUS,[23] or with straw.[24]

The cloth or ticking which covered the mattress or couch, the bed-covering,[25] was called TORAL, by later writers, *torale linteum*, or SEGESTRE, v.

1 sternebantur.
2 Serv. Virg. Æn. i. 698.
3 pulvini v. -illi.
4 in sinu recumbere, Plin. Ep. iv. 22.
5 Hor. Od. i. 27. 8. Sat. ii. 4. 39.
6 hence manus unctæ, —greasy hands, Hor. Ep. i. 16. 23.
7 ad caput lecti.
8 Virg. ib. Hor. Sat. ii.8. 20.
9 Plaut. Symp. ii. 3.

10 Cic. Pis. 27. Hor. Sat. i. 4. 86.
11 Quinct. i. 5. Plaut. Bacch. iv. 4. 69. 102.
12 Gell. xiii. 11. Plaut. Stich. iii. 2. 31. iv. 2. 12. Hor. Sat. ii. 8. 22.
Ep. i. v. 28.
13 Ov. Met. viii. 656. Suet. Jul. 49.
14 bracteæ vel laminæ.
15 Suet. Cal. 22. Mart. viii. 35. 5. Juv. v. 17. Plin. xix. 1. Ov. Fast.

vi. 680. Cic.Tusc. iii.19.
16 fœno vel acere aut palea, Var. L. L. iv. 35.
17 omnia farcimina.
18 quasi tondimentum, Suet. Tib. 54. Mart. xi. 22. xiv. 150.
19 concisa palus, i. e. arundines palustres.
20 Mart. xiv. 160. Sen. Vit. Beat. 25.
21 Ov. Fast. i. 200. 205.
22 quod herbis et frondibus lectis incubabant,

Var. L. L. iv. 35.
23 quia veteres super herbam tortam discumbebant, Serv. Virg. Æn. i. 708. v. 388. vel. ut alii dicunt, quod lectus toris, i. e. funibus tenderetur, Hor. Ep. xii. 12.
24 stramen vel stramentum, Plin. viii. 48. Hor. Sat. ii. 3. 117.
25 operimentum vel involucrum.

-trum, -trium, or LODIX, which is also put for a sheet or blanket. *Lodicula,* a small blanket or flannel coverlet for the body.[1]

On solemn occasions, the couches were covered with superb cloth, with purple and embroidery (STRAGULA VESTIS.)[2] *Textile stragulum,* an embroidered coverlet, with a beautiful mattress below (*pulcherrimo strato*), but some read here *pulcherrime ;* as, *lectus* stratus *conchyliato, peristromate,* bespread with a purple covering, also ATTALICA *peripetasmata,* much the same with what Virgil calls *superba aulæa,* fine tapestry,[3] said to have been first invented at the court[4] of Attalus king of Pergamus. *Babylonica peristromata consutaque tapetia,* wrought with needle work.[5]

Hangings (*aulæa*) used likewise to be suspended from the top of the room to receive the dust.[6]

Under the emperors, instead of three couches was introduced the use of one of a semicircular form, thus, C ; called SIGMA, from the Greek letter of that name, which usually contained seven, sometimes eight, called also STIBADIUM.[7] But in later ages the custom was introduced, which still prevails in the East, of sitting or reclining on the floor at meat, and, at other times, on cushions, ACCUBITA, covered with cloths, ACCUBITALIA.[8]

The tables (MENSÆ) of the Romans were anciently square, and called CABILLÆ ; on three sides of which were placed three couches ; the fourth side was left empty for the slaves to bring in and out the dishes. When the semicircular couch, or the *sigma,* came to be used, tables were made round.[9]

The tables of the great were usually made of citron or maple wood, and adorned with ivory.[10]

The tables were sometimes brought in and out with the dishes on them ; hence *mensam* APPONERE,[11] et AUFERRE, but some here take *mensæ* for the dishes. Sometimes the dishes were set down on the table ; hence *cibum, lances, patinas,* vel *cænam mensis,* APPONERE, *epulis mensas onerare,* DEMERE vel TOLLERE.[12]

MENSA is sometimes put for the meat or dishes ;[13] hence PRIMA MENSA, for *prima fercula,* the first course, the meat ; SECUNDA MENSA, the second course, the fruits, &c., *bellaria,* or the dessert.[14] *Mittere de mensa,* to send some dish, or part of a dish, to a person absent ; *dapes mensæ brevis,* a short meal, a frugal meal ; *mensa opima,* a rich table.[15]

Virgil uses *mensæ* for the cakes of wheaten bread[16] put under the meat, which he calls *orbes,* because of their circular figure ; and *quadræ,* because each cake was divided into four parts, quarters, of quadrants, by two straight lines drawn through the centre. Hence *aliena vivere quadra,* to live at another's expense or table ; *findetur quadra,* i. e. *frustum panis,* the piece of bread shall be shared. So *quadra placentæ* vel *casei.*[17]

A table with one foot was called MONOPODIUM. These were of a circu-

---

1 Hor. Sat. ii. 4. 84. Ep. i. 5. 22. Ver. ib. Juv. vi. 194. vii. 66. Mart. xiv. 148. 152. Suet. Aug. 83.
2 Cic. Verr. ii. 19. Liv. xxxiv. 7. Hor. Sat. ii. 2, 3. 118. picta stragula, Tibul. i. 2. 79.
3 Æn. i. 697. Cic. Ver. iv. 12. Tusc. v. 21. Phil. ii. 27.
4 in aula, hinc aulæa.
5 Plin. viii. 48. Plaut.

Stich. ii. 2. 54.
6 Hor. Sat. ii. 8. 54. Serv. Virg. Æn. i. 697.
7 Mart. ix. 48. xiv. 87.
8 Schol. Juv. v. 17. Lamprid. Heliog. 19. 25. Treb. Pol. Clau. 14.
9 Juv. i. 137. Var. L. L. iv. 25. Festus.
10 Cic. Verr. iv. 17. Mart. xiv. 89, 90. ii. 43. Plin. xiii. 15. s. 29.
11 Plaut. Asin. v. 1, 2.

Most. i. 3. 150. iii. 1. 26. Amph. ii. 2. 175. Cic. Att. xiv. 21. Ov. Met. viii. 570.
12 Virg. Æn. i. 220. 627. iv. 602. G. iv. 388. Cic. Tusc. v. 32. Ver. iv. 22. Att. vi. 1. Plaut. Mil. iii. 1. 55.
13 lanx, patina, patella, vel discus.
14 Macrob. Sat. vii. 1. Cic. Att. xiv. 6. Fam. xiv. 21. Virg. G. ii.

101. Nep. Ages. 8.
15 Cic. Att. v. 1. Hor. A. P. 198. Sil. xi. 283.
16 adorea liba vel cereale solum. Solum omne dicitur, quod aliquid sustinet. Serv. Virg. Ecl. vi. 35. Æn. v. 199. Ov. Met. l. 73.
17 Virg. Æn. vii. 116. Juv. v. 2. Hor. Ep. 1. 17. 49. Mart. vi. 75. xii. 32. 18.

41

lar figure,[1] used chiefly by the rich, and commonly adorned with ivory and sculpture.[2]

A side-board was called ABACUS, or DELPHICA, sc. *mensa*,[3] LAPIS ALBUS.[4]

The table of the poorer people commonly had three feet (TRIPES), and sometimes one of them shorter than the other two.[5] Hence *inæquales* MENSÆ, Martial i. 56. 11.

The ancient Romans did not use table-cloths,[6] but wiped the table with a sponge,[7] or with a coarse cloth.[8]

Before the guests began to eat they always washed their hands, and a towel[9] was furnished them in the house where they supped to dry them.[10] But each guest seems to have brought with him, from home, the table-napkin[11] or cloth, which he used, in time of eating, to wipe his mouth and hands, but not always.[12] The *mappa* was sometimes adorned with a purple fringe.[13]

The guests used sometimes, with the permission of the master of the feast, to put some part of the entertainment into the mappa, and give it to their slaves to carry home.[14]

Table-cloths[15] began to be used under the emperors.[16]

In later times, the Romans, before supper, used always to bathe.[17] The wealthy had baths,[18] both cold and hot, at their own houses.[19] There were public baths[20] for the use of the citizens at large,[21] where there were separate apartments for the men and women.[22] Each paid to the bath-keeper[23] a small coin (*quadrans*.)[24] Those under age paid nothing.[25]

The usual time of bathing was two o'clock[26] in summer, and three in winter; on festival days sooner.[27]

The Romans, before bathing, took various kinds of exercise;[28] as the ball or tennis (PILA), throwing the javelin, and the DISCUS or quoit, a round bullet of stone, iron, or lead, with a thong tied to it, the PALUS or PALARIA,[29] riding, running, leaping, &c.[30]

There were chiefly four kinds of balls:—1. PILA TRIGONALIS vel TRIGON, so called, because those who played at it were placed in a triangle (τϱιγωνον), and tossed it from one to another; he who first let it come to the ground was the loser.—2. FOLLIS vel *folliculus*, inflated with wind like our foot-ball, which, if large, they drove with the arms, and simply called PILA, or PILA VELOX, if smaller, with the hand, armed with a kind of gauntlet, hence called FOLLIS PUGILLATORIUS.—3. PILA PAGANICA, the village ball, stuffed with feathers, less than the *follis*, but more weighty.[31] —4. HARPASTUM,[32] the smallest of all, which they snatched from one another.[33]

Those who played at the ball were said *ludere raptim*, vel *pilam revocare*

1 orbes.
2 Juv. i. 138. xi. 123.
3 Liv. xxxix. 6. Cic. Verr. iv. 16. 25. 59. Tusc. v. 21. Vet. Schol. Juv. iii. 204. Mart. xii. 67.
4 i.e. mensa marmorea, Hor. Sat. i. 6. 116.
5 Ov. Met. viii. 661. Hor. Sat. i. 3. 13.
6 mantilia.
7 Mart. xiv. 44.
8 gausape, Hor. Sat. ii. 8. 11.
9 mantile vel -tele, -um, vel -ium.
10 Virg. Æn. i. 702. G. iv. 377.
11 mappa.

12 Mart. xii. 29. Hor. ii. 8. 63. Ep. i. 5. 22.
13 lato clavo, Mart. iv. 46. 17.
14 Mart. ii. 32.
15 lintea villosa, gausapa vel mantilia.
16 Mart. xii. 29. 12. xiv. 138.
17 Plaut. Stich. v. 2. 19.
18 balneum vel balineum, plur. -neæ vel -a.
19 Cic. Or. ii. 55.
20 balnea.
21 Cic. Cœl. 26. Hor. Ep. i. 1. 92.
22 balnea virilia et muliebria, Var. L. L. viii. 42. Vitruv. v. 10. Gell. x. 3.

23 balneator.
24 Hor. Sat. i. 3. 137. Juv. vi. 446. hence res quadrantaria for balneum, Sen. Ep. 59. quadrantaria permutatio, i. e. pro quadrante copiam sui fecit,—bestowed her favours instead of the price of the bath, Cic. Cœl. 26. so quadrantaria is put for a mean harlot, Quinct. viii. 6.
25 Juv. vi. 446.
26 octava hora.
27 Plin. Ep. iii. 1. Mart. x. 48. Juv. xi. 205.
28 exercitationes campestres, post decisa

negotia, campo, sc. Martio,—When business was over, in the Campus Martius, Hor. Ep. i. 7. 59.
29 Hor. Sat. i. 5. 48. Od. i. 8. 11.
30 Juv. vi. 246. Suet. Aug. 83. Mart. vii. 31. see p. 257.
31 Prop. iii. 12. 5. Hor. Sat. ii. 2. 11. Plaut. Rud. iii. 4. 16. Mart. xiv. 45. 47.
32 ab ἁρπάζω, rapio.
33 Mart. iv. 19. vii. 31 Suet. Aug. 83.

cadentem, when they struck it rebounding from the ground ; when a number played together in a ring, and the person who had the ball seemed to aim at one, but struck another, *ludere datatim,* vel *non sperato fugientem reddere gestu ;* when they snatched the ball from one another, and threw it aloft, without letting it fall to the ground, *ludere expulsim,* vel *pilam geminare volantem.*[1]

In country villas there was usually a tennis-court, or place for playing at the ball, and for other exercises, laid out in the form of a circus ; hence called SPHÆRISTERIUM.[2]

Young men and boys used to amuse themselves in whirling along a circle of brass or iron, set round with rings, as our children do wooden hoops. It was called TROCHUS,[3] and *Græcus trochus,* because borrowed from the Greeks. The top (TURBO vel *buxum*) was peculiar to boys.[4] Some have confounded these two, but improperly.

Those who could not join in these exercises took the air on foot, in a carriage, or a litter.

There were various places for walking,[5] both public and private, under the open air, or under covering.[6]

Covered walks (PORTICUS, porticos or piazzas,) were built in different places, chiefly round the Campus Martius and forum, supported by marble pillars, and adorned with statues and pictures, some of them of immense extent ; as those of Claudius, of Augustus, of Apollo, of Nero, of Pompey, of Livia.[7]

Porticos were employed for various other purposes besides taking exercise. Sometimes the senate was assembled, and courts of justice held in them.

A place set apart for the purpose of exercise, on horseback or in vehicles, was called GESTATIO. In villas it was generally contiguous to the garden, and laid out in the form of a circus.[8]

An enclosed gallery, with large windows to cool it in summer, was called CRYPTOPORTICUS, commonly with a double row of windows.[9]

Literary men, for the sake of exercise,[10] used to read aloud.[11]

As the Romans neither wore linen nor used stockings, frequent bathing was necessary both for cleanliness and health, especially as they took so much exercise.

Anciently they had no other bath but the Tiber. They, indeed, had no water but what they drew from thence, or from wells in the city and neighbourhood ; as the fountain of Egeria, at the foot of Mount Aventine, of Mercury, &c.[12]

The first aqueduct at Rome was built by Appius Claudius, the censor, about the year of the city 441.[13] Seven or eight aqueducts were afterwards built, which brought water to Rome, from the distance of many miles, in such abundance, that no city was better supplied.

These aqueducts were constructed at a prodigious expense ; carried through rocks and mountains, and over valleys, supported on stone or brick arches. Hence, it is supposed, the Romans were ignorant that water,

1 Luc. ad Pison. 173.
Plaut. Curc. ii. 3. 17.
Isid. i. 21.
2 Suet. Vesp. 20. Plin.
Ep. ii. 17. v. 6.
3 a τρεχω, curro.
4 Hor. Od. iii. 24. 57.
Mart. xi. 22. xiv. 169.
Virg. Æn. vii. 378. Pers.

iii. 51.
5 Ambulacra vel ambulationes, ubi spatiarontur.
6 Cic. Dom. 44. Or. ii.
20. Att. xiii. 29. Q.
Frat. iii. 17. Gell. i. 2.
Hor. Od. ii. 15, 16. Ep.
i. 10. 22. Juv. iv. 5. vi.

60.
7 Mart. Spect. ii. 9.
Suet. Aug. 31. Ner. 31.
Prop. ii. 31. 1, Plin. Ep.
i. 5. Ov. Trist. iii. 1. 59.
Art. Am. i. 67. Cic.
Frat. 4.
8 Plin. Ep. i. 3. ii. 17.
9 Id. v. 6. vii. 21.

10 stomachi causa.
11 clare et intente legere, Plin. Ep. ix. 36.
12 Liv. i. 19. Ov. F. iii.
273. v. 673. Juv. iii. 13.
13 Diod. xx. 36.

conveyed in pipes, rises to the height of its source, whatever be the distance or inequality of ground through which it passes. It is strange they did not discover this fact, considering the frequent use they made of pipes[1] in conveying water. That they were not entirely ignorant of it appears from Pliny, who says, *aqua in* vel *e plumbo subit altitudinem exortus sui*, water in leaden pipes rises to the height of its source.[2] The truth is, no pipes could have supported the weight of water conveyed to the city in the Roman aqueducts.

The waters were collected in reservoirs, called CASTELLA, and thence distributed throughout the city in leaden pipes.[3]

When the city was fully supplied with water, frequent baths were built, both by private individuals, and for the use of the public; at first, however, more for utility than show.[4]

It was under Augustus that baths first began to assume an air of grandeur, and were called THERMÆ,[5] bagnios or hot baths, although they also contained cold baths. An incredible number of these were built up and down the city. Authors reckon up above 800, many of them built by the emperors with amazing magnificence. The chief were those of Agrippa near the Pantheon, of Nero, of Titus, of Domitian,[6] of Caracalla, Antoninus, Dioclesian, &c. Of these, splendid vestiges still remain.

BATHS.

BATHING undoubtedly took place first in rivers and in the sea, but men soon learned to enjoy this pleasure in their own houses. Even Homer mentions the use of the bath as an old custom. When Ulysses enters the palace of Circe, a bath is prepared for him, after which he is anointed with costly perfumes, and dressed in rich garments. The bath, at this period, was the first refreshment offered to the guest. In later times, rooms, both public and private, were built expressly for the purpose of bathing. The public baths of the Greeks were mostly connected with the gymnasia, because they were taken immediately after the athletic exercises. The Romans, in the period of their luxury, imitated the Greeks in this point, and built magnificent baths. The following description applies both to the Greek and Roman baths :—The building which contained them was oblong, and had two divisions, the one for males, and the other for females. In both, warm or cold baths could be taken. The warm baths, in both divisions, were adjacent to each other, for the sake of being easily heated. In the midst of the building, on the ground-floor, was the heating-room, by which not only the water for bathing, but sometimes also the floors of the adjacent rooms, were warmed. Above the heating-room was an apartment in which three copper kettles were walled in, one above another, so that the lowest (*caldarium*) was immediately over the fire, the second (*tepidarium*) over the first, and the third (*frigidarium*) over the second. In this way, either boiling, luke-warm, or cold water could be obtained. A constant communication was maintained between these vessels, so that as fast as hot water was drawn off from the caldarium, the void was supplied from the tepidarium, which being already considerably heated, did but slightly reduce the temperature of the hotter boiler. The tepidarium in its turn, was supplied from the piscina or frigidarium, and that from the aqueduct; so that the heat which was not taken up by the first boiler, passed on to the second, and instead of being wasted, did its office in preparing the contents of the second for the higher temperature which it was to obtain in the first. The terms frigidarium, tepidarium, and caldarium are applied to the apartments in which the cold, tepid, and hot baths are placed, as well as to those vessels in which the operation of heating the water is carried on. The coppers and reservoir were elevated considerably above the baths, to cause the water to flow more rapidly into them.

The bathing rooms had, in the floor, a basin of masonwork, in which there were seats, and round it a gallery, where the bathers remained before they descended into the bath, and where all the attendants were. Persons going to bathe first entered the frigidarium ; they then went into the tepidarium, which prepared their bodies for the more intense heat which they were to undergo in the vapour and hot baths ; and, *vice versa*, softened the transition from the hot bath to the external air. A doorway led from the tepidarium into the caldarium. It had on one side the laconicum, where a vase for washing the hands and face was placed, called labrum. On the opposite side of the room was the hot bath, called lavacrum. Vitruvius, v. 11, explains the structure of the apartment : " Here should be placed the vaulted sweating-room (*concamerata sudatio*), twice the length of its width, which

1 fistulæ.
2 xxxi. 6. s. 31.
3 Plin. xxxvi. 15. Hor. Ep. i. 10. 20.
4 in usum, non oblectamentum, Sen. Ep. 86.
5 θέρμαι, calores, i. e.
calidæ aquæ, Liv. xxxvi. 15.
6 Plin. Ep. iv. 8. Dio. liii. 27. Mart. iii. 20. vii.
33. Stat. Sylv. i. 5. 61. Suet. 5. 7.

The basin[1] where they bathed was called BAPTISTERIUM, NATATIO or PISCINA. The cold bath was called FRIGIDARIUM, &c. *ahenum* vel *balneum* ;

should have at each extremity, on one end the *laconicum*, on the other end the hot bath." Vitruvius never mentions the laconicum as being separated from the vapour bath ; it may, therefore, be presumed to have been always connected, with it in his time, although in the thermæ constructed by the later emperors it appears always to have formed a separate apartment. In the baths of Pompeii they are united, and adjoin the tepidarium, exactly agreeing with the descriptions of Vitruvius. The laconicum is a large semicircular niche, seven feet wide, and three feet six inches deep, in the middle of which was placed a vase or labrum. The ceiling was formed by a quarter of a sphere ; it had on one side a circular opening, one foot six inches in diameter,over which, according to Vitruvius, a shield (*clypeus*) of bronze was suspended, which, by means of a chain attached to it, could be drawn over or drawn aside from the aperture, and thus regulated the temperature of the bath.

In the magnificent thermæ erected by the emperors, edifices in which architectural magnificence appears to have been carried to its extreme point, not only was accommodation provided for hundreds of bathers at once, but spacious porticos, rooms for athletic games and playing at ball, and halls for the public lectures of philosophers and rhetoricians were added one to another, to an extent which has caused them, by a strong figure, to be compared to provinces, and at an expense which could only have been supported by the inexhaustible treasures which Rome drew from a subject world. There were many of these establishments at Rome, built mostly by the emperors, for few private fortunes could suffice to so vast a charge. They were open to the public at first on the payment of the fourth of an as (*quadrans*), which is less than a farthing. Agrippa bequeathed his gardens and baths to the Roman people, and assigned particu-

lar estates for their support, that the public might enjoy them gratuitously. The splendid edifice now known as the Pantheon, served as the vestibule to his baths. At a later period the bathers in some thermæ were supplied gratuitously even with unguents ; probably it was so in all those built by the emperors. The chief were those of Agrippa, Nero, Titus, Domitian, Antoninus, Caracalla, and Diocletian ; but Ammianus Marcellinus reckons sixteen of them, and other authors eighty.

These edifices, differing of course in magnitude and splendour, and the details of the arrangement, were all constructed on a common plan. They stood among extensive gardens and walks, and often were surrounded by a portico. The main building contained extensive halls for swimming and bathing ; others for conversation ; others for various athletic and manly exercises ; others for the declamation of poets and the lectures of philosophers ; in a word, for every species of polite and manly amusement. These noble rooms were lined and paved with marble, adorned with the most valuable columns, paintings, and statues, and furnished with collections of books for the sake of the studious who resorted to them.

On entering the thermæ, where there was always a great concourse of people, the bathers first proceeded to undress, when it was necessary to hire persons to guard their clothes : these the Romans called capsarii. They next went to the unctuarium, where they anointed all over with a coarse cheap oil before they began their exercise. Here the finer odoriferous ointments which were used in coming out of the bath, were also kept, and the room was so situated as to receive a considerable degree of heat. This chamber of perfumes was quite full of pots, like an apothecary's shop ; and those who wished to anoint and perfume the body received perfumes and unguents. In the subjoined representation of a Roman

bath, copied from a painting on a wall forming part of the baths of Titus, the elæothesium appears filled with a vast number of vases. These vases contained perfumes and balsams, very different in their compositions, according to the different tastes of the persons who perfumed themselves. The rhodinum, one of those liquid perfumes, was composed of roses ; the lirinum of lily ; cyprinum of the flower of a tree called cypria, which is believed to be the same as the privet ; baccarinum, from the foxglove ; myrrhinum was composed of myrrh. Perfumes were also made of the oil of sweet marjoram, called amaracinum ; of lavender,called ed nardinum; of the wild vine, called œnanthinum. There was also the cinamominum, made of cinnamon, the composition of which was very costly ; oil made from the iris, called irinum ; the balaninum, or oil of ben ; the serpyllinum, wild thyme, with which they rubbed their eyebrows, hair, neck, and head ; they rubbed their arms with the oil of sisymbrium or watermint, and their muscles with the oil of anarcum, or others which have been mentioned. An amusing story relative to this practice of anointing is related by Spartianus. "The emperor Hadrian, who went to the public baths and bathed with the common people, seeing one day a veteran whom he had formerly known among the Roman troops, rubbing his back and other parts of his body against the marble, asked him why he did so. The veteran answered that he had no slave to rub him, whereupon the emperor gave him two slaves and wherewithal to maintain them. Another day several old men, enticed by the good fortune of the veteran, rubbed themselves also against the marble before the emperor, believing by this means to excite the liberality of Hadrian, who perceiving their drift caused them to be told to rub each other." When anointed, they immediately passed into the sphæristerium, a very light and extensive

---

[1] labrum aut lacus.

the hot, CALDARIUM, and the tepid, TEPIDARIUM : the cold bath room, CEL-
LA FRIGIDARIA ; and the hot, CELLA CALDARIA ; the stove room, HYPO-
CAUSTON, or VAPORARIUM,[1] warmed by a furnace,[2] below, adjoining to
which were sweating rooms, SUDATORIA, vel ASSA, sc. *balnea;* the un-
dressing room, APODITERIUM ; the perfuming room, UNCTUARIUM. Several improvements were made in the construction of baths in the time of
Seneca.[3]

The Romans began their bathing with hot water, and ended with cold.
The cold bath was in great repute after Antonius Musa recovered Augustus from a dangerous disease by the use of it, but fell into discredit after
the death of Marcellus, which was occasioned by the injudicious application of the same remedy.[4]

apartment, in which were performed the many kinds of exercises to which this third part
of the baths was appropriated ;
of these, the most favourite
was the ball. When its situation permitted, this apartment was exposed to the afternoon sun, otherwise it was
supplied with heat from the
furnace. After they had taken what degree of exercise
they thought necessary, they
went immediately to the adjoining warm bath, wherein
they sat and washed them-
selves. The seat was below
the surface of the water, and
upon it they used to scrape
themselves with instruments
called strigiles, most usually
of bronze, but sometimes of
iron ; or this operation was
performed by an attendant
slave, much in the way that
ostlers treat horses when they
come in hot. Young slaves
then came out of the elæothesium carrying with them little
vases of alabaster, bronze, and

terra-cotta, full of perfumed
oils, with which they had their
bodies anointed, by causing
the oil to be slightly rubbed
over every part, even to the
soles of their feet.
The subjoined cut represents
the several apartments which
we have described ; but has
the bath in a chamber sepa-

rate from the laconicum, or
concamerata sudatio ; while
at the same time the laconicum itself is represented as a
small cupola. And as the
number of figures makes it evident that the painting is intended for a public bath, we
may draw from hence a further reason for supposing that
the laconicum and hot bath itself were separated in consequence of the increasing
numbers who attended them.
Below is the hypocaustum, or
furnace ; at the side are the
boilers, as described by Vitruvius.
It is probable that the Romans resorted to the thermæ
for the purpose of bathing, at
the same time of the day that
others were accustomed to
make use of their private
baths. This was generally
from two o'clock in the afternoon till the dusk of the evening, at which time the baths
were shut till two the next
day. This practice, however,
varied at different times. Notice was given when the baths
were ready by ringing a bell ;
the people then left the exercise of the sphæristerium and
hastened to the caldarium,
lest the water should cool.
But when bathing became
more universal among the Romans, this part of the day was
insufficient, and they gradually exceeded the hours that
had been allotted for this purpose. Between two and three
in the afternoon was, however, the most eligible time for
the exercises of the palæstra
and the use of the baths. It
must be understood that we
are now speaking of the days

about the equinoxes ; for as
the Romans divided their day,
from sunrise to sunset, into
twelve hours, at all seasons of
the year, the hours of a summer's day were longer, and
those of a winter's day shorter, than the mean length, continually varying, as the sun
approached or receded from
the solstice. Hadrian forbade
any one but those who were
sick to enter the public baths
before two o'clock. The thermæ were by few emperors allowed to be continued open so
late as five in the evening.
Martial says, that after four
o'clock they demanded a hundred quadrantes of those who
bathed. This, though a hundred times the usual price, only amounted to about nineteen pence. We learn from
the same author, that the baths
were opened sometimes earlier than two o'clock. He says,
that Nero's baths were exceeding hot at twelve o'clock,
and the steam of the water
immoderate. Alexander Se-
verus, to gratify the people in
their passion for bathing, not
only suffered the thermæ to
be opened before break of day,
which had never been permitted before, but also furnished
the lamps with oil for the convenience of the people.
From this time it appears
that the Romans continued
equally attached to the practice of bathing until the removal of the seat of empire to
Constantinople ; after which
we have no account of any
new thermæ being built, and
may suppose that most of
those which were then frequented in the city of Rome,

---

1 Plin. Ep. v. 6. Vitr. v.   furnium, Plin. Ep. ii.   Q. Frat. iii. 1. Plin. Ep.   Plin. xxix. 1. Hor. Ep.
10. Cic. Q. Frat. iii. 1.   17.   ii. 17. v. 6.   i. 15. Dio. liii. 30.
2 propigneum vel præ-   3 Sen. Ep. 52. 90. Cic.   4 Suet. Aug. 59. 81.

The person who had the charge of the bath was called BALNEATOR.[1] He had slaves under him, called CAPSARII, who took care of the clothes of those who bathed.

The slaves who anointed those who bathed were called ALIPTÆ, or UNCTORES.[2]

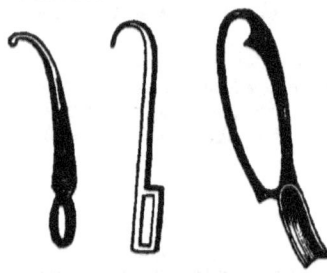

The instruments of an aliptes were a currycomb or scraper (STRIGILIS, v. -il) to rub off[3] the sweat and filth from the body, made of horn or brass, sometimes of silver or gold,[4] whence strigmenta for sordes;—towels or rubbing cloths (LINTEA);—a vial or cruet of oil (GUTTUS), usually of horn,[5] hence a large horn was called RHINOCEROS;—a jug (AMPULLA);[6]—and a small vessel called lenticula. The slave who had the care of the ointments was called UNGUENTARIUS.[7]

As there was a great concourse of people to the baths, poets sometimes read their compositions there, as they also did in the porticos and other places, chiefly in the months of July and August.[8]

Studious men used to compose, hear,. or dictate something while they were rubbed and wiped.[9]

Before bathing, the Romans sometimes used to bask themselves in the sun.[10]

Under the emperors, not only places of exercise,[11] but also libraries,[12] were annexed to the public baths.[13]

The Romans after bathing dressed for supper. They put on the SYN-

for want of the imperial patronage, gradually fell into decay. It may likewise be remarked, that the use of linen became every day more general; that great disorders were committed in the baths, a proper care and attention in the management of them not being kept up; and that the aqueducts by which they were supplied with water were many of them ruined in the frequent invasions and inroads of the barbarious nations. All these causes greatly contributed to hasten the destruction of the baths.

1 elrothesium.   3, 7 tene'arium.   5 balneum.   9 clypeus.
2, * frigidarium.   4 concamerata sudatio.   6 caldarium.   10 laconicum.

1 Cic. Cat. 26. Phil. xiii. 12.
2 Cic. Fam. i. 9. 35. Juv. iii. 76. vi. 421. Mart. vii. 31. 6. xii. 71. 3.
3 ad defricandum et destringendum vel radendum.
4 Suet. Aug. 80. Hor.

Sen. ii. 7. 110. Pers. v. 126. Mart. xiv. 51. Sen. Ep. 95. Juv. xi. 158.
5 corneus.
6 Juv. iii. 263. vii. 130. Mart xiv. 52, 53. Gel. xvii. 8. Plaut. Stich. i. 3. 77. Pers. i. 3. 44.
7 Serv. Virg. Æn. i. 697.
8 Hor. Sat i. 4. 73.

Mart. iii. 44. 10. Juv. i. 12. iii. 9. vii. 39. Plin. Ep. i. 13. iii. 18. vii. 17. viii. 12. 21. Suet. Aug. 89. Claud. 41. Domit. 2.
9 Suet. Aug. 85. Plin. Ep. iii. 5. iv. 14.
10 sole uti, Plin. Ep. iii. i. 5. vi. 16. Sen. Ep. 73.

in sole, si curet vento, ambulet nudus, &c. Spurrina, he undresses himself, and if there happens to be no wind, he walks for some time in the sun.
11 gymnasia et palestræ.
12 bibliothecæ.
13 Sen. Tranq. An. 9.

THESIS[1] and slippers ; which, when a person supped abroad, were carried to the place by a slave, with other things requisite ; a mean person sometimes carried them himself. It was thought very wrong to appear at a banquet without the proper habit, as among the Jews.[2]

After exercise and bathing, the body required rest ; hence probably the custom of reclining on couches at meat. Before they lay down, they put off their slippers that they might not stain the couches.[3]

At feasts the guests were crowned with garlands of flowers, herbs, or leaves,[4] tied and adorned with riband,[5] or with the rind or skin of the linden tree.[6] These crowns, it was thought, prevented intoxication ; hence *cum corona ebrius*.[7]

Their hair also was perfumed with various ointments, nard or spikenard,[8] MALOBATHRUM ASSYRIUM, AMOMUM, BALSAMUM *ex Judæa*. When foreign ointments, were first used at Rome is uncertain ; the selling of them was prohibited by the censors, A. U. 565.[9]

The Romans began their feasts by prayers and libations to the gods.[10] They never tasted any thing without consecrating it ; they usually threw a part into the fire as an offering to the Lares, therefore called DII PATELLARII ; hence DAPES LIBATÆ, hallowed viands ;[11] and when they drank they poured out a part in honour of some god on the table, which was held sacred as an altar, with this formula, LIBO TIBI, I make libation to thee.[12] The table was consecrated by setting on it the images of the Lares and salt-holders.[13]

Salt was held in great veneration by the ancients. It was always used in sacrifices ; thus also Moses ordained.[14] It was the chief thing eaten by the ancient Romans with bread and cheese,[15] as cresses[16] by the ancient Persians. Hence SALARIUM, a salary or pension ;[17] thus, *salaria multis subtraxit, quos otiosos videbat accipere*, sc. Antoninus Pius.[18]

A family salt-cellar[19] was kept with great care. To spill the salt at table was esteemed ominous.[20] Setting the salt before a stranger was reckoned a symbol of friendship, as it still is by some eastern nations.

From the savour which salt gives to food, and the insipidity of unsalted meat, *sal* was applied to the mind ; hence SAL, wit or humour ; *salsus*, witty ; *insulsus*, dull, insipid ; *sales*, witty sayings ; *sal Atticum, sales urbani, sales intra pomœria nati*, polite raillery or repartees ; *sal niger*, i. e. *amari sales*, bitter raillery or satire ;[21] in Hor. Sat. ii. 4. 74, *sal nigrum* means simply black salt.

Sal is metaphorically applied also to things ; thus, *tectum plus salis quam sumptus habebat*, the house displayed more of neatness, taste, and elegance, than of expense. *Nulla in corpore mica salis*.[22]

The custom of placing the images of the gods on the table, prevailed

1 vestis cœnatoria vel accubitoria.
2 Hor. Ep. 1. 13. 15. Cic. Vat. 12. Matth. xxii. 11.
3 Mart. iii. 50. Hor. Sat. ii. 8. 77.
4 serta, coronæ vel corollæ.
5 vittæ, tæniæ, vel lemnisci.
6 philyra, Hor. Od. ii. 7. 23. ii. 11. 13. Sat. ii. 3. 256. Virg. Ecl. vi. 16. Juv. v. 36. xv. 50. Mart. xiii. 127. Ov. F.

v. 337. Plin. xvi. 14.
7 Plaud. Pseud. v. 2. 2. Amph. iii. 4. 16.
8 unguenta vel aromata, nardum, vel -us.
9 Mart. iii. 12. Virg. Ecl. iii. 89. iv. 25. Plin. xiii. 25. s. 54. &c. xiii. 3. s. 5.
10 deos in vocabant, Quin. v. pr. libare diis dapes et bene precari, to offer libations to the gods, and to pray for happiness, Liv. xxxix. 43.

11 Tibul. i. 1. 19. Plaut. Cist. ii. 1. 46. Hor. Sat. ii. 6. 67.
12 Macr. Sat. iii. 11. Virg. Æn. i. 736. Sil. vii. 185. 746. Plaut. Curc. i. 2. 31. Ov. Am. i. 4. 27. Tac. Ann. xv. 64.
13 salinorum appositu, Arnob. ii.
14 Levit. ii. 13. Hor. Od. iii. 23. 90 Plin. xxvi. 7. s. 41.
15 Hor. Sat. ii. 2. 17.
16 nasturtium.

17 Cic. Tusc. v. 34. Suet. Tib. 46. Mart. iii. 7.
18 Capitolin. in vita ejus, 7.
19 paternum salinum, sc. vas.
20 Hor. Od. ii. 16. 14. Fest.
21 Plin. xxxi. 7. s. 41. Cic. Fam. ix. 15. Juv. ix. 11. Hor. Ep. ii. 2. 60.
22 Nep. Att. 13. Catul. 84. (86. of Doering's edition) 4.

also among the Greeks and Persians, particularly of Hercules ; hence EPITRAPEZIUS, and of making libations.[1]

In making an oath or a prayer, the ancients touched the table as an altar, and to violate it by an indecent word or action was esteemed impious.[2] To this Virgil alludes, Æn. vii. 114.

As the ancients had not proper inns for the accommodation of travellers, the Romans, when they were in foreign countries, or at a distance from home, used to lodge at the houses of certain persons, whom they in return entertained at their houses in Rome. This was esteemed a very intimate connection, and called HOSPITIUM, or *jus hospitii*.[3] Hence HOSPES is put both for a host or entertainer, and a guest.[4]

This connection was formed also with states, by the whole Roman people, or by particular persons. Hence *clientelæ hospitiaque provincialia*, attachments and dependencies in the provinces.[5] *Publici hospitii jura*, Plin. iii. 4.

Individuals used anciently to have a tally (TESSERA *hospitalitatis*,) or piece of wood cut into two parts, of which each party kept one. They swore fidelity to one another by Jupiter, hence called HOSPITALIS. Hence a person who had violated the rites of hospitality, and thus precluded himself access to any family, was said CONFREGISSE TESSERAM.[6]

A league of hospitality was sometimes formed by persons at a distance, by mutually sending presents to one another.[7]

The relation of *hospites* was esteemed next to that of parents and clients. To violate it was esteemed the greatest impiety.[8]

The reception of any stranger was called *hospitium*, or plur. -IA, and also the house or apartment in which he was entertained, thus, *hospitium sit tua villa meum ; divisi in hospitia*, lodgings : HOSPITALE *cubiculum*, the guest-chamber ;[9] *hospitio utebatur Tulii*, lodged at the house of, Hence Florus calls Ostia, *maritimum urbis hospitium*, the maritime store-house of the city.[10] So Virgil calls Thrace, *hospitium antiquum Trojæ*, a place in ancient hospitality with Troy. *Linquere pollutum hospitium*, to abandon a place where the laws of hospitality had been violated, i. e. *locum in quo jura hospitii violata fuerant*.[11]

The Roman nobility used to build apartments[12] for strangers, called HOSPITALIA, on the right and left end of their houses, with separate entries, that upon their arrival they might be received there, and not in the *peristyle* or principal entry ; PERISTYLIUM, so called because sourrounded with columns.[13]

The CŒNA of the Romans usually consisted of two parts, called MENSA PRIMA, the first course, consisting of different kinds of meat; and MENSA SECUNDA vel ALTERA, the second course, consisting of fruits and sweat-meats.[14]

1 Stat. Sylv. iv. 6. 60. Mart. ix. 44. Curt. v. 8. 2 Ov. Am. i. 4. 27. Juv. ii. 160. 3 Liv. i. 1. 4 Ov.,Met. x. 224. Plaut. Most. ii. 2. 48. Cic. Dejot. 3. accipere hospitem non multi cibi sed multi joci, Cic. Fam. ix. 26. divertere ad hospitem, Divin. i. 27. s. 57. Fin. v. 2. hospitium cum aliquo facere, Liv. Cic. jun-

gimus hospitio dextras, sc. in, Virg. Æn. iii. 83. hospitio conjungi, Cic. Q. Fr. i. 1. hospitio aliquem excipere et accipi ; renunciare hospitium ei, Verr. ii. 36. Liv. xxv. 18. amicitiam ei more majorum renunciare, Suet. Cal. 3. Tac. Ann. ii.70. domo interdicere, Tac. Ann. ii. 70. vi. 29. Aug. 66. 5 Liv. ii. 22. v. 28.

xxxvii. 54. Cic. Verr. iv. 65. Cat. iv. 11. Balb. 18. Cæs. B. G. i. 31. 6 Plaut. Pœn. v. 1. 22. 2. 92. Cist. ii. 1. 27. Cic. Q. Fr. ii. 11. 7 quæ mittit dona, hospitio quum jungeret absens,Cœdicus,—presents which Cœdicus sends when, in absence, he formed with him a league of hospitality, Virg. Æn. ix.

361. 8 Gell. i. 13. Virg. Æn. v. 55. Cic. Verr. v. 42. 9 Ov. F. vi. 536. Pont. i. 3. 69. Liv. i. 58. ii. 14. 10 Liv. i. 35. Flor. i. 4. 11 Virg. Æn. iii. 15. 61. 12 domunculæ. 13 Vitr. vi. 10. Suet. Aug.82. 14 Serv. Virg. Æn. i. 216. 723. viii. 283.

In later times the first part of the *cœna* was called GUSTATIO, or GUSTUS, consisting of dishes to excite the appetite, a whet, and wine mixed with water and sweetened with honey, called MULSUM ;[1] whence what was eaten and drunk[2] to whet the appetite, was named PROMULSIS,[3] and the place where these things were kept, PROMULSIDARIUM, v. *-re*, or GUSTATORIUM.[4] But *gustatio* is also put for an occasional refreshment through the day, or for breakfast.[5]

The principal dish at supper was called CŒNÆ CAPUT vel POMPA.[6]

The Romans usually began their entertainments with eggs, and ended with fruits : hence AB OVA USQUE AD MALA, from the beginning to the end of supper.[7]

The dishes[8] held in the highest estimation by the Romans are enumerated by Gellius, Macrobius, Statius, Martialis, &c.[9] a peacock, (PAVO, v. *-us*),[10] first used by Hortensius, the orator, at a supper which he gave when admitted into the college of priests ;[11] a pheasant (PHASIANA, *ex* Phasia *Colchidis fluvio*) ;[12] a bird called *attagen* vel *-ena*, from Ionia or Phrygia ; a guinea-hen (*avis Afra, gallina Numidica* vel *Africana*) ;[13] a Melian crane, an Ambracian kid ; nightingales, *lusciniæ ;* thrushes, *turdi ;* ducks, geese, &c. TOMACULUM,[14] vel ISICIUM,[15] sausages or puddings.[16]

Sometimes a whole boar was served up (hence called ANIMAL PROPTER CONVIVIA NATUM, and PORCUS TROJANUS), stuffed with the flesh of other animals.[17]

The Romans were particularly fond of fish ;[18] *mullus,* the mullet ; *rhombus,* thought to be the turbot ; *murœna,* the lamprey ; *scarus,* the scar, or schar ; *acipenser,* the sturgeon ; *lupus,* a pike, &c. ; but especially of shellfish, *pisces testacei, pectines, pectunculi,* vel CONCHYLIA, *ostrea,* oysters, &c., which they sometimes brought all the way from Britian,[19] from Rutupia, Richborough in Kent; also snails (*cochleæ*).

Oyster-beds[20] were first invented by one Sergius Arata, before the Marsic war, A. U. 660, on the shore of Baiæ,[21] and on the Lucrine lake. Hence Lucrine oysters are celebrated. Some preferred those of Brundusium ; and to settle the difference, oysters used to be brought from thence, and fed for some time on the Lucrine lake.[22]

The Romans used to weigh their fishes alive at table ; and to see them expire was reckoned a piece of high entertainment.[23]

The dishes of the second table, or the dessert, were called BELLARIA ; including fruits, *poma* vel *mala,* apples, pears, nuts, figs, olives, grapes ; *pistachiæ,* vel *-a,* pistachio nuts ; *amygdalæ,* almonds ; *uvæ passæ,* dried grapes, raisins ; *caricæ* dried figs ; *palmulæ, caryotæ,* vel *dactyli,* dates, the fruit of the palm-tree ; *boleti,* mushrooms ;[24] *nuclei pinei,* the kernels of pine-nuts ; also sweatmeats, confects, or confections, called *edulia mellita* vel *dulciaria ; cupediæ ; crustula, liba, placentæ, artologani,* cheesecakes, or the like ; *coptæ,* almond-cakes ; *scriblitæ,* tarts, &c., whence the

1 Petr. 22. 31. Mart. xi. 32. 53. Hor. Sat. ii. 4.
' 26. Cic. Tusc. iii. 10. Orat. ii. 70. Fin. ii. 5. s. 17. Plin. xxii. 24.
2 antecœna.
3 Cic. Fam. ix. 16. 23. Sen. Ep. 123. .
4 Petr. 31. Plin. ix. 12. Ep. v. 6. Mart. xiv. 68.
5 Plin. Ep. iii. 5. vi. 16. Suet. Aug. 76. Vop.

Tac. 11.
6 Mart. x. 31. Cic. Tusc. v. 34. Fin. ii. 8.
7 Hor. Sat. i. 3. 6. Cic. Fam. ix. 20.
8 edulia.
9 Gell. vii. 16. Macrob. Sat. ii. 9. Stat. Silv. iv. 6. 8. Mart. v. 79. ix. 48. xi. 53, &c.
10 Hor. Sat. ii. 2. 23. Juv. i. 143.
11 aditiali cœna sacer-

dotii, Plin. x. 20. s. 23.
12 Mart. iii. 58. xiii. 72. Sen. Helv. 9. Petr. 79. Manil. v. 372.
13 Hor. Ep. ii. 54. Mart. xiii. 61. 72. Juv. xi. ' 142.
14 a τεμνω.
15 ab inseco.
16 Juv. x. 355. Mart. i. 42. 9. Petr. 31.
17 Juv. i. 141. Macrob. Sat. ii. 2.

18 Macrob. Sat. ii. 11.
19 Rutupinoque edita fundo, Juv. iv. 141. Plin. Ep. i. 15.
20 ostrearum vivaria.
21 in Baiano.
22 Plin. ix. 54. s. 79. Hor. Ep. ii. 49.
23 Plin. ix. 17. s. 30. Sen. Nat. Q. iii. 17, 18.
24 Plin. Ep. i. 7.

maker of them, the pastry-cook, or the confectioner, was called *pistor* vel *conditor dulciarius, placentarius, libarius, crustularius,* &c.

There were various slaves who prepared the victuals, who put them in order, and served them up.

Anciently the baker and cook (*pistor* et *cpquus* vel *cocus*) were the same.[1] An expert cook was hired occasionally, whose distinguishing badge was a knife which he carried. But after the luxury of the table was converted into an art, cooks were purchased at a great price. Cooks from Sicily in particular were highly valued; hence *Siculæ dapes,* nice dishes.[2]

There were no bakers at Rome before A. U. 580 ; baking was the work of the women ; but Plutarch says, that anciently Roman women used neither to bake nor cook victuals.[3]

The chief cook who had the direction of the kitchen,[4] was called AR-CHIMAGIRUS.[5] The butler, who had the care of provisions, PROMUS CON-DUS, *procurator peni.*[6] He who put them in order, STRUCTOR, and sometimes carved, the same with CARPTOR, *corpus,* or *scissor.* He who had charge of the hall, ATRIENSIS.[7]

They were taught carving as an art, and performed it to the sound of music, hence called CHIRONOMONTES vel *gesticulatores.*[8]

The slaves who waited at table were properly called MINISTRI, lightly clothed in a tunic, and girt[9] with napkins,[10] who had their different tasks assigned them ; some put the plate in order ;[11] some gave the guests water for their hands, and towels to wipe them ;[12] some served about the bread ; some brought in the dishes,[13] and set the cups ; some carved ; some served the wine,[14] &c. In hot weather there were some to cool the room with fans,[15] and to drive away the flies.[16] Maid-servants[17] also sometimes served at table.[18]

When a master wanted a slave to bring him any thing, he made a noise with his fingers.[19]

The dishes were brought in, either on the tables themselves, or more frequently on frames (FERCULA vel REPOSITORIA), each frame containing a variety of dishes ; hence *præbere cœnam ternis* vel *senis ferculis,* i. e. *missibus,* to give a supper of three or six courses.[20] But *fercula* is also sometimes put for the dishes or the meat. So MENSÆ ; thus *mensas,* i. e. lances magnas instar mensarum, *repositoriis imponere.*[21] Sometimes the dishes[22] were brought in and set down separately.[23]

A large platter[24] containing various kinds of meat was called MAZONO-MUM ;[25] which was handed about, that each of the guests might take what he chose. Vitellius caused a dish of immense size to be made, which he called the Shield of Minerva, filled with an incredible variety of the rarest and nicest kinds of meat.[26]

1 Fest. Plaut. Aul. ii. 4. 185. iii. 2, 3. Pseud. iii. 2, 3. 30.
2 Liv. xxxix. 6. Plin. ix. 17. s. 31. Mart. xiv. 220. Athen. xiv.23. Hor. Od. iii. 1. 18.
3 Plin. xviii. 11. s. 28. Var. R. Rust. ii. 10. Quæst. Rom. 84. s. 85.
4 qui coquinæ præerat.
5 Juv. ix. 109.
6 penus autem omne quo vescuntur homines, Cic. Nat. D. ii. 27.

Plaut. Pseud. ii. 2. 14. Hor. Sat. ii. 2. 16.
7 Mart. ix. 48. Juv. v. 120. vii. 184. ix. 110. xi. 136. Cic. Par. v. 2.
8 Juv. v. 121. xi. 137. Petr. 35, 36.
9 succincti, vel alte cincti, Hor. Sat. ii. 6. 107. ; 8. 10.
10 linteis succincti, Suet. Cal. 26.
11 argentum ordinabant, Sen. Brev. Vit. 12.
12 Petron. 31.
13 opsonia inferrebant.

14 Virg. Æn. i. 705. Juv. v. 56. 59, &c.
15 flabella.
16 Mart. iii. 82.
17 famulæ.
18 Virg. Æn. i. 703. Suet. Tib. 42. Curt. v.1.
19 digitis crepuit, Mart. iii. 82. vi. 89. xiv. 119. Petr. 27.
20 Petr. 35. 66. Plin. xxviii. 2. s. 5. xxxiii. 11. s. 49. 52. Suet. Aug. 74. Juv. i. 93.
21 Hor. Sat. ii. 6. 104. Mart. iii. 50. ix. 83. xi.

32. Auson. Epigr. 8. Juv. xi. 64. Plin. xxxiii. 11. s. 49. Petr. 34. 47. 68.
22 patinæ vel catini.
23 Hor. Sat. ii. 8. 42. 2. 39.
24 lanx vel scutella.
25 a νεμω, tribuo, et μαζα, eduliom quoddam e farina lacte.
26 Hor. Sat. viii. 86. Plin. xxxv. 12. s. 46. Suet. Vit. 13.

At a supper given to that emperor by his brother upon his arrival in the city,[1] 2000 of the most choice fishes, and 7000 birds, are said to have been served up. Vitellius used to breakfast, dine, and sup with different persons on the same day, and it never cost any of them less than 400,000 sesterces, about £3229, 3*s.* 4*d.* Thus he is said to have spent in less than a year, *novies millies H. S.* i. e. £7,265,625.[2]

An uncommon dish was introduced to the sound of the flute, and the servants were crowned with flowers.[3]

In the time of supper the guests were entertained with music and dancing, sometimes with pantomimes and play-actors ;[4] with fools[5] and buffoons, and even with gladiators ;[6] but the more sober had only persons to read or repeat select passages from books (ANAGNOSTÆ vel ACROAMATA). Their highest pleasure at entertainments arose from agreeable conversation.[7]

To prevent the bad effects of repletion, some used after supper to take a vomit : thus Cæsar (*accubuit, ἐμετικὴν agebat,* i. e. *post cœnam vomere volebat, ideoque largius edebat,* wished to vomit after supper, and therefore eat heartily),[8] also before supper and at other times.[9] Even women, after bathing before supper, used to drink wine and throw it up again to sharpen their apdetite.[10]

A sumptuous entertainment[11] was called AUGURALIS ; PONTIFICALIS vel *pontificum* ; SALIARIS, because used by these priests ; or DUBIA, *ubi tu dubites, quid sumas pontissimum.*[12]

When a person proposed supping with any one without invitation, or, as we say, invited himself,[13] he was called HOSPES OBLATUS, and the entertainment, SUBITA CONDICTAQUE CŒNULA.[14]

An entertainment given to a person newly returned from abroad, was called *cœna* ADVENTITIA vel *-toria,* vel VIATICA ; by patrons to their clients, *cœna* RECTA, opposed to SPORTULA ; by a person, when he entered on an office, CŒNA ADITIALIS vel ADJICIALIS.[15]

Clients used to wait on their patrons at their houses early in the morning, to pay their respects to them,[16] and sometimes to attend them through the day wherever they went, dressed in a white toga, hence called ANTEAMBULONES, NIVEI QUIRITES ; and from their number, TURBA TOGATA, et PRÆCEDENTIA LONGI AGMINIS OFFICIA.[17] On which account, on solemn occasions, they were invited to supper, and plentifully entertained in the hall. This was called CŒNA RECTA, i. e. *justa et solemnis adeoque lauta et opipara,* a formal plentiful supper ; hence *convivari recta,* sc. *cœna, recte et dapsile,* i. e. *abundanter,* to keep a good table. So *vivere recte,* vel *cum recto apparatu.*[18]

But upon the increase of luxury, it became customary under the emperors, instead of a supper, to give each, at least of the poorer clients, a cer-

1 cœna adventitia.
2 Dio. lxv. 3. Tac. Hist. ii. 95.
3 Macrob. Sat. ii. 12.
4 Petr. 35, 36. Plaut. Stich. ii. 2. 56. Spart. Adrian. 26.
5 moriones, Plin. Ep. ix. 17. Capit. Vero. 4.
6 Cic. Att. i. 12. Fam. v. 9. Nep. Att. xiii. 14. Suet. Aug. 78. Plin. Ep. i. 15. iii. 5. vi. 31. ix. 36. Gell. iii. 19. xiii. 11. xix. 7. Mart. iii.

50.
7 Cic. Sen. 14. Hor. Sat. ii. 6. 70.
8 Cic. Att. xiii. 52. Dej. 7.
9 Suet. Vit. 13. Cic. Phil. ii. 41. Cels. i. 3. vomunt, ut edant ; edunt, ut vomant, they vomit, that they may eat ; they eat, that they may vomit, Sen. Helv. 9.
10 Falerni sextarius alter ducitur ante cibum,

rabidam facturus orexim, a second sextarius of Falernian is drunk up before meat, to provoke an eager appetite, Juv. vi. 427.
11 cœna lauta, opima vel opipara.
12 Cic. Fam. vii. 26. Att. v. 9. Hor. Od. l. 37. ii. 14. 28. Sat. ii. 2. 76. Ter. Phor. ii. 2. 28.
13 cœnam si condixit vel ad cœnam, Cic. Fam. i. 9. Suet. Tib. 42.

14 Plin. Præf. Suet Claud. 21.
15 Suet. Vit. 13. Claud. 9. Plaut. Bacch. i. 1. 61. Mart. viii. 50. Sen. Ep. 95. 123.
16 salutare, Mart. ii. 18. 3. iii. 36. iv. 8. Juv. i. 128. v. 19.
17 Juv. i. 96. vii. 142. viii. 49. x. 44. Mart. i. 56. 13. iii. 7.
18 Juv. v. 24. Suet. Aug. 74. Claud. 21. Vesp. 19. Sen. Ep. 110. 123.

tain portion or dole of meat to carry home in a pannier or small basket (SPORTULA) ; which likewise being found inconvenient, money was given in place of it, called also SPORTULA, to the amount generally of 100 *quadrantes*, or twenty-five *asses*, i. e. about 1s. 7d. each ; sometimes to persons of rank, to women as well as men. This word is put likewise for the hire given by orators to those whom they employed to applaud them, while they were pleading.[1]

SPORTULÆ, or pecuniary donations instead of suppers, were established by Nero, but abolished by Domitian, and the custom of formal suppers restored.[2]

The ordinary drink of the Romans at feasts was wine, which they mixed with water, and sometimes with aromatics or spices. They used water either cold or hot.[3]

A place where wine was sold[4] was called ŒNOPOLIUM ; where mulled wines and hot drinks were sold, THERMOPOLIUM.[5]

Wine anciently was very rare. It was used chiefly in the worship of the gods. Young men below thirty, and women all their lifetime, were forbidden 'to drink it, unless at sacrifices,' whence, according to some, the custom of saluting female relations, that it might be known whether they had drunk wine. But afterwards, when wine became more plentiful, these restrictions were removed ; which Ovid hints was the case even in the time of Tarquin the Proud.[6]

Vineyards came to be so much cultivated, that it appeared agriculture was thereby neglected ; on which account Domitian, by an edict, prohibited any new vineyards to be planted in Italy, and ordered at least the one half to be cut down in the provinces. But this edict was soon after abrogated.[7]

The Romans reared their vines by fastening them to certain trees, as the poplar and the elm ; whence these trees were said to be married[8] to the vines, and the vines to them :[9] and the plane-tree, to which they were not joined, is elegantly called CÆLEBS.[10]

Wine was made anciently much in the same manner as it is now. The grapes were picked[11] in baskets[12] made of osier, and stamped.[13] The juice was squeezed out by a machine called TORCULUM, -ar, -are,'vel -arium, or PRELUM, a press : *torcular* was properly the whole machine, and *prelum*, the beam which pressed the grapes.[14] The juice was made to pass[15] through a strainer (SACCUS vel COLUM), and received into a large vat or tub (LACUS),[16] or put into a large cask (DOLIUM),[17] made of wood or potter's earth, until the fermentation was over ;[18] hence VINUM DOLIARE. The liquor which came out without pressing was called *protropum*, or *mustum lixivium*.[19]

The must or new wine (MUSTUM) was refined,[20] by mixing it with the yolks of pigeon's eggs ;[21] the white of eggs is now used for that purpose. Then it was poured[22] into smaller vessels or casks[23] usually made of earth, hence called TESTÆ,[24] covered over with pitch or chalk,[25] and bunged or

1 Juv. i. 95. 120. Mart. i. 50. iii. 7. xi. 75. Plin. Ep. ii. 14.
2 Suet. Ner. 16. Dom. 7.
3 Juv. v. 63. vi. 302. Mart. i. 12. viii. 67. 7. xiv. 105. Plant. Curc. ii. 3. 19. Mil. iii. 2. 22.
4 taberna vinaria.
5 Plaut. Rud. ii. 6. 43. Pseud. ii. 4. 52.
6 Val. Max. ii. 1. 5. vi. 3. Gell. x. 23. Plin. xiv.

13. Plut.Q.Rom. 6. Ov. Fast. ii. 740.
7 Suet. Dom. 7. 14.
8 maritari, Hor. Ep. ii. 10.
9 duci ad arbores viduas, to be wedded to widowed trees, i. e. vitibus tanquam uxoribus per civilia bella privatas, Hor. Od. iv. 5. 30.
10 Hor. Od. ii. 15. 4.

11 decerpebantur.
12 quali, quasilli, fisci, fiscinae vel fiscellæ.
13 calcabantur.
14 trabs qua uva premitur, Serv. Virg. G. ii. 242. Vitr. vi. 9.
15 transmittebantur.
16 Mart. xii. 61. 3. xiv. 104. Ov. Fast. iv. 868. Plin. Ep. ix. 20.
17 cupa vel seria.
18 donec deferbuer it.

19 Plaut. Pseud. ii. 2. 64. Plin. xiv. 9 Colum. lxii. 41.
20 defæcabatur.
21 Hor. Sat. ii. 4. 56.
22 diffusum.
23 amphoræ vel cadi.
24 Hor. Od. i. 20. 2. iii. 21. 4.
25 oblitæ vel picatæ et gypsatæ.

stopped up;[1] hence *relinere* vel *delinere dolium* vel *cadum*, to open, to pierce, to broach.[2] Wine was also kept in leathern bags (UTRES). From new wine, a book not ripe for publication is called *musteus liber*, by Pliny.[3]

On each cask was marked the name of the consuls, or the year when it was made ; hence *nunc mihi fumosos veteris proferte Falernos consulis* (sc. *cados*), now bring for me mellow Falernian, that recalls the name of some ancient consul : and the oldest was always put farthest back in the cellar ; hence *interiore nata Falerni*, with a cup of old Falernian wine.[4]

When a cask was emptied, it was inclined to one side, and the wine poured out. The Romans did not use a siphon or spiggot, as we do ; hence *vertere cadum*, to pierce, to empty. *Invertunt Aliphanis* (sc. *poculis*) *vinaria tota* (sc. *vasa*, i. e. *cados* v. *lagenas*), they turn over whole casks into large cups made at Alifæ, a town in Samnium.[5]

Sometimes wine was ripened by being placed in the smoke above a fire,[6] or in an upper part of the house,[7] whence it was said *descendere*.

WINES.

THE application of the *fumarium* to the mellowing of wines was borrowed from the Asiatics, who were in the habit of exposing their wines to the heat of the sun on the tops of their houses, and afterwards placing them in apartments warmed from below, in order that they might be more speedily rendered fit for use. As the flues, by which the ancient dwellings were heated, were probably made to open into the apotheca, it is obvious that a tolerably steady temperature could be easily supplied, and that the vessels would be fully exposed to the action of the smoke. Although the tendency of this procedure may, according to our modern notions, appear very questionable ; yet, when attentively considered, it does not seem to differ much from that of the more recent method of mellowing Madeira, and other strong wines, by placing them in a hot-house, or in the vicinity of a kitchen-fire or baker's oven, which is found to assist the developement of their flavour, and to bring them to an early maturity. As the earthen vases, in which the ancient wines were preserved, were defended by an ample coating of pitch or plaster, it is not likely that the smoke could penetrate, so as to alloy and vitiate the genuine taste and odour of the liquor ; but the warmth which was kept up by its means would have the effect of soft-

ening the harshness of the stronger wines, and, probably, of dissipating, to a certain extent, the potent aroma of the condiments with which they were impregnated. Although Tibullus gives the epithet "smoky" to the Falernian wines thus prepared, and Horace speaks of the amphora with which he proposed to celebrate the kalends of March, as having been laid up "to imbibe the smoke," during the consulship of Tullus, they are not to be understood as alluding to the flavour of the liquor, but merely to the process by which it was brought to a high degree of mellowness. The description of Ovid, however, may be considered as more correct ; for he applies the term only to the cask in which the wine was enclosed. At the same time, it must be acknowledged, that the practice in question was liable to great abuse ; and we may readily conceive, that, from the success attending the experiment as applied to the first-rate growths, it might happen that many inferior wines, though not at all adapted for the operation, would nevertheless be made to undergo it, in the vain hope of bettering their condition ; that, from an anxiety to accelerate the process, the wines would be sometimes exposed to a destructive heat ; or that, from inattention to the corking of the vessels, the smoke might enter them, and impart a repulsive savour to

the contents. As these forced wines were in great request at Rome, and in the provinces, the dealers would often be tempted to send indifferent specimens into the market ; and it is not, perhaps, without reason that Martial inveighs so bitterly against the produce of the fumaria of Marseilles, particularly those of one Munna, who seems to have been a notorious offender in this line, and whom the poet humourously supposes to have abstained from revisiting Rome, lest he should be compelled to drink his own wines.

One certain consequence of the long exposure of the amphora to the influence of the fumarium must have been, that a portion of the contents would exhale, and that the residue would acquire a greater or less degree of consistence, for, however well the vases might have been coated and lined, or however carefully they might have been closed, yet, from the nature of the materials employed in their composition, from the action of the vinous fluid from within, and the effect of the smoke and heat from without, it was quite impossible that some degree of exudation should not take place. As the more volatile parts of the must were often evaporated by boiling, and as various solid or viscid ingredients were added to the wine previously to its introduction into the amphoræ, it is manifest that a further ex-

---

1 obturatæ.
2 Ter. Heaut. iii. i. 51. so corticem adstrictum pice demovere amphoræ, for ab amphora, to

remove the cork incrusted with pitch from the cask, Hor. iii. 8. 10.
3 Plin. xxviii. 18. Ep. viii. 21.

4 Hor. Od. i. 20. ii.[3. 8. iii. 8. 19. 28. 8. Ep. i. 5.
4. Tibull. ii. 1. 27.
5 Hor. Od. iii. 29. 2. Sat. ii. 8. 39.

6 Hor. Od. iii. 8. 11. Plin. xiv. 1. s. 3. Mart. iii. 81. x. 36.
7 in horreo vel apotheca editiore.

Often it was kept to a great age.[1] Wine made in the consulship of Opimius, A. U. 633, was to be met with in the time of Pliny, near 200 years

halation must have reduced it to the state of a syrup or extract. In the case of the finer wines, it is true, this effect would be in some measure counteracted by the influence of the insensible fermentation; and a large proportion of the original extractive matter, as well as to the heterogeneous substances suspended with it, would be precipitated on the sides and bottoms of the vessels, in the form of lees ; but, in other instances, the process of inspissation would go on, without much abatement from this cause. Hence it comes, that so many of the ancient wines have been described as thick and fat ; and that they were not deemed ripe for use, until they had acquired an oily smoothness from age. Hence, too, the practice of employing strainers (cola vinaria) to clarify them, and free them from their dregs. In fact, they often become consolidated to such a degree, that they could no longer be poured from the vessels, and it was necessary to dissolve them in hot water, before they could be drunk. We learn from Aristotle that some of the stronger wines, such as the Arcadian, were reduced to a concrete mass, when exposed in skins to the action of the smoke ; and the wine-vases, discovered among the ruins of Herculaneum and Pompeii, have generally been found to contain a quantity of earthly matter. It is clear, then, that those wines which were designed for long keeping could not have been subjected to the highest temperature of the fumarium, without being almost always reduced to an extract. Indeed, Columella warns the operator that such might be the issue of the process, and recommends that there should be a loft above the apotheca, into which the wines could be removed,— " ne rursus nimia suffitione medicata sint."

For the more precious wines, the ancients occasionally employed vessels of glass. The bottles, vases, cups, and other articles of that material, which are to be seen in every collection of antiquities, prove that

they had brought the manufacture to a great degree of perfection. We know, that, for preserving fruits, they certainly gave the preference to glass jars ; and, at the supper of Trimalcio, so admirably depicted by Petronius, even amphoræ of glass are said to have been introduced. Whether they were of the full quadrantal measure does not appear ; but, in all probability, they were of more moderate dimensions, for we are told by Martial, that the choicest Falernian was kept in small glass bottles ; and neither the number of the guests, nor the quality of the liquor, supposing it to have been genuine, would have justified the use of full-sized amphoræ, on the occasion above alluded to.

The ancients were careful to rack their wines only when the wind was northerly, as they had observed that they were apt to be turbid when it blew in an opposite direction. The weaker sorts were transferred, in the spring, to the vessels in which they were destined to remain ; the stronger kinds during summer ; but those grown on dry soils, were not drawn off until after the winter solstice. According to Plutarch, wines were most affected by the west wind ; and such as remained unchanged by it, were pronounced likely to keep well. Hence, at Athens, and in other parts of Greece, there was a feast in honour of Bacchus, on the eleventh day of the month Anthesterion, when the westerly winds had generally set in, at which the produce of the preceding vintage was first tasted. In order to allure customers, various tricks appear to have been practised by the ancient wine dealers ; some, for instance, put the new vintage into a cask that had been seasoned with an old and high flavoured wine ; others placed cheese and nuts in the cellar, that those who entered might be tempted to eat, and thus have their palates blunted, before they tasted the wine. The buyer is recommended by Florentinus to taste the wines he proposes to purchase,

during a north wind, when he will have the fairest chance of forming an accurate judgment of their qualities.

The ancient wines were, for the most part, designated according to the places where they grew ; but occasionally they borrowed the appellation of the grapes from which they were made ; and the name of the vine, or vineyard, stood indiscriminately for that of the wine. When very old, they received certain epithets indicative of that circumstance, as *sanpias, consulare, Opimianum Arvicium*. But, as it sometimes happened, that, by long keeping, they lost their original flavour, or acquired a disagreeably bitter taste, it was not unusual to introduce into them a portion of must, with the view of correcting these defects : wine thus cured was called *vinum recentatum*. The wine presented to persons of distinction was termed *γερονσιος*, or *honorarium*. Such was the rich sweet wine, of which Ulysses had twelve amphoræ given him by Maron, and which was so highly valued by the donor, that he kept it carefully concealed from all his household, save his wife and the intendant of his stores, as its attractions were not easily resisted.

None of the more generous wines were reckoned fit for drinking before the fifth year, and the majority of them were kept for a much longer period. The thin white wines are stated by Galen to have ripened soonest; acquiring, first, a certain degree of sharpness, which, by the time they were ten years old, gave place to a grateful pungency, if they did not turn acid within the first four years. Even the strong and dry white wines, he remarks, notwithstanding their body, were liable to acescency after the tenth year, unless they had been kept with due care ; but if they escaped this danger, they might be preserved for an indefinite length of time. Such was the case more especially with the Surrentine wine, which continued raw and harsh until about twenty years old, and after-

1 Hor. Od. iii. 21. 7. 14. 18. Cic. Brut. 286. Juv. v. 34. Pers. iv. 29. Vell. ii. 7.

after.[1] In order to make wine keep, they used to boil[2] the must down to one half, when it was called DEFRUTUM : to one third, SAPA ;[3] and to give

wards improved progressively, seldom contracting any unpleasant bitterness, but retaining its qualities unimpaired to the last, and disputing the palm of excellence with the growths of Falernum. The tramarine wines which were imported into Italy, were thought to have attained a moderate age in six or seven years; and such as were strong enough to bear a sea-voyage were found to be much improved by it.

The lighter red wines (vina horna fugacia) were used for common drinking, and would seldom endure longer than from one vintage to another; but, in good seasons, they would sometimes be found capable of being preserved beyond the year. Of this description we may suppose that Sabine wine to have been, which Horace calls upon his friend to broach when four years old ; although in general the proper age of the Sabinum was from seven to fifteen years ; and the poet has abundantly shown, in other parts of his works, that he knew how to value old wine, and was seldom content with it so young. The stronger dark-coloured wines, when long kept, underwent a species of decomposition (cariem vetustatis), from the precipitation of part of the extractive matter which they contained. This, and the pungency (acumen) which such wines acquired, were justly esteemed the proofs of their having arrived at their due age. The genuine flavour of the vintage was then fully developed, and all the roughness of its early condition was removed. From the mode, however, in which the ancient wines were preserved, a greater or less inspissation took place ; and, if we may depend on the statement of Pliny, this was most observable in the more generous kinds ; and the taste became disagreeably bitter, obscuring the true flavour of the liquor. Wine of a middle age, was, therefore, to be preferred, as being the most wholesome and grateful ; but in those days, as well as ours,

it was the fashion to place the highest value on whatever was rarest, and an extravagant sum was often given for wines which were literally not drinkable. Such seems to have been the case with the famous vintage of the year in which L. Opimius Nepos was consul, being the 633d from the foundation of the city ; when, from the great warmth of the summer, all the productions of the earth attained an uncommon degree of perfection. Velleius Paterculus, who flourished 150 years afterwards, denies that any of it was to be had in his time ; but both Pliny and Martial, who were considerably posterior to that historians describe it as still inexhausted at the time when they wrote. The former, indeed, admits that it was then reduced to the consistence of honey, and could only be used in small quantities for flavouring other wines, or mixing with water. Reckoning the original piece to have been one hundred nummi, or sixteen shillings and sixpence for the amphora, he calculates, that, according to the usual rate of Roman interest, a single ounce of this wine, at the time of the third consulate of Caligula, when it had reached its 160th year, must have cost at least one nummus, or twopence ; which would make the price of the quart amount to six shillings and sixpence English.

As the ordinary wines of Italy were produced in great abundance, they were often sold at very moderate prices. Columella's reduced estimate would make the cost about fourpence the gallon ; but we find from Pliny, that, when Licinius Crassus and Julius Cæsar were consuls, an edict was issued by them, prohibiting the sale of Greek and Aminean wine for eight asses the amphora, which would be less than one penny a gallon ; and the same author asserts, on the authority of Varro, that, at the time of Metellus's triumph, the congius, a somewhat similar measure than our gallon, was to be bought

for a single as, or about three farthings English.

Few parts of Italy proved unfriendly to the vine ; but it flourished most in that portion of the south-western coast, to which, from its extraordinary fertility and delightful climate, the name of Campania felix was given. The exuberant produce of the rich and inexhaustible soil of the whole of this district, which is so happily exposed to the most genial breezes, while it is sheltered by the Apennines from all the colder winds, has called forth the eulogies of every writer who has had occasion to mention it. From this district the Romans obtained those vintages which they valued so highly, and of which the fame extended to all parts of the world. In ancient times, indeed, the hills by which the surface is diversified seem to have formed one continued vineyard ; and every care was taken to maintain the choice quality of the produce. With respect to the locality and designation of particular celebrated spots, much controversy has arisen among critics. Florus speaks of Falernus as a mountain, and Martial describes it under the same title ; but Pliny, Polybius, and others denominate it a field, or territory (ager) ; and, as the best growths were styled indiscriminately Massicum and Falernium. Peregrini concurs with Vibius in deciding, that Massicus was the proper appellation of the hill which rose from the Falernian plain. By a similar mode of reasoning it might be inferred from the term "arvis," which occurs in conjunction with "Massicus," in the splendid description of the origin of the Falernian vineyards given by Silius Italicus, that the epithet Massicus was applicable to more level grounds.

The truth seems to be, that the choicest wines were produced on the southern declivities of the range of hills which commence in the neighbourhood of the ancient Sinuessa, and extend to a considerable distance inland, and which

1 In speciem asperi mellis redactum, Plin. 7. ii. 40. 5.   xiv. 4. s. 6. Mart. i. 27.   2 decoquere, Virg. G. i. 295.   3. Plin. xiv. 9. s. 11.

it a flavour,[1] they mixed with it pitch and certain herbs ; when they were said CONDIRE, MEDICARI vel *concinnare vinum*.[2]

may have taken their general name from the town or district of Falernum; but the most conspicuous, or the best exposed among them may have been the Massicus; and as, in process of time, several inferior growths were confounded under the common denomination of Falernian, correct writers would choose that epithet which most accurately denoted the finest vintages. If, however, it be allowable to appeal to the analogy of modern names, the question as to the locality will be quickly decided; for the mountain that rises from the Rocca di Mondragone, which is generally allowed to point to the site of ancient Sinuessa, is still known by the name of *Monte Massico*. That fine *Massic* wines were grown here is sufficiently proved by the testimony of Martial, who describes them as the produce of the Sinuessan vineyards. At a short distance to the east, and on the slope of the adjacent ridge, are two villages, of which the upper is called *Falciano a monte*, and the lower, *Falciano a basso*. Here was the ancient *Faustianum*, of which *Falciano* is a corruption.

The account which Pliny has furnished of the wines of Campania is the most circumstantial, and, as no one had greater opportunities of becoming familiar with the principal growths of his native country, doubtless, the most correct. "Augustus, and most of the leading men of his time," he informs us, "gave the preference to the *Setine* wine that was grown in the vineyards above Forum Appii, as being of all kinds the least apt to injure the stomach. Formerly the *Cæcuban*, which came from the poplar marshes of Amyclæ, was most esteemed; but it has lost its repute, partly from the negligence of the growers, and partly from the limited extent of the vineyard, which has been nearly destroyed by the navigable canal that was begun by Nero from Avernus to Ostia. The second rank used to be assigned to the growths of the Falernian territory, and, among them, chiefly to the Faustianum. The territory of Falernum begins from the Campanian bridge on the left hand as you go to Urbana, which has been recently colonised and placed under the jurisdiction of Capua by Sylla: the Faustian vineyards, again, are situated about four miles from the village in the vicinity of Cediæ, which village is six miles from Sinuessa. The wines produced on this soil owe their celebrity to the great care and attention bestowed on their manufacture; but latterly they have somewhat degenerated from their original excellence, in consequence of the rapacity of the farmers, who are usually more intent upon the quantity than the quality of the vintages. They continue, however, in the greatest estimation; and are, perhaps, the strongest of all wines, as they burn when approached by a flame. They are of three kinds, namely, the dry, the sweet, and the light Falernian. Some persons class them somewhat differently, giving the name of Gauranum to the wine made on the tops of the hills, of Faustianum to that which is obtained from the middle region, and reserving the appellation of Falernian for the lowest growths. It is worthy of remark that none of the grapes which yield these wines are at all pleasant to the taste."

With respect to the first of the above-mentioned wines, it is surprising that, notwithstanding the high commendation of Augustus, the *Setinum* is never once mentioned by Horace, although he has expatiated with all the fervour of an amateur, on the other first-rate growths of his time. Perhaps he took the liberty of differing from the imperial taste in this particular, as the Setine was a delicate light wine, and he seems to have had a predilection for such as were distinguished by their strength. Both Martial and Juvenal, however, make frequent mention of it; and Silius Italicus declares it to have been so choice as to be reserved for Bacchus himself,—" *ipsius mensis reposta Lyæi*." Galen commends it for its innocuous qualities. It was grown on the heights of Sezza, and though not a strong wine, possessed sufficient firmness and permanency to undergo the operation of the fumarium; for we find Juvenal alluding to some which was so old that the smoke had obliterated the mark of the jar in which it was contained.

The *Cæcuban*, on the other hand, is described by Galen as a generous, durable wine, but apt to affect the head, and ripening only after a long term of years. In another place, he remarks, that the Bithynian white wine, when very old, passed with the Romans for Cæcuban; but that in this state it was generally bitter and unfit for drinking. From this analogy we may conclude, that, when new, it belonged to the class of rough sweet wines. After the breaking up of the principal vineyards which supplied it, this wine would necessarily become very scarce and valuable; and such persons as were fortunate enough to possess any that dated from the Opimian vintage, would preserve it with extraordinary care. In fact, we are told by Pliny, in a subsequent book, that it was no longer grown,—" *Cæcuba jam non gignuntur*," and he also alludes to the Setine wine, as an article of great rarity. The *Fundanum*, which was the produce of the same territory, if, indeed, it was a distinct wine, seems to have partaken of the same characters, being, according to Galen's report, strong and full-bodied, and so heady, that it could only be drunk in small quantity.

There can be little doubt, that the excellence of these wines is to be attributed chiefly to the loose volcanic soils on which they were produced. Much also depended on the mode of culture; and it is more than probable that the great superiority of the growths of the Falernian vineyards was

1 ut odor vino contingat, et saporis quædam   acumina.   2 Plin. xiv. 20. s. 25.   Colum. xii. 19—21. Cato R. Rust. 114, 115.

43

Wines were distinguished chiefly from the places where they were produced. In Italy the most remarkable were, *vinum* FALERNUM, *Massicum*,

in the first instance, owing to the vines there being trained on *juga*, or low frames, formed of poles, instead of being raised on poplars, as was the case in several of the adjacent territories. Afterwards, when the proprietors, in consequence of the increasing demand for their wines, became desirous to augment the quantity, they probably adopted the latter practice, and forcing the vines to a great height, sacrificed the quality of the fruit.

No wine has ever acquired such extensive celebrity as the Falernian, or more truly merited the name of "immortal," which Martial has conferred upon it. At least, of all ancient wines, it is the one most generally known in modern times; for, while other eminent growths are overlooked or forgotten, few readers will be found who have not formed some acquaintance with the Falernian; and its fame must descend to the latest ages, along with the works of those mighty masters of the lyre who have sung its praises. At this distance of time, and with the imperfect data we possess, no one need expect to demonstrate the precise qualities of that or any other wine of antiquity; though by collating the few facts already stated, with some other particulars which have been handed down to us respecting the Falernian vintages, the hope may reasonably be indulged of our being able to make some approach to a more correct estimate of their true characters, and of pointing out at the same time those modern growths to which they have the greatest resemblance.

In the first place, all writers agree in describing the Falernian wine as very strong and durable, and so rough in its recent state, that it could not be drunk with pleasure, but required to be kept a great number of years, before it was sufficiently mellow. Horace even terms it a "fiery" wine, and calls for water from the spring to moderate its strength; and Persius applies to it the epithet "*indomitum*," probably in allusion to its heady quality. From Galen's account it

appears to have been in best condition from the tenth to the twentieth year; afterwards it was apt to contract an unpleasant bitterness; yet we may suppose, that when of a good vintage, and especially when preserved in glass bottles, it would keep much longer without having its flavour impaired. Horace, who was a lover of old wine, proposes in a wellknown ode, to broach an amphora which was coeval with himself, and which, therefore, was probably not less than thirty-three years old; as Torquatus Manlius was consul in the six hundred and eightyninth year from the foundation of the city, and Corvinus, in honour of whom the wine was to be drawn, did not obtain the consulate till 723 A. U. C. As he bestows the highest commendation on this sample, ascribing to it all the virtues of the choicest vintages, and pronouncing it truly worthy to be produced on a day of festivity, we must believe it to have been really of excellent quality. In general, however, it probably suffered, more or less, from the mode in which it was kept; and those whose taste was not perverted by the rage for high-dried wines, preferred it in its middle state.

Among our present wines, we have no hesitation in fixing upon those of Xeres and Madeira as the two to which the Falernian offers the most distinct features of resemblance. Both are straw-coloured wines, assuming a deeper tint from age, or from particular circumstances in the quality, or management of the vintage. Both of them present the several varieties of dry, sweet, and light. Both of them are exceedingly strong and durable wines; being, when new, very rough, harsh, and fiery, and requiring to be kept about the same length of time as the Falernian, before they attain a due degree of mellowness. Of the two, however, the more palpable dryness and bitter-sweet flavour of the Sherry might incline us to decide, that it approached most nearly to the wine under consideration; and it is worthy of remark, that the same difference in the produce of the

fermentation is observable in the Xeres vintages, as that which Galen has noticed with respect to the Falernian; it being impossible always to predict, with certainty, whether the result will be a dry wine, or a sweetish wine, resembling Paxarete. But, on the other hand, the soil of Madeira is more analagous to that of the Campagna Felice, and thence we may conclude, that the flavour and aroma of its wines are similar. Sicily, which is also a volcanic country, supplies several growths, which an inexperienced judge would very readily mistake for those of the former island, and which would, in all probability, come still nearer to them in quality, if more pains were bestowed upon the manufacture. Another point of coincidence is deserving of notice. Both Xeres and Madeira, are, it is well known, infinitely improved by being transported to a hot climate; and latterly it has become a common practice, among the dealers in the island, to force the Madeira wines by a process which is absolutely identical with the operation of the *fumarium*. It may, perhaps, be objected that the influence of heat and age upon these liquors, far from producing any disagreeable bitterness, only renders them sweeter and milder however long they may be kept; but then, in contrasting them with the superannuated wines of the Romans, we must make allowance for the previous preparations, and the effect of the different sorts of vessels in which they are preserved. If Madeira, or Sherry, but particularly the latter, were kept in earthen jars until it was reduced to the consistence of honey, there can be little doubt that the taste would become so intensely bitter, that, to use the expression of Cicero, we should condemn it as intolerable.

The Surrentine wines, which were the produce of the Aminean grapes, were, in like manner, of very durable quality,— "firmissima vina," as Virgil designates them; and on account of their lightness and wholesomeness, were much commended for the use of con-

Calenum, Cæcubum, Albanum, Setinum, Surrentinum, &c. Foreign wines, *Chium, Lesbium, Leucadium, Coum, Rhodium, Naxium, Mamertinum, Thasium, Mæonium,* vel *Lydium,.Mareoticum, &c.* Also from its colour or age, *vinum album, nigrum, rubrum, &c. ; vetus, novum, recens, hornum,* of

valescents. They are stated by Pliny to have been grown only in vineyards, and consequently the vines which yielded them could not have been high-trained.

Such were the wines of the Campania Felix, and adjacent hills, of which most frequent mention is made, and concerning which the fullest particulars have been transmitted. Respecting certain other growths, as the Cælenum, Caulinum, and Spatanum, our information is of a more imperfect nature. We only know that the vintages of Cales are much praised by Horace, and described by Galen as lighter, and more grateful to the stomach, than the Falernian; while those of the latter territories are pronounced to have been little, if at all, inferior to that celebrated wine.

The Albanum, which grew upon the hills that rise to the south, in view of the city, is ranked by Pliny only as a third-rate wine ; but from the frequent commendation of it by Juvenal and Horace, we must suppose it to have been in considerable repute, especially when matured by long keeping.

Among the lighter growths of the Roman territory, the Sabinum,· Nomentanum, and Venafranum, were among the most agreeable. The first seems to have been a thin table-wine, of a reddish colour, attaining its maturity in seven years. The Nomentan, however, which was also a delicate claret wine, but of a fuller body, is described as coming to perfection in five or six years. The wine of Spoletum, again, which was distinguished by its bright golden colour, was light and pleasant.

Amphictyon is said to have issued a law, directing that pure wine should be merely tasted at the entertainments of the Athenians ; but that the guests should be allowed to drink freely of wine mixed with water, after dedicating the first cup to Jupiter the Saviour, to remind them of the salubrious quality of the latter fluid. However much this ex-

cellent rule may have been occasionally transgressed, it is certain that the prevailing practice of the Greeks was to drink their wines in a diluted state. To drink wine unmixed was held disreputable ; and those who were guilty of such excess were said to act like Scythians (επισκυθισαι). To drink even equal parts of wine and water, or, as we familiarly term it, half and half, was thought to be unsafe ; and, in general, the dilution was more considerable ; varying, according to the taste of the drinkers, and the strength of the liquor, from one part of wine, and four of water, to two of wine, and four, or else five parts of water, which last seems to have been the favourite mixture.

From the account which Homer gives of the dilution of the Maronean wine with twenty measures of water, and from a passage in one of the books ascribed to Hippocrates, directing not less than twenty-five parts of water to be added to one part of old Thasian wine, some persons have inferred, that these wines possessed a degree of strength far surpassing any of the liquors with which we are acquainted in modern times, or of which we can well form an idea. But it must be remembered, that the wines in question were not only inspissated, but also highly seasoned with various aromatic ingredients, and had often contracted a repulsive bitterness from age, which rendered them unfit for use till they had been diffused in a large quantity of water, If they had equalled the purest alcohol in strength, such a lowering as that above described must have been more than enough ; but the strong heterogeneous taste which they had acquired would render further dilution advisable ; and, in fact, they may be said to have been used merely for the purpose of giving a flavour to the water.

Whether the Greeks and Romans were in the habit of taking draughts of hot water by itself at their meals, is a

point which, though of no great importance, has been much discussed by grammarians, without ever being satisfactorily determined. When we find the guests at an entertainment, or the interlocutors in an ancient drama, calling for hot and tepid water (θερμον και μετακεραν), it does not follow that this was to be drunk unmixed ; the water so required might be merely for diluting their wines,or for the purposes of ablution. So far indeed was mere hot water from being considered a luxury by the Romans, as some have absurdly imagined to be the fact, that we find Seneca speaking of it as fit only for the sick, and as quite insufferable to those who were accustomed to the delicacies of life.

Such of the citizens as had no regular establishment,were dependant for their daily supply of hot water on the *thermopolia,* or public-houses, in which all kinds of prepared liquors were sold. These places of entertainment,which were frequented in much the same way as our modern coffee-houses, appear to have existed in considerable number, even during the republic, as we meet with frequent allusions to them in the comedies of Plautus. In the reign of Claudius they attracted the attention of the government, having probably become obnoxious by the freedom of conversation which prevailed in them ; for an edict was issued, ordering the suppression of taverns, where people met together to drink, and forbidding the sale of hot water and boiled meats under severe penalties. This mandate, however, like many of the other arbitrary acts of that emperor, would seem to have been little regarded, and was probably soon repealed ; for, in a subsequent age, we find Ampelius, the prefect of Rome, subjecting these places of public resort to new regulations, according to which they were not allowed to be opened before ten o'clock of the forenoon, and no one was to sell hot water to the common people.

the present year's growth ; *trimum*, three years old ; *molle, lene, vetustate edentulum*, mellow ; *asperum* vel *austerum*, harsh ; *merum* vel *meracum*, pure, unmixed ; *meracius*, i. e. *fortius*, strong.[1]

The Romans set down the wine on the second table,[2] with the dessert,[3] and before they began drinking poured out libations to the gods. This, by a decree of the senate, was done also in honour of Augustus, after the battle of Actium.[4]

The wine was brought in to the guests in earthen vases (AM-PHORÆ vel *testæ*) with handles,[5] hence called DIOTÆ,[6] or in big-bellied jugs or· bottles, (AMPUL-LÆ) of glass,[7] leather,[8] or earth,[9] on each of which were affixed labels or small slips of parchment,[10] giving a short description of the quality and age of the wine ; thus, FALERNUM, OPIMI-ANUM ANNORUM CENTUM, Opimian Falernian, an hundred years old. Sometimes different kinds of wine and of fruit were set before the guests according to their different rank;[11] whence VINUM DOMINICUM, the wine drunk by the master of the house, and *cœnare civiliter*, to be on a level with one's guest.[12]

The wine was mixed[13] with water in a large vase or bowl, called CRATER, v. -era, whence it was poured into cups (PO-CULA).[14] Cups were called by different names ; *calices, phialæ, pateræ, canthari, carchesia, ciboria, scyphi, cymbia, scaphia, batiolæ, cululli, amystides*, &c., and made of various materials ; of wood, as beech, *fagina*, sc. *pocula*, of earth, *fictilia*, of glass, VITREA,[15] which when broken used to be exchanged for brimstone matches,[16] of amber, *succina*, of brass,

---

THE above drinking cups of various and peculiar construction have been found in Pompeii. They are usually of clay, but cheap as is the material, it is evident by their good workmanship that they were not made by the lowest artists. The primitive drinking vessel, as mentioned in p. 303, was the horn pierced at the smaller end, from which the liquor flowed in a small stream. Sometimes, however, the hole at the tip was

---

1 Plin. 23. 1. s. 20. xiv. 6. s. 8, &c 9. s. 11, 12. Cic. Nat. D. iii. 31.
2 alteris mensis.
3 cum bellariis.
4 Virg. Æn. 736. viii. 278. 283. G. ii. 101. Dio. li. 19. Hor. Od. iv. 5. 31.
5 ansatæ.
6 Hor. i. 9. 8.
7 vitreæ.
8 coriaceæ.
9 figlinæ, Plin. Ep. iv. 30. Suet. Dom. 21. Mart. vi. 35. 3. xiv. 110.
10 tituli vel pittacia, i.e. schedulæ e membrana excisæ, vel tabellæ.
11 Petr. 34. Juv. v. 34. 79. Plin. Ep. ii. 6. Mart. iii. 82. iv. 86. vi. 11. 49. Suet. Cæs. 48. Spart. Adr. 17.
12 Petr. 31. Juv. v. 112.
13 miscebatur vel temperabatur.
14 Ov. F. v. 522.
15 Virg. Ecl. iii. 37. Mart. i. 38. Juv. ii. 95.
16 sulphurata ramenta, Mart. i. 42. 4. x. 3. Juv. v. 49. ix. 50.

silver, and gold, sometimes beautifully engraved; hence called TOREUMA-TA,[1] or adorned with figures[2] affixed to them, called CRUSTÆ or EMBLE-MATA,[3] which might be put on and taken off at pleasure,[4] or with gems, sometimes taken off the fingers for that purpose, hence called CALICES GEMMATI vel AURUM GEMMATUM.[5]

---

closed, and one or two handles fitted to the side, and then the base formed the mouth, and sometimes the whimsical fancy of the potter fashioned it into the head of a pig, a stag, as represented above, or any other animal.

THE above cut, taken from a picture in one of the rooms of a wine shop, lately excavated at Pompeii, represents a wine-cart, and shows the way of filling the amphoræ. The clumsy transverse yoke by which the horses are fastened to the pole is worth attention. We have also to point out the large skin, occupying the whole of the waggon, and supported by a framework of three hoops. These minutiæ may of course be depended on as copied from the implements in use. The neck of the skin is closed by a ligature, and the wine is drawn off through the leg, which forms a convenient spout. Two amphoræ may be observed. They are pointed at the bottom, so that they might be stuck into the ground, and preserved in an upright position without difficulty. Amphoræ have been found several times thus arranged in the Pompeian cellars, especially in the suburban villa, where they may still be seen standing upright, in their original posture.

THE Romans possessed glass in sufficient plenty to apply it to purposes of ornament, and in the first century even for windows. The raw material appears from Pliny's account to have undergone two fusions; the first converted it into a rough mass, called ammonitrum, which was melted again, and become pure glass. We are also told of a dark coloured glass resembling obsidian, plentiful enough to be cast into solid statues. Pliny mentions having seen images of Augustus cast in this substance. It probably was some coarse kind of glass resembling the ammonitrum, or such as that in which the scoriæ of our iron furnaces abound. Glass was worked either by blowing it with a pipe, as is now practised, by turning in a lathe, by engraving and carving it, or by casting it in a mould. These two glasses of elegant form, appear to have been formed in the latter way. The ancients had certainly acquired great skill in the manufacture as appears both from the accounts which have been preserved by ancient authors,

and by the specimens which still exist; among which we may notice as pre-eminently beautiful, the Portland vase, preserved in the British Museum. A remarkable story is told by Dion Cassius, of a man who, in the time of the emperor Tiberius, brought a glass cup into the imperial presence and dashed it on the ground. To the wonder of the spectators, the vessel bent under the blow without breaking, and the ingenious artist immediately hammered out the bruise, and restored it whole and sound to its original form: in return for which display of his skill, Tiberius, it is said, ordered him to be immediately put to death. The story is a strange one, yet it is confirmed by Pliny, who both mentions the discovery itself, and gives a clue to the motives which may have urged the emperor to a cruelty apparently so unprovoked. He speaks of an artificer who had invented a method of making flexible glass, and adds, that Tiberius banished him lest this new fashion should injure the workers in metal, of whose trade the manufacture of gold, silver, and other drinking-cups, and other furniture for the table, formed an extensive and important branch.

---

1 1 e. vasa sculpta vel cælata, Cic. Ver. iv. 18. ii. 52. Pis. 27.
2 signa vel sigilla.
3 Cic. Ver. iv: 23. Juv. i. 76. Mart: viii. 51: 9.
4 exemptilia, Cic. Ver. 22. 24.
5 Juv: 5. 41. Mart. xiv. 109.

Cups were also made of precious stones, of crystal,[1] of amethyst, and *murra* or porcelain.[2]

Cups were of various forms ; some had handles (ANSÆ vel NASI), usually twisted (TORTILES),[3] hence called CALICES PTERATI.[4] Some had none.

There were slaves, usually beautiful boys,[5] who waited to mix the wine with water, and to serve it up ; for which purpose they used a small goblet, called CYATHUS, to measure it,[6] containing the twelfth part of a *sextarius*, nearly a quart English. Hence the cups were named from the parts of the Roman AS, according to the number of *cyathi* which they contained ; thus, SEXTANS, a cup which contained two *cyathi* ; TRIENS vel *triental*, three ; QUADRANS, four, &c., and those who served with wine were said AD CYATHOS STARE, AD CYATHUM STATUI, or CYATHISSARI.[7]

They also used a less measure, for filling wine and other liquors, called LIGULA or *lingula*, and COCHLEARE, vel -ar, a spoon, the fourth part of a *cyathus*.[8]

The strength of wine was sometimes lessened, by making it pass through a strainer with snow in it, COLUM NIVARIUM, vel SACCUS NIVARIUS. It was also sometimes cooled by pouring snow water upon it.[9]

The Romans used to drink to the health of one another, thus ; BENE MIHI, BENE VOBIS, &c., sometimes in honour of a friend or mistress, and used to take as many cyathi as there were letters in the name,[10] or as they wished years to them ; hence they were said, *ad numerum bibere*. A frequent number was three in honour of the Graces ; or nine, of the Muses. The Greeks drank first in honour of the gods, and then of their friends ; hence GRÆCO MORE BIBERE. They began with small cups, and ended with larger.[11] They used to name the person to whom they handed the cup ; thus, PROPINO TIBI, &c.[12]

A skeleton was sometimes introduced at feasts in the time of drinking, or the representation of one,[13] in imitation of the Egyptians, upon which the master of the feast looking at it used to say, VIVAMUS, DUM LICET ESSE BENE, let us live while it is allowed us to enjoy life; πινε τε και τερπευ, εσσεαι γαρ αποθανων τοιουτος, drink and be merry, for thus shalt thou be after death.[14]

The ancients sometimes crowned their cups with flowers. But *coronare cratera* vel *vina*, i. e. *pocula*, signifies also to fill with wine.[15]

The ancients at their feasts appointed a person to preside by throwing the dice, whom they called ARBITER BIBENDI, *magister* vel *rex convivii*, *modiperator* vel *modimperator* (συμποσιαρχος), *dictator*, *dux*, *strategus*, &c. He directed every thing at pleasure.[16]

When no director of the feast was appointed, they were said *culpo potare magistra*, to drink as much as they pleased (*culpabatur ille qui multum biberet*, excess only was blamed.)[17] Some read *cuppa* vel *cupa*, but improperly ; for *cupa* signifies either a large cask or tun which received the

1 Virg. G. ii. 506. Sen. Ira, iii. 40.
2 pocula murrina, Mart. ix. 60. 13. x. 49. Plin. xxxiii. 1. xxxvii. 2.
3 Virg. Ecl. vi. 17. Juv. v. 47. Ov. Ep. xvi. 252.
4 l. e. alati vel ansati, Plin. xxxvi. 26.
5 pueri eximia facie, Gell. xv. 12.
6 Plaut. Pers. v. 2. 16.

7 Suet. Aug. 77. Mart. viii. 51. 24. ix. 95. xi. 37. Pers. iii. 100. Suet. Jul. 49. Hor. Od. i. 26. 8. Plaut. Men. ii. 2. 29.
8 Mart. v. 20. viii. 33. 23. xiv. 121.
9 Mart. v. 65. xiv. 103, 104. 117. Plin. xix. 22. ' s. 28. xix. 4. s. 19, Sen. Ep. 79.

10 Plaut. Pers. v. 1. 20. Hor. Od. i. 27. 9. Tibul. ii. 1. 31. Mart. i. 72.
11 Ov. F. iii. 531. Hor. Od. iii. 19. 11. Auson. Eidyl. xi. 1. Cic. Ver. i. 26. Ibi Ascon.
12 Cic. Tusc. i. 40. Plaut. Stich. v. 4. 26. 30 Ter. Eun. v. 9. 57. Virg. Æn. i. 728. Mart. i. 69. vi. 44. Juv. v. 127.

13 larva argentea, Petr. 34.
14 Herodot. ii. 78. s. 74. Plut. Conv. Sapient. 6. Petr. 34.
15 Virg. Æn. i. 724. iii. 525. vii. 147. G. ii. 528. Tibul. ii. 5. 98.
16 Hor. Od. i. 4. 18. ii. 7. 25. Cic. Sen. 14. Plaut. Stich. v. 4. 20.
17 Hor. Sat. ii. 123.

must from the wine-press, or it is put for *copa* vel *caupa*, a woman who kept a tavern,[1] or for the tavern itself; whence it was thought mean for a person to be supplied with wine, or from a retailer.[2]

During the intervals of drinking they often played at dice (ALEA), of which there were two kinds, the *tesseræ* and *tali*.[3]

The TESSERÆ had six sides, marked I. II. III. IV. V. VI., like our dice. The TALI had four sides longwise, for the two ends were not regarded. On one side was marked one point (*unio*, an ace), called CANIS; on the opposite side six (SENIO, sice); on the two other sides, three and four (*ternio et quaternio*.) In playing they used three *tesseræ* and four *tali*. They were put into a box made in the form of a small tower, strait-necked, wider below than above, and fluted in ringlets,[4] called FRITILLUS,[5] and being shaken were thrown out upon the gaming-board or table (FORUS.)[6] The highest or most fortunate throw,[7] called VENUS, or JACTUS VENEREUS vel BASILICUS, was, of the tesseræ, three sixes; of the tali, when all of them came out different numbers. The worst or lowest throw,[8] called CANES vel *caniculæ*, vel *vulturii*, was, of the tesseræ, three aces; of the tali, when they were all the same. The other throws were valued from their numbers.[9] When any one of the tali fell on the end,[10] it was said *rectus cadere* vel *assistere*,[11] and the throw was to be repeated. The throw called *Venus* determined the direction of the feast.[12] While throwing the dice, it was usual for a person to express his wishes, to invoke or name a mistress, or the like.[13]

They also played at odds or evens,[14] and at a game called DUODECIM SCRIPTA vel *scriptula*, or *bis sena puncta*,[15] on a square table,[16] divided by twelve lines,[17] on which were placed counters (CALCULI, *latrones*, v. *latrunculi*) of different colours. The counters were moved[18] according to throws[19] of the dice, as with us at gammon. The lines were intersected by a transverse line, called LINEA SACRA, which they did not pass without being forced to it. When the counters had got to the last line, they were said to be *inciti* vel *immoti*, and the player *ad incitas* vel *-a redactus*, reduced to extremity; *unam calcem non posse ciere*, i. e. *unum calculum movere*, not to be able to stir. In this game there was room both for chance and art.[20]

Some exclude the tali or tesseræ from this game, and make it the same with chess among us. Perhaps it was played both ways. But several particulars concerning the private games of the Romans are not ascertained.

All games of chance were called ALEA, and forbidden by the Cornelian, Publician and Titian laws, except in the month of December. These laws, however, were not strictly observed. Old men were particularly fond of such games, as not requiring bodily exertion.[21] The character of gamesters (ALEATORES vel *aleones*) was held infamous.[22]

---

1 quæ cauponam, vel tabernam exerceret,Suet. Ner. 27.
2 de propola vel propala, Cic. Pis. 27. Suet. Claud. 40.
3 Plaut. Curc. ii. 3. 75. Cic. Sen. 16.
4 intus gradus excisos habens.
5 pyrgus, turris, turricula, phimus, orca, &c.
6 alveus, vel tabula lusoria aut aleatoria.
7 jactus, bolus vel manus.
8 jactus pessimus vel damnosus.
9 Cic. Div. i. 13. ii. 21. 59. Suet. Aug. 71. Ov. Art. Am. ii. 203. Trist. ii. 474. Prop. iv. 9. 20. Plaut. Asin. v. 2. 55. Hor. Sat. ii. 7. 17. Pers. Sat. iii. 49. Mart. xiv. 14, &c.
10 in caput.
11 Cic. Fin. iii. 16.
12 archiposia, in compotatione principatus,ma-
gisterium, Cic. Sen. 14. vel regnum vini, Hor. Od. i. 4. 18.
13 Plaut. Asin. v. 2. 55. iv. 1. 35. Capt. i. 1. 5. Curc. ii. 3. 78.
14 par impar ludebant, Suet. Aug. 71.
15 Cic. Or. i. 50. Non. Marc. ii. 781. Quinct. xi. 2. Mart. xiv. 17.
16 tabula vel alveus.
17 lineæ vel scripta.
18 promovebantur.
19 boli vel jactus.
20 Plaut. Pœn. iv. 2. 86. Trin. ii. 4. 136. Ter. Ad. iv. 7. 21. Ov. Art. Am. ii. 203. iii. 363. Auson. Prof. i. 25. Mart. vii. 71. xiv. 20.
21 Hor. Od. iii. 24. 58. Mart. iv. 14. 7. v. 85. xiv. 1. Sic. Sen. 16. Suet. Aug. 71. Juv. xiv. 4.
22 Cic. Cat. ii. 10. Phil. ii. 27.

Augustus used to introduce at entertainments a kind of diversion, similar to what we call a lottery ; by selling tickets (*sortes*), or sealed tablets, apparently equivalent, at an equal price ; which, when opened or unsealed, entitled the purchasers to things of very unequal value ;[1] as, for instance, one to 100 gold pieces, another to a pick-tooth,[2] a third to a purple robe, &c.; in like manner pictures, with the wrong side turned to the company,[3] so that, for the same price, one received the picture of an Apelles, of a Zeuxis, or a Parrhasius, and another, the first essay of a learner. Heliogabalus used to do the same.[4]

There was a game of chance (which is still common in Italy, chiefly, however, among the vulgar, called the game of *morra*), played between two persons, by suddenly raising or compressing the fingers, and, at the same instant, guessing each at the number of the other ; when doing thus, they were said MICARE DIGITIS. As the number of fingers stretched out could not be known in the dark, unless those who played had implicit confidence in one another ; hence, in praising the virtue and fidelity of a man, he was said to be DIGNUS QUICUM IN TENEBRIS MICES, a person with whom you may safely play at even and odd in the dark.[5]

The Romans ended their repasts in the same manner in which they began them, with libations and prayers. The guests drank to the health of their host, and, under the Cæsars, to that of the emperors. When about to go away, they sometimes demanded a parting cup in honour of Mercury, that he might grant them a sound sleep.[6]

The master of the house[7] used to give the guests certain presents at their departure, called *apophoreta*, or XENIA, which were sometimes sent to them. XENIUM is also put for a present sent from the provinces to an advocate at Rome, or given to the governor of a province.[8]

The presents given to guests being of different kinds, were sometimes distributed by lot, or by some ingenious contrivance.[9]

III. ROMAN RITES OF MARRIAGE.

A LEGAL marriage[10] among the Romans was made in three different ways, called *usus, confarreatio*, and *coemptio*.

1. Usus, usage or prescription, was when a woman, with the consent of her parents or guardians, lived with a man for a whole year,[11] without being absent three nights, and thus became his lawful wife, or property, by prescription.[12] If absent for three nights,[13] she was said *esse usurpata*, or *isse usurpatum*, sc. *suum jus*, to have interrupted the prescription, and thus prevented a marriage ; *usurpatio est enim usucapionis interruptio*.[14]

2. CONFARREATIO, was when a man and woman were joined in marriage by the pontifex maximus, or *flamen dialis*, in presence of at least ten witnesses, by a set form of words, and by tasting a cake made of salt, water and flour, called FAR, or PANIS FARREUS vel *farreum libum ;* which was offered with a sheep in sacrifice to the gods.[15]

This was the most solemn form of marriage, and could only be dissolved

---

1 res inæqualissimæ.
2 dentiscalpium.
3 aversas tabularum picturas in convivio venditare solebat.
4 Lamp. in Vita ejus, 21.
Suet. Aug. 75.
5 Cic. Div. ii. 41. Off. iii. 19. 23. Fin. ii. 16. s. 52.

Suet. Aug. 13.
6 Ov. F. ii. 635. Petr. 60. Mart. Delph. j. 72.
7 herus, dominus, parochus, cœnæ magister, convivator, Hor. Sat. ii. 6. 35. Mart. xii. 48. Gell. xiii. 11.
8 Suet. Aug. 75. Gal. 55.

Vesp. 19. Mart. xiii. 3. xiv. 1. Petr. 60. Plin. Ep. v. 14. vi. 31. Vitr. vi. 10. Digest.
9 Mart. xiv. 1. 5—40. 144. 170. Petr. 41.
10 justum matrimonium.
11 matrimonii causa.
12 usu capta fuit, Gell.

iii. 2.
13 trinoctium.
14 Gell. iii. 2. D. 41. 3. 2. see p. 39.
15 Diony. ii. 25. Serv. Virg. G. i. 31. Æn. iv. 104. Plin. xviii. 2.

by another kind of sacrifice, called DIFFARREATIO.[1] By it a woman was said to come into the possession or power of her husband by the sacred laws.[2] She thus became partner of all his substance and sacred rites, those of the *penates*, as well as of the *lares*.[3] If he died intestate, and without children, she inherited his whole fortune as a daughter. If he left children, she had an equal share with them. If she committed any fault, the husband judged of it in company with her relations, and punished her at pleasure. The punishment of women publicly condemned, was sometimes also left to their relations.[4]

The children of this kind of marriage were called PATRIMI et MATRIMI, often employed for particular purposes in sacred solemnities. Certain priests were chosen only from among them; as the flamen of Jupiter,[5] and the Vestal virgins. According to Festus, those were so called whose parents were both alive. If only the father was alive, *patrimi*, vel -*es*; if only the mother, *matrimi*, vel -*es*. Hence Minerva is called PATRIMA VIRGO, because she had no mother; and a man who had children while his own father was alive, PATER PATRIMUS.[6]

This ceremony of marriage in later times fell much into disuse. Hence Cicero mentions only two kinds of marriage, USUS and COEMPTIO.[7]

3. COEMPTIO was a kind of mutual purchase,[8] when a man and woman were married, by delivering to one another a small piece of money, and repeating certain words. The man asked the woman, if she was willing to be the mistress of his family, AN SIBI MATER FAMILIÆ ESSE VELLET? She answered that she was, SE VELLE. In the same manner, the woman asked the man, and he made a similar answer.[9]

The effects of this rite were the same as the former. The woman was to the husband in the place of a daughter, and he to her as a father. She assumed his name, together with her own; as Antonia Drusi, Domitia Bibuli, &c. She resigned to him all her goods,[10] and acknowledged him as her lord and master.[11] The goods which a woman brought to her husband, besides her portion, were called PARAPHERNA, -*orum* or *bona paraphernalia*. In the first days of the republic, dowries were very small; that given by the senate to the daughter of Scipio was only 11,000 *asses* of brass, £35 : 10 : 5; and one Megullia was surnamed DOTATA, or the great fortune, because she had 50,000 *asses*, i. e. £161 : 7 : 6.[12] But afterwards, upon the increase of wealth, the marriage-portions of women became greater, *decies centena*, sc. *sestertia*, £8072 : 18 : 4, the usual portion of a lady of senatorian rank. Some had *ducenties*, £161,458 : 6 : 8.[13]

Sometimes the wife reserved to herself[14] a part of the dowry; hence called DOS RECEPTICIA, and a slave, who was not subject to the power of her husband, SERVUS RECEPTICIUS, or DOTALIS.[15]

Some think that *coemptio* was used as an accessory rite to *confarreatio*, and retained when the primary rite was dropped.[16]

The rite of purchase in marriage was not peculiar to the Romans; but prevailed also among other nations; as among the Hebrews, Thracians,

---

1 Festus.
2 κατα νομους ιερους αρδη συνελθειν, in manum, i. e. potestatem viri convenire.
3 see p. 188, 189.
4 Diony. ii. 25. Plin. xiv. 13. Suet. Tib. 35. Tac. An. xiii. 32. Liv. xxxix. 18. Val. Max. vi. 3. 5.

5 Serv. Virg. G. i. 31. Liv. xxxvii. 3. Cic. Resp. Har. 11. Tac. Hist. iv. 43. An. iv. 16.
6 Gell. i. 12. Catul. i. 9. Festus.
7 Flac. 34. Tac. An. iv. 16.
8 emptio, venditio.

9 Cic. Or. i. 57. Booth. Cic. Topic. 3.
10 Serv. Virg. G. i. 31. Ter. Andr. i. 5. 61. Cic. Top. iv.
11 dominus, Virg. Æn. iv. 103. 214.
12 Val. Max. iv. 4. 10.
13 Mart. ii. 65. 5. v. 38. 34. xi. 24. 3. Juv. vi.

136. x. 355.
14 recepit, Cic. Orat. ii.
55. Topic. 26. vel excepit, i. e. in usum suum reservavit.
15 Gell. xvii. 6. Plaut. Asin. l. 72.
16 Cic. Flac. 34.

Greeks, Germans, Cantabri in Spain, and in the days of Homer,[1] to which Virgil alludes, G. i. 13.

Some say that a yoke[2] used anciently to be put on a man and woman about to be married ; whence they were called CONJUGES. But others think this expression merely metaphorical.[3]

A matrimonial union between slaves was called CONTUBERNIUM ; the slaves themselves CONTUBERNALES,[4] or when a free man lived with a woman not married (CONCUBINATUS,) in which case the woman was called CONCUBINA, PELLACA,[5] or PELLEX ;[6] thus, PELLEX REGINÆ, FILIÆ, SORORIS, JOVIS, i. e. IO.[7]

Married women were called MATRONÆ, or *matres familias*,[8] opposed to *meretrices, prostitutæ, scorta*, &c.

There could be no just or legal marriage[9] unless between Roman citizens,[10] without a particular permission for that purpose, obtained first from the people or senate, and afterwards from the emperors.[11] Anciently, a Roman citizen was not allowed even to marry a freed-woman ; hence Antony is reproached by Cicero for having married Fulvia, the daughter of a freed-man, as he afterwards was detested at Rome for marrying Cleopatra, a foreigner, before he divorced Octavia ; but this was not esteemed a legal marriage.[12]

By the LEX PAPIA POPPÆA, a greater freedom was allowed. Only senators and their sons and grandsons were forbidden to marry a freed-woman, an actress, or the daughter of an actor.[13] But it was not till Caracalla had granted the right of citizenship to the inhabitants of the whole empire, that Romans were permitted freely to intermarry with foreigners.

The Romans sometimes prohibited intermarriages between neighbouring districts of the same country, and what is still more surprising, the states of Italy were not allowed to speak the Latin language in public, nor their criers to use it in auctions, without permission.[14]

The children of a Roman citizen, whether man or woman, and a foreigner, were accounted spurious, and their condition little better than that of slaves. They were called HYBRIDÆ or *ibridæ*, vel -*des*,[15] the general name of animals of a mixed breed, or produced by animals of a different species, mongrels ;[16] as a mule from a horse and an ass, a dog from a hound and a cur ;[17] hence applied to those sprung from parents of different nations,[18] and to words compounded from different languages.

The children of a lawful marriage were called LEGITIMI ; all others, ILLEGITIMI. Of the latter there were four kinds : NATURALES, *ex concubina ;* SPURII, *ex meretrice* vel *scorto et incerto patre ;* ADULTERINI et INCESTUOSI. There were certain degrees of consanguinity, within which marriage was prohibited, as between a brother and sister, an uncle and niece, &c. Such connection was called INCESTUS, -ûs, vel -*um*, or with a Vestal virgin.[19]

1 Gen. xxix. 18. 1. Sam. xviii. 25. Xen. Anab. vii. Herodot. Ter, init. Eurip. Med. 332. Tac. Mor. G. 18, &c. Strab. iii. 165. Hom. Odys. viii. 317.
2 jugum.
3 Serv. Virg. Æn. iv. 16. Hor. Od. ii. 5. 1. iii. 8. 1. 6. Plaut. Curc. i. 1. 50,
4 see p 34.
5 Suet. Vesp. 3. Cic. Or. i. 40. Suet. Vesp. 21.
6 quæ proprie fuit ejus,

qui uxorem haberet, Fest. Plaut. Rud. v. 4. 3. Gell. iv. 3.
7 Suet. Cæs. 49. Cic. Cluent. 70. Juv. ii. 57. Ov. Met. vi. 537. Ep. 9. 132. xiv. 95. et alibi passim.
8 Gell. xviii. 6.
9 nuptiæ, justum matrimonium, connubium, conjugium, vel consortium, i. e. eadem fortuna aut conditio, for better, for worse.

10 non erat cum externo connubium, Sen. Ben. iv. 35.
11 Liv. xxxviii. 36. Ulpi. Fragm. v. 4. conjuge barbara turpis maritus vixit, he lived as a shameful husband with his barbarian wife,Hor. Od. iii. 5, 5.
12 Liv. xxxix. 19. Plin. ii. 2. iii. 6. Plut. Anto.
13 Dio. liv. 16.
14 Liv. viii. 14. ix. 43. xl. 42. xlv. 29.

15 Hor. Sat. i. 7. 2. Suet. Aug. 19. Liv. xliii. 3.
16 animalia ambigena vel bigenera, musimones, Umbri, &c.
17 canis ex venatico et gregario, Plin. viii. 61.
18 Hirt. Bell. Afr. 19. Mart. vi. 39. viii. 22.
19 Plut. Q. Rom. 101. Suet. Cl. 26. Ner. 5. Tac. An. xli. 4 — 6. Suet. Dom. 8.

These degrees were more or less extended or contracted at different times.[1]

Polygamy, or a plurality of wives, was forbidden among the Romans.[2]

The age of puberty or marriage was from fourteen for men, and twelve for girls.[3]

A custom prevailed of espousing infants to avoid the penalties of the law against bachelors : but Augustus ordained, that no nuptial engagement should be valid, which was made more than two years before the celebration of the marriage, that is, below ten. This, however, was not always observed.[4]

No young man or woman was allowed to marry without the consent of their parents or guardians. Hence a father was said *spondere*, vel *despondere filiam* aut *filium*, adding these words, QUÆ RES RECTE VERTAT: OF DII BENE VERTANT.[5]

. There was a meeting of friends, usually at the house of the woman's father, or nearest relation, to settle the articles of the marriage contract, which was written on tables,[6] and sealed. This contract was called SPONSALIA, -*orum* vel -*ium*, espousals ; the man who was betrothed or affianced, SPONSUS, and the woman SPONSA, or FACTA, as before SPERATA, and SPERATUS.[7] The contract was made in the form of a stipulation, AN SPONDES ? SPONDEO. Then likewise the dowry was promised, to be paid down on the marriage day,[8] or afterwards usually at three separate payments.[9] On this occasion there was commonly a feast ; and the man gave the woman a ring,[10] by way of pledge, which she put on her left hand, on the finger next the least ; because it was believed, a nerve reached from thence to the heart.[11]

Then also a day was fixed for the marriage.[12] Certain days were reckoned unfortunate ; as the Kalends, Nones, and Ides, and the days which followed them, paticularly the whole month of May,[13] and those days which were called ATRI, marked in the kalendar with black ; also certain festivals, as that of the *salii, parentalia*, &c. But widows might marry on those days.[14]

The most fortunate time was the middle of the month of June.[15]

If after the espousals either of the parties wished to retract,[16] which they expressed thus, CONDITIONE TUA NON UTOR, it was called REPUDIUM (hence *repudiatus repetor*, after being rejected, I am sought back ;)[17] and when a man or woman, after signing the contract, sent notice that they wished to break off the match, they were said *repudium ei* vel *amicis ejus mittere, remittere*, vel *renunciare*. But *repudiare* also signifies to divorce either a wife or a husband.[18]

On the wedding-day, the bride was dressed in a long white robe bordered with a purple fringe, or embroidered ribands,[19] thought to be the same with TUNICA RECTA, bound with a girdle[20] made of wool,[21] tied in a

---

1 Plut. Q. Rom. 6. Tac. An. xii. 6. 7. Liv. i. 42. 46. xlii. 34. Suet. Aug. 63. Claud. 26.
2 Suet. Jul. 52. Cic. Or. i. 40.
3 Festus.
4 Dio. liv. 16. lvi. 7. Suet. Aug. 34. l. 17. Digest. xxiii. tit. i. de Sponsal.
5 Cic. Flac. 35. Att. i. 3. Ter. And. l. 1. 75. Tac. Agric. 9. Plaut. Aul. ii. 2, 3, 4. 41. 49.

6 legitimæ tabellæ.
7 Juv. ii. 119. vi. 25. 199. x. 336. Gell. iv. 4. Suet. Aug. 53. Cl. 12. Plaut. Pœn. v. 3. 38. Trin. ii. 4. 99. Amp. ii. 2. 44. Ov. Ep. xi. prope finem.
8 Plaut. Trin. v. 2. 34. Ter. And. v. 4. 47. Suet. Cl. 26. Juv. x. 335.
9 tribus pensionibus, Cic. Att. xi. 4. 23. ult.

10 annulus pronubus.
11 Juv. vi. 27. Macrob. Sat. vii. 15.
12 Ter. And. l. 1. 75.
13 mense malum Majo nubere vulgus alt, Ov. F. v. 490. Plaut. Q. Rom. 85.
14 Macr. Sat. 1. 15. Plut. Q. Rom. 103.
15 Ov. F. vi. 221.
16 sponsalia dissolvere, infirmare, vel infringere.

17 Ter. And. i. 5. 15.
18 Ter. Phor. iv. 3. 72. v. 6. 35. Plaut. Aul. iv. 10. 69. Suet. Cæs. i. Quinct. vii. 8. 2.
19 segmenta et longi habitus, Juv. ii. 124.
20 Plin. viii. 48. Luc. ii. 362.
21 zona vel cingulum laneum.

knot, called *nodus Herculeus*, which the husband untied.[1] Her face was covered (NUBEBATUR) with a red or flame-coloured veil,[2] to denote her modesty ;[3] hence NUBERE, sc. *se viro*, to marry a husband ; *dare* vel *collocare filiam nuptum* v. *nuptui*, i. e. *in matrimonium dare*, to marry a daughter or dispose of her in marriage. Her hair was divided into six locks with the point of a spear, and crowned with flowers.[4] Her shoes were of the same colour with her veil.[5]

No marriage was celebrated without consulting the auspices,[6] and offering sacrifices to the gods, especially to Juno, the goddess of marriage. Anciently a hog was sacrificed. The gall of the victim was always taken out and thrown away, to signify the removal of all bitterness from marriage.[7] The marriage-ceremony was performed at the house of the bride's father, or nearest relation. In the evening, the bride was conducted[8] to her husband's house. She was taken apparently by force[9] from the arms of her mother or nearest relation, in memory of the violence used to the Sabine women. Three boys, whose parents were alive, attended her ; two of them, supporting her by the arm, and the third bearing a flambeau of pine or thorn before.[10] There were five other torches carried before her, called FACES NUPTIALES MARITÆ LEGITIMÆ. Hence TÆDA is put for marriage.[11]

Maid-servants followed with a distaff, a spindle, and wool,[12] intimating that she was to labour at spinning, as the Roman matrons did of old, and some of the most illustrious in later times. Augustus is said to have seldom worn any thing but the manufacture of his wife, sister, daughter, and nieces, at least for his domestic robes.[13]

A boy named CAMILLUS carried, in a covered vase called CUMERUM vel -*a*, the bride's utensils (NUBENTIS UTENSILIA,) and playthings for children (CREPUNDIA.)[14]

A great number of relations and friends attended the nuptial procession (*pompam nuptialem ducebant*,) which was called OFFICIUM ;[15] hence DUCERE *uxorem*, sc. *domum*, to marry a wife. The boys repeated jests and railleries[16] as she passed along.[17]

The door and door-posts of the bridegroom's house were adorned with leaves and flowers, and the rooms with tapestry.[18]

When the bride came thither, being asked who she was, she answered, UBI TU CAIUS, IBI EGO CAIA, i. e. *ubi tu dominus et pater familias, ibi ego domina et mater familias*. A new married woman was called CAIA, from Caia Cæcilia, or Tanaquil, the wife of Tarquinius Priscus, who is said to have been an excellent spinster[19] and housewife. Her distaff and spindle were kept in the temple of Sangus or Hercules.[20]

The bride bound the door-posts of her husband with woollen fillets,[21] and anointed[22] them with the fat of swine or wolves, to avert fascination or enchantments ; whence she was called UXOR, *quasi* UNXOR.[23]

1 solvebat, Ov. Ep. ii. 116. Fest.
2 luteum flammeum vel -us.
3 Luc. ii. 361. Juv. ii. 124. vi. 224. Schol. loc. x. 334. Mart. xii. 42. Plin. xii. 8.
4 Plut. Rom. Quæst. 86. vel 87. Ov. F. ii. 560. Catul. lix. 6.
5 lutei soccl, Catul. lix. 10. Plaut. Cas. prol. 89. Cic. Cluent. 5. Divin. i. 16. Liv. xlii. 12. Suet.

Cl. 26. Tac. An. xi. 27. Val. Max. ix. 1.
6 Juv. x. 336. Cic. Div. i. 16. Cluent. 5. 16. Plaut. Cas. prol. 86. Suet. Claud. 26. Tac. An. xi. 27. Luc. ii. 371.
7 Virg. Æn. iv. 59. Var. R. R. ii. 3. Plut. præcep. conjug.
8 ducebatur vel deducebatur.
9 abripiebatur.
10 tæda pinea vel spinea, Fest. Catul. lix.

17. Plin. xvi. 18. Prop. iv. 12. 46.
11 Cic. Cluent. 6. Ov. Ep. xi. 101. Met. iv. 60. Luc. ii. 356. Plut. Q. Rom. 2. Virg. Æn. iv. 18.
12 colus compta, et fusus cum stamine.
13 Plin. viii. 48. s. 47. Ov. F. ii. 741. Liv. i. 57. Suet. Aug. 73.
14 Fest. Plaut. Cist. iii. 1. 5. Rud. iv. 4. 110.
15 Juv. ii. 132. vi. 202.

Suet. Cal. 25. Claud.26. Ner. 28.
16 sales et convicia.
17 Luc. ii. 369. Festus, Catull. lix. 127.
18 Juv. vii. 51. 79. 226.
19 lanifica.
20 Cic. Mur. 12. Quinc. i. 7. Fest. Plin. viii. 48. s. 74.
21 Plin. xxix. 2. s. 9. Luc. ii. 355. Serv. Virg. Æn. iv. 458.
22 ungebat.
23 Plin. xxviii. 9. s. 37.

She was lifted over the threshold, or gently stepped over it. It was thought ominous to touch it with her feet, because the threshold was sacred to Vesta, the goddess of virgins.[1]

Upon her entry, the keys of the house were delivered to her, to denote her being entrusted with the management of the family. A sheep's skin was spread below her ; intimating that she was to work at the spinning of wool. Both she and her husband touched fire and water, because all things were supposed to be produced from these two elements, with the water they bathed their feet.[2]

The husband on this occasion gave a feast (CŒNA NUPTIALIS) to his relations and friends, to those of the bride and her attendants.[3]

Musicians attended, who sang the nuptial song,[4] HYMENÆUS vel -um, vel THALASSIO. They often repeated IO HYMEN HYMENÆE, and THALASSIO,[5] from Hymen the god of marriage among the Greeks, and Thalassus among the Romans, or from one Talassius, who lived in great happiness with his wife, as if to wish the new-married couple the like felicity, or from ταλα-σια, lanificium. These words used also to be resounded by the attendants of the bride on the way to her husband's house. Hence hymenæos canere, to sing the nuptial song, vel hymenæa, sc. carmina, hymenæi inconcessi, forbidden nuptials, vetiti.[6]

After supper the bride was conducted to her bed-chamber[7] by matrons who had been married only to one husband, called pronubæ,[8] and laid[9] in the nuptial couch,[10] which was magnificently adorned,[11] and placed in the hall[12] opposite[13] to the door, and covered with flowers, sometimes in the garden. If it had ever been used for that purpose before, the place of it was changed. There were images of certain divinities around, SUBIGUS, PERTUNDA, &c.[14] Nuptial songs were sung by young women before the door till midnight, hence called EPITHALAMIA. The husband scattered nuts among the boys, intimating that he dropped boyish amusements, and thenceforth was to act as a man. Hence nuces relinquere, to leave trifles and mind serious business,[15] or from boys playing with nuts in the time of the Saturnalia, which at other times was forbidden. Young women, when they married, consecrated their playthings, and dolls or babies (PUPÆ) to Venus.[16] The guests were dismissed with small presents.[17]

Next day another entertainment was given by the husband, called REPOTIA, -orum, when presents were sent to the bride by her friends and relations ; and she began to act as mistress of the family, by performing sacred rites.[18]

A woman after marriage retained her former name ; as Julia, Tullia, Octavia, Paulla, Valeria, &c., joined to that of her husband ; as CATONIS MARCIA,[19] Julia Pompeii, Terentia Ciceronis, Livia Augusti, &c.

Divorce,[20] or a right to dissolve the marriage, was, by the law of Romulus, permitted to the husband, but not to the wife ; as by the Jewish law,[21]

---

1 Luc. ii. 355. Plut. Rom.
Quæst. Rom. 29. Plaut.
Cas. iv. 4. 1. Serv. Virg.
Ecl. viii. 29.
2 Fest. Plut. Quæst.
Rom. 31. 1. Var. L. L.
iv. 10. Ov. F. iv. 792.
Art. Am. ii. 598. Serv.
Virg. Æn. iv. 167.
3 Plaut. Curc. v. 1. 62.
Suet. Cal. 25. Juv. vi.
201.
4 epithalamium.
5 Mart. iii. 93. 25. Catul.

61. Ter. Adel. v. 7. 7.
Stat. Sylv. ii. 7. 67.
Plaut. Cas. iv. 3. Mart.
i. 36. 6.
6 Mart. xiii. 42. 5. Fest.
Liv. i. 9. Plut. Pomp.
Rom. et Rom. Quæst.
31. Ov. Ep. xii. 143. xiv.
37. Art. Am. i. 563. Virg.
Æn. i. 651. vi. 623. vii.
398.
7 in thalamum.
8 Festus.
9 collocabatur.

10 lectus genialis.
11 Catul. lix. 188.
12 in atrio vel aula, Hor.
Ep. i. 1. 87.
13 adversus.
14 Cic. Cluent. 5. Catul.
lix. 192. Donat. Ter.
Eun. iii. 5. 45. Juv. x.
334. Tac. An. xv. 37.
Prop. iv. 11. 81. 12. 85.
9. 53. Gell. xvi. 9.
Arnob. iv. August. Civ.
Dei. vi. 9.
15 Ov. F. iii. 675. 695.

Plin. xv. 22. Serv. Ecl.
viii. 30. Catul. lix. 131.
Pers. i. 10.
16 Suet. Aug. 83. Mart.
v. 85. xiv. 1. 12. 18.
Pers. ii. 70.
17 apophoreta, Mart. xiv.
1. Juv. vi. 202.
18 Fest. Hor. Sat. ii. 2.
60. Macr. Sat. i. 15.
19 Luc. ii. 344.
20 divortium.
21 Deut. xxiv. 1.

not however without a just cause.[1] A groundless or unjust divorce was punished with the loss of effects ; of which one half fell to the wife, and the other was consecrated to Ceres.

A man might divorce his wife if she had violated the conjugal faith, used poison to destroy his offspring, or brought upon him supposititious children ; if she had counterfeited his private keys, or even drunk wine without his knowledge. In these cases, the husband judged together with his wife's relations. This law is supposed to have been copied into the Twelve Tables.[2]

Although the laws allowed husbands the liberty of divorce, there was no instance of its being exercised for about 520 years. Sp. Carvilius Ruga was the first who divorced his wife, although fond of her, because she had no children, on account of the oath he had been forced to take by the censors, in common with the other citizens, *uxorem se liberûm quærendorum gratia habiturum*, that he would marry to have children.[3]

Afterwards divorces became very frequent ; not only for important reasons, but often on the most frivolous pretexts.[4] Cæsar, when he divorced Pompeia, the niece of Sylla, because Clodius had got admission to his house in the garb of a music-girl, at the celebration of the sacred rites of the Bona Dea, declared, that he did not believe any thing that was said against her, but that he could not live with a wife who had once been suspected.[5]

If a wife was guilty of infidelity she forfeited her dowry ;[6] but if the divorce was made without any fault of hers, the dowry was restored to her. When the separation was voluntary on both sides,[7] she sometimes also retained the nuptial presents of her husband.[8]

In the later ages of the republic, the same liberty of divorce was exercised by the women as by the men. Some think that right was granted to them by the law of the Twelve Tables, in imitation of the Athenians.[9] This, however, seems not to have been the case ; for it appears they did not enjoy it even in the time of Plautus ; only if a man was absent for a certain time, his wife seems to have been at liberty to marry another.[10] Afterwards, some women deserted their husbands so frequently, and with so little shame, that Seneca says, they reckoned their years not from the number of consuls, but of husbands.[11] This desertion very frequently happened without any just cause. But a freed-woman, if married to her patron, was not permitted to divorce him.[12]

Augustus is said to have restricted this license of BONA GRATIA divorces, as they were called,[13] and likewise Domitian. They still, however, prevailed : although the women who made them were by no means respectable.[14]

The man was said ἀποπεμπειν, *dimittere uxorem;* and the woman ἀπολειπειν, *relinquere* vel *deserere virum;* both, *facere divortium cum uxore* vel *viro, a viro* vel *ab uxore.*[15]

1 Plut. Rom. Festus in Sonticum.
2 Gell. x. 23. Plin. xiv. 12. Diony. ii. 25. Cic. Phil. ii. 28.
3 Gell. iv. 3. Val. Max. ii. 1. 4. Diony. ii. 25. Plut. Rom. et Rom. Quæst. 13.
4 Suet. Aug. 62. Claud. 26. Ner. 35. Val. Max.

vi. 3. 11. 12. Dio. xlvi. 18. Plut. L. Paullo Ciceron. Juv. vi. 147.
5 Cic. Sext. 34. Att. i. 12. Dio. xxxvii. 45. Suet. Cæs. 6.
6 Val. Max. viii. 2, 3.
7 cum bona gratia a se invicem discedebant.
8 Ov. Rem. Am. 669.
9 Plut. in Alcibiade.

10 Merc. iv. 6. Plaut. Stich. i. l. 29.
11 Benef. iii. 16. so Juv. fiunt octo mariti quinque per autumnos, eight husbands are made in five autumns, vi. 228. Mart. vi. 7. Cic. Fam. viii. 7.
12 ei repudium mittere.
13 Suet. Aug. 34.

14 quæ nubit toties, non nubit · adultera lege est, she who marries so often, does not marry ; she is adulteress by law, Mart. vi. 7.
15 Cic. Fam. viii. 7. D. 24. 3. 34.

A divorce, anciently, was made with different ceremonies, according to the manner in which the marriage had been celebrated.

A marriage contracted by *confarreatio*, was dissolved by a sacrifice called DIFFARREATIO;[1] which was still in use in the time of Plutarch, when a separation[2] took place betwixt the flamen of Jupiter and his wife.[3]

A marriage contracted by *coemptio* was dissolved by a kind of release called REMANCIPATIO. In this manner Cato is supposed to have voluntarily given away his wife Marcia to Hortensius, and Tiberius Nero his wife Livia to Augustus, even when big with child.[4]

In later times, a divorce was made with fewer ceremonies. In presence of seven witnesses, the marriage-contract was torn,[5] the keys were taken from the wife,[6] then certain words were pronounced by a freed-man, or by the husband himself, RES TUAS TIBI HABE vel -ETO ; TUAS RES TIBI AGITO ; EXI, EXI OCYUS ; VADE FORAS, I FORAS, MULIER ; CEDE DO MO. Hence *exigere foras* vel *ejicere*, to divorce.[7]

If the husband was absent, he sent his wife a bill of divorce,[8] on which similar words were inscribed. This was called *matrimonii* RENUNCIATIO.

If the divorce was made without the fault of the wife, her whole portion was restored to her; sometimes all at once, but usually by three different payments.[9]

There was sometimes an action (ACTIO MALÆ TRACTATIONIS,) to determine by whose fault the divorce was made. When the divorce was made by the wife, she said VALEAS, TIBI HABEAS TUAS RES; REDDAS MEAS; farewell, keep your own things, and let me have mine.[10]

Divorces were recorded in the public registers,[11] as were marriages, births, and funerals.[12]

Widows were obliged to wear mourning for their husbands at least ten months, and if they married within that time, they were held infamous;[13] but men were under no such restriction.

M. Antoninus, the philosopher, after the death of his wife Faustina, lived with a concubine,[14] that he might not bring in a step-mother on his children.[15]

Second marriages in women were not esteemed honourable, and those who had been married but to one husband, or who remained in widowhood, were held in particular respect. Hence UNIVIRA is often found in ancient inscriptions, as an epithet of honour. So, UNI NUPTA.[16] Such as married a second time were not allowed to officiate at the annual sacred rites of Female Fortune.[17] Among the Germans second marriages were prohibited by law.[18]

IV. ROMAN FUNERALS.

THE Romans paid the greatest attention to funeral rites, because they believed that the souls of the unburied were not admitted into the abodes

1 Festus.
2 discidium.
3 flaminica, Q. Rom. 50.
4 Plut. Cat. Tac. An. v. 1. Dio. xlviii. 44. Vel. ii. 94.
5 tabulæ nuptiales vel dotales frangebantur, Tac. An. xi. 30. Juv. ix. 75.
6 claves adimebantur,

Cic. Phil. ii. 28.
7 Plaut Casin. ii. 2. 36. Amp. iii. 2. 47. Cic. Or. i. 40. Phil. ii. 28. Ov. 145. Mart. x. 42. xi. 105. 1, 2. 9. D. Div.
8 nuncium remittebat, Cic. Att. i. 10.
9 Cic. Att. xi. 4. 23. 25.
10 Cic. Top. 4. Quin.

vii. 3. Declam. viii. 18. 383. Plaut. Am. iii. 2. 47.
11 acta, Cic. Fam. viii. 7. Sen. Ben.
12 Juv. ii. 136. ix. 84. Suet. Ner. 39.
13 Sen. Ep. 63. L. 2. C. de secund. Nupt.
14 ne tot liberis superduceret novercam.

15 Capit. in Vita ejus, fin.
16 Prop. iv. ult.
17 fortuna muliebris, Diony. viii. 56. Val. Max. 1. 8. 4. Serv.Virg. Æn. iv. 19. Festus in Pudicitiæ signum.
18 Tac. Mor. Germ. 19.

of the dead, or, at least, wandered a hundred years along the river Styx, before they were allowed to cross it ; for which reason, if the bodies of their friends could not be found, they erected to them an empty tomb, (TUMULUS INANIS, κεvoταφιov, cenotaphium,) at which they performed the usual solemnities ; and if they happened to see a dead body, they always threw some earth upon it, and whoever neglected to do so, was obliged to expiate his crime by sacrificing a hog to Ceres ;[1] hence no kind of death was so much dreaded as shipwreck ; hence also *rite condere manes*, to bury in due form ; *condere animam sepulchro*, to give the soul repose in the tomb ; and to want the due rites was esteemed the greatest misfortune.[2]

When persons were at the point of death, their nearest relations present endeavoured to catch their last breath with their mouth,[3] for they believed that the soul or living principle (ANIMA,) then went out at the mouth. Hence the soul of an old person[4] was said *in primis labris esse*, or *in ore primo teneri;* so ANIMAM *agere*, to be in the agony of death.[5] *Animam dare, efflare, exhalare, exspirare, effundere*, &c., to die.

They now also pulled off their rings, which seem to have been put on again before they were placed on the funeral pile.[6]

The nearest relation closed the eyes and mouth of the deceased, proba- bly to make them appear less ghastly. The eyes were afterwards opened on the funeral pile.[7] When the eyes were closed, they called[8] upon the deceased by name several times at intervals, repeating AVE or VALE, whence *corpora nondum conclamata*, just expiring ;[9] and those who had given up their friends for lost, or supposed them dead, were said *eos conclamavisse ;* so when a thing was quite desperate, CONCLAMATUM EST, all is over.[10]

The corpse was then laid on the ground ; hence DEPOSITUS, for *in ulti- mo positus, desperatæ salutis*, desperate, dying, past hopes of recovery ;[11] or from the ancient custom of placing sick persons at the gate, to see if any that passed had ever been ill of the same disease, and what had cured them ; hence DEPONERE *aliquem vino*, to intoxicate ; *positi artus*, dead ; so *compositus vino somnoque*, overpowered with wine and sleep.[12]

The corpse was next bathed with warm water, and anointed with per- fumes,[13] by slaves called POLLINCTORES,[14] belonging to those who took care of funerals (LIBITINARII,)[15] and had the charge of the temple of Ve- nus Libitina, where the things requisite for funerals[16] were sold ; hence *vitare Libitinam*, not to die ;[17] *mirari nihil, nisi quod Libitina sacravit*, to ad- mire nobody till after his death ; *Libitinam evadere*, to escape death ; *Libi- tina* is also put for the funeral couch.[18]

In this temple was kept an account[19] of those who died, for each of whom a certain coin was paid ; hence *autumnusque gravis, Libitinæ quæstus acer- bæ*, the unwholesome autumn, ruthless Libitina's gainful season ; because autumn being unhealthful usually occasioned great mortality.[20]

1 Virg. Æn. iii. 304. iv. 326. 505. Stat. Theb. xii 162. 365. Hor. Od. i. 28. 23. 36. Festus in Præcidanea agna.
2 Ov. Trist. i. 2. 51. Ep. x. 119. Plin. Ep. vii. 27. Virg. Æn. iii. 68. Plaut. Most. ii. 2. 66. Suet. Cal. 59.
3 extremum spiritum ore excipere, Cic. Ver. v. 45. Virg. Æn. vi. 684.
4 anima sensilis.
5 Sen. Ep. 30. 101. Hor.

Fur. 1316. Liv. xxvi. 14. Cic. Fam. viii. 13.Tusc. i. 9.
6 Suet. Tib. 73. Plin. xxxi. 1. Prop. iv. 7. 9.
7 Virg. Æn. xi. 487. Ov. Her. i. 102. 113. ii. 102. x. 120. Luc. iii. 740. Suet. Ner. 49. Plin. xi. 37. s. 55.
8 inclamabant.
9 Ov. Trist. iii. 3. 43. Met. x. 62. F. iv. 852. Catul. xcviii. 10. Luc. ii. 23.
10 Liv. iv. 40. Ter. Eun.

ii. 3. 56.
11 Ov. Trist. iii. 3. 40. Pont. ii. 2. 47. Virg. Æn. xii. 395. Cic. Ver. i. 2.
12 Serv. Virg. Æn. xii. 395. Strab. iii. p. 155. xvi. 746. Herodot. i. 197. Plaut. Aul. iii. 6. 39. Ov. Her. x. 122. Amor. i. 4. 51. ii. 5. 22.
13 Virg. Æn. vi. 219. Plin. Ep. v. 16. Mart. iii. 12.
14 quasi pellis unctores,

-Plaut. Asin. v. 2. 50. Pœn. Prol. 63.
15 Sen. Ben. vi. 38.
16 necessaria funeribus.
17 Plut. Rom. Quæst. R. 23 Liv. xli.21. Hor. Od. iii. 30. 6.
18 Id. Ep. ii. 1.49. Juv. xii. 122. Mart. viii. 43. 4. Acron. in Hor. Od. iii. 30. 6.
19 ratio vel ephemeris.
20 Suet. Ner. 39. Diony. iv. 15. Hor. Sat. ii. 6. 19. Phædr. iv. 19. 25.

The money paid for the liberty of burial and other expenses was called ARBITRIUM, oftener plur. -ia ; so *arbitrium vendendi salis*, the monopoly of salt.[1]

·· The body was then dressed in the best robe which the deceased had worn when alive ; ordinary citizens in a white toga,[2] magistrates in their prætexta, &c., and laid[3] on a couch in the vestibule,[4] with the feet outwards, as if about to take its last departure. Hence *componere*, to bury.[5] Then a lamentation was made. Hence, *sic positum affati discedite corpus*, thus, with the last farewell to thy body laid out for burial, depart. The couch was sometimes decked with leaves and flowers, the bedstead of ivory. If the deceased had received a crown for his bravery, it was now placed on his head. A small coin, *triens* vel *obolus*, was put in his mouth, which he might give to Charon (*portitor* vel *porthmeus*, the ferryman of hell) for his freight.[6] Hence a person who wanted this and the other funeral oblations was said *abiisse ad Acheruntem sine viatico ;* for without them it was thought that souls could not purchase a lodging, or place of rest.[7]

A branch of cypress was placed at the door of the deceased, at least if he was a person of consequence, to prevent the pontifex maximus from entering, and thereby being polluted, for it was unlawful for him not only to touch a dead body, but even to look at it. This tree was sacred to Pluto, because when once cut it never grows again, called *atra, feralis, funerea* vel *funebris*, from its being used at funerals.[8]

The Romans at first usually interred[9] their dead, which is the most ancient and most natural method.[10] They early adopted the custom of burning[11] from the Greeks, which is mentioned in the laws of Numa, and of the Twelve Tables,[12] but it did not become general till towards the end of the republic.

Sylla was the first of the patrician branch of the *gens Cornelia* that was burned ; which he is supposed to have ordered, lest any one should dig up his body and dissipate his remains, as he did those of Marius. Pliny ascribes the first institution of burning among the Romans to their having discovered, that the bodies of those who fell in distant wars were dug up by the enemy. It appears, however, to have prevailed at an early period. The wise men among the Indians, called GYMNOSOPHISTÆ, commonly burned themselves alive, as Calanus in presence of Alexander, and Zamarus at Athens, while Augustus was there.[13]

Under the emperors, the custom of burning became almost universal, but was afterwards gradually dropped upon the introduction of Christianity, so that it had fallen into disuse about the end of the fourth century.[14]

Children before they got teeth were not burned, but buried in a place called SUGGRUNDARIUM.[15] So likewise persons struck with lightning[16] were buried in the spot where they fell, called BIDENTAL, because it was conse-

1 Cic. post Red. in Sen. 7. Dom. 37. Pis. 9. Liv. ii. 9.
2 Virg. Æn. ix. 488. Juv. iii. 172.
3 componebatur vel collocabatur.
4 locus vacuus ante januam domus, per quem a via ad ædes itur, Gel. xvi. 5.
5 Ov. Met. ix. 502. F. iii. 547. v. 426. Tac.

Agr. 45. Hist. i. 47. Sen. Ep. 12. Brev. Vit. 20. Suet. Aug. 101. Pers. iii. 104. Hor. Sat. i. 9. 28.
6 Virg. Æn. ii. 644. xi. 66. Diony. xi. 39. Cic. Legg. ii. 24. Prop. ii. 10. 21. Plin. xxi. 3. Juv. iii. 267.
7 nusquam posse diverti, Plaut. Pœn. Prol. 71.

8 Luc. iii.- 442. Fest. Hor. Od. ii. 14. 23. Plin. xvi. 33. Dio. lvi. 31. Sen. Marc. 15. liv. 28. Virg. Æn. iii. 64. iv. 507.
9 humabant.
10 Cic. Legg. ii. 22. Plin. vii. 54. Genes. iii. 19.
11 cremandi vel comburendi.
12 Plut. Num.

13 Diony. v. 47, 48. Cic. ib. Tusc. ii. 21. Plin. ib. vi. 19, s. 22. Dio. liv. 9.
14 Tac. Ann. xvi. 9. Macrob. vii. 7.
15 Fulgent. de Prisc. Serm. 7. Plin. vii. 15. s. 16. Juv. xv. 140.
16 fulguriti, Plin. ii. 55. Sen. Ira. iii. 23. Q. Nat. ii. 21.

45

crated by sacrificing sheep (*bidentes*).[1] It was enclosed with a wall, and no one was allowed to tread upon it. To remove its bounds[2] was esteemed sacrilege.[3]

The expressions SEPELIRE, *sepultura*, and *sepulchrum*, are applied to every manner of disposing[4] of a dead body. So also HUMARE, &c. JUSTA, *exsequiæ vel funus*, funeral obsequies or solemnities ; hence JUSTA *funebria*, *justa funerum vel exsequiarum*, *et justa funera alicui facere*, *solvere* vel *persolvere*, *reddere justa funeri*.[5] But EXSEQUIÆ properly denotes the funeral procession.[6] Hence EXSEQUIAS *ducere*, *deducere*, *comitari*, *frequentare*, *prosequi*, &c., to attend the funeral ; *funeri interesse*.[7]

Of funerals, there were chiefly two kinds, public and private. The public funeral was called INDICTIVUM,[8] because people were invited to it by a herald.[9] Of this kind the most remarkable were *funus* CENSORIUM, including *funus consulare*, *prætorium*, *triumphale*, &c. PUBLICUM, when a person was buried at the public expense,[10] and COLLATIVUM, by a public contribution.[11] Augustus was very liberal in granting public funerals,[12] as at first in conferring the honour of a triumph. There was also a military funeral performed at the public expense.[13]

A private funeral was called TACITUM, TRANSLATITIUM, PLEBEIUM, COMMUNE, and VULGARE.[14]

The funeral of those who died in infancy, or under age, was called ACERBUM, or *immaturum*, or EXSEQUIÆ IMMATURÆ.[15] But *funus acerbum* is applied by some only to infants, and *immaturum* to young men. Such were buried sooner than grown persons, and with less pomp.[16]

When a public funeral was intended, the corpse was kept usually for seven or eight days, with a keeper set to watch it, and sometimes boys to drive away the flies. When the funeral was private, the body was not kept so long.[17]

On the day of the funeral, when the people were assembled, the dead body was carried out with the feet foremost,[18] on a couch covered with rich cloth,[19] with gold and purple, supported commonly on the shoulders of the nearest relations of the deceased, or of his heirs, sometimes of his freedmen. Julius Cæsar was borne by the magistrates, Augustus by the senators,[20] and Germanicus by the tribunes and centurions. So Drusus, his father, who died in Germany, by the tribunes and centurions, to the winter quarters, and then by the chief men in the different cities on the road to Rome. Paulus Æmilius by the chief men of Macedonia who happened to be at Rome when he died.[21]

Poor citizens and slaves were carried to the funeral pile in a plain bier or coffin (SANDAPILA, VILIS ARCA, ORCINIANA SPONDA),[22] usually by four bear-

---

1 Pers. ii. 27. Luc. i. 606. viii. 664. Fest. Gell. xvi. 6.
2 movere bidental.
3 Hor. Art. P. 471.
4 condendi.
5 Plin. x. 2. xvii. 54. Cic. Tusc. i. 45. Flac. 38. Leg. ii. 17. 22. Sal. Jug. 11. Nep. Eum. 13. Liv. i. 20. Cæs. B. G. vi. 17.
6 officium exsequiarum, v. pompa funebris.
7 Tac. Ann. ii. 32. xvi. 6, 7. 21. Suet. Tib. 32. Ter. And. i. 100.

8 ad quod per præconem homines evocabantur.
9 Cic. Dom. 18. see p. 122.
10 Tac. Ann. iii. 48. iv. 15. vi. 11. xiii. 2. Dio. liii. 30. liv. 28. Suet. Vit. 8.
11 Liv. ii. 33. Val. Max. iv. 3. Plut. Poplic. see p. 99.
12 δημοσίαι ταφαι.
13 Liv. iii. 43. Dio. liv. 12.
14 Sen. Tranq. 1. Ov. T. i. 3. 22. Suet. Ner.

33. Prop. ii. 10. 25. Aus. Par. x. 5. Capitolin. Anton. Phil. 13.
15 Virg. Æn. vi. 429. Juv. xi. 44. Sen. Ep. 123. Tranq. An. i. 11.
16 Cic. Clu. 9. Tac. An. xiii. 17. Suet. Ner. 33. funera puerorum ad faces et cereos ducta, Sen. Brev. vi. 20. Ep. 122.
17 Serv. Virg. v. 64. vi. 218. xi. 30. Xiphilin. lxxiv. 4. Cic. Clu. 9. Suet. Oth. Tac. Ann. xiv. 3.

18 pedibus efferebatur, Plin. vii. 8.
19 stragula vestis.
20 Suet. 84. 101. Jul. 84. Plin. vii. 44. Juv. x.259. Val. Max. vii. 1. Hor. Sat. ii. 5. 86. Per. iii. 106.
21 Tac. Ann. iii. 2. Dio. iv. 2. Suet. Claud. 1. Val. Max. ii. 10. 3. Plut. Vit.
22 Mart. ii. 81. viii. 75. 14. x. 5. 9. Hor. Sat. i. 8, 9. Juv. viii. 175. Luc. viii. 736.

ers, called VESPILLONES, vel *vespæ*,[1] SANDAPILONES, vel *-arii*, and in later writers LECTICARII.

The funeral couches (LECTICÆ, *lecti*, vel *tori*) of the rich seem also to have been borne by *vespillones*. Hence a couch carried by six was called HEXAPHORUM, and by eight, OCTOPHORUM, or *lectica octophorus;* as the ordinary couches or sedans used in the city, or on a journey, were carried by slaves, called LECTICARII.[2]

These couches were sometimes open, and sometimes covered.

The general name of a bier was FERETRUM,[3] or CAPULUS, vel *-um:*[4] hence *capularis*, old, at death's door; *capuli decus*. Some make *feretrum* to be the same with *lectus;* others that on which the couch was supported.[5]

Children who died before they were weaned, were carried to the pile by their mothers.[6]

All funerals used anciently to be solemnized in the night-time with torches, that they might not fall in the way of magistrates and priests, who were supposed to be violated by seeing a corpse, so that they could not perform sacred rites, till they were purified by an expiatory sacrifice. Thus, to diminish the expense of funerals, it was ordained by Demetrius Phalereus at Athens, according to an ancient law, which seems to have fallen into desuetude. Hence FUNUS, a funeral, from *funes accensi*,[7] or *funalia*, *funales cerei*, *cereæ faces*, vel *candelæ*, torches, candles, or tapers, originally made of small ropes or cords (*funes* vel *funiculi*), covered with wax or tallow (*sevum* vel *sebum*).[8]

But in after ages, public funerals[9] were celebrated in the day-time, at an early hour in the forenoon, as it is thought from Plutarch, in Syll. fin. with torches also.[10] Private or ordinary funerals[11] were always at night.[12]

As torches were used both at funerals and marriages, hence *inter utramque facem*, for *inter nuptias et funus, et face pro thalami, fax mihi mortis adest*, and instead of the nuptial, I am threatened with the funeral torch.[13]

The order of the funeral procession was regulated, and every one's place assigned him, by a person called DESIGNATOR, an undertaker or master of ceremonies,[14] attended by lictors, dressed in black.[15]

First went musicians of various kinds: pipers (TIBICINES, vel SITICINES), trumpeters, and cornetters,[16] then mourning women (PRÆFICÆ),[17] hired to lament, and to sing the funeral song (NÆNIA vel LESSUS), or the praises of the deceased, to the sound of the flute. Boys and girls were sometimes employed for this last purpose. As these praises were often unmerited and frivolous, hence *nugæ* is put for NÆNIÆ, and *lexidia, res inanes et frivolæ*, for *voces præficarum*.[18]

The flutes and trumpets used on this occasion were larger and longer than ordinary, of a grave dismal sound. By the law of the Twelve Ta-

1 quia vespertino tempore mortuos efferebant, Fest. Suet. Dom. 17. Eutrop. vii. 34. Mart. i. 31. 48.
2 Cic. Ver. v. 11. Fam. iv. 12. Phil. 41. Nep. Att. 22.Gell. x. 3. Mart. ii. 61. vi. 67. 10. ix. 3. 11.
3 Virg. Æn. vi. 222. xi. 64. 149. Stat. Theb. vi. 55. Ov. Met. xiv. 747.

4 quod corpus capiat, Serv. Virg. xi. 64. Fest.
5 Plaut. Mil. iii. 1. 34. As. v. 2. 42. Varr. L. L. iv. 35.
6 Stat. Sylv. v. 5. 15. Ov. Her. xv. 115.
7 Serv. Virg. xi. 143. Don. Ter. And. i. 1.
81. Cic. Legg. ii. 26. Demosth. adv. Macartatum, p. 666. Laid. xi.

2. xx. 10.
6 Serv. ib. Æn. i. 727. Val. Max. iii. 6. 4. Var. Vit. Pop. R.
9 funera indictiva.
10 Serv. Virg. Æn. vi. 224. Tac. Ann. iii. 4.
11 tacita.
12 Fest. in Vespillones.
13 Ov. Ep. xxi. 172. Prop. iv. 12. 46.
14 dominus funeris.
15 Hor. Ep. i. 7. 6. Cic.

Att. iv. 2. Legg. ii. 24.
16 Hor. Sat. i. 6. 43. Ov. F. vi. 660. Gel. xx. 2. Pers. iii.103. Serv.Virg. xi. 192.
17 quæ dabant cæteris modum plangendi.
18 Festus. Lucil. 22. Hor. Art. 431. Plaut. Truc. ii. 6. 14. iv. 2. 18. Asin. iv. 62. Cic. Leg. ii. 24. Quin. viii. 2. Gel. xviii. 7.

bles, the number of players on the flute at a funeral was restricted to ten.[1]

Next came players and buffoons (*ludii* vel *histriones* et *scurræ*), who danced and sung.[2] One of them, called ARCHIMIMUS, supported the character[3] of the deceased, imitating his words and actions while alive. These players sometimes introduced apt sayings from dramatic writers.[4]

Then followed the freedmen of the deceased, with a cap on their head.[5] Some masters at their death freed all their slaves, from the vanity of having their funeral procession attended by a numerous train of freedmen.[6]

Before the corpse, were carried the images of the deceased and of his ancestors, on long poles or frames, in the same form and garb as when alive;[7] but not of such as had been condemned for any heinous crime, whose images were broken. The triumviri ordained, that the image of Cæsar, after his deification, should not be carried before the funeral of any of his relations. Sometimes there were a great many different couches carried before the corpse, on which, it is supposed, the images were placed.[8] After the funeral, these images were again set up in the hall, where they were kept.[9]

If the deceased had distinguished himself in war, the crowns and rewards which he had received for his valour were displayed, together with the spoils and standards he had taken from the enemy. At the funerals of renowned commanders were carried images or representations of the countries they had subdued, and the cities they had taken.[10] At the funeral of Sylla, above 2000 crowns are said to have been carried, which had been sent him by different cities on account of his victory. The lictors attended with their fasces inverted. Sometimes also the officers and troops, with their spears pointing to the ground, or laid aside.[11]

Behind the corpse walked the friends of the deceased in mourning;[12] his sons with their heads veiled, and his daughters with their heads bare, and their hair dishevelled, contrary to the ordinary custom of both, the magistrates without their badges, and the nobility without their ornaments.[13]

The nearest relations sometimes tore their garments, and covered their hair with dust, or pulled it out. The women in particular, who attended the funeral, beat their breasts, tore their cheeks, &c.,[14] although this was forbidden by the Twelve Tables.[15]

At the funeral of an illustrious citizen, the corpse was carried through the forum ; where the procession stopped, and a funeral oration (LAUDATIO) was delivered in praise of the deceased from the rostra, by his son, or by some near relation or friend ; sometimes by a magistrate, according to the appointment of the senate.[16]

This custom is said to have been first introduced by Poplicola, in honour of his colleague Brutus. It is first mentioned by Livy, ii. 47 ; next, ib. 61. It was an incentive to glory and virtue, but hurtful to the authenticity of historical records.[17]

1 Ov. Am. ii. 6. 6. F. vi. 664. Stat. Theb. v. 120. Cic. Legg. ii. 24.
2 Diony. vii. 72. Suet. Tib. 57.
3 personam agebat.
4 Suet. Vesp. 19. Cæs. 84.
5 pileati, Cod. de Lat. Libert. Liv. xxxviii. 55. Diony. viii.
6 Diony. iv. 24.
7 Cic. Brut. 34. Mil. xiii.

32. Hor. Ep. viii. 11. Val. Max. viii. 15. 1. Plin. xxxv. 2. Sil.x. 566. Polyb. vi. 51, 52.
8 Tac. Ann. ii. 32. iii. 76. xvi. 11. Juv. viii. 18. Serv. Virg. v. 4. vi. 862. 875. Dio. xlvii. 19.
9 see p. 21.
10 Virg. Æn. xi. 78. Tac. Ann. i. 8. Dio. lvi. 24. lxxiv. 4.

11 App. B. C. i. 417. Tac. Ann. iii. 2. Virg. xi. 92. Luc. viii. 735.
12 atra vel lugubri veste ; atrati vel pullati.
13 Plut. Q. Rom. 14. Tac. Ann. iii. 4.
14 Virg. Æn. iv. 673. xii. 609. Catul. lxii. 224. Cic. Tusc. iii. 26. Ter. And. i. 1. 90. Suet. Cæs. 84. Tibul. i. 1. 68.
15 mulieres genas ne

radunto, Cic. Legg. ii. 24. Plin. xxxvi. 11. i. s. unguibus ne scindunto, Fest.
16 Polyb. vi. 51. Quinc. iii. 7. vel 9. Cic. Or. ii. 84. Suet. Cæs. 84. Tib. vi. Aug. 101. Ner. 9. Plin. Ep. ii. 1.
17 Plut. in Popl. Diony. v. 17. ix. 54. Liv. viii. 40. Cic. Brut. 17.

The honour of a funeral oration was decreed by the senate also to women, for their readiness in resigning their golden ornaments to make up the sum agreed to be paid to the Gauls, as a ransom for leaving the city; or, according to Plutarch, to make the golden cup which was sent to Delphi, as a present to Apollo, in consequence of the vow of Camillus, after the taking of Veji.[1]

But Cicero says, that Popilia was the first to whom this honour was paid, by her son Catulus, several ages after; and, according to Plutarch, Cæsar introduced the custom of praising young matrons, upon the death of his wife Cornelia. But after that, both young and old, married and unmarried, were honoured with funeral orations.[2]

While the funeral oration was delivering, the corpse was placed before the rostra. The corpse of Cæsar was placed in a gilt pavilion, like a small temple,[3] with the robe in which he had been slain suspended on a pole or trophy, and his image exposed on a moveable machine, with the marks of all the wounds he had received, for the body itself was not seen;[4] but Dio says the contrary, xliv. 4.

Under Augustus, it became customary to deliver more than one funeral oration in praise of the same person, and in different places.[5]

From the forum, the corpse was carried to the place of burning or burial, which the law of the Twelve Tables ordered to be without the city, HOMINEM MORTUUM IN URBE NE SEPELITO, NEVE URITO, according to the custom of other nations; the Jews, the Athenians, and others.[6]

The ancients are said to have buried their dead at their own houses; whence, according to some, the origin of idolatry, and the worship of household gods, the fear of hobgoblins, or spectres in the dark (LARVÆ vel LEMURES), &c.[7] Souls separated from the body were called LEMURES vel MANES; if beneficent, LARES; if hurtful, LARVÆ vel MANIÆ.[8] Augustus, in his speech to his soldiers before the battle of Actium, says that the Egyptians embalmed their dead bodies to establish an opinion of their immortality. Several of these still exist, called mummies, from mum, the Egyptian name of wax. The manner of embalming is described by Herodotus, ii. 86. The Persians also annointed the bodies of their dead with wax, to make them keep as long as possible.[9]

The Romans prohibited burning or burying in the city, both from a sacred and civil consideration; that the priests might not be contaminated by seeing or touching a dead body, and that houses might not be endangered by the frequency of funeral fires, or the air infected by the stench.[10]

The flamen of Jupiter was not allowed to touch a dead body, nor to go where there was a grave, so the high priest among the Jews;[11] and if the pontifex maximus had to deliver a funeral oration, a veil was laid over the corpse, to keep it from his sight.[12]

The places for burial were either private or public; the private in fields or gardens, usually near the highway, to be conspicuous, and to remind those who passed of mortality.[13] Hence the frequent inscriptions, SISTE VIATOR, ASPICE VIATOR, &c. on the via Appia, Aurelia, Flaminia, Tibur-

---

1 Liv. v. 50. Plut. in. Camillo.
2 Cic. Or. ii. 11. Suet. Jul. 6. Cal. 10 Tac. Ann. v. 1. xvi. 6. Dio. xxxix. 64. 59.
3 aurata ædes.
4 Suet. Cæs. 84. App. B.

C. ii. p. 521.
5 Dio. Iv. 2.
6 Cic. Leg. ii. 23. Fam. iv. 12 Flac. 31. Tusc. v. 23. Matth. xxvii. 53. John, xix. 20. 41. Liv. xxxi. 24. Plut. Arato. Strab. x.

7 Serv. Virg. Æn. v. 64. vi. 152. Isid. xiv. 11.
8 αγαθοι και κακοι δαιμονες, Apul. de Deo Socratis.
9 Dio. 1. 24. Cic. Tusc. 1. 45.
10 Cic. Leg. ii. 22. Serv.

Virg. vi. 150. Isid. xiv. 11.
11 Gell. x. 15. Lev. xxi. 11.
12 Sen. Cons. Marc. 15. Dio. liv. 28. 35.
13 Var. L. L. v. 6.

tina, &c.[1] The public places for burial for great men were commonly in the CAMPUS MARTIUS, or CAMPUS ESQUILINUS, granted by a decree of the senate,[2] for poor people without the Esquiline gate, in places called PUTI-CULÆ, vel -i.[3]

As the vast number of bones deposited in that common burying-ground rendered the places adjoining unhealthy, Augustus, with the consent of the senate and people, gave part of it to his favourite Mæcenas, who built there a magnificent house,[4] called turris MÆCENATIANA, with extensive gardens, whence it became one of the most healthy situations in Rome.[5]

There was in the corner of the burying-ground a stone pillar, CIPPUS, on which was marked its extent towards the road,[6] and backwards to the fields ;[7] also who were to be buried in it.

If a burying-ground was intended for a person and his heirs, it was called SEPULCHRUM, vel MONUMENTUM HÆREDITARIUM, which was marked in letters, thus, H. M. H. S. i. e. HOC MONUMENTUM HÆREDES SEQUITUR ; or GEN-TILE and GENTILITIUM, PATRIUM, AVITUM.[8] If only for himself and family, FAMILIARE.[9] Freedmen were sometimes comprehended, and relations, when undeserving, excluded.[10]

The right of burying[11] was sometimes purchased by those who had no burying-ground of their own.

The Vestal virgins were buried in the city (*quia legibus non tenebantur*), and some illustrious men, as Poplicola, Tubertus, and Fabricius, (*virtutis causa, legibus soluti*) ; which right their posterity retained,[12] but did not use. To show, however, that they possessed it, when any of them died, they brought the dead body, when about to be burnt, into the forum, and setting down the couch, put a burning torch under it, which they immediately removed, and carried the corpse to another place. The right of making a sepulchre for himself within the pomœrium was decreed to Julius Cæsar as a singular privilege.[13]

When a person was burnt and buried in the same place, it was called BUSTUM ; whence this word is often put for a tomb.[14] A place where one was only burnt, USTRINA, vel -um.[15]

The funeral pile (ROGUS, vel PYRA,) was built in the form of an altar, with four equal sides, hence called ARA SEPULCHRI, FUNERIS ARA,[16] of wood which might easily catch fire, as fir, pine, cleft oak, &c.[17] unpolished, according to the law of the Twelve Tables, ROGUM ASCIA NE POLITO, but not always so, also stuffed with paper and pitch,[18] made higher or lower according to the rank of the deceased, hence ROGUS PLEBEIUS,[19] with cypress trees set around to prevent the noisome smell, at the distance of sixty feet from any house.[20]

The basilica Porcia and senate-house adjoining, contiguous to the forum, were burnt by the flames of the funeral pile of Clodius.[21]

1 Liv. vi. 36. Suet. Cal. Galb. 20. Juv. i. ult. Mart. i. 89. 115. 117. vi. 28. x. 43. xi. 14. Prop. iii. 16. 30. Nep. Att. ult. Plin. Ep. vii. 29.

2 Cic. Phil. ix. 7. Strab. v. Suet. Cæs. 84. Clau. l. Virg. Æn. vi. 873. Dio. 39. 64. 48. 53. Plut. Lucul. fin.

3 quod in pute os corpora mittebantur,—because their bodies were thrown into pits, Var. L. L. iv. 5. Fest. Hor. Sat. i. 8. 8.

4 molem propinquam nubibus arduis,—atowering mansion reaching almost to the clouds, Hor. Od. iii. 29. 10.

5 Suet. Ner. 31. 38. Aug. 72. Tib. 15.

6 in fronte.

7 in agro vel -um, Hor. ibid.

8 Suet. Ner. 50. Virg.

Æn. x. 557. Ov. Trist. iv. 3. 45. Met. xiii. 524.

9 L. 5. D. de religio.

10 Suet. Aug. 102.

11 jus inferendi.

12 Serv. Virg. Æn. ix. Cic. Legg. ii. 23.

13 Plut. Poplic. Quæst. Rom. 78. Dio. xliv. 7.

14 τυμβος, Cic. Tusc. v. 35. Att. vii. 9. Pis. 4. 7. Leg. ii. 26.

15 Festus.

16 Herodian, iv. 2. Virg. vi. 177. Sil. xv. 388.

Ov. Trist. iii. 13. 21. Ibin, 102.

17 Virg. Æn. iv. 504. vi. 180. Stat. Theb. vi 54.

18 Cic. Leg. ii. 24. Plin. xxxv. 7. Mart. viii. 44. 14. x. 97.

19 Luc. viii. 743.Virg. iv. 504. xi. 215. Ov. Ibin. 152.

20 Cic. Leg. ii. 24. Serv. loc. Sil. x. 535.

21 Asc: Cic. Mil. Dio. xi. 42.

On the funeral pile was placed the corpse with the couch. The eyes of the deceased were opened,[1] to which Virgil is thought to allude, Æn. iv. 224.

The near relations kissed the body with tears,[2] and then set fire to the pile with a lighted torch, turning away their face,[3] to show that they did it with reluctance. They prayed for a wind to assist the flames, as the Greeks did, and when that happened, it was thought fortunate.[4]

They threw into the fire various perfumes,[5] incense, myrrh, cassia, &c. which Cicero calls SUMPTUOSA RESPERSIO; forbidden by the Twelve Tables ;[6] also cups of oil and dishes,[7] with titles marking what they contained ; likewise the clothes and ornaments, not only of the deceased,[8] but their own ; every thing in short that was supposed to be agreeable to the deceased while alive. All these were called MUNERA, vel DONA.[9]

If the deceased had been a soldier, they threw on the pile his arms, rewards, and spoils ; and if a general, the soldiers sometimes threw in their own arms.[10]

At the funeral of an illustrious commander or emperor, the soldiers made a circuit[11] three times round the pile, from right to left,[12] with their ensigns inverted, and striking their weapons on one another to the sound of the trumpet,[13] all present accompanying them, as at the funeral of Sylla, and of Augustus, which custom seems to have been borrowed from the Greeks ; used also by the Cathaginians ; sometimes performed annually at the tomb.[14]

As the *manes* were supposed to be delighted with blood,[15] various animals especially such as the deceased had been fond of, were slaughtered at the pile, and thrown into it ; in ancient times, also, men, captives or slaves,[16] to which Cicero alludes, Flacc. 38. Afterwards instead of them, gladiators, called BUSTUARII, were made to fight; so among the Gauls, slaves and clients were burned on the piles of their masters ;[17] among the Indians and Thracians, wives on the piles of their husbands. As one man had several wives, there was sometimes a contest among them about the preference, which they determined by lot.[18] Thus also among the Romans, friends testified their affection ; as Plotinus to his patron, Plautius to his wife Orestilla, soldiers to Otho, Mnester, a freedman, to Agrippina[19], &c.

Instances are recorded of persons, who came to life again on the funeral pile, after it was set on fire ; so that they could not be preserved ; and of others, who, having revived before the pile was kindled, returned home on their feet.[20]

The Jews, although they interred their dead,[21] filled the couch on which the corpse was laid with sweet odours, and divers kinds of spices, and burned them.[22]

When the pile was burned down, the fire was extinguished, and the em-

1 Tibul. i. 1. 61. Plin. ii. 37.
2 Prop. ii. 13. 29. Tibul. i. 1. 62.
3 aversi.
4 Virg. Æn. vi. 223. Prop. iv. 7. 31. Homer Il. xxiii. 193. Plut. Syl.
5 odorea.
6 Legg. ii. 24. Plin. xii. 18. s. 41. Juv. iv. 109. Stat. Sylv. v. 1. 208. Mart. x. 26.
7 dapes v. fercula.
8 Virg. Æn. vi. 221. 233. Stat. Theb. vi.

126. Luc. ix. 175.
9 Tac. Ann. iii. 3. 2. Suet. Jul. 84. Donat. Virg. Æn. vi. 217. Cæs. B. G. vi. 17.
10 Virg. Æn. xi. 192. Sil. x. 562. Suet. Jul. 84. Luc. viii. 735.
11 ducurrebant, Virg. Æn. xi. 188. Tac. Ann. ii. 7.
12 orbe sinistro.
13 Stat. Theb. vi. 213. Val. Flac. iii. 346.
14 App. B. C. i. Dio. lvi. 42. Homer Il. xxiii. 13.

Liv. xxv. 17. Suet. Claud. 1.
15 Tertul. de Spect.
16 Plin. viii. 40. s. 61. Ep. iv. 2. Virg. x. 518.
, xi. 82. Æn. xi. 197. Homer Il. xviii. 166. xxi. 27.
17 Serv. Æn. x. 519. Hor. Sat. ii. 3. 85. Cæs. B. G. vi. 17. Flor. iii. 20.
18 Cic. Tusc. v. 27. Mel. Sit. Orb. ii. 2. Prop. iii. 7. Ælian. 7. 18. Serv. Æn. v. 95.

19 Plin. vii. 36. Val. Max. iv. 6. 3. Tac. Hist. ii. 49. An. xiv. 9.
20 Plin. vii. 52. s. 53. xxvi. 3. s. 8.
21 condere, quam cremare, e more Ægyptio. —they choose rather to inter them after the manner of the Egyptians, than to burn them, Tac. Hist. v. 5.
22 2 Chron. xvi. 14. Jerem. xxxiv. 5.

bers soaked with wine,[1] the bones were gathered[2] by the nearest relation, with loose robes, and sometimes bare-footed.[3]

We read also of the nearest female relations gathering the bones in
their bosom, who were called FUNERÆ, vel -eæ.[4]

The ashes and bones of the deceased are thought to have been distinguished by their particular position. Some suppose the body to have been
wrapt in a species of incombustible cloth, made of what the Greeks called
asbestos.[5] But Pliny restricts this to the kings of India, where only it
was then known.

The bones and ashes, besprinkled with the richest perfumes, were put
into a vessel called URNA, an urn ; FERALIS URNA, made of earth, brass,
marble, silver, or gold, according to the wealth or rank of every one.[6]
Sometimes also a small glass vial full of tears, called by the moderns a
lachrymatory, was put in the urn.

The urn was solemnly deposited (*componebatur*) in the sepulchre (SE-
PULCHRUM, TUMULUS, MONUMENTUM, *sedes* vel *domus*, CONDITORIUM, V.
-*tivum*, CINERARIUM, &c.) Hence *componere*, to bury, to shut up, to end ;[7]
composito die, i. e. *finito*.

When the body was not burned it was put into a coffin (*arca* vel *loculus*), with all its ornaments, usually made of stone, as that of Numa, and
of Hannibal,[8] sometimes of Assian stone, from Assos, or -us, a town in
Troas or Mysia, which consumed the body in forty days, except the teeth,
hence called SARCOPHAGUS,[9] which word is put for any coffin or tomb.[10]

The coffin was laid in the tomb on its back ; in what direction among
the Romans is uncertain ; but among the Athenians, looking to the
west.[11]

Those who died in prison were thrown out naked on the street.[12]

When the remains of the deceased were laid in the tomb, those present
were three times sprinkled by a priest with pure water;[13] from a branch
of olive or laurel,[14] to purify them, then they were dismissed by the PRÆ-
FICA, or some other person, pronouncing the solemn word ILICET, i. e. *ire
licet*, you may depart. At their departure, they asked to take a last farewell, by repeating several times VALE, or SALVE *æternum*, farewell for ever,
adding, NOS TE ORDINE, QUO NATURA PERMISERIT, CUNCTI SEQUEMUR,
we shall all follow thee, in whatever order nature may permit,[15] which
were called VERBA NOVISSIMA ; also to wish that the earth might lie light
on the person buried, which is found marked on several ancient monuments
in these letters, s. T. T. L. SIT TIBI TERRA LEVIS,[16] and the grave-stone,[17]
that his bones might rest quietly, or lie softly ;[18] PLACIDE QUIESCAS, may-
est thou rest in peace. Hence *compositus* and *positus*, buried. So *placida
compostus pace quiescit*, he, settled, now enjoys a peaceful calm, is said of
Antenor, while yet alive. We find in Ovid the contrary of this wish, *solli-
citi jaceant, terraque premantur iniqua*, may they be disquieted in their graves,
and may the earth press heavily on them, as if the dead felt these things.

1 Virg. Æn. vi. 226.
2 ossa legebantur.
3 Tibul iii. 2. 9. Suet.
Aug. 101.
4 Tibul. i. 3. 5. Sen.
Helv. 11. Luc. ix. 60.
Serv. Virg. Æn. ix. 486.
5 asbestinum, sc. li-
num, Plin. xix. l. s. 4.
6 Cic. Tusc. i. 15. Ov.
Am. iii. 9. 39. Tac. An.
iii. 1. Prop. ii. 13. 32.

Virg. Æn. vi. 228. Eu-
trop. viii. 5.
7 Prop. ii. 24. 35. Ov.
Fast. v. 426. Met. iv.
157. Hor. Sat. i. 9. 28.
Tac. Hist. i. 47. Virg.
Æn. i. 378. Plin. Ep. ii.
17.
8 Plin. vii. 2. xiii. 13.
Val. Max. i. 1. 12. Aur.
Vict. iii. 42.
9 from σαρξ, flesh ; and

φαγειν, to eat, to con-
sume, Plin. ii. 96.
xxxvi. 17.
10 Juv. x. 172.
11 Ælian. v. vii. Plut.
Solon.
12 Liv. xxxvii. 59.
13 aqua pura, vel lus-
tralis.
14 aspergillum. Serv.
Virg. Æn. vi. 239.
Festus in laurus, Juv.

ii. 158.
15 Serv. Virg. Æn. ii.
640. iii. 68. xi. 97.
16 Juv. vii. 207. Mart. i.
89. v. 35. ix. 30.
17 cippus, Pers. i. 37.
18 molliter cubarent.Ov.
Am. i. 8. 108. Ep. vii.
162. Trist. iii. 2. 75.
Virg. Ecl. x. 33.

ENTRANCE TO THE TOMB OF NAEVOLEIA TYCHE.

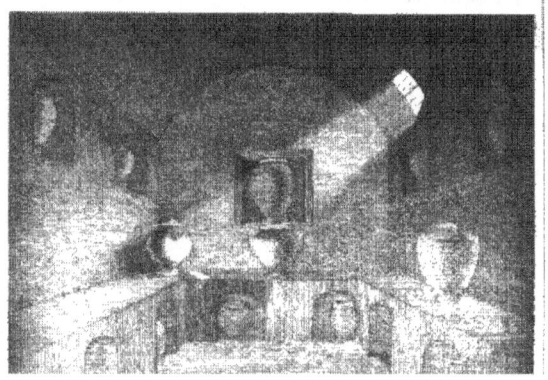

Sometimes the bones were not deposited in the earth till three days after the body was burned.[1]

The friends, when they returned home, as a further purification, after being sprinkled with water, stepped over a fire,[2] which was called SUFFI-TIO. The house itself also was purified, and swept with a certain kind of broom or besom ;[3] which purgation was called EXVERRÆ, v. *everræ ;* and he who performed it, EVERRIATOR.[4]

There were certain ceremonies for the purification of the family, called FERIÆ DENICALES ;[5] when they buried a thumb, or some part cut off from the body before it was burned, or a bone brought home from the funeral pile, on which occasion a soldier might be absent from duty.[6]

A place was held religious where a dead body, or any part of it, was buried, but not where it was burned.[7]

For nine days after the funeral, while the family was in mourning, and employed about certain solemnities at the tomb, it was unlawful to summon the heir, or any near relation of the deceased, to a court of justice, or in any other manner to molest them. On the ninth day a sacrifice was performed, called NOVENDIALE, with which these solemnities were concluded.[8]

Oblations or sacrifices to the dead (INFERIÆ, vel PARENTALIA) were afterwards made at various times, both occasionally and at stated periods, consisting of liquors, victims, and garlands,[9] called FERALIA MUNERA ; thus, ALICUI INFERIAS FERRE vel MITTERE, et PARENTARE, to perform these oblations ; *parentare regi sanguine conjuratorum,* to appease, to revenge the death of the king, by the blood of the conspirators ;[10] *Saguntinorum manibus vastatione Italiæ,* &c., *parentatum est,* an atonement was made to the

---

TOMBS.

THE annexed engraving (plate 5,) exhibits the inside and outside of the common burial place of a family, lately excavated at Pompeii, and may be supposed a fair representation of such buildings throughout the Roman empire. It consists of a square building, containing a small chamber, by the side of which is a door giving admission to a small court surrounded by a high wall. The entrance to the chamber is at the back. From the level of the outer wall there rise two steps, supporting a marble cippus richly ornamented. Its front is occupied by a bas-relief and inscription, of which we annex a copy :—

NAEVOLEIA ' 1 ' LIB. TYCHE '
SIBI ' ET
C ' MVNATIO ' FAVSTO ' AVG '
ET ' PAGANO
CVI ' DECVRIONES ' CONSENS'
' POPVLI
BISELLIVM' OB ' MERITA' EIVS

' DECREVERVNT
HOC ' MONIMENTVM ' NAEVO-
LEIA' TVCHELIBERTIS'SVIS
LIBERTABVSQ ' ET ' C ' MVNATI
' FAVSTI ' VIVA ' FECIT

The latter is to the following purport :—" Nævoleia Tyche, freed-woman of Julia Tyche, to herself and to Caius Munatius Faustus, Augustal, and chief magistrate of the suburb, to whom the Decurions, with the consent of the people, have granted the bisellium for his merits. Nævoleia Tyche erected this monument in her life-time for her freedmen and women, and for those of C. Munatius Faustus." On one of the sides is a curious bas-relief, which presents us with a view of a strangely constructed vessel. Two explanations of this sculpture are given,—one literal, that it is merely indicative of the profession of Munatius ; the other allegorical, that it symbolises the arrival of the tossed ship of life in a quiet haven.

A sort of solid bench for the reception of urns runs round the funeral chamber, and several niches for the same purpose are hollowed in the wall, called *columbaria,* from their resemblance to the holes of a pigeon house. Some lamps were found here, and many urns, three of glass, the rest of common earth. The glass urns were of large size, one of them fifteen inches in height by ten in diameter, and were protected from injury by leaden cases. They contained, when found, burnt bones, and a liquid which has been analyzed, and found to consist of mingled water, wine, and oil. In two of the urns it was of a reddish tint, in the other yellow, oily and transparent. There can be no doubt but that we have here the libations which were poured as a last tribute of friendship upon the ashes of the tenants of the tomb.

---

1 Tac. Agric. 46. Ov. Fast. v. 425. 488. Am. ii. 16. 15. Virg. Æn. i. 219. xi. 210.
2 ignem supergrediebantur, Fest.
3 scopæ, -arum.
4 Fest.
5 a nece appellatæ, Cic. Leg. ii. 22. Fest.
6 Cic. ib. 24. Quinct.viii. 5. 21. Sen. Ben. v.24. Gel. xv. xvi. 4.
7 Cic. ib.
8 Novell. 115. Porphyrio ad Hor. Epod. xvii. 48. Donat. Ter. Phorm.
9 Virg. Æn. iii. 66. v. 77. 94. ix. 215. x. 519. Tac. Hist. ii. 95. Suet. Cal. 3. 15. Claud. 11.
Ner. 11.
10 Liv. xxiv. 21. Cæs. B. G. vii. 17. Cic. Leg. ii. 21. Phil. i. 6. Flac. 38. Ov. Trist. iii. 3. 81.

ghosts of the Saguntines with the devastation of Italy, &c.; so also
LITARE.[1]

The sepulchre was then bespread with flowers, and covered with crowns
and fillets. Before it, there was a little altar, on which libations were
made, and incense burned. A keeper was appointed to watch the tomb,
which was frequently illuminated with lamps.[2]

A kind of perpetual lamps are said, by several authors, to have been
found in ancient tombs still burning, which, however, went out on the
admission of air. But this, by others, is reckoned a fiction.[3]

A feast was generally added, called SILICERNIUM,[4] both for the dead
and the living. Certain things were laid on the tomb, commonly beans,
lettuces, bread, and eggs, or the like, which it was supposed the ghosts
would come and eat: hence CŒNA FERALIS.[5] What remained was burned; for it was thought mean to take away any thing thus consecrated, or
what was thrown into the funeral pile. Hence *rapere de rogo cœnam, e
flamma cibum petere*, to snatch food from a funeral pile, i. e. to be capable
of any thing sordid or mean. *Bustirapus* is applied as a name of contempt
to a sordid person, and SILICERNIUM to an old man.[6]

After the funeral of great men, there was not only a feast for the friends
of the deceased, but also a distribution of raw meat among the people,
called VISCERATIO,[7] with shows of gladiators and games, which sometimes
continued for several days. Sometimes games were celebrated also on
the anniversary of the funeral. Faustus, the son of Sylla, exhibited a show
of gladiators in honour of his father, several years after his death, and gave
a feast to the people, according to his father's testament.[8]

The time of mourning for departed friends was appointed by Numa,[9] as
well as funeral rites,[10] and offerings to appease the *manes*.[11] There was
no limited time for men to mourn, because none was thought honourable,
as among the Germans. It usually did not exceed a few days.[12] Women
mourned for a husband or parent ten months, or a year, according to the
computation of Romulus,[13] but not longer.[14]

In a public mourning for any signal calamity, the death of a prince or
the like, there was a total cessation from business (JUSTITIUM,) either
spontaneously or by public appointment, when the courts of justice did
not sit, the shops were shut, &c.[15] In excessive grief the temples of the
gods were struck with stones,[16] and their altars overturned.[17]

Both public and private mourning was laid aside on account of the public games; for certain sacred rites, as those of Ceres, &c., and for several
other causes enumerated by Festus, in *voce* MINUITUR. After the battle
of Cannæ, by a decree of the senate, the mourning of the matrons was
limited to thirty days. Immoderate grief was supposed to be offensive to
the manes.[18]

1 Flor. ii. 5, 6. iii. 18.
parentare proprie est
parentibus justa face-
re,—parentare proper-
ly significs to perform
the funeral rites of pa-
rents, Ov. Am. i. 13.
4.
2 Suet. Ner. 57. Aug. 99.
Tac. Hist. ii. 55. Cic.
Flac. 38. Virg. Æn. iii.
63. 302. vi. 883. Prop.
iii. 16. 24. D. xl. 4. 44.
3 Klppingi Antiq. iv. 6.
14.

4 cœna funebris, quasi
in silice posita, Serv.
Virg. Æn. v. 92. vel
quod silentes, ec. um-
bræ, eam cernebant,
vel parentantes, qui
non degustabant, Don.
Ter. Adelph. iv. 2. 48.
5 Plin. xviii. 12. s. 30.
Juv. v. 85.
6 Catul. 57. 3. Tibul. i.
5. 53. Ter. Eun. iii. 2.
36. Plaut. Pseud. i. 3.
127.
7 Liv. viii. 22. see p.

214.
8 Liv. xxxvi. 46. Virg.
Æn. v. 46, &c. Cic.Syl.
19. Dio. xxxvi. 51.
9 Plut. Num.
10 justa funebria.
11 inferiæ ad placandos
manes, Liv. i. 20.
12 Sen. Ep. 63. Tac.
Mor. Ger. 27. Dio. lvi.
43.
13 see p. 216.
14 Sen. ib. Cons. Helv.
16. Ov. Fast. iii. 134.
15 Tac. An. ii. 82. iii. 3,

4. iv. 8. Suet. Cal. 24.
Liv. ix. 7. Luc. ii. 17.
Cap. in. Anton. Phil. 7.
16 lapidata, i. e. lapidibus impetita.
17 Suet. Cal. 5. Sen.Vit.
Beat. 36. Arrian. Epic-
tet. ii. 22.
18 Tac. An. iii. 6. Suet.
Cal. 6. Liv. xxii. 56.
Val. Max. i. 1. 15. Stat.
Sylv. v. 1. 179. Tibul. i.
1. 67.

The Romans in mourning kept themselves at home, avoiding every entertainment and amusement,[1] neither cutting their hair nor beard,[2] dressed in black,[3] which custom is supposed to have been borrowed from the Egyptians, sometimes in skins ;[4] laying aside every kind of ornament, not even lighting a fire, which was esteemed an ornament to the house. Hence FOCUS *perennis, i. e. sine luctu ; pervigil.*[5]

The women laid aside their gold and purple. Under the republic they dressed in black like the men ; but under the emperors, when party-coloured clothes came in fashion, they wore white in mourning.[6]

In a public mourning, the senators laid aside their *latus clavus* and rings ; the magistrates the badges of their office ;[7] and the consuls did not sit on their usual seats in the senate, which were elevated above the rest, but on a common bench.[8] Dio says, that the senators in great mourning appeared in the dress of the equites.[9]

The Romans commonly built tombs[10] for themselves during their lifetime ;[11] thus the MAUSOLEUM[12] of Augustus in the Campus Martius, between the *via Flaminia* and the bank of the Tiber, with woods and walks around. Hence these words frequently occur in ancient inscriptions, V. F., VIVUS FECIT ; V. F. C., VIVUS FACIENDUM CURAVIT ; V. S. P., VIVUS SIBI POSUIT, also SE VIVO FECIT. If they did not live to finish them, it was done by their heirs, who were often ordered by the testament to build a tomb,[13] and sometimes did it at their own expense.[14] Pliny complains bitterly of the neglect of friends in this respect.[15]

The Romans erected tombs either for themselves alone, with their wives (SEPULCHRA PRIVA, vel SINGULARIA,) or for themselves, their family, and posterity (COMMUNIA,) FAMILIARIA et HÆREDITARIA ; likewise for their friends who were buried elsewhere, or whose bodies could not be found (CENOTAPHION, vel TUMULUS HONORARIUS, vel INANIS.)[16] When a person falsely reported to have been dead returned home, he did not enter his house by the door, but was let down from the roof.[17]

The tombs of the rich were commonly built of marble,[18] the ground enclosed with a wall,[19] or an iron rail,[20] and planted around with trees, as among the Greeks.[21]

When several different persons had a right to the same burying-ground, it was sometimes divided into parts, and each part assigned to its proper owner.

But common sepulchres were usually built below ground, and called HYPOGÆA,[22] many of which still exist in different parts of Italy, under the name of catacombs. There were niches cut out in the walls, in which the urns were placed ; these, from their resemblance to the niches in a pigeon-house, were called COLUMBARIA.

Sepulchres were adorned with various figures in sculpture, which are still to be seen, with statues, columns, &c.[23]

1 Tac. Ann. iii. 3. iv. 8. Plin. Ep. ix. 13. Cic. Att. xii. 13, &c. Sen. Decl. iv. 1. Suet. Cal. 24. 45.
2 see p. 300.
3 lugubria sumebant, Juv. x. 215.
4 Fest. in pellis. Serv. Virg. Æn. xi.
5 Liv. ix. 7. Suet. Aug. 101. Schol. Juv. iii. 214. Apul. Met. ii. Homer Il. 13. Mart. x. 47. 4. Stat.

Sylv. iv. 5. 13.
6 Liv. xxxiv. 7. Ter. Heaut. ii. 3. 45. Plut. Probl. 27. Herodian. iv. 2. 6.
7 Liv. ix. 7. Cic. post Red. Sen. 5. Tac. An. iii. 4. Luc. ii. 18.
8 sede vulgari, Tac. An. iv. 8. Dio. lvi. 31.
9 xl. 46.
10 sepulchra v. conditoris.
11 Sen. Brev. Vit. 20.

12 μαυσολειον.
13 Suet. Aug. 101. Hor. Sat. ii. 3. 84. 5. 105. Strab. v. p. 236.
14 de suo vel de sua pecunia.
15 Ep. vi. 10.
16 Cic. Off. i. 17. Mart. i. 117. Cod. 13. Virg. Æn. iii. 304. Hor. Od. ii. 20, 21. Suet. Claud. i. Tac. Ann. i. 62.
17 quasi coelitus missus, Plut. Q. Rom. 5.

18 Cic. Fam. iv. 12. Tibul. iii. 2. 22.
19 maceria, Suet. Ner. 33. 50.
20 ferrea sepe, Strab. v. p. 236.
21 Mart. i. 89. 3. Paus. ii. 15.
22 Petron. 71.
23 Cic. Tusc. Q. v. 23. Virg. Æn. vi. 233. Liv. xxxviii. 56.

But what deserves particular attention, is the inscription or epitaph (TI-
TULUS, *επιγραφη*, EPITAPHIUM vel ELOGIUM,) expressed sometimes in prose,
and sometimes in verse,[1] usually beginning with these letters, D. M. S.,
DIS MANIBUS SACRUM, vel MEMORIÆ ;[2] then the name of the person followed, his character, and the principal circumstances of his life. Often these
words are used, HIC SITUS EST vel JACET, "here lies."[3] If he had lived
happily in marriage, thus, SINE QUERELA, SINE JURGIO, vel *offensa*, vel
discordia, in uninterrupted harmony.[4]

When the body was simply interred without a tomb, an inscription was
sometimes put on the stone coffin, as on that of Numa.[5]

There was an action for violating the tombs of the dead (SEPULCHRI VI-
OLATI ACTIO.)[6] The punishment was a fine, the loss of a hand,[7] working
in the mines,[8] banishment, or death.

A tomb was violated by demolition, by converting it to improper purposes, or by burying in it those who were not entitled.[9] Tombs often served
as lurking-places for the persecuted Christians, and others.[10]

The body was violated by handling, or mutilating it, which was sometimes done for magical purposes ;[11] by stripping it of any thing valuable,
as gold, arms, &c., or by transporting it to another place without leave
obtained from the pontifex maximus, from the emperor, or the magistrate
of the place.[12]

Some consecrated temples to the memory of their friends, as Cicero
proposed to his daughter Tullia ; which design he frequently mentions in
his letters to Atticus. This was a very ancient custom, and probably the
origin of idolatry.[13]

The highest honours were decreed to illustrious persons after death.
The Romans worshipped their founder Romulus as a god, under the name
of Quirinus.[14] Hence, afterwards, the solemn CONSECRATION[15] of the
emperors, by a decree of the senate,[16] who were thus said to be ranked in
the number of the gods,[17] also some empresses.[18] Temples and priests
were assigned to them.[19] They were invoked with prayers. Men swore
by their name or genius, and offered victims on their altars.[20]

The real body was burned, and the remains buried in the usual manner.
But a waxen image of the deceased was made to the life ; which, after a
variety of ridiculous ceremonies paid to it for seven days in the palace,
was carried on a couch in solemn procession, on the shoulders of young
men of equestrian and patrician rank, first to the forum, where the dirge
was sung by a choir of boys and girls of the most noble descent ; then to
the Campus Martius, where it was burned, with a vast quantity of the
richest odours and perfumes, on a lofty and magnificent pile ; from the top
of which an eagle let loose was supposed to convey the prince's soul to
heaven.[21]

---

1 Ov. Her. xiv. 128.
Mart. x. 71. Cic. Tusc.
i. 14. Arch. 11. Sen.
xvii. 20. Fin. ii. 35. Pis.
29. Virg. Ecl. v. 43.
Suet. Claud. 12. Plin.
Ep. ix. 20. Sil. xv.
44.
2 Prud. Symm. i. 402.
Gell. x. 18. Suet. Vit.
10.
3 Ov. Met. ii. 327. Fast.
iii. 3. 373. Tibul. i. 3.
55. iii. 2. 29. Sen. Ep.

78. Mart. vi. 52. Virg.
Æn. vii. 3. Plin. Ep. vi.
10.
4 Plin. Ep. viii. 5.
5 Liv. xl. 29.
6 Cic. Tusc. i. 12. Sen.
Contr. iv. 4.
7 manus amputatio.
8 damnatio ad metal-
lum.
9 alienos inferendo, Cic.
Legg. ii. 26. D. de Sep.
viol. 47. 12.
10 Chrysost. Hom. 40.

Mart. i. 35. iii. 92. 15.
11 i. 4. C. de Sep. viol.
ix. 19. Quinct. Decl. 15.
Apul. Met. ii. Tac. Ann.
ii. 69.
12 Phædr. i. 27. 3. Dig.
Cod. Plin. Ep. x. 73,
74.
13 Cic. Att. xii. 18, 19.
35, 36. 41. 43, &c. Lac.
i. 15. Plin. 27. Wisd.
xiv. 15.
14 Minuc. Felix Octav.
Liv. i. 16.

15 *αποθεωσις*.
16 Herodian. iv. 2.
17 in deorum numerum,
inter vel in deos refer-
ri, Suet. Cæs. 88. cœlo
dicari, Plin. Pan. 11.
18 Suet. Claud. 11. Tac.
Ann. v. 2. xvi. 21.
19 see p. 210.
20 Virg. G. i. 42. Hor.
Ep. ii. 1. 16.
21 Herodian. iv. 3.

ROMAN WEIGHTS AND COINS.

THE principal Roman weight was AS or *libra*, a pound ; which was divided into twelve parts or ounces (UNCIÆ). Thus, *uncia*, an ounce, or $\frac{1}{12}$ of an *as ; sextans*, 2 ounces, or $\frac{2}{12}$; *quadrans*,·3, $\frac{3}{12}$, or $\frac{1}{4}$; *triens*, 4, $\frac{4}{12}$, or $\frac{1}{3}$; *quincunx*, 5, or $\frac{5}{12}$; *semis*, 6, $\frac{6}{12}$, or $\frac{1}{2}$; *septunx*, 7, or $\frac{7}{12}$; *bes*, or *bessis*, 8, $\frac{8}{12}$, or $\frac{2}{3}$; *dodrans*, 9, $\frac{9}{12}$, or $\frac{3}{4}$; *dextans*, or *decunx*, 10, $\frac{10}{12}$, or $\frac{5}{6}$; *deunx*, 11 ounces, or $\frac{11}{12}$ of an *as.*

The UNCIA was also divided thus : *semuncia*, $\frac{1}{2}$, the half of an ounce, or $\frac{1}{24}$ of an *as; duella*, $\frac{1}{3}$; *sicilicus*, vel *-um*, $\frac{1}{4}$; *sextula*, $\frac{1}{6}$; *drachma*, $\frac{1}{8}$; *hemisescla*, i. e. *semisextula*, $\frac{1}{12}$; *tremissis, scrupulus, scriptulum* vel *scripulum*, $\frac{1}{24}$ of an ounce, or $\frac{1}{288}$ of an *as.*[1]

As was applied to any thing divided into twelve parts ; as an inheritance, an acre, liquid measure,[2] or the interest of money, &c. Hence, probably, our word *ace*, or unit.

The Roman pound was equal to 10 ounces, 18 pennyweights, $13\frac{5}{7}$ grains of English Troy weight, or nearly 12 ounces avoirdupoise.

The Greek weights, mentioned by Roman authors, are chiefly the *talent*, divided into 60 *minæ*, and the *mina* into 100 *drachmæ*. The *mina* was nearly equal to the Roman *libra*.

The English TROY weight, by which silver and gold are weighed, is as follows : 24 grains, 1 pennyweight ; 20 pwts. 1 ounce ; 12 oz. 1 pound. But apothecaries, in compounding medicines, make 20 grains 1 scruple ; 3 sc. 1 drachm ; 8 dr. 1 ounce ; 12 oz. 1 pound ; avoirdupoise weight, by which larger and coarser commodities are weighed, 16 drams, 1 oz. ; 16 oz. 1 pound.

The Romans, like other ancient nations,[3] at first had no coined money,[4] but either exchanged commodities with one another, or used a certain weight of uncoined brass,[5] or other metal. Hence the various names of money also denote weight ; so *pendere* for *solvere*, to pay ; *stipendium* (*a stipe pendenda*), soldiers' pay,[6] because at first it was weighed, and not counted. Thus, *talentum* and *mina* among the Greeks, *shekel* among the Hebrews, and *pound* among us.

Several Greek words are supposed to allude to the original custom of exchanging commodities, thus, αρνυμαι, to purchase or exchange by giving a lamb (αρς, αρνος, *agnus*) ; ωνεομαι, by giving an ass (ονος, *asinus*) ; πωλεω, by giving a foal, πωλος (*equuleus*), or the young of any animal.

Servius Tullius first stamped pieces of brass with the image of cattle, oxen, swine, &c. (PECUDES), whence PECUNIA, money.[7] Silver was first coined A. U. 484, five years before the first Punic war, or, according to others, A. U. 498 ; and gold sixty-two years after. Silver coins, however, seem to have been in use at Rome before that time, but of foreign coinage.[8] The Roman coins were then only of brass.

Hence æs, or *æra*, plur., is put for money in general ;[9] *ære mutare*, to buy or sell ; *æs alienum*, debt ; *annua æra*, yearly pay ; *ærarium*, the treasury ; *æs militare*, money for paying the soldiers, given from the treasury to the quæstor by the *tribuni ærarii*, or by them to the soldiers ; *homo æra-*

---

1 Var. L. L. iv. 36.
2 see p. 44. 325. Liv. viii. 11.
3 Strab. lii. 155.
4 pecunia signata.
5 æs rude..
6 Festus.
7 Ov. Fast. v. 261. Servius rex ovium boumque effigie primus æs
signavit, Plin. xxxiii. 3. æs pecore notavit, Var. R. R.° ii. 1. Plut. Q. Rom. 40.
8 Plin. xxxiii. 3. 40. Liv.
viii. 11. Ep. xv.
9 Hor. Art. P. 345. Ep. l. 7. 23. aureos nummos æs dicimus, Ulp.

tus, a monied man,[1] as some read the passage. So *tribuni non tam ærati*, i. e. bene nummati, *quam ut appellantur, ærarii*, i. e. ære corrupti, vel *in ærarios* aut *Cærites referendi ;*[2] *æra vetusta*, i. e. *prisca moneta*, ancient money, but *æra vetera*, old crimes or debts ; *æruscare* vel *æsculari*, to get money by any means ;[3] *æruscator* vel *æsculator*, a low beggarly fellow, a fortune-teller, or the like ; *obæratus*, oppressed with debt, a debtor ; *in meo ære est*, i. e. *in bonis meis* vel *in meo censu*, mine, my friend ;[4] *æs circumforaneum*, money borrowed from bankers,[5] who had shops in porticoes round the forum.[6]

Money was likewise called STIPS (*a stipando*), from being crammed in a cell, that it might occupy less room. But this word is usually put for a small coin, as we say a penny, or farthing, offered to the gods at games or the like,[7] or given as an alms to a beggar, or to any one as a new year's gift (STRENA), or by way of contribution for any public purpose.[8]

The first brass coin[9] was called AS, anciently *assis* (from *æs*) of a pound weight (*libralis*). The highest valuation of fortune[10] under Servius, was a 100,000 pounds weight of brass.[11]

The other brass coins, besides the *as*, were *semisses, trientes, quadrantes*, and *sextantes*. The *quadrans* is also called TERUNCIUS (*a tribus unciis*).[12]

These coins at first had the full weight which their names imported, hence in later times called ÆS GRAVE.[13]

This name was used particularly after the weight of the *as* was diminished, to denote the ancient standard,[14] because when the sum was large, the *asses* were weighed and not counted. Servius on Virgil makes *æs grave* to be lumps[15] of rough copper, or uncoined brass.[16]

In the first Punic war, on account of the scarcity of money, *asses* were struck weighing only the sixth part of a pound, or two ounces,[17] which passed for the same value as those of a pound weight had done ; whence, says Pliny, the republic gained five-sixths,[18] and thus discharged its debt. The mark of the *as* then was a double Janus on one side, and the beak or stern of a ship on the other ; of the *triens* and *quadrans*, a boat (*rates*) ; whence they were sometimes called RATITI.[19]

In the second Punic war, while Fabius was dictator, the *asses* were made to weigh only one ounce (*unciales*) ; and, afterwards by the law of Papirius, A. U. 563, half an ounce (*semunciales*).[20]

The sum of three *asses* was called *tressis ;* of ten *asses, decussis ;* of twenty, *vicessis ;* and so on to a hundred, CENTUSSIS,[21] but there were no such coins.

The silver coins were DENARIUS, the value of which was ten *asses*, or ten pounds of brass (*deni æris*, sc. *asses*), marked with the letter X.—QUINARUS, five *asses*, marked V.—and SESTERTIUS, two *asses* and a half (*quasi* SESQUITERTIUS), commonly marked by the letters L. L. S., for *libra*

1 Liv. v. 4.¦Asc. Fest. Var. L. L. iv. 36. Plaut. Most. iv. 2. 9.
2 Cic. Att. i. 16. see p. 89.
3 Ov. Fast. l. 220. Cic. Ver. v. 13. Fest. Sen. Clem. ii. 6.
4 Gel. ix. 2. xiv. 1. Liv. xxvi. 40. Cæs. B. G. i. 3. Tac. Ann. vi. 17.Cic. Fam. xiii. 62. xv. 14.
5 argentarii.
6 Cic. Att. ii. 1.
7 Var. L. L. iv. 36. Cic. Legg. ii. 16. Liv.xxv. 12. Tac. Ann. xiv. 15. Suet. Aug. 57.
8 Plin. xxxiii. 10. s. 48. xxxiv. 5. Suet.Aug. 91. Cal. 42.
9 nummus vel numus æris, a Numa rege vel a νομος lex.
10 census maximus.
11 centum millia æris,
sc. assium, vel librarum, Liv. i. 43.
12 Cic. Fam. ii. 17. Att. v. 20. Plin. xxxiii. 3. s. 13.
13 Plin. ib.
14 Liv. iv. 41. 60. v. 12. Sen. Helv. 12.
15 massæ.
16 æris rudis, Æn. vi. 862.
17 asses sextantario pondere feriebantur.
18 ita quinque partes factæ lucri.
19 Plut. Q. Rom. 40. see Ov. Fast. i. 229, &c. Festus. Plin. ib.
20 Plin. xxxiii. 3. s. 13.
21 Var. L. L. iv. 36. viii. 46. Pers. v. 76. 191. Gel. xv. 15. Macrob. Sat. ii. 13.

libra semis ; or by abbreviation, H. s., and often called absolutely NUMMUS, because it was in most frequent use.[1]

The impression on silver coins[2] was usually, on one side, carriages drawn by two or four beasts (*bigæ* vel *quadrigæ*): whence they are called BIGATI and QUADRIGATI, sc. *nummi*,[3] and on the reverse, the head of Roma with a helmet.

On some silver coins were marked the figure of Victory, hence called VICTORIATI, stamped by the Clodian law,[4] of the same value with the *quinarii*.

From every pound of silver were coined 100 *denarii ;* so that at first a pound of silver was equal in value to a thousand pounds of brass. Whence we may judge of the scarcity of silver at that time in Rome. But afterwards the case was altered. For when the weight of the *as* was diminished, it bore the same proportion to the *denarius* as before, till it was reduced to one ounce ; and then a *denarius* passed for sixteen *asses* (except in the military pay, in which it continued to pass for ten *asses*, at least under the republic, for in the time of Tiberius it appears no such exception was made),[5] a *quinarius* for eight *asses*, and a *sestertius* for four; which proportion continued when the *as* was reduced to half an ounce. Hence *argentum ære solutum*, i. e. an *as* for a *sestertius*, or the fourth part.[6]

But the weight of the silver money also varied, and was different under the emperors from what it had been under the republic.

Varro mentions silver coins of less value ; LIBELLA, worth an *as*, or the tenth part of a *denarius;* SEMBELLA (quasi *semilibella*), worth half a pound of brass, or the twentieth part of a *denarius*, and TERUNCIUS, the fortieth part of a *denarius*. But Cicero puts the *libella* for the smallest silver coin, as well as the *teruncius ;*[7] this, however, he does only proverbially ; as we may say, a penny or a farthing.

A golden coin was first struck at Rome in the second Punic war, in the consulship of C. Claudius Nero and M. Livius Salinator, A. U. 546 ; called AUREUS, or *aureus nummus*, equal in weight to two *denarii* and a *quinarius*, and in value to twenty-five *denarii*, or 100 *sestertii*. Hence the fee allowed to be taken by a lawyer is called by Tacitus *dena sestertia ;* by Pliny, *decem millia*, sc. H. s. ;[8] and by Ulpian, CENTUM AUREI,[9] all of which were equivalent.

The common rate of gold to silver under the republic was tenfold.[10] But Julius Cæsar got so much gold by plundering, that he exchanged it[11] for 3000 *sestertii*, or 750 *denarii*, the pound, i. e. a pound of gold for 7½ pounds of silver.[12]

The *aureus* in later ages was called SOLIDUS, but then greatly inferior, both in weight and beauty, to the golden coins struck under the republic and first emperors.[13]

At first forty *aurei* were made from a pound of gold, with much the same images as the silver coins. But under the late emperors they were mixed with alloy ; and thus their intrinsic value was diminished. Hence a different number of *aurei* were made from a pound of gold at different times; under Nero, 45,[14] but under Constantine, 72.

1 Cic. Ver. iii. 60, 61.
2 nota argenti.
3 Plin. xxxiii. 8. Liv. xxii. 52. xxiii. 15.
4 Cic. Font. 5. Quinct. vi. 3. 50. Plin. xxxiii. 3.
5 Tac. Ann. i. 17.

6 Plin. xxxiii. 3. Sall. Cat. 33, see p. 34.
7 Varr. L. L. iv. 36. Cic. Ver. ii. 10. Rosc. C. 4. Fin. iii. 14. Att. v. 20. Fam. ii. 17.
8 Suet. Oth. 4. Tac. Hist.

i. 24. Ann. xi. 7. Plin. Ep. v. 21.
9 D. I. 12. de extr. cog- nit. see p. 129.
10 ut pro argenteis de- cem aureus unus vale- ret,—that one piece of

gold should be deemed equivalent to ten of silver, Liv. xxxviii. 11.
11 promercale divideret.
12 Suet. Cæs. 54.
13 Lamprid. in Alex. 39.
14 Plin. xxxiii. 3.

The emperors usually impressed on their coins their own image. This was first done by Julius Cæsar, according to a decree of the senate.[1]

The essay or trial of gold was called OBRUSSA,[2] hence *aurum ad obrussam*, sc. *exactum*, the purest gold ; ARGENTUM PUSTULATUM, the finest silver,[3] vel *purum putum;* ARGENTUM *infectum* vel *rude*, bullion, unwrought or uncoined silver ; *factum*, plate ; *signatum*, coined silver ; NUMMUS *asper*, new-coined ;[4] *vetus* vel *tritus*, old, &c.

Some coins were indented (*serrati*).[5]

Besides the ordinary coins, there were various medals struck to commemorate important events, properly called MEDALLIONS ; for what we commonly term Roman medals, were their current money. When an action deserved to be recorded on a coin, it was stamped and issued out of the mint.

Money was coined in the temple of Juno MONETA ; whence *money*. The consuls at first are thought to have had the charge of it. But particular officers were afterwards created for that purpose.[6]

There are several Grecian coins mentioned by Roman writers, some of them equal to Roman coins, and some not ; DRACHMA, equal to a *denarius ;* but some make it to have been as nine to eight ; MINA, equal to 100 *drachmæ*, or to a Roman *libra* or pound of silver ; TALENTUM, equal to sixty *minæ*, or Roman pounds ; TETRA-DRACHMA vel *-um*, equal to four *drachmæ* or *denarii*, as its name imports ; but Livy, according to the common reading, makes it three *denarii;* OBOLUS, the sixth part of a *denarius* or *drachma*.[7]

METHOD OF COMPUTING MONEY.

THE Romans usually computed sums of money by SESTERTII or SESTERTIA. *Sestertium* is the name of a sum, not of a coin.

When a numeral noun is joined with *sestertii*, it means just so many sesterces ; thus, *decem sestertii*, ten sesterces : but when it is joined with *sestertia*, it means so many thousand *sestertii ;* thus, *decem sestertia*, ten thousand sesterces.

SESTERTIUM, *mille sestertii, mille nummi* vel *sestertii nummi ; mille sestertium, mille nummum* vel *sestertium, nummum mille ; H. S.* vel H̄. S̄. 2500 *æris*, sc. *asses ;* 250 *denarii* vel *drachmæ* denote the same sum.

When a numeral adverb is joined to *sestertium*, it means so many hundred thousand *sestertii ;* thus *quadragies sestertium* is the same with *quadragies centena millia sestertiorum nummorum*, or *quater millies mille sestertii*, four millions of *sestertii*. Sometimes the adverb stands by itself, and denotes the same thing ; thus, *decies, vicies* vel *vigesies*, sc. *sestertium ;* expressed more fully, *decies centena*, sc. *millia sestertium ;* and completely, Cic. Verr. i. 10. and Juv. iii. 70. So also in sums of brass, *decies æris*, sc. *centena millia assium*.[8] For when we say *deni æris, centum æris*, &c. *asses* is always to be supplied.

When sums are marked by letters, if the letters have a line over them, *centena millia* is understood, as in the case of the numeral adverbs ; thus, H. S. M. C. signifies the same with *millies centies*, i. e. 110,000,000 *sester-*

---

1 Juv. xiv. 291. Dio. 3 Suet. Ner. 44. Mart. 5 Tac. de Mor. Germ.   Cic. Fam. xii. 13.
xliv. 4.   vii. 65.   5.   8 Liv. xxiv. 11. Hor.
2 Plin. xxxiii. 3. Cic. 4 Gel. vi. 5. Liv. xxvii. 6 see p. 101.   Sat. i. 3. 15. Juv. x.
Brut. 74. Sen. Ep. 13. 18. xxxiv. 52. Suet. ib. 7 Plin. xxi. 34. Liv.   335.
s. 19.   Sen. Ep. 19.   xxxiv. 52. xxxvi. 46.

tii or *nummi*, £888,020 : 16 : 8, whereas H₁ s. m. c. without the cross line, denotes only 1100 *sestertii*, £8 : 17 : 7¼.

When the numbers are distinguished by points in two or three orders, the first towards the right hand signifies units, the second thousands, and the third hundred thousands; thus, III. XII. DC. HS. denotes 300,000, 12,000, and 600 H. s. in all making 312,600 *sestertii*, £5047 : 3 : 9.[1]

Pliny says,[2] that seven years before the first Punic war, there was in the Roman treasury *auri pondo* XVI. DCCCX., *argenti pondo*, XXII. LXX, *et in numerato*, LXII. LXXV. CCCC., that is, 16,810 pounds of gold, 22,070 pounds of silver, and in ready money, 6,275,400 *sestertii*, £50,660 : 15 : 7. But these sums are otherwise marked thus, *auri pondo* XVI. M. DCCCX.,*argenti* XXII. M. LXX., *et in numerato* LXII. LXXV. M. CCCC.

When *sestertium* neut. is used, *pondo* is understood, that is, two pounds and a half of silver, or a thousand *sestertii*.[3]

When H. s. or *sestertium* is put after *decem millia* or the like, it is in the genitive plural for *sestertiorum*, and stands for so many *sestertii*, which may be otherwise expressed by *decem sestertia*, &c. But *sestertium*, when joined with *decies* or the like, is in the nominative or accusative singular, and is a compendious way of expressing *decies centies sestertium*, i. e. *decies centum vel decies centena millia sestertium* v. *sestertiorum.*

The Romans sometimes expressed sums by talents; thus, *decem millia talentûm*, and *sestertium bis millies et quadringenties* are equivalent. So 100 talents and 600,000 *denarii ;*[4] or by pounds, LIBRÆ *pondo*, i. e. *pondere* in the ablative, for these words are often joined, as we say, pounds in weight, and when PONDO is put by itself as an indeclinable noun, for a pound or pounds, it is supposed even then, by the best critics, to be in the ablative, and to have *libra* or *libræ* understood.[5]

The Roman *libra* contained twelve ounces of silver, and was worth about £3 : 4 : 7 sterling ; the *talent*, nearly £193 : 15.

But the common computation was by *sestertii* or *nummi*.

A SESTERTIUS is reckoned to have been worth of our money one penny 3¾ farthings ; a QUINARIUS or *victoriatus* 3d. 3½q. ; a DENARIUS, 7d. 3q. ; the AUREUS, or gold coin, 16s. 1¾d. ; a SESTERTIUM, or a thousand *sestertii*, £8 : 1 : 5½,—ten *sestertii*, 1s. 7d. 1½q.—a hundred *sestertii*, 16s. 1d. 3q.— ten *sestertia*, or 10,000 *sestertii*, £80 : 14 : 7,—a hundred *sestertia*, or 100,000 *sestertii*, £807 : 5 : 10,—1000 *sestertia*, or *decies sestertium*, or *decies centena millia sestertium*, vel *nummum*, or 1,000,000 *sestertii*, £8,072 : 18 : 4, sterl.— *centies*, vel *centies* H. s., vel *centies centum millia sestertiorum*, or 10,000,000 *sestertii*, £80,729 : 3 : 4, sterl.—*millies*, vel *millies* H. s., £807,291 : 13 : 4, sterl.—*millies centies* H. s., £888,020 : 16 : 8, sterl. Hence we may form some notion of certain instances on record of Roman wealth and luxury.

Crassus is said to have possessed in lands *bis millies*, ł. e. £1,614,583 : 6 : 8, besides money, slaves, and household furniture,[6] which may be estimated at as much more.[7] In the opinion of Crassus, no one deserved to be called rich who could not maintain an army, or a legion.—Seneca, *ter millies*, £2,421,875.—Pallas, the freedman of Claudius, an equal sum.[8]—Len-

---

1 There is here an error in calculation : 312,600 sestertii reckoning to each worth 1 penny, 3¼ farthings = *l*2,523 : 11 : 10½ sterling, just one half of the amount given by the author. Several other errors of the same description in the chapter have been corrected without being pointed out in notes.—ED.
2 xxxiii. 3.
3 Liv. xxii. 23.
4 Cic. Rab. Post. 5. Liv. xxxiv. 50.

5 see Gronovius de Pec. vet. Plaut. Pseud. iii. 2. 27. Rud. iv. 2. 9. Men. iii. 3. 3. et 18. Macrob. Sat. iii. 15. Columel. xii. 20. 28. Liv. iii. 29. iv. 20. xxii. 23. xxvi. 47. Gel. ii. 24. xx. 1. Cic. Clu. 64.

Invent. ii. 40. Parad. iii. 1.
6 Plin. xxxiii. 10. s. 47.
7 alterum tantum.
8 Cic. Off. i. 8. Plin. xxxiii. 10. Tac. Ann. xii. 53. xiii. 42.

ulus the augur, *quater millies*, £3,229,166 : 13 : 4.—C. Cæcilius Claudius Isidorus, although he had lost a great part of his fortune in the civil war, left by his will 4,116 slaves, 3,600 yoke of oxen, 257,000 of other cattle ; in ready money, H. S. *sexcenties*, £484,375.[1]

Augustus received by the testaments of his friends *quater decies millies*, £32,291,666 : 13 : 4. He left in legacies to the Roman people, i. e. to the public, *quadringenties*, £322,916 : 13 : 4, and to the tribes or poor citizens,[2] TRICIES *quinquies*, £28,255 : 4 : 2.[3] Tiberius left at his death *vigesies ac septies millies*, £21,796,875, which Caligula lavished away in less than one year.[4] Vespasian, at his accession to the empire, said, that to support the commonwealth, there was need of *quadringenties millies*, £322,916,666 : 13 : 4, an immense sum ! more than the national debt of Britain ![5]

The debt of Milo is said to have amounted to H. S. *septingenties*, £565, 104 : 3 : 4.[6]

Cæsar, before he enjoyed any office, owed 1300 talents, £251,875. When, after his prætorship, he set out for Spain, he is reported to have said, *bis millies et quingenties sibi deesse, ut nihil haberet*, i. e. that he was £2,018,229 : 3 : 4 worse than nothing. A sum hardly credible ! When he first entered Rome in the beginning of the civil war, he took out of the treasury £1,095,979,[7] and brought into it, at the end of the civil war, above £4,843,750 (*amplius sexies millies*). He is said to have purchased the friendship of Curio, at the beginning of the civil war, by a bribe of *sexcenties sestertium*,[8] £484,375, and that of the consul, L. Paulus, the colleage of Marcellus, A. U. 704, by 1500 talents, about £290,625.[9] Of Curio, Lucan says, *hic vendidit urbem*, he sold the city ; *venali Curio lingua*, Curio of venal eloquence,[10] and Virgil, as it is thought, *vendidit hic auro patriam*, he sold his native country for gold. But this Curio afterwards met with the fate which as a traitor to his country he deserved, being slain by Juba in Africa.[11] *Libycas en nobile corpus pascit aves ! nullo contectus* CURIO *busto*, Lucan. iv. 809.

> See ! where, a prey, unburied Curio lies,
> To every fowl that wings the Libyan skies.—*Rowe.*

Antony, on the Ides of March, when Cæsar was killed, owed *quadringenties*, £322,916 : 13 : 4, which he paid before the kalends of April, and squandered of the public money, *sestertium septies millies*, £5,651,041 : 13 : 4.[12]

Cicero at first charged Verres with having plundered the Sicilians of *sestertium millies*, but afterwards exacted only, *quadringenties*.[13]

Apicius wasted on luxurious living *sexcenties sestertium*, £484,375 ; Seneca says, *sestertium millies in culinam consumpsit*, and being at last obliged to examine the state of his affairs, found that he had remaining only *sestertium centies*, £80,729 : 3 : 4, a sum which he thought too small to live upon, and therefore ended his days by poison.[14]

Pliny says, that in his time Lollia Paulina wore, in full dress, jewels to the value of *quadragies sestertium*, £32,291 : 13 : 4, or as others read the

---

1 Sen. Ben. ii. 27. Plin. ib.
2 tribubus vel plebi.
3 Suet. Aug. ult. Tac. Ann. i. 8.
4 Suet. Cal. 37.
5 In the year 1791, when

this work was first published.—Suet. Vesp. 16.
6 Plin. xxxvi. 15. s. 24.
7 Plut. Cæs. App. B. C. ii. 432. Plin. xxxiii. 3.
8 Vel. ii. 56. Vel. Pat. ii.

48. Dio. xl. 60. Val. Max. ix. i. 6.
9 App. B. C. ii. 443. Plut. Cæs. Pomp. et Suet. Cæs. 29.
10 Luc. i. 269. iv. ult.
11 Virg. Æn. iv. 621.

Dio. xli. 42.
12 Cic. Phil. ii. 37. v. 4. xii. 5.
13 Cæc. 5. Act. Ver. 18.
14 Sen. Cons. Helv. 10. Mart. iii. 22. Dio. lvii. 19.

passage, *quadringenties sestertium*, £322,916 : 13 : 4.[1] Julius Cæsar presented Servilia, the mother of M. Brutus, with a pearl worth *sexagis sestertio*, £48,417 : 10. Cleopatra, at a feast with Antony, swallowed a pearl dissolved in vinegar, worth *centies* H. S., £80,729 : 3 : 4. Clodius, the son of Æsopus, the tragedian, swallowed one worth *decies*, £8,072 : 18 : 4. Caligula did the same.[2]

A single dish of Æsop's is said to have cost a hundred *sestertia*, £807 : 5 : 10.[3] Caligula laid out on a supper, *centies* H. S., £80,729 : 3 : 4, and Heliogabalus *tricies* H. S., £24,218 : 15.[4] The ordinary expense of Lucullus for a supper in the hall of Apollo, was 500,000 *drachmæ*, £1,614 : 11 : 8.[5]

Even persons of a more sober character were sometimes very expensive. Cicero had a citron-table which cost him H. S. *decies*, £807 : 5 : 10 ; and bought the house of Crassus with borrowed money, for H. S. XXXV. i. e. *tricies quinquies*, £28,255 : 4 : 2.[6] This house had first belonged to the tribune M. Livius Drusus, who, when the architect promised to build it for him in such a manner that none of his neighbours should overlook him, answered, "If you have any skill, contrive it rather so, that all the world may see what I am doing."[7]

Messala bought the house of Autronius for H. S. CCCCXXXVII., £352, 786 : 2 : 9.[8] Domitius estimated his house at *sexagies sestertia*, i. e. £48,437 : 10. The house of Clodius cost *centies et quadragies octies*, £119,479.[9]

The fish-pond of C. Herius was sold for *quadragies* H. S., £32,291 : 13 : 4, and the fish of Lucullus for the same sum.[10]

The house-rent of middling people in the time of Julius Cæsar is supposed to have been *bina millia nummum*, £16 : 2 : 11. That of Cœlius was XXX *millia nummum*, £242 : 3 : 9, and thought high.[11]

The value of houses in Rome rose greatly in a few years. The house of Marius, which was bought by Cornelia for 7½ *myriads* of *drachmæ*, £2, 421 : 17 : 6, was, not long after, purchased by Lucullus for 50 *myriads*, and 200 *drachmæ*, £16,152 : 5 : 10.[12]

The house of Lepidus, which in the time of his consulship was reckoned one of the finest in Rome, in the space of 35 years was not in the hundredth rank.[13] The villa of M. Scaurus being burned by the malice of his slaves, he lost H. S. *millies*, £807,291 : 13 : 4. The golden house[14] of Nero must have cost an immense sum, since Otho laid out in finishing a part of it *quingenties* H. S., £403,645 : 16 : 8.[15]

THE INTEREST OF MONEY.

THE interest of money was called FŒNUS, vel *fenus ;* or USURA, *fructus, merces*, vel *impendium ;* the capital, CAPUT, or *sors ;* also FŒNUS, which is put for the principal as well as the interest.[16]

When one AS was paid monthly for the use of a hundred, it was called USURA CENTESIMA, because in a hundred months the interest equalled the capital ; or ASSES USURÆ. This we call 12 per cent. per annum,[17] which

1 Plin. x. 35. s. 57.
2 Suet. Cal. 34. Cæs. 50.
  Plin. ib. Macrob. Sat.
  ii. 13. Val. Max. ix. 1, 2.
  Hor. Sat. ii. 3. 239.
3 Plin. x. 51. s. 72. xxxv.
  12.
4 Sen. Helv. 9. Lampr.

27.
4 Plut. Lucul.
5 Plin. xiii. 15. [vii. 38.
  Cic. Fam. v. 6.
7 Vell. Pat. ii. 14.
8 Cic. Att. i. 13.
9 Val. Max. ix. 1. 5.
Plin. xxxvi. 15. s. 24.

10 Plin. ix. 54, 55.
11 Suet. Cæs. 38. Cic.
  Cœl. 7.
12 Plut. Mar.
13 centesimum locum
  non obtinuit, Plin.
  xxxvi. 15. s. 24.
14 aurea domus.

15 Plin. ib.
16 Tac. Ann. vi. 17. Cic.
  Att. i. 12. v. 21. vi. 1, 2.
17 duodenis assibus debere vel mutuari, Plin.
  Ep. x. 62. v. 55. centesimas computare, ix.
  28.

was usually the legal interest at Rome, at least towards the end of the republic, and under the first emperors. Sometimes the double of this was exacted, *binæ centesimæ*, 24 per cent., and even 48 per cent., *quaternæ centesimæ*. Horace mentions one who demanded 60 per cent, ; *quinas hic capiti mercedes exsecat*, i. e. *quintuplices usuras exigit*, vel *quinis centesimis fænerat*, he deducts from the capital sum five common interests.[1]

When the interest at the end of the year was added to the capital, and likewise yielded interest, it was called *centesimæ renovatæ*, or ANATOCISMUS *anniversarius*, compound interest ; if not, *centesimæ perpetuæ* ; or *fænus perpetuum*.[2]

USURÆ *semisses*, six per cent. ; *trientes*, four per cent. ; *quadrantes*, three per cent. ; *besses*, eight per cent., &c. ; *usuræ legitimæ*, vel *licitæ*, legal interest ; *illicitæ* vel *illegitimæ*, illegal.[3]

USURA is commonly used in the plural, and FŒNUS in the singular.

The interest permitted by the Twelve Tables was only one per cent., FŒNUS UNCIARIUM vel UNCIÆ USURÆ (see *lex* DUILIA MÆNIA), which some make the same with *usura centesima* ; reduced, A. U. 408, to one-half, FŒNUS SEMUNCIARIUM ;[4] but these, and other regulations, were eluded by the art of the usurers.[5] After the death of Antony and Cleopatra, A. U. 725, the interest of money at Rome fell from 12 to 4 per cent.[6]

Professed bankers or money-lenders were also called MENSARII vel *trapezitæ*, ARGENTARII, NUMMULARII, vel *collybistæ*, sometimes appointed by the public.[7]

A person who laid out money at interest was said *pecuniam alicui* v. *apud aliquem occupare, ponere, collocare*, &c. ; when he called it in, *relegere*.[8]

The Romans commonly paid money by the intervention of a banker,[9] whose account-books of debtor and creditor[10] were kept with great care ; hence *acceptum referre*, and among later writers, *acceptum ferre*, to mark on the debtor side, as received ; ACCEPTILATIO, a form of freeing one from an obligation without payment : *expensum ferre*, to mark down on the creditor side, as paid or given away ; *expensi latio*, the act of doing so ; *ratio accepti atque expensi inter nos convenit*, our accounts agree ; *in rationem inducere* vel *in tabulis rationem scribere*, to state an account. And because this was done by writing down the sum and subscribing the person's name in the banker's books, hence *scribere nummos alicui*, i. e. *se per scriptum* v. *chirographam obligure ut solvat*, to promise to pay ;[11] *rationem accepti scribere*, to borrow ; *rescribere*, to pay, or to pay back what one has received ; so, *perscribere*, to order to pay ; whence PERSCRIPTIO, an assignment or an order on a banker.[12] Hence also NOMEN is put for a debt, for the cause of a debt, or for an article of an account. NOMINA *facere*, to contract debt, to give security for payment, by subscribing the sum in a banker's books, or to accept such security ; *exigere*, to demand payment. So, *appellare denomine, dissolvere*, to discharge, to pay ; *solvere, expungere, explicare, expedire* ;[13] *transcribere nomina in alios*, to lend money in the name of others ;

---

1 Sat. i. 2. 14. Cic. Ver. iii. 70. Att. vi. 2.
2 Cic. Att. v. 21.
3 Digest. et Suet. Aug. 39. Cic. Att. iv. 15. Pers. v. 149.
4 Tac. Ann. vi. 16. Liv. vii. 27.
5 fœneratores, Cic. Att. vi. 1. Off. ii. 24, 25. Sal. Cat. 33. Liv. viii. 28.

xxxv. 7. 41.
6 Dio. li. 21.
7 Liv. vii. 21. xxiii. 21. Suet. Aug. 2—4. Cic. Flacc. 19.
8 Hor. Ep. 2. ult. Cic. Flacc. 21. Ver. i. 36.
9 Cic. Cæc. 6. in foro, et de mensæ scriptura, magis quam ex arca domoque, vel cista pe-

cunia numerabatur, Don. Ter. Adelph. ii. 4. 13.
10 tabulæ vel codices accepti et expensi ; mensæ rationes, ib. & Cic.
11 Plaut. Most. i. 3. 146. Asin. ii. 4. 34. Cic. Ver. i. 42.
12 Plaut. Truc. iv. 2. 36. Ter. Phorm. v. 7. 29,

30. Hor. Sat. ii. 3. 76. Cic. Att. iv. ult. ix. 12. xii. 51. Flacc. 19. 20. Or. i. 58. Phil. v. 4.
13 Sen. Ben. i. 1. Cic. Off. iii. 14. Fam. vii. 23. Verr. i. 10. Planc. 28. Att. v. 39. vi. 2. xiii. 29. xvi. 6. Plaut. Cist. i. 3. 41.

pecunia ei est in nominibus, is on loan ; *in codicis extrema cera nomen infimum in flagitiosa litura,* the last article at the bottom of the page shamefully blotted ; *rationum nomina,* articles of accounts ;[1] *in tabulas nomen referre,* to enter a sum received ; *multis Verri nominibus acceptum referre,* to mark down on the debtor side many articles or sums received from Verres ; *hinc ratio cum Curtiis, multis nominibus, quorum in tabulis iste habet nullum,* i. e. *Curtiis nihil expensum tulit Verres.* Hence Cicero, pleading against Verres, often says, RECITA NOMINA, i. e. *res, personas, causas, in quas ille aut quibus expensum tulit,* the accounts, or the different articles of an account ; *certis nominibus pecuniam debere,* on certain accounts ;[2] *non refert parva nomina in codices,* small sums ; *multis nominibus versuram ab aliquo facere,* to borrow many sums to pay another ; *permulta nomina,* many articles, likewise for a debtor ; *ego bonum nomen existimor,* a good debtor, one to be trusted ; *optima nomina non appellando fiunt mala,*[3] *bono nomine centesimis contentus erat, non bono quaternas centesimas, sperabat,* he was satisfied with 12 per cent. from a good debtor, he looked for 48 from a bad ; *nomina sectatur tironum nummos,* i. e. *ut debitores faciat venatur,* seeks to lend to minors, a thing forbidden by law ; *cautos nominibus certis expendere nummos,* i. e. *sub chirographo bonis nominibus* vel *debitoribus dare,* to lend on security to good debtors ; *locare nomen sponsu improbo,* to become surety with an intention to deceive.[4]

As the interest of money was usually paid on the Kalends, hence called TRISTES, and CELERES, a book in which the sums to be demanded were marked was called CALENDARIUM.[5]

ROMAN MEASURES OF LENGTH.

THE Romans measured length or distance by feet, cubits, paces, stadia, and miles.

The Romans, as other nations, derived their names of measure chiefly from the parts of the human body. DIGITUS, a digit, or finger's breadth ; POLLEX, a thumb's breadth, an inch ; PALMUS, a hand's breadth, a palm, equal to (=) 4 *digiti*, or three inches ; PES, a foot, = 16 digits or 12 inches ; PALMIPES, a foot and a hand's breadth ; CUBITUS vel *ulna*, a cubit, from the tip of the elbow, bent inwards, to the extremity of the middle finger, = 1½ foot, the fourth part of a well-proportioned man's stature ; PASSUS, a pace, = 5 feet, including a double step, or the space from the place where the foot is taken up to that where it is set down, the double of an ordinary pace, *gradus* vel *gressus.* A pole ten feet long[6] was called PERTICA, a perch.[7] The English perch or pole is 16½ feet ; *una pertica tractare,* to measure with the same ell, to treat in the same manner.[8]

Each foot (PES) was divided into 4 *palmi* or hand-breadths, 12 *pollices* or thumb-breadths, and 16 *digiti* or finger-breadths. Each digitus was supposed equal to 4 barley-corns ;[9] but the English make their inch only three barley-corns. The foot was also divided into 12 parts, denominated from the divisions of the Roman *as ;* thus, *dodrans* vel *spithama,* 9 *pollices,* or *unciæ,* inches.[10]

A cubit (CUBITUS, v. -*um*) was equal to a foot and a half (*sesquipes*), 2

1 Liv. xxxv. 7. Cic. Top. 3. Ver. i. 36. 39. Ver. 7.
2 Cic. Quinct. 11. Ver. i. 39. Asc. Cic.
3 Cic. Rosc. Com. 1.

Ver. ii. 5. 76. Fam. v. 6. Colum. i. 7.
4 Phædr. i. 16. Cic. Att. v. 21. Hor. Sat. i. 2. 16. Ep. ii. 1. 105.
5 Hor. Sat. i. 3. 87. Ov.

Rem. Am. 561. Sen. Ben. i. 2. vii. 10. Ep. 14. 87.
6 decempeda.
7 quasi portica, a portando.

8 Plin. Ep. viii. 2.
9 hordei grana, Front. de Aquæd. i. 2.
10 Suet. Aug. 79. Plin. vii. 2.

spithamæ, 6 *palmi*, 18 *pollices*, or 24 *digiti*.   PASSUS, a pace, was reckoned equal to 5 feet ; 125 *passus*, or 625 feet, made a STADIUM or furlong ; and 8 *stadia*, or 1000 paces, or 5000 feet, a mile (MILLIARIUM, vel *-re ;* vel MILLE, sc. *passus* v. *passuum*).[1]

The Greeks and Persians called 30 stadia PARASANGA ; and 2 arasangs, SCHŒNOS ; but others differ.[2]

The Roman acre (JUGERUM) contained 240 feet in length and 120 in breadth ; that is, 28,800 square feet.[3]

The half of an acre was called ACTUS QUADRATUS, consisting of 120 feet square (ACTUS, *in quo boves* agerentur *cum aratro uno impetu justo* vel *protelo*, i. e. *uno tractu* vel *tenore*, at one stretch, without stopping or turning ; *non strigantes*, without resting).   *Actus quadratus* UNDIQUE *finitur pedibus* CXX.   *Hoc duplicatum facit* jugerum, *et eb eo, quod erat* JUNCTUM. *nomen jugeri usurpavit.*   Jugum *vocabatur, quod uno jugo boum in die exarari posset.*[4]

An English acre contains 40 perches or poles, or 660 feet, in length, and four poles, or 66 feet, in breadth.   The Scottish acre is somewhat more than one-fifth larger.

The JUGERUM was divided into the same parts as an AS ; hence *uncia agri*, the twelfth part of an acre.[5]

ROMAN MEASURES OF CAPACITY.

THE measure of capacity most frequently mentioned by Roman authors is the AMPHORA,[6] called also QUADRANTAL or CADUS, and by the Greeks *metreta* or *ceramium*, a cubic foot, contained 2 *urna*, 3 *modii*, 8 *congii*, 48 *sextarii*, and 96 *heminæ* or *cotylæ*.   But the Attic *amphora*[7] contained 2 *urnæ*, and 72 *sextarii*.

The amphora was nearly equal to 9 gallons English, and the sextarius to one pint and a half English, or one mutchkin and a half Scottish.

A sextarius contained 2 heminæ, 4 quartarii, 8 acetabula, and 12 cyathi, which were denominated from the parts of the Roman *as ;* thus, *calices* or cups were called *sextantes, quadrantes, trientes,* &c., according to the number of *cyathi* which they contained.[8]

A cyathus was as much as one could easily swallow at once.   It contained 4 *ligulæ* vel *lingulæ*, or *cochlearia*, spoonfuls.[9]

CONGIUS, the eighth of an amphora, was equal to a cubic half foot, or to 6 sextarii.   This measure of oil or wine used anciently to be distributed by the magistrates or leading men among the people.   Hence CONGIARIUM, a gratuity or largess of money, corn, or oil, given to the people, chiefly by the emperors, or privately to an individual.[10]

A gratuity to the soldiers was called DONATIVUM, sometimes also CONGIARIUM.[11]   The *congiaria* of Augustus, from their smallness, used to be called HEMINARIA.[12]

The weight of rain-water contained in an amphora was 80 Roman pounds, in a congius 10 pounds, and in a sextarius 1 pound 8 ounces.

---

1 Cic. Cæc. 10. Att. iii. 4. Gell. i. 16. Plin. ii. 23.
2 Herodot. ii. 16. Plin. v. 10. xii. 14.
3 Quinct. i. 10. 42. Var. R. R. i. 10. l. Plin. xviii. 3, &c.
4 Don. Ter. Phorm. 1.

3. 36. Plin. xviii. 3. 19. s. 49. Sen. Ep. 31. Phædr. iii. 6. 9. Col. v. 1. 5. Vatr. R. R. i. 10.
5 Var. R. R. i. 10.
6 ex αμφι et φερω, quod vas ejus mensuræ utrinque ferretur, dua-

bus ansis.
7 καδος, or metreta.
8 see p. 326.
9 Columel. xii. 21. Plin. xx. 5. Mart. xiv. 120.
10 Liv. xxv. 22. xxxvii. 57. Plin. xiv. 14. Cic. Phil. ii. 45. Fam. viii. 1. Att. x. 7. Tac. Ann.

xiii. 31. Suet. Cæs. 27. 38. Aug. 42. Tib. 20. Dom. 4. Vesp. 18.
11 Suet. Cal. 46. Ner. 7. Plin. Pan. 25. Cic. Att. xvi. 8. Tac. Ann. xii. 41. Curt. vi. 2.
12 Quinct. vi. 3. 52.

The greatest measure of things liquid among the Romans was the CU-LEUS, containing 20 amphoræ.

Pliny says, the *ager Cæcubus* usually yielded 7 *culei* of wine an acre, i. e. 143 gallons 3½ pints English, worth at the vineyard 300 nummi, or 75 denarii, each *culeus*, i. e. £2 : 8 : 5¼, about a halfpenny the English pint.[1]

MODIUS was the chief measure for things dry, the third part of a cubic foot, somewhat more than a peck English. A *modius* of Gallic wheat weighed about 20 *libræ*. Five modii of wheat used to be sown in an acre, six of barley and beans, and three of pease. Six modii were called ME-DIMNUS, vel -*um*, an Attic measure.[2]

ROMAN METHOD OF WRITING.

MEN in a savage state have always been found ignorant of alphabetic characters. The knowledge of writing is a constant mark of civilization. Before the invention of this art, men employed various methods to preserve the memory of important events, and to communicate their thoughts to those at a distance.

The memory of important events was preserved by raising altars or heaps of stones, planting groves, instituting games and festivals, and, what was most universal, by historical songs.[3]

The first attempt towards the representation of thought was the painting of objects. Thus, to represent a murder, the figure of one man was drawn stretched on the ground, and of another with a deadly weapon standing over him. When the Spaniards first arrived in Mexico, the inhabitants gave notice of it to their emperor Montezuma, by sending him a large cloth, on which was painted every thing they had seen.

The Egyptians first contrived certain signs or symbols called hierogly-phics (from ἱερος, sacred, and γλυφω, to carve), whereby they represented several things by one figure. The Egyptians and Phœnicians contended about the honour of having invented letters.[4]

Cadmus, the Phœnician, first introduced letters into Greece near 1500 years before Christ, then only sixteen in number, α, β, γ, δ, ε, ι, κ, λ, μ, ν, ο, π, ρ, σ, τ, υ. To these, four were added by Palamedes, in the time of the Trojan war, θ, ζ, φ, χ; and four afterwards by Simonides, ξ, η, ψ, ω.[5]

Letters were brought into Latium by Evander from Greece. The Latin letters at first were nearly of the same form with the Greek.[6]

Some nations ranged their letters perpendicularly, from the top to the bottom of the page, but most horizontally. Some from the right to left, as the Hebrews, Assyrians, &c. Some from right to left and from left to right alternately, like cattle ploughing, as the ancient Greeks ; hence this manner of writing was called βουστροφηδον. But most, as we do, from left to right.

The most ancient materials for writing were stones and bricks. Thus the decalogue, or ten commandments, and the laws of Moses ; then plates of brass,[7] or of lead, and wooden tablets.[8] On these all public acts and monuments were preserved.[9] As the art of writing was little known, and

1 Plin. xiv. 4. Columel. iii. 3.
2 Plin. xviii. 7. 24. Nep. Attic. 2. Cic. Ver. iii. 45. 47. 49, &c.
3 Tac. Mor. Germ. 2.
4 Tac. Ann. xi. 14. Luc. iii. 220. Plin. vii. 56.
5 Hyg. Fab. 227. Herod. v. 58. Plin. vii. 56. s. 57.
6 Tac. ib. Liv. i. 7. Plin. vii. 58.
7 Joseph. Ant. Jud. i. 4. Tac. Ann. ii. 60. iv. 43. Luc. ii. 223. Liv. iii. 57. Exod. xxxiv. 1. Deut. xxvii. 8. Jos. viii. 42.
8 Isaiah, xxx. 8. Hor. Art. P. 399. Gell. ii. 12.
9 Cic. Font. 14. Liv. vi. 20. Plin. Pan. 54. Hor. Od. iv. 8. 13.

rarely practised, it behoved the materials to be durable. Capital letters only were used, as appears from ancient marbles and coins.

The materials first used in common for writing, were the leaves, or inner bark (*liber*) of trees ; whence leaves of paper (*chartæ, folia*, vel *plagulæ*), and LIBER, a book. The leaves of trees are still used for writing by several nations of India. Afterwards linen,[1] and tables covered with wax were used. About the time of Alexander the Great, paper first began to be manufactured from an Egyptian plant or reed, called PAPYRUS, vel -*um*, whence our word paper, or BIBLOS, whence βιβλος, a book.

The *papyrus* was about ten cubits high, and had several coats or skins above one another, like an onion, which they separated with a neddle. One of these membranes (*philyræ* vel *schedæ*) was spread on a table longwise, and another placed above it across. The one was called *stamen*, and the other *subtemen*, as the warp and the woof in a web. Being moistened with the muddy water of the Nile, which served instead of glue, they were put under a press, and after that dried in the sun. Then these sheets,[2] thus prepared, were joined together, end to end, but never more than twenty in what was called one SCAPUS, or roll.[3] The sheets were of different size and quality.

Paper was smoothed with a shell, or the tooth of a boar or some other animal ; hence *charta dentata*, smooth, polished.[4] The finest paper was called at Rome, after Augustus, AUGUSTA *regia ;* the next LIVIANA ; the third HIERATICA, which used anciently to be the name of the finest kind, being appropriated to the sacred volumes. The emperor Claudius introduced some alteration, so that the finest paper after him was called CLAUDIA. The inferior kinds were called Amphitheatrica, Saitica, Leneotica, from places in Egypt where paper was made ; and FANNIANA, from Fannius, who had a noted manufactory[5] for dressing Egyptian paper at Rome.[6]

Paper which served only for wrappers (*involucra* vel *segestria*, sing. -*e*) was called EMPORETICA, because used chiefly by merchants for packing goods ; coarse and spongy paper, SCABRA BIBULAQUE.[7] Fine paper of the largest size was called MACROCOLLA, sc. *charta*, as we say royal or imperial paper, and any thing written on it MACROCOLLUM, sc. *volumen*.[8]

The exportation of paper being prohibited by one of the Ptolemies, out of envy against Eumenes, king of Pergamus, who endeavoured to rival him in the magnificence of his library, the use of parchment, or the art of preparing skins for writing, was discovered at Pergamus, hence called PERGAMENA, sc. *charta*, vel MEMBRANA, parchment. Hence also Cicero calls his four books of Academics, *quatuor*, διφθεριαι, i. e. *libri e membranis facti.* Some read διφθεραι, i. e. *pelles*, by a metonymy, for *libri pellibus tecti*, vel *in pellibus scripti*.[9] DIPHTHERA, *Jovis* is the register book of Jupiter, made of the skin of the goat Amalthea, by whose milk he was nursed, on which he is supposed by the poets to have written down the actions of men. Whence the proverb, *diphtheram sero Jupiter inspexit*, Jupiter is long before he punish ; and *antiquiora diphthera*.[10] To this Plautus beautifully alludes, Rud. Prol. 21.

The skins of sheep are properly called parchment ; of calves, VELLUM.[11] Most of the ancient manuscripts which remain are written on parchment, few on the papyrus.

1 Liv. iv. 7. 13. 20. 5 officina.   8 Ib. & Cic. Att: xlii. 25. 10 Erasm. Chil. Vid.
2 plagulæ vel schedæ. 6 Plin. ib.   xvi. 3.   Pol. vii. 15.Ælian. ix. 3.
3 Plin. xiii. 11. s. 21. 7 Plin. xiii. 12. Ep. viii. 9 see Manutius, Cic. 11 quasi vitulinum, sc.
4 Cic. Q. Fr. ii. 15. 15.   Att. xlii. 24.   corium.

Egypt having fallen under the dominion of the Arabs in the seventh century, and its commerce with Europe and the Constantinopolitan empire being stopped, the manufacture of paper from the papyrus ceased. The art of making paper from cotton or silk[1] was invented in the East about the beginning of the tenth century ; and, in imitation of it, from linen rags in the fourteenth century. Coarse brown paper was first manufactured in England, A. D. 1588 ; for writing and printing, A. D. 1690 ; before which time about £100,000 are said to have been paid annually for these articles to France and Holland.

The instrument used for writing on waxen tables, the leaves or bark of trees, plates of brass or lead, &c., was an iron pencil, with a sharp point, called STYLUS, or GRAPHIUM. Hence *stylo abstineo*, I forbear writing.[2] On paper or parchment, a reed sharpened and split in the point, like our pens, called CALAMUS, ARUNDO, *fistula* vel *canna*, which they dipped in ink,[3] as we do our pens.[4]

SEPIA, the cuttle-fish, is put for ink ; because, when afraid of being caught, it emits a black matter to conceal itself, which the Romans sometimes used for ink.[5]

The ordinary writing materials of the Romans were tablets covered with wax, paper, and parchment. Their *stylus* was broad at one end ; so that when they wished to correct any thing, they turned the stylus, and smoothed the wax with the broad end, that they might write on it anew. Hence *sæpe stylum vertas*, make frequent corrections.[6]

An author, while composing, usually wrote first on these tables, for the convenience of making alterations ; and when any thing appeared sufficiently correct, it was transcribed on paper or parchment, and published.[7]

It seems one could write more quickly on waxen tables than on paper, where the hand was retarded by frequently dipping the reed in ink.[8]

The labour of correcting was compared to that of working with a file (*lima labor ;*) hence *opus limare*, to polish ; *limare de aliquo*, to lop off redundancies ; *supremam limam operiri*, to wait the last polish ; *lima mordacius uti*, to correct more carefully ;[9] *liber rasus lima amici*, polished by the correction of a friend ; *ultima lima defuit meis scriptis*, i. e. *summa manus operi defuit*, vel *non imposita est*, the last hand was not put to the work, it was not finished ; *metaph. vel translat. a pictura, quam manus complet atque ornat suprema ;* or of beating on an anvil ; thus, *et male tornatos* (some read *formatos*) *incudi reddere versus*, to alter, to correct ;[10] *uno opere eandem incudem diem noctemque tundere*, to be always teaching the same thing ; *ablatum mediis opus est incudibus illud*, the work was published in an imperfect state.[11]

The Romans used also a kind of blotting or coarse paper, or parchment (*charta deletitia*,) called PALIMPSESTOS[12] vel *palinxestus*,[13] on which they might easily erase[14] what was written, and write it anew. But it seems this might have been done on any parchment.[15] They sometimes varied the expression by interlining.[16]

1 charta bombycina.
2 Prin. Ep. vii. 21.
3 atramento intingebant.
4 Cic. Att. vi. 8. Q. Fr. ii. 15. Pers. iii. 11. 14. Hor. Art. P. 446. Plin. xvi. 36. s. 64.

5 Pers. ib. Cic. Nat. D. ii. 20. Ov. Hal. 18.
6 Hor. Sat. i. 10. 72.
7 ib. ii. 3. 2.
8 Quinct. x. 3. 30.
9 Cic. Or. i. 25. lil. Ov. Pont. i. 5. 19. Plin. Ep. viii. 5.

10 Hor. Art. P. 441. Ov. Pont. ii. 4. 17. Trist. i.
6. 30. Serv. Virg. Æn. vii. 572.
11 Ov. ibid. 29. Cic. Or. ii. 39.
12 a παλιν, rursus, et ψαω, rado.

13 a ξεω, rado.
14 delere.
15 Mart. xiv. 7. Cic. Fam. vii. 18. Hor. Art. P. 389.
16 suprascriptio, Plin. Ep. vii. 12.

The Romans used to have note-books (ADVERSARIA,) in which they marked down memorandums of any thing, that it might not be forgotten, until they wrote out a fair copy; of an account, for instance, or of any deed.[1]   Hence *referre in adversaria*, to take a memorandum of a thing.

The Romans commonly wrote only on one side of the paper or parchment, and always join-ed[2] one sheet[3] to the end of another, till they finished what they had to write, and then rolled it up on a cylinder or staff; hence VOLUMEN, a volume or scroll.   *Evolvere librum*, to open a book to read; *animi sui complicatam notionem evolvere*, to unfold, to explain the complicated conceptions of his mind.[4]

An author generally included only one book in a volume, so that usual-ly in a work there was the same number of volumes as of books.   Thus, Ovid calls his fifteen books of Metamorphoses, *mutatæ ter quinque volumina formæ*, thrice five volumes.[5]   When the book was long, it was sometimes divided into two volumes; thus, STUDIOSI *tres*, i. e. three books on Rhetoric, *in sex volumina propter amplitudinem divisi*, divided, on account of their size, into six volumes.   Sometimes a work, consisting of many books, was contained in one volume; thus, *Homerus totus in uno volumine*, i. e. forty-eight books.   Hence *annosa volumina vatum*, aged books; *peragere volumina*, to compose.[6]

When an author, in composing a book, wrote on both sides[7] of the paper or parchment, it was called OPISTOGRAPHUS, vel -*on*, i. e. *scriptus et in tergo* (ex οπισθεν, *a tergo, et* γραφω, *scribo*,) *in charta aversa*,[8] in very small characters.[9]

When a book or volume was finished, a ball or boss[10] of wood, bone, horn, or the like, was affixed to it on the outside, for security and orna-ment,[11] called UMBILICUS, from its resemblance to that part of the human body; hence *ad umbilicum adducere*, to bring to a conclusion, to finish; *ad umbilicos pervenire*, to come to the conclusion.   Some suppose this orna-ment to have been placed in the middle of the roll,[12] but others, at the end of the stick[13] on which the book was rolled, or rather at both ends, called CORNUA; hence we usually find *umbilici* in the plur.; and in Statius,[14] *binis umbilicis decoratus liber*.   UMBILICUS is also put for the centre of any thing, as navel in English; thus, *Delphi umbilicus Græciæ*, Delphi, the centre of Greece; *orbis terrarum*;[15] *Cutiliæ lacus, in quo fluctuet insula, Italiæ umbilicus*, the lake of Cutilia in which an island floats, the centre of Italy; and for a shell or pebble.[16]

The Romans usually carried with them, wherever they went, small writing tables, called PUGILLARES, vel -*ia*,[17] by Homer, πινακες; hence said to have been in use before the time of the Trojan war, on which they marked down any thing that occurred, either with their own hand, or by means of a slave, called, from his office, NOTARIUS, or TABELLARIUS.[18]

1 ut ex iis justæ tabulæ conficerentur, Cic. Ros. Com. 2. 3.
2 agglutinabant.
3 scheda.
4 Cic. Tusc. i. 11. Top. 9. Off. iii. 19.
5 Trist. i. 1. 117. Cic. Tusc. iii. 3. Att. iv. 10. Fam. xvi. 17.
6 Plin. Ep. iii. 5. Ulp. l.

62. D. de Legat. iii. Hor. Ep. li. 1. 26.
7 in utraque pagina.
8 Juv. i. 1. 6. Mart. viii. 62.
9 minutissimis, ac. lite-ris, Plin. ib.
10 bulla.
11 ad conservationem et ornatum.
12 Hor. Ep. xlv. 6. Mart. Or. li. 6.

iv. 91. Schol. in. Hor.
13 bacillus vel surculus.
14 Silv. iv. 9. 6. Mart. l. 67. iii. 2. 5, 6. viii. 61. xi. 108. Ov. Trist. i. 1.
8. Catul. xx. 7.
15 Liv. xxxv. 18—41. 32. xxxviii. 47. Cic. Div. ii. 56. Ver. iv. 48.
16 Plin. lil. 13. s. 17. Cic. Or. li. 6.

17 quod non majores erant quam quæ pug-no, vel pugillo compre-henderentur, vel quod in iis stylo pungendo scribebatur.
18 Hom. ll. vi. 169. Cic. Phil. ii. 4. Plin. iii. 5. viii. 9. xiii. 11. Ep. i. 6. Ov. Met. ix. 520.

The *pugillares* were of an oblong form, made of citron or box wood, or ivory, also of parchment, covered with coloured or white wax,[1] containing two leaves,[2] three, four, five, or more,[3] with a small margin raised all round. They wrote on them[4] with a stylus, hence *ceris et stylo incumbere*, for *in pugillaribus scribere, remittere stylum*, to give over writing.[5]

As the Romans never wore a sword or dagger in the city, they often, upon a sudden provocation, used the *graphium* or stylus as a weapon,[6] which they carried in a case.[7] Hence probably the *stiletto* of the modern Italians.

What a person wrote with his own hand was called CHIROGRAPHUS, vel -*um*, which also signifies one's hand or hand-writing. *Versus ipsius chirographo scripti*, verses written with his own hand ; *chirographum alicujus imitari*, to imitate the hand-writing of any one.[8] But *chirographum* commonly signifies a bond or obligation, which a person wrote or subscribed with his own hand, and sealed with his ring.[9] When the obligation was signed by both parties, and a copy of it kept by each, as between an undertaker and his employer, &c., it was called SYNGRAPHA, -*us*, vel -*um*, which is also put for a passport or furlough.[10]

A place where paper and instruments for writing, or books, were kept, was called SCRINIUM vel CAPSA, an escritoir, a box or case (*arcula* vel *loculus*,) commonly carried by a slave, who attended boys of rank to school, called CAPSARIUS, or LIBRARIUS, together with the private instructor, PÆDAGOGUS ;[11] also for the most part of servile condition, distinguished from the public teacher, called PRÆCEPTOR, DOCTOR, vel MAGISTER,[12] but not properly DOMINUS, unless used as a title of civility, as it sometimes was, especially to a person whose name was unknown or forgotten, as Sir among us ; thus, DOMINA is used ironically for mistress or madam. Augustus would not allow himself to be called DOMINUS, nor Tiberius,[13] because that word properly signifies a master of slaves.[14] An under teacher was called HYPODIDASCALUS.[15] Boys of inferior rank carried their satchels and books themselves.[16]

When a book was all written by an author's own hand, and not by that of a transcriber,[17] it was called AUTOGRAPHUS, or *idiographus*.[18] The memoirs which a person wrote concerning himself, or his actions, were called COMMENTARII ;[19] also put for any registers, memorials, or journals, (*diaria, ephemerides, acta diurna, &c.*)[20] Memorandums of any thing, or extracts of a book, were called *hypomnemata*. Also COMMENTARII *electorum* vel *excerptorum*, books of extracts or common-place books.[21]

1 Ov. Am. i. 12. 7.
2 duplices, δίπτυχοι.
3 Mart. xiv. 3.
4 exarabant.
5 Plin. Ep. vii. 27.
6 Plin. xxxiv. 14. s. 39. Suet. Cæs. 62. C. 98. Claud. 15. 35. Sen. Clem. i. 14.
7 theca calamaria, aut graphiaria, vel graphiarium, Mart. xiv. 21.
8 Cic. Fam. ii. 13. x. 21. xii. 1, xvi. 21. Att. ii. 20. Nat. D. ii. 74. Phil.

ii. 4. Suet. Jul. 17. Aug. 64. 67. Ner. 52. Tit. 3.
9 Juv. xiii. 137. Suet. Cal. 11.
10 Asc. Ver. i. 36. Plaut. Asin. iv. 1. Cap. ii. 3. 90.
11 Hor. Sat. i. 1. 121. iv. 22. x. 63. Juv. x. 117. Suet. Ner. 36. Claud. 35.—See cut representing the form of the crinium or capsa, p. 366.
12 Plaut. Bacch. 1, 2.

-Plin. Ep. iv. 13. Sen. Ir. ii. 22. Paneg. 47.
13 Suet. Tib. 27. Aug. 53. Claud. 21. Tac. Ann. ii. 87. Sen. Ep. iii. 47. Ter. Heaut. iv. 1. 15.
14 qui domi præest vel imperat, Ter. Eun. iii. 2. 33.
15 Cic. Fam. ix. 18.
16 lævo suspensi loculos tabulamque lacerto,—with their satchels and books of accounts hang-

ing on their left arm, Hor. Sat. i. 6. 74.
17 manu librarii.
18 Suet. Aug. 71. 87. Gell. ix. 14.
19 Cæs. & Cic. Brut. 75. Suet. Cæs. 56. Tib. 61.
20 Cic. Fam. v. 12. f. viii. 11. Phil. i. 1. Ver. v. 21. Liv. i. 31, 32. xlii. 6. Suet. Aug. 64. Plin. Ep. vi. 22. x. 96.
21 Cic. Att. xvi. 14. 21, Plin. Ep. iii, 5,

When books were exposed to sale by booksellers,[1] they were covered with skins, smoothed with pumice-stone.[2]

When a book was sent any where, the roll was tied with a thread, and wax put on the knot, and sealed; hence, *signata volumina*. The same was done with letters. The roll was usually wrapped round with coarser paper or parchment,[3] or with part of an old book, to which Horace is thought to allude, Ep. i. 20. 13. Hence the old scholiast on this place, *fient ex te* opistographa *literarum*, so called, because the inscription written on the back showed to whom the letter or book was sent.

Julius Cæsar, in his letters to the senate, introduced the custom of dividing them into pages,[4] and folding them into the form of a pocket-book or account-book,[5] with distinct pages, like our books; whereas formerly, consuls and generals, when they wrote to the senate, used to continue the line quite across the sheet,[6] without any distinction of pages, and roll them up in a volume.[7] Hence, after this, all applications or requests to the emperors, and messages from them to the senate, or public orders to the people, used to be written and folded in this form, called LIBELLI or CODICILLI,[8] rarely used in the singular; applied chiefly to a person's last will,[9] also to writing tables, the same with *pugillares*, or to letters written on them.[10]

A writ, conferring any exclusive right or privilege, was called DIPLOMA, (i. e. *libellus* duplicatus, vel *duorum foliorum*, consisting of two leaves written on one side,) granted by the emperor, or any Roman magistrate, similar to what we call letters patent, i. e. open to the inspection of all, or a patent given particularly to public couriers, or to those who wished to get the use of the public horses or carriages for despatch.[11]

Any writing, whether on paper, parchment, tablets, or whatever materials, folded like our books, with a number of distinct leaves above one another, was called CODEX,[12] particularly account-books; *tabulæ* vel CODICES, *accepti et expensi, libri* or *libelli*. Thus, we say *liber* and *volumen* of the same thing, (*liber grandi volumine*,)[13] but not *codex*. *Legere* vel *recitare suum codicem*, the crime of the tribune Cornelius, who read his own law from a book in the assembly of the people, when the herald and secretary, whose office that was,[14] were hindered to do it by the intercession of another tribune.[15] Hence, in aftertimes, *codex* was applied to any collection of laws.[16]

All kinds of writing are called LITERÆ, hence, QUAM VELLEM NESCIRE LITERAS, I wish I could not write. But *literæ* is most frequently applied to epistolary writings, (EPISTOLÆ vel *chartæ epistolares*,) used in this sense by the poets, also in the singular, so in a negative form;[17] or for one's hand-writing[18] (*manus*,) but, in prose, *litera* commonly signifies a letter of the alphabet.

1 bibliopolæ.
2 Hor. Ep. 1. 20. Plin. xxxvi. 21. s. 42. Catul. xx. 8. Tibul. iii. 1. 10.
3 Hor. Ep. 1. 13. Cic. Cat. iii. 5. Plin. xiii. 11.
4 paginæ.
5 libellus memorialis vel rationalis.
6 transversa charta.
7 Suet. Cæs. 56.
8 Tac. Ann. xvi. 24. Suet. Aug. xlv. 58.

Tib. xviii. 66. xxii. 42. Claud. 15. 29. Ner. 15. Dom. 17. Cal. 18. Mart. viii. 31. 82. see p. 16.
9 see p. 44.
10 Cic. Phil. viii. 10. Q. Fr. ii. 11. Fam. iv. 12. vi. 18. ix. 26. Suet. Claud. 5. Ner. 49.
11 Cic. Fam. vi. 12. Att. x. 17. Pis. 37. Sen. Ben. vii. 10. Suet. Aug. 50. Cal. 38. Ner. 12. Oth.

7. Plin. Ep. x. 54, 55. 121.
12 quasi caudex, plurium tabularem contextus, Sen. Brev. Vit. 13. Cic. Verr. i. 36. 46. & Asc. in loc.
13 Gell. xi. 6. Cic. Ros. Com. i. 2. Ver. ii. 61.
14 see p. 63. 121.
15 Asc. Corn. Cic. Vat. 2. Quinct. iv. 4.

16 see p. 151.
17 Cic. Att. xiii. 39. Fam. ii. 17. Arch. 8. Ver. i. 36. & passim. Suet. Ner. 10. Sen. Clem. 1. Ov. Pont. i. 7. 9. ii. 7. iv. 8. Ep. xviii. 9. xix. fin. xxi. fin.
18 manus, Cic. Att. vii. 2.

'Quinct. ix. 4. f.

EPISTOLA was always sent to those who were absent; CODICILLI and LIBELLI were also given to those present.[1]

The Romans, at least in the time of Cicero, divided their letters, if long, into pages, and folded them in the form of a little book,[2] tied them round with a thread,[3] as anciently, covered the knot with wax, or with a kind of chalk (*creta,*) and sealed it (*obsignabant,*) first wetting the ring with spittle, that the wax might not stick to it.[4] Hence *epistolam vel literas resignare, aperire,* vel *solvere,* to open,[5] *resolvere.* If any small postscript remained after the page was completed, it was written crosswise[6] on the margin.[7]

In writing letters, the Romans always put their own name first, and then that of the person to whom they wrote, sometimes with the addition of SUO, as a mark of familiarity or fondness; if he was invested with an office, that likewise was added, but no epithets, as among us, unless to particular friends, whom they sometimes called *humanissimi, optimi, dulcissimi, animæ suæ,* &c.[8]

They always annexed the letter s. for SALUTEM, sc. *dicit,* wishes health, as the Greek χαιρειν, or the like; hence *salutem alicui mittere, multam* vel *plurimam dicere, adscribere, dare, impertire, nuntiare, referre,* &c., as we express it, to send compliments, &c.[9]

They used anciently to begin with SI VALES, BENE EST *vel* GAUDEO, EGO VALEO, which they often marked with capital letters. They ended with VALE,[10] CURA UT VALEAS; sometimes AVE or SALVE to a near relation, with this addition, MI ANIME, MI SUAVISSIME, &c. They never subscribed their name as we do, but sometimes added a prayer for the prosperity of the person to whom they wrote; as, *deos obsecro ut te conservent,* I pray the gods that they preserve you, which was always done to the emperors, and called SUBSCRIPTIO. The day of the month, sometimes the hour, was annexed.[11]

Letters were sent by a messenger, commonly a slave, called TABELLARIUS, for the Romans had no established post. There sometimes was an inscription on the outside of the letter, sometimes not.[12] When Decimus Brutus was besieged by Antony at Mutina, Hirtius and Octavius wrote letters on thin plates of lead, which they sent to him by means of divers,[13] and so received his answer. Appian mentions letters inscribed on leaden bullets, and thrown by a sling into a besieged city or camp.[14]

Julius Cæsar, when he wrote to any one what he wished to keep secret, always made use of the fourth letter after that which he ought to have used; as D for A, E for B, &c. Augustus[15] used the letters following, as B for A, and C for B; for Z, AA. So that those only could understand the meaning, who were instructed in their method of writing.[16]

The Romans had slaves or freedmen who wrote their letters, called AB EPISTOLIS, (A MANU vel AMANUENSES,) and accounts (A RATIONIBUS, vel *ratiocinatores,*) also who wrote short-hand, (ACTUARII vel NOTARII,)[17] as

1 Cic. Q. Fr. i. 1. 13. iii. 1. 3. Fam. i. 7. ii. 4. Tac. Ann. iv. 39. Sen. Ep. 55. Suet. Aug. 84.
2 Cic. Att. vi. 2. Q. Fr. i. 2, 3. Fam. ii. 13. xi. 25. Sen. Ep. 45.
3 lino obligabant, Cic. Cat. iii. 5. Ov. Ep. xviii. 28.
4 Ov. Trist. v. 4, 5. Am. ii. 15. 15. Nep. Paus. 4. Curt. vii. 2. Cic. Flacc.

16. Ver. iv. 26. Plaut. Bacch. iv. 4. 64. 96. Juv. i. 68.
5 Nep. Hann. 11. Cic. Att. xi. 9. Liv. xxvi. 15.
6 transversim.
7 Cic. Att. v. 1.
8 Auson. Ep. 20. Mart. xiv. 11. Cic. & Plin. passim.
9 Plaut. Pseud. i. 1. 39. Ov. Her. xvi. 1. xviii.

1. Cic. Fam. xiv. 1. Att. xvi. 3. Hor. Ep. i. 8.
10 Ov. Trist. v. 13. 33. Sen. Ep. i. 15. Plin. Ep. i. 11. Cic. Fam. v. 9, 10. xiv. 8. 11. Hirt. B. Hisp. 26.
11 Suet. Aug. 50. Tib. 21. 32. Dio. lvii. 11.
12 Cic. Plut. in Dione.
13 urinatores.
14 Mithrid. p. 191. Dio.

xl. 9. xlvi. 36. li. 10. Frontin. iii. 13. 7.
15 Suet. Aug. 88. Cæs. 56. Dio. xl. 11. li. 3. Isid. l. 24.
16 Gell. xvii. 9.
17 Suet. Claud. 28. Cæs. 74. Aug. 67. Vesp. Tit. l. 3. Jul. 55. Sen. Ep. 90. Cic. Att. i. 12.

quickly as one could speak; *currant verba licet, manus est velocior illis,* though words flow rapidly, the hand that writes them is more rapid still; on waxen tables, sometimes put for *amanuenses* who transcribed their books (LIBRARII ;) who glued them (GLUTINATORES,[1] vulgarly called *librorum concinnatores* vel *compactores,* βιβλιοπηγοι, bookbinders ;) polished them with pumice-stone,[2] anointed them with the juice of cedar[3] to preserve them from moths and rottenness,[4] (hence *carmina cedro linenda,* worthy of immortality,)[5] and marked the titles or index with vermilion,[6] purple,[7] red earth, or red ochre ;[8] who took care of their library (A BIBLIOTHECA,) assisted them in their studies (A STUDIIS) ; read to them, (ANAGNOSTÆ, sing. *-es,* LECTORES.)[9]

The freedmen, who acted in some of these capacities under the emperors, often acquired great wealth and power. Thus Narcissus, the secretary (*ab epistolis* vel *secretis*) of Claudius, Pallas, the comptroller of the household (*a rationibus,*) and the master of requests (*a libellis.*)[10]

The place where paper was made was called OFFICINA *chartaria;* where it was sold, TABERNA ; and so OFFICINÆ ARMORUM, CYCLOPUM, workhouses, SAPIENTIÆ, *omnium artium, eloquentiæ* vel *dicendi,* schools. But *officina* and *taberna* are sometimes confounded.[11] A warehouse for paper, or books, or any merchandise, APOTHECA ; a bookseller's shop, TABERNA LIBRARIA, or simply *libraria.* LIBRARIUM, a chest for holding books.[12]

The street, in Rome, where booksellers (*bibliopolæ*) chiefly lived, was called ARGILETUS, or that part of the Forum or street called JANUS ; where was a temple or statue of the god Vertumnus.[13]

LIBRARIES.

A GREAT number of books, or the place where they were kept, were called BIBLIOTHECA, a library.[14]

The first famous library was collected by Ptolemy Philadelphus at

1 Mart. xiv. 206. Aus. Ep. 146. 17. Manil. iv. 195. Plin. Ep. iii. 5. ix. 36. Liv. xxxviii. 55. Cic. Att. ix. 4. xii. 3.
2 pumice poliebant vel lævigabant, Ov. Trist. i. 1. 9. iii. 1. 13.
3 cedro illinebant.
4 a tineis et carie, ib. Plin. xiii. 12. Mart. iii. 2. v. 6. viii. 61.
5 Hor. Art. P. 332. Pers. i. 42.
6 minium, v. cinnabaris, Ov. ib. Plin. xxxiii. 7.

7 coccus vel purpura, Mart. ib.
8 rubrica, see p. 151.
9 Cic. Fam. v. 9. xiii. 77. Att. i. 12. Nep. Att. 14. Suet. Cal. 28. Aug. 78. Plin. Ep. viii. 1.
10 Suet. Claud. 28. Dom. 14. Tac. Ann. xv. 35. xvi. 8.
11 Plin. x. 43. s. 60. xviii. 10. Hor. Od. i. 4. 6. Cic. Phil. vii. 4. Legg. i. 13. Or. 13. Fin. v. 3.
12 Gell. v. 4. Cic. Phil. ii. 9. Mil. 12.

13 Mart. i. 4. Hor. Ep. i. 20. 1.
14 Festus.
๏*๏ Above is the cylindrical box, called *scrinium* and *capsa,* or *capsula,* in which the manuscripts were placed vertically, the titles at the top. Catullus excuses himself to Manlius for not having sent him the required verses, because he had with him only one box of his books. It is evident that a great num-

ber of volumes might be comprised in this way within a small space ; and this may tend to explain the smallness of the ancient libraries, at least of the rooms which are considered to have been such. Beside the box are two tablets, which, from the money-bag and coins scattered about, had probably been used in reckoning accounts.

Alexandria, in Egypt, B. C. 284, containing 700,000 volumes; the next by Attalus, or Eumenes, king of Pergamus.[1]

Adjoining to the Alexandrian library was a building called MUSEUM,[2] for the accommodation of a college or society[3] of learned men, who were supported there at the public expense, with a covered walk and seats[4] where they might dispute. An additional museum was built there by Claudius. MUSEUM is used by us for a repository of learned curiosities, as it seems to be by Pliny.[5]

A great part of the Alexandrian library was burnt by the flames of Cæsar's fleet, when he set it on fire to save himself, but neither Cæsar himself nor Hirtius mentions this circumstance. It was again restored by Cleopatra, who, for that purpose, received from Antony the library of Pergamus, then consisting of 200,000 volumes.[6] It was totally destroyed by the Saracens, A. D. 642.

The first public library at Rome, and in the world as Pliny observes, was created by Asinius Pollio, in the *atrium* of the temple of liberty on mount Aventine.[7]

Augustus founded a Greek and Latin library in the temple of Apollo on the Palatine hill, and another in the name of his sister Octavia, adjoining to the theatre of Marcellus.[8]

There were several other libraries at Rome; in the Capitol, in the temple of Peace, in the house of Tiberius, &c. But the chief was the Ulpian library, instituted by Trajan, which Dioclesian annexed as an ornament to his *thermæ*.[9] Many private persons had good libraries, particularly in their country villas.[10]

Libraries were adorned with statues and pictures, particularly of ingenious and learned men, the walls and roof with glasses.[11] The books were put in presses or cases (ARMARIA vel CAPSÆ) along the walls, which were sometimes numbered, called also FORULI, LOCULAMENTA, NIDI,[12] but these are supposed by some to denote the lesser divisions of the cases.

The keeper of a library was called *a* BIBLIOTHECA; *bibliothecarius* is used only by later writers.

HOUSES OF THE ROMANS.

THE houses of the Romans are supposed at first to have been nothing else but cottages (*casæ* vel *tuguria*,) thatched with straw, hence CULMEN, the roof of a house (*quod culmis tegebatur*.)[13]

After the city was burnt by the Gauls, it was rebuilt in a more solid and commodious manner; but the haste in building prevented attention to the regularity of the streets.[14]*

---

* Rome was rebuilt within a year, without question in a very wretched manner. The streets in the lower parts of the city had previously been broad and straight; for the sewers ran beneath them; and even on the hills, in its gradual enlargement under the kings, the same rule which was followed in the laying out of new colonial towns, appears to have been observed, so far as the ground would allow of it: that is to say, there were

1 Gell. vi. 17. Plin. xiii. 12.
2 i. e. domicilium, specus vel templum musis dicatum, Plin. Ep. i. 9.
3 ουνοδος.
4 exedræ.
5 xxvii. 2. s. 6. Strab. 17. Suet. Claud. 42.
6 Plut. in Cæs. & Anto.

Dio. 42. 38.
7 Plin. vii. 30. xxxv. 2. Ov. Trist. iii. 1. 71. Mart. xii. 3. 5.
8 Suet. 29. Dio. liii. 1. Plut. in Marcell. Ov. Trist. iii. 1. 60. 69.
9 Suet. Dom. 20. Gell. xi. 17. xiii. 18. Vopisc. in Prob. 2.
10 Cic. Fam. vii. 28. Q.

Fr. iii. 4. Att. iv. 10. Fin. iii. 2. Plut. Lucul. Sen. Tranq. 9. Hor. Od. i. 29. 13. Mart. vii. 16. Plin. Ep. ii. 17.
11 Suet. Tib. 70. Plin. xxxv. 2. xxxvi. 25. Ep. iii. 7. iv. 28. Sen. Ep. 86. Stat. Silv. i. 5. 42. Boeth. Consol. Juv. ii. 7.

12 Vopisc. Tac. 8. Suet. Aug. 31. Juv. iii. 219. Sen. Tranq. 9. Mart. i. 118.
13 Ov. Am. ii. 9. 18. Serv. Virg. Ecl. i. 6. Æn. viii. 654.
14 Liv. v. 55. Diod. xiv. 116.

The houses were reared every where without distinction,[1] or regard to property,[2] where every one built in what part he chose, and till the war with Pyrrhus, the houses were covered only with shingles, or thin boards, (SCANDULÆ vel *scindulæ*.)[3]

It was in the time of Augustus that Rome was first adorned with magnificent buildings ; hence that emperor used to boast, that he had found it of brick, but should leave it of marble.[4] The streets, however, still were narrow and irregular, and private houses not only incommodious, but even dangerous, from their height, and being mostly built of wood. *Scalis habito tribus, sed altis*, three stories high.[5]

In the time of Nero, the city was set on fire, and more than two thirds of it burnt to the ground. Of fourteen wards[6] into which Rome was divided, only four remained entire. Nero himself was thought to have been the author of this conflagration. He beheld it from the tower of Mæcenas ; and delighted, as he said, with the beauty of the flame, played the taking of Troy, dressed like an actor.[7]

The city was rebuilt with greater regularity and splendour. The streets were made straight and broader ; the areas of the houses were measured out, and their height restricted to seventy feet, as under Augustus.[8] Each house had a portico before it, fronting the street, and did not communicate with any other by a common wall, as formerly. It behoved a certain part of every house to be built of Gabian or Alban stone, which was proof against fire.[9] These regulations were subservient to ornament as well as utility. Some, however, thought that the former narrowness of the street, and height of the houses, were more conducive to health, as preventing by their shade the excessive heat.[10]

Buildings in which several families lived were called INSULÆ ; houses

---

straight broad streets reserved to the state, while the building-ground bounded by them was regularly parcelled out and allotted as property to individuals. This right the government seems to have regarded as extinct since the enemy's conquest : hence every body was allowed to build where he chose, in order that there might be a stronger inducement to make a beginning, and that after some progress so many additional voices might be gained in favour of patience and perseverance. The Romans in after-ages, forgetting that but for this disadvantage they probably would not then have been living at Rome, complained of the precipitation with which the city was rebuilt : for, even when

it was in its greatest splendour, it was impossible, before the fire under Nero, to change the crookedness and narrowness of the streets. To lighten the task, the senate granted bricks : every body was allowed to hew stones or wood wherever he pleased, provided he gave security to finish his building within a year. By the grant of bricks must be meant that the state allowed them to be taken from buildings already existing : for how could it have found the means of paying for new ones ? Such buildings it had at Veii : and with a view of putting an end for ever to the hated scheme of migrating thither, it was wise to favour the demolition of that city, which was in fact reduced to an insignificant

place, and barely continued to exist, till it in some measure revived under Augustus as a military colony. For the substructions of the Capitol too, which were built no long time after,—and no doubt on the side beneath the citadel, where Cominius and the Gauls clumb up the grass-covered rocks— and for the repair of the walls, blocks of stone ready hewn would be supplied by Veii : in this manner its temples and city-walls disappeared. The Romans who had staid there to avoid the charge of building, were commanded by an ordinance of the senate to return before a stated day, under pain of the severest punishment.

---

1 nulla distinctione passim erectæ, Tac. Ann. xv. 43.
2 omisso sui alienique discrimine, adeo ut forma urbis esset occupatæ magis, quam divisæ similis,—all regard to distinction of property

being set aside, it was more like a city taken possession of just as each of the inhabitants could obtain a house for himself, than a city regularly distributed among its inhabitants, Liv. ib.

3 i. e. tabellæ, in parvas laminas scissæ, Plin. xvi. 10. s. 15.
4 marmoream se relinquere, quam lateritiam accepisset. Suet. Aug. 29.
5 Suet. Ner. 38. Tac. Ann. xv. 38. Juv. iii.

133. Mart. i. 118.
6 regiones.
7 Tac. Ann. xv. 39, 40.
44. Suet. Ner. 38.
8 Strab. v. p. 162.
9 ignibus   impervius, Tac. Ann. xv. 53.
10 Tac. ibid.

in which one family lived, DOMUS *vel* ÆDES PRIVATÆ.[1] We know little of the form either of the outside or inside of Roman houses, as no models of them remain. The small houses dug out of the ruins of Pompeii bear little or no resemblance to the houses of opulent Roman citizens. The principal parts were,

1. VESTIBULUM, which was not properly a part of the house, but an empty space before the gate, through which there was an access to it.[2] The vestibule of the golden palace[3] of Nero was so large that it contained three porticos, a mile long each, and a pond like a sea, surrounded with buildings like a city.[4] Here was also a colossus of himself, or statue of enormous magnitude, 120 feet high.[5]

2. JANUA, *ostium* vel *fores*, the gate (PORTA *murorum et castrorum*; JANUA *parietis et domorum*), made of various kinds of wood, cedar, or cypress, elm, oak, &c.; sometimes of iron, or brass, and especially in temples, of ivory and gold.[6] The gate was commonly raised above the ground, so that they had to ascend to it by steps. The pillars at the sides of the gates, projecting a little without the wall, were called ANTÆ, and the ornaments affixed to them, wrought in wood or stone, ANTEPAGMENTA.[7] When the gate was opened among the Romans, the folds (VALVÆ)[8] bent inwards, unless it was granted to any one by a special law to open his door outwards; as to P. Valerius Poplicola, and his brother, who had twice conquered the Sabines,[9] after the manner of the Athenians, whose doors opened to the street;[10] and when any one went out, he always made a noise, by striking the door on the inside, to give warning to those without to keep at a distance. Hence CREPUIT FORIS, *concrepuit a Glycerio ostium*, the door of Glycerium hath creaked, i. e. is about to be opened.[11] This the Greeks called ψοφειν θυραν; knocking from without, κοπτειν, *pulsare* vel *pultare*.

A slave watched[12] at the gate as porter (JANITOR), hence called OSTIARIUS, PUER AB JANUA, *claustritumus*,[13] usually in chains,[14] (which men emancipated he consecrated to the lares, or to Saturn),[15] armed with a staff or rod,[16] and attended by a dog, likewise chained. On the porter's cell was sometimes this inscription, CAVE CANEM.[17] Dogs were also employed to guard the temples, and because they failed to give warning when the Gauls attacked the Capitol, a certain number of them were annually carried through the city, and then impaled on a cross.[18] Females also were sometimes set to watch the door (JANITRICES), usually old women.[19]

On festivals, at the birth of a child, or the like, the gates were adorned with green branches, flowers, and lamps, as the windows of the Jews at Rome were on sabbaths.[20] Before the gate of Augustus, by a decree of the senate, were set up branches of laurel, as being the perpetual conqueror of his enemies; hence LAUREATÆ FORES, LAURIGERI PENATES.[21] So a crown of oak was suspended on the top of his house as being the preserver of his citizens, which honour Tiberius refused. The laurel branches seem

1 Suet. Ner. 16. 38. 44. Tac. Ann. vi. 45. xv. 41. see p. 38, 39.
2 Gell. xvi. 5. Cic. Cæc. 12. Plaut. Most. iii. 130.
3 aurea domus.
4 Suet. Ner. 30.
5 see p. 231.
6 Virg. G. ii. 442. Ov. Met. iv. 487. Ann. ii. 1. 25, Plaut. Pers. iv. 4. 21. Cic. Verr. iv. 56. Plin. viii. 10. xxxiv. 3.

7 Virg. Æn. ii. 492. Sen. Ep. 84. Festus.
8 quod intus revolvantur.
9 ut domus eorum fores extra aperirentur, Plin. xxxvi. 15.
10 in publicum.
11 Ter. And. iv. 1. 59. Hec. iv. 1. 6. Plaut. Amph. i. 2. 34.
12 servabat.
13 Ov. Fast. i. 138. Nep.

Han. 12. Gell. xii. 10.
14 catenatus, Columel. præf. 10. Ov. Am. i. 6. 1. 25.
15 Hor. i. 5. 65. Mart. iii. 29.
16 arundo vel virga, Sen. Const. 14.
17 beware of the dog, —Suet. Vit. 16. Sen. Ira, iii. 37. Petron. 29. Plaut. Most. iii. 2. 162.
18 Cic. Sext. Rosc. 20.

Arnob. vi. Liv. v. 47. Plin. xxix. 4.
19 Plaut. Curc. i. 1. 76. Tibul. i. 7. 67. Petron. 55.
20 Juv. ix. 84. xii. 91. Sen. 95. Pers. v. 180.
21 Ov. Trist. iii. 1. 39. Plin. xv. 30. s. 39. Sen. Polyb. 35. Mart. viii. 1.

to have been set up on each side of the gate, in the vestibule ; and the civic crown to have been suspended from above between them : hence Ovid says of the laurel, *mediamque tuebere quercum.*[1]

The door, when shut, was secured by bars (*obices, claustra, repagula, vectes*), iron bolts (*pessuli*), chains,[2] locks (*seræ*), and keys (*claves*) : hence *obdere pessulum foribus,* to bolt the door ; *occludere ostium pessulis,* with two bolts, one below, and another above ; *uncinum immittere,* to fix the bolt with a hook ; *obserare fores vel ostium,* to lock the door ;[3] *seram ponere, apposita janua fulta sera,* locked ; *reserare,* to open, to unlock ;[4] *excutere poste seram.* It appears, that the locks of the ancients were not fixed to the panels (*impages*) of the doors with nails like ours, but were taken off when the door was opened, as our padlocks ; hence *et jaceat tacita lapsa catena sera.*[5]

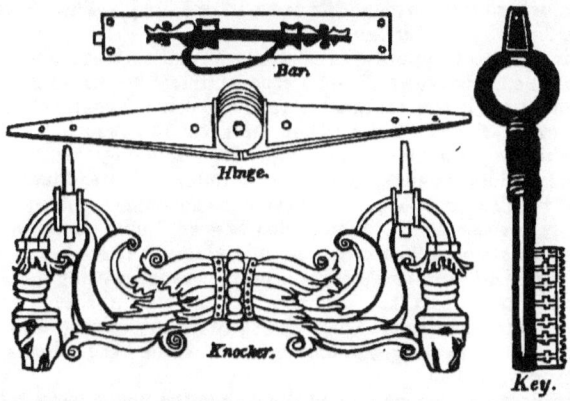

Bar.

Hinge.

Knocker.

Key.

Knockers (*marculi* v. *mallei*) were fixed to the doors, or bells (*tintinnabula*) hung up, as among us.[6]

The porter usually asked those who knocked at the gate, who they were. He admitted or excluded such as his master directed Sometimes he was ordered to deny his master's being at home.[7] Besides the *janitor,* the emperors and great men had persons who watched or kept guard in the vestibule (EXCUBIÆ vel CUSTODIA),[8] to which Virgil alludes, Æn. vi. 555, 574.

A door in the back part of the house was called POSTICUM, vel *posticum ostium,* or PSEUDOTHYRUM, v. -*on ;* that in the fore-part, ANTICUM.[9]

3. The *janua,* or principal gate, was the entrance to the ATRIUM, or AULA, the court or hall, which appears to have been a large oblong square, surrounded with covered or arched galleries.[10] Three sides of the *atrium* were supported on pillars, in later times, of marble. The side opposite to the gate was called TABLINUM ; and the other two sides, ALÆ. The *tablinum* was filled with books, and the records of what any one had done in his magistracy.[11] In the atrium, the nuptial couch was erected.[12] The

1 and thou shalt be the guardian of the oaken crown that hangs in the middle,—Met. i. 563. Suet. Tib. 26. Juv. vi. 346.
2 Juv. iii. 304.
3 Ter. Heaut. ii. 3. 37. Eun. iv. 6. 25. Plaut.

Aul. i. 2. 25. Juv. vi. 346.
4 Ov. Art. A. ii. 244. Met. x. 384. Am. i. 6. 24.
5 Prop. iv. 12. 26.
6 Suet Aug. 91. Sen. Ira. iii. 35. Dio. liv. 4.
7 Cic. Phil. ii. 31. Or.

ii. 68. Suet. Oth. 3. Sen. Ep. 47. Mart. ii. 5. v. 23. Ov. Art. Am. ii. 521.
8 Tac. Ann. xv. 52.
9 Plaut. Stich. iii. 1. 40. Hor. Ep. i. 5. 31. Cic. Verr. ii. 20. Red. Sen. 6. Festus.

10 porticus tectæ vel laqueatæ, Auson. Eidyl. x. 49.
11 Plin. xvii. 1. xxxvi. 2, 3. Vitruv. vi. 4. Plin. xxxv. 2.
12 see p. 333.
.*. The above articles were found in Pompeii.

mistress of the family, with her maid-servants, wrought at spinning and weaving.[1]

The ancient Romans used every method to encourage domestic industry in women. Spinning and weaving constituted their chief employment. To this the rites of marriage directed their attention.[2] Hence the frequent allusions to it in the poets,[3] and the atrium seems to have been the place appropriated for their working,[4] that their industry might be conspicuous : hence the qualities of a good wife ;[5] *probitas, forma, fides, fama pudicitiæ, lanificæque manus*.[6] But in aftertimes, women of rank and fortune became so luxurious and indolent, that they thought this attention below them.[7] On this account, slaves only were employed in spinning and weaving (TEXTORES et TEXTRICES, *lanifici* et *-æ*), and a particular place appropriated to them, where they wrought (TEXTRINA vel *-um*). Thus Verres appointed in Sicily, Cic. Verr. iv. 26.

The principal manufacture was of wool; for although there were those who made linen, LINTEONES,[8] and a robe of linen[9] seems to have been highly valued,[10] yet it was not much warn. The principal parts of the woollen manufacture are described by Ovid, Met. vi. 53 ; dressing the wool ; picking or teasing, combing, and carding it ;[11] spinning[12] with a distaff (COLUS) and spindle (FUSUS) ; winding or forming the thread into clues ;[13] and dying.[14] The wool seems to have been sometimes put up in round balls[15] before it was spun.[16] Wool, when new cut[17] with its natural moisture, was called SUCCIDA,[18] so *mulier succida*, plump. It used to be anointed with wine or oil, or swine's grease, to prepare it for being dyed.[19]

The loom,[20] or at least that part to which the web was tied, was called JUGUM, a cylinder or round beam across two other beams, in this form, *II*, resembling the *jugum ignominiosum*, under which vanquished enemies were made to pass.[21]

The threads or thrums which tied the web to the jugum were called LICIA ; the threads extended longwise, and alternately raised and depressed, STAMEN, the warp,[22] because the ancients stood when they wove, placing the web perpendicularly (whence *radio stantis*, i. e. *pendentis*, *percurrens stamina telæ*),[23] and wrought upwards,[24] which method was dropped, except by the linen-weavers (LINTEONES), and in weaving the *tunica recta*.

The threads inserted into the warp were called SUBTEMEN, the woof or weft,[25] some read *subtegmen*, but improperly : the instrument which separated the threads of the warp, ARUNDO, the reed ; which inserted the woof into the warp, RADIUS, the shuttle ; which fixed it when inserted, PECTEN, the lay, vel SPATHA.[26] When the web was woven upright, a thin piece of wood, like a sword, seems to have been used for this purpose ; as in the weaving of arras, of Turkey carpeting, &c., in which alone the upright mode of working is now retained, the weft is driven up with an instrument somewhat like a hand with the fingers stretched out, made of lead or iron. It is doubtful whether the ancients made use of the

1 Cic. Mil. 5. Nep. Præf. in medio ædium, i. e. in atrio, Liv. i. 57.
2 see p. 333.
3 Virg. Æn. viii. 408. ix. 488.
4 ex vetere more in atrio telæ texebantur, Asc. Cic. Mil. 5.
5 morigeræ uxoris.
6 Auson. Parent. iii. 3. xvi. 3.
7 nunc pleræque sic lu-

xu et inertia defluunt, ut ne lanificii quidem curam suscipere dignentur, Columel. xii. proœm. 9.
8 Plaut. Aul. iii. 5. 38. Serv. Æn. vii. 14.
9 vestis lintea.
10 Cic. Ver. v. 56.
11 lanam carpere, pectere vel pectinare, carminare, &c.
12 nere, poet. ducere

vel trahere.
13 glomerare.
14 tingere, fucare, fuco medicare.
15 glomerari in orbes.
16 Ov. ib. 19. Hor. Ep. i. 13, 14.
17 recens tonsa.
18 a succo, Varr.
19 Plaut. Mil. iii. 1. 193. Juv. v. 24. Plin. viii. 48. xxix. 2. Varr. R. R. ii. 11.

20 machina in qua tela texitur.
21 Festus, Liv. iii. 28.
22 a stando.
23 Ov. Met. iv. 275.
24 in altitudinem, vel sursum versum, Fest.
25 quasi subteximen vel substamen.
26 Ov. Met. vi. 53. Sen. Ep. 91.

reed and lay for driving up the weft, as the moderns do. The principal part of the machinery of a loom, vulgarly called the caam or hiddles, composed of eyed or hooked threads, through which the warp passes, and which, being alternately raised and depressed by the motion of the feet on the treadles, raises or depresses, the warp, and makes the shed for transmitting the shuttle with the weft, or something similar, seems also to have been called LICIA ; hence *licia telæ addere*, to prepare the web for weaving, to begin to weave.[1]

When figures were to be woven on cloth, several threads of the warp of different colours were alternately raised and depressed ; and in like manner, the woof was inserted. If, for instance, three rows of threads (*tria licia*) of different colours were raised or inserted together, the cloth was called TRILIX, wrought with a triple tissue or warp, which admitted the raising of threads of any particular colour or quality at pleasure ; so also BILIX. Hence the art of mixing colours or gold and silver in cloth ; thus, *fert picturatas auri subtemine vestes*, figured with a weft of gold. The warp was also called TRAMA ; hence *trama figuræ*, skin and bones, like a thread-bare coat ; but Servius makes *trama* the same with *subtemen*.[2]

The art of embroidering cloth with needle-work[3] is said to have been first invented by the Phrygians ; whence such vests were called PHRYGIONIÆ ;[4]—the interweaving of gold,[5] by king Attalus ; whence VESTES ATTALICÆ ;[6]—the interweaving of different colours[7] by the Babylonians ; hangings and furniture of which kinds of cloth for a dining-room[8] cost Nero £32,281 : 13 : 4, *quadragies sestertio ;* and even in the time of Cato cost 800,000 sestertii ;[9]—the raising of several threads at once,[10] by the people of Alexandria in Egypt, which produced a cloth similar to the Babylonian, called POLYMITA,[11] wrought, as weavers say, with a many-leaved caam or comb. The art of mixing silver in cloth[12] was not invented till under the Greek emperors, when clothes of that kind of stuff came to be much used under the name of VESTIMENTA SYRMATINA.[13]

From the operation of spinning and weaving, FILUM, a thread, is often put for a style or manner of writing, and DUCERE or DEDUCERE, to write or compose ;[14] thus, *tenui deducta poemata filo*, i. e. *subtiliore stylo scripta*, poems spun out in a fine thread ; so *deductum dicere carmen*, to sing a pastoral poem, written in a simple or humble style ; also TEXERE, and *subtexere*, to subjoin.[15]

In the atrium anciently the family used to sup, where likewise was the kitchen (CULINA).[16] In the atrium, the nobility placed the images of their ancestors,[17] the clients used to wait on their patrons, and received the *sportula*.[18] The atrium was also adorned with pictures, statues, plate, &c., and the place where these were kept was called PINACOTHECA.[19]

In later times, the atrium seems to have been divided into different parts, separated from one another by hangings or veils,[20] into which persons were admitted, according to their different degrees of favour, whence they were called *amici* ADMISSIONIS *primæ, secundæ,* vel *tertiæ ;* which distinction is

1 Virg. G. i. 285.
2 Virg. Æn. iii. 467. 483. v. 259. vii. 639. xii. 375. Sen. Ep. 91. Pers. vi. 73.
3 acu pingore. ·
4 Plin. viii. 48. s. 74.
5 aurum intexere.
6 ib. & Prop. iii. 18, 19.
7 colores diversos picturæ intexere.

8 tricliniaria Babylonica.
9 Plin. ib.
10 plurimis liciis texere.
11 ex πολυς, multus, et μιτος, filum, ib. Mart. xiv. 150. Isid. xix. 22.
12 argentum in fila deducere, et fila argenteis vestimenta contexere.

13 Salmas. ad ˙Vopisci Aurelian, 46.
14 Cic. Læl. 7. Or. ii. 22. iii. 26. Fam. ix. 12. Gell. xx. 5. Juv. vii. 74.
15 Hor. Ep. ii. 1. 225. Virg. Ecl. vi. 5. Ov. Trist. i. 10. 18. Ep. xvii. 88. Pont. i. 5. 7 13. Cic. Fam. ix. 21. Q. Fratr. iii. 5. Tibull. iv. 1.

211.
16 Serv. Virg. Æn. i. 726. iii. 353.
17 see p. 21.
18 Hor. ib. i. 5. 31. Juv. vii. 71. see p. 317.
19 Plin. xxxv. 2. Petron. 29. 83.
20 vela.

said to have been first made by C. Gracchus and Livius Drusus. Hence those who admitted persons into the presence of the emperor, were called EX OFFICIO ADMISSIONES, vel ADMISSIONALES,[1] and the chief of them, MAGISTER ADMISSIONUM, master of ceremonies, usually freedmen, who used to be very insolent under weak or wicked princes, and even to take money for admission, but not so under good princes.[2]

There was likewise an *atrium* in temples ; thus, *atrium Libertatis, atrium publicum in Capitolio.* In the hall there was a hearth (FOCUS), on which a fire was kept always burning near the gate, under the charge of the janitor, around it the images of the *lares* were placed ; whence *lar* is put for *focus.*[3]

The ancients had not chimneys for conveying the smoke through the walls as we have ; hence they were much infested with it, hence also the images in the hall are called FUMOSÆ, and December FUMOSUS, from the use of fires in that month.[4] They burnt wood, which they were at great pains to dry, and anoint with the lees of oil (*amurca*), to prevent smoke,[5] hence called *ligna* ACAPNA,[6] vel COCTA, ne *fumum facient.*[7]

The Romans used portable furnaces[8] for carrying embers and burning coals[9] to warm the different apartments of a house, which seem to have been placed in the middle of the room.[10] In the time of Seneca, a method was contrived of conveying heat from a furnace below, by means of tubes or canals affixed to the walls,[11] which warmed the rooms more equally.[12]

4. An open place in the centre of the house, where the rain water fell, and which admitted light from above, was called IMPLUVIUM, or *compluvium*, also CAVÆDIUM, or *cavum ædium*,[13] commonly uncovered ;[14] if not, from its arched roof, called TESTUDO.[15] Virtuvius directs, that it should not be more than the third, nor less than the fourth part of the breadth of the atrium. The slave who had the charge of the atrium, and what it contained, was called ATRIENSIS. He held the first rank among his fellow-slaves, and exercised authority over them.[16]

5. The sleeping apartments in a house were called CUBICULA *dormitoria* vel *nocturna, noctis, et somni ;* for there were also *cubicula diurna*, for reposing in the day-time. Each of these had commonly an ante-chamber adjoining, (PROCŒTUM vel *procestrium*).[17] There were also in bed-chambers places for holding books, inserted in the walls.[18]

Any room or apartment in the inner part of the house, under lock and key, as we say, was called CONCLAVE, vel *-ium*,[19] put also for the TRICLINIUM.[20] Among the Greeks, the women had a separate apartment from the men, called GYNÆCEUM.[21]

The slaves who took care of the bed-chamber were called CUBICULARII, or CUBICULARES, the chief of them, PRÆPOSITUS CUBICULO, vel DECURIO

---

1 Sen. Ben. vi. 32, 34. Clem. i. 10. Suet. Vesp. 14. Lamprid. in Alex. 4.

2 Vopisc. Aurelian, 12. Plin. xxxlii. 3. Pan. 47. Sen. Const. Sap. 14.

3 Cic. Mil. 22. Liv. xxiv. 10. xxxv. 7. Tac. His. i. 31. Ov. Fast. i. 135.

4 Hor. Sat. i. 5. 81. Virtuv. vii. 3. Juv. viii. 8. Cic. Pis. 1. Mart. v. 31. 5.

5 Hor. Od. i. 9. 5. iii. 17.

14. xv. 8.

6 ex a priv. et καπνος, fumus, Mart. xiii. 15.

7 Ulp. Legg. iii. 1. 53. Cato R. R. c. 133.

8 camini portatiles, fornaces, vel culæ, foculi, ignitabula vel æscharæ.

9 prunæ vel carbones igniti.

10 Cat. R. Rust. 18. Suet. Tib. 74. Vit. 8. Colum. xi. 1.

11 per tubos parietibus impressos.

12 Sen. Ep. 90. Prov. 4.

13 Festus, Varr. L. L. iv. 33. Asc. Cic. Verr. i. 23. Liv. xliii. 15. Plin. Ep. ii. 17.

14 subdivale.

15 Varr. Ibid.

16 Vitrav. vi. 4. Petron. 25. Cic. Top. 5. Plaut. Asin. ii. 3. 60. 4. 19.

17 Plin. Ep. i. 3. ii. 17. v. 6.

18 armaria parieti inserta, Id. ii. 17.

19 Ter. Heaut. v. 1. 29. a con et clavis, quod

una clavi clauditur, Festus ; vel quod intra eum locum loca multa et cubicula clausa sunt, adhærentia triclinio, Donat. Ter. Eun. iii. 5. 35.

20 Cic. Verr.iv. 26. Or. ii. 86. Quinct. ix. 2. Hor. Sat. ii. 6. 113.

21 γυναικειον, Cic. Phil. ii. 37. Ter. Phorm. v. 5. 22.

CUBICULARIORUM. They were usually in great favour with their masters,
and introduced such as wanted to see them.[1] For the emperors often
gave audience in their bed-chamber ; the doors of which had hangings or
curtains suspended before them,[2] which were drawn up[3] when any one
entered.

The eating apartments were called *cœnationes, cœnacula,* vel *triclinia.*[4]
A parlour for supping or sitting in was called DIÆTA, sometimes several
apartments joined together were called by that name, or ZETA ; and a
small apartment, or alcove, which might be joined to the principal apartment, or separated from it at pleasure, by means of curtains and windows,
ZOTHECA, vel -*cula.*[5] DIÆTA, in the civil law, is often put for a pleasure-
house, in a garden : and by Cicero, for diet, or a certain mode of living,
for the cure of a disease, Att. iv. 3. It is sometimes confounded with *cubiculum.*[6] An apartment for basking in the sun was called SOLARIUM,[7]
which Nero appointed to be made on the portico before the house, or HE-
LIOCAMINUS.[8] The apartments of a house were variously constructed, and
arranged at different times, and according to the different taste of individuals.

The Roman houses were covered with tiles[9] of a considerable breadth :
hence bricks and tiles are mentioned in Vitruvius and ancient monuments
two feet broad ;[10] and a garret[11] covered by one tile. When war was declared against Antony, the senators were taxed at 4 *oboli,* or 10 *asses,* for
every tile on their houses, whether their own property or hired.[12] In Nonius Marcellus we read, *in singulas tegulas impositis sexcentis sexcenties
confici posse,* c. iv. 93. But here, *sexcentis* is supposed to be by mistake
for *sex nummis,* or *singulas tegulas* to be put up for *singula tecta,* each roof.
The roofs[13] of the Roman houses seem to have been generally of an angu-
lar form, like ours, the top or highest part of which was called FASTIGIUM,
hence *operi fastigium imponere,* to finish ; put also for the whole roof,[14] but
particularly for a certain part on the top of the front of temples, where inscriptions were made, and statues erected. Hence it was decreed by the
senate, that Julius Cæsar might add a *fastigium* to the front of his house,
and adorn it in the same manner as a temple, which, the night before he
was slain, his wife Calpurnia dreamt had fallen down.[15]

From the sloping of the sides of the roof of a house, FASTIGIUM is put
for any declivity ; hence *cloacœ fastigio ductœ,* sloping. FATISGIATUS,
bending or sloping,[16] and from its proper signification, viz., the summit or
top, it is put for dignity or rank ; thus, *curatio altior fastigio suo,* a charge
superior to his rank, *pari fastigio stetit,* with equal dignity ; *in consulare
fastigium provectus,* to the honour of consul, or for any head of discourse ;
summa sequar fastigia rerum, I will recount the chief circumstances, also
for depth, as *altitudo.*[17] The centre of the inner part of a round roof of a
temple, where the beams joined, was called THOLUS, the front of which,
or the space above the door, was also called FASTIGIUM. But any round
roof was called THOLUS, as that of Vesta, resembling the concave hemi-

---

1 Suet. Tib. 21. Ner. 38.
Dom. 16, 17. Cic. Att.
vi. 14.
2 foribus prætenta vela,
Tac. Ann. xiii. 5. Suet.
Claud. 10.
3 levabantur, Sen. Ep.
81.
4 see p. 303.
5 Plin. Ep. ii. 17. v. 6.

Suet. Claud. 10.
6 Plin. Ep. ii. 17. vi.
16.
7 Plaut. Mil. ii. 4. 25.
Suet. Claud. 10.
8 Suet. Ner. 16. Plin. lb.
9 tegulæ.
10 bipedales.
11 cœnaculum,   Suet.
Gram. 11.

12 Dio. xlvi. 31.
13 tecta.
14 Fest. Virg. Æn. i.
442. ii. 458. 758. Cic.
Off. iii. 7. iii. 46. Q. Fr.
iii. 1. 4.
15 Plin. xxxv. 12. s. 45.
xxxvi. 5. Pan. 54. Cic.
Phil. ii. 43. Flor. iv. 2.
Suet. Jul. 81. Plut. Cæs.

p. 738.
16 Liv. i. 38. Cæs. B. C.
i. 45. ii. 24. B. G. ii. 8.
17 Serv. Virg. G. ii. 388.
Æn. i. 346. Liv. ii. 27.
Nep. xxv. 14. Vell. ii.
69.

sphere of the sky.[1] Whence Dio says, that the Pantheon of Agrippa had its name, because; from the roundness of its figure (θολοειδες . ον), it resembled heaven, the abode of the gods, liii. 27. From the *tholus* offerings consecrated to the gods, as spoils taken in war, &c. used to be suspended, or fixed to the *fastigium*, and on the top of the *tholus*, on the outside, statues were sometimes placed.[2]

The ancient Romans had only openings[3] in the walls to admit the light, FENESTRÆ, windows (from φαινω, *ostendo* ; hence *oculi et aures sunt quasi fenestræ animi*,)[4] covered with two folding leaves[5] of wood, and sometimes a curtain, hence said to be joined, when shut, *cubiculum ne diem quidem sentit, nisi apertis fenestris*,[6] sometimes covered with a net,[7] occasionally shaded by curtains.[8]

Under the first emperors, windows were contrived of a certain transparent stone, called LAPIS SPECULARIS, found first in Spain, and afterwards in Cyprus, Cappadocia, Sicily, and Africa, which might be split into thin leaves[9] like slate, but not above five feet long each.[10] What this stone was is uncertain. Windows, however, of that kind (SPECULARIA) were used only in the principal apartments of great houses, in gardens, called PERSPICUA GEMMA, in porticos,[11] in sedans,[12] or the like. Paper, linen cloth, and horn, seem likewise to have been used for windows ; hence CORNEUM SPECULAR.[13]

The Romans did not use glass for windows, although they used it for other purposes, particularly for mirrors (*specula*), nor is it yet universally used in Italy, on account of the heat. Glass was first invented in Phœnicia accidentally, by mariners burning nitre on the sand of the sea-shore.[14] Glass windows (*vitrea specularia*) are not mentioned till about the middle of the fourth century by Hieronymus (St. Jerome),[15] first used in England, A. D. 1177 ; first made there, 1558 ; but plate glass for coaches and looking glasses not till 1673.

The Romans, in later times, adorned the pavements of their houses with small pieces[16] of marble, of different colours, curiously joined together, called PAVIMENTA SECTILIA, vel EMBLEMATA VERMICULATA, or with small pebbles, (*calculi* vel *tesseræ* s. -*ulæ*), dyed in various colours ; hence called PAVIMENTA TESSELLATA,[17] used likewise, and most frequently, in ceilings,[18] in aftertimes called *opus museum* vel *musivum*, mosaic work, probably because first used in caves or grottos consecrated to the muses (*musea*). The walls also used to be covered with crusts of marble.[19]

Ceilings were often adorned with ivory, and fretted or formed into raised work and hollows.[20] LAQUEARIA vel LACUNARIA, from *lacus* or *lacuna*, the hollow interstice between the beams,[21] gilt[22] and painted. Nero made the ceiling of his dining-room to shift, and exhibit new appearances, as the different courses or dishes were removed.[23]

1 Serv. Virg. Æn. ix. 480. Ov. Fast. vi. 282. 296. Mart. ii. 59. Vitr. i. 7. 5.
2 Virg. ib. Mart. i. 71. 10.
3 foramina.
4 Cic. Tusc. 1. 20.
5 bifores valvæ.
6 Ov. Pont. iii. 5. Am. i. 5. 3. Juv. ix. 105. Hor. Od. i. 25. Plin. ii. 17. ix. 36.

7 fenestræ reticulatæ ne quod animal maleficum introire queat, Varr. R. R. iii. 7.
8 obductis velis, Plin. Ep. vii. 21.
9 finditur in quamlibet teneus crustas.—It appears that this stone the talc of Muscovy, —French Trans.
10 Sen. Ep. 90. Plin.

xxxvi. 22. s. 45.
11 Sen. Ep. 86. Nat. Q. iv. 13. Plin. xv. 16.
xix. 5. Ep. ii. 17. Mart. viii. 14. 68.
12 lecticæ, Juv. iv. 21.
13 Tertullian. Anim. 53.
14 Plin. xxxvi. 26. s. 65.
15 ad Ezech. xi. 16.
16 crustæ, vel -a.
17 Suet. Cæs. 46. λιθοστρωτα, Varr.
18 Cic. Or. iii. 43. Suet.

ib. Luc. x. 114.
19 Plin. xxxvi. 6. 21. s. 42.
20 laqueata tecta, Cic. Legg. ii. 1.
21 Serv. Virg. Æn. 1. 726.
22 aurea, Ib. & Hor. Od. ii. 18. inaurata, Plin. xxxiii. 3.
23 Plin. xxxv. 11. s. 40. Sen. Ep. 90. Suet. Ner. 31.

VILLAS AND GARDENS OF THE ROMANS.

THE magnificence of the Romans was chiefly conspicuous in their country villas.[1]

VILLA originally denoted a farm-house and its appurtenances, or the accommodations requisite for a husbandman ;[2] hence the overseer of a farm was called VILLICUS, and his wife[3] VILLICA. But when luxury was introduced, the name of villa was applied to a number of buildings reared for accommodating the family of an opulent Roman citizen in the country ;[4] hence some of them are said to have been built in the manner of cities.[5]

A villa of this kind was divided into three parts, URBANA, RUSTICA, and FRUCTUARIA. The first contained dining-rooms, parlours, bed-chambers, baths, tennis-courts, walks, terraces,[6] &c., adapted to the different seasons of the year. The villa rustica contained accommodations for the various tribes of slaves and workmen, stables, &c., and the fructuaria, wine and oil-cellars ; corn-yards,[7] barns, granaries, storehouses, reposito-

LAMPS.

No articles of ancient manufacture are more common than lamps. They are found in every variety of form and size, in clay and in metal, from the most cheap to the most costly description. We have the testimony of the celebrated antiquary, Winkelmann, to the interest of this subject : —" I place among the most curious utensils found at Herculaneum, the lamps, in which the ancients sought to display elegance, and even magnificence. Lamps of every sort will be found in the museum at Portici, both in clay and bronze, but especially the latter ; and as the ornaments of the ancients have generally some reference to some particular things, we often meet with rather remarkable subjects." A considerable number of these articles will be found in the British museum, but these are chiefly of the commoner sort. All the works, however, descriptive of Herculaneum and Pompeii, present us with specimens of the richer and more remarkable glass, which attract admiration both by the beauty of the workmanship and the whimsical variety of their designs. But beautiful as these lamps are, the light which they gave must have been weak and unsteady, and little superior to that of common street lamps, with which indeed they are identical in principle. The wick was merely a few twisted threads drawn through a hole in the upper surface of the oil-vessel ; and there was no glass to steady the light and prevent its varying with every breeze that blew. Three of different shapes, are represented above.

1 Cic. Legg. iii. 13.
2 quasi vella, quo fructus vehebant, et unde vehebant, cum venderentur, Var. R. R. i. 2.

14.
3 uxor liberi, et contubernalis servi.
4 Cic. Rosc. Com. 12.
5 in urbium modum ex

ædificatæ., Sall. Cat. 12. ædificia privata, lautitatem urbium magnarum vincentia, Sen. Ben. vii. 10. Ep. 90.

Hor. Od. ii. 15. iii. 1. 33.
6 xysti.
7 fœnilia et palearia.

ries for preserving fruits,[1] &c. Cato and Varro include both the last parts under the name of VILLA RUSTICA. But the name of villa is often applied to the first alone, without the other two, and called by Vitruvius PSEUDO-URBANA ; by others PRÆTORIUM.[2]

In every villa there commonly was a tower; in the upper part of which was a supping-room,[3] where the guests, while reclining at table, might enjoy at the same time a pleasant prospect.[4]

Adjoining to the VILLA RUSTICA, were places for keeping hens, GALLI-NARIUM ; geese, CHENOBOSCIUM ; ducks and wild fowl, NESSOTROPHIUM ; birds, *ornithon* vel AVIARIUM ; dormice, GLIRARIUM ; swine, SUILE, &c. *stabulum et haræ*, hogsties ; hares, rabbits, &c., LEPORARIUM, a warren ; bees, APIARIUM ; and even snails, COCHLEARE, &c.

There was a large park of fifty acres, or more,[5] for deer and wild beasts, THERIOTROPHIUM vel VIVARIUM, but the last word is applied also to a fish-pond (PISCINA), or an oyster-bed,[6] or any place where live animals were kept for pleasure or profit : hence *in vivaria mittere*, i. e. *lactare, muneribus et observantia omni alicujus hæreditatem captare*, to court one for his money ; *ad vivaria currunt*, to good quarters, to a place where plenty of spoil is to be had.[7]

The Romans were uncommonly fond of gardens (HORTUS vel ORTUS),[8] as, indeed, all the ancients were ; hence the fabulous gardens and golden apples of the HESPERIDES, of Adonis and Alcinous,[9] the hanging gardens[10] of Semiramis, or of Cyrus at Babylon, the gardens of Epicurus, put for his gymnasium, or school. In the laws of the Twelve Tables *villa* is not mentioned, but *hortus* in place of it.[11] The husbandmen called a garden *altera succidia*, a second dessert, or flitch of bacon,[12] which was always ready to be cut,[13] or a sallad,[14] and judged there must be a bad housewife (*nequam mater familias*, for this was her charge) in that house where the garden was in bad order.[15] Even in the city, the common people used to have representations of gardens in their windows.[16]

In ancient times, the garden was chiefly stored with fruit-trees and pot-herbs,[17] hence called HORTUS PINGUIS, the kitchen-garden, and noble families were denominated not only from the cultivation of certain kinds of pulse (*legumina*), *Fabii, Lentuli, Pisones*, &c., but also of lettuce, *Lactucini*.[18] But in after-times the chief attention was paid to the rearing of shady trees,[19] aromatic plants, flowers, and evergreens ; as the myrtle, ivy, laurel, boxwood, &c. These, for the sake of ornament, were twisted and cut into various figures by slaves trained for that purpose, called TOPIARII, who were said TOPIARIAM, SC. *artem* FACERE, vel OPUS TOPIARIUM.[20]

Gardens were adorned with the most beautiful statues. Here the Romans, when they choose it, lived in retirement, and entertained their friends.[21]

The Romans were particularly careful to have their gardens well watered (*rigui* vel *irrigui*) ; and for that purpose, if there was no water

1 oporothecæ, Columel. i. 6. 2.
2 Cat. R. R. iii. 1. ix. 1. Var. xiii. 6. Pallad. 1. 8. Suet. Aug. 72. Cal. 37. Tit. 8.
3 cœnatio.
4 Plin. Ep. ii. 17.
5 παραδεισος.
6 Gell. ii. 20. Plin. ix. 54. Juv. iv. 51.
7 Hor. Ep. i. 1. 79. Juv.

iii. 306.
8 ubi arbores et olera oriuntur.
9 Virg. Æn. iv. 484. G. ii. 87. Ov. Am. i. 10. 56. Pont. iv. 2. 10. Stat. Silv. i. 3. 81.
10 pensiles horti.
11 Plin. xix. 4. Cic. Att. xii. 23. Fin. v. 3.
12 perna, petaso vel lardum.

13 Cic. Sen. 16.
14 acetaria, -orum, faci-lis concoqui nec onera-tura sensum cibo,Plin. xix. 4. s. 19.
15 indiligens hortus, i. e. indiligenter cultus.
16 Plin. ib.
17 ex horto enim plebei macellum, ib.
18 Plin. xix. 4. s. 19. 3. Ep. ii. 17. Virg. G. iv.

118.
19 Hor. Od. ii. 14. 22.
15. 4. Ov. Nux. 29.
20 Plin. xv. 30. Ep. iii. 19. Cic. Q. Fr. iii. 1, 2.
21 Cic. Dom. 43. Art. xii. 40. Plin. Ep. viii. 16. f. Suet. Claud. 5. Tac. Ann. xvi. 34. Sen, Ep. 21. Mart. iv. 64.

in the ground, it was conveyed in pipes.[1] These aqueducts (*ductus aquarum*) were sometimes so large, that they went by the name of NILI and EURIPI.[2]

The gardens at Rome most frequently mentioned by the classics, were, *horti* CÆSARIS; LUCULLI; MARTIALIS; NERONIS; POMPEII;[3] SALUSTII, V. -IANI, the property first of Sallust the historian, then of his grand-nephew and adopted son, afterwards of the emperors; SENECÆ; TARQUINII SUPERBI, the most ancient in the city.[4] Adjoining to the garden were beautiful walks (*ambulacra*, vel -*tiones*,) shaded with trees, and a place for exercise (*palæstra.*) Trees were often reared with great care round houses in the city, and statues placed among them.[5]

AGRICULTURE OF THE ROMANS.

THE ancient Romans were so devoted to agriculture, that their most illustrious commanders were sometimes called from the plough; thus, Cincinnatus. The senators commonly resided in the country, and cultivated the ground with their own hands,[6] and the noblest families derived their surnames from cultivating particular kinds of grain; as the FABII, PISONES, LENTULI, CICERONES, &c. To be a good husbandman was accounted the highest praise (BONUS COLONUS vel AGRICOLA, was equivalent to VIR BONUS; LOCUPLES, rich, q. *loci*, hoc est, *agri plenus:* PECUNIOSUS, a. *pecorum copia;* so ASSIDUUS, ab *asse dando*); and whoever neglected his ground, or cultivated it improperly, was liable to the animadversions of the censors.[7]

At first no citizen had more ground than he could cultivate himself. Romulus allotted to each only two acres, called HÆREDIUM (*quód hæredem sequerentur*), and SORS, or *cespes fortuitus*,[8] which must have been cultivated with the spade. A hundred of these *sortes* or *hæredia* was called CENTUARIA; hence *in nullam sortem bonorum natus*, i. e. *partem hæreditatis,* to no share of his grandfather's fortune. After the expulsion of the kings, seven acres were granted to each citizen,[9] which continued for a long time to be the usual portion assigned them in the division of conquered lands. L. Quinctius Cincinnatus, Curius Dentatus, Fabricius, Regulus, &c., had no more. Cincinnatus had only four acres according to Columella and Pliny.[10]

Those whom proprietors employed to take care of those grounds, which they kept in their own hands, were called VILLICI,[11] and were usually of servile condition. Those who cultivated the public grounds of the Roman people, and paid tithes for them, were also called ARATORES, whether Roman citizens, or natives of the provinces (*provinciales*), and their farms ARATIONES.[12] But when riches increased, and the estates of individuals were enlarged, opulent proprietors let part of their grounds to other citizens, who paid a certain rent for them, as our farmers or tenants, and were properly called COLONI, CONDUCTORES, or PARTIARII, because usually they

1 inducebatur per canales, vel fistulas aquarias, Plin. Ep. v. 6. per tubos plumbeos, vel ligneos, Plin. xvi. 42. s. 81. vel fictiles, sen testaceos, xxxi. 6. s. 31.
2 Cic. Legg. ii. 1.
3 Hor. Sat. 1. 9, 18. Suet.

63. Cic. Phil. ii. 29. Tac. An. iv. 64. xi. 1. 37. xiv. 3. xv. 44.
4 Tac. Ann. iii. 30. xlii. 47. Hist. iii. 82. xiv. 52. Juv. x. 16. Liv. i. 54. Ov. Fast. ii. 703.
5 Cic. Legg. ii. 2. Ver. i. 19. Gell. i. 2. Hor. Ep. i. 10. 23. Tibul. iii.

3. 15.
6 Liv. ill. 26. Cic. Ros. Am. 16. see p. 6.
7 Plin. xviii. 1. 3. Cato, R. R. Pr. 2. Quinct. v. 10. Ov. Fast. v. 280. Gell. x. 5. Festus.
8 Varr. R. R. i. 10. Plin. xviii. 11. Hor. Od. ii. 15. 17. Festus.

9 Columel. i. 5. Liv. i. 34. Plin. xviii. 3.
10 Plin. xviii. 3. Columel. Præf. &. i. 3. Liv. v. 30. Val. Max. iv. 3—7.
11 Hor. Ep. i. 14. Cic. Ver. iii. 53. Att. xiv. 17.
12 Cic. Verr. iii. 20. 27. 53. Phil. ii. 27.

shared the produce of the ground with the proprietor. It appears that the Romans generally gave leases only for five years (*singulis lustris prædia locasse.*)[1] AGRICOLÆ was a general name, including not only those who ploughed the ground,[2] but also those who reared vines (*vinitores*), or trees (*arboratores*), and shepherds (*pastores*).

At first, the stock on the farm seems to have belonged to the proprietor, and the farmer received a certain share of the produce for his labour. A farmer of this kind was called POLÍTOR vel *polintor*, the dresser of the land, or PARTIARIUS; which name is also applied to a shepherd, or to any one who shared with another the fruits of his industry. Such farmers are only mentioned by Cato, who calls those who farmed their own grounds, COLONI. But this word is commonly used in the same general sense with *agricola : non dominus, sed colonus.*[3] In Columella, *colonus* means the same with the farmer or tenant among us, who was always of a free condition, and distinguished from VILLICUS, a bailiff or overseer of a farm; a steward, who was usually a slave or freed-man. So also shepherds. When a free-born citizen was employed as an overseer, he was called PROCURATOR; and those who acted under him, ACTORES.[4] The persons employed in rustic work, under the farmer or bailiff, were either slaves or hirelings; in later times chiefly the former, and many of them chained.[5] The younger Pliny had none such.[6]

The Romans were very attentive to every part of husbandry, as appears from the writers on that subject; Cato, Varro, Virgil, Pliny, Columella, Palladius, &c. Soils were chiefly of six kinds; fat and lean (*pingue* vel *macrum*), free and stiff (*solutum* vel *spissum, rarum* vel *densum*), wet and dry (*humidum* vel *siccum*), which were adapted to produce different crops. The free soil was most proper for vines, and the stiff for corn.[7] The qualities ascribed to the best soil 'are; that it is of a blackish colour,[8] glutinous when wet, and easily crumbled, when dry; has an agreeable smell, and a certain sweetness; imbibes water, retains a proper quantity, and discharges a superfluity; when ploughed, exhales mists and flying smoke, not hurting the plough-irons with salt rust; the ploughman followed by rooks, crows, &c., and, when at rest, carries a thick grassy turf. Land for sowing was called ARVUM (*ab arando*), anciently *arvus*, sc. *ager*; ground for pasture, PASCUUM, v. *-us*, sc. *ager*.[9]

The Romans used various kinds of manure to improve the soil, particularly dung (*fimus* vel *stercus*), which they were at great pains to collect and prepare, in dunghills (*sterquilinia* vel *fimeta*) constructed in a particular manner. They sometimes sowed pigeon's dung, or the like, on the fields like seed, and mixed it with the earth by sarcling or by weeding-hooks (*sarcula*).[10] When dung was wanting, they mixed earths of different qualities; they sowed lupines, and ploughed them down for manure (*stercorandi agri causa*). Beans were used by the Greeks for this purpose.[11]

The Romans also, for manure, burned on the ground the stubble (*stipulam urebant*), shrubs (*fruteta*), twigs and small branches (*virgas et sarmenta*). They were well acquainted with lime (*calx*), but do not seem to have

1 Cic. Cæc. 32. Colum. i. 7. Plin. Ep. vii. 30. ix. 37. x. 24. Caius, 1. 25. s. 6. ff. Locati.
2 aratores, qui terram arant, vel ipsi sua manu vel per alios, Cic. Verr. v. 38.

3 Virg. Ecl. ix. 4. Sen. Ep. 86.
4 Plin. Ep. iii. 19. Hor. Ep. i. 14. Colum. i. 7. Virg. Ecl. i. 28. 41. Cic. Cæc. 20. Att. xiv. 17. Or. i. 58. Ver. lii. 50.
5 see p. 26. Plin. xviii.

4 Mart. ix. 23. Ov. Pont. i. 6. 31.
6 Ep. iii. 19.
7 Col. lii. 2. Virg. G. ii. 229.
8 terra nigra vel pulla, Virg. G. ii. 203.
9 Plaut. Truc. 1; 2. 47.

Virg. G. ii. 203. 217. 238. 248. Plin. xvii. 5. Var. R. R. i. 29.
10 Col. i. 6. ii. 16. Plin. xvii. 9. xxiv. 19.
11 Theophrast. viii. 9. Var. R. i. 23.

.used it for manure, at least till late. Pliny mentions the use of it for that purpose in Gaul, and hence probably it was tried in Italy. He also mentions the use of marl (MARGA) of various kinds, both in Britain and Gaul, and likewise in Greece, called there *leucargillon*, but not found in Italy.[1]

To carry off the water,[2] drains (INCILIA vel *fossæ inciles*) were made, both covered and open (*cæcæ et patentes*), according to the nature of the soil, and water-furrows (*sulci aquarii* vel *elices*).[3] The instruments used in tillage were,

ARATRUM, the plough, concerning the form which authors are not agreed. Its chief parts were, TEMO, the beam, to which the *jugum*, or yoke, was fastened; STIVA, the plough-tail or handle, on the end of which was a cross bar (*transversa regula*, called MANICULA vel CAPULUS), which the ploughman (*arator* v. *bubulcus*) took hold of, and by it directed the plough; VOMER, vel -*is*, the plough-share; BURIS, a crooked piece of wood, which went between the beam and the plough-share; hence ARATRUM CURVUM,[4] represented by Virgil as the principal part of the plough, to which there seems to be nothing exactly similar in modern ploughs; to it was fitted the DENTALE, the share-beam, a piece of timber on which the share was fixed, called by Virgil, *duplici dentalia dorso*, i. e. *lato*; and by Varro, *dens*. To the *buris* were also fixed two AURES, supposed to have

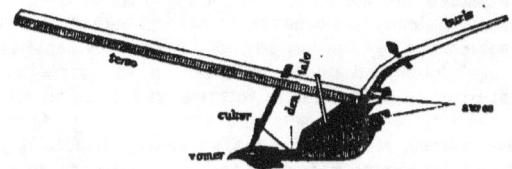

served in place of what we call mould-boards, or earth-boards, by which the furrow is enlarged, and the earth thrown back (*regeritur*); CULTER, much the same as our coulter; RALLA, or *rulla*, vel -*um*, the plough staff, used for cleaning the plough-share.[5]

The Romans had ploughs of various kinds; some with wheels, earth-boards, and coulters, others without them, &c. The common plough had neither coulter nor earth-boards.

The other instruments were, LIGO, or PALA, a spade, used chiefly in the garden and vineyard, but anciently also in corn fields;[6] RASTRUM, a rake; SARCULUM, a sarcle, a hoe, or weeding-hook; BIDENS, a kind of hoe or drag, with two hooked iron teeth for breaking the clods, and drawing up the earth around the plants, OCCA vel CRATES DENTATA, a harrow; IRPEX, a plank with several teeth, drawn by oxen as a wain, to pull roots out of the earth; MARRA, a mattock, or hand hoe, for cutting out weeds;[7] DOLABRA, an addice, or adz, with its edge athwart the handle; SECURIS, an axe, with its edge parallel to the handle, sometimes joined in one, hence called

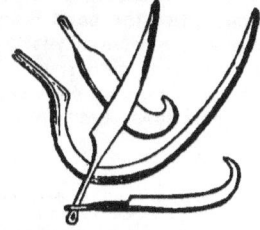

SECURIS DOLABRATA; used not only in vineyards, but in corn fields, for

1 Virg. G. 1. 84. Plin. xvii. 5. 8. xviii. 6. 25.
2 ad aquam vel uligínem nimiam deducendam.
3 quod undam eliciunt, Virg. G. 1. 169. Col. ii. 2. 8. Plin. xviii. 6.
4 Ov. Pont. i. 8. 57. Virg.
G. i. 170.
5 Plin. xviii. 18, 19.
6 Liv. iii. 26. Hor. Od. iii. 6. 38. Ep. i. 14. 27.
7 Virg. G. i. 91. ii. 400. Ov. Am. i. 13. 15. Juv. iii. 311. Plin. xviii. 18. Var. L. L. iv. 31.

cutting roots of trees, &c. The part of the pruning-knife (*falx*), made in the form of the half-formed moon (*semiformis lunæ*), was also called SECURIS.[1]

The Romans always ploughed with oxen, usually with a single pair (*singulis jugis* vel *paribus*), often more, sometimes with three in one yoke. What a yoke of oxen could plough in one day, was called JUGUM vel JU-GERUM.[2] Oxen, while young, were trained to the plough with great care.[3] The same person managed the plough, and drove the cattle[4] with a stick, sharpened at the end, called STIMULUS (πεντρον), a goad. They were usually yoked by the neck, sometimes by the horns. The common length of a furrow made without turning, was 120 feet, hence called ACTUS, which squared and doubled in length, made a JUGERUM;[5] used likewise as a measure among the Hebrews.[6] The oxen were allowed to rest a little at each turning,[7] and not at any other time.[8]

When, in ploughing, the ground was raised in the form of a ridge, it was called PORCA, or LIRA.[9] But Festus makes PORCÆ to be also the furrows on each side of the ridge for carrying off the water, properly called COLLICIÆ. Hence LIRARE, to cover the seed when sown by the plough, by fixing boards to the plough-share, when those side furrows were made. These ridges are also called SULCI; for *sulcus* denotes not only the trench made by the plough, but the earth thrown up by it.[10]

The Romans, indeed, seem never to have ploughed in ridges unless when they sowed. They did not go round when they came to the end of the field as our ploughmen do, but returned in the same track. They were at great pains to make straight furrows, and of equal breadth. The ploughman who went crooked, was said DELIRARE, (i. e. *de lira decedere ;* hence, *a recto et æquo, et a communi sensu recedere*, to dote, to have the intellect impaired by age or passion,) and PRÆVARICARI, to prevaricate ; whence this word was transferred to express a crime in judicial proceedings.[11]

To break and divide the soil, the furrows were made so narrow, that it could not be known where the plough had gone, especially when a field had been frequently ploughed. This was occasioned by the particular form of the Roman plough, which, when held upright, only stirred the ground, without turning it aside. The places where the ground was left unmoved (*crudum et immotum*), were called SCAMNA, balks.[12]

The Romans commonly cultivated their ground and left it fallow alternately (*alternis*, sc. *annis*),[13] as is still done it Switzerland, and some provinces of France. They are supposed to have been led to this from an opinion, that the earth was in some measure exhausted by carrying a crop, and needed a year's rest to enable it to produce another ; or from the culture of olive trees, which were sometimes planted in corn fields, and bore fruit only once in two years.[14]

A field sown every year was called RESTIBILIS ; after a year's rest or

---

1 Col. ii. 2. iv. 25.
2 Cic. Verr. iii. 21. Col. vi. 2. 10. Plin. xviii. 3. 18. Var. R. R. i. 10.
3 Virg. G. iii. 163. Var. I. 20. Col. vi. 2.
4 rector, Plin. Ep. viii. 17.
5 Plin. viii. 45. xviii. 3. Col. ii. 2. v. 1. 5. Var. i. 16.

6 1 Sam. xiv. 14.
7 Col. ii. 2. cum ad versuram ventum est, vel cum versus peractus est, i. e. cum sulcus ad finem perductus est.
8 nec strigare in actu spiritus, i. e. nec interquiescere in ducendo sulco, Plin. xviii. 19. nec in media parte versuræ consistere, Col. ii. 2.
9 i. e. inter duos sulcos terra elata vel eminens, Varr. R. R. i. 29. Fest. in Imporcitor, Col. ii. 4.
10 Virg. G. i. 113. Plin.

xviii. 19, 20. s. 49. Col. ii. 4. Var. i. 29.
11 Hor. Ep. i. 2. 14. Cic. Or. ii. 18. Plin. xviii. 19. s. 49. see p. 179.
12 ib. & Col. ii. 2.
13 Virg. G. i. 71.
14 Col. v. 7.—9. Varr. i. 55. Plin. xv. 3.

longer, NOVALIS, *fem.* vel *novale*, or VERVACTUM.[1] When a field, after being long uncultivated (*rudus* vel *crudus*), was ploughed for the first time, it was said PROSCINDI ; the second time *iterari* vel OFFRINGI, because then the clods were broken by ploughing across, and then harrowing ; the third time, *tertiari*, LIRARI vel *in liram redigi ;* because then the seed was sown. But four or five ploughings were given to stiff land, sometimes nine.[2] To express this they said *tertio, quarto, quinto sulco serere,* for *ter, quater, quinquies arare.* One day's ploughing, or one yoking, was called, UNA OPERA ; ten, *decem operæ.*[3] Fallow ground was usually ploughed in the spring and autumn ; dry and rich land in winter ; wet and stiff ground chiefly in summer ; hence that is called the best land,[4] BIS QUÆ SOLEM, BIS FRIGORA SENSIT,[i.] e. *bis per æstatem, bis per hiemem arata,* which has twice felt the cold and twice the heat. Thus also *seges* is used for *ager* or *terra. Locus ubi prima paretur arboribus* SEGES, i. e. *seminarium,* a nursery, but commonly for *sata,* growing corn, or the like, a crop ; as *seges lini,* a crop of flax ; or metaphorically, for a multitude of things of the same kind ; thus *seges virorum,* a crop of men ; *seges telorum,* a crop of darts ; *seges gloriæ,* a field, or harvest of glory.[5]

, The depth of the furrow in the first ploughing[6] was usually three fourths of a foot, or nine inches (*sulcus* DODRANTALIS).[7] Pliny calls ploughing four fingers or three inches deep, SCARIFICATIO.[8] The seed was sown from a basket (SATORIA, sc. corbis, *trimodia,* containing three pecks). It was scattered by the hand, and, that it might be done equally, the hand always moved with the step, as with us.[9]

The Romans either sowed above furrow (*in lira*), or under furrow (*sub sulco*), commonly in the latter way. The seed was sown on a plain surface, and then ploughed, so that it rose in rows, and admitted the operation of hoeing. It was sometimes covered with rakes and harrows (*rastris* vel *crate dentata*).[10]

The principal seed time,[11] especially for wheat and barley, was from the autumnal equinox to the winter solstice, and in spring as soon as the weather would permit.[12]

The Romans were attentive not only to the proper seasons for sowing, but also to the choice of seed, and to adapt the quantity and kind of seed to the nature of the soil.[13] When the growing corns (*segetes* vel *sata, -orum*) were too luxuriant, they were pastured upon.[14] To destroy the weeds, two methods were used ; SARCULATIO vel *sarritio,* hoeing ; and RUNCATIO, weeding, pulling the weeds with the hand, or cutting them with a hook. Sometimes the growing corns were watered.[15]

In some countries, lands are said to have been of surprising fertility,[16] yielding a hundred fold,[17] sometimes more ; as in Palestine ; in Syria and Africa ; in Hispania Bœtica, and Egypt, the Leontine plains of Sicily, around Babylon, &c. ;[18] but in Italy, in general, only ten after one,[19] as in Sicily,[20] sometimes not above four.[21]

---

1 Plin. xviii. 19. s. 49. quod vere semel aratum est.
2 Fest. Plin. xviii. 20. Ep.v. 6. Var. i. 29.Virg. G. i. 47.
3 Col. ii. 4.
4 optima seges.
5 Plin. xviii. 20. Virg. G. i. 48. 77. ii. 142. 266. iv. 129. Æn. iii. 46. Ov. Met. iii. 110. Cic. Tusc. ii. 5. Mil. 13.

6 cum sulcus altius imprimeretur.
7 Plin. xviii. 19. [1]
8 Ib. 17. tenui sulco arare, ib. 18. tenui suspendere sulco,—to turn it up lightly with a small furrow, Virg. G. i. 68.
9 Col. ii. 9. Cic. Sen. 15. Plin. vii. 24.
10 Plin. xviii. 20.
11 tempus sativum, sa-

tionis, v. seminationis, vel sementum faciendi.
12 Virg. G. i. 208. Col. ii. 8. Var. i. 34.
13 Virg. G. i. 193. Var. i. 44. Plin. xviii. 24. s. 55.
14 depascebantur, Virg. G. i. 93.
15 rigabantur, Virg. G. i. 106.
16 sata cum multo fœnore reddebant, Ov.

Pont. i. 5. 26.
17 ex uno centum.
18 Gen. xxvi. 12. Varr. i. 44. Plin. xviii. 10. 17.
19 ager cum decimo efficiebat, efferebat, v. fundebat ; decimo cum fœnore reddebat, Var. i. 44.
20 Cic. Verr. iii. 47.
21 frumenta cum quarto respondebant, Col. iii.

The grain chiefly cultivated by the Romans, was wheat of different kinds, and called by different names, TRITICUM, *siligo, robus,* also FAR, or *ador, far adoreum* vel *semen adoreum,* or simply *adoreum ;* whence ADOREA, warlike praise or glory. *Adorea aliquem afficere,* i. e. *gloria,* or victory, because a certain quantity of corn ador (*ador*) used to be given as a reward to the soldiers after a victory.[1] No kind of wheat among us exactly answers the description of the Roman *far.* What resembles it most, is what we call spelt. FAR is put for all kinds of corn, whence FARINA, meal ; *farina silignea* vel *triticea, simila,* vel *similago, flos siliginis, pollen tritici,* flour. *Cum fueris nostræ paulo ante farinæ,* i. e. *generis* vel *gregis,* since you were, but a little ago, unquestionably a person of our class.[2]

Barley, HORDEUM, vel *ordeum,* was not so much cultivated by the Romans as wheat. It was the food of horses,[3] sometimes used for bread ;[4] given to soldiers, by way of punishment, instead of wheat. In France and Spain, also in Pannonia, especially before the introduction of vineyards, it was converted into ale, as among us, called *cælia* or *ceria* in Spain, and *cervisia* in France ;[5] the froth or foam of which[6] was used for barm or yeast in baking,[7] to make the bread lighter, and by women for improving their skin.[8]

Oats, AVENA, were cultivated chiefly as food for horses ; sometimes also made into bread (*panis avenaceus*). AVENA is put for a degenerate grain,[9] or for oats which grow wild.[10] As the rustics used to play on an oaten stalk, hence *avena* is put for a pipe (*tibia* vel *fistula.*)[11] So also *calamus, stipula, arundo, ebur.*

Flax or lint (LINUM) was used chiefly for sails and cordage for ships, likewise for wearing apparel, particularly by the nations of Gaul, and those beyond the Rhine, sometimes made of surprising firmness. The rearing of flax was thought hurtful to land. Virgil joins it with oats and poppy.[12]

Willows (SALICES) were cultivated for binding the vines to the trees that supported them ; for hedges, and for making baskets. They grew chiefly in moist ground : hence *udum salictum.* So the osier, *siler ;* and broom, *genista.*[13]

Various kinds of pulse (*legumina*) were cultivated by the Romans ; FABA, the bean ; *pisum,* pease; *lupinum,* lupine ; *faselus, phaselus,* vel *phaseolus,* the kidney-bean ; *lens,* lentil ; *cicer* v. *cicercula, vicia* v. *ervum,* vetches, or tares ; *sesamum* v. -*a,* &c. These served chiefly for food to cattle ; some of them, also, for food to slaves and others, especially in times of scarcity, when not only the seed, but also the husks or pods (*siliquæ*), were eaten. The turnip (*rapum* v. -*a,* vel *rapus*) was cultivated for the same purpose.[14]

There were several things sown to be cut green, for fodder to the labouring cattle ; as *ocimum* vel *ocymum, fœnum Græcum, vicia, cicera, ervum,* &c., particularly the herb *medica* and *cytisus* for sheep.[15]

The Romans paid particular attention to meadows (PRATA),[16] for raising hay and feeding cattle, by cleaning and dunging them, sowing various grass seeds, defending them from cattle, and sometimes watering them.[17]

---

1 Plaut. Amph. i. l. 38.
v. 2. 10. Hor. Od. iv. 3.
41. Plin. xviii. 3.
2 Pers. v. 115.
3 Col. vi. 30.
4 panis hordeaceus,
Plin. xviii. 7. s. 14.
5 Liv. xxvii.13. Dio.xlix.
36. Plin. xiv. 22.

6 spuma.
7 pro fermento, Plin.
xviii. 7.
8 ad cutem nutriendam,
ib. xxii. 25. s. 62.
9 vitium frumenti, cum
hordeum in eam degeneret, Plin. xviii. 17.
Cic. Fin. v. 30.

10 steriles avenæ, i. e.
quæ non seruntur,
Serv. Virg. Ecl. v. 37.
G. i. 153. 226.
11 Virg. Ecl. i. 2. iii. 27.
Mart. viii. 3.
12 G. i. 77. Plin. xix. 1.
13 Virg. G. ii. 11. 436.
Hor. Od. ii. 5. 8. Liv.

xxv. 17. Cato. 9.
14 Plin. xviii. 13. Per. iii.
35. Hor. Ep. ii. 1. 123.
15 Plin. xiii. 24.
16 quasi semper parata,
Plin. xviii. 5.
17 Col. ii. 17.

Hay (FŒNUM) was cut and piled up in cocks, or small heaps, of a conical figure,[1] then collected into large stacks, or placed under covert. When the hay was carried off the field, the mowers (*fæniseces* vel *-cæ*) went over the meadows again (*prata siciliebant*),[2] and cut what they had at first left. This grass was called *sicilimentum*, and distinguished from *fænum*. Late hay was called FŒNUM CARDUM.[3]

The ancient Romans had various kinds of fences (*septa, sepes*, vel *sepimenta*) ; a wall (*maceria*) ; hedge, wooden fence, and ditch, for defending their marches (*limites*) and corn fields, and for enclosing their gardens and orchards, but not their meadows and pasture-grounds. Their cattle and sheep seem to have pastured in the open fields, with persons to attend them. They had parks for deer and other wild beasts ;[4] but the only enclosures mentioned for cattle, were folds for confining them in the night-time,[5] either in the open air, or under covering.[6]

Corns were cut down (*metebantur*) by a sickle, or hook, or by a scythe ; or the ears (*spicæ*) were stript off by an instrument, called BATILLUM, i. e. *serrula ferrea*, an iron saw,[7] and the straw afterwards cut. To this Virgil is thought to allude, G. i. 17, and not to binding the corn in sheaves, as some suppose, which the Romans seem not to have done. In Gaul, the corn was cut down by a machine drawn by two horses.[8] Some kinds of pulse, and also corn, were pulled up by the root.[9] The Greeks bound their corn into sheaves, as the Hebrews, who cut it down with sickles, taking the stalks in handfuls (*mergites*), as we do.[10]

The corn when cut was carried to the threshing-floor (*area*), or barn (*horreum*), or to a covered place adjoining to the threshing-floor, called NUBILARIUM. If the ears were cut off from the stalks, they were thrown into baskets.[11] When the corn was cut with part of the straw, it was carried in carts or wains,[12] as with us.

The AREA, or threshing-floor, was placed near the house, on high ground, open on all sides to the wind, of a round figure, and raised in the middle. It was sometimes paved with flint stones, but usually laid with clay, consolidated with great care, and smoothed with a huge roller.[13]

The grains of the corn were beaten out[14] by the hoofs of cattle driven over it, or by the trampling of horses ;[15] hence *area dum messes sole calente teret*, for *frumenta in area terentur* ;[16] or by flails (*baculi, fustes* vel *perticæ*) ; or by a machine, called TRAHA, v. *trahea*, a dray or sledge, a carriage without wheels ; or TRIBULA, vel *-um*, made of a board or beam, set with stones or pieces of iron,[17] with a great weight laid on it, and drawn by yoked cattle.[18]

Tribula, a threshing machine, has the first syllable long, from τρίβω, *tero*, to thresh ; but *tribulus*, a kind of thistle (or warlike machine, with three spikes or more, for throwing or fixing in the ground, called also *murex*, usually plural, *murices* v. *tribuli*, caltrops),[19] has *tri* short, from τρείς, three, and βολή, a spike or prickle.

These methods of beating out the corn were used by the Greeks and

---

1 in metus extructum, Col. ii. 22.
2 i. e. falcibus consecabant.
3 Plin. xviii. 28.
4 Virg. G. i. 270. Col. ix. Præf.
5 septa v. stabula bubilia, ovilia, caprilia, &c.
6 Virg. Æn. vii. 512.

7 Var. l. 50.falx verriculata rostrata, vel dentata, merga, vel pecten.
8 Col. ii. 21. Plin. xviii. 30.
9 vellebantur, Col. ib. et ii. 10. 12. Plin. xviii. 30. s. 72.
10 Hom. Il. xviii. 550. Ruth. ii.15.Gen.xxxvii.

7.
11 Col. ii. 21. Var. i. 1.
12 plaustra, Virg. ii.206.
13 Col. i. 6. Virg. G. i. 178. Var. i. 2.
14 excutiebantur,tundebantur, terebantur vel exterebantur.
15 equarum gressibus, Plin. xvii. 30. Virg. G.

iii. 132. Col. ii. 21.
16 Tibul. i. 5. 29.
17 tabula lapidibus, aut ferro asperato.
18 jumentis junctis, ib. et Ver. i. 52.
19 Plin. xix. 1. s. 6. Veg. iii. 24. Curt. iv. 13.

Jews.[1] Corn was winnowed[2] or cleaned from the chaff,[3] by a kind of shovel[4] which threw the corn across the wind,[5] or by a sieve,[6] which seems to have been used with or without wind, as among the Greeks and Jews.[7] The corn when cleaned[8] was laid up in granaries,[9] variously constructed,[10] sometimes in pits,[11] where it was preserved for many years; Varro says fifty.[12]

The straw was used for various purposes; for littering cattle,[13] for fodder, and for covering houses; whence CULMEN, the roof, from *culmus*, a stalk of corn. The straw cut with the ears was properly called PALEA; that left in the ground and afterwards cut, STRAMEN, vel *stramentum*, vel *stipula*, the stubble; which was sometimes burned in the fields, to meliorate the land, and destroy the weeds.[14]

As oxen were chiefly used for ploughing, so were the fleeces of sheep for clothing; hence these animals were reared by the Romans with great care. Virgil gives directions about the breeding of cattle,[15] of oxen and horses (ARMENTA,) of sheep and goats (GREGES,) also of dogs and bees,[16] as a part of husbandry.

While individuals were restricted by law to a small portion of land, and citizens themselves cultivated their own farms, there was abundance of provisions without the importation of grain; and the republic could always command the service of hardy and brave warriors when occasion required. But in after ages, especially under the emperors, when landed property was in a manner engrossed by a few, and their immense estates in a great measure cultivated by slaves,[17] Rome was forced to depend on the provinces, both for supplies of provisions, and of men to recruit her armies. Hence Pliny ascribes the ruin first of Italy, and then of the provinces, to overgrown fortunes, and too extensive possessions.[18] The price of land in Italy was increased by an edict of Trajan, that no one should be admitted as a candidate for an office who had not a third part of his estate in land.[19]

PROPAGATION OF TREES.

THE Romans propagated trees and shrubs much in the same way as we do.

Those are properly called trees (*arbores*) which shoot up in one great stem, body, or trunk,[20] and then, at a good distance from the earth, spread into branches and leaves;[21] shrubs (FRUTICES, vel *virgulta*,) which divide into branches,[22] and twigs or sprigs,[23] as soon as they rise from the root. These shrubs, which approach near to the nature of herbs, are called by Pliny *suffrutices*. Virgil enumerates the various ways of propagating trees and shrubs,[24] both natural and artificial.[25]

I. Some were thought to be produced spontaneously; as the osier (*siler*,) the broom (*genista*,) the poplar and willow (*salix*.) But the notion of spontaneous propagation is now universally exploded. Some by fortuitous seeds, as the chestnut, the *esculus*, and oak; some from the roots of

1 Isaiah xxviii. 27. Hom.
II. xx. 495.
2 ventilabatur.
3 acus, -eris.
4 vallus, pala vel ventilabrum.
5 Var. i. 52.
6 vannus vel cribrum.
7 Isaiah xxx. 24. Amos ix. 9. Luke xxii. 31. Col. ii. 21. Hom. IL xiii.

588.
8 expurgatum.
9 horrea vel granaria.
10 Plin. xviii. 30.
11 in scrobibus.
12 Id. & Var. i. 57. ·
13 pecori ovibus bubusque substernebantur, unde stramen, v. stramentum dictum, Varr. i. I. 3. Plin. xviii. 30.

14 Id. & Virg. G. i. 84.
15 qui cultus habendo sit pecori.
16 Virg. G. iii. 49. 72. iv. v. 286. 404.
17 Juv. ix. 55. Liv. vi. 12. Sen. Ep. 114.
18 latifundia, sc. nimis ampla, perdidere Italiam; jam vero et provincias, xviii. 3. 6.

19 Plin. Ep. vi. 19.
20 stirps, truncus, caudex vel stipes.
21 rami et folia.
22 rami v. -uli.
23 virgæ v. -ulæ.
24 sylvæ fructicesque.
25 G. ii. 9, &c.

other trees, as the cherry (CERASUS, first brought into Italy by Lucullus from Cerasus, a city in Pontus, A. U. 680, and 120 years after that, introduced into Britain ;)[1] the elm and laurel (*laurus*,) which some take to be the bay tree.

II, The artificial method of propagating trees were, 1. by suckers (STO-LONES,)[2] or twigs pulled from the roots of trees, and planted in furrows or trenches.[3]—2. By sets, i. e. fixing in the ground branches,[4] sharpened[5] like stakes,[6] cut into a point,[7] slit at the bottom in four ;[8] or pieces of the cleft-wood ;[9] or by planting the trunks with the roots.[10] When plants were set by the roots,[11] they were called VIVIRADICES, quicksets.[12]—3. By layers,[13] i. e. bending a branch, and fixing it in the earth, without disjoining it from the mother-tree, whence new shoots spring.[14] This method was taught by nature from the bramble.[15] It was chiefly used in vines and myrtles,[16] the former of which, however, were more frequently propagated.—4. By slips or cuttings ; small shoots cut from a tree, and planted in the ground,[17] with knops or knobs, i. e. protuberances on each side, like a small hammer.[18]—5. By grafting, or ingrafting,[19] i. e. inserting a scion, a shoot or sprout, a small branch or graff,[20] of one tree into the stock or branch of another. There were several ways of ingrafting, of which Virgil describes only one ; namely, what is called cleft grafting, which was performed by cleaving the head of a stock, and putting a scion from another tree into the cleft ;[21] thus beautifully expressed by Ovid, *fissaque adoptivas accipit arbor opes*, Medic. Fac. 6.

It is a received opinion in this country, that no graft will succeed unless it be upon the stock which bears fruit of the same kind. But Virgil and Columella say, that any scion may be grafted on any stock, *omnis surculus omni arbori inseri potest, si non est ei, cui inseritur, cortice dissimilis ;* as apples on a pear-stock, and cornels, or Cornelian cherries, on a prune or plum-stock, apples on a plane-tree, pears on a wild-ash, &c.[22]

Similar to ingrafting, is what goes by the name of inoculation, or budding.[23] The parts of the plant whence it budded,[24] were called OCULI, eyes, and when these were cut off, it was said, *occæcari*, to be blinded.[25] Inoculation was performed by making a slit in the bark of one tree, and inserting the bud[26] of another tree, which united with it, called also EMPLASTRATIO.[27] But Pliny seems to distinguish them, xvii. 16. s. 26. The part of the bark taken out[28] was called SCUTULA v. TESSELLA, the name given also to any one of the small divisions in a checkered table or pavement.[29]

Forest trees[30] were propagated chiefly by seeds ; olives by truncheons,[31] i. e. by cutting or sawing the trunk or thick branches into pieces of a foot, or a foot and a half in length, and planting them ; whence a root, and soon after a tree was formed.[32] Those trees which were reared only for cutting were called ARBORES CÆDUÆ, or which, being cut, sprout up again[33] from the stem or root. Some trees grow to an immense height. Pliny

---

1 Plin. xv. 25. s. 30.
2 unde cognomen, Stolo, Plin. xvii. I. Var. i. 2.
3 sulci v. fossæ.
4 rami v. taleæ.
5 acuminati.
6 acuto robore valli vel pali.
7 sudes quadrifidæ.
8 Virg. G. ii. 25. Plin. xvii. 17.
9 caudices secti, ib.
10 stirpes, ib.
11 cum radice sereban-tur.
12 Cic. Sen. 13.
13 propagines.
14 viva sua plantaria terra, v. 27.
15 ex rubo, Plin. xvii. 13. s. 21.
16 Virg. G. ib. v. 63.
17 surculi, et malleoli, i. e. surculi utrinque capitulati.
18 Plin. xvii. 21.
19 insitio.
20 tradux v. surculus.
21 feraces plantæ immi-tuntur,—fruitful scions are put in, ib. v. 78. alterius ramos vertere in alterius,—that the branches of one tree turn into those of an-other, 31.
22 Col. v. 11. Virg. G. ii. 33. v. 70. Plin. xv. 1. s. 17.
23 oculos imponere, in-oculare v.-atio.
24 unde germinaret.
25 Plin. xvii. 21, 22. s. 35.
26 gemma v. germen.
27 Plin. v. 73. Col. v. 11.
28 pars exempta ; an-gustus in ipso nodo si-nus.
29 Id. see p. 367.
30 arbores sylvestres.
31 trunci, caudices sec-ti, v. lignum siccum.
32 Virg. G. ii. 30. 63.
33 succisæ repullulant, Plin. xii. 19.

mentions a beam of larix, or larch, 120 feet long, and 2 feet thick, xvi. 40. s. 74.

The greatest attention was paid to the cultivation of vines. They were planted in the ground, well trenched and cleaned,[1] in furrows, or in ditches, disposed in rows, either in the form of a square, or of a *quincunx*. The outermost rows were called ANTES.[2] When a vineyard was dug up,[3] to be planted anew, it was properly said *repastinari*, from an iron instrument, with two forks ; called *pastinum*,[4] which word is put also for a field ready for planting.[5] An old vineyard thus prepared was called VINETUM RESTIBILE. The vines were supported by reeds,[6] or round stakes,[7] or by pieces of cleft oak or olive, not round,[8] which served as props,[9] round which the tendrils[10] twined. Two reeds or stakes,[11] supported each vine, with a stick,[12] or reed across, called JUGUM or CANTHERIUM, and the tying of the vines to it, CAPITUM CONJUGATIO et RELIGATIO, was effected by osier or willow twigs, many of which grew near Ameria, in Umbria.[13]

Sometimes a vine had but a single pole or prop to support it, without a *jugum* or cross-pole ; sometimes four poles, with a jugum to each ; hence called *vitis* COMPLUVIATA ;[14] if but one jugum, UNIJUGA. Concerning the fastening of vines to certain trees, see p. 317. The arches formed by the branches joined together,[15] were called FUNETA, and branches of elms extended to sustain the vines, TABULATA, stories.[16] When the branches[17] were too luxuriant, the superfluous shoots or twigs[18] were lopt off with the pruning knife.[19] Hence VITES *compescere* vel *castigare*, to restrain ; *comas stringere*, to strip the shoots ; *brachia tondere*, to prune the boughs ; *pampinare* for *pampinos decerpere*, to lop off the small branches.[20]

The highest shoots were called FLAGELLA ;[21] the branches on which the fruit grew, PALMÆ ; the ligneous or woody part of a vine, MATERIA ; a branch springing from the stock, PAMPINARIUM ; from another branch, FRUCTUARIUM ; the mark of a hack or chop, CICATRIX ; whence *cicatricosus*. The vines supported by cross stakes in dressing were usually cut in the form of the letter X, which was called DECUSSATIO.[22]

The fruit of the vine was called UVA, a grape ; put for a vine, for wine,[23] for a vine branch,[24] for a swarm[25] of bees, properly not a single berry,[26] but a cluster.[27] The stone of the grape was called VINACEUS, v. -eum, or *acinus vinaceus*.[28] Any cluster of flowers or berries,[29] particularly of ivy,[30] was called CORYMBUS, *crocei corymbi*, i. e. flores.[31] The season when the grapes were gathered was called VINDEMIA, the vintage ;[32] whence *vindemiator*, a gatherer of grapes.[33] Vineyards (VINEÆ vel *vineta*,) as fields were divided by cross paths, called LIMITES (hence *limitare*, to divide or separate, and *limes*, a boundary.) The breadth of them was determined by law.[34]

1 in pastinato, sc. agro.
2 Plin. xvii. 22. Virg. G. ii. 277. 417. Fest.
3 refodiebatur.
4 Col. iii. 18.
5 ager pastinatus.
6 arundines.
7 pali, whence vites palare, i. e. fulcire vel pedare.
8 radicæ, Plin. xvii. 22.
9 adminicula v. pedamenta.
10 clavicula v. capreoli, i. e. colliculi v. cauliculi vitei interti, ut cin-

cinni, Var. i. 31.
11 valli furcæque bidentes.
12 pertica.
13 Col. iv. 12. 30. 4. Plin. xvi. 37. s. 69. Virg. G. i. 265. Cic. Sen. 15.
14 a cavis ædium compluviis, Plin. xvii.21, 22.
15 cum palmites sarmento inter se junguntur fænium modo.
16 Plin. xvii. 22. Virg. G. ii. 361.
17 palmites v. pampini.
18 sarmenta.

19 ferro amputata, Cic. Sen. 15.
20 Virg. G. ii. 366. Plin. xviii. 27.
21 Virg. G. ii. 299.
22 Plin. xvii. 22. Col. v. 6. Colum. iv. 17.
23 Virg. G. ii. 60. Hor. Od. i. 20. 10.
24 pampinus, Ov. Met. iii. 666.
25 examen, Virg. G. iv. 558.
26 acinus v. -um, Suet. Aug. 76.
27 racemus, i. e. acino-

rum congeries, cum pe diculis, Col. xi. 2.
28 Cic. Sen. 15.
29 racemus in orbem circumactus.
30 hedera.
31 Plin. xvi. 34. Virg. Ecl. iii. 39. Ov. Met. iii. 665. Col. x. 301.
32 a vino demendo, i. e. uvis legendia.
33 Hor. Sat. i. 7. 30.
34 see Lex Mamilia, p. 142.

A path or road from east to west, was called DECIMANUS, sc. *limes* (*a mensura* denum *actuum ;*) from south to north, CARDO (*a* cardine *mundi,* i. e. the north pole ; thus, mount Taurus is called CARDO,) or *semita;* whence *semitare,* to divide by paths in this direction, because they were usually narrower than the other paths. The spaces (*areæ,*) included between two *semitæ,* were called PAGINÆ, comprehending each the breadth of five *pali,* or *capita vitium,* distinct vines.[1] Hence *agri* COMPAGINANTES, contiguous grounds.

Vines were planted[2] at different distances, according to the nature of the soil, usually at the distance of five feet, sometimes of eight ; of twenty feet by the Umbri and Marsi, who ploughed and sowed corn between the vines, which places they called PORCULETA. Vines which were transplanted,[3] bore fruit two years sooner than those that were not.[4]

The *limites* DECUMANI were called PRORSI, i. e. *porro versi,* straight ; and the CARDINES *transversi,* cross. From the *decumani* being the chief paths in a field ; hence DECUMANUS for *magnus,* thus, *ova* vel *poma decumana. Acipenser decumanus,* large.[5] So *fluctus decimanus* vel *decimus,* the greatest ; as τρικυμια, *tertius fluctus,* among the Greeks. LIMITES is also put for the streets of a city.[6]

Pliny directs the *limites decumani* in vineyards to be made eighteen feet broad, and the *cardines* or *transversi limites,* ten feet broad.[7] Vines were planted thick in fertile ground,[8] and thinner on hills, but always in exact order.[9]

The Romans in transplanting trees marked on the bark the way each stood, that it might point to the same quarter of the heaven in the place where it was set.[10]

In the different operations of husbandry, they paid the same attention to the rising and setting of the stars as sailors ; also to the winds.[11] The names of the chief winds were, *Aquilo,* or *Boreas,* the north wind ; *Zephyrus,* vel *Favonius,* the west wind ; *Auster,* v. *Notus,* the south wind ; *Eurus,* the east wind ; *Corus, Caurus,* vel *Iapix,* the north-west ; *Africus,* vel LIBS, the south-west ; *Volturnus,* the south-east, &c. But Pliny denominates and places some of these differently, ii. 47. xviii. 33, 34. Winds arising from the land were called *altani,* or *apogæi;* from the sea, *tropæi.*[12]

The ancients observed only four winds, called VENTI CARDINALES, because they blew from the four cardinal points of the world. Homer mentions no more ;[13] so in imitation of him, Ovid and Manilius.[14] Afterwards intermediate winds were added, first one, and then two, between each of the *venti cardinales.*

CARRIAGES OF THE ROMANS.

THE carriages[15] of the ancients were of various kinds, which are said to have been invented by different persons ; by Bacchus and Ceres, Minerva, Erichthonius, and the Phrygians.[16]

1 Liv. xxxvii. 34. Plin. xvii. 22.
2 serebantur.
3 translatæ.
4 satæ, Plin. ib.
5 Fest. Cic. Fin. ii. 8.
6 Ov. Trist. i. 2. 49. Met. xi. 530. Sil. xiv. 122. Luc. v. 672. Sen.

Agam. 502. Liv. xxxi. 24.
7 Plin. xvii. 22. s. 35.
8 pingui campo.
9 ad unguem, Virg. G. ii. 277.
10 Virg. G. ii. 269. Columel. de Arbor. 17. 4. Pallad. Feb. 19. 2.

11 Virg. G. i. 204. 51. iii. 273.
12 Sen. Nat. Q. v. 16. Plin. ii. 44.
13 Serv. Virg. i. 131. Plin. ii. 47. Hom. Odys. E. 295.
14 Astron. iv. 589. Ov. Met. i. 61. Trist. i. 2.

27.
15 vehicula, vectabula, v. -acula.
16 Tibul. ii. 1. 42. Cic. Nat. D. iii. 24. Virg. G. iii. 113. Plin. vii. 56.

Beasts of burden were most anciently used.[1] A dorser, dorsel, or dosser, a pannel, or pack-saddle,[2] was laid on them to enable them to bear their burden more easily, used chiefly on asses and mules; hence called CLITELLARIA, humorously applied to porters, *geruli* vel *bajuli*, but not oxen; hence CLITELLÆ BOVI SUNT IMPOSITÆ, when a task is imposed on one which he is unfit for. Bos CLITELLAS, sc. *portat*.[3] This covering was by later writers called SAGMA; put also for *sella*, or *ephippium*, a saddle for riding on; hence *jumenta* SAGMARIA, vel *sarcinaria* et SELLARIA,[4] sometimes with a coarse cloth below (CENTO, vel *centunculus*, a saddle-cloth.)

A pack-horse was called CABALLUS, or CANTHERIUS, V. -ium, sc. *jumentum (quasi* carenterius, i. e. *equus castratus*, a gelding; *qui hoc distat ab equo, quod majalis a verre*, a barrow or hog from a boar, *capus a gallo, vervex ab ariete*.[5]) Hence *minime sis cantherium in fossa*, be not a pack-horse in the ditch.[6] Some make *cantherius* the same with *clitellarius*, an ass or mule, and read, MINIME, sc. *descendam in viam ;* SCIS, CANTHERIUM IN FOSSA, sc. *equus habebat obviam*, i. e. you know the fable of the horse meeting an ass or mule in a narrow way, and being trodden down by him. See Swinburne's Travels in the South of Italy, vol. ii. sect. 66. Others suppose an allusion to be here made to the prop of a vine.[7]

He who drove a beast of burden was called AGASO, and more rarely AGITATOR.[8] A leathern bag,[9] or wallet, in which one who rode such a beast carried his necessaries, was called HIPPOPERA, MANTICA, PERA vel AVERTA, a cloak-bag or portmanteau, or BULGA.[10]

An instrument put on the back of a slave, or any other person, to help him to carry his burden, was called ÆRUMNULA (from αιρω, *tollo*,) FURCA vel FURCILLA ;[11] and because Marius, to diminish the number of waggons, which were an encumbrance to the army, appointed that the soldiers should carry their baggage (*sarcinæ, vasa et cibaria*) tied up in bundles, upon *furcæ* or forks, both the soldiers and these furcæ were called MULI MARIANI,[12] EXPELLERE, EJICERE, vel EXTRUDERE FURCA, vel *furcilla*, to drive away by force.[13]

Any thing carried, not on the back, but on the shoulders, or in the hands of men, was called FERCULUM; as the dishes at an entertainment, the spoils at a triumph, the images of the gods at sacred games, the corpse and other things carried at a funeral.[14]

When persons were carried in a chair or sedan, on which they sat, it was called SELLA *gestatoria, portatoria*, v. *fertoria*, or CATHEDRA; in a couch or litter, on which they lay extended, LECTICA, vel CUBILE, used both in the city and on journeys, sometimes open, and sometimes covered, with curtains of skin or cloth, called PLAGULÆ, which were occasionally drawn aside, sometimes with a window of glass, or transparent stone, so that they might either read or write, or sleep in them. There were commonly some footmen or lackeys, who went before the sedan (CURSORES.)[15]

The *sellæ* and *lecticæ* of women were of a different construction from those of men; hence *sella* vel *lectica muliebris :* the *cathedra* is supposed to

1 animalia vel jumenta dossuaria, vel dorsualia, from dorsum, i. e. tota posterior pars corporis ; quod ea devexa fit deorsum, Fest.
2 clitella vel stratum.
3 Plaut. Most. iii. 2. 94. Cic. Att. v. 15. Quinct. v. 11. 21.
4 Veg. ii. 10. Lampr.

Heliog. 4.
5 Varro de R. Rust. ii. 7. fin. Cic. Fam. ix. 18.
6 Liv. xxiii. 47.
7 Gronovius in Loc. Scheffer de Re Vehic.
8 Virg. G. i. 273.
9 sacculus scorteus.
10 Sen. Ep. 87. Hor. Sat. i. 6. 106. Schol. ib. Festus.

11 Fest. Plaut. Casin. ii. 8. 2.
12 Fest. in Ærumnula & Frontin. iv. 1. 7. Plut. in Mar.
13 Hor. Ep. i. 10. 24. Cic. Att. xvi. 2.
14 Suet. Aug. 74. Cæs. 37. 76. Cal. 16.
15 Suet. Ne. 26. Dom. 2. Oth. 6. Vit. 16. Tit.

10. Juv. i. 64. iii. 242. 249. iv. 20. vi. 90. Ov. Art. A. i. 487. Tac. Hist. i. 35. Ann. xiv. 4. Plin. Ep. iii. 5. Cic. Phil. ii. 41. Att. x. 13. Mart. vi. 99. ii. Sen. Ep. 123. Suas. 7. Petr. 28.

have been peculiar to women. The sella usually contained but one ; the lectica, one or more. The sella had only a small pillow (*cervical*) to recline the head on ; the lectica had a mattress stuffed with feathers ; hence *pensiles plumæ :* sometimes with roses (*pulvinus rosa farctus*,) probably with ropes below.[1]

The sellæ and lecticæ were carried by slaves, called LECTICARII, *calones*, *geruli*, v. *bajuli*, dressed commonly in a dark or red *penula*,[2] tall[3] and handsome, from different countries. They were supported on poles (ASSERES, vel *amites*,)[4] not fixed, but removable,[5] placed on the shoulders or necks of the slaves ; hence they were said *aliquem* SUCCOLARE, and those carried by them, *succolari*, who were thus greatly raised above persons on foot, particularly such as were carried in the sella or cathedra.[6] The sella was commonly carried by two, and the lectica by four ; sometimes by six, hence called *hexaphoros*, and by eight OCTOPHOROS, v. *-um*.[7]

When the lectica was set down, it had four feet to support it, usually of wood, sometimes of silver or gold. The kings of India had lecticæ of solid gold.[8] The use of lecticæ was thought to have been introduced at Rome from the nations of the East towards the end of the republic. But we find them mentioned long before, on journey, and in the army. The emperor Claudius is said first to have used a sella covered at top.[9] They do not seem to have been used in the city in the time of Plautus or of Terence ; but they were so frequent under Cæsar that he prohibited the use of them, unless to persons of a certain rank and age, and on certain days. Those who had not sedans of their own, got them to hire. Hence we read in later times of CORPORA et CASTRA *licticariorum*, who seem to have consisted not only of slaves but of plebeians of the lowest rank, particularly freedmen. SELLÆ *erant ad exonerandum ventrem aptæ, et* PRIVATÆ vel FAMILIARICÆ, et PUBLICÆ.[10]

A kind of close litter carried[11] by two mules,[12] or little horses,[13] was called BASTARNA, mentioned only by later writers.

Two horses yoked to a carriage were called BIGÆ, *bijugi*, v. *bijuges ;* three, *trigæ ;* and four, *quadrigæ, quadrijugi*, v. *-ges ;* frequently put for the chariot itself, *bijuge curriculum, quadrijugus currus ;* but *curriculum* is oftener put for *cursus*, the race.[14] We also read of a chariot drawn by six horses, joined together a-breast,[15] for so the Romans always yoked their horses in their race-chariots. Nero once drove a chariot at the Olympic games, drawn by ten horses.[16]

A carriage without wheels, drawn by any animals, was called TRAHA, v. *-ea*, vel *traga*,

1 Suet. Oth. 6. Ner. 9. Juv. i. 159. vi. 91. 352. Mart. ii. 57. 6. xii. 38. Tac. Hist. iii. 67. Cic. Verr. v. 11. Q. Fr. ii. 9. Sen. Marc. 16. Gell. x. 3.

2 Sen. Ep. 70. 113. Ben. iii. 28.

3 longi v. proceri.

4 Sen. Ep. 110. Juv. iii. 249. vi. 350. vii. 132. viii. 132. ix. 142. Mart.

ik. 23. 9.

5 exemptiles, Suet. Cal. 58.

6 Plin. Pan. 22. 24. Suet. Claud. 10. Oth. 6. Juv. iii. 240.

7 Juv. ix. 142. Mart. ii. 81. vi. 59. ix. 3. see p. 339.

8 Catul. x. 22. Athen. v. 10. Curt. viii. 9.

9 Dio. lx. 2. Liv. xxiv. 42. Gell. x. 3.

10 Mart. iii. 46. xii. 78. Suet. Cæs. 43. Claud. 28. Juv. vi. 352. ix. 142. Var. R. i. 14.

11 gestata v. deportata.

12 muli, ex equo et asino : hinni, hinnuli, v. burdones, ex equo et asina, Plin. viii. 44. s. 69.

13 manni, Ov. Am. ii. 16. 49. i. e. equi minuti, vel pumilli, s. -iones,

dwarfs.

14 Cic. Rab. 10. Marcel. 2. Hor. Od. i. 1. 3. Suet. Cal. 19. Virg. G. iii. 18.

15 ab Augusto sejuges, sicut et elephanti, Plin. xxxiv. 5. s. 10.

16 aurigavit decemjugem, sc. currum. Suet. Ner. 24. Aug. 94.

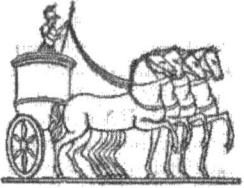

a sledge, used in rustic work in beating out the corn[1] (called by Varro, *Pœnicum plostellum*,[2] because used for that purpose by the Carthaginians,) and among northern nations in travelling on the ice and snow. Carriages with one wheel were called UNAROTA. A vehicle of this kind drawn by the hands of slaves, CHIRAMAXIUM, or ARCUMA.[3] A vehicle with two wheels, BIROTUM ; with four (*quadrirotium*.)[4]

Those who drove chariots in the circus at Rome, with whatever number of horses, were called QUADRIGARII, from the *quadrigæ* being most frequently used ; hence FACTIONES QUADRIGARIORUM. Those who rode two horses joined together, leaping quickly from the one to the other, were called DESULTORES ; hence *desultor v. desertor amoris*, inconstant ; and the horses themselves, DESULTORII, sometimes successfully used in war.[5]

The vehicles used in races were called CURRUS, or *curricula*, chariots, *a currendo*, from their velocity, having only two wheels, by whatever number of horses they were drawn : also those used in war by different nations ; of which some were armed with scythes,[6] in different forms. Also those used by the Roman magistrates, the consuls, prætors, censors, and chief ædiles, whence they were called MAGISTRATUS CURULES, and the seat on which these magistrates sat in the senate-house, the rostra, or tribunal of justice, SELLA CURULIS,[7] because they carried it with them in their chariots.[8] It was a stool or seat without a back.[9] with four crooked feet, fixed to the extremities of cross pieces of wood, joined by a common axis, somewhat in the form of the letter X (*decussatim*,) and covered with leather ; so that it might be occasionally folded together for the convenience of carriage, and set down wherever the magistrates chose to use it, adorned with ivory ; hence called CURULE EBUR, and ALTA,[10] because frequently placed on a tribunal, or because it was the emblem of dignity ; REGIA, because first used by the kings, borrowed from the Tuscans, in later times adorned with engravings ; *conspicuum signis*.[11]

A carriage in which matrons were carried to games and sacred rites, was called PILENTUM, an easy soft vehicle (*pensile*,) with four wheels ; usually painted with various colours.[12] The carriage which matrons used in common (*festo profestoque*) was called CARPENTUM, named from Carmenta, the mother of Evander, commonly with two wheels, and an arched covering ; as the flamines used (*currus arcuatus*,) sometimes without a covering.[13] Women were prohibited the use of it in the second

1 see p. 384.
2 R. R. iv. 52.
3 Hygin. ii. 14. Petron. 28. Festus.
4 τετρακυκλος σκηνη, v. τετρατροχος, quatuor rotarum currus, Hom. Il. Ω. 324.
5 Liv. xxiii. 29. xliv. 9.

Suet. Ner. 16. Cæs. 39. Ov. Am. i. 3. 15. Festus.
6 currus falcati, falcatæ quadrigæ, Liv. xxxvi. 41, 42. Curt. iv. 9.
7 See cut representing their usual form, p. 245.

8 Gell. ill. 18. Isidor. xx. 11.
9 anaclinterium, v. tabulatum a tergo sur- gens in quod reclinari posset.
10 Plut. Mar. Suet. Aug. 43. Gell. vi. 9. Hor. Ep. i. 6. 53. Sil. viii. 488.

11 Liv. i. 8. 20. Virg. Æn. xi. 334. Flor. i. 5. Ov. Pont. iv. 5. 11.
12 Serv. Virg. Æn. viii. 666. Isid. xx. 12.
13 Liv. i. 21. 34. 46. v. 25. Suet. Tib. 2. Claud. 11 Ov. Fast. i. 620.

Panic war by the Oppian law, which, however, was soon after repealed. It is sometimes put for any carriage.[1]

A splendid carriage with four wheels and four horses, adorned with ivory and silver, in which the images of the gods were led in solemn procession from their shrines (e sacrariis) at the Circensian games, to a place in the circus, called PULVINAR, where couches were prepared for placing them on, was called THENSA, from the thongs stretched before it (lora tensa,)[2] attended by persons of the first rank, in their most magnificent apparel, who were said thensam DUCERE vel DEDUCERE,[3] who delighted to touch the thongs by which the chariot was drawn (funemque manu contingere gaudent.)[4] And if a boy (puer patrimus et matrimus) happened to let go[5] the thong which he held, it behoved the procession to be renewed. Under the emperors, the decreeing of a thensa to any one was an acknowledgment of his divinity.[6]

A carriage with two wheels, for travelling expeditiously, was called CISIUM, q. citium; the driver, CISIARIUS, drawn usually by three mules; its body (capsum, v. -a) of basket-work (PLOXIMUM, v. -enum.)[7] A larger carriage, for travelling, with four wheels, was called RHEDA, a Gallic word, or CARRUCA, the driver, RHEDARIUS, or CARRUCARIUS, a hired one, MERITORIA, both also used in the city,[8] sometimes adorned with silver. An open carriage with four wheels, for persons of inferior rank, as some think, was called PETORRITUM, also a Gallic word.[9]

A kind of swift carriage used in war by the Gauls and Britons, was called ESSEDUM; the driver, or rather one who fought from it, ESSEDARIUS, adopted at Rome for common use.[10]

A carriage armed with scythes, used by the same people, COVINUS; the driver, COVINARIUS; similar to it, was probably BENNA. In the war-chariots of the ancients, there were usually but two persons, one who fought (bellator,) and another who directed the horses (auriga, the charioteer.)[11]

An open carriage for heavy burdens (vehiculum onerarium) was called PLAUSTRUM, or veha (ἅμαξα) a waggon or wain; generally with two wheels, sometimes four; drawn commonly by two oxen or more, sometimes by asses or mules. A waggon or cart with a coverlet wrought of rushes laid on it, for carrying dung or the like, was called SCIRPEA, properly the coverlet itself, sc. crates; in plaustra scirpea lata fuit.[12] A covered cart or waggon laid with cloths, for carrying the old or infirm of meaner rank, was called ARCERA, quasi arca. The load or weight which a wain could carry at once (una vectura,) was called VEHES, -is.[13]

A waggon with four wheels was also called CARRUS v. -um, by a Gallic name, or SARRACUM, or EPIRHEDIUM, and by later writers, ANGARIA, vel CLABULARE; also CARRAGIUM, and a fortification formed by a number of carriages, CARRAGO.[14]

SARRACA Bootæ, v, -tis, or plaustra, is put for two constellations, near the north pole, called the two bears (Arcti geminæ, vel duæ αρκτοι,) URSA MAJOR,

---

1 Liv. xxxiv. 1. 8. Flor. i. 18. iii. 2. 10.
2 Suet. Aug. 45. Asc. Cic. Ver. i. 59. Fest.
3 Liv. v. 41. Suet. Aug. 43. Vesp. 5.
4 and are glad to touch the rope with their hand, Asc. ib. Virg. Æn. ii. 239.
5 omittere.

6 Cic. Resp. H. 10, 11. Suet. Cæs. 76.
7 Cic. Phil. ii. 31. S. Rosc. 7. Sen. Ep. 72. Ulpian. Aus. Ep. viii. 7. Festus.
8 Quinctil. i. 9. Cic. Mil. 10. Att. v. 17. vi. 1. Suet. Ner. 30. Cæs. 57. Mart. iii. 47.
9 Plin. xxxiii. 11. Gell.

xv. 30. Hor. Sat. i. 6. 104. Festus.
10 Cæs. B. G. iv. 33. v. 19. Virg. G. iii. 204. Cic. Fam. vii. 6. Phil. ii. 58.
Suet. Cal. 26. Galb. vi. 18.
11 Tac. Agr. 35, 36. Sil. xvii. 418. Festus. Virg. Æn. ix. 330. xii. 469. 624. 737.

12 Virg. G. iii. 536. Ov. Fast. vi. 780. Varr. L. L. iv. 3.
13 Gell. xx. 1. Col. xi. 2.
14 Am. Marcellin. xxxi. 20. Cæs. B. G. i. 6. 26. Liv. x. 28. Juv. iii. 255. viii. 66. Quinct. i. 5.

named *Helicæ* (*Parrhasis*, i. e. *Arcadica*,) PARRHASIS ARCTOS,[1] from Callisto, the daughter of Lycaon, king of Arcadia, who is said to have been converted into this constellation by Jupiter, and URSA MINOR called CYNOSURA, i. e. κυνος ουρα, *canis cauda*, properly called ARCTOS, distinguished from the great bear (HELICE.)[2]

The greater bear alone was properly called PLAUSTRUM, from its resemblance to a waggon, whence we call it Charles's wain, or the Plough; and the stars which compose it, TRIONES,[3] q. TERIONES, ploughing oxen; seven in number, SEPTENTRIONES.[4] But *plaustra* in the plur. is applied to both bears; hence called GEMINI TRIONES, also *inoccidui* v. *nunquam occidentes*, because they never set; *oceani metuentes æquore tingi*, afraid of being dipped in the waters of the ocean, for a reason mentioned by Ovid; and *tardi* vel *pigri*, because, from their vicinity to the pole, they appear to move slow, *neque se quoquam in cælo commovent.*[5]

The ursa major is attended by the constellation BOOTES, q. *bubulcus*, the ox-driver, said to be retarded by the slowness of his wains, named also ARCTOPHYLAX, q. *ursæ custos,*[6] *custos Erymanthidos ursæ,*[7] into which constellation Arcas, the son of Callisto by Jupiter, was changed, and thus joined with his mother. A star in it of the first magnitude was called ARCTURUS, q. αρκτου ουρα, *ursæ cauda :* STELLA POST CAUDAM URSÆ MAJORIS, said to be the same with Bootes,[8] as its name properly implies, αρκτου ουρος, *ursæ custos.* Around the pole moved the dragon (*draco* v. *anguis*,)[9] approaching the ursa major with its tail, and surrounding the ursa minor with its body.[10]

The principal parts of a carriage were, the wheels (ROTÆ,) the body of the carriage (CAPSUM, -*us*, v. -*a*, PLOXEMUM, v. -*us*,)[11] and draught-tree (TEMO,) to which the animals which drew it were yoked.

The wheels consisted of the axletree (AXIS,) a round beam,[12] on which the wheel turns; the nave,[13] in which the axle moves, and the spokes[14] are fixed; the circumference of the wheel,[15] composed of fellies,[16] in which the spokes are fastened, commonly surrounded with an iron or brass ring.[17]

A wheel without spokes[18] was called TYMPANUM, from its resemblance to the end of a drum. It was made of solid boards,[19] fixed to a square piece of wood, as an axis, without a nave, and strengthened by cross bars,[20] with an iron ring around;[21] so that the whole turned together on the extremities of the axts, called CARDINES. Such wheels were chiefly used in rustic wains,[22] as they are still in this country, and called TUMBRELS. *Tympanum* is also put for a large wheel, moved by horses or men for raising weights from a ship, or the like, by means of pulleys,[23] ropes, and hooks, a kind of crane;[24] or for drawing water,[25] *curva* ANTLIA, ANCLA v. ANTHA (αντλημα,)[26] HAUSTUM, v. *rota aquaria,* sometimes turned by the force of water;[27] the water was raised through a siphon,[28] by the force of a sucker,[29] as in a

1 Juv. v. 23. Ov. Met. ii. 117. Trist. i. 3. 46. Luc. ii. 237. Cic. Acad. iv. 20.
2 Ov. Met. ii. 506. Ep. xviii. m. Fast. iii. 108. Cic. N. D. ii. 41.
3 Hygin. Poet. Astron. i. 2. Ov. Pont. iv. 10. 39. Mart. vi. 56. q.
4 Var. L. L. vi. 4. Gel. ii. 21. Cic. Nat. D. ii.
5 Virg. Æn. i. 744. G. i. 246. Ov. Fast. ii. 191.
6 Cic. Nat. D. ii. 42. Ov. Met. ii. 177. Man. i. 316.
7 the keeper of the Erymanthian bear, Ov. Trist. i. 3. 103.
8 Ov. Met. ii. 506 viii. 206. Serv. Virg. Æn. i. 744. iii. 516. G. i. 67.244.
9 geminas qui separat Arctos, Ov. Met. iii. 45.
10 Virg. G. i. 244.
11 Festus.
12 lignum v.stipes teres.
13 modiolus.
14 radii.
15 peripheria, vel rotæ summæ curvatura, Ov. Met. ii. 108.
16 apsides.
17 canthus, Quinct. i. 5. 8. Pers. v. 71.Virg. Æn. v. 274.
18 non radiata.
19 tabulæ.
20 transversis asseribus.
21 ferreus canthus.
22 Prob. Virg. G. i. 163. ii. 444.
23 trochleæ.
24 tolleno, grus, v. γέρανος, Lucret. iv. 903.
25 machina haustoria, Vitruv. x. 9.
26 John. vi. 11. Mart. ix. 19. Suet. Tib. 51.
27 Lucret. v. 317.
28 sipho v. -on, fistula v. canalis.
29 embolus v. -um.

pump, or by means of buckets.[1] Water-engines were also used to extinguish fires.[2]

From the supposed diurnal rotation of the heavenly bodies, AXIS is put for the line around which they were thought to turn, and the ends of the axis, CARDINES, VERTICES, vel POLI, for the north and south poles.[3] Axis and POLUS are sometimes put for *cœlum* or *æther;* thus *sub ætheris axe,*[4] i. e. *sub dio* vel *aere; lucidus polus ;*[5] *cardines mundi quatuor,* the four cardinal points; SEPTENTRIO, the north; MERIDIES, the south; ORIENS, sc. *sol,* vel *ortus solis,* the east; OCCIDENS, v. *occasus solis,* the west; *cardo eous,* the east; *occiduus* v. *hesperius,* the west. In the north Jupiter was supposed to reside ; hence it is called DOMICILIUM JOVIS,[6] SEDES DEORUM ;[7] and as some think, PORTA CŒLI :[8] thus, *tempestas a vertice,* for *septentrione.*[9]

The animals usually yoked in carriages were horses, oxen, asses, and mules, sometimes camels ; elephants, and even lions, tigers, leopards, and bears ; dogs, goats, and deer ; also men and women.[10]

Animals were joined to a carriage[11] by what was called JUGUM, a yoke ; usually made of wood, but sometimes also of metal, placed upon the neck, one yoke commonly upon two, of a crooked form, with a band (*curvatura*) for the neck of each : hence *sub* JUGO *cogere,* v. *jungere ; colla* v. *cervices jugo subjicere, subdere, submittere,* v. *supponere, & eripere :* JUGUM *subire, cervice ferre, detrectare, exuere, a cervicibus dejicere, excutere,* &c. The yoke was tied to the necks of the animals, and to the pole or team, with leathern thongs (*lora* SUBJUGIA.)[12]

When one pair of horses was not sufficient to draw a carriage, another pair was added in a straight line, before, and yoked in the same manner. If only a third horse was added, he was bound with nothing but ropes, without any yoke. When more horses than two were joined a-breast (*æquata fronte,*) a custom which is said to have been introduced by one Clisthenes of Sicyon, two horses only were yoked to the carriage, called JUGALES, *jugarii,* v. *juges* (ζυγιοι ;)[13] and the others were bound (*appensi* vel *adjuncti*) on each side with ropes ; hence called FUNALES EQUI,[14] or FUNES ; in a chariot of four (*in quadrigis,*) the horse on the right, DEXTER, v. *primus ;* on the left, SINISTER, *lævus,* v. *secundus.* This method of yoking horses was chiefly used in the Circensian games, or in a triumph.

The instruments by which animals were driven or excited, were,—1. The lash or whip (*flagrum,* V. FLAGELLUM, μαστιξ,) made of leathern thongs (SCUTICA, *loris horridis,*)[15] or twisted cords, tied at the end of a stick, sometimes sharpened (*aculeati*) with small bits of iron or lead at the end,[16] and divided into several lashes (*tæniæ* v. *lora,*) called SCORPIONS.[17] 2. A rod (VIRGA,)[18] or goad (STIMULUS,)[19] a pole, or long stick, with a sharp point : hence *stimulos alicui adhibere, admovere, addere, adjicere ; stimulis fodere, incitare, &c. Adversus stimulum calces,* sc. *jactare,* to kick against

---

1 modioli v. hamæ, Juv. xiv. 305.
2 Plin. Ep. x. 42.
3 Cic. Univ. 10. Nat. D. ii. 41. Vitruv. ix. 2. Virg. G. i. 242. Plin. ii. 15.
4 under the canopy of heaven, Virg. Æn. ii. 512. iii. 585. viii. 28.
5 Quinct. xii. 10. 67. Stat. Theb. i. 157. Luc. iv. 672. v. 71.
6 the mansion of Jove,

Serv. Virg. Æn. ii. 693.
7 the abode of the gods, Fest. in sinistræ aves.
8 the gate of heaven, Virg. G. iii. 261.
9 a tempest from the north, ib. ii. 310.
10 Suet. Ner. 11. Claud. xxxiii. 3. Curt. viii. 9. Sen. Ira, ii. 31. Luc. x. 276. Mart. i. 52. 105.

Lamprid. Heliog. 28, 29.
11 vehiculo v. ad vehiculum jungebantur, Virg. Æn. vii. 724. Cic. Att. vi. 1. Suet. Cæs. 31.
12 Hor. Od. iii. 9. 18. Jerem. xxviii. 13. Ov. Fast. iv. 216. Cato 63.
13 Festus.
14 Suet. Tib. 9. Stat. Theb. vi. 461. ζειροφοροι

στιραιοι, v. παρηοροι, Diony. vii. 73. Isid. xvii.
35. Zonar. Ann. ii. Aus. Ep. xxxv. 10.
15 σκυταλη, Mart. x. 62.
16 horribile flagellum, Hor. Sat. i. 3. 117.
17 1 Kings xii. 11.
18 Juv. iii. 317. Luc. iv. 683.
19 i. e. pertica cum cuspide acuta.

the goad.[1]—And, 3. A spur (CALCAR,)[2] used only by riders: hence *equo calcaria addere, subdere,*[3] &c. *Alter frenis eget, alter calcaribus,* the one requires the reins, the other the spurs, said by Isocrates of Ephorus and Theopompus.[4]

The instruments used for restraining and managing horses, were,—1. The bit or bridle (FRÆNUM. pl. -*i*, v. -*a*,) said to have been invented by the Lapithæ, a people of Thessaly, or by one Pelethronius; the part which went round the ears was called AUREA; that which was put into the mouth, properly the iron or bit, OREA;[5] sometimes made unequal and rough, like a wolf's teeth, particularly when the horse was headstrong (TENAX:)[6] hence *frena* LUPATA,[7] or LUPI. *Fræna injicere, concutere, accipere, mandere, detrahere, laxare,* &c. *Frenum mordere,* to be impatient under restraint or subjection; but in Martial and Statius,[8] to bear tamely. The bit was sometimes made of gold, as the collars (*monilia,*) which hung from the horses' necks; and the coverings for their backs (*strata*) were adorned with gold and purple.[9]—2. The reins (HABENÆ, vel *lora;*) hence *habenas corripere, flectere,* v. *moliri,* to manage; *dare, immittere, effundere, laxare, permittere,* to let out; *adducere,* to draw in, and *supprimere.*[10]

To certain animals, a head-stall or muzzle (CAPISTRUM) was applied, sometimes with iron spikes fixed to it, as to calves or the like, when weaned, or with a covering for the mouth (*fiscella;*) hence *fiscellis capistrare boves,* to muzzle; φιμουν,[11] *os consuere.* But *capistrum* is also put for any rope or cord; hence *vitem capistro constringere,* to bind; *jumenta capistrare,* to tie with a halter, or fasten to the stall.[12]

The person who directed the chariot and the horses, was called AURIGA,[13] or *agitator,*[14] the charioteer or driver; also MODERATOR. But these names are applied chiefly to those who contended in the circus, or directed chariots in war, and always stood upright in their chariots (*insistebant curribus;*) hence AURIGARE for *currum regere;* and AURIGARIUS, a person who kept chariots for running in the circus.[15]

Auriga is the name of a constellation in which are two stars, called HÆDI (the kids,) above the horns of Taurus. On the head of Taurus, are the Hyades (*ab ύειν, pluere,*) or Suculæ (*a suibus,*)[16] called *pluviæ* by Virgil, and *tristes* by Horace; because at their rising and sitting, they were supposed to produce rains; on the neck, or, as Servius says, *ante genua tauri; in cauda tauri septem* PLEIADES, or VERGILIÆ, the seven stars; sing. *Pleias* vel PLIAS.[17]

AGITATOR is also put for *agaso,*[18] a person who drove any beasts on foot. But drivers were commonly denominated from the name of the carriage; thus, *rhedarius, plaustrarius,* &c., or of the animals which drew it; thus, MULIO,[19] commonly put for a muleteer, who drove mules of burden;[20] as *equiso* for a person who broke or trained horses[21] to go with an ambling

1 Ter. Phorm. i. 2. 28. πρὸς κέντρα λακτίζειν, in stimulos calcitrare, —to kick against the pricks, Acts. ix. 5.
2 quod calci equitis alligetur; ferrata calce cunctantem impellebat equum, Sil. vii. 696.
3 to clap spurs to a horse.
4 Cic. Att. vi. 1. Or. iii. 9.
5 Virg. G. iii. 115. Plin. vii. 56. Festus.

6 Liv. xxxix. 5. Ov. Am. iii. 4. 13. durior oris equus, ib. ii. 9. 30.
7 Hor. Od. i. 8. 6. Virg. G. iii. 208. Ov. Am. i. 2.
15. Trist. iv. 6. 4. Stat. Achil. i. 281.
8 Mart. i. 105. Stat. Sylv. i. 2. 28. Cic. Fam. xi. 23.
9 Virg. Æn. vii. 279.
10 Ov. Am. i. 13. 10.
11 Deut. xxv. 4. Virg. G. iii. 188. 399. Plin. xviii.

19.
12 Sen. Ep. 47. Columel. vi. 20. vi. 19.
13 ἡνίοχος, qui lora tenebat.
14 ελατης.
15 Ov. Met. ii. 327. Cic. Att. xiii. 21. Acad. iv. 29. Suet. Cal. 54. Ner. xxii. 34. Plin. Ep. ix. 6. Virg. Luc. viii. 199.
16 Serv. Virg. Æn. ix. 668. Cic. Nat. D. ii. 43. Plin. ii. 39. Gell. xiii. 9.

17 Ov. Ep. xviii. 188. Plin. ii. 41. Serv. Virg. G. i. 137. Æn. iii. 516.
18 qui jumenta agebat.
19 Virg. G. i. 273. Suet. Ner. 30. Sen. Ep. 87. Mart. ix. 58. xii. 24.
20 muli clitellarii, Mart. x. 2. 76.
21 equorum domitor, qui tolutim incedere, v. badizare docebat.

pace ; under the *magister equorum*, the chief manager of horses. The horses of Alexander and Cæsar would admit no riders but themselves.[1]

The driver commonly sat behind the pole, with the whip in his right hand, and the reins in his left ; hence he was said *sedere prima sella, sedere temone*, v. *primo temone*, i. e. *in sella proxima temoni*, and *temone labi*, v. *excuti*, to be thrown from his seat ;[2] sometimes dressed in red,[3] or scarlet ;[4] sometimes he walked on foot. When he made the carriage go slower, he was said *currum equosque sustinere ;* when he drew it back or aside, *retorquere et avertere.*[5] Those who rode in a carriage or on horseback were said *vehi*, or *portari, evehi*, or *invehi ;* those carried in a hired vehicle,[6] VECTORES : so passengers in a ship ;.but *vector* is also put for one who carries : *fulminis vector*, i. e. *aquilo*, as *vehens* and *invehens*, for one who is carried.[7] When a person mounted a chariot, he was said *currum conscendere, ascendere, inscendere*, et *insilire*, which is usually applied to mounting on horseback, *saltu in currum emicare ;* when helped up, or taken up by any one, *curru* v. *in currum tolli.* The time for mounting in hired carriages was intimated by the driver's moving his rod or cracking his whip ;[8] to dismount, *descendere* v. *desilire.*

The Romans painted their carriages with different colours, and decorated them with various ornaments, with gold and silver,.and even with precious stones, as the Persians.[9]

OF THE CITY.

ROME was built on seven hills (*colles, montes, arces*, vel·*juga*, nempe, *Palatinus, Quirinalis, Aventinus, Cælius, Viminalis, Exquilinus*, et Junicularis ;) hence called *urbs* SEPTICOLLIS, or SEPTEMGEMINA ; by the Greeks, ἱπτάλοφος, and a festival was celebrated in December, called SEPTIMONTIUM, to commemorate the addition of the seventh hill.[10]

The Janiculum seems to be improperly ranked by Servius among the seven hills of Rome ; because, though built on, and fortified by Ancus, it does not appear to have been included within the city, although the contrary is asserted by several authors.[11] The collis Capitolinus, *vel* Tarpeius, which Servius omits, ought to have been put instead of it. The Janiculum, collis Hortulorum, and Vaticanus, were afterwards added.

1. *Mons* PALATINUS, vel PALATIUM, the Palatine mount, on which alone Romulus built.[12] Here Augustus had his house ; and the succeeding emperors, as Romulus had before : hence the emperor's house was called PALATIUM, a palace, DOMUS PALATINA ;[13] and in later times, those who attended the emperor were called PALATINI.

2. CAPITOLINUS, so called from the capitol built on it, formerly named SATURNIUS, from Saturn's having dwelt there, and TARPEIUS, from Tarpeia, who betrayed the citadel to the Sabines, to whom that mount was assigned to dwell in.[14]

3. AVENTINUS, the most extensive of all the hills, named from an Alban

1 Var. Curt. iv. 5. Dio. xxxvii. 54. Plin. vili. 42.
2 Virg. Æn. xii. 470. Phædr. iii. 6. Stat. Sylv. i. 2. 144. Prop. iv. 8.
3 canusinatos, i. e. veste Canusii confecta indutus, Suet. Ner. 30.
4 cocco, Mart. x. 76.
5 Liv. i. 48. Diony. iv.

39. Sen. Ep. 87. Cic. xxxvii. 54. Att. xiii. 21. Virg. Æn. xii. 465.
6 vehiculo meritorio.
7 Cic. Nat. D. i. 28. ili. 27. 3. Clar. Or. 97. Just. xi. 7. Gell. v. 6. Juv xii. 63. Ov. Fast. i. 433. Stat. Theb. ix. 855.
8 Virg. xii. 327. Juv. iii.

317.
9 Serv. Virg. Æn. viii. 666. Plin. xxxiii. 3. Juv. vii. 125. Curt. iii. 3. x. 1. Ov. Met. ii. 107.
10 Stat. Sylv. i. 2. 191. iv. 1. 6. Serv. Æn. vi. 784. G. ii. 535. Suet. Dom. 4. Plut. Q. Rom. 68. Festus.

11 Liv. i. 33. ii. 10. 51. Dio. 37. Gell. xv. 27. Eutrop. i. 5.
12 Liv. i. 5.
13 Suet. Aug. 72. Claud. 17. Vesp. 25. D. 15. Dio. lili. 16.
14 Justin. xliii. 1. Virg. ib. Diony. ii. 68. Liv. i. 11. 33.

king of that name, who was buried on it; the place which Remus chose to take the omens, therefore said not to have been included within the Pomærium[1] till the time of Claudius. But others say, it was joined to the city by Ancus, called also collis MURCIUS, from Murcia, the goddess of sleep, who had a chapel (*sacellum*) on it; collis DIANÆ, from a temple of Diana;[2] and REMONIUS, from Remus, who wished the city to be founded there.

4. QUIRINALIS is supposed to have been named from a temple of Romulus, called also Quirinus, which stood on it, or from the Sabines, who came from Cures,'and dwelt there: added to the city by Servius;[3] called in later times, mons Caballi, or Caballinus, from two marble horses placed there.

5. CÆLIUS, named from CÆLES Vibenna, a Tuscan leader, who came to the assistance of the Romans against the Sabines, with a body of men, and got this mount to dwell on; added to the city by Romulus according to Dionys. ii. 50, by Tullus Hostilius, according to Liv. i. 30, by Ancus Martius, according to Strabo, v. p. 234, by Tarquinius Priscus, according to Tacit. Ann. iv. 65; anciently called QUERQUETULANUS, from the oaks which grew on it; in the time of Tiberius ordered to be called AUGUSTUS;[4] afterwards named LATERANUS, where the popes long resided, before they removed to the Vatican.

6. VIMINALIS, named from tickets of osiers which grew there,[5] or FAGUTALIS (from *fagi*, beeches;) added to the city by Servius Tullius.[6]

7. EXQUILINUS, *Exquiliæ*, vel *Esquiliæ*, supposed to be named from thickets of oaks (*æsculeta*) which grew on it, or from watches kept there (*excubiæ*;) added to the city by Servius Tullius.[7]

JANICULUM, named from Janus, who is said to have first built on it, the most favourable place for taking a view of the city.[8] From its sparkling sands, it got the name of mons Aureus, and by corruption MONTORIUS.

VATICANUS, so called, because the Romans got possession of it by expelling the Tuscans, according to the counsel of the soothsayers (*vates*;) or from the predictions uttered there, adjoining to the Janiculum, on the north side of the Tiber,[9] disliked by the ancients, on account of its bad air,[10] noted for producing bad wine,[11] now the principal place in Rome, where are the pope's palace, called St. Angelo, the Vatican library, one of the finest in the world, and St. Peter's church.

COLLIS HORTULORUM, so called, from its being originally covered with gardens;[12] taken into the city by Aurelian; afterwards called PINCIUS, from the Pincii, a noble family who had their seat there.

The gates of Rome at the death of Romulus were three, or at most four; in the time of Pliny thirty-seven, when the circumference of the walls was thirteen miles 200 paces; it was divided by Augustus into fourteen *regiones*, wards or quarters.[13]

The principal gates were,—1. *Porta* FLAMINIA, through which the Flaminian road passed; called also FLUMENTANA, because it lay near the Tiber.—2. COLLINA (*a* collibus *Quirinali et Viminali*,) called also QUIRINALIS, AGONENSIS vel SALARIA. To this gate Hannibal rode up, and threw

1 Liv. i. 3. 6. Gell. xiii. Festus. 14.*Sen. Brev. Vit. 14.
2 Liv. i. 33. Diony. iii. 43. Stat. Silv. ii. 3. 32. Festus.
3 Hor. Ep. ii. 268. Ov. Fast. iv. 375. Liv. i. 44.
4 Var. L. L. iv. 8. Tac. An. iv. 64. Suet. Tib. 48.
5 vimineta, Varr. Ibid.
6 Plin. xvi. 10. Liv. i. 44.
7 Var. L. L. iv. 8. Ov. Fast. iii. 246. Liv. i. 44.
8 Virg. Æn. vii. 358. Ov. Fast. i. 246. Mart. iv. 64. vii. 16.
9 Hor. Od. i. 20. Gell. xvi. 17. Festus.
10 infamis aer, Frontin. Tac. Hist. ii. 93.
11 Mart. vi. 92. xii. 48. 14.
12 Suet. Ner. 50.
13 Plin. iii. 5. s. 9.

a spear within the city.[1]—3. VIMINALIS.—4. ESQUILINA, anciently Metia, Labicana, *vel* Lavicana, without which criminals were punished.[2]—5. NÆVIA, so called from one Nævius, who possessed the grounds near it.— 6. CARMENTALIS, throegh which the Fabii went, from their fate called SCELERATA.—7. CAPENA, through which the road to Capua passed.—8. TRIUMPHALIS, through which those who triumphed entered,[3] but authors are not agreed where it stood.

Between the Porta Viminalis and Esquilina, without the wall, is supposed to have been the camp of the PRÆTORIAN cohorts, or *milites* PRÆTORIANI, a body of troops instituted by Augustus to guård his person, and called by that name, in imitation of the select band which attended a Roman general in battle,[4] composed of nine cohorts, according to Dio Cassius, of ten, consisting each of a thousand men, horse and foot,[5] chosen only from Italy, chiefly from Etruria and Umbria, or ancient Latium. Under Vitellius sixteen prætorian cohorts were raised, and four to guard the city. Of these last, Augustus instituted only three.[6]

Severus new-modelled the prætorian bands, and increased them to four times the ancient number. They were composed of the soldiers draughted from all the legions on the frontier. They were finally suppressed by Constantine, and their fortified camp destroyed.[7]

Those only were allowed to enlarge the city[8] who had extended the limits of the empire. Tacitus, however, observes, that although several generals had subdued many nations, yet no one after the kings assumed the right of enlarging the pomærium, except Sylla and Augustus, to the time of Claudius. But other authors say, this was done also by Julius Cæsar. The last who did it was Aurelian.[9]

Concerning the number of inhabitants in ancient Rome, we can only form conjectures. Lipsius computes them, in its most flourishing state, at four millions.

PUBLIC BUILDINGS OF THE ROMANS.

I. TEMPLES. Of these the chief were,

1. The CAPITOL, so called because, when the foundations of it were laid, a human head is said to have been found (CAPUT *Oli* vel *Toli cujusdam*,) *with the face entire;*[10] built on the Tarpeian or Capitoline mount, by Tarquinius Superbus, and dedicated by Horatius; burned A. U. 670, rebuilt by Sylla, and dedicated by Q. Catulus, A. U. 675; again burned by the soldiers of Vitellius, A. D. 70, and rebuilt by Vespasian. At his death it was burned a third time, and restored by Domitian, with greater magnificence than ever.[11] A few vestiges of it still remain.

CAPITOLIUM is sometimes put for the mountain on which the temple stood, and sometimes for the temple itself.[12] The edifice of the Capitol was in the form of a square, extending nearly 200 feet on each side. It contained three temples,[13] consecrated to Jupiter, Minerva, and Juno. The temple of Jupiter was in the middle, whence he is called *media qui sedet*

1 Liv. v. 41. xxxvi. 10. Plin. xxxiv. 6. s. 15. Cic. Fin. iv. 9. Tac. Hist. lll. 82. Festus.
2 Plaut. Cas. ll. 6. 2. Hor. Ep. v. 99. Tac. Ann. ii. 32.
3 Cic. Pis. 23. Suet. Aug. 101. Varr. L. L. iv. 34.

Liv. ii. 49. Fest.
4 see p. 261.
5 Tac. Ann. iv. 5. Dio. iv. 24. Suet. Aug. 49. Cal. 45.
6 Tac. Ann. iv. 5. Hist. i. 84. ii. 93.
7 Herodian, iii. 44. Dio. lxxiv. 2. Aurel. Victor.

Zosim. ii. p. 89. Panegyric, 9.
8 pomærium proferre.
9 Tac. Ann. xii. 23. Cic. Att. xiii. 20. 33. 35. Dio. xliii. 49. xliv. 49. Gell. xiii. 14. Vopisc. Aurel. 21.
10 facie integra, Liv. i.

38. 55. Diony. iv. 59: Ser.Virg. Æn. viii. 345.
11 Tac. Hist. iii. 72. Liv. ii. 8. Suet. Dom. 5.
12 Liv. i. 10. 32. 38. ii. 8. lii. 18. iv. 4.
13 ædes, templa, cellæ vel delubra.

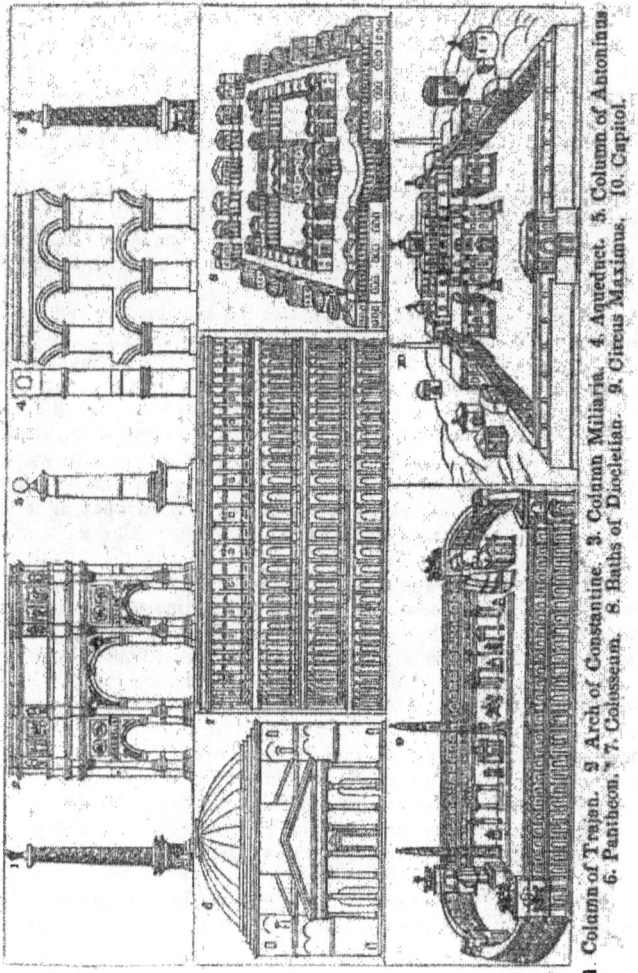

1. Column of Trajan. 2. Arch of Constantine. 3. Column Miliaria. 4. Aqueduct. 5. Column of Antoninus. 6. Pantheon. 7. Colosseum. 8. Baths of Diocletian. 9. Circus Maximus. 10. Capitol.

æde DEUS, the god who sits in the middle temple. The temple of Minerva was on the right,[1] whence she is said to have obtained the honours next to Jupiter ;[2] and the temple of Juno on the left.[3] Livy, however, places Juno first, iii. 15. So also Ovid, Trist. ii. 291.

The Capitol was the highest part in the city, and strongly fortified ; hence called ARX ;[4] *Capitolium atque arx, arx Capitolii.* The ascent to the Capitol from the forum was by 100 steps. It was most magnificently adorned ; the very gilding of it is said to have cost 12,000 talents, i. e. £1,976,250 ;[5] hence called AUREA, and FULGENS. The gates were of brass and the tiles gilt.[6]

The principal temples of other cities were also called by the name of Capitol.[7]

In the Capitol were likewise temples of Terminus,[8] of Jupiter Feretrius, &c. ; casa Romuli, the cottage of Romulus, covered with straw,[9] near the Curia Calabra.[10]

Near the ascent of the Capitol, was the ASYLUM, or sanctuary,[11] which Romulus opened,[12] in imitation of the Greeks.[13]

2. The PANTHEON, built by Agrippa, son-in-law to Augustus, and dedicated to Jupiter Ultro,[14] or to Mars and Venus, or, as its name imports, to all the gods ;[15] repaired by Adrian, consecrated by pope Boniface IV. to the Virgin Mary, and All-Saints, A. D. 607, now called the Rotunda, from its round figure, said to be 150 feet high, and of about the same breadth. The roof is curiously vaulted, void spaces being left here and there for the greater strength. It has no windows, but only an opening in the top for the admission of light, of about 25 feet diameter. The walls of the inside are either solid marble or incrusted. The front on the outside was covered with brazen plates gilt, the top with silver plates, but now it is covered with lead. The gate was of brass of extraordinary work and size. They used to ascend to it by twelve steps, but now they go down as many ; the earth around being so much raised by the demolition of houses.

3. The temple of Apollo built by Augustus on the Palatine hill, in which was a public library, where authors, particularly poets, used to recite their compositions, sitting in full dress,[16] sometimes before select judges, who passed sentence on their comparative merits. The poets were then said *committi*, to be contrasted or matched, as combatants ; and the reciters, *committere opera.* Hence Caligula said of Seneca, that he only composed COMMISSIONES, showy declamations.[17]

A particular place is said to have been built for this purpose by Hadrian, and consecrated to Minerva, called ATHENIUM.[18]

Authors used studiously to invite people to hear them recite their works, who commonly received them with acclamations ; thus, BENE, *pulchre, belle, euge ;* NON POTEST MELIUS, SOPHOS, i. e. *sapienter* (σοφως,) *scite, docte,* and sometimes expressed their fondness for the author by kissing him.[19]

1 Liv.vi. 4. Diony. iv. 61. Ov. Pont. iv. 9 32.
2 proximos illi, sc, Jovi, tamen occupavit Pallas honores, Hor. Od. i. 12. 19.
3 P. Victor. in descr. Rom. Regionis, viii.
4 Virg. Æn. viii. 652. vel ab arceo. quod is sit locus munitissimus urbis, a quo facillime possit hostis prohiberi, Var. L. L. iv. 32. vel ab

ακρος, summus.
5 Plut. Popl. Tac. Hist. iii. 71. Liv. ii. 49. iii. 15. viii. 6. Flor. iii. 21.
6 Virg. ib. 348. Plin. xxxiii. 3. Hor. Od. iii. 3. 43. Liv. x. 23.
7 Suet. Cal. 47. Sil. 267. Gell. xvi. 13. Plaut. Curc. ii. 2. 19
8 Liv. i. 54. seo p. 190.
9 Liv. iv. 20. v. 53. Nep. Att. 20. Vitruv. ii. 1. Sen. Helv. 9.

10 Macrob. Sat. i. 1. Ov. Fast. iii. 183. Sen. Contr. i. 6.
11 Liv. i. 8.
12 see p. 31.
13 Serv. Virg. Æn. viii. 342. ii. 761. Stat. Theb. xii. 498. Liv. xxxv. 51. Cic. Verr. i. 33. Tac. Ann. iv. 14.
14 Plin. xxxvi. 15. Dio. liii. 27.
15 Spart. 19. see p. 210.
16 Suet. Aug. 29. Vell.

ii. 81. Hor. Ep. i. 3. 17. Sat. i. 10. 38. Pers. i. 15.
17 Suet. Aug. 45. 89. Claud. 4. 53. Juv. vi. 435.
18 Aur. Vict. Capitol. in Gordian. 3. Pertin. 11.
19 Dialog. Or. 9. Plin. Ep. ii. 14. Cic. Or. iii. 26. Hor. Art. P. 428. Pers. i. 49. 84. Mart. i. 4. 7. 50. 37. 67. 4. 77. 9. 14. ii.

4. The temple of Diana, built on the Aventine mount, at the instigation of Servius Tullius, by the Latin states, in conjunction with the Roman people, in imitation of the temple of Diana at Ephesus, which was built at the joint expense of the Greek states in Asia.[1]

5. The temple of Janus, built by Numa,[2] with two brazen gates, one on each side, to be open in war, and shut in time of peace; shut only once during the republic, at the end of the first Punic war, A. U. 529,[3] thrice by Augustus,[4] first after the battle of Actium, and the death of Antony and Cleopatra, A. U. 725, a second time after the Cantabrian war, A. U. 729; about the third time, authors are not agreed. Some suppose this temple to have been built by Romulus, and only enlarged by Numa; hence they take Janus Quirini for the temple of Janus, built by Romulus.[5]

A temple was built to Romulus by Papirius, A. U. 459, and another by Augustus.[6]

6. The temple of Saturn, Juno, Mars, Venus, Minerva, Neptune, &c., of Fortune, of which there were many, of Concord, Peace, &c.

Augustus built a temple to Mars Ultor in the forum Augusti. Dio says in the Capitol,[7] by a mistake either of himself or his transcribers. In this temple were suspended military standards, particularly those which the Parthians took from the Romans under Crassus, A. U. 701, and which Phraates, the Parthian king, afterwards restored to Augustus, together with the captives; Suetonius[8] and Tacitus say, that Phraates also gave hostages. No event in the life of Augustus is more celebrated than this; and on account of nothing did he value himself more, than that he had recovered, without bloodshed, and by the mere terror of his name, so many citizens and warlike spoils, lost by the misconduct of former commanders. Hence it is extolled by the poets,[9] and the memory of it perpetuated by coins and inscriptions. On a stone, found at Ancyra, now Angouri in Phrygia,[10] are these words: PARTHOS TRIUM EXERCITUUM ROMANORUM (i. e. of the two armies of Crassus, both son and father, and of a third army, commanded by Oppius Statianus, the lieutenant of Antony,)[11] SPOLIA ET SIGNA REMITTERE MIHI, SUPPLICESQUE AMICITIAM POPULI ROMANI PETERE COEGI, I compelled the Parthians to restore to me the spoils and standards of three Roman armies, and to beg as suppliants the friendship of the Roman people: and on several coins the Parthian is represented on his knees delivering a military standard to Augustus, with this inscription, CIVIB. ET SIGN. MILIT. A. PARTHIS. RECEP. vel RESTIT. vel RECUP.

II. Theatres, see p. 242, amphitheatres, p. 231, and places for exercise or amusement.

ODEUM (ωδεον, from ᾀδω, cano,) a building, where musicians and actors rehearsed, or privately exercised themselves, before appearing on the stage.[12]

NYMPHÆUM, a building adorned with statues of the nymphs, and abounding, as it is thought, with fountains and waterfalls, which afforded an agreeable and refreshing coolness; borrowed from the Greeks, long of being introduced at Rome, unless we suppose it the same with the temple of the Nymphs mentioned by Cicero.[13]

1 Liv. i. 45.
2 index belli et pacis.
3 Liv. i. 19. Vell. ii. 38.
Plin. xxxiv. 7. Serv.
Virg. i. 294. vii. 607.
4 Janum Quirinum. i.
e. templum Jani belli
potentis, ter clausit,
Suet. Aug. 22. Janum

Quirini, Hor. Od. iv. 15.
9.
5 Macrob. Sat. i. 9. Dio.
ii. 20. liii. 26.
6 Liv. x. 46. Dio. liv. 19.
7 Suet. Aug. 29. Ov.
Fast. v. 551. Dio. liv. 8.
8 Dio. xl. 27. liii. 23. liv.
8. Vel. ii. 91. Just. xlii.

5. Flor. iv. 12. Eutr. vii.
5. Suet. Aug. 21. Tac.
Ann. ii. 1.
9 Hor. Od. iv. 15. 6. Ep.
i. 18. 56. Ov. Trist. ii.
227. Fast. vi. 465. Virg.
Æn. vii. 606.
10 in lapide Ancyrano.
11 Dio. xl. 21. 24. xlix.

25.
12 Cic. Att. iv. 16. Suet.
Dom. 5.
13 Mil. 27. Arusp. 27.
Plin. xxxv. 12. s. 43.
Capitol. Gord. 32.

CIRCI. The CIRCUS MAXIMUS, see p. 224. CIRCUS FLAMINIUS, laid out by one Flaminius ; called also Apolliuaris, from a temple of Apollo near it ; used not only for the celebration of games, but also for making harangues to the people.[1]

The CIRCUS MAXIMUS was much frequented by sharpers and fortune-tellers (*sortilegi*), jugglers (*præstigiatores*), &c. ; hence called FALLAX.[2]

Several new circi were added by the emperors Nero,[3] Caracalla, Heliogabalus, &c.

STADIA, places nearly in the form of circi, for the running of men and horses. HIPPODROMI, places for the running or coursing of horses, also laid out for private use, especially in country villas ;[4] but here some read Hypodromus, a shady or covered walk, which indeed seems to be meant, as Sidon. Ep. ii. 2.

PALESTRÆ, GYMNASIA, et XYSTI, places for exercising the athletæ,[5] or *pancratiastæ*, who both wrestled and boxed.[6]

These places were chiefly in the CAMPUS MARTIUS, a large plain along the Tiber, where the Roman youth performed their exercises, anciently belonging to the Tarquins ; hence called SUPERBI REGIS AGER ; and after their expulsion, consecrated to Mars : called, by way of eminence, CAMPUS : put for the comitia held there ; hence *fors domina campi :* or for the votes ; hence *venalis campus*, i. e. *suffragia ; campi nota*, a repulse : or for any thing in which a person exercises himself ; hence *latissimus dicendi campus*, *in quo liceat oratori vagari libere*, a large field for speaking ; *campus, in quo excurrere virtus, cognoscique possit*, a field wherein to display and make known your virtues.[7]

NAUMACHIÆ, places for exhibiting naval engagements, built nearly in the form of a circus ; VETUS, i. e. *Naumachia Circi Maximi ;* AUGUSTI ; DOMITIANI. These fights were exhibited also in the circus and amphitheatre.[8]

III. CURIÆ, buildings where the inhabitants of each curia met to perform divino service,[9] or where the senate assembled (SENACULA).[10]

IV. Fora, public places. Of these the chief was, FORUM ROMANUM, VETUS, vel MAGNUM, a large, oblong, open space, between the Capitoline and Palatine hills, now the cow-market, where the assemblies of the people were held, where justice was administered, and public business transacted,[11] &c., instituted by Romulus, and surrounded with porticos, shops, and buildings, by Tarquinius Priscus. These shops were chiefly occupied by bankers (*argentarii*), hence called ARGENTARIÆ, sc. *tabernæ*, VETERES ; hence *ratio pecuniarum, quæ in foro versatur*, the state of money matters ; *fidem de foro tollere*, to destroy public credit ; *in foro versari*, to trade ;[12] *foro cedere*, to become bankrupt, vel *in foro eum non habere ;* but *de foro decedere*, not to appear in public ; *in foro esse*, to be engaged in public business, vel *dare operam foro ; fori tabes*, the rage of litigation ; *in alieno foro litigare*, to follow a business one does not understand.[13]

Around the forum were built spacious halls, called BASILICÆ, where

1 Liv. iii. 54. 63. Cic. post Red. Sen. 6. Suet. 14
2 Hor. Sat. i. 6. 113.
3 Tac. Ann. xiv. 14.
4 Suet. Cæs. 39. Dom. 5. Plaut. Bacch. iii. 3.
27. Mart. xii. 50. Plin. Ep. v. 6.
5 see p. 226, 227.

6 qui pancratio certabant, i. e. omnibus viribus, παν κρατος, Sen. Ben. v. 3. Gell. iii. 15. xiii. 27. Quinct. 9.
7 Juv. vi. 523. Liv. ii. 5. Hor. Od. iii. i. 10. Cic. Cat. i. 5. Off. i 18. 29. Or. iii. 42. Acad iv. 35. Pis. 2. Mur. 8. Val.

Max. vi. 9. 14. Luc. i. 180.
8 Suet. Tit. 7. 43 Tib. 5. 72. Mart. Spect. 28. see p. 228.
9 Var. L. L. iv. 32. see p. 1.
10 see p. 6.
11 see p. 57. 73. 87. &c.
12 Diony. ii. 50. Liv. i.

35. xxvi. 11. Plaut. Curc. iv. 1. 19. Cic. Man. 7. Rul. i. 8. Flac. 29.
13 Cic. Rab. Post. 15. Nep. Att. 10. Cat. 1. Sen. Ben. iv. 39. Tac. An. xi. 6. Plaut. Asin. ii. 4. 22. Mart. Præf. xii.

courts of justice might sit, and other public business, be transacted ;[1] not used in early times, adorned with columns and porticos,[2] afterwards converted into Christian churches.   The forum was altogether surrounded by arched porticos, with proper places left for entrance.[3]

Near the rostra stood a statue of Marsyas, vel -a, who having presumed to challenge Apollo at singing, and being vanquished, was flayed alive.[4]   Hence his statue was set up in the forum, to deter unjust litigants.

There was only one forum under the republic.   Julius Cæsar added another, the area of which cost H. S. *millies*, i. e. £807,291 : 13 : 4, and Augustus a third ; hence TRINA FORA, TRIPLEX FORUM.[5]   Domitian began a fourth forum, which was finished by Nerva, and named, from him, FORUM NERVÆ ; called also TRANSITORIUM, because it served as a convenient passage to the other three.   But the most splendid forum was that built by Trajan, and adorned with the spoils he had taken in war.[6]

There were also various FORA, or market-places, where certain commodities were sold ; thus, *forum* BOARIUM, the ox and cow market, in which stood a brazen statute of a bull, adjoining to the Circus Maximus ;[7] SUARIUM, the swine-market ; PISCARIUM, the fish-market ; OLITORIUM, the green-market ; *forum* CUPEDINIS, where pastry and confections were sold ; all contiguous to one another, along the Tiber.   When joined together, called MACELLUM, from one Macellus, whose house had stood there.[8] Those who frequented this place are enumerated, Ter. Eun. ii. 2. 25.

V. PORTICUS, or piazzas, were among the most splendid ornaments of the city.   They took their names either from the edifices to which they were annexed, as porticus Concordiæ, Apollinis, Quirini, Herculis, theatri, circi, amphitheatri, &c., or from the builders of them, as porticus Pompeia, Livia, Octavia, Agrippa, &c., used chiefly for walking in, or riding under covert.   In porticos, the senate and courts of justice were sometimes held.[9] Here also those who sold jewels, pictures, or the like, exposed their goods.

Upon a sudden shower, the people retired thither from the theatre. Soldiers sometimes had their tents in porticos.   There authors recited their works, philosophers used to dispute,[10] particularly the Stoics, whence their name (from στοα, *porticus*), because Zeno, the founder of that sect, taught his scholars in a portico at Athens, called Pœcile,[11] adorned with various pictures, particularly that of the battle of Marathon.   So also *Chrysippi porticus*, the school of Chrysippus.[12]   Porticos were generally paved,[13] supported on marble pillars, and adorned with statues.[14]

VI. COLUMNÆ,[15] columns or pillars, properly denote the props or supports[16] of the roof of a house, or of the principal beam on which the roof depends ;[17] but this term came to be extended to all props or supports whatever, especially such as are ornamental, and also to those structures which support nothing, unless perhaps a statue, a globe, or the like.

A principal part of architecture consists in a knowledge of the different

1 see p. 86.
2 Cic. Ver. iv. 3. v. 58. At. iv. 16. Liv. xxvi. 27.
3 Liv. xii. 27.
4 Hor. Sat. i. 6. 120. Liv. xxxviii. 13.Ov. Fast. vi. 707.
5 Suet. Jul. 26. Plin. xxix. 31. xxxvi. 15. s. 24. Ov. Trist. iii. 12. 24.

Sen. Ira, ii. 9. Mart. iii. 38. 4.
6 Lamprid. Alex. 28. Marcellin. xvi. 6. Gell. xiii. 23. Suet. Dom. 5.
7 Tac. xii. 24. Ov. Fast. vi. 477. Festus.
8 Varr. L. L. iv. 32.
9 Ov. Art. Am. i. 67. Cic. Dom. 44. Ap. Bel.

Civ. ii. p. 500. see p. 307.
10 Vitr. v. 9. Tac. Hist. i. 31. Juv. i. 13. Cic. Or. ii. 20. Prop. ii. 33. 45.
11 τοικιλη, varia, picta.
12 Cic. Mur. 29. Pers. iii. 53. Nep. Milt. 6. Hor. Sat. ii. 3. 44. see. p.

307.
13 pavimentatæ, Cic. Dom. 44. Q. Fr. iii. 1.
14 Sen. Ep. 115. Ov. F. v. 563. Trist. iii. 1. 59. Prop. ii. 23. 5. Suet. Aug. 31.
15 στηλαι, vel στυλοι.
16 fulcra.
17 columen.

form, size, and proportions of columns. Columns are variously denominated, from the five different orders of architecture, Doric, Ionic, Corinthian, Tuscan, and Composite, i. e. composed of the first three. The foot of a column is called the base (*basis*),[1] and is always made one half of the height of the diameter of the column. That part of a column on which it stands is called its pedestal (*stylobates*, vel -*ta*), the top, its chapiter or capital, (*epistylium*, *caput* vel *capitulum*), and the straight part, its shaft (*scapus*.)

Various pillars were erected at Rome in honour of great men, and to commemorate illustrious actions. Thus, COLUMNA ÆNEA, a brazen pillar on which a league with the Latins was written;[2] COLUMNA ROSTRATA, a column adorned with figures, of ships, in honour of Duilius, in the forum,[3] of white marble, still remaining with its inscription ; another in the Capitol, erected by M. Fulvius, the consul, in the second Punic War, in honour of Cæsar, consisting of one stone of Numidian marble near twenty feet high ; another in honour of Galba.[4] But the most remarkable columns were those of Trajan and Antoninus Pius.

Trajan's pillar was erected in the middle of his forum, composed of twenty-four great pieces of marble, but so curiously cemented as to seem but one. Its height is 128 feet, according to Eutropius, 144 feet. It is about twelve feet diameter at the bottom, and ten at the top. It has in the inside 185 steps for ascending to the top, and forty windows for the admission of light. The whole pillar is encrusted with marble, on which are represented the warlike exploits of that emperor, and his army, particularly in Dacia. On the top was a colossus of Trajan, holding in his left hand a sceptre, and in his right a hollow globe of gold, in which his ashes were put ; but Eutropius affirms his ashes were deposited under the pillar.[5]

The pillar of Antoninus was erected to him by the senate after his death. It is 176 feet high, the steps of ascent 106, the windows 56. The sculpture and other ornaments are much of the same kind with those of Trajan's pillar, but the work greatly inferior.

Both these pillars are still standing, and justly reckoned among the most precious remains of antiquity. Pope Sextus V., instead of the statues of the emperors, caused the statue of St. Peter to be erected on Trajan's pillar, and of St. Paul on that of Antoninus.

The Romans were uncommonly fond of adorning their houses with pillars,[6] and placing statues between them,[7] as in temples. A tax seems to have been imposed on pillars, called COLUMNARIUM.[8]

There was a pillar in the forum called columna Mænia, from C. Mænius, who, having conquered the Antiates, A. U. 417, placed the brazen beaks of their ships on the tribunal in the forum, from which speeches were made to the people ; hence called ROSTRA.[9] Near this pillar, slaves and thieves, or fraudulent bankrupts, used to be punished. Hence insignificant, idle persons, who used to saunter about that place, were called COLUMNARII, as those who loitered about the rostra and courts of justice were called SUBROSTRANI and SUBBASILICARII,[10] comprehended in the *turba forensis*, or *plebs urbana*, which Cicero often mentions.

VII. ARCUS TRIUMPHALES, arches erected in honour of illustrious generals, who had gained signal victories in war, several of which are still

1 Plin. xxxvi. 23. s. 56.   20. Suet. Jul. 86. G. 23.   7 In intercolumniis, Cic.   9 see p. 56. Plin. xxxiv.
2 Plin. xxxiv. 5. Liv. ii.   5 Eutrop. viii. 5.   Ver. i. 19.   5. s. 11.
33.   6 Cic. Ver. i. 55. &c.   8 Ov. Trist. iii. 1. 61. Cic.   10 Cic. Cluent. 13. Fam.
3 see p. 267.   Hor. Od. ii. 18. Juv. vii.   Att. xiii. 6. Cæs. B. C.   viii. 1. 9. Plaut. Capt.
4 Sil. vi. 663. Liv. xlii.   162.   iii. 26. s. 32.   iv. 2. 35.

standing. They were at first very simple, built of brick or hewn stone, of a semi-circular figure ; hence called FORNICES by Cicero ; but afterwards more magnificent, built of the finest marble, and of a square figure, with a large arched gate in the middle, and two small ones on each side, adorned with columns and statues, and various figures done in sculpture. From the vault of the middle gate hung little winged images of Victory, with crowns in their hands, which, when let down, they put on the victor's head as he passed in triumph. This magnificence began under the first emperor's ; hence Pliny calls it NOVICIUM INVENTUM.[1]

VIII. TROPÆA, trophies, were spoils taken from the enemy, and fixed upon any thing, as signs or monuments of victory ;[2] erected[3] usually in the place where it was gained, and consecrated to some divinity, with an inscription ;[4] used chiefly among the ancient Greeks, who, for a trophy, decorated the trunk of a tree with the arms and spoils of the vanquished enemy. Those who erected metal or stone were held in detestation by the other states, nor did they repair a trophy when it decayed, to intimate, that enmities ought not to be immortal.[5]

Trophies were not much used by the Romans, who, Florus says, never insulted the vanquished. They called any monuments of a victory by that name.[6] Thus the

oak tree, with a cross piece of wood on the top, on which Romulus carried the spoils of Acron, king of the Cæninenses, is called by Livy τροπαιον ; by Livy ; FERCULUM ; or, as others read the passage, FERETRUM. Tropæum is also put by the poets for the victory itself, or the spoils.[7]

It was reckoned unlawful to overturn a trophy, as having been consecrated to the gods of war. Thus Cæsar left standing the trophies which Pompey, from a criminal vanity, had erected on the Pyrenean mountains, after his conquest of Sertorius and Perpenna in Spain, and that of Mithridates over Triarius, near Ziela in Pontus, but reared opposite to them monuments of his own victories over Afranius and Petreius in the former place, and over Pharnaces, the son of Mithridates, in the latter. The inscription on Cæsar's trophy on the Alps we have, Plin. iii. 20. s. 24. Drusus erected trophies near the Elbe, for his victories over the Germans. Ptolemy places them *inter Canduam et Luppiam*.[8]

There are two trunks of marble, decorated like trophies, still remaining at Rome, which are supposed by some to be those said to have been erect-

1 xxxiv. 6. s. 12. Dio. xlix. 15. li. 19. liv. 8. Cic. Ver. i. 7. ii. 63.Juv. x. 136.
2 a τροπη, fuga.
3 posita vel statuta.
4 Virg. Æn. iii. 268. xi.

5. Ov. Art. Am. ii. 744. Tac. Ann. ii. 22. Curt. vii. 7. viii. 1.
5 Stat. Theb. ii. 707. Juv. x. 133. Cic. Inv. ii. 23. Plut. Q. Rom. 36. Diod. Sic. 13.

6 Flor. iii. 2. Cic. Arch. 7. Dom. 37.Pis. 38.Plin. Paneg. 59. Nat. Hist. iii. s. 4. 20. 24.
7 Liv. i. 10. Hor. Od. ii. 19. Nep. Them. 5. Virg. G. iii. 32.

8 Dio. xli. 24. iv. 1. Strab iii. p. 156. xlii. 48. Flor. iv. 12. 23. Prol. ii. 11.

ed by Marius over Jugurtha, and over the Cimbri and Teutoni, *vel -es* ;[1] but this seems not to be ascertained.

IX. AQUÆDUCTUS.[2] Some of them brought water to Rome from more than the distance of sixty miles, through rocks and mountains, and over valleys,[3] supported on arches, in some places above 109 feet high, one row being placed above another. The care of them anciently belonged to the censors and ædiles. Afterwards certain officers were appointed for that purpose by the emperors, called CURATORES AQUARUM, with 720 men, paid by the public, to keep them in repair, divided into two bodies ;[4] the one called PUBLICA, first instituted by Agrippa, under Augustus, consisting of 260 ; the other FAMILIA CÆSARIS, of 460, instituted by the emperor Claudius. The slaves employed in taking care of the water were called AQUARII. AQUARIA PROVINCIA is supposed to mean the charge of the port of Ostia.[5]

A person who examined the height from which water might be brought was called LIBRATOR ; the instrument by which this was done, AQUARIA LIBRA ; hence *locus pari libra cum æquore maris est*, of the same height ; *omnes aquæ diversa in urbem libra preveniunt*, from a different height. So, *turres ad libram factæ*, of a proper height ; *locus ad libellam æquus*, quite level.[6]

The declivity of an aqueduct (*libramentum aquæ*) was at least the fourth of an inch every 100 feet ;[7] according to Vitruvius, half a foot. The moderns observe nearly that mentioned by Pliny. If the water was conveyed under ground, there were openings[8] every 240 feet.[9]

The *curator*, or *præfectus aquarum*, was invested by Augustus with considerable authority ; attending without the city by two lictors, three public slaves, an architect, secretaries, &c. ; hence, under the later emperors, he was called CONSULARIS AQUARUM.[10]

According to P. Victor, there were twenty aqueducts in Rome, but others make them only fourteen. They were named from the maker of them, the place from which the water was brought, or from some other circumstance ; thus, AQUA Claudia, Appia, Marcia, Julia, Cimina, Felix, VIRGO (vel *virgineus liquor*), so called, because a young girl pointed out certain veins, which the diggers following found a great quantity of water ; but others give a different account of the matter ; made by Agrippa, as several others were.[11]

X. CLOACÆ,[12] sewers, drains, or sinks, for carrying off the filth of the city into the Tiber ; first made by Tarquinius Priscus,[13] extending under the whole city, and divided into numerous branches. The arches which supported the streets and buildings were so high and broad, that a wain loaded with hay[14] might go below, and vessels sail in them : hence Pliny calls them *operum omnium dictu maximum, suffossis montibus, atque urbe pensili, subterque navigata.* There were in the streets, at proper distances, openings for the admission of dirty water, or any other filth, which persons were appointed always to remove, and also to keep the *cloacæ* clean. This was the more easily effected by the declivity of the ground, and the plenty of water with which the city was supplied.[15]

1 Suet. Jul. 11. Val. Max. vi. 9. 14.
2 see p. 308.
3 Plin. xxxi. 15. s. 24.
4 familiæ.
5 Front. Aquæd. Cic. Fam. viii. 6. Vat. 5. Mur. 6.
6 Plin. Ep. x. 50. 69.

Vitr. viii. 6. Columel. viii. 17. Front. i. 18. Cæs. B. C. iii. 40. Var. R. R. i. 6.
7 in centenos pedes Sicilici minimum erit, Plin. xxxi. 6. s. 31. Vitr. viii. 7.
8 lumina.

9 in binos actus, ibid.
10 Suet. Aug. 37. Front. i. 1. C. de Aquæd.
11 Ov. Pont. i. 6. 38. Front. Plin. xxxi. 3. Cassiod. vii. Ep. 6. Dio. xlviii. 32. xlix. 14. 42. liv. 14. Suet. Aug. 42.
12 a cluo vel conluo, i.e.

purgo, Fest. & Plin.
13 Liv. i. 38.
14 vehis, v. -es, fœni large onusta.
15 Plin. xxxvi. 13. 15. Ep. x. 41. Strab. v. p. 235. Hor. Sat. ii. 3. 242.

The principal sewer, with which the rest communicated, was called
CLOACA MAXIMA, the work of Tarquinius Superbus.* Various cloacæ were
afterwards made.[1] The cloacæ at first were carried through the streets;[2]
but by the want of regularity in rebuilding the city after it was burned by
the Gauls, they, in many places, went under private houses. Under the
republic, the censors had the charge of the cloacæ; but under the emperors,
CURATORES CLOACARUM were appointed, and a tax imposed for keeping
them in repair, called CLOACARIUM.[3]

XI. VIÆ.—The public ways were perhaps the greatest of all the Roman
works, made with amazing labour and expense; extending to the utmost
limits of the empire, from the pillars of Hercules to the Euphrates, and
the southern confines of Egypt.†

* Amongst the works of public utility belonging to Rome, none seem to have excited greater admiration in the ancients themselves than the Cloacæ. And from what remains of the Cloaca Maxima at the present day, we may infer that the praise which they bestowed on these works was not unremitted. The structure of this vast Cloaca is universally ascribed to Tarquinius Superbus, though it was planned and commenced by the elder Tarquin It was intended, together with its different ramifications, to carry off the waters which stagnated in the low grounds near the Forum, with the other impurities of the city. Pliny expresses his wonder at the solidity and durability of this great undertaking, which, after a lapse of 700 years, still remained uninjured and entire. So vast were the dimensions of this Cloaca, that a cart loaded with hay could easily pass under it. Dionysius informs us, that it cost the state the enormous sum of 1000 talents to have the Cloacæ cleaned and repaired. We hear also of other sewers being made from time to time on mount Aventine and other places, by the censors M. Cato and Valerius Flaccus, but more especially by Agrippa, who, according to Pliny, is said to have introduced whole rivers into these hollow channels, on which the city was as it were suspended, and thus was rendered subterraneously navigable.

† In order to afford some idea of the nature and importance of these works, we copy from the accurate account of them given in the description of ancient Italy by Cramer, so

much as may indicate their course and extent through the various provinces of that country.

"The principal way, which traversed Liguria, as well as the most ancient, was that which followed the whole length of the coast, and led in to Gaul by the Alpis Maritima. It was made by the consul Aurelius, about 605 U. C. and from him was called the VIA AURELIA. It seems to have been laid down in the first instance from Rome to Pisa, from which point it was subsequently continued, under the name of the Via Æmilia, by the consul Æmilius Scaurus, A. U. C. 639, as far as Vada Sabata: here it left the coast, and led by a circuitous rout to Acqui and Tortona. At a later period, however, this road was carried along the coast to the Maritime Alps, and even beyond them into Gaul as far as Arelate, Arles; when the name of Via Aureria, as we find from the Itinerary of Antoninus, was commonly used to designate the rout between that city and Rome.

The VIA POSTHUMIA was another great Roman road, which, beginning at Genoa, traversed the Apennines, and the part of Liguria which lies on the other side of that chain; and continued its course through a great portion of Cisalpine Gaul, as far as Verona. It has not been ascertained by whom and at what time this road was constructed; but we know that it must have existed before 636 U. C. the date of the brazen tablet of Genoa, in which mention is made of it. It may with probability be ascribed to A. Posthumius Albi-

nus, who was consul in 572 U. C. and afterwards censor in 578.

In examining the different roads which intersected the province just described, we shall commence with those which crossed the Alps, and terminated at Milan. They were constructed, as Strabo informs us, by order of Augustus; though we are not to understand the geographer as stating, that these mountain-passes were opened for the first time during the reign of that emperor, but that they were rendered more easy of access by the works which he caused to be undertaken there. That which traversed the Graian Alp, or the Little St. Bernard, led from Milan to Vienne, formerly the capitol of the Allobroges, through the country of the Centrones, now the Tarentaise; the other, which crossed the Pennine Alp, or Great St. Bernard, established a communication between the former city and Lyons. There were also two passes over the Rhætian Alps, which afforded a communication between Curia, Coire, and Milan; the one traversing the Splugen, the other Mont Septimer, and both meeting at Clavenna, Chiavenna. These roads also were probably made by Augustus, but the passes had been frequented long before, as Strabo reports on the authority of Polybius. From Milan two great roads branched off to the eastern and southern extremities of the province; the one leading to Verona and Aquileia, the latter to Placentia and Ariminum: the same name of Via Æmilia was however applied to both. Concerning this celebrated way,

1 Liv. i. 56. xxxix. 44.   2 per publicum ducta.   3 Liv. v. 55. Ulpian.

The Carthaginians are said first to have paved[1] their roads with stones ; and after them, the Romans.[2] The first road which the Romans paved[3]

we learn that it was made by M. Æmilius Lepidus, who was consul A. U. C. 567, in continuation of the Via Flaminia, which had been carried from Rome to Ariminum. The Via Æmilia was laid down in the first instance as far as Bologna, but subsequently it was continued to Placentia and Milan, and finally to Verona and Aquileia. There was another branch of it however which led from Bologna to this last city by a shorter cut, though still avoiding the marshes of the Po. and rejoining the main road at Padua. Lastly, we may notice a road which seems to have led from Parma through Liguria into Etruria. No mention is made of it in the Itineraries, but there is good historical evidence of the existence of such a rout : and we conceive that it was by this road that the Roman armies usually penetrated from Etruria into Cisalpine Gaul, before the Flaminian and Æmilian ways had been laid down. The general direction of this rout, which is now much frequented, seems to have been from Pisa to Luca, Sarzana, Pontremoli, Fornovo, and Parma.

Aquileia was the central point to which all the roads that traversed Venetia tended, and from which others diverged to pass into the neighbouring provinces of Illyria and Pannonia. The principal and most important of these was that branch of the Via Æmilia which has been described from Milan to Verona in the preceding section. At Verona, this road was joined by another, which crossed the Tridentine Alps, and terminated in Germany at Augusta Vindelicorum, Augsburg ; following precisely the same direction as the modern chaussèe which traverses the Tyrol, and descends into Italy by Trent and the valley of the Adige. From this road again we find two others branching off at different points, through the most mountainous parts of the Carnic territory, and joining the Via Æmilia, the one at Aquileia, the other at Concordia. From Aquileia, two roads

led into Pannonia and Histria. The first of these crossed the Julian Alps, or the Mons Ocra of Strabo, a passage apparently frequented from the earliest period. The road leading from Aquileia into Histria followed the coast round the peninsula as far as Tarsatica, no Tarsatsh, in Liburnia.

The Via Aurelia has already been treated of in the section which related to Liguria. The next road to be noticed as traversing Etruria was the VIA CLAUDIA, or CLODIA, which parted from the Via Flaminia a little beyond the Pons Milvius, and again from the Via Cassia a few miles farther. We are not informed by whom it was constructed, and indeed its direction is but imperfectly traced from the Itineraries ; it probably fell into disuse when the central parts of Etruria, which it seems to have crossed, became unfrequented. From Sienna, I am inclined to think that this road proceeded to Florence, where it rejoined the Via Cassia, and from thence to Luca and Luna. The Antonine. Itinerary indeed describes a rout between the two first cities, under the name of Via Clodia. We are equally ignorant by whom the Via Cassia was constructed. It is only known that it existed prior to Cicero's time ; for he informs us in the second Philippic, that it was one of the three roads which led from Rome into Cisalpine Gaul. We have seen that it joined the Via Clodin at Florence. At the station called at Novas, a road branched off to the left towards Sienna : if the distances are right, this communication must have been a circuitous one. We are inclined to think that it joined the Via Colodia near Sienna, thus connecting the central parts of Etruria with the coast. Lastly, there remains to be noticed a road which branched off from the Via Cassia at Baccano, and led to Ameria in Umbria, from which city it obtained the name of Via Amerina.

The principal road we have to notice in Umbria and Picenum, is the

VIA FLAMINIA, together with its several branches. It was constructed by C. Flaminius when consor, A. U. C. 533. and was carried in the first instance from Rome to Narnia ; from thence it branched off in two directions to Mevania and Spoletum, uniting however again at Fulginia : from this place it continued its course to Nuceria, and was there divided a second time, one branch striking off through Picenum to Ancona ; from whence it followed the coast to Fanum Fortunæ ; here it met the other branches, which passed the Apennines more to the north, and descended upon the sea by the pass of the Petra Pertusa and Forum Sempronii. These two roads thus reunited terminated at Ariminum. From Ancona there was a road which kept along the coast of Picenum, and connected the Flaminian with the Salarian way.

The first road which we have to notice in the country of the Sabini is the VIA SALARIA, which traversed the Sabine country, and terminated at Hadria in Picenum. We are told that it obtained its name from the use to which it was converted by the Sabines, for the importation of salt into their country from the sea. When or by whom it was constructed is not known ; but it appears to have existed as early as the first invasion of the Gauls ; for the battle on the Allia is said to have been fought near the eleventh milestone on that road. Strabo informs us, that it commenced at the Porta Collina, as did also the Via Nomentana, which rejoined the former near Eretum,

The VIA VALERIA is supposed, on the authority of a passage in Livy, to have been made by M. Valerius Maximus, who was censor with C. Junius Bubulcus A. U. C. 447. It commenced, as Strabo informs us, at Tibur, where the Via Tiburtina terminated, and led through the territories of the Æqui and Marsi to Corfinium ; but the Itineraries make it extend as far as Hadria in Picenum.

---

1 straviase.   2 laid. xv. 16.   3 muniverunt.

was to Capua ; first made by Appius Claudius the Censor, the same who built the first aqueduct, A. U. 441, afterwards continued to Brundusium,

In describing the different roads which traversed Latium, we shall notice them in their order as they severally branched off from Rome, their common centre. The first is the VIA OSTIENSIS, which, as its name sufficiently implies, led to Ostia, commencing at the Porta Trigemina ; or, if we take a latter period, at the Porta Ostiensis, now *Porto S. Paolo*. The Via Laurentina branched off from this road about two miles from Rome, and terminated at Laurentum. We have no account of this Roman way in the Itineraries, but we are informed of its existence from Ovid. The next road is the

VIA ARDEATINA, which evidently, was intended to establish a communication with Ardea, distant about twenty miles from Rome. There was also a road which followed the line of the coast from Ostia to Tarracina, it was called SEVERIANA, having been constructed, or more probably repaired, by order of the emperor Severus, as we learn from ancient inscriptions.

The Appian way was the most celebrated of the Roman roads, both on account of its length and the difficulties which it was necessary to overcome in its construction.

. . . . qua limite noto
Appia longarum teritur Regina viarum.
STAT. SILV. II. 2.

It was made, as Livy informs us, by the censor Appius Cæcus, A. U. C. 442. and in the first instance was only laid down as far as Capua, a distance of about a thousand stadia, or an hundred and twenty-five miles ; but even this portion of the work, according to the account of Diodorus Siculus, was executed in so expensive a manner that it exhausted the public treasury. From Capua it was subsequently carried on to Beneventum, and finally to Brundusium, when this port became the great place of resort for those who were desirous of crossing over into Greece and Asia Minor. This latter part of the Appian way is supposed to have been constructed by the consul App. Claudius Pulcher,

grandson of Cæcus, A. U. C. 504. and to have been completed by another consul of the same family thirty-six years after. We find frequent mention made of repairs done to this road by the Roman emperors, and more particularly by Trajan, both in the histories of the time and also in ancient inscriptions. This road seems to have been still in excellent order in the time of Procopius, who gives a very good account of the manner in which it was constructed. The next road which presents itself to our notice is the

VIA LATINA. It commenced at the Porta Capena, and fell into the Via Appia at Beneventum. Of its formation we have no account, but it was certainly of great antiquity, and existed probably before the Romans had conquered Latium.

The VIA LAVICANA, so called from its passing close to the ancient city of Lavicum, communicated with the Via Latina.

The VIA PRÆNESTINA, like the Via Lavicana, issued from the Porta Esquilina, and fell into the Via Latina.

So far the description of the Appian way has been confined to that portion of it which traversed the Latin plains ; we may therefore resume our statement of the stations and distances of this celebrated road from the borders of Campania, and carry it on to the limits of the Samnite territory. The Latin way, which we also left on the confines of Campania, in the last section, may be considered as falling into the Via Appia at Capua. The Appian and Latin ways were also connected by a cross rode which branched off from the former at Minturnæ, and passing through Suessa Aurunca, joined the Via Latina at Teanum. From inscriptions, we learn that it was called Via Hadriana, from having been constructed at the expense of that emperor. Another great road followed the Campanian coast from Sinuessa to Surrentum, passing through Cumæ, Puteoli, and Neapolis ; that portion of it lying between the first of these cities and Sinuessa, obtained the name of

Via Domitiana from the emperor Domitian, who caused to be constructed, as we are informed, by Statius. In the Itinerary of Antoninus this route is entitled " Iter a Terracina Neapolim." The route which led from Capua to Cumæ is termed Via Consularis by Pliny ; it is also sometimes called Via Campana. One branch of it diverged to Puteoli. From Capua also commenced a Roman way, which traversed a portion of Campania, the whole of Lucania and Bruttium, and terminated at Rhegium on the Sicilian Straits. A curious inscription, discovered at *Polla* in *Calabria*, informs us that this road was constructed by M. Aquilius Gallus, the proconsul, the same probably who is mentioned by Florus as having been prætor in Sicily. In this inscription all the distances are reckoned from the spot where it was fixed to each place or station on the road from Capua to Rhegium.

The course of the Appian way has been described through Campania as far as Capua ; from that point therefore we may resume the detail of its stations and distances as far as Beneventum, and from thence again through the different ramifications of the same route to the confines of Apulia. From Beneventum, one branch of the Appian way proceeded through the country of the Hirpini to Venusia in Apulia, and from thence to Tarentum and Brundusium. Another branch took a more northerly direction on leaving Beneventum, and passing the Apennines near Æquotuticum, led to Canusium in Apulia, and from thence along the coast to Brundusium : the latter part of this road was called Via Egnatia. The northern part of Samnium was traversed by a road which communicated with the Valerian, Latin, and Appian ways, and after crossing through part of Apulia, fell into the Via Aquilia in Lucania. There is reason for supposing this to have been the Via Numicia of which Horace says,

Brundusium Numici melius via ducat, an Appi.
I. EPIST. 18.

about 350 miles, but by whom is uncertain ; called REGINA VIARUM,[1] paved
with the hardest flint so firmly, that in several places it remains entire unto
this day, about 2000 years ; so broad, that two carriages might pass one
another, commonly, however, not exceeding fourteen feet. The stones
were of different sizes, from one to five feet every way, but so artfully
joined that they appeared but one stone. There were two *strata* below ;
the first *stratum* of rough stones cemented with mortar, and the second of
gravel ; the whole about three feet thick.

The roads were so raised as to command a prospect of the adjacent country. On each side there was usually a row of larger stones, called MAR-
GINES, a little raised for foot passengers ; hence the roads were said MAR-
GINARI.[2] Sometimes roads were only covered with gravel,[3] with a foot-
path or stone on each side.

Augustus erected a gilt pillar in the forum, called MILLIARIUM AUREUM,
where all the military ways terminated. The miles, however, were reckoned not from it, but from the gates of the city, along all the roads to the
limits of the empire, and marked on stones. Hence LAPIS is put for a mile ;
thus, *ad tertium lapidem*, the same with *tria millia passuum ab urbe*. At
smaller distances, there were stones for travellers to rest on, and to assist
those who alighted to mount their horses.[4]

The public ways (PUBLICÆ VIÆ) were named either from the persons
who first laid them out, or the places to which they led : thus VIA APPIA,
and near it, *via* NUMICIA, which also led to Brundusium. *Via* AURELIA,
along the coast of Etruria ; FLAMINIA, to Ariminum and Aquileia ; CASSIA,
in the middle between these two, through Etruria to Mutina ; ÆMILIA,
which led from Ariminum to Placentia.[5] *Via* PRÆNESTINA, to Præneste ;
TIBURTINA, vel TIBURS, to Tibur ; OSTIENSIS, to Ostia ; LAURENTINA, to
Laurentum ; SALARIA, so called because by it the Sabines carried salt
from the sea ;[6] LATINA, &c.

The principal roads were called PUBLICÆ, vel MILITARES, *consulares*,
vel *prætoriæ ;* as among the Greeks, βασιλικαι, i. e. *regiæ* ; the less frequented roads, PRIVATÆ, *agrariæ*, vel *vicinales, quia ad agros et vicos ducunt.*
The charge of the public ways was intrusted only to men of the highest
dignity. Augustus himself undertook the charge of the roads round Rome,

For Cicero speaks of a Via Minucia, which must have agreed in direction with that which I am now describing ; and early critics have remark-ed, that the true reading in this passage of Cicerowns Nu-micia. In the Itinerary of An-toninus this route is described under the head ' Iter a Medi-olano per Picenum et Cam-paniam ad Columnam.' We may here observe that a branch of the Via Latina crossed into this route from Teanum Sidicium, and thus afforded a more direct commu-nication between that town and Beneventum than by Ca-

pua. Finally, a cross-road led from Beneventum into the country of the Picentini, where it fell in with the Via Aquilia at Picentia. The on-ly route which traversed the territory of the Frentani was a continuation of the Via Sa-laria, which followed the coast as far as Brundusium. According to Romanelli it was termed Via Frentana Apula. But in the Itinerary of Antoni-nus we find it described under the head ' Via Flaminia per Picenum Brundusium.' There yet remains to be no-ticed a road which followed the whole coast of the Iapygi-

an peninsula, from Brundusi-um to Tarentum. The princi-pal road to be noticed in Lu-cania, was the Via Aquilia. We find also in the Antonine Itinerary a cross-road commu-nicating with the Via Appia and the Via Aquilia. On the eastern coast we have to fol-low the course of another Ro-man way, which terminated at Rhegium. An ancient in-scription, as cited by Roma-nelli, informs us, that this road was regarded as a branch of the Appian way, and that in consequence of its having been repaired by Trajan, it took the name of Via Trajana."

1 Liv. ix. 29. Eutr. ii. 4. Hor. Ep. i. 18. 20. Sat. i. 5. Tac. Ann. ii. 30. Stat. Sylv. ii. 2. 11. 2 Liv. xli. 27. 3 glarea, ibid. 4 Plin. iii. 5. xv. 18. Tac. Hist. i. 73. Suet. Oth. 6. Dio. liv. 8. Plut. 5 Cic. Phil. xii. 9. Cat. ii. 4. Liv. xxxix. 2. Galba, p. 1064. l. 154 D. de. V. S. Grac. Liv. xxvi. 10. 6 Hor. Sat. i. 6. 108. Plin. Ep. ii. 16. Fest. Mart. iv. 64. 18.

and appointed two men of prætorian rank to pave the roads, each of whom was attended by two lictors.[1]

From the principal ways, there were cross-roads, which led to some less noted place, to a country villa, or the like, called DIVERTICULA, which word is put also for the inns along the public roads, hence for a digression from the principal subject.[2]   But places near the road where travellers rested[3] are commonly called DIVERSORIA, whether belonging to a friend, the same with *hospitia*, or purchased on purpose,[4] or hired,[5] then properly called CAUPONÆ, or TABERNÆ DIVERSORIÆ ;[6] and the keeper[7] of such a place, of an inn or tavern, CAUPO ; those who went to it, DIVERSORES ; hence *commorandi natura diversorium nobis, non habitandi dedit*, nature has granted us an inn for our sojourning, not a home for our dwelling.[8]

In later times, the inns or stages along the roads were called MANSIONES ; commonly at the distance of half a day's journey from one another ;[9] and at a less distance, places for relays, called MUTATIONES, where the public couriers[10] changed horses.   These horses were kept in constant readiness, at the expense of the emperor, but could only be used by those employed on the public service, without a particular permission notified to the innkeepers by a *diploma*.[11]

The Romans had no public posts, as we have.   The first invention of public couriers is ascribed to Cyrus.   Augustus first introduced them among the Romans.[12]   But they were employed only to forward the public despatches, or to convey political intelligence.   It is surprising they were not sooner used for the purposes of commerce and private communication.   Lewis XI. first established them in France, in the year 1474 : but it was not till the first of Charles II., *anno* 1660, that the post-office was settled in England by act of parliament ; and three years after, the revenues arising from it, when settled on the duke of York, amounted only to £20,000.[13]

Near the public ways the Romans usually placed their sepulchres.[14] The streets of the city were also called VIÆ, the cross-streets, VIÆ TRANSVERSÆ ; thus, *via* SACRA, NOVA, &c., paved with flint, yet usually dirty.[15]*

---

* The VIA LATA was a prolongation of the Via Flaminia, and was the street through which victorious generals, who entered Rome on that side, marched their troops in triumph to the Capitol.   It is supposed to have commenced at the *Piazza Sciarra*. We bear of several triumphal arches with which this approach was adorned. Those of M. Aurelius, Verus, and Gordian are noticed by Rufus ; and Nardini is disposed to add one of Domitian, besides the temple Fortuna Redux, mentioned by Martial.

The VIA NOVA was parallel to the Vicus Tuscus, and led also from the Forum to the Velabrum.   This street existed in the time of the elder Tarquin, as appears from Livy ; unless we suppose the historian to be there speaking of it in anticipation.   Between the Campus Martius and the Tiber was a road called Via Recta, which is perhaps the same as the Triumphalis ; it seems to have followed the left bank of the Tiber, and to have run parallel with the Via Flaminia, and nearly in the same direction as the modern *Strada Giulia*.   On the eastern side of this road was a portico, which formed part of the theatre of Pompey, and another styled the portico of a hundred pillars ; also some shady walks of plane-trees.

The origin of the name, Via Sacra, seems uncertain ; but it is well known that this was the street which led directly from the southern gates of Rome to the Capitol, and that by which the Roman Generals led thither their victorious troops in triumphant procession.   The precise direction of this celebrated street has been much discussed by Roman antiquaries, but the opinion of Nardini seems to be

---

1 Ulpian, Plin. Ep. v. 15. Dio. liv. 8.
2 Suet. Ner. 48. Plin. xxxi. 3. s. 25. Serv. Æn. ix. 379. Liv. i. 51. ix. 17. Don. Ter. Eun. iv. 2. 7. Juv. xv. 72.
3 quo diverterent ad requiescendum.
4 Cic. Fam. vi. 19. vii. 23.
5 meritoria.
6 Hor. Ep. i. 11, 12. Plaut. Truc. iii. 2. 29.
7 institor.
8 Cic. Inven. i. 4. Div. 27. Sen. 23.
9 see p. 253.
10 publici cursores, vel veredarii.
11 Plin. Ep. x. 14. 121.
12 Xenop. Cyrop. viii. p. 496. edit Hutchinson. Suet. Aug. 49. Plut. Galb.
13 Plin. Ep. x. 180. Rapin. vol. ii. 623. 680. fol. ed.
14 see p. 341.
15 Cic. Ver. iv. 53. Hor. Sat. i. 9. Ov. F. vi. 395. Juv. iii. 270. 247. Mart. vii. 60. v. 23. 6.

The Roman ways were sometimes dug through mountains, as the grotto of Puzzoli, *crypta Puteolana*, between Puteoli and Naples ; and carried over the broadest rivers by bridges (hence *facere pontem in fluvio ; fluvium ponte jungere* vel *committere ; pontem fluvio imponere, indere* vel *injicere*).

The ancient bridges of Rome were eight in number :* — 1. *pons* SUBLI-CIUS vel *Æmilius ;* so called, because first made of wood (from *sublicæ*, stakes),[1] and afterwards of stone by Æmilius Lepidus ; some vestiges of it still remain at the foot of mount Aventine : 2. *pons* FABRICIUS, which led to an isle in the Tiber,[2] first built of stone, A. D. 692 ; and 3. CESTIUS, which led from the island : 4. SENATORIUS vel *Palatinus*, near mount Palatine, some arches of it are still standing : 5. *pons* JANICULI, vel *-aris ;* so named, because it led to the Janiculum; still standing : 6. *pons* TRIUMPHALIS, which those who triumphed passed in going to the Capitol ; only a few vestiges of it remain : 7. *pons* ÆLIUS, built by Ælius Hadrianus ; still standing ; the largest and most beautiful bridge in Rome : 8. *pons* MILVIUS, without the city ; now called *ponte molle*.

There are several bridges on the Anio or Teverone ; the most considerable of which is *pons* NARSIS, so called because rebuilt by the eunuch Narses, after it had been destroyed by Totila, king of the Goths.

more generally adopted. That able topographer has proved from Varro, that the Via Sacra commenced near the Colosseum, and kept near the base of the Esquiline, passing close to the ruins commonly called the temple of Peace, and terminating in the Forum through the Fabian arch.

* It may not be amiss to give some account of the Roman bridges and aqueducts. The number of the former never appears to have exceeded eight. The most ancient, and also tho first in order, if we ascend the river, was the Pons Sublicius, so called from its being constructed of wood. It was built by Ancus Martius, but was rendered more celebrated for the gallant manner in which it was defended by Horatius Cocles against the forces of Porsenna. For some centuries after, this bridge was, through motives of religious feeling, kept constantly in repair with the same materials of which it had been framed originally, without the addition of a single nail for the purpose. This continued, as we learn from Dio Cassius, till towards the conclusion of the republic, when it was rebuilt of stone by the censor Paulus Æmilius Lepidus ; whence it is also sometimes called Pons Æmilius.

Cum tibi vicinum se præbeat
Æmilius pons ?
Juv. Sat. VI. 32.

Julius Capitolinus states, that it was repaired by Antoninus Pius in marble. Next to it was the Pons Palatinus, now *Ponte di S. Maria*, or *Ponte Rotto*. This bridge is said to have been begun by M. Fulvius the censor, and to have been finished by P. Scipio Africanus and L. Mummius, who held that office, A. U. C. 611. The bridge, which connects the island in the Tiber with the left bank of that river, was anciently known by the name of Pons Fabricius. Dio Cassius speaks of it as having been built of stone soon after the conspiracy of Catiline ; from whence it might be inferred that a wooden one existed previously on the same spot. It is mentioned by Horace.

Atque a Fabricio non tristem
ponte reverti.
Il. Sat. 3. 36.

Its modern name is *Ponte di quattro Capi*. The name of Cestius was given to the bridge which connected the island with the other bank of the Tiber, it is now called *Ponte di S. Bartolomeo*. We are not informed by whom or when it was built ; but we learn from an inscription, that

it was repaired under the emperors Valentinian, Valens, and Gratian. The bridge immediately above the island is now called *Ponte Sisto*, but its ancient name,as we learn from Victor, was Pons Janiculensis. Report assigns its construction to Antoninus Pius, and an inscription mentions its having been repaired by Hadrian. Next to the Janiculensis was the Pons Triumphalis, of which we have no account in any classical writer ; but the piles on which it was raised are said to be still visible, when the bed of the river is low. The last bridge now takes its name from the castle of *S. Angelo*, in front of which it stands, and is known to have been built originally by Hadrian, after whom it was called Pons Ælius.

About two miles from Rome, we find on the Tiber a bridge called Pons Milvius, or Mulvius, a name which has been corrupted into that of *Ponte Molle*. Its construction is ascribed to M. Æmilius Scaurus, who was censor A. U. C. 644. We learn from Cicero, that the Pons Milvius existed at the time of Catiline's conspiracy, since the deputies of the Allobroges were here seized by his orders. In later times it witnessed the defeat of Maxentius by Constantine.

1 Liv. i. 33.   2 Insula, Dio. 37. 45.

About sixty miles from Rome, on the Flaminian way, in the country of the Sabines, was *pons* NARNIENSIS, which joined two mountains, near Narnia, or Narni, over the river Nar, built by Augustus, of stupendous height and size ; vestiges of it still remain ; one arch entire, about 100 feet high, and 150 feet wide.

But the most magnificent Roman bridge, and perhaps the most wonderful ever made in the world, was the bridge of Trajan over the Danube ; raised on twenty piers of hewn stone, 150 feet from the foundation, sixty feet broad, and 170 feet distant from one another, extending in length about a mile. But this stupendous work was demolished by the succeeding emperor, Hadrian, who ordered the upper part and the arches to be taken down, under pretext that it might not serve as a passage to the barbarians, if they should become masters of it ;[1] but in reality, as some writers say, through envy, because he despaired of being able to raise any work comparable to it. Some of the pillars are still standing.

There was a bridge at Nismes (*Nemausum*), in France, which supported an aqueduct over the river Gardon, consisting of three rows of arches, several of which still remain entire, and are esteemed one of the most elegant monuments of Roman magnificence. The stones are of an extraordinary size, some of them twenty feet long ; said too have been joined together, without cement, by ligaments of iron. The first row of arches was 438 feet long ; the second, 746 ; the third and highest, 805 ; the height of the three from the water, 182 feet.

In the time of Trajan, a noble bridge was built over the Tagus, or Tayo, near Alcantara, in Spain, part of which is still standing. It consisted of six arches, eighty feet broad each, and some of them 200 feet high above the water, extending in length 660 feet.

The largest single-arched bridge known is over the river Elaver, or Allier, in France, called *pons veteris Brevatis*, near the city of Brioude, in Auvergne, from Briva, the name of a bridge among the ancient Gauls. The pillars stand on two rocks, at the distance of 195 feet. The arch is eighty-four feet high above the water.

Of temporary bridges, the most famous was that of Cæsar over the Rhine, constructed of wood.[2]

The Romans often made bridges of rafts or boats, joined to one another, and sometimes of empty casks, or leathern bottles, as the Greeks.[3]

LIMITS OF THE EMPIRE.

THE limits which Augustus set to the Roman empire, and in his testament advised his successors not to go beyond, were the Atlantic ocean on the west, and the Euphrates on the east ; on the north, the Danube and the Rhine ; and on the south, the cataracts of the Nile, the deserts of Africa, and mount Atlas ; including the whole Mediterranean sea, and the best part of the then known world : so that the Romans were not without foundation called RERUM DOMINI, lords of the world, and Rome, LUX ORBIS TERRARUM, ATQUE ARX OMNIUM GENTIUM, the light of the universe, and the citadel of all nations ;[4] TERRARUM DEA GENTIUMQUE *Roma*, CUI PAR EST NIHIL, ET NIHIL SECUNDUM ; CAPUT ORBIS TERRARUM ; CAPUT RERUM ; DOMINA ROMA ; PRINCEPS URBIUM ; REGIA ; PULCHERRIMA RERUM ; MAXI-

1 Dio. lviii. 13. 14. Flor. iii. 5. Herod. iii. lvi. 33. 41. Virg. Æn.
2 Cæs. B. G. iv. 17. viii. Zosim. iii. Luc. 4 Tac. Ann. i. 11. Dio. i. 282. Cic. Cat. iv. 6.
3 Cæs. B. G. i. 12. viii. iv. 420. Xanop. Cyr.

MA RERUM ;[1] *sed quæ de septem totum circumspicit orbem montibus,* IMPERII
ROMA DEUMQUE. (i. e. *principum* v. *imperatorum*) LOCUS, but Rome, the seat
of empire and the residence of the gods, which from seven hills looks
around on the whole world. *Dumque suis victrix omnem de montibus orbem
prospiciet domitum,* MARTIA ROMA, *legar ;* while warlike Rome, victorious,
shall behold the subjugated world from her seven hills, my works shall be
read ; CAPUT MUNDI RERUMQUE POTESTAS ; *septem* URBS *ulta jugis* TOTI
QUÆ PRÆSIDET ORBI.[2]

Agreeably to the advice of Augustus, few additions were made to the
empire after his time. Trajan subdued Dacia, north of the Danube, and
Mesopotamia and Armenia, east of the Euphrates. The south of Britain
was reduced by Ostorius, under Claudius ; and the Roman dominion was
extended to the frith of Forth and the Clyde, by Agricola, under Domitian.[3]
But what is remarkable, the whole force of the empire, although exerted
to the utmost under Severus, one of its most warlike princes, could not
totally subdue the nation of the Caledonians, whose invincible ferocity in
defence of freedom[4] at last obliged that emperor, after granting them peace,
to spend near two years in building, with incredible labour, a wall of solid
stone, twelve feet high and eight feet thick, with forts and towers at proper
distances, and a rampart and ditch, from the Solway frith to the mouth
of the Tyne, above sixty-eight miles, to repress their inroads.[5]

The wall of Severus is called by some MURUS, and by others VALLUM.
Spartianus says it was 80 miles long.[6] Eutropius makes it only 32 miles.[7]
See also Victor, Epit. xx. 4. Orosius, vii. 17. Herodian, iii. 48. Beda,
Hist. i. 5. Cassiodorus, Chronicon. Camden, p. 607. edit. 1594. Gor-
don's Itinerary, c. 7—9. p. 65—93. Gough's translation of Camden, vol.
iii. p. 211.

1 Mart. xii. 8. Liv. i. 16.
45. xxi. 30. Tac. Hist.
ii. 32. Hor. Od. iii. 13.
iv. 14. 44. Ep. i. 7. 44.
Virg. G. ii, 533. Æn. vii.
602.
2 Ov. Trist. i. 4. 69. iii.
7. 51. Luc. ii. 136. Prop.

ii. 11. 57.
3 Eutrop. viii. 2. Tac.
Agric. 23.
4 devota morti pectora
liberæ, Hor. Od. iv. 14.
18.
5 Severus, in penetrat-
ing this country, is

said to have lost no
less than fifty thousand
men (πεντε μυριαδας ὁ-
λας), Dio. l. lxxvi. c.
13.—Mr. Hume must
have overlooked this
fact, when he says, that
the Romans entertain-

ed a contempt for Ca-
ledonia, Hist. of Eng-
land, vol. i. p. 10. 8vo.
edit.
6 in vita Severi, 18. 22.
7 viii. 19.

APPENDIX.

App. A, page 1.

THE origin commonly assigned to the city of Rome appears to rest on no better foundation than mere fabulous tradition. The uncertainty which prevailed on this subject, even in ancient times, is clearly evinced by the numerous and varying accounts of the origin of that city which are mentioned by Plutarch in the introduction to his life of Romulus. From that passage two conclusions are evidently to be deduced: first, that the true origin of Rome was to the ancients themselves a fertile theme of controversy; and, secondly, that from the very number of these varying statements, as well as their great discrepancy, the city of Rome must have been of very early origin ; so early, in fact, as to have been almost lost amid the darkness of fable. But whence do we obtain the commonly received account? We derive it from Fabius Pictor, who copied it from an obscure Greek author, Diocles the Peparethian; and from this tainted source have flowed all the stories concerning Mars, the Vestal, the wolf, Romulus and Remus. Of Diocles we know nothing. According to Dionysius of Halicarnassus, Fabius had no better authority for the great proportion of events which preceded his own age than vulgar tradition. He probably found that if he had confined himself to what was certain in these early times, his history would have been dry, insipid, and incomplete. This is the same Fabius, who, in the few unconnected fragments that remain of his Annals, tells us of a person who had a message brought him by a swallow, and of a party of loupgarous, who, after being transformed into wolves, recovered their own figures, and, what is more, got back their cast-off clothes, provided that they abstained for nine years from preying upon human flesh! So low, indeed, even among the Romans themselves, had the character of Fabius for historical fidelity fallen, that Polybius apologizes on one occasion for quoting Fabius as an authority. If Fabius be proved from his very narrative to have been a visionary, fabulous, and incorrect writer, his prototype Diocles must have been equally, if not more so.

We propose to offer an account of the origin of the imperial city, different, and, we hope, of a more satisfactory character; —one which will trace the foundation of Rome to a period long prior to the supposed era of Romulus; and which, advancing still farther, will show that, Rome was not the true or Latin name of the city. —Among the cities of the Pelasgi, in the land once possessed by the Siculi, that is, in Latium, mention is frequently made of one denominated Saturnia. This city, thus known by the name of Saturnia, is no other than Rome itself. Thus Pliny (3, 5,) observes, " Saturnia, where Rome now stands." So Aurelius Victor (3), " Saturnia, built on one of the hills

of Rome, was the residence of Saturn." But by whom was Saturnia built? Was it of Pelasgic origin, or founded by the ancient Siculi? The following authority will furnish a satisfactory answer. Dionysius (i. 73.) quotes an old historian, named Antiochus of Syracuse, whom he styles, at the same time, " no common or recent writer," to the following effect : " Antiochus of Syracuse says that when Morges reigned in Italy, there came to him from Rome an exile named Siculus." This passage is deserving of very close consideration. In the first place, as Morges, according to the same writer, succeeded, Italus, and as the very name of this latter prince carries us back at once to the earliest periods of Italian history, we find the name Rome applied to a city, which must of consequence have been one of the oldest in the land. In the next place, it is evident that Antiochus relates a fact not based upon his own individual knowledge, but upon an old and established tradition; for Antiochus brought down his history of Sicilian affairs to the 98th olympiad, that is, to the 388th year before the Christian era, a period when neither he himself nor any other Grecian writer knew aught of Rome, even by report, as a city actually in existence ; since only two years previous (B. C. 390.) it had been burned by the Gauls, and it was not until more than a century afterwards that the Romans became known to the Sicilian Greeks by the capture of Tarentum. It would seem, then, that Rome (Roma) was the most ancient name ; that it was displaced for a time by Saturnia, and was afterwards resumed.

We shall now enter more fully into the consideration of our subject, and endeavour to find other additional grounds for the support of the opinion which we are advocating. To the same region of Italy where Saturn had erected on the Capitoline mountain the city of Saturnia, and opposite to whom Janus had also established his residence on the Janiculum, came, according to Dionysius (i. 31.), an individual named Evander, who was received in a friendly manner by the reigning monarch Faunus. Two ships were sufficient to carry him and his followers, and a mountain was assigned him as the place of his abode, where he built a small city, and called it Pallantium, from his native city, in Arcadia. This name became gradually corrupted into Pallatium, while the mountain took the appellation of Mons Pelatinus.—Thus far Dionysius. Now, that a mere stranger, with but a handful of followers, should be received in so friendly a manner by the Pelasgi and Aborigines, as to be allowed to settle in their immediate vicinity, and in a place, too, which was, in a later age, as Dionysius informs us, the very heart of Rome, is scarcely entitled to belief ; still less is it to be credited that he wrested a settlement there by force. If, then, we are to retain this old tradition respecting Evander and his followers (and we have nothing whatever which can authorize the rejection of it), there are but two ways in which the whole can be explained. Either Evander was the leader of those very Pelasgi, who, uniting with the Aborigines, drove out the Siculi from Latium, and received for his portion the city of Rome, with its adjacent territory; or, he was a wandering Pelasgus, driven from Thessaly by the arms of the Hellenes, and after many unsuccessful attempts elsewhere, induced to come to Italy in quest of an abode. It becomes extremely difficult to decide between these two hypotheses, since they both receive considerable support from ancient authorities. The Pelasgi had already, on their very first irruption into Latium, founded a city called Pallantium in the territory of Reate, whose ancient situation Dionysius of Halicarnassus endeavours to point out. The name Pallantium was subsequently transferred by these same Pelasgi to the city of Rome, after they had become masters of it by the expulsion of the Siculi. Varro speaks in very express terms on this subject (L. L. iv. 8.): "the inhabitants of the territory of Reate, named Palatini, settled on the Roman Palatium." A passage of Festus, moreover, (v. Sacrani) is fully to the point: "the Sacrani, natives of Reate (i. e. the territory), drove the Ligures and Siculi from Septimontio (i. e. Rome)." After reading this passage, there surely can be no doubt remaining in our minds as to the early existence of the city of Rome, as well as of its occupation by a band of Pelasgi and Aborigines. It is curious, moreover, to compare the name Sacrani, which evidently means sacred, or consecrated to some deity, with the acknowledged fact of the Pelasgi being a sacerdotal caste or order; as well as with the circumstance of there being a class of priests at Ardea called Sacrani, who worshipped Cebele, a goddess whose worship is most clearly traced from the East. On the supposition, then, that Evander was the leader of the Pelasgi, we are enabled to clear up the old tradition of his having introduced into Italy the use of letters, and the knowledge of various arts. The Greeks also were indebted to the Pelasgi for an acquaintance with written characters, and with many of the arts of civilized life. The second hypothesis, namely, that Evander was a wandering Pelasgus who had come to Italy in quest of an abode, and had been hospitably received by those of his nation who were already established there, receives in its turn an air of great probability, from the concurrent testimony of all the ancient writers as to his having come to Italy by sea, as well as from the circumstance so explicitly stated, that he arrived in two ships with his band of followers. If, now, we turn our attention for a moment to the fact, that after the Hellenes had driven the Pelasgi from Thessaly, a portion of the latter retired into Epirus, while another part sailed to the western coast of Asia Minor, where Homer speaks of them as the allies of the Trojans; if, in addition to this, we call to mind that both divisions eventually settled in Italy, and laid the foundation of the Etrurian

confederacy; and if, finally, we take into consideration what Plutarch tells us in his life of Romulus, though he assigns no authority for it, that Romus, king of the Latins, drove out of the city the Tyrrheni, who had come from Thessaly to Lydia, and from Lydia to Italy, the balance preponderates considerably in favour of this second hypotheses. Perhaps, however, they may both be reconciled together by supposing that those of the Pelasgi who had come from the upper part of Italy, had changed the name of ancient Rome to that of Palatium, and that Evander came to, and was received among, them. It is most probable that Evander was one of the leaders of the Pelasgi from the coast of Asia, and bore a part in the founding of the Etrurian republic.

The question now arises as to the actual existence of Romulus. In order to answer this satisfactorily we must go a little into detail. In the district of Latium, there were, exclusive of Rome, many cities of the Aborigines or Latins, who had settled in this part of the country together with the Pelasgi. Of these Alba Longa was the most powerful. Through internal dissensions, and from the operations of other causes, the Pelasgi had lost in most places out of Etruria their original ascendancy. A leader from Alba Longa, with a band of voluntary followers, conducted an enterprize against Rome, where the power of the Pelasgi was in like manner fast diminishing. The enterprize succeeded: the conqueror became king of the ancient city, and increased its inhabitants by the number of his followers. The Pelasgi remained, but they no longer enjoyed their former power. Whether two brothers or only a single individual conducted the enterprize, whether they were previously named Romulus and Remus (i. e. Romus), or, what is far more probable, whether they received these appellations from the conquered city, is a point on which we cannot decide.

From the theory thus established, many important inferences may be drawn, which will tend to throw light on certain obscure parts of early Roman history. 1. We cease to wonder at the successful resistance which Rome, apparently in her very infancy, offered to her powerful neighbours; for even at this early period the city must be regarded as of remote and ancient origin. 2. We understand very clearly why Tuscan troops formed one of the wings of the army of Romulus; for there is very strong probability that they were in reality the old Tyrrhenian or Pelasgic inhabitants, and that Cœles Vibenna, their leader, was in truth the lucumo, or ruler, of Rome at the time of its capture by Romulus. 3. We perceive also the meaning of the Etrurian writer Volumnius, quoted by Varro (L. L. iv. 9.), when he states that the three appellations for the early Roman tribes, Ramnes and Tatienses, as well as Luceres, are all Etrurian terms; the preponderating language in Rome at the time of its capture being Tyrrhenian or Etrurian. 4. We can comprehend the close union and intercourse which subsisted at a later period between the Romans and Etrurians, Rome being, in fact, an Etrurian city. 5. The account no longer appears exaggerated of Romulus having only 3000 foot and 300 horse when he founded Rome, and of there being 46,000 foot and 4000 horse at the period of his death ; the former means the forces which accompanied him on his enterprize against the ancient city ; the latter were the combined strength of his followers and the ancient inhabitants. 6. We see, too, what to many has appeared altogether inexplicable, how the Roman kings, during their continual wars, were yet able to cherish at home the taste for building, which never can exist among a rude and early community : how it was that, even at this remote period, the Cloacæ, the Circus Maximus, the Capitol, and other public constructions were undertaken and accomplished. These stupendous structures, altogether beyond the resources of Rome, if she is to be considered as an infant state at the time of their execution, were, in fact, the work of the Etrurian part of the population of Rome. 7. We discover the reason of the most distinguished of the Roman youth being sent to the principal Etrurian cities for the purposes of education : it was done, in fact, from motives of state-policy, in order that, amid the tumult of almost incessant wars, they might still keep alive that spark of early knowledge and refinement which had distinguished Rome from the very outset, and which marks her not as the receptacle of a horde of banditti, but as an ancient and civilized city, falling by right of conquest into the hands of a military chieftain. 8. We are enabled to discover many of the secret springs which impelled the complicated and apparently discordant machinery of the Roman government. The old inhabitants being much farther advanced in civilization than their conquerors, would naturally, even after the fall of the city, be respected by the victors for their superior improvement, and the most distinguished of them would be called, from motives of policy, to some slight participation in the affairs of the government. Accordingly, we find that almost one of the first acts of Romulus was the institution of a senate, whose limited number freed him from any apprehension of their combining to overthrow his power ; while their confirmation of his decrees, in case it should be needed, would have great weight with the old population of the city. The impolitic neglect which Romulus subsequently displayed towards this order, ended in his destruction. That such indeed was his fate, and that the senate were privy to the whole affair, admits of no doubt, when we call to mind the monstrous falsehood asserted by the senator Proculus Julius, for the purpose of freeing that body from the suspicion of having taken the life of the king.—After all that has been said, we hazard little, if any thing, in asserting that the early Roman nobility were the descendants of a sacred or sacerdotal caste. That the Pelasgi were such an order, has been frequently asserted, and we trust satisfactorily established. The Etrurians, the descendants of the Pelasgi, preserved this singular feature in the form of government which they had adopted. The Etrurian confederacy was composed, indeed, of twelve independent cities, yet the government was by no means in the hands of the people ; it was the patrimony of an hereditary caste, who were at once invested with the military power, and charged

with the sacerdotal functions. This strange form of government threw the whole power into the hands of the higher classes, who were, no doubt, the immediate descendants of the Pelasgi, and subjected to their control the whole mass of the lower orders, who very probably were sprung from the early Aborigines. Now, reasoning by analogy, we must allow this very same form of government to have prevailed in Etrurian Rome before its conquest by Romulus. This arrangement would throw into the hands of the upper classes the chief power, and give them the absolute control of religious affairs ; and, on his capture of the city, Romulus would leave them in full possession of the latter, as a matter almost of necessity, while from motives of policy he would allow them to retain a small portion of the former. Hence the origin of the Roman nobility. Many circumstances combine to strengthen what has just been advanced. The nobility had for a long time in Rome the sole custody of religious affairs, and from their order all the priests were for a long series of years constantly chosen. Every patrician gens, and each individual patrician family, had certain sacred rites peculiar to itself, which went by inheritance in the same manner as effects, and which the heir was bound to perform. In this way, too, is to be explained the relation of patron and client, which in the earlier days of the Roman government was observed with so much formality and rigour. It was an artful arrangement on the part of a sacerdotal order, and may be regarded as analagous to, and no doubt derived from, the institution of castes in India. Its object was to keep the lower orders in complete dependence upon the higher, and to effect this end the terrors of religion were powerfully annexed : it was deemed unlawful for patrons and clients to accuse or bear witness against each other ; and whoever was found to have acted otherwise, might be slain with impunity as a victim devoted to Pluto and the infernal gods. A regular system of castes seems thus to have prevailed in Rome both before and a long period after its conquest by Romulus.

We come now to the true or Latin name of the Roman city. Macrobius (iii. 9.) informs us that the Romans, when they besieged a city, and thought themselves sure of taking it, used solemnly to call out the tutelary gods of the place, either because they thought that the place could not otherwise be taken, or because they regarded it as impious to hold the gods in captivity. " On this account," he adds, " the Romans themselves have willed that both the deity under whose protection Rome is, as well as the Latin name of the city, remain secret and undivulged. The name of the city is unknown even to the most learned." To the testimony of Macrobius may be added that of Pliny (iii. 5.), " Rome, whose other name it is forbidden by the secret ceremonies of religion to divulge." Now, in the sanctuary of Vesta was preserved the Palladium, " the fated pledge of Roman dominion," (fatale pignus imperii Romani, Liv. xxvi. 27.) May we not then suppose Pallas or Minerva to have been the true tutelary deity of Rome, and the real or Latin name of the city to have been Pallantium ?

AGRARIAN LAWS.—App. B, Pages 95, 149.

These laws were enacted in ancient Rome for the division of public lands. In the valuable work on Roman history by Mr. Niebuhr, it is satisfactorily shown, that these laws, which have so long been continued in the light of unjust attacks on private property, had for their object only the distribution of lands which were the property of the state, and that the troubles to which they gave rise were occasioned by the opposition of persons who had settled on these lands without having acquired any title to them.

According to Dionysius of Halicarnassus, their plan of sending out colonists, or settlers, began as early as the time of Romulus, who generally placed colonists from the city of Rome on the lands taken in war. The same policy was pursued by the kings who succeeded him; and, when the kings were expelled, it was adopted by the senate and the people, and then by the dictators. There were several reasons inducing the Roman government to pursue this policy, which was continued for a long period without any intermission; first, to have a check upon the conquered people; secondly, to have a protection against the incursions of an enemy; thirdly, to augment their population; fourthly, to free the city of Rome from an excess of inhabitants; fifthly, to quiet seditions; and, sixthly, to reward their veteran soldiers. These reasons abundantly appear in all the best ancient authorities. In the later periods of the republic, a principal motive for establishing colonies was to have the means of disposing of soldiers, and rewarding them with donations of lands; and such colonies were denominated *military* colonies.

An agrarian law contained various provisions; it described the land which was to be divided, and the classes of people among whom, and their numbers, and by whom, and in what manner, and by what bounds, the territory was to be parcelled out. The mode of dividing the lands, as far as we now understand it, was twofold; either a Roman population was distributed over the particular territory, without any formal erection of a colony, or general grants of lands were made to such citizens as were willing to form a colony there. The lands which were thus distributed were of different descriptions; which we must keep in mind, in order to have a just conception of the operation of the agrarian laws. They were either lands taken from an enemy, and not actually treated by the government as public property, or lands which were regarded and occupied by the Roman people as public property; or public lands which had been artfully and clandestinely taken possession of by rich and powerful individuals; or, lastly, lands which were bought with money from the public treasury, for the purpose of being distributed. Now, all such agrarian laws as comprehended either lands of the enemy, or those which were treated and occupied as public property, or those which had been bought with the public money, were carried into effect without any public commotions; but those

which operated to disturb the opulent and powerful citizens in the possession of the lands which they unjustly occupied, and to place colonists (or settlers) on them, were never promulgated without creating great disturbances. The first law of this kind was proposed by Spurius Cassius; and the same measure was afterwards attempted by the tribunes of the people almost every year, but was as constantly defeated by various artifices of the nobles; it was, however, at length passed. It appears, both from Dionysius and Varro (*de Re Rustica*, lib. 1), that, at first, Romulus allotted two *jugera* (about one and a fourth acre) of the public lands to each man; then Numa divided the lands which Romulus had taken in war, and also a portion of the other public lands; afterwards Tullus divided those lands which Romulus and Numa had appropriated to the private expenses of the regal establishment; then Servius distributed among those who had recently become citizens, certain lands which had been taken from the Veientes, the Cærites, and Tarquinii; and, upon the expulsion of the kings, it appears that the lands of Tarquin the Proud, with the exception of the Campus Martius, were, by a decree of the senate, granted to the people. After this period, as the republic, by means of its continual wars, received continual accessions of conquered lands, those lands were either occupied by colonists or remained public property, until the period when Spurius Cassius, twenty-four years after the expulsion of the kings, proposed a law (already mentioned), by which one part of the land taken from the Hernici was allotted to the Latins, and the other part to the Roman people; but, as this law comprehended certain lands which he accused private persons of having taken from the public, and as the senate also opposed him, he could not accomplish the passage of it. This, according to Livy, was the first proposal of an agrarian law; of which, he adds, no one was ever proposed, down to the period of his remembrance, without very great public commotions. Dionysius informs us, further, that this public land, by the negligence of the magistrates, had been suffered to fall into the possession of rich men; but that, notwithstanding this, a division of the lands would have taken place under this law, if Cassius had not included among the receivers of the bounty the Latins and Hernici, whom he had but a little while before made citizens. After much debate in the senate upon this subject, a decree was passed to the following effect: that commissioners, called decemvirs, appointed from among the persons of consular rank, should mark out, by boundaries, the public lands, and should designate how much should be let out, and how much should be distributed among the common people; that, if any land had been acquired by joint services in war, it should be divided, according to treaty, with those allies who had been admitted to citizenship; and that the choice of the commissioners, the apportionment of the lands and all other things relating to this subject, should be committed to the care of the succeeding consuls. Seventeen years after this, there was a vehement contest about the division, which the tribunes proposed to make of lands then unjustly occupied by the rich men; and, three years after that, a similar attempt on the part of the tribunes would, according to Livy, have produced a ferocious controversy, had it not been for the address of Quintus Fabius. Some years after this, the tribunes proposed another law of the same kind, by which the estates of a great part of the nobles would have been seized to the public use; but it was stopped in its progress. Appian says, that the nobles and rich men, partly by getting possession of the public lands, partly by buying out the shares of indigent owners, had made themselves owners of all the lands in Italy, and had thus, by degrees, accomplished the removal of the common people from their possessions. This abuse stim ulted Tiberius Gracchus to revive the Licinian law, which prohibited any individual from holding more than 500 *jugera*, or about 350 acres, of land; and would, consequently, compel the owners to relinquish all the surplus to the use of the public; but Gracchus proposed that the owners should be paid the value of the lands relinquished. The law, however, did not operate to any great extent, and, after having cost the Gracchi their lives, was by degrees rendered wholly inoperative. After this period, various other agrarian laws were attempted, and with various success, according to the nature of their provisions and the temper of the times in which they were proposed.

From a careful consideration of these laws, and the others of the same kind on which we have not commented, it is apparent, that the whole object of the Roman agrarian laws was,

the lands belonging to the state, the public lands or national domains, which, as already observed, were acquired by conquest or treaty, and, we may add also, by confiscations or direct seizures of private estates by different factions, either for lawful or unlawful causes; of the last of which we have a well-known example in the time of Sylla's proscriptions. The lands thus claimed by the public became naturally a subject of extensive speculation with the wealthy capitalists, both among the nobles and other classes. In our own times, we have seen, during the revolution in France, the confiscation of the lands belonging to the clergy, the nobility, and emigrants, lead to similar results. The sales and purchases of lands, by virtue of the agrarian laws of Rome, under the various complicated circumstances which must ever exist in such cases, and the attempts by the government to resume or regrant such as had been sold, whether by right or by wrong, especially after a purchaser had been long in possession, under a title which he supposed the existing laws gave him, naturally occasioned great heat and agitation; the subject itself being intrinsically one of great difficulty, even when the passions and interests of the parties concerned would permit a calm and deliberate examination of their respective rights.—From the commotions which usually attended the proposal of agrarian laws, and from a want of exact attention to their true object, there has long been a general impression, among readers of the Roman history, that those laws were always a direct and violent infringement of the rights of private property. Even such men as Machiavelli, Montesquieu, and Adam Smith, have shared in this misconception of them.

LATIN INDEX

OF

WORDS AND PHRASES.

INDEX

OF

PROPER NAMES AND THINGS.

THE END.

www.ingramcontent.com/pod-product-compliance
Lightning Source LLC
Chambersburg PA
CBHW022020110726
47901CB00006B/1601